Comprehensive

GO!

Learn | Practice | Succeed

Microsoft®
Office 365®

Access™ 2019

D1717246

Shelley Gaskin | Nancy Graviett

Series Editor: Shelley Gaskin

Pearson

VP Courseware Portfolio Management: Andrew Gilfillan
Executive Portfolio Manager: Jenifer Niles
Team Lead, Content Production: Laura Burgess
Content Producer: Shannon LeMay-Finn
Development Editor: Toni Ackley
Portfolio Management Assistant: Bridget Daly
Director of Product Marketing: Brad Parkins
Director of Field Marketing: Jonathan Cottrell
Product Marketing Manager: Heather Taylor
Field Marketing Manager: Bob Nisbet
Product Marketing Assistant: Liz Bennett
Field Marketing Assistant: Derrica Moser
Senior Operations Specialist: Diane Peirano

Senior Art Director: Mary Seiner
Interior and Cover Design: Pearson CSC
Cover Photo: Jag_cz/Shutterstock, everything possible/Shutterstock
Senior Product Model Manager: Eric Hakanson
Manager, Digital Studio: Heather Darby
Digital Content Producer, MyLab IT: Becca Golden
Course Producer, MyLab IT: Amanda Losonsky
Digital Studio Producer: Tanika Henderson
Full-Service Project Management: Pearson CSC, Katie Ostler
Composition: Pearson CSC
Printer/Binder: LSC Communications, Inc.
Cover Printer: LSC Communications

Credits and acknowledgments borrowed from other sources and reproduced, with permission, in this textbook appear on appropriate page within text.

Microsoft and/or its respective suppliers make no representations about the suitability of the information contained in the documents and related graphics published as part of the services for any purpose. all such documents and related graphics are provided "as is" without warranty of any kind. microsoft and/or its respective suppliers hereby disclaim all warranties and conditions with regard to this information, including all warranties and conditions of merchantability, whether express, implied or statutory, fitness for a particular purpose, title and non-infringement. in no event shall Microsoft and/or its respective suppliers be liable for any special, indirect or consequential damages or any damages whatsoever resulting from loss of use, data or profits, whether in an action of contract, negligence or other tortious action, arising out of or in connection with the use or performance of information available from the services.

The documents and related graphics contained herein could include technical inaccuracies or typographical errors. changes are periodically added to the information herein. microsoft and/or its respective suppliers may make improvements and/or changes in the product(s) and/or the program(s) described herein at any time. partial screen shots may be viewed in full within the software version specified.

Microsoft® and Windows® are registered trademarks of the Microsoft Corporation in the U.S.A. and other countries. Screenshots and icons reprinted with permission from the Microsoft Corporation. This book is not sponsored or endorsed by or affiliated with the Microsoft Corporation.

Many of the designations by manufacturers and seller to distinguish their products are claimed as trademarks. Where those designations appear in this book, and the publisher was aware of a trademark claim, the designations have been printed in initial caps or all caps.

Library of Congress Cataloging-in-Publication Data

On file with the Library of Congress.

4 2020

ISBN-10: 0-13-544204-4
ISBN-13: 978-0-13-544204-3

Brief Contents

Table of Contents

Access 2019   101

Chapter 1   Getting Started with Microsoft Access 2019 103

About the Authors

Shelley Gaskin, Series Editor, is a professor in the Business and Computer Technology Division at Pasadena City College in Pasadena, California. She holds a bachelor's degree in Business Administration from Robert Morris College (Pennsylvania), a master's degree in Business from Northern Illinois University, and a doctorate in Adult and Community Education from Ball State University (Indiana). Before joining Pasadena City College, she spent 12 years in the computer industry, where she was a systems analyst, sales representative, and director of Customer Education with Unisys Corporation. She also worked for Ernst & Young on the development of large systems applications for their clients. She has written and developed training materials for custom systems applications in both the public and private sector, and has also written and edited numerous computer application textbooks.

This book is dedicated to my husband Fred, and to my students, who inspire me every day.

Nancy Graviett is a professor and department chair in Business Technology at St. Charles Community College in Cottleville, Missouri. She holds a bachelor's degree in marketing and a master's degree in business education from the University of Missouri and has completed a certificate in online education. Nancy has authored textbooks on WordPerfect, Google, Microsoft Outlook, and Microsoft Access.

This book is dedicated to my husband, Dave, and my children, Matthew and Andrea. I cannot thank my family enough for the love and support they share everyday.

GO! with Microsoft Access 2019 Comprehensive

Introducing seamless digital instruction, practice, and assessment

Using GO! with MyLab IT has never been better! With the integrated etext and pre-built learning modules, instructors can assign learning easily and students can get started quickly.

▶ **Proven content and pedagogical approach of *guided instruction, guided practice,* and *mastery*** is effective for all types of learners and all types of course delivery—face-to-face in the classroom, online, and hybrid.

▶ **Students learn Microsoft Office skills by creating practical projects** they will see in their academic and professional lives.

▶ **With GO! MyLab IT students can learn, practice, and assess live or in authentic simulations of Microsoft Office.**

- **Microsoft Office autograded Grader** projects for the instructional, mastery, and assessment projects allow students to work live in Excel, Word, Access, or PPT so that during each step of the learning process, they can receive immediate, autograded feedback!

- **Microsoft Office authentic simulations** allow students to practice what they are learning in a safe environment with learning aids for instant help—*Read, Watch,* or *Practice.* Authentic simulations can also be used for assessment without learning aids.

What's New?

- The **book (print or etext) is the student's guide** to completing all autograded Grader projects for instruction, practice, and assessment.

- The **GO!** *Learn How* **videos**, integrated in the etext, give students an instructor-led, step-by-step guide through the A & B projects.

- **Improved business case connection** throughout the instruction so students always understand the *what* and *why*.

- **Mac tips** ⬜ are woven into the instruction for each project so Mac students can proceed successfully.
  - All text and Grader projects created and tested by the authors on both a Mac and a PC.
  - Content not limited by Mac compatibility! Everything students need to know for MOS exams, Excel, and Access that are not possible on the Mac are still covered!

- **MyLab IT Prebuilt Learning modules** make course setup a snap. The modules are based on research and customer use, and can be easily customized to meet your course requirements.

- **Critical Thinking assessments and badges** expand coverage of Employability Skills.

- **New combined Office Features and Windows chapter** with Grader projects and auto-graded Windows projects for a fast and concise overview of these important features. Shorter and easier to assign.

- **Regular content updates to stay current with Office 365** updates and new features:
  - New *Semester Updates* for the etext and Grader projects through MyLab IT
  - New *Lessons on the GO!* to help you teach new features

What's New for Grader Projects

- **Autograded *Integrated Projects*** covering Word, Excel, Access, and PPT.
- Projects **A & B Grader reports now include *Learning Aids*** for immediate remediation.
- Autograded Critical Thinking Quizzes and Badges
  - Critical Thinking Modules include a Capstone and Quiz that enable students to earn a Critical Thinking Badge
  - Critical Thinking quizzes for the A & B instructional projects
- A **final output image** is provided so students can visualize what their solution should look like.
- **Mac Compatibility:** All Grader projects are built for PC and Mac users, excluding Access. Only projects that have features not supported on the Mac are not 100% compatible.

What's New for Simulations

- Simulations are updated by the authors for improved reinforcement of the software navigation in each instructional project—as always, they are matched one-to-one with the text Activities.
- *Student Action Visualization* provides an immediate playback for review by students and instructors when there's a question about why an action is marked as incorrect.

The Program

The GO! series has been used for over 17 years to teach students Microsoft Office successfully because of the *Quality of Instruction*, *Ease of Implementation*, and *Excellence in Assessment*. Using the hallmark Microsoft Procedural Syntax and Teachable Moment approach, students understand how to navigate the Microsoft Office ribbon so they don't get lost, and they get additional instruction and tips *when* they need them. Learning by doing is a great approach for skill-based learning, and creating a real-world document, spreadsheet, presentation, or database puts the skills in context for effective learning!

To improve student results, we recommend pairing the text content with **MyLab IT,** which is the teaching and learning platform that empowers you to reach every student. By combining trusted author content with digital tools and a flexible platform, MyLab personalizes the learning experience and will help your students learn and retain key course concepts while developing skills that future employers are seeking in their candidates.

Solving Teaching and Learning Challenges

The GO! series continues to evolve based on author interaction and experience with real students. GO! is written to ensure students know where they are going, how to get there, and why. Today's software is cloud based and changes frequently, so students need to know how the software functions so they can adapt quickly.

Each chapter is written with two instructional projects organized around **student learning outcomes** and **numbered objectives,** so that students understand what they will learn and be able to do when they finish the chapter. The **project approach** clusters the learning objectives around the projects rather than around the software features. This tested pedagogical approach teaches students to solve real problems as they practice and learn the software features. By using the textbook (print or digital), students can complete the A & B instructional projects as autograded Grader projects in MyLab IT. The *Learn How* videos, integrated in the etext or learning modules, give students an instructor-led, step-by-step guide through the project. This unique approach enhances learning and engages students because they receive immediate feedback. Additionally, students can practice the skills they are learning in the MyLab IT simulations, where they also get immediate feedback and help when needed! Both *Graders* and *Simulations* are available in assessment form so that students can demonstrate mastery.

The **Clear Instruction** in the project steps is written following *Microsoft Procedural Syntax* to guide students where to go and *then* what to do, so they never get lost! With the **Teachable Moment** approach, students learn important concepts when they need to as they work through the instructional projects. No long paragraphs of text. And with the integrated etext in MyLab IT, students can access their book anywhere, anytime.

The page design drives effective learning; textbook pages are clean and uncluttered, with screenshots that validate the student's actions and engage visual learners. Important information is boxed within the text so that students won't miss or skip the *Mac Tips*, *Another Way*, *By Touch*, *Note*, *Alert*, or *More Knowledge* details. **Color-Coded Steps** guide students through the projects with colors coded by project and the **End-of-Project Icon** helps students know when they have completed the project, which is especially useful in self-paced or online environments.

Students can engage in a wide variety of end-of-chapter projects where they apply what they learned in outcomes-based, problem-solving, and critical thinking projects—many of which require students to create a complete project from scratch.

Within the GO! etext and MyLab IT, students also have access to the *GO! Learn How* training videos, the *GO! to Work* videos (which demonstrate how Microsoft Office is used in a variety of jobs), the GO! for Job Success videos (which teach essential employability skills), and the *Where We're Going* videos, which provide a clear and concise overview of the instructional projects to ensure student success!

This complete, highly effective offering ensures students can learn the skills they need to succeed!

Developing Employability Skills

For students to succeed in a rapidly changing job market, they should be aware of their career options and how to go about developing a variety of skills. With MyLab IT and GO! we focus on developing these skills in the following ways:

High-Demand Office Skills are taught to help students gain these skills and prepare for the Microsoft Office Specialist (MOS) certification exams. The MOS objectives are covered throughout the content and highlighted with the MOS icons.

Essential Employability Skills are taught throughout the chapters using GO! for Job Success Videos and discussions, along with the new Critical Thinking badge students can earn by successfully completing the Critical Thinking Modules.

Employability Skills Matrix (ESM)							
	Grader Projects	Project K	Project M	Project O Group Project	Critical Thinking Projects and Badge	GO! To Work and Job Success Videos	MOS Practice Exams	MOS Badges
Critical Thinking	x	x	x		x		x	x
Communication	x			x		x		
Collaboration				x		x		
Knowledge Application and Analysis	x	x	x		x		x	x
Social Responsibility						x		

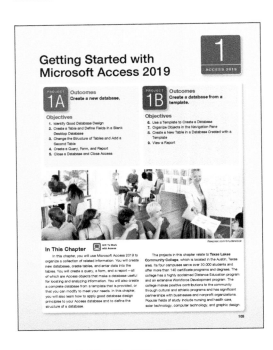

Getting Started with Microsoft Access 2019

1A Outcomes
Create a new database.

Objectives
1. Identify Good Database Design
2. Create a Table and Define Fields in a Blank Desktop Database
3. Change the Structure of Tables and Add a Second Table
4. Create a Query, Form, and Report
5. Close a Database and Close Access

1B Outcomes
Create a database from a template.

Objectives
6. Use a Template to Create a Database
7. Organize Objects in the Navigation Pane
8. Create a New Table in a Database Created with a Template
9. View a Report

In This Chapter

In this chapter, you will use Microsoft Access 2019 to organize a collection of related information. You will create new databases, create tables, and enter data into the tables. You will create a query, a form, and a report—all of which are Access objects that make a database useful for locating and analyzing information. You will also create a complete database from a template that is provided, or that you can modify to meet your needs. In this chapter, you will also learn how to apply good database design principles to your Access database and to define the structure of a database.

The projects in this chapter relate to Texas Lakes Community College, which is located in the Austin, Texas area. Its four campuses serve over 30,000 students and offer more than 140 certificate programs and degrees. The college has a highly acclaimed Distance Education program and an extensive Workforce Development program. The college makes positive contributions to the community through cultural and athletic programs and has significant partnerships with businesses and nonprofit organizations. Popular fields of study include nursing and health care, solar technology, computer technology, and graphic design.

◀ Real-World Projects and GO! To Work Videos

The projects in GO! help you learn skills you'll need in the workforce and everyday life. And the GO! to Work videos give you insight into how people in a variety of jobs put Microsoft Office into action every day.

◀ Projects in GO! are real-world projects you create from start to finish, so that you are using the software features and skills as you will on the job and in everyday life.

GO! to Work videos feature people from a variety of real jobs ◀ explaining how they use Microsoft Office every day to help you see the relevance of learning these programs.

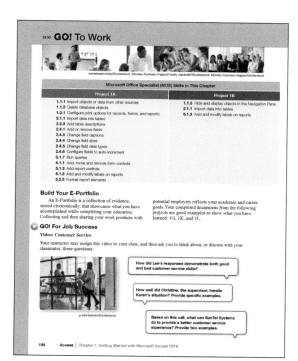

GO! for Job Success Videos and Discussions

Important professional skills you need to succeed in a work environment, such as Accepting Criticism, Customer Service, and Interview Skills, are covered in a video with discussion questions or an overall discussion topic. These are must-have skills.

Skills Badging

Within MyLab IT 2019, you can earn digital badges that demonstrate mastery of specific skills related to Office 2019 or Critical Thinking. These badges can be easily shared across social networks, such as LinkedIn, leading to real opportunities to connect with potential employers.

Applied Learning Opportunities

Throughout the chapters there are two projects for instruction, two for review, and a variety of outcomes-based projects to demonstrate mastery, critical thinking, and problem solving. In addition, within MyLab IT, GO! Learn How videos walk students through the A & B instructional project objectives. Grader projects and simulations provide hands-on instruction, training, and assessment.

▼ Live-in-the-Application Grader Projects

The MyLab IT Grader projects are autograded so students receive immediate feedback on their work. By completing these projects, students gain real-world context as they work live in the application, to learn and demonstrate an understanding of how to perform specific skills to complete a project.

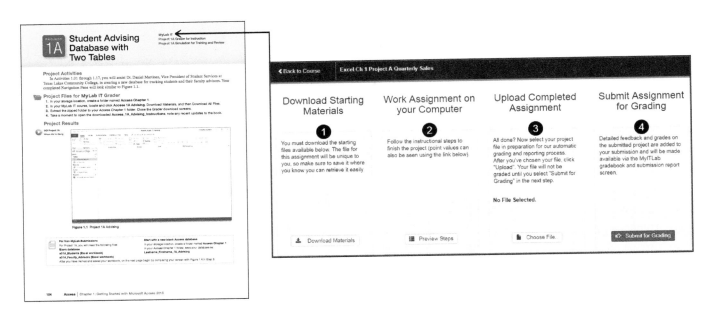

▼ Microsoft Office Simulations

The realistic and hi-fidelity simulations help students feel like they are working in the real Microsoft applications and enable them to explore, use 96% of Microsoft methods, and do so without penalty.

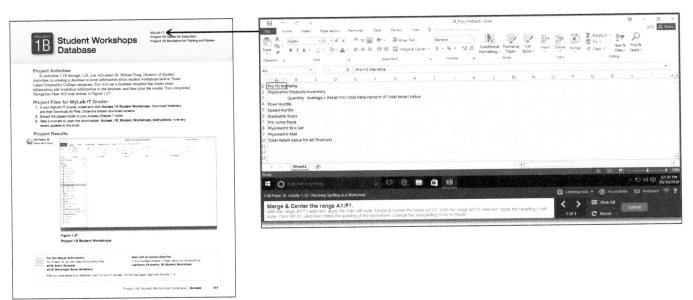

Instructor Teaching Resources

This program comes with the following teaching resources.

Resources available to instructors at www.pearsonhighered.com/go	Features of the Resources
Annotated Instructor Edition Tabs	Available for each chapter and include: • Suggested course implementation strategies and resources for the instructional portion of the chapter • Suggested strategies and resources for the Review, Practice, and Assessment portion of the chapter • Teaching tips
Annotated Solution Files	Annotated solution files in PDF feature callouts to enable easy grading.
Answer Keys for Chapter, MOS, and Critical Thinking Quizzes	Answer keys for each matching and multiple choice question in the chapter.
Application Capstones	Capstone projects for Word, Excel, Access, and PowerPoint that cover the objectives from all three chapters of each application. These are available as autograded Grader projects in MyLab IT, where students can also earn a proficiency badge if they score 90% or higher.
Collaborative Team Project	An optional exercise to assign to students to learn to work in groups.
Content Updates	A living document that features any changes in content based on Microsoft Office 365 changes as well as any errata.
Critical Thinking Quiz and Answers	Additional quiz and answers.
End-of-Chapter Online Projects H-J and M-O	Additional projects that can be assigned at instructor discretion.
Image Library	Every image in the book.
Instructor Manual	Available for each chapter and includes: • Suggested course implementation strategies and resources for the instructional portion of the chapter • Suggested strategies and resources for the Review, Practice, and Assessment portion of the chapter • Objectives • Teaching notes • Discussion questions
List of Objectives and Outcomes	Available for each chapter to help you determine what to assign • Includes every project and identifies which outcomes, objectives, and skills are included from the chapter
Lessons on the GO!	Projects created to teach new features added to Office 365. Available online only.
MOS Mapping and Additional Content	Based on the Office 2019 MOS Objectives • Includes a full guide of where each objective is covered in the textbook. • For any content not covered in the textbook, additional material is available in the Online Appendix document.
PowerPoint Presentations	PowerPoints for each chapter cover key topics, feature key images from the text, and include detailed speaker notes in addition to the slide content. PowerPoints meet accessibility standards for students with disabilities. Features include, but are not limited to: • Keyboard and screen reader access • Alternative text for images • High color contrast between background and foreground colors Audio PPTs contain spoken audio within traditional PowerPoint presentations.
Prepared Exams by Project, Chapter, and Application	An optional exercise that can be used to assess students' ability to perform the skills from each project, chapter, or across all chapters in an application • Each Prepared Exam folder includes the needed data files, instruction file, solution, annotated solution, and scorecard.

Resources available to instructors at www.pearsonhighered.com/go	Features of the Resources
Scorecards and Rubrics	Scorecards allow for easy scoring when hand-grading projects with definitive solutions. Rubrics are for projects without a definitive solution. These are available in Microsoft Word format, enabling instructors to customize the assignments for their classes.
Scripted Lectures	A lecture guide that provides the actions and language to help instructors demonstrate skills from the chapter.
Skills and Procedures Summary Charts	Concise list of key skills, including software icon and keyboard shortcut.
Solution Files, Solution File PDFs, and Solution Files with Formulas (Excel only)	Available for all exercises with definitive solutions.
Student Data Files	Files that students need to complete projects that are not delivered as Grader projects in MyLab IT.
Syllabus Template	Syllabus templates set up for 8-week, 12-week, and 16-week courses.
TestGen and Test Bank	TestGen enables instructors to: • Customize, save, and generate classroom tests • Edit, add, or delete questions from the Test Item Files • Analyze test results • Organize a database of tests and student results. The Test Gen contains approximately 75–100 total questions per chapter, made up of multiple-choice, fill-in the blank, true/false, and matching. Questions include these annotations: • Correct answer • Difficulty level • Learning objective Alternative versions of the Test Bank are available for the following LMS: Blackboard CE/Vista, Blackboard, Desire2Learn, Moodle, Sakai, and Canvas.
Transition Guide	A detailed spreadsheet that provides a clear mapping of content from GO! Microsoft Office 2016 to GO! Microsoft Office 365, 2019 Edition.

Reviewers of the GO! Series

Carmen Montanez	Allan Hancock College
Jody Derry	Allan Hancock College
Roberta McDonald	Anoka-Ramsey Community College
Paula Ruby	Arkansas State University
Buffie Schmidt	Augusta University
Julie Lewis	Baker College
Melanie Israel	Beal College
Suzanne Marks	Bellevue College
Ellen Glazer	Broward College
Charline Nixon	Calhoun Community College
Joseph Cash	California State University, Stanislaus
Shaun Sides	Catawba Valley Community College
Linda Friedel	Central Arizona College
Vicky Semple	Central Piedmont Community College
Amanda Davis	Chattanooga State Community College
Randall George	Clarion University of Pennsylvania
Beth Zboran	Clarion University of Pennsylvania
Lee Southard	College of Coastal Georgia
Susan Mazzola	College of the Sequoias
Vicki Brooks	Columbia College
Leasa Richards-Mealy	Columbia College
Heidi Eaton	Elgin Community College
Ed Pearson	Friends University
Nancy Woolridge	Fullerton College
Wayne Way	Galveston College
Leslie Martin	Gaston College
Don VanOeveren	Grand Rapids Community College

Therese ONeil	Indiana University of Pennsylvania
Bradley Howard	Itawamba Community College
Edna Tull	Itawamba Community College
Pamela Larkin	Jefferson Community and Technical College
Sonya Shockley	Madisonville Community College
Jeanne Canale	Middlesex Community College
John Meir	Midlands Technical College
Robert Huyck	Mohawk Valley Community College
Mike Maesar	Montana Tech
Julio Cuz	Moreno Valley College
Lynn Wermers	North Shore Community College
Angela Mott	Northeast Mississippi Community College
Connie Johnson	Owensboro Community & Technical College
Kungwen Chu	Purdue University Northwest
Kuan Chen	Purdue University Northwest
Janette Nichols	Randolph Community College
Steven Zhang	Roane State Community College
Elizabeth Drake	Santa Fe College
Sandy Keeter	Seminole State
Pat Dennis	South Plains College
Tamara Dawson	Southern Nazarene University
Richard Celli	SUNY Delhi
Lois Blais	Walters State Community College
Frederick MacCormack	Wilmington University
Jessica Brown	Wilmington University
Doreen Palucci	Wilmington University
Rebecca Anderson	Zane State College

Microsoft Office Features and Windows 10 File Management

1
OFFICE AND WINDOWS

PROJECT 1A

Outcomes
Use the features common across all Microsoft Office applications to create and save a Microsoft Word document.

Objectives
1. Explore Microsoft Office
2. Create a Folder for File Storage
3. Download and Extract Zipped Files, Enter and Edit Text in an Office Application, and use Editor to Check Documents
4. Perform Office Commands and Apply Office Formatting
5. Finalize an Office Document
6. Use the Office Help Features

PROJECT 1B

Outcomes
Use Windows 10 features and the File Explorer program to manage files and folders.

Objectives
7. Explore Windows 10
8. Prepare to Work with Folders and Files
9. Use File Explorer to Extract Zipped Files and to Display Locations, Folders, and Files
10. Start Programs and Open Data Files
11. Create, Rename, and Copy Files and Folders

Petar Djordjevic/Shutterstock

In This Chapter

GO! To Work
with Office Features

In this chapter, you will practice using the features of Microsoft Office that work similarly across Word, Excel, Access, and PowerPoint. These features include performing commands, adding document properties, applying formatting to text, and searching for Office commands quickly. You will also practice using the file management features of Windows 10 so that you can create folders, save files, and find your documents easily.

The projects in this chapter relate to the **Bell Orchid Hotels**, headquartered in Boston, and which own and operate restaurants, resorts, and business-oriented hotels. Resort property locations are in popular destinations, including Honolulu, Orlando, San Diego, and Santa Barbara. The resorts offer deluxe accommodations and a wide array of dining options. Other Bell Orchid hotels are located in major business centers and offer the latest technology in their meeting facilities. Bell Orchid offers extensive educational opportunities for employees. The company plans to open new properties and update existing properties over the next decade.

Chef Notes

Project Activities

In Activities 1.01 through 1.19, you will create a handout for the Executive Chef at Skyline Metro Grill to give to her staff at a meeting where they will develop new menu ideas for wedding rehearsal dinners. The restaurant is located within Bell Orchid's San Diego resort hotel. Your completed notes will look similar to Figure 1.1.

Project Files for **MyLab IT Grader**

1. For Project 1A, you will start with a blank Word document, and then you will learn how to create a folder for your **MyLab IT** files as you work through the Project instruction. At the appropriate point in the Project, you will be instructed to download your files from your **MyLab IT** course.

Project Results

GO! Project 1A

Where We're Going

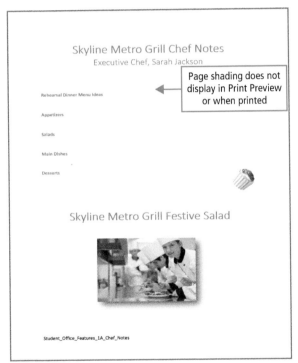

Figure 1.1 (Wavebreakmedia/Shutterstock)

For Non-MyLab Submissions   **Start with a blank Word document**

For Project 1A, you will begin with a blank Word document and then learn how to create a folder and save a Word document as you work through the Project instruction.

NOTE   If You Are Using a Touch Screen

Tap an item to click it.

Press and hold for a few seconds to right-click; release when the information or commands display.

Touch the screen with two or more fingers and then pinch together to zoom out or stretch your fingers apart to zoom in.

Slide your finger on the screen to scroll—slide left to scroll right and slide right to scroll left.

Slide to rearrange—similar to dragging with a mouse.

Swipe to select—slide an item a short distance with a quick movement—to select an item and bring up commands, if any.

Objective 1   **Explore Microsoft Office**

ALERT   Because Office 365 is a cloud-based subscription service that receives continuous updates, you may encounter some variations in what appears on your screen and what is shown in this instruction. Microsoft Office 365 is fully installed on your PC or Mac; no internet access is necessary to create or edit documents. When you *are* connected to the internet, you will receive monthly upgrades and new features, so you always have the latest versions of Office apps as soon as they are available. Your subscription gives you continuous free access to the latest innovations and refinements.

ALERT   **Is Your Screen More Colorful and a Different Size Than the Figures in This Textbook?**

Your installation of Microsoft Office may use the default Colorful theme, where the ribbon in each application is a vibrant color and the title bar displays with white text. In this textbook, figures shown use the White theme, but you can be assured that all the commands are the same. You can keep your Colorful theme, or if you prefer, you can change your theme to White to match the figures here. To do so, open any application and display a new document. On the ribbon, click the File tab, and then on the left, click Options. With General selected on the left, under Personalize your copy of Microsoft Office, click the Office Theme arrow, and then click White. Change the Office Background to No Background. (In macOS, display the menu bar, click the application name—Word, Excel, and so on—click Preferences, and then click General. Under Personalize, click the Office Theme arrow to select either Colorful or Classic.)

Additionally, the figures in this book were captured using a screen resolution of 1280 x 768. If that is not your screen resolution, your screen will closely resemble, but not match, the figures shown. To view or change your screen's resolution, on the desktop, right-click in a blank area, click Display settings, click the Resolution arrow, and then select the resolution you want.

GO! Learn How
Video OF1-1

The term ***desktop application*** or ***desktop app*** refers to a computer program that is installed on your PC and that requires a computer operating system such as Microsoft Windows to run. The programs in Office 365 and in Microsoft Office 2019 are considered to be desktop apps. A desktop app typically has hundreds of features and takes time to learn.

Activity 1.01 | Exploring Microsoft Office

1 On the computer you are using, start Microsoft Word, and then compare your screen with Figure 1.2.

Depending on which operating system you are using and how your computer is set up, you might start Word from the taskbar or from the Start menu. On an Apple Mac computer, you might start the program from the Dock.

On the left, the Home tab is active in this view, referred to as *Backstage view*, which is a centralized space for all your file management tasks such as opening, saving, printing, publishing, or sharing a file—all the things you can do *with* a file. In macOS the File tab is on the menu bar.

Documents that you have recently opened, if any, display under the Recent tab. You can also click the Pinned tab to see documents you have pinned there, or you can click the Shared with Me tab to see documents that have been shared with you by others.

On the left, you can click New to find a *template*—a preformatted document that you can use as a starting point and then change to suit your needs. Or you can click Open to navigate to your files and folders. You can also look at Account information, give feedback to Microsoft, or look at the Word Options dialog box.

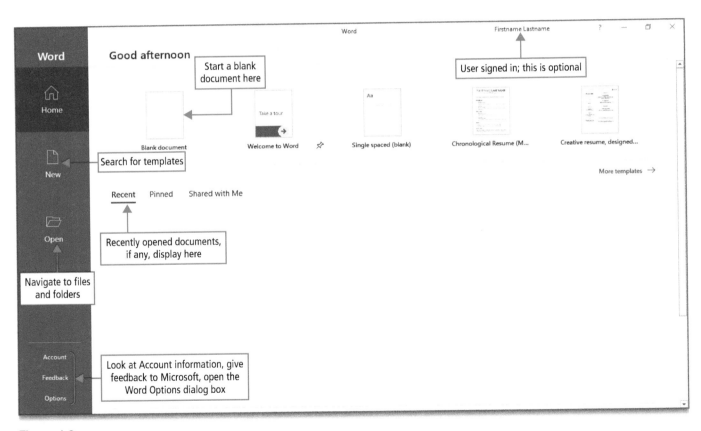

Figure 1.2

2 Click **Blank document**. Compare your screen with Figure 1.3, and then take a moment to study the description of the screen elements in the table in Figure 1.4.

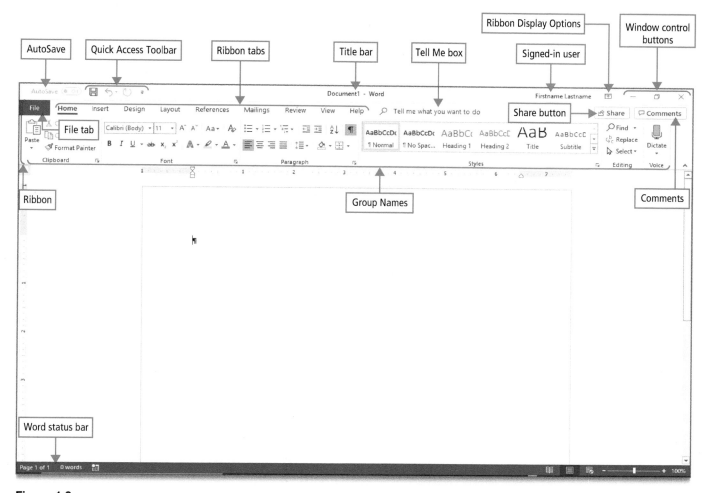

Figure 1.3

Screen Element	Description
AutoSave (off unless your document is saved to OneDrive using an Office 365 subscription)	Saves your document every few seconds so you don't have to. On a Windows system, AutoSave is available in Word, Excel, and PowerPoint for Office 365 subscribers. AutoSave is enabled only when a file is stored on OneDrive, OneDrive for Business, or SharePoint Online. Changes to your document are saved to the cloud as you are working, and if other people are working on the same file, AutoSave lets them see your changes in a matter of seconds.
Comments	Displays a short menu from which you can add a comment to your document or view other comments already in the document.
File tab	Displays Microsoft Office Backstage view, which is a centralized space for all your file management tasks such as opening, saving, printing, publishing, or sharing a file—all the things you can do *with* a file. (In macOS the File tab is on the menu bar.)
Group names	Indicate the name of the groups of related commands on the displayed ribbon tab.
Quick Access Toolbar	Displays buttons to perform frequently used commands and resources with a single click. The default commands include Save, Undo, and Redo. You can add and delete buttons to customize the Quick Access Toolbar for your convenience.
Ribbon	Displays a group of task-oriented tabs that contain the commands, styles, and resources you need to work in Microsoft Office desktop apps. The look of your ribbon depends on your screen resolution. A high resolution will display more individual items and button names on the ribbon.
Ribbon Display Options	Displays three ways you can display the ribbon: Auto-hide Ribbon, Show Tabs, or Show Tabs and Commands; typically, you will want to use Show Tabs and Commands, especially while you are learning Office.
Ribbon tabs	Display the names of the task-oriented tabs relevant to the open document.
Share	Opens the Share dialog box from which you can save your file to the cloud—your OneDrive—and then share it with others so you can collaborate. Here you can also email the Office file or a PDF of the file directly from Outlook if you are using Outlook to view and send email. A *dialog box* enables you to make decisions about an individual object or topic.
Signed-in user	Identifies the user who is signed in to Office.
Status bar	Displays file information on the left; on the right displays buttons for Read Mode, Print Layout, and Web Layout views; on the far right edge, displays Zoom controls.
Tell me what you want to do	Provides a search feature for Microsoft Office commands that you activate by typing what you are looking for in the *Tell me what you want to do* area. As you type, every keystroke refines the results so that you can click the command as soon as it displays.
Title bar	Displays the name of the file and the name of the program; the window control buttons are grouped on the right side of the title bar.
Window control buttons	Displays buttons for commands to Minimize, Restore Down, or Close the window.

Figure 1.4

Objective 2   Create a Folder for File Storage

GO! Learn How
Video OF1-2

A *location* is any disk drive, folder, or other place in which you can store files and folders. A *file* is information stored on a computer under a single name. A *folder* is a container in which you store files. Where you store your files depends on how and where you use your data. For example, for your college classes, you might decide to store your work on a removable USB flash drive so that you can carry your files to different locations and access your files on different computers.

If you do most of your work on a single computer, for example your home desktop system or your laptop computer that you take with you to school or work, then you can store your files in one of the folders on your hard drive provided by your Windows operating system—Documents, Music, Pictures, or Videos.

The best place to store files if you want them to be available anytime, anywhere, from almost any device is on your **OneDrive**, which is Microsoft's free **cloud storage** for anyone with a free Microsoft account. Cloud storage refers to online storage of data so that you can access your data from different places and devices. **Cloud computing** refers to applications and services that are accessed over the internet, rather than to applications that are installed on your local computer.

Besides being able to access your documents from any device or location, OneDrive also offers **AutoSave**, which saves your document every few seconds, so you don't have to. On a Windows system, AutoSave is available in Word, Excel, and PowerPoint for Office 365 subscribers. Changes to your document are saved to the cloud as you are working, and if other people are working on the same file—referred to as **real-time co-authoring**—AutoSave lets them see your changes in a matter of seconds.

If you have an **Office 365** subscription—one of the versions of Microsoft Office to which you subscribe for an annual fee or download for free with your college *.edu* address—your storage capacity on OneDrive is a terabyte or more, which is more than most individuals would ever require. Many colleges provide students with free Office 365 subscriptions. The advantage of subscribing to Office 365 is that you receive monthly updates with new features.

Because many people now have multiple computing devices—desktop, laptop, tablet, smartphone—it is common to store data *in the cloud* so that it is always available. **Synchronization**, also called **syncing**—pronounced SINK-ing—is the process of updating computer files that are in two or more locations according to specific rules. So, if you create and save a Word document on your OneDrive using your laptop, you can open and edit that document on your tablet in OneDrive. When you close the document again, the file is properly updated to reflect your changes. Your OneDrive account will guide you in setting options for syncing files to your specifications. You can open and edit Office files by using Office apps available on a variety of device platforms, including iOS, Android, in a web browser, and in Windows.

> **MORE KNOWLEDGE**   **Creating a Microsoft Account**
>
> Use a free Microsoft account to sign in to Microsoft Office so that you can work on different PCs and use your free OneDrive cloud storage. If you already sign in to a Windows PC or tablet, or you sign in to Xbox Live, Outlook.com, or OneDrive, use that account to sign in to Office. To create a new Microsoft account, in your browser, search for *sign up for a Microsoft account*. You can use any email address as the user name for your new Microsoft account—including addresses from Outlook.com or Gmail.

Activity 1.02 | Creating a Folder for File Storage

Your computer's operating system, either Windows or macOS, helps you to create and maintain a logical folder structure, so always take the time to name your files and folders consistently.

> **NOTE**   **This Activity is for Windows PC users. Mac users refer to the document** *Creating a Folder for File Storage on a Mac*.
>
> Mac users can refer to the document Creating a Folder for File Storage on a Mac available within **MyLab IT** or, for non-MyLab users, your instructor can provide this document to you from the Instructor Resource Center.

In this Activity, you will create a folder in the storage location you have chosen to use for your files, and then you will save your file. This example will use the Documents folder on the PC at which you are working. If you prefer to store on your OneDrive or on a USB flash drive, you can use similar steps.

1 ▶ Decide where you are going to store your files for this Project.

As the first step in saving a file, determine where you want to save the file, and if necessary, insert a storage device.

2 At the top of your screen, in the title bar, notice that *Document1 – Word* displays.

> The Blank option on the opening screen of an Office program displays a new unsaved file with a default name—*Document1, Presentation1*, and so on. As you create your file, your work is temporarily stored in the computer's memory until you initiate a Save command, at which time you must choose a file name and a location in which to save your file.

3 In the upper left corner of your screen, click the **File tab** to display **Backstage** view, and then on the left, if necessary, click **Info**. Compare your screen with Figure 1.5.

> Recall that Backstage view is a centralized space that groups commands related to *file* management; that is why the tab is labeled *File*. File management commands include opening, saving, printing, or sharing a file. The **Backstage tabs**—*Info, New, Open, Save, Save As, Print, Share, Export,* and *Close*—display along the left side. The tabs group file-related tasks together.

> Here, the **Info tab** displays information—*info*—about the current file, and file management commands display under Info. For example, if you click the Protect Document button, a list of options that you can set for this file that relate to who can open or edit the document displays.

> On the right, you can also examine the **document properties**. Document properties, also known as **metadata**, are details about a file that describe or identify it, such as the title, author name, subject, and keywords that identify the document's topic or contents.

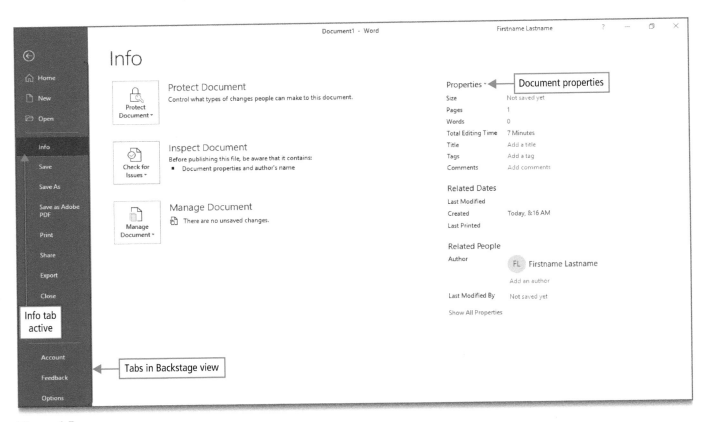

Figure 1.5

4 On the left, click **Save As**, and notice that, if you are signed into Office with a Microsoft account, one option for storing your files is your **OneDrive**. Compare your screen with Figure 1.6.

> When you are saving something for the first time, for example a new Word document, the Save and Save As commands are identical. That is, the Save As commands will display if you click Save or if you click Save As.

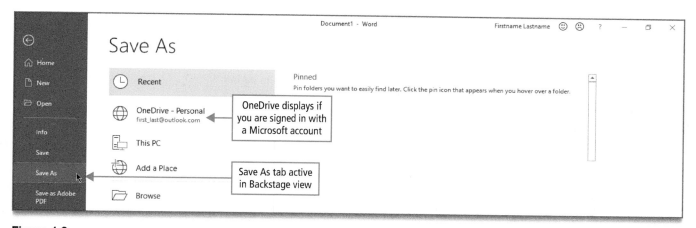

Figure 1.6

NOTE   Saving After Your File Is Named

After you name and save a file, the Save command on the Quick Access Toolbar saves any changes you make to the file without displaying Backstage view. The Save As command enables you to name and save a *new* file based on the current one—in a location that you choose. After you name and save the new document, the original document closes, and the new document—based on the original one—displays.

5 To store your Word file in the **Documents** folder on your PC, click **Browse** to display the **Save As** dialog box. On the left, in the **navigation pane**, scroll down; if necessary click > to expand This PC, and then click **Documents**. Compare your screen with Figure 1.7.

In the Save As dialog box, you must indicate the name you want for the file and the location where you want to save the file. When working with your own data, it is good practice to pause at this point and determine the logical name and location for your file.

In the Save As dialog box, a *toolbar* displays, which is a row, column, or block of buttons or icons, that displays across the top of a window and that contains commands for tasks you perform with a single click.

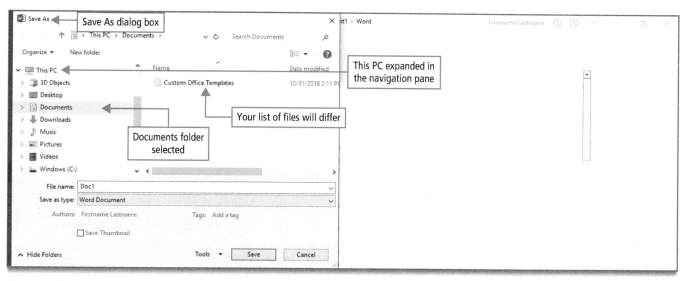

Figure 1.7

6 On the toolbar, click **New folder**.

In the file list, Windows creates a new folder, and the text *New folder* is selected.

7 Type **Office Features Chapter 1** and press [Enter]. In the **file list**, double-click the name of your new folder to open it and display its name in the **address bar**. Compare your screen with Figure 1.8.

In Windows-based programs, the [Enter] key confirms an action.

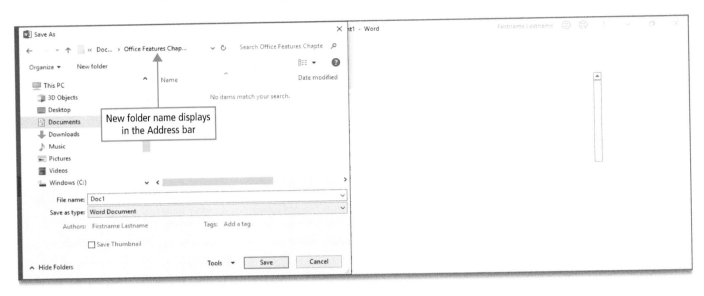

New folder name displays in the Address bar

Figure 1.8

8 In the lower right corner of the **Save As** dialog box, click **Cancel**. In the upper left corner of Backstage view, click the **Back** arrow [←].

9 In the upper right corner of the Word window, click **Close** [×]. If prompted to save your changes, click Don't Save. Close any other open windows or programs.

| Objective 3 | **Download and Extract Zipped Files, Enter and Edit Text in an Office Application, and Use Editor to Check Documents** |

GO! Learn How
Video OF1-3

Download refers to the action of transferring or copying a file from another location—such as a cloud storage location, your college's Learning Management System, or from an internet site like **MyLab IT**—to your computer. Files that you download are frequently *compressed files*, which are files that have been reduced in size, take up less storage space, and can be transferred to other computers faster than uncompressed files.

A compressed folder might contain a group of files that were combined into one compressed folder, which makes it easier to share a group of files. To *extract* means to decompress, or pull out, files from a compressed form. The terms *zip* and *unzip* refer to the process of compressing (zipping) and extracting (unzipping). Windows 10 includes *Compressed Folder Tools*, available on the ribbon, to assist you in extracting compressed files. Similar tools are available in macOS. You do not need to install a separate program to zip or unzip files; modern operating systems like Windows and macOS provide sophisticated tools for these tasks.

All programs in Microsoft Office require some typed text. Your keyboard is still the primary method of entering information into your computer. Techniques to enter text and to *edit*—make changes to—text are similar across all Microsoft Office programs.

For Non-MyLab Submissions
Start Word and click Blank document. Click the File tab, on the left click Save As, click Browse, and then navigate to your **Office Features Chapter 1 folder.** At the bottom of the **Save As** dialog box, in the **File name** box, using your own name, name the file **Lastname_Firstname_Office_Features_1A_Chef_Notes** and then click Save. Then, move to Step 3 in Activity 1.03.

Activity 1.03 | **Downloading and Extracting Zipped Files from MyLab IT and Entering and Editing Text in an Office Program**

1 ▶ Sign in to your **MyLab IT** course. Locate and click the Grader project **Office Features 1A Chef Notes**, click **Download Materials**, and then click **Download All Files**. Using the Chrome browser (if you are using a different browser see notes below), extract the zipped folder to your **Office Features Chapter 1 folder** as follows (or use your favorite method to download and extract files):

- In the lower left, next to the downloaded zipped folder, click the small **arrow**, and then click **Show in folder**. The zipped folder displays in *File Explorer*—the Windows program that displays the contents of locations, folders, and files on your computer—in the Downloads folder. (Unless you have changed default settings, downloaded files go to the Downloads folder on your computer.)
- With the zipped folder selected, on the ribbon, under **Compressed Folder Tools**, click the **Extract tab**, and then at the right end of the ribbon, click **Extract all** (you may have to wait a few seconds for the command to become active).
- In the displayed **Extract Compressed (Zipped) Folders** dialog box, click **Browse**. In the **Select a destination** dialog box, use the navigation pane on the left to navigate to your **Office Features Chapter 1 folder**, and double-click its name to open the folder and display its name in the **Address bar**.
- In the lower right, click **Select Folder**, and then in the lower right, click **Extract**; when complete, a new File Explorer window displays showing the extracted files in your chapter folder. Take a moment to open **Office_Features_1A_Chef_Notes_Instructions**; note any recent updates to the book.
- **Close** ⊠ both File Explorer windows, close any open documents, and then close the Grader download screens. You can also close **MyLab IT** and, if open, your Learning Management system.

NOTE **Using the Edge Browser or Firefox Browser to Extract Files**

Microsoft Edge: At the bottom, click Open, click Extract all, click Browse, navigate to and open your Chapter folder, click Select Folder, click Extract.

Firefox: In the displayed dialog box, click OK, click Extract all, click Browse, navigate to and open your Chapter folder, click Select Folder, and then click Extract.

🖥 **MAC TIP** Using the Chrome browser, in **MyLab IT**, after you click Download Materials, in the lower left, to the right of the zipped folder, click the arrow. Click Open. Click the blue folder containing the unzipped files. Use Finder commands to move or copy the files to your Office Features Chapter 1 folder.

2 ▶ On the Windows taskbar, click **File Explorer** 📁. Navigate to your **Office Features Chapter 1 folder**, and then double-click the Word file you downloaded from **MyLab IT** that displays your name—**Student_Office_Features_1A_Chef_Notes**. In this empty Word document, if necessary, at the top, click **Enable Editing**.

🖥 **MAC TIP** When the Word application is not open, on the Dock, use the macOS Finder commands to locate your Word document. When the Word application is open, use the File tab on the menu bar.

3 ▶ On the ribbon, on the **Home tab**, in the **Paragraph group**, if necessary, click **Show/Hide** ¶ so that it is active—shaded. On the **View tab**, if necessary, in the **Show group**, select the **Ruler** check box so that rulers display below the ribbon and on the left side of your window, and then redisplay the **Home tab**.

The *insertion point*—a blinking vertical line that indicates where text or graphics will be inserted—displays. In Office programs, the mouse *pointer*—any symbol that displays on your screen in response to moving your mouse device—displays in different shapes depending on the task you are performing and the area of the screen to which you are pointing.

When you press Enter, Spacebar, or Tab on your keyboard, characters display to represent these keystrokes. These screen characters do not print and are referred to as *formatting marks* or *nonprinting characters*.

When working in Word, display the rulers so that you can see how margin settings affect your document and how text and objects align. Additionally, if you set a tab stop or an indent, its location is visible on the ruler.

MAC TIP To display group names on the ribbon, display the menu bar, click Word, click Preferences, click View, under Ribbon, select the Show group titles check box.

NOTE   Activating Show/Hide in Word Documents

When Show/Hide is active—the button is shaded—formatting marks display. Because formatting marks guide your eye in a document—like a map and road signs guide you along a highway—these marks will display throughout this instruction. Expert Word users keep these marks displayed while creating documents.

4 Type **Skyline Grille Info** and notice how the insertion point moves to the right as you type. Point slightly to the right of the letter *e* in *Grille* and click to place the insertion point there. Compare your screen with Figure 1.9.

A *paragraph symbol* (¶) indicates the end of a paragraph and displays each time you press Enter. This is a type of formatting mark and does not print.

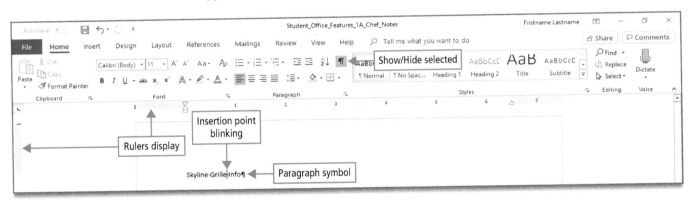

Figure 1.9

5 On your keyboard, locate and then press the Backspace key one time to delete the letter *e*.

Pressing Backspace removes a character to the left of the insertion point.

MAC TIP Press delete.

6 Press → one time to place the insertion point to the left of the *I* in *Info*. Type **Chef** and then press Spacebar one time.

By *default*, when you type text in an Office program, existing text moves to the right to make space for new typing. Default refers to the current selection or setting that is automatically used by a program unless you specify otherwise.

7 Press Del four times to delete *Info* and then type **Notes**

Pressing Del removes a character to the right of the insertion point.

MAC TIP Press fn + delete to delete characters to the right of the insertion point.

8 With your insertion point blinking after the word *Notes*, on your keyboard, hold down the Ctrl key. While holding down Ctrl, press ← three times to move the insertion point to the beginning of the word *Grill*.

> This is a ***keyboard shortcut***—a key or combination of keys that performs a task that would otherwise require a mouse. This keyboard shortcut moves the insertion point to the beginning of the previous word.

> A keyboard shortcut is indicated as Ctrl + ← (or some other combination of keys) to indicate that you hold down the first key while pressing the second key. A keyboard shortcut can also include three keys, in which case you hold down the first two and then press the third. For example, Ctrl + Shift + ← selects one word to the left.

🖥 **MAC TIP** Press option + ←.

---

9 With the insertion point blinking at the beginning of the word *Grill*, type **Metro** and press Spacebar one time.

10 Click to place the insertion point after the letter *s* in *Notes* and then press Enter one time. With the insertion point blinking, type the following and include the spelling error: **Exective Chef, Madison Dunham** (If Word autocorrects *Exective* to *Executive*, delete *u* in the word.)

11 With your mouse, point slightly to the left of the *M* in *Madison*, hold down the left mouse button, and then ***drag***—hold down the left mouse button while moving your mouse—to the right to select the text *Madison Dunham* but not the paragraph mark following it, and then release the mouse button. Compare your screen with Figure 1.10.

> The ***mini toolbar*** displays commands that are commonly used with the selected object, which places common commands close to your pointer. When you move the pointer away from the mini toolbar, it fades from view.

> ***Selecting*** refers to highlighting—by dragging or clicking with your mouse—areas of text or data or graphics so that the selection can be edited, formatted, copied, or moved. The action of dragging includes releasing the left mouse button at the end of the area you want to select.

> The Office programs recognize a selected area as one unit to which you can make changes. Selecting text may require some practice. If you are not satisfied with your result, click anywhere outside of the selection, and then begin again.

🖥 **MAC TIP** The mini toolbar may not display; use ribbon commands.

☞ **BY TOUCH** Tap once on *Madison* to display the gripper—a small circle that acts as a handle—directly below the word. This establishes the start gripper. If necessary, with your finger, drag the gripper to the beginning of the word. Then drag the gripper to the end of *Dunham* to select the text and display the end gripper.

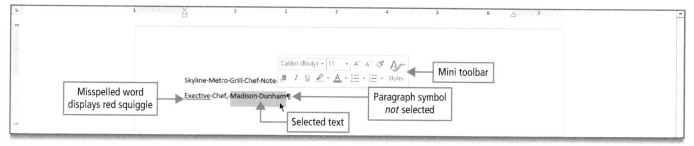

Figure 1.10

12 With the text *Madison Dunham* selected, type **Sarah Jackson**

In any Windows-based program, such as the Microsoft Office programs, selected text is deleted and then replaced when you begin to type new text. You will save time by developing good techniques for selecting and then editing or replacing selected text, which is easier than pressing Backspace or Del numerous times to delete text.

Activity 1.04 | Checking Spelling

Microsoft Office has a dictionary of words against which all entered text is checked. In Word and PowerPoint, words that are not in the dictionary display a red squiggle, indicating a possible misspelled word, a proper name, or an unusual word—none of which are in the Office dictionary. In Excel and Access, you can initiate a check of the spelling, but red squiggles do not display.

1 Notice that the misspelled word *Exective* displays with a red squiggle.

2 Point to *Exective* and then *right-click*—click your right mouse button one time.

A *shortcut menu* displays, which displays commands and options relevant to the selected text or object. These are *context-sensitive commands* because they relate to the item you right-clicked. These are also referred to as *context menus*. Here, the shortcut menu displays commands related to the misspelled word.

BY TOUCH   Tap and hold a moment—when a square displays around the misspelled word, release your finger to display the shortcut menu.

3 Press Esc two times to cancel the shortcut menus, and then in the lower left corner of your screen, on the status bar, click the **Proofing** icon, which displays an *X* because some errors are detected. In the **Editor** pane that displays on the right, if necessary, click the Results button, and then under **Suggestions**, to the right of *Executive*, click ▼, and then compare your screen with Figure 1.11.

The Editor pane displays on the right. *Editor*, according to Microsoft, is your digital writing assistant in Word and also in Outlook. Editor displays misspellings, grammatical mistakes, and writing style issues as you type by marking red squiggles for spelling, blue double underlines for grammar, and dotted underlines for writing style issues.

Here you have many more options for checking spelling than you have on the shortcut menu. The suggested correct word, *Executive*, displays under Suggestions. The displayed menu provides additional options for the suggestion. For example, you can have the word read aloud, hear it spelled out, change all occurrences in the document, or add to AutoCorrect options.

In the Editor pane, you can ignore the word one time or in all occurrences, change the word to the suggested word, select a different suggestion, or add a word to the dictionary against which Word checks.

MAC TIP   In the Spelling and Grammar dialog box, click Executive, and then click Change. The Editor pane is not available on a Mac.

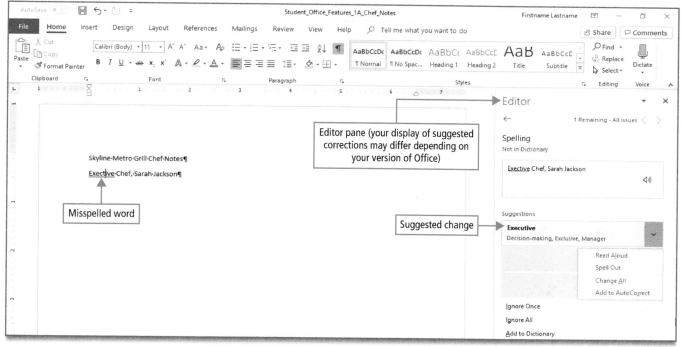

Figure 1.11

ANOTHER WAY Press [F7] to display the Editor pane; or, on the Review tab, in the Proofing group, you can check your document for Spelling.

4 In the **Editor** pane, under **Suggestions**, click *Executive* to correct the spelling. In the message box that displays, click **OK**.

5 If necessary **Close** the **Editor** pane by clicking ⊠ in the upper right corner.

Objective 4   Perform Office Commands and Apply Office Formatting

GO! Learn How
Video OF1-4

Formatting refers to applying Office commands to make your document easy to read and to add visual touches and design elements to make your document inviting to the reader. This process establishes the overall appearance of text, graphics, and pages in your document.

Activity 1.05 │ Performing Commands from a Dialog Box

MOS
1.2.4

In a dialog box, you make decisions about an individual object or topic. In some dialog boxes, you can make multiple decisions in one place.

1 On the ribbon, click the **Design tab**, and then in the **Page Background group**, click **Page Color**.

2 At the bottom of the menu, notice the command **Fill Effects** followed by an **ellipsis** (. . .). Compare your screen with Figure 1.12.

An *ellipsis* is a set of three dots indicating incompleteness. An ellipsis following a command name indicates that a dialog box will display when you click the command.

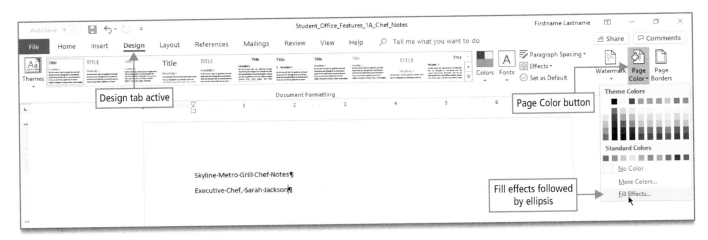

Figure 1.12

3 Click **Fill Effects** to display the **Fill Effects** dialog box. Compare your screen with Figure 1.13.

Fill is the inside color of a page or object. Here, the dialog box displays a set of tabs across the top from which you can display different sets of options. Some dialog boxes display the option group names on the left. The Gradient tab is active. In a *gradient fill*, one color fades into another.

MAC TIP Click More Colors to display the Colors dialog box.

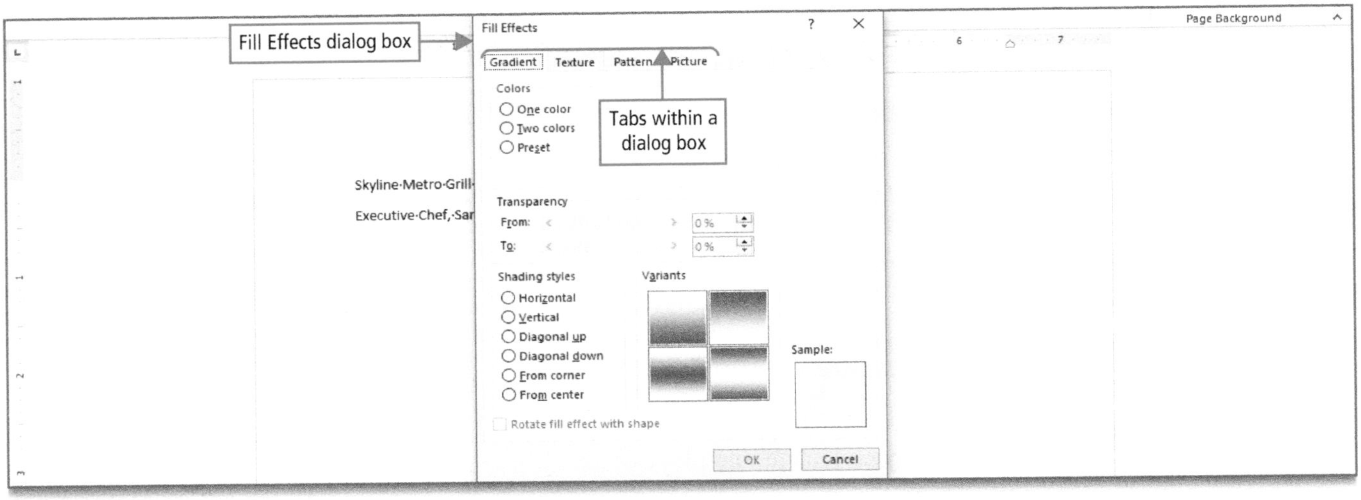

Figure 1.13

4 Under **Colors**, click the **One color** option button.

The dialog box displays settings related to the *One color* option. An ***option button*** is a round button that enables you to make one choice among two or more options.

5 Click the **Color 1 arrow**—the arrow under the text *Color 1*—and then in the eighth column, point to the second color to display a ScreenTip with the name of the color.

When you click an arrow in a dialog box, additional options display. A ***ScreenTip*** displays useful information about mouse actions, such as pointing to screen elements or dragging.

6 Click the color, and then notice that the fill color displays in the **Color 1** box. In the **Dark Light** bar, click the **Light arrow** as many times as necessary until the scroll box is all the way to the right—or drag the scroll box all the way to the right. Under **Shading styles**, click the **From corner** option button. Under **Variants**, click the **upper right variant**. Compare your screen with Figure 1.14.

This dialog box is a good example of the many different elements you may encounter in a dialog box. Here you have option buttons, an arrow that displays a menu, a slider bar, and graphic options that you can select.

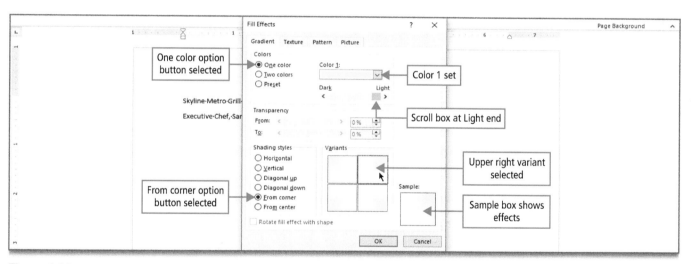

Figure 1.14

7 At the bottom of the dialog box, click **OK**, and notice the subtle page color.

In Word, the gold shading page color will not print—even on a color printer—unless you set specific options to do so. However, a subtle background page color is effective if people will be reading the document on a screen. Microsoft's research indicates that two-thirds of people who open Word documents on a screen never print or edit them; they only read them.

Activity 1.06 | Using Undo and Applying Text Effects

1 Point to the *S* in *Skyline*, and then drag down and to the right to select both paragraphs of text and include the paragraph marks. On the mini toolbar, click **Styles**, and then *point to* but do not click **Title**. Compare your screen with Figure 1.15.

> A *style* is a group of formatting commands, such as font, font size, font color, paragraph alignment, and line spacing that can be applied to a paragraph with one command.

> *Live Preview* is a technology that shows the result of applying an editing or formatting change as you point to possible results—before you actually apply it.

MAC TIP The mini toolbar and Live Preview are not available; use ribbon commands.

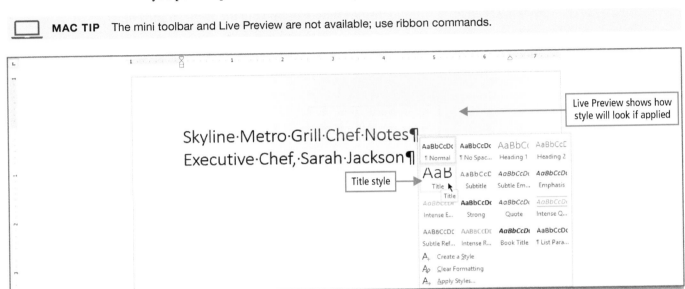

Figure 1.15

2 In the **Styles** gallery, click **Title**.

> A *gallery* is an Office feature that displays a list of potential results.

MAC TIP On the Home tab, in the Styles gallery, click Title.

3 On the ribbon, on the **Home tab**, in the **Paragraph group**, click **Center** ☰ to center the two paragraphs.

> *Alignment* refers to the placement of paragraph text relative to the left and right margins. *Center alignment* refers to text that is centered horizontally between the left and right margins. You can also align text at the left margin, which is the default alignment for text in Word, or at the right.

ANOTHER WAY Press Ctrl + E to use the Center command.

MAC TIP Press command ⌘ + E to use the Center command.

4 With the two paragraphs still selected, on the **Home tab**, in the **Font Group**, click **Text Effects and Typography** Ⓐ ▾ to display a gallery.

5 In the second row, click the first effect. Click anywhere to *deselect*—cancel the selection—the text and notice the text effect.

6 Because this effect might be difficult to read, in the upper left corner of your screen, on the **Quick Access Toolbar**, click **Undo** ↻.

The *Undo* command reverses your last action.

🔄 **ANOTHER WAY** Press Ctrl + Z as the keyboard shortcut for the Undo command.

💻 **MAC TIP** Press command ⌘ + Z as the keyboard shortcut for the Undo command.

7 Select the two paragraphs of text again, display the **Text Effects and Typography** gallery again, and then in the first row, click the fifth effect. Click anywhere to deselect the text and notice the text effect. Compare your screen with Figure 1.16.

As you progress in your study of Microsoft Office, you will practice using many dialog boxes and commands to apply interesting effects such as this to your Word documents, Excel worksheets, Access database objects, and PowerPoint slides.

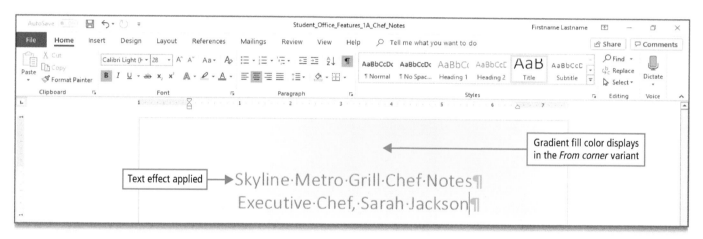

Figure 1.16

Activity 1.07 | Performing Commands from and Customizing the Quick Access Toolbar

The ribbon that displays across the top of the program window groups commands in the way that you would most logically use them. The ribbon in each Office program is slightly different, but all contain the same three elements: *tabs*, *groups*, and *commands*.

Tabs display across the top of the ribbon, and each tab relates to a type of activity; for example, laying out a page. Groups are sets of related commands for specific tasks. Commands— instructions to computer programs—are arranged in groups and might display as a button, a menu, or a box in which you type information.

You can also minimize the ribbon so only the tab names display, which is useful when working on a smaller screen such as a tablet computer where you want to maximize your screen viewing area.

1 In the upper left corner of your screen, above the ribbon, locate the **Quick Access Toolbar**.

Recall that the Quick Access Toolbar contains commands that you use frequently. By default, only the commands Save, Undo, and Redo display, but you can add and delete commands to suit your needs. Possibly the computer at which you are working already has additional commands added to the Quick Access Toolbar.

2 At the end of the **Quick Access Toolbar**, click the **Customize Quick Access Toolbar** button ⬚, and then compare your screen with Figure 1.17.

A list of commands that Office users commonly add to their Quick Access Toolbar displays, including New, Open, Email, Quick Print, and Print Preview and Print. Commands already on the Quick Access Toolbar display a check mark. Commands that you add to the Quick Access Toolbar are always just one click away.

Here you can also display the More Commands dialog box, from which you can select any command from any tab to add to the Quick Access Toolbar.

BY TOUCH Tap once on Quick Access Toolbar commands.

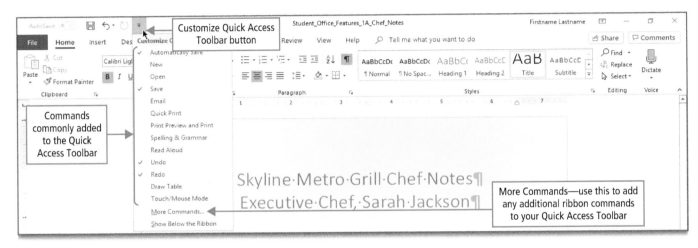

Figure 1.17

3 On the list, click **Print Preview and Print**, and then notice that the icon is added to the **Quick Access Toolbar**. Compare your screen with Figure 1.18.

The icon that represents the Print Preview command displays on the Quick Access Toolbar. Because this is a command that you will use frequently while building Office documents, you might decide to have this command remain on your Quick Access Toolbar.

ANOTHER WAY Right-click any command on the ribbon, and then on the shortcut menu, click Add to Quick Access Toolbar.

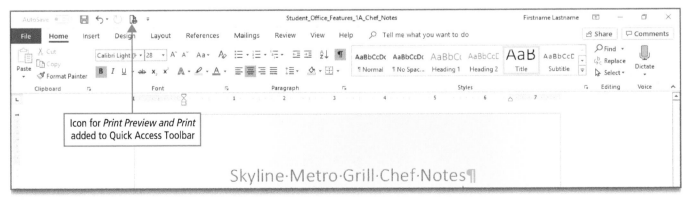

Figure 1.18

Activity 1.08 | Performing Commands from the Ribbon

1 ▶ In the second line of text, click to place the insertion point to the right of the letter *n* in *Jackson*. Press [Enter] three times. Compare your screen with Figure 1.19.

Word creates three new blank paragraphs, and no Text Effect is applied.

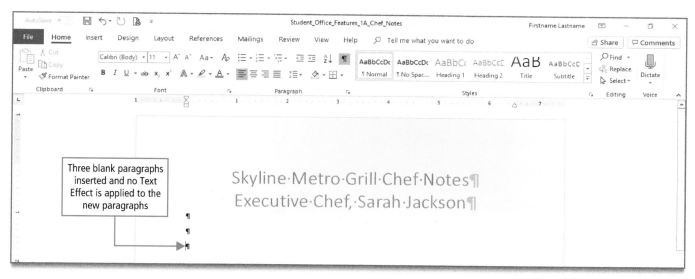

Figure 1.19

2 ▶ Click to position the insertion point to the left of the **second blank paragraph** that you just inserted. On the ribbon, click the **Insert tab**. In the **Illustrations group**, *point* to **Pictures** to display its ScreenTip.

Many buttons on the ribbon have this type of *enhanced ScreenTip*, which displays useful descriptive information about the command.

3 ▶ Click **Pictures**. In the **Insert Picture** dialog box, navigate to your **Office Features Chapter 1 folder**, double-click the **of01A_Chefs** picture, and then compare your screen with Figure 1.20.

The picture displays in your Word document.

MAC TIP Click Picture from File, then navigate to your Office Features Chapter 1 folder.

For Non-MyLab Submissions
The of01A_Chefs picture is included with this chapter's Student Data Files, which you can obtain from your instructor or by downloading the files from www.pearsonhighered.com/go

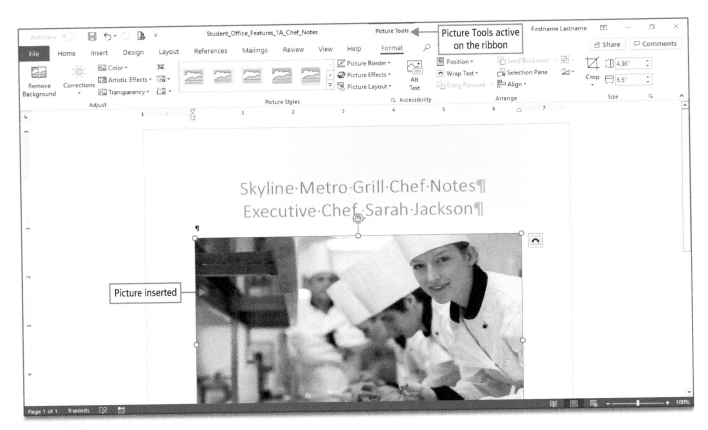

Figure 1.20

> **4** In the upper right corner of the picture, point to the **Layout Options** button ⊞ to display its ScreenTip, and then compare your screen with Figure 1.21.
>
> *Layout Options* enable you to choose how the *object*—in this instance an inserted picture—interacts with the surrounding text. An object is a picture or other graphic such as a chart or table that you can select and then move and resize.
>
> When a picture is selected, the Picture Tools become available on the ribbon. Additionally, *sizing handles*—small circles or squares that indicate an object is selected—surround the selected picture.

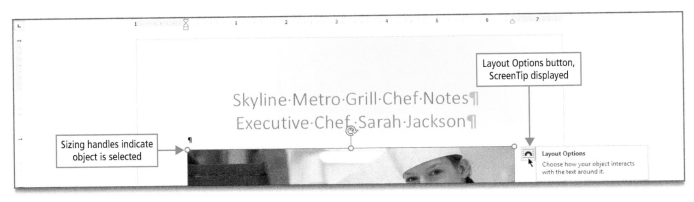

Figure 1.21

> **5** With the image selected, click **Layout Options** ⊞, and then under **With Text Wrapping**, in the second row, click the first layout—**Top and Bottom**. In the upper right corner of the **Layout Options** dialog box, click **Close** ×.

6 On the ribbon, with the **Picture Tools Format tab** active, at the right, in the **Size group**, click in the **Shape Height** box 🔲 0.29" ⬍ to select the existing text. Type **2** and press Enter.

7 On the **Picture Tools Format tab**, in the **Arrange group**, click **Align**, and then at the bottom of the list, locate **Use Alignment Guides**. If you do not see a checkmark to the left of **Use Alignment Guides**, click the command to enable the guides.

8 If necessary, click the image again to select it. Point to the image to display the 🔲 pointer, hold down the left mouse button and move your mouse slightly to display a green line at the left margin, and then drag the image to the right and down slightly until a green line displays in the center of the image as shown in Figure 1.22, and then release the left mouse button.

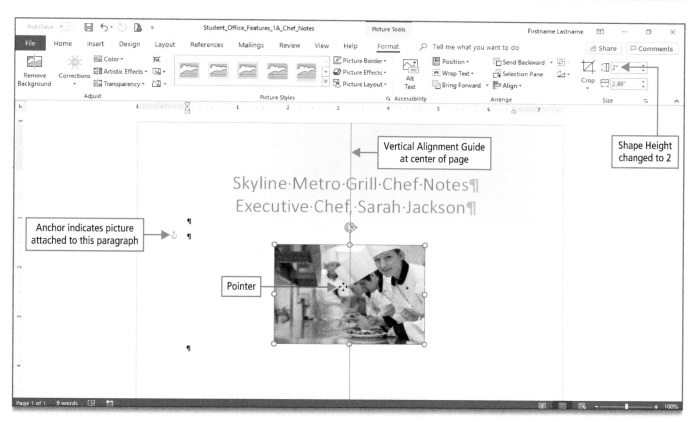

Figure 1.22

9 Be sure that there are two blank paragraphs above the image and that the anchor symbol is attached to the second blank paragraph mark—if necessary, drag the picture up slightly or down slightly. If you are not satisfied with your result, on the Quick Access Toolbar, click Undo ↺ and begin again.

> *Alignment guides* are green lines that display to help you align objects with margins or at the center of a page.

> Inserted pictures anchor—attach to—the paragraph at the insertion point location—as indicated by an anchor symbol.

10 On the ribbon, on the **Picture Tools Format tab**, in the **Picture Styles group**, point to the first style to display the ScreenTip *Simple Frame, White*, and notice that the image displays with a white frame.

⬜ **MAC TIP**   Preview may not be available.

NOTE   **The Size of Groups on the Ribbon Varies with Screen Resolution**

Your monitor's screen resolution might be set higher than the resolution used to capture the figures in this book. At a higher resolution, the ribbon expands some groups to show more commands that are available with a single click, such as those in the Picture Styles group. Or, the group expands to add descriptive text to some buttons, such as those in the Arrange group. Regardless of your screen resolution, all Office commands are available to you. In higher resolutions, you will have a more robust view of the ribbon commands.

11 Watch the image as you point to the second picture style, and then to the third, and then to the fourth.

Recall that Live Preview shows the result of applying an editing or formatting change as you point to possible results—*before* you actually apply it.

12 In the **Picture Styles group**, click the fourth style—**Drop Shadow Rectangle**. Reposition the picture up or down so that it is anchored to the second blank paragraph above the image, and then click anywhere outside of the image to deselect it. Notice that the Picture Tools no longer display on the ribbon. Compare your screen with Figure 1.23.

Contextual tabs on the ribbon display only when you need them.

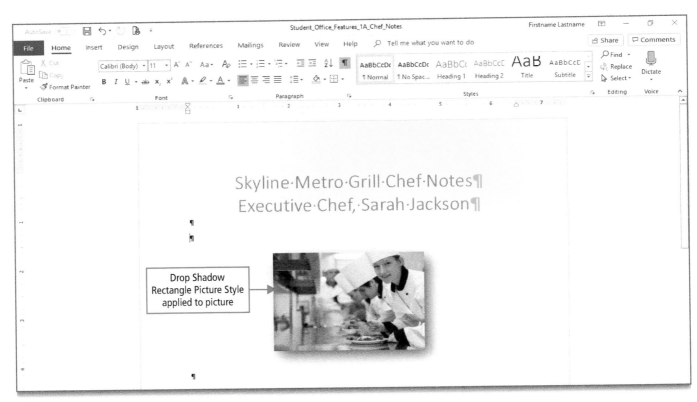

Figure 1.23

13 On the **Quick Access Toolbar**, click **Save** 🖫 to save the changes you have made.

Activity 1.09 | Minimizing the Ribbon

1 Point to any tab on the ribbon and right-click to display a shortcut menu.

Here you can choose to display the Quick Access Toolbar below the ribbon or collapse the ribbon to maximize screen space. You can also customize the ribbon by adding, removing, renaming, or reordering tabs, groups, and commands, although this is not recommended until you become an expert Word user.

2 Click **Collapse the Ribbon** and notice that only the ribbon tabs display. Click the **Home tab** to display the commands. Click in the last blank paragraph—or anywhere in the document— and notice that the ribbon goes back to the collapsed display.

MAC TIP To minimize the ribbon, click the up arrow on the top right of the screen.

---

3 Right-click any ribbon tab, and then click **Collapse the Ribbon** again to remove the check mark from this command.

Most expert Office users prefer the full ribbon display.

4 Point to any tab on the ribbon, and then on your mouse device, roll the mouse wheel. Notice that different tabs become active as you roll the mouse wheel.

You can make a tab active by using this technique, instead of clicking the tab.

MORE KNOWLEDGE **Displaying KeyTips**

Instead of a mouse, some individuals prefer to navigate the ribbon by using keys on the keyboard. You can do this by activating the *KeyTip* feature where small labels display on the ribbon tabs and also on the individual ribbon commands. Press Alt to display the KeyTips on the ribbon tabs, and then press N to display KeyTips on the ribbon commands. Press Esc to turn the feature off. NOTE: This feature is not yet available on a Mac.

Activity 1.10 | Changing Page Orientation and Zoom Level

1.2.1

1 On the ribbon, click the **Layout tab**. In the **Page Setup group**, click **Orientation**, and notice that two orientations display—*Portrait* and *Landscape*. Click **Landscape**.

In ***portrait orientation***, the paper is taller than it is wide. In ***landscape orientation***, the paper is wider than it is tall.

2 In the lower right corner of the screen, locate the **Zoom slider** ▬▬▬▬▬.

Recall that to zoom means to increase or decrease the viewing area. You can zoom in to look closely at a section of a document, and then zoom out to see an entire page on the screen. You can also zoom to view multiple pages on the screen.

3 Drag the **Zoom slider** [slider] to the left until you have zoomed to approximately *60%*. Compare your screen with Figure 1.24.

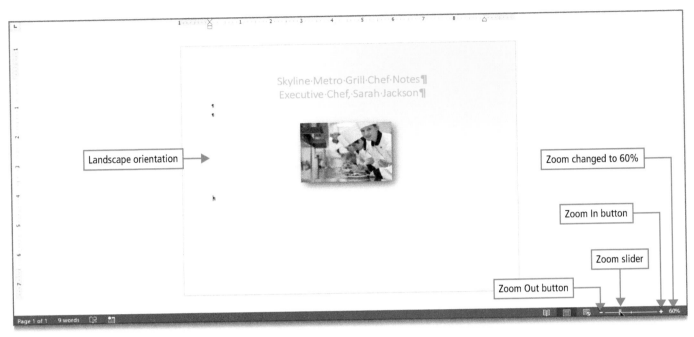

Figure 1.24

👆 **BY TOUCH**   Drag the Zoom slider with your finger.

4 Use the technique you just practiced to change the **Orientation** back to **Portrait**.

The default orientation in Word is Portrait, which is commonly used for business documents such as letters, reports, and memos.

5 In the lower right corner, click the **Zoom In** button [+] as many times as necessary to return to the **100%** zoom setting.

Use the zoom feature to adjust the view of your document for editing and for your viewing comfort.

🔄 **ANOTHER WAY**   You can also control Zoom from the ribbon. On the View tab, in the Zoom group, you can control the Zoom level and also zoom to view multiple pages.

6 On the **Quick Access Toolbar**, click **Save** [💾].

MORE KNOWLEDGE   **Zooming to Page Width**

Some Office users prefer *Page Width*, which zooms the document so that the width of the page matches the width of the window. Find this command on the View tab, in the Zoom group.

Activity 1.11 | Formatting Text by Using Fonts, Alignment, Font Colors, and Font Styles

MOS
2.2.5

1 If necessary, on the right edge of your screen, drag the vertical scroll box to the top of the scroll bar. To the left of *Executive Chef, Sarah Jackson*, point in the margin area to display the 𝄔 pointer and click one time to select the entire paragraph. Compare your screen with Figure 1.25.

Use this technique to select complete paragraphs from the margin area—drag downward to select multiple-line paragraphs—which is faster and more efficient than dragging through text.

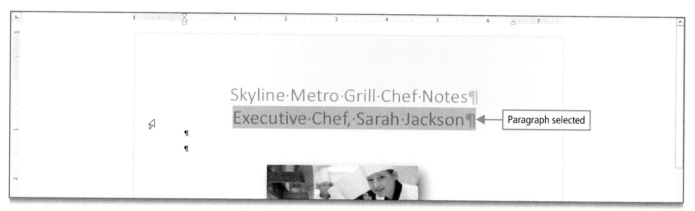

Figure 1.25

2 On the **Home tab**, in the **Font Group**, click **Clear All Formatting** 🅰◊. Compare your screen with Figure 1.26.

This command removes all formatting from the selection, leaving only the normal, unformatted text.

Figure 1.26

3 With the text still selected, on the **Home tab**, in the **Paragraph group**, click **Center** ▤.

4 With the text still selected, on the **Home tab**, in the **Font group**, click the **Font button arrow** `Calibri (Body) ▾`. On the alphabetical list of font names, scroll down and then locate and *point to* **Cambria**.

A **font** is a set of characters with the same design and shape. The default font in a Word document is Calibri, which is a **sans serif font**—a font design with no lines or extensions on the ends of characters.

The Cambria font is a **serif font**—a font design that includes small line extensions on the ends of the letters to guide the eye in reading from left to right.

The list of fonts displays as a gallery showing potential results. For example, in the Font gallery, you can point to see the actual design and format of each font as it would look if applied to text.

5 ▶ Point to several other fonts and observe the effect on the selected text. Then, scroll back to the top of the **Font** gallery. Under **Theme Fonts**, click **Calibri Light**.

A **theme** is a predesigned combination of colors, fonts, line, and fill effects that look good together and is applied to an entire document by a single selection. A theme combines two sets of fonts—one for text and one for headings. In the default Office theme, Calibri Light is the suggested font for headings.

6 ▶ With the paragraph *Executive Chef, Sarah Jackson* still selected, on the **Home tab**, in the **Font group**, click the **Font Size button arrow** [11 ▾], point to **20**, and then notice how Live Preview displays the text in the font size to which you are pointing. Compare your screen with Figure 1.27.

Figure 1.27

7 ▶ On the list of font sizes, click **20**.

Fonts are measured in **points**, with one point equal to 1/72 of an inch. A higher point size indicates a larger font size. Headings and titles are often formatted by using a larger font size. The word *point* is abbreviated as **pt**.

8 ▶ With *Executive Chef, Sarah Jackson* still selected, on the **Home tab**, in the **Font group**, click the **Font Color button arrow** [A ▾]. Under **Theme Colors**, in the sixth column, click the fifth (next to last) color, and then click in the last blank paragraph to deselect the text.

9 ▶ With your insertion point in the blank paragraph below the picture, type **Rehearsal Dinner Menu Ideas** and then press [Enter] two times.

10 Type **Appetizers** and press [Enter] two times. Type **Salads** and press [Enter] two times. Type **Main Dishes** and press [Enter] two times.

11 Type **Desserts** and press [Enter] four times. Compare your screen with Figure 1.28.

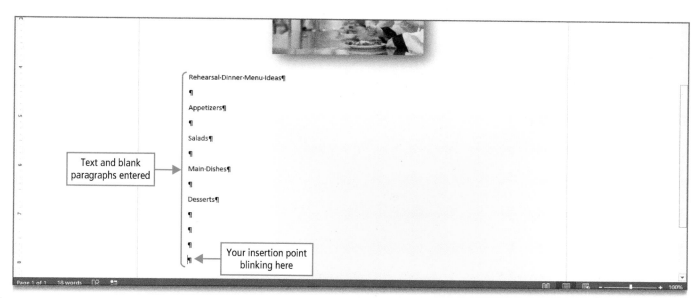

Rehearsal·Dinner·Menu·Ideas¶
¶
Appetizers¶
¶
Salads¶
¶
Main·Dishes¶
¶
Desserts¶
¶
¶
¶
¶

Text and blank paragraphs entered

Your insertion point blinking here

Page 1 of 1   18 words   100%

Figure1.28

12 Click anywhere in the word *Dinner* and then ***triple-click***—click the left mouse button three times—to select the entire paragraph. If the entire paragraph is not selected, click in the paragraph and begin again.

13 With the paragraph selected, on the mini toolbar, click the **Font Color** button [A ▾], and notice that the text color of the selected paragraph changes.

> The font color button retains its most recently used color—the color you used to format *Executive Chef, Sarah Jackson* above. As you progress in your study of Microsoft Office, you will use other commands that behave in this manner; that is, they retain their most recently used format. This is commonly referred to as *MRU*—most recently used.

> Recall that the mini toolbar places commands that are commonly used for the selected text or object close by so that you reduce the distance you must move your mouse to access a command. If you are using a touch screen device, most commands that you need are close and easy to touch.

🖥 **MAC TIP**   Use commands on the ribbon, on the Home tab.

14 With the paragraph *Rehearsal Dinner Menu Ideas* still selected and the mini toolbar displayed, on the mini toolbar, click **Bold** [B] and **Italic** [I].

> ***Font styles*** include bold, italic, and underline. Font styles emphasize text and are a visual cue to draw the reader's eye to important text.

15 On the mini toolbar, click **Italic** $\boxed{I}$ again to turn off the Italic formatting. Click anywhere to deselect, and then compare your screen with Figure 1.29.

A *toggle button* is a button that can be turned on by clicking it once, and then turned off by clicking it again.

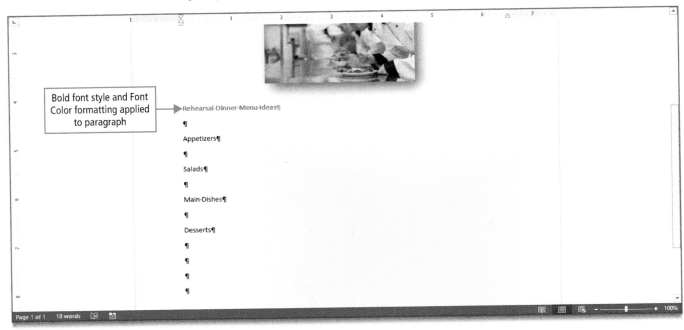

Figure 1.29

Activity 1.12 | Using Format Painter

Use the *Format Painter* to copy the formatting of specific text or copy the formatting of a paragraph and then apply it in other locations in your document.

1 To the left of *Rehearsal Dinner Menu Ideas*, point in the left margin to display the $\boxed{\nearrow}$ pointer, and then click one time to select the entire paragraph. Compare your screen with Figure 1.30.

Use this technique to select complete paragraphs from the margin area. This is particularly useful if there are many lines of text in the paragraph. You can hold down the left mouse button and drag downward instead of trying to drag through the text.

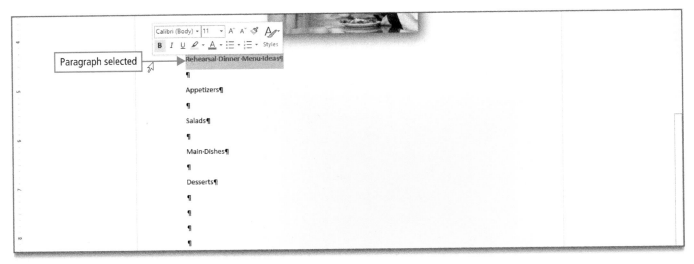

Figure 1.30

2 With *Rehearsal Dinner Menu Ideas* still selected, on the mini toolbar, click **Format Painter** 🖌. Then, move your mouse to the right of the word *Appetizers*, and notice the 🖌I mouse pointer. Compare your screen with Figure 1.31.

> The pointer takes the shape of a paintbrush and contains the formatting information from the paragraph where the insertion point is positioned or from what is selected. Information about the Format Painter and how to turn it off displays in the status bar.

MAC TIP On the Home tab, in the Clipboard group, click Format Painter.

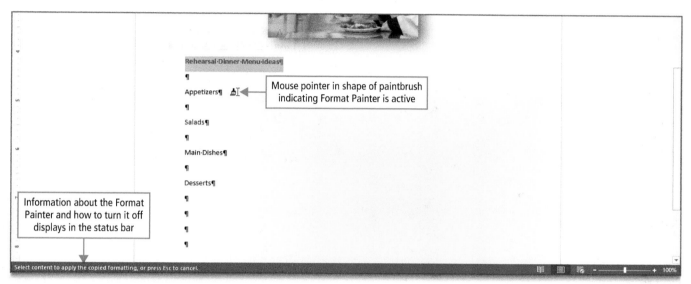

Rehearsal·Dinner·Menu·Ideas¶

¶

Appetizers¶ 🖌I ← Mouse pointer in shape of paintbrush indicating Format Painter is active

¶

Salads¶

¶

Main·Dishes¶

¶

Desserts¶

¶

Information about the Format Painter and how to turn it off displays in the status bar

¶

¶

¶

¶

Select content to apply the copied formatting, or press Esc to cancel.   100%

Figure 1.31

3 With the 🖌I pointer, drag to select the paragraph *Appetizers* and notice that the font color and Bold formatting is applied. Then, click anywhere in the word *Appetizers*, right-click to display the mini toolbar, and on the mini toolbar, *double-click* **Format Painter** 🖌.

4 Select the paragraph *Salads* to copy the font color and Bold formatting, and notice that the pointer retains the 🖌I shape. You might have to move the mouse slightly to see the paintbrush shape.

> When you *double-click* the Format Painter button, the Format Painter feature remains active until you either click the Format Painter button again, or press Esc to cancel it—as indicated on the status bar.

5 With Format Painter still active, drag to select the paragraph *Main Dishes*, and then on the ribbon, on the **Home tab**, in the **Clipboard group**, notice that **Format Painter** is selected, indicating that it is active. Compare your screen with Figure 1.32.

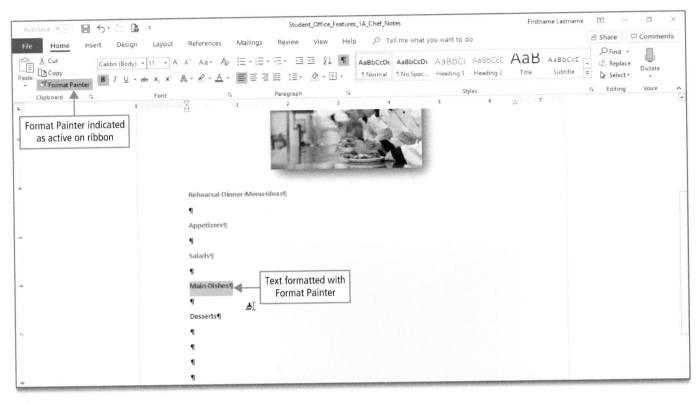

Figure 1.32

6 Select the paragraph *Desserts* to copy the format, and then on the ribbon, click **Format Painter** to turn the command off.

ANOTHER WAY Press Esc to turn off Format Painter.

7 On the **Quick Access Toolbar**, click **Save** to save the changes you have made to your document.

Activity 1.13 | Using Keyboard Shortcuts and Using the Clipboard to Copy, Cut, and Paste

The **Clipboard** is a temporary storage area that holds text or graphics that you select and then cut or copy. When you **copy** text or graphics, a copy is placed on the Clipboard and the original text or graphic remains in place. When you **cut** text or graphics, a copy is placed on the Clipboard, and the original text or graphic is removed—cut—from the document.

After copying or cutting, the contents of the Clipboard are available for you to **paste**—insert—in a new location in the current document, or into another Office file.

1 On your keyboard, hold down `Ctrl` and press `Home` to move to the beginning of your document, and then take a moment to study the table in Figure 1.33, which describes similar keyboard shortcuts with which you can navigate quickly in a document.

MAC TIP Press `command ⌘` + `fn` + to move to the top of a document.

To Move	On a Windows PC press:	On a Mac press:
To the beginning of a document	`Ctrl` + `Home`	`command ⌘` + `fn` + `←`
To the end of a document	`Ctrl` + `End`	`command ⌘` + `fn` + `→`
To the beginning of a line	`Home`	`command ⌘` + `←`
To the end of a line	`End`	`command ⌘` + `→`
To the beginning of the previous word	`Ctrl` + `←`	`option` + `←`
To the beginning of the next word	`Ctrl` + `→`	`option` + `→`
To the beginning of the current word (if insertion point is in the middle of a word)	`Ctrl` + `←`	`option` + `←`
To the beginning of the previous paragraph	`Ctrl` + `↑`	`command ⌘` + `↑`
To the beginning of the next paragraph	`Ctrl` + `↓`	`command ⌘` + `↓`
To the beginning of the current paragraph (if insertion point is in the middle of a paragraph)	`Ctrl` + `↑`	`command ⌘` + `↑`
Up one screen	`PgUp`	`fn` + `↑`
Down one screen	`PgDn`	`fn` + `↓`

Figure 1.33

2 To the left of *Skyline Metro Grill Chef Notes*, point in the left margin area to display the ⤢ pointer, and then click one time to select the entire paragraph. On the **Home tab**, in the **Clipboard group**, click **Copy** 🗋.

Because anything that you select and then copy—or cut—is placed on the Clipboard, the Copy command and the Cut command display in the Clipboard group of commands on the ribbon. There is no visible indication that your copied selection has been placed on the Clipboard.

ANOTHER WAY Right-click the selection, and then click Copy on the shortcut menu; or, use the keyboard shortcut `Ctrl` + `C`.

MAC TIP Press `command ⌘` + `C` as a keyboard shortcut for the Copy command.

3 On the **Home tab**, in the **Clipboard group**, to the right of the group name *Clipboard*, click the **Dialog Box Launcher** button ⌐, and then compare your screen with Figure 1.34.

The Clipboard pane displays with your copied text. In any ribbon group, the **Dialog Box Launcher** displays either a dialog box or a pane related to the group of commands. It is not necessary to display the Clipboard in this manner, although sometimes it is useful to do so.

🖥 **MAC TIP**   On a Mac, you cannot view or clear the Clipboard. Use the ribbon commands.

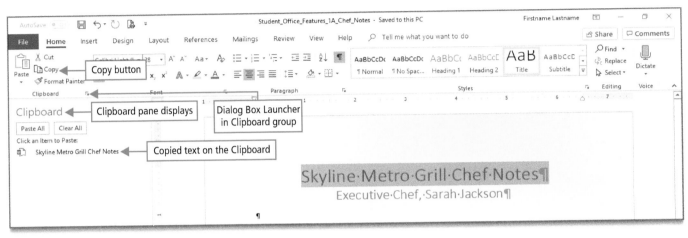

Figure 1.34

4 In the upper right corner of the **Clipboard** pane, click **Close** ☒.

5 Press Ctrl + End to move to the end of your document. On the **Home tab**, in the **Clipboard group**, point to **Paste**, and then click the *upper* portion of this split button.

The Paste command pastes the most recently copied item on the Clipboard at the insertion point location. If you click the lower portion of the Paste button, a gallery of Paste Options displays. A *split button* is divided into two parts; clicking the main part of the button performs a command, and clicking the arrow displays a list or gallery with choices.

🖥 **MAC TIP**   Press command ⌘ + fn + → to move to the end of a document. The Paste button is not split; instead, display the dropdown menu; or use command ⌘ + V to paste.

🔄 **ANOTHER WAY**   Right-click, on the shortcut menu under Paste Options, click the desired option button; or, press Control + V.

6 Below the pasted text, click **Paste Options** ▣ as shown in Figure 1.35.

Here you can view and apply various formatting options for pasting your copied or cut text. Typically, you will click Paste on the ribbon and paste the item in its original format. If you want some other format for the pasted item, you can choose another format from the *Paste Options gallery*, which provides a Live Preview of the various options for changing the format of the pasted item with a single click. The Paste Options gallery is available in three places: on the ribbon by clicking the lower portion of the Paste button—the Paste button arrow; from the Paste Options button that displays below the pasted item following the paste operation; or on the shortcut menu if you right-click the pasted item.

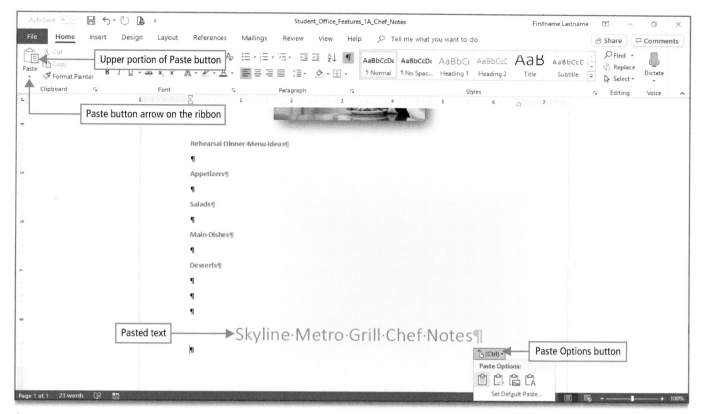

Figure 1.35

> **7** In the **Paste Options** gallery, *point* to each option to see the Live Preview of the format that would be applied if you clicked the button.

The contents of the Paste Options gallery are contextual; that is, they change based on what you copied and where you are pasting.

> **8** Press [Esc] to close the gallery; the button will remain displayed until you take some other screen action.

> **9** On your keyboard, press [Ctrl] + [Home] to move to the top of the document, and then click the **chefs image** one time to select it. While pointing to the selected image, right-click, and then on the shortcut menu, click **Cut**.

Recall that the Cut command cuts—removes—the selection from the document and places it on the Clipboard.

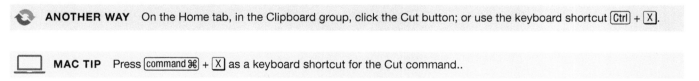

ANOTHER WAY On the Home tab, in the Clipboard group, click the Cut button; or use the keyboard shortcut [Ctrl] + [X].

MAC TIP Press [command ⌘] + [X] as a keyboard shortcut for the Cut command..

> **10** Press [Ctrl] + [End] to move to the end of the document.

11 With the insertion point blinking in the blank paragraph at the end of the document, right-click, and notice that the **Paste Options** gallery displays on the shortcut menu. Compare your screen with Figure 1.36.

Figure 1.36

12 On the shortcut menu, under **Paste Options**, click the first button—**Keep Source Formatting**.

MAC TIP On the shortcut menu, click Paste, click the Paste Options button, and then click Keep Source Formatting.

13 Point to the picture to display the ⬚ pointer, and then drag to the right until the center green **Alignment Guide** displays and the blank paragraph is above the picture. Release the left mouse button.

MAC TIP In the Arrange group, on the Picture Format tab, click Align, click Align Center.

14 Above the picture, select the text *Chef Notes*, type **Festive Salad** and then compare your screen with Figure 1.37.

Figure 1.37

15 Click **Save** 🖫.

Activity 1.14 | Adding Alternative Text for Accessibility

MOS
5.4.3

1 Point to the **chefs picture** and right-click. On the shortcut menu, click **Edit Alt Text** to display the **Alt Text** pane.

Alternative text helps people using a ***screen reader***, which is software that enables visually impaired users to read text on a computer screen to understand the content of pictures. ***Alt text*** is the term commonly used for this feature.

2 In the **Alt Text** pane, notice that Word generates a suggested description of the picture. Click in the box, select the existing text, and then type **Young chefs making salads in a restaurant kitchen** and then compare your screen with Figure 1.38.

Anyone viewing the document with a screen reader will see the alternative text displayed instead of the picture.

Figure 1.38

3 **Close** ☒ the **Alt Text** pane. Press [Ctrl] + [Home] to move to the top of your document. On the Quick Access Toolbar, click **Save** 🖫 to the changes you have made to your document.

Objective 5   Finalize an Office Document

GO! Learn How
Video OF1-5

There are steps you will want to take to finalize your documents. This typically includes inserting a footer for identifying information and adding Document Properties to facilitate searching. Recall that Document Properties—also known as metadata—are details about a file that describe or identify it, such as the title, author name, subject, and keywords that identify the document's topic or contents. You might also want to take some security measures or mark information to find later.

Activity 1.15 │ Inserting a Footer, Inserting Document Info, and Adding Document Properties

MOS
1.3.2

1 On the **Insert tab**, in the **Header & Footer group**, click **Footer**. At the bottom of the list, click **Edit Footer**, and then with the **Header & Footer Tools Design tab** active, in the **Insert group**, click **Document Info**. Click **File Name** to add the file name to the footer.

A *footer* is a reserved area for text and graphics that displays at the bottom of each page in a document. It is common in organizations to add the file name to the footer of documents so that documents are easily identified.

    MAC TIP   In the Insert group, click Field. In the dialog box, under Categories, click Document Information. Then under Field names, click FileName. Click OK.

2 On the right end of the ribbon, click **Close Header and Footer**.

3 On the **Quick Access Toolbar**, point to the **Print Preview and Print** button 🖺 you placed there, right-click, and then click **Remove from Quick Access Toolbar**.

> If you are working on your own computer and you want to do so, you can leave the icon on the toolbar; in a college lab, you should return the software to its original settings.

4 Click the **File tab** to display **Backstage** view. With the **Info tab** active, in the lower right corner, click **Show All Properties**. Click in the **Tags** box, and then type **rehearsal dinners, menus**

> *Tags*—also referred to as *keywords*—are custom file properties in the form of words that you associate with a document to give an indication of the document's content. Use tags to assist in searching for and organizing files.

MAC TIP On the menu bar, click File, click Properties, click the Summary tab, and then type the tags in the Keywords box. Click OK.

5 Click in the **Subject** box, and then type your course name and number—for example, *CIS 10, #5543*. Under **Related People**, be sure your name displays as the author. (To edit the Author, right-click the name, click Edit Property, type the new name, click in a white area to close the list, and then click OK.)

6 On the left, click **Save** to save your document and return to the Word window.

Activity 1.16 │ Inspecting a Document

Word, Excel, and PowerPoint all have the same commands to inspect a file before sharing it.

MAC TIP On the menu bar, click Tools. Here you can click Protect Document and Check Accessibility.

MOS
1.4.1,1.4.2, 1.4.3

1 With your document displayed, click the **File tab**, on the left, if necessary, click **Info**, and then on the right, click **Check for Issues**.

2 On the list, click **Inspect Document**.

> The *Inspect Document* command searches your document for hidden data or personal information that you might not want to share publicly. This information could reveal company details that should not be shared.

3 In the lower right corner of the **Document Inspector** dialog box, click **Inspect**.

> The Document Inspector runs and lists information that was found and that you could choose to remove.

4 In the lower right corner of the dialog box, click **Close**, and then click **Check for Issues** again. On the list, click **Check Accessibility**.

> The *Check Accessibility* command checks the document for content that people with disabilities might find difficult to read. The Accessibility Checker pane displays on the right and lists objects that might require attention.

5 Close ⊠ the **Accessibility Checker** pane, and then click the **File tab**.

6 Click **Check for Issues**, and then click **Check Compatibility**.

> The *Check Compatibility* command checks for features in your document that may not be supported by earlier versions of the Office program. This is only a concern if you are sharing documents with individuals with older software.

7 Click **OK**. Leave your Word document displayed for the next Activity.

Activity 1.17 | Inserting a Bookmark and a 3D Model

1.1.2, 5.2.6

A **bookmark** identifies a word, section, or place in your document so that you can find it quickly without scrolling. This is especially useful in a long document.

3D models are a new kind of shape that you can insert from an online library of ready-to-use three-dimensional graphics. A 3D model is most powerful in a PowerPoint presentation where you can add transitions and animations during your presentation, but you can also insert a 3D model into a Word document for an impactful image that you can position in various ways.

1 In the paragraph *Rehearsal Dinner Menu Items*, select the word *Menu*.

2 On the **Insert tab**, in the **Links group**, click **Bookmark**.

3 In the **Bookmark** name box, type **menu** and then click **Add**.

4 Press `Ctrl` + `Home` to move to the top of your document.

5 On the **Home tab**, at the right end of the ribbon, in the **Editing group**, click the **Find button arrow**, and then click **Go To**.

ANOTHER WAY   Press `Ctrl` + `G`, which is the keyboard shortcut for the Go To command.

MAC TIP   On the menu bar, click Edit, point to Find, click Go To. In the dialog box, click Bookmark.

---

6 Under **Go to what**, click **Bookmark**, and then with *menu* indicated as the bookmark name, click **Go To**. **Close** the **Find and Replace** dialog box, and notice that your bookmarked text is selected for you.

7 Click to position your insertion point at the end of the word *Desserts*. On the **Insert tab**, in the **Illustrations group**, click the upper portion of the **3D Models button** to open the **Online 3D Models** dialog box.

NOTE   3D Models Not Available?

If the 3D Models command is not available on your system, in the **Illustrations group**, click **Pictures**, and then from the files downloaded with this project, click of01A_Cupcake. Change the Height to .75" and then move to Step 12.

---

8 In the search box, type **cupcake** and then press `Enter`.

9 Click the image of the **cupcake in a pink and white striped wrapper**—or select any other cupcake image. At the bottom, click **Insert**.

10 Point to the **3D control** in the center of the image, hold down the left mouse button, and then rotate the image so the top of the cupcake is pointing toward the upper right corner of the page—your rotation need not be exact. Alternatively, in the 3D Model Views group, click the More button ⊡, and then locate and click Above Front Left.

11 With the cupcake image selected, on the **3D Model Tools Format tab**, in the **Size group**, click in the **Height** box, type **.75"** and press `Enter`.

12 In the **Arrange group**, click **Wrap Text**, and then click **In Front of Text**. Then, in the **Arrange group**, click **Align**, and click **Align Right** to position the cupcake at the right margin.

13 Press `Ctrl` + `Home` to move to the top of your document. On the **Quick Access Toolbar**, click **Save** ▣.

Activity 1.18 | Printing a File and Closing a Desktop App

1 Click the **File tab** to return to **Backstage** view, on the left click **Print**, and then compare your screen with Figure 1.39.

Here you can select any printer connected to your system and adjust the settings related to how you want to print. On the right, the *Print Preview* displays, which is a view of a document as it will appear on paper when you print it. Your page color effect will not display in Print Preview nor will the shading print. This effect appears only to anyone viewing the document on a screen.

At the bottom of the Print Preview area, in the center, the number of pages and page navigation arrows with which you can move among the pages in Print Preview display. On the right, the Zoom slider enables you to shrink or enlarge the Print Preview. *Zoom* is the action of increasing or decreasing the viewing area of the screen.

ANOTHER WAY From the document screen, press Ctrl + P or Ctrl + F2 to display Print in Backstage view.

MAC TIP Press command ⌘ + P.

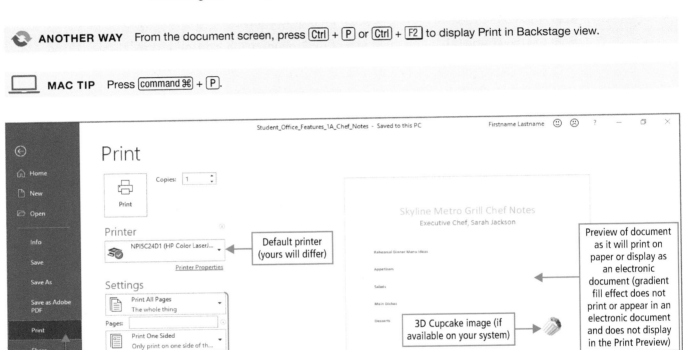

Figure 1.39

2 On the left, click **Save**. In the upper right corner of your screen, click **Close** ⊠ to close Word. If a message displays regarding copied items, click No.

MAC TIP On the menu bar, click File, click Close.

<table>
<tr><td>📄</td><td>For Non-MyLab Submissions: Determine What Your Instructor Requires as Your Submission
As directed by your instructor, submit your completed Word document.</td></tr>
</table>

3 In **MyLab IT**, locate and click the Grader Project **Office Features 1A Chef Notes**. In **step 3**, under **Upload Completed Assignment**, click **Choose File**. In the **Open** dialog box, navigate to your **Office Features Chapter 1 folder**, and then click your **Student_Office_Features_1A_ Chef_Notes** file one time to select it. In the lower right corner of the **Open** dialog box, click **Open**.

The name of your selected file displays above the Upload button.

4 To submit your file to **MyLab IT** for grading, click **Upload**, wait a moment for a green **Success!** message, and then in **step 4**, click the blue **Submit for Grading** button. Click **Close Assignment** to return to your list of **Course Materials**.

MORE KNOWLEDGE | **Creating an Electronic Image of Your Document**

You can create an electronic image of your document that looks like a printed document. To do so, in Backstage view, on the left click Export. On the right, click Create PDF/XPS, and then click the Create PDF/XPS button to display the Publish as PDF or XPS dialog box.

PDF stands for **Portable Document Format**, which is a technology that creates an image that preserves the look of your file. This is a popular format for sending documents electronically, because the document will display on most computers. **XPS** stands for **XML Paper Specification**—a Microsoft file format that also creates an image of your document and that opens in the XPS viewer.

ALERT The Remaining Activities in This Chapter Are Optional

The following Activities describing the Office Help features are recommend but are optional to complete.

Objective 6 | Use the Office Help Features

GO! Learn How
Video OF1-6

Within each Office program, you will see the *Tell Me* feature at the right end of the ribbon— to the right of the Help tab. This is a search feature for Microsoft Office commands that you activate by typing in the *Tell me what you want to do* box. Another way to use this feature is to point to a command on the ribbon, and then at the bottom of the displayed ScreenTip, click *Tell me more*.

Activity 1.19 | Using Microsoft Office Tell Me, Tell Me More, the Help Tab, and Adding Alt Text to an Excel Chart

5.3.3

1 Start Excel and open a **Blank workbook**. With cell **A1** active, type **456789** and press Enter. Click cell **A1** again to make it the active cell.

2 At the top of the screen, click in the *Tell me what you want to do* box, and then type **format as currency** In the displayed list, to the right of **Accounting Number Format**, click the ▶ arrow. Compare your screen with Figure 1.40.

As you type, every keystroke refines the results so that you can click the command as soon as it displays. This feature helps you apply the command immediately; it does not explain how to locate the command.

🖥️ **MAC TIP** Click the Help tab on the menu bar.

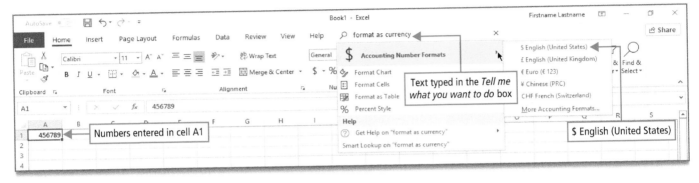

Figure 1.40

3 Click **$ English (United States)**.

4 On the **Home tab**, in the **Font group**, *point* to the **Font Color** button 🅰️▾ to display its ScreenTip, and then click **Tell me more**.

Tell me more is a prompt within a ScreenTip that opens the Office online Help system with explanations about how to perform the command referenced in the ScreenTip.

5 In the **Help** pane that displays on the right, if necessary, click **Change the color of text**. Compare your screen with Figure 1.41.

As you scroll down, you will notice that the Help pane displays extensive information about the topic of changing the color of text, including how to apply a custom color.

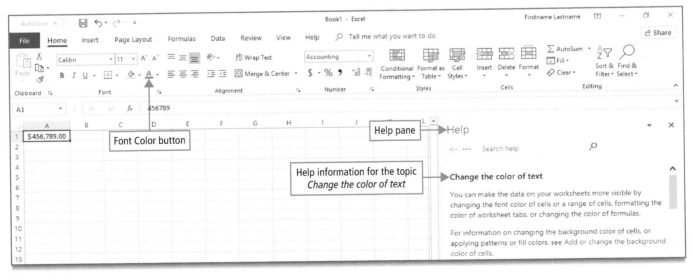

Figure 1.41

6 **Close** ✕ the **Help** pane.

7 On the ribbon, click the **Help tab**. In the **Help** group, click **Help**. In the **Help** pane, type **3D models** and then click the **Search** button. Click **Get creative with 3D models**, and then compare your screen with Figure 1.42.

Some Help topics include videos like this one to demonstrate and explain the topic.

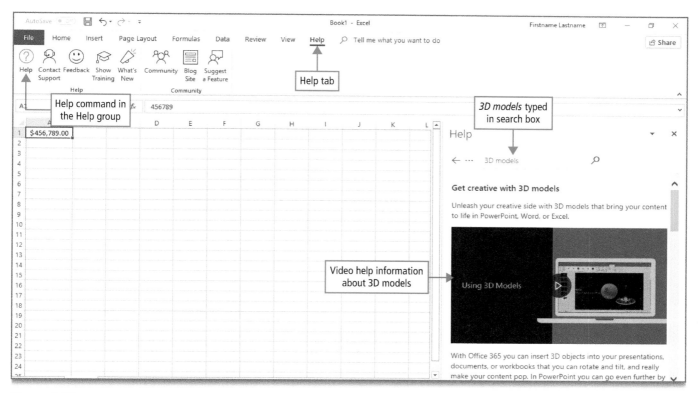

Figure 1.42

8 In the **Help** group and the **Community** group, look at the buttons.

Here you can Contact Support, send Feedback, Show Training developed by Microsoft, and see new features. In the Community group, you can visit the Excel Community, read the Excel Blog, and suggest new features.

9 ▸ Click **Show Training**, and then compare your screen with Figure 1.43.

Here you can view training videos developed by Microsoft.

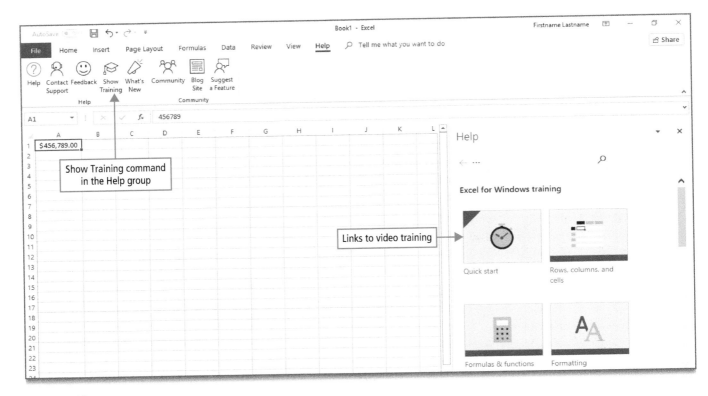

Figure 1.43

10 ▸ Click cell **A1**, and then click the **Insert tab**. In the **Charts group**, click **Recommended Charts**, and then in the **Insert Chart** dialog box, with the first chart selected, click **OK**.

11 ▸ Click the **Chart Tools Format tab**, and then in the **Accessibility group**, click **Alt Text**.

Here you can add text to describe the chart, similar to the Alt Text you added for the chef's image.

12 ▸ **Close** ⊠ the **Help** pane, **Close** ⊠ the **Alt Text** pane, and then in the upper right corner of the Excel window, click **Close** ⊠. Click **Don't Save**.

MORE KNOWLEDGE **Don't Type, Talk! With the New Dictate Feature**

Office 365 subscribers will see the *Dictate* feature in Word, PowerPoint, Outlook, and OneNote for Windows 10. When you enable Dictate, you start talking and as you talk, text appears in your document or slide. Dictate is one of Microsoft's Office Intelligent Services, which adds new cloud-enhanced features to Office. Dictate is especially useful in Outlook when you must write lengthy emails. The Dictate command is on the Home tab in Word and PowerPoint and on the Message tab in Outlook.

You have completed Project 1A **END**

Hotel Files

Project Activities

In Activities 1.20 through 1.38, you will assist Barbara Hewitt and Steven Ramos, who work for the Information Technology Department at the Boston headquarters office of the Bell Orchid Hotels. Barbara and Steven must organize some of the files and folders that comprise the corporation's computer data. As you progress through the project, you will insert screenshots of windows that you create into a PowerPoint presentation with five slides that will look similar to Figure 1.44.

Project Files for MyLab IT Grader

For Project 1B, you will start with the Windows 10 desktop displayed, and then learn how to create a folder for your **MyLab IT** files as you work through the project instruction. At the appropriate point in the project, you will be instructed to download your files from your **MyLab IT** course.

Project Results

GO! Project 1B
Where We're Going

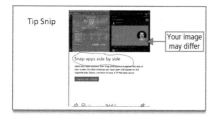

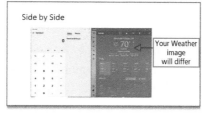

Figure 1.44

For Non-MyLab Submissions Start with the Windows 10 Desktop Displayed

For Project 1B, you will start with the Windows 10 desktop displayed and learn how to create a folder and save a new PowerPoint presentation as you work through the project instruction. Additionally, you will need the Student Data Files **win01_1B_Bell_Orchid** from your instructor or from www.pearsonhighered.com/go.

Objective 7   Explore Windows 10

ALERT   Because Windows 10 periodically checks for and then automatically downloads updates, you are assured that your device is up to date with the latest features and security improvements. Therefore, you may encounter some variations in what appears on your screen and what is shown in this instruction. Microsoft Office 365 is fully installed on your PC or Mac; no internet access is necessary to create or edit documents. When you *are* connected to the internet, you will receive monthly upgrades and new features, so you always have the latest versions of Office apps as soon as they are available. Your subscription gives you continuous free access to the latest innovations and refinements.

A *program* is a set of instructions that a computer uses to accomplish a task. A computer program that helps you perform a task for a specific purpose is referred to as an *application*. As an example, there are applications to create a document using word processing software, to play a game, to view the latest weather report, to edit photos or videos, or to manage financial information.

An *operating system* is a specific type of computer program that manages the other programs on a computing device such as a desktop computer, a laptop computer, a smartphone, a tablet computer, or a game console. You need an operating system to:

- Use application programs.
- Coordinate the use of your computer hardware such as a keyboard, mouse, touchpad, touchscreen, game controller, or printer.
- Organize data that you store on your computer and access data that you store on your own computer and in other locations.

Windows 10 is an operating system developed by Microsoft Corporation that works with mobile computing devices and also with traditional desktop and laptop PCs.

The three major tasks of an operating system are to:

- Manage your computer's hardware—the printers, scanners, disk drives, monitors, and other hardware attached to it.
- Manage the application software installed on your computer—programs like those in Microsoft Office and other programs you might install to edit photos and videos, play games, and so on.
- Manage the *data* generated from your application software. Data refers to the documents, worksheets, pictures, songs, and so on that you create and store during the day-to-day use of your computer.

The Windows 10 operating system continues to perform these three tasks, and additionally is optimized for touchscreens; for example, tablets of all sizes and convertible laptop computers. Windows 10 works equally well with any input device, including a mouse, keyboard, touchscreen, and *pen*—a pen-shaped stylus that you tap on a computer screen.

In most instances, when you purchase a computer, the operating system software is already installed. The operating system consists of many smaller programs, stored as system files, which transfer data to and from the disk and transfer data in and out of your computer's memory. Other functions performed by the operating system include hardware-specific tasks such as checking to see if a key has been pressed on the keyboard and, if it has, displaying the appropriate letter or character on the screen.

Windows 10, in the same manner as other operating systems and earlier versions of the Windows operating system, uses a *graphical user interface*—abbreviated as *GUI* and pronounced *GOO-ee*. A graphical user interface uses graphics such as an image of a file folder or wastebasket that you click to activate the item represented. A GUI commonly incorporates the following:

- A *pointer*—any symbol that displays on your screen in response to moving your mouse and with which you can select objects and commands.

- An *insertion point*—a blinking vertical line that indicates where text will be inserted when you type or where an action will take place.

- A *pointing device*, such as a mouse or touchpad, to control the pointer.

- *Icons*—small images that represent commands, files, applications, or other windows.

- A *desktop*—a simulation of a real desk that represents your work area; here you can arrange icons such as shortcuts to programs, files, folders, and various types of documents in the same manner you would arrange physical objects on top of a desk.

In Windows 10, you also have a Start menu with tiles that display when you click the Start button in the lower left corner of your screen. The array of tiles serves as a connected dashboard to all of your important programs, sites, and services. On the Start menu, your view is tailored to your information and activities.

The physical parts of your computer such as the central processing unit (CPU), memory, and any attached devices such as a printer, are collectively known as *resources*. The operating system keeps track of the status of each resource and decides when a resource needs attention and for how long.

Application programs enable you to do work on, and be entertained by, your computer—programs such as Word and Excel found in the Microsoft Office suite of products, Adobe Photoshop, and computer games. No application program, whether a larger desktop app or smaller *Microsoft Store app*—a smaller app that you download from the Store—can run on its own; it must run under the direction of an operating system.

For the everyday use of your computer, the most important and most often used function of the operating system is managing your files and folders—referred to as *data management*. In the same manner that you strive to keep your paper documents and file folders organized so that you can find information when you need it, your goal when organizing your computer files and folders is to group your files so that you can find information easily. Managing your data files so that you can find your information when you need it is one of the most important computing skills you can learn.

Activity 1.20 | Recognizing User Accounts in Windows 10

On a single computer, Windows 10 can have multiple user accounts. This is useful because you can share a computer with other people in your family or organization and each person can have his or her own information and settings—none of which others can see. Each user on a single computer is referred to as a ***user account***. Figure 1.45 shows the Settings screen where you can add additional users to your computer.

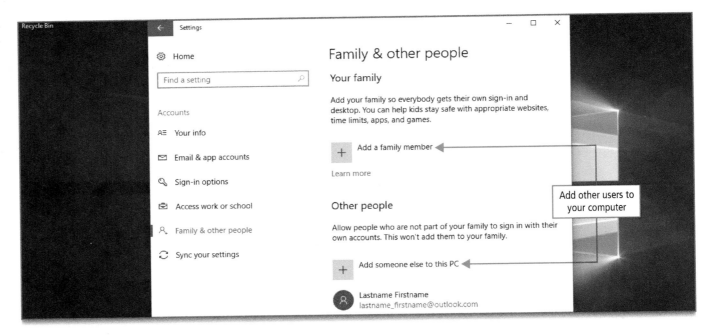

Figure 1.45

ALERT **Variations in Screen Organization, Colors, and Functionality Are Common in Windows 10**

Individuals and organizations can determine how Windows 10 displays; therefore, the colors and the organization of various elements on the screen can vary. Your college or organization may customize Windows 10 to display a college picture or company logo or restrict access to certain features. The basic functions and structure of Windows 10 are not changed by such variations. You can be confident that the skills you will practice in this instruction apply to Windows 10 regardless of available functionality or differences between the figures shown and your screen.

NOTE **Comparing Your Screen with the Figures in This Textbook**

Your screen will more closely match the figures shown in this textbook if you set your screen resolution to 1280 x 768. At other resolutions, your screen will closely resemble, but not match, the figures shown. To view your screen's resolution, on the desktop, right-click in a blank area, click *Display settings*, and then click the Resolution arrow. To adjust the resolution, select the desired setting, and then click OK.

With Windows 10, you can create a ***Microsoft account***, and then use that account to sign in to *any* Windows 10 computer on which you have, or create, a user account. By signing in with a Microsoft account you can:

- Download apps from the Microsoft Store
- Get your online content—email, social network updates, updated news—automatically displayed in an app when you sign in

Optionally, you can create a local account for use only on a specific PC. On your own Windows 10 computer, you must establish and then sign in with either a local account or a Microsoft account. Regardless of which one you select, you must provide an email address to associate with the user account name. If you create and then sign in with a local account, you can still connect to the internet, but you will not have the advantage of having your personal arrangement of apps displayed on your Start menu every time you sign in to that PC. You can use any email address to create a local account—similar to other online services where an email address is your user ID. You can also use any email address to create a Microsoft account.

To enjoy and get the full benefit of Windows 10, Microsoft Office, Skype, and free OneDrive cloud storage, if you have not already done so, create a Microsoft account. To do so, in your preferred web search engine, search for *create a Microsoft account.*

You can create an account using any email address. By signing in with a Microsoft account, your computer becomes your connected device where *you*—not your files—are the center of activity. At your college or place of employment, sign-in requirements will vary, because those computers are controlled by the organization's IT (Information Technology) professionals who are responsible for maintaining a secure computing environment for the entire organization.

Activity 1.21 | Turning On Your Computer, Signing In, and Exploring the Windows 10 Environment

Before you begin any computer activity, you must, if necessary, turn on your computer. This process is commonly referred to as ***booting the computer***. Because Windows 10 does not require you to completely shut down your computer except to install or repair a hardware device, in most instances moving the mouse or pressing a key will wake your computer in a few seconds. So, most of the time you will skip the lengthier boot process.

In this Activity, you will turn on your computer and sign in to Windows 10. Within an organization, the sign-in process may differ from that of your own computer.

ALERT   **The look and features of Windows 10 will differ between your own PC and a PC you might use at your college or workplace.**

The Activities in this project assume that you are working on your own PC and signed in with a Microsoft account, or that you are working on a PC at your college or workplace where you are permitted to sign into Windows 10 with your own Microsoft account.

If you do not have a Microsoft account, or are working at a computer where you are unable to sign in with your Microsoft account, you can still complete the Activities, but some steps will differ.

On your own computer, you created your user account when you installed Windows 10 or when you set up your new computer that came with Windows 10. In a classroom or lab, check with your instructor to see how you will sign in to Windows 10.

NOTE   **Create your Microsoft account if you have not already done so.**

To benefit from this instruction and understand your own computer, be sure that you know your Microsoft account login and password and use that to set up your user account. If you need to create a Microsoft account, in your preferred web search engine, search for *create a Microsoft account* and click the appropriate link.

1 If necessary, turn on your computer, and then examine Figure 1.46.

The Windows 10 *lock screen* fills your computer screen with a background—this might be a default picture from Microsoft such as one of the ones shown in the Lock screen settings in Figure 1.46 or a picture that you selected if you have personalized your system already. You can also choose to have a slide show of your own photos display on the lock screen.

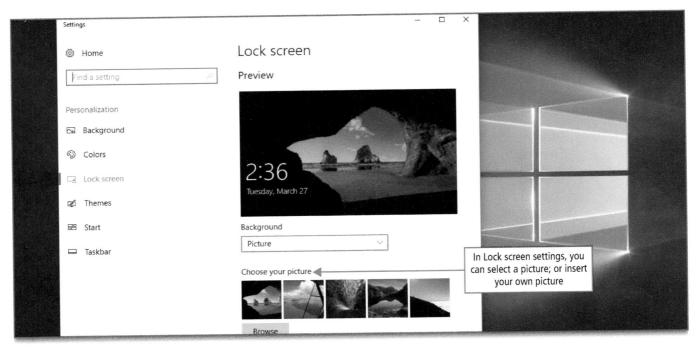

Figure 1.46

2 Determine whether you are working with a mouse and keyboard system or with a touchscreen system. If you are working with a touchscreen, determine whether you will use a stylus pen or the touch of your fingers.

NOTE   This Book Assumes You Are Using a Mouse and Keyboard, but You Can Also Use Touch

This instruction uses terminology that assumes you are using a mouse and keyboard, but you need only touch gestures (described at the beginning of Project 1A in this chapter) to move through the instruction easily using touch. If a touch gesture needs more clarification, a *By Touch* box will assist you in using the correct gesture. Because more precision is needed for desktop operations, touching with a stylus pen may be preferable to touch using your fingers. When working with Microsoft Store apps, finger gestures are usually precise enough.

3 Press Enter to display the Windows 10 sign-in screen. If you are already signed in, go to Step 5.

BY TOUCH   On the lock screen, swipe upward to display the sign-in screen. Tap your user image if necessary to display the Password box.

4 If you are the displayed user, type your password (if you have established one) and press Enter. If you are not the displayed user, click your user image if it displays or click the Switch user arrow → and then click your user image. Type your password.

The Windows 10 desktop displays with a default desktop background, a background you have selected, or perhaps a background set by your college or workplace.

BY TOUCH Tap the Password box to display the onscreen keyboard, type your password using the onscreen keyboard, and then at the right, tap the arrow.

5 In the lower left corner of your screen, move the mouse pointer over—*point to*—**Start** ▦ and then *click*—press the left button on your mouse pointing device—to display the **Start menu**. Compare your screen with Figure 1.47, and then take a moment to study the table in Figure 1.48. If your list of programs does not display, in the upper left, click the ▤ .

The *mouse pointer* is any symbol that displays on your screen in response to moving your mouse.

The Windows 10 *Start menu* displays a list of installed programs on the left and a customizable group of square and rectangular boxes—referred to as *tiles*—on the right. You can customize the arrangement of tiles from which you can access apps, websites, programs, folders, and tools for using your computer by simply clicking or tapping them.

Think of the right side of the Start menu as your connected *dashboard*—a one-screen view of links to information and programs that matter to *you*—through which you can connect with the people, activities, places, and apps that you care about.

Some tiles are referred to as *live tiles*, because they are constantly updated with fresh information relevant to you—the number of new email messages you have or new sports scores that you are interested in. Live tiles are at the center of your Windows 10 experience.

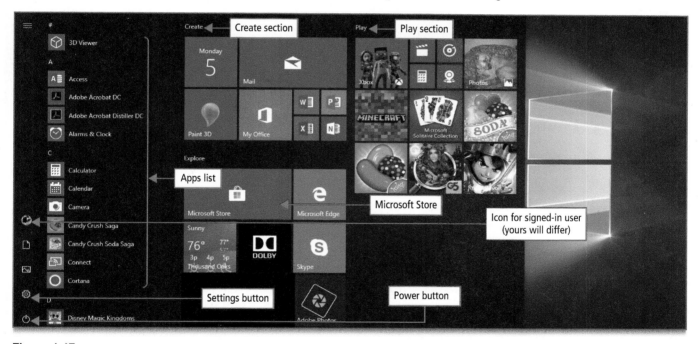

Figure 1.47

Parts of the Windows 10 Start Menu	
Create	Apps pinned to the Start menu that relate to your own information; for example, your Mail, your Calendar, and apps with which you create things; for example, your Office apps.
Apps list	Displays a list of the apps available on your system (yours will differ).
Play and Explore	Apps pinned to the Start menu that relate to games or news apps that you have installed; you can change this heading or delete it.
Power button	Enables you to set your computer to Sleep, Shut down, or Restart.
Settings	Displays the Settings menu to change any Windows 10 setting.
Signed-in User	Displays the icon for the signed-in user.

Figure 1.48

6 Click **Start** ⊞ again to close the Start menu. Compare your screen with Figure 1.49, and then take a moment to study the parts of the Windows desktop as shown in the table in Figure 1.50.

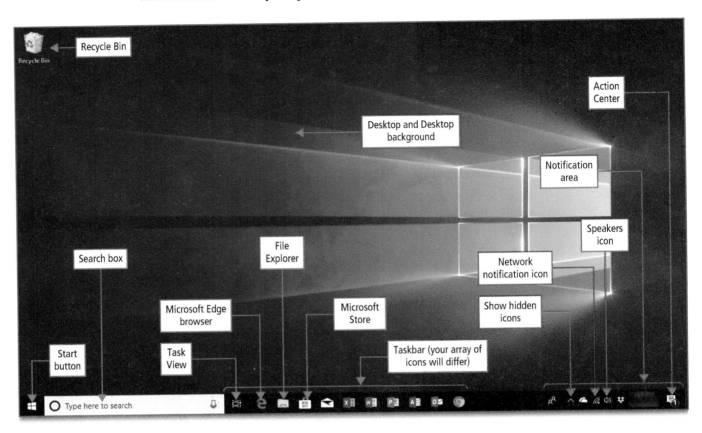

Figure 1.49

Parts of the Windows 10 Desktop

Action Center	Displays the Action Center in a vertical pane on the right of your screen where you can see notifications—such as new mail or new alerts from social networks—at the top and access commonly used settings at the bottom.
Desktop	Serves as a surface for your work, like the top of an actual desk. Here you can arrange icons—small pictures that represent a file, folder, program, or other object.
Desktop background	Displays the colors and graphics of your desktop; you can change the desktop background to look the way you want it, such as using a picture or a solid color. Also referred to as *wallpaper*.
File Explorer	Launches the File Explorer program, which displays the contents of folders and files on your computer and on connected locations and also enables you to perform tasks related to your files and folders such as copying, moving, and renaming. If your File Explorer icon does not display, search for it, right-click its name in the search results, and then click Pin to taskbar.
Microsoft Edge browser	Launches Microsoft Edge, the web browser program developed by Microsoft that is included with Windows 10.
Microsoft Store	Opens the Microsoft Store where you can select and download Microsoft Store apps.
Network notification icon	Displays the status of your network.
Notification area	Displays notification icons and the system clock and calendar; sometimes referred to as the *system tray*.
Recycle Bin	Contains files and folders that you delete. When you delete a file or folder, it is not actually deleted; it stays in the Recycle Bin if you want it back, until you take an action to empty the Recycle Bin.
Search box	If *Cortana*—Microsoft's intelligent personal assistant—is enabled, a small circle will display on the left edge of the Search box. If Cortana is not enabled, a search icon displays at the left edge.

Parts of the Windows 10 Desktop	
Show hidden icons	Displays additional icons related to your notifications.
Speakers icon	Displays the status of your computer's speakers (if any).
Start button	Displays the Start menu.
Task View	Displays your desktop background with a small image of all open programs and apps. Click once to open, click again to close. May also display the Timeline.
Taskbar	Contains buttons to launch programs and buttons for all open programs; by default, it is located at the bottom of the desktop, but you can move it. You can customize the number and arrangement of buttons.

Figure 1.50

Activity 1.22 | Pinning a Program to the Taskbar

Snipping Tool is a program within Windows 10 that captures an image of all or part of your computer's screen. A *snip*, as the captured image is called, can be annotated, saved, copied, or shared via email. Any capture of your screen is referred to as a *screenshot*, and there are many other ways to capture your screen in addition to the Snipping Tool.

NOTE   Snip & Sketch Offers Improved Snipping Capabilities

Although Snipping Tool will be available for several more years, a newer tool for snipping, called Snip & Sketch, will roll out to Windows 10 users. Find it by typing Snip & Sketch in the search box.

1 In the lower left corner of your screen, click in the **Search box**.

Search relies on *Bing*, Microsoft's search engine, which enables you to conduct a search on your PC, your apps, and the web.

2 With your insertion point in the search box, type **snipping** Compare your screen with Figure 1.51.

BY TOUCH   On a touchscreen, tap in the Search box to display the onscreen keyboard, and then begin to type *snipping*.

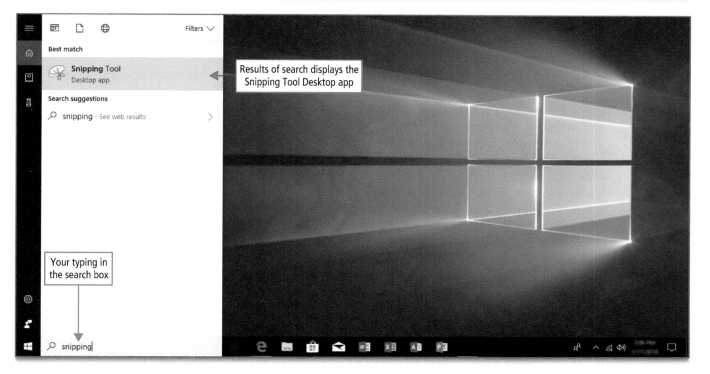

Figure 1.51

3 With the **Snipping Tool Desktop app** shaded and displayed at the top of the search results, press [Enter] one time.

The Snipping Tool program's *dialog box*—a small window that displays options for completing a task—displays on the desktop, and on the taskbar, the Snipping Tool program button displays underlined and framed in a lighter shade to indicate that the program is open.

☛ **BY TOUCH**   In the search results, tap the Snipping Tool app.

4 On the taskbar, point to the **Snipping Tool** button ▨ and then *right-click*—click the right mouse button one time. On the displayed **Jump List**, click **Pin to taskbar**.

A *Jump List* displays destinations and tasks from a program's taskbar icon when you right-click the icon.

☛ **BY TOUCH**   On the taskbar, use the *Swipe to select* technique—swipe upward with a short quick movement—to display the Jump List. On the list, tap *Pin to taskbar*.

5 Point to the upper right corner of the **Snipping Tool** dialog box, and then click **Close** ⊠.

Because Snipping Tool is a useful tool, while completing the Projects in this textbook, it is recommended that you leave Snipping Tool pinned to your taskbar.

Objective 8 | Prepare to Work with Folders and Files

A *file* is a collection of information stored on a computer under a single name. Examples of a file include a Word document, an Excel workbook, a picture, a song, or a program. A *folder* is a container in which you store files. Windows 10 organizes and keeps track of your electronic files by letting you create and label electronic folders into which you can place your files.

Activity 1.23 | Creating a New Folder to Store a File

In this Activity, you will create a new folder and save it in a location of your choice. You might decide to use a *removable storage device*, such as a USB flash drive, which is commonly used to transfer information from one computer to another. Such devices are also useful when you want to work with your files on different computers. For example, you probably have files that you work with at your college, at home, and possibly at your workplace.

A *drive* is an area of storage that is formatted with a file system compatible with your operating system and is identified by a drive letter. For example, your computer's *hard disk drive*—the primary storage device located inside your computer where some of your files and programs are typically stored—is usually designated as drive *C*. Removable storage devices that you insert into your computer will be designated with a drive letter—the letter designation varies depending on how many input ports you have on your computer.

You can also use *cloud storage*—storage space on an internet service that can also display as a drive on your computer. When you create a Microsoft account, free cloud storage called *OneDrive* is provided to you. If you are signed in with your Microsoft account, you can access OneDrive from File Explorer.

Increasingly, the use of removable storage devices for file storage is becoming less common, because having your files stored in the cloud where you can retrieve them from any device is more convenient and efficient.

ALERT   The steps in this project use the example of creating your Windows 10 Chapter 1 folder on a USB flash drive. If you want to store your folder in a different location, such as the Documents folder on your computer's hard drive or a folder on your OneDrive, you can still complete the steps, but your screens will not match exactly those shown.

1 Be sure your Windows desktop is still displayed. If you want to do so, insert your USB flash drive. If necessary, close any messages.

> Plugging in a device results in a chime sound—if sound is enabled. You might see a message in the taskbar or on the screen that the device software is being installed.

2 On your taskbar, check to see if the **File Explorer** icon ▣ displays. If it does, move to Step 3. If not, in the search box, type **file explorer** under **Best match**, point to **File Explorer Desktop app**, right-click, and then click **Pin to taskbar**.

> In an enterprise environment such as a college or business, File Explorer may not be pinned to the taskbar by default, so you might have to pin it there each time you use the computer. Windows 10 Home, the version of Windows that comes on most consumer PCs, typically has File Explorer pinned to the taskbar by default.

3 On the taskbar, click **File Explorer** ▣. If necessary, in the upper right corner of the **File Explorer** window, click Expand the Ribbon ⌄.

> *File Explorer* is the program that displays the contents of locations, folders, and files on your computer and also in your OneDrive and other cloud storage locations.
>
> The *ribbon* is a user interface in Windows 10 that groups commands for performing related tasks on tabs across the upper portion of a window. Commands for common tasks include copying and moving, creating new folders, emailing and zipping items, and changing the view.
>
> Use the *navigation pane*—the area on the left side of File Explorer window—to get to locations—your OneDrive, folders on your PC, devices and drives connected to your PC, and other PCs on your network.

4 On the ribbon at the top of the window, click the **View tab**, and then in the **Layout group**, click **Tiles**. Compare your screen with Figure 1.52, and then take a moment to study the parts of the File Explorer window as shown in the table in Figure 1.53.

NOTE **Does your ribbon show only the tab names? Does your Quick Access toolbar display below the ribbon?**

By default, the ribbon is minimized and appears as a menu bar, displaying only the ribbon tabs. If your ribbon displays only tabs, click the Expand the Ribbon arrow ⌄ on the right side to display the full ribbon. If your Quick Access toolbar displays below the ribbon, point to it, right-click, and then click Show Quick Access Toolbar above the Ribbon.

The *File Explorer window* displays with the Quick access area selected by default. A File Explorer window displays the contents of the current location and contains helpful parts so you can *navigate*—explore within the file organizing structure of Windows. A *location* is any disk drive, folder, network, or cloud storage area in which you can store files and folders.

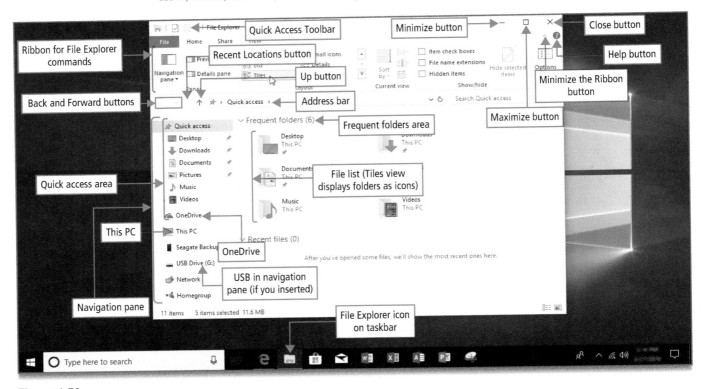

Figure 1.52

Parts of the File Explorer Window

Address bar	Displays your current location in the folder structure as a series of links separated by arrows.
Back and Forward buttons	Provides the ability to navigate to other folders you have already opened without closing the current folder window. These buttons work with the address bar; that is, after you use the address bar to change folders, you can use the Back button to return to the previous folder.
Close button	Closes the window.
File list	Displays the contents of the current folder or location; if you type text into the Search box, only the folders and files that match your search will display here—including files in subfolders.
Frequent folders area	When Quick access is selected in the navigation pane, displays the folders you use frequently.
Help button	Opens a Bing search for Windows 10 help.
Maximize button	Increases the size of a window to fill the entire screen.
Minimize button	Removes the window from the screen without closing it; minimized windows can be reopened by clicking the associated button in the taskbar.

Parts of the File Explorer Window

Minimize the Ribbon button	Collapses the ribbon so that only the tab names display.
Navigation pane	Displays—for the purpose of navigating to locations—the Quick access area, your OneDrive if you have one and are signed in, locations on the PC at which you are working, any connected storage devices, and network locations to which you might be connected.
OneDrive	Provides navigation to your free file storage and file sharing service provided by Microsoft that you get when you sign up for a Microsoft account; this is your personal cloud storage for files.
Quick access area	Displays commonly accessed locations—such as Documents and Desktop—that you want to access quickly.
Quick Access Toolbar	Displays commonly used commands; you can customize this toolbar by adding and deleting commands and by showing it below the ribbon instead of above the ribbon.
Recent Locations button	Displays the path to locations you have visited recently so that you can go back to a previously working directory quickly.
Ribbon for File Explorer commands	Groups common tasks such as copying and moving, creating new folders, emailing and zipping items, and changing views.
Search box	Locates files stored within the current folder when you type a search term.
This PC	Provides navigation to your internal storage and attached storage devices including optical media such as a DVD drive.
Up button	Opens the location where the folder you are viewing is saved—also referred to as the *parent folder*.

Figure 1.53

> **5** In the **navigation pane**, click **This PC**. On the right, under **Devices and drives**, locate **Windows (C:)**—or **OS (C:)**—point to the device name to display the ⬚ pointer, and then right-click to display a shortcut menu. Compare your screen with Figure 1.54.

A *shortcut menu* is a context-sensitive menu that displays commands and options relevant to the active object. The Windows logo on the C: drive indicates this is where the Windows 10 operating system is stored.

☛ **BY TOUCH**   Press and hold briefly to display a shaded square and then release.

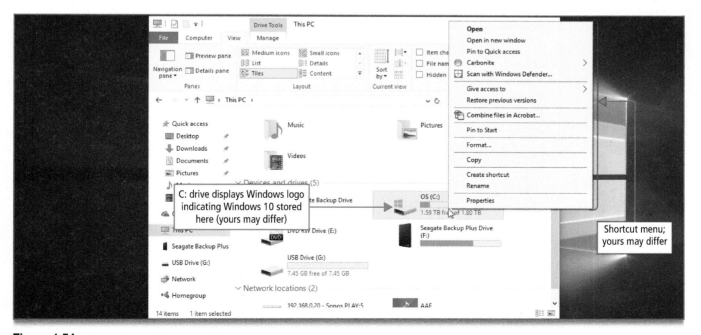

Figure 1.54

6 On the shortcut menu, click **Open** to display the *file list* for this drive.

A file list displays the contents of the current location. This area is also referred to as the ***content pane***. If you enter a search term in the search box, your results will also display here. Here, in the C: drive, Windows 10 stores various files related to your operating system.

ANOTHER WAY Point to the device name and double-click to display the file list for the device.

7 On the ribbon, notice that the **Drive Tools** tab displays above the **Manage tab**.

This is a ***contextual tab***, which is a tab added to the ribbon automatically when a specific object is selected and that contains commands relevant to the selected object.

8 To the left of the **address bar**, click **Up** ⬆ to move up one level in the drive hierarchy and close the file list.

The ***address bar*** displays your current location in the folder structure as a series of links separated by arrows. Use the address bar to enter or select a location. You can click a part of the path to go to that level. Or, click at the end of the path to select the path for copying.

9 Under **Devices and drives**, click your **USB flash drive** to select it—or click the folder or location where you want to store your file for this project—and notice that the drive or folder is highlighted in blue, indicating it is selected. At the top of the window, on the ribbon, click the **Computer tab**, and then in the **Location group**, click **Open**. Compare your screen with Figure 1.55.

The file list for the selected location displays. There may be no files or only a few files in the location you have selected. You can open a location by double-clicking its name, using the shortcut menu, or by using this ribbon command.

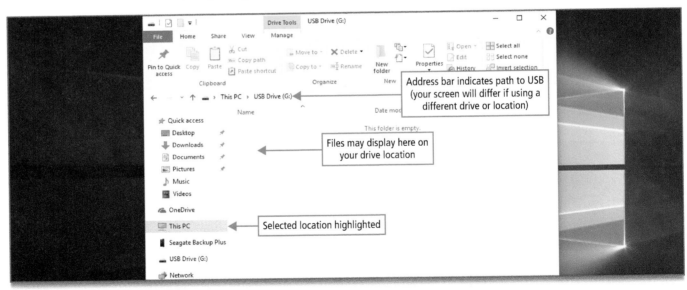

Figure 1.55

10 On the ribbon, on the **Home tab**, in the **New group**, click **New folder**.

11 With the text *New folder* highlighted, type **Windows 10 Chapter 1** and then press ⏎ to confirm the folder name and select—highlight—the new folder. With the folder selected, press ⏎ again to open the File Explorer window for your **Windows 10 Chapter 1** folder. Compare your screen with Figure 1.56.

Windows creates a new folder in the location you selected. The address bar indicates the *path* from This PC to your folder. A path is a sequence of folders that leads to a specific file or folder.

To *select* means to specify, by highlighting, a block of data or text on the screen with the intent of performing some action on the selection.

BY TOUCH You may have to tap the keyboard icon in the lower right corner of the taskbar to display the onscreen keyboard.

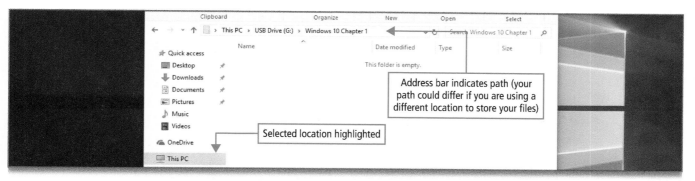

Figure 1.56

MORE KNOWLEDGE | **Use OneDrive as Cloud Storage**

OneDrive is Microsoft's *cloud storage* product. Cloud storage means that your data is stored on a remote server that is maintained by a company so that you can access your files from anywhere and from any device. The idea of having all your data on a single device—your desktop or laptop PC—has become old fashioned. Because cloud storage from large companies like Microsoft are secure, many computer users now store their information on cloud services like OneDrive. Anyone with a Microsoft account has a large amount of free storage on OneDrive, and if you have an Office 365 account—free to most college students—you have 1 terabyte or more of OneDrive storage that you can use across all Microsoft products. That amount of storage is probably all you will ever need—even if you store lots of photos on your OneDrive. OneDrive is integrated into the Windows 10 operating system.

Activity 1.24 | Creating and Saving a File

1 In the upper right corner of your **Windows 10 Chapter 1** folder window, click **Close** ☒.

2 In the lower left corner, click **Start** ⊞.

3 ▸ Point to the right side of the **apps list** to display a **scroll bar**, and then drag the **scroll box** down to view apps listed under **T**. Compare your screen with Figure 1.57.

To *drag* is to move something from one location on the screen to another while holding down the left mouse button; the action of dragging includes releasing the mouse button at the desired time or location.

A vertical *scroll bar* displays on the right side of the menu area. A scroll bar displays when the contents of a window or pane are not completely visible. A scroll bar can be vertical as shown or horizontal and displayed at the bottom of a window.

Within the scroll bar, you can move the *scroll box* to bring the contents of the window into view. The position of the scroll box within the scroll bar indicates your relative position within the window's contents. You can click the *scroll arrow* at either end of the scroll bar to move within the window in small increments.

Figure 1.57

MORE KNOWLEDGE | **Jump to a Lettered Section of the Apps List Quickly**

To move quickly to an alphabetic section of the apps list, click an alphabetic letter on the list to display an onscreen alphabet, and then click the letter of the alphabet to which you want to jump.

---

4 ▸ Click **Tips**. If necessary, in the upper right, click **Maximize** ▢ so that the **Tips** window fills your entire screen. Then, move your mouse pointer to the right edge of the screen to display the **scroll bar**. Compare your screen with Figure 1.58.

In any window, the *Maximize* button will maximize the size of the window to fill the entire screen.

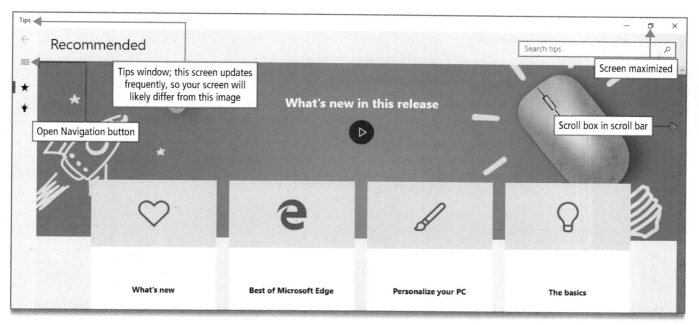

Figure 1.58

5 In the upper left corner, click **Open Navigation** ≡.

This icon is commonly referred to as a *menu icon* or a *hamburger menu* or simply a *hamburger*. The name derives from the three lines that bring to mind a hamburger on a bun. This type of button is commonly used in mobile applications because it is compact to use on smaller screens.

When you click the hamburger icon, a menu expands to identify the icons on the left—Recommended and Collections.

6 Click **Collections**, and then click **Windows**. Click **Get organized**. Move your mouse within the center right side of the screen to display a slideshow arrow ▷ , and then click the arrow until you get to the tip **Snap apps side by side**; if this tip is not available, pause at another interesting tip. Compare your screen with Figure 1.59.

To find interesting new things about Windows, Office, Microsoft Mixed Reality, and other topics, take time to explore the Tips app.

Figure 1.59

7 On the taskbar, click **Snipping Tool** 🖼 to display the small **Snipping Tool** dialog box over the screen.

8 On the **menu bar** of the **Snipping Tool** dialog box, to the right of *Mode*, click the **arrow**. Compare your screen with Figure 1.60.

> This *menu*—a list of commands within a category—displays four types of snips. A group of menus at the top of a program window is referred to as the *menu bar*.

> Use a *free-form snip* to draw an irregular line such as a circle around an area of the screen. Use a *rectangular snip* to draw a precise box by dragging the mouse pointer around an area of the screen to form a rectangle. Use a *window snip* to capture the entire displayed window. Use a *full-screen snip* to capture the entire screen.

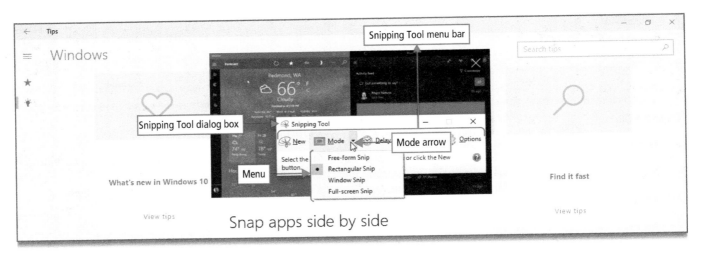

Figure 1.60

9 On the menu, click **Rectangular Snip**, and move your mouse slightly. Notice that the screen dims and your pointer takes the shape of a plus sign ➕.

10 Move the ➕ pointer to the upper left corner of the slide portion of the screen, hold down the left mouse button, and then drag down and to the right until you have captured the slide portion of the screen, as shown in Figure 1.61 and then release the mouse button. If you are not satisfied with your result, close the Snipping Tool window and begin again.

> The Snipping Tool mark-up window displays the portion of the screen that you snipped. Here you can annotate—mark or make notes on—save, copy, or share the snip.

Figure 1.61

> **11** On the toolbar of the displayed **Snipping Tool** mark-up window, click the **Pen button arrow** 🖊, and then click **Red Pen**. Notice that your mouse pointer displays as a red dot.

> **12** On the snip—remember that you are now looking at a picture of the portion of the screen you captured—use the red mouse pointer to draw a circle around the text *Snap apps side by side*—or whatever the name of the tip you selected is. The circle need not be precise. If you are not satisfied with your circle, on the toolbar, click the Eraser button 🧽, point anywhere on the red circle, click to erase, and then begin again. Compare your screen with Figure 1.62.

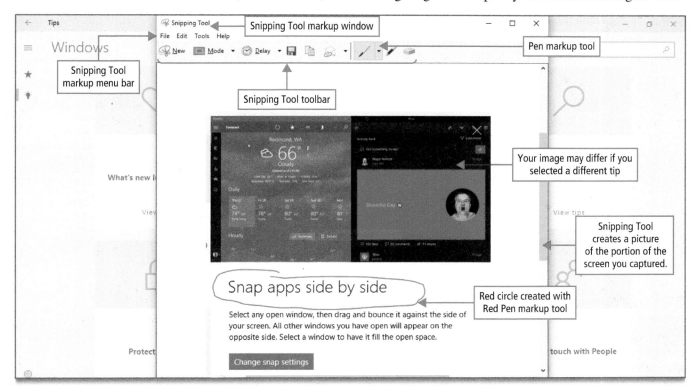

Figure 1.62

13 On the **Snipping Tool** mark-up window's toolbar, click **Save Snip**  to display the **Save As** dialog box.

14 In the **Save As** dialog box, in the **navigation pane**, drag the scroll box down as necessary to find and then click the location where you created your **Windows 10 Chapter 1** folder.

15 In the **file list**, scroll as necessary, locate and *double-click*—press the left mouse button two times in rapid succession while holding the mouse still—your **Windows 10 Chapter 1** folder. Compare your screen with Figure 1.63.

ANOTHER WAY Right-click the folder name and click Open.

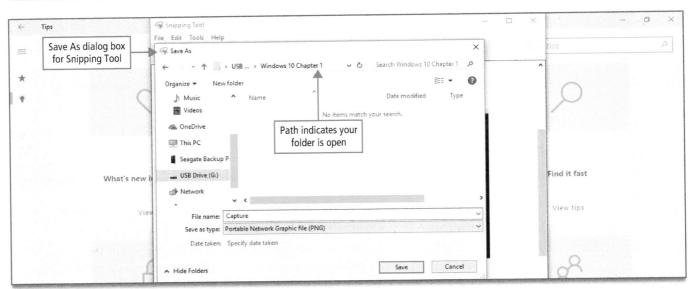

Figure 1.63

NOTE **Successful Double-Clicking Requires a Steady Hand**

Double-clicking needs a steady hand. The speed of the two clicks is not as important as holding the mouse still between the two clicks. If you are not satisfied with your result, try again.

16 At the bottom of the **Save As** dialog box, locate **Save as type**, click anywhere in the box to display a list, and then on the displayed list click **JPEG file**.

JPEG, which is commonly pronounced *JAY-peg* and stands for Joint Photographic Experts Group, is a common file type used by digital cameras and computers to store digital pictures. JPEG is popular because it can store a high-quality picture in a relatively small file.

17 At the bottom of the **Save As** dialog box, click in the **File name** box to select the text *Capture*, and then using your own name, type **Lastname_Firstname_1B_Tip_Snip**

Within any Windows-based program, text highlighted in blue—selected—in this manner will be replaced by your typing.

NOTE **File Naming in This Textbook**

Windows 10 recognizes file names with spaces. You can use spaces in file names, however, some programs, especially when transferring files over the internet, may insert the extra characters %20 in place of a space. In this instruction you will be instructed to save files using an underscore instead of a space. The underscore key is the shift of the [-] key—on most keyboards located two or three keys to the left of [Backspace].

18 In the lower right corner of the window, click **Save**.

19 **Close** ☒ the **Snipping Tool** mark-up window, and then **Close** ☒ the **Tips** window.

20 Close any open windows and display your Windows desktop.

> You have successfully created a folder and saved a file within that folder.

MORE KNOWLEDGE **The Hamburger** ≡

For a brief history of the hamburger icon, visit http://blog.placeit.net/history-of-the-hamburger-icon

---

For Non-MyLab Submissions

Start PowerPoint and click Blank Presentation. Click the File tab, on the left click Save As, click Browse, and then navigate to your Windows 10 Chapter 1 folder. At the bottom of the Save As dialog box, in the File name box, using your own name, name the file **Lastname_Firstname_Windows_10_1B_Hotel_Files** and then click Save. Move to Activity 1.26.

Activity 1.25 | Downloading and Extracting Zipped Files

1 If the Microsoft PowerPoint application is not pinned to your taskbar, use the same technique you used to search for and pin the Snipping Tool application to search for and pin the PowerPoint application to your taskbar.

2 Sign in to your **MyLab IT** course. In your course, locate and click **Windows 10 1B Hotel Files**, click Download Materials, and then click Download All Files. Using the Chrome browser (if you are using a different browser see notes below), use the steps below to extract the zipped folder to your **Windows 10 Chapter 1** (or use your favorite method to download and extract files):

- In the lower left, next to the downloaded zipped folder, click the small **arrow**, and then click **Show in folder**. The zipped folder displays in *File Explorer*—the Windows program that displays the contents of locations, folders, and files on your computer—in the Downloads folder. (Unless you have changed default settings, downloaded files go to the Downloads folder on your computer.)
- With the zipped folder selected, on the ribbon, under **Compressed Folder Tools**, click the **Extract tab**, and then at the right end of the ribbon, click **Extract all**.
- In the displayed **Extract Compressed (Zipped) Folders** dialog box, click **Browse**. In the **Select a destination** dialog box, use the navigation pane on the left to navigate to your **Windows 10 Chapter 1 folder**, and double-click its name to open the folder and display its name in the **Address bar**.
- In the lower right, click **Select Folder**, and then in the lower right, click **Extract**; when complete, a new File Explorer window displays showing the extracted files in your chapter folder. For this Project, you will see a PowerPoint file with your name and another zipped folder named **win01_1B_Bell_Orchid**, which you will extract later, a result file to check against, and an Instruction file. Take a moment to open **Windows_10_1B_Hotel_Files_Instructions**; note any recent updates to the book.
- **Close** ☒ both File Explorer windows, close the Grader download screens, and close any open documents For this Project, you should close MyLab and any other open windows in your browser.

3 ▸ From the taskbar, click **File Explorer**, navigate to and reopen your **Windows 10 Chapter 1 folder**, and then double-click the PowerPoint file you downloaded from **MyLab IT** that displays your name—**Student_Windows_10_1B_Hotel_Files**. In your blank PowerPoint presentation, if necessary, at the top click **Enable Editing**.

Activity 1.26 | Locating and Inserting a Saved File Into a PowerPoint Presentation

1 ▸ Be sure your PowerPoint presentation with your name is displayed. Then, on the **Home tab,** in the **Slides group**, click **Layout**. In the displayed gallery, click **Title Only**. If necessary, on the right, close the Design Ideas pane. Click anywhere in the text *Click to add title*, and then type **Tip Snip**

2 ▸ Click anywhere in the empty space below the title you just typed. Click the **Insert tab**, and then in the **Images group**, click **Pictures**. In the **navigation pane**, click the location of your **Windows 10 Chapter 1** folder, open the folder, and then in the **Insert Picture** dialog box, click one time to select your **Lastname_Firstname_1B_Tip_Snip** file. In the lower right corner of the dialog box, click **Insert**. If necessary, close the Design Ideas pane on the right. If necessary, drag the image to the right so that your slide title *Tip Snip* displays.

3 ▸ On the Quick Access Toolbar, click **Save** ⊟, and then in the upper right corner of the PowerPoint window, click **Minimize** ⊡ so that PowerPoint remains open but not displayed on your screen; you will need your PowerPoint presentation as you progress through this project.

4 ▸ **Close** ⊠ the File Explorer window and close any other open windows.

Activity 1.27 | Using Snap and Task View

Use **Snap** to arrange two or more open windows on your screen so that you can work with multiple screens at the same time.

Snap with the mouse by dragging the **title bar**—the bar across the top of the window that displays the program, file, or app name—of one app to the left until it snaps into place, and then dragging the title bar of another app to the right until it snaps into place.

Snap with the keyboard by selecting the window you want to snap, and then pressing ▩ + ◁. Then select another window and press ▩ + ▷. This is an example of a **keyboard shortcut**—a combination of two or more keyboard keys used to perform a task that would otherwise require a mouse.

1 From your desktop, click **Start** ⊞. In the list of apps, click the letter **A** to display the alphabet, and then click **W**. Under **W**, click **Weather**. If necessary, personalize your weather content by typing your zip code into the Search box, selecting your location, and clicking Start.

2 By using the same technique to display the alphabet, click **C**, and then click **Calculator**. On the taskbar, notice that icons display to show that the Weather app and the Calculator app are open. Notice also that on the desktop, the most recently opened app displays on top and is also framed on the taskbar. Compare your screen with Figure 1.64.

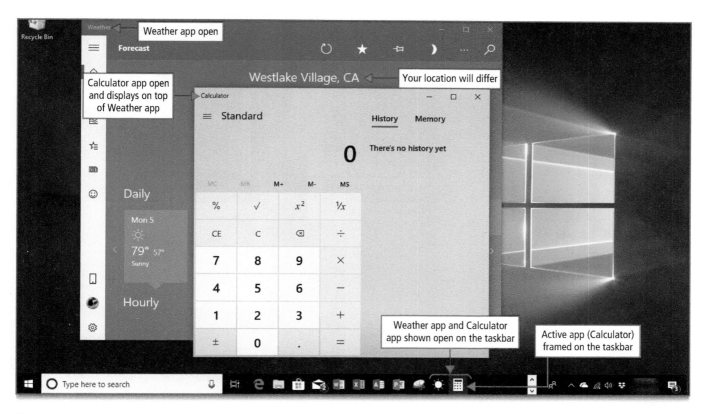

Figure 1.64

3 Point to the word *Calculator* at the top of this open app, hold down your left mouse button, drag your mouse pointer to the left edge of your screen until an outline displays to show where the window will snap, and then release the mouse button. Compare your screen with Figure 1.65.

> On the right, all open windows display—your PowerPoint presentation and the Weather app. This feature is ***Snap Assist***—after you have snapped a window, all other open windows display as ***thumbnails*** in the remaining space. A thumbnail is a reduced image of a graphic.

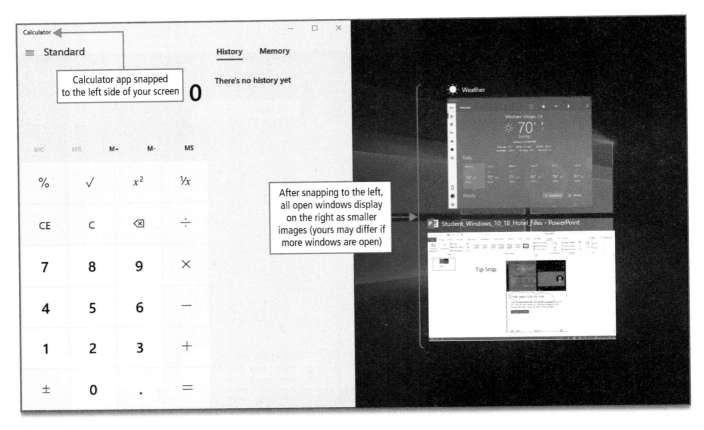

Figure 1.65

4 Click the **Weather** app to have it fill the right half of your screen.

5 In the lower left of your keyboard, press and hold down 🪟 and then in upper right of your keyboard, locate and press and release ⌈PrintScrn⌋. Notice that your screen dims momentarily.

> This is another method to create a screenshot. This screenshot file is automatically stored in the Screenshots folder in the Pictures folder of your hard drive; it is also stored on the Clipboard if you want to copy it immediately.

> A screenshot captured in this manner is saved as a *.png* file, which is commonly pronounced PING, and stands for Portable Network Graphic. This is an image file type that can be transferred over the internet.

6 On the taskbar, click **Task View** 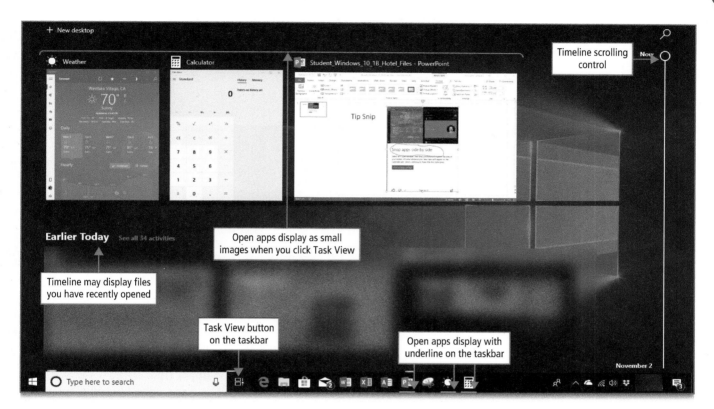, point to one of the open apps, and then compare your screen with Figure 1.66.

> Use the *Task View* button on the taskbar to see and switch between open apps—including desktop apps. You may see the Windows 10 feature *Timeline*, with which, when you click the Task View button, you can see your activities and files you have recently worked on across your devices. For example, you can find a document, image, or video you worked on yesterday or a week ago.

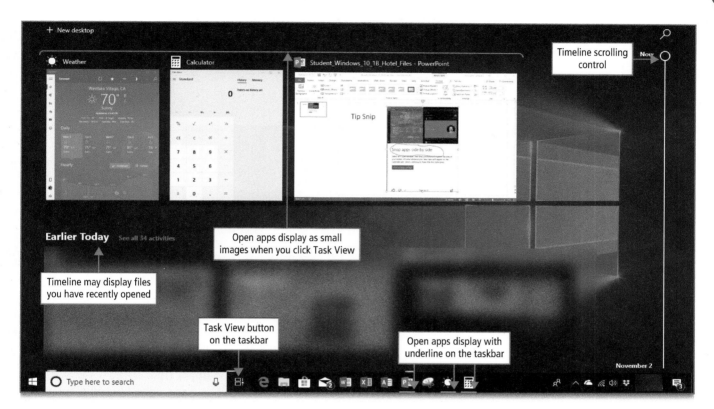

Figure 1.66

7 From **Task View**, click your **PowerPoint** window. On the **Home tab**, in the **Slides group**, click the upper portion of the **New Slide** button to insert a new slide in the same layout as your previous slide.

> An arrow attached to a button will display a menu when clicked. Such a button is referred to as a *split button*—clicking the main part of the button performs a command and clicking the arrow opens a menu with choices.

8 As the title type **Side by Side** and then click in the blank space below the title. On the ribbon, on the **Home tab**, in the **Clipboard group**, click the upper portion of the **Paste** button to paste your screenshot into the slide.

> Recall that by creating a screenshot using the ⊞ + PrintScrn command, a copy was placed on the Clipboard. A permanent copy is also stored in the Screenshots folder of your Pictures folder. This is a convenient way to create a quick screenshot.

9 ▸ With the image selected, on the ribbon, under **Picture Tools**, click **Format**. In the **Size group**, click in the **Shape Height** box ⬚ 0.05″, type 5 and press ⏎. Drag the image down and into the center of the space so that your slide title is visible. Compare your screen with Figure 1.67.

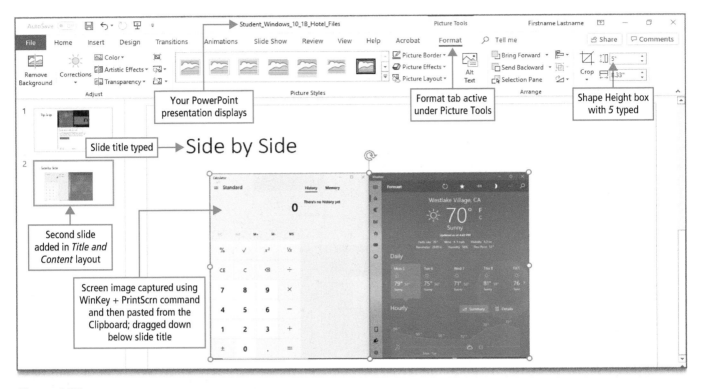

Figure 1.67

10 ▸ On the Quick Access Toolbar, click **Save** 🖫, and then in the upper right corner of the PowerPoint window, click **Minimize** ▭ so that PowerPoint remains open but not displayed on your screen.

11 ▸ **Close** ☒ the **Calculator** app and the **Weather** app to display your desktop.

Objective 9	Use File Explorer to Extract Zipped Files and to Display Locations, Folders, and Files

A file is the fundamental unit of storage that enables Windows 10 to distinguish one set of information from another. A folder is the basic organizing tool for files. In a folder, you can store files that are related to one another. You can also place a folder inside of another folder, which is then referred to as a *subfolder*.

Windows 10 arranges folders in a structure that resembles a *hierarchy*—an arrangement where items are ranked and where each level is lower in rank than the item above it. The hierarchy of folders is referred to as the *folder structure*. A sequence of folders in the folder structure that leads to a specific file or folder is a *path*.

Activity 1.28 | Navigating with File Explorer

Recall that File Explorer is the program that displays the contents of locations, folders, and files on your computer and also in your OneDrive and other cloud storage locations. File Explorer also enables you to perform tasks related to your files and folders such as copying, moving, and renaming. When you open a folder or location, a window displays to show its contents. The design of the window helps you navigate—explore within the file structure so you can find your files and folders—and so that you can save and find your files and folders efficiently.

In this Activity, you will open a folder and examine the parts of its window.

1 ▶ With your desktop displayed, on the taskbar, *point to* but do not click **File Explorer** ▢, and notice the ScreenTip *File Explorer*.

A **ScreenTip** displays useful information when you perform various mouse actions, such as pointing to screen elements.

2 ▶ Click **File Explorer** ▢ to display the **File Explorer** window.

File Explorer is at work anytime you are viewing the contents of a location or the contents of a folder stored in a specific location. By default, the File Explorer button on the taskbar opens with the **Quick access** location—a list of files you have been working on and folders you use often—selected in the navigation pane and in the address bar.

The default list will likely display the Desktop, Downloads, Documents, and Pictures folders, and then folders you worked on recently or work on frequently will be added automatically, although you can change this behavior.

The benefit of the Quick access list is that you can customize a list of folders that you go to often. To add a folder to the list quickly, you can right-click a folder in the file list and click Pin to Quick Access.

For example, if you are working on a project, you can pin it—or simply drag it—to the Quick access list. When you are done with the project and not using the folder so often, you can remove it from the list. Removing it from the list does not delete the folder, it simply removes it from the Quick access list.

3 ▶ On the left, in the **navigation pane**, scroll down if necessary, and then click **This PC** to display folders, devices, and drives in the **file list** on the right. Compare your screen with Figure 1.68.

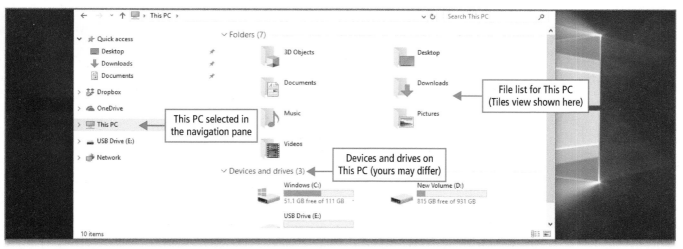

Figure 1.68

4 If necessary, in the upper right corner, click Expand the Ribbon ⌄. In the **file list**, under **Folders**—click **Documents** one time to select it, and then on the ribbon, on the **Computer tab**, in the **Location group**, click **Open**.

5 On the ribbon, click the **View tab**. In the **Show/Hide group**, be sure that **Item check boxes** is selected—select it if necessary, and then in the **Layout group**, if necessary, click **Details**.

The window for the Documents folder displays. You may or may not have files and folders already stored here. Because this window typically displays the file list for a folder, it is also referred to as the *folder window*. Item check boxes make it easier to select items in a file list and also to see which items are selected in a file list.

ANOTHER WAY Point to Documents, right-click to display a shortcut menu, and then click Open; or, point to Documents and double-click.

6 Compare your screen with Figure 1.69, and then take a moment to study the parts of the window as described in the table in Figure 1.70.

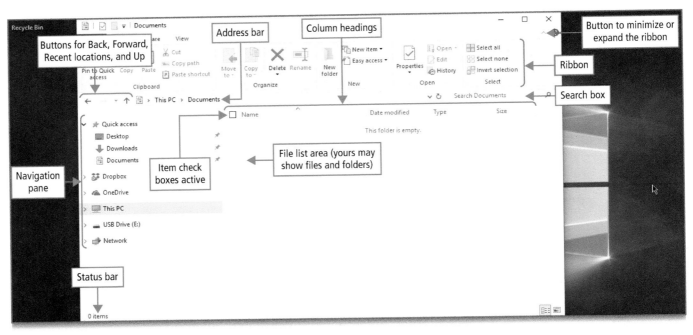

Figure 1.69

Parts of the File Explorer Window	
Window Part	**Function**
Address bar	Displays your current location in the file structure as a series of links separated by arrows. Tap or click a part of the path to go to that level or tap or click at the end to select the path for copying.
Back, Forward, Recent locations, and Up buttons	Enable you to navigate to other folders you have already opened without closing the current window. These buttons work with the address bar; that is, after you use the address bar to change folders, you can use the Back button to return to the previous folder. Use the Up button to open the location where the folder you are viewing is saved—also referred to as the *parent folder*.
Column headings	Identify the columns in Details view. By clicking the column heading name, you can change how the files in the file list are organized; by clicking the arrow on the right, you can select various sort arrangements in the file list. By right-clicking a column heading, you can select other columns to add to the file list.
File list	Displays the contents of the current folder or location. If you type text into the Search box, a search is conducted on the folder or location only, and only the folders and files that match your search will display here—including files in subfolders.
Minimize the Ribbon or Expand the Ribbon button	Changes the display of the ribbon. When minimized, the ribbon shows only the tab names and not the full ribbon.
Navigation pane	Displays locations to which you can navigate; for example, your OneDrive, folders on This PC, devices and drives connected to your PC, folders listed under Quick access, and possibly other PCs on your network. Use Quick access to open your most commonly used folders and searches. If you have a folder that you use frequently, you can drag it to the Quick access area so that it is always available.
Ribbon	Groups common tasks such as copying and moving, creating new folders, emailing and zipping items, and changing views of the items in the file list.
Search box	Enables you to type a word or phrase and then searches for a file or subfolder stored in the current folder that contains matching text. The search begins as soon as you begin typing; for example, if you type G, all the file and folder names that start with the letter G display in the file list.
Status bar	Displays the total number of items in a location, or the number of selected items and their total size.

Figure 1.70

7 ▶ Move your pointer anywhere into the **navigation pane**, and notice that a downward pointing arrow ˅ displays to the left of *Quick access* to indicate that this item is expanded, and a right-pointing arrow > displays to the left of items that are collapsed.

You can click these arrows to collapse and expand areas in the navigation pane.

Activity 1.29 | Using File Explorer to Extract Zipped Files

For Non-MyLab Users
From your instructor or from www.pearsonhighered.com/go download the zipped folder **win01_1B_Bell_Orchid** to your **Windows 10 Chapter 1** folder.

1 ▶ In the **navigation pane**, if necessary expand **This PC**, scroll down if necessary, and then click your **USB flash drive** (or the location where you have stored your chapter folder) one time to display its contents in the **file list**. Double-click to open your **Windows 10 Chapter 1 folder** and locate the zipped folder **win01_1B_Bell_Orchid**.

2 ▶ Use the steps below to extract this zipped folder to your **Windows 10 Chapter 1 folder** as follows (or use your favorite method to unzip):

- On the **Home tab**, click **New folder**, and then name the folder **win01_1B_Bell_Orchid**
- Click the zipped folder **win01_1B_Bell_Orchid** one time to select it.

- With the zipped folder selected, on the ribbon, under **Compressed Folder Tools**, click the **Extract tab**, and then at the right end of the ribbon, click **Extract all**.
- In the displayed **Extract Compressed (Zipped) Folders** dialog box, click **Browse**. In the **Select a destination** dialog box, use the navigation pane on the left to navigate to your **Windows 10 Chapter 1 folder**, and then double-click the name of the new folder you just created to open the folder and display its name in the **Address bar**.
- In the lower right, click **Select Folder**, and then in the lower right, click **Extract**. When complete, click the Up button ⬆ one time. You will see the extracted folder and the zipped folder.
- To delete the unneeded zipped version, click it one time to select it, and then on the **Home tab**, in the **Organize group**, click **Delete**. If necessary, click Yes. Now that the files are extracted, you do not need the zipped copy.

3 ▸ Close ✕ all File Explorer windows to display your desktop.

Activity 1.30 | Using File Explorer to Display Locations, Folders, and Files

1 ▸ From the taskbar, open **File Explorer** 📁. In the **navigation pane**, if necessary expand **This PC**, scroll down if necessary, and then click your **USB flash drive** (or the location where you have stored your chapter folder) one time to display its contents in the **file list**. In the **file list**, double-click your **Windows 10 Chapter 1 folder** to display its contents. Compare your screen with Figure 1.71.

In the navigation pane, *This PC* displays all of the drive letter locations attached to your computer, including the internal hard drives, CD or DVD drives, and any connected devices such as a USB flash drive.

Your PowerPoint file, your *Tip_Snip* file, and your extracted folder *win01_1B_Bell_Orchid* folder display if this is your storage location.

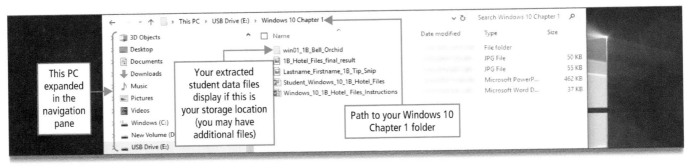

Figure 1.71

2 In the **file list**, double-click the **win01_1B_Bell_Orchid** folder to display the subfolders and files.

Recall that the corporate office of the Bell Orchid Hotels is in Boston. The corporate office maintains subfolders labeled for each of its large hotels in Honolulu, Orlando, San Diego, and Santa Barbara.

ANOTHER WAY Right-click the folder, and then click Open; or, select the folder and then on the ribbon, on the Home tab, in the Open group, click Open.

3 In the **file list**, double-click **Orlando** to display the subfolders, and then look at the **address bar** to view the path. Compare your screen with Figure 1.72.

Within each city's subfolder, there is a structure of subfolders for the Accounting, Engineering, Food and Beverage, Human Resources, Operations, and Sales and Marketing departments.

Because folders can be placed inside of other folders, such an arrangement is common when organizing files on a computer.

In the address bar, the path from the flash drive to the win01_1B_Bell_Orchid folder to the Orlando folder displays as a series of links.

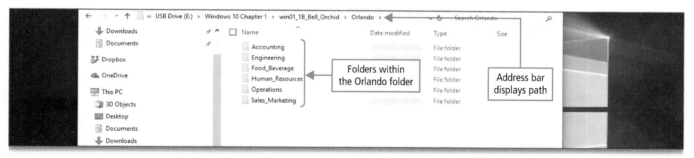

Figure 1.72

4 In the **address bar**, to the right of **win01_1B_Bell_Orchid**, click the ⟩ arrow to display a list of the subfolders in the **win01_1B_Bell_Orchid** folder. On the list that displays, notice that **Orlando** displays in bold, indicating it is open in the file list. Then, on the list, click **Honolulu**.

The subfolders within the Honolulu folder display.

5 In the **address bar**, to the right of **win01_1B_Bell_Orchid**, click the ⟩ arrow again to display the subfolders in that folder. Then, on the **address bar**—not on the list—point to **Honolulu** and notice that the list of subfolders in the **Honolulu** folder displays.

After you display one set of subfolders in the address bar, all of the links are active and you need only point to them to display the list of subfolders.

Clicking an arrow to the right of a folder name in the address bar displays a list of the subfolders in that folder. You can click a subfolder name to display its contents. In this manner, the address bar is not only a path, but it is also an active control with which you can step from the current folder directly to any other folder above it in the folder structure just by clicking a folder name.

6 On the list of subfolders for **Honolulu**, click **Sales_Marketing** to display its contents in the **file list**. On the **View tab**, in the **Layout group**, if necessary, click **Details**. Compare your screen with Figure 1.73.

ANOTHER WAY In the file list, double-click the Sales_Marketing folder.

The files in the Sales_Marketing folder for Honolulu display in the Details layout. To the left of each file name, an icon indicates the program that created each file. Here, there is one PowerPoint file, one Excel file, one Word file, and four JPEG images.

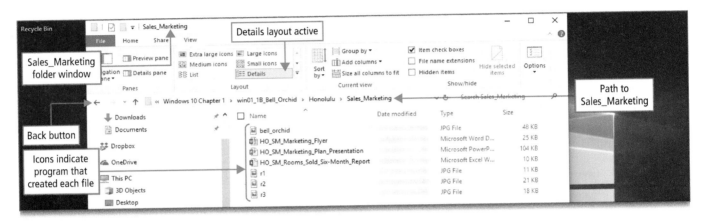

Figure 1.73

7 In the upper left portion of the window, click **Back** [←] one time.

The Back button retraces each of your clicks in the same manner as clicking the Back button when you are browsing the internet.

8 In the **file list**, point to the **Human_Resources** folder, and then double-click to open the folder.

9 In the **file list**, click one time to select the PowerPoint file **HO_HR_New_Employee_Presentation**, and then on the ribbon, click the **View tab**. In the **Panes group**, click **Details pane**, and then compare your screen with Figure 1.74.

The *Details pane* displays the most common *file properties* associated with the selected file. File properties refer to information about a file, such as the author, the date the file was last changed, and any descriptive *tags*—properties that you create to help you find and organize your files.

Additionally, a thumbnail image of the first slide in the presentation displays, and the status bar displays the number of items in the folder.

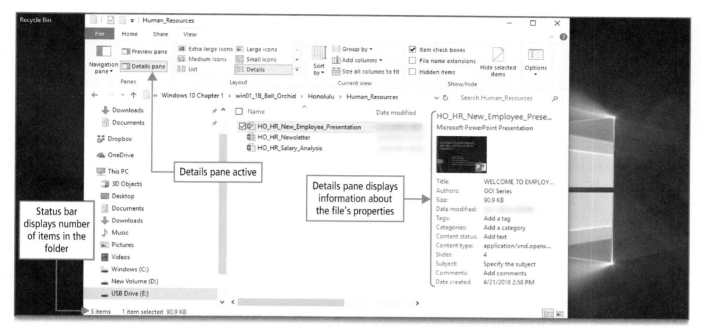

Figure 1.74

> **10** On the right, in the **Details pane**, click **Add a tag**, type **New Employee meeting** and then at the bottom of the pane click **Save**.

Because you can search for tags, adding tags to files makes them easier to find.

🔄 **ANOTHER WAY** With the file selected, on the Home tab, in the Open group, click Properties to display the Properties dialog box for the file, and then click the Details tab.

> **11** On the ribbon, on the **View tab**, in the **Panes group**, click **Preview pane** to replace the **Details pane** with the **Preview pane**. Compare your screen with Figure 1.75.

In the Preview pane that displays on the right, you can use the scroll bar to scroll through the slides in the presentation; or, you can click the up or down scroll arrow to view the slides as a miniature presentation.

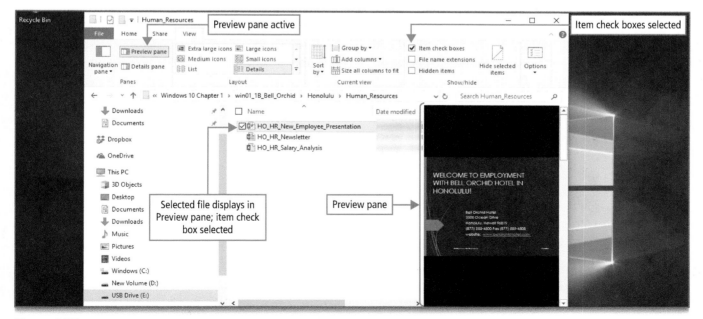

Figure 1.75

12 On the ribbon, click **Preview pane** to close the right pane.

Use the Details pane to see a file's properties and the Preview pane when you want to look at a file quickly without actually opening it.

13 Close ⨯ the **Human_Resources** window.

Objective 10 | Start Programs and Open Data Files

When you are using the software programs installed on your computer, you create and save data files—the documents, workbooks, databases, songs, pictures, and so on that you need for your job or personal use. Therefore, most of your work with Windows 10 desktop applications is concerned with locating and starting your programs and locating and opening your files.

Activity 1.31 | Starting Programs

You can start programs from the Start menu or from the taskbar by pinning a program to the taskbar. You can open your data files from within the program in which they were created, or you can open a data file from a window in File Explorer, which will simultaneously start the program and open your file.

1 Be sure your desktop displays and that your PowerPoint presentation is still open but minimized on the taskbar. You can point to the PowerPoint icon to have a small image of the active slide display. Click **Start** ⊞ to place the insertion point in the search box, type **wordpad** and then click the **WordPad Desktop app**.

2 With the insertion point blinking in the document window, type your first and last name.

3 From the taskbar, open your PowerPoint presentation. On the **Home tab**, click the upper portion of the **New Slide** button to insert a blank slide in the Title Only layout. Click anywhere in the text *Click to add title*, and then type **Wordpad**

4 Click anywhere in the lower portion of the slide. On the **Insert tab**, in the **Images group**, click **Screenshot**, and then under **Available Windows**, click the image of the WordPad program with your name typed to insert the image in the PowerPoint slide. Click in a blank area of the slide to deselect the image; if necessary, close the Design Ideas pane on the right. As necessary, drag the image down so that the title displays, and if necessary, use the Shape Height box to decrease the size of the screenshot slightly. Compare your screen with Figure 1.76.

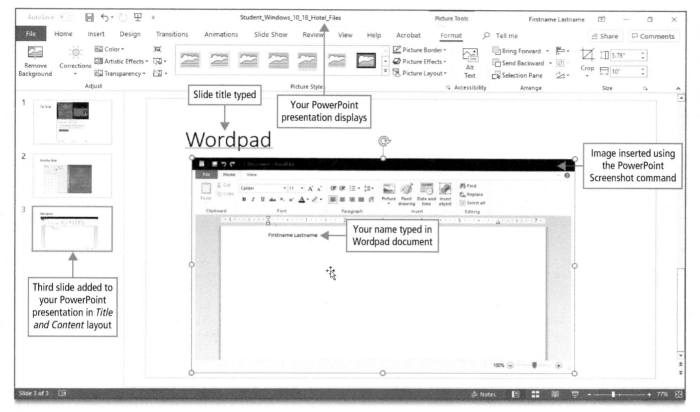

Figure 1.76

5 On the Quick Access toolbar, click **Save** ⊞ and then in the upper right corner of the PowerPoint window, click **Minimize** – so that PowerPoint remains open but not displayed on your screen.

6 Close ⊠ **WordPad**, and then click **Don't Save**.

Activity 1.32 | Opening Data Files

1 Open **Microsoft Word** from your taskbar, or click **Start** ⊞, type **Microsoft word** and then open the **Word** desktop app. Compare your screen with Figure 1.77.

The Word program window has features that are common to other programs you have opened; for example, commands are arranged on tabs. When you create and save data in Word, you create a Word document file.

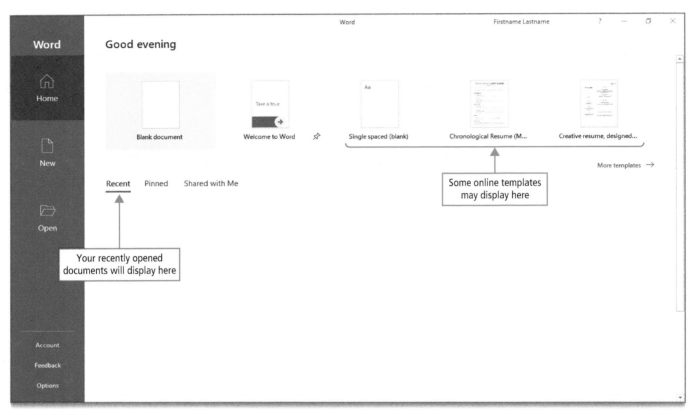

Figure 1.77

2 On the left, click **Open**. Notice the list of places from which you can open a document, including your OneDrive if you are logged in. Click **Browse** to display the **Open** dialog box. Compare your screen with Figure 1.78, and then take a moment to study the table in Figure 1.79.

Recall that a dialog box is a window containing options for completing a task; the layout of the Open dialog box is similar to that of a File Explorer window. When you are working in a desktop application, use the Open dialog box to locate and open existing files that were created in the desktop application.

When you click Browse, typically the Documents folder on This PC displays. You can use the skills you have practiced to navigate to other locations on your computer, such as your removable USB flash drive.

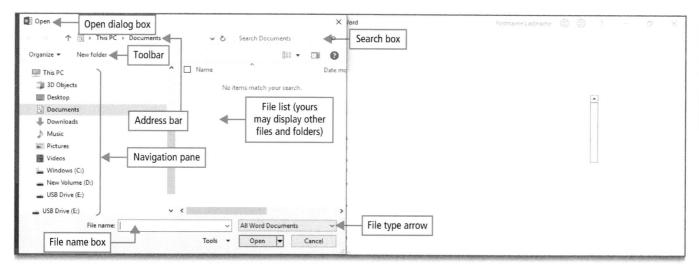

Figure 1.78

Dialog Box Element	Function
Address bar	Displays the path in the folder structure.
File list	Displays the list of files and folders that are available in the folder indicated in the address bar.
File name box	Enables you to type the name of a specific file to locate it—if you know it.
File type arrow	Enables you to restrict the type of files displayed in the file list; for example, the default *All Word Documents* restricts (filters) the type of files displayed to only Word documents. You can click the arrow and adjust the restrictions (filters) to a narrower or wider group of files.
Navigation pane	Navigate to files and folders and get access to Quick access, OneDrive, and This PC.
Search box	Search for files in the current folder. Filters the file list based on text that you type; the search is based on text in the file name (and for files on the hard drive or OneDrive, in the file itself), and on other properties that you can specify. The search takes place in the current folder, as displayed in the address bar, and in any subfolders within that folder.
Toolbar	Displays relevant tasks; for example, creating a new folder.

Figure 1.79

3 In the **navigation pane**, scroll down as necessary, and then under **This PC**, click your **USB flash drive** or whatever location where you have stored your files for this project. In the **file list**, double-click your **win01_1B_Bell_Orchid** folder to open it and display its contents.

4 In the upper right portion of the **Open** dialog box, click the **More options arrow** ⌄, and then set the view to **Large icons**. Compare your screen with Figure 1.80.

The Live Preview feature indicates that each folder contains additional subfolders.

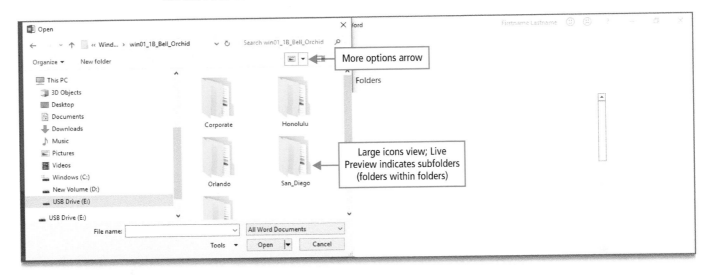

Figure 1.80

5 In the **file list**, double-click the **Corporate** folder, and then double-click the **Accounting** folder.

The view returns to the Details view.

6 In the **file list**, notice that only one document—a Word document—displays. In the lower right corner, locate the **File type** button, and notice that *All Word Documents* displays as the file type. Click the **File type arrow**, and then on the displayed list, click **All Files**. Compare your screen with Figure 1.81.

When you change the file type to *All Files*, you can see that the Word file is not the only file in this folder. By default, the Open dialog box displays only the files created in the active program; however, you can display variations of file types in this manner.

Microsoft Office file types are identified by small icons, which is a convenient way to differentiate one type of file from another. Although you can view all the files in the folder, you can open only the files that were created in the active program, which in this instance is Microsoft Word.

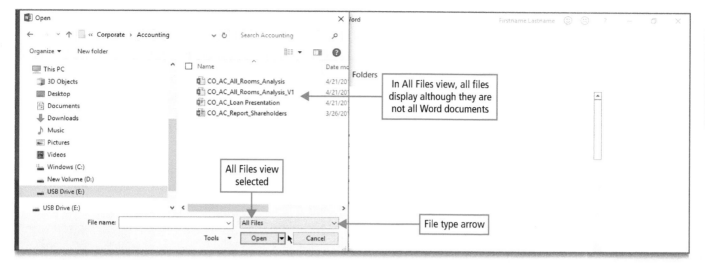

Figure 1.81

7 Change the file type back to **All Word Documents**. Then, in the **file list**, double-click the **CO_AC_Report_Shareholders** Word file to open the document. Take a moment to scroll through the document. If necessary, Maximize ▢ the window.

8 **Close** ⊠ the Word window.

9 Click **Start** ⊞, and then search for **.txt** At the top, click **Filters**, click **Documents**, and then on the list, click **Structure.txt in Future_Hotels**.

> The file opens using the Windows 10 *Notepad* desktop app—a basic text-editing program included with Windows 10 that you can use to create simple documents.
>
> In the search box, you can search for files on your computer, and you can search for a file by its *file name extension*—a set of characters at the end of a file name that helps Windows understand what kind of information is in a file and what program should open it. A *.txt file* is a simple file consisting of lines of text with no formatting that almost any computer can open and display.

10 **Close** ⊠ the Notepad program.

MORE KNOWLEDGE **Do Not Clutter Your Desktop by Creating Desktop Shortcuts or Storing Files**

On your desktop, you can add or remove *desktop shortcuts*, which are desktop icons that can link to items accessible on your computer such as a program, file, folder, disk drive, printer, or another computer. In previous versions of Windows, many computer users commonly did this.

Now the Start menu is your personal dashboard for all your programs and online activities, and increasingly you will access programs and your own files in the cloud. So do not clutter your desktop with shortcuts—doing so is more confusing than useful. Placing desktop shortcuts for frequently used programs or folders directly on your desktop may seem convenient, but as you add more icons, your desktop becomes cluttered and the shortcuts are not easy to find. A better organizing method is to use the taskbar for shortcuts to programs. For folders and files, the best organizing structure is to create a logical structure of folders within your Documents folder or your cloud-based OneDrive.

You can also drag frequently-used folders to the Quick access area in the navigation pane so that they are available any time you open File Explorer. As you progress in your use of Windows 10, you will discover techniques for using the taskbar and the Quick access area of the navigation pane to streamline your work instead of cluttering your desktop.

Activity 1.33 | Searching, Pinning, Sorting, and Filtering in File Explorer

1 From the taskbar, open **File Explorer** ▣. On the right, at the bottom, you may notice that under **Recent files**, you can see files that you have recently opened.

2 In the **navigation pane**, click your **USB flash drive**—or click the location where you have stored your files for this project. Double-click your **Windows 10 Chapter 1 folder** to open it. In the upper right, click in the **Search** box, and then type **pool** Compare your screen with Figure 1.82.

> Files that contain the word *pool* in the title display. If you are searching a folder on your hard drive or OneDrive, files that contain the word *pool* within the document will also display. Additionally, Search Tools display on the ribbon.

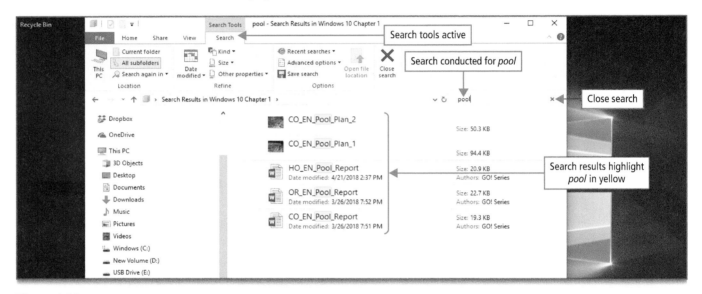

Figure 1.82

3 In the search box, clear the search by clicking ☒, and then in the search box type **Paris.jpg** Notice that you can also search by using a file extension as part of the search term.

4 **Clear** ☒ the search. Double-click your **win01_1B_Bell_Orchid** folder to open it.

5 On the **Home tab**, in the **Clipboard group**, click **Pin to Quick access**. If necessary, scroll up in the navigation pane. Compare your screen with Figure 1.83.

> You can pin frequently used folders to the Quick access area, and then unpin them when you no longer need frequent access. Folders that you access frequently will also display in the Quick access area without the pin image. Delete them by right-clicking the name and clicking Unpin from Quick access.

Figure 1.83

> 🔁 **ANOTHER WAY**   In the file list, right-click a folder name, and then click Pin to Quick access; or, drag the folder to the Quick access area in the navigation pain and release the mouse button when the ScreenTip displays Pin to Quick access.

6 In the **file list**—double-click the **Corporate** folder and then double-click the **Engineering** folder.

7 On the **View tab**, in the **Current view group**, click **Sort by**, and then click **Type**. Compare your screen with Figure 1.84.

Use this technique to sort files in the file list by type. Here, the JPG files display first, and then the Microsoft Excel files, and so on—in alphabetic order by file type.

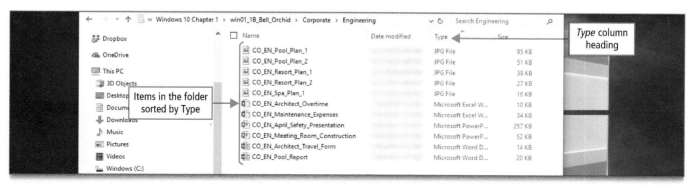

Figure 1.84

8 Point to the column heading **Type**, and then click **^**.

9 Point to the column heading **Type** again, and on the right, click ⌄. On the displayed list, click **Microsoft PowerPoint Presentation**, and notice that the file list is filtered to show only PowerPoint files.

A *filtered list* is a display of files that is limited based on specified criteria.

10 To the right of the **Type** column heading, click the check mark and then click **Microsoft PowerPoint Presentation** again to clear the Microsoft PowerPoint filter and redisplay all of the files.

11 **Close** ⊠ the File Explorer window.

ALERT   Allow Time to Complete the Remainder of This Project in One Session

If you are working on a computer that is not your own, for example in a college lab, plan your time to complete the remainder of this project in one working session. Allow 45 to 60 minutes.

Because you will need to store and then delete files on the hard disk drive of the computer at which you are working, it is recommended that you complete this project in one working session—*unless you are working on your own computer or you know that the files will be retained*. In your college lab, files you store on the computer's hard drive will not be retained after you sign off.

Objective 11   Create, Rename, and Copy Files and Folders

File management includes organizing, copying, renaming, moving, and deleting the files and folders you have stored in various locations—both locally and in the cloud.

Activity 1.34 | Copying Files from a Removable Storage Device to the Documents Folder on the Hard Disk Drive

Barbara and Steven have the assignment to transfer and then organize some of the corporation's files to a computer that will be connected to the corporate network. Data on such a computer can be accessed by employees at any of the hotel locations through the use of sharing technologies. For example, *SharePoint* is a Microsoft technology that enables employees in an organization to access information across organizational and geographic boundaries.

1 Close any open windows, but leave your open PowerPoint presentation minimized on the taskbar.

2 From the taskbar, open **File Explorer** ▣. In the **navigation pane**, if necessary expand **This PC**, and then click your USB flash drive or the location where you have stored your chapter folder to display its contents in the file list.

> Recall that in the navigation pane, under This PC, you have access to all the storage areas inside your computer, such as your hard disk drives, and to any devices with removable storage, such as CDs, DVDs, or USB flash drives.

3 Open your **Windows 10 Chapter 1** folder, and then in the **file list**, click **win01_1B_Bell_Orchid** one time to select the folder. Compare your screen with Figure 1.85.

Figure 1.85

4 With the **win01_1B_Bell_Orchid** folder selected, on the ribbon, on the **Home tab**, in the **Clipboard group**, click **Copy**.

> The Copy command places a copy of your selected file or folder on the *Clipboard* where it will be stored until you use the Paste command to place the copy somewhere else. The Clipboard is a temporary storage area for information that you have copied or moved from one place and plan to use somewhere else.

> In Windows 10, the Clipboard can hold only one piece of information at a time. Whenever something is copied to the Clipboard, it replaces whatever was there before. In Windows 10, you cannot view the contents of the Clipboard nor place multiple items there in the manner that you can in Microsoft Word.

ANOTHER WAY With the item selected in the file list, press Ctrl + C to copy the item to the clipboard.

5 To the left of the address bar, click **Up** ↑ two times. In the **file list**, double-click your **Documents** folder to open it, and then on the **Home tab**, in the **Clipboard group**, click **Paste**.

> A *progress bar* displays in a dialog box and also displays on the taskbar button with green shading. A progress bar indicates visually the progress of a task such as a copy process, a download, or a file transfer.

> The Documents folder is one of several folders within your *personal folder* stored on the hard disk drive. For each user account—even if there is only one user on the computer—Windows 10 creates a personal folder labeled with the account holder's name.

ANOTHER WAY With the destination location selected, press Ctrl + V to paste the item from the clipboard to the selected location. Or, on the Home tab, in the Organize group, click Copy to, find and then click the location to which you want to copy. If the desired location is not on the list, use the Choose location command at the bottom.

6 **Close** ☒ the **Documents** window.

Activity 1.35 | Creating Folders, Renaming Folders, and Renaming Files

Barbara and Steven can see that various managers have been placing files related to new European hotels in the *Future_Hotels* folder. They can also see that the files have not been organized into a logical structure. For example, files that are related to each other are not in separate folders; instead they are mixed in with other files that are not related to the topic.

In this Activity, you will create, name, and rename folders to begin a logical structure of folders in which to organize the files related to the European hotels project.

1▶ From the taskbar, open **File Explorer** 📁, and then use any of the techniques you have practiced to display the contents of the **Documents** folder in the **file list**.

NOTE   Using the Documents Folder and OneDrive Instead of Your USB Drive

In this modern computing era, you should limit your use of USB drives to those times when you want to quickly take some files to another computer without going online. Instead of using a USB drive, use your computer's hard drive, or better yet, your free OneDrive cloud storage that comes with your Microsoft account.

There are two good reasons to stop using USB flash drives. First, searching is limited on a USB drive—search does not look at the content inside a file. When you search files on your hard drive or OneDrive, the search extends to words and phrases actually *inside* the files. Second, if you delete a file or folder from a USB drive, it is gone and cannot be retrieved. Files you delete from your hard drive or OneDrive go to the Recycle Bin where you can retrieve them later.

2▶ In the **file list**, double-click the **win01_1B_Bell_Orchid** folder, double-click the **Corporate** folder, double-click the **Information_Technology** folder, and then double-click the **Future_Hotels** folder to display its contents in the file list; sometimes this navigation is written as *Documents > win01_1B_Bell_Orchid > Corporate > Information_Technology > Future_Hotels*.

Some computer users prefer to navigate a folder structure by double-clicking in this manner. Others prefer using the address bar as described in the following Another Way box. Use whatever method you prefer—double-clicking in the file list, clicking in the address bar, or expanding files in the Navigation pane.

🔄 ANOTHER WAY   In the navigation pane, click Documents, and expand each folder in the navigation pane. Or, In the address bar, to the right of Documents, click >, and then on the list, click win01_1B_Bell_Orchid. To the right of win01_1B_Bell_Orchid, click the > and then click Corporate. To the right of Corporate, click > and then click Information_Technology. To the right of Information_Technology, click >, and then click Future_Hotels.

3▶ In the **file list**, be sure the items are in alphabetical order by **Name**. If the items are not in alphabetical order, recall that by clicking the small arrow in the column heading name, you can change how the files in the file list are ordered.

4▶ On the ribbon, click the **View tab**, and then in the **Layout group**, be sure **Details** is selected.

The *Details view* displays a list of files or folders and their most common properties.

🔄 ANOTHER WAY   Right-click in a blank area of the file list, point to View, and then click Details.

5▶ On the ribbon, click the **Home tab**, and then in the **New group**, click **New folder**. With the text *New folder* selected, type **Paris** and press [Enter]. Click **New folder** again, type **Venice** and then press [Enter]. Create a third **New folder** named **London**

In a Windows 10 file list, folders are listed first, in alphabetic order, followed by individual files in alphabetic order.

6 Click the **Venice** folder one time to select it, and then on the ribbon, on the **Home tab**, in the **Organize group**, click **Rename**. Notice that the text *Venice* is selected. Type **Rome** and press [Enter].

↻ **ANOTHER WAY**   Point to a folder or file name, right-click, and then on the shortcut menu, click Rename.

7 In the **file list**, click one time to select the Word file **Architects**. With the file name selected, click the file name again to select all the text. Click the file name again to place the insertion point within the file name, edit the file name to **Architects_Local** and press [Enter]. Compare your screen with Figure 1.86.

You can use any of the techniques you just practiced to change the name of a file or folder.

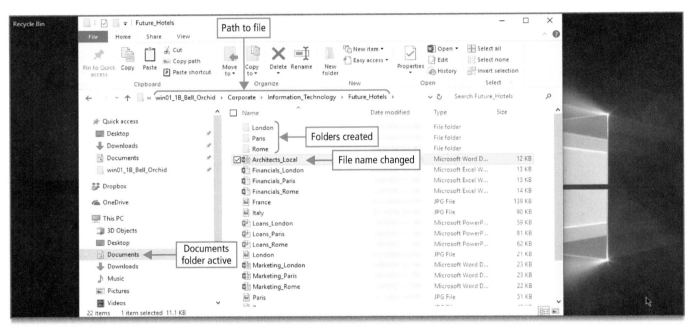

Figure 1.86

8 On the taskbar, click the **PowerPoint** icon to redisplay your **Windows_10_1B_Hotel_Files** presentation, and then on the **Home tab**, click the upper portion of the **New Slide** button to insert a new slide with the Title Only layout.

9 Click anywhere in the text *Click to add title*, type **Europe Folders** and then click anywhere in the empty space below the title.

10 On the **Insert tab**, in the **Images group**, click **Screenshot**, and then under **Available Windows**, click the image of your file list. On the **Picture Tools Format tab**, in the **Size group**, click in the **Shape Height** box, [↕ 0.05″ ÷] type **5** and then press [Enter]. As necessary, drag the image down so that the title you typed is visible; your presentation contains four slides.

11 Above the **File tab**, on the Quick Access toolbar, click **Save** [🖫], and then in the upper right corner, click **Minimize** [–] so that PowerPoint remains open but not displayed on your screen.

12 **Close** [✕] the **Future_Hotels** window.

Activity 1.36 | Copying Files

Copying, moving, renaming, and deleting files and folders comprise the most heavily used features within File Explorer. Probably half or more of the steps you complete in File Explorer relate to these tasks, so mastering these techniques will increase your efficiency.

When you *copy* a file or a folder, you make a duplicate of the original item and then store the duplicate in another location. In this Activity, you will assist Barbara and Steven in making copies of the Staffing_Plan file, and then placing the copies in each of the three folders you created—London, Paris, and Rome.

1 From the taskbar, open **File Explorer**, and then by double-clicking in the file list or following the links in the address bar, navigate to **This PC > Documents > win01_1B_Bell_ Orchid > Corporate > Information_Technology > Future_Hotels**.

2 In the upper right corner, **Maximize** ☐ the window. On the **View tab**, if necessary set the **Layout** to **Details**, and then in the **Current view group**, click **Size all columns to fit** ▦.

3 In the **file list**, click the file **Staffing_Plan** one time to select it, and then on the **Home tab**, in the **Clipboard group**, click **Copy**.

4 At the top of the **file list**, double-click the **London folder** to open it, and then in the **Clipboard group**, click **Paste**. Notice that the copy of the **Staffing_Plan** file displays. Compare your screen with Figure 1.87.

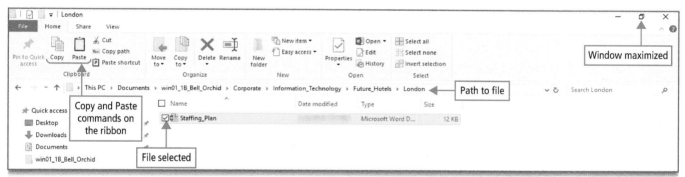

Figure 1.87

> **ANOTHER WAY** Right-click the file you want to copy, and on the menu click Copy. Then right-click the folder into which you want to place the copy, and on the menu click Paste. Or, select the file you want to copy, press Ctrl + C to activate the Copy command, open the folder into which you want to paste the file, and then press Ctrl + V to activate the Paste command.

5 With the **London** window open, by using any of the techniques you have practiced, rename this copy of the **Staffing_Plan** file to London_Staffing_Plan

6 To the left of the **address bar**, click **Up** ↑ to move up one level in the folder structure and to redisplay the **file list** for the **Future_Hotels** folder.

> **ANOTHER WAY** In the address bar, click Future_Hotels to redisplay this window and move up one level in the folder structure.

7 ▸ Click the **Staffing_Plan** file one time to select it, hold down Ctrl, and then drag the file upward over the **Paris** folder until the ScreenTip + *Copy to Paris* displays, and then release the mouse button and release Ctrl.

> When dragging a file into a folder, holding down Ctrl engages the Copy command and places a *copy* of the file at the location where you release the mouse button. This is another way to copy a file or copy a folder.

8 ▸ Open the **Paris** folder, and then rename the **Staffing_Plan** file **Paris_Staffing_Plan** Then, move up one level in the folder structure to redisplay the **Future_Hotels** window.

9 ▸ Double-click the **Rome** folder to open it. With your mouse pointer anywhere in the **file list**, right-click, and then from the shortcut menu click **Paste**.

> A copy of the Staffing_Plan file is copied to the folder. Because a copy of the Staffing_Plan file is still on the Clipboard, you can continue to paste the item until you copy another item on the Clipboard to replace it.

10 ▸ Rename the file **Rome_Staffing_Plan**

11 ▸ On the **address bar**, click **Future_Hotels** to move up one level and open the **Future_Hotels** window—or click Up ↑ to move up one level. Leave this folder open for the next Activity.

Activity 1.37 | Moving Files

When you *move* a file or folder, you remove it from the original location and store it in a new location. In this Activity, you will move items from the Future_Hotels folder into their appropriate folders.

1 ▸ With the **Future_Hotels** folder open, in the **file list**, click the Excel file **Financials_London** one time to select it. On the **Home tab**, in the **Clipboard group**, click **Cut**.

> The file's Excel icon dims. This action places the item on the Clipboard.

ANOTHER WAY Right-click the file or folder, and then on the shortcut menu, click Cut; or, select the file or folder, and then press Ctrl + X.

2 ▸ Double-click the **London** folder to open it, and then on the **Home tab**, in the **Clipboard group**, click **Paste**.

ANOTHER WAY Right-click the folder, and then on the shortcut menu, click Paste; or, select the folder, and then press Ctrl + V.

3 ▸ Click Up ↑ to move up one level and redisplay the **Future_Hotels** folder window. In the **file list**, point to **Financials_Paris**, hold down the left mouse button, and then drag the file upward over the **Paris** folder until the ScreenTip *Move to Paris* displays, and then release the mouse button.

4 ▸ Open the **Paris** folder, and notice that the file was moved to this folder. Click Up ↑—or on the address bar, click Future_Hotels to return to that folder.

5 ▶ In the **file list**, click **Loans_London** one time to select it. hold down Ctrl, and then click the photo image **London** and the Word document **Marketing_London** to select the three files. Release the Ctrl key. Compare your screen with Figure 1.88.

Use this technique to select a group of noncontiguous items in a list.

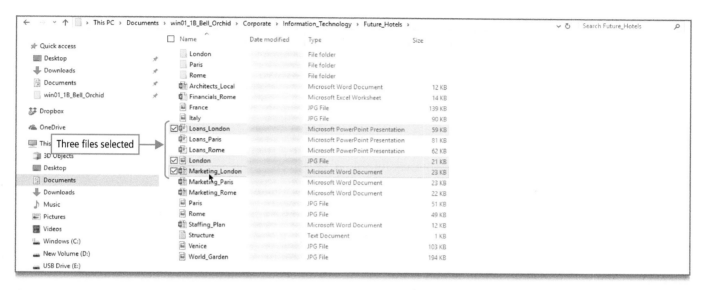

Figure 1.88

6 ▶ Point to any of the selected files, hold down the left mouse button, and then drag upward over the **London** folder until the ScreenTip →*Move to London* displays and *3* displays over the files being moved, and then release the mouse button.

You can see that by keeping related files together—for example, all the files that relate to the London hotel—in folders that have an appropriately descriptive name, it will be easier to locate information later.

7 ▶ By dragging, move the **Architects_Local** file into the **London** folder.

8 ▶ In an empty area of the file list, right-click, and then click **Undo Move**. Leave the **Future_Hotels** window open for the next Activity.

Any action that you make in a file list can be undone in this manner.

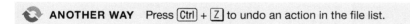

ANOTHER WAY   Press Ctrl + Z to undo an action in the file list.

MORE KNOWLEDGE   **Using Shift + Click to Select Files**

If a group of files to be selected are contiguous (next to each other in the file list), click the first file to be selected, hold down Shift and then click the left mouse button on the last file to select all of the files between the top and bottom file selections.

Activity 1.38 | Copying and Moving Files by Snapping Two Windows

Sometimes you will want to open, in a second window, another instance of a program that you are using; that is, two copies of the program will be running simultaneously. This capability is especially useful in the File Explorer program, because you are frequently moving or copying files from one location to another.

In this Activity, you will open two instances of File Explorer, and then use snap, which you have already practiced in this chapter, to display both instances on your screen.

To copy or move files or folders into a different level of a folder structure, or to a different drive location, the most efficient method is to display two windows side by side and then use drag and drop or copy (or cut) and paste commands.

In this Activity, you will assist Barbara and Steven in making copies of the Staffing_Plan files for the corporate office.

1 In the upper right corner, click **Restore Down** ▢ to restore the **Future_Hotels** window to its previous size and not maximized on the screen.

> Use the *Restore Down* command ▢ to resize a window to its previous size.

2 Hold down ⊞ and press ⬅ to snap the window so that it occupies the left half of the screen.

3 On the taskbar, *point* to **File Explorer** ▢ and then right-click. On the jump list, click **File Explorer** to open another instance of the program. With the new window active, hold down ⊞ and press ➡ to snap the window so that it occupies the right half of the screen.

4 In the window on the right, click in a blank area to make the window active. Then navigate to **Documents > win01_1B_Bell_Orchid > Corporate > Human_Resources**. Compare your screen with Figure 1.89.

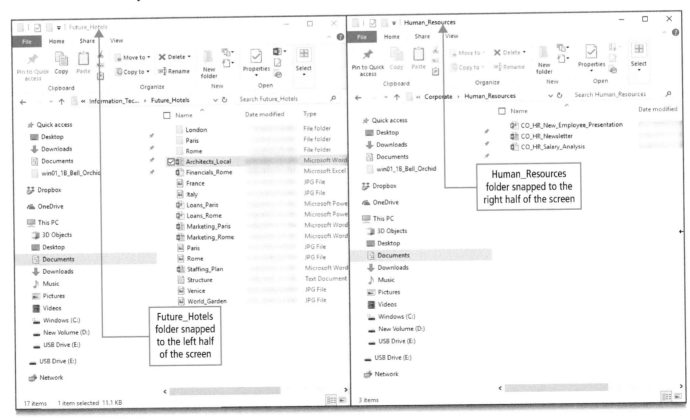

Figure 1.89

5 In the left window, double-click to open the **Rome** folder, and then click one time to select the file **Rome_Staffing_Plan**.

6 Hold down Ctrl, and then drag the file into the right window, into an empty area of the **Human_Resources file list**, until the ScreenTip + *Copy to Human_Resources* displays and then release the mouse button and Ctrl.

7 In the left window, on the **address bar**, click **Future_Hotels** to redisplay that folder. Open the **Paris** folder, point to **Paris_Staffing_Plan** and right-click, and then click **Copy**.

> You can access the Copy command in various ways; for example, from the shortcut menu, on the ribbon, or by using the keyboard shortcut Ctrl + C.

8 In the right window, point anywhere in the **file list**, right-click, and then click **Paste**.

9 On the taskbar, click the PowerPoint icon to redisplay your **Windows_10_1B_Hotel_Files** presentation, and then on the **Home tab**, click the upper portion of the **New Slide** button to insert a new slide with the **Title Only** layout; this will be your fifth slide.

10 Click anywhere in the text *Click to add title*, type **Staffing Plan Files** and then click anywhere in the empty space below the title.

11 On the **Insert tab**, in the **Images group**, click **Screenshot**, and then click **Screen Clipping**. When the dimmed screen displays, move the ⊞ pointer to the upper left corner of the screen, hold down the left mouse button, and drag to the lower right corner but do not include the taskbar. Then release the mouse button.

> Because you have two windows displayed side by side, each window displays under Available Windows. Recall that to capture an entire screen that contains more than one window, use the Screen Clipping tool with which you can capture a snapshot of your screen.

12 If necessary, close the Design Ideas pane on the right. On the **Picture Tools Format tab**, in the **Size group**, click in the **Shape Height** box, type **5** and press Enter. As necessary, drag the image down so that the title you typed is visible.

13 Click outside of the image to deselect it, and then press Ctrl + Home to display the first slide in your presentation; your presentation contains five slides.

14 In the upper right, **Close** ⊠ the **PowerPoint** window, and when prompted, click **Save**.

15 **Close** ⊠ all open windows.

For Non-MyLab Submissions Determine What Your Instructor Requires for Submission
As directed by your instructor, submit your completed PowerPoint file.

---

16 In **MyLab IT,** locate and click the Grader Project **Windows 10 1B Hotel Files**. In **step 3**, under **Upload Completed Assignment**, click **Choose File**. In the **Open** dialog box, navigate to your **Windows 10 Chapter 1 folder**, and then click your **Student_Windows_10_1B_Hotel_Files** file one time to select it. In the lower right corner of the **Open** dialog box, click **Open**.

> The name of your selected file displays above the Upload button.

17 To submit your file to **MyLab IT** for grading, click **Upload**, wait a moment for a green **Success!** message, and then in **step 4**, click the blue **Submit for Grading** button. Click **Close Assignment** to return to your list of **Course Materials**.

MORE KNOWLEDGE Deleting Files and Using the Recycle Bin

It is good practice to delete files and folders that you no longer need from your hard disk drive and removable storage devices. Doing so makes it easier to keep your data organized and also frees up storage space.

When you delete a file or folder from any area of your computer's hard disk drive or from OneDrive, the file or folder is not immediately deleted. Instead, the deleted item is stored in the **Recycle Bin** and remains there until the Recycle Bin is emptied. Thus, you can recover an item deleted from your computer's hard disk drive or OneDrive so long as the Recycle Bin has not been emptied. Items deleted from removable storage devices like a USB flash drive and from some network drives are immediately deleted and cannot be recovered from the Recycle Bin.

To permanently delete a file without first moving it to the Recycle Bin, click the item, hold down Shift, and then press Delete. A message will display indicating *Are you sure you want to permanently delete this file?* Use caution when using Shift + Delete to permanently delete a file because this action is not reversible.

You can restore items by dragging them from the file list of the Recycle Bin window to the file list of the folder window in which you want to restore. Or, you can restore them to the location they were deleted from by right-clicking the items in the file list of the Recycle Bin window and selecting Restore.

You have completed Project 1B **END**

wavebreakmedia/Shutterstock, Monkey Business Images/Fotolia, Ivanko80/Shutterstock, Monkey Business Images/Shutterstock

1

OFFICE AND
WINDOWS

Microsoft Office Specialist (MOS) Skills in this Chapter
Project 1A

Microsoft Word

1.1.1 Search for text

1.2.1 Set up document pages

1.2.4 Configure page background elements

1.2.4 Modify basic document properties

1.3.1 Modify basic document properties

1.4.1 Locate and remove hidden properties and personal information

1.4.2 Locate and correct accessibility issues

1.4.3 Locate and correct compatibility issues

2.2.5 Clear formatting

5.2.6 Format 3D models

5.4.3 Add alternative text to objects for accessibility

Microsoft Excel

5.3.3 Add alternative text to charts for accessibility

Build Your E-Portfolio

An E-Portfolio is a collection of evidence, stored electronically, that showcases what you have accomplished while completing your education. Collecting and then sharing your work products with potential employers reflects your academic and career goals. Your completed documents from the following projects are good examples to show what you have learned: 1A and 1B.

GO! for Job Success

Discussion: Managing Your Computer Files

Your instructor may assign this discussion to your class, and then ask you to think about, or discuss with your classmates, these questions:

g-stockstudio/Shutterstock

> Why do you think it is important to follow specific guidelines when naming and organizing your files?

> Why is it impractical to store files and shortcuts to programs on your desktop?

> How are you making the transition from storing all your files on physical media, such as flash drives or the hard drive of your computer, to storing your files in the cloud where you can access them from any computer with an internet connection?

End of Chapter

Summary

Many Office features and commands, such as accessing the Open and Save As dialog boxes, performing commands from the ribbon and from dialog boxes, and using the Clipboard are the same in all Office desktop apps.

A desktop app is installed on your computer and requires a computer operating system such as Microsoft Windows or Apple's macOS to run. The programs in Microsoft Office 365 and Office 2019 are considered to be desktop apps.

The Windows 10 Start menu is your connected dashboard—this is your one-screen view of information that updates continuously with new information and personal communications that are important to you.

File Explorer is at work anytime you are viewing the contents of a location, a folder, or a file. Use File Explorer to navigate your Windows 10 folder structure that stores and organizes the files you create.

GO! Learn It Online

Review the concepts, key terms, and MOS skills in this chapter by completing these online challenges, which you can find at **MyLab IT**.

Chapter Quiz: Answer matching and multiple-choice questions to test what you have learned in this chapter.

Lessons on the GO!: Learn how to use all the new apps and features as they are introduced by Microsoft.

Quiz: Answer questions to review the MOS skills that you practiced in this chapter.

Monkey Business Images/Fotolia

Glossary

Glossary of Chapter Key Terms

.png file An image file type that can be transferred over the internet, an acronym for Portable Network Graphic.

.txt file A simple file consisting of lines of text with no formatting that almost any computer can open and display.

3D models A new kind of shape that you can insert from an online library of ready-to-use three-dimensional graphics.

Address bar In a File Explorer window, the area that displays your current location in the folder structure as a series of links separated by arrows.

Alignment The placement of text or objects relative to the margins.

Alignment guides Green lines that display when you move an object to assist in alignment.

Alt text Text added to a picture or object that helps people using a screen reader understand what the object is; also called *alternative text*.

Alternative text Text added to a picture or object that helps people using a screen reader understand what the object is; also called *alt text*.

Application A computer program that helps you perform a task for a specific purpose.

AutoSave An Office 365 feature that saves your document every few seconds—if saved on OneDrive, OneDrive for Business, or SharePoint Online—and enables you to share the document with others for real-time co-authoring.

Backstage tabs The area along the left side of Backstage view with tabs to display screens with related groups of commands.

Backstage view A centralized space for file management tasks; for example, opening, saving, printing, publishing, or sharing a file.

Bing Microsoft's search engine.

Bookmark A command that marks a word, section, or place in a document so that you can jump to it quickly without scrolling.

Booting the computer The process of turning on the computer.

Center alignment The alignment of text or objects centered horizontally between the left and right margin.

Check Accessibility A command that checks a document for content that people with disabilities might find difficult to read.

Check Compatibility A command that searches your document for features that may not be supported by older versions of Office.

Click The action of pressing the left button of the mouse pointing device.

Clipboard A temporary storage area that holds text or graphics that you select and then cut or copy.

Cloud computing Applications and services that are accessed over the internet.

Cloud storage Online storage of data so that you can access your data from different places and devices.

Commands An instruction to a computer program that causes an action to be carried out.

Compressed Folder Tools A command available in File Explorer with which you can extract compressed files.

Compressed files Files that have been reduced in size, take up less storage space, and can be transferred to other computers faster than uncompressed files.

Content pane In a File Explorer window, another name for the file list.

Context menus Menus that display commands and options relevant to the selected text or object; also called *shortcut menus*.

Context-sensitive commands Commands that display on a shortcut menu that relate to the object or text that is selected.

Contextual tab A tab added to the ribbon automatically when a specific object is selected and that contains commands relevant to the selected object.

Copy A command that duplicates a selection and places it on the Clipboard.

Cortana Microsoft's intelligent personal assistant in Windows 10 and also available on other devices; named for the intelligent female character in the video game Halo.

Cut A command that removes a selection and places it on the Clipboard.

Dashboard The right side of the Start menu that is a one-screen view of links to information and programs that matter to you.

Data The documents, worksheets, pictures, songs, and so on that you create and store during the day-to-day use of your computer.

Data management The process of managing files and folders.

Default The term that refers to the current selection or setting that is automatically used by a computer program unless you specify otherwise.

Deselect The action of canceling the selection of an object or block of text by clicking outside of the selection.

Desktop A simulation of a real desk that represents your work area; here you can arrange icons such as shortcuts to files, folders, and various types of documents in the same manner you would arrange physical objects on top of a desk.

Desktop app A computer program that is installed on your PC and requires a computer operating system such as Microsoft Windows to run; also known as a *desktop application*.

Desktop application A computer program that is installed on your PC and requires a computer operating system such as Microsoft Windows to run; also known as a *desktop app*.

Desktop shortcuts Desktop icons that can link to items accessible on your computer such as a program, file, folder, disk drive, printer, or another computer.

Details pane When activated in a folder window, displays—on the right—the most common file properties associated with the selected file.

Details view A command that displays a list of files or folders and their most common properties.

Dialog box A small window that displays options for completing a task.

Dictate A feature in Word, PowerPoint, Outlook, and OneNote for Windows 10; when you enable Dictate, you start talking and as you talk, text appears in your document or slide.

Dialog Box Launcher A small icon that displays to the right of some group names on the ribbon and that opens a related dialog box or pane providing additional options and commands related to that group.

Document properties Details about a file that describe or identify it, including the title, author name, subject, and keywords that identify the document's topic or contents; also known as *metadata*.

Double-click The action of pressing the left mouse button two times in rapid succession while holding the mouse still.

Glossary

Download The action of transferring or copying a file from another location— such as a cloud storage location, your college's Learning Management System, or from an internet site—to your computer.

Drag The action of holding down the left mouse button while moving your mouse.

Drive An area of storage that is formatted with a file system compatible with your operating system and is identified by a drive letter.

Edit The process of making changes to text or graphics in an Office file.

Editor A digital writing assistant in Word and Outlook that displays misspellings, grammatical mistakes, and writing style issues.

Ellipsis A set of three dots indicating incompleteness; an ellipsis following a command name indicates that a dialog box will display if you click the command.

Enhanced ScreenTip A ScreenTip that displays useful descriptive information about the command.

Extract To decompress, or pull out, files from a compressed form.

File Information stored on a computer under a single name.

File Explorer The Windows program that displays the contents of locations, folders, and files on your computer.

File Explorer window A window that displays the contents of the current location and contains helpful parts so that you can navigate—explore within the file organizing structure of Windows.

File list In a File Explorer window, the area that displays the contents of the current location.

File name extension A set of characters at the end of a file name that helps Windows understand what kind of information is in a file and what program should open it.

File properties Information about a file, such as the author, the date the file was last changed, and any descriptive tags.

Fill The inside color of an object.

Filtered list A display of files that is limited based on specified criteria.

Folder A container in which you can store files.

Folder structure The hierarchy of folders.

Folder window A window that typically displays the File List for a folder.

Font A set of characters with the same design and shape.

Font styles Formatting emphasis such as bold, italic, and underline.

Footer A reserved area for text or graphics that displays at the bottom of each page in a document.

Format Painter The command to copy the formatting of specific text or to copy the formatting of a paragraph and then apply it in other locations in your document; when active, the pointer takes the shape of a paintbrush.

Formatting The process of applying Office commands to make your documents easy to read and to add visual touches and design elements to make your document inviting to the reader; establishes the overall appearance of text, graphics, and pages in an Office file—for example, in a Word document.

Formatting marks Characters that display on the screen, but do not print, indicating where the Enter key, the Spacebar, and the Tab key were pressed; also called *nonprinting characters*.

Free-form snip From the Snipping Tool, a command that draws an irregular line such as a circle around an area of the screen.

Full-screen snip From the Snipping Tool, a command that captures the entire screen.

Gallery An Office feature that displays a list of potential results.

Gradient fill A fill effect in which one color fades into another.

Graphical user interface Graphics such as an image of a file folder or wastebasket that you click to activate the item represented.

Groups On the Office ribbon, the sets of related commands that you might need for a specific type of task.

GUI An abbreviation of the term graphical user interface.

Hamburger Another name for a hamburger menu.

Hamburger menu Another name for a menu icon, deriving from the three lines that bring to mind a hamburger on a bun.

Hard disk drive The primary storage device located inside your computer where some of your files and programs are typically stored, usually designated as drive C.

Hierarchy An arrangement where items are ranked and where each level is lower in rank than the item above it

Icons Small images that represent commands, files, applications, or other windows.

Info tab The tab in Backstage view that displays information about the current file.

Insertion point A blinking vertical line that indicates where text or graphics will be inserted.

Inspect Document A command that searches your document for hidden data of personal information that you might not want to share publicly.

JPEG An acronym that stands for *Joint Photographic Experts Group* and that is a common file type used by digital cameras and computers to store digital pictures.

Jump List A display of destinations and tasks from a program's taskbar icon when you right-click the icon.

Keyboard shortcut A combination of two or more keyboard keys, used to perform a task that would otherwise require a mouse.

KeyTip The letter that displays on a command in the ribbon and that indicates the key you can press to activate the command when keyboard control of the ribbon is activated.

Keywords Custom file properties in the form of words that you associate with a document to give an indication of the document's content.

Landscape orientation A page orientation in which the paper is wider than it is tall.

Layout Options A button that displays when an object is selected and that has commands to choose how the object interacts with surrounding text.

Live Preview A technology that shows the result of applying an editing or formatting change as you point to possible results— *before* you actually apply it.

Live tiles Tiles that are constantly updated with fresh information.

Location Any disk drive, folder, or other place in which you can store files and folders.

Lock screen A background that fills the computer screen when the computer boots up or wakes up from sleep mode.

Maximize A window control button that will enlarge the size of the window to fill the entire screen.

Menu A list of commands within a category.

Menu bar A group of menus at the top of a program window.

Menu icon A button consisting of three lines that, when clicked, expands a menu; often used in mobile applications because it is compact to use on smaller screens— also referred to a *hamburger menu*.

Glossary

Metadata Details about a file that describe or identify it, including the title, author name, subject, and keywords that identify the document's topic or contents; also known as *document properties*.

Microsoft account A user account with which you can sign in to any Windows 10 computer on which you have, or create, an account.

Microsoft Store app A smaller app that you download from the Microsoft Store.

Mini toolbar A small toolbar containing frequently used formatting commands that displays as a result of selecting text or objects.

Minimize A window control button that will keep a program open but will remove it from screen view.

Move In File Explorer, the action of removing a file or folder from its original location and storing it in a new location.

Mouse pointer Any symbol that displays on the screen in response to moving the mouse.

MRU Acronym for *most recently used*, which refers to the state of some commands that retain the characteristic most recently applied; for example, the Font Color button retains the most recently used color until a new color is chosen.

Navigate A process for exploring within the file organizing structure of Windows.

Navigation pane The area on the left side of the File Explorer window to access your OneDrive, folders on your PC, devices and drives connected to your PC, and other PCs on your network.

Nonprinting characters Characters that display on the screen, but do not print, indicating where the Enter key, the Spacebar, and the Tab key were pressed; also called *formatting marks*.

Notepad A basic text-editing program included with Windows 10 that you can use to create simple documents.

Object A text box, picture, table, or shape that you can select and then move and resize.

Office 365 A version of Microsoft Office to which you subscribe for an annual fee.

OneDrive Microsoft's free cloud storage for anyone with a free Microsoft account.

Operating system A specific type of computer program that manages the other programs on a computing device such as a desktop computer, a laptop computer, a smartphone, a tablet computer, or a game console.

Option button In a dialog box, a round button that enables you to make one choice among two or more options.

Page Width A command that zooms the document so that the width of the page matches the width of the window.

Paragraph symbol The symbol ¶ that represents the end of a paragraph.

Parent folder The location in which the folder you are viewing is saved.

Paste The action of placing text or objects that have been copied or cut from one location to another location.

Paste Options gallery A gallery of buttons that provides a Live Preview of all the Paste options available in the current context.

Path A sequence of folders that leads to a specific file or folder.

PDF The acronym for Portable Document Format, which is a file format that creates an image that preserves the look of your file, but that cannot be easily changed; a popular format for sending documents electronically, because the document will display on most computers.

Pen A pen-shaped stylus that you tap on a computer screen.

Personal folder The folder created on the hard drive for each Windows 10 user account on a computer; for each user account—even if there is only one user on the computer—Windows 10 creates a personal folder labeled with the account holder's name.

Point to The action of moving the mouse pointer over a specific area.

Pointer Any symbol that displays on your screen in response to moving your mouse.

Pointing device A mouse or touchpad used to control the pointer.

Points A measurement of the size of a font; there are 72 points in an inch.

Portable Document Format A file format that creates an image that preserves the look of your file, but that cannot be easily changed; a popular format for sending documents electronically, because the document will display on most computers.

Portrait orientation A page orientation in which the paper is taller than it is wide.

Print Preview A view of a document as it will appear when you print it.

Program A set of instructions that a computer uses to accomplish a task.

Progress bar A bar that displays in a dialog box—and also on the taskbar button—that indicates visually the progress of a task such as a copy process, a download, or a file transfer.

pt The abbreviation for *point* when referring to a font size.

Quick access In the navigation pane in a File Explorer window, a list of files you have been working on and folders you use often.

Real-time co-authoring A process where two or more people work on the same file at the same time and see changes made by others in seconds.

Rectangular snip From the Snipping Tool, a command that draws a precise box by dragging the mouse pointer around an area of the screen to form a rectangle.

Recycle Bin The area where deleted items are stored until you empty the bin; enables you to recover deleted items until the bin is emptied.

Removable storage device A device such as a USB flash drive used to transfer information from one computer to another.

Resources The collection of the physical parts of your computer such as the central processing unit (CPU), memory, and any attached devices such as a printer.

Restore Down A command that resizes a window to its previous size.

Ribbon In Office applications, displays a group of task-oriented tabs that contain the commands, styles, and resources you need to work in an Office desktop app. In a File Explorer window, the area at the top that groups common tasks on tabs. such as copying and moving, creating new folders, emailing and zipping items, and changing the view on related tabs.

Right-click The action of clicking the right mouse button one time.

Sans serif font A font design with no lines or extensions on the ends of characters.

Screen reader Software that enables visually impaired users to read text on a computer screen to understand the content of pictures.

Screenshot Any captured image of your screen.

ScreenTip A small box that displays useful information when you perform various mouse actions such as pointing to screen elements or dragging.

Glossary

Scroll arrow An arrow found at either end of a scroll bar that can be clicked to move within the window in small increments.

Scroll bar A vertical bar that displays when the contents of a window or pane are not completely visible; a scroll bar can be vertical, displayed at the side of the window, or horizontal, displayed at the bottom of a window.

Scroll box Within a scroll bar, a box that you can move to bring the contents of the window into view.

Select To specify, by highlighting, a block of data or text on the screen with the intent of performing some action on the selection.

Selecting Highlighting, by dragging with your mouse, areas of text or data or graphics, so that the selection can be edited, formatted, copied, or moved.

Serif font A font design that includes small line extensions on the ends of the letters to guide the eye in reading from left to right.

SharePoint A Microsoft technology that enables employees in an organization to access information across organizational and geographic boundaries.

Shortcut menu A menu that displays commands and options relevant to the selected text or object; also called a *context menu*.

Sizing handles Small circles or squares that indicate a picture or object is selected.

Snap An action to arrange two or more open windows on your screen so that you can work with multiple screens at the same time.

Snap Assist A feature that displays all other open windows after one window is snapped.

Snip An image captured by the Snipping tool that can be annotated, saved, copied, or shared via email.

Snipping tool A Windows 10 program that captures an image of all or part of your computer's screen.

Split button A button divided into two parts and in which clicking the main part of the button performs a command and clicking the arrow opens a menu with choices.

Start menu A Windows 10 menu that displays as a result of clicking the Start button and that displays a list of installed programs on the left and a customizable group of tiles on the right that can act as a user dashboard.

Style A group of formatting commands, such as font, font size, font color, paragraph alignment, and line spacing that can be applied to a paragraph with one command.

Subfolder The term for a folder placed within another folder.

Synchronization The process of updating computer files that are in two or more locations according to specific rules—also called *syncing*.

Syncing The process of updating computer files that are in two or more locations according to specific rules—also called *synchronization*.

System tray Another term for the notification area on the taskbar that displays notification icons and the system clock and calendar.

Tabs (ribbon) On the Office ribbon, the name of each activity area.

Tags Custom file properties in the form of words that you associate with a document to give an indication of the document's content; used to help find and organize files. Also called keywords.

Task View A taskbar button that displays your desktop background with small images of all open programs and apps and from which you can see and switch between open apps, including desktop apps.

Taskbar The bar at the bottom of your Windows screen that contains buttons to launch programs and buttons for all open apps.

Tell Me A search feature for Microsoft Office commands that you activate by typing what you are looking for in the Tell Me box.

Tell me more A prompt within a ScreenTip that opens the Office online Help system with explanations about how to perform the command referenced in the ScreenTip.

Template A preformatted document that you can use as a starting point and then change to suit your needs.

Theme A predesigned combination of colors, fonts, and effects that look good together and that is applied to an entire document by a single selection.

Timeline A Windows 10 feature that when you click the Task view button, you can see activities you have worked on across your devices; for example, you can find a document, image, or video you worked on yesterday or a week ago.

Thumbnail A reduced image of a graphic.

Tiles A group of square and rectangular boxes that display on the start menu.

Title bar The bar across the top of the window that displays the program, file, or app name.

Toggle button A button that can be turned on by clicking it once and then turned off by clicking it again.

Toolbar A row, column, or block of buttons or icons that displays across the top of a window and that contains commands for tasks you perform with a single click.

Triple-click The action of clicking the left mouse button three times in rapid succession.

Undo On the Quick Access Toolbar, the command that reverses your last action.

Unzip The process of extracting files that have been compressed.

User account A user on a single computer.

Wallpaper Another term for the Desktop background.

Window snip From the Snipping Tool, a command that captures the entire displayed window.

Windows 10 An operating system developed by Microsoft Corporation that works with mobile computing devices and also with traditional desktop and laptop PCs.

XML Paper Specification A Microsoft file format that creates an image of your document and that opens in the XPS viewer.

XPS The acronym for *XML Paper Specification*—a Microsoft file format that creates an image of your document and that opens in the XPS viewer.

Zip The process of compressing files.

Zoom The action of increasing or decreasing the size of the viewing area on the screen.

Introduction to Microsoft Access 2019

ACCESS 2019

Mego studio/Shutterstock

Access 2019: Introduction Introduction to Access

Microsoft Access 2019 provides a convenient way to organize data that makes it easy for you to utilize and present information. Access uses tables to store the data; like Excel spreadsheets, data is stored in rows and columns in a table. So why use a database rather than an Excel spreadsheet? By using a database, you can manipulate and work with data in a more robust manner. For example, if you have thousands of records about patients in a hospital, you can easily find all of the records that pertain to the patients who received a specific type of medicine on a particular day. Information from one table can be used to retrieve information from another table.

For example, by knowing a patient's ID number, you can view immunization records or view insurance information or view hospitalization records. Having information stored in an Access database enables you to make bulk changes to data at one time even when it is stored in different tables.

It's easy to get started with Access by using one of the many prebuilt database templates. For example, a nonprofit organization can track events, donors, members, and donations for a nonprofit organization. A small business can use a prebuilt database to track inventory, create invoices, monitor projects, manage pricing, track competitors, and manage quotes.

Getting Started with Microsoft Access 2019

1
ACCESS 2019

PROJECT 1A

Outcomes
Create a new database.

Objectives

1. Identify Good Database Design
2. Create a Table and Define Fields in a Blank Desktop Database
3. Change the Structure of Tables and Add a Second Table
4. Create a Query, Form, and Report
5. Close a Database and Close Access

PROJECT 1B

Outcomes
Create a database from a template.

Objectives

6. Use a Template to Create a Database
7. Organize Objects in the Navigation Pane
8. Create a New Table in a Database Created with a Template
9. View a Report

Rawpixel.com/Shutterstock

In This Chapter

 GO! To Work with Access

In this chapter, you will use Microsoft Access 2019 to organize a collection of related information. You will create new databases, create tables, and enter data into the tables. You will create a query, a form, and a report—all of which are Access objects that make a database useful for locating and analyzing information. You will also create a complete database from a template that is provided, or that you can modify to meet your needs. In this chapter, you will also learn how to apply good database design principles to your Access database and to define the structure of a database.

The projects in this chapter relate to **Texas Lakes Community College**, which is located in the Austin, Texas area. Its four campuses serve over 30,000 students and offer more than 140 certificate programs and degrees. The college has a highly acclaimed Distance Education program and an extensive Workforce Development program. The college makes positive contributions to the community through cultural and athletic programs and has significant partnerships with businesses and nonprofit organizations. Popular fields of study include nursing and health care, solar technology, computer technology, and graphic design.

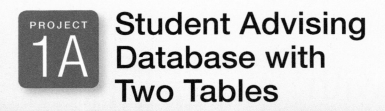

PROJECT 1A

Student Advising Database with Two Tables

MyLab IT
Project 1A Grader for Instruction
Project 1A Simulation for Training and Review

Project Activities

In Activities 1.01 through 1.17, you will assist Dr. Daniel Martinez, Vice President of Student Services at Texas Lakes Community College, in creating a new database for tracking students and their faculty advisors. Your completed Navigation Pane will look similar to Figure 1.1.

 ## Project Files for MyLab IT Grader

1. In your storage location, create a folder named **Access Chapter 1**.
2. In your **MyLab IT** course, locate and click **Access 1A Advising**, Download Materials, and then Download All Files.
3. Extract the zipped folder to your Access Chapter 1 folder. Close the Grader download screens.
4. Take a moment to open the downloaded **Access_1A_Advising_Instructions**; note any recent updates to the book.

Project Results

GO! Project 1A
Where We're Going

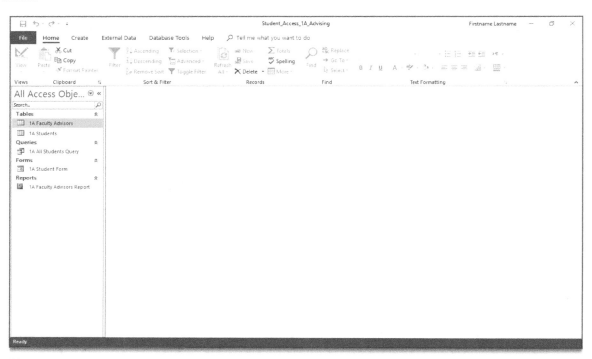

Figure 1.1 Project 1A Advising

For Non-MyLab Submissions

For Project 1A, you will need the following files:

Blank database
a01A_Students (Excel workbook)
a01A_Faculty_Advisors (Excel workbook)

Start with a new blank Access database

In your storage location, create a folder named **Access Chapter 1**
In your Access Chapter 1 folder, save your database as:
Lastname_Firstname_1A_Advising

After you have named and saved your workbook, on the next page begin by comparing your screen with Figure 1.4 in Step 3.

NOTE   If You Are Using a Touch Screen

Tap an item to click it.

Press and hold for a few seconds to right-click; release when the information or commands display.

Touch the screen with two or more fingers and then pinch together to zoom out or stretch your fingers apart to zoom in.

Slide your finger on the screen to scroll—slide left to scroll right and slide right to scroll left.

Slide to rearrange—similar to dragging with a mouse.

Swipe to select—slide an item a short distance with a quick movement—to select an item and bring up commands, if any.

Objective 1   Identify Good Database Design

ALERT   Because Office 365 is a cloud-based subscription service that receives continuous updates, you may encounter some variations in what appears on your screen and what is shown in this instruction. Microsoft Office 365 is fully installed on your PC or Mac; no internet access is necessary to create or edit documents. When you *are* connected to the internet, you will receive monthly upgrades and new features, so you always have the latest versions of Office apps as soon as they are available. Your subscription gives you continuous free access to the latest innovations and refinements.

GO! Learn How
Video A1-1

A *database* is an organized collection of *data*—facts about people, events, things, or ideas—related to a specific topic or purpose. *Information* is data that is accurate, timely, and organized in a useful manner. Your contact list is a type of database, because it is a collection of data about one topic—the people with whom you communicate. A simple database of this type is called a *flat database* because it is not related or linked to any other collection of data. Another example of a simple database is your music collection. You do not keep information about your music collection in your contact list because the data is not related to the people in your contact list.

A more sophisticated type of database is a *relational database*, because multiple collections of data in the database are related to one another—for example, data about the students, the courses, and the faculty members at a college. Microsoft Access 2019 is a relational *database management system*—also referred to as a *DBMS*—which is software that controls how related collections of data are stored, organized, retrieved, and secured.

Activity 1.01 | Using Good Design Techniques to Plan a Database

Before creating a new database, the first step is to determine the information you want to keep track of by asking yourself, *What questions should this database be able to answer?* The purpose of a database is to store the data in a manner that makes it easy to find the information you need by asking questions. For example, in a student database for Texas Lakes Community College, the questions to be answered might include:

- How many students are enrolled at the college?
- How many students have not yet been assigned a faculty advisor?
- Which students live in Austin, Texas?
- Which students owe money for tuition?
- Which students are majoring in Information Systems Technology?

Tables are the foundation of an Access database because all of the data is stored in one or more tables. A table is similar in structure to an Excel worksheet because data is organized into rows and columns. Each table row is a *record*—all of the categories of data pertaining to one person, place, event, thing, or idea. Each table column is a *field*—a single piece of information for every record. For example, in a table storing student contact information, each row forms a record for only one student. Each column forms a field for every record—for example, the student ID number or the student last name.

When organizing the fields of information in your table, break each piece of information into its smallest, most useful part. For example, create three fields for the name of a student—one field for the last name, one field for the first name, and one field for the middle name or initial.

The *first principle of good database design* is to organize data in the tables so that *redundant*—duplicate—data does not occur. For example, record the student contact information in only *one* table, so that if a student's address changes, you can change the information in just one place. This conserves space, reduces the likelihood of errors when inputting new data, and does not require remembering all of the places where a student's address is stored.

The *second principle of good database design* is to use techniques that ensure the accuracy and consistency of data as it is entered into the table. Proofreading data is critical to maintaining accuracy in a database. Typically, many different people enter data into a database—think of all the people who enter data about students at your college. When entering a state in a student contacts table, one person might enter the state as *Texas*, while another might enter the state as *TX*. Use design techniques to help those who enter data into a database to enter the data more accurately and consistently.

Normalization is the process of applying design rules and principles to ensure that your database performs as expected. Taking the time to plan and create a database that is well designed will ensure that you can retrieve meaningful information from the database.

The tables of information in a relational database are linked or joined to one another by a *common field*—a field in two or more tables that stores the same data. For example, a Students table includes the Student ID, name, and full address of every student. The Student Activities table includes the club name and the Student ID of members, but not the name or address, of each student in the club. Because the two tables share a common field—Student ID—you can use the data together to create a list of names and addresses of all of the students in a particular club. The names and addresses are stored in the Students table, and the Student IDs of the club members are stored in the Student Activities table.

Objective 2   Create a Table and Define Fields in a Blank Desktop Database

GO! Learn How
Video A1-2

Three methods are used to create a new Access database. One method is to create a new database using a *database template*—a preformatted database designed for a specific purpose. A second method is to create a new database from a *blank desktop database*. A blank desktop database is stored on your computer or other storage device. Initially, it has no data and has no database tools; you create the data and the tools as you need them. A third method is to create a *custom web app* database from scratch or by using a template that you can publish and share with others over the Internet.

Regardless of the method you use, you must name and save the database before you can create any *objects* in it. Objects are the basic parts of a database; you create objects to store your data, to work with your data, and to display your data. The most common database objects are tables, queries, forms, and reports. Think of an Access database as a container for the objects that you create.

Activity 1.02 | Starting with a Blank Database

1 Start Microsoft Access 2019. Take a moment to compare your screen with Figure 1.2 and study the parts of the Microsoft Access opening screen described in the table in Figure 1.3.

From this Access opening screen, you can open an existing database, create a blank database, or create a new database from a template.

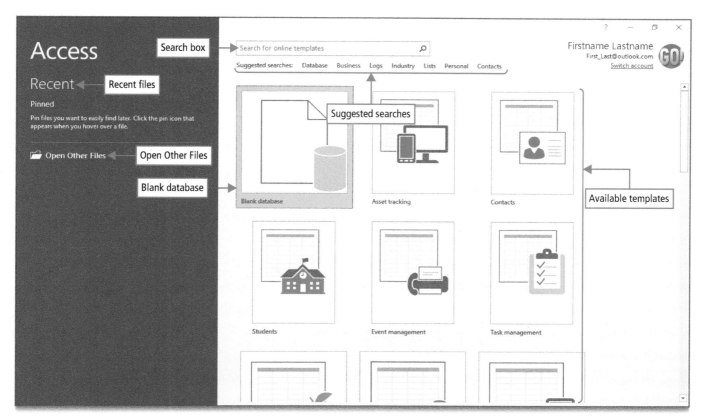

Figure 1.2

Screen Element	Description
Available templates	Starts a database for a specific purpose that includes built-in objects and tools ready for use.
Blank database	Starts a blank database that is stored on your computer or on a portable storage device.
Open Other Files	Enables you to open a database file from your computer, a shared location, or other location that you have designated.
Recent files	Displays a list of database files that have been recently opened.
Search box	Enables you to search the Microsoft Office website for templates.j
Suggested searches	Enables you to click on a category to start an online search for a template.

Figure 1.3

2 Navigate to your **Access Chapter 1 folder**, and then double-click the Access file that you downloaded from **MyLab IT** that displays your name—**Student_Access_1A_Advising**. In your blank database, if necessary, click **Enable Content** at the top.

3 ▶ Click the **Create tab**. In the **Tables group**, click **Table**. Compare your screen with Figure 1.4, and then take a moment to study the screen elements described in the table in Figure 1.5.

Recall that a table is an Access object that stores data in columns and rows, similar to the format of an Excel worksheet. Table objects are the foundation of a database because tables store data that is used by other database objects.

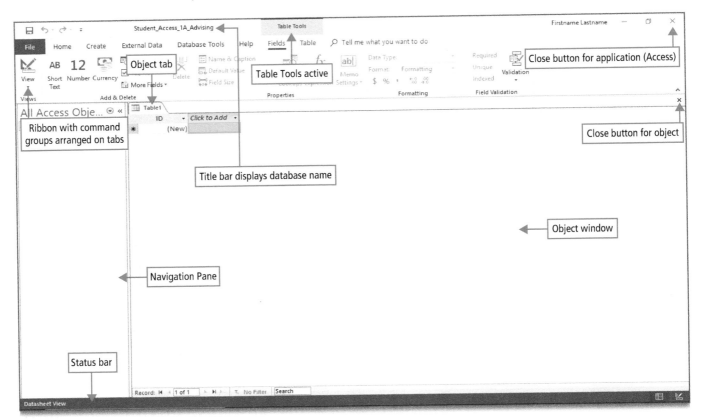

Figure 1.4

Access Window Element	Description
Navigation Pane	Displays the database objects that can be opened in the object window.
Object tab	Identifies the open object.
Object window	Displays the active or open object(s), including tables, queries, or other objects.
Close button for object	Closes the active object.
Ribbon	Displays commands grouped by related tasks and stored on different tabs.
Status bar	Indicates the active view and the status of action occurring within the database on the left; provides buttons on the right to switch between Datasheet view and Design view.
Table Tools	Provides tools on two tabs for working with the active table object, these are contextual tabs—only available when a table object is active.
Close button for application (Access)	Closes the active database and Access.

Figure 1.5   Microsoft Access Database Window Elements

Activity 1.03 | Assigning the Data Type and Name to Fields

2.4.1, 2.4.5

After you have named and saved your database, the next step is to consult your database design plan and then create the tables for your data. Limit the data in each table to *one* subject. For example, in this project, your database will have two tables—one for student information and one for faculty advisor information.

Recall that each column in a table is a field; field names display at the top of each column of the table. Recall also that each row in a table is a record—all of the data pertaining to one person, place, thing, event, or idea. Each record is broken up into its smallest usable parts—the fields. Use meaningful names for fields; for example, *Last Name*.

1 Notice the new blank table that displays in Datasheet view, and then take a moment to study the elements of the table's object window. Compare your screen with Figure 1.6.

The table displays in *Datasheet view*, which displays the data in columns and rows similar to the format of an Excel worksheet. Another way to view a table is in *Design view*, which displays the underlying design—the *structure*—of the table's fields. The *object window* displays the open object—in this instance, the table object.

In a new blank database, there is only one object—a new blank table. Because you have not yet named this table, the *object tab* displays a default name of *Table1*. Access creates the first field and names it *ID*. In the ID field, Access assigns a unique sequential number—each number incremented by one—to each record as it is entered into the table.

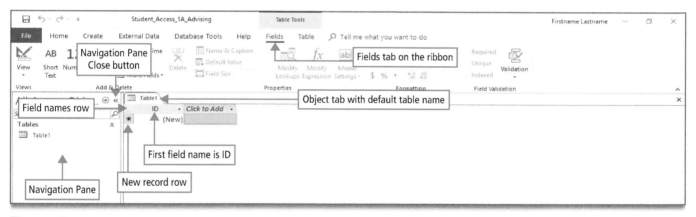

Figure 1.6

2 In the **Navigation Pane**, click **Shutter Bar Open/Close** [«] to collapse the **Navigation Pane** to a narrow bar on the left.

The *Navigation Pane* displays and organizes the names of the objects in a database. From the Navigation Pane, you can open objects. Collapse or close the Navigation Pane to display more of the object—in this case, the table.

ANOTHER WAY Press [F11] to close or open the Navigation Pane.

3 In the field names row, click anywhere in the text *Click to Add* to display a list of data types. Compare your screen with Figure 1.7.

> A ***data type*** classifies the kind of data that you can store in a field, such as numbers, text, or dates. A field in a table can have only one data type. The data type of each field should be included in your database design. After selecting the data type, you can name the field.

ANOTHER WAY   To the right of *Click to Add*, click the arrow.

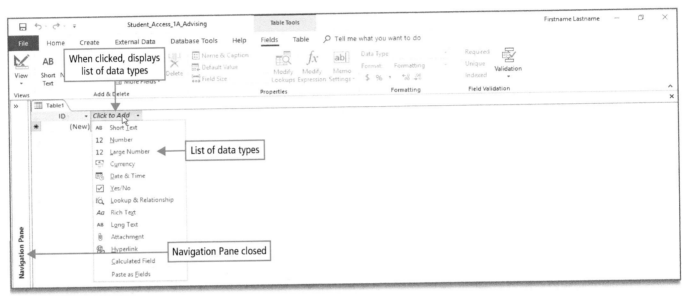

Figure 1.7

4 In the list of data types, click **Short Text**, and notice that in the second column, *Click to Add* changes to *Field1*, which is selected. Type **Last Name** and then press Enter.

> The second column displays *Last Name* as the field name, and, in the third column, the data types list displays. The ***Short Text data type*** describes text, a combination of text and numbers, or numbers that do not represent a quantity or are not used in calculations, such as the Postal Code. This data type enables you to enter up to 255 characters in the field.

ANOTHER WAY   With the list of data types displayed, type the character that is underscored to select the data type. For example, type *t* to select Short Text or type *u* to select Currency.

5 In the third field name box, type **t** to select *Short Text*, type **First Name** and then press Enter.

6 In the fourth field name box, click **Short Text**, type **Middle Initial** and then press Enter.

7 Create the remaining fields from the table below by first selecting the data type, typing the field name, and then pressing Enter. The field names in the table will display on one line–do not be concerned if the field names do not completely display in the column; you will adjust the column widths later.

Data Type		Short Text	Short Text	Short Text	Short Text	Short Text	Short Text	Short Text	Short Text	Short Text	Short Text	Currency
Field Name	ID	Last Name	First Name	Middle Initial	**Address**	**City**	**State**	**Postal Code**	**Phone**	**Email**	**Faculty Advisor ID**	**Amount Owed**

The Postal Code and Phone fields are assigned a data type of Short Text because the numbers are never used in calculations. The Amount Owed field is assigned the *Currency data type*, which describes monetary values and numeric data that can be used in calculations and that have one to four decimal places. A U.S. dollar sign ($) and two decimal places are automatically included for all of the numbers in a field with the Currency data type.

8 If necessary, scroll to bring the first column—ID—into view, and then compare your screen with Figure 1.8.

Access automatically created the ID field, and you created 11 additional fields in the table.

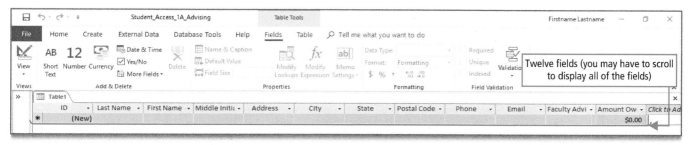

Figure 1.8

MORE KNOWLEDGE **Create Fields by Entering Data**

You can create a new field in Datasheet view by typing the data in a new column. Access automatically assigns a data type based on the data you enter. For example, if you enter a date, Access assigns the Date & Time data type. If you enter a monetary amount, Access assigns the Currency data type. If Access cannot determine the data type based on the data entered, the Short Text data type is assigned. You can always change the data type if an incorrect data type is assigned. If you use this method to create fields, you must check the assigned data types to be sure they are correct. You must also rename the fields because Access assigns the names as *Field1*, *Field2*, and so on.

Activity 1.04 | Renaming Fields, Changing Data Types, and Setting Field Size in a Table

2.4.3, 2.4.4, 2.4.5

Once a table has been created, the field structure can be edited in Datasheet view. As you change data types and field sizes, you need to be sure that any existing data meets the new restrictions. In this Activity, you will modify the default ID field that displayed when you created the new table.

1 In the first column, click anywhere in the text *ID*. On the ribbon, under **Table Tools**, on the **Fields tab**, in the **Properties group**, click **Name & Caption**. In the **Enter Field Properties** dialog box, in the **Name** box, change *ID* to **Student ID**

The field name *Student ID* is a more precise description of the data contained in this field. In the Enter Field Properties dialog box, you have the option to use the *Caption* property to display a name for a field different from the one that displays in the Name box. Many database designers do not use spaces in field names; instead, they might name a field *LastName* or *LName* and then create a caption for the field so it displays as *Last Name* in tables, forms, or reports. In the Enter Field Properties dialog box, you can also provide a description for the field.

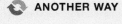 **ANOTHER WAY** Right-click the field name to display the shortcut menu, and then click Rename Field; or, double-click the field name to select the existing text, and then type the new field name.

2 Click **OK** to close the **Enter Field Properties** dialog box. On the ribbon, in the **Formatting group**, notice that the **Data Type** for the **Student ID** field is *AutoNumber*. Click the **Data Type arrow**, and then click **Short Text**.

In the new record row, the Student ID field is selected. By default, Access creates an ID field for all new tables and sets the data type for the field to AutoNumber. The *AutoNumber data type* describes a unique sequential or random number assigned by Access as each record is entered. Changing the data type of this field to Short Text enables you to enter a custom student ID number.

When records in a database have *no* unique value, such as a book ISBN or a license plate number, the AutoNumber data type is a useful way to automatically create a unique number. In this manner, you are sure that every record is different from the others.

3 On the ribbon, in the **Properties group**, click in the **Field Size** box to select the text *255*, and then type **7** Press [Enter], and then compare your screen with Figure 1.9.

This action limits the size of the Student ID field to no more than seven characters. The default field size for a Short Text field is 255. Limiting the Field Size property to seven ensures that no more than 7 characters can be entered for each Student ID. However, this does not prevent someone from entering seven characters that are incorrect or entering fewer than seven characters. Setting the proper data type for the field and limiting the field size are two ways to help reduce errors during data entry.

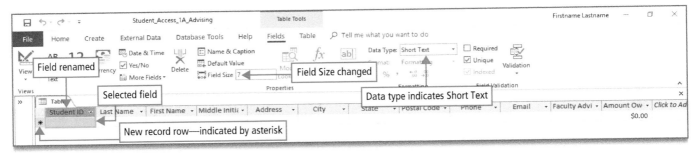

Figure 1.9

Activity 1.05 | Adding a Record to a Table

MOS
1.1.2

A new contact list is not useful until you fill it with names and phone numbers. Likewise, a new database is not useful until you *populate* it by filling one or more tables with data. You can populate a table with records by typing data directly into the table.

1 In the new record row, click in the **Student ID** field to display the insertion point, type **1023045** and then press [Enter]. Compare your screen with Figure 1.10.

The pencil icon [✏] in the *record selector box* indicates that a record is being entered or edited. The record selector box is the small box at the left of a record in Datasheet view. When clicked, the entire record is selected.

🔄 **ANOTHER WAY** Press [Tab] to move the insertion point to the next field.

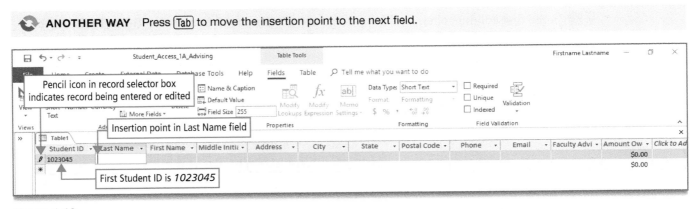

Figure 1.10

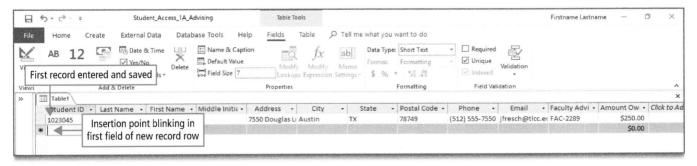

2 With the insertion point positioned in the **Last Name** field, type **Fresch** and then press `Tab`.

Pressing `Enter` or `Tab` will move the insertion point from field to field in the record.

> **NOTE** **Correcting Typing Errors**
>
> Correct any typing errors you make by using the techniques you have practiced in other Office applications. For example, use `Backspace` to remove characters to the left of the insertion point. Use `Del` to remove characters to the right of the insertion point. Or select the text you want to replace and type the correct information. Press `Esc` to exit out of a record that has not been completely entered.

3 In the **First Name** field, type **Jenna** and then press `Enter`.

4 In the **Middle Initial** field, type **A** and then press `Enter`.

5 In the **Address** field, type **7550 Douglas Ln** and then press `Enter`.

Do not be concerned if the data does not completely display in the column. As you progress in your study of Access, you will adjust column widths so that you can view all of the data.

6 Continue entering data in the fields as indicated in the table below, pressing `Enter` to move to the next field.

City	State	Postal Code	Phone	Email	Faculty Advisor ID
Austin	**TX**	**78749**	**(512) 555-7550**	**jfresch@tlcc.edu**	**FAC-2289**

> **NOTE** **Format for Typing Telephone Numbers in Access**
>
> Access does not require a specific format for typing telephone numbers in a record. The examples in this textbook use the format of Microsoft Outlook. Using such a format facilitates easy transfer of Outlook information to and from Access.

7 In the **Amount Owed** field, type **250** and then press `Enter`. Compare your screen with Figure 1.11.

Pressing `Enter` or `Tab` in the last field moves the insertion point to the next row to begin a new record. Access automatically saves the record as soon as you move to the next row; you do not have to take any specific action to save a record.

Figure 1.11

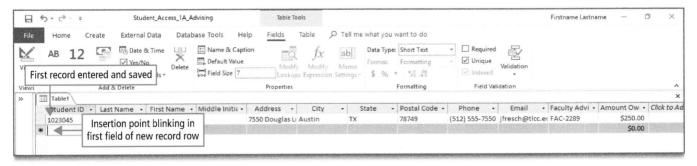

8 To give your table a meaningful name, click the **File tab**, and, on the left, click **Save As**. Under *Save As*, double-click **Save Object** As In the **Save As** dialog box, in the **Table Name** box, replace the selected text by typing **1A Students**

Save each database object with a name that identifies the data that it contains. When you save objects within a database, it is not necessary to use underscores in place of the spaces between words. Notice that the object tab—located directly above the *Student ID* field name—displays the table name.

MORE KNOWLEDGE **Renaming or Deleting a Table**

To change the name of a table, close the table, display the Navigation Pane, right-click the table name, and then click Rename. Type the new name or edit as you would any selected text. To delete a table, close the table, display the Navigation Pane, right-click the table name, and then click Delete.

Activity 1.06 | Adding Additional Records to a Table

1 In the new record row, click in the **Student ID** field, and then enter the data for two additional students as shown in the table below. Press Enter or Tab to move from field to field. The data in each field will display on one line in the table.

Student ID	Last Name	First Name	Middle Initial	Address	City	State	Postal Code	Phone	Email	Faculty Advisor ID	Amount Owed
2345677	Ingram	Joseph	S	621 Hilltop Dr	Leander	TX	78646	(512) 555-0717	jingram@tlcc.edu	FAC-2377	378.5
3456689	Snyder	Amanda	J	4786 Bluff St	Buda	TX	78610	(512) 555-9120	asnyder@tlcc.edu	FAC-9005	0

2 Press Enter, and compare your screen with Figure 1.12.

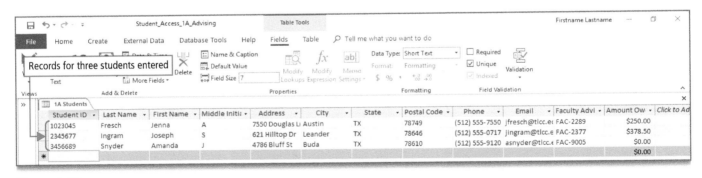

Figure 1.12

Activity 1.07 | Importing Data from an Excel Workbook into an Existing Access Table

2.1.1

You can type records directly into a table. You can also ***import*** data from a variety of sources. Importing is the process of copying data from one source or application to another application. For example, you can import data from a Word table or an Excel spreadsheet into an Access database because the data is arranged in columns and rows, similar to a table in Datasheet view.

In this Activity, you will **append**—add on—data from an Excel spreadsheet to your *1A Students* table. To append data, the table must already be created, and it should be closed.

1 In the upper right corner of the table, below the ribbon, click **Object Close** ⊠ to close your **1A Students** table. Notice that no objects are open.

2 On the ribbon, click the **External Data tab**. In the **Import & Link group**, click the **New Data Source** arrow, point to **From File**, and then click **Excel**. In the **Get External Data – Excel Spreadsheet** dialog box, click **Browse**.

3 In the **File Open** dialog box, navigate to your student files, double-click the Excel file **a01A_Students**, and then compare your screen with Figure 1.13.

> The path to the **source file**—the file being imported—displays in the File name box. There are three options for importing data from an Excel spreadsheet: import the data into a *new* table in the current database, append a copy of the records to an existing table, or link the data from the spreadsheet to a linked table in the database. A **link** is a connection to data in another file. When linking, Access creates a table that maintains a link to the source data, so that changes to the data in one file are automatically made in the other—linked—file.

🔄 **ANOTHER WAY** Click the file name, and then in the File Open dialog box, click Open.

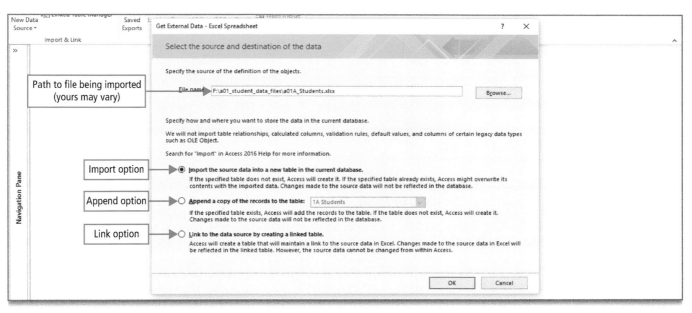

Figure 1.13

4 Click the **Append a copy of the records to the table** option button, and then, in the box to the right, click the **arrow**.

> Currently, your database has only one table, so no other tables display on the list. However, when a database has multiple tables, click the arrow to select the table to which you want to append records. The table into which you import or append data is referred to as the **destination table**.

5 Press Esc to cancel the list, and in the dialog box, click **OK**. Compare your screen with Figure 1.14.

The first screen of the Import Spreadsheet Wizard displays. A *wizard* is a feature in a Microsoft Office program that walks you step by step through a process. The presence of scroll bars in the window indicates that records and fields are out of view. To append records from an Excel workbook to an existing database table, the column headings in the Excel worksheet or spreadsheet must be identical to the field names in the table. The wizard identified the first row of the spreadsheet as column headings, which are equivalent to field names.

Figure 1.14

6 In the lower right corner of the wizard, click **Next**. Notice that the name of your table displays under **Import to Table**. In the lower right corner of the wizard, click **Finish**.

7 In the **Get External Data – Excel Spreadsheet** dialog box, click **Close**. **Open** » the **Navigation Pane**, and then compare your screen with Figure 1.15.

Figure 1.15

8 In the **Navigation Pane**, double-click your **1A Students** table to open the table in Datasheet view, and then **Close** « the **Navigation Pane**.

🔄 **ANOTHER WAY** To open an object from the Navigation Pane, right-click the object name, and then click Open.

9 In the lower left corner of your screen, locate the navigation area, and notice that there are a total of **25** records in the table—you entered three records and imported 22 additional records. Compare your screen with Figure 1.16.

The records that you entered and the records you imported from the Excel spreadsheet display in your table; the first record in the table is selected. The **navigation area** indicates the number of records in the table and has controls in the form of arrows that you click to move through the records.

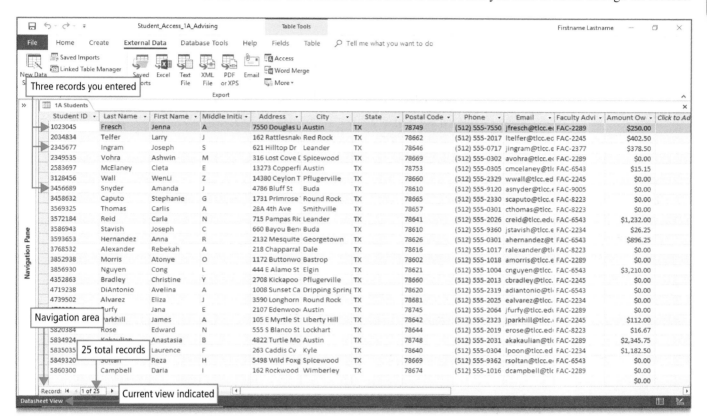

Figure 1.16

Objective 3	Change the Structure of Tables and Add a Second Table

GO! Learn How

Video A1-3

Recall that the structure of a table is the underlying design of the table and includes field names and data types. You can create or modify a table in Datasheet view. To define and modify fields, many database experts prefer to work in Design view, where you have more options for defining fields in a table.

Activity 1.08 | Deleting a Table Field in Design View

MOS

2.4.1

In a recent meeting, the Student Services department has decided that the Students table does not need to include a field for the middle initial. In this Activity, you will delete the *Middle Initial* field from the table.

1 Click the **Home tab**, and then in the **Views group**, click the **View arrow** to display a list of views.

There are two views for tables: Datasheet view and Design view. Other objects have different views. On the list, Design view is represented by a picture of a pencil, a ruler, and an angle. Datasheet view is represented by a picture of a table arranged in columns and rows. In the Views group, if the top of the View button displays the pencil, ruler, and angle, clicking View will switch your view to Design view. Likewise, clicking the top of the View button that displays as a datasheet will switch your view to Datasheet view.

2 On the list, click **Design View**, and then compare your screen with Figure 1.17.

Design view displays the underlying design—the structure—of the table and its fields. In Design view, the records in the table do not display. You can only view the information about each field's attributes. Each field name is listed, along with its data type. You can add explanatory information about a field in the Description column, but it is not required.

You can decide how each field should look and behave in the Field Properties area. For example, you can set a specific field size in the Field Properties area. In the lower right corner, information displays about the active selection—in this case, the Field Name.

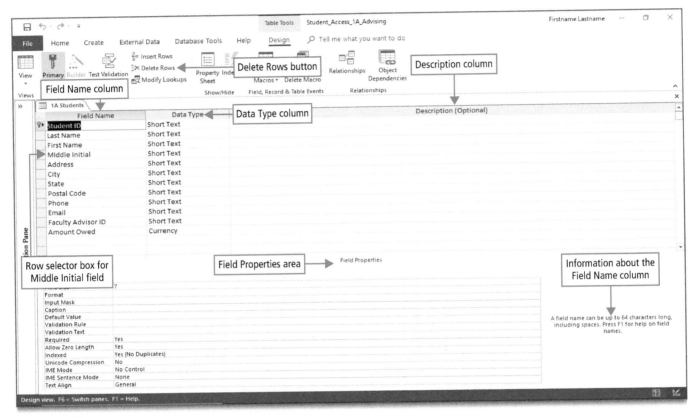

Figure 1.17

3 In the **Field Name** column, to the left of **Middle Initial**, point to the row selector box to display the ➡ pointer, and then click one time to select the entire row.

4 On the **Design tab**, in the **Tools group**, click **Delete Rows**. Read the warning in the message box, and then click **Yes**.

Deleting a field deletes both the field and its data. After you save the changes, you cannot undo this action, so Access prompts you to be sure you want to proceed. If you change your mind after deleting a field and saving the changes, you must add the field back into the table and then reenter the data for that field for every record.

🔄 **ANOTHER WAY** In Design view, right-click the selected row, and then click Delete Rows; or, in Datasheet view, select the field—column—and on the Home tab, in the Records group, click Delete.

Activity 1.09 | Adding Field Descriptions and Changing Field Size

2.2.3, 2.4.4

Typically, many different individuals have the ability to enter data into a table. For example, at your college, many Registration Assistants enter and modify student and course information daily. Two ways to help reduce errors are to restrict what can be typed in a field and to add descriptive information to help the individuals when entering the data.

1 With your table still displayed in **Design** view, in the **Field Name** column, click anywhere in the **Student ID** field name.

2 In the **Student ID** row, click in the **Description** box, type **Seven-digit Student ID number** and then press Enter. Compare your screen with Figure 1.18.

Descriptions for fields in a table are optional. Include a description if the field name does not provide an obvious explanation of the type of data to be entered. If a description is provided for a field, when data is being entered in that field in Datasheet view, the text in the Description displays on the left side of the status bar to provide additional information for the individuals who are entering the data.

When you enter a description for a field, a Property Update Options button displays below the text you typed, which enables you to copy the description for the field to all other database objects that use this table as an underlying source.

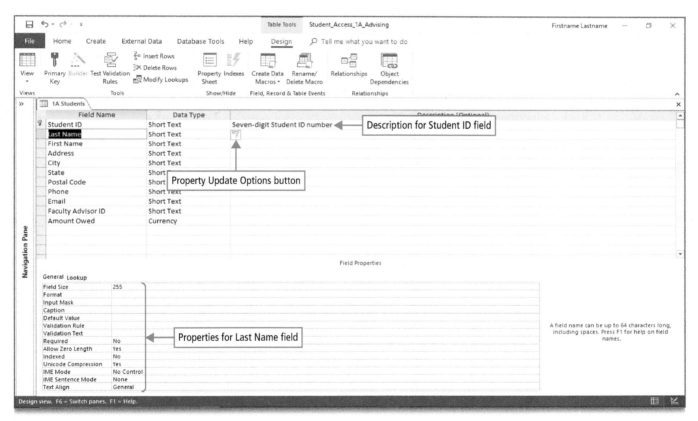

Figure 1.18

3 Click in the **State** field name box. In the lower area of the screen, under **Field Properties**, click in the **Field Size** box to select the text **255**, and type **2** Click in the **Description** box for this field, type **Two-character state abbreviation** and then press Enter.

> Recall changing the size of a field limits the number of characters that the field will accept. *Field properties* control how the field displays and how data can be entered into the field. You can define properties for each field in the Field Properties area by first clicking on the field name to display the properties for that specific data type.

4 Click in the **Faculty Advisor ID** field name box. In the **Field Properties** area, change the **Field Size** to **8** and in the **Description** box for this field, type **Eight-character ID of the instructor assigned as advisor** and then press Enter.

MORE KNOWLEDGE   **Add a Table Description**

You can create a description to provide more information to users regarding the entire table. With the table displayed in Design view, click the Design tab. In the Show/Hide group, click Property Sheet. Click in the Description box, type the table description, and then press Enter. Close the Property Sheet.

---

5 On the Quick Access Toolbar, click **Save** 🖫 to save the design changes to your table, and then notice the message.

> The message indicates that the field size property of one or more fields has changed to a shorter size. If more characters are currently present in the State, or Faculty Advisor ID fields than you have allowed, the data will be *truncated*—cut off or shortened—because the fields were not previously restricted to these specific number of characters.

6 In the message box, click **Yes**.

Activity 1.10 | Viewing the Primary Key in Design View

Primary key refers to the required field in the table that uniquely identifies a record. For example, in a college registration database, your Student ID number identifies you as a unique individual—every student has a student number and no other student at the college has your exact student number. In the 1A Students table, the Student ID uniquely identifies each student.

When you create a table using the blank database template, Access designates the first field as the primary key field and names the field ID. It is good database design practice to establish a primary key for every table, because doing so ensures that you do not enter the same record more than once. You can imagine the confusion if another student at your college had the same Student ID number as you do.

1 With your table still displayed in **Design** view, in the **Field Name** column, click in the **Student ID** box. To the left of the box, notice the small icon of a key, as shown in Figure 1.19.

Access automatically designates the first field as the primary key field, but you can set any field as the primary key by clicking the field name, and then in the Tools group, clicking Primary Key.

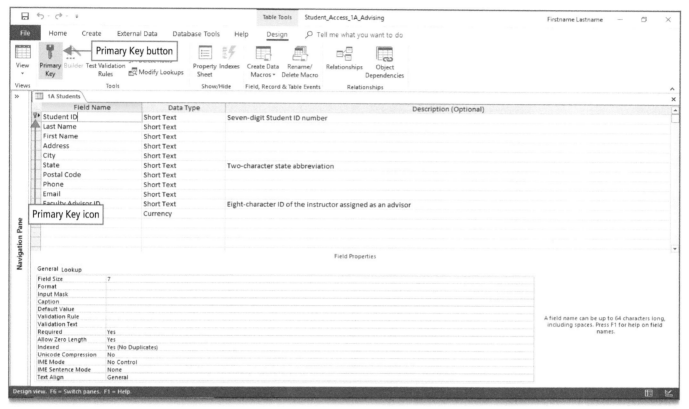

Figure 1.19

2 On the **Design tab**, in the **Views group**, notice that the View button displays a picture of a datasheet, indicating that clicking View will switch the view to Datasheet view. Click the top of the **View** button.

If you make design changes to a table and switch views without first saving the table, Access will prompt you to save the table before changing views.

Activity 1.11 | Adding a Second Table to a Database by Importing an Excel Spreadsheet

MOS
1.1.1

Many Microsoft Office users track data in an Excel spreadsheet. The sorting and filtering capabilities of Excel are useful for a simple database where all of the information resides in one large Excel spreadsheet. However, Excel is limited as a database management tool because it cannot *relate* the information in multiple spreadsheets in a way that you can ask a question and get a meaningful result. Because data in an Excel spreadsheet is arranged in columns and rows, the spreadsheet can easily convert to an Access table by importing the spreadsheet.

1 On the ribbon, click the **External Data tab**. In the **Import & Link group**, click the **New Data Source** arrow, point to **From File**, and then click **Excel**. In the **Get External Data – Excel Spreadsheet** dialog box, to the right of the **File name** box, click **Browse**.

2 In the **File Open** dialog box, navigate to the location where your student data files are stored, and then double-click **a01A_Faculty_Advisors**. Compare your screen with Figure 1.20.

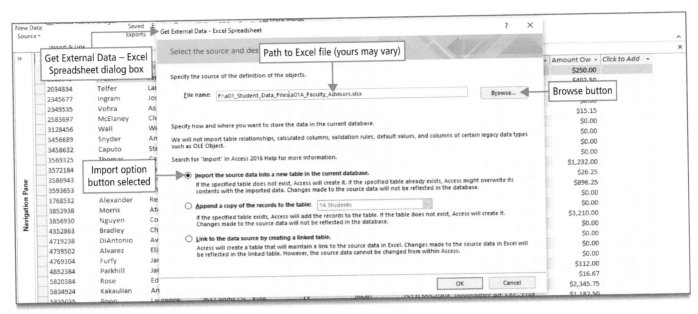

Figure 1.20

3 Be sure that the **Import the source data into a new table in the current database** option button is selected, and then click **OK**.

The Import Spreadsheet Wizard displays the spreadsheet data.

4 In the upper left corner of the wizard, select the **First Row Contains Column Headings** check box.

The Excel data is framed, indicating that the first row of Excel column titles will become the Access table field names, and the remaining rows will become the individual records in the new Access table.

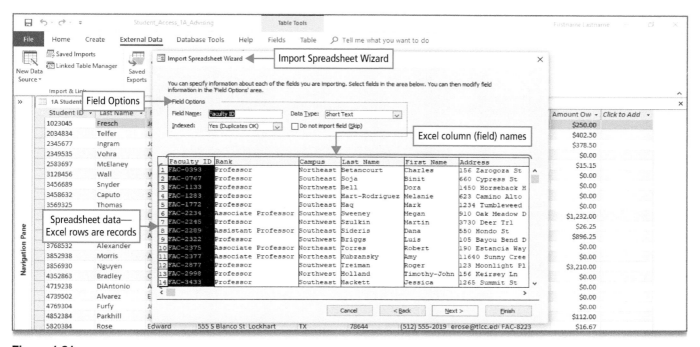

5 Click **Next**. Notice that the first column—*Faculty ID*—is selected, and in the upper area of the wizard, the **Field Name** and the **Data Type** display. Compare your screen with Figure 1.21.

In this step, under Field Options, you can review and change the name or the data type of each selected field. You can also identify fields in the spreadsheet that you do not want to import into the Access table by selecting the Do not import field (Skip) check box.

Figure 1.21

6 Click **Next**. In the upper area of the wizard, click the **Choose my own primary key** option button, and then verify that **Faculty ID** displays.

In the new table, Faculty ID will be the primary key. Every faculty member has a Faculty ID and no two faculty members have the same Faculty ID. By default, Access selects the first field as the primary key, but you can click the arrow and select a different field.

7 Click **Next**. In the **Import to Table** box, type **1A Faculty Advisors** and then click **Finish**.

8 In the **Get External Data – Excel Spreadsheet** dialog box, click **Close**. **Open** ⏵ the **Navigation Pane**.

9 In the **Navigation Pane**, double-click your **1A Faculty Advisors** table to open it in Datasheet view, and then **Close** ⏴ the **Navigation Pane**.

Two tables that are identified by their object tabs are open in the object window. Your 1A Faculty Advisors table is the active table and displays the 29 records that you imported from the Excel spreadsheet.

10 In your **1A Faculty Advisors** table, click in the **Postal Code** field in the first record. On the ribbon, under **Table Tools**, click the **Fields tab**. In the **Formatting group**, click the **Data Type arrow**, and then click **Short Text**. Compare your screen with Figure 1.22.

When you import data from an Excel spreadsheet, check the data types of all fields to ensure they are correct. Recall that if a field, such as the Postal Code, contains numbers that do not represent a quantity or are not used in calculations, the data type should be set to Short Text. To change the data type of a field, click in the field in any record.

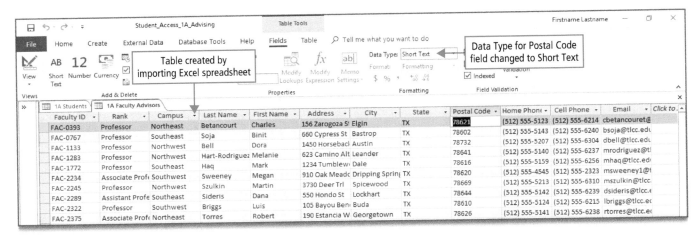

Figure 1.22

Activity 1.12 | Adjusting Column Widths and Viewing a Table in Print Preview

You can adjust the column widths in a table displayed in Datasheet view by using techniques similar to those you use for Excel spreadsheets.

1 In the object window, click the **object tab** for your **1A Students** table to make it the active object and to display it in the object window.

Clicking an object tab along the top of the object window enables you to display the open object and make it active so that you can work with it. All of the columns in the datasheet are the same width, regardless of the length of the data in the field, the length of the field name, or the field size that was set. If you print the table as currently displayed, some of the data or field names will not print completely, so you will want to adjust the column widths.

2 In the field names row, point to the right edge of the **Address** field to display the ⊞ pointer, and then compare your screen with Figure 1.23.

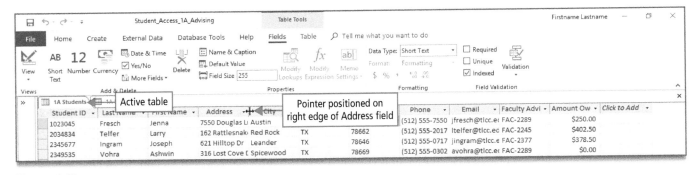

Figure 1.23

3 With the ⊞ pointer positioned as shown in Figure 1.23, double-click the right edge of the **Address** field.

> The column width of the Address field widens to display the longest entry in the field fully. In this manner, the width of a column can be increased or decreased to fit its contents in the same manner as a column in an Excel spreadsheet. In Access, adjusting the column width to fit the contents is referred to as *Best Fit*.

4 Point to the **City** field name to display the ↓ pointer, right-click to select the entire column and display the shortcut menu. Click **Field Width**, and then in the **Column Width** dialog box, click **Best Fit**.

> This is a second way to adjust column widths.

5 If necessary, scroll to the right to view the last three fields. Point to the **Email** field name to display the ↓ pointer, hold down the left mouse button, and then drag to the right to select this column, the **Faculty Advisor ID** column, and the **Amount Owed** column. Point to the right edge of any of the selected columns to display the ⊞ pointer, and then double-click to apply **Best Fit** to all three columns.

> You can select multiple columns and adjust the widths of all of them at one time by using this technique or by right-clicking any of the selected columns, clicking Field Width, and clicking Best Fit in the Column Width dialog box.

6 If necessary, scroll to the left to view the **Student ID** field. To the left of the **Student ID** field name, click **Select All** ▢. Notice that all of the fields are selected.

7 On the ribbon, click the **Home tab**. In the **Records group**, click **More**, and then click **Field Width**. In the **Column Width** dialog box, click **Best Fit**. Click anywhere in the **Student ID** field, and then compare your screen with Figure 1.24.

> Using the More command is a third way to adjust column widths. By using Select All, you can adjust the widths of all of the columns at one time. Adjusting the width of columns does not change the data in the table's records; it only changes the *display* of the data.

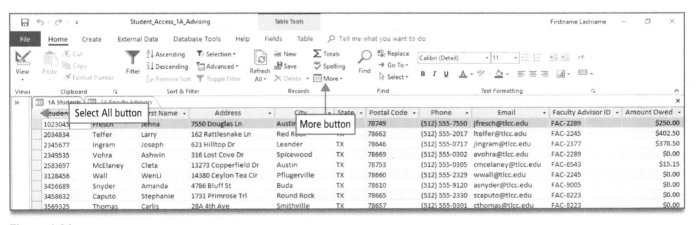

Figure 1.24

NOTE   Adjusting Column Widths

After adjusting column widths, scroll horizontally and vertically to be sure that all of the data displays in all of the fields. Access adjusts column widths to fit the screen size based on the displayed data. If data is not displayed on the screen when you adjust column widths—even if you use Select All—the column width may not be adjusted adequately to display all of the data in the field. After adjusting column widths, click in any field to remove the selection of the column or columns, and then save the table before performing other tasks.

8 On the Quick Access Toolbar, click **Save** 🖫 to save the table design changes—changing the column widths.

> If you do not save the table after making design changes, Access prompts you to save it when you close the table.

Activity 1.13 | Viewing a Table in Print Preview

MOS
1.3.1

There are times when you will want to print a table, even though a report may look more professional. For example, you may need a quick reference, or you may want to proofread the data that has been entered. In Access, it is best to preview a table before printing to make any necessary layout changes.

1 On the ribbon, click the **File tab**, click **Print**, and then click **Print Preview**. Compare your screen with Figure 1.25.

> The table displays in Print Preview with the default zoom setting of One Page, a view that enables you to see how your table will print on the page. It is a good idea to view any object in Print Preview before printing so that you can make changes to the object if needed before actually printing it. In the navigation area, the Next Page button is darker (available), an indication that more than one page will print.

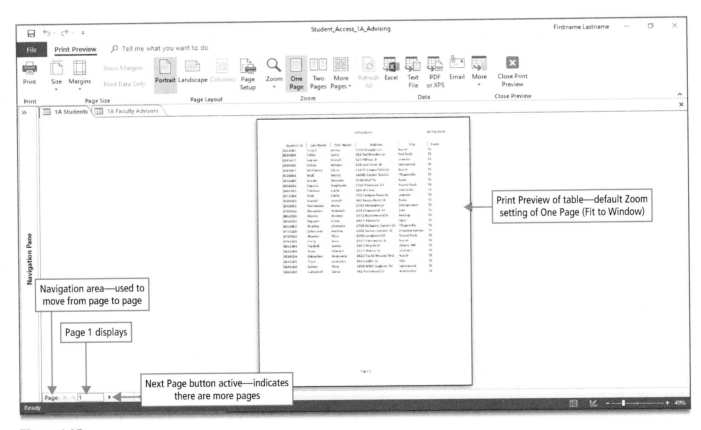

Figure 1.25

> **NOTE** **Headers and Footers in Access Objects**
>
> The headers and footers in Access tables and queries are controlled by default settings; you cannot enter additional information or edit the information. The object name displays in the center of the header area, and the current date displays on the right. Adding your name to the object name is helpful in identifying your paper printouts or electronic results. The page number displays in the center of the footer area. The headers and footers in Access forms and reports are more flexible; you can add to and edit the information.

2 In the navigation area, click **Next Page** ▸ to display Page 2. Point to the top of the page to display the 🔍 pointer, click one time to zoom in, and then compare your screen with Figure 1.26.

The Print Preview display enlarges, and the Zoom Out pointer displays. The second page of the table displays the last five fields. The Next Page button is dimmed, indicating that the button is unavailable because there are no more pages after Page 2. The Previous Page button is available, indicating that a page exists before this page.

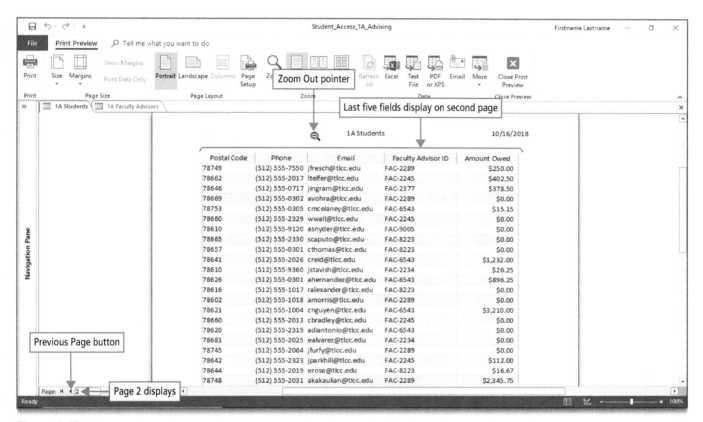

Figure 1.26

3 On the ribbon, on the **Print Preview tab**, in the **Zoom group**, click **Zoom** to change the zoom setting back to the default setting of One Page.

🔄 **ANOTHER WAY** With the 🔍 pointer displayed on the page, click to zoom back to the One Page setting.

4 In the **Page Layout group**, click **Landscape**, and notice that there are only three fields on Page 2. In the navigation area, click **Previous Page** ◀ to display Page 1, and then compare your screen with Figure 1.27.

The orientation of the page to be printed changes. The header on the page includes the table name and current date, and the footer displays the page number. The change in orientation from portrait to landscape is not saved with the table. Each time you print, you must check the page orientation, the margins, and any other print parameters so that the object prints as you intend.

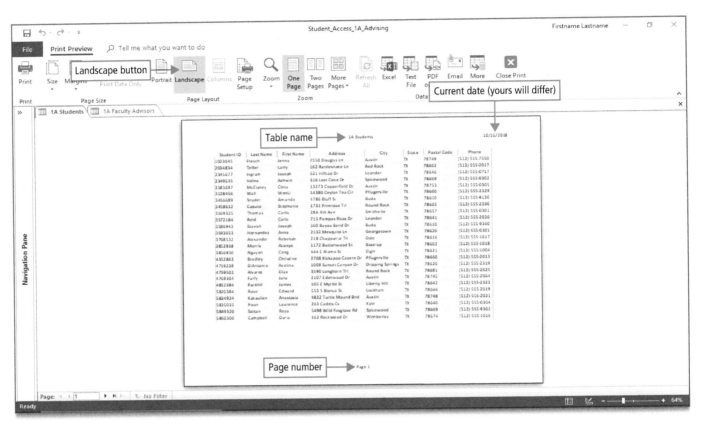

Figure 1.27

NOTE   Creating a PDF Electronic Image of Your Database Object That Looks Like a Printed Document

Display the object (table, query, form, report, and so on) in Print Preview and adjust margins and orientation as needed. On the Print Preview tab, in the Data group, click PDF or XPS. In the Publish as PDF or XPS dialog box, navigate to your chapter folder. Use the default file name, or follow your instructor's directions to name the object. If you wish to view the PDF file, in the dialog box, select the Open file after publishing check box. In the Publish as PDF or XPS dialog box, click Publish. If necessary, close any windows that try to display your PDF—Adobe Reader, Adobe Acrobat, or the Microsoft Edge browser, and then close the Export – PDF dialog box. On the ribbon, click Close Print Preview; your electronic image is saved. Close the Save Export Steps dialog box.

---

5 On the ribbon, in the **Close Preview group**, click **Close Print Preview**. In the upper right corner of the object window, click **Close Object** ✕ to close your **1A Students** table. Notice that the **1A Faculty Advisors** table is the active object in the object window.

🔄 **ANOTHER WAY**   In the object window, right-click the 1A Students object tab, and then click Close.

6 In your **1A Faculty Advisors** table, to the left of the **Faculty ID** field name, click **Select All** to select all of the columns. On the **Home tab**, in the **Records group**, click **More**, and then click **Field Width**. In the **Column Width** dialog box, click **Best Fit** to adjust the widths of all of the columns so that all of the data displays. Click in any field in the table to cancel the selection. Scroll horizontally and vertically to be sure that all of the data displays in each field; if necessary, use the techniques you practiced to apply Best Fit to individual columns. **Save** the changes you made to the table's column widths, and then click in any record to cancel the selection, if necessary.

7 On the ribbon, click the **File tab**, click **Print**, and then click **Print Preview**. On the **Print Preview tab**, in the **Page Layout group**, click **Landscape**. Notice that the table will print on more than one page. In the **Page Size group**, click **Margins**, click **Normal**, and then notice that one more column moved to the first page—your results may differ depending upon your printer's capabilities.

> In addition to changing the page orientation to Landscape, you can change the margins to Normal to see if all of the fields will print on one page. In this instance, there are still too many fields to print on one page, although the Postal Code field moved from Page 2 to Page 1.

8 On the ribbon, in the **Close Preview group**, click **Close Print Preview**. In the object window, **Close** [×] your **1A Faculty Advisors** table, saving changes if necessary.

> All of your database objects—your *1A Students* table and your *1A Faculty Advisors* table—are closed; the object window is empty.

Objective 4   Create a Query, Form, and Report

GO! Learn How
Video A1-4

Recall that tables are the foundation of an Access database because all of the data is stored in one or more tables. You can use the data stored in tables in other database objects such as queries, forms, and reports.

Activity 1.14 | Creating a Query by Using the Simple Query Wizard

MOS
3.1.7

A *query* is a database object that retrieves specific data from one or more database objects— either tables or other queries—and then, in a single datasheet, displays only the data that you specify when you design the query. Because the word *query* means *to ask a question*, think of a query as a question formed in a manner that Access can answer.

A *select query* is one type of Access query. A select query, also called a *simple select query*, retrieves (selects) data from one or more tables or queries and then displays the selected data in a datasheet. A select query creates a subset of the data to answer specific questions; for example, *Which students live in Austin, TX?*

The objects from which a query selects the data are referred to as the query's *data source*. In this Activity, you will create a simple query using a wizard that walks you step by step through the process. The process involves selecting the data source and indicating the fields that you want to include in the query results. The query—the question you want to ask—is *What is the name, email address, phone number, and Student ID of every student?*

1 On the ribbon, click the **Create tab**, and then in then in the **Queries group**, click **Query Wizard**. In the **New Query** dialog box, be sure **Simple Query Wizard** is selected, and then click **OK**. Compare your screen with Figure 1.28.

> In the wizard, the displayed table or query name is the object that was last selected on the Navigation Pane. The last object you worked with was your 1A Faculty Advisors table, so that object name displayed in the wizard.

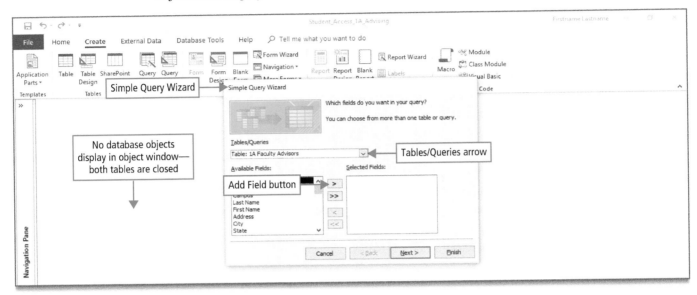

Figure 1.28

2 In the wizard, click the **Tables/Queries arrow**, and then click your **Table: 1A Students**.

> To create a query, first select the data source—the object from which the query is to select the data. The information you need to answer the question is stored in your 1A Students table, so this table is your data source.

3 Under **Available Fields**, click **Last Name**, and then click **Add Field** > to move the field to the **Selected Fields** list on the right. Double-click the **First Name** field to add the field to the **Selected Fields** list.

> Use either method to add fields to the Selected Fields list—you can add fields in any order.

4 By using **Add Field** > or by double-clicking the field name, add the following fields to the **Selected Fields** list in the order specified: **Email**, **Phone**, and **Student ID**. Compare your screen with Figure 1.29.

> Selecting these five fields will answer the question, *What is the name, email address, phone number, and Student ID of every student?*

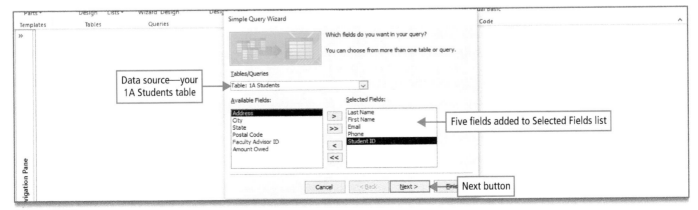

Figure 1.29

5 In the wizard, click **Next**. Click in the **What title do you want for your query?** box. Edit as necessary so that the query name is **1A All Students Query** and then compare your screen with Figure 1.30.

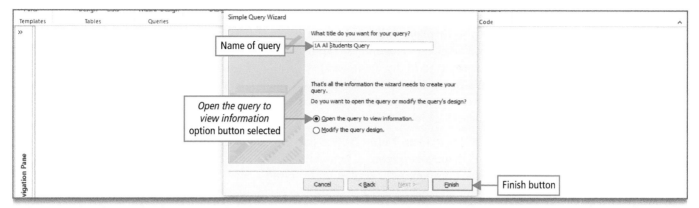

Figure 1.30

6 In the wizard, click **Finish**. Select all of the columns, apply **Best Fit**, and then **Save** 🖫 the query. In the first record, click in the **Last Name** field to cancel the selection. Compare your screen with Figure 1.31.

Access *runs* the query—performs the actions indicated in your query design—by searching the records in the specified data source, and then finds the records that match specified criteria. The records that match the criteria display in a datasheet. A select query *selects*—pulls out and displays—*only* the information from the data source that you request, including the specified fields. In the object window, Access displays every student from your 1A Students table—the data source—but displays *only* the five fields that you moved to the Selected Fields list in the Simple Query Wizard.

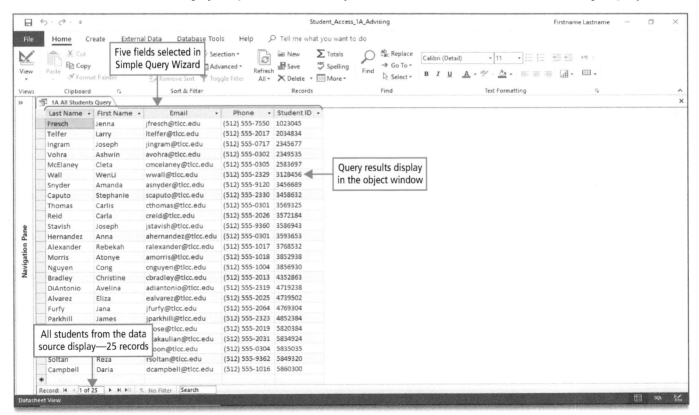

Figure 1.31

7 In the object window, **Close** ☒ the query.

Activity 1.15 | Creating a Form

1.3.1, 4.1.1

A *form* is an Access object with which you can enter data, edit data, or display data from a table or query. In a form, the fields are laid out in an attractive format on the screen, which makes working with the database easier for those who must enter and look up data.

One type of form displays only one record at a time. Such a form is useful not only to the individual who performs the data entry—typing in the records—but also to anyone who has the job of viewing information in the database. For example, when you visit the Records office at your college to obtain a transcript, someone displays your record on the screen. For the viewer, it is much easier to look at one record at a time using a form than to look at all of the student records in the database table.

1 ▶ **Open** [»] the **Navigation Pane**. Notice that a table name displays with a datasheet icon, and a query name displays an icon of two overlapping datasheets. Right-click your **1A Students** table, and then compare your screen with Figure 1.32.

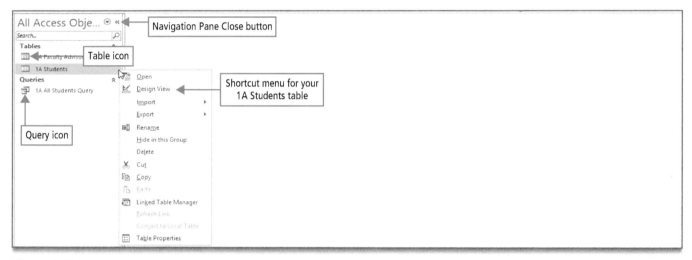

Figure 1.32

2 ▶ On the shortcut menu, click **Open** to display the table in the object window, and then **Close** [«] the **Navigation Pane** to maximize your object window space.

 ANOTHER WAY   In the Navigation Pane, double-click the object name to open it.

3 ▸ Notice that there are 11 fields in the table. On the **Create tab**, in the **Forms group**, click **Form**. Compare your screen with Figure 1.33.

The Form tool creates a form based on the currently selected object—your 1A Students table. The form displays all of the fields from the underlying data source—one record at a time—in a simple top-to-bottom format with all 11 fields in a single column. You can use this form as it displays, or you can modify it. Records that you create or edit in a form are automatically added to or updated in the underlying table or data source.

The new form displays in *Layout view*—the Access view in which you can make changes to elements of an object while it is open and displaying the data from the data source. Each field in the form displayed in Figure 1.33 displays the data for the first student record—*Jenna Fresch*—in your 1A Students table.

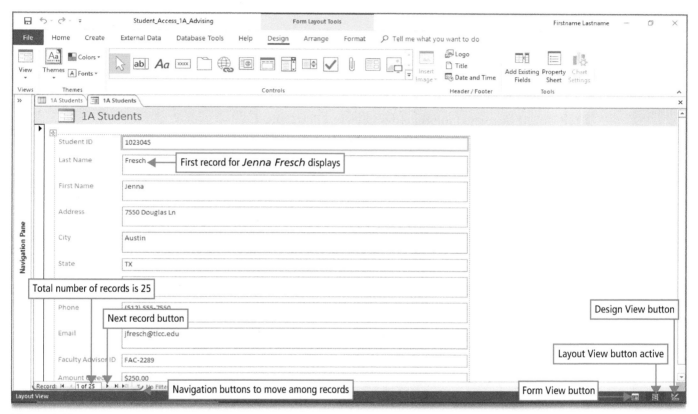

Figure 1.33

NOTE   The Property Sheet Displays

If the Property sheet was displayed the last time you were viewing a form in Access, it will display by default with the new form.

---

4 ▸ At the right side of the status bar, notice the three buttons. Point to each button to display its ScreenTip, and notice that **Layout View** 🖾 is active, indicating that the form is displayed in Layout view.

5 ▸ In the status bar, click **Form View** 🖾.

In *Form view*, you can view the records, create a new record, edit a record, and delete a record. You cannot change the layout or design of the form. Form view is useful for individuals who *access records* in your database. Layout view is useful for individuals who *design* the form.

🔁 **ANOTHER WAY**   On the Design tab, or on the Home tab, in the Views group, click View when the button displays an icon of a form.

6 In the navigation area, click **Next record** ▶ two times to display the third record—the record for *Joseph Ingram*.

> Use the navigation buttons to scroll among the records and to display any single record.

7 Save 🖫 the form as **1A Student Form**

8 On the ribbon, click the **File tab**, click **Print**, and then on the right, click **Print**—do *not* click Print Preview because you are going to print a *single* record—not all of the records.

9 In the **Print** dialog box, under **Print Range**, click the **Selected Record(s)** option button, and then click **Setup**.

10 In the **Page Setup** dialog box, click the **Columns tab**. Under **Column Size**, double-click in the **Width** box, type **7.5** and then click **OK**.

> Forms are usually not printed, so the default width for a form created with the Form command is larger than most printers can handle to print on one page. If you do not change the width, the form will print on two pages because the column flows over the margins allowed by the printer. If, after changing the Width to 7.5, your form still prints on two pages, try entering a different value for Width; for example, 7 or 6.5.

11 Unless instructed to print your objects, click Cancel.

> After printing, along the left edge of the record, the narrow bar—the *record selector bar*—displays in black, indicating that the record is selected.

NOTE   Printing a Single Form in PDF

On the File tab, click Print, and then on the right, click Print. In the Print dialog box, click Setup. In the Page Setup dialog box, click the Columns tab. Under Column Size, double-click in the Width box, type **7.5** and then click OK. In the Print dialog box, click Cancel. On the left edge of the form, click the record selector bar so that it is black—selected.

On the ribbon, click the External Data tab. In the Export group, click PDF or XPS. In the Publish as PDF or XPS dialog box, navigate to your chapter folder, and at the lower right corner of the dialog box, click Options. In the Options dialog box, under Range, click the Selected records option button, and then click OK. In the Publish as PDF or XPS dialog box, click Publish. If necessary, close Adobe Reader, Adobe Acrobat, or the Microsoft Edge browser.

---

12 Close ✕ the form object; leave your **1A Students** table open.

Activity 1.16 | Creating and Modifying a Report

MOS
5.1.1, 5.1.2, 5.2.3

A *report* is a database object that displays the fields and records from a table or query in an easy-to-read format suitable for printing. Create professional-looking reports to summarize database information.

1 Open » the **Navigation Pane**, and then open your **1A Faculty Advisors** table by double-clicking the table name or by right-clicking the table name and clicking Open. **Close** « the **Navigation Pane**.

2 On the **Create tab**, in the **Reports group**, click **Report**.

> The Report tool creates a report in Layout view and includes all of the fields and all of the records in the data source—your 1A Faculty Advisors table. Dotted lines indicate how the report would break across pages if you print it now. In Layout view, you can make quick changes to the report layout while viewing the data from the table.

3 Click the **Faculty ID** field name, and then on the ribbon, under **Report Layout Tools**, click the **Arrange tab**. In the **Rows & Columns group**, click **Select Column**, and then press Del. Using the same technique, delete the **Rank** field.

> The Faculty ID and Rank fields, along with the data, are deleted from the report. The fields readjust by moving to the left. Deleting the fields from the report does *not* delete the fields and data from the data source—your 1A Faculty Advisors table.

ANOTHER WAY   Right-click the field name, click Select Entire Column, and then press Del.

4 Click the **Address** field name, and then by using the scroll bar at the bottom of the screen, scroll to the right to display the **Cell Phone** field; be careful not to click in the report.

5 Hold down Shift, and then click the **Cell Phone** field name to select all of the fields from *Address* through *Cell Phone*. With the field names selected—surrounded by a colored border—in the **Rows & Columns group**, click **Select Column**, and then press Del.

> Use this method to select and delete multiple columns in Layout view.

6 Scroll to the left and notice that the four remaining fields display within the dotted lines— they are within the margins of the report. Click the **Campus** field name. Hold down Shift, and then click the **First Name** field name to select the first three fields. In the **Rows & Columns group**, click **Select Column** to select all three fields.

7 On the ribbon, click the **Design tab**, and then in the **Tools group**, click **Property Sheet**.

> The ***Property Sheet*** for the selected columns displays on the right side of the screen. Every object and every item in an object has an associated Property Sheet where you can make precise changes to the properties—characteristics—of selected items.

8 In the **Property Sheet**, if necessary, click the **Format tab**. Click **Width**, type **1.5** and then press Enter. Compare your screen with Figure 1.34.

> The width of the three selected fields changes to 1.5", and the fields readjust by moving to the left. You can change the Width property if you need to move columns within the margins of a report. In this report, the fields already displayed within the margins, but some reports may need this minor adjustment to print on one page.

ANOTHER WAY   Select the column, and then drag the right edge of the column to the left to decrease the width of the field, or, drag to the right to increase the width of the field.

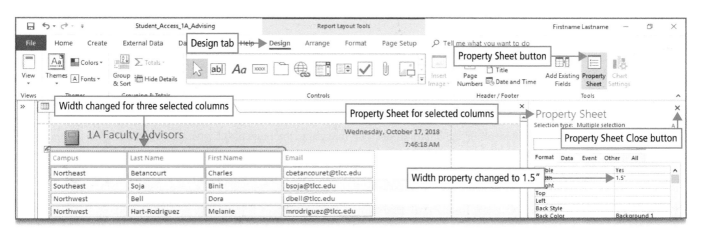

Figure 1.34

9 **Close** ⊠ the **Property Sheet**. Click the **Last Name** field name. On the ribbon, click the **Home tab**, and then in the **Sort & Filter group**, click **Ascending**.

> Access sorts the report in ascending alphabetical order by the Last Name field. By default, tables are sorted in ascending order by the primary key field—in this instance, the Faculty ID field. Changing the sort order in the report does *not* change the sort order in the underlying table.

10 At the top of the report, to the right of the green report icon, click anywhere in the title of the report to select the title. On the **Home tab**, in the **Text Formatting group**, click the **Font Size arrow**, and then click **14**. **Save** 🖫 the report. In the **Save As** dialog box, in the **Report Name** box, add **Report** to the end of *1A Faculty Advisors*, and then click **OK**.

11 On the **File tab**, click **Print**, and then click **Print Preview**. On the **Print Preview tab**, in the **Zoom group**, click **Two Pages**, and then compare your screen with Figure 1.35

> As currently formatted, the report will print on two pages, because the page number at the bottom of the report is positioned beyond the right margin of the report.

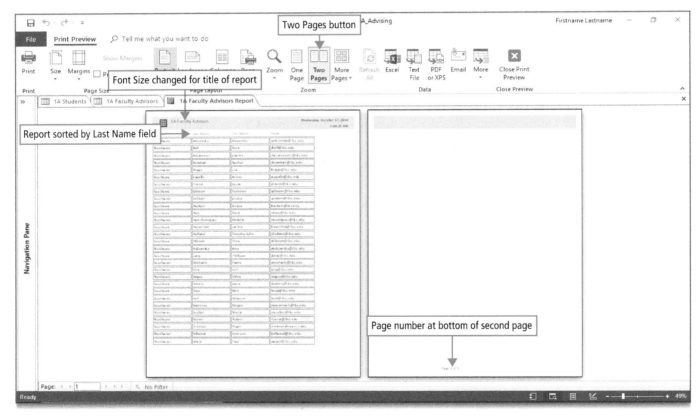

Figure 1.35

12 In the **Close Preview group**, click **Close Print Preview**. Scroll down to display the bottom of the report, and then, if necessary, scroll right to display the page number. Click the page number—**Page 1 of 1**—and then press ⌈Del⌉.

> Because all of the data will print on one page, the page number is not necessary for this report. If you want the page number to display, you can drag it within the margins of the report.

13 Display the report in **Print Preview**, and notice that the report will now print on one page. In the **Zoom group**, click **One Page**. Click **Save** 🖫 to save the changes to the design of the report. Click **Close Print Preview**.

> When you create a report by using the Report tool, the default margins are 0.25 inch. Some printers require a greater margin, so your printed report may result in two pages. As you progress

in your study of Access, you will practice making these adjustments. Also, if a printer is not installed on your system, the electronic PDF printout might result in a two-page report.

14 In the object window, right-click any **object tab**, and then click **Close All** to close all of the open objects. Notice that the object window is empty.

Objective 5 | Close a Database and Close Access

When you close a table, any changes made to the records are saved automatically. If you made changes to the structure or adjusted column widths, you will be prompted to save the table when you close the table or when you switch views. Likewise, you will be prompted to save queries, forms, and reports if you make changes to the layout or design. If the Navigation Pane is open when you close Access, it will display when you reopen the database. When you are finished using your database, close the database, and then close Access.

GO! Learn How
Video A1-5

Activity 1.17 | Closing a Database and Closing Access

1 Open 》 the **Navigation Pane**. Notice that your report object displays with a green report icon. Compare your screen with Figure 1.36.

Figure 1.36

2 On the **File tab**, click **Close** to close the database but leave Access open. This action enables you to continue working in Access with another database if you want to do so. In the Access opening screen, in the upper right corner, click **Close** ✕ to close Access.

 For Non-MyLab Submissions: Determine What Your Instructor Requires for Submission
As directed by your instructor, submit your completed database file.

---

3 In **MyLab IT**, locate and click the Grader Project **Access 1A Advising**. In **step 3**, under **Upload Completed Assignment**, click **Choose File**. In the **Open** dialog box, navigate to your **Access Chapter 1 folder**, and then click your **Student_Access_1A_Advising** file one time to select it. In the lower right corner of the **Open** dialog box, click **Open**.

The name of your selected file displays above the Upload button.

4 To submit your file to **MyLab IT** for grading, click **Upload**, wait a moment for a green **Success!** message, and then in **step 4**, click the blue **Submit for Grading** button. Click **Close Assignment** to return to your list of **Course Materials**.

You have completed Project 1A **END**

»» GO! With Google

Access web apps are designed to work with Microsoft's *SharePoint*, a service for setting up websites to share and manage documents. Your college may not have SharePoint installed, so you will use other tools to share objects from your database so that you can work collaboratively with others. Recall that Google Drive is Google's free, web-based word processor, spreadsheet, slide show, form, and data storage and sharing service. For Access, you can *export* a database object to an Excel worksheet, a PDF file, or a text file, and then save the file to Google Drive.

> **ALERT** **Working with Web-Based Applications and Services**
>
> Computer programs and services on the web receive continuous updates and improvements. Therefore, the steps to complete this web-based Activity may differ from the ones shown. You can often look at the screens and the information presented to determine how to complete the Activity.
>
> If you do not already have a Google account, you will need to create one before you begin this Activity. Go to **http://google.com** and in the upper right corner, click **Sign In**. On the Sign In screen, click **Create Account**. On the Create your Google Account page, complete the form, read and agree to the Terms of Service and Privacy Policy, and then click **Next step**. On the Welcome screen, click **Get Started**.

Activity | Exporting an Access Table to an Excel Spreadsheet, Saving the Spreadsheet to Google Drive, Editing a Record in Google Drive, and Saving to Your Computer

In this Activity, you will export your 1A Faculty Advisors table to an Excel spreadsheet, upload your Excel file to Google Drive as a Google Sheet, edit a record in the Google Sheet, and then download a copy of the edited spreadsheet to your computer.

1 Start Access, navigate to your **Access Chapter 1** folder, and then **Open** your **1A_Advising** database file. If necessary, on the Message Bar, click Enable Content. In the **Navigation Pane**, click your **1A Faculty Advisors** table to select it—do not open it.

2 On the ribbon, click the **External Data tab**, and then in the **Export group**, click **Excel**. In the **Export – Excel Spreadsheet** dialog box, click **Browse**, and then navigate to your **Access Chapter 1** folder. In the **File Save** dialog box, click in the **File name** box, type **Lastname_Firstname_a1A_Web** and then click **Save**.

3 In the **Export – Excel Spreadsheet** dialog box, under **Specify export options**, select the first two check boxes—**Export data with formatting and layout** and **Open the destination file after the export operation is complete**—and then click **OK**. Take a moment to examine the data in the file, and then **Close** Excel. In the **Export – Excel Spreadsheet** dialog box, click **Close**, and then **Close** Access.

4 Open your browser, navigate to **http://drive.google.com**, and sign in to your Google account; if necessary,

create a new Google account and then sign in. On the right side of the screen, click **Settings** ⚙, and then click **Settings**. In the **Settings** dialog box, to the right of *Convert uploads*, if necessary, select the **Convert uploaded files to Google Docs editor format** check box. In the upper right, click **Done**

> It is necessary to select this setting; otherwise, your document will upload as a pdf file and cannot be edited without further action.

5 Open your **GO! Web Projects** folder—or create and then open this folder by clicking **New** and then **Folder**. On the left, click **New**, and then click **File upload**. In the **Open** dialog box, navigate to your **Access Chapter 1** folder, and then double-click your **a1A_Web** Excel file to upload it to Google Drive. When the message *1 upload complete* displays, **Close** the message box.

6 Double-click your **Lastname_Firstname_a1A_Web** file to display the file, and then compare your screen with Figure A. The worksheet displays column letters, row numbers, and data.

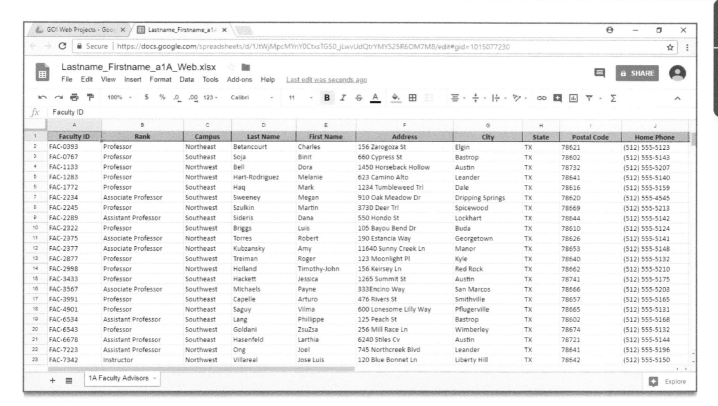

Figure A

7 Click in cell **C2** and replace the current Campus with **Southwest** Click in cell **D2** and replace Betancourt with your last name. Press Tab and then replace Charles with your first name.

8 Above row **1** and to the left of column **A**, click **Select All** ☐. On the menu bar, click **Format**, and then click **Clear formatting** so that the default font is applied to all data; the cell borders are removed, and the formatting of the field names are removed.

9 In the column headings row, click **I** to select the entire column. On the menu bar, click **Format**, point to **Number**, and then click **Plain text** to format every number in the columns as text. Click in cell **A1** to deselect the column.

Recall that in Access, numbers that are not used in calculations should be formatted as Short Text. Because the formatting is cleared, you can enter new records into the spreadsheet in the same format as the existing records.

10 Click **File** to display the menu, point to **Download as**, and then click **Microsoft Excel (.xlsx)**. Click **Enable Content**. Click **File**, and then click **Save As**. In the **Save As** dialog box, navigate to your **Access Chapter 1** folder, click in the **File name** box, and type **Lastname_ Firstname_a1A_Web_Download** and then click **Save**. **Close** the message box.

NOTE   **Saving the Downloaded File to the Access Chapter 1 Folder**

Depending on the browser you are using, you may need to open the file in Excel and then save the a1A_Web_Download worksheet to your Access Chapter 1 folder.

---

11 In Google Drive, at the top right corner of your screen, click your user name, and then click **Sign out**. **Close** your browser window.

12 Start Excel. In the Excel opening screen, click **Open Other Workbooks**, and then click **Browse**. Navigate to your **Access Chapter 1** folder, and then double-click your **a1A_Web** Excel file. Notice that this file is the original file—the record is not edited. If you

are required to print your documents, use one of the methods in the following Note. **Close** your Excel file; and, if prompted, save the changes to your worksheet. Then **Open** and print your **a1A_Web_Download** Excel file using one of the methods in the following Note. **Close** Excel; and, if prompted, save the changes to your worksheet. As directed by your instructor, submit your two workbooks and the two paper printouts or PDF electronic images that are the results of this project.

NOTE **Adding the File Name to the Footer and Printing or Creating an PDF Electronic Image of an Excel Spreadsheet on One Page**

Click the File tab, click Print, and then click Page Setup. In the Page Setup dialog box, on the Page tab, under Orientation, click Landscape. Under Scaling, click the Fit to option button. In the Page Setup dialog box, click the Header/Footer tab, and then click Custom Footer. With the insertion point blinking in the Left section box, click the Insert File Name button, and then click OK. In the Page Setup dialog box, click OK.

To print on paper, click Print. To create an electronic file of your printout, on the left side of your screen, click Export. Under Export, be sure Create PDF/XPS Document is selected, and then click Create PDF/XPS. Navigate to your Access Chapter 1 folder, and then click Publish to save the file with the default name and an extension of pdf.

Student Workshops Database

Project Activities

In Activities 1.18 through 1.24, you will assist Dr. Miriam Yong, Director of Student Activities, in creating a database to store information about student workshops held at Texas Lakes Community College campuses. You will use a database template that tracks event information, add workshop information to the database, and then print the results. Your completed Navigation Pane will look similar to Figure 1.37.

Project Files for MyLab IT Grader

1. In your **MyLab IT** course, locate and click **Access 1B Student Workshops**, Download Materials, and then Download All Files. Close the Grader download screens.
2. Extract the zipped folder to your Access Chapter 1 folder.
3. Take a moment to open the downloaded **Access_1B_Student_Workshops_Instructions**; note any recent updates to the book.

Project Results

GO! Project 1B
Where We're Going

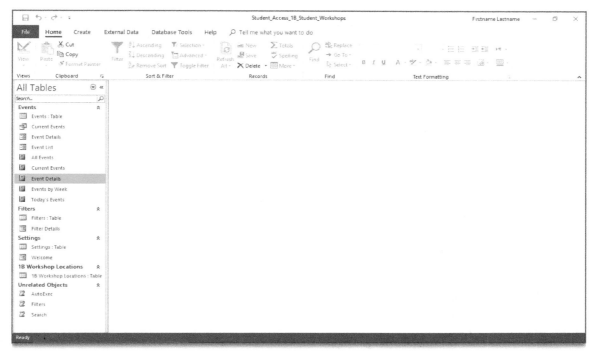

Figure 1.37
Project 1B Student Workshops

For Non-MyLab Submissions	Start with an Access Data File
For Project 1B, you will need the following files:	In your Access Chapter 1 folder, save your workbook as:
a01B_Event_Template	**Lastname_Firstname_1B_Student_Workshops**
a01B_Workshops (Excel workbook)	

After you have saved your database, open it to launch Access. On the next page, begin with Activity 1.19.

Objective 6 | Use a Template to Create a Database

GO! Learn How
Video A1-6

A database template contains prebuilt tables, queries, forms, and reports that perform a specific task, such as tracking events. For example, your college may hold events such as athletic contests, plays, lectures, concerts, and club meetings. Using a predefined template, your college's Activities Director can quickly create a database to manage these events. The advantage of using a template to start a new database is that you do not have to create the objects—all you need to do is enter the data and modify the prebuilt objects to suit your needs.

The purpose of the database in this project is to track the student workshops that are held by Texas Lakes Community College. The questions to be answered might include:

- What workshops will be offered and when will they be offered?
- In what rooms and on what campuses will the workshops be held?
- Which workshop locations have a computer projector for PowerPoint presentations?

Activity 1.18 | Using a Template to Create a Database

ALERT Because Office 365 is a cloud-based subscription service that receives continuous updates, you may encounter some variations in what appears on your screen and what is shown in this instruction. Microsoft Office 365 is fully installed on your PC or Mac; no internet access is necessary to create or edit documents. When you *are* connected to the internet, you will receive monthly upgrades and new features, so you always have the latest versions of Office apps as soon as they are available. Your subscription gives you continuous free access to the latest innovations and refinements.

These templates can be used to create databases that will be stored on your desktop. Because the templates available change so often, in this activity, you will use a previously saved template to create your database.

1 Start Access. In the Access opening screen, scroll down to display an **Inventory** template and a **Nutrition tracking** template. Compare your screen with Figure 1.38.

These templates are included with the Access program. To create a database to manage inventory on your desktop, select the *Inventory* template; to manage what you eat, select the *Nutrition tracking* template.

You can search the Microsoft Office website for more templates. You can also click on a category under the search box, where templates will be suggested.

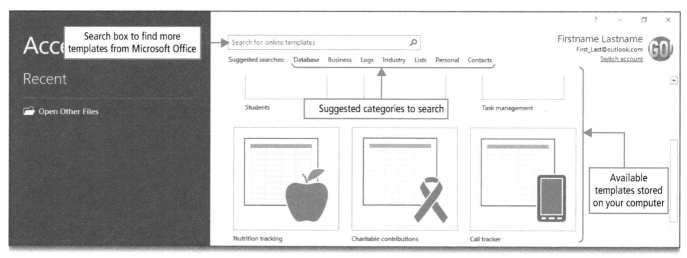

Figure 1.38

2 On the left, click **Open Other Files**, and then click **Browse**. Navigate to your **Access Chapter 1 folder**, and then double-click the Access file that you downloaded from **MyLab IT** that displays your name—**Student_Access_1B_Student_Workshops**. If necessary, at the top click **Enable Content**.

Activity 1.19 | Building a Table by Entering Records in a Multiple-Items Form and a Single-Record Form

MOS
2.3.1

One purpose of a form is to simplify the entry of data into a table—either for you or for others who enter data. In Project 1A, you created a simple form that enabled you to display or enter records in a table one record at a time. The Desktop Event management template creates a *multiple-items form* that enables you to display or enter *multiple* records in a table, but with an easier and simplified layout rather than typing directly into the table itself. The form opens when the database opens.

1 In the new record row, click in the **Title** field. Type **Your Online Reputation** and then press Tab. In the **Start Time** field, type **3/9/23 7p** and then press Tab.

Access formats the date and time. As you enter dates and times, a small calendar displays to the right of the field. You can use the calendar to select a date instead of typing it.

2 In the **End Time** field, type **3/9/23 9p** and then press Tab. In the **Description** field, type **Internet Safety** and then press Tab. In the **Location** field, type **Northeast Campus** and then press Tab three times to move to the **Title** field in the new record row. Compare your screen with Figure 1.39.

Because the workshops have no unique value, Access uses the AutoNumber data type in the ID field to assign a unique, sequential number to each record.

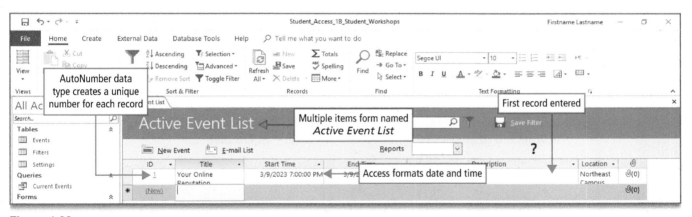

Figure 1.39

3 In the form, directly above the field names row, click **New Event**.

A *single-record form* with the name *Event Details* displays, similar to the simple form you created in Project 1A. A single-record form enables you to display or enter one record at a time into a table.

4 Using `Tab` to move from field to field, enter the following record in the **Event Details** form—press `Tab` two times to move from the **Title** field to the **Description** field, and then click the **Location** field. Then compare your screen with Figure 1.40.

Title	Description	Location	Start Time	End Time
Writing a Research Paper	Computer Skills	Southwest Campus	3/10/23 4p	3/10/23 6p

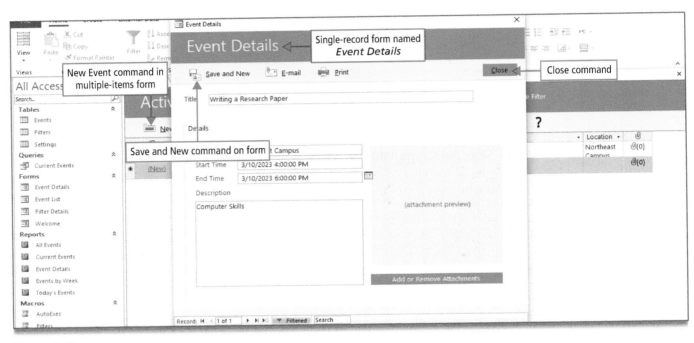

Figure 1.40

5 In the **Event Details** single-record form, in the Menu bar, click **Close**, and notice that the new record displays in the multiple-items form—*Event List*.

6 Enter the following records by using either the **Event List** form—the multiple-items form—or the **Event Details** form—the single-record form that is accessed by clicking the *New Event* command on the Event List form. Be sure the multiple-items form displays, and then compare your screen with Figure 1.41.

ID	Title	Start Time	End Time	Description	Location
3	**Resume Writing**	**3/18/23 2p**	**3/18/23 4p**	**Job Skills**	**Northwest Campus**
4	**Careers in the Legal Profession**	**3/19/23 2p**	**3/19/23 4p**	**Careers**	**Southeast Campus**

ALERT   Does a single-record form—*Event Details*—open?

In the multiple-items form, pressing [Enter] three times at the end of the row to begin a new record will display the single-record form—*Event Details*. If you prefer to use the multiple-items form—Event List—close the single-record form and continue entering records, using the [Tab] key to move from field to field.

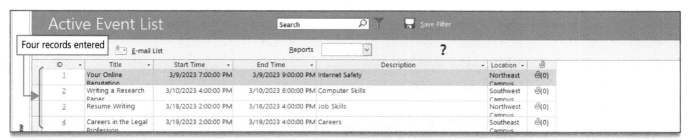

Figure 1.41

7 In the object window, click **Close** ⨉ to close the **Event List** form.

Activity 1.20 | Appending Records by Importing from an Excel Spreadsheet

MOS
2.1.1

In this Activity, you will append records to the table storing the data that displays in the Events List form. You will import the records from an Excel spreadsheet.

1 On the ribbon, click the **External Data tab**. In the **Import & Link group**, click **New Data Source**, point to **From File**, and then click **Excel**.

2 In the **Get External Data – Excel Spreadsheet** dialog box, click **Browse**. Navigate to the location where your student data files are stored, and then double-click **a01B_Workshops**.

3 Click the second option button—**Append a copy of the records to the table:**—and then click **OK**.

The table that stores the data is named *Events*. Recall that other objects, such as forms, queries, and reports, display data from tables; so the Event Details form displays data that is stored in the Events table.

4 In the **Import Spreadsheet Wizard**, click **Next**, and then click **Finish**. In the **Get External Data – Excel Spreadsheet** dialog box, click **Close**.

5 Double-click **Event List** to open the form that displays data from the Events table, and then **Close** ⟨«⟩ the **Navigation Pane**. Compare your screen with Figure 1.42.

A total of 12 records display; you entered four records, and you appended eight records from the a01B_Workshops Excel workbook. The data displays truncated in several fields because the columns are not wide enough to display all of the data.

ID	Title	Start Time	End Time	Description	Location	
1	Your Online Reputation	3/9/2023 7:00:00 PM	3/9/2023 9:00:00 PM	Internet Safety	Northeast Campus	⬤(0)
2	Writing a Research Paper	3/10/2023 4:00:00 PM	3/10/2023 6:00:00 PM	Computer Skills	Southwest Campus	⬤(0)
3	Resume Writing	3/18/2023 2:00:00 PM	3/18/2023 4:00:00 PM	Job Skills	Northwest Campus	⬤(0)
4	Careers in the Legal Profession	3/19/2023 2:00:00 PM	3/19/2023 4:00:00 PM	Careers	Southeast Campus	⬤(0)
5	Transferring to a 4-Year University	4/8/2023 11:00:00 AM	4/8/2023 12:30:00 PM	Transfer	Northeast Campus	⬤(0)
6	Financial Aid	4/14/2023 7:00:00 PM	4/14/2023 8:30:00 PM	CC Info	Southeast Campus	⬤(0)
7	Sensitivity Training	4/15/2023 8:00:00 AM	4/15/2023 9:00:00 AM	Human Behavior	Northwest Campus	⬤(0)
8	Preparing for the Job Interview	4/15/2023 12:30:00 PM	4/15/2023 2:00:00 PM	Job Skills	Northwest Campus	⬤(0)
9	Class Note Taking	4/18/2023 12:30:00 PM	4/18/2023 1:30:00 PM	Study Skills	Southeast Campus	⬤(0)
10	Managing Time and Stress	4/18/2023 6:00:00 PM	4/18/2023 7:30:00 PM	Study Skills	Southwest Campus	⬤(0)
11	Wo... Con	:00:00 AM	4/20/2023 11:00:00 AM	Computer Skills	Northeast Campus	⬤(0)
12	Pre...	:00:00 PM	4/20/2023 5:00:00 PM	Study Skills	Southeast Campus	⬤(0)

Active Event List

New Event · E-mail List · Save Filter · ?

Columns not wide enough to display all of the data

Eight records appended from Excel spreadsheet

Figure 1.42

6 To the left of the **ID** field name, click **Select All** ☐ to select all of the columns and rows.

7 In the field names row, point to the right edge of any of the selected columns to display the ⊞ pointer, and then double-click to apply Best Fit to all of the columns. Click in any field to cancel the selection, and then **Save** 🖫 the form.

Objective 7 | Organize Objects in the Navigation Pane

GO! Learn How
Video A1-7

Use the Navigation Pane to open objects, organize database objects, and perform common tasks, such as renaming an object or deleting an object.

Activity 1.21 | Grouping Database Objects in the Navigation Pane

1.1.3

The Navigation Pane groups and displays your database objects and can do so in predefined arrangements. In this Activity, you will group your database objects using the *Tables and Related Views* category, which groups objects by the table to which the objects are related. This grouping is useful because you can determine easily the table that is the data source of queries, forms, and reports.

1. **Open** » the **Navigation Pane**. At the top of the **Navigation Pane**, click **More** ⊙. On the list, under **Navigate To Category**, click **Tables and Related Views**. Compare your screen with Figure 1.43.

In the Navigation Pane, you can see the number of objects that are included in the Desktop Events Management template, including the table named *Events*. Other objects in the database that display data from the Events table include one query, two forms, and five reports. In the Navigation Pane, the Event List form is selected because it is open in the object window and is the active object.

Other objects might display on the Navigation Pane; for example, Filters and Unrelated Objects. These filters are objects created for use by the Desktop Event management template.

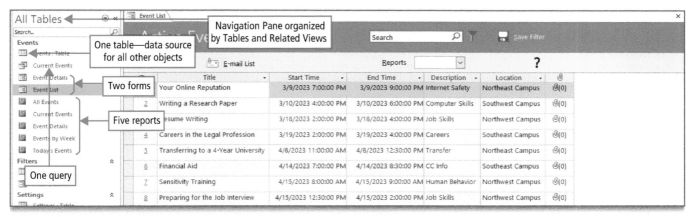

Figure 1.43

2. In the **Navigation Pane**, point to **Events: Table**, right-click, and then click **Open** to display the records in the underlying table.

The Events table is the active object in the object window. Use the Navigation Pane to open objects for use. The 12 records that display in the Event List multiple-items form are stored in this table. Recall that tables are the foundation of your database because your data must be stored in a table. You can enter records directly into a table or you can use a form to enter records.

🔄 **ANOTHER WAY**   Double-click the table name to open it in the object window.

3. In the object window, click the **Event List tab** to display the form as the active object in the object window.

Recall that a form presents a more user-friendly screen for entering records into a table.

4 In the **Navigation Pane**, double-click the **Current Events** *report* (green icon) to open the report. Compare your screen with Figure 1.44.

An advantage of using a template to create a database is that many objects, such as reports, are already designed for you.

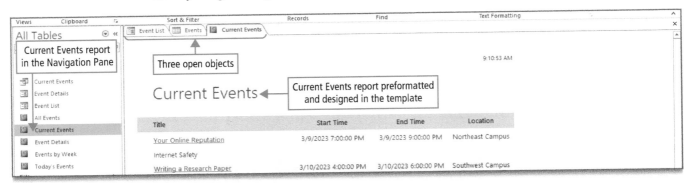

Figure 1.44

5 In the object window, **Close** ☒ the **Current Events** report.

6 By double-clicking or right-clicking, from the **Navigation Pane**, open the **Events by Week** report.

In this predesigned report, the events are displayed by week. After entering records in the form or table, the preformatted reports are updated with the records from the table.

7 In the object window, right-click any one of the **object tabs**, and then click **Close All** to close all of the objects. **Close** ☒ the **Navigation Pane**.

Objective 8   Create a New Table in a Database Created with a Template

GO! Learn How
Video A1-8

The Desktop Event management template included only one table—the *Events* table. It is easy to start a database with a template, and then you can add additional objects as needed.

Activity 1.22 | Using the Table Tool to Create a New Table

2.4.1, 2.4.5

Dr. Yong has information about the various locations where workshops are held. For example, on the Northeast Campus, she has information about the room, seating arrangements, number of seats, and multimedia equipment. In the Events table, workshops are scheduled in rooms at each of the four campuses. It would not make sense to store information about the campus rooms multiple times in the same table. It is *not* considered good database design to have duplicate information in a table.

When data becomes redundant, it is usually an indication that you need a new table to contain that information. In this Activity, you will create a table to track the workshop locations, the equipment, and the seating arrangements in each location.

1 On the ribbon, click the **Create tab**, and then in the **Tables group**, click **Table**.

2 In the field names row, click **Click to Add**, click **Short Text**, type **Campus/Location** and then press Enter.

3 In the third column, click **Short Text**, type **Room** and then press Enter. In the fourth column, click **Number**, type **Seats** and then press Enter.

The *Number data type* describes numbers that represent a quantity and may be used in calculations. For the Seats field, you may need to determine how many seats remain after reservations are booked for a room. In the new record row, a *0* displays in the field.

4 In the fifth column, type **t** to select *Short Text*, type **Room Arrangement** and then press Enter. In the sixth column, type **t** and then type **Equipment** On your keyboard, press ↓.

> With the data type list displayed, you can select the data type by either clicking it or typing the letter that is underscored for the data type.

> This table has six fields. Access automatically creates the first field in the table—the ID field—to ensure that every record has a unique value. Before naming each field, you must define the data type for the field.

5 Right-click the **ID** field name, and then click **Rename Field**. Type **Room ID** and then press Enter. On the **Fields tab**, in the **Formatting group**, click the **Data Type arrow**, and then click **Short Text**. On the ribbon, in the **Field Validation group**, notice that **Unique** is selected.

> Recall that, by default, Access creates the ID field with the AutoNumber data type so that the field can be used as the primary key. Here, this field will store a unique room ID that is a combination of letters, symbols, and numbers; therefore, it is appropriate to change the data type to Short Text. In Datasheet view, the primary key field is identified by the selection of the Unique check box.

MORE KNOWLEDGE | **Create a Table from a Template with Application Parts**

To create a table using the Application parts gallery, click the Create tab, and in the Templates group, click Application Parts. Under Quick Start, click Comments. In the Create Relationships dialog box, specify a relationship between the Comments table and an associated table, click Next to choose the lookup column, and then click Create to create the table. If you choose No relationship, click Create to create the table. The Comments table displays in the Navigation Pane.

Activity 1.23 | Entering Records Into a New Table

1 In the new record row, click in the **Room ID** field. Enter the following record, pressing Enter or Tab to move from one field to the next. Do not be concerned that all of your text does not display; you will adjust the column widths later. After entering the record, compare your screen with Figure 1.45.

> Recall that Access saves a record when you move to another row within the table. You can press either Enter or Tab to move between fields in a table.

Room ID	Campus/ Location	Room	Seats	Room Arrangement	Equipment
NE-01	**Northeast Campus**	**H265**	**150**	**Theater**	**Computer Projector, Surround Sound, Microphone**

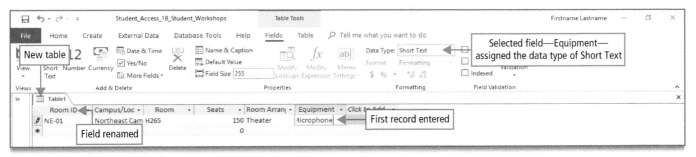

Figure 1.45

2 In the **Views group**, click the top of the **View** button to switch to **Design** view. In the **Save As** dialog box, in the **Table Name** box, using your own name, type **1B Workshop Locations** and then click **OK**.

> Recall that when you switch views or when you close a table, Access prompts you to save the table if you have not previously saved it.

ANOTHER WAY   On the right side of the status bar, click Design View 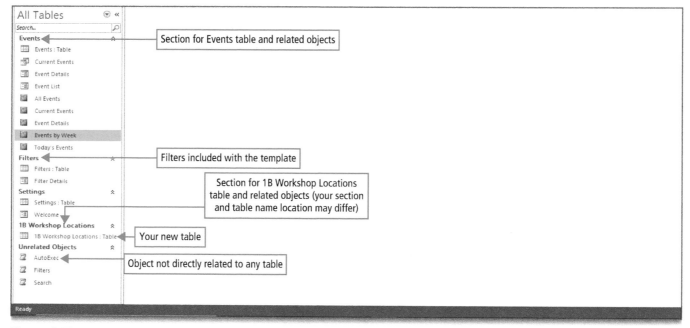 to switch to Design view.

3 In the **Field Name** column, to the left of **Room ID**, notice the key icon.

In Design view, the key icon indicates that the field—Room ID—is the primary key field.

4 In the **Views group**, click the top of the **View** button to switch back to **Datasheet** view.

ANOTHER WAY   On the right side of the status bar, click Datasheet View to switch to Datasheet view.

5 In the new record row, click in the **Room ID** field. Enter the following records, pressing Enter or Tab to move from one field to the next.

Room ID	Campus/Location	Room	Seats	Room Arrangement	Equipment
SW-01	Southwest Campus	A15	35	Lecture Classroom	Computer Projector
NW-01	Northwest Campus	C202	50	Lecture Classroom	Smart Board
SE-01	Southeast Campus	D148	20	U-shaped	White Board
NE-02	Northeast Campus	B105	25	U-shaped	25 Computers, Projector

6 To the left of the **Room ID** field name, click **Select All** to select all of the columns and rows in the table. On the **Home tab**, in the **Records group,** click **More**, and then click **Field Width**. In the **Column Width** dialog box, click **Best Fit** to display all of the data in each column. Click in any field to cancel the selection, and then **Save** the changes to the table. In the object window, **Close** your **1B Workshop Locations** table.

7 **Open** the **Navigation Pane** and notice that your new table displays in its own group. Point to the right edge of the **Navigation Pane** to display the pointer. Drag to the right to increase the width of the **Navigation Pane** so that your entire table name displays. Compare your screen with Figure 1.46.

Recall that organizing the Navigation Pane by Tables and Related Views groups the objects by each table and displays the related objects under each table name.

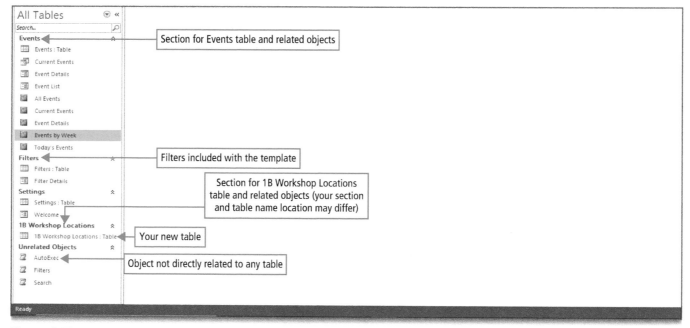

Figure 1.46

Objective 9 | View a Report

GO! Learn How
Video A1-9

Recall that one advantage to starting a new database with a template, instead of from a blank database, is that many report objects are already created for you.

Activity 1.24 | Viewing a Report

 MOS
5.1.3

1 In the **Navigation Pane**, double-click the report (not the form) name **Event Details** to open it in the object window.

> This prebuilt Event Details report displays in an attractively arranged format.

2 **Close** ⊠ the **Event Details** report. Open the **All Events** report, and then **Close** « the **Navigation Pane**. On the **Home** tab, in the **Views group**, click the top of the **View** button to switch to **Layout** view.

> Recall that Layout view enables you to make changes to an object while viewing the data in the fields. Each prebuilt report displays the records in the table in different useful formats.

 ANOTHER WAY On the right side of the status bar, click Layout View ▤ to switch to Layout view.

3 At the top of the report, click the title—*All Events*—to display a colored border around the title. Click to the left of the letter *A* to place the insertion point there. Type **1B** and then press Spacebar. Press Enter, and then **Save** 🖫 the report.

4 **Close** ⊠ your **1B All Events** report. For the convenience of the next individual opening the database, **Open** » the **Navigation Pane**.

> Notice the report name *All Events* did not change in the Navigation Pane. You changed the title of the report as it would print.

5 On the right side of the title bar, click **Close** ⊠ to close the database and to close Access.

For Non-MyLab Submissions: Determine What Your Instructor Requires for Submission
As directed by your instructor, submit your completed database file.

6 In **MyLab IT**, locate and click the Grader Project **Access 1B Student Workshops**. In **step 3**, under **Upload Completed Assignment**, click **Choose File**. In the **Open** dialog box, navigate to your **Access Chapter 1 folder**, and then click your **Student_Access_1B_Student_Workshops** file one time to select it. In the lower right corner of the **Open** dialog box, click **Open**.

> The name of your selected file displays above the Upload button.

7 To submit your file to **MyLab IT** for grading, click **Upload**, wait a moment for a green **Success!** message, and then in **step 4**, click the blue **Submit for Grading** button. Click **Close Assignment** to return to your list of **Course Materials**.

You have completed Project 1B | END

»»» GO! With Google

Access web apps are designed to work with Microsoft's SharePoint, a service for setting up websites to share and manage documents. Your college may not have SharePoint installed, so you will use other tools to share objects from your database so that you can work collaboratively with others. Recall that Google Drive is Google's free, web-based word processor, spreadsheet, slide show, form, and data storage and sharing service. For Access, you can export a database object to an Excel worksheet, a PDF file, or a text file, and then save the file to Google Drive.

> **ALERT**   **Working with Web-Based Applications and Services**
>
> Computer programs and services on the web receive continuous updates and improvements. Therefore, the steps to complete this web-based Activity may differ from the ones shown. You can often look at the screens and the information presented to determine how to complete the Activity.

Activity | Exporting an Access Table to a Word Document, Saving the Document to Google Drive, Adding a Record in Google Drive, and Saving to Your Computer

In this activity, you will export your 1B Workshop Locations table to a Word document, upload your Word file to Google Drive as a Google Doc, add a record in Google Drive, and then download a copy of the edited document to your computer.

1 Start Access, navigate to your **Access Chapter 1** folder, and then **Open** your **1B_Student_Workshops** database file. If necessary, on the Message Bar, click Enable Content, and then **Close** the **Event List** form. In the **Navigation Pane**, click your **1B Workshop Locations** table to select it—do not open it.

2 On the ribbon, click the **External Data tab**. In the **Export group**, click **More**, and then click **Word**. In the **Export – RTF File** dialog box, click **Browse**, and then navigate to your **Access Chapter 1** folder. In the **File Save** dialog box, click in the **File name** box, using your own name, type **Lastname_Firstname_a1B_Web** and then click **Save**.

3 In the **Export – RTF File** dialog box, under **Specify export options**, select the second check box—**Open the destination file after the export operation is complete**—and then click **OK**. Take a moment to examine the data in the file.

> Notice that the table is too wide to display fully with Portrait orientation.

4 **Close** Word. In the **Export – RTF File** dialog box, click **Close**, and then **Close** Access.

5 Open your browser, navigate to **http://drive.google .com**, and sign in to your Google account; if necessary, create a new Google account and then sign in. On the right side of the screen, click **Settings** ⚙, and then click **Settings**. In the **Settings** dialog box, to the right of *Convert uploads*, if necessary, select the **Convert uploaded files to Google Docs editor format** check box. In the upper right, click **Done**

> It is necessary to select this setting; otherwise, your document will upload as a pdf file and cannot be edited without further action.

6 Open your **GO! Web Projects** folder—or create and then open this folder by clicking **New** and then clicking **New folder**. On the left, click **New**, and then click **File upload**. In the **Choose File to Upload** dialog box, navigate to your **Access Chapter 1** folder, and then double-click your **a1B_Web** Word file to upload it to Google Drive. When the title bar of the message box indicates *1 upload complete*, **Close** the message box.

7 Double-click your **a1B_Web** file to open the file in Google Docs. Notice that the table is not fully displayed on the page, and compare your screen with Figure A.

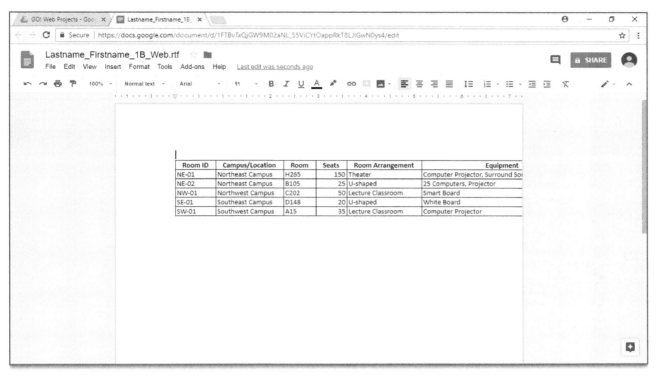

Room ID	Campus/Location	Room	Seats	Room Arrangement	Equipment
NE-01	Northeast Campus	H265	150	Theater	Computer Projector, Surround Sou
NE-02	Northeast Campus	B105	25	U-shaped	25 Computers, Projector
NW-01	Northwest Campus	C202	50	Lecture Classroom	Smart Board
SE-01	Southeast Campus	D148	20	U-shaped	White Board
SW-01	Southwest Campus	A15	35	Lecture Classroom	Computer Projector

Figure A

8 Click **File** to display a menu, and then click **Page setup**. In the **Page setup** dialog box, under **Orientation**, click **Landscape**. Click **OK**.

The table displays fully with Landscape orientation.

Field	Room ID	Campus/Location	Room	Seats	Room Arrangement	Equipment
	SE-02	**Southeast Campus**	**D120**	**20**	**Testing Lab**	**20 Computers**

9 Click in the last cell in the table, and press ⊞Tab. Add the following record.

10 On the menu, click **File**, point to **Download as**, and then click **Microsoft Word (.docx)**. In the message box—usually displays at the bottom of your screen—click the **Save arrow**, and then click **Save as**. In the **Save As** dialog box, navigate to your **Access Chapter 1** folder, click in the **File name** box, and type **Lastname_Firstname_a1B_Web_Download** and then click **Save**. If necessary, click OK to upgrade to the newest file format.

11 In Google Drive, at the top right corner of your screen, click your user name, and then click **Sign out**. **Close** your browser window.

12 Start Word. In the Word opening screen, click **Open**. Under **Open**, click **Browse**. Navigate to your **Access Chapter 1** folder, and then double-click your **a1B_Web** Word file. Notice that this file is the original file—the new record is not entered. If you are required to print your documents, use one of the methods in following Note. **Close** your Word file; and, if prompted, save the changes to your document. Then **Open** and print your **a1B_Web_Download** Word file using one of the methods in the following Note. **Close** Word; and, if prompted, save the changes to your document. As directed by your instructor, submit your two documents and the two paper printouts or PDF electronic images that are the results of this project.

NOTE   Adding the File Name to the Footer and Printing or Creating a PDF Electronic Image

Click the Insert tab. In the Header & Footer group, click Footer, and then click Blank. With Type here selected, in the Insert group, click Document Info, and then click File Name. Close the Footer window. Click the Layout tab. In the Page Setup group, click Orientation, and then click Landscape.

To print on paper, click File, and then click Print. To create a pdf electronic image of your printout, click File, and then click Export. Under Export, be sure Create PDF/XPS Document is selected, and then click Create PDF/XPS. Navigate to your Access Chapter 1 folder, and then click Publish to save the file with the default name and an extension of pdf.

»»» GO! To Work

Microsoft Office Specialist (MOS) Skills in This Chapter

Project 1A	Project 1B
1.1.1 Import objects or data from other sources	**1.1.3** Hide and display objects in the Navigation Par
1.1.2 Delete database objects	**2.1.1** Import data into tables
1.3.1 Configure print options for records, forms, and reports	**5.1.3** Add and modify labels on reports
2.1.1 Import data into tables	
2.2.3 Add table descriptions	
2.4.1 Add or remove fields	
2.4.3 Change field captions	
2.4.4 Change field sizes	
2.4.5 Change field data types	
2.4.6 Configure fields to auto-increment	
3.1.7 Run queries	
4.1.1 Add, move and remove form controls	
5.1.2 Add report controls	
5.1.3 Add and modify labels on reports	
5.2.3 Format report elements	

Build Your E-Portfolio

An E-Portfolio is a collection of evidence, stored electronically, that showcases what you have accomplished while completing your education. Collecting and then sharing your work products with potential employers reflects your academic and career goals. Your completed documents from the following projects are good examples to show what you have learned: 1G, 1K, and 1L.

 ## GO! For Job Success

Video: Customer Service

Your instructor may assign this video to your class, and then ask you to think about, or discuss with your classmates, these questions:

g-stockstudio/Shutterstock

How did Lee's responses demonstrate both good and bad customer service skills?

How well did Christine, the supervisor, handle Karen's situation? Provide specific examples.

Based on this call, what can SunTel Systems do to provide a better customer service experience? Provide two examples.

End of Chapter

Summary

Principles of good database design, also known as normalization, help ensure that the data in your database is accurate and organized in a way that you can retrieve information that is useful.

You can create databases from scratch by using the blank desktop database template or a custom web app or by using a template that contains prebuilt tables, queries, forms, reports, and other objects.

Tables are the foundation of a database, but before entering records in a table, you must define the data type and name the field. Common data types are Short Text, Number, Currency, and Date/Time.

Use forms to enter data into a table or view the data in a table. Use queries to retrieve information from tables. Reports display information from tables in a professional-looking format.

GO! Learn It Online

Review the concepts, key terms, and MOS skills in this chapter by completing these online challenges, which you can find at **MyLab IT**.

Chapter Quiz: Answer matching and multiple-choice questions to test what you learned in this chapter.

Lessons on the GO!: Learn how to use all the new apps and features as they are introduced by Microsoft.

MOS Prep Quiz: Answer questions to review the MOS skills that you practiced in this chapter.

GO! Collaborative Team Project (Available in Instructor Resource Center)

If your instructor assigns this project to your class, you can expect to work with one or more of your classmates—either in person or by using Internet tools—to create work products similar to those that you created in this chapter. A team is a group of workers who work together to solve a problem, make a decision, or create a work product. Collaboration is when you work together with others as a team in an intellectual endeavor to complete a shared task or achieve a shared goal.

Monkey Business Images/ Fotolia

Project Guide for Access Chapter 1

Your instructor will assign Projects from this list to ensure your learning and assess your knowledge.

	Review and Assessment Guide for Access Chapter 1		
Project	**Apply Skills from These Chapter Objectives**	**Project Type**	**Project Location**
1A MyLab IT	Objectives 1–5 from Project 1A	**1A Instructional Project (Grader Project)**　　　　**Instruction** A guided review of the skills from Project 1A.	In **MyLab IT** and in text
1B MyLab IT	Objectives 6–9 from Project 1B	**1B Instructional Project (Grader Project)**　　　　**Instruction** A guided review of the skills from Project 1B.	In **MyLab IT** and in text
1C	Objectives 1–5 from Project 1A	**1C Chapter Review (Scorecard Grading)**　　　　**Review** A guided review of the skills from Project 1A.	In text
1D	Objectives 6–9 from Project 1B	**1D Chapter Review (Scorecard Grading)**　　　　**Review** A guided review of the skills from Project 1B.	In text
1E MyLab IT	Objectives 1–5 from Project 1A	**1E Mastery (Grader Project)**　　　**Mastery and Transfer of Learning** A demonstration of your mastery of the skills in Project 1A with extensive decision-making.	In **MyLab IT** and in text
1F MyLab IT	Objectives 6–9 from Project 1B	**1F Mastery (Grader Project)**　　　**Mastery and Transfer of Learning** A demonstration of your mastery of the skills in Project 1B with extensive decision-making.	In **MyLab IT** and in text
1G MyLab IT	Combination of Objectives from Projects 1A and 1B	**1G Mastery (Grader Project)**　　　**Mastery and Transfer of Learning** A demonstration of your mastery of the skills in Projects 1A and 1B with extensive decision-making.	In **MyLab IT** and in text
1H	Combination of Objectives from Projects 1A and 1B	**1H GO! Fix It (Scorecard Grading)**　　　**Critical Thinking** A demonstration of your mastery of the skills in Projects 1A and 1B by creating a correct result from a document that contains errors you must find.	IRC
1I	Combination of Objectives from Projects 1A and 1B	**1I GO! Make It (Scorecard Grading)**　　　**Critical Thinking** A demonstration of your mastery of the skills in Projects 1A and 1B by creating a result from a supplied picture.	IRC
1J	Combination of Objectives from Projects 1A and 1B	**1J GO! Solve It (Rubric Grading)**　　　**Critical Thinking** A demonstration of your mastery of the skills in Projects 1A and 1B, your decision-making skills, and your critical thinking skills. A task-specific rubric helps you self-assess your result.	IRC
1K	Combination of Objectives from Projects 1A and 1B	**1K GO! Solve It (Rubric Grading)**　　　**Critical Thinking** A demonstration of your mastery of the skills in Projects 1A and 1B, your decision-making skills, and your critical thinking skills. A task-specific rubric helps you self-assess your result.	In text
1L	Combination of Objectives from Projects 1A and 1B	**1L GO! Think (Rubric Grading)**　　　**Critical Thinking** A demonstration of your understanding of the Chapter concepts applied in a manner that you would outside of college. An analytic rubric helps you and your instructor grade the quality of your work by comparing it to the work an expert in the discipline would create.	In text
1M	Combination of Objectives from Projects 1A and 1B	**1M GO! Think (Rubric Grading)**　　　**Critical Thinking** A demonstration of your understanding of the Chapter concepts applied in a manner that you would outside of college. An analytic rubric helps you and your instructor grade the quality of your work by comparing it to the work an expert in the discipline would create.	IRC
1N	Combination of Objectives from Projects 1A and 1B	**1N You and GO! (Rubric Grading)**　　　**Critical Thinking** A demonstration of your understanding of the Chapter concepts applied in a manner that you would in a personal situation. An analytic rubric helps you and your instructor grade the quality of your work.	IRC
1O	Combination of Objectives from Projects 1A and 1B	**1O Cumulative Team Project for Access Chapter 1** A demonstration of your understanding of concepts and your ability to work collaboratively in a group role-playing assessment, requiring both collaboration and self-management.	IRC

Glossary

Glossary of Chapter Key Terms

Append To add on to the end of an object; for example, to add records to the end of an existing table.

AutoNumber data type A data type that describes a unique sequential or random number assigned by Access as each record is entered and that is useful for data that has no distinct field that can be considered unique.

Best Fit An Access command that adjusts the width of a column to accommodate the column's longest entry.

Blank desktop database A database that has no data and has no database tools—you must create the data and tools as you need them; the database is stored on your computer or other storage device.

Caption A property setting that displays a name for a field in a table, query, form, or report different from the one listed as the field name.

Common field A field included in two or more tables that stores the same data.

Currency data type An Access data type that describes monetary values and numeric data that can be used in mathematical calculations involving values with one to four decimal places.

Custom web app A database that you can publish and share with others over the Internet.

Data Facts about people, events, things, or ideas.

Data source The table or tables from which a query, form, or reports gathers its data.

Data type Classification identifying the kind of data that can be stored in a field, such as numbers, text, or dates.

Database An organized collection of facts about people, events, things, or ideas related to a specific topic or purpose.

Database management system (DBMS) Database software that controls how related collections of data are stored, organized, retrieved, and secured; also known as a DBMS.

Database template A preformatted database that contains prebuilt tables, queries, forms, and reports that perform a specific task, such as tracking events.

Datasheet view The Access view that displays data organized in columns and rows similar to an Excel worksheet.

DBMS An acronym for database management system.

Design view An Access view that displays the detailed structure of a table, query, form, or report. For forms and reports, may be the view in which some tasks must be performed, and only the controls, and not the data, display in this view.

Destination table The table to which you import or append data.

Export The process of copying data from one file into another file, such as an Access table into an Excel spreadsheet.

Field A single piece of information that is stored in every record; represented by a column in a database table.

Field properties Characteristics of a field that control how the field displays and how data can be entered in the field; vary for different data types.

First principle of good database design A principle of good database design stating that data is organized in tables so that there is no redundant data.

Flat database A simple database file that is not related or linked to any other collection of data.

Form An Access object you can use to enter new records into a table, edit or delete existing records in a table, or display existing records.

Form view The Access view in which you can view records, but you cannot change the layout or design of the form.

Import The process of copying data from another file, such as a Word table or an Excel workbook, into a separate file, such as an Access database.

Information Data that is accurate, timely, and organized in a useful manner.

Layout view The Access view in which you can make changes to a form or report while the data from the underlying data source displays.

Link A connection to data in another file.

Multiple-items form A form that enables you to display or enter multiple records in a table.

Navigation area An area at the bottom of the Access window that indicates the number of records in the table and contains controls in the form of arrows that you click to move among the records.

Navigation Pane An area of the Access window that displays and organizes the names of the objects in a database; from here, you open objects for use.

Normalization The process of applying design rules and principles to ensure that your database performs as expected.

Number data type An Access data type that represents a quantity, how much or how many, and may be used in calculations.

Object tab In the object window, a tab that identifies the object and which enables you to make an open object active.

Object window An area of the Access window that displays open objects, such as tables, queries, forms, or reports; by default, each object displays on its own tab.

Objects The basic parts of a database that you create to store your data and to work with your data; for example, tables, queries, forms, and reports.

Populate The action of filling a database table with records.

Primary key A required field that uniquely identifies a record in a table; for example, a Student ID number at a college.

Property Sheet A list of characteristics—properties—for fields or controls on a form or report in which you can make precise changes to each property associated with the field or control.

Query A database object that retrieves specific data from one or more database objects—either tables or other queries—and then, in a single datasheet, displays only the data you specify.

Record All of the categories of data pertaining to one person, place, event, thing, or idea; represented by a row in a database table.

Record selector bar The bar at the left edge of a record when it is displayed in a form, and which is used to select an entire record.

Record selector box The small box at the left of a record in Datasheet view that, when clicked, selects the entire record.

Redundant In a database, information that is duplicated in a manner that indicates poor database design.

Relational database A sophisticated type of database that has multiple collections of data within the file that are related to one another.

Report A database object that summarizes the fields and records from a table or query in an easy-to-read format suitable for printing.

Glossary

Run The process in which Access searches the records in the table(s) included in the query design, finds the records that match the specified criteria, and then displays the records in a datasheet; only the fields that have been included in the query design display.

Second principle of good database design A principle stating that appropriate database techniques are used to ensure the accuracy and consistency of data as it is entered into the table.

Select query A type of Access query that retrieves (selects) data from one or more tables or queries, displaying the selected data in a datasheet; also known as a simple select query.

SharePoint A Microsoft application used for setting up web sites to share and manage documents.

Short Text data type An Access data type that describes text, a combination of text and numbers, or numbers that are not used in calculations, such as the Postal Code.

Simple select query Another name for a select query.

Single-record form A form that enables you to display or enter one record at a time from a table.

Source file When importing a file, refers to the file being imported.

Structure In Access, the underlying design of a table, including field names, data types, descriptions, and field properties.

Table A format for information that organizes and presents text and data in columns and rows; the foundation of a database.

Tables and Related Views An arrangement in the Navigation Pane that groups objects by the table to which they are related.

Truncated Data that is cut off or shortened because the field or column is not wide enough to display all of the data or the field size is too small to contain all of the data.

Wizard A feature in Microsoft Office that walks you step by step through a process.

Chapter Review

Skills Review Project 1C College Administrators

Apply 1A skills from these Objectives:

1. Identify Good Database Design
2. Create a Table and Define Fields in a Blank Desktop Database
3. Change the Structure of Tables and Add a Second Table
4. Create a Query, Form, and Report
5. Close a Database and Close Access

In the following Skills Review, you will create a database to store information about the administrators of Texas Lakes Community College and their departments. Your completed Navigation Pane will look similar to Figure 1.47.

Project Files

For Project 1C, you will need the following files:

Blank database
a01C_Administrators (Excel workbook)
a01C_Departments (Excel workbook)

You will save your database as:

Lastname_Firstname_1C_College_Administrators

Project Results

Figure 1.47

(continues on next page)

Chapter Review

1 Start Access. In the Access opening screen, click **Blank database**. In the **Blank database** dialog box, to the right of the **File Name** box, click **Browse**. In the **File New Database** dialog box, navigate to your **Access Chapter 1** folder. In the **File New Database** dialog box, click in the **File name** box, type **Lastname_Firstname_1C_College_Administrators** and then press Enter. In the **Blank database** dialog box, click **Create**.

a. **Close** the **Navigation Pane**. In the field names row, click in the text *Click to Add*, and then click **Short Text**. Type **Title** and then press Enter.

b. In the third field name box, click **Short Text**, type **Last Name** and then press Enter. In the fourth field name box, click **Short Text**, type **First Name** and then press Enter. Create the remaining fields shown in Table 1, pressing Enter after the last field name. All of the data is typed on one line.

Table 1

Data Type		Short Text	Short Text	Short Text	Short Text	Short Text	Short Text	Short Text	Short Text	Short Text	Short Text	Currency
Field Name	ID	Title	Last Name	First Name	**Middle Initial**	**Address**	City	State	Postal Code	Phone Number	Department ID	Salary

c. If necessary, scroll to bring the first column into view, and then click the **ID** field name. On the **Fields tab**, in the **Properties group**, click **Name & Caption**. In the **Name** box, change *ID* to **Employee ID** and then click **OK**. On the ribbon, in the **Formatting group**, click the **Data Type arrow**, and then click **Short Text**.

d. In the new record row, click in the **Employee ID** field, type, **ADM-9200** and press Enter. In the **Title** field, type **Vice President** and press Enter. Continue entering data in the fields shown in Table 2, pressing Enter or Tab to move to the next field and to the next row.

Table 2

Last Name	First Name	Middle Initial	Address	City	State	Postal Code	Phone Number	Department ID	Salary
Shaffer	**Lonnie**	**J**	**489 Ben Ave**	**Austin**	**TX**	**78734**	**(512) 555-6185**	**AS**	**123500**

e. On the Quick Access Toolbar, click **Save**. In the **Save As** dialog box, in the **Table Name** box, using your own name, replace the selected text by typing **Lastname Firstname 1C Administrators** and then click **OK**.

f. In the new record row, enter the data for two college administrators shown in Table 3, pressing Enter or Tab to move from field to field and to the next row.

Table 3

Employee ID	Title	Last Name	First Name	Middle Initial	Address	City	State	Postal Code	Phone Number	Department ID	Salary
ADM-9201	Associate Vice President	Holtz	Diann	S	8416 Spencer Ln	George town	TX	78627	(512) 555-1069	AS	101524
ADM-9202	Director, Enrollment Services	Fitchette	Sean	H	3245 Deer Trl	Spice wood	TX	78669	(512) 555-9012	SS	45070

g. **Close** your **1C Administrators** table. On the **External Data tab**, in the **Import & Link group**, click **New Data Source**, point to **From File**, and then click **Excel**. In the **Get External Data – Excel Spreadsheet** dialog box, click **Browse**. In the **File Open** dialog box, navigate to your student data files, and then double-click the **a01C_Administrators** Excel file.

h. Click the **Append a copy of the records to the table** option button, and then click **OK**. In the **Import Spreadsheet Wizard**, click **Next**, and then click **Finish**. In the **Get External Data – Excel Spreadsheet** dialog box, click **Close**.

(continues on next page)

Chapter Review

Skills Review: Project 1C College Administrators (continued)

i. **Open** the **Navigation Pane**. Resize the Navigation Pane so that the entire table name displays. In the **Navigation Pane**, double-click your **1C Administrators** table to open it, and then **Close** the **Navigation Pane**—there are 30 records in this table.

2 Click the **Home tab**, and then in the **Views group**, click the top of the **View** button to switch to **Design** view. In the **Field Name** column, to the left of **Middle Initial**, click the row selector box to select the entire row. On the **Design tab**, in the **Tools group**, click **Delete Rows**. In the message box, click **Yes**.

a. Click in the **Employee ID** field name box. Under **Field Properties**, click **Field Size** to select the existing text. Type **8** and then in the **Employee ID** field row, click in the **Description** box. Type **Eight-character Employee ID** and then press Enter.

b. Click in the **State** field name box. In the **Field Properties** area, click **Field Size**, and then type **2** In the **State Description** box, type **Two-character state abbreviation** and then press Enter.

c. **Save** the design changes to your table, and in the message box, click **Yes**. On the **Design tab**, in the **Views group**, click the top of the **View** button to switch to **Datasheet** view.

d. On the ribbon, click the **External Data tab**, and then in the **Import & Link group**, click **New Data Source**, point to **From File**, and then click **Excel**. In the **Get External Data – Excel Spreadsheet** dialog box, to the right of the **File name** box, click **Browse**. In the **File Open** dialog box, navigate to your student data files, and then double-click **a01C_Departments**. Be sure that the **Import the source data into a new table in the current database** option button is selected, and then click **OK**.

e. In the upper left corner of the wizard, select the **First Row Contains Column Headings** check box, and then click **Next**. Click **Next** again. Click the **Choose my own primary key** option button, be sure that **Department ID** displays, and then click **Next**. In the **Import to Table** box, type **1C Departments** and then click **Finish**. In the **Get External Data – Excel Spreadsheet** dialog box, click **Close**.

f. **Open** the **Navigation Pane**, double-click your **1C Departments** table, and then **Close** the **Navigation Pane**. There are 12 records in your **1C Departments** table.

g. To the left of the **Department** field name, click **Select All**. On the ribbon, click the **Home tab**, and in the **Records group**, click **More**, and then click **Field Width**. In the **Column Width** dialog box, click **Best Fit**. Click in any field to cancel the selection, and then **Save** your table. In the object window, click the **object tab** for your **1C Administrators** table. Using the techniques you just practiced, apply **Best Fit** to the columns, cancel the selection, and then **Save** the table.

h. With your **1C Administrators** table displayed, on the ribbon, click the **File tab**, click **Print**, and then click **Print Preview**. On the **Print Preview tab**, in the **Page Layout group**, click **Landscape**. Click **Close Print Preview**, and then **Close** your **1C Administrators** table.

i. With your **1C Departments** table displayed, view the table in **Print Preview**. Change the orientation to **Landscape**, and then create a paper printout or PDF electronic image as directed by your instructor—one page results. Click **Close Print Preview**, and then **Close** your **1C Departments** table.

3 On the ribbon, click the **Create tab**, and then in the **Queries group**, click **Query Wizard**. In the **New Query** dialog box, be sure **Simple Query Wizard** is selected, and then click **OK**. In the wizard, click the **Tables/Queries arrow**, and then click your **Table: 1C Administrators**.

a. Under **Available Fields**, click **Last Name**, and then click **Add Field** to move the field to the **Selected Fields** list on the right. Double-click the **First Name** field to move it to the **Selected Fields** list. By using **Add Field** or by double-clicking the field name, add the following fields to the **Selected Fields** list in the order specified: **Title**, **Department ID**, and **Phone Number**. This query will answer the question, *What is the last name, first name, title, Department ID, and phone number of every administrator?*

b. In the wizard, click **Next**. Click in the **What title do you want for your query?** box. Using your own name, edit as necessary so that the query name is **1C All Administrators Query** and then click **Finish**. If necessary, apply Best Fit to the columns, and then Save the query. Display the query in **Print**. Click **Close Print Preview**, and then **Close** the query.

(continues on next page)

Chapter Review

c. **Open** the **Navigation Pane**, right-click your **1C Administrators** table, and then click **Open** to display the table in the object window. **Close** the **Navigation Pane**. Notice that the table has 11 fields. On the ribbon, click the **Create tab**, and in the **Forms group**, click **Form**. On the Quick Access Toolbar, click **Save**. In the **Save As** dialog box, click in the **Form Name** box, edit to name the form **Lastname Firstname 1C Administrator Form** and then click **OK**.

d. In the navigation area, click **Last record**, and then click **Previous record** two times to display the record for *Diann Holtz*. By using the instructions in Activity 1.15, print or create an PDF electronic image of only this record on one page. **Close** the form object, saving it if prompted. Your **1C Administrators** table object remains open.

e. **Open** the **Navigation Pane**, open your **1C Departments** table by double-clicking the table name or by right-clicking the table name and clicking Open. **Close** the **Navigation Pane**. On the **Create tab**, in the **Reports group**, click **Report**.

f. Click the **Department ID** field name, and then on the ribbon, under **Report Layout Tools**, click the **Arrange tab**. In the **Rows & Columns group**, click **Select Column**, and then press Del. Using the same technique, delete the **Department Email** field.

g. Click the **Department Phone** field name. Hold down Shift, and then click the **Suite Number** field name to select the last three field names. In the **Rows & Columns group**, click **Select Column**. On the ribbon, click the **Design tab**, and then in the **Tools group**, click **Property Sheet**. In the **Property Sheet**, on the **Format tab**, click **Width**, type **1.5** and then press Enter. **Close** the **Property Sheet**.

h. Click the **Department Name** field name. On the ribbon, click the **Home tab.** In the **Sort & Filter group**, click **Ascending** to sort the report in alphabetic order by *Department Name*. At the bottom of the report, on the right side, click **Page 1 of 1**, and then press Del.

i. **Save** the report as **Lastname Firstname 1C Departments Report** and then click **OK**. Display the report in **Print**. Click **Close Print Preview**. In the object window, right-click any **object tab**, and then click **Close All** to close all open objects, leaving the object window empty.

4 **Open** the **Navigation Pane**. If necessary, increase the width of the Navigation Pane so that all object names display fully. On the right side of the title bar, click **Close** to close the database and to close Access. As directed by your instructor, submit your database for grading.

You have completed Project 1C **END**

Chapter Review

Skills Review	Project 1D Certification Events

Apply 1B skills from these Objectives:

6. Use a Template to Create a Database
7. Organize Objects in the Navigation Pane
8. Create a New Table in a Database Created with a Template
9. View a Report

In the following Skills Review, you will create a database to store information about certification test preparation events at Texas Lakes Community College. Your completed Navigation Pane will look similar to Figure 1.48.

Project Files

For Project 1D, you will need the following files:

a01D_Certification_Template
a01D_Certification_Events (Excel workbook)

You will save your database as:

Lastname_Firstname_1D_Certification_Events

Project Results

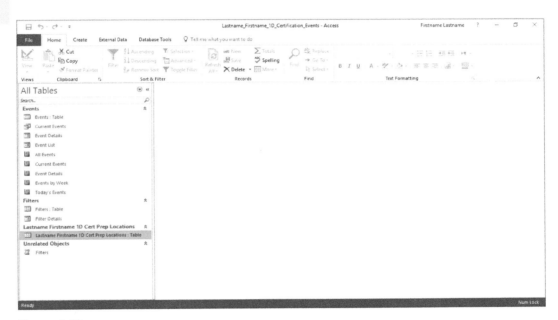

Figure 1.48

(continues on next page)

Chapter Review

1 Start Access. On the left, click **Open Other Files**, and then click **Browse**. Navigate to your student data for this chapter, and open the database named **a01D_Certification_Template**. On the ribbon, click the **File tab**, on the left, click **Save As**, and then, under *Save Database As*, click **Save As**. In the **Save As dialog** box, navigate to your **Access Chapter 1** folder, and then using your own name, type **Lastname_Firstname_1D_Certification_Events** and then click **Save**. Under the ribbon, on the **Message Bar**, click **Enable Content**.

a. In the first row, click in the **Title** field, type **Word 2019** and then press [Tab]. In the **Start Time** field, type **7/9/23 10a** and then press [Tab]. In the **End Time** field, type **7/9/23 4p** and then press [Tab]. In the **Description** field, type **Office 2019** and then press [Tab]. In the **Location** field, type **Southwest Campus** and then press [Tab] three times to move to the **Title** field in the new record row.

b. In the form, directly above the field names row, click **New Event** to open the **Event Details** single-record form. Using [Tab] to move from field to field, enter the record shown in **Table 1**. Press [Tab] three times to move from the **End Time** field to the **Description** field.

Table 1

Title	Location	Start Time	End Time	Description
Excel 2019	Northeast Campus	7/16/23 10a	7/16/23 4p	Office 2019

c. In the **Events Detail** form, click **Close**. Using either the **Event List** multiple-items form or the **Event Details** single-record form, enter the records shown in **Table 2**. If you use the Event Details form, be sure to close it after entering records to display the records in the Event List form.

Table 2

ID	Title	Start Time	End Time	Description	Location
3	Access 2019	7/23/23 12p	7/23/23 6p	Office 2019	Southeast Campus
4	PowerPoint 2019	7/30/23 9a	7/30/23 3p	Office 2019	Northwest Campus

d. **Close** the **Event List** form. On the ribbon, click the **External Data tab**, in the **Import & Link group**, click **New Data Source**, point to **From File**, and then click **Excel**. In the **Get External Data – Excel Spreadsheet** dialog box, click **Browse**. Navigate to your student data files, and then double-click **a01D_Certification_Events**. Click the second option button—**Append a copy of the records to the table: Events**—and then click **OK**.

e. In the **Import Spreadsheet Wizard**, click **Next**, and then click **Finish**. In the **Get External Data – Excel Spreadsheet** dialog box, click **Close**. Open the **Navigation Pane**, and then double-click **Event List** to open the form that displays data stored in the Events table—12 total records display. **Close** the **Navigation Pane**.

f. To the left of the **ID** field name, click **Select All**. In the field names row, point to the right edge of any of the selected columns to display the ⊞ pointer, and then double-click to apply **Best Fit** to all of the columns. Click in any field to cancel the selection, and then **Save** the form.

2 Open the Navigation Pane. At the top of the Navigation Pane, click **More**. On the list, under **Navigate To Category**, click **Tables and Related Views**.

a. In the **Navigation Pane**, point to **Events: Table**, right-click, and then click **Open** to display the records in the underlying table. In the **Navigation Pane**, double-click the **Current Events** *report* (green icon) to view this predesigned report. From the **Navigation Pane**, open the **Events by Week** report to view this predesigned report.

b. In the object window, right-click any of the **object tabs**, and then click **Close All**. **Close** the **Navigation Pane**.

3 On the ribbon, click the **Create tab**, and in the **Tables group**, click **Table**.

a. In the field names row, click **Click to Add**, click **Short Text**, type **Campus Location** and then press [Enter]. In the third column, click **Short Text**, type **Lab** and then press [Enter]. In the fourth column, click **Number**, type **# Computers** and then press [Enter]. In the fifth column, click **Short Text**, type **Additional Equipment** and then press [↓].

(continues on next page)

Chapter Review

b. Right-click the **ID** field name, and then click **Rename Field**. Type **Lab ID** and then press Enter. On the **Fields tab**, in the **Formatting group**, click the **Data Type arrow**, and then click **Short Text**.

c. In the new record row, click in the **Lab ID** field, and then enter the records shown in **Table 3**, pressing Enter or Tab to move from one field to the next.

Table 3

Lab ID	Campus Location	Lab	# Computers	Additional Equipment
NW-L01	Northwest Campus	H202	35	3 printers, DVD player
SE-L01	Southeast Campus	E145	25	Projector, document camera, smart board
NE-L01	Northeast Campus	F32	40	4 printers, smart board, instructor touch screen
SW-L01	Southwest Campus	G332	30	Projector, 4 digital displays
SE-L02	Southeast Campus	A225	25	Projector, white board, instructor touch screen

d. In the **Views group**, click the upper portion of the **View** button to switch to **Design** view. In the **Save As** dialog box, in the **Table Name** box, using your own name, type **Lastname Firstname1D Cert Prep Locations** and then click **OK**. Notice that the **Lab ID** field is the **Primary Key**. On the **Design tab**, in the **Views group**, click the upper portion of the **View** button to switch to **Datasheet** view.

e. To the left of the **Lab ID** field name, click **Select All** to select all of the columns and rows in the table. On the **Home tab**, in the **Records group**, click **More**, and then click **Field Width**. In the **Column Width** dialog box, click **Best Fit**. Click in any field to cancel the selection, and then **Save** the changes to the table. **Close** the table, and then **Open** the Navigation Pane. Increase the width of the **Navigation Pane** so that your entire table name displays.

4 In the Navigation Pane, double-click the **All Events** report to open it in the object window. **Close** the **Navigation Pane**. On the **Home tab**, in the **Views group**, click the top of the **View** button to switch to **Layout** view. At the top of the report, click the title—*All Events*—to display a colored border around the title. Click to the left of the letter *A* to place the insertion point there. Using your name, type **Lastname Firstname 1D** and then press Spacebar. Press Enter, and then **Save** the report.

a. On the right side of the status bar, click **Print Preview**, and notice that the report will print on one page. Click **Close Print Preview**, and then **Close** the report.

b. **Open** the **Navigation Pane**, double-click your **1D Cert Prep Locations** table, and then **Close** the **Navigation Pane**. On the ribbon, click the **File tab**, click **Print**, and then click **Print Preview**. On the **Print Preview tab**, in the **Page Layout group**, click **Landscape**. **Close Print Preview**. Close your **1D Cert Prep Locations** table.

c. **Open** the **Navigation Pane**. On the right side of the title bar, click **Close** to close the database and to close Access. As directed by your instructor, submit your database for grading.

You have completed Project 1D   **END**

Mastering Access   **Project 1E Kiosk Inventory**

Apply 1A skills from these Objectives:

1. Identify Good Database Design
2. Create a Table and Define Fields in a Blank Desktop Database
3. Change the Structure of Tables and Add a Second Table
4. Create a Query, Form, and Report
5. Close a Database and Close Access

In the following Mastering Access project, you will create a database to track information about the inventory of items for sale in the kiosk located in the Snack Bar at the Southeast Campus of Texas Lakes Community College. Your completed Navigation Pane will look similar to Figure 1.49.

Project Files for MyLab IT Grader

1. In your **MyLab IT** course, locate and click **Access 1E Kiosk Inventory**, Download Materials, and then Download All Files. Close the Grader download screens.
2. Extract the zipped folder to your Access Chapter 1 folder.
3. Take a moment to open the downloaded **Access_1E_Kiosk_Inventory_Instructions**; note any recent updates to the book.

Project Results

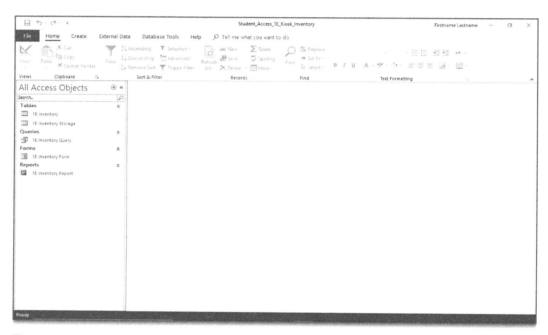

Figure 1.49

For Non-MyLab Submissions
For Project 1E, you will need these starting file:
Blank database
a01E_Inventory (Excel workbook)
a01E_Inventory_Storage (Excel workbook)

Start with a New Blank Access Database
In your Access Chapter 1 folder, save your database as:
Lastname_Firstname_1E_Kiosk_Inventory

After you have saved your database, open it to launch Access. On the next page, begin with Step 2.
After Step 11, submit your database as directed by your instructor.

(continues on next page)

Content-Based Assessments (Mastery and Transfer of Learning)

Mastering Access: Project 1E Kiosk Inventory (continued)

1 Start Access. Navigate to your **Access Chapter 1 folder**, and then double-click the downloaded file that displays your name—**Student_1E_Kiosk_Inventory**. If necessary, at the top, click Enable Content.

2 **Close** the **Navigation Pane**. Create a new table in Datasheet view, and create the fields shown in **Table 1**.

Table 1

Data Type		Short Text	Short Text	Short Text	Short Text	Currency	Number
Field Name	ID	**Item**	**Category**	**Campus**	**Storage Location**	**Price**	**Quantity in Stock**

3 For the **ID** field, change the **Data Type** to **Short Text**, rename the field to **Item ID** and then enter the records shown in **Table 2.**

Table 2

Item ID	Item	Category	Campus	Storage Location	Price	Quantity in Stock
C-1	Chocolate Bar	Candy	Southeast	SE100A	.89	250
C-2	Lollipop	Candy	Southeast	SE100A	.5	500
T-1	T-shirt	Clothing	Southeast	SE100B	17.5	100

4 **Save** the table as **1E Inventory** and **Close** the table. From your student data files, import and then **Append** the data in the Excel file **a01E_Inventory** to your **1E Inventory** table. After importing, open your **1E Inventory** table—17 records display.

5 In **Design** view, delete the **Campus** field, which is redundant data. For the **Category** field, change the **Field Size** to **25** and enter a **Description** of **Enter the category of the item** For the **Item ID** field, change the **Field Size** to **10** and then **Save** the changes to your table. Switch to **Datasheet** view, apply **Best Fit** to all of the fields in the table, and then **Save** your changes. Display the table in **Print Preview**, change the orientation to **Landscape**. **Close Print Preview**, and then **Close** the table.

6 From your student data files, import the **Excel** file **a01E_Inventory_Storage** into the database as a new table; designate the first row as column headings and the **Category** field as the primary key. In the wizard, name the table **1E Inventory Storage** and then open your **1E Inventory Storage** table—five records display. In **Design** view, for the **Location Detail** field, change the **Field Size** to **35** and enter a **Description** of **Room and bin number or alternate location of inventory item Save** the design changes, switch to **Datasheet** view, apply **Best Fit** to all of the fields, and then **Save** your changes. **Close** the table.

7 **Create** a **Simple Query**, by using the **Query Wizard**, based on your **1E Inventory** table. Include only the three fields that will answer the question, *For all items, what is the storage location and quantity in stock?* In the wizard, accept the default name for the query. Display the query in **Print Preview**, create a paper printout or PDF electronic image as directed, **Close Print Preview**, and then **Close** the query.

8 Open your **1E Inventory** table, and then **Create** a **Form** for this table. **Save** the form as **1E Inventory Form** and then view the records. **Close** the form object, saving changes if prompted.

9 With your **1E Inventory** table open, **Create** a **Report**. Delete the **Category** and **Price** fields, and then sort the **Item ID** field in **Ascending** order. Using the **Property Sheet**, for the **Item ID** field, change the **Width** to **0.75** and then for the **Storage Location** field, change the **Width** to **1.5** Scroll to display the bottom of the report, if necessary, and then delete the page number— **Page 1 of 1**. **Save** the report as **1E Inventory Report Close** the report.

10 **Close All** open objects. **Open** the **Navigation Pane** and be sure that all object names display fully.

11 **Close** the database, and then **Close** Access.

(continues on next page)

Content-Based Assessments (Mastery and Transfer of Learning)

12 In **MyLab IT**, locate and click the Grader Project **Access 1E Kiosk Inventory**. In **step 3**, under **Upload Completed Assignment**, click **Choose File**. In the **Open** dialog box, navigate to your **Access Chapter 1 folder**, and then click your **Student_Access_1E_Kiosk_Inventory** file one time to select it. In the lower right corner of the **Open** dialog box, click **Open.**

13 To submit your file to **MyLab IT** for grading, click Upload, wait a moment for a green **Success!** message, and then in **step 4**, click the blue **Submit for Grading** button. Click **Close Assignment** to return to your list of **Course Materials**.

You have completed Project 1E   END

Content-Based Assessments (Mastery and Transfer of Learning)

Mastering Access · Project 1F Recruitment Events

Apply 1B skills from these Objectives:

6. Use a Template to Create a Database
7. Organize Objects in the Navigation Pane
8. Create a New Table in a Database Created with a Template
9. View a Report

In the following Mastering Access project, you will create a database to store information about the recruiting events that are scheduled to attract new students to Texas Lakes Community College. Your completed Navigation Pane will look similar to Figure 1.50.

Project Files for MyLab IT Grader

1. In your **MyLab IT** course, locate and click **Access 1F Recruitment Events**, Download Materials, and then Download All Files. Close the Grader download screens.
2. Extract the zipped folder to your Access Chapter 1 folder.
3. Take a moment to open the downloaded **Access_1F_Recruitment_Events_Instructions**; note any recent updates to the book.

Project Results

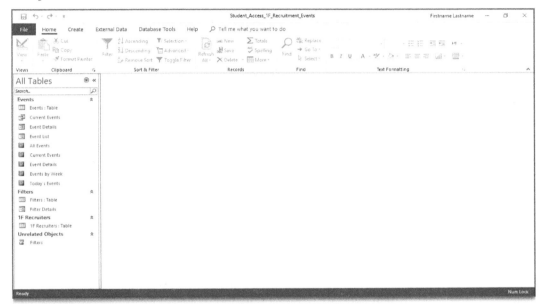

Figure 1.50

For Non-MyLab Submissions	Start with an Access Data File
For Project 1F, you will need these starting files:	In your Access Chapter 1 folder, save your database as:
a01F_Recruitment_Template	**Lastname_Firstname_1F_Recruitment_Events**
a01F_Recruiting_Events (Excel workbook)	

After you have saved your database, open it to launch Access. On the next page, begin with Step 2.
After Step 9, submit your database as directed by your instructor.

(continues on next page)

Content-Based Assessments (Mastery and Transfer of Learning)

1 Start Access. Navigate to your **Access Chapter 1 folder**, and then double-click the downloaded file that displays your name—**Student_1F_Recruitment_ Events**. If necessary, at the top, click Enable Content.

2 In the **Event List** multiple-items form or the **Event Details** single-record form—open by clicking **New Event** on the Event List form—enter the records shown in **Table 1**.

Table 1

ID	Title	Start Time	End Time	Description	Location
1	Health Professions	6/1/23 8a	6/1/23 12p	Science Students	Hill Country High School
2	New Students	6/1/23 10a	6/1/23 3p	College Fair	Brazos Convention Center
3	Information Technology	6/2/23 9a	6/2/23 12p	Technical Students	Round Rock Technical Center
4	International Students	6/2/23 2p	6/2/23 5p	Open House	Southeast Campus

3 **Close** the **Event List** form. From your student data files, import and **Append** the data from the **Excel** file **a01F_Recruiting_Events** to the **Events** table. **Open** the **Navigation Pane**, organize the objects by **Tables and Related Views**, and then open the **Events** table to display 13 records. **Close** the table, and then **Close** the **Navigation Pane**.

4 **Create** a new **Table** defining the new fields shown in **Table 2**.

Table 2

Data Type		Short Text	Short Text	Short Text	Short Text	Short Text
Field Name	ID	Location	Last Name	First Name	Email Address	Business Phone

5 For the **ID** field, change the **Data Type** to **Short Text**, rename the field to **Recruiter ID** and then enter the records shown in **Table 3**.

Table 3

Recruiter ID	Location	Last Name	First Name	Email Address	Business Phone
R-01	Hill Country High School	Rostamo	Robyn	rrostamo@hillcohs.sch	(512) 555-3410
R-02	Brazos Convention Center	Hart	Roberto	rlhart@brazosconv.ctr	(512) 555-1938
R-03	Round Rock Technical Center	Sedlacek	Belinda	bsedlacek@rrocktech.sch	(512) 555-0471
R-04	Southeast Campus	Nguyen	Thao	tnguyen@tlcc.edu	(512) 555-2387

6 Apply **Best Fit** to all of the columns. **Save** the table as **1F Recruiters** and then **Close** the table.

7 From the **Navigation Pane**, open the **Event Details** *report* (green icon). Switch to **Layout** view. In the report, click in the title—*Event Details*—and then click to position the insertion point to the left of the word *Event*. **1F** and then press Spacebar and Enter. **Save** and **Close** the report.

8 From the **Navigation Pane**, open the **Events** table, select all of the columns, and then apply **Best Fit** to all of the columns by double-clicking the right edge of any of the selected columns. Cancel the selection, and then **Save** the table. Display the table in **Print Preview**, change the orientation to **Landscape**, change the **Margins** to **Normal**. **Save** and **Close** the table.

(continues on next page)

Content-Based Assessments (Mastery and Transfer of Learning)

Mastering Access: Project 1F Recruitment Events (continued)

9 In the **Navigation Pane**, be sure that all object names display fully. **Close** the database and **Close** Access.

10 In In **MyLab IT**, locate and click the Grader Project **Access 1F Recruitment Events**. In **step 3**, under **Upload Completed Assignment**, click **Choose File**. In the **Open** dialog box, navigate to your **Access Chapter 1 folder**, and then click your **Student_Access_1F_ Recruitment_Events** file one time to select it. In the lower right corner of the **Open** dialog box, click **Open**.

11 To submit your file to **MyLab IT** for grading, click **Upload**, wait a moment for a green **Success!** message, and then in **step 4**, click the blue **Submit for Grading** button. Click **Close Assignment** to return to your list of **Course Materials**.

You have completed Project 1F   **END**

Content-Based Assessments (Mastery and Transfer of Learning)

Mastering Access   **Project 1G College Construction**

Apply 1A and 1B skills from these Objectives:

1. Identify Good Database Design
2. Create a Table and Define Fields in a Blank Desktop Database
3. Change the Structure of Tables and Add a Second Table
4. Create a Query, Form, and Report
5. Close a Database and Close Access
6. Use a Template to Create a Database
7. Organize Objects in the Navigation Pane
8. Create a New Table in a Database Created with a Template
9. View a Report

In the following Mastering Access project, you will create one database to store information about construction projects for Texas Lakes Community College and a second database to store information about the public events related to the construction projects. Your completed Navigation Pane will look similar to Figure 1.51.

Project Files for MyLab IT Grader

1. In your **MyLab IT** course, locate and click **Access 1G College Construction** Download Materials, and then Download All Files. Close the Grader download screens.
2. Extract the zipped folder to your Access Chapter 1 folder.
3. Take a moment to open the downloaded **Access_1G_College_Construction_Instructions**; note any recent updates to the book.

Project Results

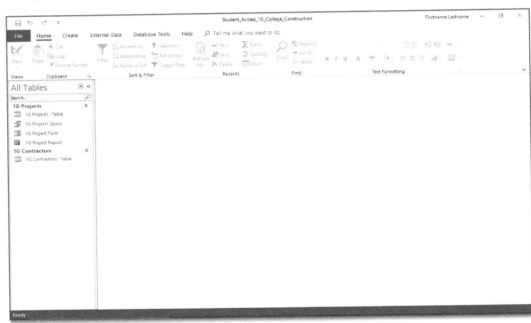

Figure 1.51

For Non-MyLab Submissions
For Project 1G, you will need these starting files:
a01G_College_Construction
a01G_Projects (Excel workbook)
a01G_Contractors (Excel workbook)

Start with an Access Data File
In your Access Chapter 1 folder, save your database as:
Lastname_Firstname_1G_College_Construction

After you have saved your database, open it to launch Access. On the next page, begin with Step 2.
After Step 13, submit your database as directed by your instructor.

(continues on next page)

Mastering Access: Project 1G College Construction (continued)

1 Navigate to your **Access Chapter 1 folder**, and then double-click the downloaded file that displays your name—**Student_Access_1G_College_Construction**. If necessary, at the top, click Enable Content.

2 **Close** the **Navigation Pane**. Create a new table with the fields shown in **Table 1**.

Table 1

Data Type		Short Text	Short Text	Short Text	Currency
Field Name	ID	**Building Project**	**Site**	**Contractor**	**Budget Amount**

3 For the **ID** field, change the **Data Type** to **Short Text**, rename the field to **Project ID** and change the **Field Size** to **5** Enter the three records shown in **Table 2**.

Table 2

Project ID	Building Project	Site	Contractor	Budget Amount
P-356	**Student Center, 3-story**	**Northeast Campus**	**RR Construction**	**61450000**
P-823	**Student Center, 2-story**	**Southeast Campus**	**RR Construction**	**41960000**
P-157	**Health Professions Center**	**Northwest Campus**	**Marshall Ellis Construction**	**42630000**

4 Save the table as **1G Projects** and **Close** the table. From your student data files, import and then **Append** the data in the **Excel** file **a01G_Projects** to your **1G Projects** table. After importing, open your **1G Projects** table—eight records display.

5 In **Design** view, for the **Project ID** field, enter a **Description** of **Enter the Project ID using the format P-###** For the **Site** field, change the field size to **25** and enter a **Description** of **Campus location Save** the changes to your table. Switch to **Datasheet** view, apply **Best Fit** to all of the fields in the table, and then **Save** your changes. Display the table in **Print Preview**, change the orientation to **Landscape**. **Close Print Preview**, and then **Close** the table.

6 From your student data files, import the **Excel** file **a01G_Contractors** into the database as a new table; designate the first row as column headings and the **CO ID** field as the primary key. In the wizard, name the table **1G Contractors** and then open your **1G Contractors** table—four records display. Apply **Best Fit** to all of the fields, and then **Save** your changes. Display the table in **Print Preview**, change the orientation to **Landscape. Close Print Preview**, and then **Close** the table.

7 **Create**, by using the **Query Wizard**, a **Simple Query** based on your **1G Projects** table. Include only the three fields that will answer the question, *For every site, what is the building project and the budget amount?* In the wizard, accept the default name for the query. **Close** the query.

8 Open your **1G Projects** table, and then **Create** a **Form** for this table. **Save** the form as **1G Project Form** and **Close** the form object.

9 With your **1G Projects** table open, **Create** a **Report**. Delete the **Budget Amount** field, and then sort the **Building Project** field in **Ascending** order. For the **Building Project**, **Site**, and **Contractor** fields, using the **Property Sheet**, change the **Width** of all three fields to **2** At the bottom of the report, delete the page number— **Page 1 of 1**. Change the **Report title** to **1G Project Report Save** the report as **1G Project Report**

10 Open the Navigation Pane, open the **Event List** form, and then close the Navigation Pane. In the Event List multiple-items form, enter the following two records (the Start Time and End Time data will reformat automatically):

Table 3

ID	Title	Start Time	End Time	Location	Description
1	**Groundbreaking**	**6/13/22 10a**	**6/13/22 11a**	**Northeast Campus**	**Student Center groundbreaking**
2	**Dedication**	**8/26/22 12:30p**	**8/26/22 2p**	**Southwest Campus**	**Gymnasium building dedication**

(continues on next page)

Mastering Access: Project 1G College Construction (continued)

11 In the **Event List** form, click **New Event**, and in the **Event Details** single-record form, enter the following record (the Start Time and End Time data will reformat automatically):

Table 4

ID	Title	Start Time	End Time	Location	Description
3	**Community Arts Expo**	**10/5/21 6p**	**10/5/22 9p**	**Southeast Campus**	**Book and Art Expo at Library Location**

12 **Close All** open objects. **Open** the **Navigation Pane**, arrange the objects by **Tables and Related Views**, and be sure that all object names display fully.

13 In the **Navigation Pane**, be sure that all object names display fully. **Close** the database and **Close** Access.

14 In In **MyLab IT**, locate and click the Grader Project **Access 1G College Construction**. In **step 3**, unde **Upload Completed Assignment**, click **Choose File**. In the **Open** dialog box, navigate to your **Access Chapter 1 folder**, and then click your **Student_Access_1G_College_ Construction** file one time to select it. In the lower right corner of the **Open** dialog box, click **Open**.

15 To submit your file to **MyLab IT** for grading, click **Upload**, wait a moment for a green **Success!** message, and then in **step 4**, click the blue **Submit for Grading** button. Click **Close Assignment** to return to your list of **Course Materials**.

You have completed Project 1G **END**

Content-Based Assessments (Critical Thinking)

Apply a combination of the 1A and 1B skills.			
	GO! Fix It	Project 1H Scholarships	IRC
	GO! Make It	Project 1I Theater Events	IRC
	GO! Solve It	Project 1J Athletic Scholarships	IRC
	GO! Solve It	Project 1K Student Activities	

Project Files

For Project 1K, you will need the following files:

Event management template
a01K_Student_Activities (Word document)
You will save your database as:
Lastname_Firstname_1K_Student_Activities

Use the Event management template to create a database, and then save it in your Access Chapter 1 folder as **Lastname_Firstname_1K_Student_Activities** From your student data files, use the information in the Word document a01K_Student_Activities to enter data into the Event List multiple-items form. Each event begins at 7 p.m. and ends at 10 p.m.

After entering the records, close the form, and arrange the Navigation Pane by Tables and Related Views. Open the Event Details *report*, and then add your **Firstname Lastname 1K** to the beginning of the report title. Decrease the font size of the title so that it displays on one line. Create a paper printout or PDF electronic image as directed—two pages result. As directed, submit your database for grading.

		Performance Level		
		Exemplary	**Proficient**	**Developing**
Performance Criteria	**Create database using Event management template and enter data**	Database created using the correct template, named correctly, and all data entered correctly.	Database created using the correct template, named correctly, but not all data entered correctly.	Database created using the correct template, but numerous errors in database name and data.
	Modify report	Event Details report title includes name and project on one line.	Event Details report title includes name and project, but not on one line.	Event Details report title does not include name and project and does not display on one line.
	Create report printout	Event Details report printout is correct.	Event Details printout is incorrect.	Event Details report printout not created.

You have completed Project 1K | END

Outcomes-Based Assessments (Critical Thinking)

Rubric

The following outcomes-based assessments are *open-ended assessments*. That is, there is no specific correct result; your result will depend on your approach to the information provided. Make *Professional Quality* your goal. Use the following scoring rubric to guide you in how to approach the problem and then to evaluate how well your approach solves the problem.

The *criteria*—Software Mastery, Content, Format & Layout, and Process—represent the knowledge and skills you have gained that you can apply to solving the problem. The *levels of performance*—Professional Quality, Approaching Professional Quality, or Needs Quality Improvements—help you and your instructor evaluate your result.

	Your completed project is of Professional Quality if you:	Your completed project is Approaching Professional Quality if you:	Your completed project Needs Quality Improvements if you:
1-Software Mastery	Choose and apply the most appropriate skills, tools, and features and identify efficient methods to solve the problem.	Choose and apply some appropriate skills, tools, and features, but not in the most efficient manner.	Choose inappropriate skills, tools, or features, or are inefficient in solving the problem.
2-Content	Construct a solution that is clear and well organized, contains content that is accurate, appropriate to the audience and purpose, and is complete. Provide a solution that contains no errors of spelling, grammar, or style.	Construct a solution in which some components are unclear, poorly organized, inconsistent, or incomplete. Misjudge the needs of the audience. Have some errors in spelling, grammar, or style, but the errors do not detract from comprehension.	Construct a solution that is unclear, incomplete, or poorly organized, contains some inaccurate or inappropriate content, and contains many errors of spelling, grammar, or style. Do not solve the problem.
3-Format and Layout	Format and arrange all elements to communicate information and ideas, clarify function, illustrate relationships, and indicate relative importance.	Apply appropriate format and layout features to some elements, but not others. Overuse features, causing minor distraction.	Apply format and layout that does not communicate information or ideas clearly. Do not use format and layout features to clarify function, illustrate relationships, or indicate relative importance. Use available features excessively, causing distraction.
4-Process	Use an organized approach that integrates planning, development, self-assessment, revision, and reflection.	Demonstrate an organized approach in some areas, but not others; or, use an insufficient process of organization throughout.	Do not use an organized approach to solve the problem.

Outcomes-Based Assessments (Critical Thinking)

Apply a combination of the 1A and 1B skills.

| GO! Think | Project 1L Student Clubs |

Project Files

For Project 1L, you will need the following files:

Blank database
a01L_Clubs (Word document)
a01L_Student_Clubs (Excel workbook)
a01L_Club_Presidents (Excel workbook)
You will save your database as
Lastname_Firstname_1L_Student_Clubs

Dr. Daniel Martinez, Vice President of Student Services, needs a database that tracks information about student clubs. The database should contain two tables—one for club information and one for contact information for the club presidents.

Create a desktop database, and then save the database in your Access Chapter 1 folder as **Lastname_Firstname_1L_Student_Clubs** From your student data files, use the information in the Word document a01L_Clubs to create the first table and to enter two records. Name the table appropriately to include your name and 1L, and then append the 23 records from the Excel workbook a01L_Student_Clubs to your table. For the Club ID and President ID fields, add a description and change the field size.

Create a second table in the database by importing 25 records from the Excel workbook a01L_Club_Presidents, and then name the table appropriately to include your name and 1L. For the State and Postal Code fields, add a description and change the field size. Be sure that the field data types are correct—recall that numbers that are not used in calculations should have a data type of Short Text. Be sure all of the data and field names display in each table.

Create a simple query based on the Clubs table that answers the question, *What is the club name, meeting day, meeting time, campus, and Room ID for all of the clubs?* Create a form based on the Clubs table, saving it with an appropriate name that includes your name and 1L. Create a report based on the Presidents table, saving it with an appropriate name that includes your name and 1L, that displays the president's last name (in ascending order), the president's first name, and the phone number of every president. Change the width of the three fields so that there is less space between them, but being sure that each record prints on a single line.

Create paper printout or PDF electronic images of the two tables, the query, only Record 21 of the form, and the report as directed being sure that each object prints on one page. Organize the objects on the Navigation Pane by Tables and Related Views, and be sure that all object names display fully. As directed, submit your database for grading.

| | You have completed Project 1L | END |

GO! Think	Project 1M Faculty Training Online	IRC
You and GO!	Project 1N Personal Contacts Online	IRC
GO! Cumulative Group Project	Project 1O Bell Orchid Hotels Online	IRC

Sort and Query a Database

2
ACCESS 2019

PROJECT 2A

Outcomes
Sort and query a database

Objectives
1. Open and Save an Existing Database
2. Create Table Relationships
3. Sort Records in a Table
4. Create a Query in Design View
5. Create a New Query From an Existing Query
6. Sort Query Results
7. Specify Criteria in a Query

PROJECT 2B

Outcomes
Create complex queries

Objectives
8. Specify Numeric Criteria in a Query
9. Use Compound Criteria in a Query
10. Create a Query Based on More Than One Table
11. Use Wildcards in a Query
12. Create Calculated Fields in a Query
13. Calculate Statistics and Group Data in a Query
14. Create a Crosstab Query
15. Create a Parameter Query

Spiroview Inc./Shutterstock

In This Chapter

GO! to Work
with Access

In this chapter, you will sort Access database tables and create and modify queries. To convert data into meaningful information, you must manipulate your data in a way that you can answer questions. One question might be: *Which students have a grade point average of 3.0 or higher?* With this information, you could send information about scholarships or internships to students who meet the grade point average criteria.

The projects in this chapter relate to **Texas Lakes Community College**, which is located in the Austin,

Texas, area. Its four campuses serve over 30,000 students and offer more than 140 certificate programs and degrees. The college has a highly acclaimed Distance Education program and an extensive Workforce Development program. The college makes positive contributions to the community through cultural and athletic programs and has maintained partnerships with businesses and non-profit organizations.

PROJECT
2A

Instructors and Courses

MyLab IT
Project 2A Grader for Instruction
Project 2A Simulation for Training and Review

Project Activities

In Activities 2.01 through 2.16, you will assist Dr. Carolyn Judkins, Dean of the Business Division at the Northeast Campus of Texas Lakes Community College, in locating information about instructors and summer courses offered in the Division. Your completed Navigation Pane will look similar to Figure 2.1.

Project Files for MyLab IT Grader

1. In your storage location, create a folder named **Access Chapter 2**.
2. In your **MyLab IT** course, locate and click **Access 2A Instructors and Courses**, Download Materials, and then Download All Files.
3. Extract the zipped folder to your Access Chapter 2 folder. Close the Grader download screens.
4. Take a moment to open the downloaded **Access_2A_Instructors_Courses_Instructions**; note any recent updates to the book.

Project Results

GO! Project 2A
Where We're Going

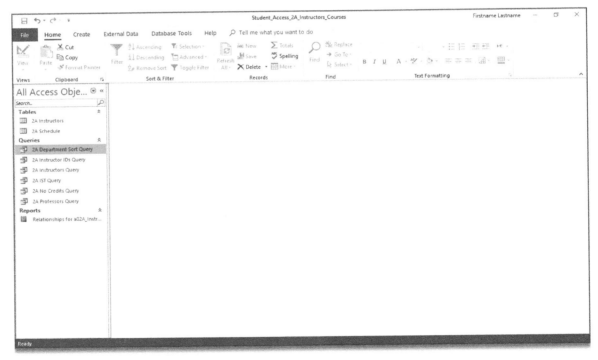

Figure 2.1 Project 2A Instructors and Courses

For Non-MyLab Submissions

For Project 2A, you will need this starting file:
a02A_Instructors_Courses

Start with an Access Data File

In your storage location, create a folder named **Access Chapter 2**
In your Access Chapter 2 folder, save your database as:
Lastname_Firstname_2A_Instructors_Courses

After you have saved your database, launch Access and open the database. On the next page, begin with Step 2.

Objective 1   Open and Save an Existing Database

GO! Learn How
Video A2-1

There will be instances where you need to work with a database and still keep the original, unaltered version of the database. Like the other Microsoft Office 2019 applications, you can open a database file and save it with another name.

Activity 2.01 | Opening an Existing Database and Resolving Security Alerts

1 Start Access. In the Access opening screen, click **Open Other Files**. Navigate to your **Access Chapter 2 folder**, and then double-click the Access file that you downloaded from **MyLab IT** that displays your name—**Student_Access_2A_Instructors_Courses**.

2 In the **Navigation Pane**, notice that this database contains two table objects.

The 2A Instructors table contains information about the instructors at Texas Lakes Community College. The 2A Schedule table outlines the course schedule information.

3 On the **Message Bar**, notice the **SECURITY WARNING**. Compare your screen with Figure 2.2.

The *Message Bar* is the area directly below the ribbon that displays information such as security alerts when there is potentially unsafe, active content in an Office document that you open. Settings that determine the alerts that display on your Message Bar are set in the Access *Trust Center*, an area in Access where you can view the security and privacy settings for your Access installation.

Figure 2.2

4 On the **Message Bar**, click **Enable Content**.

When working with the student data files that accompany this textbook, repeat this action each time you see the security warning. Databases for this textbook are safe to use on your computer.

Objective 2 — Create Table Relationships

GO! Learn How
Video A2-2

Access databases are relational databases because the tables in the database can relate— actually connect—to other tables through common fields. Recall that common fields are fields in one or more tables that store the same data; for example, a Student ID number may be stored in two tables in the same database.

After you have a table for each subject in your database, you must provide a way to connect the data in the tables when you need to obtain meaningful information from the stored data. To do this, create common fields in the related tables, and then define table *relationships*. A relationship is an association that you establish between two tables based on common fields. After the relationship is established, you can create a query, form, or report that displays information from more than one related table.

Activity 2.02 | Selecting the Tables and Common Field to Establish the Table Relationship

1.2.1, 1.2.5

In this Activity, you will select the two tables in the database that will be used to establish the table relationship and identify the common field that is used to connect the tables.

1 In the **Navigation Pane**, double-click your **2A Instructors** table to open it in the object window. Examine the fields in the table. Double-click your **2A Schedule** table to open it and examine the fields in the table.

In the 2A Instructors table, *Instructor ID* is the primary key field, which ensures that each instructor has only one record in the table. No two instructors have the same Instructor ID, and the table is sorted by Instructor ID.

In the 2A Schedule table, *Schedule ID* is the primary key field. Every scheduled course section during an academic term has a unique Schedule ID. The courses are sorted by Schedule ID.

2 In the **2A Schedule** table, scroll to display the **Instructor ID** field, and then compare your screen with Figure 2.3.

Both the 2A Instructors table and the 2A Schedule table include the *Instructor ID* field, which is the common field of the two tables. Because *one* instructor can teach *many* different courses, *one* Instructor ID can be present *many* times in the 2A Schedule table. When the relationship is established, it will be a ***one-to-many relationship***, which is the most common type of relationship in Access.

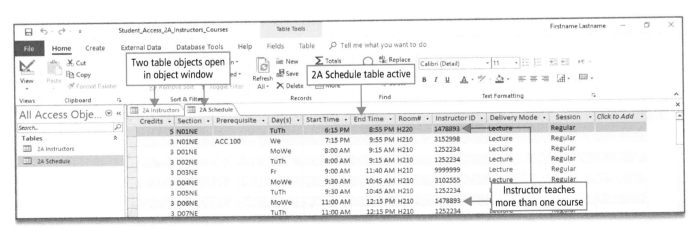

Figure 2.3

3 In the object window, right-click either **object tab**, and then click **Close All** to close both tables. Click the **Database Tools tab**, and then in the **Relationships group**, click **Relationships**. Compare your screen with Figure 2.4.

The Show Table dialog box displays in the Relationships window. In the Show Table dialog box, the Tables tab displays the two tables that are in this database.

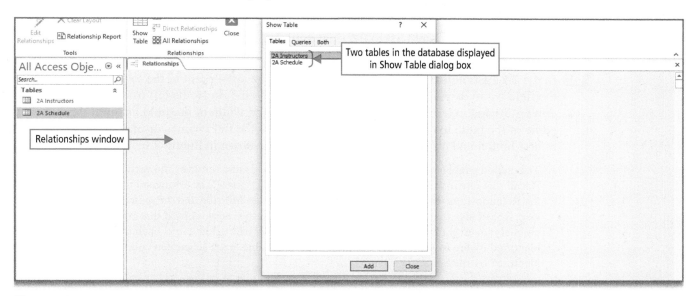

Figure 2.4

4 Point to the title bar of the **Show Table** dialog box, and then, holding down the left mouse button, drag downward and slightly to the right to move the dialog box away from the top of the **Relationships** window. Release the mouse button.

Moving the Show Table dialog box enables you to see the tables as they are added to the Relationships window.

5 In the **Show Table** dialog box, if necessary, click your **2A Instructors** table, and then click **Add**. In the **Show Table** dialog box, double-click your **2A Schedule** table to add it to the **Relationships** window. In the **Show Table** dialog box, click **Close**, and then compare your screen with Figure 2.5.

You can use either technique to add a table to the Relationships window; tables are displayed in the order in which they are added. A *field list*—a list of the field names in a table—for each of the two table objects displays, and each table's primary key is identified by a key icon. Although this database has only two tables, it is not uncommon for larger databases to have many tables. Scroll bars in a field list indicate that there are fields in the table that are not currently in view.

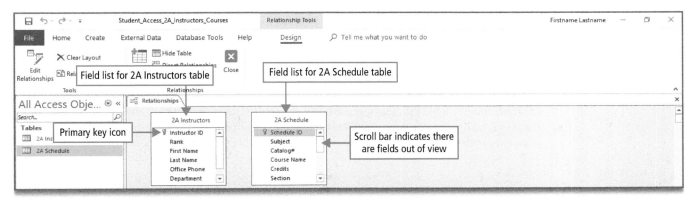

Figure 2.5

6 In the **2A Schedule** field list—the field list on the right—point to the title bar to display the ⬉ pointer. Drag the field list to the right until there is about one inch of space between the field lists.

7 In the **2A Instructors** field list—the field list on the left—point to the lower right corner of the field list to display the ⬉ pointer, and then, holding down the left mouse button, drag downward and to the right to increase the height and width of the field list until the entire name of the table in the title bar displays and all of the field names display. Release the mouse button and all of the field names display as shown in Figure 2.6.

This action enables you to see all of the available fields and removes the vertical scroll bar. Recall that *one* instructor can teach *many* scheduled courses. The arrangement of field lists in the Relationships window displays the *one table* on the left side and the *many table* on the right side. Recall also that the primary key in each table is the required field that contains the data that uniquely identifies each record in the table. In the 2A Instructors table, each instructor is uniquely identified by the Instructor ID. In the 2A Schedule table, each scheduled course section is uniquely identified by the Schedule ID.

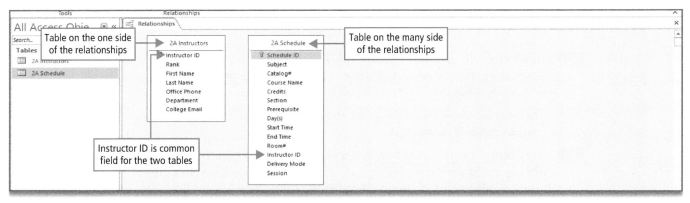

Figure 2.6

8 In the **2A Instructors** field list, point to **Instructor ID**, and then, holding down the left mouse button, drag the field name downward and to the right into the **2A Schedule** field list until the ⬉ pointer's arrow is on top of **Instructor ID**. Release the mouse button to display the **Edit Relationships** dialog box.

As you drag, a small graphic displays to indicate that you are dragging a field name from one field list to another. A table relationship works by matching data in two fields—the common field. In these two tables, the common field has the same name—*Instructor ID*. Common fields are not required to have the same name; however, they must have the same data type and field size.

ANOTHER WAY   On the Design tab, in the Tools group, click Edit Relationships. In the Edit Relationships dialog box, click Create New. In the Create New dialog box, designate the tables and fields that will create the relationship.

9 ▶ Point to the title bar of the **Edit Relationships** dialog box, and then, holding down the left mouse button, drag the dialog box to the right below the two field lists as shown in Figure 2.7. Release the mouse button.

By dragging the common field, you create the *one-to-many* relationship. In the 2A Instructors table, Instructor ID is the primary key. In the 2A Schedule table, Instructor ID is the *foreign key* field. The foreign key is the field in the related table used to connect to the primary key in another table. The field on the *one* side of the relationship is typically the primary key.

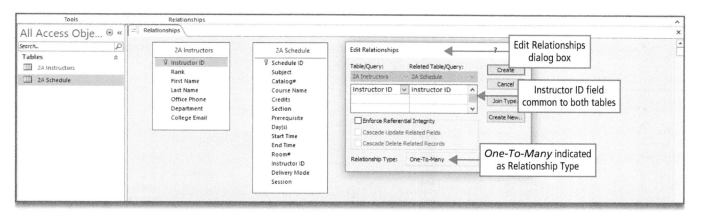

Figure 2.7

Activity 2.03 | Setting Relationship Options

In this Activity, you will set relationship options that will enable you to work with records in the related tables.

1 ▶ In the **Edit Relationships** dialog box, click to select the **Enforce Referential Integrity** check box. Notice that the two options under **Enforce Referential Integrity** are now available.

Referential integrity is a set of rules that Access uses to ensure that the data between related tables is valid. Enforcing referential integrity ensures that an Instructor ID cannot be added to a course in the 2A Schedule table if the Instructor ID is *not* included in the 2A Instructors table first. Similarly, enforcing referential integrity ensures that you cannot delete an instructor from the 2A Instructors table if there is a course that has been assigned to that instructor in the 2A Schedule table. After selecting Enforce Referential Integrity, *cascade options*—relationship options that enable you to update records in related tables when referential integrity is enforced—become available for use.

2 ▶ In the **Edit Relationships** dialog box, click to select the **Cascade Update Related Fields** check box.

The *Cascade Update Related Fields* option enables you to change the data in the primary key field for the table on the *one* side of the relationship, and updates automatically change any fields in the related table that store the same data. For example, in the 2A Instructors table, if you change the data in the Instructor ID field for one instructor, Access automatically finds every scheduled course assigned to that instructor in the 2A Schedule table and changes the data in the common field, in this case, the Instructor ID field. Without this option, if you try to change the ID number for an instructor, an error message displays if there is a related record in the related table on the *many* side of the relationship.

3 In the **Edit Relationships** dialog box, click to select the **Cascade Delete Related Records** check box, and then compare your screen with Figure 2.8.

The *Cascade Delete Related Records* option enables you to delete a record in the table on the *one* side of the relationship and also delete all of the related records in related tables. For example, if an instructor retires or leaves the college and the courses that the instructor teaches must be canceled because no other instructor can be found, you can delete the instructor's record from the 2A Instructors table, and then all of the courses that are assigned to that instructor in the 2A Schedule table are also deleted. Without this option, an error message displays if you try to delete the instructor's record from the 2A Instructors table. Use caution when applying this option; in many instances another instructor would be found so you would not want the course to be deleted. In this instance, you would need to change the Instructor ID in the related records before deleting the original instructor from the 2A Instructors table.

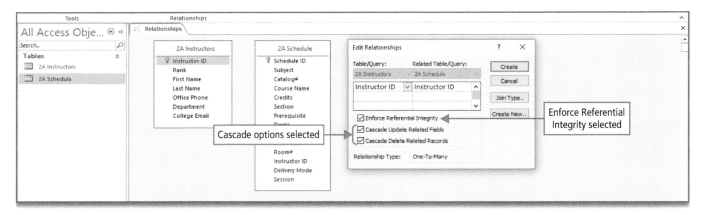

Figure 2.8

4 In the **Edit Relationships** dialog box, click **Create**, and then compare your screen with Figure 2.9.

A *join line*—the line connecting or joining the two tables—displays between the two tables. The join line connects the primary key field—Instructor ID—in the 2A Instructors field list to the common field—Instructor ID—in the 2A Schedule field list. On the join line, *1* indicates the *one* side of the relationship, and the infinity symbol (∞) indicates the *many* side of the relationship. These symbols display when referential integrity is enforced.

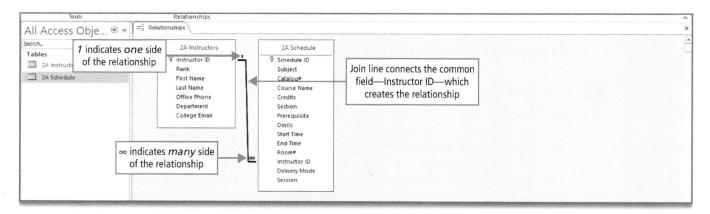

Figure 2.9

MORE KNOWLEDGE | **Edit or Delete a Relationship**

To modify or delete an existing relationship, right-click the join line. On the shortcut menu, click Delete to remove the join line and the relationship. If you want to edit the relationship options, click Edit Relationship to display the Edit Relationships dialog box.

Activity 2.04 | Saving a Relationship Report

1.3.1, 1.2.2

The Relationships window provides a map of how your database tables are related, and you can print and save this information as a report.

1 On the **Design tab**, in the **Tools group**, click **Relationship Report**.

The report is created and displays in the object window in Print Preview.

2 On the **Print Preview tab**, in the **Page Size group**, click **Margins**, and then click **Normal** to increase the margins slightly—some printers cannot print with narrow margins. Compare your screen with Figure 2.10.

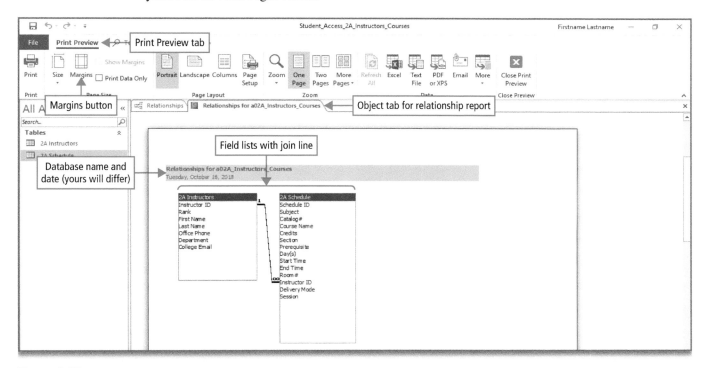

Figure 2.10

3 On the **Quick Access Toolbar**, click **Save** 🖫. In the **Save As** dialog box, click **OK** to accept the default report name. On the **Print Preview** tab, click **Close Print Preview**.

The report name displays in the Navigation Pane under *Unrelated Objects*. Because the report is just a map of the relationship between the tables, and not a report containing records from a table, it is not associated or related with any tables.

4 In the object window, click **Close** ⊠ to close the report, and then **Close** ⊠ the **Relationships** window.

NOTE   **Close Print Preview and the Relationship Report**

If you click Close Print Preview when the report is displayed in Print Preview, the Relationship report will display in Design view in the object window. If this happens, you can Close the object while it is displayed in this view.

Activity 2.05 | Displaying Subdatasheet Records

When you open the table on the *one* side of the relationship, the related records from the table on the *many* side are available for you to view and to modify.

1 In the **Navigation Pane**, double-click your **2A Instructors** table to open it in the object window, and then **Close** ⊠ the **Navigation Pane**.

2 On the left side of the first record—*Instructor ID* of *1224567*—click **+**, and then compare your screen with Figure 2.11.

A plus sign (+) to the left of a record in a table indicates that *related* records may exist in another table. Click the plus sign to display the related records in a ***subdatasheet***. In the first record for *Craig Fresch*, you can see that related records exist in the 2A Schedule table—he is scheduled to teach five LGL (Legal) courses. The plus signs display because you created a relationship between the two tables using the Instructor ID field—the common field.

When you click + to display the subdatasheet, the symbol changes to a minus sign (-), an indication that the subdatasheet is expanded. Click - to collapse the subdatasheet.

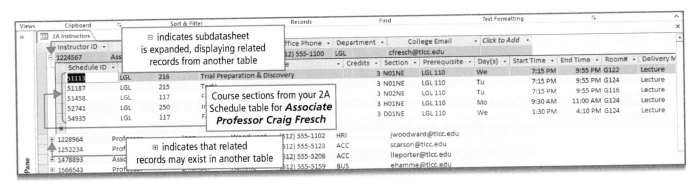

Figure 2.11

MORE KNOWLEDGE | **Other Types of Relationships: One-to-One and Many-to-Many**

The type of relationship is determined by the placement of the primary key field. A one-to-one relationship exists between two tables when a record in one table is related to only one record in a second table. In this case, both tables use the same field as the primary key. This is most often used when data is placed in a separate table because access to that information is restricted; for example, using an Employee ID field as the primary key field, there is one table for contact information, and a second table with payroll information.

A many-to-many relationship between tables exists where many records in one table can be related to many records in another table. For example, many students can enroll in many courses. To create a many-to-many relationship, you must create a third table that contains the primary key fields from both tables. In the Relationships window, you create a join line from this table to the other two tables. In effect, you create multiple one-to-many relationships.

Activity 2.06 | Testing Cascade Options

Recall that cascade options enable you to make changes to records on the *one* side table of the relationship and update or delete records in the table on the *many* side of the relationship. In this Activity, you will change the data in the Instructor ID field—the primary key field—for one instructor, and then delete all of the records associated with another instructor from both tables.

1 In the subdatasheet for the first record—*Instructor ID* of *1224567*—notice that the first course that the instructor is scheduled to teach has a *Schedule ID* of *51113—LGL 216*. In the **2A Instructors** table, to the left of the first record, click **–** (minus sign) to collapse the subdatasheet.

2 If necessary, in the first record, in the **Instructor ID** field, select the data—**1224567**. Type **8224567** and then press ⬇ to save the record.

If you had not enabled Cascade Update Related Fields in the Edit Relationships dialog box, an error message would have displayed.

3 Open ⟫ the **Navigation Pane**. In the **Navigation Pane**, double-click your **2A Schedule** table to open it, and then **Close** ⟪ the **Navigation Pane**.

ANOTHER WAY   Press F11 to open or close the Navigation Pane.

4 Scroll to locate the record with a **Schedule ID** of **51113**—*LGL 216*. If necessary, scroll to the right to display the **Instructor ID** field, and notice that for this record, the **Instructor ID** is **8224567**. Compare your screen with Figure 2.12.

The Cascade Update Related Fields option enables you to change the data in the primary key field in your 2A Instructors table, and the five related records for *Craig Fresch* in the 2A Schedule table were updated to store his Instructor ID of *8224567*.

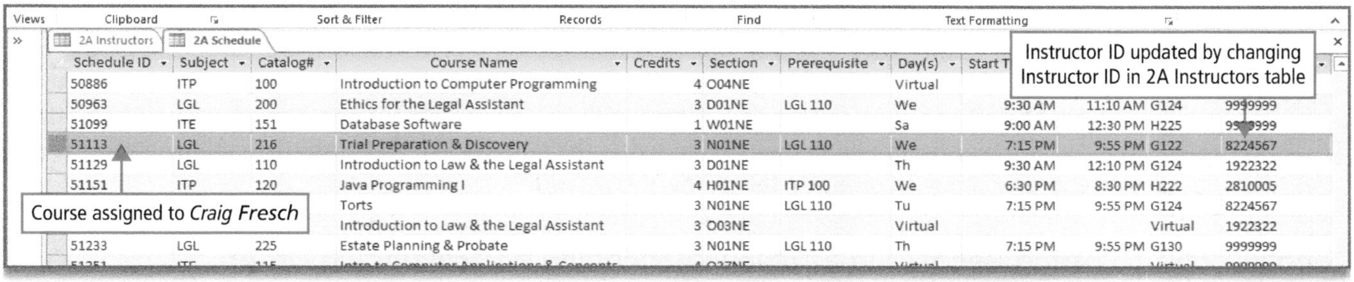

Figure 2.12

5 **Close** ✕ your **2A Schedule** table. In your **2A Instructors** table, scroll to display the last few records. On the left side of the record for **Instructor ID** of **6145288**—*Professor Ivey Clarke*— click ⊞ to display the subdatasheet. Notice that this instructor is scheduled to teach two courses—*Schedule ID* of *42837* and *42930*.

6 Click ⊟ to collapse the subdatasheet. For the same record—**Instructor ID** of **6145288**— point to the record selector box to display the ➡ pointer, and then click to select the record. On the **Home tab**, in the **Records group**, click **Delete**.

A message displays warning you that this record and related records in related tables will be deleted. The record you selected does not display in the table, and the next record is selected. If you had not enabled Cascade Delete Related Records, an error message would have displayed, and you would not be able to delete the record for Professor Ivey Clarke without assigning her courses to another instructor first.

ANOTHER WAY   With the record selected, press Del or with the record selected, right-click, and then click Delete Record.

7 In the message box, click **Yes**.

The record for *Instructor ID* of *6145288* is deleted. On the Quick Access Toolbar, the Undo button is unavailable—if you mistakenly delete the wrong record and the related records, you must enter them again in both tables. Access cannot use Undo to undo a Delete.

8 Open ⟫ the **Navigation Pane**, open your **2A Schedule** table, and then **Close** ⟪ the **Navigation Pane**. Scroll through the records and notice that the records for a **Schedule ID** of **42837** and **42930** have been deleted from the table.

The Cascade Delete Related Records option in the Edit Relationships dialog box enables you to delete a record in the table on the *one* side of the relationship—2A Instructors—and simultaneously delete the records in the table on the *many* side of the relationship—2A Schedule—that are related to the deleted record.

9 ▶ In the object window, right-click either **object tab**, and then click **Close All** to close both tables.

NOTE   **Cascade Options—Record Must Be Edited or Deleted in Correct Table**

Changes in the data in the common field must be made in the primary key field in the table on the *one* side of the relationship—you cannot change the data in the common field in the table on the *many* side of the relationship. To delete a record and all of its associated records in another table, you must delete the record in the table on the *one* side of the relationship. You can, however, delete a related record from the table on the *many* side of the relationship—the related record in the table on the *one* side of the relationship is not deleted.

Objective 3	**Sort Records in a Table**

GO! Learn How
Video A2-3

Sorting is the process of arranging data in a specific order based on the value in a field. For example, you can sort the names in your contact list alphabetically by each person's last name, or you can sort your music collection by the artist. As records are entered into an Access table, they display in the order in which they are added to the table. After you close the table and reopen it, the records display in order by the primary key field.

Activity 2.07 | **Sorting Records in a Table in Ascending or Descending Order**

2.3.2

In this Activity, you will determine the departments of the faculty in the Business Division by sorting the data. Data can be sorted in either *ascending order* or *descending order*. Ascending order sorts text alphabetically (A to Z) and sorts numbers from the lowest number to the highest number. Descending order sorts text in reverse alphabetical order (Z to A) and sorts numbers from the highest number to the lowest number.

1 ▶ **Open** ⟩ the **Navigation Pane**, open your **2A Instructors** table, and then **Close** ⟨ the **Navigation Pane**. Notice that the records in the table are sorted in ascending order by the **Instructor ID** field, which is the primary key field.

2 ▶ In the field names row, click the **Department arrow**, click **Sort A to Z**, and then compare your screen with Figure 2.13.

> To sort records in a table, click the arrow to the right of the field name in the column on which you want to sort, and then click the sort order. After a field is sorted, a small arrow in the field name box indicates the sort order. For the Department field, the small arrow points up, indicating an ascending sort, and on the ribbon, Ascending is selected.

> The records display in alphabetical order by the Department field. Because the department names are now grouped together, you can quickly scroll through the table to see the instructors for each department. The first record in the table has no data in the Department field because the *Instructor ID* of *9999999* is reserved for *Staff*, a designation that is used until a scheduled course has been assigned to a specific instructor.

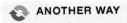 **ANOTHER WAY**   Click in the field in any record, and then on the Home tab, in the Sort & Filter group, click Ascending; or right-click in the field in any record, and then click Sort A to Z.

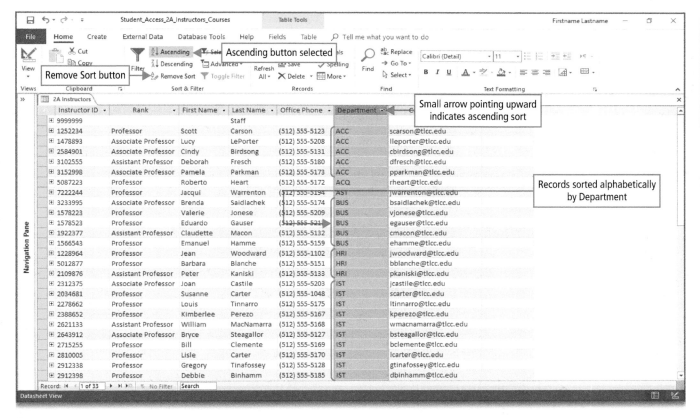

Figure 2.13

> **3** On the **Home tab**, in the **Sort & Filter group**, click **Remove Sort** to clear the sort and return the records to the default sort order, which is by the primary key field—*Instructor ID*.

> **4** Click the **Last Name arrow**, and then click **Sort Z to A**.

>> The records in the table are sorted by the Last Name field in reverse alphabetical order. The small arrow in the field name box points down, indicating a descending sort. On the ribbon, Descending is selected.

> **5** In the **Sort & Filter group**, click **Remove Sort** to clear the sort.

Activity 2.08 | Sorting Records in a Table on Multiple Fields

MOS
2.3.2

To sort a table on two or more fields, first identify the fields that will act as the ***outermost sort field*** and the ***innermost sort field***. The outermost sort field is the first level of sorting, and the innermost sort field is the second or final level of sorting. To alphabetize a table by Last Name and then First Name (also called First Name within Last Name), the Last Name field is identified as the outermost sort field. If there are duplicate last names, the records should be further sorted by the First Name field—the innermost sort field. For tables, you sort the innermost field first and then sort the outermost field.

In this Activity, you will sort the records by Last Name (innermost sort field) within the Department (outermost sort field).

> **1** In the **Last Name** field, click in any record. On the **Home tab**, in the **Sort & Filter group**, click **Ascending**.

>> The records are sorted in ascending order by Last Name—the innermost sort field.

2 Point anywhere in the **Department** field, right-click, and then click **Sort Z to A**. Compare your screen with Figure 2.14.

> The records are sorted in descending order first by Department—the outermost sort field. Within each Department grouping, the records are sorted in ascending order by Last Name—the innermost sort field. Records can be sorted on multiple fields using both ascending and descending order.

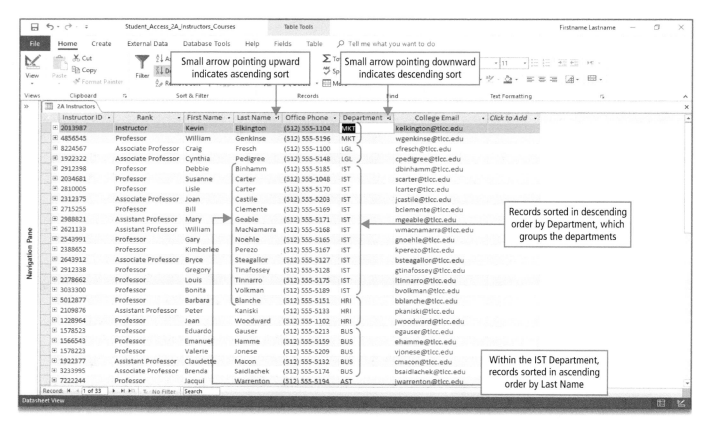

Figure 2.14

3 On the ribbon, click the **File tab**, click **Print**, and then click **Print Preview**. In the **Page Layout** group, click **Landscape**. In the **Zoom group**, click **Two Pages**, and notice that the table will print on two pages.

4 In the **Close Preview group**, click **Close Print Preview**. In the object window, **Close** ☒ the table. In the message box, click **Yes** to save the changes to the sort order.

> Tables are not always stored with the data sorted. In some cases, queries are created that sort the data, and then reports are created to display the sorted data.

Objective 4   Create a Query in Design View

GO! Learn How
Video A2-4

Recall that a select query is a database object that retrieves (selects) specific data from one or more tables and then displays the specified data in a table in Datasheet view. A query answers a question such as *Which instructors teach courses in the IST department?* Unless a query has already been designed to ask this question, you must create a new query.

Database users rarely need to see all of the records in all of the tables. That is why a query is so useful; it creates a **subset** of records—a portion of the total records—according to your specifications, and then displays only those records.

Activity 2.09 | Creating a New Select Query in Design View

MOS
3.1.1, 3.2.1

Previously, you created a query using the Query Wizard. To create queries with more control over the results that are displayed, use Query Design view. The table or tables from which a query selects its data is referred to as the *data source*.

1 On the ribbon, click the **Create tab**, and then in the **Queries group**, click **Query Design**. Compare your screen with Figure 2.15.

A new query opens in Design view, and the Show Table dialog box displays, which lists both tables in the database.

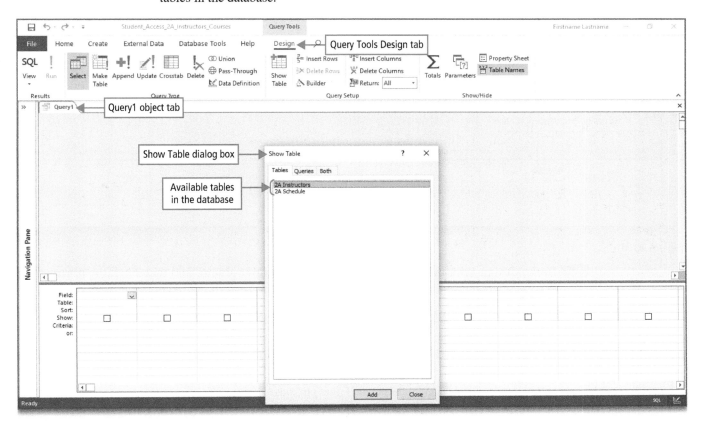

Figure 2.15

2 In the **Show Table** dialog box, double-click **2A Instructors**, and then, in the dialog box, click **Close**.

A field list for your 2A Instructors table displays in the upper area of the Query window. Instructor ID is the primary key field in this table. The Query window has two parts: the *table area* (upper area), which displays the field lists for tables that are used in the query, and the *design grid* (lower area), which displays the design of the query.

ALERT   Is there more than one field list in the table area?

If you double-click a table more than one time, a duplicate field list displays in the table area of the Query window. To remove a field list from the Query window, right-click the title bar of the field list, and then click Remove Table.

---

3 Point to the lower right corner of the field list to display the ⬚ pointer, and then, holding down the left mouse button, drag downward and to the right to resize the field list, displaying all of the field names and the entire table name. Release the mouse button. In the **2A Instructors** field list, double-click **Rank**, and then look at the design grid.

The Rank field name displays in the design grid in the Field row. You limit the fields that display in the query results by placing only the desired field names in the design grid.

4 In the **2A Instructors** field list, point to **First Name**, holding down the left mouse button, drag the field name down into the design grid until the pointer displays in the **Field** row in the second column, and then release the mouse button. Compare your screen with Figure 2.16.

This is a second way to add field names to the design grid. When you release the mouse button, the field name displays in the Field row.

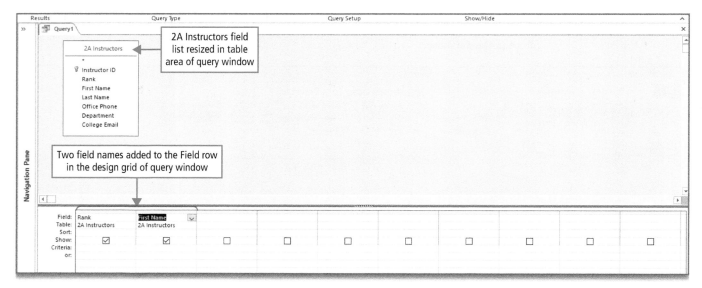

Figure 2.16

5 In the design grid, in the **Field** row, click in the third column, and then click the **arrow** that displays. From the list, click **Last Name** to add the field to the design grid.

This is a third way to add field names to the design grid.

6 Using one of the three techniques you just practiced, add the **Office Phone** field to the fourth column and the **Department** field to the fifth column in the design grid.

ALERT **Is there a duplicate field name or an incorrect field name in the design grid?**

If you double-click a field name more than one time, a duplicate field name displays in the design grid. To remove a duplicate field name, in the design grid, in the Field row, right-click the duplicate field name, and then click Cut. Use this same method to delete a field name that you placed in the design grid by mistake. As you progress in your study of query design, you will learn alternate ways to delete field names from the design grid.

Activity 2.10 | Running, Saving, and Closing a Query

MOS
3.1.1, 3.1.6, 3.1.7
Once a query is designed, you **run** it to display the results. When you run a query, Access looks at the records in the table (or tables) you have included in the query, finds the records that match the specified conditions (if any), and displays only those records in a datasheet. Only the fields that you have added to the design grid display in the query results. The query always runs using the current table or tables, presenting the most up-to-date information.

1 On the **Design tab**, in the **Results group**, click **Run**, and then compare your screen with Figure 2.17.

This query answers the question, *What is the rank, first name, last name, office phone number, and department of all of the instructors in the 2A Instructors table?* A query is a subgroup of the records in the table, arranged in Datasheet view, using the fields and conditions that you specify in the design grid. The five fields you specified in the design grid display in columns, and the records from the 2A Instructors table display in rows.

ANOTHER WAY On the Design tab, in the Results group, click the upper portion of the View button, which runs the query by switching to Datasheet view.

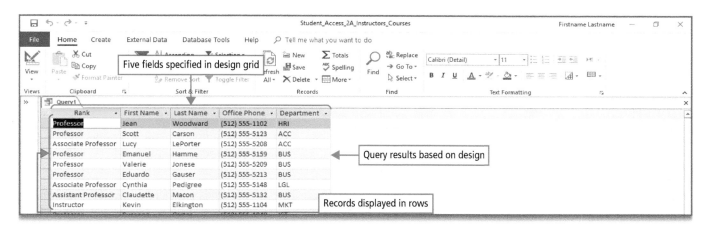

Figure 2.17

2 On the **Quick Access Toolbar**, click **Save** 🖫. In the **Save As** dialog box, type **2A Instructors Query** and then click **OK**.

The query name displays on the object tab in the object window. Save your queries if you are likely to ask the same question again; doing so will save you the effort of creating the query again to answer the same question—just run the query again.

3 Click the **File tab**, click **Print**, and then click **Print Preview**.

Queries answer questions and gather information from the data in tables. Typically, queries are created as a basis for a report, but query results can be printed like any table of data.

4 **Close** Print Preview. **Close** ☒ the query. **Open** ⏩ the **Navigation** Pane. At the top of the **Navigation Pane**, click **More** 🔘. On the list, under **Navigate To Category**, click **Tables and Related Views**. Notice that your **2A Instructors Query** object displays under your **2A Instructors** table object.

The new query name displays in the Navigation Pane under the table with which it is related—the 2A Instructors table, which is the data source. Only the design of the query is saved; the records reside in the table object. Each time you open a query, Access runs it and displays the results based on the data stored in the data source. Thus, the results of the query always reflect the most up-to-date information.

Objective 5 | Create a New Query From an Existing Query

GO! Learn How
Video A2-5

You can create a new query from scratch or you can open an existing query, save it with a new name, and modify the design to answer another question. Using an existing query saves you time if your new query uses all or some of the same fields and conditions in an existing query.

Activity 2.11 | Copying an Existing Query

1 In the **Navigation Pane**, right-click your **2A Instructors Query**, and then click **Copy**.

2 In the **Navigation Pane**, point to a blank area, right-click, and then click Paste.

The Paste As dialog box displays, which enables you to name the copied query.

ANOTHER WAY To create a copy of the query, in the Navigation Pane, click the query name to select it. On the Home tab, in the Clipboard group, click Copy. On the Home tab, in the Clipboard group, click the upper portion of the Paste button.

3 In the **Paste As** dialog box, type **2A Instructor IDs Query** and then click **OK**.

A new query, based on a copy of your 2A Instructors Query, is created and displays in the object window and in the Navigation Pane under its data source—your 2A Instructors table.

> **MORE KNOWLEDGE** **Rename a Query**
>
> If the query name is not correct, you can rename it as long as the query is closed. In the Navigation Pane, right-click the query name, and then click Rename. Edit the current name or type a new name, and then press Enter to accept the change.

4 In the **Navigation Pane**, double-click your **2A Instructor IDs Query** to run the query and display the query results in **Datasheet** view. **Close** « the **Navigation Pane**.

ANOTHER WAY To create a copy of a query using a new name, click the File tab, and then click Save As. Under Save As, double-click Save Object As. In the Save As dialog box, click in the Name box and type the name of the new query.

Activity 2.12 | Modifying the Design of a Query

1 On the **Home tab**, in the **Views group**, click **View** to switch to **Design** view.

ANOTHER WAY On the Home tab, in the Views group, click the View arrow, and then click Design View; or on the right side of the status bar, click the Design View button.

2 In the design grid, point to the thin gray selection bar above the **Office Phone** field name to display the ↓ pointer, and then compare your screen with Figure 2.18.

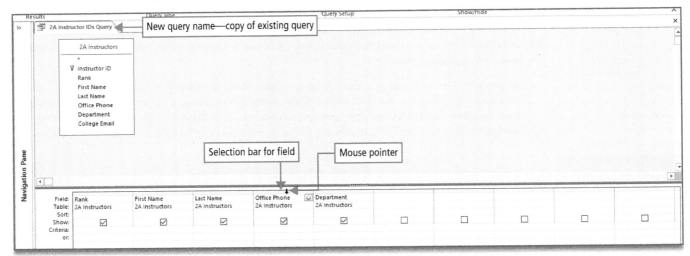

Figure 2.18

3 With the ⬇ pointer displayed in the selection bar above the **Office Phone** field name, click to select the column, and then press Del.

> This action deletes the field from the query design only—it has no effect on the field in the data source—2A Instructors table. The Department field moves to the left. Similarly, by using the selection bar, you can drag to select multiple fields and delete them at one time.

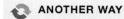 **ANOTHER WAY** In the design grid, click in the field name. On the Design tab, in the Query Setup group, click Delete Columns; or right-click the field name, and then click Cut; or click in the field name, and on the Home tab, in the Records group, click Delete.

4 Point to the selection bar above the **First Name** column, and then click to select the column. In the selected column, point to the selection bar to display the ⬉ pointer, and then drag to the right until a dark vertical line displays on the right side of the **Last Name** column. Release the mouse button to position the **First Name** field in the third column.

> To rearrange fields in a query, first select the field to move, and then drag it to a new position in the design grid.

5 Using the technique you just practiced, move the **Department** field to the left of the **Rank** field.

6 From the field list, drag the **Instructor ID** field down to the first column in the design grid until the ⬚ pointer displays, and then release the mouse button. Compare your screen with Figure 2.19.

> The Instructor ID field displays in the first column, and the remaining four fields move to the right. Use this method to insert a field to the left of a field already displayed in the design grid.

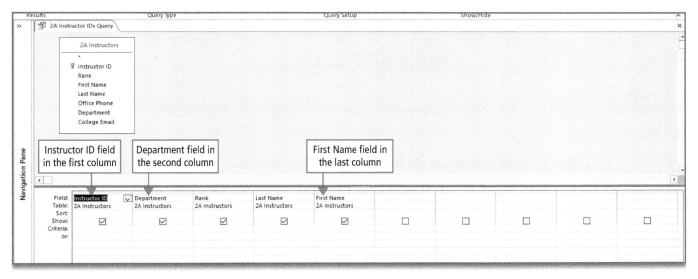

Figure 2.19

7 On the **Design tab**, in the **Results group**, click **Run**.

> This query answers the question, *What is the instructor ID, department, rank, last name, and first name of every instructor in the 2A Instructors table?* The results of the query are a subgroup of the records stored in the 2A Instructors table. The records are sorted by the table's primary key field—Instructor ID.

8 **Close** ⨯ the query. In the message box, click **Yes** to save the changes to the query design—deleting a field, moving two fields, and adding a field. **Open** » the **Navigation Pane**.

> The query is saved and closed, and the query name displays in the Navigation Pane under the related table. Recall that only the *design* of the query is saved; the records reside in the related table or tables.

Objective 6 Sort Query Results

GO! Learn How
Video A2-6

You can sort the results of a query in ascending or descending order in either Datasheet view or Design view. Use Design view if your query results should always display in a specified sort order, or if you intend to use the sorted results in a report.

Activity 2.13 | Sorting Query Results

3.2.2, 3.1.7, 3.1.6

In this Activity, you will save an existing query with a new name, and then sort the query results by using the Sort row in Design view.

1 ▶ In the **Navigation Pane**, right-click your **2A Instructor IDs Query**, and then click **Copy**. In the **Navigation Pane**, point to a blank area, right-click, and then click **Paste**.

2 ▶ In the **Paste As** dialog box, type **2A Department Sort Query** and then click **OK**.

A new query is created based on a copy of your 2A Instructor IDs Query; that is, the new query includes the same fields in the same order as the query on which it is based. The query does not need to be open to save it with another name; you can select the object name in the Navigation Pane.

3 ▶ In the **Navigation Pane**, right-click your **2A Department Sort Query**, and then click **Design View**. **Close** « the **Navigation Pane**.

Use this technique to display the query in Design view if you are redesigning the query. Recall that if you double-click a query name in the Navigation Pane, Access runs the query and displays the query results in Datasheet view.

4 ▶ In the design grid, in the **Sort** row, under **Last Name**, click to display the insertion point and an arrow. Click the **arrow**, click **Ascending**, and then compare your screen with Figure 2.20.

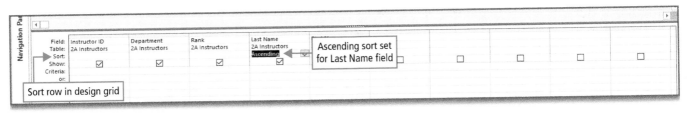

Figure 2.20

5 ▶ On the **Design tab**, in the **Results group**, click **Run**.

In the query results, the records are sorted in ascending order by the Last Name field, and two instructors have the same last name of *Carter—Susanne* and *Lisle*.

6 ▶ On the **Home tab**, in the **Views group**, click the upper portion of the **View** button to switch to **Design** view.

7 ▶ In the design grid, click in the **Sort** row under **First Name**, click the **arrow**, and then click **Ascending**. **Run** the query.

In the query results, the records are sorted first by the Last Name field. If two instructors have the same last name, then those records are sorted by the First Name field. The two instructors with the same last name of *Carter* are sorted by their first names, and the two records with the same last name of *Fresch* are sorted by their first names.

8 ▶ Switch to **Design** view. In the design grid, click in the **Sort** row under **Department**, click the **arrow**, and then click **Descending**. **Run** the query, and then compare your screen with Figure 2.21.

In Design view, fields with a Sort setting are sorted from left to right. That is, the sorted field on the left becomes the outermost sort field, and the sorted field on the right becomes the innermost sort field. Thus, the records in this query are sorted first in descending order by the Department field—the leftmost sort field. Then, within each department, the records are sorted in ascending order by the Last Name field. And, finally, within each duplicate last name, the records are sorted in ascending order by the First Name field.

If you run a query and the sorted results are not what you intended, be sure the fields are displayed from left to right according to the groupings that you desire.

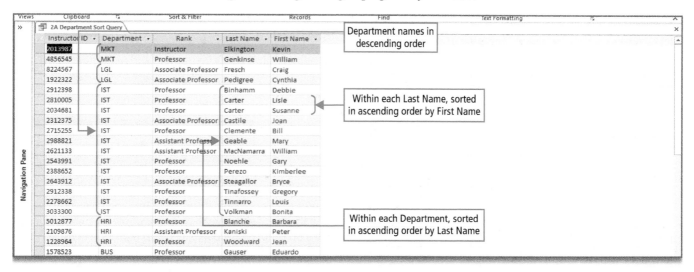

Figure 2.21

9 ▶ **Close** ☒ the query. In the message box, click **Yes** to save the changes to the query design.

MORE KNOWLEDGE **Sorting in Design View or Datasheet View**

If you add a sort order to the *design* of a query, it remains as a permanent part of the query design. If you use the sort buttons in Datasheet view, the sort order will override the sort order of the query design and can be saved as part of the query.

A sort order designated in Datasheet view does not display in the Sort row of the query design grid. As with sorting tables, in Datasheet view, a small arrow displays to the right of the field name to indicate the sort order of the field.

Objective 7 **Specify Criteria in a Query**

GO! Learn How
Video A2-7

Queries locate information in a table based on ***criteria*** that you specify as part of the query design. Criteria are conditions that identify the specific records for which you are looking. Criteria enable you to ask a more specific question; therefore, you will get a more specific result. For example, to find out how many instructors are in the IST department, limit the results to display only that specific department by entering criteria in the design grid.

Activity 2.14 | **Specifying Text Criteria in a Query**

MOS
3.1.1, 3.2.1, 3.2.3,
3.1.6, 3.1.7

In this Activity, you will assist Dean Judkins by creating a query to answer the question, *Which instructors are in the IST Department?*

1 ▶ On the ribbon, click the **Create tab**, and then in the **Queries group**, click **Query Design**.

2 In the **Show Table** dialog box, double-click your **2A Instructors** table to add it to the table area, and then **Close** the **Show Table** dialog box.

3 By dragging the lower right corner, resize the field list to display all of the field names and the table name. Add the following fields to the design grid in the order given: **Department**, **Instructor ID**, **Rank**, **First Name**, and **Last Name**.

4 In the design grid, click in the **Criteria** row under **Department**, type **IST** and then press Enter. Compare your screen with Figure 2.22.

Access places quotation marks around the criteria to indicate that this is a ***text string***—a sequence of characters. Use the Criteria row to specify the criteria that will limit the results of the query to your exact specifications. The criteria is not case sensitive; you can type *ist* instead of *IST*.

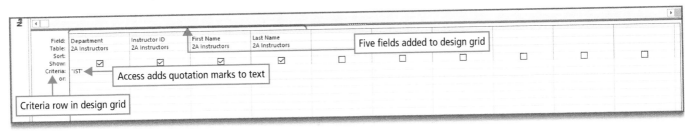

Figure 2.22

5 **Run** the query, and then compare your screen with Figure 2.23.

Thirteen records display. There are 13 instructors in the IST Department; or, more specifically, there are 13 records that have *IST* in the Department field.

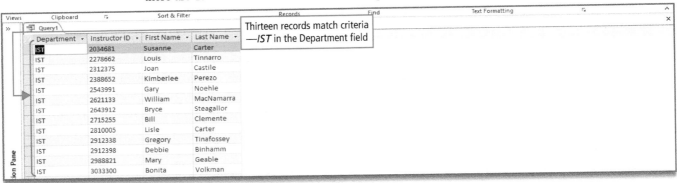

Figure 2.23

6 **Save** 💾 the query as **2A IST Query**

7 **Close** ✕ the query, **Open** » the **Navigation Pane**, and then notice your **2A IST Query** object.

Recall that in the Navigation Pane, queries display an icon of two overlapping datasheets.

Activity 2.15 | Specifying Criteria and Hiding the Field in the Query Results

So far, all of the fields that you included in the query design have also been included in the query results. There are times when you need to use the field in the query design, but you do not need to display that field in the results—usually, when the data in the field is the same for all of the records. In this Activity, you will create a query to answer the question, *Which instructors have a rank of Professor?*

1 **Close** « the **Navigation Pane.** On the **Create tab**, in the **Queries group**, click **Query Design**.

2 In the **Show Table** dialog box, double-click your **2A Instructors** table to add it to the table area, and then **Close** the **Show Table** dialog box.

3 Resize the field list, and then add the following fields to the design grid in the order given: **Instructor ID**, **First Name**, **Last Name**, and **Rank**.

4 Click in the **Sort** row under **Last Name**, click the **arrow**, and then click **Ascending**.

5 Click in the **Criteria** row under **Rank**, type **professor** and then press Enter. Compare your screen with Figure 2.24.

> Recall that criteria is not case sensitive. As you start typing *professor*, a list of functions displays, from which you can select if a function is included in your criteria. After pressing Enter, the insertion point moves to the next criteria box, and quotation marks are added around the text string that you entered.

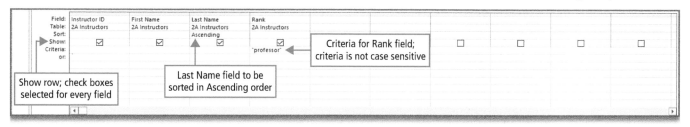

Figure 2.24

6 In the design grid, in the **Show** row, notice that a check box is selected for every field. **Run** the query.

> Eighteen records meet the criteria—*professor* in the *Rank* field. In the Rank column, every record displays *Professor*, and the records are sorted in ascending order by the Last Name field.

7 Switch to **Design** view. In the design grid, in the **Show** row under **Rank**, click to clear the check box.

> Because it is repetitive and not particularly useful to display *Professor* for every record in the query results, clear the Show check box so that the field is hidden or does not display. You should, however, always run the query first before clearing the Show check box to be sure that the correct records display.

8 **Run** the query, and then notice that the *Rank* field does not display even though it was used to specify criteria in the query.

> The same 18 records display, but the *Rank* field is hidden from the query results. Although the Rank field is included in the query design so that you could specify the criteria of *professor*, it is not necessary to display the field in the results. When appropriate, clear the Show check box to avoid cluttering the query results with data that is not useful.

9 **Save** 🖫 the query as 2A Professors Query **Close** ✕ the query.

Activity 2.16 | Using *Is Null* Criteria to Find Empty Fields

MOS
3.1.1, 3.2.1,
3.2.2, 3.2.3,
3.1.6, 3.1.7, 3.2.3

Sometimes you must locate records where data is missing. You can locate such records by using *Is Null* as the criteria in a field. *Is Null* is used to find empty fields. Additionally, you can display only the records where data has been entered in the field by using the criteria of *Is Not Null*, which excludes records where the specified field is empty. In this Activity, you will design a query to answer the question, *Which scheduled courses have no credits listed?*

1 On the **Create tab**, in the **Queries group**, click **Query Design**. In the **Show Table** dialog box, double-click your **2A Schedule** table to add it to the table area, and then **Close** the **Show Table** dialog box.

2 Resize the field list, and then add the following fields to the design grid in the order given: **Subject**, **Catalog#**, **Section**, **Course Name**, and **Credits**.

3 Click in the **Criteria** row under **Credits**, type **is null** and then press Enter.

Access capitalizes *is null*. The criteria *Is Null* examines the Credits field and locates records that do *not* have data entered in the field.

4 Click in the **Sort** row under **Subject**, click the **arrow**, and then click **Ascending**. **Sort** the **Catalog#** field in **Ascending** order, and then **Sort** the **Section** field in **Ascending** order. Compare your screen with Figure 2.25.

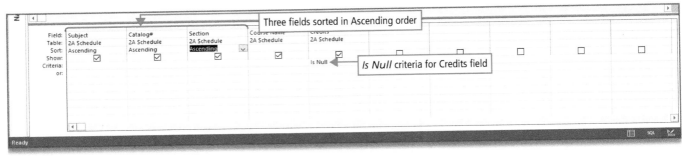

Figure 2.25

5 **Run** the query, and then compare your screen with Figure 2.26.

Four scheduled courses do not have credits listed—the Credits field is empty. The records are sorted in ascending order first by the Subject field, then by the Catalog# field, and then by the Section field. Using the information displayed in the query results, a course scheduler can more easily locate the records in the table and enter the credits for these courses.

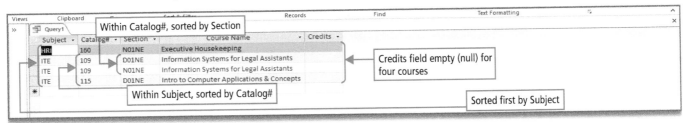

Figure 2.26

6 **Save** the query as **2A No Credits Query**

7 **Close** the query. **Open** the **Navigation Pane**, and then notice that your **2A No Credits Query** object displays under your **2A Schedule** table object, its data source. At the top of the **Navigation Pane**, click **More**. On the list, under **Navigate To Category**, click **Object Type**. Notice that the queries are now grouped together.

8 **Close** the database and **Close** Access.

For Non-MyLab Submissions: Determine What Your Instructor Requires for Submission
As directed by your instructor, submit your completed database file.

9 In **MyLab IT**, locate and click the Grader Project **Access 2A Instructors and Courses**. In **step 3**, under **Upload Completed Assignment**, click **Choose File**. In the **Open** dialog box, navigate to your **Access Chapter 2 folder**, and then click your **Student_Access_2A_Instructors_Courses** file one time to select it. In the lower right corner of the **Open** dialog box, click **Open**.

The name of your selected file displays above the Upload button.

10 To submit your file to **MyLab IT** for grading, click **Upload**, wait a moment for a green **Success!** message, and then in **step 4**, click the blue **Submit for Grading** button. Click **Close Assignment** to return to your list of **Course Materials**.

You have completed Project 2A | **END**

»» GO! With Google

Objective	Export a Relationship Report to a PDF File, Save the PDF File to Google Drive, and then Share the File

Access web apps are designed to work with Microsoft's SharePoint, a service for setting up websites to share and manage documents. Your college may not have SharePoint installed, so you will use other tools to share objects from your database so that you can work collaboratively with others. Recall that Google Drive is Google's free, web-based word processor, spreadsheet, slide show, form, and data storage and sharing service. For Access, you can export a database object to an Excel worksheet, a PDF file, or a text file, and then save the file to Google Drive.

ALERT   **Working with Web-Based Applications and Services**

Computer programs and services on the web receive continuous updates and improvements, so the steps to complete this web-based Activity may differ from the ones shown. You can often look at the screens and the information presented to determine how to complete the Activity.

If you do not already have a Google account, you will need to create one before you begin this Activity. Go to **http://google.com** and in the upper right corner, click **Sign In**. On the Sign In screen, click **Create Account**. On the Create your Google Account page, complete the form, read and agree to the Terms of Service and Privacy Policy, and then click **Next step**. On the Welcome screen, click **Get Started**.

Activity | Exporting a Relationship Report to a PDF File, Saving the PDF file to Google Drive, and Sharing the File

In this Activity, you will export your Relationships Report object to a PDF file, upload your PDF file to Google Drive, and then share the file.

1 Start Access, navigate to your **Access Chapter 2** folder, and then open your **2A_Instructors_Courses** database file. On the **Message Bar**, click **Enable Content**. In the **Navigation Pane**, click your **Relationships for 2A_Instructors_Courses** object to select it.

2 On the ribbon, click the **External Data tab**, and then in the **Export group**, click **PDF or XPS**. In the **Publish as PDF or XPS** dialog box, navigate to your **Access Chapter 2** folder. In the **Publish as PDF or XPS** dialog box, click in the **File name** box, and then using your own name, type **Lastname_Firstname_AC_2A_Web** and be sure that the **Open file after publishing** check box is selected and the **Minimum size (publishing online)** option button is selected. Click **Publish**.

The PDF file is created and opens in your browser, Adobe Reader, or Adobe Acrobat, depending on the software that is installed on your computer.

3 If necessary, close the view of the PDF file. In the **Export – PDF** dialog box, click **Close**, and then **Close** ⌧ Access.

4 From the desktop, open your browser, navigate to **http://google.com**, and then sign in to your Google account. Click the **Google Apps** menu ⊞, and then click **Drive** ☁. Open your **GO! Web Projects** folder—or click New to create and then open this folder if necessary.

5 On the left, click **New**, click **File upload**. In the **Open** dialog box, navigate to your **Access Chapter 2** folder, and then double-click your **Lastname_Firstname_AC_2A_Web** file to upload it to Google Drive. When the title bar of the message box indicates *1 upload complete*, **Close** the message box. A second message box may display t emporarily.

6 In the file list, click your **Lastname_Firstname_AC_2A_Web** PDF file one time to select it.

7 Right-click the file name. On the shortcut menu, click **Share**.

8 In the **Share with others** dialog box, with your insertion point blinking in the **Enter names or email addresses** box, type the email address that you use at your college. To the right of the email address, click **Edit files directly** ✏, and click **Can comment.** Click in the **Add a note** box, and then type **This relationship report identifies tables that can be used together to create other objects in the database.** Compare your screen with Figure A.

If you upload a table that you exported as an Excel spreadsheet or Word document and that you want to enable others to add records, be sure that you set the Sharing permission to *Can edit.*

9 Start the **Snipping Tool.** In the **Snipping Tool** dialog box, click the **New arrow,** and then click **Full-screen Snip.**

10 On the **Snipping Tool** toolbar, click the **Save Snip** button 💾. In the **Save As** dialog box, navigate to your **Access Chapter 2** folder. Click in the **File name** box, type **Lastname_Firstname_AC_2A_Web_Snip** be sure that the **Save as type** box displays **JPEG file,** and then click **Save. Close** ⊠ the **Snipping Tool** window.

11 In the **Share with others** dialog box, click **Send.**

If your college is not using Google accounts, you may have to confirm sending the message with a link.

12 In Google Drive, click your Google Drive name, and then click **Sign out. Close** your browser window.

13 If directed to submit a paper printout of your PDF and snip file, follow the directions given in the Note below. As directed by your instructor, submit your pdf file and your snip file that are the results of this project. Your instructor may also request that you submit a copy of the email that was sent to you notifying you of the shared file.

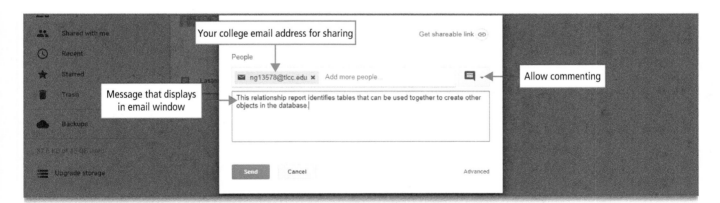

Figure A

NOTE   Printing your PDF and Snip .JPG File

Using File Explorer, navigate to your Access Chapter 2 folder. Locate and double-click your AC_2A_Web file. On the toolbar, click the Print file button. Then Close your default PDF reader. In your Access Chapter 2 folder, locate and double-click your AC_2A_Web_Snip file. If this is the first time you have tried to open a .jpg file, you will be asked to identify a program. If you are not sure which program to use, select Paint or Windows Photo Viewer. From the ribbon, menu bar, or toolbar, click the Print command, and then Close the program window.

PROJECT 2B
Athletic Scholarships Database

Project Activities

In Activities 2.17 through 2.32, you will assist Roberto Garza, Athletic Director for Texas Lakes Community College, in creating queries to locate information about athletic scholarships that have awarded to students. Your completed Navigation Pane will look similar to Figure 2.27.

Project Files for MyLab IT Grader

1. In your **MyLab IT** course, locate and click **Access 2B Athletes and Scholarships**, Download Materials, and then Download All Files.
2. Extract the zipped folder to your Access Chapter 2 folder. Close the Grader download screens.
3. Take a moment to open the downloaded **Access 2B_Athletes_Scholarships_Instructions**; note any recent updates to the book.

Project Results

GO! Project 2B
Where We're Going

Figure 2.27 Project 2B Athletic Scholarships

For Non-MyLab Submissions

For Project 2B, you will need:
a02B_Athletes_Scholarships
a02B_Athletes (Excel workbook)

Start with an Access Data File

In your Access Chapter 2 folder, save your database as:
Lastname_Firstname_2B_Athletes_Scholarships

After you have saved your database, launch Access and open the database. On the next page, begin with Step 2.

GO! Learn How
Video A2-8

Criteria can be set for fields containing numeric data. When you design your table, set the appropriate data type for fields that will contain numbers, currency, or dates so that mathematical calculations can be performed.

Activity 2.17 | Opening an Existing Database and Importing a Spreadsheet as a New Table

MOS
1.1.1, 1.2.3, 2.4.5

In this Activity, you will import an Excel spreadsheet as a new table in the database.

1 Start Access. In the Access opening screen, click **Open Other Files**. Navigate to your **Access Chapter 2 folder**, and then double-click the Access file that you downloaded from **MyLab IT** that displays your name—**Student_Access_2B_Athletes_Scholarships**.

2 On the **Message Bar**, click **Enable Content**. Double-click the **2B Scholarships Awarded** table to open it in **Datasheet** view. **Close** [«] the **Navigation Pane**, and then examine the data in the table. Compare your screen with Figure 2.28.

In this table, Mr. Garza tracks the names and amounts of scholarships awarded to student athletes. Students are identified only by their Student ID numbers, and the primary key is the Scholarship ID field.

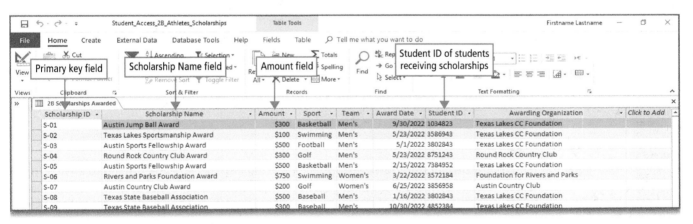

Figure 2.28

3 **Close** [×] the table. On the ribbon, click the **External Data tab**. In the **Import & Link group**, click the **New Data Source** arrow, point to **From File**, and then click **Excel**. In the **Get External Data – Excel Spreadsheet** dialog box, to the right of the **File name** box, click **Browse**.

4 In the **File Open** dialog box, navigate to your student data files, and then double-click **a02B_Athletes**. Be sure that the **Import the source data into a new table in the current database** option button is selected, and then click **OK**.

The Import Spreadsheet Wizard opens and displays the spreadsheet data.

5 In the upper left area of the wizard, select the **First Row Contains Column Headings** check box. In the wizard, click **Next**, and then click **Next** again.

6 In the wizard, click the **Choose my own primary key** option button, and then verify that **Student ID** displays in the box.

In the new table, Student ID will be designated as the primary key. No two students have the same Student ID.

7 Click **Next**. With the text selected in the **Import to Table** box, type **2B Athletes** and then click **Finish**. In the **Get External Data – Excel Spreadsheet** dialog box, click **Close**.

8 **Open** ▸ the **Navigation Pane**. In the **Navigation Pane**, right-click your **2B Athletes** table, and then click **Design View**. **Close** ◂ the **Navigation Pane**.

9 To the right of **Student ID**, click in the **Data Type** box, click the **arrow**, and then click **Short Text**. For the **Postal Code** field, change the **Data Type** to **Short Text**, and in the **Field Properties** area, click **Field Size**, type **5** and then press Enter. In the **Field Name** column, click **State**, set the **Field Size** to **2** and then press Enter. Compare your screen with Figure 2.29.

Recall that numeric data that does not represent a quantity and is not used in a calculation, such as the Student ID and Postal Code, should be assigned a data type of Short Text.

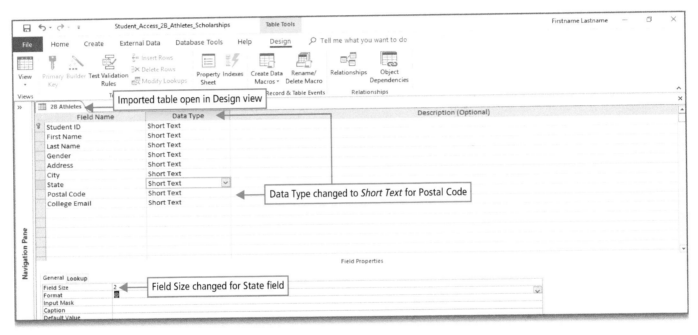

Figure 2.29

10 On the **Design tab**, in the **Views group**, click the top half of the **View button** to switch to **Datasheet** view. In the message box, click **Yes** to save the table. In the second message box, click **Yes**—no data will be lost. Take a moment to examine the data in the imported table.

11 In the datasheet, to the left of the **Student ID** field name, click the **Select All** ☐ button. On the **Home tab**, in the **Records group**, click **More**, and then click **Field Width**. In the **Column Width** dialog box, click **Best Fit**. Click in any record to cancel the selection, **Save** ☐ the layout changes to the table, and then **Close** × the table.

Activity 2.18 | Creating a One-to-Many Table Relationship

MOS
1.2.1, 1.2.2,
1.2.4, 1.2.5

In this Activity, you will create a one-to-many relationship between your 2B Athletes table and your 2B Scholarships Awarded table by using the common field—*Student ID*.

1 Click the **Database Tools tab**, and then in the **Relationships group**, click **Relationships**.

2 In the **Show Table** dialog box, double-click your **2B Athletes** table, and then double-click your **2B Scholarships Awarded** table to add both tables to the **Relationships** window. **Close** the **Show Table** dialog box.

3 Point to the title bar of the field list on the right, and then drag the field list to the right until there is approximately one inch of space between the field lists. By dragging the lower right corner of the field list, resize each field list to display all of the field names and the entire table name.

Repositioning and resizing the field lists are not required but doing so makes it easier for you to view the field names and the join line when creating relationships.

4 In the **2B Athletes** field list, point to **Student ID**, and then, holding down the left mouse button, drag the field name into the **2B Scholarships Awarded** field list on top of **Student ID**. Release the mouse button to display the **Edit Relationships** dialog box.

5 Point to the title bar of the **Edit Relationships** dialog box, and then drag it to the right of the two field lists. In the **Edit Relationships** dialog box, verify that **Student ID** displays as the common field for both tables.

Repositioning the Edit Relationships dialog box is not required but doing so enables you to see the field lists. The Relationship Type is *One-To-Many*—one athlete can have *many* scholarships. The common field in both tables is the *Student ID* field. In the 2B Athletes table, Student ID is the primary key. In the 2B Scholarships Awarded table, Student ID is the foreign key.

6 In the **Edit Relationships** dialog box, click to select the **Enforce Referential Integrity** check box, the **Cascade Update Related Fields** check box, and the **Cascade Delete Related Records** check box. Click **Create**, and then compare your screen with Figure 2.30.

The one-to-many relationship is established. The *1* and ∞ symbols indicate that referential integrity is enforced, which ensures that a scholarship cannot be awarded to a student whose Student ID is not included in the 2B Athletes table. Recall that the Cascade options enable you to update and delete records automatically on the *many* side of the relationship when changes are made in the table on the *one* side of the relationship.

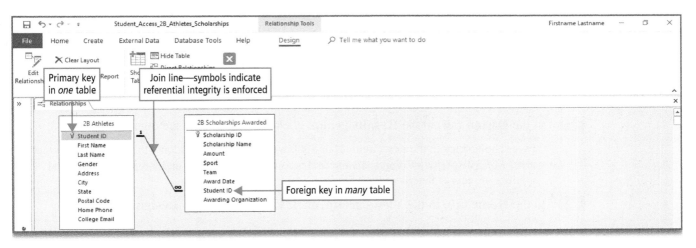

Figure 2.30

7 On the **Design tab**, in the **Tools group**, click **Relationship Report**. On the **Print Preview tab**, in the **Page Size group**, click **Margins**, and then click **Normal. Save** 🖫 the report as **2B Relationships**

8 In the object window, right-click either **object tab**, and then click **Close All** to close the Relationships Report and the Relationships window.

9 **Open** ⟫ the **Navigation Pane**, double-click your **2B Athletes** table to open it, and then **Close** ⟪ the **Navigation Pane**. On the left side of the first record, click **+** (plus sign) to display the subdatasheet for the record.

In the first record, for *Joel Barthmaier*, one related record exists in the 2B Scholarships Awarded table. Joel has been awarded the *Austin Jump Ball Award* in the amount of *$300*. The subdatasheet displays because you created a relationship between the two tables using Student ID as the common field.

10 Close ⊠ the **2B Athletes** table.

When you close the table, the subdatasheet will collapse—you do not need to click – (minus sign) before closing a table.

Activity 2.19 | Specifying Numeric Criteria in a Query

MOS
3.1.1, 3.2.1, 3.2.2, 3.2.3, 3.1.7

In this Activity, you will create a query to answer the question regarding scholarships awarded, *Which scholarships are in the amount of $300, and for which sports?*

1 Click the **Create tab**. In the **Queries group**, click **Query Design**.

2 In the **Show Table** dialog box, double-click your **2B Scholarships Awarded** table to add it to the table area, and then **Close** the **Show Table** dialog box. Resize the field list to display all of the fields and the entire table name.

3 Add the following fields to the design grid in the order given: **Scholarship Name**, **Sport**, and **Amount**.

4 Click in the **Sort** row under **Sport**, click the **arrow**, and then click **Ascending**.

5 Click in the **Criteria** row under **Amount**, type **300** and then press Enter. Compare your screen with Figure 2.31.

When you enter currency values as criteria, do not type the dollar sign. Include a decimal point only if you are looking for a specific amount that includes cents; for example, 300.49. Access does not insert quotation marks around the criteria because the data type of the field is Currency, which is a numeric format.

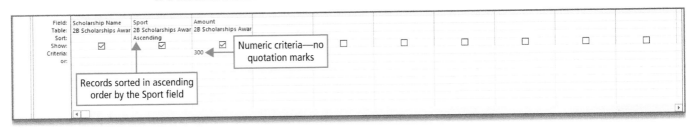

Figure 2.31

6 On the **Design tab**, in the **Results group**, click **Run** to display the query results.

Five scholarships in the exact amount of $300 were awarded to student athletes. In the navigation area, *1 of 5* displays—1 represents the first record that is selected, and 5 represents the total number of records that meet the criteria.

7 On the **Home tab**, in the **Views group**, click **View** to switch to **Design** view.

Activity 2.20 | Using Comparison Operators in Criteria

MOS
3.1.6, 3.2.3

Comparison operators are symbols that are used to evaluate data in the field to determine whether it is the same (=), greater than (>), less than (<), or in between a range of values as specified by the criteria. If no comparison operator is specified, equal (=) is assumed. For example, in the previous Activity, you created a query to display only those records where the *Amount* is *300*. The comparison operator of = was assumed, and the query results displayed only those records that had values in the Amount field equal to 300.

1 In the design grid, in the **Criteria** row under **Amount**, select the existing criteria—*300*— and then type **>300** and press Enter. **Run** the query.

Fourteen records display, and each has a value *greater than* $300 in the Amount field; there are no records for which the Amount is *equal to* $300.

2 Switch to **Design** view. In the **Criteria** row under **Amount**, select the existing criteria—*>300*. Type **<300** and then press Enter. **Run** the query.

Eleven records display, and each has a value *less than* $300 in the Amount field; there are no records for which the Amount is *equal to* $300.

3 Switch to **Design** view. In the **Criteria** row under **Amount**, select the existing criteria–*<300*. Type **>=300** and then press Enter. **Run** the query, and then compare your screen with Figure 2.32.

Nineteen records display, including the records for scholarships in the exact amount of $300. The records include scholarships *greater than* or *equal to* $300. In this manner, comparison operators can be combined. This query answers the question, *Which scholarships have been awarded in the amount of $300 or more, and for which sports, arranged alphabetically by sport?*

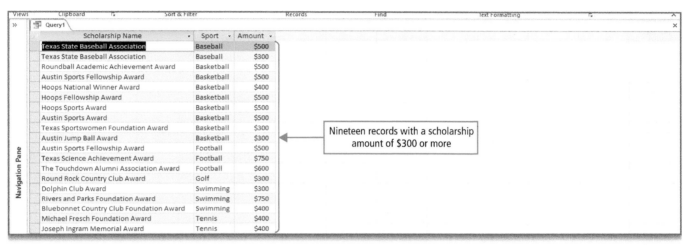

Figure 2.32

4 Save 🖫 the query as **2B $300 or More Query** and then display the query results in **Print Preview**.

5 Click **Close Print Preview**. **Close** ⊠ the query. **Open** ⏵⏵ the **Navigation Pane**, and notice that this new query displays under *2B Scholarships Awarded*, its data source.

Activity 2.21 | **Using the Between . . . And Comparison Operator**

3.1.6, 3.1.7, 3.2.3

The ***Between . . . And operator*** is a comparison operator that looks for values within a range. It is useful when you need to locate records that are within a range of dates; for example, scholarships awarded between May 1 and June 30.

In this Activity, you will create a new query from an existing query, and then add criteria to look for values within a range of dates. The query will answer the question, *Which scholarships were awarded between May 1 and June 30?*

1 In the **Navigation Pane**, click your **2B $300 or More Query** object to select it. On the **Home tab**, in the **Clipboard** group, click **Copy**. In the **Navigation Pane**, point to a blank area, right-click, and then click **Paste**.

2 In the **Paste As** dialog box, type **2B Awards May-June Query** and then click **OK**.

A new query, based on a copy of your 2B $300 or More Query, is created and displays in the Navigation Pane under its data source—your 2B Scholarships Awarded table.

3 In the **Navigation Pane**, right-click your **2B Awards May-June Query**, click **Design View**, and then **Close** ⏴⏴ the **Navigation Pane**.

4 In the **2B Scholarships Awarded** field list, double-click **Award Date** to add it to the fourth column in the design grid.

5 > In the **Criteria** row under **Amount**, select the existing criteria—>=*300*—and then press ⌈Del⌋ so that the query is not restricted by a monetary value.

6 > Click in the **Criteria** row under **Award Date**, type **between 5/1/22 and 6/30/22** and then press ⌈Enter⌋.

7 > In the selection bar of the design grid, point to the right edge of the **Award Date** column to display the ⊞ pointer, and then double-click to apply Best Fit to this column. Compare your screen with Figure 2.33.

> The width of the Award Date column is increased to fit the longest entry in the column, which enables you to see all of the criteria. Access places pound signs (#) around the dates and capitalizes *between* and *and*. This criteria instructs Access to look for values in the Award Date field that begin with 5/1/22 and end with 6/30/22. Both the beginning and ending dates will be included in the query results.

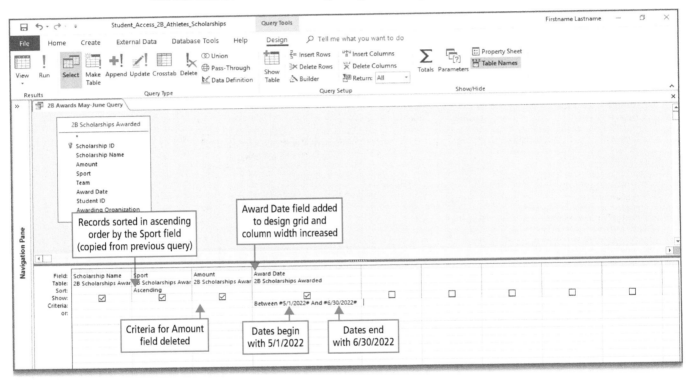

Figure 2.33

8 > **Run** the query, and notice that eight scholarships were awarded between 5/1/2022 and 6/30/2022.

9 > **Close** ⌈×⌋ the query, and in the message box, click **Yes** to save the changes to the query design.

Objective 9 | Use Compound Criteria in a Query

GO! Learn How
Video A2-9

You can specify more than one condition—criteria—in a query; this is called *compound criteria*. Compound criteria use AND and OR *logical operators*. Logical operators enable you to enter multiple criteria for the same field or for different fields.

Activity 2.22 | Using AND Criteria in a Query

MOS
3.1.1, 3.2.1,
3.2.3, 3.1.6, 3.1.7

The *AND condition* is an example of a compound criteria used to display records that match all parts of the specified criteria. In this Activity, you will help Mr. Garza answer the question, *Which scholarships over $500 were awarded for football?*

1 > Click the **Create tab**, and in the **Queries group**, click **Query Design**. In the **Show Table** dialog box, double-click your **2B Scholarships Awarded** table to add it to the table area, and then **Close** the **Show Table** dialog box. Resize the field list to display all of the fields and the table name.

2 Add the following fields to the design grid in the order given: **Scholarship Name**, **Sport**, and **Amount**.

3 Click in the **Criteria** row under **Sport**, type **football** and then press Enter.

4 In the **Criteria** row under **Amount**, type **>500** and then press Enter. Compare your screen with Figure 2.34.

> You create the AND condition by placing the criteria for both fields on the same line in the Criteria row. The criteria indicates that records should be located that contain *Football* in the Sport field AND a value greater than *500* in the Amount field. Both conditions must exist or be true for the records to display in the query results.

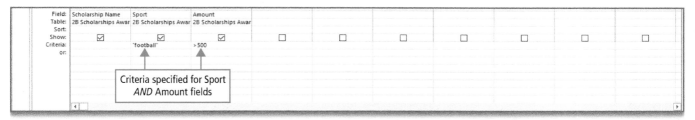

Figure 2.34

5 **Run** the query, and notice that two records display that match both conditions—*Football* in the Sport field AND a value greater than *$500* in the Amount field.

6 **Save** 🖫 the query as **2B Football AND Over $500 Query** and then **Close** ✕ the query.

7 **Open** » the **Navigation Pane**, and then click to select the **2B Football AND Over $500 Query** object. Click the **File tab**, click **Print**, and then click **Print Preview**.

> You can view an object in Print Preview or print any selected object in the Navigation Pane—the object does not need to be open in the object window to print it.

8 Click **Close Print Preview**. **Close** the query. **Close** « the **Navigation Pane**.

Activity 2.23 | Using OR Criteria in a Query

MOS
3.1.1, 3.2.1, 3.2.3, 3.1.6, 3.1.7

The *OR condition* is an example of a compound criteria used to display records that meet one or more parts of the specified criteria. The OR condition can specify criteria in a single field or in different fields. In this Activity, you will help Mr. Garza answer the question, *Which scholarships over $200 were awarded for volleyball or golf, and what is the award date of each?*

1 On the **Create tab**, in the **Queries group**, click **Query Design**.

2 In the **Show Table** dialog box, double-click your **2B Scholarships Awarded** table to add it to the table area, and then **Close** the **Show Table** dialog box. Resize the field list, and then add the following fields to the design grid in the order given: **Scholarship Name**, **Sport**, **Amount**, and **Award Date**.

3 In the design grid, click in the **Criteria** row under **Sport**, type **volleyball** and then press ↓.

> The insertion point is blinking in the *or* row under Sport.

4 In the **or** row under **Sport**, type **golf** and then press Enter. **Run** the query.

> Six records were located in the 2B Scholarships Awarded table that have either *volleyball* OR *golf* stored in the Sport field. This is an example of using the OR condition to locate records that meet one or more parts of the specified criteria in a single field—*Sport*.

5 Switch to **Design** view. In the **or** row under **Sport**, select *"golf"* and then press Del. In the **Criteria** row under **Sport**, select and delete *"volleyball"*. Type **volleyball or golf** and then press Enter.

6 In the **Criteria** row under **Amount**, type **>200** and then press [Enter]. Compare your screen with Figure 2.35.

This is an alternative way to enter the OR condition in the Sport field and is a good method to use when you add an AND condition to the criteria. Access will locate records where the Sport field contains *volleyball* OR *golf* AND where the Amount field contains a value greater than *200*.

If you enter *volleyball* in the Criteria row, and *golf* in the or row for the Sport field, then you must enter *>200* in both the Criteria row and the or row for the Amount field so that the correct records are located when the query is run.

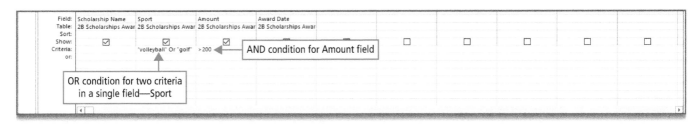

Figure 2.35

7 **Run** the query.

Two records were located in the 2B Scholarships Awarded table that have either *Volleyball* OR *Golf* stored in the Sport field AND a value greater than $200 in the Amount field. This is an example of using the OR condition in combination with an AND condition.

8 **Save** 🖫 the query as **2B Volleyball OR Golf AND Over $200 Query Close** ✕ the query.

Objective 10   Create a Query Based on More Than One Table

GO! Learn How
Video A2-10

In a relational database, you can retrieve information from more than one table. Recall that a table in a relational database contains all of the records about a single topic. Tables are joined to one another by relating the primary key in one table to the foreign key in another table. This common field is used to create the relationship and is used to find records from multiple tables when the query is created and run.

For example, the Athletes table stores all of the data about the student athletes—name, address, and so on. The Scholarships Awarded table stores data about the scholarship name, the amount, and so on. When an athlete receives a scholarship, only the Student ID of the athlete is used to identify the athlete in the Scholarships Awarded table. It is not necessary to include any other data about the athlete in the Scholarships Awarded table; doing so would result in redundant data.

Activity 2.24 | Creating a Query Based on More Than One Table

3.1.1, 3.2.1,
3.2.3, 3.2.2,
3.1.5, 3.1.6, 3.1.7

In this Activity, you will create a query that selects records from two tables. This is possible because you created a relationship between the two tables in the database. The query will answer the questions, *What is the name, email address, and phone number of athletes who have received a scholarship for tennis or swimming, and what is the name and amount of the scholarship?*

1 On the **Create tab**, in the **Queries group**, click **Query Design**. In the **Show Table** dialog box, double-click your **2B Athletes** table, and then double-click your **2B Scholarships Awarded** table to add both tables to the table area. In the **Show Table** dialog box, click **Close**. Resize each field list to display all of the field names and the entire table name.

The join line displays because you created a one-to-many relationship between the two tables using the common field of Student ID; *one* athlete can have *many* scholarships.

2 From the **2B Athletes** field list, add the following fields to the design grid in the order given: **First Name**, **Last Name**, **College Email**, and **Home Phone**.

3 From the **2B Scholarships Awarded** field list, add the following fields to the design grid in the order given: **Scholarship Name**, **Sport**, and **Amount**.

4 Click in the **Sort** row under **Last Name**, click the **arrow**, and then click **Ascending** to sort the records in alphabetical order by the last names of the athletes.

5 Click in the **Criteria** row under **Sport**, type **tennis or swimming** and then press Enter.

6 In the selection bar of the design grid, point to the right edge of the **Scholarship Name** column to display the ⊞ pointer, and then double-click to increase the width of the column and to display the entire table name on the **Table** row. Using the same technique, increase the width of the **Sport** column. Compare your screen with Figure 2.36.

> When locating data from multiple tables, the information in the Table row is helpful, especially when different tables include the same field name, such as Address. Although the field name is the same, the data may be different—for example, an athlete's address or a coach's address from two different related tables.

Figure 2.36

7 **Run** the query, and then compare your screen with Figure 2.37.

> Eight records display for athletes who received either a Swimming *or* Tennis scholarship, and the records are sorted in ascending order by the Last Name field. Because the common field of Student ID is included in both tables, Access can locate the specified fields in both tables by using one query. Two students—*Carla Reid* and *Florence Zimmerman*—received two scholarships, one for swimming and one for tennis. Recall that *one* student athlete can receive *many* scholarships.

Figure 2.37

8 **Save** 🖫 the query as **2B Tennis OR Swimming Query** and then display the query results in **Print Preview**. Change the orientation to **Landscape**, and the **Margins** to **Normal**. **Close** Print Preview.

9 ▸ **Close** ⊠ the query, **Open** » the **Navigation Pane**. If necessary, resize the Navigation Pane so all object names are visible, and then compare your screen with Figure 2.38.

Your *2B Tennis OR Swimming Query* object name displays under both tables from which it selected records.

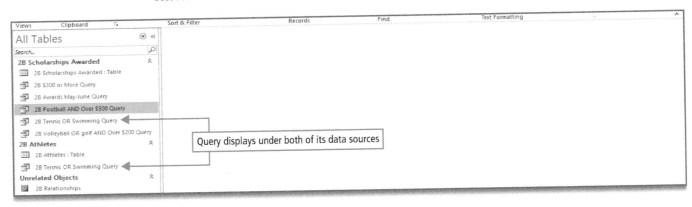

Figure 2.38

10 ▸ **Close** « the **Navigation Pane**.

Objective 11 | Use Wildcards in a Query

GO! Learn How
Video A2-11

A ***wildcard character*** is used to represent one or more unknown characters in a string. When you are unsure of the specific character or set of character to include in the criteria for a query, use a wildcard character in place of the character.

Activity 2.25 | Using a Wildcard in a Query

MOS
3.1.1, 3.1.5,
3.2.1, 3.2.3,
3.1.6, 3.1.7

Use the asterisk (*) wildcard character to represent one or more unknown characters. For example, entering Fo* as the criteria in a last name field will result in displaying records containing last names of Foster, Forrester, Fossil, or any other last name that begins with *Fo*. In this Activity, you will use the asterisk (*) wildcard character in criteria to answer the question related to organizations that award scholarships, *Which athletes received scholarships from local rotary clubs, country clubs, or foundations?*

1 ▸ On the **Create tab**, in the **Queries group**, click **Query Design**. In the **Show Table** dialog box, double-click your **2B Athletes** table, and then double-click your **2B Scholarships Awarded** table to add both tables to the table area. In the **Show Table** dialog box, click **Close**. Resize each field list to display all of the field names and the entire table name.

2 ▸ From the **2B Athletes** field list, add the following fields to the design grid in the order given: **First Name** and **Last Name**. From the **2B Scholarships Awarded** field list, add the **Awarding Organization** field to the design grid.

3 ▸ Click in the **Sort** row under **Last Name**, click the **arrow**, and then click **Ascending** to sort the records in alphabetical order by the last names of the athletes.

4 ▸ Click in the **Criteria** row under **Awarding Organization**, type **rotary*** and then press Enter.

The * wildcard character is a placeholder used to match one or more unknown characters. After pressing Enter, Access adds *Like* to the beginning of the criteria.

5 **Run** the query, and then compare your screen with Figure 2.39.

Three athletes received scholarships from a rotary club from different cities. The results are sorted alphabetically by the Last Name field.

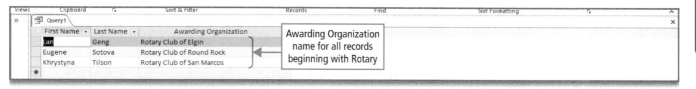

Figure 2.39

6 Switch to **Design** view. Click in the **or** row under **Awarding Organization**, type ***country club** and then press Enter.

The * wildcard character can be used at the beginning, middle, or end of the criteria. The position of the * determines the location of the unknown characters. By entering *country club*, you will locate records where the Awarding Organization name ends in *Country Club*.

7 **Run** the query.

Six records display for students receiving scholarships; three from organizations with a name that begins with *Rotary*, and three from organizations with a name that ends with *Country Club*.

8 Switch to **Design** view. In the design grid under **Awarding Organization** and under **Like "*country club"**, type ***foundation*** and then press Enter. Compare your screen with Figure 2.40.

This query will also display records where the Awarding Organization has *Foundation* anywhere in the organization name—at the beginning, middle, or end. Three *OR* criteria have been entered for the Awarding Organization field. When run, this query will locate records where the Awarding Organization has a name that begins with *Rotary*, OR ends with *Country Club*, OR that has *Foundation* anywhere in its name.

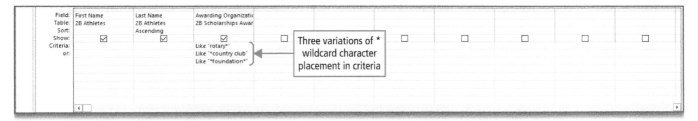

Figure 2.40

9 **Run** the query.

Twenty-eight scholarships were awarded from organizations where the name of the organization begins with Rotary, ends with Country Club, or has Foundation anywhere in its name. The records are sorted alphabetically by the Last Name field.

10 **Save** 🖫 the query as **2B Wildcard Query** and then display the query results in **Print Preview**. Click **Close Print Preview**.

11 **Close** ✕ the query, and then **Open** » the **Navigation Pane**. Notice that your **2B Wildcard Query** displays under both tables because the query selected data from both tables—the data sources.

MORE KNOWLEDGE **Using the ? Wildcard Character to Search for a Single Unknown Character**

The question mark (?) wildcard character is used to search for a single unknown character. For each question mark included in the criteria, any character can be located. For example, entering *b?d* as the criteria will result in the display of words such as *bed*, *bid*, or *bud*, or any three-character word that begins with *b* and ends with *d*. Entering *b??d* as the criteria will results in the display of words such as *bard*, *bend*, or *bind*, or any four-character word that begins with *b* and ends with *d*.

Objective 12 | Create Calculated Fields in a Query

GO! Learn How
Video A2-12

Queries can create calculated values that are stored in a *calculated field*. A calculated field stores the value of a mathematical operation. For example, you can multiply the value stored in a field named Total Hours Worked by the value stored in a field named Hourly Pay to display the Gross Pay value for each work study student.

There are two steps to create a calculated field in a query. First, name the field that will store the results of the calculation. Second, enter the *expression*—the formula—that will perform the calculation. When entering the information for the calculated field in the query, the new field name must be followed by a colon (:), and each field name from the table used in the expression must be enclosed within its own pair of brackets.

Activity 2.26 | Creating a Calculated Field in a Query

3.1.1, 3.2.1,
3.2.2, 3.1.6, 3.1.7

For each scholarship received by student athletes, the Texas Lakes Community College Alumni Association will donate an amount equal to 50 percent of each scholarship. In this Activity, you will create a calculated field to determine the amount that the alumni association will donate for each scholarship. The query will answer the question, *How much money will the alumni association donate for each student athlete who is awarded a scholarship?*

1 ▶ Close « the **Navigation Pane**. On the **Create tab**, in the **Queries group**, click **Query Design**. In the **Show Table** dialog box, double-click your **2B Scholarships Awarded** table to add the table to the table area, **Close** the **Show Table** dialog box, and then resize the field list.

2 ▶ Add the following fields to the design grid in the order given: **Student ID**, **Scholarship Name**, and **Amount**. Click in the **Sort** row under **Student ID**, click the **arrow**, and then click **Ascending**.

3 ▶ In the **Field** row, right-click in the first empty column to display a shortcut menu, and then click **Zoom**.

Although the calculation can be typed directly in the empty Field box, the Zoom dialog box gives you more working space and enables you to see the entire calculation as you enter it.

4 ▶ In the **Zoom** dialog box, type **Alumni Donation:[Amount]*0.5** and then compare your screen with Figure 2.41.

The first element, *Alumni Donation*, is the new field name that will identify the result of the calculation when the query is run; the field is not added back to the table. The new field name is followed by a colon (:), which separates the new field name from the expression. *Amount* is enclosed in brackets because it is an existing field name in your 2B Scholarships Awarded table; it contains the numeric data on which the calculation is performed. Following the right square bracket is the asterisk (*), the mathematical operator for multiplication. Finally, the percentage expressed as a decimal—*0.5*—displays.

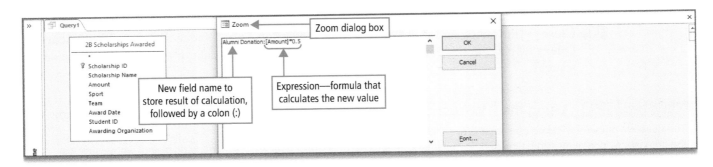

Figure 2.41

5 In the **Zoom** dialog box, click **OK**, **Run** the query, and then compare your screen with Figure 2.42.

The query results display three fields from your 2B Scholarships Awarded table and a fourth field—*Alumni Donation*—that displays a calculated value. Each calculated value equals the value in the Amount field multiplied by 0.5 or 50%.

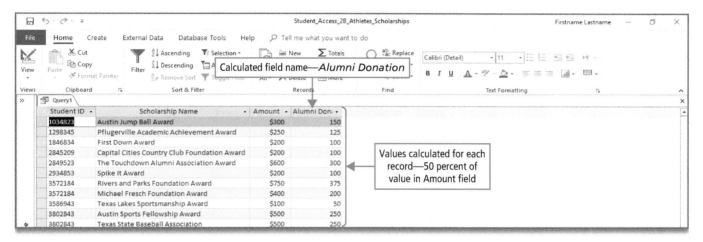

Figure 2.42

> **ALERT   Do your query results differ from Figure 2.42?**
>
> If your new field name does not display or if the results of the calculation do not display as shown in Figure 2.42, switch to Design view and carefully examine the expression you entered. Spelling or syntax errors prevent calculated fields from working properly.

6 Notice the formatting of the values in the **Alumni Donation** field—there are no dollar signs to match the formatting in the **Amount** field; you will adjust the formatting of this field later.

When using a number, such as 0.5, in an expression, the values that display in the calculated field may not be formatted the same as the existing field that was part of the calculation.

Activity 2.27 | Creating a Second Calculated Field in a Query

3.2.1, 3.1.7

In this Activity, you will create a calculated field to determine the total value of each scholarship after the alumni association donates an additional 50% based on the amount awarded by various organizations. The query will answer the question, *What is the total value of each scholarship after the alumni association donates an additional 50%?*

1 Switch to **Design** view. In the **Field** row, right-click in the first empty column to display a shortcut menu, and then click **Zoom**.

2 In the **Zoom** dialog box, type **Total Scholarship:[Amount]+[Alumni Donation]** and then compare your screen with Figure 2.43.

Each existing field name—*Amount* and *Alumni Donation*—must be enclosed in separate pairs of brackets.

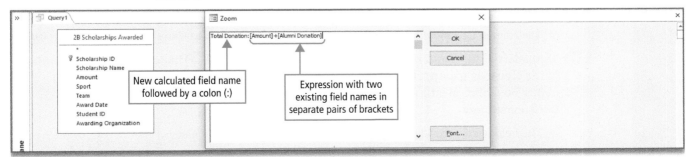

Figure 2.43

3 In the **Zoom** dialog box, click **OK**, and then **Run** the query.

The value in the *Total Scholarship* field is calculated by adding together the values in the Amount field and the Matching Donation field. The values in the Total Scholarship field are formatted with dollar signs, commas, and decimal points, which is carried over from the Currency format in the Amount field.

Activity 2.28 | Formatting Calculated Fields

MOS
3.1.6, 3.1.7, 3.2.4

In this Activity, you will format the calculated fields so that the values display in a consistent manner as currency.

1 Switch to **Design** view. In the **Field** row, click in the **Alumni Donation** field name box.

2 On the **Design tab**, in the **Show/Hide group**, click **Property Sheet**.

The Property Sheet displays on the right side of your screen. Recall that a Property Sheet enables you to make precise changes to the properties—characteristics—of selected items, in this case, a field.

ANOTHER WAY In the design grid, on the Field row, right-click in the Alumni Donation field name box, and then click Properties.

3 In the **Property Sheet**, with the **General tab** active, click **Format**. In the property setting box, click the **arrow**, and then compare your screen with Figure 2.44.

A list of available formats for the Alumni Donation field displays.

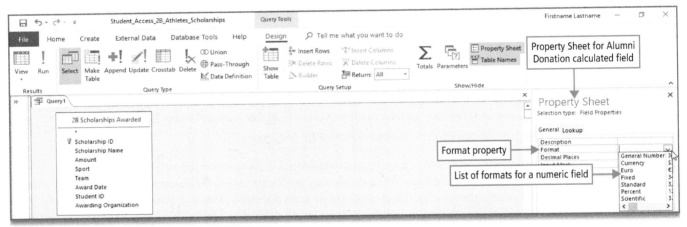

Figure 2.44

4 In the list, click **Currency**. In the **Property Sheet**, click **Decimal Places**. In the property setting box, click the **arrow**, and then click **0**.

5 In the design grid, in the **Field** row, click in the **Total Scholarship** field name. In the **Property Sheet**, set the **Format** property setting to **Currency** and the **Decimal Places** property setting to **0**.

6 Close ⊠ the **Property Sheet**, and then **Run** the query.

The Alumni Donation and Total Scholarship fields are formatted as Currency with 0 decimal places.

7 To the left of the **Student ID** field name, click the **Select All** ▢ button. On the **Home tab**, in the **Records group**, click **More**, and then click **Field Width**. In the **Column Width** dialog box, click **Best Fit**. Click in any field, and then **Save** 🖫 the query as **2B Alumni Donations Query**

The field widths are adjusted to display fully the calculated field names.

8 Close ⊠ the query.

Objective 13 Calculate Statistics and Group Data in a Query

GO! Learn How
Video A2-13

Queries can be used to perform statistical calculations known as *aggregate functions* on a group of records. For example, you can find the total or average amount for a group of records, or you can find the lowest or highest number in a group of records.

Activity 2.29 | Using the Min, Max, Avg, and Sum Functions in a Query

MOS
3.1.1, 3.1.7, 3.2.4

In this Activity, you will use aggregate functions to find the lowest and highest scholarships amounts and the average and total scholarship amounts. The last query in this Activity will answer the question, *What is the total dollar amount of all scholarships awarded?*

1 On the **Create tab**, in the **Queries group**, click **Query Design**. In the **Show Table** dialog box, double-click your **2B Scholarships Awarded** table to add the table to the table area, **Close** the **Show Table** dialog box, and then resize the field list.

2 Add the **Amount** field to the design grid.

Include only the field to summarize in the design grid, so that the aggregate function is applied only to that field.

3 On the **Design tab**, in the **Show/Hide group**, click **Totals** to add a **Total** row as the third row in the design grid. Notice that in the design grid, on the **Total** row under **Amount**, *Group By* displays.

Use the Total row to select an aggregate function for the selected field.

4 In the **Total** row under **Amount**, click in the box that displays *Group By*, and then click the **arrow** to display a list of aggregate functions. Compare your screen with Figure 2.45, and then take a moment to review the available aggregate functions and the purpose of each function as shown in the table in Figure 2.46.

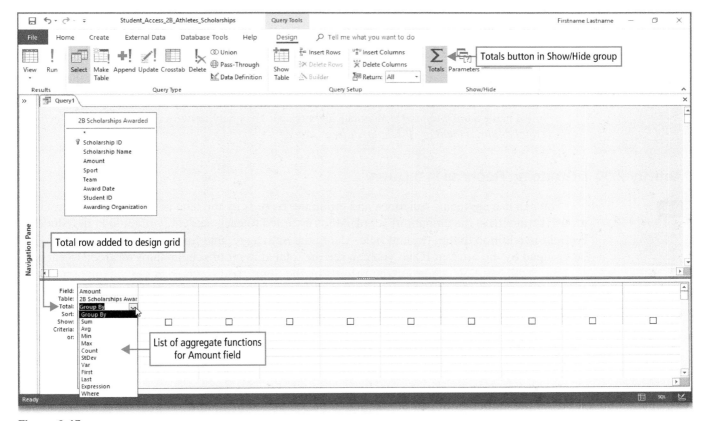

Figure 2.45

Function Name	Purpose
Group By	Combines data based on matching data in the selected field.
Sum	Totals the values in a field.
Avg	Averages the values in a field.
Min	Locates the smallest value in a field.
Max	Locates the largest value in a field.
Count	Displays the number of records based on a field.
StDev	Calculates the standard deviation for the values in a field.
Var	Calculates the variance for the values in a field.
First	Displays the first value in a field for the first record.
Last	Displays the last value in a field for the last record.
Expression	Creates a calculated field that includes an aggregate function.
Where	Limits the records to those that match a condition specified in the Criteria row of a field.

Figure 2.46

5 In the list of functions, click **Min**, and then **Run** the query. Point to the right edge of the first column to display the ⊞ pointer, and then double-click to apply Best Fit to the field.

Access locates the minimum (smallest) value--*$100*—in the Amount field for all of the records in the 2B Scholarships Awarded table. The field name *MinOfAmount* is automatically created. This query answers the question, *What is the minimum (smallest) scholarship amount awarded to athletes?*

6 Switch to **Design** view. In the **Total** row under **Amount**, click the **arrow**, and then click **Max**. **Run** the query.

The maximum (largest) value for a scholarship award amount is *$750.00*.

7 Switch to **Design** view. In the **Total** row, select the **Avg** function, and then **Run** the query.

The average scholarship award amount is *$358.33*.

8 Switch to **Design** view. In the **Total** row, select the **Sum** function, and then **Run** the query.

The values in the Amount field for all records is summed and displays a result of *$10,750.00*. The field name *SumOfAmount* is automatically created. The query answers the question, *What is the total dollar amount of all scholarships awarded?*

Activity 2.30 | Grouping Records in a Query

MOS
3.2.4, 3.2.2,
3.1.6, 3.1.7

You can use aggregate functions and group the records by the data in a field. For example, to group (summarize) the amount of scholarships awarded to each student, you include the Student ID field in addition to the Amount field. Using the Sum aggregate function, the records will be grouped by the Student ID so you can see the total amount of scholarships awarded to each student. Similarly, you can group the records by the Sport field so you can see the total amount of scholarships awarded for each sport.

1 Switch to **Design** view. From the field list, drag the **Student ID** field to the first column of the design grid—the **Amount** field moves to the second column. In the **Total** row under **Student ID**, notice that *Group By* displays.

This query will group—organize—the records by Student ID and will calculate a total amount for each student.

2 ▶ **Run** the query, and then compare your screen with Figure 2.47.

The query calculates the total amount of all scholarships for each student.

Figure 2.47

3 ▶ Switch to **Design** view. In the design grid, above **Student ID**, point to the selection bar to display the ⬇ pointer. Click to select the column, and then press `Del` to remove the **Student ID** field from the design grid.

4 ▶ From the field list, drag the **Sport** field to the first column in the design grid—the **Amount** field moves to the second column. Click in the **Sort** row under **Amount**, click the **arrow**, and then click **Descending**.

5 ▶ On the **Design tab**, in the **Show/Hide group**, click **Property Sheet**. In the **Property Sheet**, set the **Format** property to **Currency**, and then set the **Decimal Places** property to **0**. **Close** ⎽×⎽ the **Property Sheet**.

6 ▶ **Run** the query, and then compare your screen with Figure 2.48.

Access groups—summarizes—the records by each sport and displays the groupings in descending order by the total amount of scholarships awarded for each sport. Basketball scholarships were awarded the largest total amount--*$3,500*—and Volleyball scholarships were awarded the smallest total amount--*$650*.

Figure 2.48

7 ▶ **Save** 🖫 the query as **2B Total by Sport Query** and then **Close** ⎽×⎽ the query.

Objective 14 Create a Crosstab Query

GO! Learn How
Video A2-14

A *crosstab query* uses an aggregate function for data that can be grouped by two types of information, and displays the data in a compact, spreadsheet-like format with column headings and row headings. A crosstab query always has at least one row heading, one column heading, and one summary field. Use a crosstab query to summarize a large amount of data in a compact space that is easy to read.

Activity 2.31 │ Creating a Crosstab Query Using the Query Wizard

MOS
3.1.2, 3.2.4

In this Activity, you will create a crosstab query that displays the total amount of scholarships awarded for each sport and for each type of team—men's or women's.

1 ▶ On the **Create tab**, in the **Queries group**, click **Query Wizard**.

2 ▶ In the **New Query** dialog box, click **Crosstab Query Wizard**, and then click **OK**.

3 In the **Crosstab Query Wizard**, click your **Table: 2B Scholarships Awarded**, and then click **Next**.

4 In the wizard under **Available Fields**, double-click **Sport** to group the scholarship amounts by the sports—the sports will display as row headings. Click **Next**, and then compare your screen with Figure 2.49.

> The sport names will be grouped and displayed as row headings, and you are prompted to select column headings.

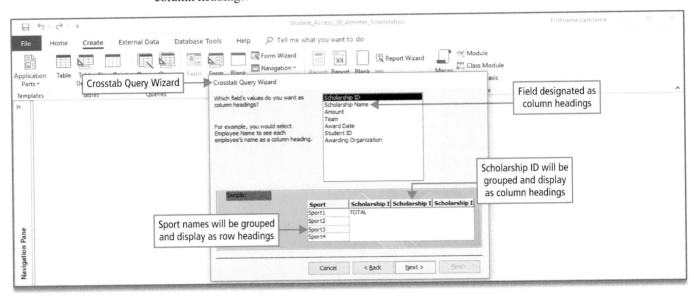

Figure 2.49

5 In the wizard, in the field list, click **Team** to select the column headings. Click **Next**, and then compare your screen with Figure 2.50.

> The Team types—*Men's* and *Women's*—will display as column headings, and you are prompted to select a field to summarize.

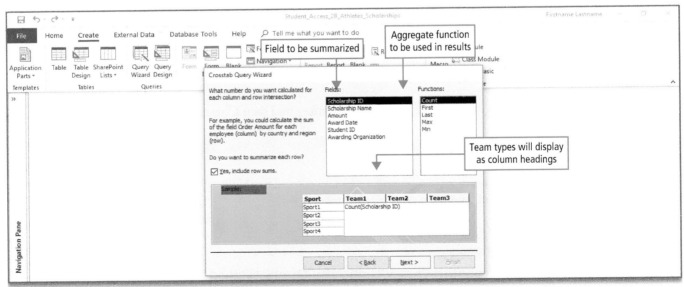

Figure 2.50

6 In the wizard under **Fields**, click **Amount**. Under **Functions**, click **Sum**.

> The crosstab query will calculate the total scholarship amount for each sport and for each type of team.

7 Click **Next**. In the **What do you want to name your query?** box, select the existing text, type **2B Sport and Team Crosstab Query** and then click **Finish**. Apply **Best Fit** to the datasheet, click in any field to cancel the selection, **Save** 🖫 the query, and then compare your screen with Figure 2.51.

The field widths are adjusted to display fully the calculated field names.

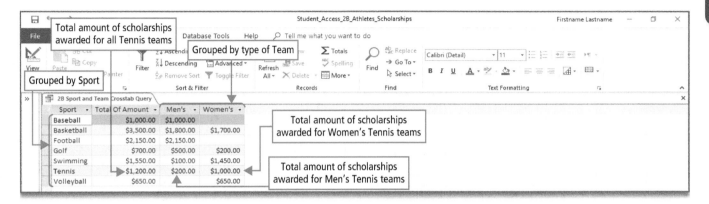

Figure 2.51

8 **Close** ⨉ the query.

MORE KNOWLEDGE | **Creating a Crosstab Query Using Data From Two Related Tables**

To create a crosstab query using fields from more than one table, you must first create a select query with the fields from both tables, and then use the query as the data source for the crosstab query.

Objective 15 | Create a Parameter Query

GO! Learn How
Video A2-15

A *parameter query* prompts you for criteria before running the query. For example, you need to display the records for students who live in different cities serviced by Texas Lakes Community College. You can create a select query and enter the criteria for a city such as Austin, but when you open the query, only the records for those students who live in Austin will display. To find the students who live in Round Rock, you must open the query in Design view, change the criteria, and then run the query again.

A parameter query eliminates the need to change the design of a select query. You create a single query that prompts you to enter the city; the results are based upon the criteria you enter when prompted.

Activity 2.32 | Creating a Parameter Query With One Criteria

MOS
3.1.3, 3.2.2,
3.1.6, 3.1.7

In this Activity, you will create a parameter query that displays student athletes from a specific city in the areas serviced by Texas Lakes Community College each time it is run.

1 On the **Create tab**, in the **Queries group**, click **Query Design**.

2 In the **Show Table** dialog box, double-click your **2B Athletes** table to add it to the table area, **Close** the **Show Table** dialog box, and then resize the field list.

3 Add the following fields to the design grid in the order given: **First Name**, **Last Name** **Address**, **City**, **State**, and **Postal Code**.

4 In the **Sort** row under **Last Name**, click the **arrow**, and then click **Ascending**.

5 In the **Criteria** row under **City**, type **[Enter a City]** and then press `Enter`. Compare your screen with Figure 2.52.

> The bracketed text indicates a *parameter*—a value that can be changed—rather than specific criteria.

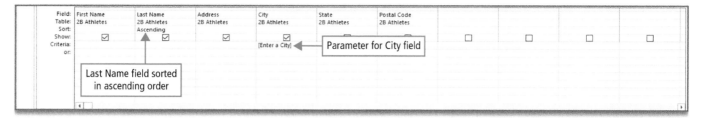

Figure 2.52

6 **Run** the query. In the **Enter Parameter Value** dialog box, type **austin** and then compare your screen with Figure 2.53.

> The Enter Parameter Value dialog box prompts you to *Enter a City*, which is the text enclosed in brackets that you entered in the criteria row under City. The city you enter will be set as the criteria for the query. Because you are prompted for the criteria, you can reuse this query without having to edit the criteria row in Design view. The value you enter is not case sensitive—you can enter *austin*, *Austin*, or *AUSTIN*.

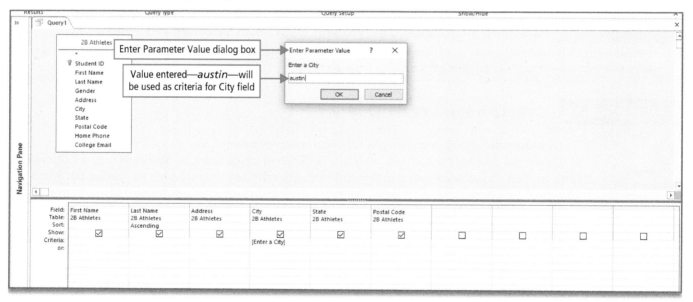

Figure 2.53

ALERT   Did the Enter Parameter Value dialog box not display?

If the Enter Parameter Value dialog box does not display, you may have typed the parameter incorrectly in the design grid. Common errors include using parentheses or curly braces instead of brackets around the parameter text, which Access interprets as specific criteria, resulting in no records matching the criteria. If you typed curly braces instead of brackets, the query will not run. To correct, display the query in Design view and change the parameter entered in the Criteria row.

---

7 In the **Enter Parameter Value** dialog box, click **OK**.

> Twenty-three students live in the city of Austin, and the records are sorted in alphabetical order by the Last Name field.

8 **Save** 🖫 the query as **2B City Parameter Query**, and then **Close** ⊠ the query.

9 **Open** » the **Navigation Pane**. In the **Navigation Pane**, under your **2B Athletes** table, double-click your **2B City Parameter Query**. In the **Enter Parameter Value** dialog box, type **round rock** and then click **OK**. **Close** « the **Navigation Pane**. Compare your screen with Figure 2.54.

Nine students live in the city of Round Rock. Every time you open a parameter query, you are prompted to enter criteria. You may have to apply Best Fit to the columns if all of the data in the fields does not display and you wish to print the query results—the length of the data in the fields changes as new records display depending upon the criteria entered. Recall that only the query design is saved; each time you open a query, it is run using the most up-to-date information in the data source.

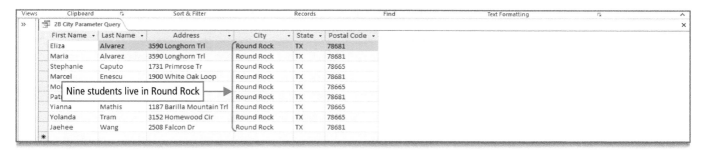

Figure 2.54

10 **Close** × the query.

MORE KNOWLEDGE **Parameter Query Prompts**

Be sure that the parameter you enter in the Criteria row as a prompt is not the same as the field name. For example, do not use *[City]* as the parameter. Access interprets this as the field name of *City*. Recall that you entered a field name in brackets when creating a calculated field in a query. If you use a field name as the parameter, the Enter Parameter Value dialog box will not display, and all of the records will display.

The parameter should inform the individual running the query of the data required to display the correct results. If you want to use the field name by itself as the prompt, type a question mark at the end of the text; for example, *[City?]*. You cannot use a period, exclamation mark (!), curly braces ({ }), another set of brackets ([ ]), or the ampersand (&) as part of the parameter.

11 **Open** » the **Navigation Pane**, and, if necessary increase the width of the pane so that all object names display fully. **Close** × the database and **Close** Access.

For Non-MyLab Submissions: Determine What Your Instructor Requires for Submission
As directed by your instructor, submit your completed database file.

12 In **MyLab IT**, locate and click the Grader Project **Access 2B Athletes and Scholarships**. In **step 3**, under **Upload Completed Assignment**, click **Choose File**. In the **Open** dialog box, navigate to your **Access Chapter 2 folder**, and then click your **Student_Access_2B_Athletes_Scholarships** file one time to select it. In the lower right corner of the **Open** dialog box, click **Open**.

The name of your selected file displays above the Upload button.

13 To submit your file to **MyLab IT** for grading, click **Upload**, wait a moment for a green **Success!** message, and then in **step 4**, click the blue **Submit for Grading** button. Click **Close Assignment** to return to your list of **Course Materials**.

You have completed Project 2B   END

»» GO! With Google

Objective	Export an Access Query to an Excel Spreadsheet, Save it in Google Drive, and Create a Chart

Access web apps are designed to work with Microsoft's SharePoint, a service for setting up websites to share and manage documents. Your college may not have SharePoint installed, so you will use other tools to share objects from your database so that you can work collaboratively with others. Recall that Google Drive is Google's free, web-based word processor, spreadsheet, slide show, form, and data storage and sharing service. For Access, you can export a database object to an Excel worksheet, a PDF file, or a text file, and then save the file to Google Drive.

ALERT   **Working with Web-Based Applications and Services**

Computer programs and services on the web receive continuous updates and improvements, so the steps to complete this web-based Activity may differ from the ones shown. You can often look at the screens and the information presented to determine how to complete the Activity.

If you do not already have a Google account, you will need to create one before you begin this Activity. Go to **http://google.com** and in the upper right corner, click **Sign In**. On the Sign In screen, click **Create Account**. On the Create your Google Account page, complete the form, read and agree to the Terms of Service and Privacy Policy, and then click **Next step**. On the Welcome screen, click **Get Started**.

Activity | Exporting an Access Query to an Excel Spreadsheet, Saving the Spreadsheet to Google Drive, Editing a Record in Google Drive, and Saving to Your Computer

In this Activity, you will export your 2B Sport and Team Crosstab Query table to an Excel spreadsheet, upload the Excel file to your Google Drive as a Google Sheet, edit a record in Google Drive, and then download a copy of the edited spreadsheet to your computer.

1 Start Access, navigate to your **Access Chapter 2** folder, and then open your **2B_Athletes_Scholarships** database file. If necessary, on the Message Bar, click **Enable Content**. In the **Navigation Pane**, click your **2B Sport and Team Crosstab Query** one time to select it—do not open it.

2 Click the **External Data tab**, and then in the **Export group**, click **Excel**. In the **Export – Excel Spreadsheet** dialog box, click **Browse**, and then navigate to your **Access Chapter 2** folder. In the **File Save** dialog box, click in the **File name** box, type **Lastname_Firstname_AC_2B_Web** and then click **Save**.

3 In the **Export – Excel Spreadsheet** dialog box, under **Specify export options**, select the first two check boxes—**Export data with formatting and layout** and **Open the destination file after the export operation is complete**—and then click **OK**. Take a moment to examine the data in the file, and then **Close** Excel. In the **Export – Excel Spreadsheet** dialog box, click **Close**, and then **Close Access**.

4 From the desktop, open your browser, navigate to **http://google.com**, and then sign in to your Google account. Click the **Google Apps** menu, and then click **Drive**. Open your **GO! Web Projects** folder—or click New to create and then open this folder if necessary.

5 In the upper right corner, click **Settings**, and then on the menu click **Settings**. In the **Settings** dialog box, next to *Convert uploads*, be sure that **Convert uploaded files to Google Docs editor format** is selected. In the upper right, click **Done**.

> If this setting is not selected, your document will upload as a pdf file and cannot be edited without further action.

6 On the left, click **New**, and then click **File upload**. In the **Open** dialog box, navigate to your **Access Chapter 2** folder, and then double-click your **AC_2B_Web** Excel file to upload it to Google Drive. In the lower right corner, when the title bar of the message box indicates *Uploads completed*, **Close** the message box. A second message box may display temporarily.

---

7 In the file list, double-click your **Lastname_Firstname_AC_2B_Web** file to open it in Google Sheets. Compare your screen with Figure A.

The worksheet displays column letters, row numbers, and data.

8 Select the range **A1:B8**. On the menu bar, click **Insert**, and then click **Chart**.

The chart is placed in the spreadsheet, covering some of the data.

Figure A

9 Click the **Chart title**, type **Total Scholarships by Sport**. In the **Chart editor**, click **Legend**. Click the arrow next to *Right*, and then click **None**.

10 Click to select the chart, if necessary. Point to the top of the chart window until the [⬚] pointer displays. Hold down the left mouse button, and then drag the chart below the data in the spreadsheet.

11 On the menu, click **File**, point to **Download as**, and then click **Microsoft Excel (.xlsx)**. Use your browser commands to save the file in your **Access Chapter 2** folder as **Lastname_Firstname_AC_2B_Web_Download**

> **NOTE**   Saving The Downloaded File to the Access Chapter 2 Folder
>
> Depending on the browser you are using, you may need to open the file in Excel and then save the AC_2B_Web_Download worksheet to your Access Chapter 2 folder.

12 On the Taskbar, click the icon for your browser. In Google Drive, in the upper right corner, click your name, and then click **Sign out**. **Close** your browser window.

13 If necessary, start Excel. In the Excel opening screen, in the lower left corner, click **Open Other Workbooks**. Navigate to your **Lastname_Firstname_AC_2B_Web_Download** file and then open the file.

14 If directed to submit a paper printout of your Lastname_Firstname_AC_2B_Web_Download file, follow the directions given in the Note below. As directed by your instructor, submit your Excel file created of this project.

> **NOTE**   Printing or Creating an PDF electronic image of an Excel Spreadsheet
>
> To print on paper, click Print. To create a PDF electronic image of your printout, on the left side of your screen, click Export. Under Export, be sure Create PDF/XPS Document is selected, and then click Create PDF/XPS. Navigate to your Access Chapter 2 folder, and then click Publish to save the file with the default name and an extension of pdf.

»»» GO! To Work

wavebreakmedia/Shutterstock, Monkey Business Images/Fotolia, Ivanko80/Shutterstock, Monkey Business Images/Shutterstock

Microsoft Office Specialist (MOS) Skills in this Chapter	
Project 2A	**Project 2B**
1.2.1 Understand relationships	**1.1.1** Import objects or data from other sources
1.2.2 Display relationships	**1.2.1** Understand relationships
1.2.4 Enforce referential integrity	**1.2.2** Display relationships
1.2.5 Set foreign keys	**1.2.3** Set Primary Keys
1.3.1 Configure print options for records, forms, and reports	**1.2.4** Enforce referential integrity
2.3.2 Sort records	**1.2.5** Set foreign keys
3.1.1 Create simple queries	**3.1.1** Create simple queries
3.1.6 Save queries	**3.1.2** Create basic crosstab queries
3.1.7 Run queries	**3.1.3** Create basic parameter queries
3.2.1 Add, hide, and remove fields in queries	**3.1.5** Create basic multi-table queries
3.2.2 Sort data within queries	**3.1.6** Save queries
3.2.3 Filter data within queries	**3.1.7** Run queries
	3.2.1 Add, hide, and remove fields in queries
	3.2.2 Sort data within queries
	3.2.3 Filter data within queries
	3.2.4 Format fields within queries

Build Your E-Portfolio

An E-Portfolio is a collection of evidence, stored electronically, that showcases what you have accomplished while completing your education. Collecting and then sharing your work products with potential employers reflects your academic and career goals. Your completed documents from the following projects are good examples to show what you have learned: 2G, 2K, and 2L.

GO! For Job Success

Video: Preparing for Meetings

Your instructor may assign this video to your class, and then ask you to think about, or discuss with your classmates, these questions:

g-stockstudio/Shutterstock

> Out of the four employees, which one demonstrated appropriate meeting behavior? Provide specific examples.

> How did technology assist the meeting and how did technology hinder the meeting?

> What perception of the company may the client have from the conference call? Provide two examples.

End of Chapter

Summary

Table relationships are created by joining the common fields in tables providing a means for you to modify data simultaneously and use data from multiple tables to create queries, forms, and reports.

Queries are created to answer questions and to extract information from your database tables; saving a query with your database saves you time when you need to answer the question many times.

Queries range from simple queries where you ask a single question to complex queries where you use compound criteria, wildcard characters, logical operators, and create calculated fields.

A crosstab query displays information grouped by two fields, an easy way to display complex data, and a parameter query prompts you to enter the criteria each time you open or run the query.

GO! Learn It Online

Review the concepts and key terms in this chapter by completing these online challenges, which you can find at **MyLab IT**.

Chapter Quiz: Answer matching and multiple choice questions to test what you learned in this chapter.

Lessons on the GO!: Learn how to use all the new apps and features as they are introduced by Microsoft.

MOS Prep Quiz: Answer questions to review the MOS skills that you practiced in this chapter.

GO! Collaborative Team Project (available in Instructor Resource Center)

If your instructor assigns the project to your class, you can expect to work with one or more of your classmates—either in class or by using Internet tools—to create work products similar to those you created in this chapter. A team is a group of workers who work together to solve a problem, make a decision, or create a work product. Collaboration is when you work together with others as a team in an intellectual endeavor to complete a shared task or achieve a shared goal.

Monkey Business Images/Fotolia

Project Guide for Access Chapter 2

Your instructor will assign Projects from this list to ensure your learning and assess your knowledge.

	Project Guide for Access Chapter 2		
Project	**Apply Skills from These Chapter Objectives**	**Project Type**	**Project Location**
2A MyLab IT	Objectives 1–7 from Project 2A	**2A Instructional Project (Grader Project)** **Instruction** A guided review of the skills from Project.	**MyLab IT** and in text
2B MyLab IT	Objectives 8–15 from Project 2B	**2B Instructional Project (Grader Project)** **Instruction** A guided review of the skills from Project.	**MyLab IT** and in text
2C	Objectives 1–7 from Project 2A	**2C Chapter Review (Scorecard Grading)** **Review** A guided review of the skills from Project 2A.	In text
2D	Objectives 8–15 from Project 2B	**2D Chapter Review (Scorecard Grading)** **Review** A guided review of the skills from Project 2B.	In text
2E MyLab IT	Objectives 1–7 from Project 2A	**2E Mastery (Grader Project)** **Mastery and Transfer of Learning** A demonstration of your mastery of the skills in Project 2A with extensive decision-making.	**MyLab IT** and in text
2F MyLab IT	Objectives 8–15 from Project 2B	**2F Mastery (Grader Project)** **Mastery and Transfer of Learning** A demonstration of your mastery of the skills in Project 2B with extensive decision-making.	**MyLab IT** and in text
2G MyLab IT	Combination of Objectives from Projects 2A and 2B	**2G Mastery (Grader Project)** **Mastery and Transfer of Learning** A demonstration of your mastery of the skills in Projects 2A and 2B with extensive decision-making.	**MyLab IT** and in text
2H	Combination of Objectives from Projects 2A and 2B	**2H GO! Fix It (Scorecard Grading)** **Critical Thinking** A demonstration of your mastery of the skills in Projects 2A and 2B by creating a correct result from a document that contains errors you must find.	IRC
2I	Combination of Objectives from Projects 2A and 2B	**2I GO! Make It (Scorecard Grading)** **Critical Thinking** A demonstration of your mastery of the skills in Projects 2A and 2B by creating a result from a supplied picture.	IRC
2J	Combination of Objectives from Projects 2A and 2B	**2J GO! Solve It (Rubric Grading)** **Critical Thinking** A demonstration of your mastery of the skills in Projects 2A and 2B, your decision-making skills, and your critical thinking skills. A task-specific rubric helps you self-assess your result.	IRC
2K	Combination of Objectives from Projects 2A and 2B	**2K GO! Solve It (Rubric Grading)** **Critical Thinking** A demonstration of your mastery of the skills in Projects 2A and 2B, your decision-making skills, and your critical thinking skills. A task-specific rubric helps you self-assess your result.	In text
2L	Combination of Objectives from Projects 2A and 2B	**2L GO! Think (Rubric Grading)** **Critical Thinking** A demonstration of your understanding of the Chapter concepts applied in a manner that you would outside of college. An analytic rubric helps you and your instructor grade the quality of your work by comparing it to the work an expert in the discipline would create.	In text
2M	Combination of Objectives from Projects 2A and 2B	**2M GO! Think (Rubric Grading)** **Critical Thinking** A demonstration of your understanding of the Chapter concepts applied in a manner that you would outside of college. An analytic rubric helps you and your instructor grade the quality of your work by comparing it to the work an expert in the discipline would create.	IRC
2N	Combination of Objectives from Projects 2A and 2B	**2N You and GO! (Rubric Grading)** **Critical Thinking** A demonstration of your understanding of the Chapter concepts applied in a manner that you would in a personal situation. An analytic rubric helps you and your instructor grade the quality of your work.	IRC
2O	Combination of Objectives from Projects 2A and 2B	**2O Cumulative Group Project for Access Chapter 2** A demonstration of your understanding of concepts and your ability to work collaboratively in a group role-playing assessment, requiring both collaboration and self-management.	IRC

Glossary

Glossary of Chapter Key Terms

Aggregate functions Calculations such as Min, Max, Avg, and Sum that are performed on a group of records.

AND condition A compound criteria used to display records that match all parts of the specified criteria.

Ascending order A sorting order that arranges text alphabetically (A to Z) and numbers from the lowest number to the highest number.

Between . . . And operator A comparison operator that looks for values within a range.

Calculated field A field that stores the value of a mathematical operation.

Cascade Delete Related Records A cascade option that enables you to delete a record in a table and also delete all of the related records in related tables.

Cascade options Relationship options that enable you to update records in related tables when referential integrity is enforced.

Cascade Update Related Fields A cascade option that enables you to change the data in the primary key field in the table on the *one* side of the relationship and update that change to any fields storing that same data in related tables.

Comparison operators Symbols that are used to evaluate data in the field to determine if it is the same (=), greater than (>), less than (<), or in between a range of values as specified by the criteria.

Compound criteria Multiple conditions in a query or filter.

Criteria Conditions in a query that identify the specific records you are looking for.

Crosstab query A query that uses an aggregate function for data that can be grouped by two types of information and displays the data in a compact, spreadsheet-like format with column headings and row headings.

Data source The table or tables from which a form, query, or report retrieves its data.

Descending order A sorting order that arranges text in reverse alphabetical order (Z to A) and numbers from the highest number to the lowest number.

Design grid The lower area of the query window that displays the design of the query.

Expression A formula that will perform the calculation.

Field list A list of field names in a table.

Foreign key The field that is included in the related table so the field can be joined with the primary key in another table for the purpose of creating a relationship.

Innermost sort field When sorting on multiple fields in Datasheet view, the field that will be used for the second level of sorting.

Is Not Null A criteria that searches for fields that are not empty.

Is Null A criteria that searches for fields that are empty.

Join line In the Relationships window, the line joining two tables that visually indicates the common fields and the type of relationship.

Logical operators Operators that combine criteria using AND and OR. With two criteria, AND requires that both conditions be met and OR requires that either condition be met for the record to display in the query results.

Message Bar The area directly below the ribbon that displays information such as security alerts when there is potentially unsafe, active content in an Office document that you open.

One-to-many relationship A relationship between two tables where one record in the first table corresponds to many records in the second table—the most common type of relationship in Access.

OR condition A compound criteria used to display records that match at least one of the specified criteria.

Outermost sort field When sorting on multiple fields in Datasheet view, the field that will be used for the first level of sorting.

Parameter A value that can be changed.

Parameter query A query that prompts you for criteria before running the query.

Referential integrity A set of rules that Access uses to ensure that the data between related tables is valid.

Relationship An association that you establish between two tables based on common fields.

Run The process in which Access looks at the records in the table(s) included in the query design, finds the records that match the specified criteria, and then displays the records in a datasheet; only the fields included in the query design display.

Sorting The process of arranging data in a specific order based on the value in a field.

Subdatasheet A format for displaying related records when you click the plus sign (+) next to a record in a table on the *one* side of the relationship.

Subset A portion of the total records available.

Table area The upper area of the query window that displays field lists for the tables that are used in a query.

Text string A sequence of characters.

Trust Center An area of Access where you can view the security and privacy settings for your Access installation.

Wildcard character In a query, a character that represents one or more unknown characters in criteria; an asterisk (*) represents one or more unknown characters, and a question mark (?) represents a single unknown character.

Chapter Review

Project 2C Freshman Orientation

Apply 2A skills from these Objectives:

1. Open and Save an Existing Database
2. Create Table Relationships
3. Sort Records in a Table
4. Create a Query in Design View
5. Create a New Query From an Existing Query
6. Sort Query Results
7. Specify Criteria in a Query

In the following Skills Review, you will assist Dr. Wendy Bowie, the Director of Counseling at the Southwest Campus, in using her database to answer several questions about the freshman orientation sessions that will be held prior to class registration. Your completed Navigation Pane will look similar to Figure 2.55.

Project Files

For Project 2C, you will need the following file:

a02C_Freshman_Orientation

You will save your database as:

Lastname_Firstname_2C_Freshman_Orientation

Project Results

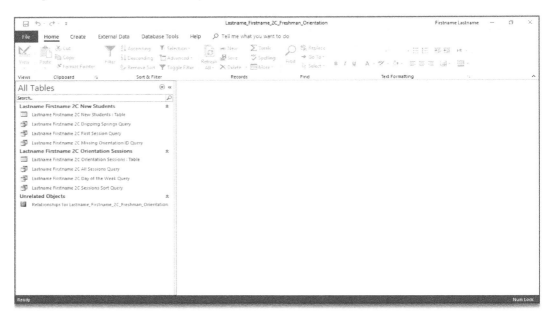

Figure 2.55

(continues on next page)

Chapter Review

1 Start Access. In the Access opening screen, click **Open Other Files**. Under **Open**, click Browse, and then navigate to the location where your student data files are stored. Double-click **a02C_Freshman_Orientation** to open the database.

a. Click the **File tab**, and then click **Save As**. Under **File Types**, be sure **Save Database As** is selected. On the right, under **Database File Types**, be sure **Access Database** is selected, and then click **Save As**.

b. In the **Save As** dialog box, navigate to your **Access Chapter 2** folder. Click in the **File name** box, type **Lastname_Firstname_2C_Freshman_Orientation** and then press [Enter]. On the **Message Bar**, click **Enable Content**.

c. In the **Navigation Pane**, right-click **2C New Students**, and then click **Rename**. With the table name selected and using your own name, type **2C New Students** and then press [Enter]. **Rename** the **2C Orientation Sessions** table to **Lastname Firstname 2C Orientation Sessions** and resize the **Navigation Pane** to display both tables names fully.

2 In the **Navigation Pane**, double-click your **Lastname Firstname 2C New Students** table to open it in the object window, and examine the fields in the table. Double-click your **Lastname Firstname 2C Orientation Sessions** table and examine the fields in the table. In the object window, right-click either **object tab**, and then click **Close All** to close both tables. **Close** the **Navigation Pane**.

a. Click the **Database Tools tab**, and then in the **Relationships group**, click **Relationships**.

b. In the **Show Table** dialog box, click your **Lastname Firstname 2C Orientation Sessions** table, and then click **Add**. In the **Show Table** dialog box, double-click your **Lastname Firstname 2C New Students** table to add it to the **Relationships** window. In the **Show Table** dialog box, click **Close**.

c. In the **Lastname Firstname 2C New Students** field list, point to the lower right corner of the field list to display the pointer, and then drag downward and to the right to resize the field list and display all of the field names and the entire table name. Use the same technique to resize the **Lastname Firstname 2C Orientation Sessions** field list—the field list on the left—so that the table name displays fully. In the

Lastname Firstname 2C New Students field list—the field list on the right—point to the title bar, and holding down the left mouse button, drag the field list to the right until there are approximately one inch of space between the field lists.

d. In the **Lastname Firstname 2C Orientation Sessions** field list, point to **Orientation ID**, and, holding down the left mouse button, drag the field name downward and to the right into the **Lastname Firstname 2C New Students** field list until the pointer's arrow is on top of **Orientation ID**. Release the mouse button to display the **Edit Relationships** dialog box. Drag the **Edit Relationships** dialog box downward and to the right below the two field lists.

e. In the **Edit Relationships** dialog box, click to select the **Enforce Referential Integrity** check box, the **Cascade Update Related Fields** check box, and the **Cascade Delete Related Records** check box. In the **Edit Relationships** dialog box, click **Create** to create a one-to-many relationship—*one* orientation session can be scheduled for *many* new students.

f. On the **Design tab**, in the **Tools group**, click **Relationship Report**. On the **Print Preview tab**, in the **Page Size group**, click **Margins**, and then click **Normal**. On the **Quick Access Toolbar**, click the **Save** button. In the **Save As** dialog box, click **OK** to accept the default report name. In the object window, **Close** the report, and then **Close** the **Relationships** window.

g. **Open** the Navigation Pane, double-click your **Lastname Firstname 2C Orientation Sessions** table to open it in the object window, and then **Close** the **Navigation Pane**. On the left side of the last record—*Orientation ID* of *OS-01*—click **+** to display the subdatasheet and notice that 13 new students are scheduled to attend this orientation session. Click **-** to collapse the subdatasheet.

h. In the last record, in the **Orientation ID** field, select the existing data—*OS-01*—and then type **OS-001** to make the data consistent with the Orientation IDs of the other sessions; the 13 related records are updated with the new Orientation ID because you selected Cascade Update Related Fields in the Edit Relationships dialog box.

(continues on next page)

Chapter Review

i. Display the subdatasheet for the record with an **Orientation ID** of **OS-010** and notice that one student—*Student ID* of *8273485*—is scheduled for this orientation session. Collapse the subdatasheet. To the left of the record, point to the record selector box to display the → pointer, and then click to select the record. On the **Home tab**, in the **Records group**, click **Delete**. In the message box, click **Yes** to delete this record and the related student record in the **Lastname Firstname 2C New Students** table.

3 In the **Date** field, click in any record. On the **Home tab**, in the **Sort & Filter group**, click **Ascending** to sort the records by the date. In the field names row, click the **Room arrow**, and then click **Sort Z to A** to sort the rooms from Room 203 to Room 201. The records are sorted first by the Room and then by the Date. On the **File tab**, click **Print**, and then click **Print Preview**. Create a paper or PDF electronic image as directed, and then click **Close Print Preview**. On the **Home tab**, in the **Sort & Filter group**, click **Remove Sort**. **Close** the table, and in the message box, click **No**; you do not need to save any design changes to the table.

4 Click the **Create tab**, and then in the **Queries group**, click **Query Design**. In the **Show Table** dialog box, double-click your **Lastname Firstname 2C Orientation Sessions** table, and then **Close** the **Show Table** dialog box. Resize the field list, displaying all of the field names and the entire table name.

a. In the field list, double-click **Date** to add the field to the first column in the design grid. In the design grid, in the **Field** row, click in the second column, click the **arrow**, and then click **Day of Week** to add the field to the design grid. In the field list, point to **Room**, drag the field name down into the design grid until the ⬚ pointer displays in the **Field** row in the first column, and then release the mouse button. Using one of the three techniques you just practiced, add the **Time** field to the fourth column

b. On the **Design tab**, in the **Results group**, click **Run**. This query answers the question, *What is the room, date, day of week, and time for all of the orientation sessions in the Lastname Firstname 2C Orientation Sessions table?*

c. On the **Quick Access Toolbar**, click **Save**. In the **Save As** dialog box, type **Lastname Firstname 2C All Sessions Query** and then click **OK**. **Close** the query.

5 **Open** the **Navigation Pane**. Right-click the **Lastname Firstname 2C All Sessions Query** and click **Copy**. Right-click in a blank area of the **Navigation Pane**, and then click **Paste**. In the **Paste As** dialog box, type **Lastname Firstname 2C Day of Week Query** and then click **OK** to create a new query based on an existing query. **Close** the **Navigation Pane**.

a. In the **Navigation Pane**, right-click the **Lastname Firstname 2C Day of the Week Query** and click **Design View**. In the design grid, point to the thin gray selection bar above the **Room** field name to display the ↓ pointer, click to select the column, and then press Delete.

b. Point to the selection bar above the **Day of Week** field name to display the ⬚ pointer, and then drag to the left until a dark vertical line displays on the left side of the **Date** column. Release the mouse button to position the **Day of Week** field in the first column.

c. **Run** the query. The query results display three fields. This query answers the question, *What is the day of week, date, and time for every orientation session in the Lastname Firstname 2C Orientation Sessions table?*

d. **Close** the query, and in the message box, click **Yes** to save the changes to the design—you deleted one field and moved another field. **Open** the **Navigation Pane**.

6 Right-click the **Lastname Firstname 2C Day of the Week Query** and click **Copy**. Right-click in a blank area of the **Navigation Pane**, and then click **Paste**. In the **Paste As** dialog box, type **Lastname Firstname 2C Sessions Sort Query** and then click **OK** to create a new query based on an existing query. Increase the width of the **Navigation Pane** so that the names of all of the objects display fully.

a. In the **Navigation Pane**, right-click your **Lastname Firstname 2C Sessions Sort Query**, click **Design View**, and then **Close** the **Navigation Pane**. In the field list, drag the **Room** field to the left of the **Day of Week** field to position it in the first column. In the design grid, in the **Sort** row under **Room**, click the **arrow**, and then click **Descending**. In the **Sort** row under **Date**, click the **arrow**, and then click **Ascending**.

b. **Run** the query. This query answers the question, *For every session, within each room (with the Room field sorted in descending order), what is the day of week, date (with the Date field sorted in ascending order), and time?*

c. **Close** the query, and in the message box, click **Yes** to save the changes to the query design.

(continues on next page)

Chapter Review

7 ▶ Click the **Create tab**, and then in the **Queries group**, click **Query Design**. In the **Show Table** dialog box, double-click your **Lastname Firstname 2C New Students** table to add it to the table area, and then **Close** the **Show Table** dialog box. Resize the field list to display all of the field names and the table name. Add the following fields to the design grid in the order given: **Student ID**, **Last Name**, **First Name**, and **Orientation ID**.

a. In the design grid, click in the **Criteria** row under **Orientation ID**, type **OS-001**—the first character is the letters *O* and *S* followed by a hyphen, two zeros, and the number *1*—and then press Enter.

b. **Run** the query to display 13 records that meet the specified criteria—records that have *OS-001* in the *Orientation ID* field. **Save** the query as **Lastname Firstname 2C First Session Query** and then **Close** the query.

c. On the **Create tab**, in the **Queries group**, click **Query Design**. In the **Show Table** dialog box, double-click your **Lastname Firstname 2C New Students** table to add it to the table area, and then **Close** the **Show Table** dialog box. Resize the field list, and then add the following fields to the design grid in the order given: **Student ID**, **First Name**, **Last Name**, **Phone Number**, **Email Address**, and **City**. Click in the **Criteria** row under **City**, type **dripping springs** and then press Enter.

d. **Run** the query to display the five new students who live in *Dripping Springs*. Switch to **Design** view. In the design grid, in the **Show** row under **City**, click to clear the check box. Recall that if all of the results use the same criteria, such as *dripping springs*, it is not necessary to display that field in the query results. **Run** the query again. **Save** the query as **Lastname Firstname 2C Dripping Springs Query** and then **Close** the query.

e. On the **Create tab**, in the **Queries group**, click **Query Design**. In the **Show Table** dialog box, double-click your **Lastname Firstname 2C New Students** table to add it to the table area, and then **Close** the **Show Table** dialog box. Resize the field list, and then add the following fields to the design grid in the order given: **Student ID**, **First Name**, **Last Name**, **Email Address**, **Phone Number**, and **Orientation ID**. Click in the **Sort** row under **Last Name**, click the **arrow**, and then click **Ascending**. Click in the **Criteria** row under **Orientation ID**, type **is null** and then press Enter.

f. **Run** the query to display the three new students who have not signed up for an orientation session. **Save** the query as **Lastname Firstname 2C Missing Orientation ID Query** and then **Close** the query.

g. **Open** the **Navigation Pane**. If necessary, increase the width of the pane so that all object names display fully. On the right side of the title bar, click **Close** to close the database and to close Access. As directed by your instructor, submit your database for grading.

You have completed Project 2C **END**

Chapter Review

In the following Skills Review, you will assist Dr. Michael Bransford, the Student Activities Director for Texas Lakes Community College, in answering his questions about fundraisers, clubs, donations, dates of fundraiser events, and fundraiser locations. Your completed Navigation Pane will look similar to Figure 2.56.

Apply 2B skills from these Objectives:

8. Specify Numeric Criteria in a Query
9. Use Compound Criteria in a Query
10. Create a Query Based on More Than One Table
11. Use Wildcards in a Query
12. Create Calculated Fields in a Query
13. Calculate Statistics and Group Data in a Query
14. Create a Crosstab Query
15. Create a Parameter Query

Project Files

For Project 2D, you will need the following files:

a02D_Club_Fundraisers

a02D_Club (Excel workbook)

You will save your database as:

Lastname_Firstname_2D_Club_Fundraisers

Project Results

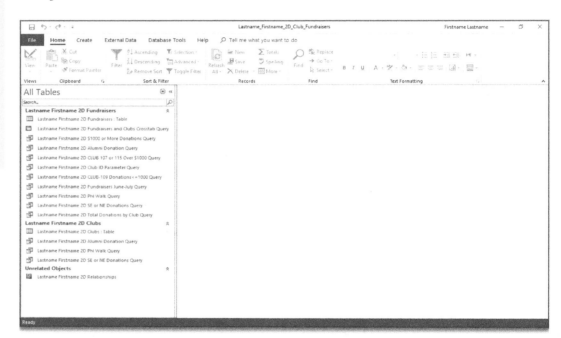

Figure 2.56

(continues on next page)

Chapter Review

1 ▶ Start Access. In the Access opening screen, click **Open Other Files**. Under **Open**, click **Browse** and then navigate to the location where your student data files are stored. Double-click **a02D_Club_Fundraisers** to open the database.

a. Click the **File tab**, and then click **Save As**. Under **File Types**, be sure **Save Database As** is selected. On the right, under **Database File Types**, be sure **Access Database** is selected, and then at the bottom of the screen, click **Save As**. In the **Save As** dialog box, navigate to your **Access Chapter 2** folder. Click in the **File name** box, type **Lastname_ Firstname_2D_Club_Fundraisers** and then press Enter. On the **Message Bar**, click **Enable Content**.

b. In the **Navigation Pane**, right-click **2D Fundraisers**, click **Rename**, type **Lastname Firstname 2D Fundraisers** and then press Enter. Increase the width of the **Navigation Pane** to display the entire table name. Double-click the table name to open it, examine the fields in the table, and then **Close** the table.

c. Click the **External Data tab**, and then in the **Import & Link group**, click **Excel**. In the **Get External Data – Excel Spreadsheet** dialog box, to the right of the **File name** box, click **Browse**. In the **File Open** dialog box, navigate to your student data files, and then double-click **a02D_Clubs**. Be sure that the **Import the source data into a new table in the current database** option button is selected, and then click **OK**.

d. In the upper left area of the wizard, select the **First Row Contains Column Headings** check box. In the wizard, click **Next**, and then click **Next** again. In the wizard, click the **Choose my own primary key** option button, be sure that **Club ID** displays, and then click **Next**. With the text selected in the **Import to Table** box, type **Lastname Firstname 2D Clubs**, and then click **Finish**. In the **Import Spreadsheet Wizard**, click **Next**, and then click **Finish**. In the **Get External Data – Excel Spreadsheet** dialog box, click **Close**.

e. In the **Navigation Pane**, right-click your **Lastname Firstname 2D Clubs** table, and then click **Design View**. **Close** the **Navigation Pane**. In the **Field Name** column, click **Club ID**. In the **Field Properties** area, click **Field Size**, type **8** and then press Enter. On the **Design tab**, in the **Views group**,

click **View** to switch to **Datasheet** view. In the message box, click **Yes** to save the design changes. In the second message box, click **Yes**—no data will be lost. Examine the fields and data in the table. To the left of the **Club ID** field name, click the **Select All** button. On the **Home tab**, in the **Records group**, click **More**, and then click **Field Width**. In the **Column Width** dialog box, click **Best Fit**. Click in any record to cancel the selection, **Save** the table, and then **Close** the table.

f. Click the **Database Tools tab**, and then in the **Relationships group**, click **Relationships**. In the **Show Table** dialog box, double-click your **Lastname Firstname 2D Clubs** table, and then double-click your **Lastname Firstname 2D Fundraisers** table to add both tables to the **Relationships** window. **Close** the **Show Table** dialog box. By dragging the lower right corner of the field list, resize each field list to display all of the field names and the entire table name. Point to the title bar of the field list on the right, and drag the field list to the right until there are approximately one inch of space between the field lists.

g. In the **Lastname Firstname 2D Clubs** field list, point to **Club ID**, drag the field name into the **Lastname Firstname 2D Fundraisers** table on top of **Club ID**, and then release the mouse button. Point to the title bar of the **Edit Relationships** dialog box, and then drag it downward below the two field lists. In the **Edit Relationships** dialog box, select the **Enforce Referential Integrity** check box, the **Cascade Update Related Fields** check box, the **Cascade Delete Related Records** check box, and then click **Create**. A *one-to-many* relationship is established; *one* student club can raise money for *many* fundraising events.

h. On the **Design tab**, in the **Tools group**, click **Relationship Report**. On the **Print Preview tab**, in the **Page Size group**, click **Margins**, and then click **Normal**. **Save** the report as **Lastname Firstname 2D Relationships** and then click **Close All**.

2 ▶ Click the **Create tab**. In the **Queries group**, click **Query Design**. In the **Show Table** dialog box, double-click your **Lastname Firstname 2D Fundraisers** table to add it to the table area, and then **Close** the **Show Table** dialog box. Resize the field list. Add the following fields to the design grid in the order given: **Fundraiser Name**, **Donation**, and **Fundraiser Location**.

(continues on next page)

Chapter Review

a. Click in the **Sort** row under **Fundraiser Name**, click the **arrow**, and then click **Ascending**. Click in the **Criteria** row under **Donations**, type **>=1000** and then press ⏎. **Run** the query and notice that seven records match the criteria. This query answers the question, *Where was each fundraiser held (in alphabetical order by the Fundraiser Name field) for fundraisers with donations greater than or equal to $1,000?*

b. **Save** the query as **Lastname Firstname 2D $1000 or More Donations Query**. **Close** the query.

c. In the **Navigation Pane**, right-click your **Lastname Firstname 2D $1000 or More Donations Query**, and click **Copy**. In a blank area in the Navigation Pane, right-click and click **Paste**. In the **Paste As** dialog box, type **Lastname Firstname 2D Fundraisers June-July Query** and then click **OK**. In the **Navigation Pane**, right-click your **Lastname Firstname 2D Fundraisers June-July Query** query, and then click **Design View**.

d. In the **Lastname Firstname 2D Fundraisers** field list, double-click **Date** to add it to the fourth column in the design grid. Click in the **Sort** row under **Fundraiser Name**, click the **arrow**, and then click **(not sorted)**. Click in the **Sort** row under **Date**, click the **arrow**, and then click **Ascending**.

e. In the **Criteria** row under **Donation**, select the existing criteria, *>=1000*, and then press ⌦ so that the query results are not restricted by a monetary value. Click in the **Criteria** row under **Date**, type **between 6/1/22 and 7/31/22** and then press ⏎. **Run** the query, and notice that four records match the criteria. This query answers the question, *What is the fundraiser name, donation, fundraiser location, and date (in chronological order) for events held between June 1, 2022 and July 31, 2022?*

f. **Close** the query, and in the message box, click **Yes** to save the changes to the query design.

3 ▶ Click the **Create tab**, and in the **Queries group**, click **Query Design**. In the **Show Table** dialog box, double-click your **Lastname Firstname 2D Fundraisers** table to add it to the table area, and then **Close** the **Show Table** dialog box. Resize the field list. Add the following fields to the design grid in the order given: **Fundraiser Name**, **Fundraiser Location**, **Donation**, and **Club ID**.

a. Click in the **Sort** row under **Fundraiser Name**, click the **arrow**, and then click **Ascending**. Click in the **Criteria** row under **Club ID**, type **club-109**

and then press ⏎. Click in the **Criteria** row under **Donation**, type **<=1000** and then press ⏎. **Run** the query, and notice that two records match the criteria. Switch back to **Design** view, and in the **Show** row under **Club ID**, clear the check box. **Run** the query again. This query answers the question, *Which fundraiser events with their locations listed had donations of $1,000 or less raised by CLUB-109?*

b. **Save** the query as **Lastname Firstname 2D CLUB-109 Donations <=1000 Query** and **Close** the query.

c. On the **Create tab**, in the **Queries group**, click **Query Design**. In the **Show Table** dialog box, double-click your **Lastname Firstname 2D Fundraisers** table to add it to the table area, and then **Close** the **Show Table** dialog box. Resize the field list. Add the following fields to the design grid in the order given: **Club ID**, **Fundraiser Name**, **Date**, and **Donation**.

d. Click in the **Sort** row under **Date**, click the **arrow**, and then click **Ascending**. Click in the **Criteria** row under **Club ID**, type **club-107 or club-115** and then press ⏎. Click in the **Criteria** row under **Donation**, type **>1000** and then press ⏎. **Run** the query, and notice that two records match the criteria. This query answers the question, *Which fundraiser events received donations over $1,000 from either CLUB-107 or CLUB-115, and on what dates (in chronological order) were the fundraiser events held?*

e. **Save** the query as **Lastname Firstname 2D CLUB 107 or 115 Over $1000 Query** and **Close** the query.

4 ▶ On the **Create tab**, in the **Queries group**, click **Query Design**. In the **Show Table** dialog box, double-click your **Lastname Firstname 2D Clubs** table, and then double-click your **Lastname Firstname 2D Fundraisers** table to add both tables to the table area. **Close** the **Show Table** dialog box. Drag the field list on the right side to the right until there are approximately one inch of space between the field lists, and then resize each field list.

a. From the **Lastname Firstname 2D Clubs** field list, add the following fields to the design grid in the order given: **Club Name**, **Campus**, and **Club Email**. From the **Lastname Firstname 2D Fundraisers** field list, add the following fields to the design grid in the order given: **Fundraiser Name**, **Date**, and **Donation**. In the design grid, drag the **Donation** field to position it as the first column.

(continues on next page)

Chapter Review

Mastering Access: Project 2D Club Fundraisers (continued)

b. Click in the **Sort** row under **Donation**, click the **arrow**, and then click **Descending**. Click in the **Criteria** row under **Campus**, type **southeast** and then press Enter. Click in the **or** row under **Campus**, type **northeast** and then press Enter. **Run** the query, and notice that 10 records match the criteria. This query answers the question, *For the Southeast and Northeast campuses, what is the donation (in descending order), club name, campus name, club email address, fundraiser name, and date of all fundraising events?*

c. **Save** the query as **Lastname Firstname 2D SE or NE Donations Query** and then display the query results in **Print Preview**. In the **Page Layout group**, click **Landscape**. In the **Page Size group**, click **Margins**, and then click **Normal**. **Close** the query.

5 On the **Create tab**, in the **Queries group**, click **Query Design**. In the **Show Table** dialog box, double-click your **Lastname Firstname 2D Clubs** table, and then double-click your **Lastname Firstname 2D Fundraisers** table to add both tables to the table area. **Close** the **Show Table** dialog box. Drag the field list on the right side to the right until there are approximately two inches of space between the field lists, and then resize each field list. From the **Lastname Firstname 2D Clubs** field list, add the **Club Name** field to the design grid. From the **Lastname Firstname 2D Fundraisers** field list, add the **Fundraiser Name** field to the design grid.

a. Click in the **Sort** row under **Club Name**, click the **arrow**, and then click **Ascending**. Click in the **Criteria** row under **Club Name**, type **phi*** and then press Enter. In the **Criteria** row under **Fundraiser Name**, type ***walk*** and then press Enter. **Run** the query, and notice that two records match the criteria—Club Name begins with *Phi* and Fundraiser Name has *Walk* anywhere in its name. This query answers the question, *Which clubs (in alphabetical order) that have names starting with Phi have raised money for fundraisers that involve walking?*

b. **Save** the query as **Lastname Firstname 2D Phi Walk Query** and then **Close** the query.

6 On the **Create tab**, in the **Queries group**, click **Query Design**. In the **Show Table** dialog box, double-click your **Lastname Firstname 2D Clubs** table, and then double-click your **Lastname Firstname 2D Fundraisers** table to add both tables to the table area. **Close** the **Show Table** dialog box. Drag the field list on

the right side to the right until there are approximately two inches of space between the field lists, and then resize each field list. From the field lists, add the following fields to the design grid in the order given: **Fundraiser ID**, **Club Name**, and **Donation**.

a. Click in the **Sort** row under **Fundraiser ID**, click the **arrow**, and then click **Ascending**. Alumni will donate an additional 25 percent based on the value in the Donation field. In the **Field** row, right-click in the fourth column, and then click **Zoom**. In the **Zoom** dialog box, type **Alumni Donation:[Donation]*0.25** and then click **OK**. **Run** the query to be sure the new field—*Alumni Donation*—displays. In the first record, the *Alumni Donation* displays as *156.25*.

b. Switch to **Design** view. In the **Field** row, right-click in the first empty column, and then click **Zoom**. In the **Zoom** dialog box, type **Total Donation:[Donation]+[Alumni Donation]** and then click **OK**. **Run** the query to be sure that the new field—*Total Donation*—displays. In the first record, the *Total Donation* displays as *$781.25*.

c. Switch to **Design** view. In the **Field** row, click in the **Alumni Donation** field name box. On the **Design tab**, in the **Show/Hide group**, click **Property Sheet**. In the **Property Sheet**, click **Format**. In the property setting box, click the **arrow**, and then click **Currency**. **Close** the **Property Sheet**, and then **Run** the query. This query answers the question, *In ascending order by Fundraiser ID, what is the club name, donation, alumni donation, and total donation for each fundraising event if the alumni donate an additional 25 percent based on the value in the Donation field?*

d. To the left of the **Fundraiser ID** field name, click the **Select All** button. On the **Home tab**, in the **Records group**, click **More**, and then click **Field Width**. In the **Column Width** dialog box, click **Best Fit**. Click in any field to cancel the selection, **Save** the query as **Lastname Firstname 2D Alumni Donation Query** and **Close** the query.

7 On the **Create tab**, in the **Queries group**, click **Query Design**. In the **Show Table** dialog box, double-click your **Lastname Firstname 2D Fundraisers** table to add the table to the table area. **Close** the **Show Table** dialog box. Resize the field list, and then add the **Donation** field to the design grid.

(continues on next page)

Chapter Review

a. On the **Design tab**, in the **Show/Hide group**, click **Totals** to add a **Total** row as the third row in the design grid. In the **Total** row under **Donation**, click in the box that displays *Group By*, click the **arrow**, and then click **Sum**. In the **Show/Hide group**, click **Property Sheet**. In the **Property Sheet**, set **Decimal Places** to **0**, and then **Close** the **Property Sheet**. **Run** the query. Apply Best Fit to the field. The sum of the Donations field is *$20,259*.

b. Switch to **Design** view. From the field list, drag the **Club ID** field to the first column in the design grid—the **Donation** field moves to the second column. **Run** the query. This query answers the question, *For each club ID, what are the total donations?*

c. **Save** the query as **Lastname Firstname 2D Total Donations by Club Query** and then **Close** the query.

8 On the **Create tab**, in the **Queries group**, click **Query Wizard**. In the **New Query** dialog box, click **Crosstab Query Wizard**, and then click **OK**. In the **Crosstab Query Wizard**, click your **Table: Lastname Firstname 2D Fundraisers**, and then click **Next**. In the wizard under **Available Fields**, double-click **Fundraiser ID** to group the records by this field and display the Fundraiser IDs as row headings. Click **Next**.

a. In the wizard, in the field list, click **Club ID** to select the column headings, and then click **Next**. Under **Fields**, click **Donation**. Under **Functions**, click **Sum**, and then click **Next**. In the **What do you want to name your query?** box, select the existing text, type **Lastname Firstname 2D Fundraisers and Clubs Crosstab Query** and then click **Finish**.

b. Click the **Home** tab, and then switch to **Design** view. In the design grid, click in the **Donation** column. On the **Design tab**, in the **Show/Hide group**, click **Property Sheet**. In the **Property Sheet**, set **Decimal Places** to **0**, and then **Close** the **Property Sheet**. **Run** the query. Select all of the columns, apply **Best Fit**, and then **Save** the query. This query answers the question, *Grouped by Fundraiser ID and Club ID, what are the total donations?*

c. **Close** the query.

9 On the **Create tab**, in the **Queries group**, click **Query Design**. In the **Show Table** dialog box, double-click your **Lastname Firstname 2D Fundraisers** table to add the table to the table area. **Close** the **Show Table** dialog box, and then resize the field list. Add the following fields to the design grid in the order given: **Club ID**, **Fundraiser Location**, and **Date**.

a. In the **Sort** row under **Date**, click the **arrow**, and then click **Ascending**. In the **Criteria** row under **Club ID**, right-click, and then click **Zoom**. In the **Zoom** dialog box, type **[Enter a Club ID in the format club-###]** and then click **OK**. **Save** the query as **Lastname Firstname 2D Club ID Parameter Query**

b. **Run** the query. In the **Enter Parameter Value** dialog box, type **club-109** and then click **OK**. Three records match the criteria. **Close** the query.

c. **Open** the **Navigation Pane**, and increase the width of the pane so that all object names display fully. On the right side of the title bar, click **Close** to close the database and **Close** Access. As directed by your instructor, submit your database for grading.

You have completed Project 2D **END**

Content-Based Assessments (Mastery and Transfer of Learning)

MyLab IT Grader

Mastering Access **Project 2E Biology Supplies**

Apply 2A skills from these Objectives:

1. Open and Save an Existing Database
2. Create Table Relationships
3. Sort Records in a Table
4. Create a Query in Design View
5. Create a New Query From an Existing Query
6. Sort Query Results
7. Specify Criteria in a Query

In the following Mastering Access project, you will assist Greg Franklin, Chair of the Biology Department at the Southwest Campus, in using his database to answer questions about biology laboratory supplies. Your completed Navigation Pane will look similar to Figure 2.57.

Project Files for MyLab IT Grader

1. In your **MyLab IT** course, locate and click **Access 2E Biology Supplies**, Download Materials, and then Download All Files.
2. Extract the zipped folder to your Access Chapter 2 folder. Close the Grader download screens.
3. Take a moment to open the downloaded **Access_2E_Biology_Supplies_Instructions**; note any recent updates to the book.

Project Results

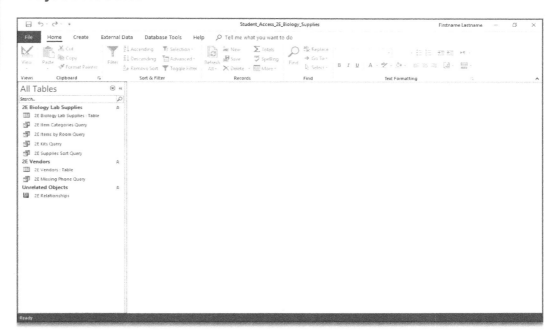

Figure 2.57

For Non-MyLab Submissions

For Project 2E, you will need:

a02E_Biology_Supplies

Start with an Access Data File

In your Access Chapter 2 folder, save your database as:

Lastname_Firstname_2E_Biology_Supplies

After you have saved your database, open it to launch Access. On the next page, begin with Step 2.
After Step 10, submit your file as directed by your instructor.

(continues on next page)

Mastering Access: Project 2E Biology Supplies (continued)

1 Navigate to your **Access Chapter 2 folder**, and then double-click the downloaded file that displays your name—**Student_2E_Biology Supplies** and then enable the content.

2 Open both tables to examine the fields and data, and then **Close** both tables. Create a *one-to-many* relationship between your **2E Vendors** table and your **2E Biology Lab Supplies** table using the common field **Vendor ID**. **Enforce Referential Integrity**, and enable both cascade options. *One* vendor can supply *many* supplies. Create a **Relationship Report** with **Normal Margins**. Save it as **2E Relationships**

3 **Close All** open objects. Open your **2E Vendors** table. In the last record, in the **Vendor ID** field, select **V-100**, type **V-001** and then press ⬇ to save the record. **Close** the table.

4 Open your **2E Biology Lab Supplies** table. Sort the records first in **Descending** order by **Price Per Item** and then in **Ascending** order by **Category**. **Close** the table, saving changes to the table.

5 **Create** a query in **Query Design** view using your **2E Biology Lab Supplies** table to answer the question, *What is the item ID, item name, room, location, and quantity in stock for all of the items, sorted in ascending order by the Room field and the Location field?* Display the fields in the order listed in the question. **Save** the query as **2E Items by Room Query Close** the query.

6 In the **Navigation Pane**, use your **2E Items by Room Query** to create a new query object named **2E Item Categories Query** and then redesign the query to answer the question, *What is the item ID, item name, category, vendor ID, and quantity in stock for all items, sorted in ascending order by the Category field and the Vendor ID field?* Display only the fields necessary to answer the question and in the order listed in the question. **Close** the query, saving the design changes.

7 In the **Navigation Pane**, use your **2E Items by Room Query** to create a new query object named **2E Supplies Sort Query** and then open the new query in **Design** view. Redesign the query to answer the question,

What is the item name, category, price per item, and quantity in stock for all supplies, sorted in ascending order by the Category field and then in descending order by the Price Per Item field? Display only the fields necessary to answer the question and in the order listed in the question. **Close** the query, saving the design changes.

8 Using your **2E Supplies Sort Query**, create a new query object named **2E Kits Query** and then redesign the query to answer the question, *What is item name, category, price per item, quantity in stock, and vendor ID for all items that have a category of kits, sorted in ascending order by the Item Name field?* Do not display the **Category** field in the query results. Display the rest of the fields in the order listed in the question. Six records match the criteria. **Close** the query, saving the design changes.

9 **Create** a query in **Query Design** view using your **2E Vendors** table to answer the question, *What is the vendor ID, vendor name, and phone number where the phone number is blank, sorted in ascending order by the Vendor Name field?* Display the fields in the order listed in the question. Two records match the criteria. **Save** the query as **2E Missing Phone Query Close** the query.

10 Be sure all objects are closed. **Open** the **Navigation Pane**, be sure that all object names display fully, and then **Close** Access.

11 In **MyLab IT**, locate and click the Grader Project **Access 2E Biology Supplies**. In **step 3**, under **Upload Completed Assignment**, click **Choose File**. In the **Open** dialog box, navigate to your **Access Chapter 2 folder**, and then click your **Student_Access_2E_Biology_Supplies** file one time to select it. In the lower right corner of the **Open** dialog box, click **Open**. The name of your selected file displays above the Upload button.

12 To submit your file to **MyLab IT** for grading, click **Upload**, wait a moment for a green **Success!** message, and then in **step 4**, click the blue **Submit for Grading** button. Click **Close Assignment** to return to your list of **Course Materials**.

You have completed Project 2E **END**

Content-Based Assessments (Mastery and Transfer of Learning)

| MyLab IT Grader | **Mastering Access** | **Project 2F Student Publications** |

Apply 2B skills from these Objectives:

8. Specify Numeric Criteria in a Query
9. Use Compound Criteria in a Query
10. Create a Query Based on More Than One Table
11. Use Wildcards in a Query
12. Create Calculated Fields in a Query
13. Calculate Statistics and Group Data in a Query
14. Create a Crosstab Query
15. Create a Parameter Query

In the following Mastering Access project, you will assist Siabhon Reiss, the English Writing Lab Coordinator, in using her database to answer questions about student publications. Your completed Navigation Pane will look similar to Figure 2.58.

Project Files for MyLab IT Grader

1. In your **MyLab IT** course, locate and click **Access 2F Student Publications**, Download Materials, and then Download All Files.
2. Extract the zipped folder to your Access Chapter 2 folder. Close the Grader download screens.
3. Take a moment to open the downloaded **Access_2F_Student_Publications_Instructions**; note any recent updates to the book.

Project Results

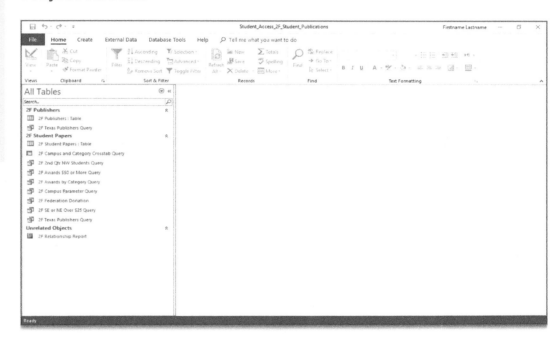

Figure 2.58

For Non-MyLab Submissions	**Start with an Access Data File**
For Project 2F, you will need:	In your Access Chapter 2 folder, save your database as:
a02F_Student_Publications	**Lastname_Firstname_2F_Student_Publications**
a02F_Student_Papers (Excel workbook)	

After you have saved your database, open it to launch Access. On the next page, begin with Step 2.
After Step 10, submit your file as directed by your instructor.

(continues on next page)

Content-Based Assessments (Mastery and Transfer of Learning)

1 Navigate to your **Access Chapter 2 folder**, and then double-click the downloaded file that displays your name—**Student_2F_Student_Publications** and then enable the content.

2 From your student data files, import **a02F_Student_Papers** as a new table in the database. Designate the first row of the spreadsheet as column headings, and designate **Paper ID** as the primary key. Name the new table **2F Student Papers**

Open your **2F Student Papers** table in **Design** view. For the **Student ID** field, change the **Data Type** to **Short Text**. Switch to **Datasheet** view, apply **Best Fit** to all of the columns, and then **Save** the table. Examine the fields and data in this table. Open your **2F Publishers** table, examine the fields and data, and then **Close All** open objects.

Create a *one-to-many* relationship between your **2F Publishers** table and your **2F Student Papers** table using the common field **Publisher ID**. **Enforce Referential Integrity** and enable both cascade options. *One* publisher can publish *many* student papers. Create a **Relationship Report** with **Normal Margins**, saving it as **2F Relationship Report Close All** open objects.

3 Create a query in **Query Design** view using your **2F Student Papers** table to answer the question, *What is the student ID, home campus, award paid, and publisher ID for awards greater than or equal to $50, sorted in ascending order by the Student ID field?* Display the fields in the order listed in the question. Five records match the criteria. **Save** the query as **2F Awards $50 or More Query**

4 Using your **2F Awards $50 or More Query**, create a new query object named **2F 2nd Qtr NW Students Query** and then redesign the query to answer the questions, *Which students (Student ID) from the Northwest campus had papers published between 4/1/22 and 6/30/22, and what was the paper name, the award paid, and the category, sorted in ascending order by the Publication Date field?* Do not display the **Home Campus** field in the query results. Display the rest of the fields in the order listed in the question. Three records match the criteria. **Close** the query, saving the design changes.

5 Create a query in **Query Design** view using your **2F Student Papers** table to answer the question, *Which paper IDs, paper names, and category for students from the Southeast and Northeast campuses were published that had an award paid greater than $25, sorted in descending order by the Award Paid field?* Display the fields in the order listed in the question. Six records match the criteria. **Save** the query as **2F SE or NE Over $25 Query Close** the query.

6 Create a query in **Query Design** view using both tables to answer the questions, *Which paper names were published with a publisher name that has Texas as part of its name, what is the contact name and contact phone number, and what was the award paid, sorted in descending order by the Award Paid field?* (Hint: Use a wildcard character in the criteria row.) Display the fields in the order listed in the question. Eight records match the criteria. **Save** the query as **2F Texas Publishers Query Close** the query.

7 The college's Federation of English Faculty will donate money to the English Writing Lab based on 50 percent of the awards paid to the students. **Create** a query in **Query Design** view using your **2F Student Papers** table to answer the question, *In ascending order by the Paper ID field, what will be the total of each donation to the Writing Lab if the Federation donates an additional 50 percent of each award paid to students?* (Hint: First calculate the amount of the donation, naming the new field **Federation Donation**, and then run the query to be sure the correct results display. Then calculate the total donation, naming the new field **Total Donation**.) Change the property settings of the **Federation Donation** field to display with a **Format** of **Currency** and with **Decimal Places** set to **2**. For the **Publisher ID** of **P-20**, the *Federation Donation* is *$22.50*, and the *Total Donation* is *$67.50*. Apply **Best Fit** to all of the columns, **Save** the query as **2F Federation Donation Query Close** the query.

8 Create a query in **Query Design** view using your **2F Student Papers** table and the **Sum** aggregate function to answer the question, *What are the total awards paid for each category, sorted in descending order by the Award Paid field?* Display the fields in the order listed in the question. Change the property settings of the **Award Paid** field to display with a **Format** of **Currency** and with **Decimal Places** set to **0**. For the **Category** of **Student Life**, total awards paid are *$265*. Apply **Best Fit** to the **SumOfAward Paid** column. **Save** the query as **2F Awards by Category Query Close** the query.

(continues on next page)

Content-Based Assessments (Mastery and Transfer of Learning)

Mastering Access: Project 2F Student Publications (continued)

9 By using the **Query Wizard**, create a crosstab query based on your **2F Student Papers** table. Select **Home Campus** as the row headings and **Category** as the column headings. **Sum** the **Award Paid** field. Name the query **2F Campus and Category Crosstab Query** In **Design** view, change the property settings of the last two fields to display with a **Format** of **Currency** and with **Decimal Places** set to **0**. This query answers the question, *What are the total awards paid for student publications by each home campus and by each category?* Apply **Best Fit** to all of the columns, and then **Save** the query. **Close** the query.

10 **Create** a query in **Query Design** view using your **2F Student Papers** table that prompts you to **Enter the Home Campus**, and then answers the question, *What is the home campus, student ID, paper name, category, and publication date for student publications, sorted in ascending order by the Publication Date field?* Display the fields in the order listed in the question. **Run** the

query, entering **southwest** when prompted for criteria. Seven records match the criteria. **Save** the query as **2F Campus Parameter Query Close** the query.

11 Open the **Navigation Pane** and be sure that all object names display fully. **Close** Access.

12 In **MyLab IT**, locate and click the Grader Project **Access 2F Student Publications**. In **step 3**, under **Upload Completed Assignment**, click **Choose File**. In the **Open** dialog box, navigate to your **Access Chapter 2 folder**, and then click your **Student_Access_2F_Student_Publications** file one time to select it. In the lower right corner of the **Open** dialog box, click **Open**. The name of your selected file displays above the Upload button.

13 To submit your file to **MyLab IT** for grading, click **Upload**, wait a moment for a green **Success!** message, and then in **step 4**, click the blue **Submit for Grading** button. Click **Close Assignment** to return to your list of **Course Materials**.

You have completed Project 2F   **END**

Content-Based Assessments (Mastery and Transfer of Learning)

Mastering Access **Project 2G Student Scholarships**

Apply 2A and 2B skills from these Objectives:

1. Open and Save an Existing Database
2. Create Table Relationships
3. Sort Records in a Table
4. Create a Query in Design View
5. Create a New Query From an Existing Query
6. Sort Query Results
7. Specify Criteria in a Query
8. Specify Numeric Criteria in a Query
9. Use Compound Criteria in a Query
10. Create a Query Based on More Than One Table
11. Use Wildcards in a Query
12. Create Calculated Fields in a Query
13. Calculate Statistics and Group Data in a Query
14. Create a Crosstab Query
15. Create a Parameter Query

In the following Mastering Access project, you will assist Kim Ngo, Director of Academic Scholarships, in using her database to answer questions about scholarships awarded to students. Your completed Navigation Pane will look similar to Figure 2.59.

Project Files for MyLab IT Grader

1. In your **MyLab IT** course, locate and click **Access 2G Student Scholarships**, Download Materials, and then Download All Files.
2. Extract the zipped folder to your Access Chapter 2 folder. Close the Grader download screens.
3. Take a moment to open the downloaded **Access_2G_Student_Scholarships_Instructions**; note any recent updates to the book.

Project Results

Figure 2.59

For Non-MyLab Submissions

For Project 2G you will need:
a02G_Student_Scholarships

Start with an Access Data File

In your Access Chapter 2 folder, save your Access as:
Lastname_Firstname_2G_Student_Scholarships

After you have saved your database, open it to launch Access. On the next page, begin with Step 2.
After Step 12, submit your file as directed by your instructor.

(continues on next page)

Content-Based Assessments (Mastery and Transfer of Learning)

Mastering Access: Project 2G Student Scholarships (continued)

1 ▶ Navigate to your **Access Chapter 2 folder**, and then double-click the downloaded file that displays your name—**Student_2G_Student_Scholarships** and then enable the content.

2 ▶ Open both tables to examine the fields and data, and then **Close** both tables. Create a *one-to-many* relationship between your **2G Students** table and your **2G Scholarships Awarded** table using the common field **Student ID**. **Enforce Referential Integrity** and enable both cascade options. *One* student can have *many* scholarships. Create a **Relationship Report** with **Normal Margins**, saving it as **2G Relationships**. Create a paper or PDF electronic image as directed, and then **Close All** open objects. Open your **2G Students** table. In the last record, in the **Student ID** field, select **9999999**, type **2839403** and then press ⬇ to save the record. **Close** the table.

3 ▶ Create a query in **Query Design** view using your **2G Scholarships Awarded** table to answer the question, *What is the scholarship name, amount, and major for scholarships greater than or equal to $500, sorted in ascending order by the Scholarship Name field?* Display the fields in the order listed in the question. Eight records match the criteria. **Save** the query as **2G Amount $500 or More Query Close** the query.

4 ▶ Use your **2G Amount $500 or More Query** to create a new query object named **2G Awards 4th Qtr Query** and then redesign the query to answer the question, *Which scholarships (Scholarship Name) were awarded between 10/1/22 and 12/31/22, for what amount, and for which student (Student ID), sorted in ascending order by the Award Date field?* Display only the fields necessary to answer the question and in the order listed in the question. Do not restrict the results by amount, and sort only by the field designated in the question. Five records match the criteria. **Close** the query, saving the design changes.

5 ▶ Create a query in **Query Design** view using your **2G Scholarships Awarded** table to answer the question, *Which scholarships (Scholarship Name) were awarded for either Math or Business majors for amounts of more than $200, sorted in descending order by the Amount field?* Display the fields in the order listed in the question. Four records match the criteria. (Hint: If six records display, switch to Design view and combine the majors on one criteria line using OR.) **Save** the query as **2G Math or Business More Than $200 Query Close** the query.

6 ▶ Create a query in **Query Design** view using your **2G Students** table to answer the question, *What is the city, student ID, first name, and last name of students from cities that begin with the letter L, sorted in ascending order by the City field and by the Last Name field?* Display the fields in the order listed in the question. Five records match the criteria. **Save** the query as **2G L Cities Query Close** the query.

7 ▶ Create a query in **Query Design** view using your **2G Students** table and all of the fields to answer the question, *For which students is the Postal Code missing?* Three records match the criteria. **Save** the query as **2G Missing Postal Code Query** and **Close** the query.

8 ▶ The Board of Trustees for the college will donate an amount equal to 50 percent of each scholarship amount. **Create** a query in **Query Design** view using both tables to answer the question, *In ascending order by the Scholarship Name field, and including the first name and last name of the scholarship recipient, what will be the total value of each scholarship if the Board of Trustees donates an additional 50 percent of each award paid to students?* (Hint: First calculate the amount of the donation, naming the new field **Board Donation**, and then run the query to be sure the correct results display. Then calculate the total donation, naming the new field **Total Donation**.) Change the property settings of the appropriate fields to display with a **Format** of **Currency** and with **Decimal Places** set to **0**. For the **Scholarship Name** of **Amanda Snyder Foundation Scholarship**, the *Board Donation* is *$125*, and the *Total Donation* is *$375*. Apply **Best Fit** to all of the columns, **Save** the query as **2G Board Donation Query** and **Close** the query.

9 ▶ Create a query in **Query Design** view using your **2G Scholarships Awarded** table and the **Sum** aggregate function to answer the question, *For each major, what is the total scholarship amount, sorted in descending order by the Amount field?* Display the fields in the order listed in the question. Change the property settings of the **Amount** field to display with a **Format** of **Currency** and with **Decimal Places** set to **0**. For the **Major** of **History**, the total scholarship amount is *$1,850*. Apply **Best Fit** to all of the columns. **Save** the query as **2G Amount by Major Query** and **Close** the query.

(continues on next page)

Mastering Access: Project 2G Student Scholarships (continued)

10 By using the **Query Wizard**, create a crosstab query based on your **2G Scholarships Awarded** table. Select **Student ID** as the row headings and **Major** as the column headings. **Sum** the **Amount** field. Name the query **2G Student ID and Major Crosstab Query** In **Design** view, change the property settings of the last two fields to display with a **Format** of **Currency** and with **Decimal Places** set to **0**. This query answers the question, *What are the total scholarship amounts paid by each student ID and by each major?* Apply **Best Fit** to all of the columns, and then **Save** the query. **Close** the query.

11 **Create** a query in **Query Design** view using your **2G Scholarships Awarded** table that prompts you to enter the **Major** of the student, and then answers the question, *What is the scholarship name and amount for a major, sorted in ascending order by the Scholarship Name field?* Display the fields in the order listed in the question. **Run** the query, entering **history** when prompted for criteria. Four records match the criteria. Hide the **Major** field from the results, and then **Run** the query again, entering **history** when prompted for criteria. **Save** the query as **2G Major Parameter Query** and **Close** the query.

12 Open the **Navigation Pane** and be sure that all object names display fully. **Close** Access.

13 In **MyLab IT**, locate and click the Grader Project **Access 2G Student Scholarships**. In **step 3**, under **Upload Completed Assignment**, click **Choose File**. In the **Open** dialog box, navigate to your **Access Chapter 2 folder**, and then click your **Student_Access_2G_Student_Scholarships** file one time to select it. In the lower right corner of the **Open** dialog box, click **Open**. The name of your selected file displays above the Upload button.

14 To submit your file to **MyLab IT** for grading, click **Upload**, wait a moment for a green **Success!** message, and then in **step 4**, click the blue **Submit for Grading** button. Click **Close Assignment** to return to your list of **Course Materials**.

You have completed Project 2G **END**

Content-Based Assessments (Critical Thinking)

<table>
<tr><td>Apply a combination of the 2A and 2B skills.</td><td>**GO! Fix It**</td><td>**Project 2H Social Sciences**</td><td>IRC</td></tr>
<tr><td></td><td>**GO! Make It**</td><td>**Project 2I Faculty Awards**</td><td>IRC</td></tr>
<tr><td></td><td>**GO! Solve It**</td><td>**Project 2J Student Refunds**</td><td>IRC</td></tr>
<tr><td></td><td>**GO! Solve It**</td><td>**Project 2K Leave**</td><td></td></tr>
</table>

Project Files

For Project 2K, you will need the following file:

a02K_Leave

You will save your database as:

Lastname_Firstname_2K_Leave

Start Access, navigate to your student data files, open a02K_Leave, and then save the database in your Access Chapter 2 folder as **Lastname_Firstname_2K_Leave** Add your Lastname Firstname to the beginning of both table names, create a one-to-many relationship with cascade options between the two tables—*one* employee can receive *many* leave transactions—and then create a relationship report saving it as **Lastname Firstname 2K Relationships**

Create and save four queries to answer the following questions; be sure that all data displays fully:

- What is the last name and first name of employees who have used personal leave, sorted in ascending order by the Last Name field? Do not display the Leave field in the query results.

- What is the last name, first name, and email address of employees who have no phone number listed, sorted in ascending order by the Last Name and First Name fields?

- Grouped by the Leave Classification field, what is the total of each type of leave used? (Hint: Use the aggregate function Count.)

- What is the total number of leave transactions grouped in rows by the Employee# field and grouped in columns by the Leave Classification field?

Verify that the object names display fully in the Navigation Pane. As directed, submit your database for grading.

(continues on next page)

Content-Based Assessments (Critical Thinking)

		Performance Level		
		Exemplary	**Proficient**	**Developing**
Performance Criteria	**Create relationship and relationship report**	Relationship and relationship report created correctly.	Relationship and relationship report created with one error.	Relationship and relationship report created with two or more errors, or missing entirely.
	Create Personal Leave query	Query created with correct name, fields, sorting, and criteria.	Query created with one element incorrect.	Query created with two or more elements incorrect, or missing entirely.
	Create Missing Phone query	Query created with correct name, fields, sorting, and criteria.	Query created with one element incorrect.	Query created with two or more elements incorrect, or missing entirely.
	Create Type of Leave query	Query created with correct name, fields, and aggregate function.	Query created with one element incorrect.	Query created with two or more elements incorrect, or missing entirely.
	Create Crosstab query	Query created with correct name, row headings, column headings, and aggregate function.	Query created with one element incorrect.	Query created with two or more two elements incorrect, or missing entirely.

You have completed Project 2K | END

Outcomes-Based Assessments (Critical Thinking)

Rubric

The following outcomes-based assessments are open-ended assessments. That is, there is no specific correct result; your result will depend on your approach to the information provided. Make Professional Quality your goal. Use the following scoring rubric to guide you in how to approach the problem and then to evaluate how well your approach solves the problem.

The *criteria*—Software Mastery, Content, Format and Layout, and Process—represent the knowledge and skills you have gained that you can apply to solving the problem. The *levels of performance*—Professional Quality, Approaching Professional Quality, or Needs Quality Improvements—help you and your instructor evaluate your result.

	Your completed project is of Professional Quality if you:	Your completed project is Approaching Professional Quality if you:	Your completed project Needs Quality Improvements if you:
1-Software Mastery	Choose and apply the most appropriate skills, tools, and features and identify efficient methods to solve the problem.	Choose and apply some appropriate skills, tools, and features, but not in the most efficient manner.	Choose inappropriate skills, tools, or features, or are inefficient in solving the problem.
2-Content	Construct a solution that is clear and well organized, contains content that is accurate, appropriate to the audience and purpose, and is complete. Provide a solution that contains no errors of spelling, grammar, or style.	Construct a solution in which some components are unclear, poorly organized, inconsistent, or incomplete. Misjudge the needs of the audience. Have some errors in spelling, grammar, or style, but the errors do not detract from comprehension.	Construct a solution that is unclear, incomplete, or poorly organized, contains some inaccurate or inappropriate content, and contains many errors of spelling, grammar, or style. Do not solve the problem.
3-Format and Layout	Format and arrange all elements to communicate information and ideas, clarify function, illustrate relationships, and indicate relative importance.	Apply appropriate format and layout features to some elements, but not others. Overuse features, causing minor distraction.	Apply format and layout that does not communicate information or ideas clearly. Do not use format and layout features to clarify function, illustrate relationships, or indicate relative importance. Use available features excessively, causing distraction.
4-Process	Use an organized approach that integrates planning, development, self-assessment, revision, and reflection.	Demonstrate an organized approach in some areas, but not others; or, use an insufficient process of organization throughout.	Do not use an organized approach to solve the problem.

Apply a combination of the 2A and 2B skills.

GO! Think	Project 2L Coaches

Project Files

For Project 2L, you will need the following file:

a02L_Coaches

You will save your database as

Lastname_Firstname_2L_Coaches

Start Access, navigate to your student data files, open a02L_Coaches, and then save the database in your Access Chapter 2 folder as **Lastname_Firstname_2L_Coaches** Add to the beginning of both table names, create a one-to-many relationship with cascade options between the two tables—*one* coach can participate in *many* activities—and then create a relationship report saving it as **Lastname Firstname 2L Relationships**

Create queries to assist Randy Garza, the Athletic Director, answer the following questions about the coaches at Texas Lakes Community College:

- What is the last name and first name of every coach involved in *Dive* activities, sorted in ascending order by the Last Name field? Do not display the activity name.
- What is the last name and first name of every coach involved in basketball or football activities, sorted in ascending first by the Activity Name field and then by the Last Name field?
- Grouped by division, what is the total number of activity names, sorted in descending order by the total number? (Hint: Use the Count aggregate function.)
- What is the skill specialty, first name, last name, and phone number for coaches in a specified position that is entered when prompted for the Position, sorted in ascending order first by the Skill Specialty field and then by the Last Name field? (When prompted, enter the position of *director*)

Verify that the object names display fully in the Navigation Pane. As directed, submit your database for grading.

	You have completed Project 2L	END

GO! Think	Project 2M Club Donations	IRC
You and GO!	Project 2N Personal Inventory	IRC
GO! Cumulative Group Project	Project 2O Bell Orchid Hotels	IRC

Forms, Filters, and Reports

3
ACCESS 2019

PROJECT 3A

Outcomes
Create forms to enter and delete records and to display data in a database.

Objectives

1. Create and Use a Form to Add and Delete Records
2. Filter Records
3. Create a Form by Using the Form Wizard
4. Modify a Form in Layout View and in Design View

PROJECT 3B

Outcomes
Create reports to display database information.

Objectives

5. Create a Report by Using the Report Tool and Modify the Report in Layout View
6. Create a Report by Using the Report Wizard
7. Modify the Design of a Report
8. Keep Grouped Data Together in a Printed Report

nd3000/Shutterstock

In This Chapter

GO! To Work with Access

In this chapter, you will create forms to enter and delete data and to view data in database tables. Forms can display one record at a time with fields placed in the same order to match a paper source document. Records in a form or table can be filtered to display a subset of the records based on matching specific values. You will modify forms by adding fields, changing field widths, and adding labels to the forms. You will create professional-looking reports that summarize the data from query or table. You will modify the reports by changing the fields in the report, by changing the layout of the report, by grouping data, and by making sure that groupings of data stay together on the printed page.

The projects in this chapter relate to **Texas Lakes Community College**, which is located in the Austin, Texas area. Its four campuses serve over 30,000 students and offer more than 140 certificate programs and degrees. The college has a highly acclaimed Distance Education program and an extensive Workforce Development program. The college makes positive contributions to the community through cultural and athletic programs, and has significant partnerships with businesses and nonprofit organizations. Popular fields of study include nursing and health care, solar technology, computer technology, and graphic design.

PROJECT 3A · Students and Majors Database

MyLab IT
Project 3A Grader for Instruction
Project 3A Simulation for Training and Review

Project Activities

In Activities 3.01 through 3.15, you will assist Sean Fitchette, Director of Enrollment Services at Texas Lakes Community College, in using his Access database to track new students and their major fields of study. Your completed Navigation Pane will look similar to Figure 3.1.

Project Files for MyLab IT Grader

1. In your storage location, create a folder named **Access Chapter 3**.
2. In your **MyLab IT** course, locate and click **Access 3A Students and Majors**, Download Materials, and then Download All Files.
3. Extract the zipped folder to your Access Chapter 3 folder. Close the Grader download screens.
4. Take a moment to open the downloaded **Access_3A_Students_Majors_Instructions**; note any recent updates to the book.

Project Results

GO! Project 3A
Where We're Going

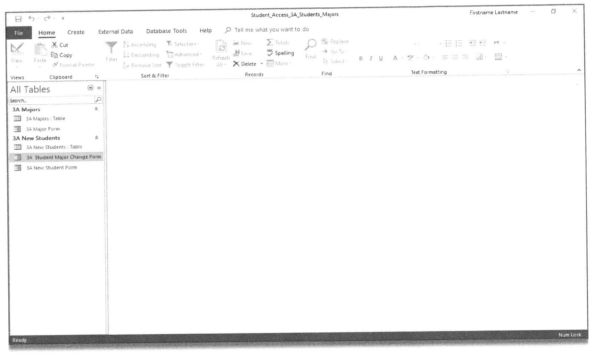

Figure 3.1 Project 3A Students and Majors

For Non-MyLab Submissions
For Project 3A, you will need this starting file:
a03A_Students_Majors

Start with an Access Data File
In your storage location, create a folder named **Access Chapter 3**
In your Access Chapter 3 folder, save your database as:
Lastname_Firstname_3A_Students_Majors

After you have saved your database, launch Access and open the database. On the next page, begin with Step 2.

ALERT   Because Office 365 is a cloud-based subscription service that receives continuous updates, you may encounter some variations in what appears on your screen and what is shown in this instruction. Microsoft Office 365 is fully installed on your PC or Mac; no internet access is necessary to create or edit documents. When you *are* connected to the internet, you will receive monthly upgrades and new features, so you always have the latest versions of Office apps as soon as they are available. Your subscription gives you continuous free access to the latest innovations and refinements.

GO! Learn How
Video A3-1

A *form* is a database object that you can use to display existing records in a table, or to edit, delete, or enter new records into a table. A form is useful to control access to the data. For example, you can design a form for college registration assistants so that they can see and enter the courses scheduled and fees paid by an individual student. However, they cannot see or enter grades for a student.

Some forms display only one record at a time; other forms display multiple records at the same time. A form that displays only one record at a time is useful not only to the individual who performs the *data entry*—entering the actual records—but also to anyone who has the job of viewing information in a database. For example, when you request a transcript from your college, someone displays your record on the screen. For the individual viewing your transcript, it is much easier to look at one record at a time, using a form, than to look at all of the student transcripts in the database.

Activity 3.01 | Opening and Saving an Existing Database and Viewing a Table Relationship

1.2.2

1 Start Access. In the Access opening screen, click **Open Other Files**. Navigate to your **Access Chapter 3 folder**, and then double-click the Access file that you downloaded from **MyLab IT** that displays your name—**Student_Access_3A_Students_Majors**. On the **Message Bar**, click **Enable Content**.

2 On the ribbon, click the **Database Tools tab**. In the **Relationships group**, click **Relationships**. If the relationships do not display, under Relationship Tools, on the Design tab, in the Relationships group, click All Relationships.

> If you rename the tables, the field lists do not automatically display in the Relationships window.

3 In the **Relationships** window, click the **join line** between the two field lists. In the **Tools group**, click **Edit Relationships**. Point to the title bar of the **Edit Relationships** dialog box and drag the dialog box to the right of the two field lists. Compare your screen with Figure 3.2.

> *One* major is associated with *many* students. A one-to-many relationship is established between your 3A Majors table and your 3A New Students table using the Major ID field as the common field. Recall that Cascade Update Related Fields enables you to change the primary key in the 3A Majors table, and then the data in the foreign key field in the 3A New Students field is automatically updated. Recall that Cascade Delete Related Records enables you to delete a record in the 3A Majors table, and then all related records in the 3A New Students table are automatically deleted.

ANOTHER WAY In the Relationships window, double-click the join line to display the Edit Relationships dialog box.

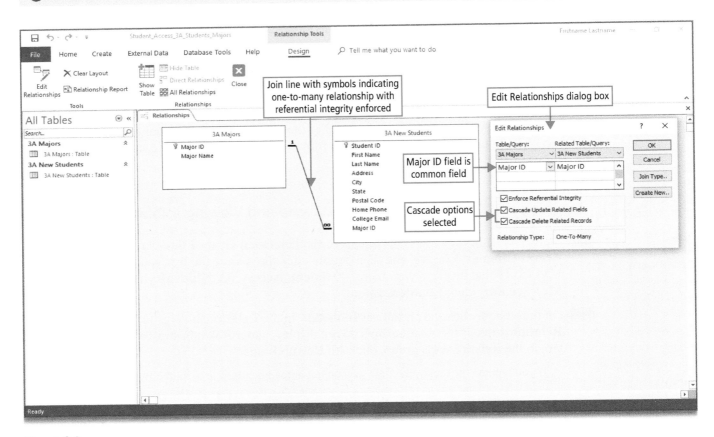

Figure 3.2

ALERT   Is your Edit Relationships dialog box empty?

The Edit Relationships dialog box does not display any information if you do not first click the join line. If this happens, close the Edit Relationships dialog box, and then be sure that you click the join line—when selected, the join line is darker.

4 **Close** ⊠ the **Edit Relationships** dialog box, and then **Close** ⊠ the **Relationships** window. If necessary, in the message box, click Yes to save changes to the layout of the relationships.

Activity 3.02 | Creating a Form and Viewing Records

4.2.2

There are several ways to create a form in Access, but the fastest and easiest way is to use the ***Form tool***. With a single mouse click, all fields from the data source are placed on the form. You can modify the form in Layout view or in Design view, or you can switch to Form view and use the new form immediately.

The Form tool uses all of the field names and all of the records from an existing table or query. Records that you create or edit using a form are automatically updated in the underlying table or tables. In this Activity, you will create a form and then view records from the underlying New Students table—the data source—so the staff can access information easily.

1 In the **Navigation Pane**, double-click your **3A New Students** table to open it. Scroll as needed to view all 10 fields—*Student ID*, *First Name*, *Last Name*, *Address*, *City*, *State*, *Postal Code*, *Home Phone*, *College Email*, and *Major ID*. **Close** ⌧ the table.

2 In the **Navigation Pane**, be sure your **3A New Students** table is selected. On the ribbon, click the **Create tab**, and then in the **Forms group**, click **Form**. **Close** « the **Navigation Pane**, and then compare your screen with Figure 3.3.

The form is created based on the currently selected object—your 3A New Students table—and displays in *Layout view*. In Layout view, you can modify the form with the data displayed in the fields. For example, you can adjust the size of the text boxes to fit the data.

The form is created in a simple top-to-bottom layout, with all 10 fields from your 3A New Students table lined up in a single column. The data for the first record in the data source displays.

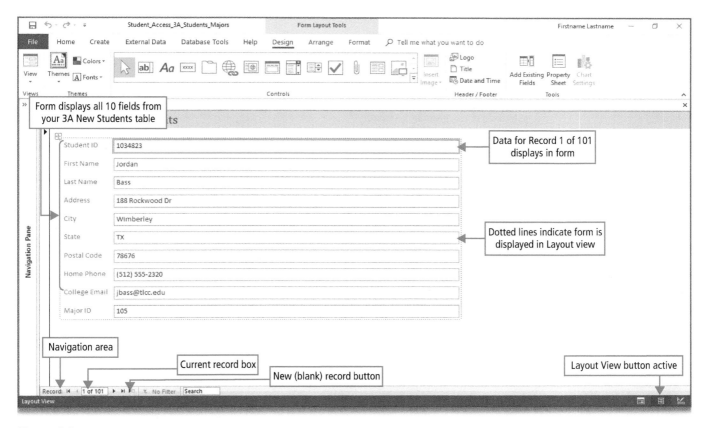

Figure 3.3

3 In the navigation area, click **Next record** ▶ four times to display the fifth record—*Student ID 1298345*. In the navigation area, select the text in the Current record box, type **62** and then press Enter to display the record for *Student ID 5720358*. In the navigation area, click **Last record** ▶| to display the record for *Student ID 9583924*, and then click **First record** |◀ to display the record for *Student ID 1034823*.

Use the navigation buttons to scroll among the records or the Current record box to display any single record.

4 ▶ Save 🖫 the form as **3A New Student Form** and then **Close** ⊠ the form object.

5 ▶ Open ⧉ the **Navigation Pane**. Notice that your new form displays under the table with which it is related—your **3A New Students** table.

Activity 3.03 | Creating a Second Form

MOS
4.2.2

In this Activity, you will use the Form tool to create a form for your 3A Majors table so the enrollment services staff can review student information relative to his or her major.

1 ▶ In the **Navigation Pane**, click your **3A Majors** table to select it. On the ribbon, click the **Create tab**, and then in the **Forms group**, click **Form**. **Close** ⧉ the **Navigation Pane**, and then compare your screen with Figure 3.4.

Because a one-to-many relationship is established, the form displays related records in the 3A New Students table for each record in the 3A Majors table. Five new students have selected a major of *Diagnostic Medical Sonography—Major ID 105*.

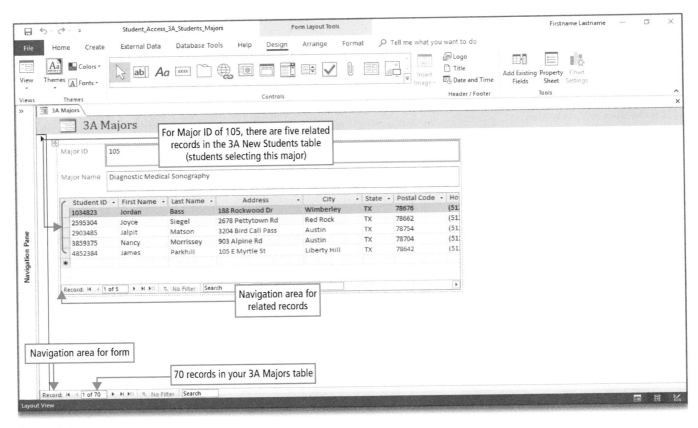

Figure 3.4

2 ▶ **Close** ⊠ your **3A Majors** form. In the message box, click **Yes**. In the **Save As** dialog box, in the **Form Name** box, type **3A Major Form** and then click **OK**.

Recall that if you do not save an object, you are prompted to do so when you close the object.

3 ▶ Open ⧉ the **Navigation Pane**. Notice that your new form displays under the table with which it is related—your **3A Majors** table.

By using a single-record form to add, modify, and delete records, you can reduce the number of data entry errors, because the individual performing the data entry is looking at only one record at a time. Recall that your database is useful only if the information is accurate—just like your contact list is useful only if it contains accurate phone numbers and email addresses.

Forms are based on—also referred to as ***bound*** to—the table where the records are stored. When a record is entered in a form, the new record is added to the underlying table. The reverse is also true—when a record is added to the table, the new record can be viewed in the related form.

In this Activity, you will add a new record to both tables by using the forms that you just created.

1 In the **Navigation Pane**, double-click your **3A New Student Form** object to open it, and then **Close** «⟨ the **Navigation Pane**. In the navigation area, click **New (blank) record** ▶⁑ to display a new blank form.

When you double-click to open a form, the first record in the underlying table displays in ***Form view***, which is used to view, add, modify, and delete records stored in the table.

2 In the **Student ID** field, type **9712345** and then press Tab.

Use the Tab key to move from field to field in a form. ***Tab order*** is the order in which the insertion point moves from one field to the next when you press the Tab key. As you start typing, the pencil icon displays in the ***record selector bar*** at the left—the bar used to select an entire record. The pencil icon displays when a record is being created or edited.

ANOTHER WAY   Press the Enter key, provided there are no special links on the form, such as a link to create a new form or a link to print the form.

3 Using your own first name and last name and using the first initial of your first name and your last name for the *College Email* field, continue entering the data shown in the following table, and then compare your screen with Figure 3.5.

Student ID	First Name	Last Name	Address	City	State	Postal Code	Home Phone	College Email	Major ID
9712345	**First Name**	**Last Name**	**5820 Sweet Basil Ct**	**Austin**	**TX**	**78726**	**(512) 555-5712**	**flastname@ tlcc.edu**	**339**

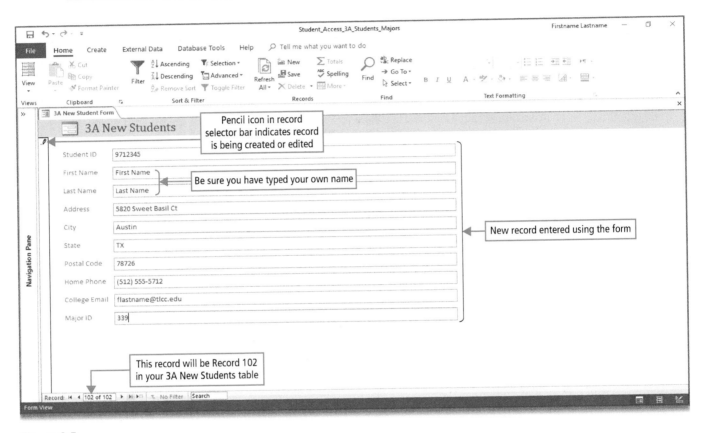

Figure 3.5

4 With the insertion point positioned in the last field, press [Enter] to save the record and display a new blank record. **Close** ⊠ your **3A New Student Form** object.

5 **Open** ⊠ the **Navigation Pane**, and then double-click your **3A New Students** table to open it. In the navigation area, click **Last record** ⊠ to verify that the record you entered in the form is stored in the underlying table. **Close** ⊠ your **3A New Students** table.

6 In the **Navigation Pane**, double-click your **3A Major Form** object to open it. At the bottom of the screen, in the navigation area for the form—*not* the navigation area for the subdatasheet— click **New (blank) record** ⊠. In the blank form, enter the data shown in the following table:

Major ID	Major Name
339.555.22	**Network Security**

7 **Close** ⊠ your **3A Major Form** object. In the **Navigation Pane**, double-click your **3A Majors** table, and then scroll to verify that the record for *Major ID 339.555.22 Network Security* displays in the table—records are sorted by the *Major ID* field. **Close** ⊠ the table.

Activity 3.05 | Deleting Records from a Table by Using a Form

MOS
2.3.1

You can delete records from a database table by using a form. In this Activity, you will delete the record for *Major ID 800.03* because the program has been discontinued.

1 In the **Navigation Pane**, double-click your **3A Major Form** object to open it, and then **Close** « the **Navigation Pane**. On the **Home tab**, in the **Find group**, click **Find** to open the **Find and Replace** dialog box.

> **ANOTHER WAY** Press Ctrl + F to open the Find and Replace dialog box.

2 In the **Look In** box, notice that *Current field* displays. In the **Find What** box, type **800.03** and then click **Find Next**. Compare your screen with Figure 3.6, and then verify that the record for *Major ID 800.03* displays.

Because the insertion point was positioned in the *Major ID* field before opening the dialog box, Access will search for data in this field—the *Current field*.

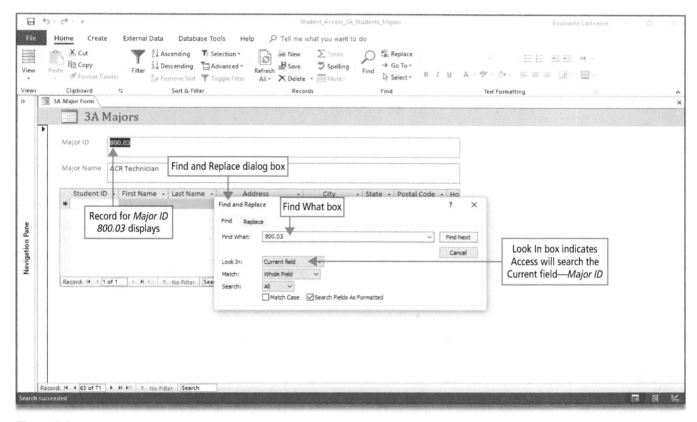

Figure 3.6

3 **Close** × the **Find and Replace** dialog box. On the **Home tab**, in the **Records group**, click the **Delete arrow**, and then click **Delete Record**.

The record is removed from the screen, and a message displays alerting you that you are about to delete *1 record(s)*. Once you click *Yes*, you cannot click Undo to reverse this action. If you delete a record by mistake, you must re-create the record by reentering the data. Because no students are associated with this major and the program is being discontinued, you can delete it from the table.

4 In the message box, click **Yes** to delete the record. In the navigation area for the form, notice that the total number of records in the table is *70*. **Close** × your **3A Major Form** object.

5 **Open** >> the **Navigation Pane**, and then double-click your **3A Majors** table to open it. Examine the table to verify that the *Major ID 800.03* record has been deleted from the table, and then **Close** × the table.

> Adding and deleting records in a form updates the records stored in the underlying table.

Objective 2 | Filter Records

GO! Learn How
Video A3-2

Filtering records in a form displays only a portion of the total records—a *subset*—based on matching specific values. Filters are commonly used to provide a quick answer to a question, and the result is not generally saved for future use. For example, by filtering records in a form, you can quickly display a subset of records for students majoring in Information Systems Technology, which is identified by the Major ID of 339.

A form provides an interface for the database. For example, because of security reasons, the registration assistants at your college may not have access to the entire student database. Rather, by using a form, they can access and edit only some information—the information necessary for them to do their jobs. Filtering records within a form provides individuals who do not have access to the entire database a way to ask questions of the database without constructing a query. You can save the filter with the form if you are going to use the filter frequently.

Activity 3.06 | Filtering Data by Selection of One Field

2.3.3

In this Activity, you will assist a counselor at the college who wants to see records for students majoring in Information Systems Technology. In a form, you can use the *Filter By Selection* command to display only the records that contain the value in the selected field and to hide the records that do *not* contain the value in the selected field.

1 **Open** >> the **Navigation Pane**, double-click your **3A New Student Form** object to open it in **Form** view, and then **Close** « the **Navigation Pane**.

2 In the first record, click the **Major ID** field name—or you can click in the text box. Press Ctrl + F to display the **Find and Replace** dialog box. In the **Find What** box, type **339** If necessary, in the Match box, click the arrow, and then click Whole Field. Click **Find Next**, and then compare your screen with Figure 3.7.

> This action finds and displays a record with a *Major ID* of *339*—the major of *Information Systems Technology*. You will use this action to filter the records using the value of *339*.

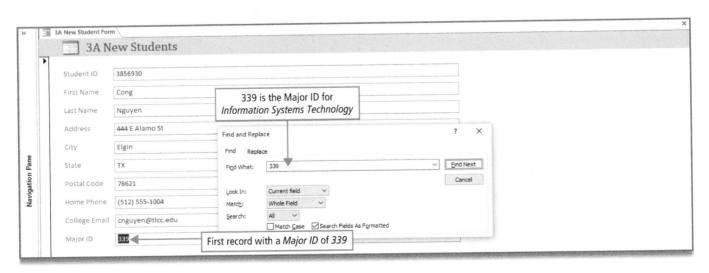

Figure 3.7

3 ▶ **Close** ⊠ the **Find and Replace** dialog box. On the **Home tab**, in the **Sort & Filter group**, click **Selection**, and then click **Equals "339"**. Compare your screen with Figure 3.8.

Seven records match the contents of the selected Major ID field—*339*—the Major ID for the Information Systems Technology major. In the navigation area, *Filtered* with a funnel icon displays next to the number of records. *Filtered* also displays on the right side of the status bar to indicate that a filter is applied. On the Home tab, in the Sort & Filter group, Toggle Filter is active.

ANOTHER WAY   With the data selected in the field, right-click the selection, and then click Equals "339".

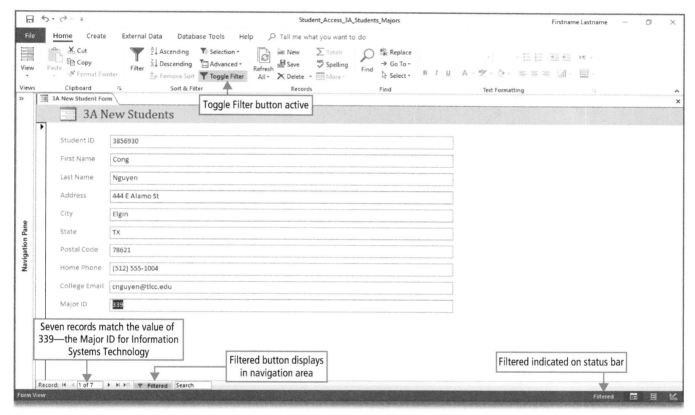

Figure 3.8

4 ▶ On the **Home tab**, in the **Sort & Filter group**, click **Toggle Filter** to remove the filter and display all 102 records. Notice *Unfiltered* in the navigation area, which indicates a filter is created but is not active.

ANOTHER WAY   Click Filtered in the navigation area to remove the filter.

NOTE   The Toggle Filter Button

On the Home tab, in the Sort & Filter group, the Toggle Filter button is used to apply or remove a filter. If no filter is created, the button is not available. After a filter is created, the button becomes available. Because it is a toggle button used to apply or remove a filter, the ScreenTip that displays for this button alternates between Apply Filter—when a filter is created but is not currently applied—and Remove Filter—when a filter is applied.

5 Be sure that the first record—for *Jordan Bass*—displays. On the **Home tab**, in the **Sort & Filter group**, click **Toggle Filter** to reapply the filter. In the navigation area, click **Last record** to display the last of the seven records that match a Major ID of *339*.

The record for *Student ID 9712345* displays—the record with your name. Use Toggle Filter to apply or remove filters as needed.

6 In the navigation area, click **Filtered** to remove the filter and display all of the records.

In the navigation area, *Filtered* changes to *Unfiltered*.

7 In the first record for *Jordan Bass*, in the **Last Name** field, select the first letter—**B**—in *Bass*. In the **Sort & Filter group**, click **Selection**, and then click **Begins with "B"**.

A new filter is applied that displays eight records in which the *Last Name* begins with the letter *B*.

ANOTHER WAY With the letter *B* selected, right-click the selection, and then click Begins with "B".

8 Use either **Toggle Filter** in the **Sort & Filter group** or **Filtered** in the navigation area to remove the filter and display all of the records.

9 In the **Sort & Filter group**, click **Advanced**, and then click **Clear All Filters**. Notice, that in the navigation area, *Unfiltered* changed to *No Filter*.

The filter is removed from the form and must be recreated to apply it. If you toggle the filter off and save the form, the filter is saved with the form even though the filter is not currently applied.

Activity 3.07 | Using Filter By Form

MOS
2.3.3

Use the *Filter By Form* command to filter the records based on one or more fields, or based on more than one value in the same field. The Filter By Form command offers greater flexibility than the Filter By Selection command and can be used to answer a question that requires matching multiple values. In this Activity, you will filter records to help Mr. Fitchette determine how many students live in Dripping Springs or Austin.

1 On the **Home tab**, in the **Sort & Filter group**, click **Advanced**, and then click **Filter By Form**. Compare your screen with Figure 3.9.

The Filter by Form window displays all of the field names, but without any data. In the empty text box for each field, you can type a value or select a value from a list. The *Look for* and *Or* tabs display at the bottom.

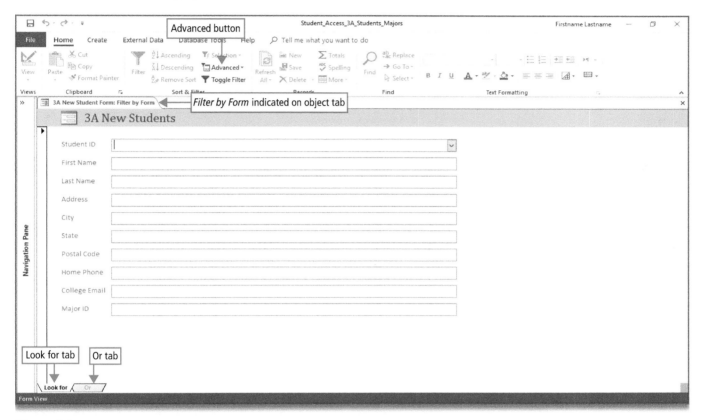

Figure 3.9

2 In the form, click the **City** field name to position the insertion point in the **City** field box. At the right edge of the **City** field box, click the **arrow**, and then click **Dripping Springs**. In the **Sort & Filter group**, click **Toggle Filter**.

As displayed in the navigation area, four student records have *Dripping Springs* stored in the City field.

3 In the **Sort & Filter group**, click **Advanced**, and then click **Filter By Form**. In the lower left corner of the form, click the **Or tab**. Click the **City** field box **arrow**, and then click **Austin**. In the **Sort & Filter group**, click **Toggle Filter**, and then compare your screen with Figure 3.10.

As displayed in the navigation area, 28 student records have either *Dripping Springs* OR *Austin* stored in the City field. You have created an *OR condition*; that is, records display where, in this instance, either of two values—Dripping Springs *or* Austin—is present in the selected field.

> **ANOTHER WAY** Click in the field box, and type the criteria separated by the word *or*. For example, in the City field box, type *Dripping Springs or Austin*.

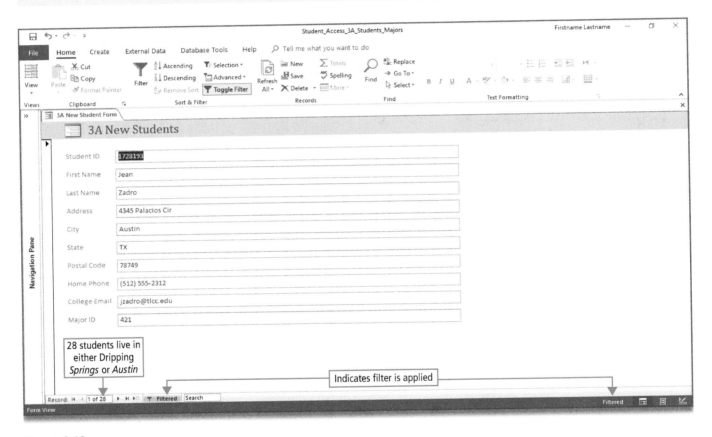

Figure 3.10

4 In the **Sort & Filter group**, click **Advanced**, and then click **Clear All Filters** to display all 102 records.

Activity 3.08 | Using Advanced Filter/Sort

MOS
2.3.3

In this Activity, you will assist the enrollment services assistant by using the Advanced Filter/Sort command to filter records to locate students who live in Austin with a Major ID of *339*—Information Systems Technology.

1 In the **Sort & Filter group**, click **Advanced**, and then click **Advanced Filter/Sort**. In the table area, resize the field list so that the entire table name and all of the field names display.

The Advanced Filter design grid displays, which is similar to the query design grid, although not all rows display in the bottom half of the window. A field list for the underlying table of the form displays.

2 In the **3A New Students** field list, double-click **City**, and then double-click **Major ID** to add both fields to the design grid. In the **Criteria** row, under **City**, type **Austin** and then press [Enter]. In the **Criteria** row, under **Major ID**, type **339** and then press [Enter]. Compare your screen with Figure 3.11.

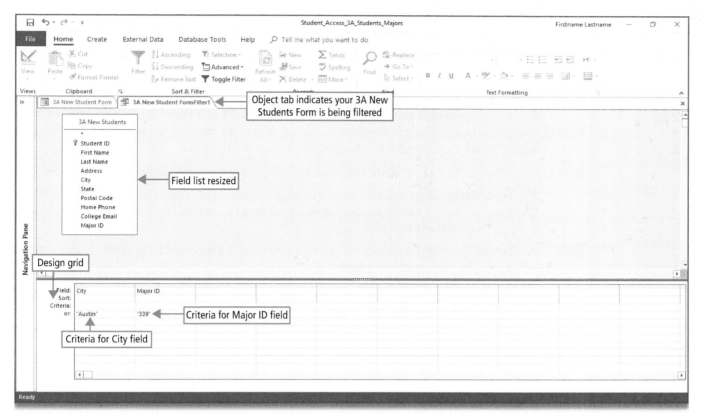

Figure 3.11

3 In the **Sort & Filter group**, click **Toggle Filter** to display the filtered records.

Three records match the criteria. You have created an ***AND condition***; that is, only records where both values—Austin *and* 339—are present in the selected fields display. There are three students who live in Austin who have declared a major of Information Systems Technology.

4 In the **Sort & Filter group**, click **Toggle Filter** to remove the filter and to display all of the records.

In the navigation area, *Unfiltered* displays, which indicates that a filter has been created for this form. Unless you click Clear All Filters, the filter is saved with the form when the form is closed. When you reopen the form, you can click Toggle Filtered or Unfiltered to reapply the filter.

5 **Close** ⊠ your **3A New Student Form** object and notice that the Advanced Filter grid also closes.

MORE KNOWLEDGE **Using the Filter Button**

You can filter a table in a manner similar to the way you filter records in a form. With a table open in Datasheet view, click in the field you wish to use for the filter. On the Home tab, in the Sort & Filter group, click Filter to display a shortcut menu. Select the (Select All) check box to clear the option, and then select the data by which you want to filter your records by clicking the check boxes preceding the data. To remove the filter, redisplay the menu, and then select the (Select All) check box.

GO! Learn How
Video A3-3

Objective 3 | Create a Form by Using the Form Wizard

The *Form Wizard* walks you step by step through the creation of a form and gives you more flexibility in the design, layout, and number of fields in a form than the Form tool. Design a form for the individuals who use the form—either for entering new records or viewing records. For example, when your college counselor displays student information, it may be easier for the counselor to view the information if the fields are arranged in a layout that more closely matches a paper form.

Activity 3.09 | Creating a Form by Using the Form Wizard

4.1.1

In this Activity, you will create a form to match the layout of a paper form that a student at Texas Lakes Community College completes when that student changes his or her major. This will make it easier for the individual who changes the data in the database.

1 On the ribbon, click the **Create tab**, and then in the **Forms group**, click **Form Wizard**.

The Form Wizard walks you step by step through the process of creating a form by asking questions. In the first wizard screen, you select the fields to include on the form. The fields can come from more than one table or query.

2 In the **Tables/Queries** box, click the **arrow** to display a list of available tables and queries from which you can create the form.

There are two tables in the database from which you can create a new form. The selected table is the one that you last worked with.

3 Click **Table: 3A New Students**, and then compare your screen with Figure 3.12.

In the Available Fields list, the field names from your 3A New Students table display.

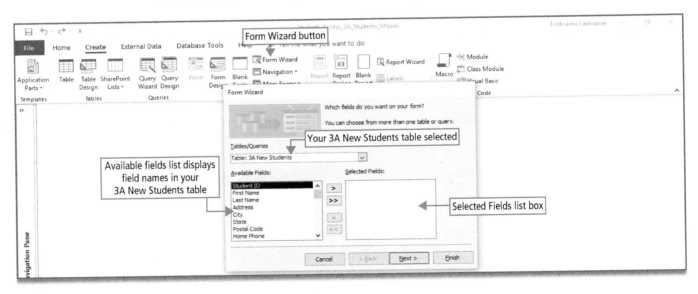

Figure 3.12

> **4** In the **Available Fields** list, double-click the following field names in the order given to move them to the **Selected Fields** list: **First Name**, **Last Name**, and **Major ID**. Compare your screen with Figure 3.13.

> Three field names from your 3A New Students table display in the Selected Fields list.

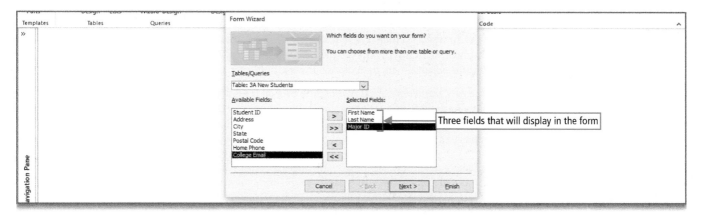

Figure 3.13

> **5** Click **Next**. In the wizard, be sure **Columnar** is selected as the layout, and then click **Next**. In the **What title do you want for your form?** box, select the existing text, type **3A Student Major Change Form** and then click **Finish** to close the wizard and create the form.

> The three fields and the data from the first record in your 3A New Students table display in Form view.

> **6** **Open** `»` the **Navigation Pane**. Compare your screen with Figure 3.14.

> In the Navigation Pane, the form displays under its data source—your 3A New Students table.

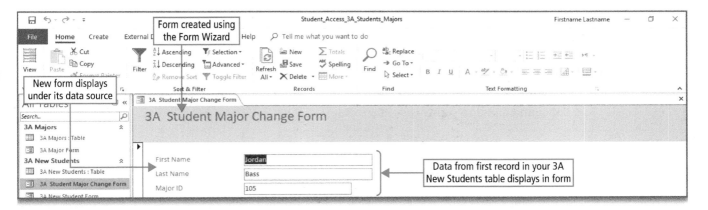

Figure 3.14

Objective 4	Modify a Form in Layout View and in Design View

GO! Learn How
Video A3-4

After you create a form, you can make changes to it. For example, you can group the fields, resize the fields, add more fields to the form, and change the style of the form. Layout view enables you to see the data in the form as you modify the form. Most changes to a form can be made in Layout view.

Activity 3.10 | Grouping Controls in Layout View

MOS
4.1.2

In this Activity, you will group *controls* in the form so that you can work with them as one unit. Controls are objects on a form that display data or text, perform actions, and let you view and work with information.

> **1** ▶ **Close** « the **Navigation Pane** and be sure that your **3A Student Major Change Form** object displays in the object window. On the **Home tab**, in the **Views group**, click the top portion of the **View** button to switch to **Layout** view. If the Field List pane displays on the right side of your screen, click Close ✕ to close the pane. Compare your screen with Figure 3.15.

The field names and data for the first record in your 3A New Students record display in controls. The data for the first record displays in *text box controls*. The most commonly used control is the text box control, which typically displays data from a field in the underlying table. A text box control is a *bound control*—its data comes from a field in a table or query.

The field names—*First Name*, *Last Name*, and *Major ID*—display in *label controls*. A label control displays to the left of a text box control and contains descriptive information that displays on the form, usually the field name. A control that does not have a data source is an *unbound control*. Another example of an unbound control is a label control that displays the title of a form.

🔄 **ANOTHER WAY** On the right side of the status bar, click Layout View ▤ to switch from Form view to Layout view.

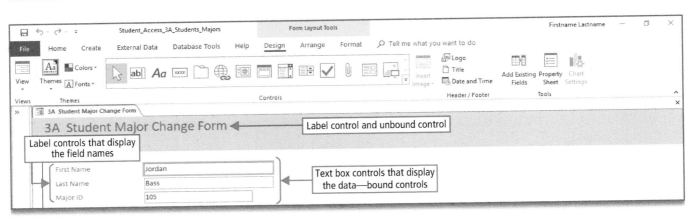

Figure 3.15

> **2** ▶ Click the **First Name label control**. Hold down Shift, and then click the **Last Name label control**, the **Major ID label control**, and the three **text box controls** to select all of the label and text box controls on the form.

ALERT **Do your controls change order when selecting?**

If, when selecting multiple controls, the controls change order, click Undo, and then select the controls again. Be careful not to drag the mouse when you are selecting multiple controls.

3 With all six controls selected—surrounded by a colored border—on the ribbon, under **Form Layout Tools**, click the **Arrange tab**. In the **Table group**, click **Stacked**. Click the **First Name label control** to cancel the selection of all of the controls and to surround the **First Name label control** with a colored border. Compare your screen with Figure 3.16.

This action groups the controls together in the *Stacked layout* format—a layout similar to a paper form, with labels to the left of each field. Because the controls are grouped, you can move and edit the controls more easily as you redesign your form.

A dotted line forms a border around the controls, which indicates that the controls are grouped together. Above and to the left of the first label control that displays *First Name*, the *layout selector* displays. The layout selector is used to select and move or format the entire group of controls.

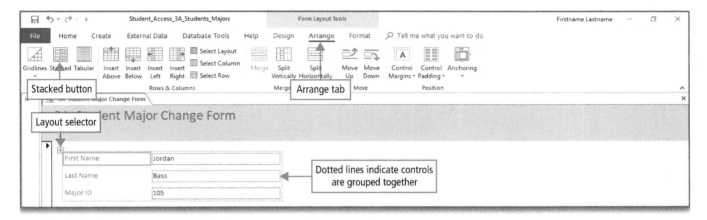

Figure 3.16

Activity 3.11 | Applying a Theme and Formatting a Form in Layout View

4.1.3

In this Activity, you will apply a *theme* to the form in Layout view. A theme is a predesigned set of colors, fonts, lines, and fill effects that look good together and that can be applied to all of the objects in the database or to individual objects in the database.

1 Under **Form Layout Tools**, click the **Design tab**. In the **Themes group**, click **Themes**. In the **Themes** gallery, using the ScreenTips, point to the **Retrospect** theme, right-click, and then click **Apply Theme to This Object Only**.

Right-click a theme so that you can apply the theme to an individual object within the database. Apply a theme before formatting any other controls in your form.

NOTE Applying a Theme to an Object and Determining the Applied Theme

If you click a theme rather than right-clicking it and selecting an option, the theme is applied to all objects in the database. You cannot click Undo to cancel the application of the theme to all objects. To determine the applied theme, in the Themes group, point to Themes. The ScreenTip displays the name of the current theme.

2 Click anywhere in the title of the form—*3A Student Major Change Form*—to select the title. Under **Form Layout Tools**, click the **Format tab**. In the **Font group**, click the **Font Size arrow**, and then click **14**. In the **Font group**, click **Bold** B. Click the **Font Color arrow**, and then under **Theme Colors**, in the fourth column, click the last color.

Activity 3.12 | Adding, Resizing, and Moving Controls in Layout View

4.1.1, 4.1.2, 4.1.3

In Layout view, you can change the form's *control layout*—the grouped arrangement of controls. After reviewing this form, Sean has requested a few changes. In this Activity, you will add the Student ID field and reorganize the form.

> **1** Be sure that your **3A Student Major Change Form** object displays in **Layout** view. On the **Design tab**, and in the **Tools group**, click **Add Existing Fields**. Compare your screen with Figure 3.17.

> The Field List pane displays, which lists the fields in the underlying table—your 3A New Students table.

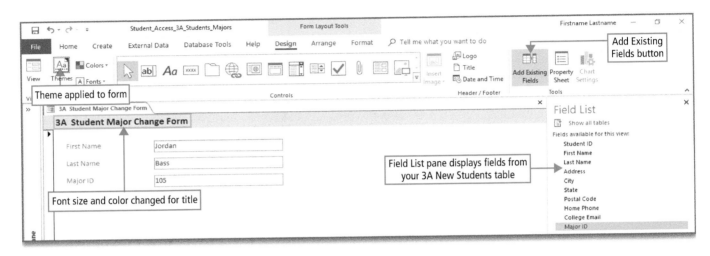

Figure 3.17

> **2** In the **Field List** pane, click **Student ID**, and then drag the field name to the left until the pointer displays above the **First Name label control** and a colored line displays above the control. Release the mouse button, and then compare your screen with Figure 3.18. If you are not satisfied with the result, click Undo, and begin again.

> This action adds the Student ID label control and text box control to the form above the First Name controls.

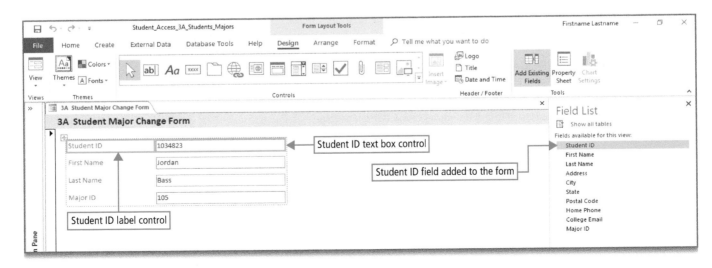

Figure 3.18

3 ▶ Close ☒ the **Field List** pane. Click the **Student ID text box control**, which displays *1034823*, to surround it with a border and to remove the border from the label control.

4 ▶ On the **Design tab**, in the **Tools group**, click **Property Sheet**.

The Property Sheet for the Student ID text box control displays. Recall that each control has an associated Property Sheet where precise changes to the properties—characteristics—of selected controls can be made. At the top of the Property Sheet, to the right of *Selection type: Text Box* displays because you selected the Student ID text box control.

5 ▶ In the **Property Sheet**, if necessary, click the **Format tab**. Click **Width** to select the property setting, type **1.5** and then press Enter to decrease the width of the text box controls. Compare your screen with Figure 3.19.

All four text box controls are resized simultaneously. Because the controls are grouped together in a stacked layout, you can adjust the width of all of the text box controls at one time without having to select all of the controls. By decreasing the width of the text box controls, you have more space in which to rearrange the form controls. Because you can see the data in Layout view, you can determine visually that the space you have allotted is adequate to display all of the data in every field for every record.

🔄 **ANOTHER WAY** With the text box control selected, point to the right edge of the text box control until the ⟷ pointer displays, and then drag left to the desired location.

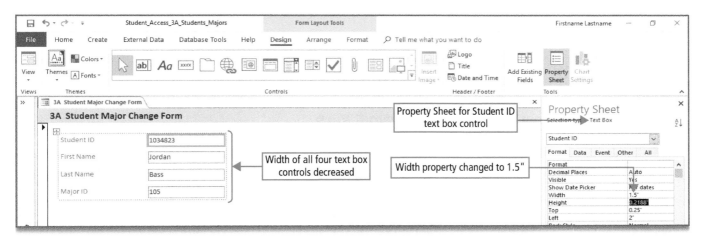

Figure 3.19

6 ▶ Close ☒ the **Property Sheet**. Click the **Last Name text box control**, which displays *Bass*. Under **Form Layout Tools**, click the **Arrange tab**, and in the **Rows & Columns group**, click **Select Row** to select the text box control and its associated label control.

7 In the **Move group**, click **Move Up** to move both controls above the **First Name** controls, and then compare your screen with Figure 3.20.

ANOTHER WAY Drag the selected controls to the desired location and then release the mouse button.

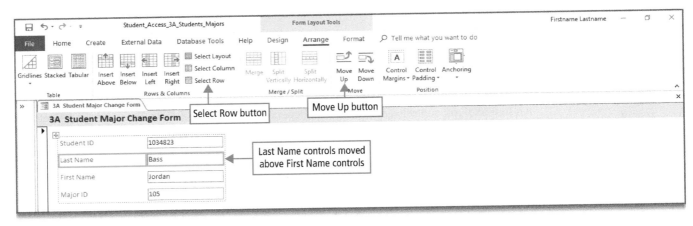

Figure 3.20

ALERT   **Did the Last Name Label Control not move with the Last Name Text Box Control?**
Be sure to select both the text box control and the label control before moving the controls; otherwise, only one of the controls will move. If this happens, click Undo, select both controls, and try again. Controls are stacked from top to bottom, not right to left.

8 **Save** 🖫 the changes you have made to the design of your form.

Activity 3.13 | Formatting Controls in Layout View

MOS
4.1.2, 4.1.3

In this Activity, you will format and change the property settings for multiple controls.

1 With the form displayed in **Layout** view, click the **Student ID text box control**, which displays *1034823*. On the **Arrange tab**, in the **Rows & Columns group**, click **Select Column** to select all four text box controls.

ANOTHER WAY Click the first text box control, hold down Shift, and then click the last text box control to select all four text box controls.

2 With all four text box controls selected, on the **Format tab**, in the **Font group**, click the **Background Color arrow** 🎨 ▾. Under **Theme Colors**, in the last column, click the second color.

All of the text box controls display a background color. This formatting is not applied to the label controls on the left.

3 Click the **Student ID label control**. On the ribbon, click the **Arrange tab**, and then in the **Rows & Columns group**, click **Select Column**. On the **Format tab**, click the **Font Color arrow**—*not* the Background Color arrow. Under **Theme Colors**, in the fourth column, click the first color. Click **Bold** Ⓑ. Click in a blank area of the form to cancel the selection, and then compare your screen with Figure 3.21.

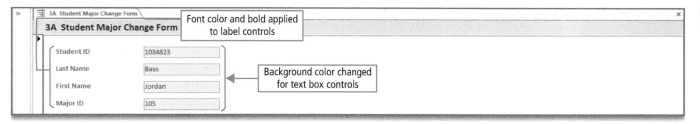

Figure 3.21

4 Click any **label control** to display the **layout selector** ⊞, and then click the **layout selector** ⊞ to select all of the grouped controls.

Recall that the layout selector, which displays to the left and above the Student ID label control, enables you to select and move the entire group of controls in Layout view.

ANOTHER WAY Click any control, and then on the Arrange tab, in the Rows & Columns group, click Select Layout.

5 On the **Format tab**, in the **Font group**, click the **Font Size arrow**, and then click **12** to change the font size of all of the text in all of the controls.

6 With all of the controls still selected, click the **Design tab**. In the **Tools group**, click **Property Sheet**, and then compare your screen with Figure 3.22.

The Property Sheet for the selected controls displays. At the top of the Property Sheet, to the right of *Selection type: Multiple selection* displays because you have more than one control selected.

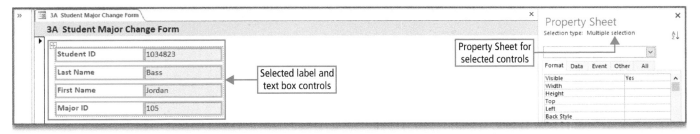

Figure 3.22

7 In the **Property Sheet**, click **Height**, type **0.25** and then press Enter to change the height of each selected control.

8 Click the **Student ID label control** to cancel the selection of all of the controls and to select only this label control. In the **Property Sheet**, click **Width**, type **1.25** and then press Enter.

The width of every label control changed to 1.25 inches. Recall that because the label controls are arranged in a stacked layout, you can change the width of all controls by selecting only one control. This is one of the few properties that can be changed without first selecting the column.

9 Close ✕ the **Property Sheet**, and then Save 🖫 the design changes to your form.

Activity 3.14 | Modifying a Form in Design View

4.1.2, 4.2.4,
4.1.1, 4.1.3

Design view presents a detailed view of the structure of your form. Because the form is not actually running when displayed in Design view, the data does not display in the text box controls. However, some tasks, such as resizing sections, must be completed in Design view.

1 On the status bar, click **Design View** 🖾, and then compare your screen with Figure 3.23.

The form in Design view displays three sections, each designated by a ***section bar*** at the top of each section. The ***Form Header*** contains information, such as the form title, that displays at the top of the screen in Form view or Layout view and is printed at the top of the first page when records are printed as forms. The ***Detail section*** displays the records from the underlying table, and the ***Form Footer*** displays at the bottom of the screen in Form view or Layout view and is printed after the last detail section on the last page of a printout.

> 🔄 **ANOTHER WAY** On the Home tab, in the Views group, click the View arrow, and then click Design view; or right-click the object tab, and then click Design View.

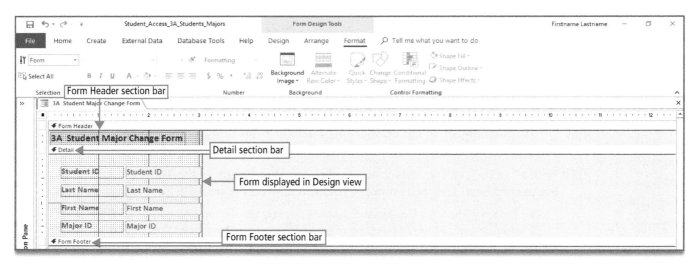

Figure 3.23

2 At the bottom of the form, click the **Form Footer section bar** to select it. On the ribbon, click the **Design tab**, and in the **Tools group**, click **Property Sheet**. In the **Property Sheet**, on the **Format tab**, click **Height**, type **0.5** and then press Enter. Compare your screen with Figure 3.24.

In addition to properties for controls, you can make precise changes to sections of the form. Because you selected the Form Footer section bar, the Property Sheet displays a *Selection type* of *Section*, and the section is identified as *Form Footer*.

🔄 **ANOTHER WAY** At the bottom of the form, point to the lower edge of the Form Footer section bar to display the ➕ pointer, and then drag downward approximately 0.5 inch to increase the height of the section.

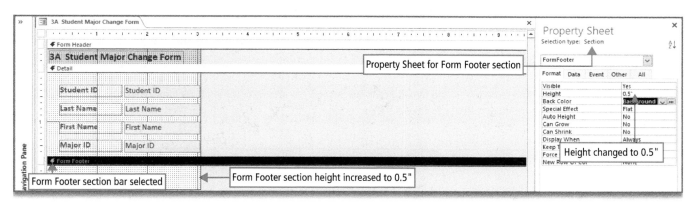

Figure 3.24

3 On the **Design tab**, in the **Controls group**, click **Label** Aa. Move the ⁺A pointer into the **Form Footer** section and then position the plus sign of the ⁺A pointer at approximately **0.25 inch on the horizontal ruler** and even with the lower edge of the **Form Footer section bar**—the position does not need to be precise. Compare your screen with Figure 3.25.

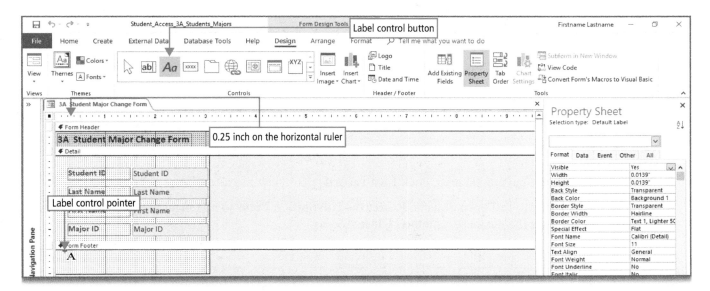

Figure 3.25

4 ▶ Click one time. Type **Texas Lakes Community College** and then press Enter. With the **label control** selected, click the **Format tab**. In the **Font group**, click **Bold** B. Click the **Font Color arrow**, and then under **Theme Colors**, in the fourth column, click the first color.

5 ▶ With the **label control** still selected, in the **Property Sheet**, click **Top**, type **0.1** and then press Enter. In the **Property Sheet**, in the **Left** property setting, type **0.6** and then press Enter. **Close** ✕ the **Property Sheet**, and then **Save** 💾 the design changes to your form.

> The top edge of the label control in the Form Footer section displays 0.1 inch from the lower edge of the Form Footer section bar. The left edge of the label control aligns at 0.6 inch from the left margin of the form. In this manner, you can place a control in a specific location on the form.

6 ▶ On the right side of the status bar, click **Form View** 🖽, and then compare your screen with Figure 3.26.

> Form Footer text displays on the screen at the bottom of the form and prints only on the last page if all of the forms are printed. Recall, that in Form view, you can add, modify, or delete records stored in the underlying table.

🔄 **ANOTHER WAY**   On the Home tab, in the Views group, click the View arrow, and then click Form View; or right-click the object tab, and then click Form View.

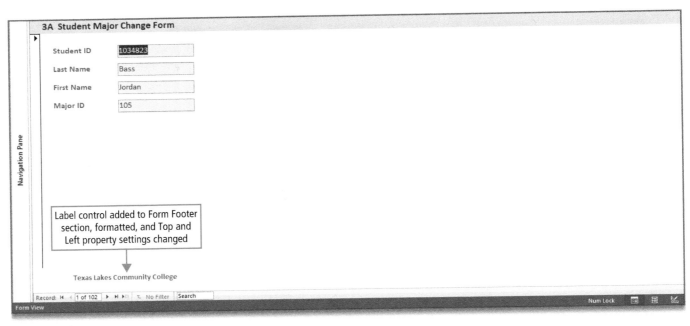

Figure 3.26

7 ▶ In the navigation area, click **Last record** ▶❙ to view the record containing your name.

8 ▶ **Close** ✕ all open objects. **Resize** the **Navigation Pane** so all object names display fully. **Close** the database, and then **Close** Access.

For Non-MyLab Submissions: Determine What Your Instructor Requires for Submission
As directed by your instructor, submit your completed database file. If you are completing the optional activity, do so before submitting your database to your instructor.

9 In **MyLab IT**, locate and click the Grader Project **Access 3A Students and Majors**. In **step 3**, under **Upload Completed Assignment**, click **Choose File**. In the **Open** dialog box, navigate to your **Access Chapter 3 folder**, and then click your **Student_Access_3A_Students_Majors** file one time to select it. In the lower right corner of the **Open** dialog box, click **Open**.

The name of your selected file displays above the Upload button.

10 To submit your file to **MyLab IT** for grading, click **Upload**, wait a moment for a green **Success!** message, and then in **step 4**, click the blue **Submit for Grading** button. Click **Close Assignment** to return to your list of **Course Materials**.

You have completed Project 3A | END

Activity 3.15 | Printing a Single Form

ALERT   This Activity is optional

This Activity is optional. Check with your instructor to see if you should complete this Activity. This Activity is not included in the **MyLab IT** Grader system for this project; however, you may want to practice this on your own to learn how to print a form for a single record within your database.

4.2.3

When a form is displayed, clicking Print causes *all* of the records to print in the form layout. In this Activity, you will print only *one* record.

1 Start Access. Under *Recent*, click your **3A_Students_Majors** database to open it.

2 **Open** ▸ the **Navigation Pane**. In the **Navigation Pane**, double-click your **3A New Student Form** object to open it. Press Ctrl + F to open the **Find and Replace** dialog box. In the **Find What** box, type **9712345** and then click **Find Next** to display the record with your name. **Close** × the **Find and Replace** dialog box.

3 On the **File tab**, click **Print**, and then on the right, click **Print**. In the **Print** dialog box, under **Print Range**, click the **Selected Record(s)** option button. In the lower left corner of the dialog box, click **Setup**.

4 In the **Page Setup** dialog box, click the **Columns tab**. Under **Column Size**, double-click in the **Width** box to select the existing value, type **7.5** and then compare your screen with Figure 3.27.

Change the width of the column in this manner so that the form prints on one page. Forms are not typically printed, so the width of the column in a form might be greater than the width of the paper on which you are printing. The maximum column width that you can enter is dependent upon the printer that is installed on your system. This setting is saved when you save or close the form.

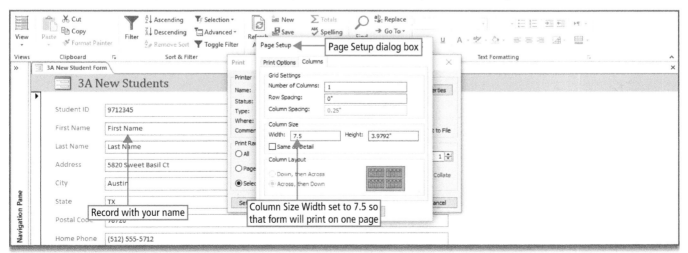

Figure 3.27

5 In the **Page Setup** dialog box, click **OK**. To create a paper printout, in the **Print** dialog box click **OK**. To create a PDF electronic image of this single form, click **Cancel** and then follow the instructions in the Note below.

NOTE   Printing a Single Form as a PDF Electronic Image

To create a PDF electronic image of a single form as a PDF electronic image, change the column width to 7.5 as described in Step 3 above, and then in the Print dialog box, click Cancel. On the left side of the form, click the Record Selector bar so that it is black—selected. Click the External Data tab. In the Export group, click PDF or XPS.

In the Publish as PDF or XPS dialog box, navigate to your chapter folder. In the File name box, the file has the same name as the form. Be sure that the Open file after publishing check box is selected, and that the Minimum size (publishing online) option button is selected. In the Publish as PDF or XPS dialog box, click Options. In the Options dialog box, under Range, click the Selected records option button, click OK, and then click Publish. Close the Windows Edge Reader, Adobe Reader or Adobe Acrobat window, and then submit the file as directed by your instructor.

---

6 Open »| the **Navigation Pane**, and then double-click your **3A Major Form** object to open it.

7 Use the techniques you just practiced to **Find** the record for the **Major ID** of **339.555.22**, and then create a paper or electronic printout as directed by your instructor of that record only on one page.

> If there are no related records in the subdatasheet, the empty subdatasheet does not display in the printed form.

8 In the **Navigation Pane**, double-click your **3A Student Major Change Form** object to open it. With the first record displayed, create a paper or electronic printout as directed by your instructor of that record only on one page.

9 **Close** |×| all open objects, and then **Open** |»| the **Navigation Pane**. If necessary, resize the **Navigation Pane** so all object names display fully. On the right side of the title bar, click Close |×| to close the database and to close Access. As directed by your instructor, submit your database for grading.

You have completed the optional portion of Project 3A   END

| Objective | Export an Access Form to an Excel Spreadsheet, Save to Google Drive as a Google Sheet, Edit a Record, and Save to Your Computer |

Access web apps are designed to work with Microsoft's SharePoint, a service for setting up websites to share and manage documents. Your college may not have SharePoint installed, so you will use other tools to share objects from your database so that you can work collaboratively with others. Recall that Google Drive is Google's free, web-based word processor, spreadsheet, slide show, form, and data storage and sharing service. For Access, you can export a database object to an Excel worksheet, a PDF file, or a text file, and then save the file to Google Drive.

ALERT   Working with Web-Based Applications and Services

Computer programs and services on the web receive continuous updates and improvements, so the steps to complete this web-based activity may differ from the ones shown. You can often look at the screens and the information presented to determine how to complete the activity.

If you do not already have a Google account, you will need to create one before you begin this activity. Go to http://google.com and in the upper-right corner, click Sign In. On the Sign In screen, click Create account. On the Create your Google Account page, complete the form, read and agree to the Terms of Service and Privacy Policy, and then click Next step. On the Welcome screen, click Get Started.

Activity | Exporting an Access Form to an Excel Spreadsheet, Saving the Spreadsheet to Google Drive, Editing a Record in Google Sheets, and Saving to Your Computer

In this Activity, you will export your 3A Student Major Change Form object to an Excel spreadsheet, upload your Excel file to Google Drive, edit a record in Google Sheets, and then download a copy of the edited spreadsheet to your computer.

1 Start Access, on the left click **Open Other Files**, navigate to your **Access Chapter 3** folder, and then **Open** your **3A_Students_Majors** database file. If necessary, on the **Message Bar**, click **Enable Content**. In the **Navigation Pane**, click your **3A Student Major Change Form** object to select it.

2 On the **External Data tab**, in the **Export group**, click **Excel**. In the **Export – Excel Spreadsheet** dialog box, click **Browse**, and then navigate to your **Access Chapter 3** folder. In the **File Save** dialog box, click in the **File name** box, type **Lastname_Firstname_AC_3A_Web** and then click **Save**.

3 In the **Export – Excel Spreadsheet** dialog box, under **Specify export options**, select the second check box—**Open the destination file after the export operation is complete**—and then click **OK**.

The records from the underlying table of the form display in Excel. When you export a form to Excel, the formatting and layout are automatically saved. For example, notice the olive green background color of the cells, which was the color that was applied to the text box controls in the form.

4 In the **Microsoft Excel** window, in the column headings row, to the left of column A, click **Select All**. On the **Home tab**, in the **Cells group**, click **Format**, and then click **AutoFit Column Width**. Click in cell **A1** to cancel the selection, and then compare your screen with Figure A.

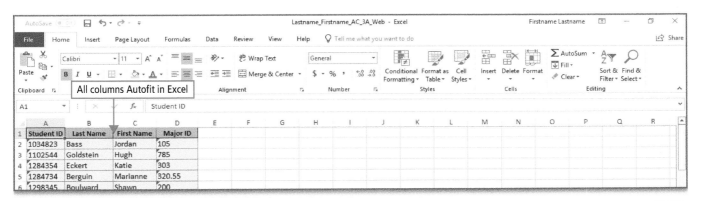

Figure A

»»» **GO!** With Google continues on next page

5 **Save** the workbook, and then **Close** Excel. In the **Export – Excel Spreadsheet** dialog box, click **Close**, and then **Close** Access.

6 From the desktop, open your browser, navigate to http://google.com, and then sign in to your Google account. Click the Google Apps menu ⊞, and then click Drive ▲. Open your **GO! Web Projects** folder—or click New to create and then open this folder if necessary.

7 In the upper right corner, click **Settings** ⚙, and then on the menu click **Settings**. In the **Settings** dialog box, next to **Convert uploads**, be sure that **Convert uploaded files to Google Docs editor format** is selected. In the upper right, click **Done**.

If this setting is not selected, your document will upload as a pdf file and cannot be edited without further action.

8 On the left, click **New**, and then click **File upload**. In the **Open** dialog box, navigate to your **Access Chapter 3** folder, and then double-click your **Lastname_Firstname_AC_3A_Web** file to upload it to Google Drive. When the title bar of the message box indicates *1 upload complete*, **Close** the message box.

9 In your **GO! Web Projects** folder, double-click your **Lastname_Firstname_AC_3A_Web** file to open it in Google Sheets.

10 In the second record (row 3), click in the **Last Name** field, using your own last name, type **Lastname** and then press Enter. In the **First Name** field, using your own first name, type Firstname and then press Enter to save the record. Compare your screen with Figure B.

Figure B

11 On the menu bar, click **File**, point to **Download as**, and then click **Microsoft Excel (.xlsx)**. As necessary, open the downloaded file in Excel, enable editing, and then **Save** the file in your **Access Chapter 3** folder as **Lastname_Firstname_AC_3A_Web_Download**

12 Close Excel. In Google Drive, in the upper right corner, click your user name, and then click **Sign out**. **Close** your browser window.

13 As directed by your instructor, submit your two workbooks.

NOTE Printing or Creating an PDF electronic image of an Excel Spreadsheet

To print on paper, click Print. To create a PDF electronic image of your printout, on the left side of your screen, click Export. Under Export, be sure Create PDF/XPS Document is selected, and then click Create PDF/XPS. Navigate to your Access Chapter 3 folder, and then click Publish to save the file with the default name and an extension of pdf.

PROJECT 3B Job Openings Database

MyLab IT
Project 3B Grader for Instruction
Project 3B Simulation for Training and Review

Project Activities

In Activities 3.16 through 3.23, you will assist Jack Woods, director of the Career Center for Texas Lakes Community College, in using his Access database to track the employees and job openings advertised for the annual job fair. Your completed Navigation Pane will look similar to Figure 3.28.

Project Files for MyLab IT Grader

1. In your **MyLab IT** course, locate and click **Access 3B Job Openings**, Download Materials, and then Download All Files.
2. Extract the zipped folder to your Access Chapter 3 folder. Close the Grader download screens.
3. Take a moment to open the downloaded **Access_3B_Job_Openings_Instructions**; note any recent updates to the book.

Project Results

GO! Project 3B
Where We're Going

Figure 3.28 Project 3B Job Openings

For Non-MyLab Submissions
For Project 3B, you will need this starting file:
a03B_Job_Openings

Start with an Access Data File
In your Access Chapter 3 folder, save your database as:
Lastname_Firstname_3B_Job_Openings

After you have saved your database, launch Access and open the database. On the next page, begin with Step 2.

Create a Report by Using the Report Tool and Modify the Report in Layout View

ALERT   Because Office 365 is a cloud-based subscription service that receives continuous updates, you may encounter some variations in what appears on your screen and what is shown in this instruction. Microsoft Office 365 is fully installed on your PC or Mac; no internet access is necessary to create or edit documents. When you *are* connected to the internet, you will receive monthly upgrades and new features, so you always have the latest versions of Office apps as soon as they are available. Your subscription gives you continuous free access to the latest innovations and refinements.

GO! Learn How
Video A3-5

A *report* is a database object that summarizes the fields and records from a query or from a table in an easy-to-read format suitable for printing. A report consists of information extracted from queries or tables and report design controls, such as labels, headings, and graphics. The queries or tables that provide the underlying data for a report are referred to as the report's *record source*.

Activity 3.16 | **Opening and Saving an Existing Database, Renaming Objects, and Viewing a Table Relationship**

1.2.2

1 Start Access. In the Access opening screen, click **Open Other Files**. Under **Open**, click **Browse**, navigate to your **Access Chapter 3 folder**, and then double-click the Access file that you downloaded from **MyLab IT** that displays your name—**Student_Access_3B_Job_Openings**. On the **Message Bar**, click **Enable Content**.

2 On the **Database Tools tab**, in the **Relationships group**, click **Relationships**. If the relationships do not display, under Relationship Tools, on the Design tab, in the Relationships group, click All Relationships. If necessary, resize and move the field lists so that the entire table name and fields display for each field list.

3 In the **Relationships** window, click the **join line** between the two field lists. In the **Tools group**, click **Edit Relationships**. Point to the title bar of the **Edit Relationships** dialog box, and then drag the dialog box to the right of the **3B Job Openings** field list. Compare your screen with Figure 3.29.

One employer is associated with *many* job openings. Thus, a one-to-many relationship is established between the 3B Employers table and the 3B Job Openings table by using Employer ID as the common field. Referential integrity is enforced, and cascade options are selected.

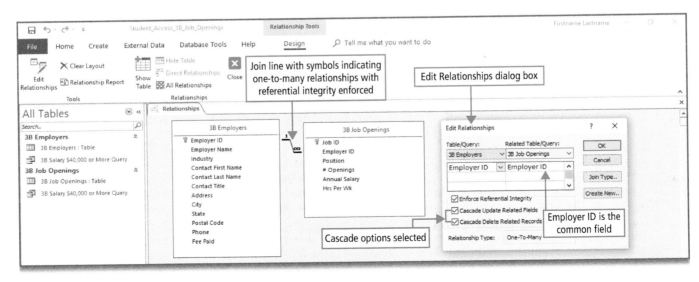

Figure 3.29

4 Close ✕ the **Edit Relationships** dialog box, and then **Close** ✕ the **Relationships** window. If necessary, in the message box, click Yes to save changes to the layout of the relationships.

5 In the **Navigation Pane**, double-click each table, and then examine the fields and data in each table. Double-click the query object to run the query and examine the query results, apply **Best Fit** to the query results, and then **Save** the query. Switch to **Design** view to examine the design grid.

> The query answers the question, *What is the Job ID, position, employer name, number of job openings, and annual salary for job openings that have an annual salary of $40,000 or more, in ascending order by the Employer Name field within the Position field?*

6 In the object window, right-click any **object tab**, and then click **Close All**.

Activity 3.17 | Creating a Report by Using the Report Tool and Applying a Theme to the Report

5.1.2, 5.2.3

The ***Report tool*** is the fastest way to create a report, because it displays all of the fields and records from the record source that you select. You can use the Report tool to look at the underlying data quickly in an easy-to-read format, after which you can save the report and modify it in Layout view or in Design view.

In this Activity, you will use the Report tool to create a report from a query that lists all of the job openings with an annual salary of at least $40,000 and apply a theme to the report.

1 In the **Navigation Pane**, if necessary, click to select your **3B Salary $40,000 or More Query** object. On the **Create tab**, in the **Reports group**, click **Report**. **Close** « the **Navigation Pane**, and then compare your screen with Figure 3.30.

> The report is created using the query as the record source and displays in Layout view. The report includes all of the fields and all of the records from the query and the title of the query. In Layout view, the broken lines indicate the page margins in the report.

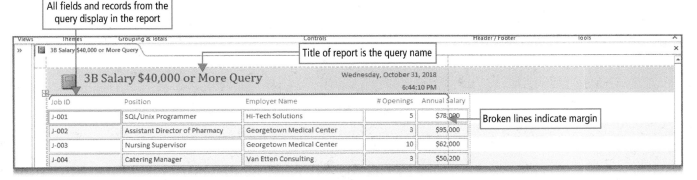

Figure 3.30

2 Under **Report Layout Tools**, on the **Design tab**, in the **Themes group**, click **Themes**. In the **Themes** gallery, use the ScreenTips to locate the **Integral** theme, right-click the **Integral** theme, and then click **Apply Theme to This Object Only**.

> Recall that right-clicking a theme enables you to apply a predefined format to the active object only, which is a quick way to apply a professional look to a report. Apply a theme before formatting any other controls on the report.

ALERT **You applied the theme to the entire database instead of a single object.**

If you applied the theme to the entire database, you cannot undo that selection. To correct the theme, under Report Layout Tools, on the Design tab, in the Themes group, click Themes. In the Themes gallery, click the Office theme to apply it to the entire database. Return to Step 2 above to apply the Integral theme to a single object.

Activity 3.18 | Modifying a Report in Layout View

5.2.1, 5.1.2,
5.2.5, 5.1.1, 5.2.3

After you create a report, you can make changes to it. For example, you can add or delete fields, resize the fields, and change the style of the report. Layout view enables you to see the data in the report as you modify the report. Most changes to a report can be made in Layout view.

1 Click the **Job ID** field name. On the **Report Layout Tools**, click the **Arrange tab**, in the **Rows & Columns group**, click **Select Column** to select the field name and all of the data for each record in the field. Press Del to remove the field from the report.

> The Job ID field is deleted, and the remaining fields move to the left. No fields extend beyond the right margin of the report.

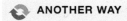 **ANOTHER WAY** With the column selected, on the Home tab, in the Records group, click Delete; or right-click the selected column, and then click Delete or Delete Column.

2 In the **Employer Name** field, click in the **text box control** that displays *Monroe Heating & Air Conditioning* to select all of the text box controls in this field.

3 On the **Report Layout Tools**, click the **Design tab**, and in the **Tools group**, click **Property Sheet**. In the **Property Sheet**, on the **Format tab**, click **Width**, type **2.5** and then press Enter. Compare your screen with Figure 3.31.

> Recall that you can use the Property Sheet to make precise changes to control properties.

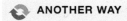 **ANOTHER WAY** Point to the right edge of the text box control to display the pointer. Drag to the right slightly until the data in the text box control displays on correctly.

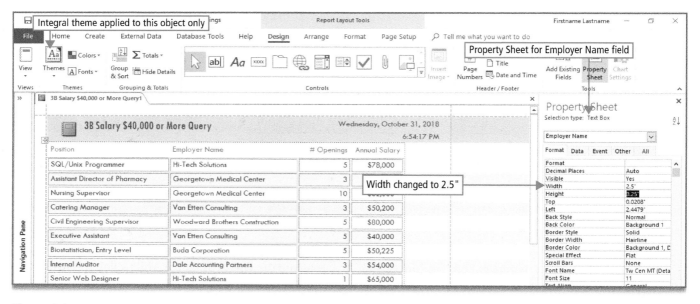

Figure 3.31

4 Close ☒ the **Property Sheet**. Click the **Position** field name, and then on the **Home tab**, in the **Sort & Filter group**, click **Ascending** to sort the records in ascending order by the Position field.

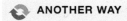 **ANOTHER WAY** Right-click the selected field name and then click Sort A to Z.

5 Scroll to the bottom of the report, and then click the **calculated control** that displays *$2,157,625*, which is shortened at the bottom cutting off part of the data. Press Del to remove this control.

In a report created by using the Report tool, a **calculated control** is automatically created to sum any field that is formatted as currency. A calculated control contains an expression, often a formula or a function. Here, the total is not a useful number and thus can be deleted.

6 Scroll to the bottom of the report again, and then under the last column, click the horizontal line that is the border between the last record and the calculated control that you deleted. Press Del to remove this line, and then scroll to the bottom of the report to verify that the line has been deleted.

7 Scroll to the top of the report, and then click the **# Openings** field name. On the **Design tab**, in the **Grouping & Totals group**, click **Totals**, and then click **Sum**.

8 Scroll to the bottom of the report, and then click the **calculated control** that displays *100*. On the **Design tab**, in the **Tools group**, click **Property Sheet**. In the **Property Sheet**, on the **Format tab**, click **Height**, type **0.25** and then press Enter. Compare your screen with Figure 3.32.

The total number of job openings for positions with a salary of $40,000 or more is 100.

ANOTHER WAY Point to the lower edge of the text box control to display the ↕ pointer, and then double-click to resize the control, or drag downward to increase the height of the control.

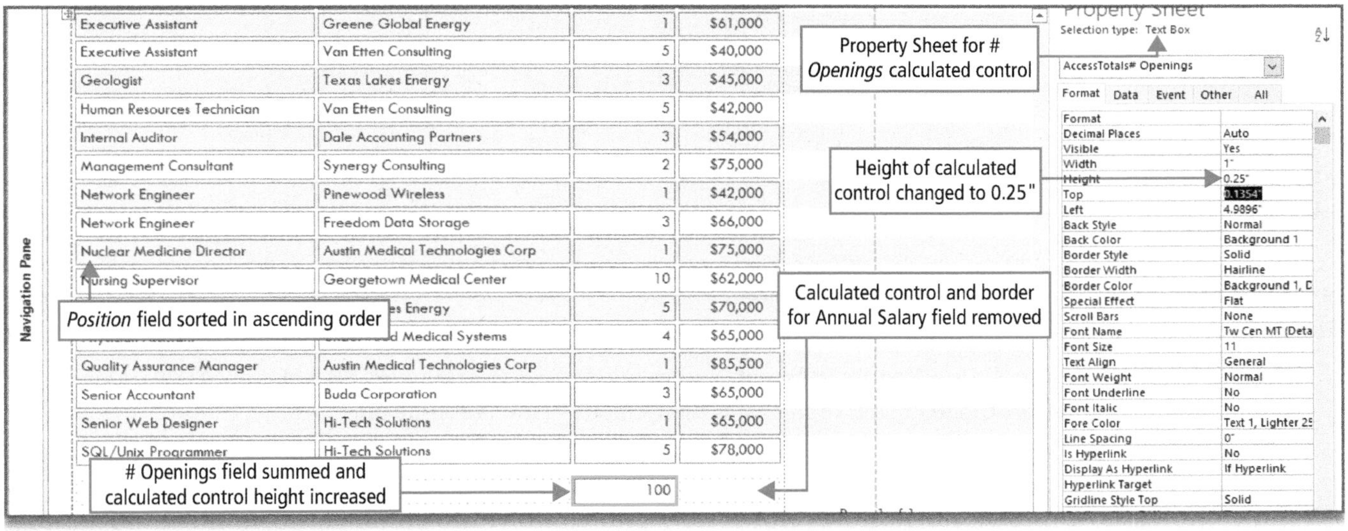

Figure 3.32

9 At the bottom of the report to the right of the calculated control, notice that the control that displays the page number does not fit entirely within the margins of the report. Click the **control** that displays *Page 1 of 1*. In the **Property Sheet**, click **Left**, type **2.5** and then press Enter.

The control moves within the margins of the report with the left edge of the control 2.5 inches in from the left margin of the report. When you click on different controls in a report or form, the Property Sheet changes to match the selected control. Before printing, always scroll through the report to be sure that all of the controls display on one page and not outside of the margins.

ANOTHER WAY Click the control, point to the selected control to display the pointer, and then drag the control to the left within the margins of the report.

10 Scroll to the top of the report, and then click the **label control** that displays the title of the report—*3B Salary $40,000 or More Query*. On the **Report Layout Tools**, click the **Format tab**. In the **Font group**, click the **Font Size arrow**, and then click **14**.

11 With the **label control** for the title still selected, double-click **Query** to select the word, type **Report** and then press [Enter] to change the name of the report to *3B Salary $40,000 or More Report*.

12 Click the **Position** field name. In the **Property Sheet**, click **Left**, type **0.5** and then press [Enter] to move this field 0.5 inch in from the left margin of the report. Compare your screen with Figure 3.33.

The other fields adjust by moving to the right. The fields are centered approximately within the margins of the report.

ANOTHER WAY Click the layout selector ⊞ to select all of the controls, and then drag it slightly downward and to the right until the columns are visually centered between the margins of the report. If your columns rearrange, click Undo and begin again.

Left edge of first field moved in 0.5 inch from left margin

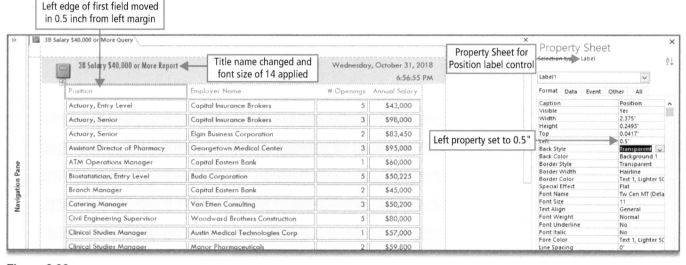

Figure 3.33

13 Close × the **Property Sheet**, and then **Save** 🖫 the report as **3B Salary $40,000 or More Report** Close × the report, and then Open » the **Navigation Pane**.

The report displays under both tables from which the query was created. The report object name displays with a small green notebook icon.

14 Close « the **Navigation Pane**.

Objective 6   Create a Report by Using the Report Wizard

GO! Learn How
Video A3-6

Use the ***Report Wizard*** when you need more flexibility in the design of your report. You can group and sort data by using the wizard and use fields from more than one table or query if you have created the relationships between tables. The Report Wizard is similar to the Form Wizard; the wizard walks you step by step through the process of creating the report by asking you questions and then designs the report based on your answers.

Activity 3.19 | Creating a Report by Using the Report Wizard

In this Activity, you will prepare a report for Mr. Woods that displays the employers, grouped by industry, and the total fees paid by employers for renting a booth at the Job Fair.

1 On the **Create tab**, in the **Reports group**, click **Report Wizard**.

In the first wizard screen, you select the fields to include on the report. The fields can come from more than one table or query.

2 In the **Tables/Queries** box, click the **arrow**, and then click **Table: 3B Employers**. In the **Available Fields** list, double-click the following field names in the order given to move them to the **Selected Fields** list: **Industry**, **Employer Name**, and **Fee Paid** (scroll as necessary to locate the *Fee Paid* field). Compare your screen with Figure 3.34.

Three field names from your 3B Employers table display in the Selected Fields list.

↻ **ANOTHER WAY**   Click the field name, and then click One Field `>` to move a field from the Available Fields list to the Selected Fields list.

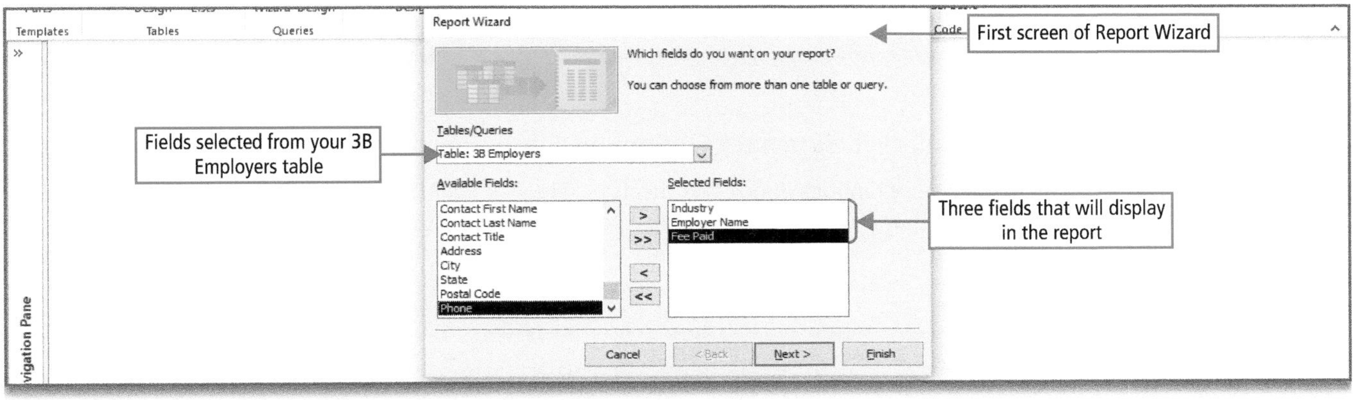

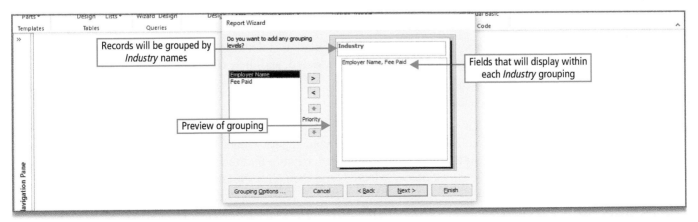

Figure 3.34

3 Click **Next**. In the wizard, notice that you can add grouping levels and that a preview of the grouping level displays on the right.

Grouping data helps to organize and summarize the data in your report.

4 On the left, double-click **Industry**, and then compare your screen with Figure 3.35.

The preview displays how the data will be grouped in the report. Grouping data in a report places all of the records that have the same data in a field together as a group—in this instance, the records will be grouped by *Industry*. Within each Industry name, the Employer Name and Fee Paid will display.

Figure 3.35

5 Click **Next**. Click the **1** box **arrow**, click **Employer Name**, and then compare your screen with Figure 3.36.

In this step of the wizard, you indicate how you want to sort the records and summarize the information. You can sort up to four fields. The Summary Options button displays because the data is grouped, and at least one of the fields—*Fee Paid*—contains numerical or currency data. Within each Industry grouping, the records will be sorted alphabetically by the Employer Name. Sorting records in a report presents a more organized view of the records.

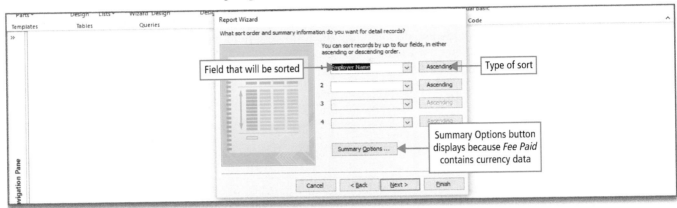

Figure 3.36

6 In the wizard, click **Summary Options**, and then compare your screen with Figure 3.37.

The Summary Options dialog box displays. The *Fee Paid* field can be summarized by selecting one of the four check boxes for Sum, Avg, Min, or Max. You can also display only summary information or display both the details—each record—and the summary information. The default setting is to display *Detail and Summary*.

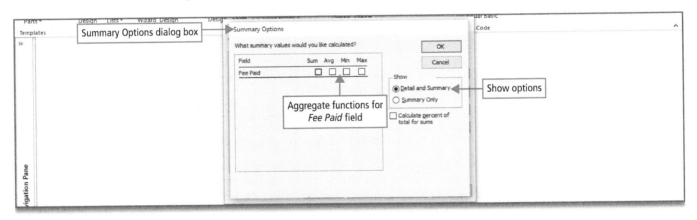

Figure 3.37

7 In the **Summary Options** dialog box, click to select the **Sum** check box. Under **Show**, verify that **Detail and Summary** is selected, and then click **OK**. In the wizard, click **Next**.

In this step of the wizard, you select the layout and page orientation. A preview of the layout displays on the left.

8 Click each **Layout** option button, noticing the changes in the preview, and then click **Stepped** to select it as the layout for your report. Under **Orientation**, be sure that **Portrait** is selected. At the bottom of the wizard, be sure that the **Adjust the field width so all fields fit on a page** check box is selected, and then click **Next**.

9 In the **What title do you want for your report?** box, select the existing text, type **3B Booth Fees by Industry Report** and then click **Finish**. Compare your screen with Figure 3.38.

The report is saved and displays in Print Preview using the specifications you defined in the Report Wizard. The records are grouped by Industry. Within each Industry, the records display in ascending order by the Employer Name. Within each Industry grouping, the Fee paid is summed or totaled—the word *Sum* displays at the end of each grouping.

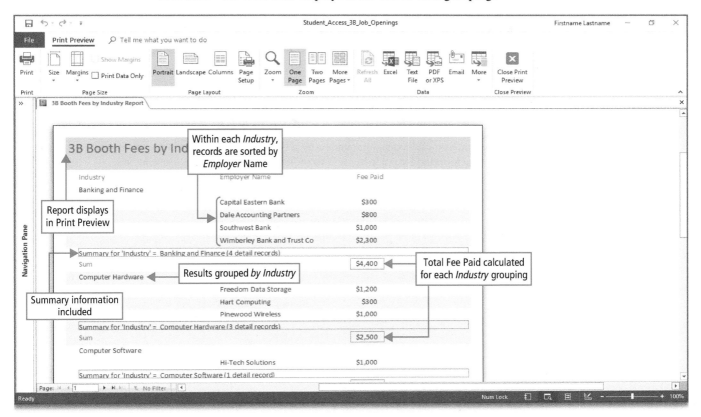

Figure 3.38

10 In the object window, right-click the **object tab** for the report, and then click **Layout View**.

ANOTHER WAY On the status bar, click Layout View 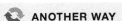; or click Close Print Preview, and then on the Home tab or the Design tab, click the View arrow, and then click Layout View.

Objective 7 | Modify the Design of a Report

GO! Learn How
Video A3-7

You can modify the design of a report that is created using the Report Wizard by using the same techniques and tools that you use to modify a report created with the Report tool. Recall that most report modifications can be made in Layout view.

Activity 3.20 | Formatting and Deleting Controls in Layout View

MOS
5.2.3

In this Activity, you will apply a theme to the report, format the title of the report, and delete the summary information controls.

1 Be sure that your **3B Booth Fees by Industry Report** object is displayed in **Layout** view. Under **Report Layout Tools**, on the **Design tab**, in the **Themes group**, click **Themes**. In the **Themes** gallery, use the ScreenTips to locate the **Ion Boardroom** theme, right-click the **Ion Boardroom** theme, and then click **Apply Theme to This Object Only**.

Recall that you should apply a theme before applying any other formatting changes. Also, recall that if you click a theme—instead of right-clicking—the theme is applied to all of the objects in the database.

2 At the top of the report, click the title—*3B Booth Fees by Industry Report*—to display a border around the label control. On the **Report Layout Tools**, click the **Format tab**. In the **Font group**, click the **Font Size arrow**, and then click **14**. In the **Font group**, click **Bold** [B].

By changing the font size, the report name is no longer truncated and includes the word *Report*.

3 Within each *Industry* grouping, notice the **Summary for 'Industry'** information.

Because you selected Summary Options, a summary line is included at the end of each grouping that details what is being summarized—in this case, summed—and the number of records that are included in the summary total. Now that Mr. Woods has viewed the report, he has decided that this information is not necessary and can be removed.

4 Click any one of the controls that begins with **Summary for 'Industry'**.

The control that you clicked is surrounded by a border, and all of the other summary information controls are surrounded by paler borders to indicate that all controls are selected.

5 Press [Del] to remove the controls from the report, and then compare your screen with Figure 3.39.

ANOTHER WAY   Right-click any of the selected controls, and then click Delete to remove the controls from the report.

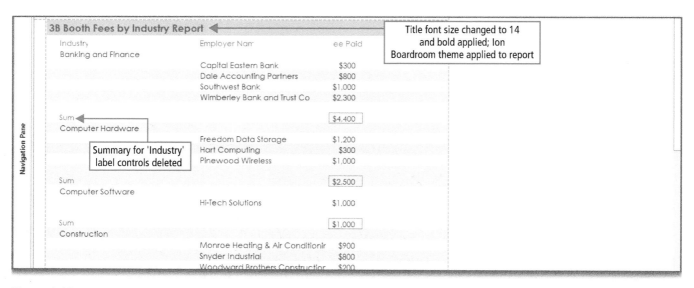

Figure 3.39

6 **Save** [💾] the changes you have made to the design of the report.

Activity 3.21 | Modifying Controls in Layout View

MOS

5.2.2, 5.2.3, 5.1.3

In this Activity, you will modify the text in controls, move controls, resize controls, and add a control to the report in Layout view.

1 ▶ On the left side of the report, click a **Sum label control**, which selects all of the related controls. Double-click the control to select the text—*Sum*. Type **Total Booth Fees by Industry** and then press Enter. Compare your screen with Figure 3.40.

This text states more clearly what is being summed.

Figure 3.40

2 ▶ At the top of the report, click the **Industry label control** to select it. Hold down Shift, click the **Employer Name label control**, and then click the **Fee Paid label control** to select all three field names. On the **Format tab**, in the **Font group**, click **Bold** B.

Applying bold also increases the size of the controls so that the text is no longer truncated.

3 ▶ At the top of the report, under the **Fee Paid label control**, click the **text box control** that displays *$300* to select the text box controls for all of the records for this field. On the **Design tab**, in the **Tools group**, click **Property Sheet**. In the **Property Sheet**, on the **Format tab**, click **Left**, type **7** and then press Enter. Compare your screen with Figure 3.41.

All of the Fee Paid text box controls move to the right—7" in from the left margin. Do not be concerned that the summary total and the field name are not aligned with the data; you will correct this in the next Activity. The field is moved to the right so that you can increase the width of the Employer Name text box controls so that all of the data for every record displays.

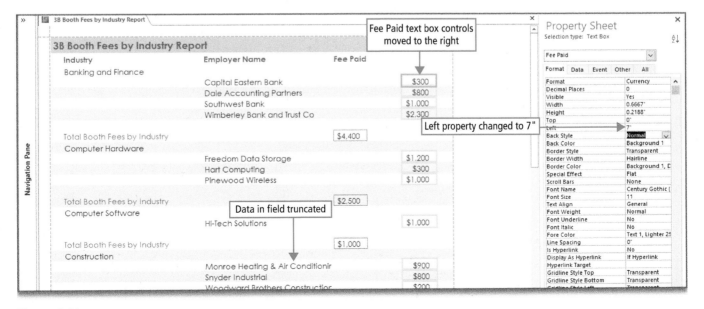

Figure 3.41

4 Scroll to view the bottom of the report. Click to select the **calculated control** for the **Grand Total**, which displays *20,400* and part of the dollar symbol. In the **Property Sheet**, click **Width**, type **0.8** and then press Enter.

> The width of the calculated control increases to display the dollar symbol. Do not be concerned that the right edge of the control no longer aligns with the control above it; you will correct this in the next Activity. Recall that a calculated control contains an expression—a formula or function—that displays the result of the expression when the report is displayed in Report view, Print Preview, or Layout view.

ANOTHER WAY Point to the left edge of the control to display the ↔ pointer. Drag to the left slightly to increase the width of the calculated control.

5 At the bottom of the report, on the left side, click the **Grand Total label control**. In the **Property Sheet**, click **Width**, type **1** and then press Enter. Compare your screen with Figure 3.42.

> The width of the label control is increased so that all of the text displays.

ANOTHER WAY Point to the right edge of the control to display the ↔ pointer, and then double-click to resize the control.

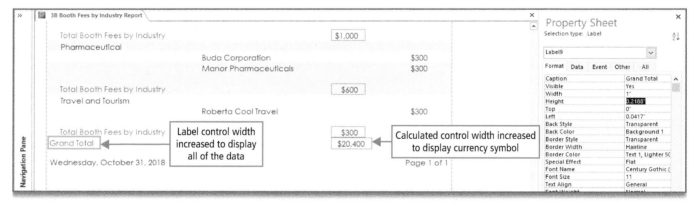

Figure 3.42

6 Scroll to the top to display the Industry grouping of **Construction**, and then notice that the first and third records have truncated data in the **Employer Name** field. In the **Construction** grouping, click the **Employer Name text box control** that starts with *Monroe Heating* to select all of the text box controls for this field.

7 In the **Property Sheet**, click **Width**, type **3** and then press Enter. **Save** 🖫 the design changes to your report, and then compare your screen with Figure 3.43.

> The width of the Employer Name text box controls is increased so that all of the data in this field for every record displays. Recall that you moved the Fee Paid text box controls to the right to make room for the increased width of these controls.

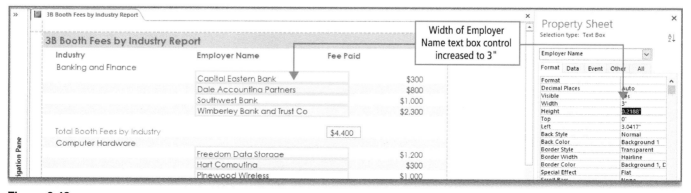

Figure 3.43

Activity 3.22 | Aligning Controls in Design View

5.2.2, 5.2.3, 5.1.3

Design view gives you a more detailed view of the structure of your report. You can see the header and footer sections for the report, for the page, and for groups. In Design view, your report is not running, so you cannot see the data from the table in the controls. In the same manner as forms, you can add labels to the Page Footer section or increase the height of sections. Some tasks, such as aligning controls, must be completed in Design view.

1 **Close** ☒ the **Property Sheet**. On the status bar, click **Design View** 📝, and then compare your screen with Figure 3.44.

Design view for a report is similar to Design view for a form. You can modify the layout of the report in this view, and then use the dotted grid pattern to align controls. This report has several sections. The ***Report Header*** displays information at the top of the *first page* of a report. The ***Page Header*** displays information at the top of *every page* of a report. The ***Group Header*** displays the name of data in the field by which the records are grouped; in this case, the *Industry* name. The Detail section displays the data for each record. The ***Group Footer*** displays the summary information for each grouping; in this case, the Industry name. The ***Page Footer*** displays information at the bottom of *every page* of the report. The ***Report Footer*** displays information at the bottom of the *last page* of the report.

If you do not group data in a report, the Group Header section and Group Footer section will not display. If you do not summarize the data, the Group Footer section will not display.

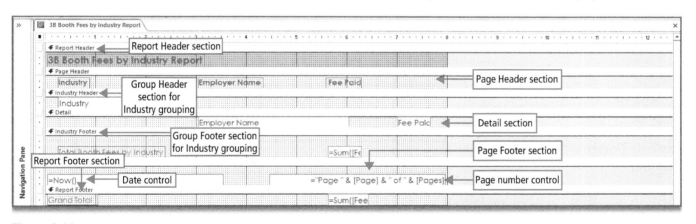

Figure 3.44

2 In the **Page Footer** section of the report, examine the two controls in this section. Recall that information in the Page Footer section displays at the bottom of every page in the report.

On the left side, the ***date control*** displays *=Now( )*, which inserts the current date each time the report is opened. On the right side, the ***page number control*** displays *="Page " & [Page] & " of " & [Pages]*, which inserts the page number, for example *Page 1 of 2*, when the report is displayed in Print Preview or when printed. Both of these controls contain examples of functions that are used by Access to create controls in a report.

3 In the **Industry Footer** section, click the **Total Booth Fees by Industry label control**. Hold down Shift, and in the **Report Footer** section, click the **Grand Total label control** to select both label controls.

4 Under **Report Design Tools**, click the **Arrange tab**. In the **Sizing & Ordering group**, click **Align**, and then click **Left**.

The left edge of the *Grand Total label control* is aligned with the left edge of the *Total Booth Fees by Industry label control*. When using the Align Left command, the left edges of the selected controls are aligned with the control that is the farthest to the left in the report.

5 In the **Page Header** section, click the **Fee Paid label control**. Hold down Shift while you click the following: in the **Detail** section, click the **Fee Paid text box control**; in the **Industry Footer** section, click the **calculated control** that begins with =*Sum*; and in the **Report Footer** section, click the **calculated control** that begins with =*Sum*.

Four controls are selected.

6 On the **Arrange tab**, in the **Sizing & Ordering group**, click **Align**, and then click **Right**. **Save** 🖫 the design changes to your report, and then compare your screen with Figure 3.45.

The right edges of the four selected controls are aligned with the right edge of the *Fee Paid text box control*. When using the Align Right command, the right edges of the selected controls are aligned with the control that is the farthest to the right in the report.

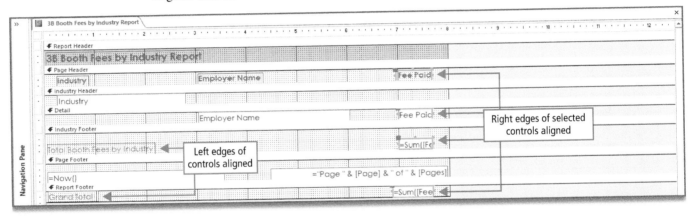

Figure 3.45

7 On the status bar, click **Layout View** 🖽 to display the underlying data in the controls. Scroll to view the bottom of the report. On the left side, notice that the **Total Booth Fees by Industry label control** and the **Grand Total label control** are left aligned. Also, notice the right alignment of the controls in the **Fee Paid** column.

Objective 8   Keep Grouped Data Together in a Printed Report

GO! Learn How
Video A3-8

Before you print a report, examine the report in Print Preview to be sure that all of the labels and data display fully and to be sure that all of the data is properly grouped. Sometimes a page break occurs in the middle of a group of data, leaving the labels on one page and the data or summary information on another page.

Activity 3.23 | Keeping Grouped Data Together in a Printed Report

In this Activity, you will preview the document and then will keep the data in each group together so a grouping is not split between two pages of the report. This is possible if the data in a grouping does not exceed the length of a page.

1 On the status bar, click **Print Preview** 🔍. On the **Print Preview tab**, in the **Zoom group**, click **Two Pages**, and then compare your screen with Figure 3.46.

The report will print on two pages. For the Industry grouping of *Hotel and Food Service*, one record and the summary data display at the top of Page 2 and is separated from the rest of the grouping that displays at the bottom of Page 1. Your display may differ depending upon your printer configuration.

In Print Preview, the One Page or Two Pages Zoom view causes the records to be compressed slightly and might display with the bottoms of records truncated. The records, however, will print correctly.

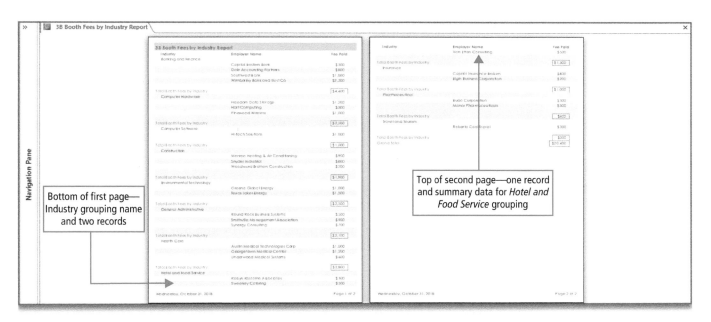

Figure 3.46

2 Click **Close Print Preview** to return to **Layout** view. On the **Design tab**, in the **Grouping & Totals group**, click **Group & Sort**.

At the bottom of the screen, the *Group, Sort, and Total pane* displays. This pane is used to control how information is grouped, sorted, or totaled. Layout view is the preferred view in which to accomplish these tasks because you can see how the changes affect the display of the data in the report.

3 In the **Group, Sort, and Total** pane, on the **Group on Industry** bar, click **More**. To the right of **do not keep group together on one page**, click the **arrow**, and then compare your screen with Figure 3.47.

The *keep whole group together on one page* command keeps each industry group together, from the name in the Group Header section through the summary information in the Group Footer section. The default setting is *do not keep group together on one page*. Next to *Group on Industry*, *with A on top* indicates that the industry names are sorted in ascending order.

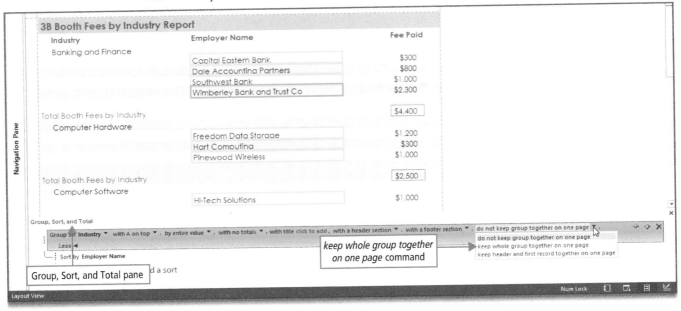

Figure 3.47

4 Click **keep whole group together on one page**. On the **Design tab**, in the **Grouping & Totals group**, click **Group & Sort** to close the **Group, Sort, and Total** pane.

5 On the status bar, click **Print Preview** . If necessary, in the **Zoom group**, click **Two Pages**. Compare your screen with Figure 3.48.

The entire grouping for the Industry of *Hotel and Food Service* displays at the top of page 2. The grouping no longer breaks between page 1 and page 2. Recall that even though the bottoms of records display truncated because of the compressed Print Preview setting of Two Pages, the records will print correctly.

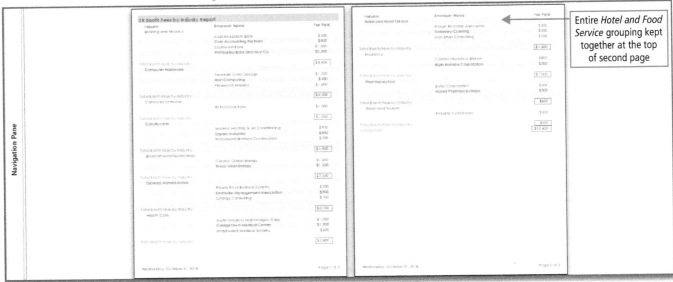

Entire *Hotel and Food Service* grouping kept together at the top of second page

Figure 3.48

6 **Save** 🖫 the design changes to your report.

7 **Close** ⌧ the report, and then **Open** » the **Navigation Pane**. If necessary, increase the width of the Navigation Pane so that all object names display fully.

8 On the right side of the title bar, click **Close** ⌧ to close the database and to close Access.

For Non-MyLab Submissions: Determine What Your Instructor Requires for Submission

As directed by your instructor, submit your completed database file.

---

9 In **MyLab IT**, locate and click the Grader Project **Access 3B Job Openings**. In **step 3**, under **Upload Completed Assignment**, click **Choose File**. In the **Open** dialog box, navigate to your **Access Chapter 3 folder**, and then click your **Student_Access_3B_Job_Openings** file one time to select it. In the lower right corner of the **Open** dialog box, click **Open**.

The name of your selected file displays above the Upload button.

10 To submit your file to **MyLab IT** for grading, click **Upload**, wait a moment for a green **Success!** message, and then in **step 4**, click the blue **Submit for Grading** button. Click **Close Assignment** to return to your list of **Course Materials**.

You have completed Project 3B **END**

»»» GO! With Google

Access web apps are designed to work with Microsoft's SharePoint, a service for setting up websites to share and manage documents. Your college may not have SharePoint installed, so you will use other tools to share objects from your database so that you can work collaboratively with others. Recall that Google Drive is Google's free, web-based word processor, spreadsheet, slide show, form, and data storage and sharing service. For Access, you can export a database object to an Excel worksheet, a PDF file, or a text file, and then save the file to Google Drive.

> **ALERT**   **Working with Web-Based Applications and Services**
>
> Computer programs and services on the web receive continuous updates and improvements, so the steps to complete this web-based activity may differ from the ones shown. You can often look at the screens and the information presented to determine how to complete the activity.
>
> If you do not already have a Google account, you will need to create one before you begin this activity. Go to http://google.com and in the upper-right corner, click Sign In. On the Sign In screen, click Create account. On the Create your Google Account page, complete the form, read and agree to the Terms of Service and Privacy Policy, and then click Next step. On the Welcome screen, click Get Started.

Activity | Exporting an Access Report to a Word File, Uploading the Word File to OneDrive, and Editing the Report in Google Docs

In this Activity, you will export your 3B Salary $40,000 or More Report object to a Word file, upload your Word file to OneDrive, and then edit the report in Google Docs.

1 Start Access, on the left click **Open Other Databases**, navigate to your **Access Chapter 3** folder, and then open your **3B_Job_Openings** database file. If necessary, on the Message Bar, click Enable Content. In the **Navigation Pane**, click one time to select the report **3B Salary $40,000 or More Report** object to select it.

2 On the **External Data tab**, in the **Export group**, click **More**, and then click **Word**.

The report will be exported as a ***Rich Text Format (RTF)***—a standard file format that contains text and some formatting such as underline, bold, italic, font sizes, and colors. RTF documents can be opened in many word processing programs and text editors.

3 In the **Export – RTF File** dialog box, click **Browse**, and then navigate to your **Access Chapter**

3 folder. In the **File Save** dialog box, click in the **File name** box to select the existing text. Type **Lastname_Firstname_AC_3B_Web** and then click **Save**. In the **Export – RTF File** dialog box, select the **Open the destination file after the export operation is complete** check box, and then click **OK**.

4 In Word, click the **File tab,** click **Save As,** and then click **Browse**. In the **Save As** dialog box, navigate to your **Access Chapter 3** folder. In the **File name** box, type **Lastname_Firstname_AC_3B_Web_Word** and then in the **Save as type** box, click the arrow and select **Word Document**. In the **Save As** dialog box, click **Save**. In the message box, click **OK**, and then compare your screen with Figure A.

The file is saved as a Word document in the .docx format to preserve the formatting of the document originally created in Access.

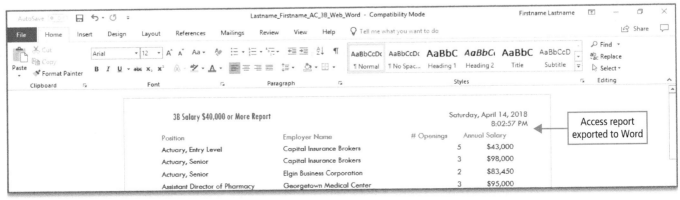

Figure A

5 Close Word. In the **Export – RTF File** dialog box, click **Close**, and then **Close** Access.

6 From the desktop, open your browser, navigate to http://google.com, and then sign in to your Google account. Click the **Google Apps** menu ▦, and then click **Drive** ☁. Open your **GO! Web Projects** folder—or click New to create and then open this folder if necessary.

7 In the upper right, click **Settings** ⚙, and then on the menu click **Settings**. In the **Settings** dialog box, next to *Convert uploads*, be sure that **Convert uploaded files to Google Docs editor format** is selected. In the upper right, click **Done**.

If this setting is not selected, your document will upload as a pdf file and cannot be edited without further action.

8 On the left, click **New**, and then click **File upload**. In the **Open** dialog box, navigate to your **Access Chapter 3** folder, and then double-click your **Lastname_Firstname_AC_3B_Web_Word** file to upload it to Google Drive. In the lower right corner, when the title bar of the message box indicates *1 upload complete*, **Close** the message box.

9 In the file list, double-click your **AC_3B_Web_Word** file to open it in Google Docs.

10 Drag across the four column headings—**Position**, **Employer Name**, **# Openings**, and **Annual Salary**—to select them, and then on the toolbar, click **Bold** B and **Underline** U. Click in the report title to deselect the row, and compare your screen with Figure B.

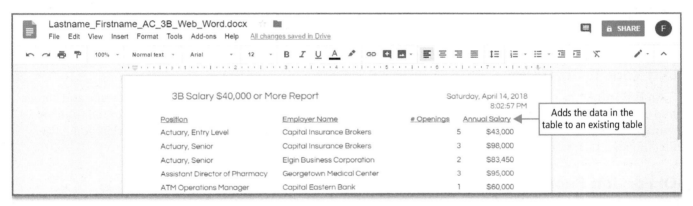

Figure B

11 Start the **Snipping Tool**. In the Snipping Tool dialog box, click the **New arrow**, and then click **Full-screen Snip**.

12 On the Snipping Tool toolbar, click **Save Snip** 💾. In the **Save As** dialog box, navigate to your **Access Chapter 3** folder. Click in the **File name** box, type **Lastname_Firstname_AC_3B_Web_Snip** and then be sure

that the **Save as type** box displays **JPEG file**. Click **Save**. **Close** ✕ the Snipping Tool window.

13 In **Google Drive**, at the upper right, click your user name, and then click **Sign out**. **Close** your browser window.

14 Submit your file as directed by your instructor.

»» GO! To Work

wavebreakmedia/Shutterstock, Monkey Business Images/Fotolia, Ivanko80/Shutterstock, Monkey Business Images/Shutterstock

Microsoft Office Specialist (MOS) Skills in This Chapter	
Project 3A	**Project 3B**
1.2.2 Display relationships	**1.2.2** Display relationships
2.3.1 Find and replace data	**5.1.1** Group and sort fields on reports
2.3.3 Filter records	**5.1.2** Add report controls
4.1.1 Add, move, and remove form controls	**5.1.3** Add and modify labels on reports
4.1.2 Set form control properties	**5.2.2** Modify report positioning
4.1.3 Add and modify form labels	**5.2.3** Format report elements
4.2.2 Set records by form field	**5.2.5** Insert information in report headers and footers
4.2.3 Modify form positioning	
4.2.4 Insert images in form headers and footers	

Build Your E-Portfolio

An E-Portfolio is a collection of evidence, stored electronically, that showcases what you have accomplished while completing your education. Collecting and then sharing your work products with potential employers reflects your academic and career goals. Your completed documents from the following projects are good examples to show what you have learned: 3G, 3K, and 3L.

GO! For Job Success

Video: Tough Interview Questions

Your instructor may assign this video to your class, and then ask you to think about, or discuss with your classmates, these questions:

g-stockstudio/Shutterstock

> How would you answer an illegal interview question like *Are you married or single*?

> How would you handle an interview question about a missing reference?

> Why is it important to always be open, honest, and to the point in an interview?

End of Chapter

ACCESS 3

Summary

A form is a database object that you can use to enter new records into a table, or to edit, delete, or display existing records in a table and can be used to control access to the data in a database.

Filter records in a form to display only a subset of the total records based on matching specific values to provide a quick answer to a question. Filters are generally not saved with a form.

A report is a database object that summarizes the fields and records from a query or from a table, in an easy-to-read format suitable for printing. You can group records and summarize the data in a report.

Most changes to forms and reports can be done in Layout view where the underlying data displays in the controls; however, some modifications, such as aligning controls, must be done in Design view.

GO! Learn It Online

Review the concepts and key terms in this chapter by completing these online challenges, which you can find at **MyLab IT**.

Chapter Quiz: Answer matching and multiple choice questions to test what you learned in this chapter.

Learn it on the GO!: Learn how to use all the new apps and features as they are introduced by Microsoft.

MOS Prep Quiz: Answer questions to review the MOS skills that you practiced in this chapter.

GO! Collaborative Team Project (Available in Instructor Resource Center)

If your instructor assigns this project to your class, you can expect to work with one or more of your classmates—either in person or by using internet tools—to create work products similar to those that you created in this chapter. A team is a group of workers who work together to solve a problem, make a decision, or create a work product. Collaboration is when you work together with others as a team in an intellectual endeavor to complete a shared task or achieve a shared goal.

Monkey Business Images/ Fotolia

Project Guide for Access Chapter 3

Your instructor will assign Projects from this list to ensure your learning and assess your knowledge.

	Projetct Guide for Access Chapter 3		
Project	**Apply Skills from These Chapter Objectives**	**Project Type**	**Project Location**
3A MyLab IT	Objectives 1–4 from Project 3A	**3A Instructional Project (Grader Project)** Instruction A guided review of the skills from Project 3A.	In **MyLab IT** and in text
3B MyLab IT	Objectives 5–8 from Project 3B	**3B Instructional Project (Grader Project)** Instruction A guided review of the skills from Project 3B.	In **MyLab IT** and in text
3C	Objectives 1–4 from Project 3A	**3C Chapter Review (Scorecard Grading)** Review A guided review of the skills from Project 3A.	In text
3D	Objectives 5–8 from Project 3B	**3D Chapter Review (Scorecard Grading)** Review A guided review of the skills from Project 3B.	In text
3E MyLab IT	Objectives 1–4 from Project 3A	**3E Mastery (Grader Project)** Mastery and Transfer of Learning A demonstration of your mastery of the skills in Project 3A with extensive decision-making.	In **MyLab IT** and in text
3F MyLab IT	Objectives 5–8 from Project 3B	**3F Mastery (Grader Project)** Mastery and Transfer of Learning A demonstration of your mastery of the skills in Project 3B with extensive decision-making.	In **MyLab IT** and in text
3G MyLab IT	Combination of Objectives from Projects 3A and 3B	**3G Mastery (Grader Project)** Mastery and Transfer of Learning A demonstration of your mastery of the skills in Projects 3A and 3B with extensive decision-making.	In **MyLab IT** and in text
3H	Combination of Objectives from Projects 3A and 3B	**3H GO! Fix It (Scorecard Grading)** Critical Thinking A demonstration of your mastery of the skills in Projects 3A and 3B by creating a correct result from a document that contains errors you must find.	IRC
3I	Combination of Objectives from Projects 3A and 3B	**3I GO! Make It (Scorecard Grading)** Critical Thinking A demonstration of your mastery of the skills in Projects 3A and 3B by creating a result from a supplied picture.	IRC
3J	Combination of Objectives from Projects 3A and 3B	**3J GO! Solve It (Rubric Grading)** Critical Thinking A demonstration of your mastery of the skills in Projects 3A and 3B, your decision-making skills, and your critical thinking skills. A task-specific rubric helps you self-assess your result.	IRC
3K	Combination of Objectives from Projects 3A and 3B	**3K GO! Solve It (Rubric Grading)** Critical Thinking A demonstration of your mastery of the skills in Projects 3A and 3B, your decision-making skills, and your critical thinking skills. A task-specific rubric helps you self-assess your result.	In text
3L	Combination of Objectives from Projects 3A and 3B	**3L GO! Think (Rubric Grading)** Critical Thinking A demonstration of your understanding of the Chapter concepts applied in a manner that you would outside of college. An analytic rubric helps you and your instructor grade the quality of your work by comparing it to the work an expert in the discipline would create.	In text
3M	Combination of Objectives from Projects 3A and 3B	**3M GO! Think (Rubric Grading)** Critical Thinking A demonstration of your understanding of the Chapter concepts applied in a manner that you would outside of college. An analytic rubric helps you and your instructor grade the quality of your work by comparing it to the work an expert in the discipline would create.	IRC
3N	Combination of Objectives from Projects 3A and 3B	**3N You and GO! (Rubric Grading)** Critical Thinking A demonstration of your understanding of the Chapter concepts applied in a manner that you would in a personal situation. An analytic rubric helps you and your instructor grade the quality of your work.	IRC
3O	Combination of Objectives from Projects 3A and 3B	**3O Cumulative Team Project for Access Chapter 1** A demonstration of your understanding of concepts and your ability to work collaboratively in a group role-playing assessment, requiring both collaboration and self-management.	IRC
Capstone Project for Access Chapters 1-3	Combination of Objectives from Projects 1A, 1B, 2A, 2B, 3A, and 3B	A demonstration of your mastery of the skills in Chapters 1-3 with extensive decision making. **(Grader Project)**	In **MyLab IT** and IRC

Glossary

Glossary of Chapter Key Terms

AND condition A condition in which records display only when all of the specified values are present in the selected fields.

Bound A term used to describe objects and controls that are based on data that is stored in tables.

Bound control A control that retrieves its data from an underlying table or query; a text box control is an example of a bound control.

Calculated control A control that contains an expression, often a formula or function, that most often summarizes a field that contains numerical data.

Control An object on a form or report that displays data or text, performs actions, and lets you view and work with information.

Control layout The grouped arrangement of controls on a form or report; for example, the Stacked layout.

Data entry The action of entering the data into a record in a database table or form.

Date control A control on a form or report that inserts the current date each time the form or report is opened.

Design view The Access view that displays the detailed structure of a query, form, or report; for forms and reports, may be the view in which some tasks must be performed, and displays only the controls, not the data.

Detail section The section of a form or report that displays the records from the underlying table or query.

Filter by Form An Access command that filters the records in a form based on one or more fields, or based on more than one value in the field.

Filter by Selection An Access command that displays only the records that contain the value in the selected field and hides the records that do not contain the value.

Filtering The process of displaying only a portion of the total records (a subset) based on matching specific values to provide a quick answer to a question.

Form A database object that you can use to enter new records into a table, or to edit, delete, and display existing records in a table.

Form Footer Information displayed at the bottom of the screen in Form view or Layout view that is printed after the last detail section on the last page of a printout.

Form Header Information such as a form's title that displays at the top of the screen in Form view or Layout view and is printed at the top of the first page when records are printed as forms.

Form tool An Access tool that creates a form with a single mouse click, which includes all of the fields from the underlying data source (table or query).

Form view The Access view in which you can view, modify, delete, or add records in a table but you cannot change the layout or design of the form.

Form Wizard An Access tool that walks you step by step through the creation of a form and that gives you more flexibility in the design, layout, and number of fields in a form.

Group Footer Information printed at the end of each group of records to display summary information for the group.

Group Header Information printed at the beginning of each new group of records; for example, the group name.

Group, Sort, and Total pane A pane that displays at the bottom of the window in Design view in which you can control how information is sorted and grouped in a report; provides the most flexibility for adding or modifying groups, sort orders, or totals options on a report.

Label control A control on a form or report that contains descriptive information, usually a field name or title.

Layout selector A small symbol that displays in the upper left corner of a selected control layout in a form or report that is displayed in Layout view or Design view and is used to move or format an entire group of controls.

Layout view The Access view in which you can make changes to a form or report while the data from the underlying data source displays.

OR condition A condition in which records display that match at least one of the specified values.

Page Footer Information printed at the bottom of every page in a report and most often includes the page number.

Page Header Information printed at the top of every page in a report.

Page number control A control on a form or report that inserts the page number when displayed in Print Preview or when printed.

Record selector bar The vertical bar at the left edge of a record used to select an entire record in Form view.

Record source The tables or queries that provide the underlying data for a form or report.

Report A database object that summarizes the fields and records from a query or table in an easy-to-read format suitable for printing.

Report Footer Information printed at the bottom of the last page of a report.

Report Header Information printed on the first page of a report that is used for logos, titles, and dates.

Report tool An Access tool that creates a report with one mouse click and displays all of the fields and records from the record source that you select.

Report Wizard An Access tool that walks you step by step through the creation of a report and that gives you more flexibility in the design, layout, and number of fields in a report.

Rich Text Format (RTF) A standard file format that contains some formatting such as underline, bold, font sizes, and colors. RTF documents can be opened in many applications.

Section bar In Design view, a bar in a form or report that identifies and separates one section from another; used to select the section and to change the size of the section.

Stacked layout A control layout format that is similar to a paper form, with label controls placed to the left of each text box control; the controls are grouped together for easy editing.

Subset A portion of the total records available.

Tab order The order in which the insertion point moves from one field to another in a form when you press the Tab key.

Text box control A bound control on a form or report that displays the data from the underlying table or query.

Theme A predesigned set of colors, fonts, lines, and fill effects that look good together and that can be applied to all of the objects in the database or to individual objects in the database.

Unbound control A control that does not have a source of data, such as the title in a form or report.

Chapter Review

Skills Review **Project 3C Student Internships**

Apply 3A skills from these Objectives:

1. Create and Use a Form to Add and Delete Records
2. Filter Records
3. Create a Form by Using the Form Wizard
4. Modify a Form in Layout View and in Design View

In the following Skills Review, you will assist Erinique Jerlin, the Dean of Business at the Northwest Campus, in using her database to track business students and their internship placements for the current semester. Your completed Navigation Pane will look similar to Figure 3.49.

Project Files

For Project 3C, you will need the following file:

a03C_Student_Internships

You will save your database as:

Lastname_Firstname_3C_Student_Internships

Project Results

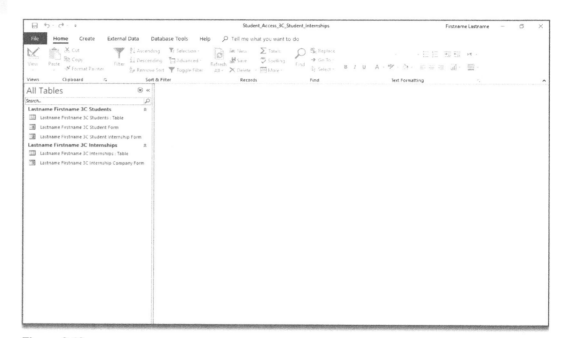

Figure 3.49

(continues on next page)

Chapter Review

Skills Review: Project 3C Student Internships (continued)

1 ▶ Start Access. In the Access opening screen, click **Open Other Files**. Under **Open**, click **Browse** and then navigate to the location where your student data files are stored. Double-click **a03C_Student_Internships** to open the database.

a. On the **File tab**, click **Save As**. Under **File Types**, be sure **Save Database As** is selected. On the right, under **Database File Types**, be sure **Access Database** is selected, and then click **Save As**.

b. In the **Save As** dialog box, navigate to your **Access Chapter 3** folder. In the **File name** box, replace the existing text with **Lastname_Firstname_3C_ Student_Internships** and then press [Enter]. On the **Message Bar**, click **Enable Content**.

c. In the **Navigation Pane**, right-click **3C Students**, and then click **Rename**. With the table name selected and using your own name, type **Lastname Firstname 3C Students** and then press [Enter]. **Rename** the **3C Internships** table to **Lastname Firstname 3C Internships** and then point to the right edge of the **Navigation Pane** to display the ⟷ pointer. Drag to the right to increase the width of the pane until both tables names display fully.

d. On the **Database Tools tab**, in the **Relationships group**, click **Relationships**. Under **Relationship Tools**, on the **Design tab**, in the **Relationships group**, click **All Relationships**. Resize and move the field lists so that the entire table name and fields display for each field list. In the **Relationships** window, click the **join line** between the two field lists. In the **Tools group**, click **Edit Relationships**. Point to the title bar of the **Edit Relationships**

dialog box, and then drag the dialog box downward below the two field lists. Notice that a *one-to-many* relationship is established between the two tables by using *Internship ID* as the common field. **Close** the **Edit Relationships** dialog box, and then **Close** the **Relationships** window. In the message box, click **Yes** to save changes to the layout of the relationships.

e. In the **Navigation Pane**, click your **3C Students** table to select it. On the **Create tab**, and then in the **Forms group**, click **Form**. **Save** the form as **Lastname Firstname 3C Student Form** and then **Close** the form object.

f. In the **Navigation Pane**, click your **3C Internships** table to select it. On the **Create tab**, and then in the **Forms group**, click **Form**. Notice that for the first record—*Internship ID INTERN-1000* for *Lakes Realty Inc*—there are two student records in the subdatasheet—two students have been assigned internships for this employer. **Close** the form, and in the message box, click **Yes** to save the form. In the **Save As** dialog box, type **Lastname Firstname 3C Internship Company Form** and then press [Enter]. If necessary, increase the width of the Navigation Pane so that all object names display fully.

g. In the **Navigation Pane**, double-click your **3C Student Form** object to open it, and then **Close** the **Navigation Pane**. In the navigation area, click **New (blank) record** to display a new blank form. In the **Student ID** field, type **3120045** and then press [Enter]. Using your own last name and first name, continue entering the data as shown in **Table 1**.

Table 1

Student ID	Last Name	First Name	Phone Number	Email	Internship ID
3120045	**Lastname**	**Firstname**	**(512) 555-3263**	**ns3120@tlcc.edu**	**INTERN-1000**

h. With the insertion point positioned in the last field, press [Enter] to save the record and display a new blank record. **Close** your **3C Student Form** object, and then **Open** the **Navigation Pane**. Double-click your **3C Internship Company Form** object to open it, and then **Close** the **Navigation Pane**. Notice that for the

first record, in the subdatasheet, the record you just entered displays. Scroll to view the bottom of the form. In the navigation area for the form—*not* the navigation area for the subdatasheet—click **New (blank) record**. In the blank form, using your own first name and last name, enter the data as shown in **Table 2**.

Table 2

Internship ID	Employer Name	Contact First Name	Contact Last Name	Address	City	State	Postal Code	Phone	Hrs Per Week
INTERN-1027	**College Suppliers**	**Firstname**	**Lastname**	**1700 College Cres**	**Austin**	**TX**	**78755**	**(512) 555-3133**	**10**

(continues on next page)

Chapter Review

i. In the navigation area for the form, click **First record**. Click in the **Employer Name** field, and then on the **Home tab**, in the **Find group**, click **Find**. In the **Find and Replace** dialog box, in the **Find What** box, type **Jones Consulting** and then click **Find Next**. **Close** the **Find and Replace** dialog box. On the **Home tab**, in the **Records group**, click the **Delete arrow**, and then click **Delete Record**. In the message box, click **Yes** to delete the record. In the navigation area for the form, notice that the total number of records is *27*.

j. Use the technique you just practiced to **Find** the form for the **Internship ID** of **INTERN-1027**, and then **Close** the **Find and Replace** dialog box. On the **File tab**, click **Print**, and then on the right, click **Print**. In the **Print** dialog box, under **Print Range**, click the **Selected Record(s)** option button. In the lower left corner of the dialog box, click **Setup**. In the **Page Setup** dialog box, click the **Columns tab**. Under **Column Size**, double-click in the **Width** box to select the existing value, type **7.5** and then click **OK**.

k. **Close** your **3C Internship Company Form** object, and then **Open** the **Navigation Pane**. In the **Navigation Pane**, double-click your **3C Student Form** object to open it, and then **Close** the **Navigation Pane**. Use the **Find** command to display the record where the **Last Name** field contains your last name, and then create a paper or electronic printout of only that record, being sure to change the **Column Size Width** to **7.5**

2 With your **3C Student Form** object displayed in **Form** view, in the navigation area, click **First record**, and then click the **Internship ID** field name to select the text in the field box. Press Ctrl + F to display the **Find and Replace** dialog box. In the **Find What** box, type **INTERN-1009** and then click **Find Next** to find and display the record for *Michael Fresch*. **Close** the **Find and Replace** dialog box. On the **Home tab**, in the **Sort & Filter group**, click **Selection**, and then click **Equals "INTERN-1009"**. In the navigation area, notice that two students are assigned internships with the company identified as INTERN-1009.

a. In the **Sort & Filter group**, click **Toggle Filter** to remove the filter and display all 52 records. **Close** the form. If prompted, click **Yes** to save the form.

b. **Open** the **Navigation Pane**, double-click your **3C Internship Company Form** object to open it, and then **Close** the **Navigation Pane**. On the **Home tab**, in the **Sort & Filter group**, click **Advanced**, and then click **Filter By Form**. In the form, click the **City** field name to position the insertion point in the **City** field box, click the **arrow**, and then click **Georgetown**. In the **Sort & Filter group**, click **Toggle Filter** to display the filtered records. In the navigation area for the form, notice that three internships are located in the *City* of *Georgetown*.

c. In the **Sort & Filter group**, click **Advanced**, and then click **Filter By Form**. In the lower left corner of the form, click the **Or tab**. Click the **City** field box **arrow**, and then click **Elgin**. In the **Sort & Filter group**, click **Toggle Filter**. In the navigation area for the form, notice that five internships are located in either *Georgetown* or *Elgin*. In the **Sort & Filter group**, click **Advanced**, and then click **Clear All Filters** to display all 27 records.

d. In the **Sort & Filter group**, click **Advanced**, and then click **Advanced Filter/Sort**. Resize the field list. In the **3C Internships** field list, double-click **City**, and then double-click **Hrs Per Week** to add both fields to the design grid. Click in the **Criteria** row under **City**, type **Austin** In the **Criteria** row under **Hrs Per Week**, type **>10** In the **Sort & Filter group**, click **Toggle Filter** to display the filtered records, and notice that that there are five internships in the *City* of *Austin* offering *more than 10* hours per week of work. In the **Sort & Filter group**, click **Toggle Filter** to remove the filter and display all 27 records. **Save** and then **Close** your **3C Internship Company Form** object, which also closes the Advanced Filter grid.

3 On the **Create tab**, and in the **Forms group**, click **Form Wizard**. In the **Tables/Queries** box, click the **arrow**, and then click **Table: Lastname Firstname 3C Students**. In the **Available Fields** list, double-click the following field names in the order given to move them to the **Selected Fields** list: **First Name**, **Last Name**, and **Internship ID**. Click **Next**. In the wizard, be sure **Columnar** is selected as the layout, and then click **Next**. In the **What title do you want for your form?** box, select the existing text, type **Lastname Firstname 3C Student Internship Form** and then click **Finish** to close the wizard and create the form.

4 On the **Home tab**, in the **Views group**, click the top portion of the **View** button to switch to **Layout** view. If the **Field List** pane displays on the right side of your screen, close the pane. If the Property Sheet displays, Close it. Click the **First Name label control**. Hold down Shift, and then click the **Last Name label control**, the **Internship ID label**

(continues on next page)

Chapter Review

control, and the three **text box controls** to select all of the controls. On the **Form Layout Tools**, click the **Arrange tab**. In the **Table group**, click **Stacked** to group all of the controls. Click the **First Name label control** to cancel the selection of all of the controls.

a. On the **Form Layout Tools**, click the **Design tab**. In the **Themes group** click **Themes**. In the **Themes** gallery, using the ScreenTips, point to the **Wisp** theme, right-click, and then click **Apply Theme to This Object Only**. Click anywhere in the title—*Lastname Firstname 3C Student Internship Form*—to select the title. On the **Form Layout Tools**, click the **Format tab**, and in the **Font group**, click the **Font Size arrow**, and then click **14**. In the **Font group**, click **Bold**. Click the **Font Color arrow**, and then under **Theme Colors**, in the sixth column, click the last color.

b. On the **Design tab**, in the **Tools group**, click **Add Existing Fields**. In the **Field List** pane, click **Student ID**, and then drag the field name to the left until the pointer displays above the **First Name label control** and a colored line displays above the control. Release the mouse button to add the *Student ID* controls to the form, and then **Close** the **Field List** pane.

c. Click the **First Name text box control**, which displays *Jordan*, to select it. On the **Design tab**, in the **Tools group**, click **Property Sheet**. In the **Property Sheet**, on the **Format tab**, click **Width**, type **1.75** and then press Enter to decrease the width of the text box controls. **Close** the **Property Sheet**. Be sure that the **First Name text box control** is still selected. On the **Arrange tab**, in the **Rows & Columns group**, click **Select Row**. In the **Move group**, click **Move Down** to move both controls below the **Last Name** controls. **Save** the changes you have made to the design of your form.

d. Click the **Student ID text box control**, which displays *1010101*. On the **Arrange tab**, in the **Rows & Columns group**, click **Select Column** to select all four text box controls. On the **Format tab**, in the **Font group**, click the **Background Color arrow**. Under **Theme Colors**, in the fourth column, click the second color.

e. Click the **Student ID label control**, and then click the **Arrange tab**. In the **Rows & Columns group**, click **Select Column** to select all four label controls. Click the **Format tab**, and then click the **Font Color arrow**—*not* the **Background Color arrow**. Under **Theme Colors**, in the fourth column, click the first color. In the **Font group**, click **Bold**.

f. Click the **layout selector** to select all of the controls. In the **Font group**, click the **Font Size arrow**, and then click **12**. With all of the controls still selected, on the ribbon, click the **Design tab**, and in the **Tools group**, click **Property Sheet**. In the **Property Sheet**, on the **Format tab**, click **Height**, type **0.25** and then press Enter to change the height of each selected control.

g. Click the **Student ID label control** to select only that control. In the **Property Sheet**, click **Width**, type **1.75** and then press Enter to change the width of all of the label controls. **Save** the design changes to your form.

h. On the status bar, click **Design View**. At the bottom of the form, click the **Form Footer section bar** to select it. In the **Property Sheet**, click **Height**, type **0.5** and then press Enter to increase the height of the **Form Footer** section.

i. Under **Form Layout Tools**, click the **Design tab**. In the **Controls group**, click **Label**. Move the pointer into the **Form Footer** section and then position the plus sign of the pointer at approximately **0.25 inch on the horizontal ruler** and even with the lower edge of the **Form Footer section bar**—the placement does not need to be precise. Click one time, type **Texas Lakes Community College** and then press Enter.

j. With the **label control** selected, click the **Format tab**. In the **Font group**, click **Bold**. Click the **Font Color arrow**, and then under **Theme Colors**, in the fourth column, click the first color. If necessary, double-click the right edge of the label control to resize the control so that all of the data displays.

k. With the **label control** still selected, in the **Property Sheet**, click **Top**, type **0.1** and then press Enter. In the **Property Sheet**, in the **Left** property setting box, type **0.9** and then press Enter. **Close** the **Property Sheet**, and then **Save** the design changes to your form.

l. On the right side of the status bar, click **Form View**. In the navigation area, click **Last record** to display the record containing your name. On the **File tab**, click **Print**. In the **Print** dialog box, under **Print Range**, click the **Selected Records(s)** option button. Because you changed the field widths, you do not need to change the Column Size Width in the **Print** dialog box.

5 **Close** all open objects, and then **Open** the **Navigation Pane**. If necessary, increase the width of the pane so that all object names display fully. On the right side of the title bar, click **Close** to close the database and to close Access.

6 As directed by your instructor, submit your database for grading.

You have completed Project 3C **END**

Chapter Review

Skills Review | Project 3D Student Parking

Apply 3B skills from these Objectives:

5. Create a Report by Using the Report Tool and Modify the Report in Layout View
6. Create a Report by Using the Report Wizard
7. Modify the Design of a Report
8. Keep Grouped Data Together in a Printed Report

In the following Skills Review, you will assist Carlos Medina, Chief of Security, in using his Access database to track the details about students who have paid for parking in designated lots at the Southeast Campus of Texas Lakes Community College. Your completed Navigation Pane will look similar to Figure 3.50.

Project Files

For Project 3D, you will need the following file:

a03D_Student_Parking

You will save your database as:

Lastname_Firstname_3D_Student_Parking

Project Results

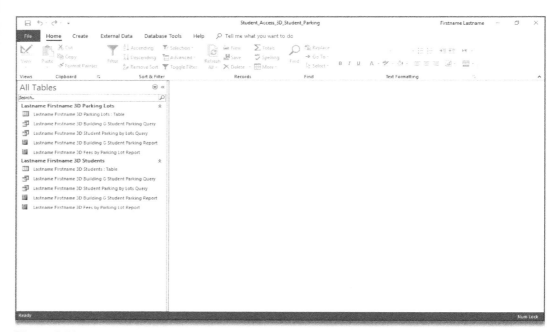

Figure 3.50

(continues on next page)

Chapter Review

Skills Review: Project 3D Student Parking (continued)

1 ▶ Start Access. In the Access opening screen, click **Open Other Files**. Under **Open**, click **Browse** and then navigate to the location where your student data files are stored. Double-click **a03D_Student_Parking** to open the database.

a. On the **File tab**, click **Save As**. Under **File Types**, be sure **Save Database As** is selected. On the right, under **Database File Types**, be sure **Access Database** is selected, and then at the bottom of the screen, click **Save As**. In the **Save As** dialog box, navigate to your **Access Chapter 3** folder. In the **File name** box, replace the existing text with **Lastname_Firstname_3D_Student_Parking** and then press [Enter]. On the **Message Bar**, click **Enable Content**.

b. In the **Navigation Pane**, right-click the **3D Parking Lots** table, and then click **Rename**. Using your own name, type **Lastname Firstname 3D Parking Lots** and then press [Enter]. Use this same technique to add your last name and first name to the beginning of the names of the two queries and the **3D Students** table. Increase the width of the **Navigation Pane** so that all object names display fully.

c. On the **Database Tools tab**, in the **Relationships group**, click **Relationships**. On the **Design tab**, in the **Relationships group**, click **All Relationships**. Resize and move the field lists so that the entire table name and fields display for each field list. In the **Relationships** window, click the **join line** between the two field lists. In the **Tools group**, click **Edit Relationships**. Point to the title bar of the **Edit Relationships** dialog box, and then drag the dialog box downward below the two field lists. Notice that a *one-to-many* relationship is established between the two tables by using *Lot ID* as the common field. **Close** the **Edit Relationships** dialog box, and then **Close** the **Relationships** window. In the message box, click **Yes** to save changes to the layout of the relationships.

d. In the **Navigation Pane**, double-click each table to open them, and then examine the fields and data in each table. In the **Navigation Pane**, double-click your **3D Building G Student Parking Query** object to run the query and view the results. Apply **Best Fit** to the query results, and then **Save** the query. Switch to **Design** view to examine the design grid. This query answers the question, *What is the lot ID, lot location, student ID, student last name, student first name, license plate, and semester fee for students who have paid for parking in front of Building G, in ascending order by the Last Name field?*

In the **Navigation Pane**, double-click your **3D Student Parking by Lots Query** object, apply **Best Fit** to the query results, **Save** the query, and then switch to **Design** view to examine the design grid. This query answers the question, *What is the lot ID, student ID, student last name, student first name, license plate, state, and semester fee for all students?* In the object window, right-click any **object tab**, and then click **Close All**.

e. In the **Navigation Pane**, click to select your **3D Building G Student Parking Query** object. On the **Create tab**, in the **Reports group**, click **Report**. **Close** the Navigation Pane. Under **Report Layout Tools**, on the **Design tab**, in the **Themes group**, click **Themes**. In the **Themes** gallery, use the ScreenTips to locate the **Retrospect** theme, right-click the **Retrospect** theme, and then click **Apply Theme to This Object Only**.

f. Click the **Lot Location** field name. On the **Report Layout Tools**, click the **Arrange tab**. In the **Rows & Columns group**, click **Select Column** to select the field name and all of the data for each record in the field. Press [Del] to remove the field from the report.

g. Click the **Last Name** field name, hold down [Shift], and then click the **First Name** field name. On the **Design tab**, in the **Tools group**, click **Property Sheet**. In the **Property Sheet**, on the **Format tab**, click **Width**, type **1.25** and then press [Enter] to decrease the width of the two fields. **Close** the **Property Sheet**.

h. Click the **Last Name** field name to cancel the selection of both fields and to select only this field. On the **Home tab**, in the **Sort & Filter group**, click **Ascending** to sort the records in ascending order by the Last Name field.

i. If necessary, scroll to the bottom of the report, and notice that the *Semester Fee* column is automatically totaled. At the top of the report, click the **Student ID** field name. On the **Design tab**, in the **Grouping & Totals group**, click **Totals**, and then click **Count Records**. If necessary, scroll to the bottom of the report, and notice that *14* students have paid for parking in front of Building G.

(continues on next page)

Chapter Review

j. At the bottom of the report, under **Student ID**, click the **calculated control** that displays *14*. Hold down Ctrl, and then under **Semester Fee**, click the **calculated control** that displays *$1,075*—the two calculated controls are selected. On the **Design tab**, in the **Tools group**, click **Property Sheet**. In the **Property Sheet**, click **Height**, type **0.25** and then press Enter to increase the height of both controls. At the bottom of the report, to the right of the **calculated control** that displays *$1,075*, click the **control** that displays *Page 1 of 1*. In the **Property Sheet**, click **Left**, type **2.5** and then press Enter to move the page number within the margins of the report.

k. At the top of the report, click the **label control** that displays the title of the report—*Lastname Firstname 3D Building G Student Parking Query*. On the **Report Layout Tools**, click the **Format tab**. In the **Font group**, click the **Font Size arrow**, and then click **14**. With the **label control** still selected, double-click **Query** to select the word, type **Report** and then press Enter to change the title of the report to *Lastname Firstname 3D Building G Student Parking Report*.

l. Click the **Lot ID** field name. In the **Property Sheet**, click **Left**, type **0.25** and then press Enter to move all of the fields slightly to the right from the left margin. **Close** the **Property Sheet**, and then **Save** the report as **Lastname Firstname 3D Building G Student Parking Report**.

m. On the right side of the status bar, click **Print Preview**. On the **Print Preview tab**, in the **Zoom group**, click **Two Pages**, and notice that the report will print on one page. **Close Print Preview**, and then **Close** the report.

2 On the **Create tab**, in the **Reports group**, click **Report Wizard**. In the **Tables/Queries** box, click the **arrow**, and then click **Query: Lastname Firstname 3D Student Parking by Lots Query**. In the **Available Fields** list, double-click the following field names in the order given to move them to the **Selected Fields** list: **Lot ID**, **Last Name**, **First Name**, **Student ID**, and **Semester Fee**.

a. Click **Next**. In the **How do you want to view your data?** box, click **by Lastname Firstname 3D Students**, and then click **Next**. In the list on the left, double-click **Lot ID** to group the records by this field, and then click **Next**. Click the **1** box **arrow**, and then click **Last Name** to sort the records by the student's last name within each Lot ID.

b. In the wizard, click **Summary Options**. In the **Summary Options** dialog box, to the right of **Semester Fee**, click to select the **Sum** check box. Under **Show**, be sure that **Detail and Summary** is selected, and then click **OK**. In the wizard, click **Next**.

c. In the wizard, under **Layout**, be sure that **Stepped** is selected. Under **Orientation**, click **Landscape**. At the bottom of the wizard, be sure that the **Adjust the field width so all fields fit on a page** check box is selected, and then click **Next**. In the **What title do you want for your report?** box, select the existing text, type **Lastname Firstname 3D Fees by Parking Lot Report** and then click **Finish**. In the object window, right-click the **object tab** for the report, and then click **Layout View**.

3 Under **Report Layout Tools**, on the **Design tab**, in the **Themes group**, click **Themes**. In the **Themes** gallery, use the ScreenTips to locate the **Ion Boardroom** theme, right-click the **Ion Boardroom** theme, and then click **Apply Theme to This Object Only**. In the report, click the title—*Lastname Firstname 3D Fees by Parking Lot*—to display a border around the label control. On the **Report Layout Tools**, click the **Format tab**. In the **Font group**, click the **Font Size arrow**, and then click **14**. In the **Font group**, click **Bold**. In the body of the report, click any one of the controls that begins with **Summary for 'Lot ID'**, and then press Del. **Save** the design changes to your report.

a. On the left side of the report, click a **Sum label control**, which will select all of the related controls. Double-click the control to select the text—*Sum*. Type **Total Fees by Parking Lot** and then press Enter.

b. At the top of the report, click the **Lot ID label control** to select it. Hold down Shift, and then click each one of the four other label controls that display the field names to select all five label controls. On the **Format tab**, in the **Font group**, click **Bold**.

c. In the report, under **Last Name**, click the **text box control** that displays *Dolensky*. Hold down Shift, and then under **First Name**, click the **text box control** that displays *Adam*. On the **Design tab**, in the **Tools group**, click **Property Sheet**. In the **Property Sheet**, click **Width**, type **1.5** and then press Enter.

(continues on next page)

Chapter Review

d. In the report, click the **Student ID label control**. In the **Property Sheet**, click **Left**, type **7.25** and then press Enter. Do not be concerned that the data in the field is not aligned with the field name; you will adjust this later in this project. Scroll to the bottom of the report, and then click the **Grand Total label control**. In the **Property Sheet**, click **Width**, type **1** and then press Enter. **Close** the **Property Sheet**, and then **Save** the design changes to your report.

e. On the status bar, click **Design View**. In the **Lot ID Footer** section, click the **Total Fees by Parking Lot label control**. Hold down Shift, and in the **Report Footer** section, click the **Grand Total label control** to select both controls. Under **Report Design Tools**, click the **Arrange tab**. In the **Sizing & Ordering group**, click **Align**, and then click **Left**.

f. In the report, in the **Page Header** section, click the **Student ID label control**. Hold down Shift, and in the **Detail** section, click the **Student ID text box control**. On the **Arrange tab**, in the **Sizing & Ordering group**, click **Align**, and then click **Left**. On the status bar, click **Layout View** and notice the left alignment of the two sets of controls.

4 On the status bar, click **Print Preview**. On the **Print Preview tab**, in the **Zoom group**, click **More Pages**, and then click **Four Pages** to view how your report is currently laid out. In the **Zoom group**, click the **Zoom arrow**, and then click **50%**. Notice at the bottom of Page 1 and the top of Page 2, that the grouping for **LOT-2B** breaks across these two pages. Notice at the bottom of Page 2 and the top of Page 3, that the grouping for **LOT-6A** breaks across these two pages. Your pages may display differently depending upon the printer that is installed on your system.

a. **Close Print Preview** to return to **Layout** view. On the **Design tab**, in the **Grouping & Totals group**, click **Group & Sort**. In the **Group, Sort, and Total** pane, on the **Group on Lot ID** bar, click **More**. Click the **do not keep group together on one page arrow**, and then click **keep whole group together on one page**. On the **Design tab**, in the **Grouping & Totals group**, click **Group & Sort** to close the **Group, Sort, and Total** pane. **Save** the design changes to your report.

b. On the status bar, click **Print Preview**. Notice that the entire grouping for **LOT-2B** displays at the top of Page 2. Keeping this group together forced the groupings for **LOT-5C** and **LOT-6A** to move to the top of Page 3—your groupings may display differently depending upon the printer that is installed on your system.

c. **Close** the report, and then **Open** the **Navigation Pane**. If necessary, increase the width of the pane so that all object names display fully. On the right side of the title bar, click **Close** to close the database and to close Access.

5 As directed by your instructor, submit your database for grading.

You have completed Project 3D **END**

Content-Based Assessments (Mastery and Transfer of Learning)

Mastering Access   **Project 3E Textbook Publishers**

Apply 3A skills from these Objectives:

1. Create and Use a Form to Add and Delete Records
2. Filter Records
3. Create a Form by Using the Form Wizard
4. Modify a Form in Layout View and Design view

In the following Mastering Access project, you will assist Donna Rider, Bookstore Manager, in using her database to track textbooks and publishers for courses being offered by the Science Department at the Northeast Campus of Texas Lakes Community College. Your completed Navigation Pane will look similar to Figure 3.51.

Project Files for MyLab IT Grader

1. In your **MyLab IT** course, locate and click **Access 3E Textbook Publishers**, Download Materials, and then Download All Files.
2. Extract the zipped folder to your Access Chapter 3 folder. Close the Grader download screens.
3. Take a moment to open the downloaded **Access_3E_Textbook_Publishers_Instructions**; note any recent updates to the book.

Project Results

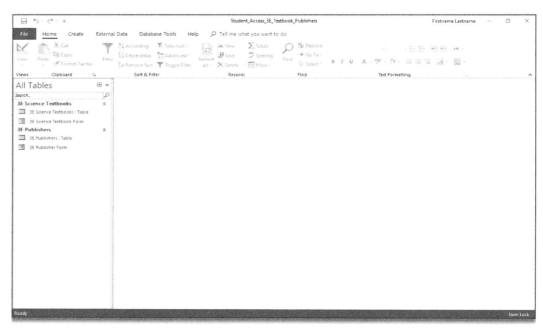

Figure 3.51

For Non-MyLab Submissions

For Project 3E, you will need this starting file:
a03E_Textbook_Publishers

Start with an Access Data File

In your Access Chapter 3 folder, save your database as:
Lastname_Firstname_3E_Textbook_Publishers

After you have saved your database, open it to launch Access. On the next page, begin with Step 2.
After Step 12, save and submit your file as directed by your instructor.

(continues on next page)

Content-Based Assessments (Mastery and Transfer of Learning)

Mastering Access: Project 3E Textbook Publishers (continued)

1 Start Access. From your student data files, open **Student_Access_3E_Textbook_Publishers** and **Enable Content**.

2 View the relationship between the *3E Publishers* table and the *3E Science Textbooks* table; *one* publisher can provide *many* textbooks for the science courses. If necessary, resize the field lists so all table and field names are fully visible. Save the changes to the layout of the relationships.

3 Based on your **3E Publishers** table, use the **Form** tool to create a form. **Save** the form as **3E Publisher Form** and then switch to **Form** view. Using the form, add a new record to the underlying table as shown in **Table 1**.

Table 1

Publisher ID	Publisher Name	Address	City	State	Postal Code	Phone Number	Publisher Web Site
PUB-1008	**Hidden Hills Publishing Co**	**5100 Live Oak St**	**Dallas**	**TX**	**75201**	**(214) 555-0857**	**http://www.hhpubco.pub**

4 Display the first record, and then click in the **Publisher ID** field. **Find** the record for the **Publisher ID** of **PUB-1006**, and then **Delete** the record. **Find** the record for the **Publisher ID** of **PUB-1008**, and change the **Column Size Width** in the **Print** dialog box to **7.5**. **Save** the design changes to your form.

5 Use the **Filter By Form** tool in your **3E Publisher Form** object to create a filter that displays records with a **State** of **CA** or **TX**. After verifying that three records match this criteria, click **Toggle Filter** to display all seven records. **Save** your form, and then **Close** your form.

6 Use the **Form Wizard** to create a form based on your **3E Science Textbooks** table that includes the following fields in the order given: **Course(s)**, **Textbook Name**, **Publisher ID**, **Price Per Book**, and **# Books**. Apply a **Columnar** layout, and then name the form **3E Science Textbook Form**.

7 In **Layout** view, apply the **Stacked** layout to all of the controls, and then apply the **Ion Boardroom** theme to this object (Form) only. For the title of the form, change the **Font Size** to **16**, apply **Bold**, and then change the **Font Color** to **Dark Purple, Text 2**—under **Theme Colors**, in the fourth column, the first color. **Save** the design changes to the form.

8 From the **Field List** pane, add the **Textbook ID** field to the form directly above the **Textbook Name** field. Move the **# Books** controls directly above the **Price Per Book** controls. **Close** the **Field List** pane. Display Record 9—this record's textbook name is the longest entry of all records. Click the **Textbook Name text box control**, set the **Width** property to **4** and then **Save** the design changes to your form.

9 Select all six **text box controls**, and, change the **Background Color**. Under **Theme colors**, in the eighth column, select the second color. Select all six **label controls**, and change the **Font Color**. Under **Theme Colors**, in the eighth column, select the last color. With the **label controls** still selected, set the **Width** property to **1.75** and then select all of the **label controls** and all of the **text box controls**. Change the **Font Size** to **12**, set the **Height** property to **0.25** and then **Save** the design changes to your form.

10 In **Design** view, set the **Form Footer** section **Height** property to **0.5** Add a **Label control** to the **Form Footer** section that displays **Texas Lakes Science Books** For this **label control**, change the **Font Color**; under **Theme Colors**, in the eighth column, select the last color—and then apply **Bold**. For this **label control**, set the **Width** property to **2.25** set the **Top** property to **0.1** and then set the **Left** property to **1.95**

11 **Close** the **Property Sheet**. **Save** your form.

12 **Close** all open objects, and then **Open** the **Navigation Pane**. If necessary, increase the width of the pane so that all object names display fully. **Close** Access.

13 In **MyLab IT**, locate and click the Grader Project **Access 3E Textbook Publishers**. In **step 3**, under **Upload Completed Assignment**, click **Choose File**. In the **Open** dialog box, navigate to your **Access Chapter 3 folder**, and then click your **Student_Access_3E_Textbook_Publishers** file one time to select it. In the lower right corner of the **Open** dialog box, click **Open**.

14 To submit your file to **MyLab IT** for grading, click **Upload**, wait a moment for a green **Success!** message, and then in **step 4**, click the blue **Submit for Grading** button. Click **Close Assignment** to return to your list of **Course Materials**.

You have completed Project 3E **END**

Mastering Access   **Project 3F Degrees and Students**

In the following Mastering Access project, you will assist Tom Catogrides, the Registrar, in using his database to track degrees and grade point averages for honor students in the health professions program in preparation for graduation. Your completed Navigation Pane will look similar to Figure 3.52.

Project Files for MyLab IT Grader

1. In your **MyLab IT** course, locate and click **Access 3F Degrees and Students**, Download Materials, and then Download All Files.
2. Extract the zipped folder to your Access Chapter 3 folder. Close the Grader download screens.
3. Take a moment to open the downloaded **Access_3F_Degrees_Students_Instructions**; note any recent updates to the book.

Project Results

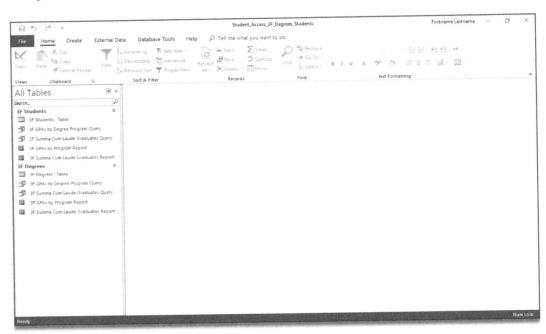

Figure 3.52

For Non-MyLab Submissions
For Project 3F, you will need this starting file:
a03F_Degrees_Students

Start with an Access Data File
In your Access Chapter 3 folder, save your database as:
Lastname_Firstname_3F_Degrees_Students

After you have saved your database, open it to launch Access. On the next page, begin with Step 2.
After Step 7, save and submit your file as directed by your instructor.

(continues on next page)

Content-Based Assessments (Mastery and Transfer of Learning)

1 Start Access. From your student data files, open **Student_Access_3F_Degrees_Students** and then **Enable Content**.

2 View the relationship that is established between the *3F Degrees* tables and the *3F Students* table—*one* type of degree can be awarded to *many* students. If necessary, resize the field lists so all table and field names are fully visible. Save the changes to the layout of the relationships. **Run** each query to display the query results, apply **Best Fit**, and then **Save** each query.

Open each query in **Design** view to examine the design grid. The *3F Summa Cum Laude Graduates Query* answers the question, *What is the GPA, student ID, last name, first name, degree, and program for students graduating with a grade point average of 3.8 or higher, in descending order by GPA and ascending order by Last Name?* The *3F GPAs by Degree Program Query* answers the question, *What is the program, last name, first name, and GPA for all students, in ascending order by the Last Name field within the Program field?* **Close All** objects.

3 Based on your **3F Summa Cum Laude Graduates Query** object, use the **Report** tool to create a report. Apply the **Facet** theme to only this object (report). Delete the **Student ID** field from the report. For the **Last Name**, **First Name**, and **Degree text box controls**, set the **Width** property to **1.25** and then **Sort** the **Last Name** field in **Ascending** order. For the **Program text box controls**, set the **Width** property to **2.5**

At the bottom of the report, for the **calculated control**, which displays *8*, set the **Height** to **0.25** and then for the **page number control**, set the **Left** property to **5** For the title of the report, set the **Font Size** to **14** and change the word *Query* to **Report** For the **GPA** field, set the **Left** property to **0.25** to approximately center the fields within the margins of the report. **Save** the report as **3F Summa Cum Laude Graduates Report Close Print Preview**, **Close** the **Property Sheet**, and then **Close** the report.

4 Use the **Report Wizard** to create a report based on your **3F GPAs by Degree Program Query** object that includes the following fields in the order given: **Program, GPA, Last Name**, and **First Name**. View your data by **3F Degrees** and do not apply any additional grouping. Sort first in **Descending** order by **GPA**, and second in **Ascending** order by **Last Name**. Summarize the report by averaging the **GPA** field for each degree. Be sure the layout is **Stepped** and the orientation is **Portrait**. For the report title, type **3F GPAs by Program Report** and then switch to **Layout** view.

5 Apply the **Wisp** theme to only this object (report). For the report title, change the **Font Size** to **16**, and then apply **Bold**. Delete the controls that begin with *Summary for 'Program'*. Under **Program**, for the **text box controls**, set the **Width** property to **2.75** At the top of the report, select the four **label controls** that display the field names, and then apply **Bold**. Select the **GPA label control**, the **GPA text box controls**, and the **calculated controls** for the average GPA, and then set the **Width** property to **1** and the **Left** property to **3 Close** the **Property Sheet**. Display the report in **Design** view. Under **Program Header**, click the **Program text box control**, hold down Shift, and under **Program Footer**, click the **Average GPA by Program label control**. **Align** the controls on the **Right**, and then **Save** the design changes to your report.

6 Switch to **Print Preview**, **Zoom** to display **Two Pages** of the report, and examine how the groupings break across the pages. Switch to **Layout** view, display the **Group, Sort, and Total** pane, select **keep whole group together on one page**, and then close the **Group, Sort, and Total** pane. Switch to **Print Preview**, and then notice that the groupings are not split between pages. **Save** the report.

7 **Close Print Preview**, and then **Close** the report. **Open** the **Navigation Pane**, and, if necessary, increase the width of the pane so that all object names display fully.

8 In **MyLab IT**, locate and click the Grader Project **Access 3F Degrees and Students**. In **step 3**, under **Upload Completed Assignment**, click **Choose File**. In the **Open** dialog box, navigate to your **Access Chapter 3 folder**, and then click your **Student_Access_3F_Degrees_Students** file one time to select it. In the lower right corner of the **Open** dialog box, click **Open**.

9 To submit your file to **MyLab IT** for grading, click **Upload**, wait a moment for a green **Success!** message, and then in **step 4**, click the blue **Submit for Grading** button. Click **Close Assignment** to return to your list of **Course Materials**.

You have completed Project 3F END

Content-Based Assessments (Mastery and Transfer of Learning)

| **Mastering Access** **Project 3G Career Books**

1. Create and Use a Form to Add and Delete Records
2. Filter Records
3. Create a Form by Using the Form Wizard
4. Modify a Form in Layout View and in Design View
5. Create a Report by Using the Report Tool and Modify the Report in Layout View
6. Create a Report by Using the Report Wizard
7. Modify the Design of a Report
8. Keep Grouped Data Together in a Printed Report

In the following Mastering Access project, you will assist Rebecca Hennelly, Head Librarian at the Southwest Campus of Texas Lakes Community College, in using her database to track publishers and book titles that assist students in finding employment. Your completed Navigation Pane will look similar to Figure 3.53.

Project Files for MyLab IT Grader

1. In your **MyLab IT** course, locate and click **Access 3G Career Books**, Download Materials, and then Download All Files.
2. Extract the zipped folder to your Access Chapter 3 folder. Close the Grader download screens.
3. Take a moment to open the downloaded **Access_3G_Career_Books_Instructions**; note any recent updates to the book.

Project Results

Figure 3.53

For Non-MyLab Submissions
For Project 3G, you will need this starting file:
a03G_Career_Books

Start with an Access Data File
In your Access Chapter 3 folder, save your database as:
Lastname_Firstname_3G_Career_Books

After you have saved your database, open it to launch Access. On the next page, begin with Step 2.
After Step 20, save and submit your file as directed by your instructor.

(continues on next page)

Content-Based Assessments (Mastery and Transfer of Learning)

ACCESS

3

Mastering Access: Project 3G Career Books (continued)

1 Start Access. From your student data files, open **Student_Access_3G_Career_Books.** and then **Enable Content**.

2 View the relationship that is established between the *3G Publishers* table and the *3G Career Books* table—*one* publisher can publish *many* career books. If necessary, resize the field lists so all table and field names are fully visible. Save the changes to the layout of the relationships.

3 Open the **3G Resume or Interview Books Query**, apply **Best Fit**, and then **Save** the query. Switch the query to **Design** view, examine the design of the query, and then **Close** the query object.

4 Based on your **3G Career Books** table, use the **Form** tool to create a form. **Save** the form as **3G Career Book Form** and then switch to **Form** view. Using the form, add a new record to the underlying table as shown in **Table 1**.

Table 1

Title ID	Title	Author Last Name	Author First Name	Publisher ID	Category	Copies On Hand	Value of Books
T-25	Effective Networking	Nunez	Charlene	PUB-109	Job Search	6	180

5 Display the first record and click in the **Title ID** field. **Find** the record for the **Title ID** of **T-19**, and then **Delete** the record. Display the record you entered for **T-25** and change the **Column Size Width** in the **Print** dialog box to **7.5 Save** the design changes to your form.

6 Use the **Filter By Form** tool in your **3G Career Book Form** object to create a filter that displays records with a **Category** of **Interviewing Strategies** or **Resumes**. After verifying that 10 records match this criteria, click **Toggle Filter** to display all 24 records. **Save** the form, and then **Close** the form.

7 Use the **Form Wizard** to create a form based on your **3G Publishers** table that includes the following fields in the order given: **Company Name**, **Rep Last Name**, **Rep First Name**, **Job Title**, and **Phone Number**. Apply a **Columnar** layout, and name the form **3G Publisher Form**

8 In **Layout** view, apply the **Stacked** layout to all of the controls, and then apply the **Integral** theme to this form only. For the title of the form, change the **Font Size** to **16**, apply **Bold**, and then change the **Font Color**— under **Theme Colors**, in the fourth column, select the last color. **Save** the design changes to the form.

9 From the **Field List** pane, add the **Publisher ID** field to the form directly above the **Company Name** field. **Close** the **Field List** pane. Move the **Rep First Name** controls directly above the **Rep Last Name** controls. Click the **Job Title text box control**, set the **Width** property to **2.5** and then **Save** the design changes to your form.

10 Select all six **text box controls**, and change the **Background Color**; under **Theme Colors**, in the fifth column, select the second color. Select all six **label controls**, and change the **Font Color**— under **Theme Colors**, in the fourth column, select the last color. Apply **Bold** to the **label controls**. With the **label controls** still selected, set the **Width** property to **1.75** and then select all of the **label controls** and all of the **text box controls**. Change the **Font Size** to **12**, set the **Height** property to **0.25** and then **Save** the design changes to your form.

11 In **Design** view, set the **Form Footer** section **Height** property to **0.5** Add a **Label** control to the **Form Footer** section that displays **Texas Lakes Southwest Campus**. For this **label control**, change the **Font Color**; under **Theme Colors**, in the fourth column, select the last color —and then apply **Bold**. For this **label control**, set the **Width** property to **2.2** set the **Top** property to **0.1** and then set the **Left** property to **1.25 Close** the **Property Sheet**, **Save** your form, and then switch to **Form** view. Using the form, add a new record to the underlying table as shown in **Table 2**.

Table 2

Publisher ID	Company Name	Rep First Name	Rep Last Name	Job Title	Phone Number
PUB-111	Associated Publishers	Marquis	Sullivan	Sales Associate	(512) 555-7373

(continues on next page)

Project 3G: Career Books | Access   321

12 View the record that you just created. **Close** the form.

13 Based on your **3G Resume or Interview Books Query** object, use the **Report** tool to create a report. Apply the **Retrospect** theme to only this report. Delete the following fields from the report: **Publisher ID**, **Category**, and **Company Name**. For the **Title text box controls**, set the **Width** property to **3** and then **Sort** the **Title** field in **Ascending** order. For the **Author Last Name text box controls** and the **Author First Name text box controls**, set the **Width** property to **1.5**

14 Click the **Title** field name, and then add a calculated control that counts the number of records. At the bottom of the report, for the **calculated control**, which displays *10*, set the **Height** to **0.25** and then for the **page number control**, set the **Left** property to **5** For the title of the report, set the **Font Size** to **14** and change the word *Query* to **Report**. Click the **Title** field name, and then set the **Left** property to **0.75** to move all of the controls to the right. **Save** the report as **3G Resume or Interview Books Report Close** the **Property Sheet**, and then **Close** the report.

15 Use the **Report Wizard** to create a report based on your **3G Career Books** table that includes the following fields in the order given: **Category**, **Title**, and **Value of Books**. Group your data by **Category**, sort in **Ascending** order by **Title**, and then summarize the report by summing the **Value of Books** field. Be sure the layout is **Stepped** and the orientation is **Portrait**. For the report title, type **3G Book Values by Category Report** and then switch to **Layout** view.

16 Apply the **Ion Boardroom** theme to only this report. For the report title, change the **Font Size** to **14**, and then apply **Bold**. Delete the controls that begin with **Summary for 'Category'**. Select the **Category**, **Title**, and **Value of Books label controls**, and then apply **Bold**. Under **Title**, for the **text box controls**, set the **Width** property to **3.5** For the **Value of Books label control**, set the **Left** property to **6** and then **Save** the design changes to your report.

17 At the bottom of the report in the last column, select the following three controls: **text box control** that displays *$420*, **calculated control** that displays *$945*, and the **calculated control** that displays *7,730 (Grand Total control, may be too small to view number)*. Set the **Width** property to **1.25** and the **Left** property to **6** For the **Grand Total label control**, set the **Width** property to **1** and then change the text in the **Sum label control** to **Total Value of Books by Category** Click any **Title text box control**, set the **Height** property to **0.35** and then **Save** your report.

18 **Close** the **Property Sheet**, and then display your report in **Design** view. Under **Category Footer**, click the **label control** that displays *Total Value of Books by Category*, hold down Shift, and then under **Report Footer**, click the **Grand Total label control**. **Align** the controls on the **Left**, and then **Save** the design changes to your report.

19 Switch to **Print Preview**, **Zoom** to display **Two Pages** of the report, and examine how the groupings break across the pages. Switch to **Layout** view, display the **Group, Sort, and Total** pane, select **keep whole group together on one page**, and then close the **Group, Sort, and Total** pane. Switch to **Print Preview** and notice that the groupings are no longer split between pages. **Save** the report.

20 **Close Print Preview**, and then **Close** the report. **Open** the **Navigation Pane**, and, if necessary, increase the width of the pane so that all object names display fully. On the right side of the title bar, click **Close** to close the database and to close Access.

21 In **MyLab IT**, locate and click the Grader Project **Access 3G Career Book**. In **step 3**, under **Upload Completed Assignment**, click **Choose File**. In the **Open** dialog box, navigate to your **Access Chapter 3 folder**, and then click your **Student_Access_3G_Career_Books** file one time to select it. In the lower right corner of the **Open** dialog box, click **Open**.

22 To submit your file to **MyLab IT** for grading, click **Upload**, wait a moment for a green **Success!** message, and then in **step 4**, click the blue **Submit for Grading** button. Click **Close Assignment** to return to your list of **Course Materials**.

You have completed Project 3G ⬛ END

Content-Based Assessments (Critical Thinking)

ACCESS

3

Apply a combination of the 3A and 3B skills.

GO! Fix It	Project 3H Resume Workshops	IRC
GO! Make It	Project 3I Study Abroad	IRC
GO! Solve It	Project 3J Job Offers	IRC
GO! Solve It	Project 3K Financial Aid	

Project Files

For Project 3K, you will need the following file:

a03K_Financial_Aid

You will save your database as:

Lastname_Firstname_3K_Financial_Aid

Start Access, navigate to your student data files, open **a03K_Financial_Aid**, and then save the database in your **Access Chapter 3** folder as **Lastname_Firstname_3K_Financial_Aid**. Using your own name, add **Lastname Firstname** to the beginning of both table names and the query name. Sivia Long, the Financial Aid Director, would like you to create an attractive form and a report for this database, using the following guidelines:

- The form will be used to update student records in the 3K FA Students table. Be sure that the Last Name field displays above the First Name field. After the form is created, enter a new record using your own information with a Student ID of **9091246** and Financial Aid ID of **FA-07** and a Home Phone of **(512) 555-9876** and a College Email of **ns246@tlcc.edu** Create a filter that when toggled on displays the records for those students whose last names begin with the letter *S*. Add a footer to the form that displays **Texas Lakes Community College Financial Aid** Save the form as **Lastname Firstname 3K FA Student Update Form**.

- The report should use the query and list the Award Name, the Student ID, and the Award Amount for financial aid offered to students, viewed by students, grouped by the Award Name field, and sorted in ascending order by Student ID. Include a total for the Award Amount field, save the report as **Lastname Firstname 3K FA Amount by Award Report** and be sure the groupings do not break across pages when the report is printed.

Open the Navigation Pane, be sure that all object names display fully, and then close Access. As directed, submit your database for grading.

	Performance Level		
	Exemplary: You consistently applied the relevant skills	**Proficient:** You sometimes, but not always, applied the relevant skills	**Developing:** You rarely or never applied the relevant skills
Create 3K FA Student Update Form	Form created with correct fields, new record, footer, and filter in an attractive format.	Form created with no more than two missing elements.	Form created with more than two missing elements.
Create 3K FA Amount by Award Report	Report created with correct fields, grouped, sorted, and summarized correctly, with groupings kept together in an attractive format.	Report created with no more than two missing elements.	Report created with more than two missing elements.

Performance Criteria

You have completed Project 3K | END

Outcomes-Based Assessments (Critical Thinking)

Rubric

The following outcomes-based assessments are *open-ended assessments*. That is, there is no specific correct result; your result will depend on your approach to the information provided. Make *Professional Quality* your goal. Use the following scoring rubric to guide you in *how* to approach the problem and then to evaluate *how well* your approach solves the problem.

The *criteria*—Software Mastery, Content, Format and Layout, and Process—represent the knowledge and skills you have gained that you can apply to solving the problem. The *levels of performance*—Professional Quality, Approaching Professional Quality, or Needs Quality Improvements—help you and your instructor evaluate your result.

	Your completed project is of Professional Quality if you:	Your completed project is Approaching Professional Quality if you:	Your completed project Needs Quality Improvements if you:
1-Software Mastery	Choose and apply the most appropriate skills, tools, and features and identify efficient methods to solve the problem.	Choose and apply some appropriate skills, tools, and features, but not in the most efficient manner.	Choose inappropriate skills, tools, or features, or are inefficient in solving the problem.
2-Content	Construct a solution that is clear and well organized, contains content that is accurate, appropriate to the audience and purpose, and is complete. Provide a solution that contains no errors of spelling, grammar, or style.	Construct a solution in which some components are unclear, poorly organized, inconsistent, or incomplete. Misjudge the needs of the audience. Have some errors in spelling, grammar, or style, but the errors do not detract from comprehension.	Construct a solution that is unclear, incomplete, or poorly organized, contains some inaccurate or inappropriate content, and contains many errors of spelling, grammar, or style. Do not solve the problem.
3-Format and Layout	Format and arrange all elements to communicate information and ideas, clarify function, illustrate relationships, and indicate relative importance.	Apply appropriate format and layout features to some elements, but not others. Overuse features, causing minor distraction.	Apply format and layout that does not communicate information or ideas clearly. Do not use format and layout features to clarify function, illustrate relationships, or indicate relative importance. Use available features excessively, causing distraction.
4-Process	Use an organized approach that integrates planning, development, self-assessment, revision, and reflection.	Demonstrate an organized approach in some areas, but not others; or, use an insufficient process of organization throughout.	Do not use an organized approach to solve the problem.

Outcomes-Based Assessments (Critical Thinking)

ACCESS

3

Apply a combination of the 3A and 3B skills.

GO! Think	**Project 3L Food Services**

Project Files

For Project 3L, you will need the following file:

a03L_Food_Services

You will save your database as:

Lastname_Firstname_3L_Food_Services

Start Access, navigate to your student data files, open **a03L_Food_Services**, save the database in your **Access Chapter 3** folder as **Lastname_Firstname_3L_Food_Services** and then enable the content. Using your own name, add **Lastname Firstname** to the beginning of both table names. Luciano Gonzalez, the Hospitality Director, would like you to create to create an attractive form and a report to assist him with the staff scheduling of food services for a two-day student orientation workshop using the following guidelines:

- The form will be used to update records in the 3L Staff table. Be sure that the Last Name field displays above the First Name field. After the form is created, enter a new record using your own last name and first name with a Staff ID of **STAFF-1119** and a Phone Number of **(512) 555-0845** and a Title of **Server** Create a filter that when toggled on displays the records for staff with a Title of *Server*. Add a footer to the form that displays **Texas Lakes Community College Hospitality Services** Save the form as **Lastname Firstname 3L Staff Update Form** and then create a paper or PDF electronic image of your record only.

- The report will be used by Mr. Gonzalez to call staff members when the schedule changes, so it should be grouped by title. Add a report footer that displays **Texas Lakes Community College Hospitality Services** and then save the report as **Lastname Firstname 3L Staff Phone List** Create a paper or PDF electronic image as directed.

Open the Navigation Pane, be sure that all object names display fully, and then close Access. As directed, submit your database for grading.

You have completed Project 3L | END

GO! Think	**Project 3M Donor Gifts**	IRC

You and GO!	**Project 3N Personal Inventory**	IRC

GO! Cumulative Group Project	**Project 3O Bell Orchid Hotels**	IRC

Enhancing Tables

4

ACCESS 2019

PROJECT 4A

Outcomes
Maneuver and manage data

Objectives
1. Manage Existing Tables
2. Modify Existing Tables
3. Change Data Types
4. Attach Files to Records

PROJECT 4B

Outcomes
Format tables and validate data entry

Objectives
5. Create a Table in Design View
6. Create a Lookup Field
7. Set Field Properties
8. Create Data Validation Rules and Validation Text

Lux Blue/Shutterstock

In This Chapter

GO! To Work with Access

In this chapter, you will enhance tables and improve data accuracy and data entry. You will begin by identifying secure locations where databases will be stored and by backing up existing databases to protect the data. You will edit existing tables for more effective design and copy data and table design across tables. You will create a new table in Design view and determine the best data type for each field based on its characteristics. You will use the field properties to enhance the table and to improve data accuracy and data entry, including looking up data in another table and attaching an existing document to a record.

Golden Grove, California, is a growing city located between Los Angeles and San Diego. Just 10 years ago the population was under 100,000; today it has grown to almost 300,000. Its growth in population is based on its growth as a community. Community leaders have always focused on quality of life and economic development in decisions on housing, open space, education, and infrastructure, making the city a model for other communities its size around the United States. The city provides many recreational and cultural opportunities with a large park system and library system, thriving arts, and a friendly business atmosphere.

PROJECT 4A City Directory

Project Activities

Dario Soto, the new City Manager of Golden Grove, has a database of city directory information. This database has three tables that have duplicate information in them. In Activities 4.01 through 4.12, you will redesign the tables, edit and proofread data, change data types, and attach files to records. Your completed Navigation Pane will look similar to those in Figure 4.1.

Project Files for MyLab IT Grader

1. In your storage location, create a folder named **Access Chapter 4**.
2. In your **MyLab IT** course, locate and click **Access 4A GG Directory**, Download Materials, and then Download All Files.
3. Extract the zipped folder to your Access Chapter 4 folder. Close the Grader download screens.
4. Take a moment to open the downloaded **Access_4A_GG_Directory_Instructions**; note any recent updates to the book.

Project Results

GO! Project 4A
Where We're Going

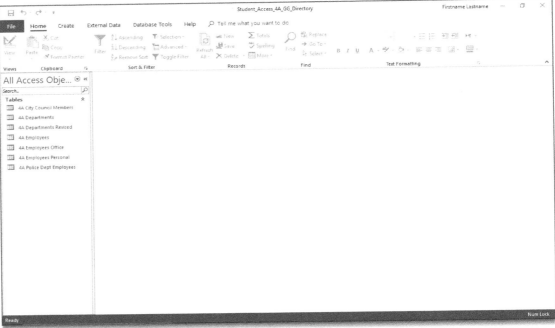

Figure 4.1 Project 4A City Directory

For Non-MyLab Submissions	Start with an Access Data File
For Project 4A, you will need these starting files:	In your storage location, create a folder named **Access Chapter 4**.
a04A_GG_Directory	In your Access Chapter 4 folder, save your databases as:
a04A_GG_Employees	**Lastname_Firstname_4A_GG_Directory**
a04A_PZ_Schedule	**Lastname_Firstname_4A_GG_Directory_2021_04_23 (date will vary)**
a04A_Bldg_Permit_App	

After you have saved your database, launch Access and open the database. In Activity 4.01, begin with Step 2.

Objective 1   Manage Existing Tables

ALERT   Because Office 365 is a cloud-based subscription service that receives continuous updates, you may encounter some variations in what appears on your screen and what is shown in this instruction. Microsoft Office 365 is fully installed on your PC or Mac; no internet access is necessary to create or edit documents. When you *are* connected to the internet, you will receive monthly upgrades and new features, so you always have the latest versions of Office apps as soon as they are available. Your subscription gives you continuous free access to the latest innovations and refinements.

GO! Learn How

Video A4-1

A database is most effective when the data is maintained accurately and efficiently. It is important to back up your database often to be sure you can always obtain a clean copy if the data is corrupted or lost. Maintaining the accuracy of the field design and data is also critical for a useful database; regular reviews and updates of design and data are necessary. It is also helpful to avoid retyping data that already exists in a database; using copy/paste or appending records reduces the chances for additional errors as long as the source data is accurate.

Activity 4.01 | Backing Up a Database

Before modifying the structure of an existing database, it is important to **back up** the database so that a copy of the original database will be available if you need it. It is also important to back up databases regularly to avoid losing data. In this Activity, you will be creating a back-up copy of your database.

1 Start Access. In the Access opening screen, click **Open Other Files**. Navigate to your **Access Chapter 4 folder**, and then double-click the Access file that you downloaded from **MyLab IT** that displays your name—**Student_Access_4A_GG_Directory**.

2 Click **File**, click **Save As**, and then, under *Save Database As*, double-click **Back Up Database**. In the **Save As** dialog box, navigate to the location where you will be saving your folders and projects for this chapter. and then compare your screen with Figure 4.2.

Access appends the date to the file name as a suggested name for the backed-up database. Having the date as part of the file name assists you in determining the copy that is the most current.

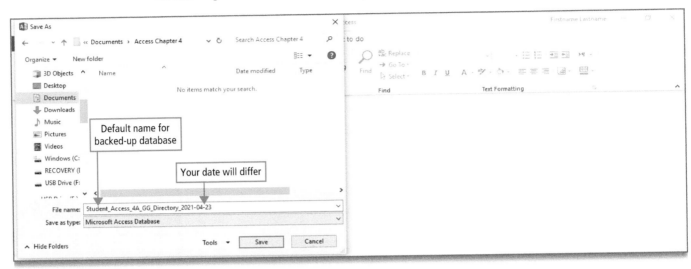

Figure 4.2

3 In the **Save As** dialog box, click **Save**. In the title bar, notice that the original database file—not the backed-up file—is open.

ALERT **A backup file is kept for safe keeping in case data is corrupted or lost.**
It is important to maintain a database in an accurate and efficient way. If there is an error or corruption of the database, you will need to recover data from your backup file. It is important to set a regular schedule for backing up your files to protect your files in case of file failure. This file will not be submitted in **MyLab IT** for grading; however, check with your instructor to see if it should be submitted another way.

4 On the taskbar, click **File Explorer** , and then navigate to the location of your **Access Chapter 4** folder. Open the folder to verify that the backed-up database exists, but do not open the file. **Close** the Access Chapter 4 File Explorer window.

MORE KNOWLEDGE **Recover Data from a Backup**
If your database is damaged, restore a backup to replace the damaged file.
• Open File Explorer, and browse to the location where the good copy (backup) is stored.
• Copy the backup file to the location where the damaged file is located, replacing the existing file if necessary.

Activity 4.02 | Adding File Locations to Trusted Locations

In this Activity, you will add the location of your database files for this chapter and the location of the student data files to the *Trust Center*—a security feature that checks documents for macros and digital signatures. When you open any database from a location displayed in the Trust Center, no security warning will display. You should not designate the Documents folder as a trusted location because others may try to gain access to this known folder.

1 Display **Backstage** view, and click **Enable Content**. Click **Advanced Options** to display the **Microsoft Office Security Options** dialog box. In the lower left corner, click **Open the Trust Center**.

2 In the **Trust Center** window, in the left pane, click **Trusted Locations**. Compare your screen with Figure 4.3.

The right pane displays the locations that are trusted sources. A ***trusted source*** is a person or organization that you know will not send you databases with malicious code. Under Path and User Locations, there is already an entry. A ***path*** is the location of a folder or file on your computer or storage device.

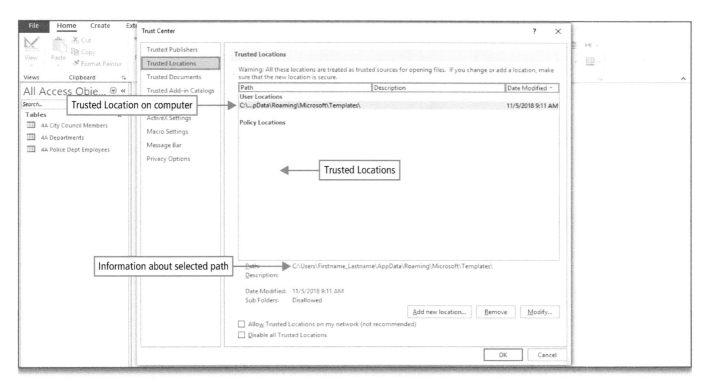

Figure 4.3

3 In the **Trusted Locations** pane, at the lower right, click **Add new location**. In the **Microsoft Office Trusted Location** dialog box, click **Browse**. In the **Browse** dialog box, navigate to where you saved your *Access Chapter 4* folder, double-click **Access Chapter 4**, and then click **OK**. Compare your screen with Figure 4.4.

The Microsoft Office Trusted Location dialog box displays the path to a trusted source of databases. Notice that you can trust any subfolders in the *Access Chapter 4* folder by checking the *Subfolders of this location are also trusted* option. Only locations that you know are secure should be added to the Trust Center. If other people have access to the databases and can change the information in the database, the location is not secure.

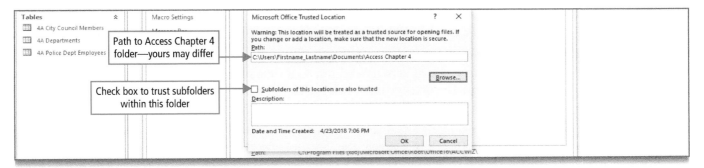

Figure 4.4

4 In the **Microsoft Office Trusted Location** dialog box, under **Description**, type **Databases created in GO! Activities** and then click **OK**.

The Trusted Locations pane displays the path of the *Access Chapter 4* folder. You will no longer receive a security warning when you open databases from this location.

5 At the lower right corner of the **Trust Center** dialog box, click **OK**. In the displayed **Microsoft Office Security Options** dialog box, click **OK**.

The message bar no longer displays—you opened the database from a trusted location.

6 Display **Backstage** view, and then click **Close**. Open your **Student_Access_4A_GG_Directory** database.

The database opens, and the message bar with the Security Alert does not display. Using the Trust Center button is an efficient way to open databases that are saved in a safe location.

MORE KNOWLEDGE **Remove a Trusted Location**

Display Backstage view, and then click Options. In the Access Options dialog box, in the left pane, click Trust Center. In the right pane, click the Trust Center Settings button, and then click Trusted Locations. Under Path, click the trusted location that you want to remove, and then click the Remove button. Click OK to close the dialog box.

Activity 4.03 | Duplicating a Table and Modifying the Structure

1.2.3, 2.4.1, 2.4.5, 2.3.2

Making a copy of the original table before modifying the structure of a table is a good idea to protect the original information. In this Activity, you will duplicate the *4A Departments* table, modify the structure by deleting fields and data that are duplicated in other tables, and then designate a primary key field.

1 In the **Navigation Pane**, double-click **4A Departments** to open the table. **Close** ‹‹ the **Navigation Pane**. Click the **File tab**, and then click **Save As**. Under *File Types*, double-click **Save Object As**. Compare your screen to Figure 4.5.

The Save As command displays the Save As dialog box where you can name and save a new object based on the currently displayed object. After you name and save the new table, the original table closes, and the new table—based on the original one—displays.

Figure 4.5

2 In the displayed **Save As** dialog box, under **Save '4A Departments' to:**, type **4A Departments Revised** and then click **OK**.

The *4A Departments Revised* table is open; it is an exact duplicate of the *4A Departments* table. Working with a duplicate table ensures that the original table will be available if needed.

3 Point to the **Dept Head** field name until the ↓ pointer displays. Hold down the left mouse button, and drag to the right to the **Admin Asst** field name to select both fields. On the **Home tab**, in the **Records group**, click **Delete**. In the displayed message box, click **Yes** to permanently delete the fields and the data.

The names of the employees are deleted from this table to avoid having employee data in more than one table. Recall that a table should store data about one subject—this table now stores only departmental data. In addition to removing duplicate data, the fields that you deleted were also poorly designed. They combined both the first and last names in the same field, limiting the use of the data to entire names only.

4 Switch to **Design** view. To the left of **Department**, click the **row selector** box. Under **Table Tools**, on the **Design tab**, in the **Tools group**, click **Insert Rows** to insert a blank row (field) above the *Department* field.

5 Under **Field Name**, click in the blank field name box, type **Dept ID** and then press `Tab`. In the **Data Type** box, type **a** and then press `Tab`. Alternatively, click the Data Type arrow, and then select the AutoNumber data type. Under **Table Tools**, on the **Design tab**, in the **Tools group**, click **Primary Key**, and then compare your screen with Figure 4.6.

> Recall that a primary key field is used to ensure that each record is unique. Because each department has a unique name, you might question why the *Department* field is not designated as the primary key field. Primary key fields should be data that does not change often. When organizations or companies are reorganized, department names are often changed.

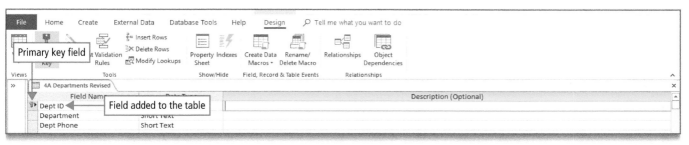

Figure 4.6

6 Switch to **Datasheet** view, and in the displayed message box, click **Yes** to save the table.

> Because the *Dept ID* field has a data type of AutoNumber, each record is sequentially numbered. The data in this field cannot be changed because it is generated by Access.

7 In the datasheet, next to **Department**, click the **Sort and Filter arrow** ▾, and then click **Sort A to Z**.

> Sorting the records by the department name makes it easier to locate a department.

8 **Save** 🖫 the table. **Close** ✕ the table. **Open** ⏵⏵ the **Navigation Pane**.

> Because the sorted table is saved, the records will be in alphabetical order by Department the next time you open the table. This overrides the default sort in primary key order.

Activity 4.04 | Copying and Appending Records to a Table

2.1.1, 2.2.3

> In this Activity, you will copy the *4A City Council Members* table to use as the basis for a single employees table. You will then copy the data in the *4A Police Dept Employees* table and *append*—add on—the data to the new employees table.

1 In the **Navigation Pane**, click **4A City Council Members**. On the **Home tab**, in the **Clipboard group**, click **Copy**. In the **Clipboard group**, click **Paste**.

> *Copy* sends a duplicate version of the selected table to the Clipboard, leaving the original table intact. The *Clipboard* is a temporary storage area in Office that can store up to 24 items. *Paste* moves the copy of the selected table from the Clipboard into a new location. Because two tables cannot have the same name in a database, you must rename the pasted version.

2 In the displayed **Paste Table As** dialog box, under **Table Name**, type **4A Employees** and then compare your screen with Figure 4.7.

Under Paste Options, you can copy the structure only, including all the items that are displayed in Design view—field names, data types, descriptions, and field properties. To make an exact duplicate of the table, click Structure and Data. To copy the data from the table into another existing table, click Append Data to Existing Table.

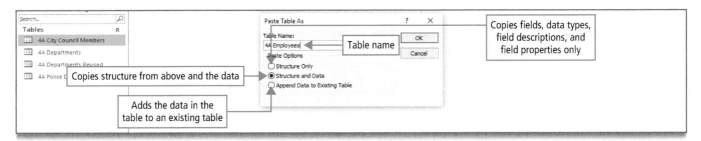

Figure 4.7

↻ **ANOTHER WAY** There are two other methods to copy and paste selected tables:

• In the Navigation Pane, right-click the table, and from the displayed list, click Copy. To paste the table, right-click the Navigation Pane, and click Paste from the options listed.

• In the Navigation Pane, click the table, hold down [Ctrl], and then press [C]. To paste the table, hold down [Ctrl], and then press [V].

---

3 Under **Paste Options**, be sure that the **Structure and Data** option button is selected, and then click **OK**. Notice that the copied table displays in the **Navigation Pane**.

An exact duplicate of the *4A City Council Members* table is created. The *4A Employees* table will be used to build a table of all employees.

MORE KNOWLEDGE **Add a Table Description**

A table description can also be added to the table properties to provide more information about the table. With the table displayed in Design view, under Table Tools, click the Design tab. In the Show/Hide group, click Property Sheet. Alternatively, in the Navigation Pane, right-click the table name, and then click Table Properties. On the Property sheet, click in the Description box, and type a description of the table. Close the Property Sheet.

---

4 Open the **4A Employees** table, and notice the duplicate records that were copied from the *4A City Council Members* table.

5 Copy the **4A Police Dept Employees** table, and then click **Paste**. In the **Paste Table As** dialog box, under **Table Name**, type **4A Employees** Under **Paste Options**, click the **Append Data to Existing Table** option button, and then click **OK**. With the **4A Employees table** active, on the **Home tab**, in the **Records group**, click **Refresh All**, and then compare your screen with Figure 4.8.

The table to which you are appending the records must exist before using the Append option. Clicking the Refresh All button causes Access to refresh or update the view of the table, displaying the newly appended records. The *4A Employees* table then displays the two records for the police department employees—last names of *Farmer* and *Forbes*—and the records are arranged in ascending order by the first field. The records still exist in the *4A Police Dept Employees* table. If separate tables existed for the employees for each department, you would repeat these steps until every employee's record was appended to the *4A Employees* table.

Figure 4.8

ALERT   Does a message box display?

If a message box displays stating that the Microsoft Office Access database engine could not find the object, you probably mistyped the name of the table in the Paste Table As dialog box. In the Navigation Pane, note the spelling of the table name to which you are copying the records. In the message box, click OK, and then in the Paste Table As dialog box, under Table Name, correctly type the table name.

MORE KNOWLEDGE   Append Records

Access appends all records from the *source table*—the table from which you are copying records—into the *destination table*—the table to which the records are appended—as long as the field names and data types are the same in both tables. Exceptions include:

- If the source table does not have all of the fields that the destination table has, Access will still append the records, leaving the data in the missing fields blank in the destination table.
- If the source table has a field name that does not exist in the destination table or the data type is incompatible, the append procedure will fail.

Before performing an append procedure, carefully analyze the structure of both the source table and the destination table.

Activity 4.05 | Splitting a Table into Two Tables

2.4.1, 2.4.5

The *4A Employees* table stores personal data and office data about the employees. Although the table contains data about one subject—employees—you will split the table into two separate tables to keep the personal information separate from the office information.

1 With the **4A Employees** table open in **Datasheet** view, **Close** ⟪ the **Navigation Pane**. Click the **File tab**, and then in **Backstage** view, click **Save As**. Under *File Types*, double-click **Save Object As**.

2 In the **Save As** dialog box, in the **Save to** box, type **4A Employees Office** Notice the *As* box displays *Table*, and then click **OK**. Using the technique you just practiced, create a copy of the open table named **4A Employees Personal**

These two new tables will be used to split the *4A Employees* table into two separate tables, one storing personal data and the other storing office data.

3 In the **4A Employees Personal** table, scroll to the right, if needed, to display the **Date Hired**, **Office Phone**, **Position**, **Office Email**, and **Notes** fields. Select all five fields. On the **Home tab**, in the **Records group**, click **Delete**. In the displayed message box, click **Yes** to permanently delete the fields and data.

Because these fields contain office data, they are deleted from the *4A Employees Personal* table. These fields will be stored in the *4A Employees Office* table.

4 Select the **Title**, **First Name**, **MI**, and **Last Name** fields, and then delete the fields. **Close** ⊠ the table.

The fields you deleted are stored in the *4A Employees Office* table. You have deleted redundant data from the *4A Employees Personal* table.

5 **Open** » the **Navigation Pane**. Open the **4A Employees Office** table. **Close** « the **Navigation Pane**. Point to the **Street** field name until the ↓ pointer displays. Hold down the left mouse button and drag to the right to the **Home Phone** field name, and then compare your screen with Figure 4.9.

Five fields are selected and will be deleted from this table. This is duplicate data that exists in the *4A Employees Personal* table. The *Empl ID* field will be the common field between the two tables.

Figure 4.9

6 Delete the selected fields and data from the table.

The *4A Employees Office* table now stores only office data about the employees and can be linked to the *4A Employees Personal* table through the common field, *Empl ID*.

7 Click the **Position** field name. Under **Table Tools**, on the **Fields tab**, in the **Add & Delete group**, click **Number**.

A blank field is inserted between the *Position* field and the *Office Email* field, and it holds numeric data. Because this field will be used to link to the *4A Departments Revised* Dept ID field, which has a data type of AutoNumber, this field must use a data type of Number, even though it will not be used in a calculation.

8 The default name *Field1* is currently selected; type **Dept** to replace it and name the new field. Press Enter.

9 **Open** » the **Navigation Pane**. Open the **4A Departments Revised** table.

The *4A Departments Revised* table opens in Datasheet view, and the records are sorted in ascending order by the *Department* field.

10 Locate the **Dept ID** for the **City Police** department. On the **tab row**, click the **4A Employees Office tab** to make the table active. In the record for *Andrew Farmer*, enter the City Police Dept ID **14** in the **Dept** field. Press ↓ two times. In the third record, for **Colette Forbes**, type **14**

11 Using the techniques you just practiced, find the **Dept ID** for the **City Council** department, and then enter that number in the **Dept** field for the second and fourth records in the **4A Employees Office** table. Compare your screen with Figure 4.10.

The *Dept* field is a common field with the *Dept ID* field in the *4A Departments Revised* table and will be used to link or join the two tables.

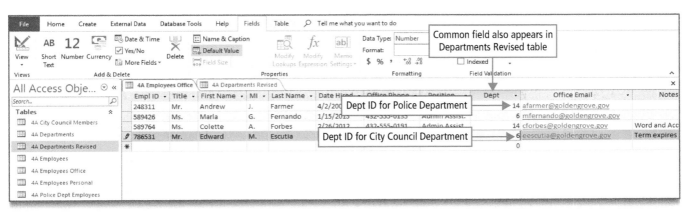

Figure 4.10

12 On the **tab row**, right-click any table tab, and then click **Close All**.

Activity 4.06 | Appending Records from Another Database

2.1.3

Additional employee records are stored in another database. In this Activity, you will open a second database to copy and paste records from tables in the second database to tables in the *4A_GG_Directory* database.

1 Point to the **Start** button ⊞ in the lower left corner of your screen, and then click one time to display the menu. In the **Search box**, type **Acc**, and then click **Access 2019** to open a second instance of Access.

2 On the left side of the Access startup window, at the bottom, click **Open Other Files**. Under **Open**, click **Browse**. In the **Open** dialog box, navigate to the location where the student data files for this textbook are saved. Locate and open the **a04A_GG_Employees** file.

3 In the **4A_GG_Employees** database window, in the **Navigation Pane**, right-click **4A Office**, and then click **Copy**. Click the **Access** icon in the taskbar to see two instances of Access open. Compare your screen with Figure 4.11.

Each time you start Access, you open an instance of it. Two instances of Access are open, and each instance displays in the taskbar. You cannot open multiple databases in one instance of Access. If you open a second database in the same instance, Access closes the first database. You can, however, open multiple instances of Access that display different databases. The number of times you can start Access at the same time is limited by the amount of your computer's available RAM.

Two instances of Access open

Current database— 4A_GG_Employees

Figure 4.11

4 Point to each thumbnail to display the ScreenTip, and then click the thumbnail for the **4A_GG_Directory** database. In the **4A_GG_Directory** database window, right-click the **Navigation Pane**, and then click **Paste**—recall that you copied the *4A Office* table. In the **Paste Table As** dialog box, under **Table Name**, type **4A Employees Office** being careful to type the table name exactly as it displays in the **Navigation Pane**. Under **Paste Options**, click the **Append Data to Existing Table** option button, and then click **OK**.

The records from the *4A Office* table in the source database—*4A_GG_Employees*—are copied and pasted into the *4A Employees Office* table in the destination database—*4A_GG_Directory*.

5 Using the techniques you just practiced, append the records from the **4A Personal** table in the **4A_GG_Employees** database to the **4A Employees Personal** table in the **4A_GG_Directory** database.

6 Click the **Access** icon in the taskbar to see both open databases. Point to the **4A_GG_Employees** database, and in the upper right corner, click **Close** ☒. If a message displays, click **Yes**.

7 If the **4A_GG_Directory** database is not active, on the taskbar, click the **Microsoft Access** button. Open the **4A Employees Personal** table, and then open the **4A Employees Office** table. **Close** ☒ the **Navigation Pane**.

8 If necessary, on the **tab row**, click the **4A Employees Office tab** to make the table active, and then compare your screen with Figure 4.12.

In addition to appending records, you can copy a single record or data in a field from a table in the source database file to a table in the destination database file. Now that you have finished restructuring the database, you can see that it is wise to plan your database before creating the tables and entering data.

Empl ID	Title	First Name	MI	Last Name	Date Hired	Office Phone	Position	Dept	Office Email	Notes	Click to Add
248311	Mr.	Andrew	J.	Farmer	4/2/2009	432-555-0190	Police Chief	14	afarmer@goldengrove.gov		
456789	Ms.	Sheila	J.	Kehoe	11/1/2012	714-555-0100	Mayor	35	skehoe@goldengrove.gov	Term expires 2022	
532268	Miss	Katherine	C.	Bothski	3/17/2015	714-555-0135	Director	1	kbothski@goldengrove.gov		
589426	Ms.	Marla	G.	Fernando	1/15/2015	432-555-0135	Admin Assist.	6	mfernando@goldengrove.gov		
589764	Ms.	Colette	A.	Forbes	2/26/2012	432-555-0191	Admin Assist.	14	cforbes@goldengrove.gov	Word and Access certifie	
689444	Mr.	Dario	T.	Soto	11/10/2014	714-555-0101	City Manager	7	dsoto@goldengrove.gov		
786531				Escutia	11/1/2018	432-555-0138	Presient	6	eescutia@goldengrove.gov	Term expires May 2021	
								0			

4A Employees Personal   4A Employees Office

Three appended records

Figure 4.12

9 On the **tab row**, right-click any table tab, and then click **Close All**.

Objective 2 | Modify Existing Tables

Data in a database is usually ***dynamic***—changing. Records can be created, deleted, and edited in a table. It is important that the data is always up-to-date and accurate in order for the database to provide useful information.

GO! Learn How
Video A4-2

Activity 4.07 | Finding and Deleting Records

MOS
2.3.1

1 ▶ **Open** ⟫ the **Navigation Pane**. Open the **4A Departments Revised** table. **Close** ⟪ the **Navigation Pane**.

2 ▶ In the table, scroll to the bottom of the table, and then click in the last record for *Waste Management* in the **Department** field, On the **Home tab**, in the **Find group**, click **Find**. Alternatively, hold down Ctrl, and then press F.

The Find and Replace dialog box displays with the Find tab active.

3 ▶ In the **Find and Replace** dialog box, in the **Find What** box, type **assessor**

The Look In box displays *Current field*, which refers to the Department field because you clicked in that field before you clicked the Find button. Access will search the current field in the entire table, whether the entry displays before or after the active cell in the table.

4 ▶ In the **Find and Replace** dialog box, click the **Look In box arrow**. Notice that Access can search for the data in the entire Departments Revised table instead of only the Department field. Leaving the entry as **Current field**, click the **Look In box arrow** one time to close the list, and then click **Find Next**. Compare your screen with Figure 4.13.

If Access did not locate Record 2, ensure that you typed *assessor* correctly in the Find What box. Notice it is not case sensitive. If you misspelled *assessor* in the table, type the misspelled version in the Find What box. This is an example of how important accuracy is when entering data in your tables.

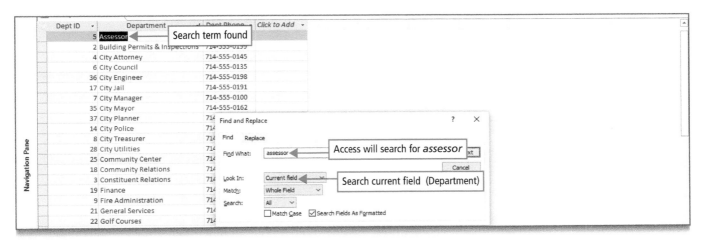

Figure 4.13

5 ▶ In the **Find and Replace** dialog box, click **Cancel** to close the dialog box.

The table displays with *Assessor* selected in Record 2. Even though you can locate this record easily in the table because there are a limited number of records, keep in mind that most database tables contain many more records. Using the Find button is an efficient way to locate a record in the table.

6 Point to the **Record Selector** box for the *Assessor* record until the ➡ pointer displays. Click one time to ensure that the entire record is selected, and then compare your screen with Figure 4.14.

Figure 4.14

7 On the **Home tab**, in the **Records group**, click **Delete** to delete the active record, and then compare your screen with Figure 4.15.

Notice that Access displays a message stating that you are about to delete one record and will be unable to undo the Delete operation.

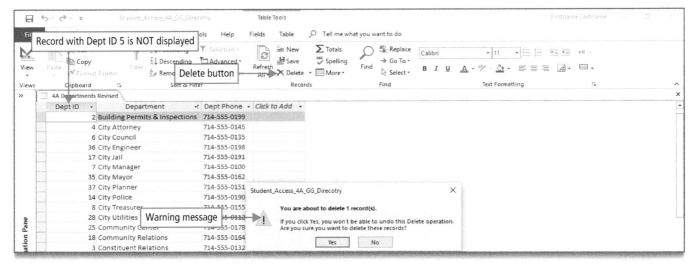

Figure 4.15

ANOTHER WAY   There are two other methods to delete selected records in a table:

- On the selected record, right-click and then click Delete Record.
- From the keyboard, press Delete.

8 In the message box, click **Yes** to confirm the deletion.

The record holding information for *Assessor* no longer displays in the table; it has been permanently deleted from the table and will no longer display in any other objects that were created using the Departments Revised table. The record number of Dept ID 2—Building Permits & Inspections—is now record 2 and is the current record.

MORE KNOWLEDGE   **Why the Dept ID Field Data Did Not Renumber Sequentially**

You added the Dept ID field with an AutoNumber data type. Because of this, when data is entered into the table, Dept ID is automatically numbered sequentially, and those numbers are not changed as records are added, deleted, or modified.

Activity 4.08 | Finding and Modifying Records

MOS
2.3.1

When data needs to be changed or updated, you must locate and modify the record with the data. Recall that you can move among records in a table using the navigation buttons at the bottom of the window and that you can use Find to locate specific data. Other navigation methods include using keys on the keyboard and using the Search box in the navigation area.

1 Take a moment to review the table in Figure 4.16, which lists the key combinations you can use to navigate within an Access table.

Keystroke	Movement
↑	Moves the selection up one record at a time.
↓	Moves the selection down one record at a time.
PgUp	Moves the selection up one screen at a time.
PgDn	Moves the selection down one screen at a time.
Ctrl + Home	Moves the selection to the first field in the table or the beginning of the selected field.
Ctrl + End	Moves the selection to the last field in the table or the end of the selected field.
Tab	Moves the selection to the next field in the table.
Shift + Tab	Moves the selection to the previous field in the table.
Enter	Moves the selection to the next field in the table.

Figure 4.16

2 On the keyboard, press ↓ to move the selection down one record. Record 3—*City Attorney*—is now the current record.

3 On the keyboard, hold down Ctrl, and then press Home to move to the first field of the first record in the table—Dept ID *1*.

4 In the navigation area, click **Next record** ▶ six times to navigate to Record 7—Dept ID *7*.

5 On the keyboard, hold down Ctrl, and then press End to move to the last field in the last record in the table—Dept Phone *714-555-0175*.

6 On the keyboard, hold down Shift, and then press Tab to move to the previous field in the same record in the table—*Waste Management* in the Department field.

7 In the navigation area, click in the **Search** box. In the **Search** box, type **b**

Record 2 is selected, and the letter *B* in *Building Permits & Inspections* is highlighted. Search found the first occurrence of the letter *b*. It is not necessary to type capital letters in the Search box; Access will locate the words regardless of capitalization.

8 Double-click in the **Search** box to select the *b*, and type **sani**

Record 30 is selected, and the letters *Sani* in *Sanitation* are highlighted. Search found the first occurrence of the letters *sani*. This is the record that needs to be modified. It is not necessary to type an entire word into the Search box to locate a record containing that word.

9 In the Department field box, double-click the word *Sanitation* to select it. Type **Trash Pickup** to replace the current entry. The Small Pencil icon in the Record Selector box means that the record is being edited. Press ↓ to move to the next record.

If you must edit part of a name, drag through letters or words to select them. You can then type the new letters or words over the selection to replace the text without having to press Delete or Backspace.

10 In the field name row, next to **Department**, click the **Sort and Filter arrow** ⏷, and then click **Sort A to Z**.

> Sorting the records by the department name again is necessary because a department changed its name.

11 **Save** 🖫 and **Close** the table. **Open** » the **Navigation Pane**.

Activity 4.09 | **Adding and Moving Fields in Design View and Datasheet View**

MOS
2.4.1, 2.4.5

In this Activity, you will add and move fields in Design view and in Datasheet view.

1 Right-click the **4A Employees Personal** table to display a shortcut menu, and click **Design View** to open the table in Design view. Alternatively, double-click the table name in the Navigation pane to open the table in Datasheet view, and then click the View button to switch to Design view. **Close** « the **Navigation Pane**.

2 In the **Field Name** column, click the **Home Phone** Field Name box. Under **Table Tools**, on the **Design tab**, in the **Tools** group, click **Insert Rows**.

> A new row is inserted above the *Home Phone* field. Recall that a row in Design view is a field.

3 In the empty **Field Name** box, type **Birthdate** and then press `Tab` to move to the **Data Type** column. Click the **Data Type arrow** to display the list of data types, and then click **Date/Time** to set the data type for this field. Compare your screen with Figure 4.17.

> A new field to display the employee's date of birth has been created in the *4A Employees Personal* table. An advantage of adding a field in Design view is that you name the field and set the data type when you insert the field.

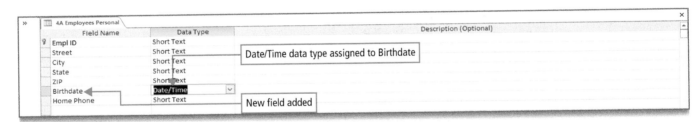

Figure 4.17

4 In the **Field Name** column, locate **Home Phone**, and then click the **Row Selector** box to select the field. Point to the **Row Selector** box to display the ➡ pointer. Hold down the left mouse button and drag the field up until you see a dark horizontal line following *Empl ID*, and then release the mouse button. Compare your screen with Figure 4.18.

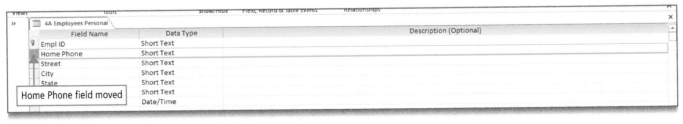

Figure 4.18

5 Switch the **4A Employees Personal** table to **Datasheet** view. In the displayed message box, click **Yes** to save the design changes.

The *Home Phone* field displays to the left of the *Street* field.

6 In the first record—248311—click in the **Birthdate** field. Using the techniques you have practiced, enter the birthdate for each record shown in the following list, pressing ⬇ after each entry to move to the next record.

Empl ID	Birthdate
248311	4/21/1955
456789	6/1/1964
532268	12/14/1984
589426	7/27/1990
589764	12/30/1972
689444	8/13/1980
786531	10/6/1966

7 Apply **Best Fit** to all columns, ensuring that all of the field names and all of the field data display. View the table in **Print Preview**. On the **Print Preview tab**, in the **Page Size group**, click **Margins** and then click **Normal**.

8 On the **Print Preview tab**, in the **Close Preview group,** click **Close Print Preview**. Close the **4A Employees Personal** table, saving changes. Open [»] the **Navigation Pane**. Open the **4A Employees Office** table in **Datasheet** view. Close [«] the **Navigation Pane**.

9 Select the **Office Phone** column. Under **Table Tools**, on the **Fields tab**, in the **Add & Delete group**, click **Short Text**. Alternatively, right-click the selected field and, from the shortcut menu, click Insert Field. A new column is inserted to the right of *Office Phone*.

10 If necessary, double-click **Field1**—the name of your field may differ if you have been experimenting with adding fields—to select the field name. Type **Work Site** and press Enter.

11 In the first record—248311—click in the **Work Site** field. Using the techniques you have practiced, enter the work site for each record shown in the following list, pressing ⬇ after each entry to move to the next record.

Empl ID	Work Site
248311	Justice Center
456789	City Hall
532268	B-121
589426	A-214
589764	Justice Center
689444	City Hall
786531	A-214

12 Point to **Position** until the ⬇ pointer displays, and then click one time to select the column. Hold down the left mouse button and drag the field left until you see a dark vertical line between *Date Hired* and *Office Phone*, and then release the mouse button. Compare your screen with Figure 4.19.

The *Position* field is moved after the *Date Hired* field and before the *Office Phone* field. If you move a field to the wrong position, select the field again, and then drag it to the correct position. Alternatively, on the Quick Access Toolbar, click Undo to place the field back in its previous position.

Figure 4.19

MORE KNOWLEDGE **Hide/Unhide Fields in a Table**

If you do not want a field to display in Datasheet view or on a printed copy of the table, you can hide the field.

- Right-click the field name at the top of the column.
- On the shortcut menu, click Hide Fields.
- To display the field again, right-click any field name. On the shortcut menu, click Unhide Fields. In the dialog box, click the fields to unhide, and then click OK.

Activity 4.10 | Checking Spelling

In this exercise, you will use the Spell Check feature to find spelling errors in your data. It is important to realize that Spell Check will not find all data entry mistakes, so you will need to use additional proofreading methods to ensure the accuracy of the data.

1 In the first record—248311—click in the **Empl ID** field. On the **Home tab**, in the **Records group**, click **Spelling**. Alternatively, press F7. Compare your screen with Figure 4.20.

The Spelling dialog box displays, and *Bothski* is highlighted because it is not in the Office dictionary. Many proper names will be *flagged*—highlighted—by the spelling checker. Take a moment to review the options in the Spelling dialog box; these are described in Figure 4.21.

Figure 4.20

Button	Action
Ignore 'Last Name' Field	Ignores any words in the selected field.
Ignore	Ignores this one occurrence of the word but continues to flag other instances of the word.
Ignore All	Discontinues flagging any instance of the word anywhere in the table.
Change	Changes the identified word to the word highlighted under Suggestions.
Change All	Changes every instance of the word in the table to the word highlighted under Suggestions.
Add	Adds the highlighted word to a custom dictionary, which can be edited. This option does not change the built-in Office dictionary.
AutoCorrect	Adds the flagged word to the AutoCorrect list, which will subsequently correct the word automatically if misspelled in the future.
Options	Displays the Access Options dialog box.
Undo Last	Undoes the last change.
Cancel	Closes the Spelling dialog box without making any changes.

Figure 4.21

2 In the **Spelling** dialog box, click **Ignore 'Last Name' Field**.

Present, which displays in the Position field, is flagged by the spelling checker. In the Spelling dialog box under Suggestions, *President* is highlighted.

3 In the **Spelling** dialog box, click **Change** to change the word from *Present* to *President*.

When the spelling checker has completed checking the table and has found no other words missing from its dictionary, a message displays stating *The spelling check is complete*.

4 In the message box, click **OK**.

Objective 3 Change Data Types

GO! Learn How
Video A4-3

Before creating a table, it is important to decide on the data types for the fields in the table. Setting a specific data type helps to ensure that the proper data will be entered into a field; for example, it is not possible to enter text into a field with a Currency data type. It is also important to choose a number data type when it is appropriate to avoid problems with calculations and sorting.

Activity 4.11 | Changing Data Types

MOS
2.4.5

Once data is entered into a field, caution must be exercised when changing the data type—existing data may not be completely visible or may be deleted. You can change the data type in either Datasheet view or Design view.

1 With the **4A Employees Office** table open, switch to **Design** view. Change the **Data Type** for the **Date Hired** field to **Date/Time**. Press F6 to move to the **Field Properties** pane at the bottom of the screen. Click in the **Format** property and select **Short Date**.

The data type of Date/Time is more appropriate for this field because it will display dates and restrict other entries. This will also allow the field to be accurately used in calculations, comparisons, and sorts.

2 Change the data type for the **Notes** field to **Long Text**, and then compare your screen with Figure 4.22.

The data type of Long Text is more appropriate for this field because it may require more than 255 characters and spaces to effectively describe notes associated with an employee.

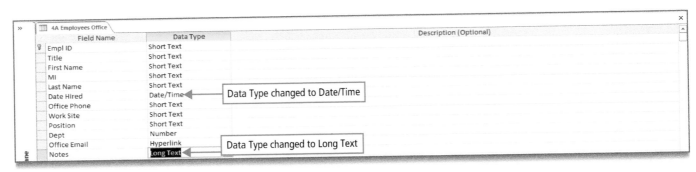

Figure 4.22

3 Switch to **Datasheet** view, saving changes to the table. Apply **Best Fit** to all columns, ensuring that all of the field names and all of the field data display. View the table in **Print Preview**. In the **Page Layout group**, click **Landscape** to change the orientation. Change the **Margins** to **Normal**.

Notice that the table will print on two pages.

4 **Close** Print Preview. **Close** the **4A Employees Office** table, saving changes.

 Objective 4 **Attach Files to Records**

GO! Learn How
Video A4-4

The Attachment data type can be used to add one or more files to the records in a database. For example, if you have a database for an antique collection, you can attach a picture of each antique and a Word document that contains a description of the item. Access stores the attached files in their native formats—if you attach a Word document, it is saved as a Word document. By default, fields contain only one piece of data; however, you can attach more than one file by using the Attachment data type. As you attach files to a record, Access creates one or more *system tables* to keep track of the multiple entries in the field. You cannot view or work with these system tables.

Activity 4.12 | **Attaching a Word Document to a Record**

MOS
2.4.5

In this Activity, you will attach documents to records in the *4A Departments Revised* table.

1 **Open** ≫ the **Navigation Pane**. Open the **4A Departments Revised** table, and then switch to **Design** view. **Close** ≪ the **Navigation Pane**. Click in the empty **Field Name** box under **Dept Phone**, type Information and then press [Tab] to move to the **Data Type** box. Click the **Data Type arrow**, click **Attachment**, and then press [Enter]. Under **Field Properties**, on the **General tab**, notice that only two field properties—**Caption** and **Required**—are displayed for an Attachment field.

2 Switch to **Datasheet** view, saving changes to the table. In the **Attachment** field, notice that the field name of *Information* does not display; instead, a paper clip symbol displays. In each record, *(0)* displays after the paper clip symbol, indicating that there are no attachments for this record.

Because multiple files can be attached to a record, the name of the field displays the paper clip symbol.

3 In record 12 for *Planning & Zoning*, double-click in the **Attachment** field. In the displayed **Attachments** dialog box, click **Add**. In the **Choose File** dialog box, navigate to the location where the student data files for this textbook are saved. Double-click **a04A_PZ_Schedule**, and then compare your screen with Figure 4.23.

> The Word document will be added to the Attachments dialog box. You can attach multiple files to the same record.

Figure 4.23

4 In the **Attachments** dialog box, click **OK**. Notice that the **Attachment** field now indicates there is *1* attachment for record 12. Double-click in the **Attachment** field. In the **Attachments** dialog box, click **a04A_PZ_Schedule.docx**, and then click **Open**.

> Word opens, and the document displays. You can make changes to the document, and then save it in the database.

5 **Close** Word. In the **Attachments** dialog box, click **OK**.

6 In record 2 for *Building Permits & Inspections*, double-click in the **Attachment** field. In the displayed **Attachments** dialog box, click **Add**. In the **Choose File** dialog box, navigate to the location where the student data files for this textbook are saved. Double-click **a04A_Bldg_Permit_App**. In the **Attachments** dialog box, click **OK**.

> The PDF document is added to the field in record 2.

NOTE   Saving Changes to an Attached File

When you open an attached file in the program that was used to create it, Access places a temporary copy of the file in a temporary folder on the hard drive of your computer. If you change the file and save changes, Access saves the changes in the temporary copy. Closing the program used to view the attachment returns you to Access. When you click OK to close the Attachments dialog box, Access prompts you to save the attached file again. Click Yes to save the changes to the attached file in the database, or click No to keep the original, unedited version in the database.

---

7 Apply **Best Fit** to all columns, ensuring that all of the field names and all of the field data display.

8 **Close** the table, saving changes. **Open** [»] the **Navigation Pane**. **Close** the database, and **Close** Access.

For Non-MyLab Submissions: Determine What Your Instructor Requires for Submission

As directed by your instructor, submit your completed database file.

9 In **MyLab IT**, locate and click the Grader Project **Access 4A City Directory**. In **step 3**, under **Upload Completed Assignment**, click **Choose File**. In the **Open** dialog box, navigate to your **Access Chapter 4 folder**, and then click your **Student_Access_4A_GG_Directory** file one time to select it. In the lower right corner of the **Open** dialog box, click **Open**.

The name of your selected file displays above the Upload button.

10 To submit your file to **MyLab IT** for grading, click **Upload**, wait a moment for a green **Success!** message, and then in **step 4**, click the blue **Submit for Grading** button. Click **Close Assignment** to return to your list of **Course Materials**.

You have completed Project 4A   END

PROJECT
4B

IT Tasks

MyLab IT
Project 4B Grader for Instruction
Project 4B Simulation for Training and Review

Project Activities

Matthew Shoaf, Director of the Information Technology department, has created a table to keep track of tasks that he has assigned to the employees in his department. In Activities 4.13 through 4.23, you will create a table in Design view that stores records about assigned tasks, modify its properties, and customize its fields. You will add features to the database table that will help to reduce data entry errors and that will make data entry easier. Your completed Navigation Pane will look similar to the tables shown in Figure 4.24.

Project Files for MyLab IT Grader

1. In your **MyLab IT** course, locate and click **Access 4B IT Workload**, Download Materials, and then Download All Files.
2. Extract the zipped folder to your Access Chapter 4 folder. Close the Grader download screens.
3. Take a moment to open the downloaded **Access_4B_IT_Workload_Instructions**; note any recent updates to the book.

Project Results

GO! Project 4B

Where We're Going

Figure 4.24 Project 4B IT Tasks

For Non-MyLab Submissions	**Start with an Access Data File**
For Project 4B, you will need the following file:	In your Access Chapter 4 folder, save your workbook as:
a04B_IT_Workload	**Lastname_Firstname_4B_IT_Workload**

After you have saved your database, launch Access and open the database. On the next page, begin with Step 2.

Objective 5 Create a Table in Design View

GO! Learn How

Video A4-5

Creating a table in Design view gives you the most control over the characteristics of the table and the fields. Most database designers use Design view to create tables, setting the data types and formats before entering any records. Design view is a good way to create a table when you know exactly how you want to set up your fields.

Activity 4.13 │ Creating a Table in Design View

1.2.3, 2.4.5,
2.4.4, 2.4.3

In this Activity, you will create a table to keep track of the tasks that the IT department will be completing.

1 **Start** Access. In the Access opening screen, click **Open Other Files**. Navigate to your **Access Chapter 4 folder**, and then double-click the Access file that you downloaded from **MyLab IT** that displays your name—**Student_Access_4B_IT_Workload**.

2 If you did not add the **Access Chapter 4** folder to the Trust Center, enable the content. **Close** [«] the **Navigation Pane**.

3 On the ribbon, click the **Create tab**. In the **Tables group**, click **Table Design** to open an empty table in Design view, and then compare your screen with Figure 4.25.

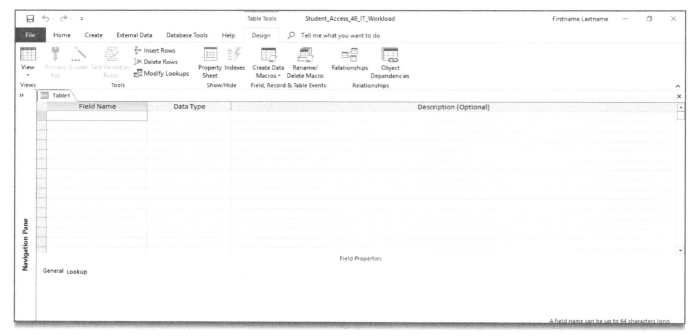

Figure 4.25

4 In the first **Field Name** box, type **WO#** press [Tab], and then, under **Table Tools**, on the **Design tab**, in the **Tools group**, click **Primary Key**.

5 ▸ Click the **Data Type arrow** to display a list of data types, as shown in Figure 4.26. Take a moment to study the table in Figure 4.27 that describes the choices.

In Design view, all the data types are displayed. In Datasheet view, the list depends on the data entered in the field and does not display all available data types. Those unavailable in Datasheet view include AutoNumber, Calculated, and Lookup Wizard.

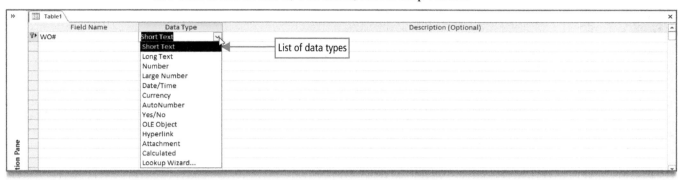

Figure 4.26

Data Type	Description	Example
Short Text	Text or combinations of text and numbers; also, numbers that are not used in calculations. Limited to 255 characters or length set on field, whichever is less. Access does not reserve space for unused portions of the text field. This is the default data type.	An inventory item, such as towels, or a phone number or postal code that is not used in calculations and that may contain characters other than numbers
Long Text	Lengthy text or combinations of text and numbers that can hold up to 65,535 characters depending on the size of the database.	A description of a product
Number	Numeric data used in mathematical calculations with varying field sizes.	A quantity, such as 500
Date/Time	Date and time values for the years 100 through 9999.	An order date, such as 11/10/2021 3:30 p.m.
Currency	Monetary values and numeric data that can be used in mathematical calculations involving data with one to four decimal places. Accurate to 15 digits on the left side of the decimal separator and to 4 digits on the right side. Use this data type to store financial data and when you do not want Access to round values.	An item price, such as $8.50
AutoNumber	Available in Design view. A unique sequential or random number assigned by Access as each record is entered that cannot be updated.	An inventory item number, such as 1, 2, 3, or a randomly assigned employee number, such as 38527
Yes/No	Contains only one of two values—Yes/No, True/False, or On/Off. Access assigns 1 for all Yes values and 0 for all No values.	Whether an item was ordered—Yes or No
OLE Object	An object created by a program other than Access that is linked to or embedded in the table. *OLE* is an abbreviation for *object linking and embedding*, a technology for transferring and sharing information among programs. Stores up to two gigabytes of data (the size limit for all Access databases). Must have an OLE server registered on the server that runs the database. Should usually use Attachment data type instead.	A graphics file, such as a picture of a product, a sound file, a Word document, or an Excel spreadsheet stored as a bitmap image
Hyperlink	Web or email address.	An email address, such as dwalker@ityourway.com, or a Web page, such as http://www.ityourway.com
Attachment	Any supported type of file—images, spreadsheet files, documents, or charts. Similar to email attachments.	Same as OLE Object
Calculated	Available in Design view. Opens the Expression Builder to create an expression based on existing fields or numbers. Field must be designated as a Calculated field when it is inserted into the table; the expression can be edited in the Field Properties.	Adding two existing fields such as [field1]+[field2], or performing a calculation with a field and a number such as [field3]*.5
Lookup Wizard	Available in Design view. Not really a data type, but will display in the list of data types. Links to fields in other tables to display a list of data instead of having to manually type the data.	Link to another field in the same or another table

Figure 4.27

6 From the displayed list, click **Short Text**, and then press ⌨Tab to move to the **Description** box. In the **Description** box, type **Identification number assigned to task reported on work order form**

Field names should be short; use the description box to display more information about the contents of the field. A description is not necessary if the field name is self-explanatory.

7 Press ⌨F6 to move to the **Field Properties** pane at the bottom of the screen. In the **Field Size** box, type **8** to replace the 255. Compare your screen with Figure 4.28.

Pressing ⌨F6 while in the Data Type column moves the insertion point to the first field property box in the Field Properties pane. Alternatively, click in the Field Size property box.

Recall that a field with a data type of Short Text can store up to 255 characters. You can change the field size to limit the number of characters that can be entered into the field to ensure accuracy. For example, if you use the two-letter state abbreviations for a state field, limit the size of the field to two characters. When entering a state in the field, you will be unable to type more than two characters.

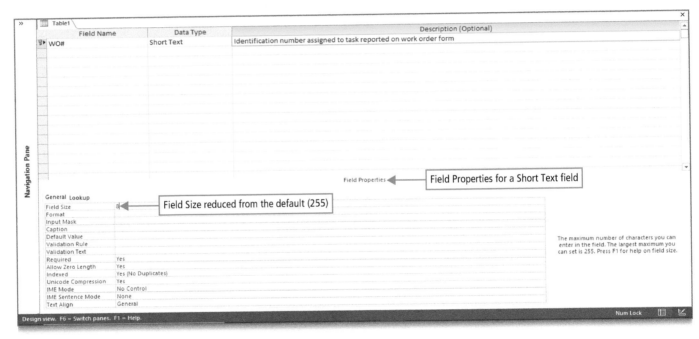

Figure 4.28

8 Click in the second **Field Name** box, type **Priority** and then press ⌨Tab twice to move to the **Description** box. Type **Indicate the priority level of this task** Press ⌨F6 to move to the **Field Properties** pane at the bottom of the screen. Click in the **Format** box and type **>**

Because Short Text is the default data type, you do not have to select it if it is the correct data type for the field. Additionally, if the field name is descriptive enough, the Description box is optional.

A greater than symbol (>) in the Format property box in a Text field converts all entries in the field to uppercase. Using a less than symbol (<) will force all entries to be lowercase.

MORE KNOWLEDGE **The Caption Property**

The Caption property is used to give a name to fields used on forms and reports. Many database administrators create short and abbreviated field names in tables. In a form or report based on the table, a more descriptive name is desired. The value in the Caption property is used in label controls on forms and reports instead of the field name. If the Caption property is blank, the field name is used in the label control. A caption can contain up to 2,048 characters.

---

9 In the third **Field Name** box, type **Status** and then press [Tab] three times to move to the next **Field Name** box.

The default Short Text data type is applied, and the Description is blank.

10 In the fourth **Field Name** box, type **%Complete** Press [Tab] and then click the **Data Type arrow**. From the displayed list, click **Number**. Press [Tab] to move to the **Description** box, and then type **Percentage of the task that has been completed** Press [F6] to move to the **Field Properties** pane. Click the **Field Size** property arrow and select **Single**. Click the **Format** property arrow and select **Percent**. Click the **Decimal Places** property arrow and select 0.

The data type of Number is appropriate for this field because it will display only the amount of a task that has been completed. Defining the number as a percent with zero decimal places further restricts the entries. This allows the field to be used accurately in calculations, comparisons, and sorts.

11 In the fifth **Field Name** box, type **Parts** Press [Tab] and then click the **Data Type arrow**. From the displayed list, click **Yes/No**. Press [Tab] to move to the **Description** box. Type **Click the field to indicate parts have been ordered to complete the task**

The data type of Yes/No is appropriate for this field because there are only two choices: parts are on order (yes) or parts are not on order (no). In Datasheet view, click the check box to indicate yes with a checkmark.

Activity 4.14 | **Adding Fields to a Table in Design View**

2.4.1, 2.4.4, 2.4.5

1 In the sixth **Field Name** box, type **Tech** and then press [Tab] three times to move to the next Field Name box.

2 In the seventh **Field Name** box, type **Phone#** Press [Tab] two times to move to the **Description** box, type **Enter as ###-####** and then change the **Field Size** property to **8**

3 Click in the eighth **Field Name** box, and then type **Problem** Press [Tab] and then click the **Data Type arrow**. From the displayed list, click **Long Text**. Press [Tab] to move to the **Description** box, and then type **Description of the IT problem**

The data type of Long Text is appropriate for this field because it may require more than 255 characters and spaces to effectively describe the IT problem that needs attention.

4 Click in the ninth **Field Name** box, and then type **Start Date** Press [Tab] and then click the **Data Type arrow**. From the displayed list, click **Date/Time**.

The data type of Date/Time is appropriate for this field because it will only display date information. Because Date/Time is a type of number, this field can be used in calculations.

5 Click in the tenth **Field Name** box and then type **End Date** Press [Tab] and then click the **Data Type arrow**. From the displayed list, click **Date/Time**.

6 Click in the eleventh **Field Name** box and then type **Task Duration** Press ⟨Tab⟩ and then click the **Data Type arrow**. From the displayed list, click **Calculated**. In the **Expression Builder** dialog box, type **[End Date]-[Start Date]** and then compare your screen to Figure 4.29.

> The data type of Calculated is appropriate for this field because the entry is calculated with an expression—subtracting *Start Date* from *End Date*. The *Task Duration* field will remain blank if the task has not yet been completed; nothing can be entered in the field.

> The ***Expression Builder*** is a feature used to create formulas (expressions) in calculated fields, query criteria, form and report controls, and table validation rules. An expression can be entered using field names or numbers, and the only spaces included are those that separate words in field names. Any time a field name is used in the expression, it should be enclosed in square brackets. An existing field cannot be changed to a Calculated data type; it must be assigned when the field is added to the table. Otherwise, you would need to delete the field and reinsert it. The expression can be edited in the Field Properties.

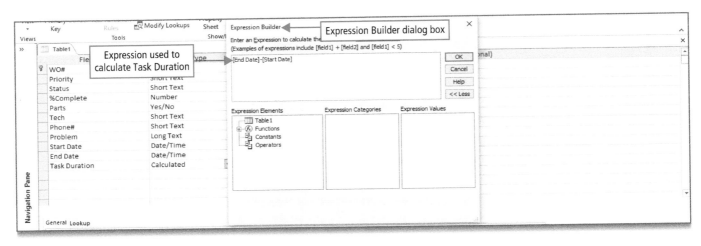

Figure 4.29

7 Click **OK**. In the **Description** box, type **Number of days necessary to complete the task** Press ⟨F6⟩ to move to the **Field Properties** pane at the bottom of the screen. Click in the **Result Type** property arrow, and then select **Single**.

8 On the **Quick Access** toolbar, click **Save** 🖫. In the **Save As** dialog box, type **4B Tasks** and then click **OK**. Switch to **Datasheet** view to view the table you have just created; there are no records in the table yet.

Objective 6 | Create a Lookup Field

GO! Learn How
Video A4-6

Creating a ***lookup field*** can restrict the data entered in a field because the person entering data selects that data from a list retrieved from another table, query, or list of entered values. The choices can be displayed in a ***list box***—a box containing a restrictive list of choices—or a ***combo box***—a box that is a combination of a list box and a text box. You can create a lookup field by using the Lookup Wizard or manually by setting the field's lookup field properties. Whenever possible, use the Lookup Wizard because it simplifies the process, ensures consistent data entry, automatically populates the associated field properties, and creates the needed table relationships.

Activity 4.15 | Creating a Lookup Field Based on a List of Values

2.4.5

In this Activity, you will create a lookup field for the Status field.

1 With the **4B Tasks** table open, switch to **Design** view. In the **Status** field, click in the **Data Type** box, and then click the **arrow**. From the displayed list of data types, click **Lookup Wizard**.

2 In the first **Lookup Wizard** dialog box, click the **I will type in the values that I want** option button, and then click **Next**. Compare your screen with Figure 4.30.

The first step of the Lookup Wizard enables you to choose whether you want Access to locate the information from another table or query or whether you would like to type the information to create a list.

The second step enables you to select the number of columns you want to include in the lookup field. The values are typed in the grid, and you can adjust the column width of the displayed list.

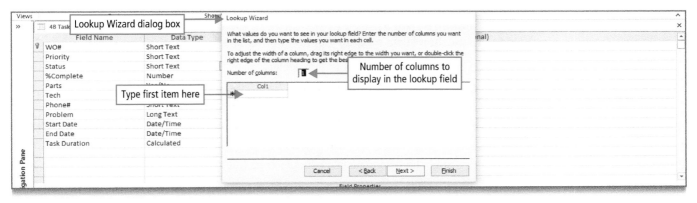

Figure 4.30

3 Be sure the number of columns is **1**. Under **Col1**, click in the first row, type **Not Started** and then press [Tab] or [↓] to save the first item.

If you mistakenly press [Enter], the next dialog box of the wizard displays. If that happens, click Back.

4 Type the following data, and then compare your screen with Figure 4.31.

In Progress
Completed
Reassigned

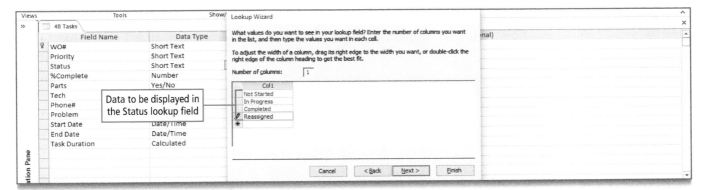

Figure 4.31

5 Double-click the right edge of **Col1** to apply Best Fit, adjusting the column width so it is just wide enough for all entries to display, and then click **Next**. In the final dialog box, click **Finish**. With the **Status** field selected, under **Field Properties**, click the **Lookup tab**.

> The Lookup Wizard populates the Lookup property boxes. The *Row Source Type* property indicates that the data is retrieved from a Value List, a list that you created. The *Row Source* property displays the data you entered in the list. The *Limit to List* property displays No, so you can type alternative data in the field if necessary.

6 **Save** the changes, and switch to **Datasheet** view. Click the **Status** field in the first record, and then click the **arrow** to view the lookup list. Press Esc to return to a blank field.

Activity 4.16 | Creating a Lookup Field Based on Data in Another Table

In this Activity, you will create a lookup field for the Tech field.

MOS
2.4.5

1 In the **4B Tasks** table, switch to **Design** view. In the **Tech** field, click in the **Data Type** box, and then click the **Data Type arrow**. From the displayed list of data types, click **Lookup Wizard**.

2 In the first **Lookup Wizard** dialog box, verify that the **I want the lookup field to get the values from another table or query** option button is selected.

3 Click **Next**. The **4B Employees** table is selected.

4 Click **Next** to display the third **Lookup Wizard** dialog box. Under **Available Fields**, click **Last Name**, and then click **Add Field** (>) to move the field to the **Selected Fields** box. Move the **First Name** and **Job Title** fields from the **Available Fields** box to the **Selected Fields** box. Compare your screen with Figure 4.32.

> Because there might be several people with the same last name, the First Name field and the Job Title field are included.

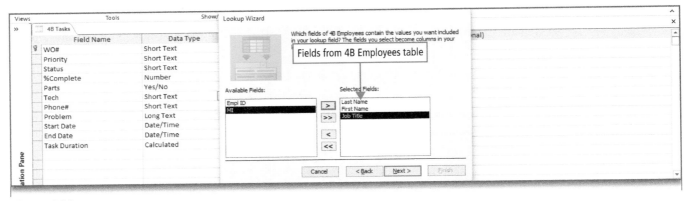

Figure 4.32

5 Click **Next** to display the fourth **Lookup Wizard** dialog box. In the **1** box, click the **arrow**, and then click **Last Name**. In the **2** box, click the **arrow**, and then click **First Name**. In the **3** box, click the **arrow**, and then click **Job Title**. Leave all three sort orders as **Ascending**.

> The list will first display last names in ascending order. If there are duplicate last names, then the duplicate last names will be sorted by the first name in ascending order. If there are duplicate last names and first names, then those names will be sorted in ascending order by the job title.

6 ▶ Click **Next** to display the fifth **Lookup Wizard** dialog box. This screen enables you to change the width of the lookup field and to display the primary key field. Be sure the **Hide key column** (**recommended**) check box is selected, and then click **Next** to display the sixth and final **Lookup Wizard** dialog box.

> The actual data that is stored in the lookup field is the data in the primary key field.

7 ▶ Under **What label would you like for your lookup field?**, leave the default of **Tech** and be sure that **Enable Data Integrity** and **Allow Multiple Values** are *not* selected.

> Because you have already named the field, the default name is appropriate. If you were creating a new field that had not yet been named, a label should be entered on this screen. If you want to add Cascade options to the relationship built between the two tables, select the Enable Data Integrity option to display the cascade options. If you want to allow the selection of more than one last name when the lookup field displays and then store the multiple values, select the Allow Multiple Values check box, which changes the lookup field to a multivalued field. A *multivalued field* holds multiple values, such as a list of people to whom you have assigned the same task.

8 ▶ Click **Finish**. A message displays stating that the table must be saved before Access can create the needed relationship between the *4B Tasks* table and the *4B Employees* table. Click **Yes**.

9 ▶ With the **Tech** field selected, under **Field Properties**, click the **Lookup tab**, if necessary.

> The Lookup Wizard populates the Lookup properties boxes. The *Row Source Type* property indicates that the data is retrieved from a table or query. The *Row Source* property displays the SQL statement that is used to retrieve the data from the fields in the *4B Employees* table. The *Limit to List* property displays Yes, which means you must select the data from the list and cannot type data in the field.

10 ▶ Click the **General tab** to display the list of general field properties.

<table>
<tr><td>**Objective 7**</td><td>**Set Field Properties**</td></tr>
</table>

GO! Learn How
Video A4-7

A *field property* is an attribute or characteristic of a field that controls the display and input of data. You previously used field properties to change the size of a field and to specify a specific format for data types. When you click in any of the property boxes, a description of the property displays to the right. Available field properties depend on the data type of each field.

Activity 4.17 | **Creating an Input Mask Using the Input Mask Wizard**

2.4.8

An *input mask* is a field property that determines the data that can be entered, how the data displays, and how the data is stored. For example, an input mask can require individuals to enter telephone numbers in a specific format like (636) 555-1212. If you enter the telephone number without supplying an area code, you will be unable to save the record until the area code is entered. Input masks provide *data validation*—rules that help prevent individuals from entering invalid data—and help ensure that individuals enter data in a consistent manner. By default, you can apply input masks to fields with a data type of Short Text, Number, Currency, and Date/Time. The Input Mask Wizard can be used to apply input masks to fields with a data type of Short Text or Date/Time only.

1 Under **Field Name**, click **Phone#**. Under **Field Properties**, click in the **Input Mask** box. At the right side of the Field Properties, notice the description given for this property. In the **Input Mask** box, click **Build** [...]. Compare your screen with Figure 4.33.

The Build button displays after you click in a field property box so you can further define the property. The Input Mask Wizard starts, which enables you to create an input mask using one of several standard masks that Access has designed, such as Phone Number, Social Security Number, Zip Code, and so on. Clicking in the Try It box enables you to enter data to test the input mask.

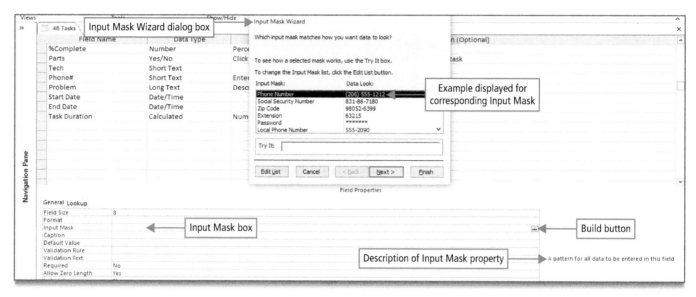

Figure 4.33

2 In the displayed **Input Mask Wizard** dialog box, with **Phone Number** selected, click **Next**, and then compare your screen with Figure 4.34. In the **Input Mask Wizard** dialog box, notice the entry in the **Input Mask** box.

A *0* indicates a required digit; a *9* indicates an optional digit or space. The area code is enclosed in parentheses, and a hyphen (-) separates the three-digit prefix from the four-digit number. The exclamation point (!) causes the input mask to fill in from left to right. The Placeholder character indicates that the field will display an underscore character (_) for each digit before data is entered in Datasheet view.

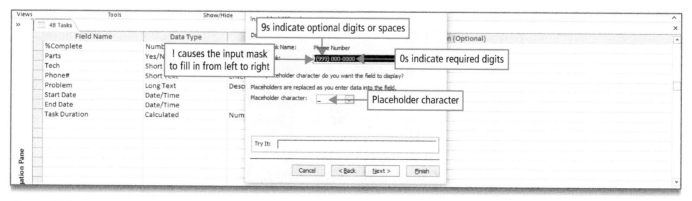

Figure 4.34

3 In the **Input Mask Wizard** dialog box, click **Back**, and then click **Edit List**.

The Customize Input Mask Wizard dialog box displays, which enables you to edit the default input mask or add an input mask.

4 In the **Customize Input Mask Wizard** dialog box, in the navigation area, click **New (blank) record** ▸*. In the **Description** box, type **Local Phone Number** Press Tab to move to the **Input Mask** box, and type **!000-0000** Press Tab to move to the **Placeholder** box, and type **#** Press Tab to move to the **Sample Data** box, and type **555-2090** Compare your screen with Figure 4.35.

Because tasks are assigned to local personnel, the area code is unnecessary. Instead of displaying an underscore as the placeholder in the field, the number sign (#) displays.

Figure 4.35

5 In the **Customize Input Mask Wizard** dialog box, click **Close**.

The newly created input mask for Local Phone Number displays below the input mask for Password.

6 Under **Input Mask**, click **Local Phone Number**, and then click **Next**. Click the **Placeholder character arrow** to display other symbols that can be used as placeholders. Be sure that **#** is displayed as the placeholder character, and then click **Next**.

After creating an input mask to be used with the Input Mask Wizard, you can change the placeholder character for individual fields.

7 The next wizard screen enables you to decide how you want to store the data. Be sure that the **Without the symbols in the mask, like this:** option button is selected, as shown in Figure 4.36.

Saving the data without the symbols makes the database size smaller.

Figure 4.36

8 Click **Next**. In the final wizard screen, click **Finish**. Notice that the entry in the *Input Mask* box displays as *!000\-0000;;#*. **Save** the table.

Recall that the exclamation point (!) fills the input mask from left to right, and the 0s indicate required digits. The two semicolons (;) are used by Access to separate the input mask into three sections. This input mask has data in the first section—the 0s—and in the third section—the placeholder of *#*.

The second and third sections of an input mask are optional. The second section, which is not used in this input mask, determines whether the literal characters—in this case, the hyphen (-)—are stored with the data. A *0* in the second section will store the literal characters; a *1* or leaving it blank stores only the characters entered in the field. The third section of the input mask indicates the placeholder character—in this case, the # sign. If you want to leave the fill-in spaces blank instead of using a placeholder, type " "—there is a space between the quotation marks—in the third section.

9 Take a moment to study the table shown in Figure 4.37, which describes the most common characters that can be used to create a custom input mask.

Character	Description
0	Required digit (0 through 9).
9	Optional digit or space.
#	Optional digit, space, plus sign, or minus sign; blank positions are converted to spaces.
L	Required letter (A through Z).
?	Optional letter.
A	Required digit or letter.
a	Optional digit or letter.
&	Any character or space; required.
C	Any character or space; optional.
<	All characters that follow are converted to lowercase.
>	All characters that follow are converted to uppercase.
!	Characters typed into the mask are filled from left to right. The exclamation point can be included anywhere in the input mask.
\	Character that follows is displayed as text. This is the same as enclosing a character in quotation marks.
Password	Creates a password entry box that displays asterisks (*) as you type. Access stores the characters.
" "	Used to enclose displayed text.
.	Decimal separator.
,	Thousands separator.
: ; - /	Date and time separators. Character used depends on your regional settings.

Figure 4.37

Activity 4.18 | Creating an Input Mask Using the Input Mask Properties Box

MOS
2.4.8, 2.4.5

In addition to using the wizard, input masks can be created directly in the Input Mask Properties box. In this Activity, you will use the Input Mask Properties box to create a mask that will ensure the Work Order # is entered according to departmental policy. An example of a work order number used by the Information Technology department is WO CM-46341. WO is an abbreviation for Work Order. CM represents the initials of the person entering the work order data. A hyphen separates the initials from a number assigned to the work order.

1 With the **4B Tasks** table displayed in **Design** view, click in the **WO#** field. Under **Field Properties**, click in the **Input Mask** box, type **WO** press ⎵Spacebar, type **>LL-99** and then compare your screen with Figure 4.38.

The letters *WO* and a space will display at the beginning of every Work Order # (WO#). The greater than (>) sign converts any text following it to uppercase. Each *L* indicates that a letter (not a number) is required. A hyphen (-) follows the two letters, and the two 9s indicate optional numbers.

Take a moment to study the examples of input masks shown in Figure 4.39.

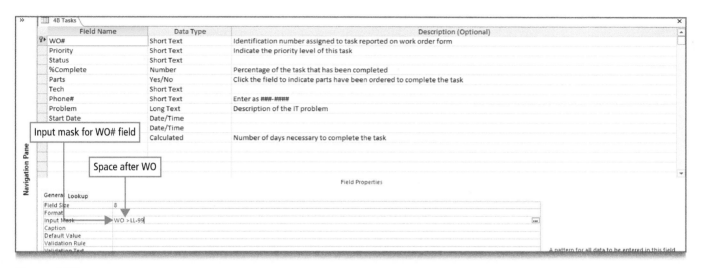

Figure 4.38

Input Mask	Sample Data	Description
(000) 000-0000	(712) 555-5011	Must enter an area code because of the 0s enclosed in parentheses.
(999) 000-0000!	(702) 555-6331 ( ) 555-6331	Area code is optional because of the 9s enclosed in parentheses. Exclamation point causes mask to fill in from left to right.
(000) AAA-AAAA	(712) 555-TELE	Enables you to substitute the last seven digits of a U.S.-style phone number with letters. Area code is required.
#999	-20 2009	Can accept any positive or negative number of no more than four characters and no thousands separator or decimal places.
>L????L?000L0	GREENGR339M3 MAY R 452B7	Allows a combination of required (L) and optional (?) letters and required numbers (0). The greater than (>) sign changes letters to uppercase.
00000-9999	23703-5100	Requires the five-digit postal code (0) and makes the plus-four section (9) optional.
>L<???????????????	Elizabeth Rose	Enables up to 15 letters in which the first letter is required and is capitalized; all other letters are lowercase.
ISBN 0-&&&&&&&&&-0	ISBN 0-13-232762-7	Allows a book number with text of ISBN, required first and last digits, and any combination of characters between those digits.
>LL00000-0000	AG23703-0323	Accepts a combination of two required letters, both uppercase, followed by five required numbers, a hyphen, and then four required numbers. Could be used with part or inventory numbers.

Figure 4.39

2 Click in the **Start Date** field to make the field active. Under **Field Properties**, click in the **Format** box, and then click the **arrow**. From the displayed list, click **Short Date**. Also set the format of **End Date** to **Short Date**.

MORE KNOWLEDGE **The Differences Between Input Masks and Display Formats**

You can define input masks to control how data is entered into a field and then apply a separate display format to the same data. For example, you can require individuals to enter dates in a format such as 30 Dec. 2022 by using an input mask of DD MMM. YYYY. By using the Format property, you can specify a format of Short Date, which will display the data as 12/30/2022, regardless of how the data was entered.

---

3 Switch to **Datasheet** view, and click **Yes** to save the table. In the **WO#** field in the first record, type **da3** and then press Tab or Enter to go to the next field.

The input mask adds the WO and a space. The *da* is automatically capitalized, and the hyphen is inserted before the 3.

4 In the **Priority** field, type **High** and then press Tab or Enter to go to the next field.

5 In the **Status** field, type **C** to display the **Completed** item in the lookup list, and then press Tab or Enter to move to the next field.

6 In the **%Complete** field, type **100** and then press Tab or Enter three times to bypass the **Parts** and **Tech** fields.

Leaving the Yes/No field blank assigns a No value in the Parts field, so parts are not on order for this task.

7 In the **Phone#** field, type **5558735** and then press Tab or Enter to move to the next field.

8 In the **Problem** field, type **Computer 14 has a computer virus** and then press Tab or Enter to move to the next field.

9 In the **Start Date** field, type **3/28/2022** and then press Tab or Enter to move to the next field.

10 In the **End Date** field, type **3/29/22** and then press Tab or Enter to move to the **Task Duration** field. Notice the calculated field now displays a *1*. Apply **Best Fit** to adjust the width of all columns, and then compare your screen with Figure 4.40.

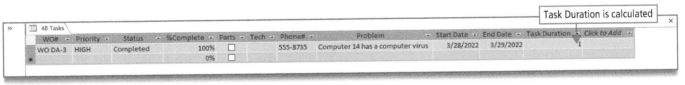

Figure 4.40

11 Switch to **Design** view. The data entry is automatically saved when the record is complete.

Activity 4.19 | Specifying a Required Field

Recall that if a table has a field designated as the primary key field, an entry for the field is *required*; it cannot be left empty. You can set this requirement on other fields in either Design view or Datasheet view. In this Activity, you will require an entry in the Status field. Use the Required field property to ensure that a field contains data and is not left blank.

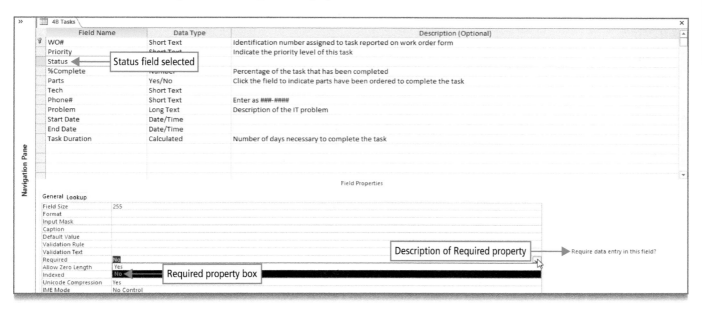

1 Under **Field Name**, click in the **Status** field, and then under **Field Properties**, click in the **Required** box. Click the **Required arrow**, and then compare your screen with Figure 4.41.

Only Yes and No options display in the list.

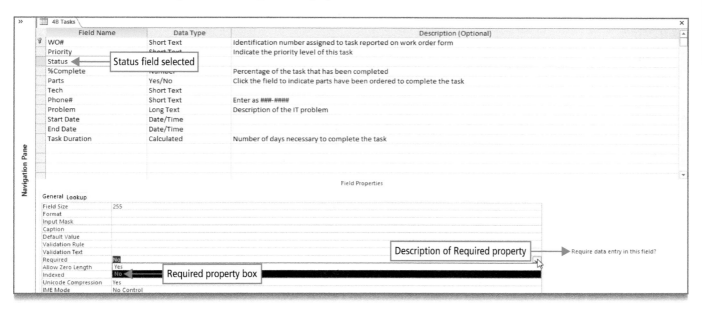

Figure 4.41

2 Click **Yes** to require an individual to enter the status for each record. **Save** 🖫 the changes to the table.

A message displays stating that data integrity rules have been changed and that existing data may not be valid for the new rules. This message displays when you change field properties where data exists in the field. Clicking Yes requires Access to examine the field in every record to see if the existing data meets the new data validation rule. For each record Access finds in which data does not meet the new validation rule, a new message displays that prompts you to keep testing with the new setting. You also can revert to the prior validation setting and continue testing or cancel testing of the data.

3 In the message box, click **No**. Switch to **Datasheet** view. Click in the **Status** field. Under **Table Tools**, on the **Fields tab**, in the **Field Validation group**, notice that the **Required** check box is selected.

4 In the table, click in the **Tech** field. On the **Fields tab**, in the **Field Validation group**, click the **Required** check box. Compare your screen with Figure 4.42.

A message displays stating that the existing data violates the Required property for the Tech field because the field is currently blank.

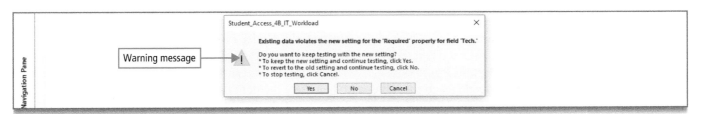

Figure 4.42

5 In the message box, click Cancel. Click the arrow at the right of the **Tech** field, and then select **Ron Lee**.

Activity 4.20 | Setting Default Values for Fields

2.4.7

You can use the Default Value field property to display a value in a field for new records. As you enter data, you can change the ***default value*** in the field to another value within the parameters of any validation rules. Setting a default value for fields that contain the same data for multiple records increases the efficiency of data entry. For example, if all of the employees in the organization live in California, set the default value of the state field to CA. If most of the employees in your organization live in the city of Golden Grove, set the default value of the city field to Golden Grove. If an employee lives in another city, you can type the new value over the displayed default value.

1 Switch to **Design** view. Under **Field Name**, click the **Priority** field. Under **Field Properties**, click in the **Default Value** box, and then type **Low** Switch to **Datasheet** view, and then **Save** 🔲 changes to the table. Notice that the Priority field displays *LOW* in the New Record row.

Setting a default value does not change the data in saved records; the default value will display in new records and will be saved only if nothing else is typed in the field.

2 Switch back to **Design** view. Using the technique you just practiced, for the **Status** field, set the **Default Value** property to **Not Started** If necessary, for the **%Complete** field, set the **Default Value** property to **0**

3 For the **Start Date** field, set the **Default Value** to **3/30/22** Switch to **Datasheet** view, saving changes to the table. Compare your screen with Figure 4.43.

The Status field shows a default value of *Not "Started"*. *Not* is an Access logical operator; therefore, Access excluded the word *Not* from the text expression.

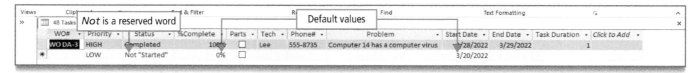

Figure 4.43

4 Switch to **Design** view. Click in the **Status** field. Under **Field Properties**, in the **Default Value** box, select the text, and then type **"Not Started"** Click in the **Start Date** field, and notice that in the **Default Value** box, Access displays the date as **#3/30/2022#**. Switch to **Datasheet** view, saving changes to the table, and then view the default value in the **Status** field.

Inserting quotation marks around *Not Started* informs Access that both words are part of the text expression.

Activity 4.21 | Indexing Fields in a Table

An *index* is a special list created in Access to speed up searches and sorting—such as the index at the back of a book. The index is visible only to Access and not to you, but it helps Access find items much faster. You should index fields that you search frequently, fields that you sort, or fields used to join tables in relationships. Indexes, however, can slow down the creation and deletion of records because the data must be added to or deleted from the index.

1 Switch to **Design** view. Under **Field Name**, click **WO#**. Under **Field Properties**, locate the **Indexed** property box, and notice the entry of **Yes (No Duplicates)**.

> By default, primary key fields are indexed. Because WO# is the primary key field, the field is automatically indexed, and no duplicate values are permitted in this field.

2 Under **Field Name**, click **Tech**. Under **Field Properties**, click in the **Indexed** property box, and then click the displayed **arrow**. Compare your screen with Figure 4.44.

> Three options display for the Indexed property—No, Yes (Duplicates OK), and Yes (No Duplicates).

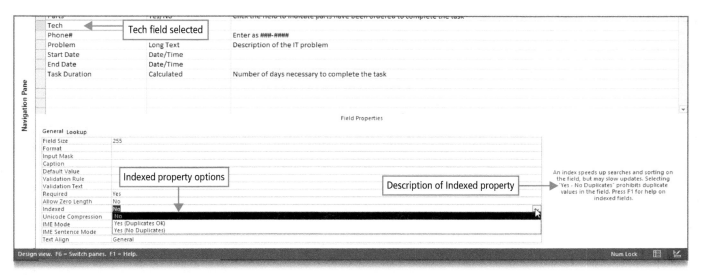

Figure 4.44

3 Click **Yes (Duplicates OK)**.

> By adding an index to the field and allowing duplicates, you create faster searches and sorts on this field, while allowing duplicate data. Because a person may be assigned more than one task, allowing duplicate data is appropriate.

4 Save 🖫 the table design.

5 Under **Table Tools**, on the **Design tab**, in the **Show/Hide group**, click **Indexes**.

> An Indexes dialog box displays the indexes in the current table. Opening the Indexes dialog box is an efficient way to determine the fields that have been indexed in a table.

6 In the **Indexes: 4B Tasks** dialog box, click **Close** ⊠.

Objective 8 | Create Data Validation Rules and Validation Text

GO! Learn How
Video A4-8

You have practiced different techniques to help ensure that data entered into a field is valid. Data types restrict the type of data that can be entered into a field. Field sizes control the number of characters that can be entered into a field. Field properties further control how data is entered into a field, including the use of input masks to require individuals to enter data in a specific way.

Another way to ensure the accuracy of data is by using the Validation Rule property. A *validation rule* is an expression that precisely defines the range of data that will be accepted in a field. An *expression* is a combination of functions, field values, constants, and operators that brings about a result. *Validation text* is the error message that displays when an individual enters a value prohibited by the validation rule.

Activity 4.22 | Creating Data Validation Rules and Validation Text

MOS
2.4.2

In this Activity, you will create data validation rules and validation text for the %Complete field, the Start Date field, and the Priority field.

1 Under **Field Name**, click **%Complete**. Under **Field Properties**, click in the **Validation Rule** box, and then click **Build** ⬚.

The Expression Builder dialog box displays. Recall that the Expression Builder is a feature used to create formulas (expressions) in query criteria, form and report controls, and table validation rules. Take a moment to study the table shown in Figure 4.45, which describes the operators that can be used in building expressions.

Operator	Function	Example
Not	Tests for values NOT meeting a condition.	**Not** > 10 (the same as <=10)
In	Tests for values equal to existing members in a list.	**In** ("High","Normal","Low")
Between . . . And	Tests for a range of values, including the values on each end.	**Between** 0 **And** 100 (the same as >=0 **And** <=100)
Like	Matches pattern strings in Text and Memo fields.	**Like** "Car*"
Is Not Null	Requires individuals to enter values in the field. If used in place of the Required field, you can create validation text that better describes what should be entered in the field.	**Is Not Null** (the same as setting Required property to Yes)
And	Specifies that all of the entered data must fall within the specified limits.	>=#01/01 /2022# **And** <=#03/01 /2022# (date must be between 01/01/2022 and 03/01/2022). Can use And to combine validation rules; for example, **Not** "USA" **And Like** "U*"
Or	Specifies that one of many entries can be accepted.	"High" **Or** "Normal" **Or** "Low"
<	Less than.	<100
<=	Less than or equal to.	<=100
>	Greater than.	>0
>=	Greater than or equal to.	>=0
=	Equal to.	=Date()
<>	Not equal to.	<>#12/24/53#

Figure 4.45

2 In the upper box of the **Expression Builder** dialog box, type **>=0 and <=1** In the **Expression Builder** dialog box, click **OK**. Alternatively, type the expression in the Validation Rule property box.

The %Complete field has a data type of Number and is formatted as a percent. Recall that the Format property changes the way the stored data displays. To convert the display of a number to a percent, Access multiplies the value by 100 and appends the percent sign (%). Therefore, 100% is stored as 1—Access multiples 1 by 100, resulting in 100. A job that is halfway completed—50%—has the value stored as .5 because .5 times 100 equals 50.

ANOTHER WAY When using the Expression Builder to create an expression, you can either type the entire expression or, on the small toolbar in the dialog box, click an existing button, such as the > button, to insert operators into the expression.

3 Click in the **Validation Text** box, and then type **Enter a value between 0 and 100** so that the percentages are reflected accurately. Compare your screen with Figure 4.46.

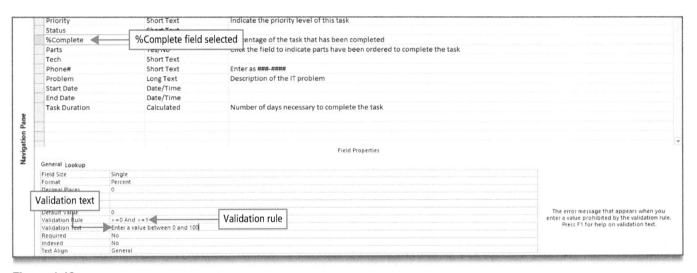

Figure 4.46

4 Under **Field Name**, click **Start Date** to make the field active. Under **Field Properties**, click in the **Validation Rule** box, and then type **>=3/15/2022** Click in the **Validation Text** box, and then type **You must enter a date 3/15/2022 or after** Compare your screen with Figure 4.47.

In expressions, Access inserts a number or pound sign (#) before and after a date. This validation rule ensures that the person entering data cannot enter a date prior to 3/15/2022.

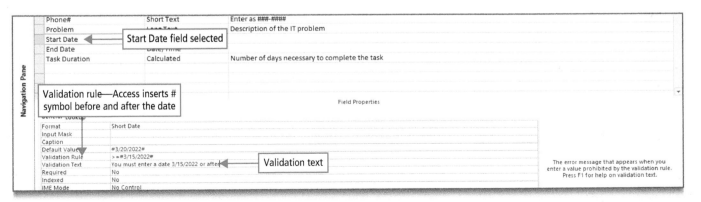

Figure 4.47

5 Under **Field Name**, click **Priority**. Under **Field Properties**, click in the **Validation Rule** box, and then type **in ("High","Normal","Low")** Click in the **Validation Text** box, and then type **You must enter High, Normal, or Low** Compare your screen with Figure 4.48.

The operators are not case sensitive; Access will capitalize the operators when you click in another property box. With the *In* operator, the members of the list must be enclosed in parentheses, and each member must be enclosed in quotation marks and separated from each other by commas. Another way to specify the same validation rule is: "High" Or "Normal" Or "Low".

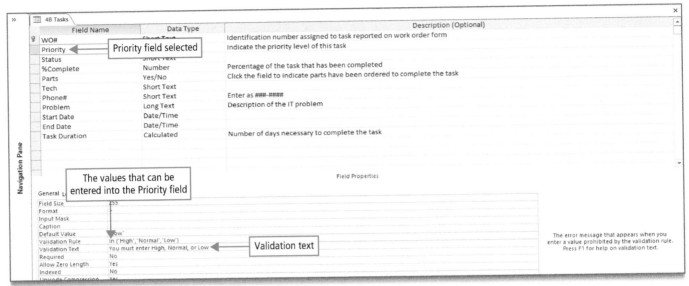

Figure 4.48

6 **Save** ⊟ the changes to the table. Switch to **Datasheet** view. A message displays stating that data integrity rules have changed. Even though you have clicked No in previous message boxes, click **Yes**.

In a large database, you should click Yes to have Access check the data in all of the records before moving on.

Activity 4.23 | **Testing Table Design and Field Properties**

In this Activity, you will add records to the *4B Tasks* table to test the design and field properties.

1 With the **4B Tasks** table open in **Datasheet** view, in the second record in the **WO#** field, type **sk1** and then press ⟨Tab⟩ or ⟨Enter⟩ to go to the next field.

2 In the **Priority** field, type **Medium** to replace the default entry *Low*, and then press ⟨Tab⟩ or ⟨Enter⟩ to go to the next field. The message *You must enter High, Normal, or Low* appears on your screen because the validation rule limits the entry in this field. Compare your screen with Figure 4.49.

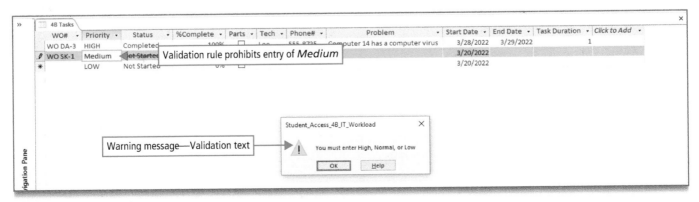

Figure 4.49

3 Click **OK** and type **Normal** in the **Priority** field to replace *Medium*. Press ⌷Tab⌷ or ⌷Enter⌷ to go to the next field.

4 In the **Status** field, **Not Started** automatically appears because it is the default entry. Type **Backordered** and then press ⌷Tab⌷ or ⌷Enter⌷ to move to the next field.

Recall that the Limit to List property setting is set to No for the lookup field, enabling you to type data other than that displayed in the list box. If the purpose of the lookup field is to restrict individuals to entering only certain data, then the Limit to List property setting should be set to Yes.

5 In the **%Complete** field, with the **0%** selected, type **50** and then press ⌷Tab⌷ or ⌷Enter⌷ to move to the next field.

6 In the **Parts** field, click in the check box to add a checkmark and indicate parts are on order to complete the task. Press ⌷Tab⌷ or ⌷Enter⌷ to move to the next field.

7 In the **Tech** field, select **William McCamara**. Press ⌷Tab⌷ or ⌷Enter⌷ to move to the next field.

 ANOTHER WAY   You can locate an entry in a long list faster if you type the first letter of the data for which you are searching. For example, if you are searching for a last name that begins with the letter *m*, when the list displays, type **m** or **M** The selection will move down to the first entry that begins with the letter.

8 In the **Phone#** field, type **aaa** and notice that Access will not allow a letter entry because the input mask you just created requires numbers in this field. Type **5556798** and then press ⌷Tab⌷ or ⌷Enter⌷ to move to the next field.

9 In the **Problem** field, type **Printer B will not print** Press ⌷Tab⌷ or ⌷Enter⌷ to move to the next field.

10 In the **Start Date** field, type **4/5/2022** Press ⌷Tab⌷ or ⌷Enter⌷ three times to move past **Task Duration** and move to the next record.

Notice the calendar icon that appears to the right of the date fields. Clicking the icon enables you to choose a date from a calendar.

End Date is not a required field, so it accepts a blank entry. Because End Date is blank, there is nothing to calculate in the Task Duration field.

11 In the third record, in the **WO#** field, type **da4** and then press ⌷Tab⌷ or ⌷Enter⌷ twice to move to the **Status** field.

12 In the **Status** field, select **Completed**. Press ⌷Tab⌷ or ⌷Enter⌷ to move to the next field.

13 In the **%Complete** field, with the *0%* selected, type **110** and then press ⌷Tab⌷ or ⌷Enter⌷ to move to the next field.

A message *Enter a value between 0 and 100* appears on your screen because the validation rule limits the entry in this field.

14 Click **OK** to close the dialog box. Select the *110%* and type **100** Press [Tab] or [Enter] twice. In the **Tech** field, type **Rukstad** Press [Tab] or [Enter] to move to the next field. Compare your screen with Figure 4.50.

A message *The text you entered isn't an item in the list* appears on your screen. Recall that the Limit to List property setting is set to Yes for the lookup field, which restricts you from entering anything that is not on the list.

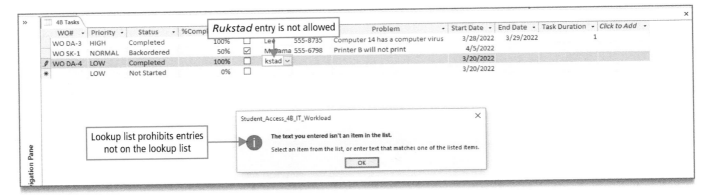

Figure 4.50

15 Click **OK** and select **Angelina Perry** from the lookup list. Press [Tab] or [Enter] to move to the next field.

16 In the **Phone#** field, type **5556313** Press [Tab] or [Enter] to move to the next field. In the **Problem** field, type **Computer 3 needs updates** Press [Tab] or [Enter] to move to the next field.

17 In the **Start Date** field, notice the default date of 3/30/2022, and press [Tab] or [Enter] to move to the next field. In the **End Date** field, type **4/2/2022** Press [Tab] or [Enter] to move to the next field.

Notice the change to the Task Duration field.

18 Apply **Best Fit**, ensuring that all of the field names and all of the field data display. View the table in **Print Preview**, and then change the orientation to **Landscape**. The table will print on two pages.

19 **Close** Print Preview. **Close** the table, saving changes, if necessary. **Close** the database, and **Close** Access.

For Non-MyLab Submissions: Determine What Your Instructor Requires for Submission
As directed by your instructor, submit your completed database file.

20 In **MyLab IT**, locate and click the Grader Project **Access 4B IT Workload**. In **step 3**, under **Upload Completed Assignment**, click **Choose File**. In the **Open** dialog box, navigate to your **Access Chapter 4 folder**, and then click your **Student_Access_4B_IT_Workload** file one time to select it. In the lower right corner of the **Open** dialog box, click **Open**.

The name of your selected file displays above the Upload button.

21 To submit your file to **MyLab IT** for grading, click **Upload**, wait a moment for a green **Success!** message, and then in **step 4**, click the blue **Submit for Grading** button. Click **Close Assignment** to return to your list of **Course Materials**.

You have completed Project 4B **END**

wavebreakmedia/Shutterstock, Monkey Business Images/Fotolia, Ivanko80/Shutterstock, Monkey Business Images/Shutterstock

4

ACCESS

Microsoft Office Specialist (MOS) Skills in This Chapter	
Project 4A	**Project 4B**
2.1.1 Import data into tables	**1.2.3** Set Primary Keys
2.1.3 Import tables from other databases	**2.4.1** Add or remove fields
2.2.3 Add table descriptions	**2.4.2** Add validation rules to fields
2.3.1 Find and replace data	**2.4.3** Change field captions
2.3.2 Sort records	**2.4.4** Change field sizes
2.4.1 Add or remove fields	**2.4.5** Change field data types
2.4.5 Change field data types	**2.4.7** Set default values
	2.4.8 Apply built-in input masks

Build Your E-Portfolio

An E-Portfolio is a collection of evidence, stored electronically, that showcases what you have accomplished while completing your education. Collecting and then sharing your work products with potential employers reflects your academic and career goals. Your completed documents from the following projects are good examples to show what you have learned: 4G, 4K, and 4L.

GO! For Job Success

Topic: Social Media

You know that you should avoid making social media posts about your employer and never post anything negative about your boss or coworkers. There have been incidents, however, when people lost their jobs over social media posts made on their personal accounts during non-work hours that had nothing to do with their employers. Employers who take this action usually do so in response to an employee post that degrades others or involves illegal activity.

g-stockstudio/Shutterstock

Do you think an employer should have the right to fire an employee for making a personal social media post that makes negative comments about coworkers or about the company?

What would you do if you saw a coworker's post that made negative comments about the company?

What is your employer's or school's policy on social media?

End of Chapter

Summary

Backup files are copies of a database created to protect the data. Adding trustworthy storage locations to the Trust Center as secure locations allows the user full use of the content in the database.

Using existing tables as the basis to create new ones eliminates the chances of mistakes in table design, and they can be continually modified and updated to keep the data useful over time.

Creating a table in Design view allows control over the fields in the table, the choice of the data type based on the content, and the ability to set field properties to minimize errors in data entry.

Reducing errors starts with a lookup or calculated data type to minimize manual entry, formatting properties and input masks to ensure accurate presentation, and validation rules to restrict data entry.

GO! Learn It Online

Review the concepts, key terms, and MOS skills in this chapter by completing these online challenges, which you can find at **MyLab IT**.

Chapter Quiz: Answer matching and multiple choice questions to test what you learned in this chapter.

Lessons on the GO!: Learn how to use all the new apps and features as they are introduced by Microsoft.

MOS Prep Quiz: Answer questions to review the MOS skills that you practiced in this chapter.

Project Guide for Access Chapter 4

Your instructor will assign Projects from this list to ensure your learning and assess your knowledge.

	Project Guide for Access Chapter 4		
Project	**Apply Skills from These Chapter Objectives**	**Project Type**	**Project Location**
4A MyLab IT	Objectives 1–4 from Project 4A	**4A Instructional Project (Grader Project)** **Instruction** A guided review of the skills from Project 4A.	In **MyLab IT** and in text
4B MyLab IT	Objectives 5–8 from Project 4B	**4B Instructional Project (Grader Project)** **Instruction** A guided review of the skills from Project 4B.	In **MyLab IT** and in text
4C	Objectives 1–4 from Project 4A	**4C Skills Review (Scorecard Grading)** **Review** A guided review of the skills from Project 4A.	In text
4D	Objectives 5–8 from Project 4B	**4D Skills Review (Scorecard Grading)** **Review** A guided review of the skills from Project 4B.	In text
4E	Objectives 1–4 from Project 4A	**4E Mastery (Scorecard Grading)** **Mastery and Transfer of Learning** A demonstration of your mastery of the skills in Project 4A with extensive decision making.	In text
4F	Objectives 5–8 from Project 4B	**4F Mastery (Scorecard Grading)** **Mastery and Transfer of Learning** A demonstration of your mastery of the skills in Project 4B with extensive decision making.	In text
4G MyLab IT	Objectives 1–8 from Projects 4A and 4B	**4G Mastery (Grader Project)** **Mastery and Transfer of Learning** A demonstration of your mastery of the skills in Projects 4A and 4B with extensive decision making.	In **MyLab IT** and in text
4H	Combination of Objectives from Projects 4A and 4B	**4H GO! Fix It (Scorecard Grading)** **Critical Thinking** A demonstration of your mastery of the skills in Projects 4A and 4B by creating a correct result from a document that contains errors you must find.	IRC
4I	Combination of Objectives from Projects 4A and 4B	**4I GO! Make It (Rubric Grading)** **Critical Thinking** A demonstration of your mastery of the skills in Projects 4A and 4B by creating a result from a supplied picture.	IRC
4J	Combination of Objectives from Projects 4A and 4B	**4J GO! Solve It (Rubric Grading)** **Critical Thinking** A demonstration of your mastery of the skills in Projects 4A and 4B, your decision-making skills, and your critical thinking skills. A task-specific rubric helps you self-assess your result.	IRC
4K	Combination of Objectives from Projects 4A and 4B	**4K GO! Solve It (Rubric Grading)** **Critical Thinking** A demonstration of your mastery of the skills in Projects 4A and 4B, your decision-making skills, and your critical thinking skills. A task-specific rubric helps you self-assess your result.	In text
4L	Combination of Objectives from Projects 4A and 4B	**4L GO! Think (Rubric Grading)** **Critical Thinking** A demonstration of your understanding of the chapter concepts applied in a manner that you would use outside of college. An analytic rubric helps you and your instructor grade the quality of your work by comparing it to the work an expert in the discipline would create.	In text
4M	Combination of Objectives from Projects 4A and 4B	**4M GO! Think (Rubric Grading)** **Critical Thinking** A demonstration of your understanding of the chapter concepts applied in a manner that you would use outside of college. An analytic rubric helps you and your instructor grade the quality of your work by comparing it to the work an expert in the discipline would create.	IRC
4N	Combination of Objectives from Projects 4A and 4B	**4N You and GO! (Rubric Grading)** **Critical Thinking** A demonstration of your understanding of the chapter concepts applied in a manner that you would use in a personal situation. An analytic rubric helps you and your instructor grade the quality of your work.	IRC

Glossary

Glossary of Chapter Key Terms

Append An action that allows you to add data to an existing table.

Back up A feature that creates a copy of the original database to protect against lost data.

Clipboard A temporary storage area in Windows that can hold up to 24 items.

Combo box A box that is a combination of a list box and a text box in a lookup field.

Copy A command that duplicates a selection and places it on the Clipboard.

Data validation Rules that help prevent invalid data entries and ensure data is entered consistently.

Default value A specified value to be automatically entered in a field in new records.

Destination table The table to which records are appended.

Dynamic An attribute applied to data in a database that changes.

Expression A combination of functions, field values, constants, and operators that produces a result.

Expression Builder A feature used to create formulas (expressions) in calculated fields, query criteria, form and report controls, and table validation rules.

Field property An attribute or a characteristic of a field that controls the display and input of data.

Flagged Action of highlighting a word that Spell Check does not recognize from the Office dictionary.

Index A special list created in Access to speed up searches and sorting.

Input Mask A field property that determines the data that can be entered, how the data displays, and how the data is stored.

List Box A control that enables individuals to select from a list but does not allow individuals to type anything that is not on the list.

Lookup Field A list retrieved from another table, query, or list of entered values from which a user can enter data in a table or form; the list may restrict entries in the field.

Multivalued field A field that holds multiple values.

Paste An action of placing text or other objects that have been copied or cut from one location to a new location.

Path The location of a folder or file on your computer or storage device.

Required A field property that ensures a field cannot be left empty.

Source table The table from which records are being extracted or copied.

System tables Tables used to keep track of multiple entries in an attachment field that you cannot work with or view.

Trust Center A security feature that checks documents for macros and digital signatures.

Trusted source A person or organization that you know will not send you databases with malicious content.

Validation rule An expression that precisely defines the range of data that will be accepted in a field.

Validation text The error message that displays when an individual enters a value prohibited by the validation rule.

Zero-length string An entry created by typing two quotation marks with no spaces between them ("") to indicate that no value exists for a required text or memo field.

Chapter Review

Skills Review | Project 4C Commerce

Apply 4A skills from these Objectives:

1. Manage Existing Tables
2. Modify Existing Tables
3. Change Data Types
4. Attach Files to Records

Dario Soto, the City Manager of Golden Grove, has a database of the city's industry information. This database has five tables. The Industries table contains summary information from the other four tables. Each update to an individual industry table would require updates to the summary table. In the following Skills Review, you will redesign the tables, taking advantage of table relationships to avoid entering and storing redundant data. Your completed Navigation Pane will look similar Figure 4.51.

Project Files

For Project 4C, you will need the following files:

a04C_Commerce

a04C_GCH_Contacts

You will save your databases as:

Lastname_Firstname_4C_Commerce

Lastname_Firstname_4C_Commerce_2022-4-30 (date will vary)

Project Results

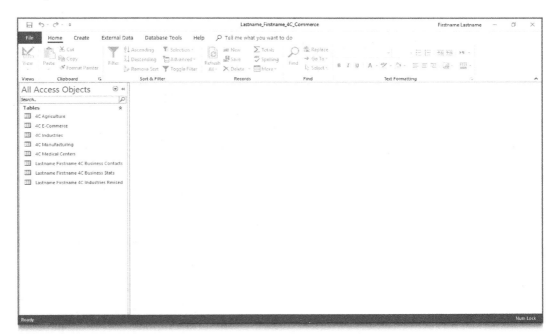

Figure 4.51

(continues on next page)

Chapter Review

1 Start Access. Locate and open the **a04C_ Commerce** database.

a. **Save** the database in the **Microsoft Access Database** format in your **Access Chapter 4** folder as **Lastname_Firstname_4C_Commerce**

b. On the **File tab**, click **Save As**, and then, under **Save Database As**, double-click **Back Up Database**. In the **Save As** dialog box, navigate to the drive on which you will be storing your folders and projects for this chapter, and then click **Save** to accept the default name.

2 In the **Navigation Pane**, double-click **4C Industries**. Take a moment to review the contents of the table. Close the **Navigation Pane**.

a. Click the **File tab**, and click **Save As**. Under **File Types**, double-click **Save Object As**.

b. In the displayed **Save As** dialog box, under **Save '4C Industries' to**, type **Lastname Firstname 4C Industries Revised** and then click **OK**.

3 Point to the **Business #5** field name until the ↓ pointer displays. Hold down the left mouse button and drag to the left to the **Business #1** field name to select the five fields. On the **Home tab**, in the **Records group**, click **Delete**. In the displayed message box, click **Yes** to permanently delete the fields and the data.

4 Switch to **Design** view. To the left of **Industry Code**, click the **row selector** box, and then, under **Table Tools**, on the **Design tab**, in the **Tools group**, click **Primary Key**. **Close** the table, saving any changes. **Open** the **Navigation Pane**.

5 In the Navigation Pane, click **4C Agriculture**.

a. On the **Home tab**, in the **Clipboard group**, click **Copy**.

b. On the **Home tab**, in the **Clipboard group**, click **Paste**.

c. In the **Paste Table As** dialog box, under **Table Name**, type **Lastname Firstname 4C Business Contacts** Under **Paste Options**, verify that the **Structure and Data** option button is selected, and then click **OK**.

6 In the Navigation Pane, click **4C Manufacturing**.

a. On the **Home tab**, in the **Clipboard group**, click **Copy**, and then click **Paste**.

b. In the **Paste Table As** dialog box, under **Table Name**, type **Lastname Firstname 4C Business Contacts** Under **Paste Options**, click the **Append Data to Existing Table** option button, and then click **OK**.

c. Using the same procedure, append the **4C Medical Centers** table and the **4C E-Commerce** table to the **Lastname Firstname 4C Business Contacts** table.

7 Open the **4C Business Contacts** table and **Save As Lastname Firstname 4C Business Statistics** One table will contain only contact information, and the other table will contain only statistical information.

8 In the **4C Business Statistics** table, select the **Business Name** field, and then press Delete. Click **Yes** to delete the field and data. If necessary, scroll to the right to display the **Address, City, State, ZIP, Contact,** and **Phone#** fields. Select all six fields, and then press Delete. Click **Yes** to delete the fields and data.

a. Switch to **Design** view, and click in the **Business ID** field. Under **Table Tools**, on the **Design tab**, in the **Tools group**, click **Primary Key**. Change the data type of the **First Year** field to **Number**. **Save** the changes, and then switch to **Datasheet** view.

b. Click in the **Employees** field in the first record. On the **Home tab**, in the **Find group**, click **Find**. In the **Find What** box, type **12** In the Look In box, select **Current field**, if necessary. Click **Find Next** to select the next occurrence in the current field. Click **Cancel** in the **Find and Replace** dialog box.

c. Click the **Record Selector** box to select the record containing *12*. On the **Home tab**, in the **Records group**, click **Delete**. In the displayed message box, click **Yes** to permanently delete the record.

d. Apply **Best Fit** to all columns. Close the table, saving changes if necessary.

9 Open the **4C Business Contacts** table. Close the **Navigation Pane**. Select the **Employees, Gross Sales,** and **First Year** fields. On the **Home tab**, in the **Records group**, click **Delete**. In the displayed message box, click **Yes** to permanently delete the fields and data.

10 Click the **Business Name** field name. Under **Table Tools**, on the **Fields tab**, in the **Add & Delete group**, click **Short Text**. Type **Industry Code** to replace **Field1**, and then press Enter. **Save** your work.

a. In the first record, click in the **Industry Code** field. **Open** the **Navigation Pane**, and open the **4C Industries Revised** table. Under **Industry Category**, locate the record for **Agriculture**, and notice the **Industry Code** of AGR. On the **tab row**, click the **4C Business Contacts tab** to make the table active. In the **Business ID** of **189018**, in the **Industry Code** field, type **AGR** Locate the **Business ID** of **675234**, and then in the **Industry Code** field, type **AGR** Locate the **Business ID** of **234155**, type **AGR**

(continues on next page)

Chapter Review

b. Using the techniques you just practiced, locate the **Industry Codes** for the **Manufacturing, Medical Center**, and **E-Commerce** Industry Categories. In Business IDs **479728, 966657, 399740, 927685,** and **258679**, type **MAN** In Business IDs **295738, 252479, 420879,** and **362149**, type **MED** and then in Business IDs **420943, 129741,** and **329718**, type **INT**

11 In the navigation area at the bottom of the window, in the **Search** box, type **adv** Click at the end of **AdventuCom**. Press ⎵Spacebar and type **Resources** Move to the next record to save the changes.

12 Switch the **4C Business Contacts** table to **Design** view. With the insertion point in the **Business ID** field, under **Table Tools**, on the **Design tab**, in the **Tools group**, click **Primary Key**. **Save** the changes.

13 To the left of **Contact**, click the **row selector** box. Hold down the left mouse button and drag the field up until you see a dark horizontal line between *Industry Code* and *Address*, and then release the mouse button. **Save** the changes.

14 Click in the blank field name box under **Phone#**, type **Contact List** and then press ⌧Tab to move to the **Data Type** box. Click the **Data Type arrow**, and click **Attachment**.

15 Switch to **Datasheet** view, saving changes to the table.

a. In the fourth record (*Greater Community Hospital*), double-click in the **Attachment** field. In the displayed **Attachments** dialog box, click **Add**.

b. Navigate to the location where the student data files for this textbook are stored. In the **Choose File** dialog box, double-click **a04C_GCH_Contacts**. In the **Attachments** dialog box, click **OK**.

16 On the **Home tab**, in the **Records group**, click **Spelling**. Ignore the entries until it selects *Makets*, and **Change** the spelling to *Markets*. Ignore the other names it selects as the process continues. Click **OK** to continue.

17 Apply **Best Fit** to all columns to view the field names and data. View the table in **Print Preview**, and then change the orientation to **Landscape**.

18 On the **tab row**, right-click any table tab, and then click **Close All**, saving changes if necessary. Resize the **Navigation pane** so all object names display fully. **Close** the database, and **Close** Access.

19 As directed by your instructor, submit your database for grading.

You have completed Project 4C **END**

Chapter Review

Skills Review	**Project 4D City Airport**

Apply 4B skills from these Objectives:

5. Create a Table in Design View
6. Create a Lookup Field
7. Set Field Properties
8. Create Data Validation Rules and Validation Text

Dario Soto, City Manager of Golden Grove, California, has created a table to keep track of airport personnel. In the following Skills Review, you will add a table that stores records about the employees, modify the properties, and customize the fields in the table. You will add features to the database table that will help to reduce data entry errors and that will make data entry easier. Your completed Navigation Pane will look similar to the table shown in Figure 4.52.

Project Files

For Project 4D, you will need the following file:

a04D_City_Airport

You will save your database as:

Lastname_Firstname_4D_City_Airport

Project Results

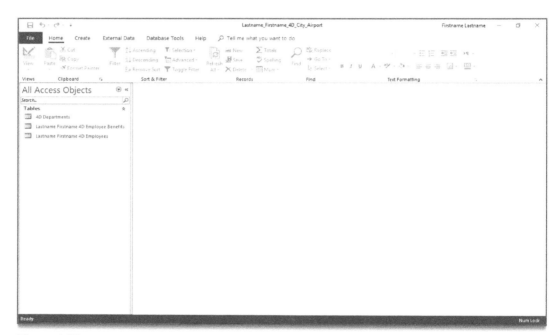

Figure 4.52

(continues on next page)

Chapter Review

1 Start Access. Locate and open the **a04D_City_ Airport** database. **Save** the database in the **Microsoft Access Database** format in your **Access Chapter 4** folder as **Lastname_Firstname_4D_City_Airport**

2 Close the **Navigation Pane**. On the **Create tab**, in the **Tables group**, click **Table Design** to open an empty table in Design view.

a. In the first **Field Name** box, type **Empl ID** and press Tab.Under **Table Tools**, on the **Design tab**, in the **Tools group**, click **Primary Key**. Press F6 to move to the **Field Properties** pane at the bottom of the screen. In the **Field Size** box, type **6** to replace the 255.

b. In the second **Field Name** box, type **Vacation** In the **Data Type** box, click the **arrow**, and then click **Number**. Press Tab to move to the **Description** box. Type **Indicate how many weeks of vacation the employee receives per year** Press Tab or Enter to move to the next field.

c. In the third **Field Name** box, type **Coverage** In the **Data Type** box, click the **arrow**, and from the displayed list of data types, click **Lookup Wizard**. In the first **Lookup Wizard** dialog box, click **I will type in the values that I want** option button, and then click **Next**. Verify the number of columns is **1**. Click in the first row under **Col1**, type **Emp** and then press Tab or ↓ to save the first item. In the next three rows type the following data: **Emp+C** and **Fam** and **None** and then click **Next**. In the final dialog box, click **Finish**.

d. Click in the **Description** box, and type **Indicate the type of insurance coverage the employee has selected**

e. Click in the fourth **Field Name** box, and type **LT Care** Click the **Data Type arrow**, and then click **Number**. Press Tab to move to the **Description** box. Type **Indicate the benefit period option selected by the employee**

f. Press F6 to move to the **Field Properties** pane at the bottom of the screen, and then click in the **Validation Rule** box. Click **Build**. In the upper box of the **Expression Builder** dialog box, type **>=0 and <=2** and then click **OK**. Click in the **Validation Text** box, and then type **Enter a value between 0 and 2** and press Enter.

g. Click in the fifth **Field Name** box, and type **401K** Click the **Data Type arrow**, and then click **Yes/ No**. Press Tab to move to the **Description** box. Type **Indicate whether or not the employee participates in the 401K plan**

h. Save the table as **Lastname Firstname 4D Employee Benefits** Switch to **Datasheet** view and enter these records. **Close** the table.

Empl ID	Vacation	Coverage	LT Care	401K
589734	3	Emp	0	Yes
986458	2	None	1	No
564897	2	Emp+C	2	Yes
233311	4	Fam	1	Yes
722859	2	Fam	2	Yes

3 In the **Navigation Pane**, under **Tables**, rename the **4D Employees** table by adding your **Lastname Firstname** to the beginning of the table name. Double-click **4D Employees** to open the table. **Close** the **Navigation Pane**.

a. Switch to **Design** view. Make **Empl ID** the **Primary Key** field. Change the data type for the **Date Hired** field to **Date/Time**. Change the data type for the **Annual Salary** field to **Currency**. Change the data type for the **Office E-mail** field to **Hyperlink**. **Save** your work. You will see two message boxes warning about data. Click **Yes** to continue in both.

b. In the **Dept** field, click in the **Data Type** box, click the **arrow**, and then click **Lookup Wizard**. In the first **Lookup Wizard** dialog box, verify that **I want the lookup field to get the values from another table or query** option button is selected. Click **Next**. Select the **4D Departments** table. Click **Next** to display the third **Lookup Wizard** dialog box. Under **Available Fields**, with **Department** selected, click **Add Field** to move the field to the **Selected Fields** box.

(continues on next page)

ACCESS

4

Chapter Review

c. Click **Next** to display the fourth **Lookup Wizard** dialog box. In the **1** box, click the **arrow**, and then click **Department**. Leave the sort order as **Ascending**. Click **Next** twice to display the sixth and final **Lookup Wizard** dialog box. Under **What label would you like for your lookup field?**, leave the default of **Dept** and be sure that **Allow Multiple Values** is *not* selected. Click **Finish**. Click **Yes** to save the table. Click **Yes** to close the message box.

d. Under **Field Name**, click **Office Phone**. Under **Field Properties**, click in the **Input Mask** box and then click **Build**.

e. In the displayed **Input Mask Wizard** dialog box, with **Phone Number** selected, click **Edit List**. In the **Customize Input Mask Wizard** dialog box, click **New (blank) record**. In the **Description** box, type **Phone Number with Extension** In the **Input Mask** box, type **!(999) 000-0000 \X999** Click in the **Placeholder** box, and then change _ to # Click in the **Sample Data** box, and type **714 5551234236** In the **Customize Input Mask Wizard** dialog box, click **Close**.

f. Under **Input Mask**, scroll down, click **Phone Number with Extension**, and then click **Next**. Verify that # is displayed as the placeholder character, and then click **Next**. The next wizard screen enables you to decide how you want to store the data. Verify that the **Without the symbols in the mask, like this** option button is selected, and then click **Next**. In the final wizard screen, click **Finish**.

g. Click in the **Date Hired** field. Under **Field Properties**, click in the **Format** box, and then click the **Format arrow**. From the displayed list, click **Medium Date**. Click in the **Required** box. Click the **Required arrow**, and then click **Yes**. Click in the **Monthly Earn** field. Under **Field Properties**, click in the **Expression** box, and edit the expression to read **[Annual Salary]/12** Click the **Result Type arrow**, and then select **Currency** from the displayed list.

h. Under **Field Name**, click **State**. Under **Field Properties**, click in the **Format** box, and then type **>** Click in the **Default Value** box, and then type **CA** Using the same technique, set the **Default Value** of the **City** field to **Golden Grove**

i. Under **Field Name**, click **Last Name**. Under **Field Properties**, click in the **Indexed** property box, and then click the displayed **arrow**. Click **Yes (Duplicates OK)**. **Save** your work. In the message box, click **Yes** to test the existing data with the new rules. Under **Table Tools**, on the **Design tab**, in the **Show/Hide group**, click the **Indexes** button.

4 Switch to **Datasheet** view, saving changes to the table if necessary. You will see a message box warning that some data may be lost. Click **Yes** to continue.

a. Click **New (blank) record**. Type the following data:

Empl ID	543655
Title	Mr.
First Name	Mark
Last Name	Roberts
Street	1320 Woodbriar Court
City	Golden Grove
State	CA
Postal Code	96265
Dept	Operations
Date Hired	9/23/2019
Salary	92000
Office Phone	7145550167101
Office E-Mail	mroberts@goldengrove.gov

b. Apply **Best Fit** to all columns so all data displays fully.

5 **Open** the **Navigation Pane**. Resize the Navigation Pane so all object names display fully. **Close** the database, saving changes if necessary, and **Close** Access.

6 As directed by your instructor, submit your database for grading.

You have completed Project 4D **END**

Mastering Access | Project 4E Cultural Events

Apply 4A skills from these Objectives:

1. Manage Existing Tables
2. Modify Existing Tables
3. Change Data Types
4. Attach Files to Records

In the following Mastering Access project, you will manage and modify tables in a database that contains cultural information about the city of Golden Grove. The database will be used by the arts council. Your completed Navigation Pane will look similar to Figure 4.53.

Project Files

For Project 4E, you will need the following files:

a04E_Cultural_Events
a04E_Concert_Flyer
a04E_Quilts_Flyer

You will save your database as:

Lastname_Firstname_4E_Cultural_Events

Project Results

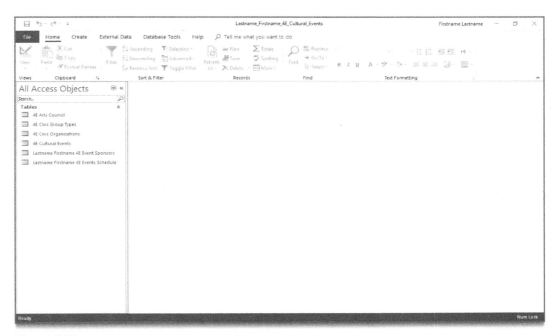

Figure 4.53

(continues on next page)

Content-Based Assessments (Mastery and Transfer of Learning)

1 Start Access. Locate and open the **a04E_Cultural_Events** file. **Save** the database in the **Microsoft Access Database** format in your **Access Chapter 4** folder as **Lastname_Firstname_4E_Cultural_Events**

2 Open the **4E Cultural Events** table. In **Backstage** view, click **Save As**. Under **File Types**, double-click **Save Object As**. In the **Save As** dialog box, type **Lastname Firstname 4E Events Schedule** Click **OK**.

3 Make a second copy of the table. Name the table **Lastname Firstname 4E Event Sponsors**

4 With the **4E Event Sponsors** table open in **Datasheet** view, select the first four columns, the **Event Name** field through the **Cost** field. Press Delete, and then click **Yes** to delete the fields and data. Switch to **Design** view, and then make the **Org ID** field the **Primary Key** field.

5 Insert a row above the **Members** field, and add a field named **Chamber** with a data type of **Yes/No**. Switch to **Datasheet** view, saving the changes.

6 In **Datasheet** view, click the **Chamber** field to place a checkmark for the **Downtown Merchants Association**, **Quilt Guild**, and **Garden Club of Golden Grove**. If you are instructed to submit this result, create a paper printout or PDF electronic image of the **4E Event Sponsors** table in **Landscape** orientation. It will print on two pages.

7 Open the **4E Events Schedule** table in **Datasheet** view. **Close the Navigation Pane**. Select and delete the following fields: **Civic Name**, **Org Type**, **Members**, **Address**, **City**, **State**, **Postal Code**, **Contact**, and **Phone#**.

8 Using **Find**, find **1876** in the **Event Name** field; in the **Match** field, select **Any Part of Field**, if necessary. Select and delete the record. On the **Home tab**, in the **Records group**, click **Spelling**. Make any spelling corrections necessary in the table.

9 In the navigation area at the bottom of the window, search for *k* in the records. When it stops at *Make Golden Grove Beautiful*, delete the word **Make** and the space following the word from the Event Name.

10 Switch to **Design** view. Select the **Event Date** field, and, holding down the left mouse button, drag it up until it is between **Event Name** and **Location**. Add a **Flyer** field at the bottom of the field list using an **Attachment** data type.

11 Switch to **Datasheet** view, saving the changes to the table design. Attach the **a04E_Concert_Flyer** to the *Beachside Singers Holiday Concert* record, and add the **a04E_Quilts_Flyer** to the *Annual Quilt Show* record. Apply **Best Fit** to all columns to display all of the data and field names. **Close** the table, saving changes if necessary.

12 **Open** the **Navigation Pane** and resize it so all object names display fully. **Close** the database, and **Close** Access.

13 As directed by your instructor, submit your database for grading.

You have completed Project 4E | **END**

Content-Based Assessments (Mastery and Transfer of Learning)

Mastering Access | Project 4F Library System

Dario Soto, City Manager, has asked Ron Singer, Database Manager for the city, to improve the library database. In the following Mastering Access project, you will create a table that stores records about the library programs in Design view, and then modify the properties and customize the fields in the table. You will add features to the database table that will help to reduce data entry errors and that will make data entry easier. Your completed Navigation Pane will look similar to the table shown in Figure 4.54.

Apply 4B skills from these Objectives:

5. Create a Table in Design View
6. Create a Lookup Field
7. Set Field Properties
8. Create Data Validation Rules and Validation Text

Project Files

For Project 4F, you will need the following file:

a04F_Library_System

You will save your database as:

Lastname_Firstname_4F_Library_System

Project Results

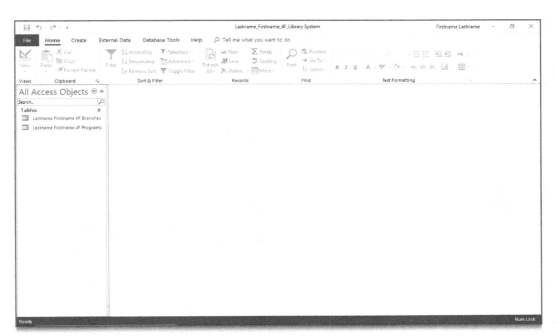

Figure 4.54

(continues on next page)

Content-Based Assessments (Mastery and Transfer of Learning)

1 Start Access. Locate and open the **a04F_Library_System** file. **Save** the database in the **Microsoft Access Database** format in your **Access Chapter 4** folder as **Lastname_Firstname_4F_Library_System** Rename the table by adding your **Lastname Firstname** to the beginning of the table name. **Close** the **Navigation Pane**.

2 Create a table in **Design** view. In the first **Field Name** box, type **Program ID** and set the field as the **Primary Key**. Change the **Field size** to **5**

3 In the second **Field Name** box, type **Activity** In the **Field Properties**, click the **Indexed arrow**, and then select **Yes (Duplicates OK)**. Make it a **Required** field.

4 In the third **Field Name** box, type **Branch** and select **Lookup Wizard** as the data type. Verify that **I want the lookup field to get the values from another table or query** is selected. Click **Next**. There is only one other table in this database from which to choose—*4F Branches*—and it is selected. Click **Next**. Add **Branch** to the Selected Fields. Click **Next**. In the **1** box, click the **arrow**, and then click **Branch**. Leave the sort order as **Ascending**. Click **Next** two times. Under **What label would you like for your lookup field?**, accept the

default of **Branch**, and then verify that **Enable Data Integrity** and **Allow Multiple Values** are *not* selected. Click **Finish**. In the message box, click **Yes**.

5 **Save** the table as **Lastname Firstname 4F Programs**

6 In the fourth **Field Name** box, type **Activity Date** and then select the **Date/Time** data type. Click in the **Format** box, and select **Long Date**.

7 In the fifth **Field Name** box, type **Age Group** Set the **Default Value** to **Teen** In the **Validation Rule** box, type **"Child" OR "Teen" OR "Adult"** For the **Validation Text**, type **Entry must be Child, Teen, or Adult**

8 In the sixth **Field Name** box, type **Prereq** Select the **Yes/No** data type. In the **Description** box, type **Click to indicate a prerequisite is required before enrolling in this activity**

9 In the seventh **Field Name** box, type **Max** and select **Number** data type. Change the **Field Size** to **Integer**. In the **Validation Rule** box, type **<=20** In the **Validation Text** box, type **Participation is limited to 20**

10 Switch to **Datasheet** view, saving the changes to the design. Populate the table with the following data:

Program ID	Activity	Branch	Activity Date	Age Group	Prereq	Max
CC23	Mystery Book Club	Central	3/16/22	Adult	Yes	8
MM15	FrightFest	Memorial	10/31/22	Teen	No	20
WA63	Laptime Stories	West Side	9/8/22	Child	No	10
MM21	Young Writer	Memorial	7/15/22	Teen	No	12
CC44	Holiday History	Central	12/1/22	Adult	No	10

11 Apply **Best Fit** to all columns so all data is fully visible. If you are instructed to submit this result, create a paper printout or PDF electronic image of the **4F Programs** table in **Landscape** orientation. **Close** the table, saving the changes. **Open** the **Navigation Pane**.

12 Open the **4F Branches** table in **Design** view. In the **Postal Code** field, under **Input Mask**, click **Build**. If prompted, **Save** the table. In the **Input Mask Wizard** dialog box, under **Input Mask**, select **Zip Code**, and then click **Next**. Accept the default "_" as the placeholder character. Click **Next**. Store the data without the symbols in the mask, click **Next**, and then click **Finish**.

13 Switch to **Datasheet** view, saving the changes to the table design. Update the **Postal Code** for each branch as shown.

Central	962650001
Memorial	962700030
West Side	962680010

14 Apply **Best Fit** to all columns to display all of the data and field names. **Save** the changes. **Close** the table.

15 Resize the **Navigation Pane** so all object names are fully visible, if necessary. **Close** the database, and **Close** Access.

16 As directed by your instructor, submit your database for grading.

You have completed Project 4F | END

4
ACCESS

Apply 4A and 4B skills from these Objectives:

1. Manage Existing Tables
2. Modify Existing Tables
3. Change Data Types
4. Attach Files to Records
5. Create a Table in Design View
6. Create a Lookup Field
7. Set Field Properties
8. Create Data Validation Rules and Validation Text

Yvonne Guillen is the Chair of the Parks and Recreation Commission for Golden Grove, California. The database she is using has separate tables that should be combined. In the following Mastering Access project, you will combine these tables into a facilities table. You will modify the existing tables, set field properties to ensure more accurate data entry, and add driving directions to the facilities as an attached document. You will also create a table to organize youth sports programs that use the facilities. Your completed Navigation Pane will look similar to Figure 4.55.

Project Files for MyLab IT Grader

1. In your **MyLab IT** course, locate and click **Access 4G Parks and Recreation**, Download Materials, and then Download All Files.
2. Extract the zipped folder to your Access Chapter 4 folder. Close the Grader download screens.
3. Take a moment to open the downloaded **Access_4G_Parks_Recreation_Instructions**; note any recent updates to the book.

Project Results

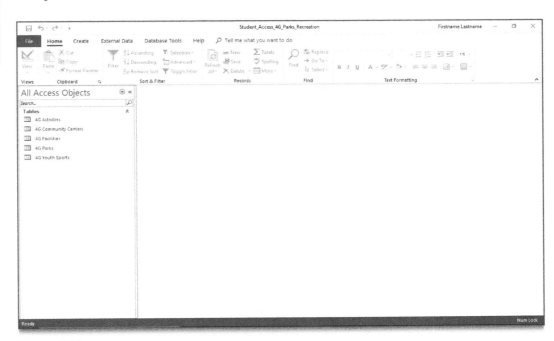

Figure 4.55

For Non-MyLab Submissions
For Project 4G, you will need the following files:
a04G_Parks_Recreation
a04G_Biscayne_Park
a04G_Hugo_West
After you have saved your database, open it to launch Access. On the next page, begin with Step 2.
After Step 15, submit your file as directed by your instructor.

Start with an Access Data File
In your Access Chapter 4 folder, save your workbook as:
Lastname_Firstname_4G_Parks_Recreation

(continues on next page)

Content-Based Assessments (Mastery and Transfer of Learning)

1 Start Access. Navigate to your **Access Chapter 4 folder**, and then double-click the Access file that you downloaded from **MyLab IT** that displays your name—**Student_Access_4G_Parks_Recreation**.

2 Select the **4G Community Centers** table. **Copy** and **Paste** the table. Name the table **4G Facilities** In the **Paste Table As** dialog box, verify the **Structure and Data** option is selected, and then click **OK**.

3 Select the **4G Parks** table. **Copy** and **Paste** the table. In the **Table Name** box, type **4G Facilities** Under **Paste Options**, select **Append Data to Existing Table**, and then click **OK** to create one table that contains all of the facility information for the Parks and Recreation Department.

4 Open the **4G Facilities** table in **Design** view. **Close** the **Navigation Pane**. Change the **Data Type** for the **Entry Fee** field to **Currency**. In the **Contact** field, change the field size to **20**

5 Add a new **Monthly Pass** field between the **Entry Fee** and **Contact** fields, and use a data type of **Calculated**. In the **Expression Builder** dialog box, type **[Entry Fee]*15** Change the **Result Type** to **Currency**.

6 Below the **Phone#** field add a new **Directions** field to the table and assign a data type of **Attachment**. In the description box, type **Directions to facility**

7 Select the **Phone#** field. In the **Input Mask** box, type **!000-0000** Change the field size to **8** Set the **Field Property** of **Required** to **Yes**.

8 Switch to **Datasheet** view. Save your changes. You will see a message box warning that some data may be lost. Click **Yes** to continue. You will also see a message explaining that data integrity rules have changed. Click **No** to testing the data with the new rules.

9 In the **Biscayne Park** record, double-click in the **Attachment** field, and then from the student data files, attach **a04G_Biscayne_Park**. Click **OK**.

10 Using the same technique, for the **Hugo West Center**, add the directions that are in the **a04G_Hugo_West** file.

11 Create a table in **Design** view. In the first **Field Name** box, type **Sport ID** Select an **AutoNumber** data type. Set this as the primary key.

12 In the second **Field Name** box, type **Sport** In the third **Field Name** box, type **Season** and select the **Lookup Wizard** data type. Type the following four items into the first column in the lookup list: **Winter Spring Summer** and **Fall** Save the table as **4G Youth Sports**

13 Switch to **Datasheet** view, and populate the table with the following data.

Sport ID	Sport	Season
1	**t-ball**	**Spring**
2	**baseball**	**Summer**
3	**fast pitch softball**	**Fall**
4	**basketball**	**Winter**
5	**volleyball**	**Fall**

14 Apply **Best Fit** to all columns to display all of the data and field names.

15 **Close** the tables, saving changes if necessary. **Close** the database, and **Close** Access.

16 In **MyLab IT**, locate and click the Grader Project **Access 4G Parks and Recreation**. In **step 3**, under **Upload Completed Assignment**, click **Choose File**. In the **Open** dialog box, navigate to your **Access Chapter 4 folder**, and then click your **Student_Access_4G_Parks_Recreation** file one time to select it. In the lower right corner of the **Open** dialog box, click **Open**.

17 To submit your file to **MyLab IT** for grading, click **Upload**, wait a moment for a green **Success!** message, and then in **step 4**, click the blue **Submit for Grading** button. Click **Close Assignment** to return to your list of **Course Materials**.

You have completed Project 4G END

Content-Based Assessments (Critical Thinking)

Apply a combination of the 4A and 4B skills.

GO! Fix It	Project 4H Permit Applications	IRC
GO! Make It	Project 4I Medical Centers	IRC
GO! Solve It	Project 4J Fire Department	IRC
GO! Solve It	Project 4K City Zoo	

Project Files

For Project 4K, you will need the following files:

a04K_City_Zoo
a04K_Dragonfly

You will save your database as:

Lastname_Firstname_4K_City_Zoo

Mandi Cartwright, Public Relations Director of Golden Grove, California, and City Manager Dario Soto are meeting with Mayor Sheila Kehoe to discuss the funding for the city zoo. The Corporate and Foundation Council provides citizens and corporations with a partnering opportunity to support the city zoo. Mandi has outlined a database to organize the sponsorships. From the student files that accompany this textbook, open the **a04K_City_Zoo** database file, and then save the database in your **Access Chapter 4** folder as **Lastname_Firstname_4K_City_Zoo**

In this project, you will open the **a04K_City_Zoo** database and examine the tables. Rename the tables by adding your **Lastname Firstname** to each table name. Resize the Navigation Pane so all object names are fully visible. Modify the *4K Sponsored Events* table to eliminate redundancy between it and the *4K Sponsors* table. Also, change data types to match the data, including a lookup field for the Sponsor field, and apply an applicable input mask to the Event Date. In the *4K Sponsors* table, create data validation for sponsor type; it must be Individual, Family, or Corporate. In the *4K Sponsors* table, use the *4K Sponsor Levels* table as a lookup field. To the *4K Sponsor Levels* table, add an attachment field named Logo. Add the **a04K_Dragonfly** file from the student data files to the appropriate record. As directed by your instructor, submit your database for grading.

		Performance Level		
		Exemplary	**Proficient**	**Developing**
Performance Element	**Modify the 4K Sponsored Events table to eliminate redundancy**	Table was modified with correct fields in easy-to-follow format.	Table was modified with no more than two missing elements.	Table was modified with more than two missing elements.
	Change data types and field properties in the 4K Sponsored Events and 4K Sponsors tables	Data types and field properties were assigned effectively for the data that each field will hold.	Data types and field properties were assigned with no more than two missing or incorrect elements.	Data types and field properties were assigned with more than two missing or incorrect elements.
	Add field to 4K Sponsor Levels table and populate field	Field was added with correct data type and correct data was added to the table.	Field was added with no more than two missing or incorrect elements.	Field was added with more than two missing or incorrect elements.

You have completed Project 4K | END

Outcomes-Based Assessments (Critical Thinking)

Rubric

The following outcomes-based assessments are open-ended assessments. That is, there is no specific correct result; your result will depend on your approach to the information provided. Make Professional Quality your goal. Use the following scoring rubric to guide you in how to approach the problem, and then to evaluate how well your approach solves the problem.

The *criteria*—Software Mastery, Content, Format and Layout, and Process—represent the knowledge and skills you have gained that you can apply to solving the problem. The *levels of performance*—Professional Quality, Approaching Professional Quality, or Needs Quality Improvements—help you and your instructor evaluate your result.

	Your completed project is of Professional Quality if you:	Your completed project is Approaching Professional Quality if you:	Your completed project Needs Quality Improvements if you:
1-Software Mastery	Choose and apply the most appropriate skills, tools, and features and identify efficient methods to solve the problem.	Choose and apply some appropriate skills, tools, and features, but not in the most efficient manner.	Choose inappropriate skills, tools, or features, or are inefficient in solving the problem.
2-Content	Construct a solution that is clear and well organized, contains content that is accurate, appropriate to the audience and purpose, and is complete. Provide a solution that contains no errors of spelling, grammar, or style.	Construct a solution in which some components are unclear, poorly organized, inconsistent, or incomplete. Misjudge the needs of the audience. Have some errors in spelling, grammar, or style, but the errors do not detract from comprehension.	Construct a solution that is unclear, incomplete, or poorly organized, contains some inaccurate or inappropriate content, and contains many errors of spelling, grammar, or style. Do not solve the problem.
3-Format and Layout	Format and arrange all elements to communicate information and ideas, clarify function, illustrate relationships, and indicate relative importance.	Apply appropriate format and layout features to some elements, but not others. Overuse features, causing minor distraction.	Apply format and layout that does not communicate information or ideas clearly. Do not use format and layout features to clarify function, illustrate relationships, or indicate relative importance. Use available features excessively, causing distraction.
4-Process	Use an organized approach that integrates planning, development, self-assessment, revision, and reflection.	Demonstrate an organized approach in some areas, but not others; or, use an insufficient process of organization throughout.	Do not use an organized approach to solve the problem.

Apply a combination of the 4A and 4B skills.

GO! Think   Project 4L Streets Department

Project Files

For Project 4L, you will need the following files:

a04L_Streets_Department

a04L_Work_Order

You will save your database as:

Lastname_Firstname_4L_Streets_Department

    In this project, you will examine the database that has been created to help the Deputy City Manager of Infrastructure Services organize and track the constituent work requests for the city street repairs. Save the database as **Lastname_Firstname_4L_ Streets_Department** Rename all of the tables by adding your **Lastname Firstname** to the beginning of each table name. Resize the Navigation Pane so all object names display fully. Modify the design of the *4L Work Requests* table. Set the Work Order # field as the primary key field, and then create an input mask to match the data for that field in the first record. For the Type field, create a lookup table using the *4L Repair Types* table. In the Repair Team field, create a Lookup Wizard data type using the *4L Repair Teams* table. In the Priority field, create a validation rule requiring an entry of A, B, or C. Explain this rule with appropriate validation text. Add a long text field called Description between Type and Repair Team. Open **a04L_Work_Order**, and then use the data to add information to the first record in the table. Use today's date as the start date, and leave the completion date blank. Add an attachment field to the table, and then add **a04L_ Work_Order** as the attachment. As directed by your instructor, submit your database for grading.

You have completed Project 4L | END |

GO! Think   Project 4M Police Department   IRC

You and GO!   Project 4N Club Directory   IRC

Enhancing Queries

5
ACCESS 2019

Imfoto/Shutterstock

In This Chapter   GO! To Work with Access

Queries can do more than extract data from tables and other queries. You can create queries to perform special functions, such as calculate and summarize numeric data. Queries can also be used to find duplicate and unmatched records in tables, which is useful for maintaining data integrity. You can create a parameter query, where an individual is prompted for the criteria each time the query is run, for more flexibility in the data extracted. Queries can create additional tables in the database, append records to an existing table, delete records from a table, and modify data in the tables based on specific criteria.

S-Boards, Inc., a surf and snowboard shop, combines the expertise and favorite sports of two friends after they graduated from college. Gina Pollard and Steven Michaels grew up in the sun of Southern California, but they also spent time in the mountain snow. The store carries top brands of men's and women's apparel, goggles and sunglasses, boards, and gear. The surfboard selection includes both classic boards and the latest high-tech boards. Snowboarding gear can be purchased in packages or customized for the most experienced boarders. Pollard and Michaels are proud to serve Southern California's board enthusiasts.

PROJECT 5A Store Inventory

MyLab IT
Project 5A Grader for Instruction
Project 5A Simulation for Training and Review

Project Activities

In Activities 5.01 through 5.10, you will help Miles Gorden, purchasing manager of S-Boards, Inc., a surf and snowboard shop, create special-purpose queries to perform calculations, summarize and group data, display data in a spreadsheet-like format, and find duplicate and unmatched records. You will also create a query that prompts individuals to enter the query criteria. Your completed Navigation Pane will look similar to Figure 5.1.

Project Files for MyLab IT Grader

1. In your storage location, create a folder named **Access Chapter 5**.
2. In your **MyLab IT** course, locate and click **Access 5A Store Inventory**, Download Materials, and then Download All Files.
3. Extract the zipped folder to your Access Chapter 5 folder. Close the Grader download screens.
4. Take a moment to open the downloaded **Access_5A_Store_Inventory_Instructions**; note any recent updates to the book.

Project Results

GO! Project 5A
Where We're Going

Figure 5.1 Project 5A Store Inventory

For Non-MyLab Submissions
For Project 5A, you will need:
a05A_Store_Inventory

Start with an Access Data File
In your storage location, create a folder named **Access Chapter 5**
In your Access Chapter 5 folder, save your database as:
Lastname_Firstname_5A_Store_Inventory

After you have saved your database, open it to launch Access. On the next page, begin with Step 2.

Objective 1 | Create Calculated Fields in a Query

ALERT Because Office 365 is a cloud-based subscription service that receives continuous updates, you may encounter some variations in what appears on your screen and what is shown in this instruction. Microsoft Office 365 is fully installed on your PC or Mac; no internet access is necessary to create or edit documents. When you *are* connected to the internet, you will receive monthly upgrades and new features, so you always have the latest versions of Office apps as soon as they are available. Your subscription gives you continuous free access to the latest innovations and refinements.

GO! Learn How
Video A5-1

Queries can be used to create a ***calculated field***—a field that obtains its data by performing a calculation or computation, using a formula. For example, to determine the profit that will be made from the sale of an item, subtract the cost of the item from the sale price of the item. Another example is to create a calculated field that computes the gross pay for an employee. Two steps are needed to produce a calculated field in a query. First, in the design grid of the query, in a blank column, type the name of the field that will store the results of the calculated field—the name must be followed by a colon (:). Second, type the ***expression***—the formula—that will perform the calculation. *Each field name* used in the expression must be enclosed within *its own pair* of square brackets, []. If you are using a number in the expression—for example, a decimal—type only the decimal; do not enclose it in brackets.

Activity 5.01 | Creating a Calculated Field Based on Two Existing Fields

MOS

3.1.6, 3.1.7,
3.2.1

In this Activity, you will create a calculated field to determine the profit for each item in the inventory table for S-Boards, Inc.

1 **Start** Access. In the Access opening screen, click **Open Other Files**. Navigate to your **Access Chapter 5 folder**, and then double-click the Access file that you downloaded from **MyLab IT** that displays your name—**Student_Access_5A_Store_Inventory**.

2 If necessary, enable the content or add the Access Chapter 5 folder to the Trust Center.

3 In the **Navigation Pane**, double-click **5A Inventory**. If the Field List pane opens, close it. Take a moment to study the fields in the table.

Snowboarding items have a catalog number beginning with 8; surfing items have a catalog number beginning with 9. The Category field is a Lookup column. If you click in the Category field, and then click the arrow, a list of category numbers and their descriptions display. The Supplier field identifies the supplier numbers. Cost is the price the company pays to a supplier for each item. Selling Price is what the company will charge its customers for each item. On Hand refers to the current inventory for each item.

4 Switch to **Design** view, and then take a moment to study the data structure. Notice the Category field has a data type of Number; this reflects the AutoNumber field (ID field) in the Category table used in the Lookup field. When you are finished, **Close** ⌧ the table, and then **Close** ⌫ the **Navigation Pane**.

5 On the ribbon, click the **Create tab**, and then, in the **Queries group**, click **Query Design**. In the **Show Table** dialog box, double-click **5A Inventory** to add the table to the query design workspace, and then click **Close**. Resize the list so the table name and all fields are fully displayed.

If you add the wrong table to the workspace or have two copies of the same table, right-click the extra table, and click Remove Table.

6 From the **5A Inventory** field list, add the following fields, in the order specified, to the design grid: **Catalog#**, **Item**, **Cost**, and **Selling Price**.

Recall that you can double-click a field name to add it to the design grid, or you can drag the field name to the field box on the design grid. You can also click in the field box, click the arrow, and click the field name from the displayed list.

7 Under **Query Tools**, on the **Design tab**, in the **Results group**, click **Run** to display the four fields used in the query, and then compare your screen with Figure 5.2.

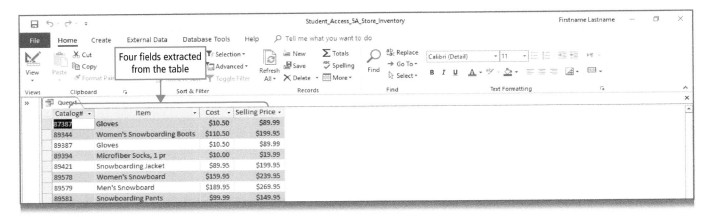

Figure 5.2

8 Switch to **Design** view. In the **Field row**, right-click in the first empty column—the fifth column—to display a shortcut menu, and then click **Zoom** to display the **Zoom** dialog box. *Arithmetic operators* are mathematical symbols used to build expressions in calculated fields. Take a moment to study the arithmetic operators as described in Figure 5.3.

Operator	Description	Example	Result
+	Addition	Cost:[Price]+[Tax]	Adds the value in the Price field to the value in the Tax field and displays the result in the Cost field.
−	Subtraction	Cost:[Price]-[Markdown]	Subtracts the value in the Markdown field from the value in the Price field and displays the result in the Cost field.
*	Multiplication	Tax:[Price]*.05	Multiplies the value in the Price field by .05 (5%) and displays the result in the Tax field. (Note: This is an asterisk, not an x.)
/	Division	Average:[Total]/3	Divides the value in the Total field by 3 and displays the result in the Average field.
^	Exponentiation	Required:2^[Bits]	Raises 2 to the power of the value in the Bits field and stores the result in the Required field.
\	Integer division	Average:[Children]\ [Families]	Divides the value in the Children field by the value in the Families field and displays the integer portion—the digits to the left of the decimal point—in the Average field.

Figure 5.3

9 In the **Zoom** dialog box, type **Per Item Profit:[Selling Price]-[Cost]** and then compare your screen with Figure 5.4.

The first element of the calculated field—*Per Item Profit*—is the new field name that will display the calculated value. The field name must be unique for the table being used in the query. Following the new field name is a colon (:). A colon in a calculated field separates the new field name from the expression. *Selling Price* is enclosed in square brackets because it is an existing field name in the *5A Inventory* table and contains data that will be used in the calculation. Following *[Selling Price]* is a hyphen (-), which, in math calculations, signifies subtraction. Finally, *Cost*, an existing field in the *5A Inventory* table, is enclosed in square brackets. This field also contains data that will be used in the calculation.

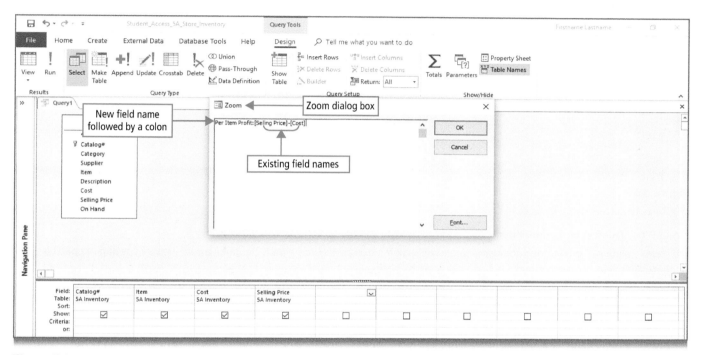

Figure 5.4

NOTE **Using Square Brackets Around Field Names in Expressions**

Square brackets are not required around a field name in an expression if the field name is only one word. For example, if the field name is Cost, it is not necessary to type brackets around it—Access will automatically insert the square brackets. If a field name has a space in it, however, you must type the square brackets around the field name. Otherwise, Access will display a message stating that the expression you entered contains invalid syntax.

10 In the **Zoom** dialog box, click **OK**, and then **Run** the query. Adjust the column width of the *Per Item Profit* field to display the entire field name, and then compare your screen with Figure 5.5.

A fifth column—the calculated field—with a field name of *Per Item Profit* displays. For each record, the value in the Per Item Profit field is calculated by subtracting the value in the Cost field from the value in the Selling Price field.

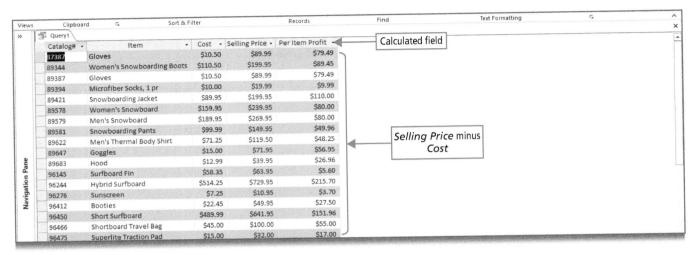

Figure 5.5

ALERT   Does your screen differ?

If a calculation in a query does not work, carefully check the expression you typed. Common errors include spelling or spacing the existing field name incorrectly, not enclosing each existing field name in square brackets, using an existing field name from a table that is not included in the query workspace, enclosing numbers in square brackets, and forgetting to type the colon after the new field name.

---

11 On the tab row, right-click the **Query1 tab**, and then click **Save** 🖫. In the **Save As** dialog box, under **Query Name**, type **5A Per Item Profit Query** and then click **OK**.

12 **Close** ⊠ the query.

Activity 5.02 | Creating a Calculated Field Based on One Existing Field and a Number

3.1.6, 3.1.7,
3.2.1, 3.2.3,
3.2.4

Each year S-Boards, Inc. has a sale on its surfboarding items. In this Activity, you will calculate the sale prices of each surfboarding item for the annual sale. During this event, all surfboarding supplies are discounted by 15 percent.

1 On the ribbon, click the **Create tab**. In the **Queries group**, click **Query Design**. Add the **5A Inventory** table to the Query design workspace, and then **Close** ⊠ the **Show Table** dialog box. Resize the field list.

2 From the **5A Inventory** field list, add the following fields, in the order specified, to the design grid: **Catalog#**, **Item**, and **Selling Price**.

3 In the **Field row**, right-click in the field cell in the first empty column—the fourth column—to display a shortcut menu, and then click **Zoom**. In the **Zoom** dialog box, type **Discount:[Selling Price]*.15** and then compare your screen with Figure 5.6.

The value in the Discount field is calculated by multiplying the value in the Selling Price field by .15—15%. Recall that only field names are enclosed in square brackets.

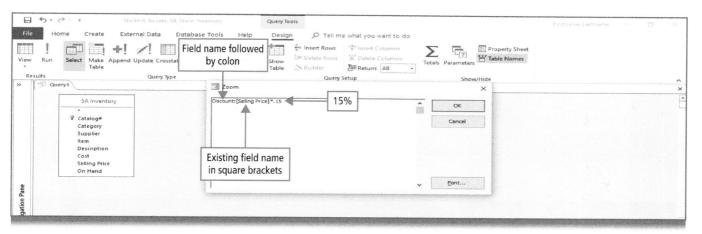

Figure 5.6

4 In the **Zoom** dialog box, click **OK**, and then **Run** the query.

The Discount field displays the results of the calculation. The data is not formatted with a dollar sign, and the first record displays a discount of 13.4985. When using a number in an expression, the values in the calculated field may not be formatted the same as in the existing field used in the expression.

5 Switch to **Design** view. Under **Query Tools**, on the **Design tab**, in the **Show/Hide group**, click **Table Names**.

In the design grid, the Table row no longer displays. If all of the fields in the design grid are from one table, you can hide the Table row. The Table Names button is a toggle button; if you click it again, the Table row displays in the design grid.

6 In the **Field row**, click in the **Discount** field box. Under **Query Tools**, on the **Design tab**, in the **Show/Hide group**, click **Property Sheet**. Alternatively, right-click in the field box and click Properties, or hold down ⌐Alt⌐ and press ⌐Enter⌐.

The Property Sheet for the selected field—Discount—displays on the right side of the screen. In the Property Sheet, under the title of Property Sheet, is the subtitle—Selection type: Field Properties.

ALERT **Does the Property Sheet display a subtitle of Selection Type: Query Properties?**

To display the Property Sheet for a field, you must first click in the field; otherwise, the Property Sheet for the query might display. If this occurs, in the Field row, click the Discount field box to change the Property Sheet to this field.

7 In the **Property Sheet**, on the **General tab**, click in the **Format** box, and then click the displayed **arrow**. If necessary, resize the Property Sheet so all formats are visible, and compare your screen with Figure 5.7.

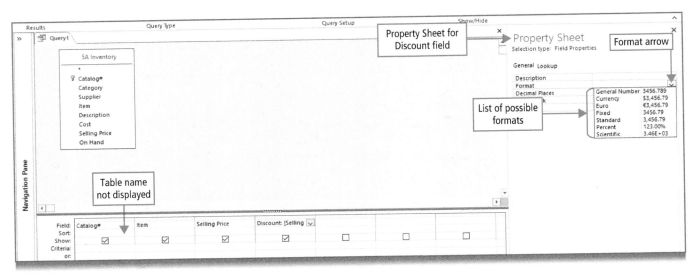

Figure 5.7

8 From the list of formats, click **Currency**. On the **Property Sheet** title bar, click **Close** ⟨×⟩. **Run** the query to display the results.

The values in the Discount field now display with a dollar sign, and the first record's discount—$13.50—displays with two decimal places.

9 Switch to **Design** view. In the **Field row**, right-click in the first empty column, and then click **Zoom**. In the **Zoom** dialog box, type **Sale Price:[Selling Price]-[Discount]** and then click **OK**. **Run** the query to display the results.

The Sale Price for Catalog #87387, Gloves, is $76.49. The value in the Sale Price field is calculated by subtracting the value in the Discount field from the value in the Selling Price field. The field names are not case sensitive—you can type a field name in lower case, such as [selling price]. Because you used only existing fields in the expression that were formatted as currency, the values in the Sale Price field are formatted as currency.

10 Switch to **Design** view. In the design grid, click in the **Criteria row** under **Catalog#**, type **9*** and then press ⟨Enter⟩.

Recall that the asterisk (*) is a wildcard. With the criteria, Access will extract those records where the catalog number begins with 9 followed by one or more characters. Also, recall that Access formats the criteria. For example, you typed 9*, and Access formatted the criteria as Like "9*".

11 **Run** the query. Notice that only the records with a **Catalog#** beginning with a **9** display—surfboarding items.

12 Save ⟨💾⟩ the query as **5A Surfboarding Sale Query**

13 Close ⟨×⟩ the query.

Objective 2 — Use Aggregate Functions in a Query

GO! Learn How
Video A5-2

In Access queries, you can use *aggregate functions* to perform a calculation on a column of data and return a single value. Examples are the Sum function, which adds a column of numbers, and the Average function, which adds a column of numbers and divides by the number of records with values, ignoring null values. Access provides two ways to use aggregate functions in a query—you can add a total row in Datasheet view or create a totals query in Design view.

Activity 5.03 | Adding a Total Row to a Query

MOS
3.1.1, 3.1.6,
3.1.7, 3.2.1

In this Activity, you will create and run a query. In Datasheet view, you will add a Total row to insert an aggregate function in one or more columns without having to change the design of the query.

1 Create a new query in **Query Design**. Add the **5A Inventory** table to the query design workspace, and then **Close** ⊠ the **Show Table** dialog box. Resize the field list. From the **5A Inventory** field list, add the following fields, in the order specified, to the design grid: **Catalog#**, **Item**, **Cost**, and **On Hand**.

2 In the **Field row**, right-click in the first empty column, and then click **Zoom**. In the **Zoom** dialog box, type **Inventory Cost:[Cost]*[On Hand]**

The value in the Inventory Cost field is calculated by multiplying the value in the Cost field by the value in the On Hand field. This field will display the cost of all of the inventory items, not just the cost per item.

3 In the **Zoom** dialog box, click **OK**, and then **Run** the query to display the results in Datasheet view. Adjust the column width of the **Inventory Cost** field to display the entire field name, and then compare your screen with Figure 5.8.

If the *Inventory Cost* for Catalog #87387, Gloves, is not $525.00, switch to Design view and edit the expression you entered for the calculated field.

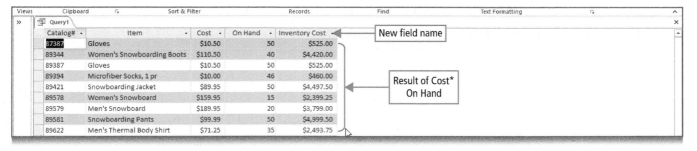

Figure 5.8

4 On the **Home tab**, in the **Records group**, click **Totals**. If necessary, scroll down until the newly created Total row displays. In the **Total row** under **Inventory Cost**, click in the empty box to display an arrow at the left edge. Click the **arrow**, and then compare your screen with Figure 5.9. Take a moment to study the aggregate functions that can be used with both the Total row and the design grid, as described in the table in Figure 5.10.

> The Total row displays after the New record row. The first field in a Total row contains the word Total. The Total row is not a record. The list of aggregate functions displayed will vary depending on the data type for each field or column; for example, number types display a full list of functions, whereas a text field will display only the Count function.

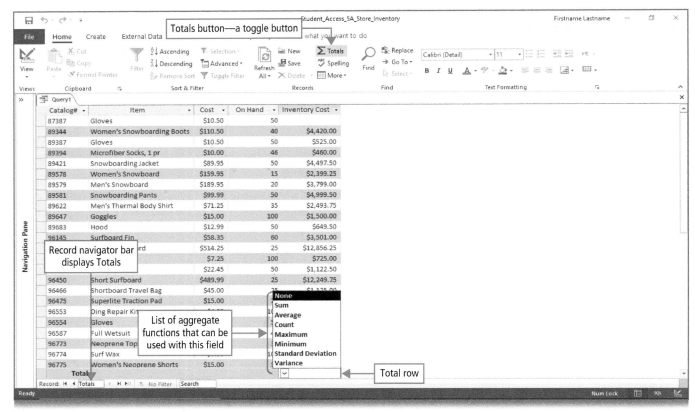

Figure 5.9

Function	Description	Can Be Used with Data Type(s)
Sum	Adds the values in a column.	Currency, Decimal, Number
Average	Calculates the average value for a column, ignoring null values.	Currency, Decimal, Number
Count	Counts the number of items in a column, ignoring null values.	All data types, except complex repeating scalar data, such as a column of multivalued lists
Maximum	Displays the item with the highest value. Can be used with text data only in Design view. With text data, the highest value is *Z*. Case and null values are ignored.	Currency, Date/Time, Decimal, Number, Text
Minimum	Displays the item with the lowest value. Can be used with text data only in Design view. For text data, the lowest value is *A*. Case and null values are ignored.	Currency, Date/Time, Decimal, Number, Text
Standard Deviation	Measures how widely values are dispersed from the mean value.	Currency, Decimal, Number
Variance	Measures the statistical variance of all values in the column. If the table has less than two rows, a null value is displayed.	Currency, Decimal, Number

Figure 5.10

5 From the displayed list, click **Sum**, and then compare your screen with Figure 5.11.

A sum of $67,186.25 displays, which is the total of all the data in the Inventory Cost field.

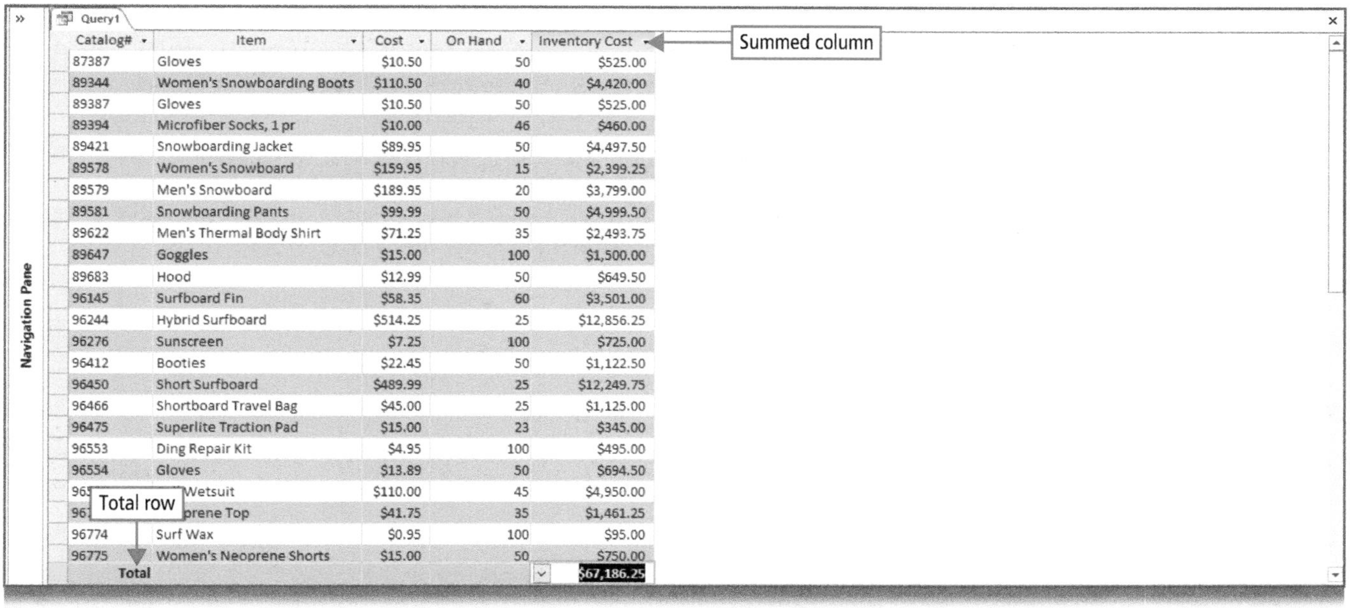

Figure 5.11

You can apply aggregate functions to more than one field by clicking in the Total row for the field, clicking the arrow, and then clicking the function. The functions for multiple fields can be different functions.

6 ▶ **Save** 🖫 the query as **5A Total Inventory Cost Query**

7 ▶ **Close** ☒ the query.

MORE KNOWLEDGE   **Removing the Aggregate Function and Removing the Total Row**

To remove an aggregate function from a column, on the Total row under the field, click the arrow and then click None. To remove the Total row, on the Home tab, in the Records group, click Totals. You cannot cut or delete a Total row; you can only turn it on or off. You can copy a Total row and paste it into another file—for example, an Excel worksheet or a Word document.

Activity 5.04 | Creating a Totals Query

3.1.1, 3.1.5,
3.1.6, 3.1.7,
3.2.1

In this Activity, you will create a ***totals query***—a query that calculates subtotals across groups of records. For example, to subtotal the number of inventory items by suppliers, use a totals query to group the records by the supplier and then apply an aggregate function to the On Hand field. In the previous activity, you created a Total row, which applied an aggregate function to one column—field—of data. A totals query is used when you need to apply an aggregate function to some or all of the records in a query. A totals query can then be used as a source for another database object, such as a report.

1 ▶ Create a new query in **Query Design**. Add the **5A Suppliers** table and the **5A Inventory** table to the query design workspace, and then **Close** ☒ the **Show Table** dialog box. Resize both field lists. Notice that there is a one-to-many relationship between the tables—*one* supplier can supply *many* items. From the **5A Inventory** field list, add **On Hand** to the first field box in the design grid.

2 ▶ Under **Query Tools**, on the **Design tab**, in the **Show/Hide group**, click **Totals**.

Like the Totals button on the Home tab, this button is a toggle button. In the design grid, a Total row displays under the Table row, and Group By displays in the box.

3 In the design grid, click in the **Total row** under **On Hand** to display the arrow. Click the **arrow**, and then compare your screen with Figure 5.12.

A list of aggregate functions displays. This list displays more functions than the list in Datasheet view, and the function names are abbreviated.

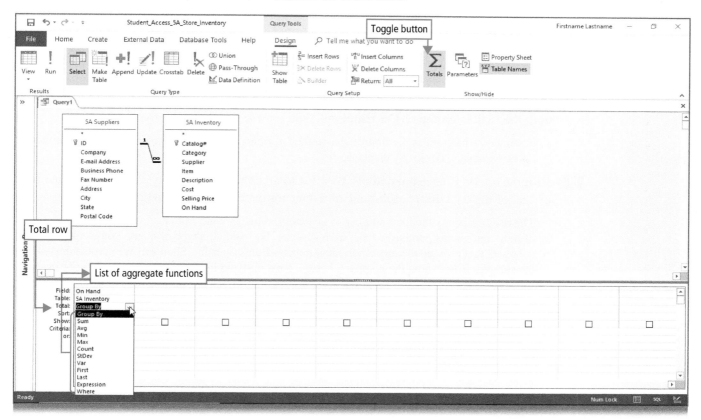

Figure 5.12

4 From the displayed list, click **Sum**. **Run** the query, and then adjust the width of the column to display the entire field name. Compare your screen with Figure 5.13.

When you run a totals query, the result of the aggregate function—*1244*—is displayed; the records are not displayed. The name of the function and the field used are displayed in the column heading.

Figure 5.13

MORE KNOWLEDGE | **Changing the Name of the Totals Query Result**

To change the name from the combination aggregate function and field name to something more concise and descriptive, in Design view, in the Field row, click in the On Hand field box. Under Query Tools, on the Design tab, in the Show/Hide group, click Property Sheet. In the Property Sheet, on the General tab, click in the Caption box, and type the new name for the result.

5 ▶ Switch to **Design** view. In the **5A Inventory** field list, double-click **Item** to insert the field in the second column in the design grid. In the design grid, click in the **Total row** under **Item**, click the displayed **arrow**, and then click **Count**. **Run** the query. Adjust the width of the second column to display the entire field name.

The number of records—25—displays. You can include multiple fields in a totals query, but each field in the query must have an aggregate function applied to it. If you include a field but do not apply an aggregate function, the query results will display every record and will not display a single value for the field or fields. The exception to this is when you group records by a category, such as supplier name.

6 ▶ Switch to **Design** view. From the **5A Suppliers** field list, drag **Company** to the design grid until the field is on top of **On Hand** and then release the mouse button.

Company is inserted as the first field, and the On Hand field moves to the right. In the Total row under Company, *Group By* displays.

7 ▶ **Run** the query. If necessary, apply **Best Fit** to all columns to display all of the field names and all of the data under each field, and then compare your screen with Figure 5.14.

The results display the total number of inventory items on hand from each supplier and the number of individual items purchased from each supplier. By using this type of query, you can identify the suppliers that provide the most individual items—Bob's Sporting Shop and Wetsuit Country—and the supplier from whom the company has the most on-hand inventory items—Bob's Sporting Shop.

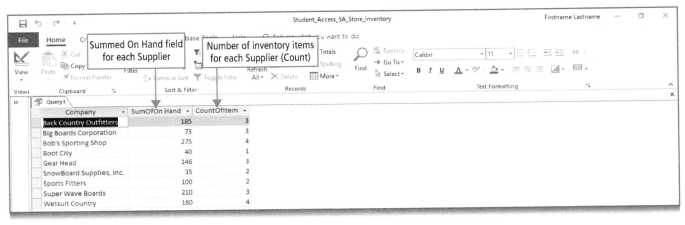

Figure 5.14

8 ▶ **Save** 🖫 the query as **5A Inventory By Supplier Query**

9 ▶ **Close** ⊠ the query.

Objective 3 | Create a Crosstab Query

GO! Learn How
Video A5-3

A *crosstab query* uses an aggregate function for data that is grouped by two types of information and displays the data in a compact, spreadsheet-like format. A crosstab query always has at least one row heading, one column heading, and one summary field. Use a crosstab query to summarize a large amount of data in a small space that is easy to read.

Activity 5.05 | Creating a Select Query as the Source for a Crosstab Query

MOS
3.1.1, 3.1.6,
3.1.7, 3.2.1,
3.1.5, 3.2.2

In this Activity, you will create a select query displaying suppliers, the category of the inventory item, the inventory item, and the number on hand. Recall that a select query is the most common type of query, and it extracts data from one or more tables or queries, displaying the results in a datasheet. After creating the select query, you will use it to create a crosstab query to display the data in a format that is easier to analyze. Because most crosstab queries extract data from more than one table or query, it is helpful to create a select query containing all of the fields necessary for the crosstab query.

1 Create a new query in **Query Design**. Add the following tables to the query design workspace: **5A Category**, **5A Inventory**, and **5A Suppliers**. In the **Show Table** dialog box, click **Close**. Resize the field lists.

2 In the **5A Suppliers** field list, double-click **Company** to add it to the first field box in the design grid. In the **5A Category** field list, double-click **CatName** to add it to the second field box in the design grid. In the **5A Inventory** field list, double-click **On Hand** to add it to the third field box in the design grid. In the design grid, click in the **Sort** box under **Company**. Click the **arrow**, and then click **Ascending**. Sort the **CatName** field in **Ascending** order.

3 Under **Query Tools**, on the **Design tab**, in the **Show/Hide group**, click **Totals**. Click in the **Total row** under **On Hand**, click the **arrow**, and then click **Sum**. Compare your screen with Figure 5.15.

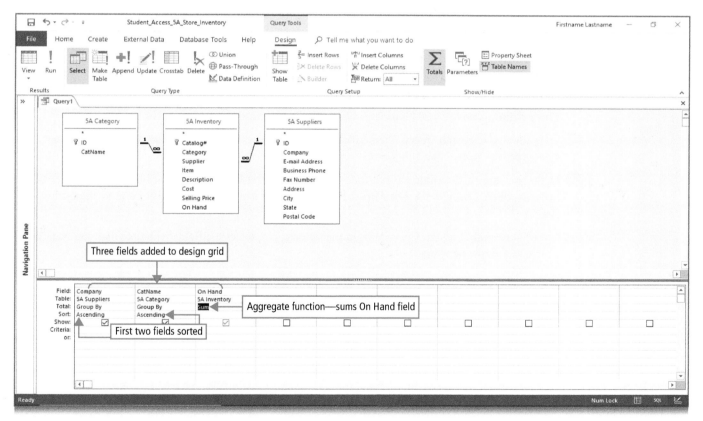

Figure 5.15

NOTE Selecting Multiple Fields for Row Headings

You can select up to three fields for row headings in a crosstab query. An example would be sorting first by state, then by city, and then by postal code. State would be the first row heading, city would be the second row heading, and postal code would be the third row heading. Regardless of the number of fields used for row headings, at least two fields must remain available to complete the crosstab query.

4 ▶ **Run** the query. In the datasheet, apply **Best Fit** to all columns to display the entire field name and the data for each record, and then compare your screen with Figure 5.16.

The select query groups the totals vertically by company and then by category.

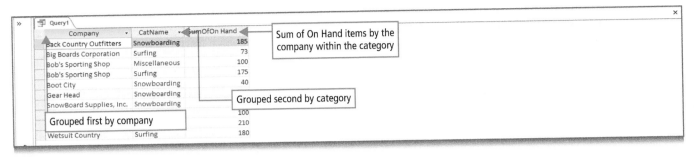

Figure 5.16

5 ▶ Switch to **Design** view. Under **Query Tools**, on the **Design tab**, in the **Show/Hide group**, click **Totals** to remove the **Total row** from the design grid.

This select query will be used to create the crosstab query. When you create a crosstab query, you will be prompted to use an aggregate function on a field, so it should not be summed prior to creating the query.

6 ▶ **Save** 🖫 the query as **5A On Hand Per Company and Category Query** and then **Close** ⊠ the query.

Activity 5.06 | Creating a Crosstab Query

3.1.2

In this Activity, you will create a crosstab query using the 5A On Hand Per Company and Category query as the source.

1 ▶ On the ribbon, click the **Create tab**, in the **Queries group**, click **Query Wizard**. In the **New Query** dialog box, click **Crosstab Query Wizard**, and then click **OK**.

In the first Crosstab Query Wizard dialog box, you select the table or query to be used as the source for the crosstab query.

2 ▶ In the middle of the dialog box, under **View**, click the **Queries** option button. In the list of queries, click **Query: 5A On Hand Per Company and Category Query**, and then click **Next**.

In the second Crosstab Query Wizard dialog box, you select the fields with data that you want to use as the row headings.

3 Under **Available Fields**, double-click **Company**, and then compare your screen with Figure 5.17.

Company displays under Selected Fields. At the bottom of the dialog box, in the Sample area, a preview of the row headings displays. Each company name will be listed on a separate row in the first column.

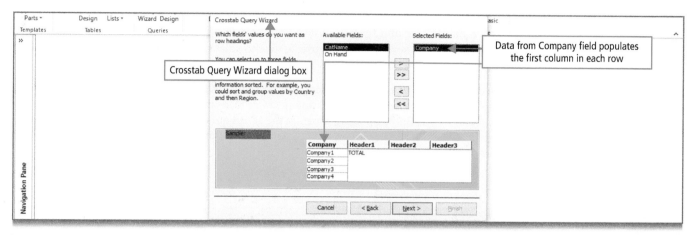

Figure 5.17

4 In the **Crosstab Query Wizard** dialog box, click **Next**.

In the third dialog box, you select the fields with data that you want to use as column headings.

5 In the displayed list of fields, **CatName** is selected; notice in the sample area that the category names display in separate columns. Click **Next**. Under **Functions**, click **Sum**, and then compare your screen with Figure 5.18.

This dialog box enables you to apply an aggregate function to one or more fields. The function will add the number on hand for every item sold by each company for each category. Every row can also be summed.

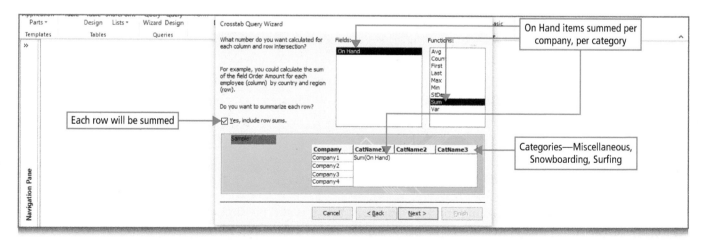

Figure 5.18

6 On the left side of the **Crosstab Query Wizard** dialog box, above the **Sample** area, clear the **Yes, include row sums** check box, and then click **Next**.

> If the check box is selected, a column will be inserted between the first and second column that sums all of the numeric data per row.

7 Under **What do you want to name your query?**, select the existing text, type **5A Crosstab Query** and then click **Finish**. Apply **Best Fit** to all columns to display the entire field name and the data in each field, and then compare your screen with Figure 5.19. Then take a moment to compare this screen with Figure 5.16, the select query you created with the same extracted data.

> The same data is extracted using the select query as shown in Figure 5.16; however, the crosstab query displays the data differently. A crosstab query reduces the number of records displayed, as shown by the entry for Bob's Sporting Shop. In the select query, there are two records displayed, one for the Miscellaneous category and one for the Surfing category. The crosstab query combines the data into one record.

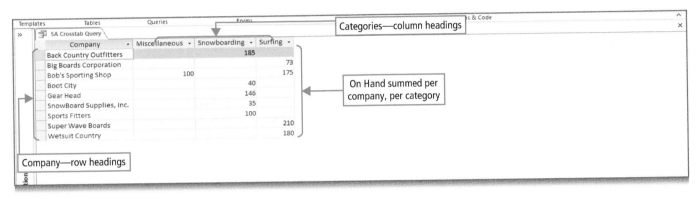

Figure 5.19

NOTE   Including Row Sums

If you include row sums in a crosstab query, the sum will display in a column following the column for the row headings. In this Activity, the row sums column would display following the Company column. For Bob's Sporting Shop, the row sum would be 275—100 plus 175.

---

8 **Close** ☒ the query, saving changes—you adjusted the column widths.

Objective 4	Find Duplicate and Unmatched Records

GO! Learn How
Video A5-4

Even when a table contains a primary key, it is still possible to have duplicate records in a table. For example, the same inventory item can be entered with different catalog numbers. You can use the *Find Duplicates Query* Wizard to locate duplicate records in a table. As databases grow, you may have records in one table that have no matching records in a related table; these are *unmatched records*. For example, there may be a record for a supplier in the Suppliers table, but no inventory items are ordered from that supplier. You can use the *Find Unmatched Query* Wizard to locate unmatched records.

Activity 5.07 | Finding Duplicate Records

3.2.1, 3.2.3

Miles is concerned that there may be duplicate records in the Inventory table, which would lead to inaccurate inventory reports. In this Activity, you will find duplicate records in the *5A Inventory* table by using the Find Duplicates Query Wizard.

1 On the **Create tab**, in the **Queries group**, click **Query Wizard**. In the **New Query** dialog box, click **Find Duplicates Query Wizard**, and then click **OK**.

2 In the first **Find Duplicates Query Wizard** dialog box, in the list of tables, click **Table: 5A Inventory**, and then click **Next**.

The second dialog box displays, enabling you to select the field or fields that may contain duplicate data. If you select all of the fields, then every field must contain the same data, which cannot be the case for a primary key field.

3 Under **Available fields**, double-click **Item** to move it under **Duplicate-value fields**, and then click **Next**.

The third dialog box displays, enabling you to select one or more fields that will help you distinguish duplicate from nonduplicate records.

4 Under **Available fields**, add the following fields, in the order specified, to the **Additional query fields** box: **Catalog#**, **Category**, **Supplier**, **Cost**, and **Selling Price**. Compare your screen with Figure 5.20.

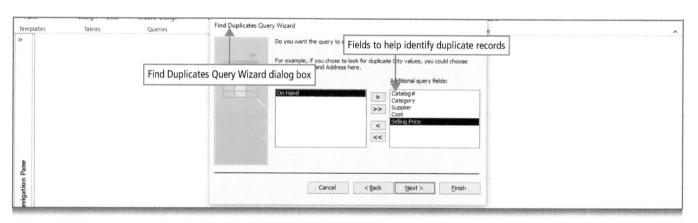

Figure 5.20

5 Click **Next**. Click **Finish** to accept the suggested query name—*Find duplicates for 5A Inventory*. If all data is not visible, apply **Best Fit** to all columns, and then compare your screen with Figure 5.21.

Three records display with a duplicate value in the *Item* field. Using the displayed fields, you can determine that the second and third records are duplicates; the *Catalog#* was entered incorrectly for one of the records. By examining the *5A Inventory* table, you can determine that Category 1 is Snowboarding and Category 2 is Surfing. Be careful when using the Find Duplicates Query Wizard. If you do not include additional fields to help determine whether the records are duplicates or not, you might mistakenly identify them as duplicates.

Normally, you would delete the duplicate record, but your instructor needs to verify that you have found the duplicate record by using a query.

Figure 5.21

6 **Close** ⊠ the query, saving changes.

Activity 5.08 | Finding Unmatched Records

3.2.1, 3.2.3

In this Activity, you will find unmatched records in related tables—*5A Suppliers* and *5A Inventory*—by using the Find Unmatched Query Wizard.

1 On the **Create tab**, in the **Queries group**, click **Query Wizard**. In the **New Query** dialog box, click **Find Unmatched Query Wizard**, and then click **OK**.

2 In the first **Find Unmatched Query Wizard** dialog box, in the list of tables, click **Table: 5A Suppliers**, and then click **Next**.

The second dialog box displays, enabling you to select the related table or query that you would like Access to compare to the first table to find unmatched records.

3 In the list of tables, click **Table: 5A Inventory**, and then click **Next**.

The third dialog box displays, enabling you to select the matching fields in each table.

4 Under **Fields in '5A Suppliers'**, if necessary, click **ID**. Under **Fields in '5A Inventory'**, if necessary, click **Supplier**. Between the two fields columns, click the button that displays **<=>**. Click **Next**.

Your table names may require two lines, depending on the length of your name. At the bottom of the dialog box, Access displays the matching fields of ID and Supplier.

5 Under **Available fields**, double-click **ID**, and then double-click **Company** to move the field names under **Selected fields**. Notice that these fields will display in the query results, and then compare your screen with Figure 5.22.

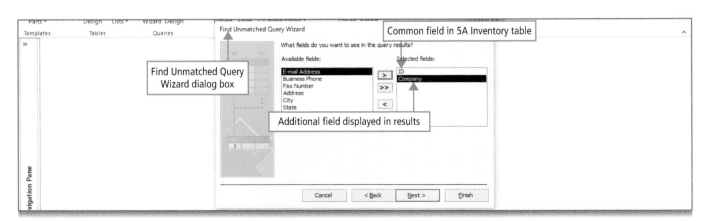

Figure 5.22

---

6 ▶ Click **Next**. In the last dialog box, under **What would you like to name your query?**, type **5A Find Unmatched Query** and then click **Finish**. Compare your screen with Figure 5.23.

The query results display one company—*Cold Sports Club*—that has no inventory items in the *5A Inventory* table. Normally, you would either delete the Cold Sports Club record from the *5A Suppliers* table or add inventory items in the related *5A Inventory* table for the Cold Sports Club, but your instructor needs to verify that you have located an unmatched record by using a query.

Figure 5.23

7 ▶ **Close** ☒ the query, saving changes.

MORE KNOWLEDGE **Finding Unmatched Records in a Table with Multivalued Fields**

You cannot use the Find Unmatched Query Wizard with a table that has *multivalued fields*—fields that appear to hold multiple values. If your table contains multivalued fields, you must first create a query to extract all of the fields except the multivalued fields, and then create the query to find unmatched records.

Objective 5 **Create a Parameter Query**

GO! Learn How
Video A5-5

A *parameter query* prompts you for criteria before running the query. For example, if you had a database of snowboarding events, you might need to find all of the snowboarding events in a particular state. You can create a select query for a state, but when you need to find information about snowboarding events in another state, you must open the original select query in Design view, change the criteria, and then run the query again. With a parameter query, you can create one query—Access will prompt you to enter the state and then display the results based upon the criteria you enter in the dialog box.

Activity 5.09 | **Creating a Parameter Query Using One Criterion**

MOS
3.1.3, 3.1.5,
3.2.3, 3.1.6,
3.1.7

In this Activity, you will create a parameter query to display a specific category of inventory items. You can enter a parameter anywhere you use text, number, or date criteria.

1 ▶ **Open** ⟫ the **Navigation Pane**. Under **Tables**, double-click **5A Inventory** to open the table in **Datasheet** view. In any record, click in the **Category** field, and then click the **arrow** to display the list of categories. Take a moment to study the four categories used in this table. Be sure you do not change the category for the selected record. **Close** ☒ the table, and **Close** ⟪ the **Navigation Pane**.

2 ▶ Create a new query in **Query Design**. Add the **5A Category** table, the **5A Inventory** table, and the **5A Suppliers** table to the query design workspace, and then **Close** ☒ the **Show Table** dialog box. Resize the field lists. From the **5A Category** field list, add **CatName** to the first column in the design grid. From the **5A Inventory** field list, add **Catalog#** and **Item** to the second and third columns in the design grid. From the **5A Suppliers** field list, add **Company** to the fourth column in the design grid.

3 In the **Criteria row** under **CatName**, type **[Enter a Category]** and then compare your screen with Figure 5.24.

> The brackets indicate a *parameter*—a value that can be changed—rather than specific criteria. When you run the query, a dialog box will display, prompting you to *Enter a Category*. The category you type will be set as the criteria for the query. Because you are prompted for the criteria, you can reuse this query without resetting the criteria in Design view.

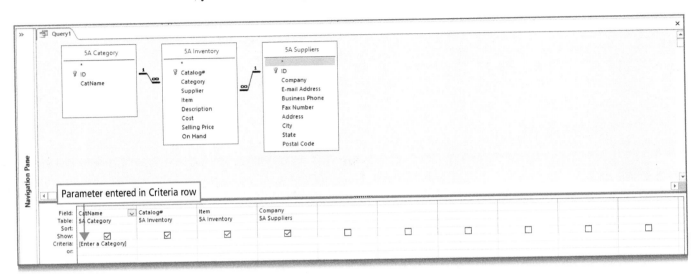

Figure 5.24

4 **Run** the query. In the **Enter Parameter Value** dialog box, type **Surfing** and then compare your screen with Figure 5.25.

Figure 5.25

ALERT **Does your screen differ?**

If the Enter Parameter Value dialog box does not display, you may have typed the parameter incorrectly in the design grid. Common errors include using parentheses or curly braces instead of square brackets around the parameter text, causing Access to interpret the text as specific criteria. If you use parentheses, when you run the query no records will display. If you use curly braces, the query will not run. To correct this, display the query in Design view, and then correct the parameter entered in the Criteria row.

---

5 In the **Enter Parameter Value** dialog box, click **OK**.

> Thirteen records display where the CatName field is Surfing.

6 Apply **Best Fit** to all columns, if necessary, and **Save** 🖫 the query as **5A Category Parameter Query Close** ✕ the query, and then **Open** » the **Navigation Pane**.

7 In the **Navigation Pane**, under **Queries**, double-click **5A Category Parameter Query**. In the **Enter Parameter Value** dialog box, type **Snowboarding** and then click **OK**.

Eleven items categorized as Snowboarding display. Recall that when you open a query, Access runs the query so that the most up-to-date data is extracted from the underlying table or query. When you have entered a parameter as the criteria, you will be prompted to enter the criteria every time you open the query.

8 Switch to **Design** view. Notice that the parameter—[Enter a Category]—is stored with the query. Access does not store the criteria entered in the Enter Parameter Value dialog box.

9 **Run** the query, and in the **Enter Parameter Value** dialog box, type **Miscellaneous** being careful to spell it correctly. Click **OK** to display one record. Apply **Best Fit** to all columns.

10 **Close** ⊠ the query, saving changes, and then **Close** ⟪ the **Navigation Pane**.

MORE KNOWLEDGE | **Parameter Query Prompts**

When you enter the parameter in the Criteria row, make sure that the prompt—the text enclosed in the square brackets—is not the same as the field name. For example, if the field name is Category, do not enter [Category] as the parameter. Because Access uses field names in square brackets for calculations, no prompt will display. If you want to use the field name by itself as a prompt, type a question mark at the end of the prompt; for example, [Category?]. You cannot use a period, exclamation mark (!), square brackets ([]), or the ampersand (&) as part of the prompt.

Activity 5.10 | Creating a Parameter Query Using Multiple Criteria

MOS
3.1.3, 3.1.5,
3.2.3, 3.1.6,
3.1.7

In this Activity, you will create a parameter query to display the inventory items that fall within a certain range in the On Hand field.

1 Create a new query in **Query Design**. Add the **5A Suppliers** table and the **5A Inventory** table to the query design workspace, and then **Close** ⊠ the **Show Table** dialog box. Resize the field lists. From the **5A Inventory** field list, add **Item** and **On Hand** to the first and second columns in the design grid. From the **5A Suppliers** field list box, add **Company** to the third column in the design grid.

2 In the **Criteria row**, right-click in the **On Hand** field, and then click **Zoom**. In the **Zoom** dialog box, type **Between [Enter the lower On Hand number] and [Enter the higher On Hand number]** and then compare your screen with Figure 5.26.

The Zoom dialog box enables you to see the entire parameter. The parameter includes *Between* and, which will display a range of data. Two dialog boxes will display when you run the query. You will be prompted to enter the lower number first and then the higher number.

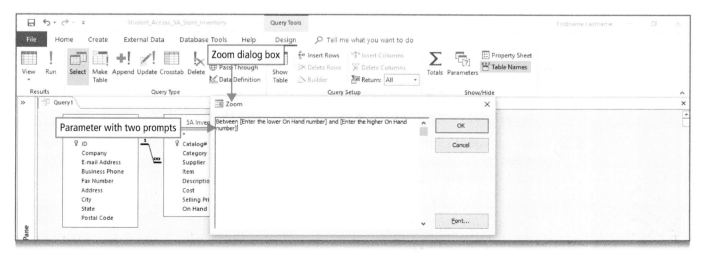

Figure 5.26

3 After verifying that you have entered the correct parameter, in the **Zoom** dialog box, click **OK**, and then **Run** the query. In the first **Enter Parameter Value** dialog box, type **10** and then click **OK**. In the second **Enter Parameter Value** dialog box, type **25** and then click **OK**. Compare your screen with Figure 5.27.

Six records have On Hand items in the range of 10 to 25. These might be inventory items that need to be ordered soon.

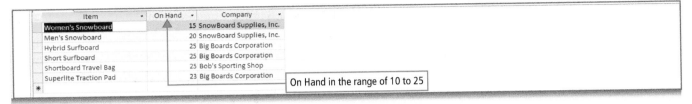

Figure 5.27

MORE KNOWLEDGE **Creating a Parameter Query Using Multiple Criteria**

When you create a query using more than one field with parameters, the individual sees the prompts in the order that the fields are arranged from left to right in the design grid. When you create a query using more than one parameter in a single field, the individual sees the prompts in the order displayed, from left to right, in the Criteria box.

If you want the prompts to display in a different order, under Query Tools, on the Design tab, in the Show/Hide group, click Parameters. In the Parameter column, type the prompt for each parameter exactly as it was typed in the design grid. Enter the parameters in the order you want the dialog boxes to display when the query is run. In the Data Type column, next to each entered parameter, specify the data type by clicking the arrow and displaying the list of data types. Click OK, and then run the query.

---

4 Apply **Best Fit** to all columns, and **Save** ⊟ the query as **5A On Hand Parameter Query**

5 **Close** ✕ the query.

6 **Open** » the **Navigation Pane**. If necessary, resize the **Navigation Pane** so all object names are fully visible. **Close** the database, and **Close** Access.

For Non-MyLab Submissions: Determine What Your Instructor Requires for Submission
As directed by your instructor, submit your completed database file.

---

7 In **MyLab IT**, locate and click the Grader Project **Access 5A Store Inventory**. In **step 3**, under **Upload Completed Assignment**, click **Choose File**. In the **Open** dialog box, navigate to your **Access Chapter 5 folder**, and then click your **Student_Access_5A_Store_Inventory** file one time to select it. In the lower right corner of the **Open** dialog box, click **Open**.

The name of your selected file displays above the Upload button.

8 To submit your file to **MyLab IT** for grading, click **Upload**, wait a moment for a green **Success!** message, and then in **step 4**, click the blue **Submit for Grading** button. Click **Close Assignment** to return to your list of **Course Materials**.

You have completed Project 5A **END**

PROJECT 5B Customer Orders

MyLab IT
Project 5B Grader for Instruction
Project 5B Simulation for Training and Review

Project Activities

In Activities 5.11 through 5.19, you will help Miko Adai, sales associate for S-Boards, Inc., a surf and snowboard shop, keep the tables in the database up to date and ensure that the queries display pertinent information. You will create action queries that will create a new table, update records in a table, append records to a table, and delete records from a table. You will also modify the join type of relationships to display different subsets of the data when the query is run. Your completed Navigation Pane will look similar to Figure 5.28.

Project Files for MyLab IT Grader

1. In your **MyLab IT** course, locate and click **Access 5B Customer Orders**, Download Materials, and then Download All Files.
2. Extract the zipped folder to your Access Chapter 5 folder. Close the Grader download screens.
3. Take a moment to open the downloaded **Access_5B_Customer_Orders_Instructions**; note any recent updates to the book.

Project Results

GO! Project 5B
Where We're Going

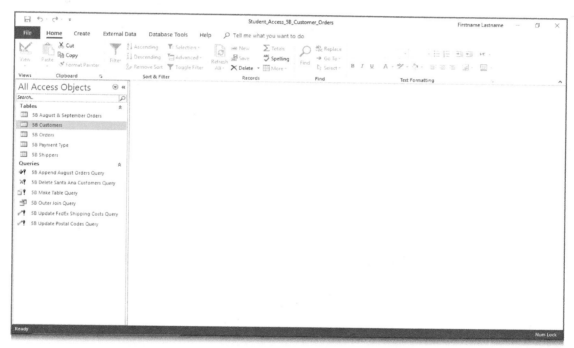

Figure 5.28 Project 5B Customer Orders

For Non-MyLab Submissions
For Project 5B, you will need:
a05B_Customer_Orders
a05B_Potential_Customers

Start with an Access Data File
In your Access Chapter 5 folder, save your databases as:
Lastname_Firstname_5B_Customer_Orders
Lastname_Firstname_5B_Potential_Customers

After you have saved your database, open it to launch Access. On the next page, begin with Step 2.

Objective 6 | Create a Make Table Query

GO! Learn How
Video A5-6

An *action query* enables you to create a new table or change data in an existing table. A *make table query* is an action query that creates a new table by extracting data from one or more tables. Creating a new table from existing tables is useful when you need to copy or back up data. For example, you may wish to create a table that displays the orders for the past month. You can extract that data and store it in another table, using the new table as a source for reports or queries. Extracting data and storing it in a new table reduces the time to retrieve *static data*—data that does not change—and creates a convenient backup of the data.

Activity 5.11 | Creating a Select Query

MOS
1.2.2, 3.1.5,
3.2.1, 3.2.3,
3.1.7

In this Activity, you will create a select query to extract the fields you wish to store in the new table.

1▶ Start Access. In the Access opening screen, click **Open Other Files**. Navigate to your **Access Chapter 5 folder**, and then double-click the Access file that you downloaded from **MyLab IT** that displays your name—**Student_Access_5B_Customer_Orders**.

2▶ If you did not add the **Access Chapter 5** folder to the Trust Center, enable the content. Take a moment to open each table and observe the data in each. In the **5B Orders** table, make a note of the data type for the **Order#** field and the pattern of data entered in the field. When you are finished, close all of the tables, and **Close** ⟪ the **Navigation Pane**.

In the *5B Orders* table, the first record contains an Order# of 7-11-17-0002. The first section of the order number is the month of the order and the second section is the day of the month. The last section is a sequential number. Records with orders for July, August, and September are contained in this table.

3▶ Create a new query in **Query Design**. From the **Show Table** dialog box, add the following tables to the query design workspace: **5B Customers**, **5B Orders**, and **5B Shippers**. **Close** ✕ the **Show Table** dialog box, and then resize the field lists. Notice the relationships between the tables.

The *5B Customers* table has a one-to-many relationship with the *5B Orders* table—*one* customer can have *many* orders. The *5B Shippers* table has a one-to-many relationship with the *5B Orders* table—*one* shipper can ship *more* than one order.

4▶ From the **5B Orders** field list, add **Order#** to the first column of the design grid. From the **5B Customers** field list, add **Last Name** and **First Name** to the second and third columns of the design grid. From the **5B Shippers** field list, add **Shipping Company** to the fourth column of the design grid.

5 In the design grid, click in the **Criteria row** under **Order#**, type **9*** and then compare your screen with Figure 5.29.

Recall that the asterisk is a wildcard that stands for one or more characters—Access will extract the records where the Order# starts with a 9, and it does not matter what the following characters are. The first section of the Order# contains the month the order was placed without any regard for the year; all September orders will display no matter what year they were placed. You do not need criteria in a select query to convert it to a make table query.

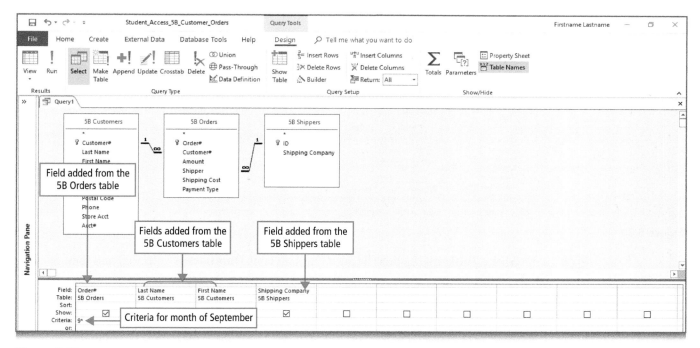

Figure 5.29

6 **Run** the query, and notice that four orders were placed in September.

The select query displays the records that will be stored in the new table.

NOTE **Using Expressions and Aggregate Functions in a Make Table Query**

In addition to using criteria in a select query upon which a make table query is based, you can use expressions to create a calculated field; for example, *Gross Pay:[Hourly Wage]*[Hours Worked]*. You can also use aggregate functions; for example, you may want to sum the *Hours Worked* field.

Activity 5.12 | Converting a Select Query to a Make Table Query

3.1.4, 3.1.6,
3.1.7, 1.1.3

In this Activity, you will convert the select query you just created to a make table query.

1 Switch to **Design** view. Under **Query Tools**, on the **Design tab**, in the **Query Type group**, click **Make Table**. Notice the exclamation point (!) in several of the buttons in the Query Type group—these are action queries. In the **Make Table** dialog box, in the **Table Name** box, type **5B September Orders** and then compare your screen with Figure 5.30.

> The table name should be a unique table name for the database in which the table will be saved. If it is not, you will be prompted to delete the first table before the new table can be created. You can save a make table query in the current database or in another existing database.

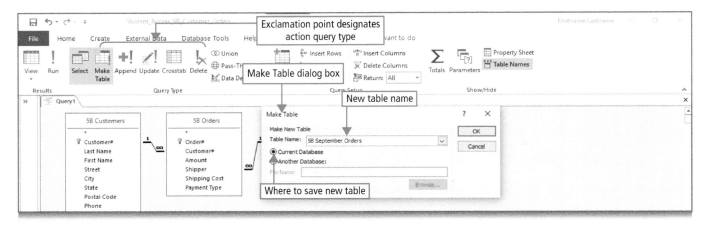

Figure 5.30

2 In the **Make Table** dialog box, be sure that **Current Database** is selected, and then click **OK**. **Run** the query.

> A message displays indicating that *You are about to paste 4 row(s) into a new table* and that you cannot use the Undo command.

3 In the displayed message box, click **Yes**. **Close** ☒ the query, click **Yes** in the message box prompting you to save changes, and then name the query **5B Make Table Query**

4 **Open** ☒ the **Navigation Pane**. Notice that under Tables, the new table you created—*5B September Orders*—is displayed. Under Queries, the *5B Make Table Query* is displayed.

5 In the **Navigation Pane**, click the title—**All Access Objects**. Under **Navigate To Category**, click **Tables and Related Views**, and then compare your screen with Figure 5.31.

> The Navigation Pane is grouped by tables and related objects. Because the 5B Make Table Query extracted records from three tables—*5B Customers*, *5B Orders*, and *5B Shippers*—it is displayed under all three tables. Changing the grouping in the Navigation Pane to Tables and Related Views enables you to easily determine which objects are dependent upon other objects in the database.

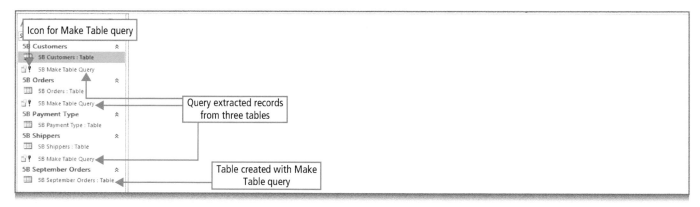

Figure 5.31

6 In the **Navigation Pane**, double-click **5B September Orders** to open the table in **Datasheet** view.

If you click the category title instead of the table, the category will close—if that happens, double-click the category title to redisplay the table, and then double-click the table.

7 Switch to **Design** view. Notice that the *Order#* field does not have an input mask associated with it and that there is no Primary Key field defined in this table.

When using a make table query to create a new table, the data in the new table does not inherit the field properties or the Primary Key field setting from the original table.

8 Switch to **Datasheet** view, and then adjust all column widths. **Close** ⊠ the table, saving changes.

NOTE Updating a Table Created with a Make Table Query

The data stored in a table created with a make table query is not automatically updated when records in the original tables are modified. To keep the new table up to date, you must run the make table query periodically to be sure the information is current.

Objective 7   Create an Append Query

GO! Learn How
Video A5-7

An ***append query*** is an action query that adds new records to an existing table by adding data from another Access database or from a table in the same database. An append query can be limited by criteria. Use an append query when the data already exists and you do not want to manually enter it into an existing table. Like the make table query, you first create a select query and then convert it to an append query.

Activity 5.13 │ Creating an Append Query for a Table in the Current Database

MOS
3.1.4, 3.1.5,
3.2.1, 3.2.3,
3.1.6, 3.1.7,
1.1.3

In this Activity, you will create a select query to extract the records for customers who have placed orders in August and then append the records to the *5B September Orders* table.

1 **Close** ⊠ the **Navigation Pane**. Create a new query in **Query Design**. From the **Show Table** dialog box, add the following tables to the Query design workspace: **5B Customers**, **5B Orders**, and **5B Shippers**. **Close** ⊠ the **Show Table** dialog box, and then resize the field lists.

2 From the **5B Customers** field list, add **First Name** and **Last Name**, in the order specified, to the first and second columns of the design grid. From the **5B Orders** field list, add **Order#** and **Shipping Cost**, in the order specified, to the third and fourth columns of the design grid. From the **5B Shippers** field list, add **Shipping Company** to the fifth column of the design grid.

3 In the design grid, click in the **Criteria row** under **Order#**, type **8*** and then press ⬇.
Compare your screen with Figure 5.32.

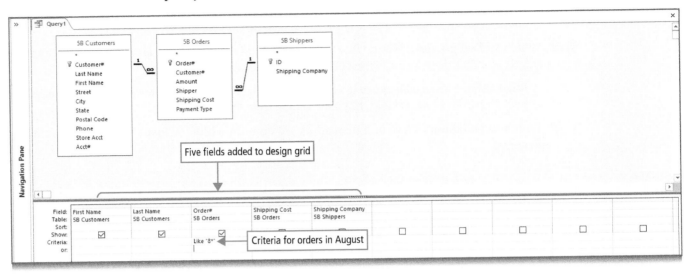

Figure 5.32

4 **Run** the query, and notice that four customers placed orders in August.

5 Switch to **Design** view. Under **Query Tools**, on the **Design tab**, in the **Query Type group**, click **Append**. In the **Append** dialog box, click the **Table Name arrow**, and then from the displayed list, click **5B September Orders**. Click **OK**. Compare your screen with Figure 5.33.

In the design grid, Access inserts an *Append To* row above the Criteria row. Access compares the fields in the query with the fields in the *destination table*—the table to which you are appending the fields—and attempts to match fields. If a match is found, Access adds the name of the destination field to the Append To row in the query. If no match is found, Access leaves the destination field blank. You can click the box in the Append To row and select a destination field.

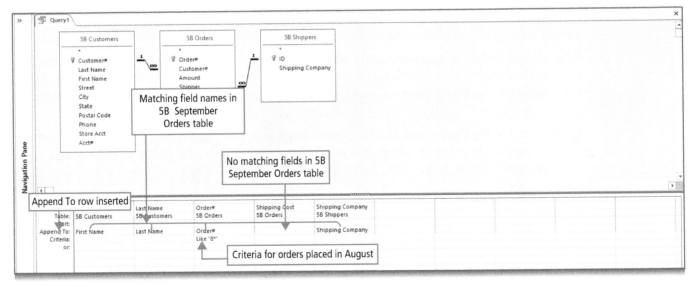

Figure 5.33

6 **Run** the query. In the displayed message box, click **Yes** to append the four rows to the *5B September Orders* table.

7 **Close** ⊠ the query, and then save it as **5B Append August Orders Query**

8 **Open** ⟫ the **Navigation Pane**. Notice that **5B Append August Orders Query** displays under the three tables from which data was extracted.

9 In the **Navigation Pane**, click the title—**All Tables**. Under **Navigate To Category**, click **Object Type** to group the Navigation Pane objects by type. Under **Queries**, notice the icon that displays for **5B Append August Orders Query**. Recall that this icon indicates the query is an action query.

10 Under **Tables**, double-click **5B September Orders** to open the table in **Datasheet** view, and then compare your screen with Figure 5.34.

> Four orders for August are appended to the *5B September Orders* table. Because there is no match in the *5B September Orders* table for the Shipping Cost field in the 5B Append August Orders Query, the field is ignored when the records are appended. Notice that the formatting is not applied to the Order# in the last record.

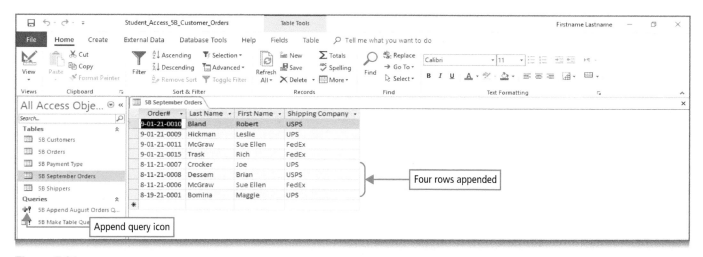

Figure 5.34

11 **Close** the table. In the **Navigation Pane**, under **Tables**, right-click **5B September Orders**, and then click **Rename**. **Rename** the table as **5B August & September Orders**

Activity 5.14 | Creating an Append Query for a Table in Another Database

MOS
2.1.1, 3.1.4,
3.2.1, 3.1.6,
3.1.7

Miko Adai recently discovered that the marketing manager has been keeping a database of persons who have requested information about S-Boards, Inc. These names need to be added to the *5B Customers* table so those potential clients can receive catalogs when they are distributed. In this Activity, you will create an append query to add the records from the marketing manager's table to the *5B Customers* table.

1 On the Access window title bar, click **Minimize** ☐. Display the **Start screen**, and then open **Access**. Navigate to your **Access Chapter 5** folder. Locate and open the **a05B_Potential_ Customers** file.

2 If you did not add the **Access Chapter 5** folder to the Trust Center, enable the content. Take a moment to open the table, noticing the fields and field names. When you are finished, **Close** the table, and **Close** ☒ the **Navigation Pane**.

> The *5B Potential Customers* table in this database contains fields similar to those in the *5B Customers* table in the *5B_Customer_Orders* database.

3 Create a new query in **Query Design**. From the **Show Table** dialog box, add the **5B Potential Customers** table to the query design workspace, and then **Close** ☒ the **Show Table** dialog box. Resize the field list.

4 In the **5B Potential Customers** field list, click **Customer#**, hold down Shift, and then click **Phone** to select all of the fields. Drag the selection down into the first column of the design grid.

> Although you could click the asterisk (*) in the field list to add all of the fields to the design grid, it is easier to detect which fields have no match in the destination table when the field names are listed individually in the design grid.

5 Under **Query Tools**, on the **Design tab**, in the **Query Type group**, click **Append**. In the **Append** dialog box, click the **Another Database** option button, and then click **Browse**. Navigate to your **Access Chapter 5** folder, and then double-click **5B Customer Orders**. (Be sure to use the version of the file that you worked on and saved earlier.)

> The *5B Customer Orders* database contains the destination table.

6 In the **Append** dialog box, click the **Table Name arrow**, click **5B Customers**, and then compare your screen with Figure 5.35.

> Once you select the name of another database, the tables contained in that database display.

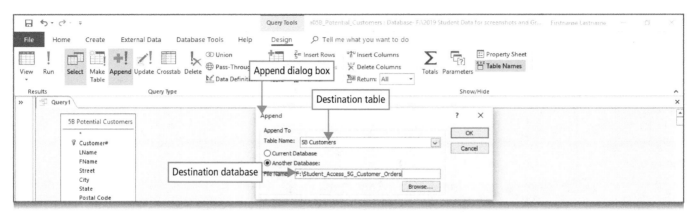

Figure 5.35

7 Click **OK**. In the design grid, notice that in the **Append To row**, Access found field name matches for all fields except **LName** and **FName**.

8 In the design grid, click in the **Append To row** under **LName**, click the **arrow**, and then compare your screen with Figure 5.36.

> A list displays the field names contained in the *5B Customers* table. If the field names are not exactly the same in the source and destination tables, Access will not designate them as matched fields. A *source table* is the table from which records are being extracted.

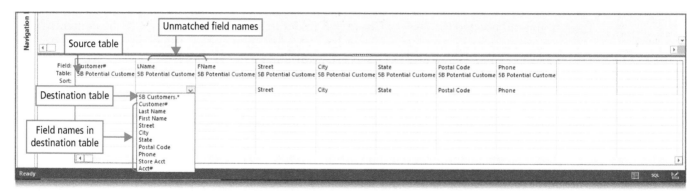

Figure 5.36

9 From the displayed list, click **Last Name**. Click in the **Append To** row under **FName**, and then click the **arrow**. In the displayed list, click **First Name**.

10 **Save** 🖫 the query as **5B Append to 5B Customers Query** and then **Run** the query, clicking **Yes** to append nine rows. **Close** ⊠ the query, and then **Open** ⧉ the **Navigation Pane**, resizing it if necessary. **Close** the database, and then **Close** this instance of Access.

ALERT   To trust or not to trust? That is the question!

When you allow someone else to run an action query that will modify a table in your database, be sure that you can trust that individual. One mistake in the action query could destroy your table. A better way of running an action query that is dependent upon someone else's table is to obtain a copy of the table, place it in a database that you have created, and examine the table for malicious code. Once you are satisfied that the table is safe, you can create the action query to modify the data in your tables. Be sure to make a backup copy of the destination database before running action queries.

---

11 If necessary, on the taskbar, click the button for your **5B_Customer_Orders** database. If you mistakenly closed the *5B_Customer_Orders* database, reopen it. In the **Navigation Pane**, under **Tables**, double-click **5B Customers** to open the table in **Datasheet** view. **Close** ⟪ the **Navigation Pane**. Scroll down until Customer# 9908 is displayed, and then compare your screen with Figure 5.37.

> The last nine records—Customer#s 9900 through 9908—have been appended to the *5B Customers* table. The last two fields—Store Acct and Acct#—are blank because there were no corresponding fields in the *5B Potential Customers* table.

Figure 5.37

MORE KNOWLEDGE   Running the Same Append Query a Second Time

If you run the same append query a second time with the same records in the source table and no primary key field is involved in the appending of records, you will have duplicate records in the destination table. If a primary key field is part of the records being duplicated, a message will display stating that Access cannot append all of the records due to one of several rule violations. If new records were added to the source table that were not originally appended to the destination table, clicking Yes in the message dialog box will enable those records to be added without adding duplicate records.

Objective 8 | Create a Delete Query

GO! Learn How
Video A5-8

A *delete query* is an action query that removes records from an existing table in the same database. When information becomes outdated or is no longer needed, the records should be deleted from your database. Recall that one method you can use to find unnecessary records is to create a find unmatched query. Assuming outdated records have common criteria, you can create a select query, convert it to a delete query, and then delete all of the records at one time rather than deleting the records one by one. Use delete queries only when you need to remove many records quickly. Before running a delete query, you should back up the database because you cannot undo the deletion.

Activity 5.15 | Creating a Delete Query

2.3.2, 1.2.2,
3.1.4, 3.2.1,
3.2.3, 3.1.6,
3.1.7

A competing store has opened in Santa Ana, and the former customers living in that city have decided to do business with that store. In this Activity, you will create a select query and then convert it to a delete query to remove records for clients living in Santa Ana.

1 With the **5B Customers** table open in **Datasheet** view, under **City**, click in any row. On the **Home tab**, in the **Sort & Filter group**, click **Descending** to arrange the cities in descending alphabetical order.

2 At the top of the datasheet, in the record for **Customer# 1060**, click the **plus (+) sign** to display the subdatasheet. Notice that this customer has placed one order that has been shipped.

3 Display the subdatasheets for the four customers residing in **Santa Ana**, and then compare your screen with Figure 5.38.

The four customers residing in Santa Ana have not placed orders.

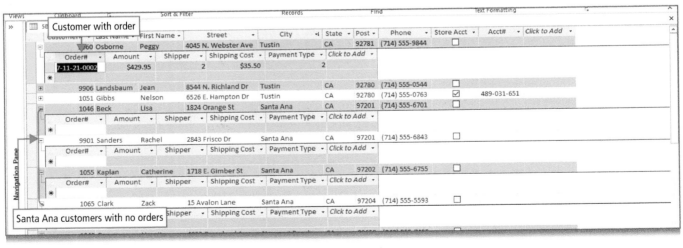

Figure 5.38

4 Collapse all of the subdatasheets by clicking each **minus (–) sign**.

5 On the ribbon, click the **Database Tools tab**. In the **Relationships group**, click **Relationships**. If the relationships do not display, under **Relationship Tools**, on the **Design tab**, in the **Relationships group**, click **All Relationships**. Resize the field lists and rearrange the field lists to match the layout displayed in Figure 5.39.

The *5B Customers* table has a one-to-many relationship with the *5B Orders* table, and referential integrity has been enforced. By default, Access will prevent the deletion of records from the table on the *one* side of the relationship if related records are contained in the table on the *many* side of the relationship. Because the records for the Santa Ana customers do not have related records in the related table, you will be able to delete the records from the *5B Customers* table, which is on the *one* side of the relationship.

To delete records from the table on the *one* side of the relationship that have related records in the table on the *many* side of the relationship, you must either delete the relationship or enable Cascade Delete Related Records. If you need to delete records on the *many* side of the relationship, you can do so without changing or deleting the relationship.

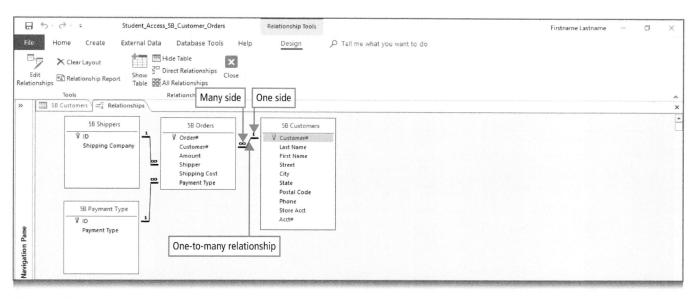

Figure 5.39

6 On the **tab row**, right-click any tab, and then click **Close All**, saving changes to the table and to the layout of the Relationships window.

7 Create a new query in **Query Design**. Add the **5B Customers** table to the query design workspace, and then **Close** ⌧ the **Show Table** dialog box. Resize the field list. From the field list, add **Customer#** and **City**, in the order specified, to the first and second columns in the design grid.

Since you are deleting existing records based on criteria, you need to add only the field that has criteria attached to it—the City field. However, it is easier to analyze the results if you include another field in the design grid.

8 In the design grid, click in the **Criteria** row under **City**, type **Santa Ana** and then press ⬇.

Access inserts the criteria in quotation marks because this is a Text field.

9 **Run** the query, and then compare your screen with Figure 5.40.

Four records for customers in Santa Ana are displayed. If your query results display an empty record, switch to Design view and be sure that you typed the criteria correctly.

Figure 5.40

10 Switch to **Design** view. In the query design workspace, to the right of the field list, right-click in the empty space. From the displayed shortcut menu, point to **Query Type**, and click **Delete Query**. Alternatively, under **Query Tools**, on the **Design tab**, in the **Query Type** group, click **Delete**. Compare your screen with Figure 5.41.

In the design grid, a Delete row is inserted above the Criteria row with the word *Where* in both columns. Access will delete all records *Where* the City is Santa Ana. If you include all of the fields in the query using the asterisk (*), Access inserts the word *From* in the Delete row, and all of the records will be deleted.

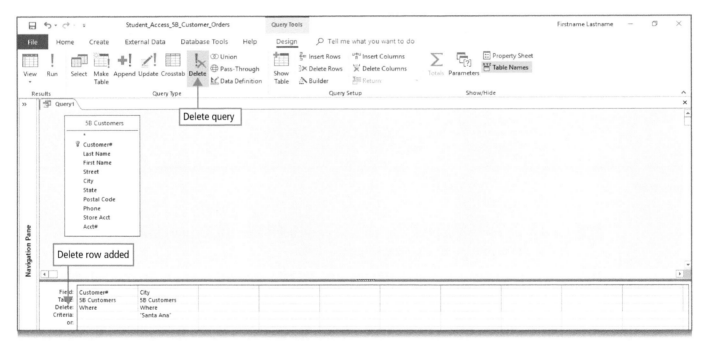

Figure 5.41

11 **Save** 🖫 the query as **5B Delete Santa Ana Customers Query** and then **Run** the query. In the message box stating that *You are about to delete 4 row(s) from the specified table*, click **Yes**.

12 Close ⊠ the query, and then **Open** ⏵⏵ the **Navigation Pane**. Under **Queries**, notice the icon that is associated with a delete query—**5B Delete Santa Ana Customers Query**. Under **Tables**, open the **5B Customers** table in **Datasheet** view. Notice that the records are still in descending order by the **City** field, and notice that the four records for customers living in **Santa Ana** have been deleted from the table.

13 Close ⏴⏴ the **Navigation Pane**, leaving the table open for the next activity. On the **Home tab**, in the **Sort & Filter group**, click **Remove Sort** to clear all sorts from the **City** field.

Objective 9 | Create an Update Query

GO! Learn How
Video A5-9

An *update query* is an action query that is used to add, change, or delete data in fields of one or more existing records. Combined with criteria, an update query is an efficient way to change data for a large number of records at one time, and you can change records in more than one table at a time. If you need to change data in a few records, you can use the Find and Replace dialog box. You are unable to use update queries to add or delete records in a table; use an append query or delete query as needed. Because you are changing data with an update query, you should back up your database before running one.

Activity 5.16 | Creating an Update Query

MOS
2.3.2, 3.1.4,
3.2.1, 3.2.3,
3.1.6, 3.1.7

The postal codes for all of the customers living in Irvine or East Irvine are changing to a consolidated postal code. In this Activity, you will create a select query to extract the records from the *5B Customers* table for customers living in these cities, and then convert the query to an update query so that you change the postal codes for all of the records at one time.

1 With the **5B Customers** table open in **Datasheet** view, click in the **City** field in any row. Sort the **City** field in **Ascending** order. Notice that there are five customers living in **East Irvine** with postal codes of **92650** and five customers living in **Irvine** with postal codes of **92602**, **92603**, and **92604**.

2 Close the table, saving changes. Create a new query in **Query Design**. Add the **5B Customers** table to the query design workspace, and then **Close** ⊠ the **Show Table** dialog box. Resize the field list.

3 In the **5B Customers** field list, double-click **City** to add the field to the first column of the design grid. Then add the **Postal Code** field to the second column of the design grid. In the design grid, click in the **Criteria row** under **City**, and then type **Irvine or East Irvine** Alternatively, type **Irvine** in the Criteria row, and then type **East Irvine** in the Or row. **Run** the query.

Ten records display for the cities of Irvine or East Irvine. If your screen does not display ten records, switch to Design view and be sure you typed the criteria correctly. Then run the query again.

4 Switch to **Design** view, and then notice how Access changed the criteria under the **City** field, placing quotation marks around the text and capitalizing *or*. Under **Query Tools**, on the **Design tab**, in the **Query Type group**, click **Update**.

In the design grid, an Update To row is inserted above the Criteria row.

5 In the design grid, click in the **Update To** row under **Postal Code**, type **92601** and then compare your screen with Figure 5.42.

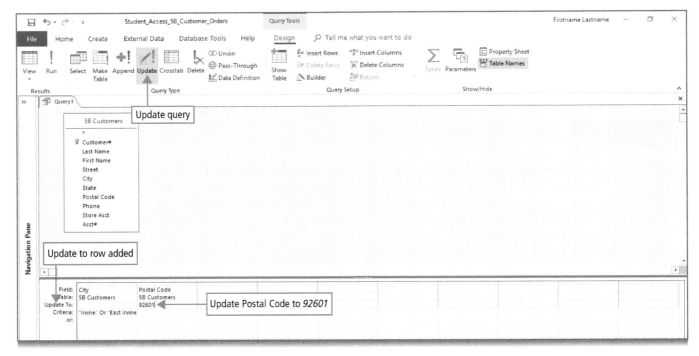

Figure 5.42

6 Save 🔲 the query as **5B Update Postal Codes Query** and then **Run** the query. In the message box stating that *You are about to update 10 row(s)*, click **Yes**.

7 **Close** the query, and then **Open** 》 the **Navigation Pane**. Under **Queries**, notice the icon that is associated with an update query—**5B Update Postal Codes Query**. Under **Tables**, open the **5B Customers** table in **Datasheet** view. Notice that the 10 records for customers living in **East Irvine** and **Irvine** have a **Postal Code** of **92601**.

8 **Close** ⨉ the table.

Activity 5.17 | Creating an Update Query with an Expression

MOS

2.3.2, 3.1.4,
3.1.5, 3.2.1,
3.2.3, 3.1.6,
3.1.7

There was a computer problem, and customers were overcharged for items shipped by FedEx. In this Activity, you will create an update query to correct the field to reflect an accurate shipping cost. Any item shipped by FedEx will be discounted 7 percent.

1 Open the **5B Orders** table in **Datasheet** view, and **Close** « the **Navigation Pane**. Click the right side of the **Shipper** field to see the lookup list. Notice an entry of **1** means the order was shipped using FedEx. Press Esc to return to the field box. Sort the **Shipper** field from **Smallest to Largest**. Notice that there are five orders that were shipped using FedEx. Make note of the shipping cost for each of those items.

2 **Close** the table, saving changes. Create a new query in **Query Design**. From the **Show Table** dialog box, add the **5B Shippers** table and the **5B Orders** table to the query design workspace, and then **Close** ⨉ the **Show Table** dialog box. Resize the field lists.

3 From the **5B Shippers** field list, add **Shipping Company** to the design grid. From the **5B Orders** field list, add **Shipping Cost** to the design grid. In the **Criteria row** under **Shipping Company**, type **FedEx Run** the query.

Five records display for FedEx. If your screen does not display five records, switch to Design view and be sure you typed the criteria correctly. Then run the query again.

4 Switch to **Design** view. Under **Query Tools**, on the **Design tab**, in the **Query Type group**, click **Update**.

In the design grid, an Update To row is inserted above the Criteria row.

5 In the design grid, under **Shipping Cost**, click in the **Update To row**, type **[Shipping Cost]*.93** and then compare your screen with Figure 5.43.

Recall that square brackets surround existing fields in an expression, and numbers do not include any brackets. This expression will reduce the current shipping cost by 7%, so the customers will pay 93% of the original cost. Currency, Date/Time, and Number fields can be updated using an expression. For example, a selling price field can be increased by 15% by typing [Selling Price]*1.15 in the Update To box, and an invoice due date can be extended by 3 days by typing [Invoice Date]+3 in the Update To box.

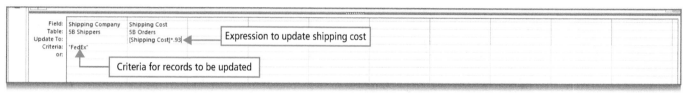

Figure 5.43

6 Save 🖫 the query as **5B Update FedEx Shipping Costs Query** and then **Run** the query. In the message box stating that *You are about to update 5 row(s)*, click **Yes**.

The update query runs every time the query is opened, unless it is opened directly in Design view. To review or modify the query, right-click the query name, and then click Design View.

7 **Close** ⊠ the query, and then **Open** �» the **Navigation Pane**. Under **Tables**, open the **5B Orders** table in **Datasheet** view. Notice that the five records for orders shipped via FedEx have lower shipping costs than they did prior to running the query—93 percent of the original cost, or 7 percent less.

8 **Close** ⊠ the **5B Orders** table.

MORE KNOWLEDGE **Restrictions for Update Queries**

It is not possible to run an update query with these types of table fields:

- Calculated fields, created in a table or in a query
- Fields that use total queries or crosstab queries as their source
- AutoNumber fields, which can change only when you add a record to a table
- Fields in union queries
- Fields in unique-values or unique-records queries
- Primary key fields that are common fields in table relationships, unless you set Cascade Update Related Fields

You cannot cascade updates for tables that use a data type of AutoNumber to generate the primary key field.

Objective 10 | Modify the Join Type

GO! Learn How
Video A5-10

When multiple tables are included in a query, a *join* helps you extract the correct records from the related tables. The relationship between the tables, based on common fields, is represented in a query by a join, which is displayed as the join line between the related tables. When you add tables to the query design workspace, Access creates the joins based on the defined relationships. If you add queries to the query design workspace or tables where the relationship has not been defined, you can manually create joins between the objects by dragging a common field from one object to the common field in the second. Joins establish rules about records to be included in the query results and combine the data from multiple sources on one record row in the query results.

Activity 5.18 | Viewing the Results of a Query Using an Inner Join

1.2.2, 3.1.5,
3.2.1, 3.2.2,
1.2.1, 3.1.7

The default join type is the *inner join*, which is the most common type of join. When a query with an inner join is run, only the records where the common field exists in both related tables are displayed in the query results. All of the queries you have previously run have used an inner join. In this Activity, you will view the results of a query that uses an inner join.

1 Close ⊘ the **Navigation Pane**. On the ribbon, click the **Database Tools tab**, and then in the **Relationships group** click **Relationships**. Notice the relationship between the **5B Customers** table and the **5B Orders** table.

Because referential integrity has been enforced, it is easy to determine that the *5B Customers* table is on the *one* side of the relationship, and the *5B Orders* table is on the *many* side of the relationship. *One* customer can have *many* orders. The common field is Customer#.

2 In the **Relationships** window, double-click the **join line** between the **5B Customers** table and the **5B Orders** table. Alternatively, right-click the join line, and then click **Edit Relationship**, or click the line, and then in the **Tools** group, click **Edit Relationships**. Compare your screen with Figure 5.44.

The Edit Relationships dialog box displays, indicating that referential integrity has been enforced and that the relationship type is *One-to-Many*. Because the relationship has been established for the tables, you can view relationship properties in the Relationships window.

ALERT   Is your Edit Relationships dialog box empty?

If your Edit Relationships dialog box does not display as shown in Figure 5.44, you may have double-clicked *near* the join line and not *on* the join line. In the Edit Relationships dialog box, click Cancel, and then try again.

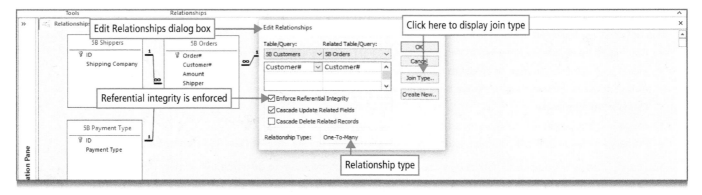

Figure 5.44

3 In the **Edit Relationships** dialog box, click **Join Type**, and then compare your screen with Figure 5.45. In the displayed **Join Properties** dialog box, notice that option **1** is selected—*Only include rows where the joined fields from both tables are equal.*

Option 1 is the default join type, which is an inner join. Options 2 and 3 are outer join types.

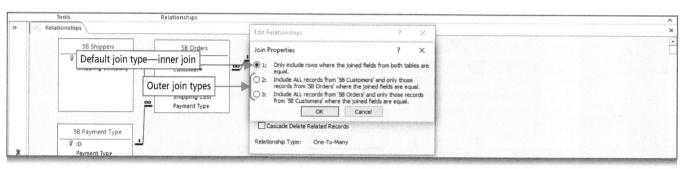

Figure 5.45

4 In the **Join Properties** dialog box, click **Cancel**. In the **Edit Relationships** dialog box, click **Cancel**. **Close** ⊠ the **Relationships** window.

Because the relationships have been established and saved in the database, you should not change the join properties in the Relationships window. You should only change join properties in the query design workspace.

5 **Open** ⟩⟩ the **Navigation Pane**. In the **Navigation Pane**, open the **5B Orders** table and the **5B Customers** table, in the order specified, and then **Close** ⟨⟨ the **Navigation Pane**.

6 With the **5B Customers** table active, on the **Home tab**, in the **Sort & Filter group**, click **Remove Sort** to remove the ascending sort from the **City** field. Notice that the records are now sorted by the **Customer#** field—the primary key field.

7 In the third record, click the **plus (+) sign** to expand the subdatasheet—the related record in the *5B Orders* table—and then notice that **Willie Smith** has no related records—he has not placed any orders. Click the **minus (–) sign** to collapse the subdatasheet.

8 Expand the subdatasheet for **Customer# 1045**, and then notice that **Joe Crocker** has one related record in the *5B Orders* table—he has placed one order. Collapse the subdatasheet.

9 Expand the subdatasheet for **Customer# 1047**, and then notice that **Robert Bland** has two related records in the *5B Orders* table—he has placed *many* orders. Collapse the subdatasheet.

10 On the **tab row**, click the **5B Orders tab** to make the datasheet active, and then notice that 15 orders have been placed. On the **tab row**, right-click any tab, and then click **Close All**, saving changes, if prompted.

11 Create a new query in **Query Design**. From the **Show Table** dialog box, add the **5B Customers** table and the **5B Orders** table to the query design workspace, and then **Close** ⊠ the **Show Table** dialog box. Resize both field lists.

12 From the **5B Customers** field list, add **Customer#**, **Last Name**, and **First Name**, in the order specified, to the design grid. In the design grid, under **Customer#**, click in the **Sort row**, click the **arrow**, and then click **Ascending**. **Run** the query, and then compare your screen with Figure 5.46. There is no record for Willie Smith, there is one record for Customer# 1045—Joe Crocker—and there are two records for Customer# 1047—Robert Bland.

Because the default join type is an inner join, the query results display records only where there is a matching Customer#—the common field—in both related tables, even though you did not add any fields from the *5B Orders* table to the design grid. All of the records display for the table on the *many* side of the relationship—*5B Orders*. For the table on the *one* side of the relationship—*5B Customers*—only those records that have matching records in the related table display. Recall that there were 30 records in the *5B Customers* table and 15 records in the *5B Orders* table.

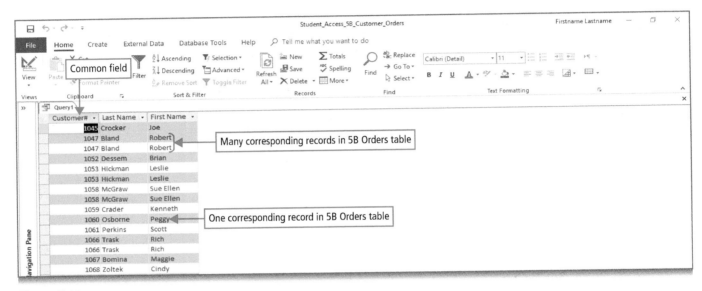

Figure 5.46

13 Switch to **Design** view. From the **5B Orders** field list, add **Order#** to the fourth column of the design grid, and then add **Amount** to the fifth column of the design grid. **Run** the query to display the results.

The same 15 records display but with two additional fields.

Activity 5.19 | Changing the Join Type to an Outer Join

1.2.1, 3.1.6, 3.1.7

An *outer join* is typically used to display records from both tables, regardless of whether there are matching records. In this Activity, you will modify the join type to display all of the records from the *5B Customers* table, regardless of whether the customer has placed an order.

1 Switch to **Design** view. In the query design workspace, double-click the **join line** to display the **Join Properties** dialog box. Alternatively, right-click the join line, and then click **Join Properties**. Compare your screen with Figure 5.47.

The Join Properties dialog box displays the tables used in the join and the common field from both tables. Option 1—inner join type—is selected by default. Options 2 and 3 are two different types of outer joins.

Option 2 is a *left outer join*. Select a left outer join when you want to display all of the records on the *one* side of the relationship, whether or not there are matching records in the table on the *many* side of the relationship. Option 3 is a *right outer join*. Selecting a right outer join will display all of the records on the *many* side of the relationship, whether or not there are matching records in the table on the *one* side of the relationship. This should not occur if referential integrity has been enforced because all orders should have a related customer.

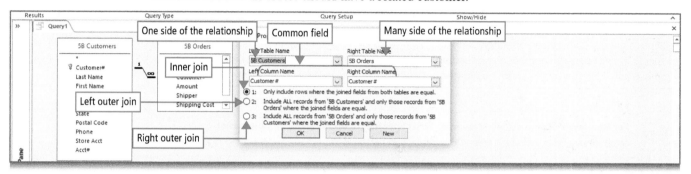

Figure 5.47

2 In the **Join Properties** dialog box, click the option button next to **2**, and then click **OK**. **Run** the query, and then compare your screen with Figure 5.48.

Thirty-four records display. There are thirty records in the *5B Customers* table; however, four customers have two orders, so there are two separate records for each of these customers. If a customer does not have a matching record in the *5B Orders* table, the Order# and Amount fields are left empty in the query results.

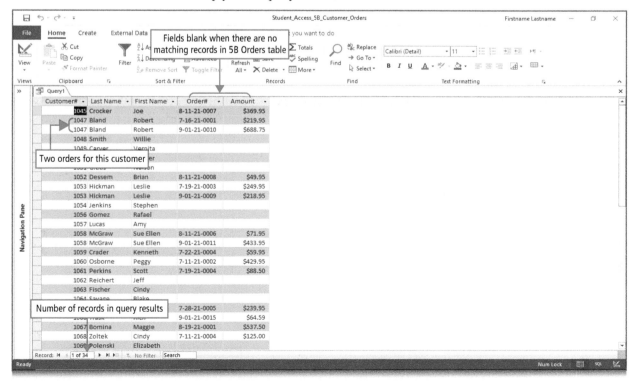

Figure 5.48

3 Save 🖫 the query as **5B Outer Join Query**

4 **Close** the query, and then **Open** the **Navigation Pane**. Resize the **Navigation Pane** so all object names are fully displayed. **Close** the database, and then **Close** Access.

MORE KNOWLEDGE **Other Types of Joins**

There are two other types of joins: cross joins and unequal joins. A *cross join* is not explicitly set in Access 2019. In a cross join, each row from one table is combined with each row in a related table. Cross joins are usually created unintentionally when you do not create a join line between related tables in a query. In fact, the results of the query will probably not make much sense. In the previous query, you would create a cross join by deleting the join line between the 5B Customers table and the 5B Orders table. A cross join produces many records; depending on the number of records in both tables, the cross join can take a long time to run. A cross join using the aforementioned tables would result in 348 displayed records when the query is run (29 customers × 12 orders = 348 records).

An *unequal join* is used to combine rows from two data sources based on field values that are not equal. The join can be based on any comparison operator, such as greater than (>), less than (<), or not equal to (<>). The results in an unequal join using the not equal to comparison operator are difficult to interpret and can display as many records as those displayed in a cross join. Unequal joins cannot be created in Design view; they can be created only in SQL view.

For Non-MyLab Submissions: Determine What Your Instructor Requires for Submission
As directed by your instructor, submit your completed database file.

---

5 In **MyLab IT**, locate and click the Grader Project **Access 5B Customer Orders**. In **step 3**, under **Upload Completed Assignment**, click **Choose File**. In the **Open** dialog box, navigate to your **Access Chapter 5 folder**, and then click your **Student_Access_5B_ Customer_Orders** file one time to select it. In the lower right corner of the **Open** dialog box, click **Open**.

The name of your selected file displays above the Upload button.

6 To submit your file to **MyLab IT** for grading, click **Upload**, wait a moment for a green **Success!** message, and then in **step 4**, click the blue **Submit for Grading** button. Click **Close Assignment** to return to your list of **Course Materials**.

You have completed Project 5B **END**

wavebreakmedia/Shutterstock, Monkey Business Images/Fotolia, Ivanko80/Shutterstock, Monkey Business Images/Shutterstock

Microsoft Office Specialist (MOS) Skills in This Chapter	
Project 5A	**Project 5B**
3.1.1 Create simple queries	**1.1.3** Hide and display objects in the Navigation Pane
3.1.2 Create basic crosstab queries	**1.2.1** Understand relationships
3.1.3 Create basic parameter queries	**1.2.2** Display relationships
3.1.5 Create basic multi-table queries	**2.1.1** Import data into tables
3.1.6 Save queries	**2.3.2** Sort records
3.1.7 Run queries	**3.1.4** Create basic action queries
3.2.1 Add, hide, and remove fields in a query	**3.1.5** Create basic multi-table queries
3.2.2 Sort data within queries	**3.1.6** Save queries
3.2.3 Filter data within queries	**3.1.7** Run queries
3.2.4 Format fields within queries	**3.2.1** Add, hide, and remove fields in a query
	3.2.3 Filter data within queries

Build Your E-Portfolio

An E-Portfolio is a collection of evidence, stored electronically, that showcases what you have accomplished while completing your education. Collecting and then sharing your work products with potential employers reflects your academic and career goals. Your completed documents from the following projects are good examples to show what you have learned: 5G, 5K, and 5L.

GO! for Job Success

Topic: Agile Business Culture

Markets and technologies move fast in today's high-tech environment. Companies that need to adapt to changes quickly are adopting an agile business culture. Evolved from a software development technique, agile businesses put their focus on customer needs and welcome the changes to products or services that customers request. Constant innovation toward more effective strategies is seen as the norm.

g-stockstudio/Shutterstock

What are some businesses that you interact with, either at a physical location or online, that might benefit from the quicker innovation and response to customer input provided by an agile culture?

Do you see areas at your college that you think would benefit from a more agile culture?

Are there areas of your personal or professional life where an agile approach to change and innovation might be beneficial?

End of Chapter

Summary

Queries are powerful database objects created to do more than extract data from tables and other queries; results can provide tools for analyzing, updating, and maintaining the integrity of the data.

Special-purpose queries are created to calculate fields, use aggregate functions, display data for easier analysis, find duplicate and unmatched records to avoid problems, and create prompts to use.

Action queries are used to create new tables, append records from source data in the same and other databases, delete records, and update data in tables. The results must be viewed in the original table.

Query results can be modified to display additional records by changing from the default inner join to an outer join between tables.

GO! Learn It Online

Review the concepts, key terms, and MOS skills in this chapter by completing these online challenges, which you can find at **MyLab IT**.

Chapter Quiz: Answer matching and multiple choice questions to test what you learned in this chapter.

Lessons on the GO!: Learn how to use all the new apps and features as they are introduced by Microsoft.

MOS Prep Quiz: Answer questions to review the MOS skills that you practiced in this chapter.

Project Guide for Access Chapter 5

Your instructor will assign Projects from this list to ensure your learning and assess your knowledge.

		Project Guide for Access Chapter 5		
Project	**Apply Skills from These Chapter Objectives**	**Project Type**		**Project Location**
5A MyLab IT	Objectives 1–5 from Project 5A	**5A Instructional Project (Grader Project)** **Instruction** A guided review of the skills from Project 5A.		MyLab IT and in the text
5B MyLab IT	Objectives 6–10 from Project 5B	**5B Instructional Project (Grader Project)** **Instruction** A guided review of the skills from Project 5B.		MyLab IT and in the text
5C	Objectives 1–5 from Project 5A	**5C Chapter Review (Scorecard Grading)** **Review** A guided review of the skills from Project 5A.		In the text
5D	Objectives 6–10 from Project 5B	**5D Chapter Review (Scorecard Grading)** **Review** A guided review of the skills from Project 5B.		In the text
5E	Objectives 1–5 from Project 5A	**5E Mastery (Scorecard Grading)** **Mastery and Transfer of Learning** A demonstration of your mastery of the skills in Project 5A with extensive decision making.		In the text
5F	Objectives 6–10 from Project 5B	**5F Mastery (Scorecard Grading)** **Mastery and Transfer of Learning** A demonstration of your mastery of the skills in Project 5B with extensive decision making.		In the text
5G MyLab IT	Objectives 1–10 from Projects 5A and 5B	**5G Mastery (Grader Project)** **Mastery and Transfer of Learning** A demonstration of your mastery of the skills in Projects 5A and 5B with extensive decision making.		MyLab IT and in the text
5H	Combination of Objectives from Projects 5A and 5B	**5H GO! Fix It (Scorecard Grading)** **Critical Thinking** A demonstration of your mastery of the skills in Projects 5A and 5B by creating a correct result from a document that contains errors you must find.		Instructor Resource Center (IRC)
5I	Combination of Objectives from Projects 5A and 5B	**5I GO! Make It (Scorecard Grading)** **Critical Thinking** A demonstration of your mastery of the skills in Projects 5A and 5B by creating a result from a supplied picture.		IRC
5J	Combination of Objectives from Projects 5A and 5B	**5J GO! Solve It (Rubric Grading)** **Critical Thinking** A demonstration of your mastery of the skills in Projects 5A and 5B, your decision-making skills, and your critical thinking skills. A task-specific rubric helps you self-assess your result.		IRC
5K	Combination of Objectives from Projects 5A and 5B	**5K GO! Solve It (Rubric Grading)** **Critical Thinking** A demonstration of your mastery of the skills in Projects 5A and 5B, your decision-making skills, and your critical thinking skills. A task-specific rubric helps you self-assess your result.		In the text
5L	Combination of Objectives from Projects 5A and 5B	**5L GO! Think (Rubric Grading)** **Critical Thinking** A demonstration of your understanding of the chapter concepts applied in a manner that you would use outside of college. An analytic rubric helps you and your instructor grade the quality of your work by comparing it to the work an expert in the discipline would create.		In the text
5M	Combination of Objectives from Projects 5A and 5B	**5M GO! Think (Rubric Grading)** **Critical Thinking** A demonstration of your understanding of the chapter concepts applied in a manner that you would use outside of college. An analytic rubric helps you and your instructor grade the quality of your work by comparing it to the work an expert in the discipline would create.		IRC
5N	Combination of Objectives from Projects 5A and 5B	**5N You and GO! (Rubric Grading)** **Critical Thinking** A demonstration of your understanding of the chapter concepts applied in a manner that you would use in a personal situation. An analytic rubric helps you and your instructor grade the quality of your work.		IRC

Glossary

Glossary of Chapter Key Terms

Action query A query that creates a new table or changes data in an existing table.

Aggregate function A function that performs a calculation on a column of data and returns a single value.

Append query An action query that adds new records to an existing table by adding data from another Access database or from a table in the same database.

Arithmetic operators Mathematical symbols used in building expressions.

Calculated field A field that obtains its data by using a formula to perform a calculation or computation.

Cross join A join that displays when each row from one table is combined with each row in a related table, usually created unintentionally when you do not create a join line between related tables.

Crosstab query A query that uses an aggregate function for data that is grouped by two types of information and displays the data in a compact, spreadsheet-like format. A crosstab query always has at least one row heading, one column heading, and one summary field.

Delete query An action query that removes records from an existing table in the same database.

Destination table In an append query, the table to which you are appending records, attempting to match the fields.

Expression The formula that will perform a calculation.

Find Duplicates Query A query used to locate duplicate records in a table.

Find Unmatched Query A query used to locate unmatched records so they can be deleted from the table.

Inner join A join that allows only the records where the common field exists in both related tables to be displayed in query results.

Join A relationship that helps a query return only the records from each table you want to see, based on how those tables are related to other tables in the query.

Left outer join A join used when you want to display all of the records on the *one* side of a one-to-many relationship, whether or not there are matching records in the table on the *many* side of the relationship.

Make table query An action query that creates a new table by extracting data from one or more tables.

Multivalued fields Fields that hold multiple values.

Outer join A join that is typically used to display records from both tables, regardless of whether there are matching records.

Parameter A value that can be changed.

Parameter query A query that prompts you for one or more criteria before running.

Right outer join A join used when you want to display all of the records on the *many* side of a one-to-many relationship, whether or not there are matching records in the table on the *one* side of the relationship.

Source table In a make table or append query, the table from which records are being extracted.

Static data Data that does not change.

Totals query A query that calculates subtotals across groups of records.

Unequal join A join used to combine rows from two data sources based on field values that are not equal; can be created only in SQL view.

Unmatched records Records in one table that have no matching records in a related table.

Update query An action query used to add, change, or delete data in fields of one or more existing records.

Chapter Review

Skills Review | **Project 5C Employee Payroll**

Apply 5A skills from these Objectives:

1. Create Calculated Fields in a Query
2. Use Aggregate Functions in a Query
3. Create a Crosstab Query
4. Find Duplicate and Unmatched Records
5. Create a Parameter Query

Derek Finkel, Human Resource Specialist at S-Boards, Inc., a surf and snowboard shop, has a database containing employee data and payroll data. In the following Skills Review, you will create special-purpose queries to perform calculations on data, summarize and group data, display data in a spreadsheet-like format, and find duplicate and unmatched records. You will also create a query that prompts an individual to enter the criteria. Your completed Navigation Pane will look similar to Figure 5.49.

Project Files

For Project 5C, you will need the following file:

a05C_Employee_Payroll

You will save your database as:

Lastname_Firstname_5C_Employee_Payroll

Project Results

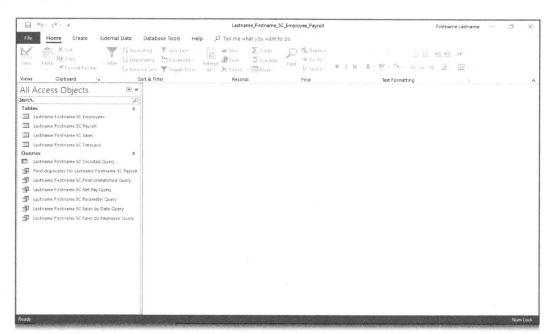

Figure 5.49

(continues on next page)

Chapter Review

1 Start Access. Locate and open the **a05C_Employee_Payroll** file. **Save** the database in your **Access Chapter 5** folder as **Lastname_Firstname_5C_Employee_Payroll**

a. If necessary, enable the content or add the Access Chapter 5 folder to the Trust Center.

b. Rename the tables by adding your **Lastname Firstname** to the beginning of each table name. **Close** the **Navigation Pane**.

2 On the ribbon, click the **Create tab**. In the **Queries group**, click **Query Design**. In the **Show Table** dialog box, add the following three tables to the query design workspace—**5C Employees**, **5C Payroll**, and **5C Timecard**—and then click **Close**. Resize the field lists.

a. From the **5C Employees** field list, add the following fields, in the order specified, to the design grid: **EmpID**, **Last Name**, and **First Name**.

b. From the **5C Payroll** field list, add the **Pay Rate** field.

c. From the **5C Timecard** field list, add the **Timecard Date** and **Hours** fields in this order. Under **Timecard Date**, in the **Criteria row**, type **6/29/2022**

d. In the **Field row**, right-click in the first cell in the first empty column to display a shortcut menu, and then click **Zoom**. In the **Zoom** dialog box, type **Gross Pay:[Pay Rate]*[Hours]** and then click **OK**. **Run** the query. Return to **Design** view.

e. If the **Gross Pay** does not show as **Currency**, click in the **Gross Pay** field that you just added. On the **Design tab**, in the **Show/Hide group**, click **Property Sheet**, if necessary. In the **Property Sheet**, on the **General tab**, click in the **Format** box, and then click the displayed **arrow**. In the list of formats, click **Currency**. On the **Property Sheet** title bar, click **Close**.

f. In the **Field row**, right-click in the first cell in the first empty column to display a shortcut menu, and then click **Zoom**. In the **Zoom** dialog box, type **Social Security:[Gross Pay]*0.042** and then click **OK**. Using the technique you just practiced, set a Currency format for this field, if necessary. **Close** the Property Sheet.

g. In the **Field row**, right-click in the first cell in the first empty column to display a shortcut menu, and then click **Zoom**. In the **Zoom** dialog box, type **Net Pay:[Gross Pay]-[Social Security]** and then click **OK**. **Run** the query to display the payroll calculations. Adjust column widths to display all field names and all data under each field.

h. On the **Home tab**, in the **Records group**, click **Totals**. In the **Total row**, under **Net Pay**, click in the empty box, and then click the **arrow** at the left edge. From the displayed list, click **Sum**.

i. On the **tab row**, right-click the **Query1 tab**, and then click **Save**. In the **Save As** dialog box, under **Query Name**, type **Lastname Firstname 5C Net Pay Query** and then click **OK**. View the query in **Print Preview**. Change the orientation to **Landscape** to ensure the table prints on one page. **Close** the query.

3 Create a new query in **Query Design**. Add the **5C Employees** table and the **5C Sales** table to the query design workspace, and then **Close** the **Show Table** dialog box. Resize both field lists.

a. From the **5C Employees** field list, add **Last Name** to the first field box in the design grid. From the **5C Sales** table, add **Sales** to both the second and third field boxes.

b. On the **Design tab**, in the **Show/Hide group**, click **Totals**. In the design grid, in the **Total row** under the first **Sales** field, click in the box displaying *Group By* to display the arrow, and then click the **arrow**. From the displayed list, click **Count**.

c. Under the second **Sales** field, click in the box displaying *Group By* to display the arrow, and then click the **arrow**. From the displayed list, click **Sum**.

d. In the design grid, in the **Sort row** under **Last Name**, click in the box to display the arrow, and then click the **arrow**. From the displayed list, click **Ascending**. **Run** the query to display the total number of sales and the total amount of the sales for each associate.

e. If necessary, adjust column widths to display all field names and all data under each field. **Save** the query as **Lastname Firstname 5C Sales by Employee Query** View the query in **Print Preview**, ensuring that the query prints on one page. **Close** the query.

4 Create a new query in **Query Design**. Add the following tables to the query design workspace: **5C Employees** and **5C Sales**. In the **Show Table** dialog box, click **Close**. Resize the field lists.

a. From the **5C Employees** table, add the **Last Name** and **First Name** fields. From the **5C Sales** table, add the **Timecard Date** and **Sales** fields. **Run** the query to display the sales by date. **Save** the query as **Lastname Firstname 5C Sales by Date Query** and then **Close** the query.

(continues on next page)

Chapter Review

Skills Review: Project 5C Employee Payroll (continued)

b. On the ribbon, click the **Create tab**. In the **Queries group**, click **Query Wizard**. In the **New Query** dialog box, click **Crosstab Query Wizard**, and then click **OK**. In the middle of the **Crosstab Query Wizard** dialog box, under **View**, click the **Queries** option button. In the list of queries, click **Query: 5C Sales by Date Query**, and then click **Next**.

c. Under **Available Fields**, double-click **Last Name** and **First Name**, and then click **Next**. In the displayed list of fields, double-click **Timecard Date**. Select an interval of **Date**, and then click **Next**. Under **Functions**, click **Sum**. On the left side of the **Crosstab Query Wizard** dialog box, above the **Sample** area, clear the **Yes, include row sums** check box, and then click **Next**.

d. Under **What do you want to name your query?**, select the existing text, type **Lastname Firstname 5C Crosstab Query** and then click **Finish**. Adjust all of the column widths to display the entire field name and the data in each field. The result is a spreadsheet view of total sales by employee by payroll date. View the query in **Print Preview**, ensuring that the query prints on one page. **Close** the query, saving changes.

5 On the **Create tab**, in the **Queries group**, click **Query Wizard**. In the **New Query** dialog box, click **Find Duplicates Query Wizard**, and then click **OK**.

a. In the first **Find Duplicates Query Wizard** dialog box, in the list of tables, click **Table: 5C Payroll**, and then click **Next**. Under **Available fields**, double-click **EmpID** to move it under **Duplicate-value fields**, and then click **Next**.

b. Under **Available fields**, add all of the fields to the **Additional query fields** box. Click **Next**. Click **Finish** to accept the suggested query name—*Find duplicates for Lastname Firstname 5C Payroll*. Adjust all column widths. View the query in **Print Preview**, ensuring that the query prints on one **Landscape** page. **Close** the query, saving changes.

6 On the **Create tab**, in the **Queries group**, click **Query Wizard**. In the **New Query** dialog box, click **Find Unmatched Query Wizard**, and then click **OK**.

a. In the first **Find Unmatched Query Wizard** dialog box, in the list of tables, click **Table: 5C Employees**, if necessary, and then click **Next**.

In the list of tables, click **Table: 5C Payroll**, if necessary, and then click **Next**. Under **Fields in '5C Employees'**, if necessary, click **EmpID**. Under **Fields in 5C Payroll**, if necessary, click **EmpID**. Click the **<=>** button. Click **Next**.

b. Under **Available fields**, double-click **EmpID**, **Last Name**, and **First Name** to move the field names under **Selected fields**. Click **Next**. In the last dialog box, under **What would you like to name your query?**, type **Lastname Firstname 5C Find Unmatched Query** and then click **Finish**.

c. Adjust all column widths. View the query in **Print Preview**, ensuring that the query prints on one page. **Close** the query, saving changes if necessary.

7 **Create** a new query in **Query Design**. Add the **5C Employees** table and the **5C Timecard** table to the query design workspace, and then **Close** the **Show Table** dialog box. Resize the field lists.

a. From the **5C Employees** field list, add **Last Name** and **First Name** to the first and second columns in the design grid. From the **5C Timecard** field list, add **Timecard Date** and **Hours** to the third and fourth columns in the design grid.

b. In the **Criteria row** under **Timecard Date** field, type **[Enter date]**

c. In the **Criteria row**, right-click in the **Hours** field, and then click **Zoom**. In the **Zoom** dialog box, type **Between [Enter the minimum Hours] And [Enter the maximum Hours]** and then click **OK**.

d. **Run** the query. In the **Enter Parameter Value** dialog box, type **6/29/22** and then click **OK**. Type **60** and then click **OK**. Type **80** and then click **OK**. Three employees have worked between 60 and 80 hours during the pay period for 6/29/22.

e. Adjust all column widths, and **Save** the query as **Lastname Firstname 5C Parameter Query** View the query in **Print Preview**, ensuring that the query prints on one page. **Close** the query.

8 Open the **Navigation Pane**, and resize it so all object names are fully visible. **Close** the database, and then **Close** Access.

9 As directed by your instructor, submit your database for grading.

Chapter Review

Apply 5B skills from these Objectives:

6. Create a Make Table Query
7. Create an Append Query
8. Create a Delete Query
9. Create an Update Query
10. Modify the Join Type

Miles Gorden, Purchasing Manager for S-Boards, Inc., a surf and snowboard shop, must keep the tables in the database up to date and ensure that the queries display pertinent information. Two of the suppliers, Super Wave Boards and Boot City, will no longer provide merchandise for S-Boards, Inc. This merchandise must be moved to a new discontinued items table. In the following Skills Review, you will create action queries that will create a new table, update records in a table, append records to a table, and delete records from a table. You will also modify the join type of relationships to display different subsets of the data when the query is run. Your completed Navigation Pane will look similar to Figure 5.50.

Project Files

For Project 5D, you will need the following files:

a05D_Store_Items
a05D_Warehouse_Items

You will save your databases as:

Lastname_Firstname_5D_Store_Items
Lastname_Firstname_5D_Warehouse_Items

Project Results

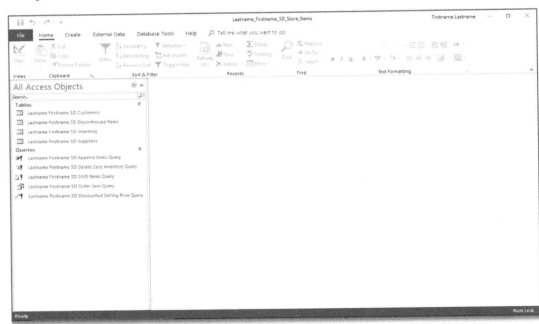

Figure 5.50

(continues on next page)

Chapter Review

Skills Review: Project 5D Clearance Sale (continued)

1 Start Access. Locate and open the **a05D_Store_Items** file. **Save** the database in your **Access Chapter 5** folder as **Lastname_Firstname_5D_Store_Items**

a. If necessary, enable the content or add the Access Chapter 5 folder to the Trust Center.

b. Rename the tables by adding your **Lastname Firstname** to the beginning of each table name. **Close** the **Navigation Pane**.

2 Create a new query in **Query Design**. From the **Show Table** dialog box, add the following tables to the query design workspace: **5D Suppliers** and **5D Inventory**. **Close** the **Show Table** dialog box, and then resize the field lists.

a. From the **5D Suppliers** field list, add **Company** to the first column of the design grid. From the **5D Inventory** field list, double-click each field to add them all to the design grid.

b. In the design grid, click in the **Criteria row** under **Supplier**, type **8** and then **Run** the query. Notice that three items are supplied by *Super Wave Boards*.

c. Switch to **Design** view. On the **Design tab**, in the **Query Type group**, click **Make Table**. In the **Make Table** dialog box, in the **Table Name** box, type **Lastname Firstname 5D Discontinued Items** In the **Make Table** dialog box, be sure that **Current Database** is selected, and then click **OK**. **Run** the query. In the displayed message box, click **Yes** to paste the rows to the new table.

d. **Close** the query, click **Yes** in the message box asking if you want to save changes, and then name the query **Lastname Firstname 5D SWB Items Query**

3 Create a new query in **Query Design**. From the **Show Table** dialog box, add the following tables, in the order specified, to the query design workspace: **5D Suppliers** and **5D Inventory**. **Close** the **Show Table** dialog box, and then resize the field lists.

a. From the **5D Suppliers** field list, add **Company** to the first column of the design grid. From the **5D Inventory** field list, add all the fields in the field list to the design grid.

b. In the design grid, click in the **Criteria row** under **Supplier**, type **3** and then **Run** the query. Notice that one item is supplied by *Boot City*.

c. Switch to **Design** view. On the **Design tab**, in the **Query Type group**, click **Append**. In the **Append** dialog box, click the **Table Name arrow**, and from the displayed list, click **5D Discontinued Items**. Click **OK**.

d. **Run** the query. In the displayed message box, click **Yes** to append one row. **Close** the query, and then save it as **Lastname Firstname 5D Append Items Query**

4 On the Access window title bar, click **Minimize**. **Start** a second instance of Access. Navigate to the location where the student data files for this textbook are saved. Locate and open the **a05D_Warehouse_Items** file. Save the database in your **Access Chapter 5** folder as **Lastname_Firstname_5D_Warehouse_Items** If necessary, enable the content or add the Access Chapter 5 folder to the Trust Center.

5 Create a new query in **Query Design**. From the **Show Table** dialog box, add the **5D Suppliers** table and the **5D Discontinued Items** table to the query design workspace, and then **Close** the **Show Table** dialog box. Resize the field lists. From the **5D Suppliers** field list, add **Company** to the first column of the design grid. From the **5D Discontinued Items** field list, add all of the fields to the design grid in the order listed.

a. On the **Design tab**, in the **Query Type group**, click **Append**. In the **Append** dialog box, click the **Another Database** option button, and then click **Browse**. Navigate to your **Access Chapter 5** folder, and then double-click **Lastname_Firstname_5D_Store_Items**.

b. In the **Append** dialog box, click the **Table Name arrow**, click **5D Discontinued Items**, and then click **OK**. **Save** the query as **Lastname Firstname 5D Append Warehouse Query** and then **Run** the query. In the displayed message box, click **Yes** to append three rows. **Close** the query. **Close** the database, and then **Close** this instance of Access.

c. If necessary, from the Windows taskbar, click the **5D_Store_Items** database. Verify that the **5D Discontinued Items** table now contains seven records. Apply **Best Fit** to all columns. **Close** the table, saving changes.

6 Create a new query in **Query Design**. Add the **5D Inventory** table to the query design workspace, and then **Close** the **Show Table** dialog box.

a. Resize the field list. From the field list, add **Catalog#** and **On Hand**, in this order, to the first and second columns in the design grid. In the design grid, click in the **Criteria row** under **On Hand**, type **0** and then **Run** the query to display one record.

b. Switch to **Design** view. In the query design workspace, right-click in the empty space. From the displayed shortcut menu, point to **Query Type**, and then click **Delete Query**.

(continues on next page)

ACCESS

5

Chapter Review

c. **Save** the query as **Lastname Firstname 5D Delete Zero Inventory Query** and then **Run** the query. In the message box stating that *You are about to delete 1 row(s) from the specified table*, click **Yes**. **Close** the query. You have removed this item from the inventory.

7 ▶ Create a new query in **Query Design**. Add the **5D Discontinued Items** table to the query design workspace, and then **Close** the **Show Table** dialog box. Resize the field list.

a. In the **5D Discontinued Items** field list, double-click **Catalog#** to add the field to the first column of the design grid. Then add the **Selling Price** field to the second column of the design grid.

b. On the **Design tab**, in the **Query Type group**, click **Update**. In the design grid, click in the **Update To row** under **Selling Price**, and then type **[Selling Price]*0.75**

c. **Save** the query as **Lastname Firstname 5D Discounted Selling Price Query** and then **Run** the query. In the message box stating that *You are about to update 7 row(s)*, click **Yes**. **Close** the query.

d. Open the **Navigation Pane**, and then double-click the **5D Discontinued Items** table to open it in **Datasheet** view. Close the **Navigation Pane**. Adjust all column widths. **Close** the table, saving changes.

8 ▶ Create a new query in **Query Design**. From the **Show Table** dialog box, add the **5D Suppliers** table and the **5D Discontinued Items** table to the query design workspace, and then **Close** the **Show Table** dialog box.

a. Resize both field lists. From the **5D Suppliers** table, drag the **ID** field to the **5D Discontinued Items** table **Supplier** field to create a join between the tables.

b. From the **5D Suppliers** field list, add **Company** and **Business Phone** to the first and second columns in the design grid. From the **5D Discontinued Items** field list, add **Catalog#**, **Item**, and **On Hand**, in this order, to the design grid. In the design grid, click in the **Sort row** under **Company**, click the **arrow**, and then click **Ascending**. **Run** the query.

c. Switch to **Design** view. Verify that the **5D Suppliers** table appears on the left, and the **5D Discontinued Items** table is on the right. Correct as necessary. In the query design workspace, double-click the **join line** to display the **Join Properties** dialog box. Click the option button next to **2**, and then click **OK**. **Run** the query. Adjust all column widths. This query displays all of the supplier companies used by the shop, not just those with discontinued items.

d. **Save** the query as **Lastname Firstname 5D Outer Join Query Close** the query.

9 ▶ Open the **Navigation Pane**, and resize it so all object names are fully displayed. **Close** the database, and then **Close** Access.

10 ▶ As directed by your instructor, submit your databases for grading.

You have completed Project 5D   **END**

Content-Based Assessments (Mastery and Transfer of Learning)

Mastering Access **Project 5E Surfing Lessons**

Apply 5A skills from these Objectives:

1. Create Calculated Fields in a Query
2. Use Aggregate Functions in a Query
3. Create a Crosstab Query
4. Find Duplicate and Unmatched Records
5. Create a Parameter Query

Gina Pollard, one of the owners of S-Boards, Inc., a surf and snowboard shop, has a database containing student, instructor, and surfing lesson data. In the following Mastering Access project, you will create special-purpose queries to calculate data, summarize and group data, display data in a spreadsheet-like format, and find duplicate and unmatched records. You will also create a query that prompts an individual to enter the criteria. Your completed Navigation Pane will look similar to Figure 5.51.

Project Files

For Project 5E, you will need the following file:

a05E_Surfing_Lessons

You will save your database as:

Lastname_Firstname_5E_Surfing_Lessons

Project Results

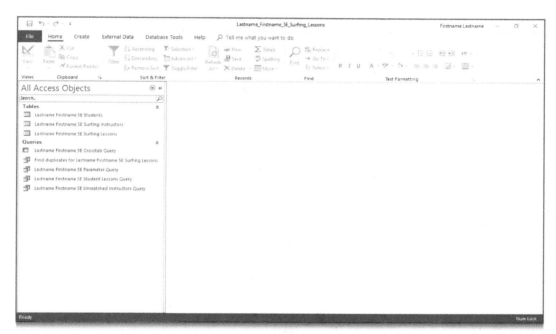

Figure 5.51

(continues on next page)

Mastering Access: Project 5E Surfing Lessons (continued)

1 Start Access. Locate and open the **a05E_Surfing_Lessons** file. Save the database in your **Access Chapter 5** folder as **Lastname_Firstname_5E_Surfing_Lessons** If necessary, enable the content or add the Access Chapter 5 folder to the Trust Center. Rename the tables by adding your **Lastname Firstname** to the beginning of each table name.

2 **Create** a query in **Query Design** using the **5E Surfing Lessons** table and the **5E Students** table. From the **5E Surfing Lessons** table, add the **Instructor** field, the **Lesson Time** field, and the **Duration** field to the first, second, and third columns of the design grid. From the **5E Students** table, add the **Last Name** and **First Name** fields to the fourth and fifth columns.

3 In the sixth column of the design grid, add a calculated field **End Time:[Duration]/24+[Lesson Time]** Display the **Field Properties** property sheet, and then format this field as **Medium Time**. This field will display the time the lesson ends.

4 In the first blank column, in the field name row, add the calculated field **Fee:[Duration]*80** Display the **Field Properties** property sheet, and then format this field as **Currency**. Surfing lessons cost $80.00 an hour.

5 In the **Instructor** field, in the **Sort row**, click **Ascending**. In the **Lesson Time** field, in the **Sort row**, click **Ascending**. **Run** the query.

6 On the **Home tab**, in the **Records group**, click **Totals**. In the **Fee** column, in the **Total row**, click the **arrow**, and then click **Average**. Adjust field widths as necessary.

7 **Save** the query as **Lastname Firstname 5E Student Lessons Query Close** the query.

8 **Create** a new query using the **Crosstab Query Wizard**. Select the **Query: 5E Student Lessons Query**. Click **Next**. From the **Available Fields**, add **Instructor** to the **Selected Fields** column. Click **Next**. Double-click **Lesson Time**, and then click **Date**. Click **Next**. From the **Fields column**, select **Duration**, and then from **Functions**, select **Sum**. Clear the **Yes, include row sums** check box.

9 Click **Next**. Name the query **Lastname Firstname 5E Crosstab Query** Select **View the query**, and then

click **Finish**. This query displays each instructor and the number of hours he or she taught by date. Adjust field widths as necessary. **Close** the query, saving changes.

10 Create a new query using the **Find Duplicates Query Wizard**. Select **Table: 5E Surfing Lessons**, click **Next**, and then select the **Lesson Time** field for duplicate information. Click **Next**. From **Available fields**, add the **Instructor** and **Duration** fields to the **Additional query fields** column. Click **Next**, and then accept the default name for the query. Click **Finish**. The query results show that there are duplicate lesson times. Adjust field widths as necessary. **Close** and **Save** the query.

11 Create a new query in the **Find Unmatched Query Wizard**. Select **Table: 5E Surfing Instructors**. From the **Which table or query contains the related records?** dialog box, click **Table: 5E Surfing Lessons**. Click **Instructor** as the **Matching** field. Display the one field **Instructor** in the query results. Name the query **Lastname Firstname 5E Unmatched Instructors Query** and then click **Finish**. Ralph is the only instructor who has no students. **Close** the query.

12 **Create** a query in **Design** view using the **5E Surfing Lessons** table and the **5E Students** table. From the **5E Surfing Lessons** table, add the **Instructor** field. From the **5E Students** table, add the **Last Name**, **First Name**, and **Phone#** fields in that order to the design grid. In the **Criteria row** under **Instructor**, type **[Enter Instructor's First Name]**

13 **Run** the query. In the **Enter Parameter Value** dialog box, type **Andrea** and then press Enter. The query displays Andrea's students and their phone numbers.

14 **Save** the query as **Lastname Firstname 5E Parameter Query** Adjust field widths as necessary. **Close** the query.

15 Open the **Navigation Pane**, and resize it so all object names are fully displayed. **Close** the database, and then **Close** Access.

16 As directed by your instructor, submit your database for grading.

You have completed Project 5E **END**

Content-Based Assessments (Mastery and Transfer of Learning)

Project 5F Gift Cards

Apply 5B skills from these Objectives:

6. Create a Make Table Query
7. Create an Append Query
8. Create a Delete Query
9. Create an Update Query
10. Modify the Join Type

Andrea Fierro, Sales Manager for S-Boards, Inc., a surf and snowboard shop, has decided to offer gift cards for purchase at the shop. She has a database of the employees and the details of the cards they have sold. In the following Mastering Access project, you will create action queries that will create a new table, update records in a table, append records to a table, and delete records from a table. You will also modify the join type of the relationship to display a different subset of the data when the query is run. Your completed Navigation Pane will look similar to Figure 5.52.

Project Files

For Project 5F, you will need the following file:

a05F_Gift_Cards

You will save your database as:

Lastname_Firstname_5F_Gift_Cards

Project Results

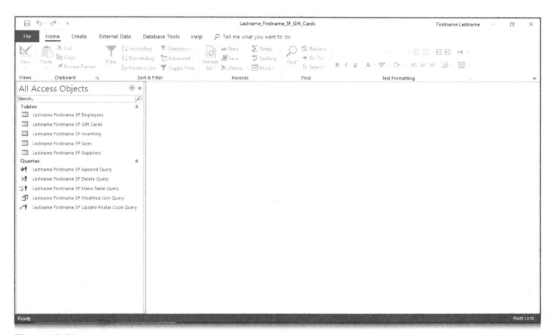

Figure 5.52

(continues on next page)

Content-Based Assessments

1 Start Access. Locate and open the **a05F_Gift_Cards** file. Save the database in your **Access Chapter 5** folder as **Lastname_Firstname_5F_Gift_Cards** If necessary, enable the content or add the Access Chapter 5 folder to the Trust Center. Rename the tables by adding your **Lastname Firstname** to the beginning of each table name.

2 Create a new query in **Query Design**. To the query design workspace, add the **5F Employees**, **5F Sales**, and the **5F Inventory** tables. From the **5F Employees** table, add the **First Name** and **Last Name** fields to the first and second columns of the design grid. From the **5F Sales** table, add the following fields to the design grid in the order specified: **Sales Date** and **Quantity**. From the **5F Inventory** table, add the **Item** and **Cost** fields.

3 In the **Criteria row** under **Item**, type **gift cards** In the **Criteria row** under **Cost**, type **25 Or 50 Sort** the **Last Name** field in **Ascending** order.

4 Change the **Query Type** to **Make Table**. Name the table **Lastname Firstname 5F $25 or $50 Gift Cards** Select **Current Database**, click **OK**, and then **Run** the query to add two records. **Close** the query, saving it as **Lastname Firstname 5F Make Table Query** Open the **5F $25 or $50 Gift Cards** table to display the two gift card purchases. **Close** the table.

5 Create a new query in **Query Design**. To the query design workspace, add the **5F Employees**, **5F Sales**, and the **5F Inventory** tables. From the **5F Employees** table, add the **First Name** and **Last Name** fields to the first and second columns of the design grid. From the **5F Sales** table, add the following fields to the design grid in the following order: **Sales Date** and **Quantity**. From the **5F Inventory** table, add the **Item** and **Cost** fields.

6 In the **Criteria row** under **Item**, type **Gift Cards** In the **Criteria row** under **Cost**, type **100 Or 250 Sort** the **Last Name** field in **Ascending** order.

7 Change the **Query Type** to **Append**, and then append the records to the **5F $25 or $50 Gift Cards** table. Click **OK**. **Run** the query. Click **Yes** to append three rows. **Close** the query, saving it as **Lastname Firstname 5F Append Query** Rename the **5F $25 or $50 Gift Cards** table as **Lastname Firstname 5F Gift Cards** Open the table to display all gift card purchases.

8 View the table in **Print Preview**, ensuring that the table prints on one page. **Close** the table.

9 Create a new query in **Query Design**. Add the **5F Inventory** table to the query design workspace. From the **5F Inventory** table, add the **Catalog#** and **Item** fields to the first and second columns of the design grid. In the design grid, click in the **Criteria row** under **Item**, and type **Gift Cards**

10 **Run** the query to view the results. Switch to **Design** view, change the **Query Type** to **Delete**, and then **Run** the query. Click **Yes** to delete four gift cards from the **5F Inventory** table. The gift cards are not to be counted as inventory items. **Close** and **Save** the query, naming it **Lastname Firstname 5F Delete Query**

11 Open the **5F Inventory** table to verify the gift cards are no longer listed in inventory. **Close** the table.

12 Create a new query in **Query Design**. Add the **5F Employees** table to the query design workspace. From the **5F Employees** table, add **Postal Code** to the first column of the design grid. In the design grid, click in the **Criteria row** under **Postal Code**, and then type **972*** **Run** the query to view the results. Switch to **Design** view, and change the **Query Type** to **Update**.

13 In the design grid, click in the **Update To row** under **Postal Code**, and then type **92710**

14 **Run** the query. Click **Yes** to update two rows. **Close** the query, saving it as **Lastname Firstname 5F Update Postal Code Query** Open the **5F Employees** table to verify the updated records. **Close** the table.

15 Create a new query in **Query Design**. Add the **5F Employees** and **5F Gift Cards** tables to the query design workspace. From the **5F Employees** field list, click **Last Name**, and then drag to the **5F Gift Cards Last Name** field. Double-click the **join line**, and then select option **2**.

16 From the **5F Employees** field list, add **First Name** and **Last Name** to the first two columns of the design grid. From the **5F Gift Cards** field list, add the **Cost** and **Quantity** fields, in that order, to the design grid. **Run** the query to display the results, which include all 14 employees and not just gift card sellers. **Save** the query as **Lastname Firstname 5F Modified Join Query**. **Close** the query.

17 Open the **Navigation Pane**, and resize it so all object names are displayed fully. **Close** the database, and then **Close** Access.

18 As directed by your instructor, submit your database for grading.

You have completed Project 5F **END**

<table>
<tr><td>

MyLab IT Grader

Apply 5A and 5B skills from these Objectives:

1. Create Calculated Fields in a Query
2. Use Aggregate Functions in a Query
3. Create a Crosstab Query
4. Find Duplicate and Unmatched Records
5. Create a Parameter Query
6. Create a Make Table Query
7. Create an Append Query
8. Create a Delete Query
9. Create an Update Query
10. Modify the Join Type

</td><td>

Mastering Access   Project 5G Advertising Options

    Steven Michaels, one of the owners of S-Boards, Inc., a surf and snowboard shop, is responsible for all of the advertising for the business. In the following Mastering Access project, you will create special-purpose queries to perform calculations on data, and then summarize and group data for advertising cost analysis. You will also create a query that prompts an individual to enter the criteria for a specific type of advertisement media. Your completed Navigation Pane will look similar to Figure 5.53.

Project Files for MyLab IT Grader

1. In your **MyLab IT** course, locate and click **Access 5G Advertising Options**, Download Materials, and then Download All Files.
2. Extract the zipped folder to your **Access Chapter 5** folder. Close the Grader download screens.
3. Take a moment to open the downloaded **Access_5G_Advertising_Options_Instructions**; note any recent updates to the book.

Project Results

</td></tr>
</table>

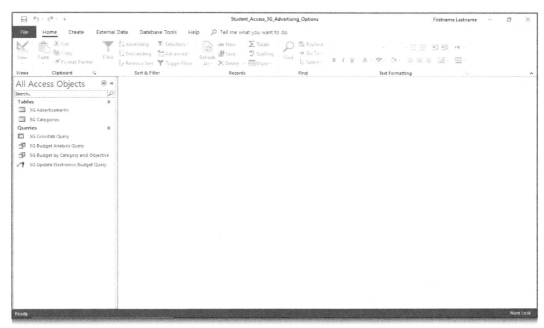

Figure 5.53

For Non-MyLab Submissions
For Project 5G, you will need:
a05G_Advertising_Options

Start with an Access Data File
In your Access Chapter 5 folder, save your database as:
Lastname_Firstname_5G_Advertising_Options

After you have saved your database, open it to launch Access. On the next page, begin with Step 2.
After Step 12, submit your database as directed by your instructor.

(continues on next page)

Content-Based Assessments

1 Start Access. Navigate to your **Access Chapter 5 folder**, and then double-click the Access file that you downloaded from **MyLab IT** that displays your name—**Student_Access_5G_Advertising_Options**.

2 **Close** the **Navigation Pane**. Create a new query in **Query Design**. From the **5G Categories** table, add the **Category** field to the design grid. From the **5G Advertisements** table, add the **Type**, **Budget Amount**, **Design Fee**, and **Production Fee** fields to the design grid in this order.

3 In the first blank field column, add a calculated field to display the total cost: **Cost:[Design Fee]+[Production Fee]** In the next blank field column, add a second calculated field: **Variance:[Cost]-[Budget Amount]** to display the amount over or under budget.

4 **Run** the query. Save it as **5G Budget Analysis Query** View the results in **Print Preview**, ensuring that it fits on one page in **Landscape** orientation. **Close** the query.

5 Create a new query in **Query Design**. From the **5G Categories** table, add the **Category** field to the design grid. From the **5G Advertisements** table, add the **Objective** and **Budget Amount** fields to the design grid. On the **Design tab**, in the **Show/Hide group**, click **Totals**. In the design grid, in the **Total row** under **Budget Amount**, click **Sum**.

6 **Run** the query. Save it as **5G Budget by Category and Objective Query** View the results in **Print Preview**, ensuring that it fits on one page. **Close** the query.

7 Create a new crosstab query using the **Query Wizard**. Select **Query: 5G Budget Analysis Query**. For row headings, use **Type**, and for column headings, use **Category**. Select **Cost** for the calculated field, using the **Sum** function. Do not summarize each row. Save it as **5G Crosstab Query** and then click **Finish**.

8 **Close** the query.

9 Create a new query in **Query Design**. From the **5G Categories** table, add the **Category** field to the design grid. From the **5G Advertisements** table, add the **Budget Amount** field to the design grid. In the design grid, click in the **Criteria row** under **Category**, and type **Electronic**

10 Change the **Query Type** to **Update**. In the design grid, click in the **Update To row** under **Budget Amount**, write an expression to increase the Budget Amount by 15%.

11 **Run** the query. Click **Yes** to update five rows. **Close** the query, saving it as **5G Update Electronics Budget Query Open** the **Navigation Pane**. **Open** the **5G Advertisements** table to verify the updates.

12 **Close** the table. **Open** the **Navigation Pane**, and resize it so all object names are displayed fully. **Close** the database, and then **Close** Access.

13 In **MyLab IT**, locate and click the Grader Project **Access 5G Advertising Options**. In **step 3**, under **Upload Completed Assignment**, click **Choose File**. In the **Open** dialog box, navigate to your **Access Chapter 5 folder**, and then click your **Student_Access_5G_ Advertising_Options** file one time to select it. In the lower right corner of the **Open** dialog box, click **Open**.

14 To submit your file to **MyLab IT** for grading, click **Upload**, wait a moment for a green **Success!** message, and then in **step 4**, click the blue **Submit for Grading** button. Click **Close Assignment** to return to your list of **Course Materials**.

You have completed Project 5G   **END**

Content-Based Assessments (Critical Thinking)

Apply a combination of the 5A and 5B skills.

GO! Fix It	**Project 5H Contests**	IRC
GO! Make It	**Project 5I Ski Trips**	IRC
GO! Solve It	**Project 5J Applications**	IRC
GO! Solve It	**Project 5K Ski Apparel**	

Project Files

For Project 5K, you will need the following file:

a05K_Ski_Apparel

You will save your database as:

Lastname_Firstname_5K_Ski_Apparel

Miles Gorden is the Purchasing Manager for S-Boards, Inc., a surf and snowboard shop. It is his responsibility to keep the clothing inventory current and fashionable. You have been asked to help him with this task. From the student files that accompany this textbook, open the **a05K_Ski_Apparel** database file, and then save the database in your Access Chapter 5 folder as **Lastname_Firstname_5K_Ski_Apparel**

The database consists of a table of ski apparel for youth, women, and men. Create a query to identify the inventory by status of the items (promotional, in stock, and discontinued clothing), and the number of items that are in each category. Update the selling price of the discontinued items to 80 percent of the current selling price. Use a make table query to place the promotional items into their own table and a delete query to remove those items from the 5K Ski Apparel table. Save your queries using your last and first names followed by the query type. View the queries in Print Preview, ensuring that each query prints on one page. As directed by your instructor, submit your database for grading.

		Performance Level		
		Exemplary	**Proficient**	**Developing**
Performance Criteria	**Create 5K Totals Query**	Query created to display inventory by status.	Query created with no more than two missing elements.	Query created with more than two missing elements.
	Create 5K Update Query	Query created to update clearance discontinued sale prices.	Query created with no more than two missing elements.	Query created with more than two missing elements.
	Create 5K Make Table Query	Query created to make a table for promotional items.	Query created with no more than two missing elements.	Query created with more than two missing elements.
	Create 5K Delete Query	Query created to delete promotional items from the Ski Apparel table.	Query created with no more than two missing elements.	Query created with more than two missing elements.

You have completed Project 5K | END

Outcomes-Based Assessments (Critical Thinking)

Rubric

The following outcomes-based assessments are open-ended assessments. That is, there is no specific correct result; your result will depend on your approach to the information provided. Make Professional Quality your goal. Use the following scoring rubric to guide you in how to approach the problem and then to evaluate how well your approach solves the problem.

The *criteria*—Software Mastery, Content, Format and Layout, and Process—represent the knowledge and skills you have gained that you can apply to solving the problem. The *levels of performance*—Professional Quality, Approaching Professional Quality, or Needs Quality Improvements—help you and your instructor evaluate your result.

	Your completed project is of Professional Quality if you:	Your completed project is Approaching Professional Quality if you:	Your completed project Needs Quality Improvements if you:
1-Software Mastery	Choose and apply the most appropriate skills, tools, and features and identify efficient methods to solve the problem.	Choose and apply some appropriate skills, tools, and features, but not in the most efficient manner.	Choose inappropriate skills, tools, or features, or are inefficient in solving the problem.
2-Content	Construct a solution that is clear and well organized, contains content that is accurate, appropriate to the audience and purpose, and is complete. Provide a solution that contains no errors of spelling, grammar, or style.	Construct a solution in which some components are unclear, poorly organized, inconsistent, or incomplete. Misjudge the needs of the audience. Have some errors in spelling, grammar, or style, but the errors do not detract from comprehension.	Construct a solution that is unclear, incomplete, or poorly organized, contains some inaccurate or inappropriate content, and contains many errors of spelling, grammar, or style. Do not solve the problem.
3-Format and Layout	Format and arrange all elements to communicate information and ideas, clarify function, illustrate relationships, and indicate relative importance.	Apply appropriate format and layout features to some elements, but not others. Overuse features, causing minor distraction.	Apply format and layout that does not communicate information or ideas clearly. Do not use format and layout features to clarify function, illustrate relationships, or indicate relative importance. Use available features excessively, causing distraction.
4-Process	Use an organized approach that integrates planning, development, self-assessment, revision, and reflection.	Demonstrate an organized approach in some areas, but not others; or, use an insufficient process of organization throughout.	Do not use an organized approach to solve the problem.

Outcomes-Based Assessments (Critical Thinking)

Apply a combination of the 5A and 5B skills.	**GO! Think** **Project 5L Surfboards**

Project Files

For Project 5L, you will need the following file:

a05L_Surfboards

You will save your database as

Lastname_Firstname_5L_Surfboards

    Miles Gorden, Purchasing Manager for S-Boards, Inc., a surf and snowboard shop, is stocking the shop with a variety of surfboards and accessories for the upcoming season. In this project, you will open the **a05L_Surfboards** database and create queries to perform special functions. Save the database as **Lastname_Firstname_5L_Surfboards** Create a query to display the item, cost, selling price, on hand, and two calculated fields: Item Profit by subtracting the cost from the selling price, and Inventory Profit by multiplying Item Profit by the number on hand for each item. Be sure both fields display as Currency. Include a sum for the Inventory Profit column at the bottom of the query results. Check the supplier against the inventory using a find unmatched records query; display all fields in the supplier table. Create a query to show the company that supplies each item, its email address, and then the Item and On Hand fields for each item in the inventory. Before running the query, create an outer join query using the *5L Suppliers* table and the *5L Inventory* table. Save your queries using your last and first names followed by the query type. View the queries in Print Preview, ensuring that the queries print on one page. As directed by your instructor, submit your database for grading.

You have completed Project 5L   **END**

GO! Think	**Project 5M Shop Promotions** **IRC**
You and GO!	**Project 5N Club Directory** **IRC**

Customizing Forms and Reports

6

ACCESS 2019

PROJECT 6A

Outcomes
Customize forms.

Objectives
1. Create a Form in Design View
2. Change and Add Controls
3. Format a Form
4. Make a Form User Friendly

PROJECT 6B

Outcomes
Customize reports.

Objectives
5. Create a Report Based on a Query Using a Wizard
6. Create a Report in Design View
7. Add Controls to a Report
8. Group, Sort, and Total Records in Design View

Olena Yakobchuk/Shutterstock

In This Chapter

 GO! To Work with Access

Forms provide a way to enter, edit, and display data from underlying tables. You have created forms using the Form tool and wizard. Forms can also be created in Design view. Access provides tools to enhance the appearance of forms, like adding color, backgrounds, borders, or guidelines to assist the person using the form. Forms can also be created from multiple tables if a relationship exists between the tables.

Reports display data in a professional-looking format suitable for printing. Like forms, reports can be created using the Report tool or a wizard, or in Design view, and they can all be enhanced using Access tools. Reports can be based on tables or queries in the database.

Rosebud Cafe is a "fast casual" franchise restaurant chain with headquarters in Florida and locations throughout the United States. The founders wanted to create a restaurant where fresh flavors would be available at reasonable prices in a comfortable atmosphere. The menu features quality ingredients in offerings that include grilled meat and vegetable skewers, wraps, salads, frozen yogurt, smoothies, coffee drinks, and seasonal favorites. All 81 outlets offer wireless internet connections and meeting space, making Rosebud Cafe the perfect place for groups and people who want some quiet time or to work with others.

PROJECT 6A Locations

Project Activities

In Activities 6.01 through 6.10, you will help Linda Kay, president, and James Cecil, vice president of franchising, create robust forms to match the needs of Rosebud Cafe. For example, forms can include color and different types of controls and can manipulate data from several tables. You will customize your form to make it easier to use and more attractive. Your completed Navigation Pane will look similar to Figure 6.1.

Project Files for MyLab IT Grader

1. In your storage location, create a folder named **Access Chapter 6**.
2. In your **MyLab IT** course, locate and click **Access 6A Locations**, Download Materials, and then Download All Files.
3. Extract the zipped folder to your Access Chapter 6 folder. Close the Grader download screens.
4. Take a moment to open the downloaded **Access_6A_Locations_Instructions**; note any recent updates to the book.

Project Results

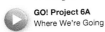

GO! Project 6A
Where We're Going

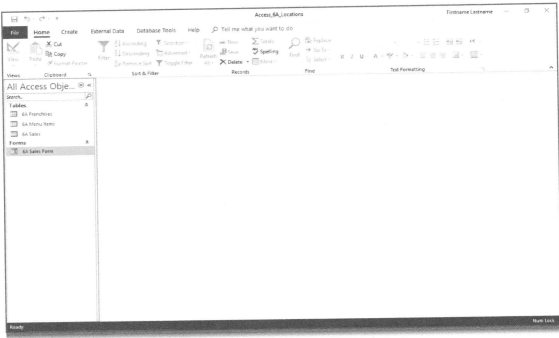

Figure 6.1 Project 6A Locations

For Non-MyLab Submissions	**Start with an Access Data File**
For Project 6A, you will need:	In your storage location, create a folder named **Access Chapter 6**
a06A_Locations	In your Access Chapter 6 folder, save your database as:
a06A_Logo	**Lastname_Firstname_6A_Locations**
a06A_Background	

After you have saved your database, open it to launch Access. On the next page, begin with step 2.

GO! Learn How
Video A6-1

Forms are usually created using the Form tool or the Form Wizard and then modified in Design view to suit your needs. Use Design view to create a form when these tools do not meet your needs or if you want more control in the creation of a form. Creating or modifying a form in Design view is a common technique when additional controls, such as combo boxes or images, need to be added to the form.

Activity 6.01 | Creating a Form in Design View

4.1.1, 4.1.2,
4.2.2

In this Activity, you will create a form in Design view that will enable employees to enter the daily sales data for each franchise of Rosebud Cafe.

1 Start Access. In the Access opening screen, click **Open Other Files**. Navigate to your **Access Chapter 6 folder**, and then double-click the Access file that you downloaded from **MyLab IT** that displays your name—**Student_Access_6A_Locations.**

2 If necessary, enable the content or add the Access Chapter 6 folder to the Trust Center.

3 In the **Navigation Pane**, double-click **6A Sales** to open the table in **Datasheet** view. Take a moment to examine the fields in the table. In any record, click in the **Franchise#** field, and then click the **arrow**. This field is a Lookup field—the values are looked up in the *6A Franchises* table. The Menu Item field is also a Lookup field—the values are looked up in the *6A Menu Items* table.

4 Close ⊠ the table, and then **Close** « the **Navigation Pane**. On the **Create tab**, in the **Forms group**, click **Form Design**.

The design grid for the Detail section displays.

5 Under **Form Design Tools**, on the **Design tab**, in the **Tools group**, click **Property Sheet**. Compare your screen with Figure 6.2. Notice that the *Selection type* box displays *Form*— this is the Property Sheet for the entire form.

Every object on a form, including the form itself, has an associated *Property Sheet* that can be used to further enhance the object. *Properties* are characteristics that determine the appearance, structure, and behavior of an object. This Property Sheet displays the properties that affect the appearance and behavior of the form. The left column displays the property name, and the right column displays the property setting. Some of the text in the property setting boxes may be truncated.

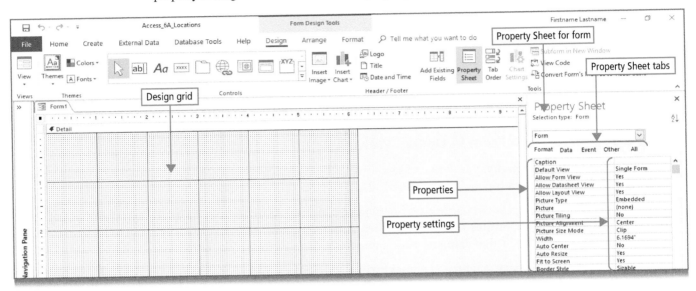

Figure 6.2

6 On the **Property Sheet**, with the **Format tab** displayed, scroll down, if necessary, to display the **Split Form Orientation** property box. If necessary, point to the left edge of the **Property Sheet** until the ⟷ pointer displays, and then drag to the left until the setting in the **Split Form Orientation** property box—*Datasheet on Top*—displays entirely.

7 On the **Property Sheet**, click the **Data tab**. Click the **Record Source** property setting box **arrow**, and then click **6A Sales**.

The *Record Source property* enables you to specify the source of the data for a form or a report. The property setting can be a table name, a query name, or an SQL statement.

8 **Close** ⊠ the **Property Sheet**. Under **Form Design Tools**, on the **Design tab**, in the **Tools group**, click **Add Existing Fields**, and then compare your screen with Figure 6.3.

The Field List for the record source—6A Sales—displays.

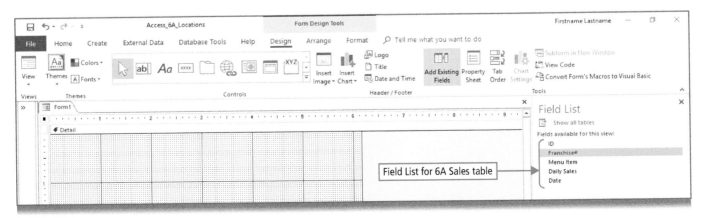

Figure 6.3

9 In the **Field List**, click **Franchise#**, if necessary. To select multiple fields, hold down Shift, and then click **Date**. Drag the selected fields onto the design grid until the top of the arrow of the pointer is **three dots** below the bottom edge of the **Detail section bar** and aligned with the **1.5-inch mark on the horizontal ruler**, as shown in Figure 6.4, and then release the mouse button.

Drag the fields to where the text box controls should display. If you drag to where the label controls should display, the label controls and text box controls will overlap. If you move the controls to an incorrect position, click Undo, and move them again.

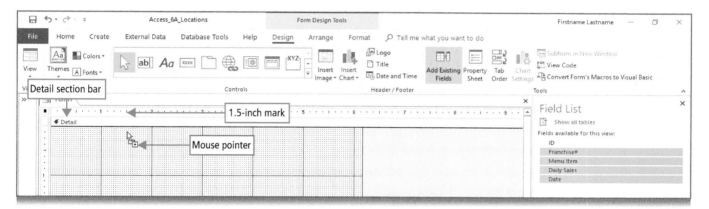

Figure 6.4

🔄 **ANOTHER WAY**   In the Field List, double-click each field name to add the fields to the form. It is not possible to select all the fields and then double-click. Alternatively, in the Field List, right-click a field name, and then click Add Field to View.

10 Close ⊠ the Field List.

MORE KNOWLEDGE   **Remove Unnecessary Form Controls**

If controls that you no longer need are displayed, click to select one of the controls. Holding down Shift, select all extra controls at one time, and then press Delete.

11 With all controls selected, under **Form Design Tools**, click the **Arrange tab**. In the **Table group**, click **Stacked**.

When you create a form in Design view, the controls are not automatically grouped in a stacked or tabular layout. Grouping the controls makes it easier to format the controls and keeps the controls aligned.

12 Save 🖫 the form as **6A Sales Form**

MORE KNOWLEDGE   **Horizontal and Vertical Spacing Between Controls**

If the controls on a form are not grouped in a tabular or stacked layout, you can change the spacing between the controls. With the controls selected, click the Arrange tab. In the Sizing & Ordering group, click Size/Space, and then click the appropriate button to control spacing. Spacing options include Equal Horizontal, Increase Horizontal, Decrease Horizontal, Equal Vertical, Increase Vertical, and Decrease Vertical.

Activity 6.02 | Adding Sections to a Form

4.2.4, 4.2.5,
4.2.3

The only section that is automatically added to a form when it is created in Design view is the Detail section. In this Activity, you will add a Form Header section and a Form Footer section.

1 Switch to **Form** view, and notice that the form displays only the data. There is no header section with a logo or name of the form.

2 Switch to **Design** view. Under **Form Design Tools**, on the **Design tab**, in the **Header/Footer group**, click **Logo**. In the **Insert Picture** dialog box, navigate to your **Access Chapter 6** folder. Locate and double-click **a06A_Logo** to insert the logo in the Form Header section.

> Two sections—the Form Header and the Form Footer—are added to the form along with the logo. Sections can be added only in Design view.

3 On the selected logo, point to the right middle sizing handle until the pointer ⟷ displays. Drag to the right until the right edge of the logo is aligned with the **1.5-inch mark on the horizontal ruler**.

4 In the **Header/Footer group**, click **Title** to insert the title in the Form Header section. Compare your screen with Figure 6.5.

> The name of the form is inserted as a title into the Form Header section, and the label control is the same height as the logo.

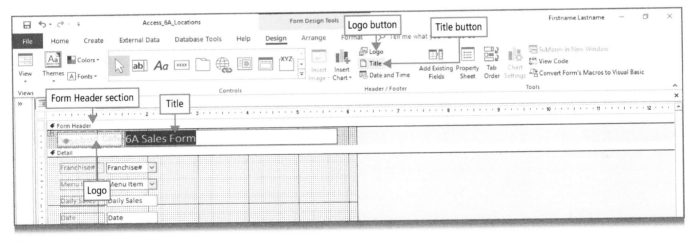

Figure 6.5

5 Scroll down until the **Form Footer** section bar displays. Point to the top of the **Form Footer** section bar until the pointer ⊞ displays. Drag upward until the top of the Form Footer section bar aligns with the **2-inch mark on the vertical ruler**.

> The height of the Detail section is decreased. Extra space at the bottom of the Detail section will cause blank space to display between records if the form is printed.

6 Under **Form Design Tools**, on the **Design tab**, in the **Controls group**, click **Label** `Aa`. Point to the **Form Footer** section until the plus sign (+) of the pointer aligns with the bottom of the **Form Footer** section bar and with the left edge of the **Date label control** in the Detail section. Click and drag downward to the bottom of the **Form Footer** section and to the right to **3 inches on the horizontal ruler**. Type **Designed for Rosebud Cafe** Press Enter, and then compare your screen with Figure 6.6.

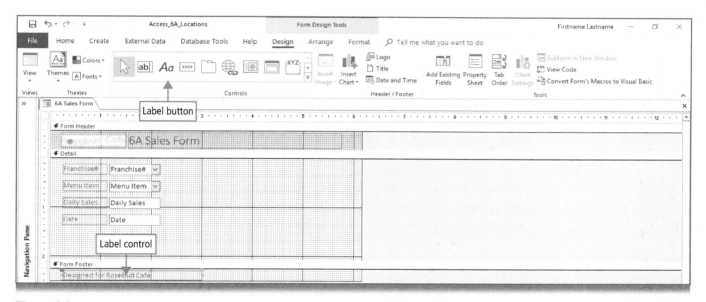

Figure 6.6

7 With the label control in the Form Footer section selected, hold down Shift, and then click each of the label controls in the Detail section. Under **Form Design Tools,** click the **Arrange tab**. In the **Sizing & Ordering group**, click **Align**, and then select **Left**. Save `□` the form, and then switch to **Form** view.

> The Form Header section displays the logo and the title of the form. The Form Footer section displays the label control that is aligned with the label controls in the Detail section. Both the Form Header and Form Footer sections display on every form page.

Objective 2 Change and Add Controls

GO! Learn How

Video A6-2

A ***control*** is an object, such as a label or text box, in a form or report that enables you to view or manipulate information stored in tables or queries. You have worked with label controls, text box controls, and logo controls, but there are more controls that can be added to a form. More controls are available in Design view than in Layout view. By default, when you create a form, Access uses the same field definitions as those in the underlying table or query.

Activity 6.03 | Changing Controls on a Form

4.1.1, 4.1.2, 4.2.2

To use the form more efficiently, you will change the controls. In this Activity, you will change a combo box control to a list box control.

1 Click the **Menu Item field arrow**.

> Because the underlying table—*6A Sales*—designated this field as a lookup field, Access inserted a combo box control for this field instead of a text box control. The Franchise# field is also a combo box control. A ***combo box*** enables individuals to select from a list or to type a value.

2 Switch to **Design** view. In the **Detail** section, click the **Menu Item label control**, hold down Shift, and then click the **Menu Item combo box control**. Under **Form Design Tools**, click the **Arrange tab**. In the **Table group**, click **Remove Layout**.

Remove Layout is used to remove a field from a stacked or tabular layout—it does not delete the field or remove it from the form. If fields are in the middle of a stacked layout column and are removed from the layout, the remaining fields in the column will display over the removed field. To avoid the clutter, first move the fields that you want to remove from the layout to the bottom of the column.

3 Click **Undo** 🔄. Point to the **Menu Item label control** until the pointer 🔯 displays. Click and drag downward until a thin orange line displays on the bottom edges of the **Date** controls. Release the mouse button.

ALERT   **Did the control stay in the same location?**

In Design view, the orange line that indicates the location where controls will be moved is much thinner than—and not as noticeable as—the line in Layout view. If you drag downward too far, Access will not move the selected fields.

4 In the **Table group**, click **Remove Layout** to remove the Menu Item field from the stacked layout. Point to the selected controls, and then drag to the right and upward until the **Menu Item label control** is aligned with the **Franchise#** controls and with the **3.25-inch mark on the horizontal ruler**. Compare your screen with Figure 6.7.

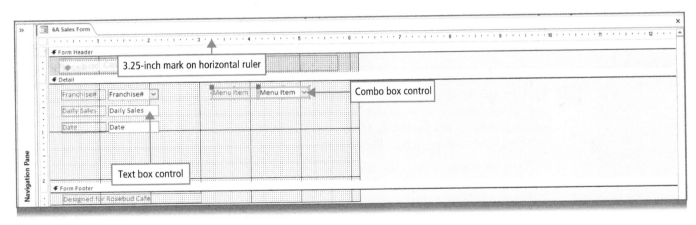

Figure 6.7

5 With the **Menu Item controls** selected, in the **Table group**, click **Stacked**. Click anywhere in the **Detail** section to deselect the second column.

The Menu Item controls display in the second column and are grouped in a stacked layout. Recall that a stacked layout keeps the controls aligned and makes it easier to edit and move the controls.

6 Right-click the **Menu Item combo box control**. From the shortcut menu, point to **Change To**, and then click **List Box**.

A *list box* enables individuals to select from a list but does not enable individuals to type anything that is not in the list. Based on the data in the underlying table or query, Access displays the control types to which you can change a field. The control type can be changed in Design view only.

7 **Save** 💾 the form, and then switch to **Form** view. Notice the **Menu Item list box control** is not wide enough to display both columns and that there are horizontal and vertical scroll bars to indicate there is more data.

8 Click the **Menu Item list box control**. Scroll down until Menu Item *7839* displays. Switch to **Layout** view. Point to the right edge of the control until the pointer ↔ displays. Drag to the right until all of the Menu Item *7839* displays. Release the mouse button to display the resized list box. Click anywhere in the **Detail** section to deselect the control.

> Switching to Layout view allows you to view the data while resizing the control without switching back and forth between views.

9 Save 🖫 the form, and switch to **Design** view.

MORE KNOWLEDGE | **Validate or Restrict Data in Forms**

When you design tables, set field properties to ensure the entry of valid data by using input masks, validation rules, and default values. Any field in a form created with a table having these properties inherits the validation properties from the underlying table. Setting these properties in the table is the preferred method; however, you can also set the properties on controls in the form. If conflicting settings occur, the setting on the bound control in the form will override the field property setting in the table.

Activity 6.04 | Adding Controls to a Form

MOS
4.1.3, 4.1.1,
4.2.5, 4.1.2

In this Activity, you will add an image control and button controls to the form to perform actions with a single mouse click. An *image control* enables you to insert an image into any section of a form or report. A *button control* enables you to add a command button to a form or report that will perform an action when the button is clicked.

1 Under **Form Design Tools**, click the **Design tab**. In the **Controls group**, click **Insert Image**, and then click **Browse**. In the displayed **Insert Picture** dialog box, navigate to your **Access Chapter 6** folder and double-click **a06A_Logo**. Align the plus sign (+) of the pointer with the bottom of the **Form Header** section bar at **5.5 inches on the horizontal ruler**, as shown in Figure 6.8.

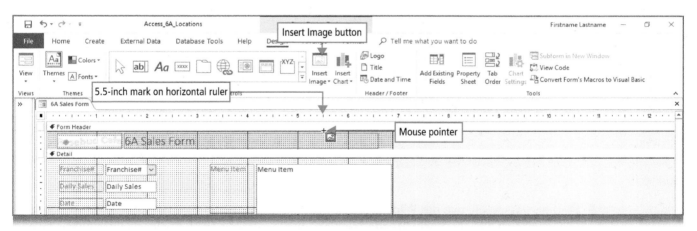

Figure 6.8

2 Click and drag the pointer downward to the bottom of the **Form Header** section and to the right to **6.75 inches on the horizontal ruler**. Release the mouse button to insert the picture in the Form Header section.

> Using the logo control inserts a picture in a predetermined location—the left side—of the Form Header section. The image control is used to insert a picture anywhere in the form. There is a second image control in the Controls gallery under Form Design Tools, on the Design tab.

3 Click the **title's label control**. Point to the right edge of the label control until the pointer ⟨⟩ displays. Drag to the left until there is **one dot** displayed between the right edge of the label control and the left edge of the image control. Under **Form Design Tools**, click the **Format tab**. In the **Font group**, click **Center** 🔲. Switch to **Form** view, and then compare your screen with Figure 6.9.

> The title is centered between the logo on the left and the image on the right, but the logo and the image are not the same size.

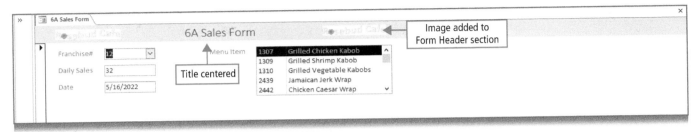

Figure 6.9

4 Switch to **Design** view, and then click the **image control**—the Rosebud Cafe image on the right side in the Form Header section. Under **Form Design Tools**, on the **Design tab**, in the **Tools group**, click **Property Sheet**. If necessary, on the **Property Sheet**, click the **Format tab**, and then compare your screen with Figure 6.10. Notice the **Width** and **Height** property settings.

> Your Width property setting and Height property setting may differ.

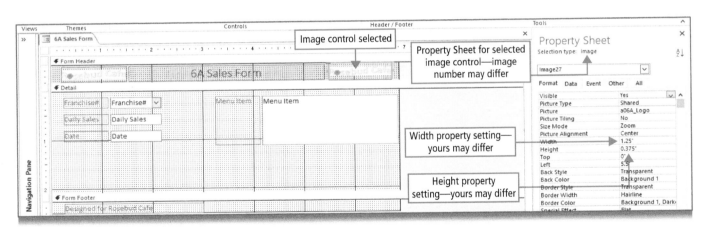

Figure 6.10

5 If necessary, change the **Width** property setting to **1.25** and then change the **Height** property setting to **0.5** In the **Form Header** section, on the left side, click the **logo control**, and then notice that the Property Sheet for the logo control displays. On the **Property Sheet**, change the **Width** property setting to **1.25** and then change the **Height** property setting to **0.5 Close** ✕ the **Property Sheet**.

> The width and height of the two controls are now the same.

6 With the image control selected, hold down Shift, and then click the **logo control**. Under **Form Design Tools**, click the **Arrange tab**. In the **Sizing & Ordering group**, click **Align**, and then click **Bottom**.

> The logo control and the image control are aligned at the bottom.

7 Under **Form Design Tools**, click the **Design tab**. In the **Controls group**, at the right edge of the **Controls gallery**, click **More** ⊡, and verify that the **Use Control Wizards** option is active. Click **Button** ⌷. Move the mouse pointer down into the **Detail** section. Align the plus sign (**+**) of the pointer at **1.5 inches on the vertical ruler** and **1.5 inches on the horizontal ruler**, and then click. If a security message displays, click Open. Compare your screen with Figure 6.11.

> The Command Button Wizard dialog box displays. The first dialog box enables you to select an action for the button based on the selected category.

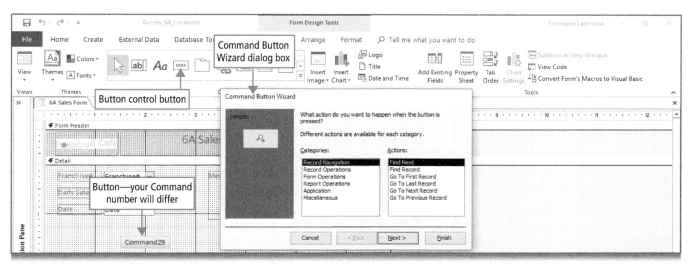

Figure 6.11

8 Take a moment to click the different categories to display the actions associated with each category. When you are finished, under **Categories**, if necessary, click **Record Navigation**. Under **Actions**, click **Go To Previous Record**, and then click **Next**.

> The second Command Button Wizard dialog box displays, which enables you to select what will display on the button—either text or a picture. If you select Picture, you can then click Browse to navigate to a location on your computer where pictures are saved, and then select any picture. If you select Text, you can accept the default text or type new text. A preview of the button displays on the left side of the dialog box.

9 Next to **Picture**, verify **Go To Previous** is selected, and then click **Next**.

> The third Command Button Wizard dialog box displays, which enables you to name the button. If you need to refer to the button later—usually in creating macros—a meaningful name is helpful. The buttons created with the Command Button Wizard are linked to macros or programs.

10 In the text box, type **btnPrevRecord** and then click **Finish**.

> When you are creating controls that can later be used in programming, it is a good idea to start the name of the control with an abbreviation of the type of control—btn—and then a descriptive abbreviation of the purpose of the control.

11 Using the techniques you have just practiced, add a **button control** about **1 inch** to the right of the **Previous Record button control**. Under **Categories**, click **Record Navigation**, if necessary. Under **Actions**, click **Go To Next Record**. For **Picture**, click **Go To Next**, name the button **btnNxtRecord** and then click **Finish**. Do not be concerned if the button controls are not exactly aligned.

12 With the **Next Record button control** selected, hold down Shift, and then click the **Previous Record button control**. Under **Form Design Tools,** click the **Arrange tab**. In the **Sizing & Ordering group**, click **Align**, and then click **Top**. Click **Size/Space**, and then, under **Spacing**, click either **Increase Horizontal** or **Decrease Horizontal** until there is approximately **1 inch** of space between the two controls. Compare your screen with Figure 6.12.

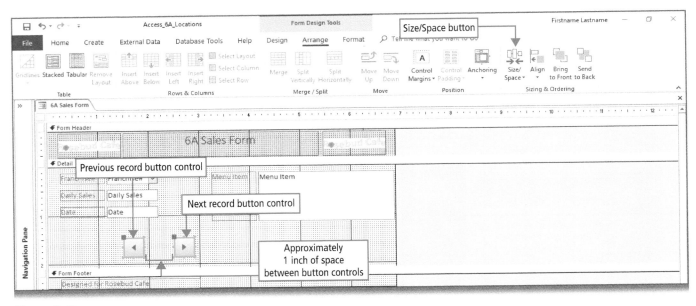

Figure 6.12

13 Save 🖫 the form, and then switch to **Form** view. Experiment by clicking the **Next Record** button and the **Previous Record** button, and notice in the record navigator that you are displaying different records.

14 Switch to **Design** view. Under **Form Design Tools**, on the **Design tab**, in the **Controls group**, click **Button** 🔲 Align the plus sign (+) of the pointer at **1.5 inches on the vertical ruler** and at **5.5 inches on the horizontal ruler**, and then click.

15 In the **Command Button Wizard** dialog box, under **Categories**, click **Form Operations**. Under **Actions**, click **Print Current Form**, and then click **Next**. Click the **Text** option button to accept *Print Form*, and then click **Next**. Name the button **btnPrtForm** and then click **Finish**.

> You will use this button to print one record when you are finished formatting the form.

16 Save 🖫 the form.

Objective 3   Format a Form

GO! Learn How
Video A6-3

There are several methods you can use to modify the appearance of a form. Each section and control on a form has properties. Some properties can be modified by using buttons in the groups on a tab or by changing the property setting on the Property Sheet.

Activity 6.05 | Adding a Background Color

4.1.2

In this Activity, you will apply a color to the background of the entire form.

1 With **6A Sales Form** open in **Design** view, click the **Form Header** section bar.

> The darkened bar indicates that the entire Form Header section of the form is selected.

2 Under **Form Design Tools**, click the **Format tab**. In the **Font group**, click the **Background Color arrow**. Under **Theme Colors**, in the second row, click the sixth color.

> The background color for the Form Header section changes.

3 Double-click the **Form Footer** section bar to display the Property Sheet for the Form Footer section. On the **Property Sheet**, click the **Format tab**, if necessary, and then click in the **Back Color** property setting box—it displays Background 1. Click **Build** […].

> The color palette displays. Background 1 is a code used by Access to represent the color white. You can select an Access Theme Color, a Standard Color, a Recent Color, or click More Colors to select shades of colors.

4 Click **More Colors**. In the displayed **Colors** dialog box, click the **Custom tab**.

> All colors use varying amounts of Red, Green, and Blue.

5 In the **Colors** dialog box, click **Cancel**. On the **Property Sheet**, click the **Back Color property setting arrow**.

> A list of color schemes display. These colors also display on the color palette under Access Theme Colors.

MORE KNOWLEDGE | **Changing the Theme Colors**

If you want to change the theme applied to this form (or object) only, display the object in Design or Layout view. On the Design tab, in the Themes group, click Themes to display a list of available themes. Right-click the theme you want to apply, and click Apply Theme to This Object Only.

---

6 From the displayed list, experiment by clicking on different color schemes and viewing the effects of the background color change. You will have to click the property setting arrow each time to select another color scheme. When you are finished, click **Build** […]. Under **Theme Colors**, in the second row, click the sixth color. **Close** [×] the **Property Sheet**.

> You can change the background color either by using the Background Color button in the Font group or by changing the Back Color property setting on the Property Sheet.

ANOTHER WAY Open the form in Layout view. To select a section, click in an empty area of the section. On the Home tab, in the Text Formatting group, click the Background Color button.

---

7 Using one of the techniques you have just practiced, change the background color of the **Detail** section to match the header and footer. Switch to **Form** view, and then compare your screen with Figure 6.13.

Figure 6.13

8 Save 🖫 the form, and then switch to **Design** view.

MORE KNOWLEDGE | **Adding a Shape Fill to Controls**

You can also add fill color to controls. First, click the control or controls to which you want to add a fill color. If you want to use color schemes, open the Property Sheet, and then click the Back Color property setting arrow. If you want to use the color palette, in Design view, under Form Design Tools, on the Format tab, in the Font group, click Background Color.

Activity 6.06 | Adding a Background Picture to a Form

4.1.2, 4.2.5

In order to make the form more representative of the franchise name, you have been asked to apply a background image to the form. In this Activity, you will add a picture to the background of *6A Sales Form*.

1 With **6A Sales Form** open in **Design** view, locate the **Form selector**, as shown in Figure 6.14.

The *Form selector* is the box where the rulers meet, in the upper left corner of a form in Design view. Use the Form selector to select the entire form.

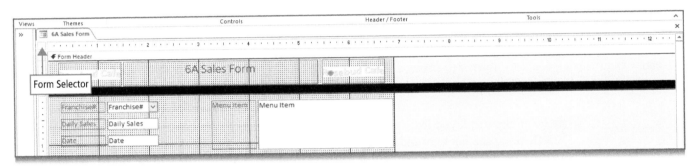

Figure 6.14

2 Double-click the **Form selector** to open the **Property Sheet** for the form.

3 On the **Property Sheet**, on the **Format tab**, click in the **Picture** property setting box. Click **Build** ⬛. Navigate to the location where the student data files for this textbook are saved. Locate and double-click **a06A_Background** to insert the picture in the form, and then compare your screen with Figure 6.15.

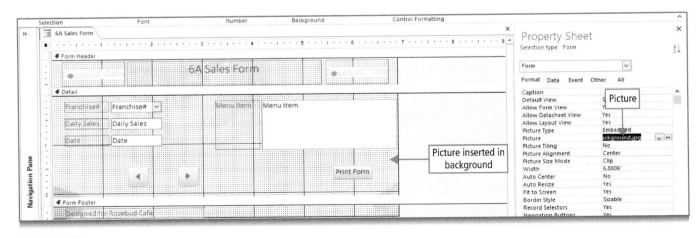

Figure 6.15

---

4 ▶ Click in the **Picture Alignment** property setting box, click the **arrow**, and then click **Form Center**.

The *Picture Alignment property* determines where the background picture for a form displays on the form. Center places the picture in the center of the page when the form is printed. Form Center places the picture in the center of the form data when the form is printed.

5 ▶ Click in the **Picture Size Mode** property setting box, and then click the **arrow** to display the options. From the displayed list, click **Stretch**.

The *Picture Size Mode property* determines the size of the picture in the form. The Clip setting retains the original size of the image. The Stretch setting stretches the image both vertically and horizontally to match the size of the form—the image may be distorted. The Zoom setting adjusts the image to be as large as possible without distorting the image. Both Stretch Horizontal and Stretch Vertical can distort the image. If you have a background color and set the Picture Type property setting to Stretch, the background color will not display.

6 ▶ **Close** ☒ the **Property Sheet**, **Save** 🖫 the form, and then switch to **Layout** view. Compare your screen with Figure 6.16.

Figure 6.16

Activity 6.07 | Modifying the Borders of Controls

4.1.2, 4.1.3

With the background image applied, you have been asked to make the controls stand out more. In this Activity, you will modify the borders of some of the controls on *6A Sales Form*. There are related property settings on the Property Sheet.

1 With **6A Sales Form** open in **Layout** view, click the **Franchise#** combo box control. Holding down Shift, click the **Daily Sales** text box control, and then click the **Date** text box control. Under **Form Layout Tools**, on the **Format tab**, in the **Control Formatting group**, click **Shape Outline**. Notice the options that are used to modify borders—Colors, Line Thickness, and Line Type. Compare your screen with Figure 6.17.

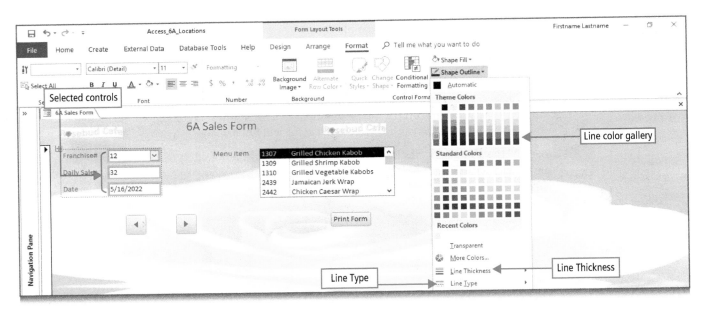

Figure 6.17

2 Point to **Line Type** and point to each line type to display the **ScreenTip**. The second line type—Solid—is the default line type. Click the fifth line type—**Dots**—and then switch to **Form** view to display the results. Notice that the borders of the three controls display a dotted line. Switch to **Layout** view.

You can review the results in Layout view, but you would have to deselect the three controls.

3 With the three controls still selected, under **Form Layout Tools**, on the **Format tab**, in the **Control Formatting group**, click **Shape Outline**. Point to **Line Thickness** and point to each line thickness to display the **ScreenTip**. The first line thickness—Hairline—is the default line thickness. Click the second line type—**1 pt**.

4 In the **Control Formatting group**, click **Shape Outline**. Under **Theme Colors**, point to a few colors to display the **ScreenTip**, and then in the last row, click the last color. Switch to **Form** view to display the results.

The borders of the three controls display a line thickness of 1 point, and the color of the borders is a dark green shade. A *point* is 1/72 of an inch.

5 Switch to **Layout** view. With the three controls still selected, under **Form Layout Tools**, on the **Design tab**, in the **Tools group**, click **Property Sheet**, and then compare your screen with Figure 6.18. Notice the properties that are associated with the buttons on the ribbon with which you changed the borders of the selected controls.

Because multiple items on the form are selected, the Property Sheet displays *Selection type: Multiple selection*. You changed the property settings of the controls by using buttons, and the Property Sheet displays the results of those changes. You can also select multiple controls, open the Property Sheet, and make the changes to the properties. The Property Sheet displays more settings than those available through the use of buttons.

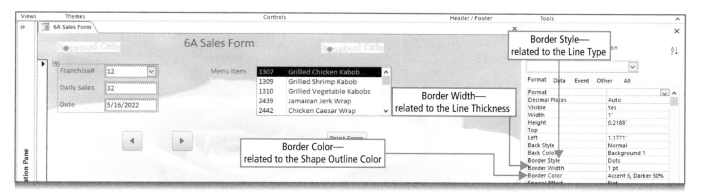

Figure 6.18

6 **Close** ⊠ the **Property Sheet**, and then **Save** 🖫 the form. Switch to **Form** view.

MORE KNOWLEDGE **Adding Borders to Label Controls**

By default, the line type of a label control is transparent, effectively hiding the border from the display. Because borders display around bound controls that contain data, it is recommended that you do not add borders to label controls so that individuals can easily distinguish the control that holds data.

Objective 4 Make a Form User Friendly

GO! Learn How
Video A6-4

To make forms easy to use, you can add instructions to the status bar while data is being entered and custom *ControlTips* that display when an individual points to a control on a form. Additionally, you can change the tab order of the fields on a form. *Tab order* refers to the order in which the fields are selected when the Tab key is pressed. By default, the tab order is created based on the order in which the fields are added to the form.

Activity 6.08 | Adding a Message to the Status Bar

MOS
4.1.2

When you created tables, you may have added a description to the field, and the description displayed in the status bar of the Access window. If a description is included for a field in the underlying table of a form, the text of the description will also display in the status bar when an individual clicks in the field on the form. In this Activity, you will add a description to the Daily Sales field in the *6A Sales* table, and then *propagate*—disseminate or apply—the changes to *6A Sales Form*. You will also add status bar text to a field on a form using the Property Sheet of the control.

1 With **6A Sales Form** open in **Form** view, click in the **Daily Sales** field. On the left side of the status bar, *Form View* displays—there is no text to assist an individual entering data.

2 Close ⊠ the form, and then **Open** » the **Navigation Pane**. Under **Tables**, right-click **6A Sales**, and then from the shortcut menu, click **Design View**. In the **Daily Sales** field, click in the **Description** box. Type **How many items were sold?** and then press Enter. Compare your screen with Figure 6.19.

> A *Property Update Options button* displays in the Description box for the Date field. When you make changes to the design of a table, Access displays this button, which enables individuals to update the Property Sheet for this field in all objects that use this table as the record source.

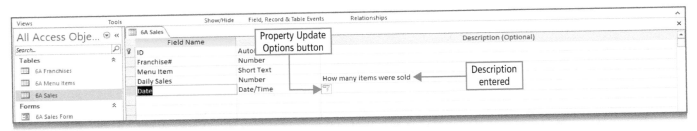

Figure 6.19

3 Click **Property Update Options** 📝, and then click **Update Status Bar Text everywhere Daily Sales is used**. In the displayed **Update Properties** dialog box, under **Update the following objects?**, notice that only one object—*Form: 6A Sales Form*—displays, and it is selected. In the **Update Properties** dialog box, click **Yes**. **Close** ⊠ the table, saving changes.

> The changes in the Description field in the table will be propagated to *6A Sales Form*. If multiple objects use the *6A Sales* table as the underlying object, you can propagate the change to all of the objects.

4 In the **Navigation Pane**, under **Forms**, double-click **6A Sales Form** to open it in **Form** view. **Close** « the **Navigation Pane**. Click in the **Daily Sales** field, and then notice that on the left side of the status bar, *How many items were sold?* displays.

> Access propagated the change made in the underlying table to the form.

5 Switch to **Design** view. Click the **Daily Sales text box control**. Under **Form Design Tools**, on the **Design tab**, in the **Tools group**, click **Property Sheet**.

6 On the **Property Sheet**, click the **Other tab**. Locate the **Status Bar Text** property, and notice the setting *How many items were sold?*

> When Access propagated the change to the form, it populated the Status Bar Text property setting. The *Status Bar Text property* enables individuals to add descriptive text that will display in the status bar for a selected control.

7 In the **Detail** section, click the **Date text box control**, and then notice that the **Property Sheet** changes to display the properties for the Date text box control. Click in the **Status Bar Text** property setting box, type **Enter the date of the sales report** and then press Enter.

> Entering a Status Bar Text on the Text Box Property Sheet does not display Property Update Options to propagate changes to the underlying table or add the information to the Description box for the field in the table.

8 **Save** 🖫 the form, and then switch to **Form** view. Click in the **Date** field, and then compare your screen with Figure 6.20.

> The status bar displays the text you entered in the Status Bar Text property setting box.

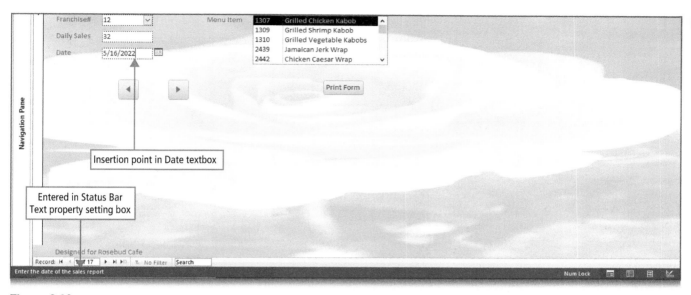

Figure 6.20

9 Switch to **Design** view.

MORE KNOWLEDGE **Conflicting Field Description and Status Bar Text Property Setting**

When you create a form, the fields inherit the property settings from the underlying table. You can change the Status Bar Text property setting for the form, and it will override the setting that is inherited from the table. If you later change field properties in Table Design view, Property Update Options displays—you must manually propagate those changes to the table's related objects; propagation is not automatic. An exception to this is entering Validation Rules—changes are automatically propagated.

Activity 6.09 | Creating Custom ControlTips

4.1.2

Another way to make a form easier to use is to add custom ControlTips to objects on the form. A ControlTip is similar to a ScreenTip, and temporarily displays descriptive text while the mouse pointer is paused over the control. This method is somewhat limited because most individuals press Tab or Enter to move from field to field and thus do not see the ControlTip. However, a ControlTip is a useful tool in a training situation when an individual is learning how to use the data entry form. In this Activity, you will add a ControlTip to the Print Form button control.

1 With **6A Sales Form** open in **Design** view and the **Property Sheet** displayed, click the **Print Form** button. If necessary, click the **Other tab** to make it active. Notice the **Property Sheet** displays *Selection type: Command Button* and the Selection type box displays *btnPrtForm*, the name you gave to the button when you added it to the form.

2 Click in the **ControlTip Text** property setting box, type **Prints the selected record** and then press Enter. Compare your screen with Figure 6.21.

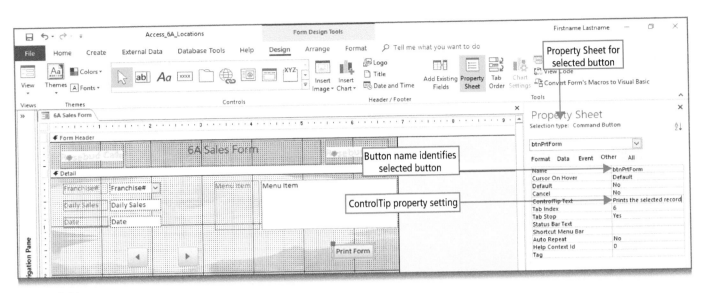

Figure 6.21

3 **Close** ⊠ the **Property Sheet**, **Save** 🖫 the form, and then switch to **Form** view. Point to the **Print Form** button, and then compare your screen with Figure 6.22.

A ControlTip displays the message you typed for the ControlTip Text property setting.

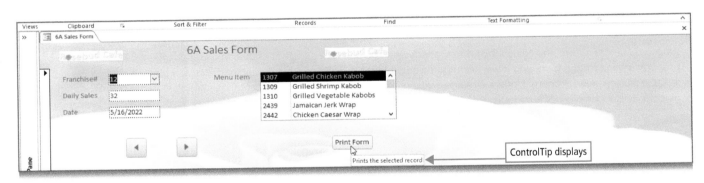

Figure 6.22

Activity 6.10 │ Changing the Tab Order

MOS
4.2.1, 4.1.2,
4.2.3, 4.2.2

You can customize the order in which you enter data on a form by changing the tab order. Recall that tab order refers to the order in which the fields are selected each time Tab is pressed. As you press Tab, the focus of the form changes from one control to another control. *Focus* refers to the control that is selected and currently being acted upon.

1 With **6A Sales Form** open in **Form** view, in the record navigator, click **New (blank) record**. If necessary, click in the **Franchise#** combo box. Press Tab three times, and then notice that the insertion point moves from field to field, ending with the **Date** text box. Press Tab three more times, and then notice the **Print Form** button is the focus. The button displays with a darker border. Press Enter.

Because the focus is on the Print Form button, the Print dialog box displays.

> **2** In the **Print** dialog box, click **Cancel**. Switch to **Design** view.

> **3** Under **Form Design Tools**, on the **Design tab**, in the **Tools group**, click **Tab Order**, and then compare your screen with Figure 6.23.

> The Tab Order dialog box displays. Under Section, Detail is selected. Under Custom Order, the fields and controls display in the order they were added to the form. To the left of each field name or button name is a row selector button.

> As you rearrange fields on a form, the tab order does not change from the original tab order. This can make data entry chaotic because the focus is changed in what appears to be an illogical order. The Auto Order button will change the tab order based on the position of the controls in the form from left to right and top to bottom.

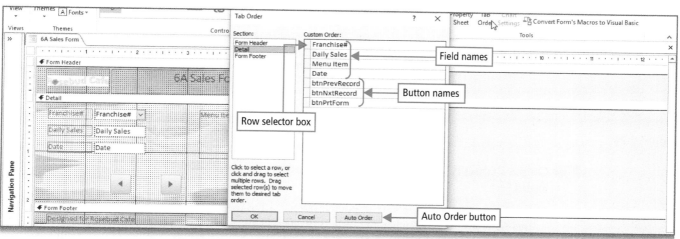

Figure 6.23

> **4** To the left of **Menu Item**, click the **row selector** box. Point to the **row selector** box, and then drag downward until a dark horizontal line displays between **Date** and **btnPrevRecord**.

> The Menu Item field will now receive the focus after the Date field.

ALERT   Did the field stay in the same location?

You must point to the row selector box before dragging the field. If you point to the field name, the field will not move.

> **5** In the **Tab Order** dialog box, click **OK**. Save 🖫 the form, and then switch to **Form** view. In the record navigator, click **Last record**. When the Menu Item field has the focus, it is easier to see it on a blank record. In the record navigator, click **New (blank) record**.

> The insertion point displays in the Franchise# field.

> **6** Press Tab three times. Even though it is difficult to see, the focus changes to the **Menu Item** list box. Press Tab again, and then notice that the focus changes to the **btnPrevRecord** button.

> Before allowing individuals to enter data into a form, you should always test the tab order to ensure that the data will be easy to enter.

7 Switch to **Design** view. In the **Detail** section, right-click the **Date text box control**, and click **Properties**. If necessary, click the **Other** tab, and then compare your screen with Figure 6.24.

Text box controls have three properties relating to tab order: Tab Index, Tab Stop, and Auto Tab. Combo box controls and list box controls do not have an Auto Tab property.

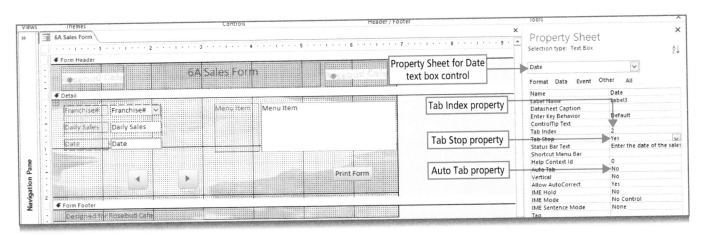

Figure 6.24

8 On the **Property Sheet**, click in the **Tab Index** property setting box, which displays *2*. Click **Build** [...].

Tab Index settings begin with 0. Franchise# has a Tab Index setting of 0, which indicates that this field has the focus when the form is opened. Daily Sales has a Tab Index setting of 1—it will receive the focus when Tab is pressed one time. Date has a Tab Index setting of 2—it will receive the focus when Tab is pressed a second time. Menu Item has a Tab Index setting of 3—it will receive the focus when Tab is pressed a third time.

9 In the **Tab Order** dialog box, click **Cancel**. On the **Property Sheet**, notice that the **Tab Stop** property setting is **Yes**, which means individuals can press Tab to move to this field.

The Auto Tab property setting is No. It should be changed to Yes only when a text field has an input mask. Recall that an input mask controls how the data is entered into a field; for example, the formatting of a phone number.

10 In the **Detail** section, click the **Franchise# combo box control**, and then on the **Property Sheet**, notice the settings for the **Tab Index** and **Tab Stop** properties.

The Tab Index setting is 0, which means this field has the focus when the form page is displayed—it is first on the tab order list. The Tab Stop setting is Yes. Because an input mask cannot be applied to a combo box, there is no Auto Tab property. The Auto Tab property applies only to a text box control.

11 In the **Detail** section, click the **Previous Record** button control. On the **Property Sheet**, click in the **Tab Stop** property setting box, click the **arrow**, and then click **No**.

Changing the Tab Stop property setting to No means that the focus will not be changed to the button by pressing Tab.

12 Save ⊟ the form, and then switch to **Form** view. In the record navigator, click **Last record**. Press Tab two times, watching the focus change from the **Franchise#** field to the **Date** field. Press Tab two more times, and then compare your screen with Figure 6.25.

Because the Tab Stop property setting for the Previous Record button control was changed to No, the button does not receive the focus by pressing the Tab key.

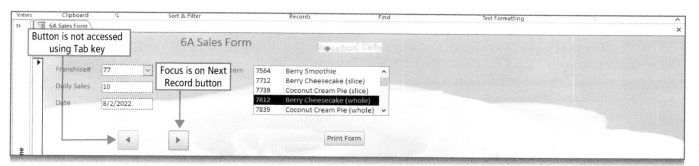

Figure 6.25

13 In the **Detail** section, click the **Previous Record** button.

The previous record displays—you can still use the button by clicking on it.

14 Switch to **Design** view. Using the techniques you have just practiced, for the **Next Record** button and the **Print Form** button, change the **Tab Stop** property setting to **No**.

15 **Close** ✕ the **Property Sheet**. **Save** ⊟ the form, and then switch to **Form** view. Test the tab order by pressing Tab, making sure that the focus does not change to any of the buttons.

When the focus is on the Menu Item field, pressing the Tab key moves the focus to the Franchise# field in the next record.

16 **Close** ✕ the form, and then **Open** » the **Navigation Pane**. **Close** the database, and then **Close** Access.

For Non-MyLab Submissions: Determine What Your Instructor Requires for Submission
As directed by your instructor, submit your completed database file.

17 In **MyLab IT**, locate and click the Grader Project **Access 6A Locations**. In **step 3**, under **Upload Completed Assignment**, click **Choose File**. In the **Open** dialog box, navigate to your **Access Chapter 6 folder**, and then click your **Student_Access_6A_Locations** file one time to select it. In the lower right corner of the **Open** dialog box, click **Open**.

The name of your selected file displays above the Upload button.

18 To submit your file to **MyLab IT** for grading, click **Upload**, wait a moment for a green **Success!** message, and then in **step 4**, click the blue **Submit for Grading** button. Click **Close Assignment** to return to your list of **Course Materials**.

You have completed Project 6A | END

Rosebud Cafe

MyLab IT
Project 6B Grader for Instruction
Project 6B Simulation for Training and Review

Project Activities

In Activities 6.11 through 6.18, you will create customized reports for Jane Chin. The corporate office of Rosebud Cafe (RBC) maintains a database about the franchises, including daily sales of menu items per franchise, the franchise owners, and franchise fees and payments. Reports are often run to summarize data in the tables or queries. Creating customized reports will help the owners and officers of the company view the information in the database in a meaningful way. Your completed Navigation Pane will look similar to Figure 6.26.

Project Files for MyLab IT Grader

1. In your **MyLab IT** course, locate and click **Access 6B Rosebud Cafe**, Download Materials, and then Download All Files.
2. Extract the zipped folder to your Access Chapter 6 folder. Close the Grader download screens.
3. Take a moment to open the downloaded **Access_6B_Rosebud_Cafe_Instructions**; note any recent updates to the book.

Project Results

GO! Project 6B
Where We're Going

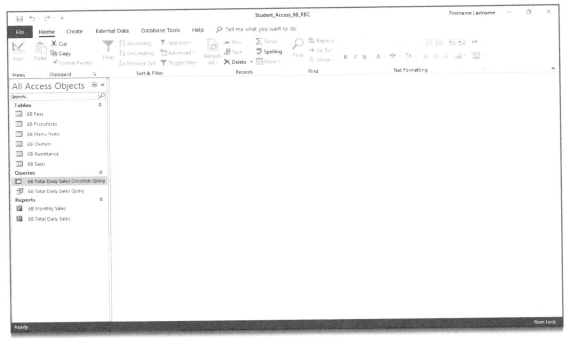

Figure 6.26 Project 6B Rosebud Cafe

For Non-MyLab Submissions	Start with an Access Data File
For Project 6B, you will need:	In your Access Chapter 6 folder, save your database as:
a06B_RBC	**Lastname_Firstname_6B_RBC**
a06B_Logo	

After you have saved your database, launch Access and open the database. On the next page, begin with Step 2.

Create a Report Based on a Query Using a Wizard

GO! Learn How
Video A6-5

A report wizard is a more efficient way to start a report, although Design view does offer more control as you create your report. Once the report has been created, its appearance can be modified in Design or Layout view.

Activity 6.11 | Creating a Report Using a Wizard

2.2.1, 5.1.2,
5.2.1

In this Activity, you will use a wizard to create a report for Rosebud Cafe that displays the data from the 6B Total Daily Sales Crosstab Query.

1 Start Access. In the Access opening screen, click **Open Other Files**. Navigate to your **Access Chapter 6 folder**, and then double-click the Access file that you downloaded from **MyLab IT** that displays your name—**Student_Access_6B_RBC**.

2 If you did not add the Access Chapter 6 folder to the Trust Center, enable the content. In the **Navigation Pane**, under **Queries**, double-click **6B Total Daily Sales Crosstab Query**. Take a moment to study the data in the query, as shown in Figure 6.27.

The data is grouped by Item Name and Month. The Sum function calculates the total daily sales for each item per month.

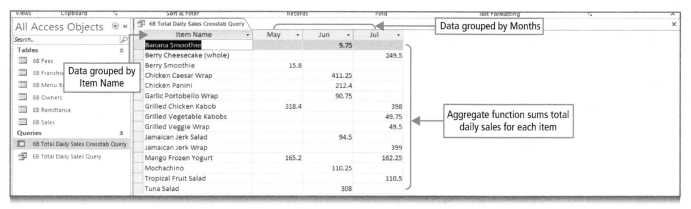

Figure 6.27

ALERT **Are blank columns displayed for months besides May, June, and July?**

If blank columns are displayed for months besides May, June, and July, select the blank columns for Jan, Feb, Mar, and Apr and right-click. From the shortcut menu, click Hide Fields. Using the same technique, hide the columns for Aug, Sep, Oct, Nov, and Dec.

3 Close ⊠ the query, saving if necessary. With **6B Total Daily Sales Crosstab Query** still selected, **Close** ⊠ the **Navigation Pane**.

4 On the **Create tab**, in the **Reports group**, click **Report Wizard**.

5 Because the crosstab query was selected in the Navigation Pane, in the **Report Wizard** dialog box, in the **Tables/Queries** box, **Query: 6B Total Daily Sales Crosstab Query** displays. If it does not display, click the Tables/Queries arrow, and then click Query: 6B Total Daily Sales Crosstab Query.

6 Under **Available Fields**, notice there are more months than those that were displayed in 6B Total Daily Sales Crosstab Query.

> Because there was data for the months of May, June, and July only, the other months may have been hidden from the display in the query.

7 Under **Available Fields**, double-click each field name, in the order specified, to add the field names to the Selected Fields box: **Item Name**, **May**, **Jun**, and **Jul**.

8 In the **Report Wizard** dialog box, click **Next**. Because no grouping levels will be used, click **Next**.

9 To sort the records within the report by Item Name, click the **arrow** next to the **1** box. From the displayed list, click **Item Name**. Leave the sort order as **Ascending**, and then click **Next**.

10 Under **Layout**, verify the **Tabular** option button is selected. Under **Orientation**, verify the **Portrait** option button is selected, and then click **Next**.

> Choose Landscape orientation to display more data across the page.

11 In the **What title do you want for your report?** box, type **6B Monthly Sales** and then click **Finish**. Compare your screen with Figure 6.28.

> The report displays in Print Preview. Because this report uses a crosstab query as the record source, it displays calculated data grouped by two different types of information.

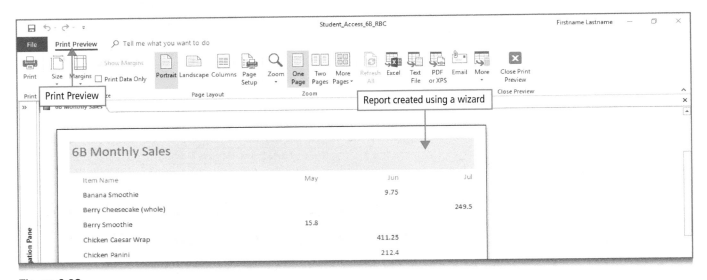

Figure 6.28

Activity 6.12 | Modifying a Report Created Using a Wizard

5.1.3, 5.2.3

In this Activity, you will modify controls in the report to change its appearance. Although the report was created using a wizard, its appearance can be modified in Design view and Layout view.

1 On the **Print Preview tab**, in the **Close Preview group**, click **Close Print Preview**. If the **Field List** or **Property Sheet** displays, **Close** ⊠ it.

2 Under **Report Design Tools**, on the **Design tab**, in the **Themes group**, click **Themes** to display a list of available themes. Under **Office**, click **Organic** to apply the theme to the entire database.

> ***Themes*** simplify the process of creating professional-looking objects within one program or across multiple programs. A theme includes theme colors and theme fonts that will be applied consistently throughout the objects in the database. It is a simple way to provide professional, consistent formatting in a database.

3 Click the **Report title text box control** to select it. Under **Report Design Tools**, click the **Format tab**, and in the **Font group**, click the **Font Color arrow** Ⓐ⁻. Under **Theme Colors**, in the first row, click the eighth color.

4 Select all of the controls in the **Page Header** section by pointing to the top left of the **Page Header** section, holding down your mouse button, dragging the mouse across the Page Header controls and to the bottom of the Page Header section, and then releasing the mouse button. Under **Report Design Tools**, on the **Format tab**, in the **Font group**, click the **Font Color button** Ⓐ⁻ to apply the same font color as you used for the title. Click anywhere in the **Detail** section to deselect the **Page Header** controls.

> Any group of controls can be selected using this lasso method. It can be more efficient than holding down Shift while clicking each control.

5 In the **Detail** section, click the **Item Name** control. Hold down Shift and, in the Page **Header** section, click the **Item Name label control**. Point to the right edge of any control until the pointer ↔ displays. Drag to the left until the box is approximately **2.5 inches** wide.

6 **Save** 🖫 the report, and then switch to **Layout** view. Be sure none of the data in the **Item Name** column is truncated or cut off.

7 To select all of the text box controls, in the **May** column, click any cell. Holding down Shift, in the **Jun** and **Jul** columns, click a **text box control**. Compare your screen with Figure 6.29.

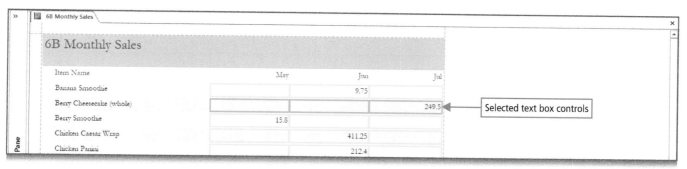

Figure 6.29

8 Under **Report Layout Tools**, on the **Design tab**, in the **Tools group**, click **Property Sheet**. Notice that the Selection Type is *Multiple selection*.

9 On the **Property Sheet**, click the **Format tab**. Click the **Format** property setting arrow. From the displayed list, select **Currency**. Click the **Border Style** property setting arrow, and click **Short Dashes**. **Close** ⓧ the **Property Sheet**.

10 **Save** 🖫 the report, and then switch to **Print Preview** view.

11 On the **Print Preview tab**, in the **Close Preview group**, click **Close Print Preview**. **Close** ⓧ the report, and then **Open** » the **Navigation Pane**.

Objective 6 Create a Report in Design View

GO! Learn How
Video A6-6

You usually create a report using the Report tool or the Report Wizard, and then modify the report in Design view to suit your needs. Use Design view to create a report when these tools do not meet your needs or if you want more control in the creation of a report. Creating or modifying a report in Design view is a common technique when additional controls, such as calculated controls, need to be added to the report or properties need to be changed.

Activity 6.13 | Creating a Report in Design View

5.1.2, 5.2.2,
5.2.3

Creating a report with the Report tool or the Report Wizard is the easiest way to start the creation of a customized report, but you can also create a report from scratch in Design view. Once you understand the sections of a report and how to manipulate the controls within the sections, it is easier to modify a report that has been created using the report tools. Jane Chin and her staff have asked for a report that displays information about daily sales.

1 ▶ In the **Navigation Pane**, open **6B Total Daily Sales Query** in **Design** view, and then notice the underlying tables that were used in the creation of the query. Notice the calculated field—*Total Cost.*

> Recall that a calculated field contains the field name, followed by a colon, and then an expression. In the expression, the existing field names must be enclosed in square brackets. The Total Cost was calculated by multiplying the value in the Cost field by the value in the Daily Sales field.

2 ▶ When you are finished, **Close** ⌧ the query, and **Close** « the **Navigation Pane**. Click the **Create tab**, and then, in the **Reports group**, click **Report Design**. When the design grid displays, scroll down to display all of the report sections.

> Three sections are included in the blank design grid: the Page Header section, the Detail section, and the Page Footer section. A page header displays at the top of every printed page, and a page footer displays at the bottom of every printed page.

3 ▶ Double-click the report selector to display the **Property Sheet**. On the **Property Sheet**, click the **Data tab**. Click the **Record Source property setting box arrow**, and then compare your screen with Figure 6.30. If necessary, increase the width of the Property Sheet.

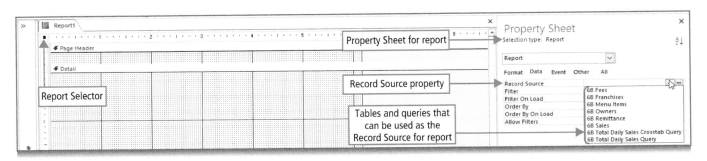

Figure 6.30

4 ▶ From the displayed list of tables and queries, click **6B Total Daily Sales Query**, and then **Close** ⌧ the **Property Sheet**.

> 6B Total Daily Sales Query is the record source—underlying query—for this report.

5 ▶ Under **Report Design Tools**, on the **Design tab**, in the **Tools group**, click **Add Existing Fields** to display the fields in 6B Total Daily Sales Query.

6 ▶ In the **Field List**, click **Date**. Hold down Shift, and then click **Franchise#** to select all of the fields.

ALERT **Are multiple tables displayed in the field list?**

If all tables display in the field list, click Show only fields in the current record source at the bottom of the Field List box.

---

7 Drag the selected fields into the **Detail** section of the design grid until the top of the arrow of the pointer is **one dot** below the bottom edge of the **Detail** section bar and aligned with the **3-inch mark on the horizontal ruler**. **Close** ⊠ the **Field List**, and then compare your screen with Figure 6.31.

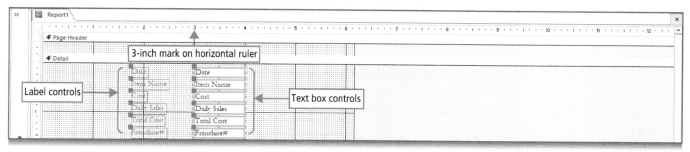

Figure 6.31

8 With the label controls and text box controls for the fields selected, under **Report Design Tools** click the **Arrange tab**. In the **Table group**, click **Stacked** to group the fields together for easier formatting.

MORE KNOWLEDGE | **Using the Tabular Arrangement**

When you want your data to display professionally in a report, on the Arrange tab, in the Table group, click the Tabular button. This will place the labels in the Page Header and the data in the Detail section for a table-like appearance.

---

9 Under **Report Design Tools**, on the **Design tab**, in the **Themes group**, click **Themes**. Under **In This Database**, notice the theme used in this database—**Organic**. Press Esc to close the gallery.

10 Save 🖫 the report as **6B Total Daily Sales**

Activity 6.14 | Modifying the Sections of a Report

5.1.3, 5.2.6

By default, a report created in Design view includes a Page Header section and a Page Footer section. Reports can also include a Report Header section and a Report Footer section. In this Activity, you will add the Report Header and Report Footer sections and hide the Page Header section. Recall that a Report Header displays at the top of the first printed page of a report, and the Report Footer displays at the bottom of the last printed page of a report.

1 Right-click in the **Detail** section of the report, and click **Report Header/Footer**. Notice that the **Report Header** section displays at the top of the design grid. Scroll down to display the **Report Footer** section.

2 Scroll up to display the **Report Header** section. Under **Report Design Tools**, click the **Design tab**, and then, in the **Header/Footer group**, click **Logo**. Locate and double-click **a06B_Logo** to insert the logo in the Report Header section. On the selected logo, point to the right middle sizing handle until the pointer ↔ displays. Drag to the right until the right edge of the logo is aligned with the **1.5-inch mark on the horizontal ruler**.

3 Under **Report Design Tools**, on the **Design tab**, in the **Header/Footer group**, click **Title**. On the **title's label control**, point to the right middle sizing handle until the pointer displays ↔, and then double-click to adjust the size of the label control to fit the text.

4 Scroll down until the **Page Footer** section bar displays. Point to the top edge of the **Page Footer** section bar until the pointer ↕ displays. Drag upward until the top of the **Page Footer** section bar aligns with the **2.25-inch mark on the vertical ruler**.

This prevents extra blank space from printing between the records.

5 Scroll up until the **Report Header** section displays. Point to the top edge of the **Detail** section bar until the pointer ⬍ displays. Drag upward until the top edge of the **Detail** section bar aligns with the bottom edge of the **Page Header** section bar, and then compare your screen with Figure 6.32.

The Page Header and Page Footer sections are paired together. Likewise, the Report Header and Report Footer sections are paired together. You cannot remove only one section of the pair. If you wish to remove one section of a paired header/footer, decrease the height of the section. Alternatively, set the Height property for the section to 0. Because there is no space in the Page Header section, nothing will print at the top of every page. To remove both of the paired header/footer sections, right click in the Detail section, and click Page Header/Footer to deselect it.

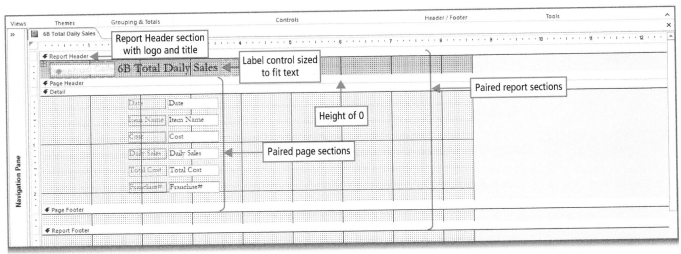

Figure 6.32

6 Drag the right edge of the design grid to the left until it aligns with the **6.5-inch mark on the horizontal ruler. Save** 🖫 the report.

The width of the report page is decreased, which will enable the report to fit within the margins of paper in portrait orientation.

MORE KNOWLEDGE **Formatting a Report**

You can add a background picture to a report or change the background color of a report using the same techniques you used for forms.

| Objective 7 | Add Controls to a Report |

GO! Learn How
Video A6-7

Reports are not used to manipulate data in the underlying table or query, so they contain fewer types of controls. You can add label controls, text box controls, images, hyperlinks, or calculated controls to a report.

Activity 6.15 | **Adding Label and Text Box Controls to a Report**

5.1.2, 5.1.3

In this Activity, you will add controls to the report that will contain the page numbering, the date, and submission information.

1 Under **Report Design Tools**, on the **Design tab**, in the **Header/Footer group**, click **Page Numbers**. In the **Page Numbers** dialog box, under **Format**, click **Page N of M**. Under **Position**, click **Bottom of Page [Footer]**. Alignment should remain **Center**; click **OK**.

> A text box control displays in the center of the Page Footer section. The control displays an expression that will display the page number. Every expression begins with an equal sign (=). "Page " is enclosed in quotation marks. Access interprets anything enclosed in quotation marks as text and will display it exactly as it is typed within the quotation marks, including the space. The & symbol is used for *concatenation*—linking or joining—of strings. A *string* is a series of characters. The word *Page* followed by a space will be concatenated—joined—to the string that follows the & symbol. [Page] is a reserved name that retrieves the current page number. This is followed by another & symbol that concatenates the page number to the next string—" of ". The & symbol continues concatenation of [Pages], a reserved name that retrieves the total number of pages in the report.

2 Save the report. Under **Report Design Tools**, on the **Design tab**, in the **Views group**, click the **View button arrow**, and then click **Print Preview**. On the **Print Preview tab**, in the **Zoom group**, click **Two Pages**.

3 In the **Close Preview group**, click **Close Print Preview**.

4 Under **Report Design Tools**, on the **Design tab**, in the **Controls group**, click **Label** Aa. Point to the **Report Footer** section until the plus sign (+) of the pointer aligns with the bottom edge of the **Report Footer** section bar and with the left edge of the **Report Footer** section. Click and drag downward to the bottom of the **Report Footer** section and to the right to the **2.5-inch mark on the horizontal ruler**. Type Prepared for Jane Chin and then compare your screen with Figure 6.33.

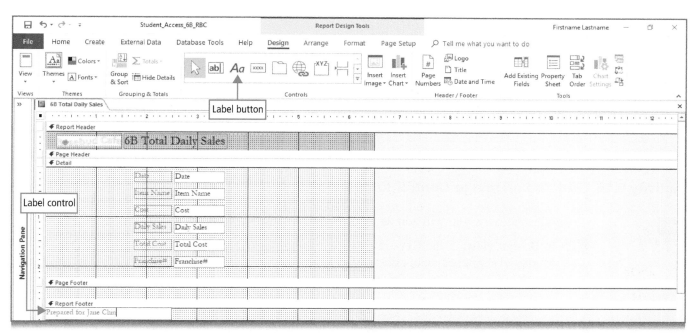

Figure 6.33

5 Click away from the label box, and then **Save** the report. Under **Report Design Tools**, on the **Design tab**, in the **Header/Footer group**, click **Date and Time**. In the **Date and Time** dialog box, under **Include Date**, click the third option button, which displays the date as mm/dd/yyyy. Click to clear the **Include Time** check box, and then click **OK**.

> A text box control with an expression for the current date displays in the Report Header section. It may display over the Report title.

6 In the **Report Header**, click the **Date text box control** to select it. Under **Report Design Tools**, click the **Arrange tab**, and, in the **Table group**, click **Remove Layout** so the Date text box control can be moved. Right-click the selected control, and click **Cut**. Point to the **Report Footer** section bar, right-click, and then click **Paste**. Drag the text box control until the right edge of the text box control aligns with the **6.25-inch mark on the horizontal ruler**. Click the **Title label control** which has been resized to a bar next to the logo, to select it, point to the right middle sizing handle until the pointer ⟷ displays, and then drag to the right until the right edge of the text box control aligns with the **4.5-inch mark on the horizontal ruler**.

When the Date control was removed from the layout, the Title label control was resized.

7 Save 🖫 the report, and then switch to **Layout** view. Notice that, for the first record, the data for the **Item Name** field does not fully display. Click the **Item Name text box control**, which partially displays *Banana Smoothie*. Point to the right edge of the **Item Name text box control** until the pointer ⟷ displays. Drag to the right approximately **1.5 inches**. Because no ruler displays in Layout view, you will have to estimate the distance to drag.

Because the controls are in a stacked layout, the widths of all of the text box controls are increased.

8 Scroll down, observing the data in the **Item Name** field. Ensure that all of the data displays. If the data is not all visible in a record, use the technique you just practiced to increase the width of the text box control until all of the data displays.

9 Switch to **Design** view. Point to the right edge of the design grid until the pointer ⟷ displays. If necessary, drag to the left until the right edge of the design grid aligns with the **6.5-inch mark on the horizontal ruler**. Save 🖫 the report.

The width of the report page will change with the addition of more text boxes, making it necessary to readjust the width so the report will fit within the margins of paper in portrait orientation.

MORE KNOWLEDGE **Adding a Hyperlink to a Report**

Add a hyperlink to a report in Design view by clicking Insert Hyperlink in the Controls group and then specifying the complete URL. To test the hyperlink, in Design view, right-click the hyperlink, click Hyperlink, and then click Open Hyperlink. The hyperlink is active—jumps to the target—in Design view, Report view, and Layout view. The hyperlink is not active in Print Preview view. If the report is exported to another Office application, the hyperlink is active when it is opened in that application. An application that can export data can create a file in a format that another application understands, enabling the two programs to share the same data.

Activity 6.16 | Adding an Image Control to a Report

MOS

5.2.6, 5.2.3,
5.2.2

In this Activity, you will add an image control to the report header.

1 In **Design view**, in the **Report Header** section, right-click the **logo control**. From the displayed shortcut menu, click **Copy**. Right-click anywhere in the **Report Header** section, and then from the shortcut menu, click **Paste**.

A copy of the image displays on top and slightly to the left of the original logo control.

2 Point to the selected logo until the pointer ⟨k displays. Drag to the right until the left edge of the outlined control is the same distance from the title as the logo control on the left. Point to the top edge of the **Page Header** section bar until the pointer ✛ displays. Drag upward until the top of the **Page Header** section bar aligns with the **0.5-inch mark on the vertical ruler**.

Recall that when you created a form in Design view, you clicked Insert Image and selected the location in the header section. You then had to change the properties of the image to match the size of the image in the logo control. Because you copied the original image from the logo, the images are the same size.

3 With the image control on the right selected, hold down Ctrl, and then click the **logo control**. Under **Report Design Tools**, click the **Arrange tab**, and, in the **Sizing & Ordering group**, click **Align**, and select **Bottom**. Compare your screen with Figure 6.34.

Both the logo control and the image control are aligned along the bottom edges.

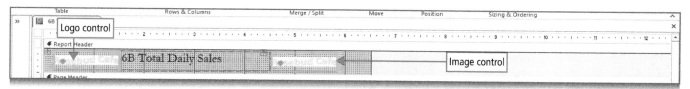

Figure 6.34

4 Under **Report Design Tools**, click the **Design tab**, and, in the **Controls group**, click the **More** button ⊽, and then click **Line** ◻. Point to the **Detail** section until the middle of the plus sign (**+**) of the pointer aligns at **2 inches on the vertical ruler** and **0 inches on the horizontal ruler**, as shown in Figure 6.35.

A *line control* enables an individual to insert a line in a form or report.

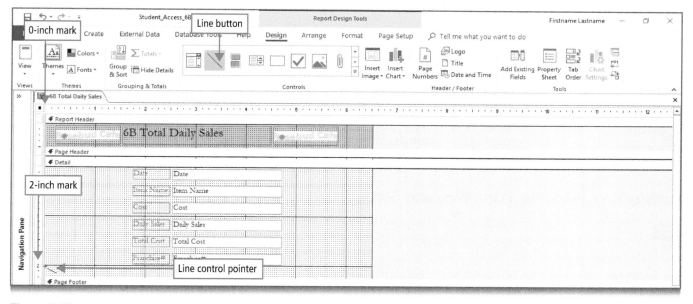

Figure 6.35

5 Hold down Shift, drag to the right to **6.5 inches on the horizontal ruler**, and then release the mouse button.

An orange line control displays. Holding down the Shift key ensures that the line will be straight.

6 Under **Report Design Tools**, click the **Format tab**, and, in the **Control Formatting group**, click **Shape Outline**. Point to **Line Thickness** and then click the third line—**2 pt**. In the **Control Formatting group**, click **Shape Outline**. Under **Theme Colors**, on the fifth row, click the sixth color.

7 **Save** 💾 the report, and then switch to **Report** view. Compare your screen with Figure 6.36. Notice the horizontal line that displays between the records.

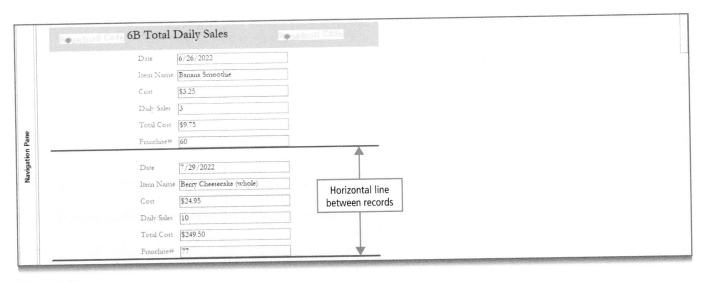

Figure 6.36

8 Switch to **Design** view. Click anywhere in the **Detail** area to deselect the line.

Objective 8 | **Group, Sort, and Total Records in Design View**

GO! Learn How
Video A6-8

If a report has been created that was not grouped, you can modify the report in Design view to include grouping and summary data. Calculated controls are often added to reports to display summary information in reports with grouped records.

Activity 6.17 | Adding a Grouping and Sort Level to a Report

5.1.1, 5.2.2

In this Activity, you will add a grouping and sort order to the report, and then move a control from the Detail section to the Header section to make it easier for the staff to read.

1 Under **Report Design Tools**, on the **Design tab**, in the **Grouping & Totals group**, click **Group & Sort**, and then compare your screen with Figure 6.37.

The Group, Sort, and Total pane displays at the bottom of the screen. Because no grouping or sorting has been applied to the report, two buttons relating to these functions display in the Group, Sort, and Total pane.

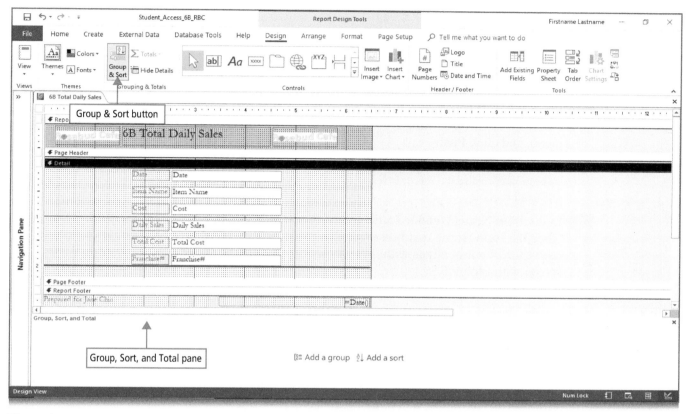

Figure 6.37

2 In the **Group, Sort, and Total pane**, click **Add a group**. A list of fields that are used in the report displays, as shown in Figure 6.38.

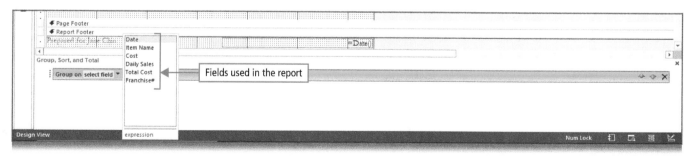

Figure 6.38

3 From the displayed list, click **Item Name**.

An empty Item Name Header section is inserted above the Detail section. The report will be grouped by the Item Name, and the Item Names will be sorted in ascending order.

4 In the **Detail** section, click the **Item Name text box control**. Point to the selected text box control until the pointer displays. Drag downward until a thin orange line displays below the **Franchise#** controls.

> The text box control for this field will be moved to the Item Name Header section in the report. Recall that moving the controls to the bottom of the stacked layout makes it easier to remove the controls from the stacked layout.

5 Under **Report Design Tools**, click the **Arrange tab**, and, in the **Table group**, click **Remove Layout**.

> The label control and the text box control for the Item Name field are removed from the stacked layout.

6 Right-click the selected **Item Name text box control** to display the shortcut menu, and click **Cut**. Click the **Item Name Header** section bar to select it, right-click to display the shortcut menu, and click **Paste**.

> The controls for the Item Name are moved from the Detail section to the Item Name Header section. Because the report is being grouped by this field, the controls should be moved out of the Detail section.

7 In the **Item Name Header** section, click the **Item Name label control**, and then press Delete. Click the **Item Name text box control** to select it, and then drag it to the right until the left edge of the control aligns with the **1-inch mark on the horizontal ruler**. Compare your screen with Figure 6.39.

> Because the records are grouped by the data in the Item Name field, the name of the field is unnecessary.

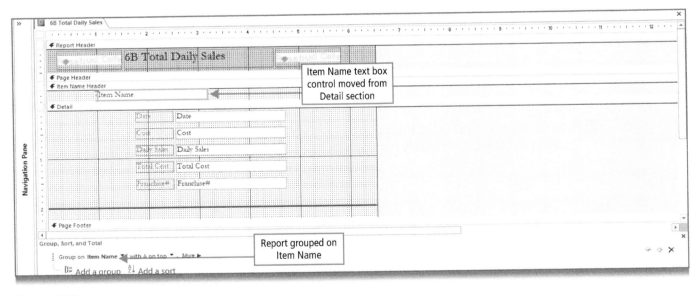

Figure 6.39

8 Save the report, and then switch to **Report** view. Scroll down, noticing the grouping of records, until the grouping for **Grilled Chicken Kabob** displays. Notice that there are two records, one for Franchise# 62 and another for Franchise# 12. For these two records, notice the dates.

9 Switch back to **Design** view. In the **Group, Sort, and Total pane**, click **Add a sort**, and then click **Date**. Notice that the Date will be sorted from oldest to newest.

10 Save 🖫 the report, and then switch to **Report** view. Scroll down until the **Grilled Chicken Kabob** grouping displays. Within the grouping, the two records are arranged in order by the date with the oldest date listed first.

11 Switch to **Design** view, and then **Close** ⊠ the **Group, Sort, and Total pane**. Be sure to click the Close button located in the title bar and not the Delete button that is inside the pane. Alternatively, to close the Group & Sort pane, on the Design tab, in the Grouping & Totals group, click Group & Sort.

Activity 6.18 | Adding Calculated Controls to a Report

5.1.2, 5.1.3,
5.2.3, 5.2.2

A report can be used to summarize information for specific fields. In this Activity, you will add an aggregate function and appropriate section to the report.

1 In the **Detail** section, click the **Total Cost text box control**. Under **Report Design Tools**, on the **Design tab**, in the **Grouping & Totals group**, click **Totals**, and then compare your screen with Figure 6.40.

A list of *aggregate functions*—functions that group and perform calculations on multiple fields—displays. Before selecting Totals, the field that will be used in the aggregate function must be selected. If you wish to perform aggregate functions on multiple fields, you must select each field individually, and then select the aggregate function to apply to the field.

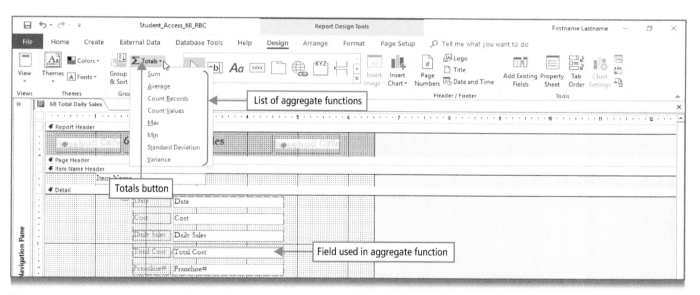

Figure 6.40

2 In the displayed list of aggregate functions, click **Sum**, and then compare your screen with Figure 6.41. If necessary scroll down so the bottom of the report is visible.

The Item Name Footer section is added to the report. A calculated control is added to the section that contains the expression that will display the sum of the Total Cost field for each grouping. A calculated control is also added to the Report Footer section that contains the expression that will display the grand total of the Total Cost field for the report. Recall that an expression begins with an equal sign (=). The Sum function adds or totals numeric data. Field names are included in square brackets.

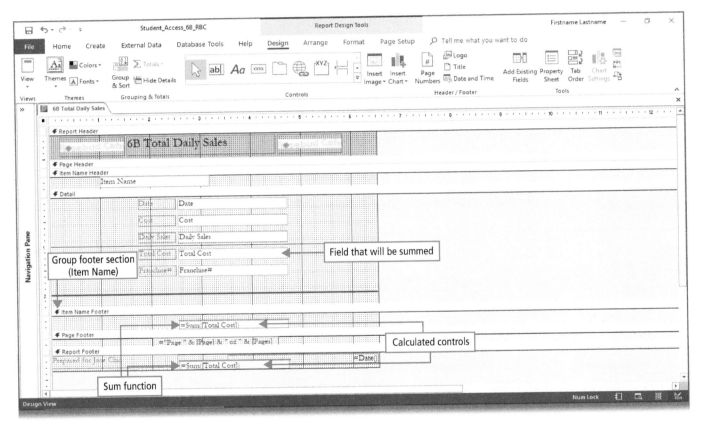

Figure 6.41

3 Save ⊟ the report, and then switch to **Report** view. Notice that for the first grouping—Banana Smoothie—which only contains one record—the sum of the grouping displays below the horizontal line. Scroll down to the **Grilled Chicken Kabob** grouping, and then notice that the total for the grouping—**$716.40**—displays below the horizontal line for the second record in the grouping.

The placement of the horizontal line is distracting in the report, and there is no label attached to the grouping total.

4 Switch to **Design** view. Under **Report Design Tools**, on the **Design tab**, in the **Controls group**, click **Text Box** [ab]. Point to the **Item Name Footer** section until the plus sign (+) of the pointer aligns with the bottom edge of the **Item Name Footer** section bar and with the **0.25-inch mark on the horizontal ruler**. Drag downward to the bottom of the **Item Name Footer** section and to the right to the **2.5-inch mark on the horizontal ruler**.

5 Click inside the text box, and type **=[Item Name] & " Total Cost:"** ensuring that you include a space between the quotation mark and *Total* and that *Item Name* is enclosed in square brackets. Compare your screen with Figure 6.42.

> Because a field name is included in the description of the total, a text box control must be used. This binds the control to the Item Name field in the underlying query, which makes this control a bound control. If you wish to insert only string characters as a description—for example, Total Cost—add a label control, which is an unbound control.

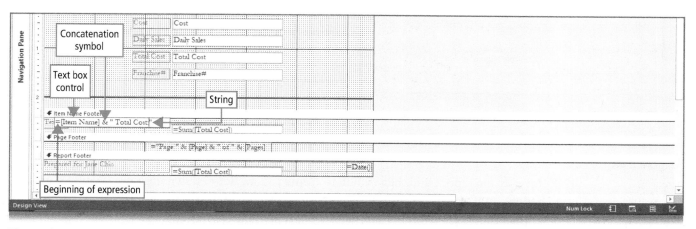

Figure 6.42

6 In the **Item Name Footer** section, click the **label control** that displays to the left of the text box control where you typed the expression. Press [Delete] to delete the text box control's associated label control.

> The data in the text box control is descriptive and does not require an additional label control.

7 In the **Item Name Footer** section, click the **text box control** that contains the expression you typed. Point to the left middle sizing handle until the pointer displays. Drag to the left until the left edge of the text box control aligns with the left edge of the design grid. With the text box control selected, hold down [Shift]. In the **Item Name Footer** section, click the **calculated control** for the sum. Under **Report Design Tools**, click the **Arrange tab**. In the **Sizing & Ordering group**, click **Size/Space**, and then click **To Tallest**. In the **Sizing & Ordering group**, click **Align**, and then click **Bottom** to align both controls at the bottom.

> The two controls are now the same height and aligned at the top edges of the controls.

8 Point to the top of the **Page Footer** section bar until the pointer ⊞ displays. Drag downward to the top of the **Report Footer** section bar to increase the height of the Item Name Footer section so **four dots** display below the **Total Cost** controls.

9 In the **Detail** section, click the **line control**. Point to the line control until the pointer displays. Drag downward into the **Item Name Footer** section under the controls until there are approximately **two dots** displayed between the text box controls and the line control, and then release the mouse button.

> The line control is moved from the Detail section to the Item Name Footer section.

10 Point to the top of the **Item Name Footer** section bar until the pointer ⊞ displays. Drag upward until approximately **two dots** display between the **Franchise#** controls and the top edge of the **Item Name Footer** section bar. Compare your screen with Figure 6.43.

The height of the Detail section is changed.

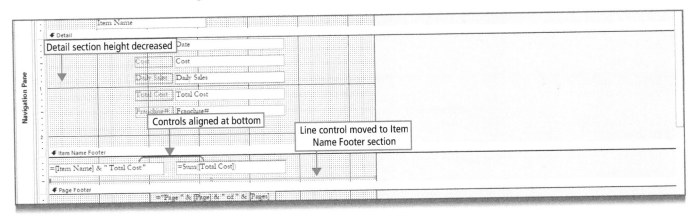

Figure 6.43

11 Save 🖫 the report, and then switch to **Report** view. Scroll down until the **Grilled Chicken Kabob** grouping displays, and then compare your screen with Figure 6.44.

The report is easier to read with the horizontal line moved to the grouping footer section and with an explanation of the total for the grouping.

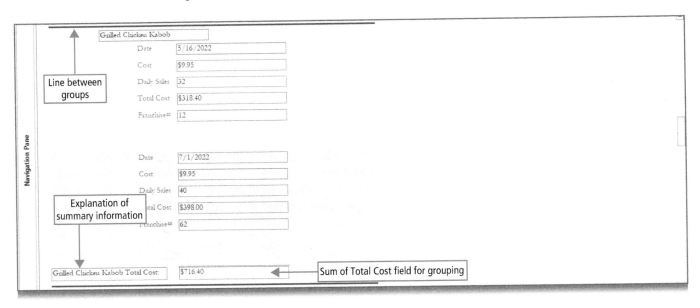

Figure 6.44

12 Hold down Ctrl, and then press End to move to the end of the report. Notice the sum of **$3,154.80**.

By default, when you insert an aggregate function into a report, a calculated control for the grand total is inserted in the Report Footer section. The control is aligned with the text box control that is being used in the aggregate function. If the Report Footer section is not tall enough and multiple aggregate functions are used, the controls will display on top of one another.

13 Switch to **Design** view. In the **Report Footer** section, the calculated control displays *=Sum([Total Cost])*. Point to the bottom of the **Report Footer** section—not the section bar—until the pointer ⊞ displays. Drag downward until the height of the **Report Footer** section is approximately **1 inch**.

14 Click the label control that displays **Prepared for Jane Chin**. Hold down Shift, and then click the text box control that displays the **Date** expression. Under **Report Design Tools**, click the **Arrange tab**. In the **Sizing & Ordering group**, click **Size/Space**, and then click **To Tallest**. In the **Sizing & Ordering group**, click **Align**, and then click **Bottom**.

The two controls are the same height and aligned at the bottom edges of the controls.

15 Point to either of the selected controls until the pointer displays. Drag downward until the bottom edges of the controls align with the bottom edge of the Report Footer section. Click in the Report Footer to deselect the controls, and then compare your screen with Figure 6.45.

The controls are moved to the bottom of the Report Footer section to increase readability and to make space to insert a label control for the grand total.

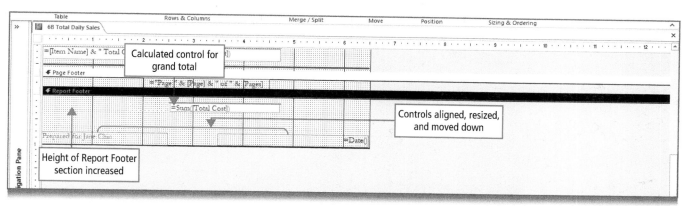

Figure 6.45

16 Under **Report Design Tools**, click the **Design tab**. Use the techniques you have practiced previously to add a **label control** in the **Report Footer** section to the left of the calculated control—the left edge of the control should be aligned with the **0-inch mark on the horizontal ruler** and the right edge should be **one dot** to the left of the calculated control. In the label control, type **Grand Total Cost of All Items:** Align the label control with the calculated control and be sure that the controls are the same height. Click in the Report Footer to deselect the controls, and then compare your screen with Figure 6.46.

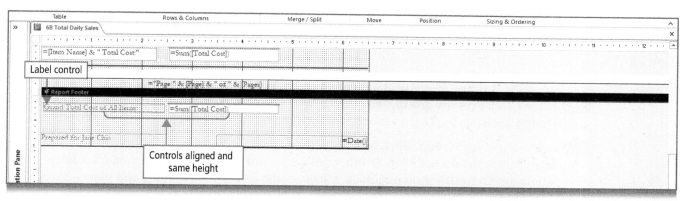

Figure 6.46

ALERT   Does your control display with two boxes?

If your control displays with two boxes—one that displays text and a number, for example Text35, and one that displays Unbound—you selected the Text Box button instead of the Label button. If that happens, click Undo, and then begin again.

17 Save ⊟ the report, and then switch to **Report** view. Hold down Ctrl, and then press End to move to the end of the report. Notice that the grand total is now easier to distinguish because a description of the control has been added and the other controls are moved down.

18 Display the report in **Print Preview** view. If necessary, on the **Print Preview tab**, in the **Zoom group**, click **Two Pages**. Look at the bottom of Page 1 and the top of Page 2, and notice that the grouping breaks across two pages. In the navigation area, click **Next Page** ▶ to display Pages 3 and 4. Groupings are split between these pages. Compare your screen with Figure 6.47.

For a more professional-looking report, avoid splitting groupings between pages.

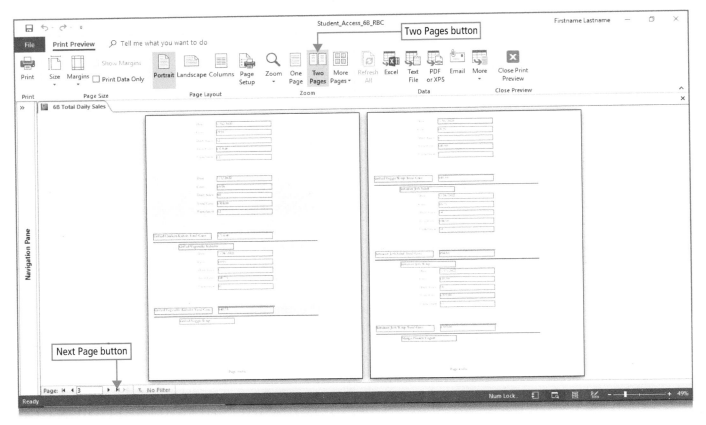

Figure 6.47

19 In the **Close Preview group**, click **Close Print Preview**. Switch to **Design** view. Under **Report Design Tools**, on the **Design tab**, in the **Grouping & Totals group**, click **Group & Sort**.

20 In the displayed **Group, Sort, and Total pane**, on the **Group on Item Name** bar, click **More**. Click the **do not keep group together on one page arrow**, and then click **keep whole group together on one page. Close** ☒ the **Group, Sort, and Total pane**—do not click the Delete button.

21 Save the report, and then switch to **Print Preview** view. In the navigation area, click the buttons to display pages in the report, and then notice that groupings are no longer split between pages. Also notice that more blank space displays at the bottom of some pages. **Close Print Preview. Close** the report, **Close** the database, and **Close** Access.

MORE KNOWLEDGE **Changing the Margins in Print Preview**

On the Print Preview tab, in the Print Layout group, click Page Setup. On the Print Options tab, adjust the left and right margins to balance the report across the page, and then click OK.

For Non-MyLab Submissions: Determine What Your Instructor Requires for Submission
As directed by your instructor, submit your completed database file.

---

22 In **MyLab IT**, locate and click the Grader Project **Access 6B Rosebud Cafe**. In **step 3**, under **Upload Completed Assignment**, click **Choose File**. In the **Open** dialog box, navigate to your **Access Chapter 6 folder**, and then click your **Student_Access_6B_RBC** file one time to select it. In the lower right corner of the **Open** dialog box, click **Open**.

The name of your selected file displays above the Upload button.

23 To submit your file to **MyLab IT** for grading, click **Upload**, wait a moment for a green **Success!** message, and then in **step 4**, click the blue **Submit for Grading** button. Click **Close Assignment** to return to your list of **Course Materials**.

You have completed Project 6B **END**

>>> GO! To Work

Microsoft Office Specialist (MOS) Skills in This Chapter	
Project 6A	**Project 6B**
4.1.1 Add, move, and remove form controls	**2.2.1** Hide fields in tables
4.1.2 Set form control properties	**5.1.1** Group and sort fields on reports
4.1.3 Add and modify form labels	**5.1.2** Add report controls
4.2.1 Modify tab order on forms	**5.1.3** Add and modify labels on reports
4.2.2 Set records by form field	**5.2.1** Format a report into multiple columns
4.2.4 Insert information in form headers and footers	**5.2.2** Change report orientation
4.2.5 Insert images on forms	**5.2.3** Format report elements
	5.2.5 Insert information in report headers and footers
	5.2.6 Insert images on reports

Build Your E-Portfolio

An E-Portfolio is a collection of evidence, stored electronically, that showcases what you have accomplished while completing your education. Collecting and then sharing your work products with potential employers reflects your academic and career goals. Your completed documents from the following projects are good examples to show what you have learned: 6G, 6K, and 6L.

GO! For Job Success

Topic: More Effective Meetings

Meetings are a common source of frustration in most organizations. There are too many meetings that go on too long and include too many people and don't result in any actionable ideas or decisions. Many organizations are implementing new rules that are designed to make meetings a valuable use of time rather than becoming time wasters. At Apple, meeting attendees are expected to come to meetings with ideas and be prepared to challenge and question the ideas presented. At Google, meetings must have a clearly designated decision maker. Some organizations strongly encourage collaborative brainstorming in meetings and require that attendees respond to all suggestions with Yes, AND . . . , not No, or Yes, BUT. This encourages meeting attendees to find the positive in an idea and try to build on it, rather than immediately identifying the reasons why it won't work.

g-stockstudio/Shutterstock

> Have you ever been in a meeting at work, school, or for a volunteer organization where you wanted to challenge an idea, but did not feel the meeting leader or attendees wanted an open discussion?

> What are the benefits of ensuring that every meeting has a decision maker, and what are some outcomes of a meeting that does not have a decision maker?

> Have you been in situations where an idea of yours was killed with a No? How would you have felt if the response had been Yes, BUT?

End of Chapter

Summary

Forms are database objects used to interact with the data in tables; however, specific records can be printed. Sections and controls can be added, formatted, and modified to make the form user friendly.

Reports are database objects used to present data from tables or queries in a professional format. Grouping and sorting levels are added for organization, and then aggregate functions can summarize the data.

Forms and reports can be created in Design view or by using a wizard. Some editing can be done in Layout view, but specific modifications can be done only in Design view.

Controls added to forms and reports include label controls, image controls, command button controls, and line controls. Text box controls with expressions and concatenated strings are used to clarify data.

GO! Learn It Online

Review the concepts, key terms, and MOS skills in this chapter by completing these online challenges, which you can find at **MyLab IT**.

Chapter Quiz: Answer matching and multiple choice questions to test what you learned in this chapter.

Lessons on the GO!: Learn how to use all the new apps and features as they are introduced by Microsoft.

MOS Quiz: Answer questions to review the MOS skills that you practiced in this chapter.

Project Guide for Access Chapter 6

Your instructor will assign Projects from this list to ensure your learning and assess your knowledge.

Project Guide for Access Chapter 6

Project	Apply Skills from These Chapter Objectives	Project Type		Project Location
6A MyLab IT	Objectives 1–4 from Project 6A	**6A Instructional Project (Grader Project)** A guided review of the skills from Project 6A.	**Instruction**	In **MyLab IT** and in text
6B MyLab IT	Objectives 5–8 from Project 6B	**6B Instructional Project (Grader Project)** A guided review of the skills from Project 6B.	**Instruction**	In **MyLab IT** and in text
6C	Objectives 1–4 from Project 6A	**6C Chapter Review (Scorecard Grading)** A guided review of the skills from Project 6A.	**Review**	In text
6D	Objectives 5–8 from Project 6B	**6D Chapter Review (Scorecard Grading)** A guided review of the skills from Project 6B.	**Review**	In text
6E	Objectives 1–4 from Project 6A	**6E Mastery (Scorecard Grading)** A demonstration of your mastery of the skills in Project 6A with extensive decision making.	**Mastery and Transfer of Learning**	In text
6F	Objectives 5–8 from Project 6B	**6F Mastery (Scorecard Grading)** A demonstration of your mastery of the skills in Project 6B with extensive decision making.	**Mastery and Transfer of Learning**	In text
6G MyLab IT	Objectives 1–8 from Projects 6A and 6B	**6G Mastery (Grader Project)** A demonstration of your mastery of the skills in Projects 6A and 6B with extensive decision making.	**Mastery and Transfer of Learning**	In **MyLab IT** and in text
6H	Combination of Objectives from Projects 6A and 6B	**6H GO! Fix It (Scorecard Grading)** A demonstration of your mastery of the skills in Projects 6A and 6B by creating a correct result from a document that contains errors you must find.	**Critical Thinking**	Instructor Resource Center (IRC)
6I	Combination of Objectives from Projects 6A and 6B	**6I GO! Make It (Scorecard Grading)** A demonstration of your mastery of the skills in Projects 6A and 6B by creating a result from a supplied picture.	**Critical Thinking**	IRC
6J	Combination of Objectives from Projects 6A and 6B	**6J GO! Solve It (Rubric Grading)** A demonstration of your mastery of the skills in Projects 6A and 6B, your decision-making skills, and your critical thinking skills. A task-specific rubric helps you self-assess your result.	**Critical Thinking**	IRC
6K	Combination of Objectives from Projects 6A and 6B	**6K GO! Solve It (Rubric Grading)** A demonstration of your mastery of the skills in Projects 6A and 6B, your decision-making skills, and your critical thinking skills. A task-specific rubric helps you self-assess your result.	**Critical Thinking**	In text
6L	Combination of Objectives from Projects 6A and 6B	**6L GO! Think (Rubric Grading)** A demonstration of your understanding of the chapter concepts applied in a manner that you would use outside of college. An analytic rubric helps you and your instructor grade the quality of your work by comparing it to the work an expert in the discipline would create.	**Critical Thinking**	In text
6M	Combination of Objectives from Projects 6A and 6B	**6M GO! Think (Rubric Grading)** A demonstration of your understanding of the chapter concepts applied in a manner that you would use outside of college. An analytic rubric helps you and your instructor grade the quality of your work by comparing it to the work an expert in the discipline would create.	**Critical Thinking**	IRC
6N	Combination of Objectives from Projects 6A and 6B	**6N You and GO! (Rubric Grading)** A demonstration of your understanding of the chapter concepts applied in a manner that you would use in a personal situation. An analytic rubric helps you and your instructor grade the quality of your work.	**Critical Thinking**	IRC

Glossary

Glossary of Chapter Key Terms

Aggregate function A function that groups and performs calculations on multiple values.

Button control A control that enables individuals to add a command button to a form or report that will perform an action when the button is clicked.

Combo box A control that enables individuals to select from a list or to type a value.

Concatenation Linking or joining strings.

Control An object, such as a label or text box, in a form or report that enables individuals to view or manipulate information stored in tables or queries.

ControlTip A message that displays descriptive text when the mouse pointer is paused over the control.

Focus A control that is selected and currently being acted upon.

Form selector The box in the upper left corner of a form in Design view where the rulers meet; used to select the entire form.

Image control A control that enables individuals to insert an image into any section of a form or report.

Line control A control that enables an individual to insert a line into a form or report.

List box A control that enables individuals to select from a list but does not enable individuals to type anything that is not in the list.

Picture Alignment property A property that determines where the background picture for a form displays on the form.

Picture Size Mode property A property that determines the proportion of a picture in a form.

Point A measurement that is 1/72 of an inch.

Propagate To disseminate or apply changes to an object.

Properties The characteristics that determine the appearance, structure, and behavior of an object.

Property Sheet A pane that is available for every object on a form, including the form itself, to further enhance the object.

Property Update Options button An option button that displays when you make changes to the design of a table; it enables individuals to update the Property Sheet for a field in all objects that use a table as the record source.

Record Source property A property that enables you to specify the source of the data for a form or a report; the property setting can be a table name, a query name, or an SQL statement.

Status Bar Text property A form property that enables individuals to enter text that will display in the status bar for a selected control.

String A series of characters.

Tab order A setting that refers to the order in which the fields are selected when the Tab key is pressed.

Theme A design tool that simplifies the process of creating professional-looking objects within one program or across multiple programs; includes theme colors and theme fonts that will be applied consistently throughout the objects in a database.

Chapter Review

Apply 6A skills from these Objectives:

1. Create a Form in Design View
2. Change and Add Controls
3. Format a Form
4. Make a Form User Friendly

Marty Kress, vice president of marketing for the Rosebud Cafe franchise restaurant chain, wants to expand the chain's offerings to include party trays for advance order and delivery. In the following project, you will create a form to use for the data entry of these party order items. Your completed Navigation Pane will look similar to Figure 6.48.

Project Files

For Project 6C, you will need the following files:

a06C_Party_Orders

a06C_Logo

a06C_Rose

You will save your database as:

Lastname_Firstname_6C_Party_Orders

Project Results

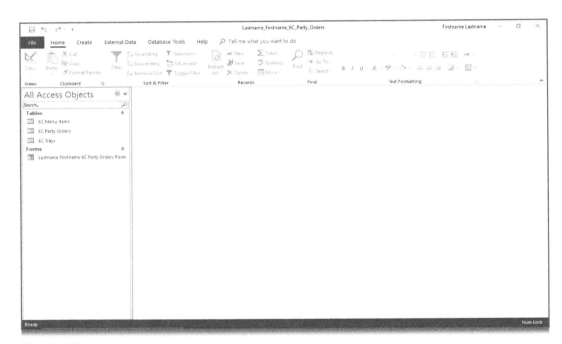

Figure 6.48

(continues on next page)

Chapter Review

Skills Review: Project 6C Party Orders (continued)

1 Start Access. Locate and open the **a06C_Party_Orders** file. Save the database in your **Access Chapter 6** folder as **Lastname_Firstname_6C_Party_Orders** If necessary, click **Enable Content**.

2 Double-click **6C Party Orders** to open the table in **Datasheet** view. Take a moment to examine the fields in the table.

a. In any record, click in the **Party Tray** field, and then click the **arrow**. This field is a Lookup field in the *6C Trays* table. In any record, click in the **Extras** field, and then click the **arrow**. This field is a Lookup field in the *6C Menu Items* table.

b. **Close** the table, and then **Close** the **Navigation Pane**.

3 On the **Create tab**, in the **Forms group**, click **Form Design**.

a. If necessary, under **Form Design Tools**, on the **Design tab**, in the **Tools group**, click **Property Sheet**. On the **Property Sheet**, click the **Data tab**. Click the **Record Source arrow**, and then click **6C Party Orders**. Close the **Property Sheet**.

4 Under **Form Design Tools**, on the **Design tab**, in the **Tools group**, click **Add Existing Fields**.

a. In the **Field List**, click **Order ID**, hold down Shift, and then click **Extras**. Drag the selected fields onto the design grid until the top of the pointer arrow is aligned at **0.25 inch on the vertical ruler** and **2 inches on the horizontal ruler**, and then release the mouse button. **Close** the **Field List**.

b. With all of the controls still selected, under **Form Design Tools**, on the **Arrange tab**, in the **Table group**, click **Stacked**.

c. Drag the left edge of the label controls to the **0.5-inch mark on the horizontal ruler**. Increase the width of the text boxes by approximately **0.5 inches**. **Save** the form as **Lastname Firstname 6C Party Orders Form**

5 Under **Form Design Tools**, on the **Design tab**, in the **Header/Footer group**, click **Logo**.

a. Navigate to the location where the student data files for this textbook are saved. Locate and double-click **a06C_Logo** to insert the logo in the **Form Header**.

b. On the selected logo, point to the right middle sizing handle until the pointer displays. Drag to the right until the right edge of the logo is aligned with the **1.5-inch mark on the horizontal ruler**.

6 In the **Header/Footer group**, click **Title**.

a. In the **label control** for the title, replace the text with **6C Party Orders** and then press Enter.

b. Drag the right edge of the title to align it with the **4-inch mark on the horizontal ruler**.

c. With the title selected, under **Form Design Tools**, on the **Format tab**, in the **Font group**, click **Center**.

7 Scroll down until the **Form Footer** section bar displays. Point to the top of the **Form Footer** section bar until the pointer displays. Drag upward until the top of the **Form Footer** section bar aligns with the **2.5-inch mark on the vertical ruler**.

a. Under **Form Design Tools**, on the **Design tab**, in the **Controls group**, click **Label**. Point to the **Form Footer** section until the plus sign (+) of the pointer aligns with the bottom of the **Form Footer** section bar and the **0.25-inch mark on the horizontal ruler**. Drag downward to the bottom of the **Form Footer** section and to the right to the **3.25-inch mark on the horizontal ruler**.

b. Type **Order online at www.rosebudcafe.net** and then press Enter.

c. With the **label control** in the **Form Footer** section selected, hold down Shift, and then click the **Logo control** and the **Extras label control**. Under **Form Design Tools**, on the **Arrange tab**, in the **Sizing & Ordering group**, click **Align**, and then click **Left**. **Save** the form.

8 Click and hold the **Party Tray list box control** until the pointer displays. Drag downward until a thin orange line displays on the bottom edges of the **Extras** controls and then release the mouse button.

a. With the **Party Tray combo box control** selected, hold down Shift, and then click the **Party Tray label control**, **Extras combo box control**, and **Extras label control**.

b. Under **Form Design Tools**, on the **Arrange tab**, in the **Table group**, click **Remove Layout** to remove the *Extras* field and the *Party Tray* field from the stacked layout.

c. Click in a blank area in the **Detail** section to deselect the controls. Right-click the **Party Tray combo box control**. From the shortcut menu, point to **Change To**, and then click **List Box**.

(continues on next page)

Chapter Review

d. **Save** the form, and then switch to **Form** view. Notice that the **Party Tray list box control** is not wide enough to display all columns and that there are horizontal and vertical scroll bars to indicate there is more data. Click the **Extras combo box arrow** to see if any menu item names or prices are cut off. Press Esc.

e. Switch to **Design** view, and click the **Party Tray list box control**, if necessary. Point to the right edge of the control until the pointer displays. Drag to the right until the right edge of the control aligns with the **4.25-inch mark on the horizontal ruler**.

f. Switch to **Layout** view. Resize the **Extras combo box control** to be the same size as the **Party Tray list box control**. **Save** the form and switch to **Design** view.

9 Click the **Form Header section bar**. Under **Form Design Tools**, on the **Design tab**, in the **Controls group**, click **Insert Image**, and then click **Browse**. In the displayed **Insert Picture** dialog box, navigate to the location where the student data files for this textbook are saved.

a. Locate and double-click **a06C_Logo**.

b. Align the plus sign (+) with the bottom of the **Form Header** section bar and with the **4-inch mark on the horizontal ruler**. Drag downward to the top of the **Detail** section bar and to the right to the **5.25-inch mark on the horizontal ruler**.

c. Click the **image control**—the Rosebud Cafe image on the right side in the **Form Header** section—if necessary. On the **Design tab**, in the **Tools group**, click **Property Sheet**. If necessary, on the **Format tab**, change the **Width** property setting to **1.25** and then change the **Height** property setting to **0.5**.

d. In the **Form Header** section, click the **logo control**. On the **Property Sheet**, change the **Width** property setting to **1.25** and change the **Height** property setting to **0.5**. **Close** the **Property Sheet**.

e. With the logo control selected, hold down Shift, and then click the **image control**. On the **Arrange tab**, in the **Sizing & Ordering group**, click **Align**, and then click **Top**.

10 Under **Form Design Tools**, on the **Design tab**, in the **Controls group**, click **Button**.

a. Move the mouse pointer down into the **Detail** section. Align the plus sign (+) of the pointer at **0.25 inches on the vertical ruler** and **3.25 inches on the horizontal ruler**, and then click.

b. Under **Categories**, verify **Record Navigation** is selected. Under **Actions**, click **Find Record**, and then click **Next** two times. In the text box, type **btnFindRcrd** and then click **Finish**.

c. Using the technique you just practiced, add a **button control** right next to the **Find Record button**. Under **Categories**, click **Record Operations**. Under **Actions**, click **Print Record**, and then click **Next** two times. Name the button **btnPrtForm** Click **Finish**.

d. With the **Print Current Form button control** selected, hold down Shift, and then click the **Find Record button control**. Under **Form Design Tools**, on the **Arrange tab**, in the **Sizing & Ordering group**, click **Align**, and then click **Top**.

11 Switch to **Layout** view. Click in the **Form Footer** section to the right of the label control to select the entire section.

a. Under **Form Layout Tools**, on the **Format tab**, in the **Control Formatting group**, click **Shape Fill**. Under **Theme Colors**, in the third row, click the seventh color.

b. Using the technique you just practiced, change the color of the **Form Header** section to match the **Form Footer** section.

12 Switch to **Design** view, and then double-click the **Form selector** to open the Property Sheet for the form.

a. On the **Property Sheet**, on the **Format tab**, click in the **Picture** property setting box, and then click **Build**. Navigate to where the student data files for this textbook are saved. Locate and double-click **a06C_Rose** to insert the picture in the form.

b. Click in the **Picture Alignment** property setting box, click the **arrow**, and then click **Form Center**. **Close** the **Property Sheet**, and then **Save** the form.

13 Switch to **Layout** view, click the **Order ID text box control**, hold down Shift, and then click the **Cust Name text box control** and the **Cust Phone# text box control**.

a. Under **Form Layout Tools**, on the **Format tab**, in the **Control Formatting group**, click **Shape Outline**. Point to **Line Type**, and click the fifth line type—**Dots**.

b. Under **Form Layout Tools**, on the **Format tab**, in the **Control Formatting group**, click **Shape Outline**. Point to **Line Thickness**, and then click the second line type—**1 pt**.

(continues on next page)

Chapter Review

c. In the **Control Formatting group**, click **Shape Outline**. Under **Theme Colors**, in the fifth row, click the seventh color.

14 Switch to **Form** view, and then click in the **Cust Phone# text box control**. On the left side of the status bar, *Form View* displays—there is no text that helps an individual enter data. **Close** the form, **Save** your changes, and open the **Navigation Pane**.

a. Under **Tables**, right-click **6C Party Orders**; from the shortcut menu, click **Design View**. In the **Cust Phone#** field, click in the **Description** box. Type **Include area code for 10-digit dialing** and then press Enter.

b. Click the **Property Update Options** button, and then click **Update Status Bar Text everywhere Cust Phone# is used**. In the displayed **Update Properties** dialog box, click **Yes**. **Close** the table, saving changes.

15 Open **6C Party Orders Form** in **Design** view. **Close** the **Navigation Pane**. If necessary, on the **Design tab**, in the **Tools** group, click **Property Sheet**.

a. In the **Detail** section, click the **Print Form** button. Notice that the **Property Sheet** is displayed for the button you selected.

b. On the **Other tab**, click in the **ControlTip Text** property setting box, type **Prints the Current Form** to replace the existing **Print Form** text, and then press Enter.

c. **Close** the **Property Sheet**, **Save** the form, and then switch to **Form** view. Point to the **Print Form** button to display the ControlTip.

16 Switch to **Design** view. In the **Detail** section, click the **Order ID text box control**, hold down Shift, and then click the **Find Record button control** and the **Print Current Form button control**.

a. Under **Form Design Tools**, on the **Design tab**, in the **Tools group**, click the **Property Sheet** button. If necessary, on the **Property Sheet**, click the **Other tab**. On the **Property Sheet**, click in the **Tab Stop** property setting box, click the **arrow**, and then click **No**.

b. Click the **Cust Name text box control**. Click in the **Tab Index** property setting box, and then type **0** **Close** the **Property Sheet**.

17 Switch to **Form** view. With the **Cust Name** control selected, click the **Find Record** button.

a. In the **Find and Replace** dialog box, in the **Find What** box, type **Gonzalez, Ricardo** Click **Find Next**. **Close** the Find and Replace dialog box.

b. In the **Cust Name text box**, type your **Lastname, Firstname** replacing Ricardo's name. Press Tab. In the **Cust Phone#** field, enter your phone number, and then press Enter. **Save** the form.

18 **Close** the form, **Open** the **Navigation Pane**, and resize it so all object names are fully visible. **Close** the database, and then **Close** Access.

19 As directed by your instructor, submit your database for grading.

You have completed Project 6C | **END**

Chapter Review

Apply 6B skills from these Objectives:

5. Create a Report Based on a Query Using a Wizard
6. Create a Report in Design View
7. Add Controls to a Report
8. Group, Sort, and Total Records in Design View

Each Rosebud Cafe location maintains a database about the orders that are placed for the catering entity of the business. Reports are run to summarize data in the tables or queries. Creating customized reports will help the managers of each location view the information in the database in a meaningful way. In this project, you will create customized reports. Your completed Navigation Pane will look similar to Figure 6.49.

Project Files

For Project 6D, you will need the following files:

a06D_Catering

a06D_Logo

You will save your database as:

Lastname_Firstname_6D_Catering

Project Results

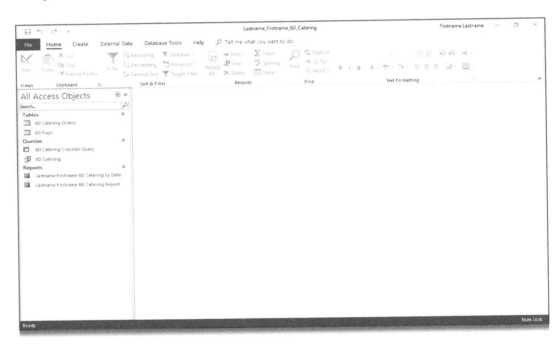

Figure 6.49

(continues on next page)

Chapter Review

1 Start Access. Locate and open the **a06D_Catering** file. Save the database in your **Access Chapter 6** folder as **Lastname_Firstname_6D_Catering** If necessary, click **Enable Content**.

2 In the Navigation Pane, under **Queries**, double-click **6D Catering Crosstab Query**. Take a moment to study the data in the query. **Close** the query, and then **Close** the **Navigation Pane**.

3 On the **Create tab**, in the **Reports group**, click **Report Wizard**.

  a. Under **Tables/Queries**, verify **Query: 6D Catering Crosstab Query** is displayed. Under **Available Fields**, add all of the field names to the **Selected Fields** box. Click **Next** twice.

  b. Click the **arrow** next to the **1** box, and then click **Cust Name**. Leave the sort order as **Ascending**, and then click **Next**.

  c. Under **Layout**, verify the **Tabular** option button is selected. Under **Orientation**, verify the **Portrait** option button is selected. Verify the **Adjust the field width so all fields fit on a page** check box is selected. Click **Next**.

  d. For the title of the report, type **Lastname Firstname 6D Catering by Date** Select **Modify the report's design**, and then click **Finish**.

4 Under **Report Design Tools**, on the **Design tab**, in the **Themes group**, click **Themes**, and then in the first row click the fourth theme.

5 Switch to **Layout** view. If necessary, click in the 3/16/2022 cell and select the column, point to the left edge of the column so the middle sizing handle displays, and drag to the right approximately 0.5 inches, resizing the column. Point to the right edge of the **Cust Phone#** column and drag to the right until all of the data in the **Cust Phone#** column displays. Click in a blank area of the report to deselect the column. Switch to **Design** view. Drag the right edge of the report to the **8-inch mark on the horizontal ruler**, resizing the right column as necessary.

6 Select all of the controls in the **Page Header** section by pointing to the top left of the **Page Header** section, holding down your mouse button, and then dragging the mouse across the **Page Header controls** and to the bottom of the **Page Header** section. Release the mouse button.

  a. Under **Report Design Tools**, on the **Format tab**, in the **Font group**, click the **Font color arrow**. Under **Theme Colors**, on the first row, click the fourth color. In the **Font group**, click **Bold**.

7 **Save** the report. **Close** the report.

8 On the **Create tab**, in the **Reports group**, click **Report Design**.

  a. Under **Report Design Tools**, on the **Design tab**, in the **Tools group**, click **Property Sheet**. On the **Property Sheet**, click the **Data tab**. Click the **Record Source arrow**, click **6D Catering**, and then **Close** the **Property Sheet**.

  b. Under **Report Design Tools**, on the **Design tab**, in the **Tools group**, click **Add Existing Fields**.

  c. In the **Field List**, click **Pickup Time**. Hold down ⇧ Shift, and then click **Price** to select all of the fields. Drag the selected fields into the **Detail** section until the top of the arrow of the pointer is aligned with the **0.25-inch mark on the vertical ruler** and with the **1.5-inch mark on the horizontal ruler**.

  d. With the controls still selected, under **Report Design Tools**, on the **Arrange tab**, in the **Table group**, click **Stacked**. **Close** the **Field List**, and then **Save** the report as **Lastname Firstname 6D Catering Report**

9 Under **Report Design Tools**, on the **Design tab**, in the **Header/Footer group**, click **Logo**.

  a. Locate and double-click **a06D_Logo** to insert the logo in the Report Header section.

  b. On the selected logo, point to the right middle sizing handle until the pointer displays. Drag to the right until the right edge of the logo is aligned with the **1.5-inch mark on the horizontal ruler**.

10 Under **Report Design Tools**, on the **Design tab**, in the **Header/Footer group**, click **Title**. In the **title's label control**, select **Lastname Firstname**, and then press ⌦ Delete.

11 Point to the top edge of the **Page Footer** section bar until the pointer displays. Drag upward until the top of the **Page Footer** section bar aligns with the **2-inch mark on the vertical ruler**.

12 Point to the top edge of the **Detail** section bar until the pointer displays. Drag upward until the top edge of the **Detail** section bar aligns with the bottom edge of the **Page Header** section bar. **Save** the report.

(continues on next page)

Chapter Review

13 Under **Report Design Tools**, on the **Design tab**, in the **Header/Footer group**, click **Page Numbers**.

a. In the displayed **Page Numbers** dialog box, under **Format**, click **Page N**, if necessary. Under **Position**, click **Bottom of Page [Footer]**, if necessary, and then click **OK**.

b. Resize and move the **Page Number control box** until it fits between the **2-inch and 4-inch marks on the horizontal ruler**.

14 Under **Report Design Tools**, on the **Design tab**, in the **Controls group**, click **Label**.

a. Drag the plus sign (+) from the bottom edge of the **Report Footer** section bar at the **0.25-inch mark on the horizontal ruler** to the bottom of the **Report Footer** section at the **3-inch mark on the horizontal ruler**.

b. Using your own first and last names, type **Catering Manager: Firstname Lastname** Press Enter.

15 Under **Report Design Tools**, on the **Design tab**, in the **Header/Footer group**, click **Date and Time**. In the **Date and Time** dialog box, under **Include Date**, click the second option button. Under **Include Time**, remove the check mark, if necessary, and then click **OK**. **Save** the report.

a. Click the **Date text box control**. On the **Arrange tab**, in the **Table group**, click **Remove Layout**.

b. Right-click the selected control, and click **Cut**. Right-click the **Page Footer** section, and click **Paste**.

c. Move the **Date text box control** and resize it until it fits between the **4.5-inch and 6.25-inch marks on the horizontal ruler**.

d. Click the **Title text box control** to select it, point to the right middle sizing handle until the pointer displays, and then drag to the left until the right edge of the text box control aligns with the **4.75-inch mark on the horizontal ruler**.

16 Drag the right edge of the design grid to the left until it aligns with the **6.5-inch mark on the horizontal ruler**. **Save** the report.

a. Switch to **Layout** view. In the first record, click the **Tray Desc text box control**, and then point to the right edge of the control until the pointer displays. Drag to the right until all of the text displays in the **Tray Desc text box control**—*Grilled Chicken Skewer Tray*.

17 Switch to **Design** view. In the **Report Header** section, right-click the **logo control**. From the displayed shortcut menu, click **Copy**. Right-click anywhere in the **Report Header** section, and then from the shortcut menu, click **Paste**.

a. Point to the selected logo, and then drag to the right until the left edge of the outlined control aligns with the **4.75-inch mark on the horizontal ruler**.

b. With the image control on the right selected, hold down Ctrl, and then click the **logo control**. Under **Report Design Tools**, on the **Arrange tab**, in the **Sizing & Ordering group**, click **Align**, and then click **Bottom**.

c. Resize the **Title text box control** so the right edge is **one dot** away from the image on its right. **Center** the title in the control. Drag the **Page Header section bar** up to the **0.5-inch mark on the vertical ruler**.

18 Under **Report Design Tools**, on the **Design tab**, in the **Grouping & Totals group**, click **Group & Sort**.

a. In the **Group, Sort, and Total Pane**, click **Add a group**. From the displayed list, click **Pickup Time**.

b. Click the **by quarter arrow**, and then click **by entire value**. Click in a blank area of the **Group, Sort, and Total Pane**. Click the **More arrow**, click the **do not keep group together on one page arrow**, and then click **keep whole group together on one page**.

c. In the **Group, Sort, and Total Pane**, click **Add a sort**, and then click **Cust Name**. **Close** the **Group, Sort, and Total Pane**.

19 In the **Detail** section, click the **Pickup Time text box control**. Drag downward until a thin orange line displays at the bottom of the **Price** controls, and then release the mouse button.

a. On the **Arrange tab**, in the **Table group**, click **Remove Layout**.

b. Move the **Pickup Time text box control** into the **Pickup Time Header** section so the left edge of the text box control aligns with the **1-inch mark on the horizontal ruler**.

c. In the **Pickup Time Header** section, select the **Pickup Time label control**, and then press Delete.

20 In the **Detail** section, click the **Tray Desc text box control**. On the **Design tab**, in the **Grouping & Totals group**, click **Totals**. In the displayed list of aggregate functions, click **Count Records**.

(continues on next page)

Chapter Review

Skills Review: Project 6D Catering (continued)

21 In the **Pickup Time Footer** section, select the **Count text box control**, and then holding down Shift, in the **Report Footer** select the **Count text box control**.

a. Under **Report Design Tools**, on the **Arrange tab**, in the **Table group**, click **Remove Layout**.

b. Align and resize each control so the left edge of each control is even with the **5.5-inch marker on the horizontal ruler** and the right edge of each control is even with the **6-inch marker on the horizontal ruler**.

c. Under **Report Design Tools**, on the **Design tab**, in the **Controls group**, click **Text Box**. Drag the plus sign (+) from the bottom edge of the **Pickup Time Footer** section bar at the **2.75-inch mark on the horizontal ruler** to the bottom of the **Pickup Time Footer** section and to the right to the **5.5-inch mark on the horizontal ruler**.

d. In the unbound text box, type **=[Pickup Time] & "# of Orders:"** In the **Pickup Time Footer** section, click the **label control** that displays to the left of the text box control, and then press Delete.

e. In the **Pickup Time Footer** section, click the **text box control** that contains the expression you typed. Hold down Shift and click the **Count calculated control** in the **Pickup Time Footer**. On the **Arrange tab**, in the **Sizing & Ordering group**, click **Size/Space**, and then click **To Tallest**. In the **Sizing & Ordering group**, click **Align**, and then click **Top**.

22 Drag the right edge of the design grid to the left until it aligns with the **6.5-inch mark on the horizontal ruler**. Switch to **Report** view. Hold down Ctrl, and then press End to move to the end of the report.

23 Switch to **Design** view. Point to the bottom of the **Report Footer** section, and then drag downward until it reaches the **0.5-inch mark on the vertical ruler**.

a. In the **Report Footer** section, click the **Count text box control**, and then drag downward until the bottom edge of the control aligns with the bottom edge of the **Report Footer** section.

b. Use the techniques you have practiced to add a label control in the **Report Footer** section to the left of the calculated control—the left edge of the control should be aligned with the **4-inch mark on the horizontal ruler**. In the **label control**, type **Total # of Orders:**

c. Align the label control with the calculated control at the bottom and then be sure that the controls are the same height.

24 Under **Report Design Tools**, on the **Design tab**, in the **Controls group**, click **Line**. Point to the bottom of the **Pickup Time Footer** section until the middle of the plus sign (+) of the pointer aligns with the top of the **Page Footer** section bar and the **0-inch mark on the horizontal ruler**. Click, hold down Shift, drag to the right to the **6.5-inch mark on the horizontal ruler**, and then release the mouse button and Shift.

25 Under **Report Design Tools**, on the **Format tab**, in the **Control Formatting group**, click **Shape Outline**. Click **Line Thickness**, and then click the third line—**2 pt**. In the **Control Formatting group**, click **Shape Outline**. Under **Theme Colors**, in the first row, click the eighth color. **Save** the report.

26 Switch to **Print Preview**. Adjust the margins or report width as needed. **Close Print Preview**.

27 **Close** the report. **Open** the **Navigation Pane** and resize so all object names display fully. **Close** the database, and then **Close** Access.

28 As directed by your instructor, submit your database for grading.

You have completed Project 6D   **END**

Mastering Access   Project 6E Monthly Promotions

Apply 6A skills from these Objectives:

1. Create a Form in Design View
2. Change and Add Controls
3. Format a Form
4. Make a Form User Friendly

In the following project, you will create a form that will be used to enter the data for the monthly promotions that are offered to guests at the Rosebud Cafe restaurant franchise. Your task includes designing a form that will be attractive and provide easy data entry for the staff. Your completed Navigation Pane will look similar to Figure 6.50.

Project Files

For Project 6E, you will need the following files:

a06E_Monthly_Promotions

a06E_Logo

a06E_Dollar

You will save your database as:

Lastname_Firstname_6E_Monthly_Promotions

Project Results

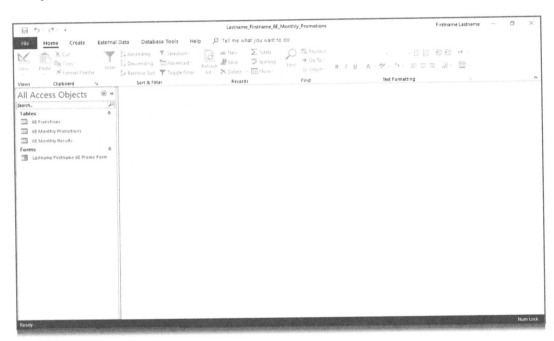

Figure 6.50

(continues on next page)

Content-Based Assessments (Mastery and Transfer of Learning)

Mastering Access: Project 6E Monthly Promotions (continued)

1 Start Access. Locate and open the **a06E_Monthly_ Promotions** file. Save the database in your **Access Chapter 6** folder as **Lastname_Firstname_6E_Monthly_ Promotions** If necessary, click **Enable Content**.

2 Create a form in **Form Design**. For the **Record Source**, use the **6E Monthly Results** table. Select all of the fields, and then drag them onto the design grid until the top of the arrow is aligned with the **1-inch mark on the horizontal ruler** and the **0.25-inch mark on the vertical ruler**. **Save** the form as **Lastname Firstname 6E Promo Form**

3 With all of the text box controls selected, display the **Property Sheet**, and then click the **Format tab**. In the **Left** property box, type **1.5** and press Enter. Click anywhere in the **Detail** section to deselect the controls. Select the **Franchise text box control**, and then drag the right edge to the **3-inch mark on the horizontal ruler**. Select the **# Redeemed text box control**, and in the **Property Sheet**, change the **Width** to **0.75 Close** the Property Sheet. **Save** the form. Switch to **Form** view, and then click the **Promo Month** text box control to view the entries. Switch to **Design** view.

4 In the **Form Header**, insert the **a06E_Logo**. Widen the selected logo to the **1.5-inch mark on the horizontal ruler**.

5 In the **Header/Footer group**, add a **Title**, and then, if necessary, resize the **Title label control** so the entire title is visible. With the title selected, select all of the label controls. Under **Form Design Tools**, on the **Format tab**, in the **Font group**, click the **Font Color** arrow, Under **Theme Colors**, in the fifth row click the sixth color.

6 Scroll down until the **Form Footer** section bar displays. Point to the top of the **Form Footer**, and drag up until the top of the **Form Footer** section bar aligns with the **1.5-inch mark on the vertical ruler**.

7 In the **Form Footer**, insert a **Label** control so the left aligns with the **0-inch mark on the horizontal ruler** and the right aligns with the **4-inch mark on the horizontal ruler**. Type **Coupons may be redeemed at any Rosebud Cafe location** Press Enter. Click the **Font Color** arrow, and then, under **Theme Colors**, in the fifth row click the sixth color.

8 In the **Form Footer**, insert the **a06E_Dollar** image at the top of the **Form Footer** section and at the **4.25-inch mark on the horizontal ruler**.

9 With the image selected display the **Property Sheet**, and change the **Width** and **Height** to **0.35** Point to the bottom of the **Form Footer** and drag up until the bottom of the Form Footer section bar aligns with the **0.5-inch mark on the vertical ruler**. **Close** the Property Sheet.

10 In the **Detail** section, insert a **Button** control aligning the plus sign (+) of the pointer with the **0.5-inch mark on the vertical ruler** and the **3.5-inch mark on the horizontal ruler**.

11 Under **Categories**, click **Form Operations**. Under **Actions**, click **Close Form**. Select the **Text** option button. Name the button **btnCloseFrm** With the button selected, change the **Font Color** to match the title and the Form Footer.

12 With the **Close Form** button selected, open the **Property Sheet**. Change the **Tab Stop** property to **No**. **Close** the **Property Sheet**.

13 Click the **Close Form** button, saving changes. **Open** the **Navigation Pane**, and resize to display all objects fully. **Close** the database, and then **Close** Access.

14 As directed by your instructor, submit your database for grading.

You have completed Project 6E **END**

Mastering Access	Project 6F Promotional Results

Apply 6B skills from these Objectives:

5. Create a Report Based on a Query Using a Wizard
6. Create a Report in Design View
7. Add Controls to a Report
8. Group, Sort, and Total Records in Design View

In the following project, you will create a report that will display the promotions that are offered to guests of the Rosebud Cafe restaurant franchise. You will also create a crosstab report that will summarize the results of the promotions. Creating customized reports will help the managers of each location view the information in the database in a meaningful way. Your completed Navigation Pane will look similar to Figure 6.51.

Project Files

For Project 6F, you will need the following files:

a06F_Promotional_Results

a06F_Logo

You will save your database as:

Lastname_Firstname_6F_Promotional_Results

Project Results

Figure 6.51

(continues on next page)

Mastering Access: Project 6F Promotional Results (continued)

1 Start Access. Locate and open the **a06F_ Promotional_Results** file. Save the database in your **Access Chapter 6** folder as **Lastname_Firstname_6F_ Promotional_Results** If necessary, click **Enable Content**.

2 Under **Queries**, open the **6F Coupons Crosstab Query**. Take a moment to study the data in the query. **Close** the query, and then **Close** the **Navigation Pane**.

3 **Create** a report using the **Report Wizard**. From the **Query: 6F Coupons Crosstab Query**, select all of the fields. Under **Do you want to add any grouping levels?**, select **City**. Do not apply any additional sorting. Under **Layout**, be sure the **Blocked** option button is selected. Under **Orientation**, click the **Landscape** option button. Be sure the **Adjust the field width so all fields fit on a page** check box is selected. For the title of the report, type **Lastname Firstname 6F Coupons Redeemed** Select **Modify the report's design**, and then click **Finish**. If necessary, **Close** the Field List.

4 Switch to **Layout** view, and then apply the **Organic** theme. Click in the **Total Redeemed** control to the left of the R, and then press Shift + Enter to create a two-line title. Move the **City label and text box controls** to the left margin. If any data is cut off in the controls, select the label control and drag to widen the column to display all data. Reduce the width of any columns that display a lot of blank space to allow for the widened columns.

5 Switch to **Design** view. Insert the **a06F_Logo** image so it appears from the **5.25-inch mark on the horizontal ruler** to the **7-inch mark**, and is the height of the Report Header section.

6 Select the seven **Date label controls and textbox controls**. Change the width to **0.75**. Change the **Font Color** to the sixth row in the seventh column under **Theme Colors**.

7 If necessary, resize and move controls so you can resize the report to print on one landscape page. **Save** the report. **Close** the report.

8 Open the **6F Coupons** query in **Design** view, and notice the underlying tables that were used in the creation of the query. **Close** the query, and then **Close** the **Navigation Pane**.

9 Create a new report using **Report Design**. Display the **Property Sheet**. On the **Data tab**, click the **Record Source property setting box arrow**, and then select **6F Coupons**. **Close** the **Property Sheet**.

10 Display the **Field List**. From the **Field List**, select all fields included in the query. Drag the selected fields into the **Detail** section of the design grid until the top of the pointer is aligned with the **0.25-inch mark on the vertical ruler** and the **1-inch mark on the horizontal ruler**. With the controls selected, under **Report Design Tools**, on the **Arrange tab**, in the **Table group**, click **Tabular**. **Close** the **Field List**. Drag the **Page Footer section bar** up to the **0.5-inch mark on the vertical ruler**.

11 **Save** the report as **Lastname Firstname 6F Promotions** Switch to **Layout** view to be sure all data is visible in the report. If necessary, adjust the width of any columns where data is cut off. Switch to **Design** view.

12 Under **Report Design Tools**, on the **Design tab**, click the **Group & Sort** button. Click **Add a group**, and then from the displayed list, click **City**. Apply **Keep whole group together on one page**. Click **Add a sort**, and then click **Visit Date**. **Close** the **Group, Sort, and Total Pane**.

13 In the **Page Header** section, click the **City** label control, and then press Delete. In the **Detail** section, right-click the **City text box control** to display the shortcut menu, and click **Cut**. Click the **City Header** section bar to select it, right-click to display the shortcut menu, and click **Paste**.

14 In the **Detail** section, click the **# Redeemed text box control**. On the **Design tab**, click the **Totals** button, and then click **Sum**.

15 In the **Report Header**, insert the **a06F_Logo**. On the **Property Sheet**, increase the width to **1.75 inches**. Insert a **Title**. Delete your **Lastname Firstname** from the beginning of the title.

16 Add a **label control** to the **Report Footer**. Position the plus sign of the pointer at the bottom of the **Report Footer** section bar and the **4.5-inch mark on the horizontal ruler**. Drag upward to the top of the **Report Footer** section and to the right to the left edge of the Sum control box. Type **Total # Redeemed Coupons**

(continues on next page)

Mastering Access: Project 6F Promotional Results (continued)

17 Click the **Date and Time** button. Under **Include Date**, click the second option button. Do not **Include Time**. Remove the **Date text box control** from the layout.

18 Cut and **paste** the control to the left edge of the **Report Footer**. Click the **Date text box control** two times. Position the insertion point between the equal sign and the D. Type **"Prepared by Firstname Lastname on"&** and then press [Enter]. Click the **Title label control**, and resize it so the right edge aligns with the **3-inch mark on the horizontal ruler**. **Center** the text in the control. Resize the report to **7.75 inches wide**.

19 Select all of the controls in the **Report Footer**. Be sure they are all the same height and aligned at the bottom.

20 Switch to **Layout** view, and then adjust all controls to fit the data without extending beyond the right margin. **Save** the report. **Close** the report.

21 **Open** the **Navigation Pane**, and resize to display all objects fully. **Close** the database, and then **Close** Access.

22 As directed by your instructor, submit your database for grading.

You have completed Project 6F **END**

Content-Based Assessments (Mastery and Transfer of Learning)

Mastering Access | Project 6G Wireless Usage

Apply 6A and 6B skills from these Objectives:

1. Create a Form in Design View
2. Change and Add Controls
3. Format a Form
4. Make a Form User Friendly
5. Create a Report Based on a Query Using a Wizard
6. Create a Report in Design View
7. Add Controls to a Report
8. Group, Sort, and Total Records in Design View

Marty Kress, vice president of marketing for Rosebud Cafe franchises, keeps a database on the wireless usage per franchise on a monthly basis. The individual restaurants report the number of customers using the wireless connections and the average length of usage per customer. In this project, you will design a form for the data entry of this data and design a report that can be used by Mr. Kress to plan next year's marketing strategies. Your completed work will look similar to Figure 6.52.

Project Files for MyLab IT Grader

1. In your **MyLab IT** course, locate and click **Access 6G Wireless Usage**, Download Materials, and then Download All Files.
2. Extract the zipped folder to your Access Chapter 6 folder. Close the Grader download screens.
3. Take a moment to open the downloaded **Access_6G_Wireless_Usage_Instructions**; note any recent updates to the book.

Project Results

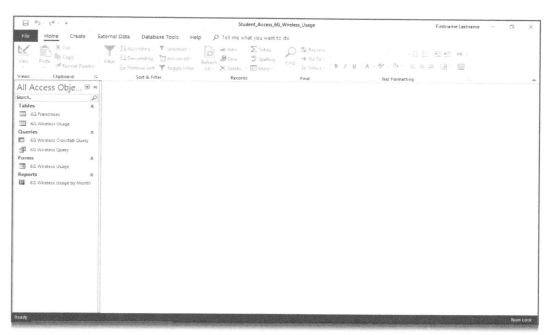

Figure 6.52

For Non-MyLab Submissions
For Project 6G, you will need the following files:
a06G_Wireless_Usage
a06G_Logo

Start with an Access Data File
In your Access Chapter 6 folder, save your database as:
Lastname_Firstname_6G_Wireless_Usage

After you have saved your database, open it to launch Access. On the next page, begin with Step 2.
After Step 14, submit your database as directed by your instructor.

(continues on next page)

Mastering Access: Project 6G Wireless Usage (continued)

1 Start Access. Navigate to your **Access Chapter 6 folder**, and then double-click the Access file that you downloaded from **MyLab IT** that displays your name—**Student_Access_6G_Wireless_Usage**.

2 If necessary, click **Enable Content**. Create a form in **Form Design**. For the **Record Source**, use the **6G Wireless Usage** table. Select all of the fields, and then drag them onto the design grid until the top of the arrow is aligned with the **1-inch mark on the horizontal ruler** and the **0.25-inch mark on the vertical ruler**. **Save** the form as **6G Wireless Usage**

3 Apply a **Stacked** layout. Apply a dashed outline to the text box and combo box controls in the **Detail** section. Change the border color to the color in the sixth row in the fifth column under **Theme Colors**.

4 Insert the **a06G_Logo**. Widen the selected logo to the **1.5-inch mark on the horizontal ruler**.

5 Insert a **Title**. Adjust the right edge of the title label control to just fit the text.

6 In the **Detail** section, add a **Button** at the **0.5-inch mark on the vertical ruler** and the **2.5-inch mark on the horizontal ruler** to add a new record. Select **Go To New** Picture, and then name the button **btnNewRcrd** In the **Detail** section, insert a **Button** at the **2.5-inch mark on the horizontal ruler** and the **1-inch mark on the vertical ruler** to print the current record. Place a picture on it, and name it **btnPrtRcrd**

7 With the **New Record** and **Print Record** buttons selected, change the **Tab Stop** property to **No**. If necessary, **Align** the buttons at the **Right**.

8 Drag the top of the **Form Footer** section bar until it aligns with the **2-inch mark on the vertical ruler**. In the **Form Footer** section, insert a label aligned with the bottom of the **Form Footer** section bar and the left edge of the form. Type **Created for Marty Kress** and then press ⏎.

9 Switch to **Form** view. Click the **New Record** button. From the list of **Franchises**, select **Holland MI**. In the **Wireless Month text box control**, select **June 1, 2022**. In the **# of Customers text box control**, type **757** In the **Avg Minutes text box control**, type **25**

10 Create a report using the **Report Wizard**. From the **Query: 6G Wireless Crosstab Query**, select the **City, Total Of # of Customers, Jul, Aug**, and **Sep** fields. Do not add any grouping levels. **Sort** records within the report by **City**, in **Ascending** order. Use a **Tabular** layout and a **Landscape** orientation. Name your report as **6G Wireless Usage by Month**

11 Switch to **Design** view. Select the **Title** label control and all of the label controls in the **Page Header** section. Change the font color to the color in the sixth row in the fifth column under **Theme Colors**. Reduce the width of the **Page # control** so the right edge aligns with the **8-inch mark on the horizontal ruler**.

12 Resize the **Jul, Aug**, and **Sep textbox controls** and **label controls** to **1 inch**. Move the controls to the left so there is one dot between the monthly columns. Resize the report to **9.5 inches** wide.

13 Modify the **Page Footer** by adding **Prepared for Rosebud Cafe on** before **Now()**.Be sure to use correct syntax when adding the text. Widen the control to the **5-inch mark on the horizontal ruler**. Switch to **Print Preview**.

14 Open the **Navigation Pane**, and resize to display all objects fully. **Close** the database, and then **Close** Access.

15 In **MyLab IT**, locate and click the Grader Project **Access 6G Wireless Usage**. In **step 3**, under **Upload Completed Assignment**, click **Choose File**. In the **Open** dialog box, navigate to your **Access Chapter 6 folder**, and then click your **Student_Access_6G_Wireless_Usage** file one time to select it. In the lower right corner of the **Open** dialog box, click **Open**.

16 To submit your file to **MyLab IT** for grading, click **Upload**, wait a moment for a green **Success!** message, and then in **step 4**, click the blue **Submit for Grading** button. Click **Close Assignment** to return to your list of **Course Materials**.

You have completed Project 6G **END**

Content-Based Assessments (Critical Thinking)

Apply a combination of the 6A and 6B skills.

GO! Fix It	**Project 6H Advertising Contracts**	IRC
GO! Make It	**Project 6I Supply Orders**	IRC
GO! Solve It	**Project 6J Menu Items**	IRC
GO! Solve It	**Project 6K Birthday Coupons**	

Project Files

For Project 6K, you will need the following files:

a06K_Birthday_Coupons
a06K_Rose
a06K_Birthday
a06K_Cupcake
a06_Logo

You will save your database as:

Lastname_Firstname_6K_Birthday_Coupons

The Vice President of Marketing, Marty Kress, encourages each location of the Rosebud Cafe franchise to offer birthday coupons to its customers as a promotional venture. Open the **a06K_Birthday_Coupons** database, and then save it as **Lastname_ Firstname_6K_Birthday_Coupons** Use the *6K Birthdates* table to create a form to enter the names, birthday months, and email addresses of the customers visiting one of the restaurants. Save the form as **Lastname Firstname 6K Birthday Form** Add a button control to print the current record. Include the Rose image as the logo, and title the form **6K Happy Birthday** Remove the background from the Form Header. Resize the Detail area to 1.5 inches. Be sure all data is visible on the form. Add a new record using the form and your own information.

Create a report to display the customer name and email address grouped by birthday month using the months as a section header and sorted by customer name. Add the **a06K_Birthday** image as the logo, resized to 1 inch tall and wide. Add a title. Draw a line above the Birthday Month header control to separate the months; apply a Line Color and Line Type. Add a footer that includes your name. Save the report as **Lastname Firstname 6K Birthdate Report**

Create a report based on the *6K First Quarter Birthdays* query. Include both of the fields arranged in a tabular format. Save the report as **Lastname Firstname 6K First Quarter Birthdays** Add a title to the report, **Lastname Firstname 6K First Quarter Birthdays** Add the current date and time to the Report Header section. Delete the Page Footer controls, and resize the Page Footer section to 0. Apply a solid outline to the label controls in the Page Header section; choose a Line Color and Line Thickness. Add a count of how many first quarter birthdays there are to the Report Footer. Include a descriptive label to the right of the count. Be sure the controls are the same size and aligned. Adjust the width of the report to 7.5 inches, making necessary adjustments to textbox controls. Add the **a06K_Cupcake** image and place it in the bottom right of the Report Footer. Resize it to 1 inch tall and wide. Save the changes. As directed by your instructor, submit your database for grading.

(continues on next page)

Content-Based Assessments (Critical Thinking)

Mastering Access: Project 6K Birthday Coupons (continued)

		Performance Level		
		Exemplary	**Proficient**	**Developing**
Performance Criteria	Create 6K Birthday Form	Form created with the correct fields and formatted as directed.	Form created with no more than two missing elements.	Form created with more than two missing elements.
	Create 6K Birthdate Report	Report created with the correct fields and formatted as directed.	Report created with no more than two missing elements.	Report created with more than two missing elements.
	Create 6K First Quarter Birthdays Report	Report created with the correct fields and formatted as directed.	Report created with no more than two missing elements.	Report created with more than two missing elements.

You have completed Project 6K | END

Rubric

The following outcomes-based assessments are open-ended assessments. That is, there is no specific correct result; your result will depend on your approach to the information provided. Make Professional Quality your goal. Use the following scoring rubric to guide you in how to approach the problem and then to evaluate how well your approach solves the problem.

The *criteria*—Software Mastery, Content, Format and Layout, and Process—represent the knowledge and skills you have gained that you can apply to solving the problem. The *levels of performance*—Professional Quality, Approaching Professional Quality, or Needs Quality Improvements—help you and your instructor evaluate your result.

	Your completed project is of Professional Quality if you:	Your completed project is Approaching Professional Quality if you:	Your completed project Needs Quality Improvements if you:
1-Software Mastery	Choose and apply the most appropriate skills, tools, and features and identify efficient methods to solve the problem.	Choose and apply some appropriate skills, tools, and features, but not in the most efficient manner.	Choose inappropriate skills, tools, or features, or are inefficient in solving the problem.
2-Content	Construct a solution that is clear and well organized, contains content that is accurate, appropriate to the audience and purpose, and is complete. Provide a solution that contains no errors of spelling, grammar, or style.	Construct a solution in which some components are unclear, poorly organized, inconsistent, or incomplete. Misjudge the needs of the audience. Have some errors in spelling, grammar, or style, but the errors do not detract from comprehension.	Construct a solution that is unclear, incomplete, or poorly organized, contains some inaccurate or inappropriate content, and contains many errors of spelling, grammar, or style. Do not solve the problem.
3-Format and Layout	Format and arrange all elements to communicate information and ideas, clarify function, illustrate relationships, and indicate relative importance.	Apply appropriate format and layout features to some elements, but not others. Overuse features, causing minor distraction.	Apply format and layout that does not communicate information or ideas clearly. Do not use format and layout features to clarify function, illustrate relationships, or indicate relative importance. Use available features excessively, causing distraction.
4-Process	Use an organized approach that integrates planning, development, self-assessment, revision, and reflection.	Demonstrate an organized approach in some areas, but not others; or, use an insufficient process of organization throughout.	Do not use an organized approach to solve the problem.

Outcomes-Based Assessments (Critical Thinking)

Apply a combination of the 6A and 6B skills.

GO! Think	Project 6L Vacation Days

Project Files

For Project 6L, you will need the following files:

a06L_Vacation_Days

a06L_Logo

You will save your database as:

Lastname_Firstname_6L_Vacation_Days

In this project, you will create a report to display the information for the Rosebud Cafe employees and their vacation days. Open the **a06L_Vacation_Days** database and save it as **Lastname_Firstname_6L_Vacation_Days** From the *6L Vacation Days* table, add the following fields to the report: Employee Name, Days Allotted, and Days Taken. Add a calculated text box control to display the number of vacation days each employee has remaining (Days Allotted-Days Taken) with a label control to describe the field, and format the result as a General Number. Change the Theme to Retrospect. In the Report Header section, add the Rosebud Cafe logo and a descriptive title. Add a label control to the Report Footer section that reads **Report Designed by Firstname Lastname** Align the left edge with the label controls in the Detail section. Change the background color and font color used in the Report Header and Report Footer sections so they are easy to read. Sort the report on Employee Name. Adjust all label and text controls to display all field names and data. Adjust the width of the report so it is 6 inches wide. Add a dotted line between employees to make it easier to read. Center page numbers in the page footer. Resize the Detail section to reduce the blank space. Close the space for the Page Header. Save the report as **Lastname Firstname 6L Vacation Days Report** As directed by your instructor, submit your database for grading.

You have completed Project 6L | END

GO! Think	Project 6M Seasonal Items	IRC

You and GO!	Project 6N Club Directory	IRC

Creating Advanced Forms and Reports

7
ACCESS 2019

PROJECT 7A

Outcomes
Create advanced forms.

Objectives
1. Create a Split Form
2. Create a Form and a Subform
3. Create a Multi-Page Form

PROJECT 7B

Outcomes
Create advanced reports.

Objectives
4. Create and Modify a Subreport
5. Create a Report Based on a Parameter Query
6. Create an Alphabetic Index

Mark Baldwin/Shutterstock

In This Chapter

 GO! To Work with Access

Forms provide a way to enter, edit, and display data; reports display the data in a professional manner. Access 2019 enables you to create a form that also displays the data in Datasheet view or to create multiple-page forms. If a one-to-many relationship exists between the underlying tables, forms can be used to manipulate data from multiple tables, and reports can display data from multiple tables. You have also practiced creating a parameter query, which, in turn, can be used to create a report based on the criteria entered when the report is opened. Specialty reports, like an alphabetic index, can also be created.

Gardening has increased in popularity in many areas of the country. The stylish simplicity and use of indigenous, hardy plants make for beautiful, environmentally friendly gardens in any region of the country. Gardeners also enjoy learning about plants and gardens in other parts of the country and the world. Produced by MWB Productions, **Midwest Botanicals** is a syndicated television show that is broadcast nationwide. The show and its website provide tips and tricks for beautiful plants and gardens, highlight new tools and techniques, and present tours of public and private gardens to inspire home gardeners.

Project Activities

In Activities 7.01 through 7.07, you will help Gina Donaldson, office manager of MWB Productions, customize the company's forms. She wants the database forms to display related data. For example, she is interested in displaying the advertisers of the television shows on one form. You will display data in two ways on the same form, display data from multiple tables on one form, and display data on multiple pages on a form. Your completed Navigation Pane will look similar to Figure 7.1.

Project Files for MyLab IT Grader

1. In Your storage location, create a folder named **Access Chapter 7**.
2. In your **MyLab IT** course, locate and click **Access 7A MWB Schedule**, Download Materials, and then Download All Files.
3. Extract the zipped folder to your Access Chapter 7 folder. Close the Grader download screens.
4. Take a moment to open the downloaded **Access_7A_MWB_Schedule_Instructions**; note any recent updates to the book.

Project Results

GO! Project 7A
Where We're Going

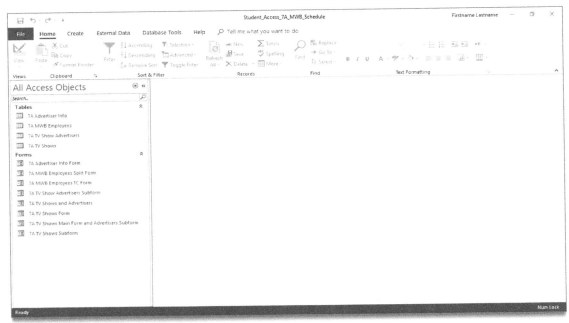

Figure 7.1 Project 7A MWB Schedule

For Non-MyLab Submissions

For Project 7A, you will need:

a07A_MWB_Schedule
a07A_MWB_Logo

Start with an Access Data File

In your storage location, create a folder named **Access Chapter 7**

In your Access Chapter 7 folder, save your database as:

Lastname_Firstname_7A_MWB_Schedule

After you have saved your database, open it to launch Access. On the next page, begin with Step 2.

NOTE   If You Are Using a Touch Screen

Tap an item to click it.

Press and hold for a few seconds to right-click; release when the information or commands displays.

Touch the screen with two or more fingers and then pinch together to zoom in or stretch your fingers apart to zoom out.

Slide your finger on the screen to scroll—slide left to scroll right and slide right to scroll left.

Slide to rearrange—similar to dragging with a mouse.

Swipe to select—slide an item a short distance with a quick movement—to select an item and bring up commands, if any.

Objective 1   Create a Split Form

ALERT   Because Office 365 is a cloud-based subscription service that receives continuous updates, you may encounter some variations in what appears on your screen and what is shown in this instruction. Microsoft Office 365 is fully installed on your PC or Mac; no internet access is necessary to create or edit documents. When you *are* connected to the internet, you will receive monthly upgrades and new features, so you always have the latest versions of Office apps as soon as they are available. Your subscription gives you continuous free access to the latest innovations and refinements.

GO! Learn How
Video A7-1

A *split form* displays data in two views—Form view and Datasheet view—on a single form. The two views display data from the same source and are synchronized with each other at all times. When you select a field in one of the views, the same field displays in the other view. You can add, delete, or edit data in either view. An advantage of displaying data in a split form is the flexibility of finding a record in Datasheet view and then editing the same record in Form view.

Activity 7.01 | Creating a Split Form Using the Split Form Tool

Gina would like to be able to view each record in a form and be able to refer to other records in the datasheet at the same time. In this Activity, you will create a split form.

1 Start Access. In the Access opening screen, click **Open Other Files**. Navigate to your **Access Chapter 7 folder**, and then double-click the Access file that you downloaded from **MyLab IT** that displays your name—**Student_Access_7A_MWB_Schedule**.

2 Enable the content or add the Access Chapter 7 folder to the Trust Center.

3 In the **Navigation Pane**, double-click **7A TV Show Advertisers** to open the table in Datasheet view. In the first record, in the **TV Show #** field, click the **arrow** to the right of *MWB001-01* to display a list of television show codes. In the first record, click in the **Advertiser** field, and then click the **arrow** to the right of *A-Z Home Products* to display a list of advertisers.

Both of these fields are lookup fields. The TV Show # field looks up data in the 7A TV Shows table. The Advertiser field looks up data in the 7A Advertiser Info table. Because these fields look up data in specific tables, you will not change the names of the existing tables and forms in this database. If you did rename the tables, the lookup fields would not be able to locate the related tables.

4 ▶ Press Esc to close the list. If the small pencil displays in the record selector box, press Esc one more time. **Close** ⊠ the table.

5 ▶ In the **Navigation Pane**, double-click **7A MWB Employees** to open the table in Datasheet view. Take a moment to review the fields in the table. **Close** ⊠ the table.

6 ▶ With the **7A MWB Employees** table selected, **Close** « the **Navigation Pane**. On the **Create tab**, in the **Forms group**, click **More Forms**, and then click **Split Form**. Compare your screen with Figure 7.2.

> The underlying table or query does not need to be open to create a split form as long as it is selected before clicking the Create tab on the ribbon.
> The split form displays in Layout view. The top section of the split form displays the data in Form view, and the bottom section of the split form displays the data in Datasheet view.

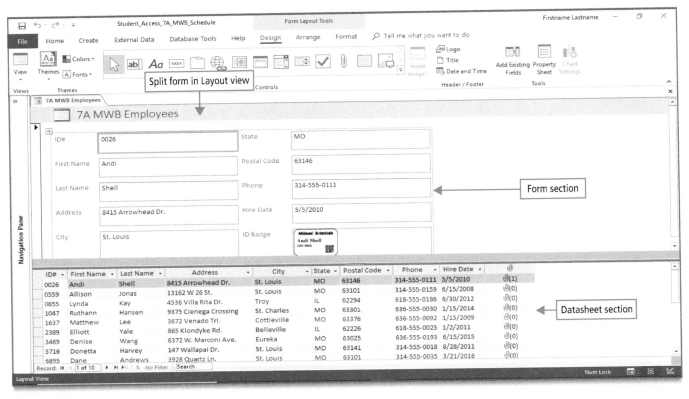

Figure 7.2

7 ▶ In the datasheet section of the split form, click anywhere in the first record, and then press ↓. Notice that the form section displays the data for the second record—the two sections are synchronized.

8 ▶ Save ⊟ the split form as **7A MWB Employees Split Form**

MORE KNOWLEDGE **Converting an Existing Form to a Split Form**

To convert a form to a split form, display the form in Design view. Display the Property sheet for the Form. On the Property Sheet Format tab, click in the Default View property setting box—Single Form is displayed. Click the arrow, and then click Split Form. Switch to Layout view to display the split form.

Activity 7.02 | Formatting a Split Form

MWB is currently implementing a new employee badge program, and that badge will be attached to each employee's record. To prepare the form to align with implementation of the badge program, only one badge has currently been attached to the first employee's record. In this Activity, you will enhance the split form by modifying the fields and form properties.

1 ▶ In the datasheet section of the split form, click anywhere in the first record. In the form section of the split form, click the **ID Badge** for *Andi Shell*, and then compare your screen with Figure 7.3.

A mini toolbar displays above Andi's badge. If the mini toolbar does not display, point to the picture. A *mini toolbar* is a miniature, semi-transparent toolbar that is used to work with objects on the screen. In this case, the mini toolbar displays a Back button, a Forward button, and a Manage Attachments button. If there were multiple attachments for this record, clicking the Forward button would display the next attachment, and clicking the Back button would display the previous attachment. Clicking the Manage Attachments button would display the Attachments dialog box. Recall that the Layout Selector is used to select all of the fields in the current layout. Clicking any field in a column displays the Layout Selector for the column.

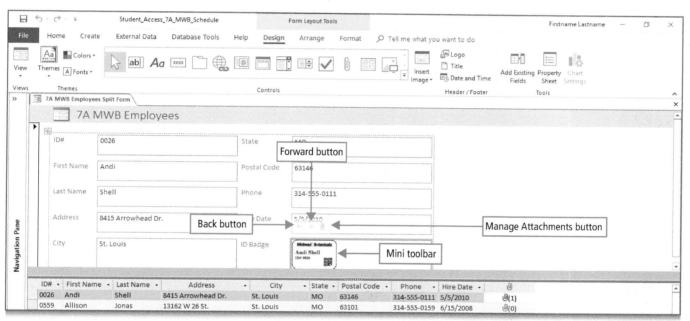

Figure 7.3

2 ▶ Select the **Attachment control**—the box displaying the image—and **Attachment label control**, and then on the ribbon, under **Form Layout Tools**, click the **Arrange tab**. In the **Table group**, click **Stacked**. Notice that both controls have been removed from the stacked layout.

The ID Badge field is moved outside of the form arrangement, to the left margin, because it was removed from the stacked layout. A dotted placeholder displays the original position in the stacked layout.

3 ▶ Click in the **Attachment control**. Under **Form Layout Tools**, on the **Design tab**, in the **Tools group**, click **Property Sheet**. Verify that the Property Sheet displays *Selection type: Attachment*. On the **Property Sheet Format tab**, click in the **Picture Alignment** property setting box, and then click the **arrow** to review the options. Click **Bottom Left**, and then **Close** [×] the **Property Sheet**.

Aligning the image at the left edge of the attachment control makes it easier to adjust the width of the control. Recall that you must remove a field from the predefined layout to resize only that field.

4 Point to the right edge of the **Attachment control** until the ↔ pointer displays. Drag to the left until the border aligns with the right edge of the ID badge, and then compare your screen with Figure 7.4.

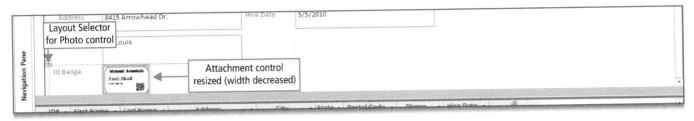

Figure 7.4

5 **Save** 🖫 the split form. With the **Attachment control** selected, right-click and then click **Form Properties** to display the form's Property Sheet.

6 On the **Property Sheet Format tab**, scroll down until the properties that relate to split forms display, and then compare your screen with Figure 7.5. Take a moment to study the six properties that directly relate to split forms, as described in the table in Figure 7.6.

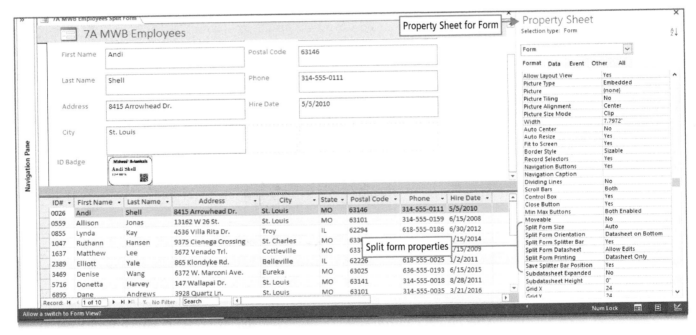

Figure 7.5

Property	Description	View(s) in Which the Property Can Be Set
Split Form Size	Specify an exact height or width, depending on whether the form is split vertically or horizontally, for the form section of the split form. For example, type *1* to set the form height or width to 1 inch. Type *Auto* to set the size by other means, such as dragging the splitter bar in Layout view. The default is *Auto*.	Design or Layout
Split Form Orientation	Define whether the datasheet displays above, below, to the left, or to the right of the form. The default is *Datasheet on Bottom*.	Design
Split Form Splitter Bar	If set to *Yes*, the form and datasheet can be resized by moving the splitter bar that separates the two sections. If set to *No*, the splitter bar is hidden, and the form and datasheet cannot be resized. The default is *Yes*.	Design
Split Form Datasheet	If set to *Allow Edits* and the form's source can be updated, editing can be done in the datasheet section. If set to *Read Only*, editing cannot be done in the datasheet section. The default is *Allow Edits*.	Design or Layout
Split Form Printing	Define which section of the form is printed. If set to *Form Only*, only the form section is printed. If set to *Datasheet Only*, only the datasheet section is printed. The default is *Datasheet Only*.	Design or Layout
Save Splitter Bar Position	If set to *Yes*, the form opens with the splitter bar in the same position in which it was saved. If set to *No*, the form and datasheet cannot be resized, and the splitter bar is hidden. The default is *Yes*.	Design

Figure 7.6

7 On the **Property Sheet**, click in the property setting box for **Split Form Printing**, click the **arrow**, and then click **Form Only**. Notice that you can print either the Form or the Datasheet, but not both.

8 On the **tab row**, right-click **7A MWB Employees Split Form**, and then click **Design View**. On the **Property Sheet** for the form, click in the **Split Form Orientation** property setting box, and then click the **arrow**. Compare your screen with Figure 7.7. If necessary, increase the width of the Property Sheet to display all four of the property settings.

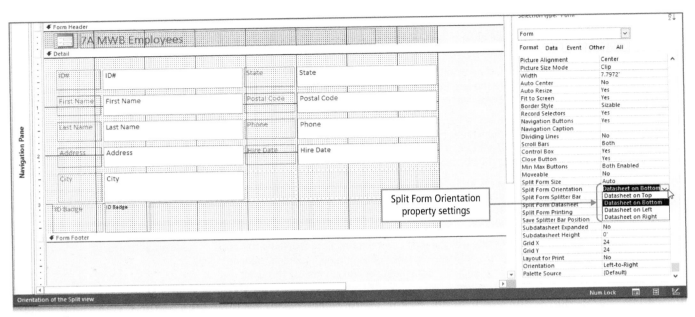

Figure 7.7

9 Click **Datasheet on Top**, and then **Close** ⊠ the Property Sheet.

ALERT   Does a message display, prompting you to change to Design View?

If you try to change a property that can only be changed in Design view, Access displays a message prompting you to change to Design view. If you then try to change a property that can only be changed in Layout view, Access will display the same message. If this happens, switch to Design view and then switch back to Layout view, or change to Design view, and then change the property settings. All split form properties can be changed in Design view.

10 Switch to **Layout** view. Click the **Attachment label control**, and press Delete. Click the **Attachment control**, and drag it to the right until the left edge aligns with the left edge of the City text box control.

Some editing in the form can be done in Layout view. The datasheet section displays above the form section of the split form. A splitter bar divides the two sections.

11 Point to the splitter bar until the ➕ pointer displays. Drag upward until the dark horizontal line displays between the records with an **ID#** of **0855** and **1047**.

In the datasheet section, Records 1 through 3 display, and the height of the form section is increased.

12 Switch to **Design** view. Under **Form Design Tools**, on the **Design tab**, in the **Header/ Footer group**, click **Logo**. Navigate to the location where the student data files are saved, and then double-click **a07A_MWB_Logo**. In the **Tools group**, click **Property Sheet** to display the Property Sheet for the logo. Click in the **Size Mode** setting box—*Clip* is displayed. Click the arrow, and then click **Zoom**. **Close** ⊠ the **Property Sheet**.

When the logo is inserted in a form or report that includes a logo placeholder, the Size Mode property is set to *Clip*, and the image may be too large to display in the control. By setting the property to *Zoom*, the image is resized to fit the control while maintaining the proportions of the object.

13 Increase the width of the **logo control** to the **1.5-inch mark on the horizontal ruler**. Click in the title's **label control**, and then click at the end of the line. Press Spacebar and type **Split Form** after the title of the form and press Enter to accept the changes. Switch to **Form** view, and then compare your screen with Figure 7.8.

Figure 7.8

14 Save 🖫 the form. Press PageDown until **Record 6** is displayed. In the form section, change the **First Name** from *Elliott* to **Phillip** and then press Tab. Notice that in the datasheet section, the same record—*ID# 2389*—is selected and is in the editing mode. Also notice that the **First Name** field has been updated in the datasheet section.

Recall that you can only make changes to the data in the fields with the form displayed in Form view. Notice the empty attachment field. As soon as the ID Badge program is fully implemented, all badges will display as they do in Record 1.

15 Close ✕ the form, saving changes if necessary. **Open** 》 the **Navigation Pane**.

MORE KNOWLEDGE **Adding or Deleting a Field**

To add a field to a split form in Layout view, display the Field List—on the Design tab, in the Tools group, click Add Existing Fields. Drag the field from the Field List to the datasheet section or the form section. The field will be added to both sections of the split form.

To delete a field from a split form, you must delete it from the form section. The field will then be removed automatically from the datasheet section.

Objective 2 **Create a Form and a Subform**

GO! Learn How
Video A7-2

In the previous activities, you created a split form that displayed the datasheet of the underlying table—the data in the form section was the same data as that displayed in the datasheet section. A *subform* is a form that is embedded within another form—the *main form*—and is used to view, enter, and edit data that is related to data in the main form. A subform is similar to a subdatasheet—the data in the related table is displayed without having to open another table or form.

Activity 7.03 | Creating a Form and a Subform Using the Form Tool

1.2.2, 4.1.1,
4.2.2, 4.2.4,
4.2.3

If Access finds a single table that has a one-to-many relationship with the table used to create a form, Access adds the datasheet as a subform to display the related records. In this Activity, you will create the main form using the 7A TV Shows table. Because a one-to-many relationship has been created between this table and the 7A TV Show Advertisers table, the datasheet for the 7A TV Show Advertisers table will be inserted as a subform.

1 ▶ Click the **Database Tools tab**, and then in the **Relationships group**, click **Relationships**. If the tables do not display in the Relationships window, under **Relationship Tools**, on the **Design tab**, in the **Relationships group**, click **All Relationships**. If necessary, expand the table boxes and rearrange them so that it is easier to view the relationships as shown in Figure 7.9. Take a moment to study the established relationships.

This is an example of a *many-to-many relationship* between the *7A TV Shows* table and the *7A Advertiser Info* table. *Many* television shows can have *many* advertisers. Conversely, *many* advertisers can advertise on *many* television shows.

To create the *many-to-many relationship* between *7A TV Shows* and *7A Advertiser Info*, the *7A TV Show Advertisers* table was created. This table is known as a *junction table*. It breaks down the many-to-many relationship into two *one-to-many relationships*. The data from the primary key fields—*TV Show #* and *Advertiser*—from the two tables are added to the junction table, which records each instance of the relationship. The primary key fields from the two tables are connected to the foreign key fields in the junction table.

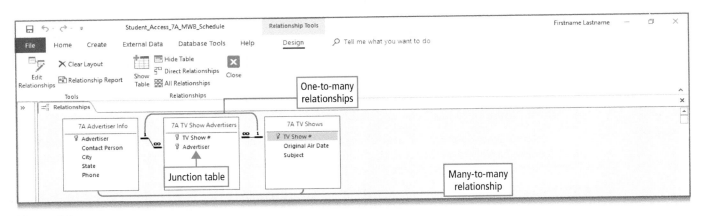

Figure 7.9

NOTE   **Specifying Multiple Primary Key Fields**

A junction table contains data from the primary key fields in two tables. The fields in the junction table are designated as primary key fields. In Design view, to specify multiple fields as primary key fields, hold down the Ctrl key, and then click the row selector boxes for each primary key field. Under Table Tools, on the Design tab, in the Tools group, click Primary Key. A junction table can include fields other than the common fields from the two related tables.

2 **Close** ⊠ the Relationships window, saving changes if prompted. **Open** » the **Navigation Pane**. Under **Tables**, click **7A TV Shows**. On the **Create tab**, in the **Forms group**, click **Form**. **Close** « the **Navigation Pane**, and then compare your screen with Figure 7.10.

> The data in the *7A TV Shows* table displays in the main form and the subform displays the Advertiser information from the related table, *7A TV Show Advertisers*.

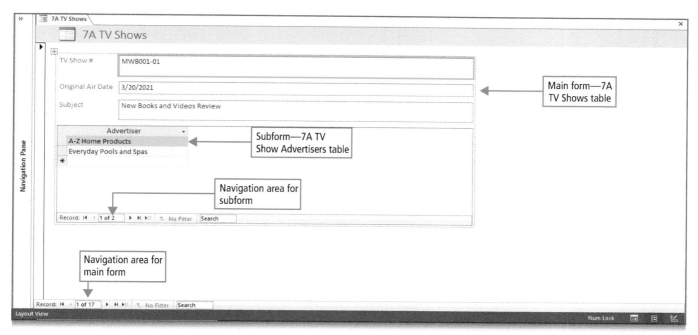

Figure 7.10

3 In the main form, click the **TV Show # text box control**, if necessary, and then press PageDown until Record **5** is displayed, observing changes in the subform and in the two record navigators.

> As you scroll through the records in the *7A TV Shows* table, the subform displays the related records for each television show. For example, in Record 5, the TV Show # is *MWB001-06*, and three advertisers support this show.

4 In the main form, click the **Subject text box control**. Point to the right edge of the text box control until the ↔ pointer displays, and then drag the right edge of the text box control to the left until there is approximately **1 inch** of space between *Devices* and the right edge of the text box control.

> Because the controls are part of the same stacked layout, the width of all of the text box controls is decreased.

5 Click anywhere in the subform. Notice that the Layout Selector ⊞ displays above the upper left corner of the subform and the datasheet is selected with a border around it. The Layout Selector also displays above the upper left corner of the main form because the forms are stacked. Switch to **Design** view. Click the *Table.7A TV Show Advertisers* subform placeholder. Under **Form Design Tools**, click the **Arrange tab**. In the **Table group**, click **Remove Layout** to remove the subform from the stacked layout.

6 ▶ Switch to **Layout** view. Click the subform, and then compare your screen with Figure 7.11.

Notice that the Layout Selector only displays above the upper left corner of the form because the forms are no longer stacked.

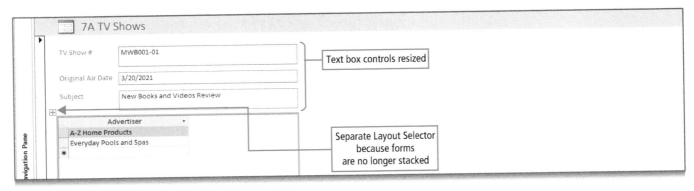

Figure 7.11

MORE KNOWLEDGE **Sort Records in a Form**

In a form or subform, records are sorted by the primary key field. To modify the sort order, click the text box control for the field to be sorted. On the Home tab, in the Sort & Filter group, click Ascending or Descending (depending on the sort you want to perform). To remove the sort, on the Home tab, in the Sort & Filter group, click Remove Sort.

7 ▶ With the subform selected, point to the right edge of the subform until the ↔ pointer displays, and then drag the right edge of the subform to the left until it aligns with the right edge of the **Advertiser** control box. Point to the subform **Layout Selector** ⊞ until the ⁂ pointer displays, and then drag to the right until the subform is centered under the text box controls in the main form. **Save** 🖫 the form as **7A TV Shows and Advertisers**

Be sure to leave some space between the main form and the subform so it is not returned to the Stacked Layout. If it returns to that layout, click Undo, and move the subform again.

8 ▶ Switch to **Design** view. Under **Form Design Tools**, on the **Design tab**, in the **Header/Footer group**, click **Logo**. Navigate to the location where the student data files for this chapter are saved. Locate and double-click **a07A_MWB_Logo** to insert the logo in the form header. In the **Tools group**, click **Property Sheet** to display the Property Sheet for the logo. Click in the **Size Mode** property box, click the arrow, and then click **Zoom. Close** ⊠ the **Property Sheet**. Point to the center right edge of the control until the ↔ pointer displays; click and drag to the right until it is between the *S* and *h* in *Shows*, and then compare your screen to Figure 7.12.

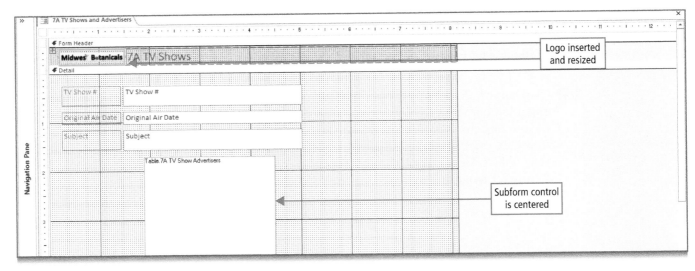

Figure 7.12

9 Click at the end of the title label control, hold down Shift, and then press Enter. Type **and Advertiser Subform** Press Enter.

Pressing Shift + Enter creates a line break so the title displays on two lines in the label control.

10 Point to the right edge of the **title's label control** until the ↔ pointer displays—the right edge may display at the very right side of your screen. Drag to the left until the right edge aligns with the **5.75-inch mark on the horizontal ruler**. With the **title's label control** selected, under **Form Design Tools**, click the **Format tab**. In the **Font group**, click **Center** ≡ and **Bold** B.

11 Resize the width of the form to **7 inches**. Compare your screen with Figure 7.13. Notice that the subform control displays the related table's name—*Table.7A TV Show Advertisers*. Also, notice that the title's label control may not display the entire title. Be sure it is visible before moving on.

Although you can make most adjustments to a form in Layout view, you should adjust the title's control in Design view to ensure the form's title will print as desired. With narrow margins for a form and with Portrait orientation, the right edge of the form should not exceed 7.5 inches on the horizontal ruler; otherwise, pages will print with only the background color in the form header.

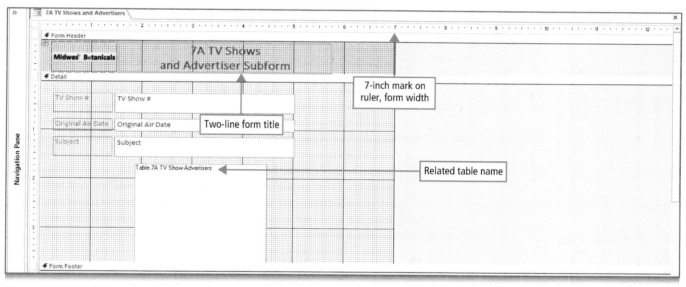

Figure 7.13

12 Save ⊟ the form, and then switch to **Form** view and scroll through the records. Notice the main form and the subform. **Close** × the form.

MORE KNOWLEDGE **Create Forms with Application Parts**

Create a form using application parts by clicking the Create tab. In the Templates group, click the Application Parts arrow, and then click the template you want to use for the form. Once you assign the Record Source to the form, you can add fields to the form.

Activity 7.04 | Creating a Form and a Subform Using the Form Wizard

MOS
4.1.1

Use the Form Wizard to create a form and a subform when you want to have more control over the design of the subform or if the underlying table or query has more than one relationship established. If the underlying table or query that is on the *one* side of the relationship is related to more than one table or query on the *many* side of the relationship, the subform will not automatically be created when the form is created. The same technique can be used to create a split form between two tables that have a many-to-many relationship.

1 On the **Create tab**, in the **Forms group**, click **Form Wizard**. In the **Form Wizard** dialog box, if necessary, click the **Tables/Queries arrow**, and then click **Table: 7A TV Shows**, which is on the *one* side of the relationship with **7A Advertiser Info** using the junction table.

It does not matter which table you select first; in a later dialog box, you can select the table that displays in the main form and the table that displays in the subform.

2 Under **Available Fields**, click **All Fields** [>>] to add all of the fields to the **Selected Fields** box. In the same dialog box, click the **Tables/Queries arrow**, and from the displayed list, click **Table: 7A Advertiser Info**, which is on the *many* side of the relationship with the **7A TV Shows** table. Again, add **All Fields** to the **Selected Fields** box. Click **Next**, and then compare your screen with Figure 7.14.

The second Form Wizard dialog box displays with a preview of how the data will be arranged. The order in which you select the tables or queries to be included in the main form and subform does not matter because you can change the way the data is displayed in this Form Wizard dialog box. If a relationship between the tables has not been established, this Form Wizard dialog box will not display.

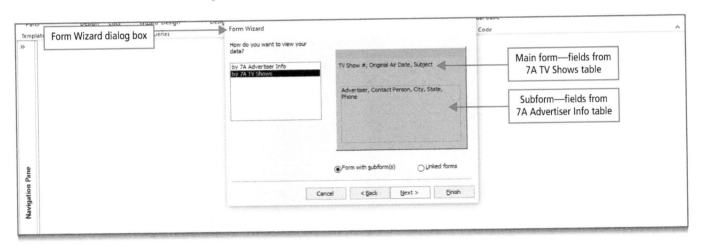

Figure 7.14

3 Under **How do you want to view your data?**, click **by 7A Advertiser Info**, and notice that the form will display with the *7A Advertiser Info* table as the main form and the *7A TV Shows* table as the subform. Under the preview of the form, click **Linked forms**, and notice the preview displays two separate forms with a button on the main form that represents the link between the two forms.

A *linked form* is a related form that is not stored within the main form. To view the data in a linked form, click on the link that is displayed on the main form.

NOTE **Switching Main Form and Subform Tables**

If the tables have a one-to-many relationship, and you switch the view to display the many side as the main form and the one side as the subform, the form will display as a single form instead of a main form with a subform. With a one-to-many relationship, the main form should display the table on the one side of the relationship, and the subform should display the table on the many side of the relationship.

---

4 ▶ Click **Form with subform(s)**, and then click **Next** to display the third **Form Wizard** dialog box, where you can select the subform layout. Notice the two layouts are *Tabular* and *Datasheet*, with Datasheet being the default layout.

Both layouts arrange the subform data in rows and columns, but the tabular layout is more customizable. You can add color, graphics, and other elements to a tabular subform. The subform you created in the previous activity used the datasheet layout, which is more compact than the tabular layout.

5 ▶ Click **Tabular**, and then click **Next** to display the last **Form Wizard** dialog box. In the **Form** text box, select the existing text, and then type **7A Advertiser Info Form** In the **Subform** text box, notice the title *7A TV Shows Subform,* and then click **Finish**. Compare your screen to Figure 7.15.

The form and subform display in Form view. Notice that all of the fields and data are not visible in the subform.

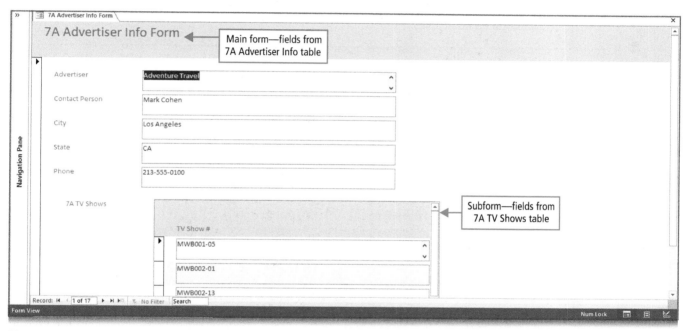

Figure 7.15

6 ▶ Switch to **Design** view. If necessary, Close the Field list pane. Using the lasso technique you have practiced, select all of the controls in the main form. Under **Form Design Tools**, click the **Arrange tab**. In the **Table** group, click **Stacked**.

7 ▶ Save 🖫 the form.

Activity 7.05 | Modifying a Form and a Subform

1 ▶ Switch the **7A Advertiser Info Form** to **Layout** view. In the subform, click the **TV Show # label control**. Hold down Shift, and then click the **TV Show # text box control** to select both controls. Point to the right edge of the **TV Show # text box control** until the ↔ pointer displays. Drag the right edge of the control to the left until there are approximately **0.25 inches** of space between the first show # and the right edge of the **TV Show # text box control**.

2 Scroll to the right, and click the **Subject label control**; hold down Shift and click the **Subject text box control**. Under **Form Layout Tools**, on the **Design tab**, in the **Tools** group, click **Property Sheet** to display the Property Sheet for *Multiple selection*. On the **Format tab**, select the **Width** property. Type **3** and press Enter. With the **Subject** controls still selected, hold down Shift and click the **Original Air Date text box** and **label controls**. Drag the controls to the left until the **Original Air Date** appears immediately to the right of **TV Show #**.

> The widths of the Subject controls are decreased and all four controls are right next to one another.

3 In the upper left corner of the subform, click the **Layout Selector** ⊞. On the Property Sheet, the **Selection Type** should now read *Subform/Subreport*. Select the **Width** property setting, and then type **6.15** Press Enter, and then type **3.5** in the **Height** property setting. **Close** × the Property Sheet. Scroll down to display the entire subform, and then compare your screen with Figure 7.16.

> The width and height of the subform are adjusted, and the vertical and horizontal scroll bars in the subform do not display.

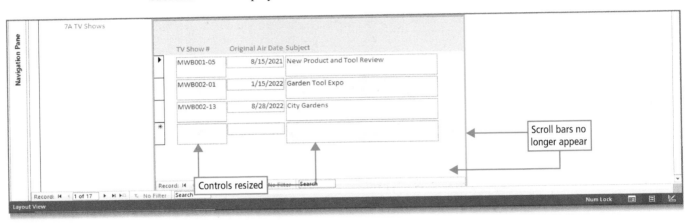

Figure 7.16

4 Click the main form, and navigate to **Record 17**—*Advertiser* of *Very Green Lawns Inc.* In the main form, click the **Advertiser text box control**. Point to the right edge of the text box control until the ↔ pointer displays. Drag to the left until there is approximately **0.5 inches** of space between the data in the **Advertiser** field and the right edge of the text box control. Recall that the controls are grouped together in a stacked layout, so adjusting the size of one control adjusts the size of all of the controls.

5 Click the **Phone text box control**, hold down Shift, and click the **Phone label control**. Point to the **Phone text box control** until the ⬚ pointer displays. Drag upward until an orange horizontal line displays between the **Contact Person** field and the **City** field, and then release the mouse button. Click the **City text box control**. Hold down Shift, and then click the **City label control**, the **State text box control,** and the **State label control** to select all four controls. Under **Form Layout Tools**, click the **Arrange tab**. In the **Table group**, click **Stacked** to remove the controls from the Stacked Layout. Click the original location of the **City text box control**. Hold down Shift, and then click the original location of the **City label control**, the **State text box control,** and the **State label control** to select all four placeholders. Press Delete to remove the placeholders from the stacked layout.

> Recall that it is easier to remove fields from a stacked layout when they are at the bottom of the layout, but the placeholders remain once the controls are removed from the stacked layout.

6 Click the **City label control** to display the **Layout Selector** ⊞ for the controls. Point to the **Layout Selector** until the 🔄 pointer displays, and then drag upward and to the right until the **City** field aligns with the **Contact Person** field and there is approximately **0.5 inches** of space between the **Contact Person text box control** and the **City label control**. Click in a blank area of the form to deselect the controls. Click the **City label control**, and then point to the right edge of the **City label control** until the ↔ pointer displays. Drag the right edge of the **City label control** to the left until there is approximately **0.5 inches** of space between the word *City* and the right edge of the **City label control**. Using the same technique, resize the **City text box control**. **Save** 🖫 the form. Compare your screen with Figure 7.17.

> After removing the fields from the stacked layout, they are grouped as a separate layout for ease in making adjustments to the controls. The widths of the City and State label controls are decreased so that the text box controls will not exceed the allowable width when printed.

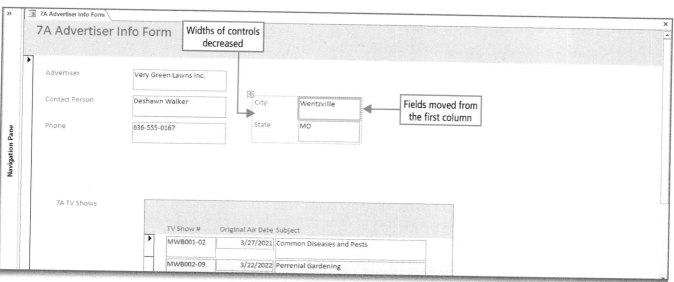

Figure 7.17

7 Using the techniques you have practiced, remove the **Advertiser textbox control** and the **Advertiser label control** from the stacked layout, and then delete the placeholders from the stacked layout. Move the left column down so the **Contact Person** field aligns with the **City** field. Click the **Advertiser label control**. Hold down Shift, and then click the **Advertiser text box control** to select both controls. Point to one of the selected controls until the 🔄 pointer displays. Drag upward and to the right until the controls are approximately centered above the controls on the left and the controls on the right.

> The Advertiser field is contained in its own stacked layout.

8 Click the **subform label control**—*7A TV Shows*—and press Delete to remove the label from the subform control. Click the **subform** to display the **Layout Selector** for the subform. Point to the **Layout Selector** until the pointer displays. Drag the subform upward until there is approximately **0.5 inches** of space between the **Phone** field and the subform, and the right edge of the subform aligns with the right edge of the **State text box control**. Compare your screen with Figure 7.18.

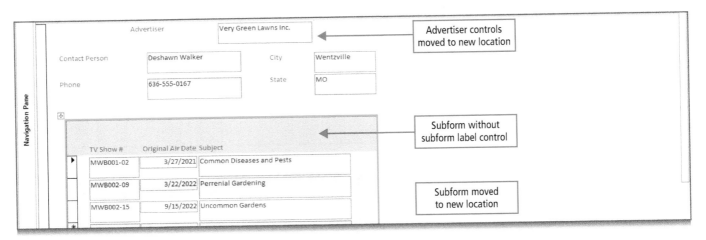

Figure 7.18

9 **Save** the form, and switch to **Design** view. Using the techniques you have practiced, in the main form, add a **Logo** to the **Form Header** section using **a07A_MWB_Logo**, and then **Delete** the accompanying label control that displays to the right of the logo. Move the **form title's label control** so the left edge aligns with the **2-inch mark on the horizontal rule**. Click before the space in front of *Form* in the title and press Shift + Enter to move *Form* to the second line of the control. Type **and TV Shows** and press Enter. Resize the **title label control** by aligning the right edge of the form title's label control with the right edge of the subform. **Center** the text in the form title's label control. Adjust the size of the logo so there is one dot between it and the title label control and it is the same height as the title. Compare your screen with Figure 7.19.

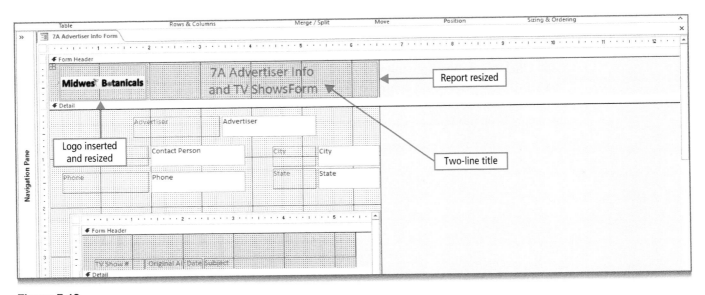

Figure 7.19

10 Switch to **Form** view. Press PageDown until the record for **A-Z Home Products**—*Record 4*—displays.

11 **Close** ✕ the form, saving changes. **Open** » the **Navigation Pane**. Under **Forms**, **7A Advertiser Info Form** and **7A TV Shows Subform** display. Double-click **7A Advertiser Info Form** to open it in Form view. The subform is embedded in the form. Double-click the **7A TV Shows Subform** to open it in Form view. This form displays the fields from the *TV Shows* table that are used in the subform of *7A Advertiser Info Form*.

> When a subform is created in a main form, a separate form object is created and displays in the Navigation Pane under Forms.

12 **Close** ✕ all forms.

MORE KNOWLEDGE **Adding the Table Name to the Subform**

To add the name of the table used to create the subform at the top of the subform, add a label control to the Form Header section of the subform, and then type the name of the table. If the table name is added to the Form Header section, the label control with the table name that displays to the left of the subform should be deleted.

Objective 3 | Create a Multi-Page Form

GO! Learn How
Video A7-3

A ***multi-page form*** displays the data from the underlying table or query on more than one page. Creating a multi-page form enables you to divide a long form into sections that display on separate pages or to display subforms on different tabs within the main form. A multi-page form enables the user to display only the data that needs to be accessed and displays the form in a more organized format.

Activity 7.06 | Creating a Multi-Page Form Using the Tab Control

4.1.1, 4.1.2

In this Activity, you will modify a form to create a multi-page form using the tab control. A ***tab control*** is used to display data on the main form on different tabs, similar to the way database objects, such as forms and tables, display on different tabs.

1 In the **Navigation Pane**, under **Forms**, open **7A MWB Employees TC Form** in Design view, and then **Close** « the **Navigation Pane**. Point to the top of the **Form Footer section bar** until the ✛ pointer displays. Drag downward to the **2.5-inch mark on the vertical ruler** to increase the height of the Detail section.

2 Under **Form Design Tools**, on the **Design tab**, in the **Controls group**, click **Tab Control** ▢. Move the pointer into the **Detail** section until the plus (+) sign of the pointer is aligned approximately with the **0.25-inch mark on the horizontal ruler** and with the **0.25-inch mark on the vertical ruler**. Click one time, and then compare your screen with Figure 7.20.

A tab control is inserted into the Detail section of the form. There are two tabs on the tab control. Each tab represents a separate page on the form. Do not be concerned if the page numbers on your tabs differ from those displayed in Figure 7.20.

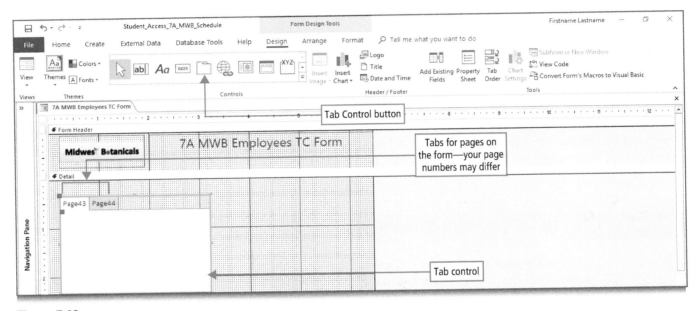

Figure 7.20

3 In the selected **tab control**, point to the **right middle sizing handle** until the ↔ pointer displays. Drag to the right until the right edge of the tab control aligns with the **6-inch mark on the horizontal ruler**.

4 Under **Form Design Tools**, on the **Design tab**, in the **Tools group**, click **Add Existing Fields**.

The Field List for the *7A MWB Employees* table displays.

5 In the **Field List**, click **ID#**. Hold down ⇧Shift, and then click **Last Name** to select three fields. Hold down Ctrl, click **Hire Date**, and then click **ID Badge** to select two additional fields. Point to a selected field, and then drag downward and to the left onto the first tab until the top of the arrow of the pointer aligns with the **1.5-inch mark on the horizontal ruler** and with the **0.75-inch mark on the vertical ruler**. Release the mouse button. Compare your screen with Figure 7.21.

> The controls for the fields are arranged in a column on the first tab in the tab control, and Access automatically adjusts the height of the tab control so that all of the controls display. The controls are not grouped together.

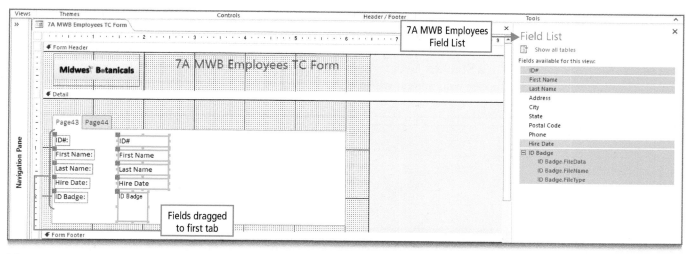

Figure 7.21

6 Close ✕ the **Field List**. Click in an empty area of the tab control to deselect the controls. Hold down ⇧Shift, and then click the **label controls** for the **Hire Date** and **ID Badge** fields, the **text box control** for **Hire Date**, and the **attachment control** for the **ID Badge**. Point to the selected controls until the pointer displays. Drag to the right and upward until the *Hire Date* controls align with the *ID#* controls and there is approximately **0.5 inches** of space between the two columns. Do not be concerned if the controls do not exactly align.

7 With the controls selected, under **Form Design Tools**, click the **Arrange tab**. In the **Table group**, click **Stacked** to group the controls together. Click the **ID# label control** to deselect the controls in the second column. Using the techniques you have just practiced, select all of the controls in the first column, and then group them together in a **Stacked** layout.

8 Click the **Layout Selector** for the first column. Hold down ⇧Shift, click the **Hire Date label control**, and then click the **Layout Selector** above the second column to select both columns. Under **Form Design Tools**, on the **Arrange tab**, in the **Sizing & Ordering group**, click **Align**, and then click **Top**. Compare your screen with Figure 7.22.

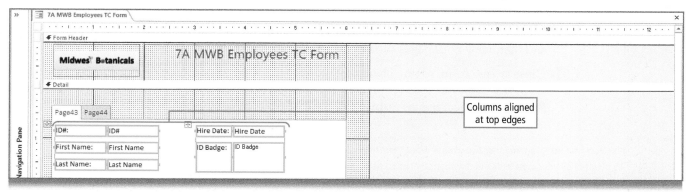

Figure 7.22

9 Save 🖫 the form, and then switch to **Layout** view. Press PageDown several times to display the other records in the table, ensuring that all of the data displays in all of the fields.

10 Switch to **Design** view. In the **Detail** section, click the **tab control** to select it, and then click the **second tab**, which has no controls added to it. Under **Form Design Tools**, click the **Design tab**, and then, in the **Tools group**, click **Add Existing Fields**. In the **Field List**, click **Address**. Hold down Shift, and then click **Phone** to select five fields. Point to the selected fields, and then drag downward and to the left onto the second tab until the top of the arrow of the pointer aligns with the **1.5-inch mark on the horizontal ruler** and with the **0.75-inch mark on the vertical ruler**.

11 Using the techniques you have practiced, move the **Phone label control** and **Phone text box control** upward and to the right until the controls are aligned with the **Address** controls. Arrange the **Phone controls** in a **Stacked** layout. Arrange the eight controls in the first column in a **Stacked** layout. Align the tops of both columns. **Close** ⊠ the **Field List**, and then compare your screen with Figure 7.23.

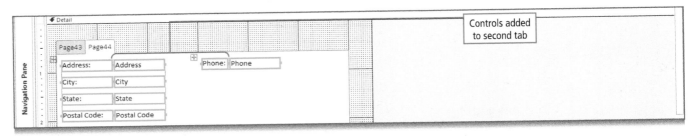

Figure 7.23

12 Save 🖫 the form, and then switch to **Layout** view. Click the **second tab** and notice that the data in the **Address** field is truncated. Press PageDown three times to display **Record 4**. Point to the right edge of the **Address text box control** until the ↔ pointer displays, and then drag to the right until the entire address displays in the text box control. Move the **Phone label control** to the right so the columns are about 0.5 inches apart, if necessary. Click the **first tab** of the form.

13 Right-click in the **first page** of the form, and then click **Properties**. The Property Sheet should display *Selection type: Page*, and the Selection type box should display the tab's page number. If necessary, change the Selection type. On the **Property Sheet Format tab**, click in the **Caption** property setting box, type **Employee Name and ID** and then press Enter.

The first tab displays the text you entered in the Caption property setting box.

14 In the form, click the **second tab** to display the Property Sheet for the second tab. Click in the **Caption** property setting box, type **Address and Phone** and then press Enter to change the text on the second tab. **Close** ⊠ the **Property Sheet**. In the form, click the **Employee Name and ID tab** to display the first page of the form.

15 Change the **title** of the form to **7A MWB Employees Tab Control Form** Switch to **Form** view, and then view both pages of the first record.

16 **Close** ⊠ the form, saving changes. **Open** ≫ the **Navigation Pane**. Under **Forms, Rename** *7A MWB Employees TC Form* as **7A MWB Employees Tab Control Form Resize** the **Navigation Pane** so all object names display fully. **Close** the database, and then **Close** Access.

For Non-MyLab Submissions: Determine What Your Instructor Requires for Submission

As directed by your instructor, submit your completed database file. If you are completing the optional activity, do so before submitting your database to your instructor.

17 In **MyLab IT**, locate and click the Grader Project **Access 7A MWB Schedule**. In **step 3**, under **Upload Completed Assignment**, click **Choose File**. In the **Open** dialog box, navigate to your **Access Chapter 7 folder**, and then click your **Student_Access_7A_ MWB_Schedule** file one time to select it. In the lower right corner of the **Open** dialog box, click **Open**.

> The name of your selected file displays above the Upload button.

18 To submit your file to **MyLab IT** for grading, click **Upload**, wait a moment for a green **Success!** message, and then in **step 4**, click the blue **Submit for Grading** button. Click **Close Assignment** to return to your list of **Course Materials**.

You have completed Project 7A | **END**

Activity 7.07 | **Creating a Subform by Dragging a Related Table onto an Existing Form**

4.1.1, 4.1.3

In this Activity, you will create a subform by dragging an existing table—*7A TV Show Advertisers*—on the *many* side of the relationship onto an existing form—*7A TV Shows Form*—on the *one* side of the relationship. When a table has more than one relationship with other tables, this method is helpful in adding a subform to a form.

1 Start Access. Under *Recent*, click your **7A_MWB_Schedule** database to open it.

2 In the **Navigation Pane**, under **Tables**, click the **7A TV Shows** table to select it. On the **Create tab**, in the **Forms group**, click **Form Wizard**. Verify that the **7A TV Shows** table displays in the **Tables/Queries** box. Click **Add all fields** >> to move all of the fields to the **Selected Fields** column. Click **Next**.

3 In the **Form Wizard** dialog box, verify that **Columnar** is selected as the layout, and then click **Next**. In the **What title do you want for your form?** Box, select the existing text, and type **7A TV Shows Main Form and Advertisers Subform** In the wizard, click the button next to **Modify the form's design** and click **Finish**.

4 In the form, point to the top of the **Form Footer section bar** until the ⊹ pointer displays. Drag downward until the Detail section is **3 inches** high.

5 Under **Form Design Tools**, on the **Design tab**, in the **Controls group**, click the **More** ⁼ button, and verify that the **Use Control Wizards** ⬚ option is active.

> The existing form must be open in Design view before you drag a related table onto it. If you try to drag a related table onto a form in Layout view, an error message displays.

6 In the **Navigation Pane**, under **Tables**, drag **7A TV Show Advertisers** onto *7A TV Shows Main Form* to the **1.75-inch mark on the vertical ruler** and **0.25-inch mark on the horizontal ruler**. The first **SubForm Wizard** dialog box displays. Compare your screen with Figure 7.24.

Notice at the bottom of the dialog box that Access will display records from the *7A TV Show Advertisers* table for each record in the *7A TV Shows* table using the *TV Show #* field—the common field.

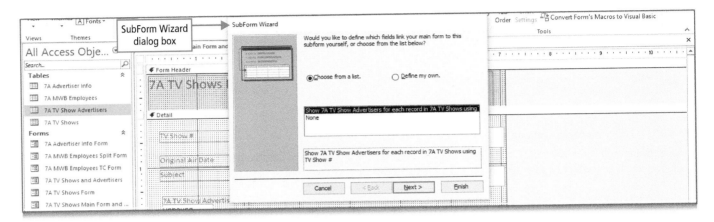

Figure 7.24

7 In the **SubForm Wizard** dialog box, click **Define my own**.

The SubForm Wizard dialog box changes to display list boxes in which you can select the fields that link the main form to the subform.

8 Under **Form/report fields**, in the **first list box**, click the **arrow**, and then click **TV Show #**. Under **Subform/subreport fields**, in the **first list box**, click the **arrow**, and then click **TV Show #**. Compare your screen with Figure 7.25.

The same field is used to link the form and the subform as when *Choose from a list* was selected. By default, Access uses the fields that are used to create the join line in the relationship between the tables. You should select *Define my own* when you want to use fields other than the common fields as defined in the relationship.

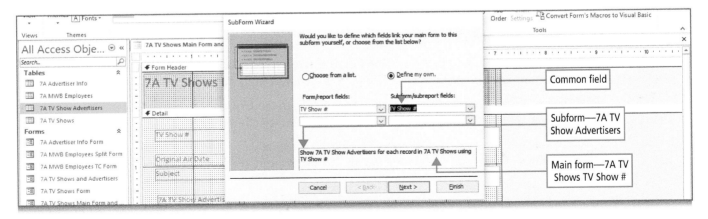

Figure 7.25

9 Click **Next**. Under **What name would you like for your subform or subreport?**, type **7A TV Show Advertisers Subform** and then click **Finish**. **Close** « the **Navigation Pane** and compare your screen with Figure 7.26.

> The subform displays under the label and text box controls of the main form, and a subform label control displays above the subform.

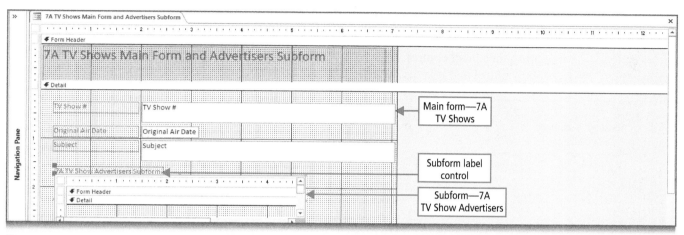

Figure 7.26

10 With the subform control selected, point to the **bottom middle sizing handle** of the subform control until the ↕ pointer displays. Drag downward about **0.5 inches**. If necessary, point to the top of the **Form Footer section bar** until the ⊕ pointer displays, and then drag upward to the bottom of the subform control. **Close** × the **Field List**, if necessary. **Save** 🖫 the form.

11 Switch to **Layout** view. If necessary, resize controls so both fields are visible in the subform. Press PageDown to display the record for each television show and the related record(s) in the subform. Notice that the **TV Show #** field displays in both the main form and the subform.

12 In the record navigator for the main form, click **First Record** ◄. Switch to **Design** view. In the subform control, click the **TV Show # label control**, hold down Shift, and click the **TV Show # text box control**. Press Delete, and then switch to **Layout** view. Press PageDown until the record for **MWB001-09**—*Record 7*—displays. Double-click the right edge of the **Advertiser label control** to resize for the longest item in the list.

> The *TV Show #* field is removed from the subform.

13 With the **subform control** selected, click the displayed **Layout Selector** ⊞. Point to the bottom right corner of the **subform control** until the ⬈ pointer displays. Drag upward and to the left until there is approximately **0.25 inches** of blank space between the **Advertiser** controls and the right edges of the subform. Compare your screen with Figure 7.27.

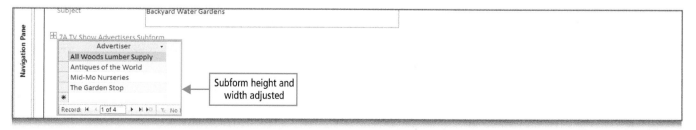

Figure 7.27

14 Click the **subform label control**, which displays *7A TV Show Advertisers Subform*, and then press Delete to remove the label control from the subform.

15 Click anywhere in the subform, and then point to the displayed **Layout Selector** ⊞ until the ⬚ pointer displays. Drag to the right until the subform is centered under the form text box controls.

16 Switch to **Design** view, saving changes to both objects. Using the techniques you have practiced, in the main form, add a **Logo** to the **Form Header** section using **a07A_MWB_ Logo**, and then **Delete** the accompanying label control. Change the title of the form to **7A TV Shows and Advertisers** Move the **form title's label control** so the left edge aligns with the **2.25-inch mark on the horizontal rule**. Apply **Bold** B and then **Center** ≡ the text in the form title's label control. Adjust the size of the logo so there is one dot between it and the title label control and it is the same height as the title. Compare your screen with Figure 7.28.

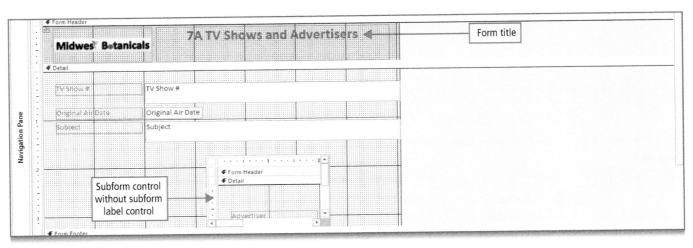

Figure 7.28

17 Save 🖫 the form, and in the **Microsoft Access** dialog box, click **Yes**. Switch to **Form** view to view the form.

18 Close ✕ the form and **Open** » the **Navigation Pane**. Resize the Navigation Pane so all objects display fully. **Close** Access.

MORE KNOWLEDGE   **Creating a Form with Two Subforms or Nested Subforms**

A form can contain more than one subform. The main form should have a one-to-many relationship with the first subform. The first subform should have a one-to-many relationship with the second subform. The main form would contain both subform controls. To create a form with two subforms, use the Form Wizard, selecting each table from the Tables/Queries list and each table's fields.

A form can also contain *nested subforms*. The main form should have a one-to-many relationship with the first subform. The first subform should have a one-to-many relationship with the second subform. Instead of the main form containing both subform controls, the first subform would contain the second subform control. You can have a maximum of seven levels of subforms.

 For Non-MyLab Submissions: Determine What Your Instructor Requires for Submission
As directed by your instructor, submit your completed database file.

PROJECT 7B Online Orders

Project Activities

In Activities 7.08 through 7.14, you will create advanced reports that will help the president and officers of the production company view the information in a database in a different way. MWB Productions maintains a website where customers can order gardening supplies that are featured in the *Midwest Botanicals* television show. You will create advanced reports that display data from multiple tables and from a parameter query. You will also create an alphabetic index of garden suppliers. Your completed Navigation Pane will look similar to Figure 7.29.

Project Files for MyLab IT Grader

1. In your **MyLab IT** course, locate and click **Access 7B Online Orders**, Download Materials, and then Download All Files.
2. Extract the zipped folder to your Access Chapter 7 folder. Close the Grader download screens.
3. Take a moment to open the downloaded **Access_7B_Online_Orders_Instructions**; note any recent updates to the book.

Project Results

GO! Project 7B
Where We're Going

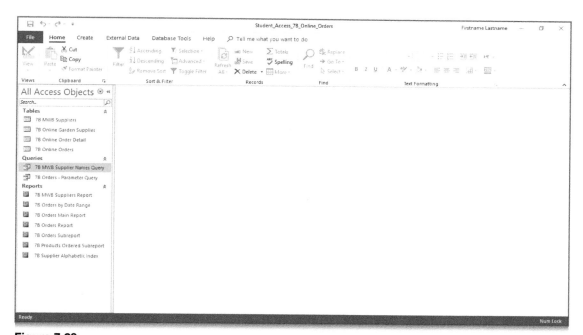

Figure 7.29

For Non-MyLab Submissions
For Project 7B, you will need:
a07B_Online_Orders

Start with an Access Data File
In your Access Chapter 7 folder, save your database as:
Lastname_Firstname_7B_Online_Orders

After you have saved your database, launch Access and open the database. On the next page, begin with Step 2.

ALERT   Because Office 365 is a cloud-based subscription service that receives continuous updates, you may encounter some variations in what appears on your screen and what is shown in this instruction. Microsoft Office 365 is fully installed on your PC or Mac; no internet access is necessary to create or edit documents. When you *are* connected to the internet, you will receive monthly upgrades and new features, so you always have the latest versions of Office apps as soon as they are available. Your subscription gives you continuous free access to the latest innovations and refinements.

GO! Learn How
Video A7-4

A *subreport* is a report that is embedded within another report—the *main report*. The main report is either bound or unbound. A *bound report* displays data from an underlying table, query, or SQL statement as specified in the report's Record Source property; an *unbound report* does not. An *SQL statement* is an instruction using Structured Query Language. An example of an unbound report being used as the main form would be a report that displays a title, logo, and date, similar to a report header. A main report can also contain a subform instead of a subreport. A main report can contain up to seven levels of subforms and subreports.

Activity 7.08 │ Using the SubReport Wizard to Create a Subreport

MOS
1.2.1, 1.2.2,
5.1.3, 5.1.2

In this Activity, you will create a subreport using the SubReport Wizard. The main report will display the online orders, and the subreport will display the products that were ordered. Before creating a subreport using the SubReport Wizard, the underlying tables or queries should have established relationships.

1▶ Start Access. In the Access opening screen, click **Open Other Files**. Navigate to your **Access Chapter 7 folder**, and then double-click the Access file that you downloaded from **MyLab IT** that displays your name—**Student_Access_7B_Online_Orders**.

2▶ If you did not add the Access Chapter 7 folder to the Trust Center, enable the content. **Close** « the **Navigation Pane**.

3▶ On the **Database Tools tab**, in the **Relationships group**, click **Relationships**. Take a moment to review the relationships between the tables.

There is a *one-to-many* relationship between the *7B MWB Suppliers* table and the *7B Online Orders* table. There is a *one-to-many* relationship between the *7B Online Orders* table and the *7B Online Order Detail* table. There is a *one-to-many* relationship between the *7B Online Garden Supplies* table and the *7B Online Order Detail* table. The *7B Online Order Detail* table is a junction table that is used to create a *many-to-many* relationship between the *7B Online Orders* table and the *7B Online Garden Supplies* table.

4▶ **Close** × the **Relationships tab**, and then **Open** » the **Navigation Pane**. Under **Reports**, right-click **7B Orders Report**, and then click **Copy**. On the **Home tab**, in the **Clipboard group**, click **Paste**. In the **Paste As** dialog box, under **Report Name**, and with the existing text selected, type **7B Orders Main Report** and then click **OK**.

In the Navigation Pane under Reports, the newly named copy of the *7B Orders Report* displays.

5▶ Open **7B Orders Main Report** in **Design** view, and then **Close** « the **Navigation Pane**. Click the **small box** in the upper left corner of the report, where the top and left margins intersect. Recall that clicking this box selects the report. Under **Report Design Tools**, on the **Design tab**, in the **Tools group**, click **Property Sheet**.

The Property Sheet should display *Selection type: Report*.

6 Click the **Property Sheet Data tab**. Notice that the **Record Source** property setting is *7B Online Orders*. **Close** ⊠ the **Property Sheet**.

> *7B Orders Main Report* is bound to the *7B Online Orders* table.

7 In the report, point to the top of the **Page Footer section bar** until the ⊕ pointer displays. Drag downward to the **1-inch mark on the vertical ruler** to make room in the Detail section for the subreport.

8 Under **Report Design Tools**, on the **Design tab**, in the **Controls group**, click the **More** ⊽ arrow, and verify that the **Use Control Wizards** option is active. In the **Controls group**, click **Subform/Subreport** ▦. Move the mouse pointer down into the **Detail** section until the top of the plus (+) sign of the pointer aligns with the **1-inch mark on the horizontal ruler** and with the **0.5-inch mark on the vertical ruler**, and then click. Compare your screen with Figure 7.30.

> A subreport control is inserted into the Detail section of the report, and the SubReport Wizard dialog box displays. The control displays *Unbound* because the control has not yet been linked to a record source.

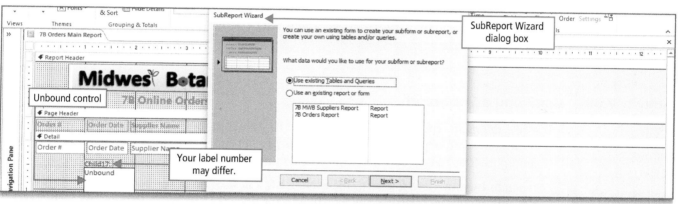

Figure 7.30

9 In the **SubReport Wizard** dialog box, verify that **Use existing Tables and Queries** is selected, and then click **Next**.

> The second SubReport Wizard dialog box enables you to select the table or query and the fields to use in the subreport.

10 Click the **Tables/Queries box arrow**, and from the displayed list, click **Table: 7B Online Order Detail**. Under **Available Fields**, double-click **Product**, and then double-click **Quantity** to move the fields to the **Selected Fields** box. Click **Next**.

> The third SubReport Wizard dialog box enables you to define the fields that link the main form to the subreport. Because there is a one-to-many relationship between the two tables, the default setting is to show the data in the *7B Online Order Detail* table for each record in the *7B Online Orders* table.

11 Click **Next**, name the report **7B Products Ordered Subreport** and then click **Finish**. Switch to **Report** view, and then compare your screen with Figure 7.31.

The subreport data displays under each record from the *7B Online Orders* table. For example, for *Order # MWB100*, two Border Rakes were ordered.

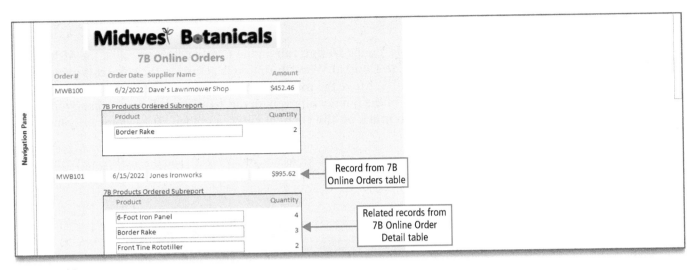

Figure 7.31

Activity 7.09 | Modifying a Subreport

MOS
5.1.2, 5.1.3

Just like the main report, the subreport can be modified. In this Activity, you will remove the name of the subreport, apply conditional formatting in the subreport, and change the border color of the subreport. You can modify the subreport in either Layout view or Design view.

1 Switch to **Layout** view. **Close** ☒ the **Field List**, if necessary. In any subreport control, click the **subreport label control**, which displays *7B Products Ordered Subreport*, and then press Delete.

The label control for the subreport no longer displays.

2 In any subreport control, click the **Quantity text box control**. Under **Report Layout Tools**, click the **Format tab**. In the **Control Formatting group**, click **Conditional Formatting**. The **Conditional Formatting Rules Manager** dialog box displays to show formatting rules for the *Quantity* field. Click **New Rule**, and compare your screen with Figure 7.32.

Conditional formatting is a way to apply formatting to specific controls based on a comparison to a rule set in the New Rule dialog box. It is one way to draw attention to an entry that might require additional action.

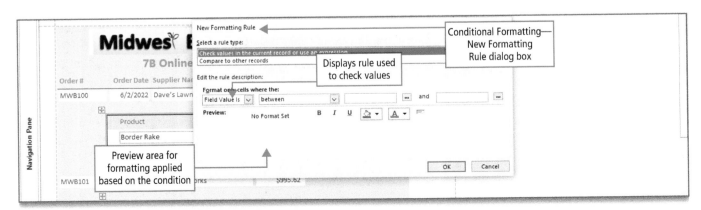

Figure 7.32

3 Click the arrow to the right of the box that displays *between*, and select **less than or equal to**. Click in the empty text box, and type **3** The rule will format only cells where the *Field Value is less than or equal to 3.*

The rule has now been set; however, no format options have been set. These settings are applied using the buttons below the rule.

4 Click **Bold** B , and then click the **Background color** 🎨 button arrow. Under **Standard Colors**, on the fourth row, click the sixth color. Click **OK** to close the **New Formatting Rule** dialog box. Click **OK** to close the **Conditional Formatting Rules Manager**.

For any items ordered, if the quantity is 3 or less, the quantity will display bold with a light background. This will alert the staff to determine if special marketing strategies might be helpful to increase sales.

5 Click anywhere in the subreport, if necessary, and then click the **Layout Selector**. Under **Report Layout Tools**, on the **Format tab**, in the **Control Formatting group**, click the **Shape Outline button arrow**. Under **Theme Colors**, on the first row, click the sixth color. Again, click the **Shape Outline button arrow**, and then point to **Line Thickness**. In the displayed list, click the third line—**2 pt**—and then click anywhere in the main report to display the results of the formatting. Switch to **Report** view. Compare your screen with Figure 7.33.

The subreport displays with a thicker border.

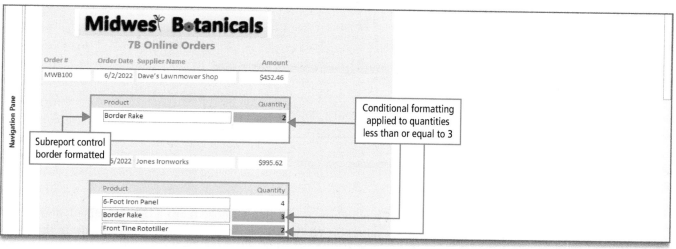

Figure 7.33

NOTE **Removing a Horizontal Scroll Bar**

Adding the thicker border decreased the area where the data displays, and it may cause a horizontal scroll bar to display at the bottom of the subreport. If so, in Layout view, click the subreport control—not a field label control or text box control in the subreport—and then point to the right edge of the subreport control until the pointer displays. Drag the right edge of the subreport control to the right until the horizontal scroll bar no longer displays.

---

6 Save 💾 the report. View the report in **Print Preview**.

7 **Close** the **Print Preview** window and **Close** the report, and then **Open** » the **Navigation Pane**.

Activity 7.10 | Creating a Subreport by Adding an Object to an Existing Report

5.1.2, 5.2.3

In this Activity, you will drag the *7B Online Orders* table onto the *7B MWB Suppliers Report* to create a subreport. For the subreport to be linked to the main report, the underlying tables should have an established relationship. You can also create a subreport by dragging an existing form, subform, query, report, or subreport onto a report.

1 In the **Navigation Pane**, under **Reports**, locate **7B MWB Suppliers Report**, and then open the report in **Design** view. In the report, point to the top of the **Page Footer section bar** until the ⊞ pointer displays. Drag downward to the **1.25-inch mark on the vertical ruler** to make room in the Detail section for the subreport.

2 In the **Navigation Pane**, under **Tables**, click **7B Online Orders**, and then drag the table to the right onto the **Detail** section until the top of the pointer aligns with the **1-inch mark on the horizontal ruler** and the **0.5-inch mark on the vertical ruler**. The **SubReport Wizard** dialog box displays, as shown in Figure 7.34.

The SubReport Wizard suggests that the report shows the Online Orders for each record in the Suppliers using Supplier Name. If you were dragging an existing report onto this report that had an established relationship between the underlying tables, the SubReport Wizard dialog box would not display.

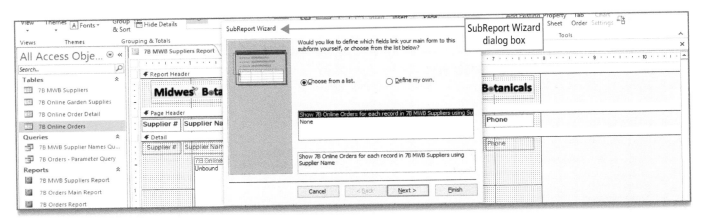

Figure 7.34

3 In the **SubReport Wizard** dialog box, verify that **Choose from a list** is selected, and then click **Next**. Name the subreport **7B Orders Subreport** and then click **Finish**. In the **Navigation Pane**, notice that the newly created subreport displays under **Reports**.

4 Close ✕ the **Field List**, if necessary. Press F4 to display the Property Sheet for the subreport, and then **Close** ≪ the **Navigation Pane**. If necessary, click the **Property Sheet Data tab**, click in the **Link Master Fields** property setting box, and then click **Build** ….

The Subreport Field Linker dialog box displays. The fields that are used to link the two underlying record sources are displayed; the Master Fields property setting box displays the linked field in the main report, and the Child Fields property setting box displays the linked field in the subreport. Use the Subreport Field Linker dialog box to change the linked fields if the subreport does not display the data in the manner you intended. If you are unsure of which fields to link, click Suggest.

5 In the **Subreport Field Linker** dialog box, click **OK. Close** ✕ the **Property Sheet**, and then switch to **Layout** view. Notice that **Record 1** displays no data in the subreport; no orders have been placed with A&S Garden Supply.

6 In the main report, locate Record 2—**Martinez Nurseries**. Notice that Record 2 displays one order in the subreport and displays the name of the supplier in the third field. In the **subreport control** for **Record 2**, click **Martinez Nurseries**, press Shift, and click the **Supplier Name label control**. Press Delete to remove the label and text box controls and the redundant data. Resize the other three controls so they are wide enough to just view the data. Move the controls to close large gaps between fields.

7 Click the **subreport's Layout Selector** ⊞, and then press F4 to display the Property Sheet for the subreport. Click the **Property Sheet Format tab**, select the text in the **Width** property setting box, type **3.5** and then press Enter to change the width of the subreport control. **Close** ✕ the **Property Sheet**.

> The subreport has been modified, and the redundant field has been removed. A horizontal scroll bar displays in the subreport.

8 Click the **subreport label control**—*7B Orders Subreport*—to select it, and then, under **Report Design Tools**, on the **Format tab**, in the **Font group**, click the **Font Color button** A⋅ arrow. Under **Theme Colors**, in the fifth row, click the sixth color, and then click **Bold** B. Point to the selected label control until the 🤚 pointer displays, and then drag the control to the right until it is approximately centered between the margins of the subreport control.

9 Switch to **Design** view, saving changes to the main report and subreport. Select the **Subreport Header**, and under **Report Design Tools**, click the **Format tab**. Click the **Background color button** 🎨⋅ arrow. Under **Standard Colors**, on the third row, click the sixth color Click the **Order # label control**, hold down Shift, click the **Order Date label control**, and then click the **Amount label control** to select all three label controls, scrolling to the right as necessary. Change the **Font color** to match the subreport label control, and apply **Bold**. Switch to **Layout** view, and then compare your screen with Figure 7.35.

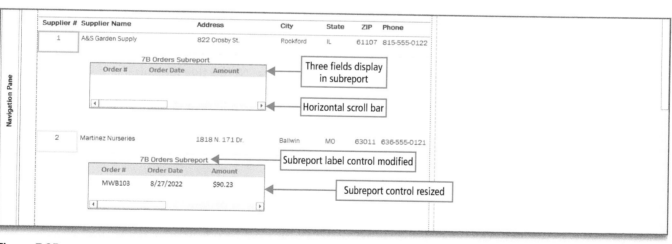

Figure 7.35

10 **Save** 💾 the report.

Activity 7.11 | Displaying a Total from a Subreport on the Main Report

MOS
5.1.2, 5.2.2,
5.2.5, 5.2.3

In this Activity, you will display a total from the subreport on the main report.

1 Switch to **Design** view. Click the subreport to select it. Under **Report Design Tools**, on the **Design tab**, in the **Tools group**, click **Subreport in New Window** 🖼.

> The subreport displays on its own tab, and all of the controls are displayed, which makes it easier to edit.

2 Under **Report Design Tools**, on the **Design tab**, in the **Tools group**, click **Property Sheet**. Verify that the Property Sheet displays *Selection type: Report*. On the **Property Sheet Format tab**, change the **Width** property setting to **3.45** and press Enter. Compare your screen with Figure 7.36.

Recall that the subreport control displayed a horizontal scroll bar—this is because the actual subreport's width was wider than the size of the control. By making the width of the report smaller than the width of the subreport control, the scroll bar will no longer display in the *7B MWB Suppliers Report* because it is not really necessary to view data.

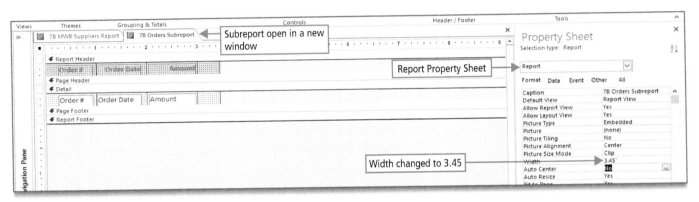

Figure 7.36

3 Close ⌧ the **Property Sheet**. In the **Detail** section, click the **Amount text box control**. Under **Report Design Tools**, on the **Design tab**, in the **Grouping & Totals group**, click **Totals**, and then click **Sum** to insert a calculated control into the Report Footer section.

4 Save 🖫 the subreport, and then **Close** ⌧ *7B Orders Subreport*.

To view the results of the changes made to the subreport in the main report, you first must close the subreport.

5 Switch *7B MWB Suppliers Report* to **Report** view. Notice that the horizontal scroll bar no longer displays, and in the subreport controls, **Record 1** displays a total Amount of **$0.00** and **Record 2** displays a total Amount of **$90.23**. Scroll down to display **Record 5**, which displays a total Amount of **$535.33**.

Adding a sum to a field in the subreport causes the sum to display in the subreport control on the main form.

6 Switch to **Design** view, and verify that the subreport is still selected. Under **Report Design Tools**, on the **Design tab**, in the **Tools group**, click **Subreport in New Window** 🔲. Click the **Report Footer section bar**, and then press F4 to display the Property Sheet for the Report Footer section. On the **Property Sheet Format tab**, click in the **Visible** property setting box, which displays **Yes**. Click the **arrow**, and then click **No**.

The data in the Report Footer section will not display when the report is displayed in any view other than Design view. You will be displaying the calculated field in the main form, so it is being hidden from view.

7 In the **Report Footer** section, click the **calculated control**. The **Property Sheet** displays *Selection type: Text Box*, and the **Selection type** box displays *AccessTotalsAmount*. Click the **Property Sheet Other tab**, and then click in the **Name** property setting box. Select **AccessTotalsAmount**, type **Total Amount** and then press [Enter]. Compare your screen with Figure 7.37.

> The Selection type box displays Total Amount, which is the new name of the text box control that displays the sum of the amount field. Rename controls to easily remember the name, especially if the control name is used somewhere else in the form. You will be using this control name to display the total of the amount field in the main form.

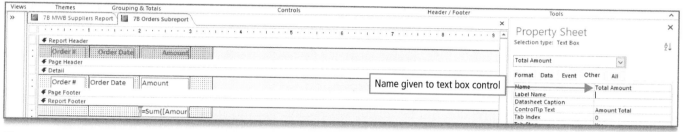

Figure 7.37

8 **Close** ⊠ the **Property Sheet**, **Save** 🖫 the report, and then **Close** ⊠ *7B Orders Subreport*. Switch *7B MWB Suppliers Report* to **Report** view, and notice that the sum of the Amount field no longer displays in the subreport control.

9 Switch to **Design** view. Under **Report Design Tools**, on the **Design tab**, in the **Controls group**, click **Text Box** ⓐⓑ. Move the mouse pointer down to the **Detail** section until the top of the plus (+) sign aligns with the **6-inch mark on the horizontal ruler** and with the **1-inch mark on the vertical ruler**, and then click. Compare your screen with Figure 7.38.

> A text box control with an associated label control displays in the Detail section. The text box control displays Unbound because the control is not linked to a field.

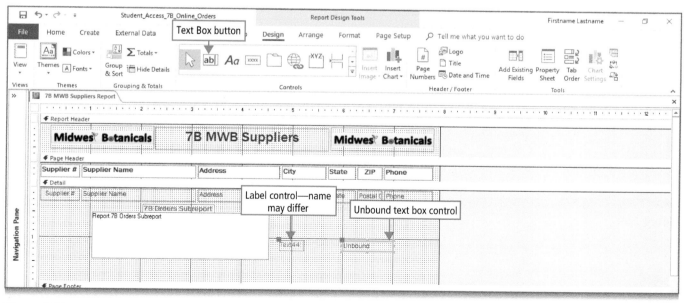

Figure 7.38

10 In the **Detail** section, click the **label control** that is associated with the unbound text box control, and then press F4 to display the Property Sheet for the label control. Click the **Property Sheet Format tab**, select the text in the **Caption** property setting box, and then type **Total Amt:** Select the text in the **Width** property setting box, type **.75** and then press Enter to increase the width of the label control.

> The Caption property setting controls the text that is displayed in the label control associated with the unbound text box control.

11 In the **Detail** section, click the **unbound text box control**. If the control is hidden behind the Property Sheet, decrease the width of the Property Sheet by dragging the left edge of the Property Sheet to the right. Click the **Property Sheet Data tab**, and then in the **Control Source** property setting box, click **Build** [...].

> The Expression Builder dialog box displays. Although you can type the expression directly in the Control Source property setting box, the Expression Builder dialog box is similar to the Zoom dialog box, where you can see the entire typed expression. The Control Source property setting is used to link the text box control to a field.

12 In the **Expression Builder** dialog box, double-clicking the correct objects as they appear in the list, type **=IIf(IsError([7B Orders Subreport].[Report]![Total Amount]),0,[7B Orders Subreport].[Report]![Total Amount])** and then compare your screen with Figure 7.39.

> The expression starts with an equal (=) sign and is followed by the IsError function within the IIf function. The IIf function checks for the #Error message in the Total Amount field of 7B Orders Subreport. If #Error is found, 0 is displayed in the field; otherwise, the data in the Total Amount field is displayed. A period separates the report name from the object name, which is also enclosed in brackets. The object name, in this case [Report], is only necessary if the name of the report is the same as the underlying record source. The exclamation (!) mark is called the ***bang operator***. The bang operator tells Access that what follows it is an object that belongs to the object that precedes it in the expression. In this expression, Total Amount is an object in the 7B Orders Subreport report.

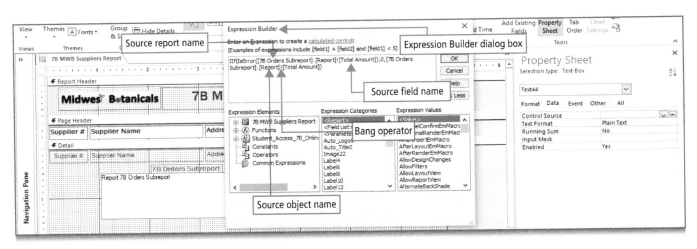

Figure 7.39

ANOTHER WAY If the subreport contained data for each control on the main report, you could have typed a simpler expression of =[7B Online Orders Subreport].[Report]![Total Amount]. The expression starts with an equal (=) sign and is followed by the name of the report enclosed in brackets. A period separates the report name from the object name—Report—which is also enclosed in brackets. The bang operator is used to identify Total Amount as an object in the 7B Orders Subreport report. If the subreport does not contain any data for any control on the main report, the control on the main report displays #Error when printed using the simplified expression.

13 In the **Expression Builder** dialog box, click **OK**.

The expression displays in the Control Source property setting box.

ALERT **Does a message box display?**

If a message box displays stating that the expression contains invalid syntax, click OK. In the Control Source property setting box, click Build, and correct the expression. *Syntax* is the set of rules by which words and symbols in an expression are combined.

14 Click the **Property Sheet Format tab**. Click in the **Format** property setting box, click the displayed **arrow**, and then select **Currency**. **Close** ⊠ the **Property Sheet**.

The data that was typed in the Control Source property setting box displays in the text box control.

15 With the **text box control selected**, point to the small gray box that displays in the upper left corner of the text box control until the pointer displays. Drag to the left until the left edge of the text box control aligns with the right edge of the label control that displays *Total Amt:*.

Dragging the small box that displays in the upper left corner of a control enables you to move only that control. If you point to any other part of the control before dragging, the control and its associated controls are moved.

16 **Save** 🖫 the report, and click **Yes** in the dialog box if necessary. Switch to **Report** view. Scroll down to display **Records 6 and 7**, and then compare your screen with Figure 7.40.

The sum of the Amount field in the subreport is displayed in the main report and is formatted as Currency.

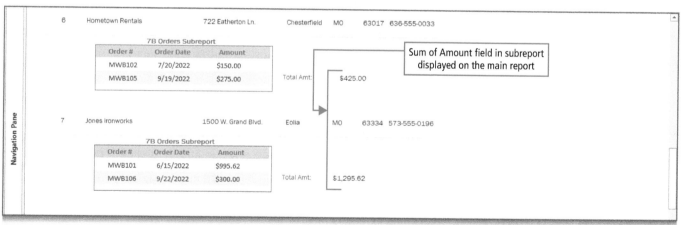

Figure 7.40

ALERT **Does an Enter Parameter Value message box display?**

If an Enter Parameter Value message box displays, you probably typed the name of the subreport or the name of the field incorrectly. If this occurs, repeat Steps 11 and 12, ensuring that you type the expression correctly.

17 **Close** ⊠ the report, and then **Open** « the **Navigation Pane**.

Objective 5   Create a Report Based on a Parameter Query

GO! Learn How

Video A7-5

Recall that a *parameter query* prompts you for criteria before running the query. Using a parameter query as the record source for a report enables the user to set the criteria for the report when the report is opened. Recall that when a report is opened, the underlying table or query in the report is read to ensure that the report displays the most current data. MWB Productions maintains a table to keep track of the website orders. A parameter query was created to display the orders between a range of dates.

Activity 7.12 | Creating a Report Based on a Parameter Query

5.1.2, 5.1.3,
5.2.3

In this Activity, you will view the design of the *7B Orders Parameter Query*, and then create a report based on the parameter query.

1 In the **Navigation Pane**, under **Tables**, double-click **7B Online Orders** to open the table in **Datasheet** view. Notice that the **Order Date** data ranges from 6/2/2022 to 9/22/2022.

> When you run the parameter query, if you enter a range for which there is no data or if you enter the data incorrectly, the resulting fields will be empty.

2 **Close** ☒ the table. In the **Navigation Pane**, under **Queries**, double-click **7B Orders - Parameter Query**. In the **Enter Parameter Value** message box, under **Enter first date**, type **6/1/22** and then click **OK**. In the second message box, under **Enter second date**, type **July 31, 2022** and then click **OK**.

> Because the Order Date field has a data type of Date, you can enter the date in several formats. The query is run and displays orders between June 1, 2022, and July 31, 2022.

3 **Close** ☒ the query, and then **Close** ☒ the **Navigation Pane**. On the **Create tab**, in the **Reports group**, click **Report Wizard**.

> Because the query was selected in the Navigation Pane, the *7B Orders - Parameter Query* displays in the Tables/Queries box.

4 In the **Report Wizard** dialog box, click **All Fields** ⏩ to move all of the fields from the Available Fields box to the Selected Fields box, and then click **Next**.

5 In the second **Report Wizard** dialog box, click **Next**. In the third **Report Wizard** dialog box, **sort** the records by **Order Date** in **Ascending** order, and then click **Next** two times.

6 In the last **Report Wizard** dialog box, name the report **7B Orders by Date Range** and then click **Finish**.

> An Enter Parameter Value message box displays. Because the report is based on a parameter query, you must enter the parameter values.

7 For the first date, type **6/1/22** and click **OK**. For the second date, type **7/31/22** Click **OK**, and then compare your screen with Figure 7.41.

> Six records are extracted from the underlying tables based on the parameter values entered. Five fields are included in the report, but all data may not be visible on this page. In that case, adjustments will need to be made to controls so all data is visible and the report prints on one page.

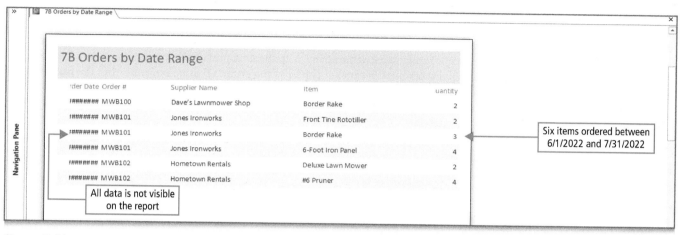

Figure 7.41

8 Right-click the object tab, and click **Layout View**. Close the Field List, if necessary. Resize the text box controls and label controls for the **Item** and **Supplier Name** so they are just wide enough to display the longest item in each column. Resize the **Order Date** field to fully display the data, and then resize the **Quantity** field to fit the label control.

9 Switch to **Design** view. Adjust the field placement so all fields display on the page and the right edge of the **Quantity** field aligns at the **7-inch mark on the horizontal ruler**.

10 In the **Page Footer** section, click to select the **Page Numbering** text box. Point to the right middle sizing handle until the ↔ pointer displays. Drag to the left until the right edge of the text box control aligns with the right edge of the **Quantity** controls. Resize the width of the report to **7.25 inches**. **Save** 🖫 the report.

Activity 7.13 | Placing the Parameters in the Report

5.2.5, 5.1.3, 5.2.6

The parameters used in the creation of the report can be printed as a part of the report by adding a text box control to a section. In this Activity, you will add a text box control to the Report Header section to display the parameter values as a subtitle.

1 Point to the top of the **Page Header section bar** until the ✛ pointer displays. Drag downward to the top of the **Detail section bar** to increase the size of the **Report Header**.

2 Under **Report Design Tools**, on the **Design tab**, in the **Controls group**, click **Text Box** ⓐⓑ. In the **Report Header** section, align the top of the plus (+) sign of the pointer **one dot** from the left margin and **three dots** below the label control for the report title, and then click.

> Recall that adding a text box control to the design also adds an associated label control that can be used to describe the data in the text box control.

3 Click the **label control** that is associated with the newly added text box control, and then press Delete.

4 Click the unbound **text box control**, and then press F4 to display the Property Sheet for the control. Click the **Property Sheet Data tab**, click in the **Control Source** property setting box, and then click **Build** ⌐⌐⌐. In the displayed **Expression Builder** dialog box, type **="Between** press Spacebar, and then continue typing **"&[Enter first date]&"** Press Spacebar, and then type **and** Press Spacebar again, and then continue typing **"&[Enter second date]** Compare your screen with Figure 7.42.

Recall that an expression must begin with an equal sign (=). The word *Between* and a space will print. The & symbol concatenates the string with the next part of the expression. *Enter first date* is enclosed in square brackets because it is part of the criteria that is retrieved from the parameter query. You must type the criteria exactly as it displays in the criteria of the parameter query. The criteria will be concatenated with the space, the word *and*, and another space. This is concatenated with the second criteria.

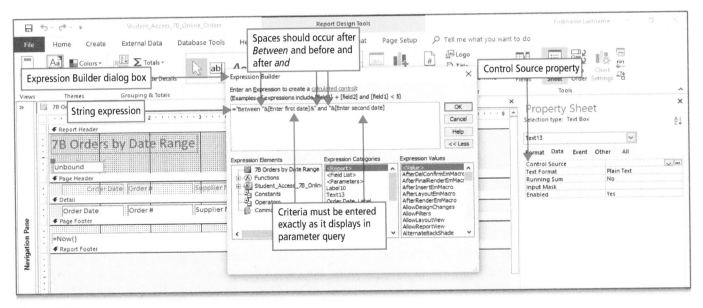

Figure 7.42

5 In the **Expression Builder** dialog box, click **OK**, and then press Enter to save the property setting.

ALERT **Did a message box display?**

If a message box displays stating that the expression you entered contains invalid syntax, click OK. Click the Control Source Build button, and then view Figure 7.42 to be sure that you typed the expression correctly. Common errors include not typing the equal sign, using parentheses instead of square brackets, leaving out the beginning or ending quotation marks, or leaving out one of the & symbols.

6 **Close** ✕ the **Property Sheet**. Under **Report Design Tools**, on the **Format tab**, in the **Font group**, click the **Font Color button arrow** Ⓐ▾. Under **Theme Colors**, on the sixth row, click the fourth color.

7 With the text box control selected, in the **Font group**, click the **Font Size button arrow** ⌷, and from the displayed list, click **14**. Increase the width of the text box until the entire expression displays.

8 Under **Report Design Tools**, click the **Arrange tab**, and then, in the **Sizing & Ordering group**, click **Size/Space**, and then click **To Fit**.

> The height of the text box control is increased to fit the size of the text, and the width of the text box control will adjust to fit the title that displays in Layout view, Report view, and Print Preview view.

9 Save 🖫 the report, and switch to **Report** view. For the first date, enter **6/1/22** and for the second date, enter **7/31/22**

> The report displays with a subtitle of *Between 6/1/22 and 7/31/22*. When the criteria is displayed in the report, be sure to enter the criteria in a consistent manner. For example, do not enter 6/1/22 for the first date and July 31, 2022, for the second date. If you do, the subtitle will display as *Between 6/1/22 and July 31, 2022*.

ALERT   Did another message box display?

If an unexpected Enter Parameter Value message box displays when you try to print or preview a report, you may have misspelled one of the criteria or a field name in the expression. If this happens, click Cancel to return to Design view and correct the error. The parameter criteria in this report must match exactly to the parameter criteria used in the query.

---

10 Close ✕ the **report**, and then Open ⟩⟩ the **Navigation Pane**.

MORE KNOWLEDGE   Inserting an Image in a Report

Under Report Layout Tools, click the Design tab. Click Insert Image, and then click Browse. Navigate to the location where the image is stored, and double-click the file name to insert it in the report.

Objective 6   Create an Alphabetic Index

GO! Learn How
Video A7-6

A report can display an ***alphabetic index***, similar to the grouping of addresses in an address book. An alphabetic index groups items by a common first character. For example, all of your contacts can be sorted by last name in ascending order. All of the last names beginning with the letter *A* are grouped together under the letter *A*. All of the last names beginning with the letter *B* are grouped together under the letter *B*, and so on.

Activity 7.14 | Creating an Alphabetic Index

5.1.1, 5.1.3

Midwest Botanicals would like to produce a report that displays all of the suppliers from which they purchase. In this Activity, you will create an alphabetic index of the suppliers' names from the *7B MWB Suppliers* table, using the *7B MWB Supplier Names Query*.

1 In the **Navigation Pane**, under **Queries**, double-click **7B MWB Supplier Names Query**. Take a moment to review the data in the query, and then switch to **Design** view.

> The query displays the Supplier Name field in ascending order from the *7B MWB Suppliers* table.

2 ▸ **Close** ⊠ the query, and then **Close** ⊠ the **Navigation Pane**.

3 ▸ On the **Create tab**, in the **Reports group**, click **Report Wizard**.

4 ▸ Because the query was selected in the Navigation Pane, in the **Report Wizard** dialog box, in the **Tables/Queries** box, **Query: 7B MWB Supplier Names Query** displays. If it does not display, click the **Tables/Queries arrow**, and then click **Query: 7B MWB Supplier Names Query**.

5 ▸ Under **Available Fields**, double-click **Supplier Name** to add the field name to the **Selected Fields** box, and then click **Next**.

> Because the query sorts the Supplier Name in ascending order, the field will automatically be sorted in the same manner in the report.

6 ▸ Click **Next**. Under **Layout**, verify that the **Tabular** option button is selected. Under **Orientation**, verify that the **Portrait** option button is selected, and then click **Next**.

7 ▸ For the title of the report, type **7B Supplier Alphabetic Index** and then click **Finish**. Compare your screen with Figure 7.43.

> The report displays in Print Preview.

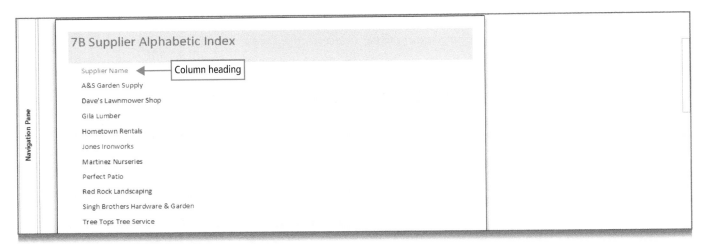

Figure 7.43

8 ▸ **Close** Print Preview. In **Design** view, click anywhere in an empty area of the design grid to deselect the controls, if necessary, and then click the **Supplier Name label control**. Be sure that the orange border only displays around the Supplier Name label control. Press Delete to remove the Supplier Name label control from the report.

9 ▸ **Save** 🖫 the report, and then switch to **Layout** view.

10 ▸ Under **Report Layout Tools**, on the **Design tab**, in the **Grouping & Totals group**, click **Group & Sort**. In the **Group, Sort, and Total pane**, click **Add a group**. From the displayed list, click **Supplier Name**.

> The report must be grouped by Supplier Name to create an alphabetic index of the names.

11 In the **Group, Sort, and Total pane**, on the **Group bar**, click the **More arrow**. Click the **by entire value arrow**, and from the displayed list, click the **by first character** option button. Verify that the third option from the right displays **with a header section**. Click in an empty area of the report, and then compare your screen with Figure 7.44.

The first letter of the Supplier Name displays above the supplier names along with a label control that displays Supplier Name. You can select more than one character for the index.

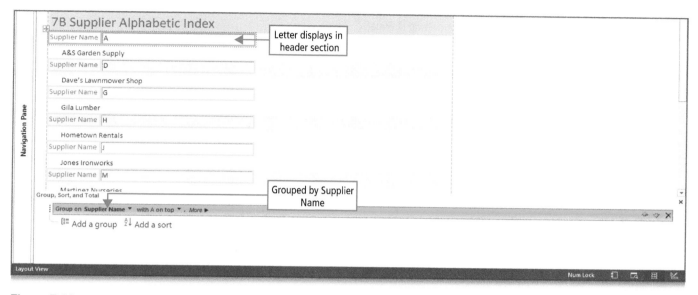

Figure 7.44

12 In the **Group, Sort, and Total pane**, on the **Group bar**, click the **More arrow**. To the right of **with title**, click the **Supplier Name** link. With *Supplier Name* selected, in the displayed **Zoom** dialog box, press Delete, and then click **OK**. In the report, delete the placeholder from the **Supplier Name control**. Under **Report Layout Tools**, on the **Design tab**, in the **Grouping & Totals group**, click **Group & Sort** to close the pane.

13 Click the **Supplier text box control** for the first record—*A&S Garden Supply*. Point to the left edge of the control until the ↔ pointer displays. Drag to the right until the left edge of the text box control is approximately **0.5 inches** to the right of the letter *A* in the **Supplier Name header**. Change the **Font Size** to **12**, and then compare your screen with Figure 7.45.

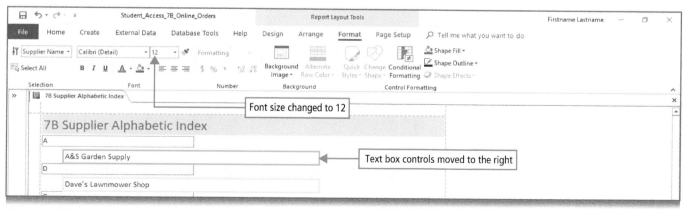

Figure 7.45

14 Click the **text box control** that displays the letter *A*, and change the **Font Size** to **16**. Click the **Font Color** A ⁻ arrow. Under **Theme Colors**, on the first row, click the fourth color, and then click **Bold** B .

15 **Save** 🖫 the report, and then switch to **Report** view. Compare your screen with Figure 7.46.

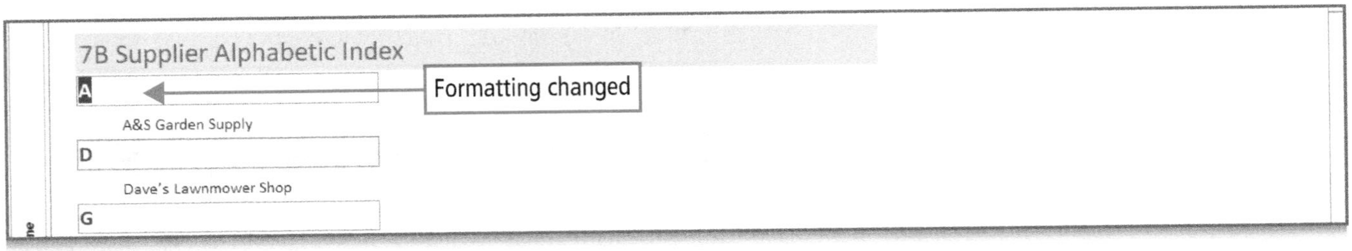

7B Supplier Alphabetic Index

A ◄————— Formatting changed

A&S Garden Supply

D

Dave's Lawnmower Shop

G

Figure 7.46

16 **Close** × the report. **Open** » the **Navigation Pane**. If necessary, resize the **Navigation Pane** to be sure all object names display fully. **Close** the database. **Close** Access.

For Non-MyLab Submissions: Determine What Your Instructor Requires for Submission
As directed by your instructor, submit your completed database file.

17 In **MyLab IT**, locate and click the Grader Project **7B Online Orders**. In **step 3**, under **Upload Completed Assignment**, click **Choose File**. In the **Open** dialog box, navigate to your **Access Chapter 7 folder**, and then click your **Student_Access_7B_Online_Orders** file one time to select it. In the lower right corner of the **Open** dialog box, click **Open**.

The name of your selected file displays above the Upload button.

18 To submit your file to **MyLab IT** for grading, click **Upload**, wait a moment for a green **Success!** message, and then in **step 4**, click the blue **Submit for Grading** button. Click **Close Assignment** to return to your list of **Course Materials**.

You have completed Project 7B   **END**

wavebreakmedia/Shutterstock, Monkey Business Images/Fotolia, Ivanko80/Shutterstock, Monkey Business Images/Shutterstock

7

ACCESS

Microsoft Office Specialist (MOS) Skills in This Chapter	
Project 7A	**Project 7B**
1.2.2 Display relationships	**1.2.1** Understand relationships
4.1.1 Add, move, and remove form controls	**1.2.2** Display relationships
4.1.2 Set form control properties	**5.1.1** Group and sort fields on reports
4.1.3 Add and modify form controls	**5.1.2** Add report controls
4.2.2 Set records by form field	**5.1.3** Add and modify labels on reports
4.2.3 Modify form positioning	**5.2.2** Modify report positioning
4.2.4 Insert information in form headers and footers	**5.2.3** Format report elements
4.2.5 Insert images on forms	**5.2.5** Insert information in report headers and footers
	5.2.6 Insert images on reports

Build Your E-Portfolio

An E-Portfolio is a collection of evidence, stored electronically, that showcases what you have accomplished while completing your education. Collecting and then sharing your work products with potential employers reflects your academic and career goals. Your completed documents from the following projects are good examples to show what you have learned: 7G, 7K, and 7L.

GO! For Job Success

Topic: Job Satisfaction

Satisfied employees add value to businesses. They work harder, produce better results, and reduce costs related to hiring and training replacement workers. Especially in technology, companies provide benefits beyond great pay to keep employees happy and engaged. Beyond pay, opportunities for career growth and good relationships contribute to happy workers in all fields. Work/life balance—having a fulfilling personal life as well as a satisfying job—is also a motivator for many employees.

g-stockstudio/Shutterstock

Do employers have a responsibility to provide work/life balance to employees? What responsibilities do employees have?

What can managers do to ensure that workers have opportunities to meet and interact with their coworkers?

Beyond employee motivation, why would a supervisor want regular, open communications with their direct reports?

End of Chapter

Summary

Advanced forms can display data from one or more record sources. Split forms display data from one table in two different ways in the same form: Form view and Datasheet view.

Subforms display data from related tables on one form; they can be created using the Form Tool and the Form Wizard or by dragging a related table onto an existing form. Forms can be displayed on multiple pages by using the tab control.

Reports can be simple or complex; advanced reports use some of the same techniques as advanced forms. Subreports can be created using the SubReport Wizard and by dragging a related table onto a report.

A report can be created from a parameter query, and the criteria can be displayed in an unbound control in the report. A report can also use grouping and sorting features to display an alphabetic index.

GO! Learn It Online

Review the concepts, key terms, and MOS skills in this chapter by completing these online challenges, which you can find at **MyLab IT**.

Chapter Quiz: Answer matching and multiple choice questions to test what you learned in this chapter.

Learn it on the GO!: Learn how to use all the new apps and features as they are introduced by Microsoft.

MOS Prep Quiz: Answer questions to review the MOS skills that you practiced in this chapter.

Project Guide for Access Chapter 7

Your instructor will assign Projects from this list to ensure your learning and assess your knowledge.

Project	Apply Skills from These Chapter Objectives	Project Type		Project Location
7A MyLab IT	Objectives 1–3 from Project 7A	**7A Instructional Project (Grader Project)** A guided review of the skills from Project 7A.	**Instruction**	In **MyLab IT** and in text
7B MyLab IT	Objectives 4–6 from Project 7B	**7B Instructional Project (Grader Project)** A guided review of the skills from Project 7B.	**Instruction**	In **MyLab IT** and in text
7C	Objectives 1–3 from Project 7A	**7C Chapter Review (Scorecard Grading)** A guided review of the skills from Project 7A.	**Review**	In text
7D	Objectives 4–6 from Project 7B	**7D Chapter Review (Scorecard Grading)** A guided review of the skills from Project 7B.	**Review**	In text
7E	Objectives 1–3 from Project 7A	**7E Mastery (Scorecard Grading)** A demonstration of your mastery of the skills in Project 7A with extensive decision making.	**Mastery and Transfer of Learning**	In text
7F	Objectives 4–6 from Project 7B	**7F Mastery (Scorecard Grading)** A demonstration of your mastery of the skills in Project 7B with extensive decision making.	**Mastery and Transfer of Learning**	In text
7G MyLab IT	Objectives 1–6 from Projects 7A and 7B	**7G Mastery (Grader Project)** A demonstration of your mastery of the skills in Projects 7A and 7B with extensive decision making.	**Mastery and Transfer of Learning**	In **MyLab IT** and in text
7H	Combination of Objectives from Projects 7A and 7B	**7H GO! Fix It (Scorecard Grading)** A demonstration of your mastery of the skills in Projects 7A and 7B by creating a correct result from a document that contains errors you must find.	**Critical Thinking**	Instructor Resource Center (IRC)
7I	Combination of Objectives from Projects 7A and 7B	**7I GO! Make It (Scorecard Grading)** A demonstration of your mastery of the skills in Projects 7A and 7B by creating a result from a supplied picture.	**Critical Thinking**	IRC
7J	Combination of Objectives from Projects 7A and 7B	**7J GO! Solve It (Rubric Grading)** A demonstration of your mastery of the skills in Projects 7A and 7B, your decision-making skills, and your critical thinking skills. A task-specific rubric helps you self-assess your result.	**Critical Thinking**	IRC
7K	Combination of Objectives from Projects 7A and 7B	**7K GO! Solve It (Rubric Grading)** A demonstration of your mastery of the skills in Projects 7A and 7B, your decision-making skills, and your critical thinking skills. A task-specific rubric helps you self-assess your result.	**Critical Thinking**	In text
7L	Combination of Objectives from Projects 7A and 7B	**7L GO! Think (Rubric Grading)** A demonstration of your understanding of the chapter concepts applied in a manner that you would use outside of college. An analytic rubric helps you and your instructor grade the quality of your work by comparing it to the work an expert in the discipline would create.	**Critical Thinking**	In text
7M	Combination of Objectives from Projects 7A and 7B	**7M GO! Think (Rubric Grading)** A demonstration of your understanding of the chapter concepts applied in a manner that you would use outside of college. An analytic rubric helps you and your instructor grade the quality of your work by comparing it to the work an expert in the discipline would create.	**Critical Thinking**	IRC
7N	Combination of Objectives from Projects 7A and 7B	**7N You and GO! (Rubric Grading)** A demonstration of your understanding of the chapter concepts applied in a manner that you would use in a personal situation. An analytic rubric helps you and your instructor grade the quality of your work.	**Critical Thinking**	IRC

Glossary

Glossary of Chapter Key Terms

Alphabetic index Grouping of items by a common first character.

Bang operator The exclamation (!) mark that tells Access that what follows is an object that belongs to the object that precedes it in the expression.

Bound report A report that displays data from an underlying table, query, or SQL statement as specified in the report's Record Source property.

Conditional formatting A way to apply formatting to specific controls based on a comparison to a rule set.

Junction table A table that breaks down the many-to-many relationship into two one-to-many relationships.

Linked form A form related to the main form that is not stored within the main form.

Main form A form that contains a subform.

Main report A report that contains a subreport.

Many-to-many relationship A relationship between tables where one record in one table has many matching records in a second table, and a single record in the related table has many matching records in the first table.

Mini toolbar A miniature, semitransparent toolbar that is used to work with objects on the screen.

Multi-page form A form that displays the data from the underlying table or query on more than one page.

Nested subform A subform that is embedded within another subform.

Parameter query A query that prompts an individual for criteria before running the query.

Split form An object that displays data in two views—Form view and Datasheet view—on a single form.

SQL statement An instruction using Structured Query Language.

Subform A form that is embedded within another form.

Subreport A report that is embedded within another report.

Syntax The set of rules by which words and symbols in an expression are combined.

Tab control A control that is used to display data on the main form on different tabs, similar to the way database objects, such as forms and tables, display on different tabs.

Unbound report A report that does not display data from an underlying table, query, or SQL statement and has an empty Record Source property setting.

Chapter Review

Apply **7A skills** from these Objectives:

1. Create a Split Form
2. Create a Form and a Subform
3. Create a Multi-Page Form

| Skills Review | Project 7C Historical Gardens |

Matthew Lee, coordinator for cultural and historical events of MWB Productions, wants the database forms to display related data. For example, he is interested in displaying the contacts for the historical gardens on one form. In this project, you will customize the company's forms to display data in two ways on the same form, to display data from multiple tables on one form, and to display data on multiple pages on a form. Your completed Navigation Pane will look similar to Figure 7.47.

Project Files

For Project 7C, you will need the following files:

a07C_Historical_Gardens
a07C_MWB_Logo

You will save your database as:

Lastname_Firstname_7C_Historical_Gardens

Project Results

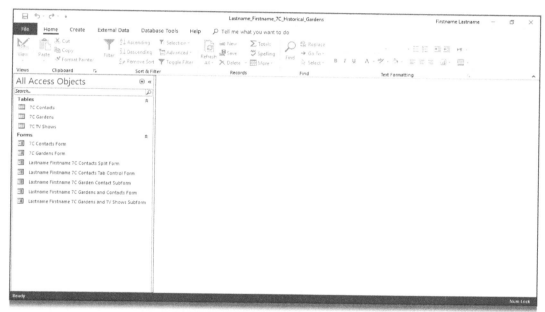

Figure 7.47

(continues on next page)

Chapter Review

1 Start Access. Open the **a07C_Historical_Gardens** file. Save the database in your **Access Chapter 7** folder as **Lastname_Firstname_7C_Historical_Gardens** If necessary, enable the content.

2 In the **Navigation Pane**, click **7C Contacts** to select the table. **Close** the **Navigation Pane**.

a. On the **Create tab**, in the **Forms group**, click **More Forms**, and then click **Split Form**. **Save** the split form as **Lastname Firstname 7C Contacts Split Form**

b. Under **Form Layout Tools**, on the **Design tab**, in the **Tools group**, click **Property Sheet**. Click the **Selection type arrow**, and then click **Form**.

c. Click the **Form Property Sheet Format tab**, if necessary. In the property setting box for **Split Form Printing**, click the **arrow**, and then click **Form Only**.

d. Switch to **Design** view. Click in the **Split Form Orientation** property setting box, and then click the **arrow**. Click **Datasheet on Top**, and then **Close** the **Property Sheet**. Select the **title's label control**. Point to the right edge of the **title's label control** until the pointer displays. Drag to the left until the right edge of the label control aligns with the **7-inch mark on the horizontal ruler**. Repeat the process with the text box controls in the form. Point to the right edge of the main form until the pointer displays. Drag to the left until the edge aligns with the **7.25-inch mark on the horizontal ruler**.

e. Switch to **Layout** view. Point to the splitter bar until the pointer displays. Drag upward until the dark line displays between the fourth and fifth records.

f. Under **Form Layout Tools**, on the **Design tab**, in the **Header/Footer group**, click **Logo**. Navigate to the student data files, and then double-click **a07C_MWB_Logo**. Display the **Property Sheet**. Click in the **Size Mode** property box, click the arrow, and then click **Zoom**. Increase the **Width** of the **logo control** to **1.5 inches**. **Close** the **Property Sheet**.

g. Click the **title's label control**. Click at the beginning of the title, and then type your **Lastname Firstname**

h. **Save** the form, and then switch to **Form** view. Press (PageDown) until **Record 4** displays. In the form section, change the **Phone Number** for *Chicago Botanic Garden* to **800-555-1136**

i. **Close** the form. **Open** the **Navigation Pane**.

3 Under **Tables**, click **7C Gardens**. On the **Create tab**, in the **Forms group**, click **Form**. **Close** the **Navigation Pane**.

a. Switch to **Design** view. In the **Detail** section, click on the **Layout Selector** to select the controls in the main form and subform. Under **Form Design Tools**, click the **Arrange tab**. In the **Table group**, click **Remove Layout**. Click an empty area of the design grid to deselect the controls.

b. Switch to **Layout** view. In the main form, click the **Garden Name text box control**. Press (Shift) and then click each of the text boxes in the main form. Point to the right edge of one of the text box controls until the pointer displays, and then drag to the left until there is approximately **1 inch** of space between *Gardens* and the right edge of the text box control. Click the **subform control** to select it. Point to the right edge of the **subform control** until the pointer displays. Drag to the left until there is approximately **0.25 inches** of space after the **Subject control** in the subform.

c. Switch to **Design** view. Change the form title to **Lastname Firstname 7C Gardens and TV Shows Subform** Click to the right of **Gardens**, and delete the space. Hold down (Shift), and then press (Enter). **Save** the form as **Lastname Firstname 7C Gardens and TV Shows Subform**

d. Using the techniques you have practiced, insert **a07C_MWB_Logo** in the **Form Header** section, and change the **Picture Size Mode** property to **Zoom**.

e. Point to the middle right sizing handle of the **logo control** until the pointer displays. Drag to the right between *TV* and *Shows*.

f. Click in an empty area of the design grid, and then click the **title's label control**. Point to the right edge of the **title's label control** until the pointer displays. Drag to the left until the right edge of the label control aligns with the **6-inch mark on the horizontal ruler**. With the **title's label control** selected, under **Form Design Tools**, click the **Format tab**. In the **Font group**, click **Center**.

g. Point to the right edge of the main form until the pointer displays. Drag to the left until the edge aligns with the **6.5-inch mark on the horizontal ruler**.

h. **Save** the form, and then switch to **Form** view. **Close** the form.

(continues on next page)

Chapter Review

4 **Open** the **Navigation Pane**. Under **Forms**, open **7C Gardens Form** in **Design** view.

a. Under **Form Design Tools**, on the **Design tab**, in the **Controls group**, verify that the **Use Control Wizards** option is active. In the form, point to the top of the **Form Footer section bar** until the pointer displays. Drag downward **1 inch**.

b. In the **Navigation Pane**, under **Tables**, drag **7C Contacts** onto **7C Gardens Main Form** at the **1.75-inch mark on the vertical ruler** and even with the left edge of the form.

c. In the **SubForm Wizard** dialog box, click **Define my own**. Under **Form/report fields**, in the **first list box**, click the **arrow**, and then click **Garden Name**. Under **Subform/subreport fields**, in the **first list box**, click the **arrow**, and then click **Garden Name**. Click **Next**. Under **What name would you like for your subform or subreport?**, type **Lastname Firstname 7C Garden Contact Subform** and then click **Finish**. **Close** the **Navigation Pane**. Close the **Field List**, if necessary.

d. **Save** the form. With the subform selected, under **Form Design Tools**, on the **Design tab**, in the **Tools group**, click **Property Sheet**. Verify that the Selection type is *Form*. Change the **Default View** property to **Single Form**. **Close** the **Property Sheet**.

e. In the subform, click the **Garden Name label control**, press (Shift), click the **Garden Name combo box control**, and then press (Delete). Move the other controls up to close the empty space. Switch to **Layout** view.

f. Reduce the size of the **First Name**, **Last Name**, and **Phone Number** controls so there is approximately **0.5 inches** of blank space to the right of the data. Point to the lower right corner of the **subform control** until the pointer displays. Drag to the left and up until the **right edge of the subform control** aligns with the **right edge of the text box controls** and the **bottom edge of the subform control** aligns with the **bottom of the E-mail controls**.

g. Delete the **subform label control**, which displays *Lastname Firstname 7C Garden Contact Subform*.

h. Switch to **Design** view, saving changes if necessary. Change the title of the form to **Lastname Firstname 7C Gardens and Contacts** and then place *7C Gardens and Contacts* on the second line. Adjust the width of the **title's label control** so that the **right edge of the title's label control** aligns with the **right edge of the main form field's text box controls**.

i. **Save** the form. Switch to **Form** view. **Close** the form. **Open** the **Navigation Pane**. In the **Navigation Pane**, under **Forms**, **Rename** *7C Gardens Form* to **Lastname Firstname 7C Gardens and Contacts Form**

5 In the **Navigation Pane**, under **Forms**, open **7C Contacts TC Form** in **Design** view, and then **Close** the **Navigation Pane**.

a. Point to the top of the **Form Footer section bar**, and drag downward to the **3-inch mark on the vertical ruler**. Under **Form Design Tools**, on the **Design tab**, in the **Controls group**, click **Tab Control**. Move the pointer into the **Detail** section until the plus (**+**) sign of the pointer is aligned approximately with the **0.25-inch mark on the horizontal and vertical rulers**, and then click.

b. In the selected **tab control**, point to the **right middle sizing handle** until the pointer displays. Drag to the right until the right edge of the tab control aligns with the **6-inch mark on the horizontal ruler**.

c. Under **Form Design Tools**, on the **Design tab**, in the **Tools group**, click **Add Existing Fields**. In the **Field List**, click **Garden Name**. Hold down (Shift), and then click **Last Name**. Point to a selected field, and then drag onto the first tab until the top of the arrow of the pointer aligns with the **1.5-inch mark on the horizontal ruler** and with the **0.75-inch mark on the vertical ruler**. **Close** the **Field List**.

d. Click anywhere in the form to deselect the controls. Click the **Garden Name combo box control**, and point to the **right edge** of the control until the pointer displays. Drag to the right until the right edge aligns with the **5-inch mark on the horizontal ruler**.

e. Click to select the **Last Name label control**, press (Shift), and click to select the **Last Name text box control**. Drag the controls to the right and upward until they align with the **First Name controls** and there is approximately **0.5 inches** of space between the two controls.

(continues on next page)

Chapter Review

f. In the **Detail** section, click the **second tab**, which has no controls. Under **Form Design Tools**, on the **Design tab**, in the **Tools group**, click **Add Existing Fields**. In the **Field List**, click **Phone Number**. Hold down ⌈Shift⌉, and then click **E-mail**. Point to the selected fields, and then drag onto the second tab until the top of the pointer arrow aligns with the **1.5-inch mark on the horizontal ruler** and the **0.75-inch mark on the vertical ruler**. **Close** the **Field List**. **Save** the form.

g. Click the **first page tab.** Right-click the **first page**, and then click **Properties**. The Property Sheet displays *Selection type: Page*. Click in the **Caption** property setting box, type **Contact Name** and then press ⌈Enter⌉.

h. Click the **second tab** to display its **Property Sheet**. Click in the **Caption** property setting box, type **Contact Information** and then press ⌈Enter⌉. **Close** the **Property Sheet**.

i. In the form, click the **Contact Name** to display the first page of the form. Change the form's **title** to **Lastname Firstname 7C Contacts Tab Control Form** and then place *7C Contacts Tab Control Form* on the second line. Switch to **Form** view.

j. **Save** and **Close** the form.

6 ▶ **Open** the **Navigation Pane**. Rename the *7C Contacts TC Form* as **Lastname Firstname 7C Contacts Tab Control Form**

7 ▶ Resize the **Navigation Pane** so all object names display fully. **Close** the database, and then **Close** Access.

8 ▶ As directed by your instructor, submit your database for grading.

You have completed Project 7C ▐ **END**

Chapter Review

Skills Review | **Project 7D Featured Gardens**

MWB Productions maintains a database of the historic gardens that are featured in the *Midwest Botanicals* television show. Creating advanced reports will help the president and officers of the production company view the information in the database in a different way. In this project, you will create advanced reports that display data from multiple tables and from a parameter query. You will also create an alphabetic index of historic gardens. Your completed Navigation Pane will look similar to Figure 7.48.

Project Files

For Project 7D, you will need the following file:

a07D_Featured_Gardens

You will save your database as:

Lastname_Firstname_7D_Featured_Gardens

Project Results

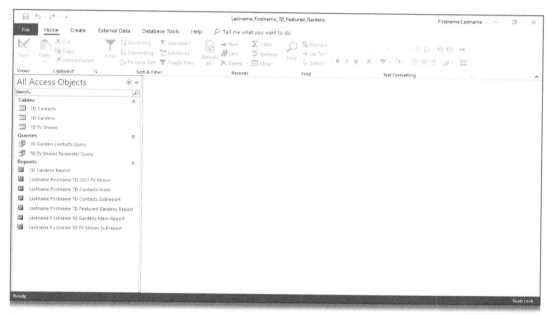

Figure 7.48

(continues on next page)

Chapter Review

1 ▶ Start Access. Open the **a07D_Featured_Gardens** file. Save the database in your **Access Chapter 7** folder as **Lastname_Firstname_7D_Featured_Gardens** If necessary, enable the content.

2 ▶ Make a copy of the *7D Gardens Report*, name it **Lastname Firstname 7D Gardens Main Report** and then open in **Design** view. **Close** the **Navigation Pane**.

a. In the **Report Header** section, click the **title label control**. Add your **Lastname Firstname** before the title.

b. In the report, point to the top of the **Page Footer section bar**, and then drag it downward to the **1-inch mark on the vertical ruler**.

c. Under **Report Design Tools**, on the **Design tab**, in the **Controls group**, verify that the **Use Controls Wizard** option is active. In the **Controls group**, click **Subform/Subreport**. Point to the **Detail** section so the plus sign (+) aligns with the **0.25-inch mark on the horizontal ruler** and the **0.5-inch mark on the vertical ruler**, and then click.

d. In the dialog box, verify that **Use existing Tables and Queries** is selected, and then click **Next**. Select **Table: 7D TV Shows**. Under **Available Fields**, double-click **TV Show #**, **Original Air Date**, and **Subject**. Click **Next** two times. Name the report **Lastname Firstname 7D TV Shows Subreport** Click **Finish**.

e. Delete the **subreport label control**. Select the **label controls** in the subreport **Report Header**, and then, under **Report Design Tools**, on the **Format tab**, in the **Font group**, click the **Font Color arrow**. Under **Theme Colors**, on the first row, click the first color. In the subreport, right-click the **Report Header** and point to the **Fill/Back Color arrow**. Under **Standard Colors**, on the sixth row, click the seventh color. **Save** the report.

f. Switch to **Layout** view. Close the **Field List**, if necessary. In the subreport, click the **Original Air Date** text box control. Under **Report Layout Tools**, click the **Format tab**. In the **Control Formatting group**, click **Conditional Formatting**. In the dialog box, click **New Rule**. Click the arrow to the right of the box that displays *between*, and select **less than**. Click inside the empty text box, and type **1/1/22**

g. Click **Bold**, and then click the **Font color arrow.** Under **Standard Colors**, on the sixth row, click the sixth color. Click **OK** two times.

h. Scroll down to the subreport for *Missouri Botanical Garden*, and select the **TV Show # label** and **text box controls**. Resize them so they are just wide enough to display the data. Select the **Original Air Date label** and **text box controls**. Resize them so they are just wide enough to display the data, and then drag to the left until there is approximately **0.25 inches** after *TV Show #*. Select the **Subject label** and **text box controls**, and then drag to the left until there is approximately **0.25 inches** after *Original Air Date*. Resize the **subreport control** so it is just wide enough to display the data. **Save** the changes.

i. Switch to **Design** view. Select the **subreport control**. Under **Report Design Tools**, click the **Format tab**. In the **Control Formatting group**, click **Shape Outline**. Under **Theme Colors**, on the first row, click the eighth color. **Save** the report. If a message box appears, click **OK**.

j. Click any **subreport control**, and then under **Report Design Tools**, on the **Design tab**, in the **Tools group**, click **Subreport in New Window**. Resize the subreport to **5.75 inches wide**. In the **Detail** section, click the **TV Show # text box control**. Under **Report Design Tools**, on the **Design tab**, in the **Grouping & Totals group**, click **Totals**, and then click **Count Records** to insert a calculated control.

k. Click the **Report Footer section bar**, and then press F4 . On the **Property Sheet Format tab**, click in the **Visible** property setting box. Set it to **No**.

l. Click the **Count calculated control**, and then click the **Property Sheet Other tab**. In the **Name** property setting box, type **Count of Shows Close** the **Property Sheet**. **Save** and **Close** the subreport.

m. Under **Report Design Tools**, on the **Design tab**, in the **Controls group**, click **Text Box**. Move the mouse pointer to the **Detail** section until it aligns with the **6.5-inch mark on the horizontal ruler** and the **1.5-inch mark on the vertical ruler**, and then click.

n. Click the associated **label control**, and then press F4 . Click the **Property Sheet Format tab**, and in the **Caption** property setting box, type **# of TV Shows:** In the **Width** property setting box, type **1** and then press Enter . Drag the **# of TV Shows unbound control** until it aligns with the right edge of the label control.

(continues on next page)

Chapter Review

o. Click the **unbound text box control**. Click the **Property Sheet Data tab**, and then click in the **Control Source** property setting box. Click **Build**. In the dialog box, using your own first and last names and double-clicking objects from the list, type **=IIf(IsError([Lastname Firstname 7D TV Shows Subreport].[Report]![Count of Shows]),0,[Lastname Firstname 7D TV Shows Subreport].[Report]![Count of Shows])** In the **Expression Builder** dialog box, click **OK**. **Close** the **Property Sheet**. Resize the textbox control so the right edge aligns with the **7-inch mark on the horizontal ruler**. Resize the report to **7.25 inches wide**.

p. **Save** the report. View the report in **Print Preview**, and view the report. **Close** the **Print Preview** window and the **report**.

3 **Open** the **Navigation Pane**. Make a copy of **7D Gardens Report**, name it **Lastname Firstname 7D Featured Gardens Report** and then open in **Design** view.

a. In the **Report Header** section, click the **title label control**. Select the text, type **Lastname Firstname 7D Featured Gardens** and then press Enter.

b. Point to the top of the **Page Footer section bar**, and drag downward to the **1-inch mark on the vertical ruler**.

c. In the **Navigation Pane**, under **Tables**, click **7D Contacts**, and then drag the table onto the **Detail** section until the pointer aligns with the **0.5-inch mark on the horizontal and vertical rulers**. In the **SubReport Wizard** dialog box, verify that **Choose from a list** is selected and **Show 7D Contacts for each record in 7D Gardens using Garden Name** is selected, and then click **Next**. Name the subreport **Lastname Firstname 7D Contacts Subreport** and then click **Finish**.

d. If necessary, select the subreport, press F4, and then **Close** the **Navigation Pane**. If necessary, click the **Property Sheet Data tab**, click in the **Link Master Fields** property setting box, and then click **Build**. In the **Subreport Field Linker** dialog box, click **OK**. On the **Property Sheet Format tab**, in the **Width** property setting box, type **8.5 Close** the **Property Sheet**.

e. Switch to **Layout** view. In the subreport, delete the controls for **Garden Name**. Adjust the widths and positions of the remaining controls to fit data without gaps of blank space between fields.

f. Switch to **Design** view, saving changes. Resize the **subreport control** to **6.25 inches wide**. Select the **subreport label control**, and drag to the right until it is approximately centered across the subreport control.

g. With the label control selected, click **Font Color**. Under Theme Colors, on the sixth row, click the fourth color, and then **Bold** the text.

h. In the subreport, in the **Page Header**, from the Theme Colors, apply a **Background Color** using the first row, the fourth color. Select the **label controls** in **Page Header**, and change the **Font Color** to **White**.

i. Adjust the width of the report to **7 inches wide**. **Save** the report, click **Yes** in the dialog box, and then switch to **Report** view. **Close** the report.

4 On the **Create tab**, in the **Reports group**, click **Report Wizard**.

a. In the **Report Wizard** dialog box, select the **Query: 7D TV Shows Parameter Query**. Move all of the fields to the **Selected Fields** box, and then click **Next** two times. Sort the records by **Original Air Date** in **Ascending** order, and then click **Next**. Under **Orientation**, click **Landscape**, and then click **Next**. Name the report **Lastname Firstname 7D 2022 TV Shows** and then click **Finish**. For the first date, type **1/1/22** and for the second date, type **12/31/22**

b. Switch to **Layout View**. Resize and move all label and text box controls to fit the data within the page constraints. **Save** the report, and then switch to **Design** view.

c. Point to the top of the **Page Header section bar**, and drag downward to the top of the **Detail section bar**.

d. Under **Report Design Tools**, on the **Design tab**, in the **Controls group**, click **Text Box**. In the **Report Header** section, align the top of the plus (**+**) sign of the pointer with the **0.25-inch mark on the horizontal ruler** and the **0.5-inch mark on the vertical ruler**, and then click. Click the associated **label control**, and then press Delete.

e. Click the **unbound text box control**, and then press F4. Click the **Property Sheet Data tab**, click in the **Control Source** property setting box, and then click **Build**. In the displayed **Expression Builder** dialog box, type **="Original Air Date Between "&[Enter first date]&" and "&[Enter second date]** making sure that you press Spacebar after *Between* and before and after *and*. Click **OK**. **Close** the Property Sheet.

(continues on next page)

7
ACCESS

Chapter Review

f. With the text box control selected, under **Report Design Tools**, click the **Format tab**. In the **Font group**, click **Center**. In the **Font group**, click the **Font Size arrow**, and click **14**. Increase the size of the text box control until it is the same size and aligns with the right edge of the report title or to the **5-inch mark on the horizontal ruler** (whichever is greater).

g. **Save** the report, and switch to **Report** view. For the first date, enter **1/1/22** and for the second date, enter **12/31/22** Switch to **Print Preview** view to view the parameters in the report. **Close** the **Print Preview** window and the **report**, and then **Open** the **Navigation Pane**.

5 In the **Navigation Pane**, under **Queries**, click **7D Garden Contacts Query**, and then **Close** the **Navigation Pane**. On the **Create tab**, in the **Reports group**, click **Report Wizard**.

a. In the **Report Wizard** dialog box, **Query: 7D Garden Contacts Query** should display. Move all of the fields to the **Selected Fields** box, and then click **Next**. Click **Remove Field** to remove the grouping. Click **Next** three times. For the title of the report, type **Lastname Firstname 7D Contacts Index** and then click **Finish**. **Close** Print Preview.

b. **Save** the report, and then switch to **Layout** view. Adjust the width of all controls so that all of the data displays for every record.

c. Under **Report Layout Tools**, on the **Design tab**, in the **Grouping & Totals group**, click **Group & Sort**. In the **Group, Sort, and Total pane**, click **Add a group**. From the displayed list, click **Last Name**. On the **Group bar**, click the **More arrow**. Click the **by entire value arrow**, and click the **by first character** option button. Click in an empty area of the report.

d. In the **Group, Sort, and Total pane**, on the **Group bar**, click **More**, and then to the right of **with title**, click the **Last Name** link. With *Last Name* selected in the displayed **Zoom** dialog box, press Delete, and then click **OK**. Delete the empty label control box placeholder. **Close** the **Group, Sort, and Total pane**.

e. Click the **text box control** that displays the letter *B*. Under **Report Layout Tools**, click the **Format tab**, in the **Font group**, change the **Font Size** to **16**. Resize the control to approximately **1 inch**.

f. **Save** the report, and then switch to **Report** view.

g. **Close** the report, and then **Open** the **Navigation Pane**. **Resize** the **Navigation Pane** so all object names display fully. **Close** the database, and **Close** Access.

6 As directed by your instructor, submit your database for grading.

You have completed Project 7D `END`

Content-Based Assessments (Mastery and Transfer of Learning)

Apply **7A** skills from these Objectives:

1. Create a Split Form
2. Create a Form and a Subform
3. Create a Multi-Page Form

Mastering Access   Project 7E Phone Orders

MWB Productions maintains a database where customers can place telephone orders for the gardening supplies that are featured in the *Midwest Botanicals* television show. Ruthann Hansen, president of MWB Productions, wants the database forms to display related data. For example, she is interested in displaying the orders on one form. She also wants to display the CSR (customer service representative) information in a tab control form. In the following project, you will customize the company's forms to display data in two ways on the same form, to display data from multiple tables on one form, and to display data on multiple pages on a form. Your completed Navigation Pane will look similar to Figure 7.49.

Project Files

For Project 7E, you will need the following files:

a07E_Phone_Orders
a07E_MWB_Logo
You will save your database as:
Lastname_Firstname_7E_Phone_Orders

Project Results

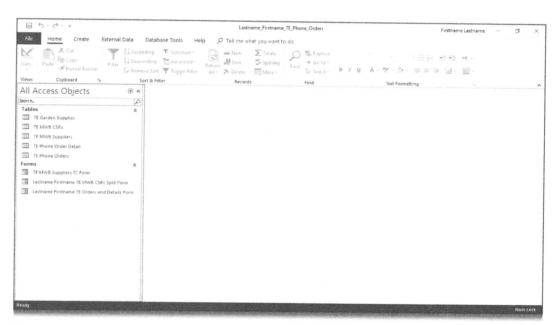

Figure 7.49

(continues on next page)

Content-Based Assessments (Mastery and Transfer of Learning)

Mastering Access: Project 7E Phone Orders (continued)

1 Start Access. Locate and open the **a07E_Phone_ Orders** file. **Save** the database in your **Access Chapter 7** folder as **Lastname_Firstname_7E_Phone_Orders** If necessary, enable the content.

2 In the **Navigation Pane**, click **7E MWB CSRs** and then **Close** the **Navigation Pane**. Create a split form, and **Save** it as **Lastname Firstname 7E MWB CSRs Split Form**

3 Switch to **Design** view. In the **Property Sheet**, click the **Selection type arrow**. Click **Form** to display the Form Property Sheet. Click the **Split Form Printing** property setting box arrow, and then click **Form Only**. Click the **Split Form Orientation** property setting box arrow, and then click **Datasheet on Top**. **Close** the **Property Sheet**.

4 Switch to **Layout** view. Move the **Split Form Splitter Bar** between records 3 and 4. Select the **Photo controls** for *Andi Shell*. Under **Form Layout Tools**, on the **Arrange tab**, click **Tabular** to remove the Photo field from the layout. Delete the **Photo label control**. Click the **Photo control**. In the **Property Sheet**, click the **Picture Alignment** property setting box arrow, and then click **Top Right**. Close the **Property Sheet**. Align the left edge of the **Photo control** with the left edge of the photograph. **Save** the form.

5 Add the **a07E_MWB_Logo** to the form, and change the **Picture Size Mode** property to **Zoom**. Increase the width of the logo control to **2** Close the **Property Sheet**. Click the **title's label control**, and then type your **Lastname Firstname** at the beginning. Resize the **label control** to fit the title. **Save** the form.

6 Switch to **Form** view, and then navigate to Record 3. In the form section, change the **Last Name** from *Kay* to **Martin Save** the form. **Close** the form. **Open** the Navigation Pane.

7 Click the **7E Phone Orders** table. Click the **Create tab**, and then click **Form**. **Close** the Navigation Pane. In the main form, click the **Supplier Name combo box control**. Resize the **combo box control** so there is approximately **1 inch** of space between *Shop* and the right edge of the text box control.

8 Switch to **Design** view. Remove the subform from the stacked layout. Drag the right edge of the subform to the left until it aligns with the **3-inch mark on the horizontal ruler**. Move the subform under and to the center of the bottom of the main form. Drag the bottom edge upward until it aligns with the **3-inch mark on the vertical ruler**.

9 **Save** the form as **Lastname Firstname 7E Orders and Details Form** Drag the right bottom corner of the control downward to the top of the **Detail** section bar and to the right until it aligns with the **2-inch mark on the horizontal ruler**.

10 Select the **Title label control** box and resize the placeholder so the right edge aligns with the **6.25-inch mark on the horizontal ruler**. Edit the **title** to be **Lastname Firstname 7E Phone Orders and Details Form** with only your name on the first line. **Center** the title text.

11 Point to the right edge of the form. Drag to the left until the right edge of the form aligns with the **6.5-inch mark on the horizontal ruler**.

12 **Save** the form, and then switch to **Form** view and view the records. **Close** the form. **Open** the Navigation Pane.

13 Open **7E MWB Suppliers TC Form** in **Design** view. Drag the **Form footer section bar** downward **2 inches**. Insert a tab control at the **0.5-inch mark on the horizontal ruler** and the **0.25-inch mark on the vertical ruler**. Increase the size of the tab control by dragging to the right until the right edge aligns with the **6-inch mark on the horizontal ruler**.

14 To the **first page** of the **tab control**, at the **1.5-inch mark on the horizontal ruler** and the **1.25-inch mark on the vertical ruler**, add the **Supplier #** and **Supplier Name** fields. Resize the **Supplier # text box control** so the right edge aligns at the **2-inch mark on the horizontal ruler**. Position the **Supplier Name** controls so the left edge of the **Supplier Name label control** is at the **2.25-inch mark on the horizontal ruler** and the top edge of the controls are aligned with the top edge of the **Supplier # text box control**. Resize the **Supplier Name text box control** so the right edge aligns at the **6-inch mark on the horizontal ruler**. On the first page of the tab control, change the **Caption** property to **Supplier**

15 To the **second page** of the **tab control**, at the **1.5-inch mark on the horizontal ruler** and the **1.25-inch mark on the vertical ruler**, add the following fields: **Address, City, State, Postal Code,** and **Phone.** Extend the widths of all text box controls to the **4-inch mark on the horizontal ruler**. Edit the **Caption** property to display **Directory Information**

16 Change the **title** of the form to **Lastname Firstname 7E Suppliers Tab Control Form** placing *Tab Control Form* on a second line. Align the right edge of the title's label control with the **5.5-inch mark on the horizontal ruler**. **Center** the text of the title. Resize the form to **6.5 inches** wide. Switch to **Form** view.

17 **Save** and **Close** the form. **Resize** the **Navigation Pane** so all object names display fully. **Close** the database, and then **Close** Access.

18 As directed by your instructor, submit your database for grading.

You have completed Project 7E | END

Content-Based Assessments (Mastery and Transfer of Learning)

Apply 7B skills from these Objectives:

4. Create and Modify a Subreport
5. Create a Report Based on a Parameter Query
6. Create an Alphabetic Index

Mastering Access	Project 7F Customer Service

MWB Productions maintains a customer service phone line where viewers can order gardening supplies that are featured in the *Midwest Botanicals* television show. Creating advanced reports will help the president and officers of the production company study the information in the database in a different way. In the following project, you will create advanced reports that display data from multiple tables and from a parameter query. You will also create an alphabetic index of the last names of the customer service representatives. Your completed Navigation Pane will look similar to Figure 7.50.

Project Files

For Project 7F, you will need the following files:

a07F_Customer_Service

a07F_MWB_Logo

You will save your database as:

Lastname_Firstname_7F_Customer_Service

Project Results

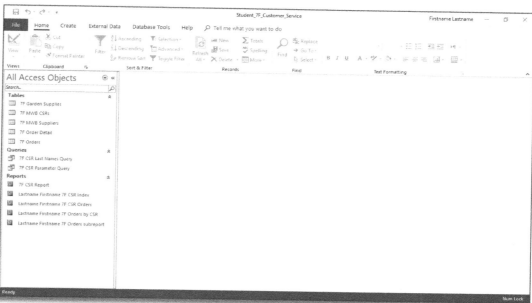

Figure 7.50

(continues on next page)

Mastering Access: Project 7F Customer Service (continued)

1 Start Access. Open the **a07F_Customer_Service** file. Save the database in your **Access Chapter 7** folder as **Lastname_Firstname_7F_Customer_Service** If necessary, enable the content.

2 Make a copy of the **7F CSR Report** and save it as **Lastname Firstname 7F CSR Orders** Open the report in **Design** view. **Close** the **Field List**, if necessary. **Close** the **Navigation Pane**.

3 Edit the **Title** of the report by changing *Lastname Firstname* to your first and last names. **Center** the text in the control.

4 Drag the **Page Footer section bar** down to the **1.5-inch mark on the vertical ruler**. Insert a **Subform/Subreport** control at the **0.5-inch mark on the horizontal and vertical rulers**.

5 Using the **SubReport Wizard**, select **Use existing Tables and Queries**. From the **7F Orders** table, select the following fields in this order: **Order #**, **Order Date**, **Supplier Name**, and **Amount**. Show **7F Orders** for each record in **7F MWB CSRs** using **ID#**. Add your **Lastname Firstname** to the beginning of the subreport's default name.

6 Switch to **Layout** view. Delete the **subreport label control**. Scroll down to see the subreport for *Singh Brothers Hardware & Garden*. In the subreport, resize the label and text box controls to just fit the data. Move the controls to close blank space between fields. Add a border of **Green 5** under **Standard Colors** and **2 pt Thickness** to the subreport. **Save** the report.

7 Switch to **Design** view. Select the subreport, and open it in its own window. Resize the subreport control to **5.0 inches wide**. Change the **Background Color** of the report header in the subreport to a shade of brown under **Standard Colors**. Select the label controls, and then change the **Font Color** to **White, Background 1**. **Save** and **Close** the subreport. Resize the **subreport control** until it is **5.25 inches wide**. If necessary, drag the **Page Footer section bar** back up to the **1.5-inch mark on the horizontal ruler**. Resize the report to **7.5 inches wide**.

8 Switch to **Layout** view. In any subreport control, click the **Amount text box control**. Display the **Conditional Formatting** dialog box, and create a **New Rule** to format the font for any **Amount** greater than **500** as a shade of green and apply **Bold**. **Save** the report.

9 **Close** the report, and then **Open** the **Navigation Pane**.

10 Click to select the **7F CSR Parameter Query**. Using the **Report Wizard**, add all **Available Fields** to the **Selected Fields** list. View the data by **7F Orders**. **Group** on the **ID#** field. **Sort Ascending** by **Order Date**. Use **Stepped** layout and **Portrait** orientation. Name the report **Lastname Firstname 7F Orders by CSR** Select **Modify the report's design**, and then click **Finish**. **Close** the **Navigation Pane**. **Save** the report.

11 Delete the **label** and **textbox controls** for the **ID** field. Resize the **Order Date** controls so the entire label is visible. Resize the **First Name** and **Last Name** controls to **1.25 inches** each. Move the fields to remove the blank space between them.

12 Delete the **report title control box**. To the **Report Header section**, add the **a07F_MWB_Logo**. Expand the width of the logo to the **2-inch mark on the horizontal ruler** and to the bottom of the **Report Header section**. Delete the **Title** placeholder. Add a **text box control** at the **2.25-inch mark on the horizontal ruler** and **0.25-inch mark on the vertical ruler**. Delete the **text box label control**. Click the **unbound text box control**. Click the **Property Sheet Data tab**, and then click in the **Control Source** property setting box. Open the **Expression Builder** dialog box. Type the following concatenated string in the text control box: **="7F Orders Taken by "&[First Name]&" "&[Last Name]** Align and resize the title between the **2.25-** and **6-inch marks on the horizontal ruler**. Change the font size to **14**. Size the text box **To Fit**.

13 In the **Page Footer section**, click in the **Now()** control box to the right of the equal sign. Type **"Report prepared by Firstname Lastname on "&** Widen the control so the right edge aligns with the **4.5-inch mark on the horizontal ruler**. Resize the **Page number control** so it displays between the **5.5-inch** and **7-inch mark on the horizontal ruler**. Resize the report to **7 inches wide**. **Save** the report.

14 Switch to **Report** view. In the **Enter Parameter Value** message box, under **Enter CSR #**, type **0559**

15 **Close** the report, saving changes. **Open** the **Navigation Pane**.

16 Click **7F CSR Last Names Query**. Create a report using the **Report Wizard**. From the **Available Fields** list, add **Last Name** to the **Selected Fields** list. No sorting is required. Use **Tabular** layout and **Portrait** orientation. Title the report **Lastname Firstname 7F CSR Index Close** Print Preview. **Close** the **Navigation Pane**.

(continues on next page)

Mastering Access: Project 7F Customer Service (continued)

17 Switch to **Layout** view. In the **Group, Sort, and Total** pane, click **Add a group**, and then click **Last Name**. On the **Group bar**, click the **More arrow**. Click the **by entire value arrow**, and click the **by first character** option button. Click in an empty area of the report. On the **Group bar**, click **do not keep group together on one page arrow**, and from the displayed list, click **keep whole group together on one page**. Remove the **Lastname Firstname** title and placeholder. **Save** the report.

18 Click the **text box control** that displays the letter *A*, and change the **Font Size** to **16**. Click the **Font Color arrow**. Under **Theme Colors**, on the first line, click the sixth color and then apply **Bold** and **Italic**.

19 **Save** the report, and then switch to **Print Preview** and page through the report.

20 **Close** the report, and then **Open** the **Navigation Pane. Resize** the **Navigation Pane** so all object names display fully. **Close** the database, and then **Close** Access.

21 As directed by your instructor, submit your database for grading.

You have completed Project 7F END

Content-Based Assessments (Mastery and Transfer of Learning)

MyLab IT Grader

Mastering Access | **Project 7G Garden Tours**

Apply 7A and 7B skills from these Objectives:

1. Create a Split Form
2. Create a Form and a Subform
3. Create a Multi-Page Form
4. Create and Modify a Subreport
5. Create a Report Based on a Parameter Query
6. Create an Alphabetic Index

MWB Productions produces the television show *Midwest Botanicals*. The show's hosts present tours of public and private gardens that showcase the various styles. Matthew Lee maintains an updated database about the tours of the featured historic gardens. In this project, you will design a multi-page form for the gardens and tour information that will be used to update this part of the production. You will also create a report based on a parameter query using the name of the garden. Your completed Navigation Pane will look similar to Figure 7.51.

Project Files for MyLab IT Grader

1. In your **MyLab IT** course, locate and click **Access 7G Garden Tours**, Download Materials, and then Download All Files.
2. Extract the zipped folder to your Access Chapter 7 folder. Close the Grader download screens.
3. Take a moment to open the downloaded **Access_7G_Garden_Tours_Instructions**; note any recent updates to the book.

Project Results

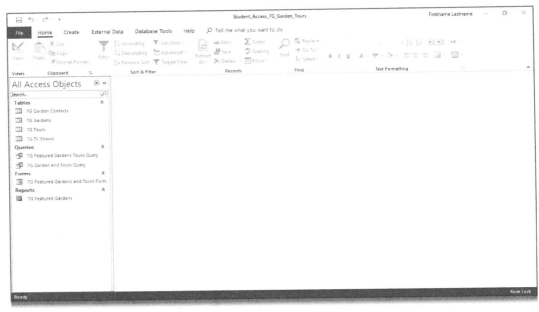

Figure 7.51

For Non-MyLab Submissions
For Project 7G, you will need:
a07G_Garden_Tours

Start with an Access Data File
In your Access Chapter 7 folder, save your database as:
Lastname_Firstname_7G_Garden_Tours

After you have saved your database, launch Access and open the database. On the next page, begin with Step 2.
After Step 8, submit your database as directed by your instructor.

(continues on next page)

Content-Based Assessments (Mastery and Transfer of Learning)

1 Start Access. Navigate to your **Access Chapter 7 folder**, and then double-click the Access file that you downloaded from **MyLab IT** that displays your name—**Student_Access_7G_Garden_Tours**.

2 If necessary, enable the content. Open **7G Featured Gardens and Tours Form** in **Design** view, and then **Close** the **Navigation Pane**. Drag the top of the **Form footer section bar** down to the **2.5-inch mark on the vertical ruler**. In the Detail section, add a **tab control** at the **0.25-inch mark on the vertical and horizontal rulers**.

3 Extend the right edge of the **tab control** to the **5-inch mark on the horizontal ruler**. To the first page of the **tab control**, on the **Property Sheet**, add a caption of **Garden** From the **Field List**, add the **Garden Name**, **Location**, and **State/Country** field at the **1.5-inch mark on the horizontal ruler** and the **1-inch mark on the vertical ruler**. Extend the **text box controls** to the **4.5-inch mark on the horizontal ruler**. To the second page of the **tab control**, add a caption of **Tours** Add the **Times**, **Cost**, and **Reservations** fields to the same position as the first page.

4 View the form in **Form** view. **Save** and **Close** the form, and then **Open** the **Navigation Pane**

5 Click the **7G Garden and Tours Query**. **Close** the **Navigation Pane**. Create a report using the **Report Wizard**. Use all of the fields. Do not add any grouping levels. **Sort** by **Subject** in **Ascending** order. Use **Tabular** layout and **Landscape** orientation. Title the report **7G Featured Gardens** Modify the report's design.

6 Select the **title control** and change the font color. Under Theme Colors, in the fifth row, click the tenth color and change the font size to **24**. Set the width of the **title control** to **9** and center it in the control. Resize the controls so the report width can be adjusted to **9 inches** wide. Change the report width to **9**.

7 Switch to **Layout** view. In the **Enter Parameter Value** message box, type **Missouri Botanical Garden Save** the report.

8 Close the report, and then **Open** the **Navigation Pane**. **Resize the Navigation Pane** so all object names display fully. **Close** the database, and then **Close Access**.

9 In **MyLab IT**, locate and click the Grader Project **7G Garden Tours**. In **step 3**, under **Upload Completed Assignment**, click **Choose File**. In the **Open** dialog box, navigate to your **Word Chapter 7 folder**, and then click your **Student_Access_7G_Garden_Tours** file one time to select it. In the lower right corner of the **Open** dialog box, click **Open**.

10 To submit your file to **MyLab IT** for grading, click **Upload**, wait a moment for a green **Success!** message, and then in **step 4**, click the blue **Submit for Grading** button. Click **Close Assignment** to return to your list of **Course Materials**.

You have completed Project 7G **END**

Content-Based Assessments (Critical Thinking)

Apply a combination of the 7A and 7B skills.

GO! Fix It	Project 7H Contests	IRC
GO! Make It	Project 7I Advertising	IRC
GO! Solve It	Project 7J Host Travel	IRC
GO! Solve It	Project 7K Special Programming	

Project Files

For Project 7K, you will need the following files:

a07K_Special_Programming
a07K_MWB_Logo

You will save your database as:

Lastname_Firstname_7K_Special_Programming

Ruthann Hansen, president of MWB Productions, has scheduled special programming segments for the *Midwest Botanicals* television show. These segments will focus on holiday and seasonal topics.

Open the **a07K_Special_Programming** database and save it as **Lastname_Firstname_7K_Special_Programming** In this project, you will use the *7K TV Shows Form* to create a multi-page form. To the first tab, add the TV Show # and the Original Air Date fields with a caption of **Show** To the second tab, add the Subject, Featured Garden, and Program fields with a caption of **Programming** Adjust all controls to display all data. In the title, replace *Lastname Firstname* with your first and last names. Rename the form as **Lastname Firstname 7K TV Shows Form**

Open the *7K Special Programs* report in Design view. Add the *7K Show Sponsors* table as a subreport. Link the reports using the TV Show # field. Accept the default name for the subreport. Remove the TV Show # controls from the subreport and reduce the width to 3 inches. Delete the subreport label control. Add a logo and two-line title including your Lastname Firstname to the report. Apply color in backgrounds, outlines, and fonts to create a well-formatted report on a portrait page. Save the report.

Create an alphabetic index on *7K Special Programs* using the Program field sorted in ascending order. Format the text box controls containing the letters. Arrange and adjust label and text box controls to display all data. Save as **Lastname Firstname 7K Special Programming Index**

As directed by your instructor, submit your database for grading.

		Performance Level		
		Exemplary	**Proficient**	**Developing**
Performance Criteria	**Create 7K TV Shows Form**	Form created with the correct controls and formatted as directed	Form created with no more than two missing elements	Report modified with more than two missing elements
	Modify 7K Special Programs report	Report modified and formatted correctly	Report modified with no more than two missing elements	Form created with more than two missing elements
	Create 7K Special Programming Index	Index created to include the correct controls, grouping, sorting, and formatting	Index created with no more than two missing elements	Index created with more than two missing elements

You have completed Project 7K | END

Outcomes-Based Assessments (Critical Thinking)

Rubric

The following outcomes-based assessments are open-ended assessments. That is, there is no specific correct result; your result will depend on your approach to the information provided. Make Professional Quality your goal. Use the following scoring rubric to guide you in how to approach the problem and then to evaluate how well your approach solves the problem.

The *criteria*—Software Mastery, Content, Format and Layout, and Process—represent the knowledge and skills you have gained that you can apply to solving the problem. The *levels of performance*—Professional Quality, Approaching Professional Quality, or Needs Quality Improvements—help you and your instructor evaluate your result.

	Your completed project is of Professional Quality if you:	Your completed project is Approaching Professional Quality if you:	Your completed project Needs Quality Improvements if you:
1-Software Mastery	Choose and apply the most appropriate skills, tools, and features and identify efficient methods to solve the problem.	Choose and apply some appropriate skills, tools, and features, but not in the most efficient manner.	Choose inappropriate skills, tools, or features, or are inefficient in solving the problem.
2-Content	Construct a solution that is clear and well organized, contains content that is accurate, appropriate to the audience and purpose, and is complete. Provide a solution that contains no errors of spelling, grammar, or style.	Construct a solution in which some components are unclear, poorly organized, inconsistent, or incomplete. Misjudge the needs of the audience. Have some errors in spelling, grammar, or style, but the errors do not detract from comprehension.	Construct a solution that is unclear, incomplete, or poorly organized, contains some inaccurate or inappropriate content, and contains many errors of spelling, grammar, or style. Do not solve the problem.
3-Format and Layout	Format and arrange all elements to communicate information and ideas, clarify function, illustrate relationships, and indicate relative importance.	Apply appropriate format and layout features to some elements, but not others. Overuse features, causing minor distraction.	Apply format and layout that does not communicate information or ideas clearly. Do not use format and layout features to clarify function, illustrate relationships, or indicate relative importance. Use available features excessively, causing distraction.
4-Process	Use an organized approach that integrates planning, development, self-assessment, revision, and reflection.	Demonstrate an organized approach in some areas, but not others; or, use an insufficient process of organization throughout.	Do not use an organized approach to solve the problem.

Outcomes-Based Assessments (Critical Thinking)

Apply a combination of the 7A and 7B skills.

GO! Think	Project 7L Plants

Project Files

For Project 7L, you will need the following files:

a07L_Plants
a07L_MWB_Logo

You will save your database as:

Lastname_Firstname_7L_Plants

As a promotion for the *Midwest Botanicals* television show, Ruthann Hansen, president of MWB Productions, is always looking for ways to increase the attendance in the live studio audience. She has decided to offer a featured plant to the guests in the audience.

Open the **a07L_Plants** database and save it as **Lastname_Firstname_7L_Plants** In this project, you will create a split form based on the *7L Flower/Plant* table. In the form, adjust the label and text box controls to display all data. Delete the Photo label control and arrange the label and text box controls so that the first column contains the ID#, Common Name, Scientific Name, and Photo fields. The photo should align with the left edge of the text boxes in the first column. The second column should display the other four fields. Add the **a07L_MWB_Logo** to the form header, change the Size Mode to Zoom, and resize the logo. Edit the form title to include your last and first names. Select the option to print the form only. Save the form as **Lastname Firstname 7L Flower/Plant Split Form**

Open the *7L TV Shows and Featured Plants* report in Design view. Create a subreport using the 7L Flower/Plant table linking the Featured Plant with the ID# fields. In the subreport, delete the ID#, Scientific Name, and Description fields. Resize and move the controls so all data is visible, and resize the subreport to 5.5 inches. Delete the subreport label control. In the Navigation Pane, rename the report to include your **Lastname Firstname**.

As directed by your instructor, submit your database for grading.

	You have completed Project 7L	END

GO! Think	Project 7M Seminars	IRC

You and GO!	Project 7N Club Directory	IRC

Creating Macros

ACCESS 2019

PROJECT
8A
Outcomes
Create and modify macros.

Objectives
1. Create a Standalone Macro with One Action
2. Add Multiple Actions to a Standalone Macro
3. Create an Embedded Macro
4. Print Macro Details

PROJECT
8B
Outcomes
Build macro groups.

Objectives
5. Create a Macro Group
6. Associate a Macro with an Event
7. Create a Data Macro

cunaplus/Shutterstock

In This Chapter

 GO! to Work with Access

Macros provide a way to automate tasks that you may need to perform repeatedly. For example, you may create a report or query that you open and print on a weekly basis. You can create a macro that prints the query or report when the user clicks a command button. You may also use a macro to perform a set of actions every time a database is opened. Related macros can be created in a group. Macros can be run automatically, through the Navigation Pane, or by associating them with other actions like clicking a button on a form or report. Data macros are created to validate and ensure the accuracy of data in a table.

Providence & Warwick Hospital serves the metropolitan area of Providence, Rhode Island, and the surrounding cities that include Warwick, Rhode Island, and Fall River, Massachusetts. It is a world-class medical facility providing care to adults and children through the hospital as well as a number of social service and multidisciplinary facilities, such as the Asthma Center and Adult Metabolism Clinic. Scientists at the hospital conduct research and clinical trials of new drugs. The hospital's medical staff focuses on innovation and new technologies to provide quality patient care to patients at every stage of life.

PROJECT 8A Employee Records

Project Activities

In Activities 8.01 through 8.07, you will help Jordan Jones, human resources director for Providence & Warwick Hospital, customize the employee records database to make it easier for his staff to use. You will create macros to automatically display a form and message box when an individual opens the database. The form will be ready for the staff to edit and update employment data for the hospital. Mr. Jones also wants you to add a button with an embedded macro to a form and embed a macro within a report. Finally, you will display and print a report that documents the details of the macros you created. When completed, your Navigation Pane will look similar to Figure 8.1.

Project Files for MyLab IT Grader

1. In your storage location, create a folder named **Access Chapter 8**.
2. In your **MyLab IT** course, locate and click **Access 8A Employee Records**, Download Materials, and then Download All Files.
3. Extract the zipped folder to your Access Chapter 8 folder. Close the Grader download screens.
4. Take a moment to open the downloaded **Access_8A_Employee_Records_Instructions**; note any recent updates to the book.

Project Results

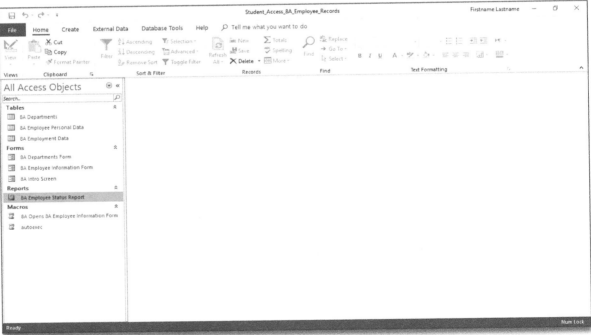

Figure 8.1 Project 8A Employee Records

For Non-MyLab Submissions

For Project 8A, you will need:

a08A_Employee_Records

Start with an Access Data File

In your storage location, create a folder named **Access Chapter 8**

In your Access Chapter 8 folder, save your database as:

Lastname_Firstname_8A_Employee_Records

After you have saved your database, open it to launch Access. On the next page, begin with Step 2.

Objective 1   Create a Standalone Macro with One Action

GO! Learn How
Video A8-1

A ***macro*** is a series of actions grouped as a single command to accomplish a task or multiple tasks automatically, adding functionality to your object or control. A ***standalone macro*** is an object displayed under Macros in the Navigation Pane. Some of the more commonly used actions are to open a report, find a record, or apply a filter to an object. An ***action*** is a self-contained instruction that can be combined with other actions to automate tasks.

Before creating a macro, you should list the actions you want to occur and in what order. You should determine if an argument applies to the action. An ***argument*** is a value that provides information to the action, such as the words to display in a message box. You should also determine if any conditions should be specified. A ***condition*** specifies that certain criteria must be met before the macro executes. A ***comment*** is used to provide explanatory information about the macro or the action.

Activity 8.01 | Creating a Standalone Macro

In this Activity, you will create a standalone macro that will display the *8A Employee Information Form* when the macro is run.

1 Start Access. In the Access opening screen, click **Open**. Navigate to your **Access Chapter 8 folder**, and then double-click the Access file that you downloaded from **MyLab IT** that displays your name—**Student_Access_8A_Employee_Records**.

2 If necessary, add the Access Chapter 8 folder to the Trust Center.

For this chapter, you must add the Access Chapter 8 folder to the Trust Center—you cannot just enable the content, because some of the macros will not execute properly if the database is not trusted.

3 In the **Navigation Pane**, under **Forms**, click **8A Employee Information Form** to select the form. **Close** [«] the **Navigation Pane**.

4 On the **Create tab**, in the **Macros & Code group**, click **Macro**, and then compare your screen with Figure 8.2.

The ***Macro Designer*** displays, which allows you to build the list of actions to be carried out when the macro runs. The Add New Action bar displays in the Macro Designer window, and the Action Catalog task pane displays on the right side of the screen. The buttons under Macro Tools on the Design tab are used to run, test, or modify a macro; to expand or collapse actions; and to display panes in the Macro Designer or to display more actions.

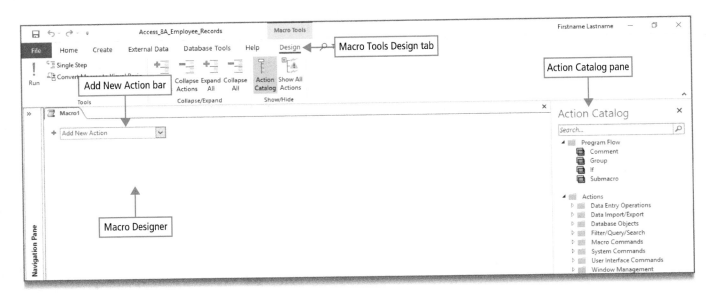

Figure 8.2

5 In the **Macro Designer**, in the **Add New Action bar**, click the **arrow**, and then compare your screen with Figure 8.3.

Because the Show All Actions button is not active, a shorter list of macro actions displays. These macro actions can be used in a database that is not trusted. You can click the Show All Actions button to display a longer list of macro actions; however, if the database is not trusted and you select a macro action that requires the database to be trusted, the macro will not execute. Instead, a message box will display.

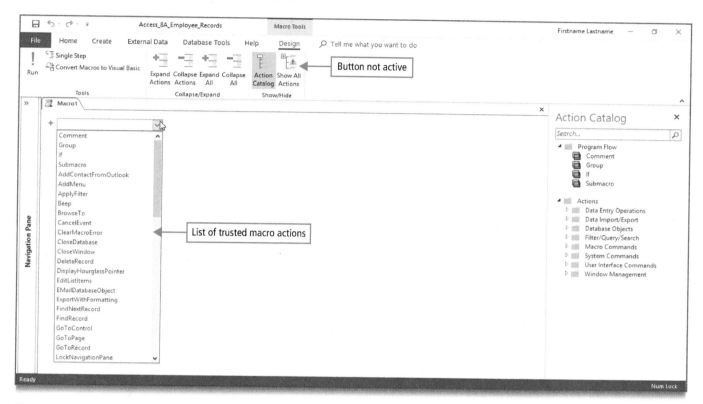

Figure 8.3

6 Scroll down the displayed list, and then click **OpenForm** to display the **OpenForm** action block. Compare your screen with Figure 8.4.

Notice the Form Name is a required argument and default settings display in the View box and Window Mode box.

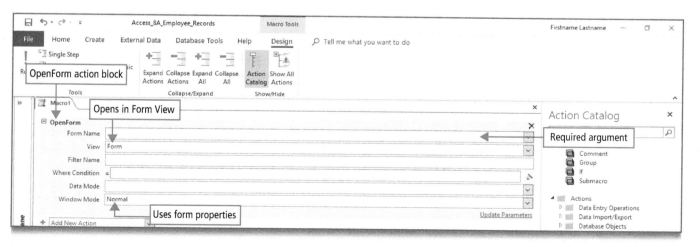

Figure 8.4

7 In the **Form Name** box, click the **arrow** to display all forms in the database, and then click **8A Employee Information Form**.

This is a required argument in the macro action.

8 In the **View** box, click the **arrow**. Notice that you can open the form in Form view, Design view, Print Preview, Datasheet view, PivotTable view, PivotChart view, or Layout view. Be sure that **Form** is selected.

The OpenForm action opens a form in Form view by default.

9 Point to the **Filter Name** box until the ScreenTip appears; read the description. Read the descriptions in the **Where Condition** box and the **Data Mode** box. Be sure that these arguments are left blank.

The Data Mode argument is used for forms that open in either Form view or Datasheet view. If left blank, Access opens the form in the data entry mode set in the form's Allow Edits, Allow Deletions, Allow Additions, and Data Entry property settings.

10 Point to the **Window Mode** box, and then read the description. Click the arrow, and notice the options for displaying the form. Be sure that the Window Mode setting is **Normal**.

11 In the **Action Catalog pane**, under **Program Flow**, double-click **Comment**. In the **Comment** text box that displays below the **OpenForm** action block, type **Displays the 8A Employee Information Form when the macro is run** Compare your screen with Figure 8.5.

You should always enter a description of a macro so that you and others can easily determine the actions that will occur when the macro runs. A green arrow displays to the right of the Comments dialog box; clicking it will move the comment above the action arguments.

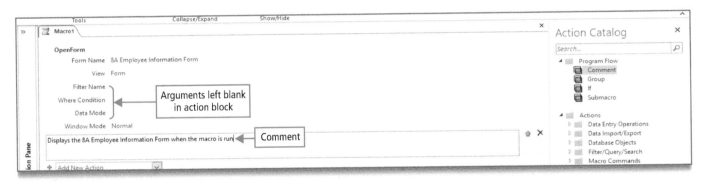

Figure 8.5

12 Under **Macro Tools**, on the **Design tab**, in the **Tools** group, click **Run**.

A message displays stating that you must save the macro before you run it.

13 In the displayed message box, click **Yes** to save the macro. In the **Save As** dialog box, type **8A Open 8A Employee Information Form** and then click **OK**.

The macro is saved and runs. When the macro runs, it displays the 8A Employee Information Form.

14 Close ☒ the **8A Employee Information Form**, and then **Close** ☒ the Macro Designer. **Open** ⟩⟩ the **Navigation Pane**, resize it so all object names display fully, and then compare your screen with Figure 8.6.

> In the Navigation Pane, a new group—Macros—displays, and the newly created macro object displays under the group name.

All Access Objects

Search...

Tables
- 8A Departments
- 8A Employee Personal Data
- 8A Employment Data

Forms
- 8A Departments Form
- Macros group ⟶ rmation Form
- 8A Intro Screen

Reports
- 8A Employee Status Report

Macros
- 8A Opens 8A Employee Information Form ⟵ Macro object

Figure 8.6

15 In the **Navigation Pane**, under **Macros**, double-click **8A Open 8A Employee Information Form**.

> Double-clicking a macro object causes the macro to run.

16 Close ☒ the form.

Activity 8.02 | Opening a Form in Its Own Window

MOS
4.1.2

  In this Activity, you will modify the properties of a form to create a pop-up, modal window. A *pop-up window* displays (pops up), usually contains a menu of commands, and stays on the screen until the user selects one of the commands. A *modal window* is a child (secondary window) to a parent window—the original window that opened the modal window—that takes over control of the parent window. A user cannot press any controls or enter any information in the parent window until the modal window is closed. Both pop-up and modal windows are commonly used when the database designer wants to direct a user's focus to the information in the window.

1 In the **Navigation Pane**, under **Forms**, double-click **8A Intro Screen** to open the form in **Form** view.

> Like most of the objects you have opened, the form displays with its own tab.

2 Switch to **Design** view. Under **Form Design Tools**, on the **Design tab**, in the **Tools group**, click **Property Sheet**. If the Property Sheet does not display *Selection type: Form*, click the **Selection type** arrow, and then click **Form**.

3 On the **Property Sheet**, click the **Other tab**. Click the **Pop Up property setting arrow**, and then click **Yes**. Click in the **Modal property setting box**, click the **arrow**, and then click **Yes**. Compare your screen with Figure 8.7.

The Pop Up property setting of Yes displays the object in its own window on top of all other opened objects. A setting of No displays the object as a tabbed object. Changing the Pop Up setting to Yes is most common for objects that you want to get the attention of the individual using the database. The Modal property setting is used to keep the focus on the opened form, because you cannot change the focus to another database object until the form is closed.

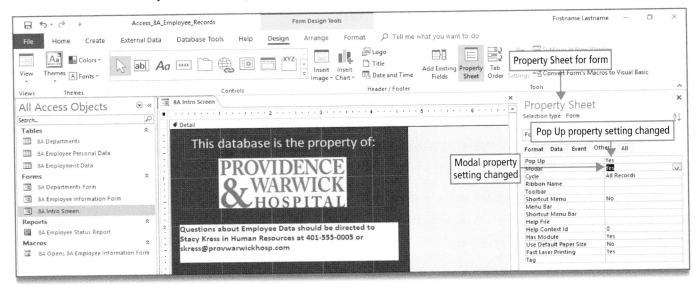

Figure 8.7

4 **Close** ⊠ the **Property Sheet**, and then **Close** ⊠ the form, saving changes when prompted. In the **Navigation Pane**, under **Macros**, double-click **8A Open 8A Employee Information Form**, and then under **Forms**, double-click **8A Intro Screen** to open both forms in Form view. Notice the text in the title bar of the pop-up window. In the **Navigation Pane**, under **Forms**, double-click **8A Departments Form**, and notice that the form does not open. Compare your screen with Figure 8.8.

8A Employee Information opens as a tabbed object, and *8A Intro Screen* opens in its own pop-up window. The pop-up window can be moved or closed. Until it is closed, the focus cannot be changed to another database object; that is why you cannot open *8A Departments Form*. The *8A Intro Screen* form displays a Close button, but no Minimize or Maximize buttons, because the Modal property setting is Yes. A Modal property setting of No means the screen can display the Minimize and Maximize buttons.

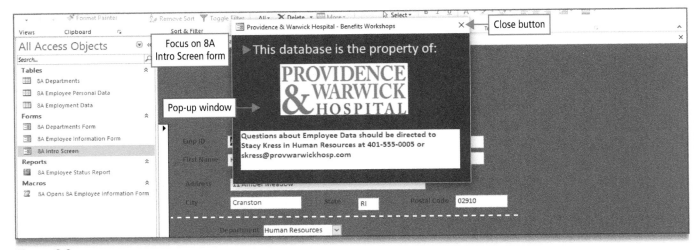

Figure 8.8

5 Close ⊠ the **8A Intro Screen** form, and then **Close** ⊠ the **8A Employee Information Form**. In the **Navigation Pane**, open the **8A Intro Screen** form in **Design** view.

6 Under **Form Design Tools**, on the **Design tab**, in the **Tools group**, click **Property Sheet**. Verify that the **Selection type** box displays **Form**. On the **Property Sheet**, click the **Format tab**, and then take a moment to review some of the property settings for this form while comparing your screen with Figure 8.9.

The text entered in the Caption property displays on the title bar of the form when in Form view. The Allow Form View property setting is Yes, while all of the other views are disabled. The Border Style property setting is Dialog, which is a thick border that can include a title bar with a Close button. The form cannot be resized, maximized, or minimized with this border style. Because this is a custom form that does not display any records from an underlying table or query, the Record Selectors, Navigation Buttons, and Scroll Bars property settings have been set to No or Neither.

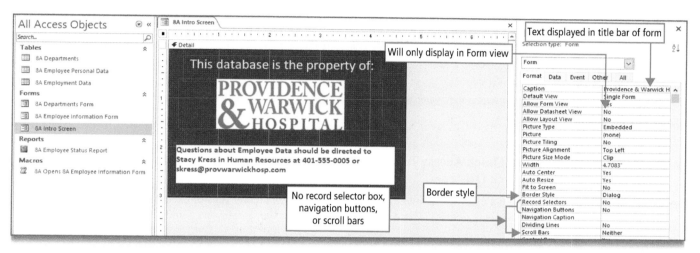

Figure 8.9

7 Close ⊠ the **Property Sheet**, **Close** ⊠ the form, and then **Close** « the **Navigation Pane**.

Activity 8.03 | Creating a Standalone Macro That Executes Automatically

In this Activity, you will create another standalone macro that will open the *8A Intro Screen* form when the database is opened.

1 On the **Create tab**, in the **Macros & Code group**, click **Macro** to display the **Macro Designer**.

2 In the **Macro Designer**, in the **Add New Action bar**, click the **arrow**, scroll down, and then click **OpenForm**. In the **OpenForm** action block, click the **Form Name arrow**, and then click **8A Intro Screen**.

3 If necessary, under Macro Tools, on the Design tab, in the Show/Hide group, click Action Catalog to display the Action Catalog pane. In the **Action Catalog pane**, point to **Comment**, and, holding down the left mouse button, drag it below the **OpenForm** action. Release the mouse button. In the **Comment** box, type **Opens the 8A Intro Screen form** Compare your screen with Figure 8.10.

> In addition to double-clicking an action in the Action Catalog, an action can also be added by dragging it to the correct position. Comments are also used to identify or explain a macro action.

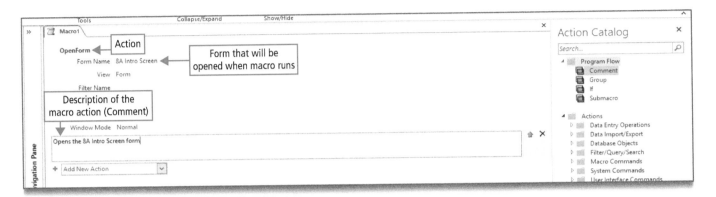

Figure 8.10

4 On the **Quick Access Toolbar**, click **Save**. In the **Save As** dialog box, type **autoexec** and then click **OK**.

> When a macro is named *autoexec*, Access automatically runs or executes the macro each time the database is opened. There can be only one macro in a database named *autoexec*.

5 **Close** ☒ the Macro Designer, and then **Open** ☒ the **Navigation Pane**. Notice that in the **Navigation Pane**, under **Macros**, **autoexec** displays. Double-click **autoexec** to run the macro.

> The *8A Intro Screen* form displays in its own pop-up, modal window.

6 **Close** the form. Display **Backstage** view, and then click **Close**. In **Backstage** view, click **Open**. Under *Open*, verify **Recent** is selected, and then, on the right, click your **Access_8A_Employee_Records** file.

> The macro automatically executes or runs when the *8A_Employee_Records* database opens, and it displays the pop-up, modal *8A Intro Screen* form. Because this is a trusted macro action, the macro will execute even if the database has not been trusted or the content enabled.

🔄 **ANOTHER WAY** The preferred method to open an object when the database is opened is the following. Display Backstage view, and then click Options. In the Access Options window, on the left side, click Current Database. Under Application Options, click the Display Form arrow, and then click the form that should be displayed when the database is opened. Because you will add more actions to the standalone macro, it is appropriate to open the 8A Intro Screen form as an auto executable action.

---

7 **Close** ☒ the form.

Objective 2   Add Multiple Actions to a Standalone Macro

GO! Learn How
Video A8-2

In the previous activities, you created macros that each contained only one action—opening a form. A macro can contain multiple actions that are executed in a specified order. For example, you can display a busy icon as the macro executes, which is especially useful for macros with multiple actions, to let the user know that Access is working on a process. This can be followed by an action that runs another standalone macro—for example, opening a form. And then you can select the title bar on the form, maximize the form, and then turn off the busy icon.

Activity 8.04 | Adding Multiple Actions to an Existing Standalone Macro

In this Activity, you will modify the autoexec macro and add more actions to the macro.

1 In the **Navigation Pane**, under **Macros**, right-click **autoexec**, and then click **Design View**. Close **«** the **Navigation Pane**.

2 In the **Action Catalog pane**, click in the **Search** box, and then type **dis** Under **System Commands**, click **DisplayHourglassPointer** to display a description in the lower section of the Action Catalog.

When you search for an action using the Action Catalog pane, a description of the macro you selected appears at the bottom of the pane. The Hourglass action changes the normal pointer to a busy icon to inform the user that some action is taking place. On a slower computer, the icon will keep the user from thinking that something is wrong with the database. If the computer is fast, the busy icon may not display. When the macro finishes running, the normal mouse pointer displays.

3 In the **Action Catalog pane**, double-click **DisplayHourglassPointer** to display the **DisplayHourglassPointer** action block. Notice that the default argument is *Yes*. Compare your screen with Figure 8.11.

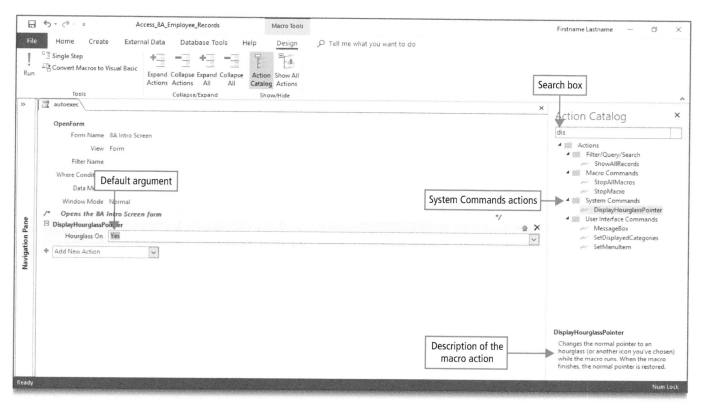

Figure 8.11

4 Click inside the **Add New Action bar**, and type **'Turns mouse pointer to a busy icon to show that the macro may take a few seconds to execute** and then press [Enter].

> Typing a single quote before the comment identifies the text that follows as a comment. The Comment block displays after you press [Enter].

5 Under **Macro Tools**, on the **Design tab**, in the **Show/Hide** group, click **Show All Actions**.

> Recall that the default list of macros displays only trusted macro actions. The next macro action that you will add to the macro is not a trusted macro action. For the macro to execute properly, you must add the location of the database to Trusted Locations or enable the content. Because this macro is used to open a pop-up, modal window, the database location must be trusted. The modal form will open automatically when the database is opened, and you cannot enable the content until the form is closed.

6 In the **Action Catalog pane**, click in the **Search** box, and then replace any existing text with **ech** Under **Macro Commands**, double-click **Echo**. In the **Echo** action block, in the **Echo On** box, click the **arrow**, and then click **No**. Click in the **Status Bar Text** box, and type **Macro is running** Click inside the **Add New Action bar** and type **'Hides the flickering screen as the macro actions execute** and then press [Enter]. Compare your screen with Figure 8.12.

> The Echo macro action hides or displays the results of the macro while it runs; however, it will not hide error messages or property sheets. Changing the Echo On argument to No hides the results. The Status Bar Text argument displays text on the status bar while the macro is running with Echo On set to No. The icon that displays in the Action Argument box indicates that the macro action is not safe.

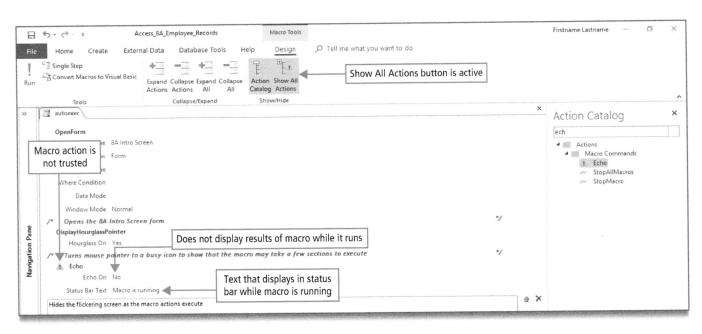

Figure 8.12

7 In the **Action Catalog pane**, click in the **Search** box, and then replace any existing text with **run** Under **Macro Commands**, double-click **RunMacro**.

> The RunMacro action is used to run a macro from within another macro.

8 In the **RunMacro** action block, click the **Macro Name box arrow**, and then click **8A Open 8A Employee Information Form**. Point to the **Repeat Count** box, and then read the description. Point to the **Repeat Expression** box, and then read the description.

> The Repeat Count and Repeat Expression action arguments are used when the macro should be run more than one time. Left blank, the macro will run only one time.

9 Click inside the **Add New Action bar**, type **'Opens the 8A Employee Information Form** and then press Enter.

10 In the **Action Catalog pane**, click in the **Search** box, and then replace any existing text with **mes** Under **User Interface Commands**, double-click **MessageBox**.

> The MessageBox macro action is a trusted action that displays a message box that contains a warning or informational message. The MessageBox macro action can contain up to four arguments.

11 In the argument block, click in the **Message** box, and then type **Only employees of Providence & Warwick Hospital are authorized to access this database. Unauthorized use will result in legal action.**

12 Point to the **Beep** box, and read the description of the **Beep** argument. Verify that the **Beep** argument is **Yes**. Click the **Type arrow**, and then compare your screen with Figure 8.13.

> There are five different message types listed. Each has a different icon that is displayed in the message box. None is the default message type because no icon displays in the message box.

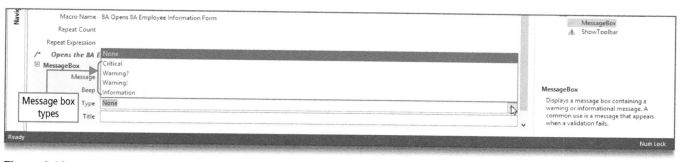

Figure 8.13

13 In the displayed list, click **Warning!** Point to the **Title** box, and read the description of the argument. Click in the **Title** box, and type **For Use by Providence & Warwick Hospital Employees Only!**

14 Click inside the **Add New Action bar**, type **'Displays a warning message box** and press Enter.

15 Scroll to the top of the **Macro Designer** window. Click the **OpenForm** action to make it active. At the right edge of the title, click the green **Move down arrow** two times to move the action below the **DisplayHourglassPointer** action. (Be sure to click twice, not double-click.) Click the green **Move down arrow** in the **OpenForm** action box five more times or until it appears below the comment *Opens the 8A Employee Information Form.* Compare your screen with Figure 8.14.

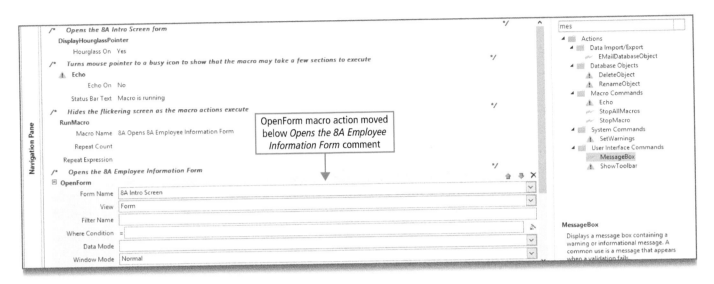

Figure 8.14

 **ANOTHER WAY** Alternatively, you can point to the right edge of the Action or Comment block and drag it to a new position. When you point to the top edge of an Action or Comment block to move it, the mouse pointer does not change in appearance. As you drag the box, an orange line will appear at positions where the box can be dropped.

16 Click the green **Move down arrow** to the right of the **OpenForm macro comment** until you move it below the **OpenForm macro action**. In the **Designer** window, scroll down until the **Add New Action bar** is displayed.

17 In the **Action Catalog pane**, click in the **Search** box, and then replace any existing text with **dis** Under **System Commands**, drag **DisplayHourglassPointer** above the **Add New Action bar**, and release the mouse button. In the **Action Arguments** box, click the **Hourglass On arrow**, and then click **No**.

Dragging an action into the Designer window gives the user more control over the placement of the action in the macro.

18 Click inside the **Add New Action bar**, type **'Restores the normal mouse pointer** and then press Enter.

The normal mouse pointer will be displayed to let the user know that the macro is finished executing.

19 In the **Action Catalog pane**, click in the **Search** box, and then replace any existing text with **ech** Under **Macro Commands**, double-click **Echo**. Notice that in the action block, in the **Echo On** box, the setting is **Yes**. Click inside the **Add New Action bar**, type **'Displays screen results** and then press Enter.

> Screen actions will no longer be hidden from the individual using the database. Status Bar Text is not displayed because the Echo On argument is set to Yes.

NOTE **Turning Off Macro Actions**

Access automatically restores Hourglass and Echo to the default settings after a macro has finished running to protect inexperienced macro programmers from causing the system to continue displaying the hourglass icon, which might lead the user to think that the database is operating incorrectly or is frozen. Even though Access restores these settings, it is good practice to always restore what you turn off. This will lead to better coding if you write Visual Basic code to execute commands.

---

20 On the **Quick Access Toolbar**, click **Save** 🖫. Under **Macro Tools**, on the **Design tab**, in the **Tools group**, click **Run**. Compare your screen with Figure 8.15.

> Access does not always wait for one action to complete before going on to the next action. Notice that the *8A Employee Information Form* is not yet open; however, the *8A Intro Screen* is open with a message box displayed on top of it. A beep sounded when the message box displayed. The busy icon displays, and the status bar displays *Macro is running*.

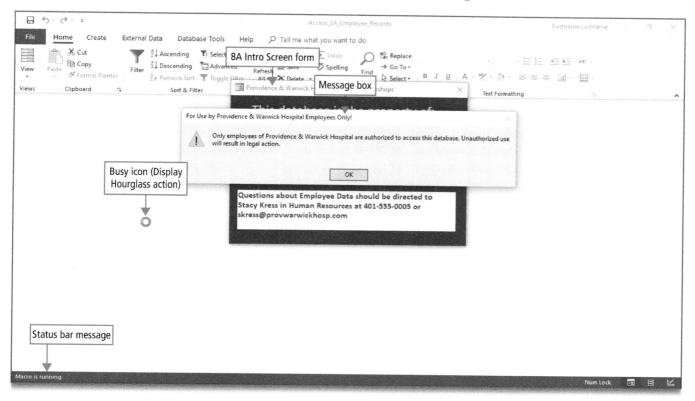

Figure 8.15

ALERT **Did a message box display?**

If a message box displays stating that the Echo macro action cannot be run in disabled mode, you did not add the Access Chapter 8 folder to Trust Center. The Echo macro action is not trusted by default. To correct this, click OK, click Stop All Macros, and then add the Access Chapter 8 folder to the Trust Center.

21 In the displayed message box, click **OK**. The **8A Employee Information Form** displays underneath the **8A Intro Screen** form. **Close** ⊠ the **8A Intro Screen** form. On the **tab row**, right-click any tab, and then click **Close All**.

22 Display **Backstage** view, and then click **Close**. Display **Backstage** view, click **Open** and then, under **Recent**, click your **8A_Employee_Records** file.

The Autoexec macro automatically executes or runs when the *8A_Employee_Records* database opens, and it displays the pop-up, modal *8A Intro Screen* form with the message box on top of it.

23 In the displayed message box, click **OK**. **Close** ⊠ the **8A Intro Screen** form. Leave the **8A Employee Information Form** open for the next Activity.

MORE KNOWLEDGE | **Debugging a Macro**

Debugging is using a logical process to find and reduce the number of errors in a program. To debug a macro, you can use *single stepping*, which executes one action at a time. Single stepping allows you to observe the results of each macro action to isolate an action that may be causing an error or producing unwanted results.

To single step through a macro, open the macro in Design view. Under Macro Tools, on the Design tab, in the Tools group, click Single Step. In the Tools group, click Run. The Macro Single Step dialog box displays information about the macro, including the macro name, condition, action name, arguments, and an error number. An error number of 0 indicates that no error has occurred. In this dialog box, you can carry out the macro action by clicking Step. You can stop the macro and close the dialog box by clicking Stop All Macros, or you can turn off single stepping and run the rest of the macro by clicking Continue. When the macro has fully executed, be sure to turn off single stepping. Under Macro Tools, on the Design tab, in the Tools group, click Single Step.

Objective 3 | **Create an Embedded Macro**

GO! Learn How
Video A8-3

An *embedded macro* is a macro that is stored in the Event properties of forms, reports, or controls. Embedded macros are not displayed in the Navigation Pane under Macros. They are easier to manage because you do not have to keep track of the separate macro objects. Unlike standalone macros, when objects containing embedded macros are copied, imported, or exported, the macros are also copied, imported, or exported. Any standalone macro can be created as an embedded macro.

Activity 8.05 | Creating an Embedded Macro on a Form

4.1.1, 4.1.2

In this Activity, you will create an embedded macro that will execute when the *Dept Info* button is clicked on the *8A Employee Information Form*.

1 ▸ Switch the **8A Employee Information Form** to **Design** view. Under **Form Design Tools**, on the **Design tab**, in the **Controls group**, click **Button** ⌷⌷⌷⌷. In the **Detail** section, align the plus sign (+) of the pointer at **4.5 inches on the horizontal ruler** and **2.5 inches on the vertical ruler**, and then click. Compare your screen with Figure 8.16.

The button displays at the set position, and the Command Button Wizard dialog box displays.

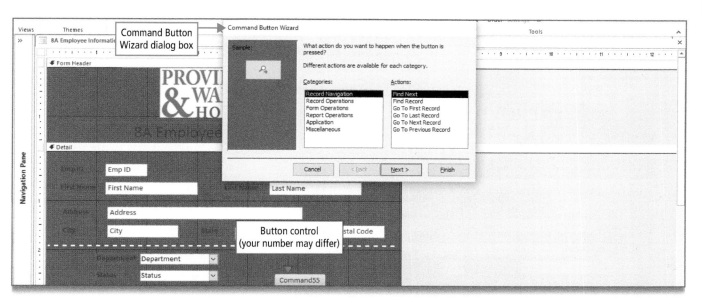

Figure 8.16

2 ▸ In the **Command Button Wizard** dialog box, click **Cancel**.

Recall that the Command Button Wizard can be used to associate a button with a preset action. Cancel the wizard to embed or assign a macro to the button. Because no name or picture has been associated with the button, it displays Command55. The number following the word *Command* may differ.

3 ▸ Right-click the button, and then click **Properties**. Verify that the **Property Sheet** displays *Selection type: Command Button* and the **Selection type** box displays *Command55*, identifying your command button. On the **Property Sheet Other tab**, in the **Name** property box, select the existing text and type **btnDeptInfo** and press ⏎.

The button name has been updated to *btnDeptInfo*. The button name will now display in the Selection type box for easy identification.

4 On the **Property Sheet Format tab**, in the **Caption** property box, select the existing text and type **Dept Info** and press Enter. Compare your screen with Figure 8.17.

The button label has been updated to *Dept Info*, reflecting the caption property. However, no actions have been associated with the button.

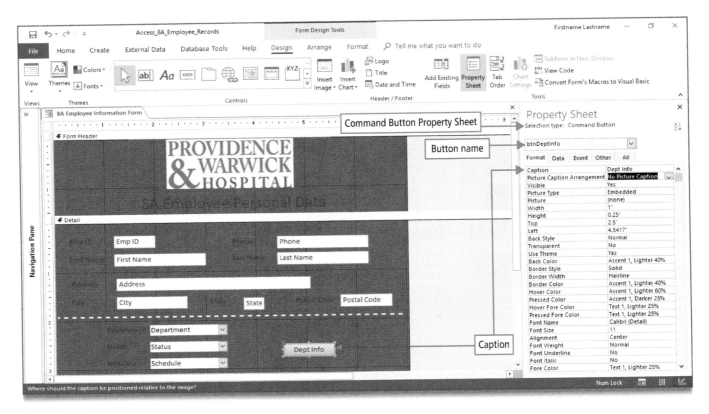

Figure 8.17

5 On the **Property Sheet**, click the **Event tab**. In the **On Click** property setting box, click **Build**, and then compare your screen with Figure 8.18.

The Choose Builder dialog box displays for you to select the Macro Builder, the Expression Builder, or the Code Builder. You have previously used the Macro Builder and the Expression Builder. The *Code Builder* is used for programming in Microsoft Visual Basic.

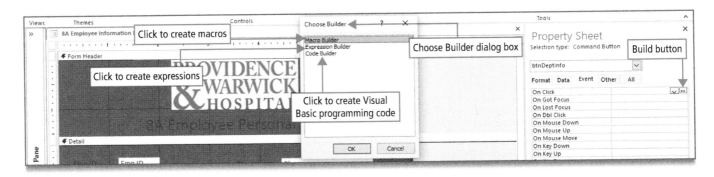

Figure 8.18

6 In the **Choose Builder** dialog box, if necessary, click **Macro Builder**, and then click **OK** to display the Macro Designer.

7 In the **Macro Designer**, add the **OpenForm** action using one of the techniques you have learned. In the **OpenForm** action block, click the **Form Name arrow**, and then click **8A Departments Form**. Click in the **Where Condition** box, type **[Dept ID]=[Forms]![8A Employee Information Form]![Department]** selecting items as they appear in the list to reduce errors, and then compare your screen with Figure 8.19.

> The Where Condition property selects the records from the *8A Departments Form* for the Department displayed on the *8A Employee Information Form*.

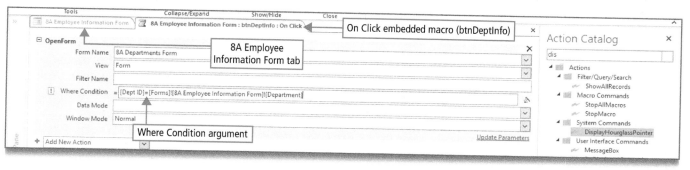

Figure 8.19

8 In the **OpenForm** action block, click the **Data Mode arrow**, and then click **Read Only** to enable the user to only view the data in the *8A Departments Form*. Add the following comment: **Opens 8A Departments Form for department indicated on 8A Employee Information Form**

9 **Close** ⊠ the **Macro Designer**. In the displayed message box, click **Yes** to save the changes made to the macro and to update the On Click property. Compare your screen with Figure 8.20.

> In the Property Sheet, the On Click property displays *[Embedded Macro]*. To display the macro, click Build.

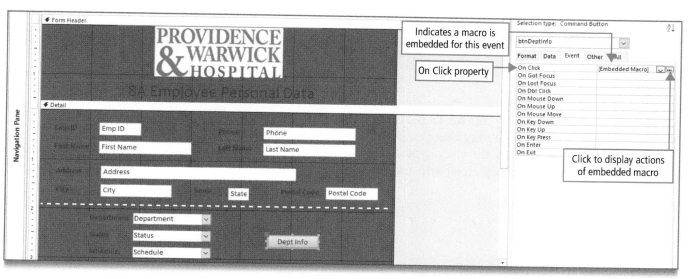

Figure 8.20

10 On the **Property Sheet**, click the **Format tab**. In the **Caption** box, click to the left of **Dept Info**, and then type **&** to create a shortcut key using the letter *D*. **Close** ⊠ the **Property Sheet**, **Save** 🖫 the form, and then switch the *8A Employee Information Form* to **Form** view.

> The ampersand (&) causes the letter that follows it to be underlined on the button, which will enable the user to use a shortcut key combination to access the button instead of clicking on the button. The user presses ⌨Alt + the letter to activate the button. For this button, the shortcut is ⌨Alt + ⌨D.

11 On the **8A Employee Information Form**, click the **Dept Info** button or press ⌨Alt + ⌨D.

> The *8A Departments Form* displays as a pop-up window and provides directory information about the Human Resources department, the Department listed on the *8A Employee Information Form*.

12 **Close** ⊠ the **8A Departments Form**. In the **8A Employee Information Form**, in the record navigator, click **Last record** ⏭. In the **8A Employee Information Form**, click the **Dept Info** button, and then compare your screen with Figure 8.21.

> The pop-up window displays directory information for the Facilities department, the same department displayed on the *8A Employee Information Form*, as indicated by the Filtered button to the right of the record navigator in the *8A Departments Form*.

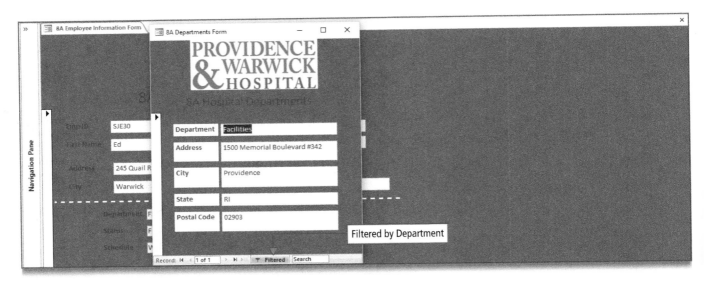

Figure 8.21

13 **Close** ⊠ the **8A Departments Form**, and then **Close** ⊠ the **8A Employee Information Form**, saving changes, if necessary. **Open** ⏩ the **Navigation Pane**. Notice that under **Macros**, the macro you created to display the *8A Departments Form* does not display—embedded macros do not display in the Navigation Pane.

Activity 8.06 | Creating an Embedded Macro on a Report

4.1.1, 4.1.2

In this Activity, you will create an embedded macro that will execute when the *Emp ID* text box is clicked on the *8A Employee Status Report*.

1 Open the **8A Employee Status Report** in **Design** view. **Close** ☒ the **Navigation Pane**. In the **Detail** section, right-click the **Emp ID** text box, and then click **Properties**. Verify that the **Property Sheet** displays *Selection type: Text Box* and the **Selection type** box displays *Emp ID*.

2 On the **Property Sheet Event tab**, in the **On Click** property setting box, click **Build** ⋯. In the **Choose Builder** dialog box, verify that **Macro Builder** is selected, and then click **OK** to display the Macro Designer.

3 In the **Macro Designer**, add the **OpenForm** action using one of the techniques you have learned. In the **OpenForm** action block, click the **Form Name arrow**, and then click **8A Employee Information Form**. Click in the **Where Condition** box, type **[Emp ID]=[Reports]![8A Employee Status Report]![Emp ID]** selecting items as they appear in the list to reduce errors, and then compare your screen with Figure 8.22.

The Where Condition property selects the records from the *8A Employee Information Form* for the Employee selected on the *8A Employee Status Report*.

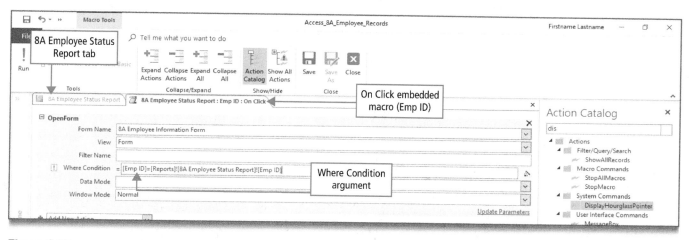

Figure 8.22

4 In the **OpenForm** action block, click the **Data Mode arrow**, and then click **Read Only**. Add the following comment: **Opens 8A Employee Information Form for the employee selected on 8A Employee Status Report**

5 **Close** ☒ the **Macro Designer**. In the displayed message box, click **Yes** to save the changes made to the macro and to update the On Click property. **Close** ☒ the **Property Sheet**. **Save** 🖫 the report.

6 Switch to **Report** view. On the **8A Employee Status Report**, click the **Empl ID** text box for *BOM22* to run the macro.

The *8A Employee Information Form* displays and provides information about Maria Bartello, the employee whose Emp ID was selected on the *8A Employee Status Report*.

7 **Close** ☒ the **8A Employee Information Form**. **Close** ☒ the **8A Employee Status Report**, saving changes if necessary. **Open** ☒ the **Navigation Pane**. Notice that under **Macros**, the macro you created to display the *8A Employee Information Form* does not display because embedded macros do not display in the Navigation Pane.

8 Close the database, and then **Close** Access.

For Non-MyLab Submissions: Determine What Your Instructor Requires for Submission
As directed by your instructor, submit your completed database file. If you are completing the optional activity, do so before submitting your database to your instructor.

9 In **MyLab IT**, locate and click the Grader Project **Access 8A Employee Records**. In **step 3**, under **Upload Completed Assignment**, click **Choose File**. In the **Open** dialog box, navigate to your **Access Chapter 8 folder**, and then click your **Student_Access_8A_ Employee_Records** file one time to select it. In the lower right corner of the **Open** dialog box, click **Open**.

The name of your selected file displays above the Upload button.

10 To submit your file to **MyLab IT** for grading, click **Upload**, wait a moment for a green **Success!** message, and then in **step 4**, click the blue **Submit for Grading** button. Click **Close Assignment** to return to your list of **Course Materials**.

ALERT   The Activity in Objective 4 Is Optional
The following Activity is optional. Check with your instructor to see if you should complete this Activity. This Activity is not included in the **MyLab IT** Grader system for this project; however, you may want to practice this on your own.

Objective 4 | Print Macro Details

GO! Learn How
Video A8-4

Use the *Database Documenter* to create a report that contains detailed information about the objects in a database, including macros, and to create a paper record.

Activity 8.07 | Printing Macro Details

In this Activity, you will use the Database Documenter to print out the details of the macros that you have created in this project.

1 Start Access. Under *Recent*, click your **Access_8A_Employee_Records** file to open it.

2 **Close** « the **Navigation Pane**. On the **Database Tools tab**, in the **Analyze group**, click **Database Documenter**. In the displayed **Documenter** dialog box, click the **Macros tab**, and then compare your screen with Figure 8.23.

The Documenter dialog box displays tabs for each object type and a tab for the current database. Only standalone macros display on the Macros tab. Macros that are embedded with an object will display as a property of the object.

Figure 8.23

3 In the **Documenter** dialog box, click **Options**, and then compare your screen with Figure 8.24.

The Print Macro Definition dialog box displays. Properties, actions, arguments, and permissions by user and group can be displayed in the printed report.

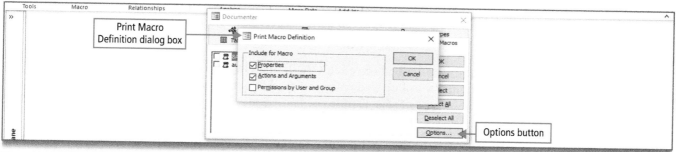

Figure 8.24

4 If necessary, click the **Permissions by User and Group** check box to clear it, and then click **OK**. In the **Documenter** dialog box, click **Select All**, and then click **OK**. Click in the middle of the document to zoom in, scroll up to display the top section of the report, and then compare your screen with Figure 8.25.

The Object Definition opens in Print Preview and displays the first page of information about the macro named *autoexec*, including actions, arguments, conditions, and comments.

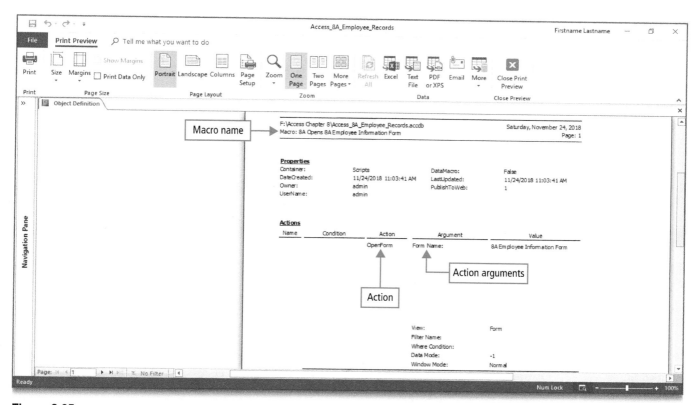

Figure 8.25

5 On the **Print Preview tab**, in the **Close Preview group**, click **Close Print Preview**.

6 On the **Database Tools tab**, in the **Analyze group**, click **Database Documenter**. In the **Documenter** dialog box, click the **Forms tab**. Click **Options**. In the **Print Form Definition** dialog box, if necessary, clear the check boxes for **Properties** and **Permissions by User and Group**, and then click **OK**.

7 In the **Documenter** dialog box, click the **8A Employee Information Form** check box.

This form has an embedded macro.

8 In the **Documenter** dialog box, click **OK**. In the **Object Definition** print preview, zoom in, and then scroll up to display the top of the first page, noticing that the report displays properties of the **8A Employee Information Form**. Click **Next Page** until the **OnClickEmMacro** data is displayed Compare your screen with Figure 8.26.

The properties of the Dept Info button—Command Button: btnDeptInfo—display.

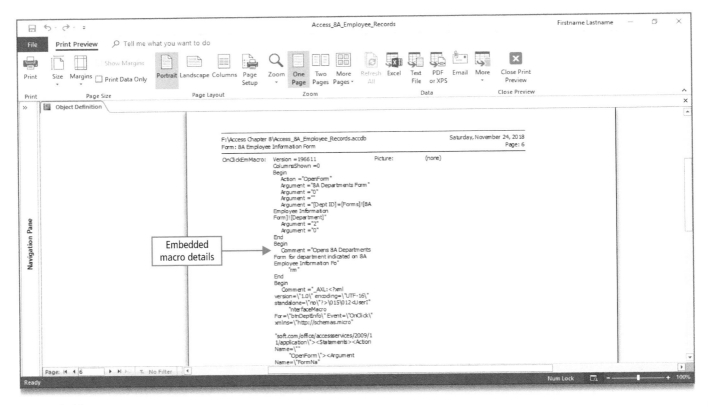

Figure 8.26

9 On the **Print Preview tab**, in the **Close Preview group**, click the **Close Print Preview** button.

10 On the **Database Tools tab**, in the **Analyze group**, click **Database Documenter**. In the **Documenter** dialog box, if necessary, click the **Reports tab**. Click **Options**. In the **Print Report Definition** dialog box, if necessary, clear the check boxes for **Properties** and **Permissions by User and Group**, and then click **OK**.

11 In the **Documenter** dialog box, click the **8A Employee Status Report** check box, and then click **OK**.

12 In the **Object Definition** print preview, zoom in, and click **Next Page five** times. Scroll down to display the bottom of the page.

> The OnClick property displays the embedded macro.

13 On the **Print Preview tab**, in the **Close Preview group**, click **Close Print Preview**.

14 Open ⟩⟩ the **Navigation Pane**. Resize the **Navigation Pane** so all object names display fully. **Close** the database, and then **Close** Access.

For Non-MyLab Submissions: Determine What Your Instructor Requires for Submission

As directed by your instructor, submit your completed database file.

You have completed Project 8A | END

Employee Benefits

Project Activities

In Activities 8.08 through 8.13, you will help Maria Diaz, vice president of operations for Providence & Warwick Hospital, create a macro group. She also wants to add buttons on the form to automate some of the most common tasks, such as finding a training session. When completed, your Navigation Pane will look similar to Figure 8.27.

Project Files for MyLab IT Grader

1. In your **MyLab IT** course, locate and click **Access 8B Employee Benefits**, Download Materials, and then Download All Files.
2. Extract the zipped folder to your Access Chapter 8 folder. Close the Grader download screens.
3. Take a moment to open the downloaded **Access_8B_Employee_Benefits_Instructions**; note any recent updates to the book.

Project Results

GO! Project 8B
Where We're Going

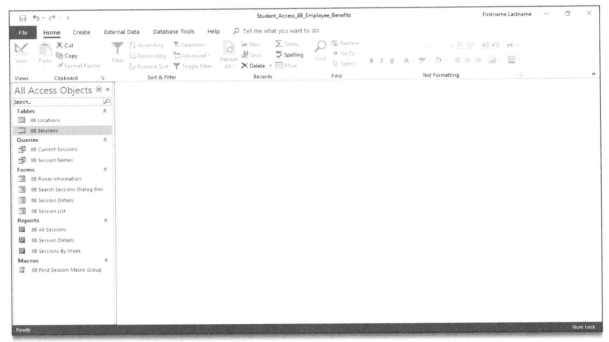

Figure 8.27 Project 8B Employee Benefits

For Non-MyLab Submissions	Start with an Access Data File
For Project 8B, you will need:	In your Access Chapter 8 folder, save your database as:
a08B_Employee_Benefits	**Lastname_Firstname_8B_Employee_Benefits**

After you have saved your database, open it to launch Access. On the next page, begin with Step 2.

Objective 5 | Create a Macro Group

GO! Learn How
Video A8-5

In the previous activities, you created a standalone macro with one action and another standalone macro with multiple actions. As you continue to create more macros, you may want to group related macros by creating a ***macro group***. A macro group is a set of submacros grouped by a common name that displays as one macro object in the Navigation Pane. For example, you might want to create a macro group that opens several forms or reports in a database.

Activity 8.08 | Creating the First Macro in a Macro Group

In this Activity, you will create the first macro in the macro group that will open the *8B Search Sessions Dialog Box* form.

1 Start Access. In the Access opening screen, click **Open**. Navigate to your **Access Chapter 8 folder**, and then double-click the Access file that you downloaded from **MyLab IT** that displays your name—**Student_Access_8B_Employee_Benefits**. If necessary, add Access Chapter 8 to the Trust Center.

2 In the **Navigation Pane**, under **Forms**, double-click **8B Session Details**, and then double-click **8B Search Sessions Dialog Box** to open the forms in **Form** view. If necessary, point to the title bar of the **Search Sessions Dialog Box**, and then drag the pop-up form downward and to the right until, on the **8B Session Details** form, the Find Session button under the title displays. Compare your screen with Figure 8.28.

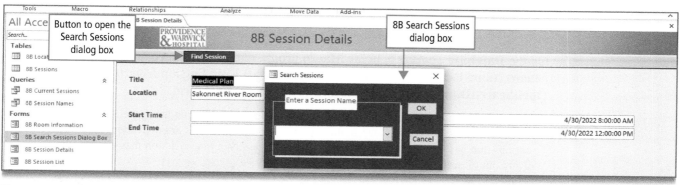

Figure 8.28

3 Close ⊠ the **Search Sessions Dialog Box** form, and then Close ⊠ the **8B Session Details** form. Close « the **Navigation Pane**.

4 On the **Create tab**, in the **Macros & Code group**, click **Macro**. Under **Macro Tools**, on the **Design tab**, in the **Show/Hide group**, click **Show All Actions**.

Recall that the Show All Actions button displays trusted and untrusted macro actions.

5 In the **Action Catalog pane**, double-click **Group**. In the **Macro Designer**, in the **Group** box, type **8B Find Session Macro Group** to identify the group. Add the following comment: **Purpose: To enable the user to search for a specific session in the 8B Session Details form**

It is a good practice to start a macro group with a name and the purpose of the macro group.

6 In the **Action Catalog pane**, double-click **Submacro** and then in the **Submacro** box, delete any text that is there and type **OpenSearchDialogBox**

> In macro groups, submacro names are needed to distinguish the individual macros from one another. Within a macro group, the submacro name is entered before the macro actions in each submacro. The macro ends when *End Submacro* is encountered. Macro names are limited to 64 characters. Because macros perform an action or actions, it is good practice to start the name of the macro with a verb—in this case, *Open*.

7 In the **Submacro**, using one of the techniques you have learned, add an **OpenForm** action. In the **OpenForm** action block, click the **Form Name arrow**, and then click **8B Search Sessions Dialog Box**. Click the **Data Mode arrow**, and then click **Edit**. Add the following comment: **Opens the 8B Search Sessions Dialog Box form** Compare your screen with Figure 8.29.

> Editing is enabled so that the user can enter a Session name in the combo box on the *8B Search Sessions Dialog Box* form. Because the form property has been set to open as a pop-up window, the Window Mode setting of Normal is appropriate.

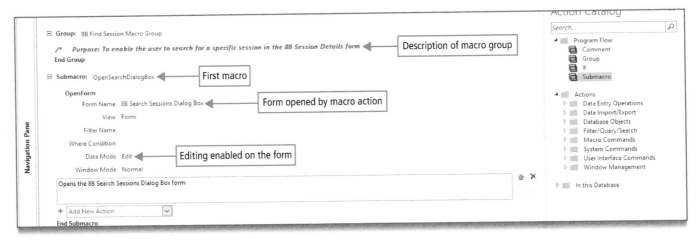

Figure 8.29

8 Save the macro group as **8B Find Session Macro Group**

9 On the **Database Tools tab**, in the **Macro group**, click **Run Macro**, and then, in the **Macro Name** list, click the arrow, and then click **8B Find Session Macro Group. OpenSearchDialogBox**. Click **OK**, and then **Close** × the form.

> Because the macro is associated with a macro group, it must be run using the Run Macro button on the Database Tools tab. Keep in mind that some macro actions are dependent upon other macro actions that have previously executed, and independently, a macro action may not execute properly if run out of order.

Activity 8.09 | Creating a Second Macro in a Macro Group

In this Activity, you will create a second macro in the macro group that will check to see if a value is entered for the Session name in the *8B Search Sessions Dialog Box* form, hide the *8B Search Sessions Dialog Box* form, change the focus to the *8B Session Details* form, select the title of the Session on the *8B Session Details* form, sort the records by the Session name, find the requested Session, close the *8B Search Sessions Dialog Box* form, and display a message to the user with a reminder to display all of the records.

1 In the **Macro Designer**, in the **Action Catalog pane**, double-click **Submacro**, and in the **Submacro** box type **SearchForSession** In the **Action Catalog pane**, double-click **If**.

> The If action block displays in the SearchForSession submacro to control the program flow. In some macros, an action should execute only if a condition is true. For example, if the user does not select a value in the combo box on the *8B Search Sessions Dialog Box* form, the macro should not execute.

2 In the **Submacro**, to the right of the **If** textbox, click **Builder** ⬛. In the **Expression Builder** dialog box, type **IsNull([Forms]![8B Search Sessions Dialog Box]![SessionName])** selecting items as they appear in the list to reduce errors. Compare your screen with Figure 8.30.

> The expression used for the condition checks the SessionName combo box in the *8B Search Sessions Dialog Box* form to determine if the combo box is blank—IsNull. Recall that the exclamation mark (!) is the bang operator that separates the object type from the object name.

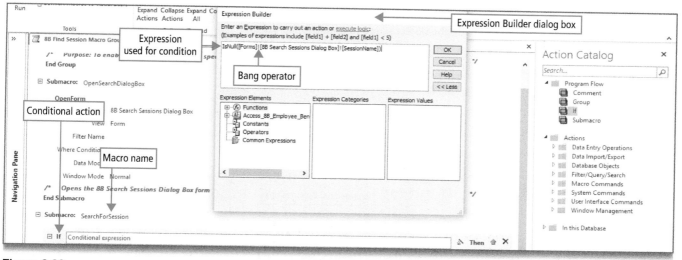

Figure 8.30

3 In the **Expression Builder** dialog box, click **OK**. In the **If** action block, add the **CloseWindow** action using one of the techniques you have learned. In the **CloseWindow** action block, click the **Object Type arrow**, and then click **Form**. Click the **Object Name arrow**, and then click **8B Search Sessions Dialog Box**. Click the **Save arrow**, and then click **No**. Add the following comment: **If a session is not selected, then close the 8B Search Sessions Dialog Box form**

> If Access finds that the Sessions combo box is blank, it will close the *8B Search Sessions Dialog Box* form without saving changes made to the form. Recall that the warning symbol in the row selector box indicates that this macro action is not trusted.

4 In the **If Arguments Block**, add the **StopMacro** action. Notice that there are no action arguments for the StopMacro action. Add the following comment: **Exits the macro**

> If the Sessions combo box is blank, and the form closes, the macro stops executing.

5 In the **Macro Designer**, click the **Submacro:SearchForSession** text box to activate the **Add New Action bar** below the **End If** label. Add the **SetValue** action. In the **SetValue** action block, to the right of the **Item** text box, click **Builder** 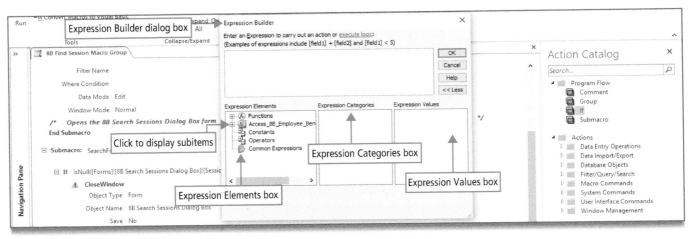 to open the **Expression Builder**. Compare your screen with Figure 8.31.

The SetValue macro action is an untrusted action used to set the value of a field, control, or property on a form, a form datasheet, or a report. The item is the name of the field, control, or property whose value you want to set. You must use the full syntax to refer to the item—do not just type the field, control, or property name. *Syntax* refers to the spelling, grammar, and sequence of characters of a programming language.

The operator buttons and list boxes in the Expression Builder can help you build the expression using correct syntax. As you select an object in the first list box, the second and third list boxes will be populated. In the first list box, the plus sign (+) next to an object indicates that more items display under the object; click the plus sign (+) or double-click the object name to expand the list. The minus sign (–) indicates that the list under the object is fully expanded. Click the minus sign (–) or double-click the object name to collapse the list.

Figure 8.31

ALERT   Did the SetValue action appear before the End If label?

If the SetValue action appears before the End If label, you didn't click the Submacro SearchForSession Action Block before adding the new action. To correct this, move the SetValue action below the End If label using either technique practiced in the chapter.

---

6 In the **Expression Builder** dialog box, in the **Expression Elements** list box, click the plus sign to the left of file name to display the list of objects in the database. Click the plus sign (+) next to **Forms** to expand the list, and click the plus sign next to **All Forms**. Scroll down, and then click **8B Search Sessions Dialog Box**—use the horizontal scroll bar to display the entire name of the form.

The Expression Categories list box displays controls on the form. The Expression Values list box displays property settings and events that can be associated with the form or the controls on the form. An *event* is any action that can be detected by a program or computer system, such as clicking a button or closing an object. Selecting an object in the Expression Categories list box causes the values or events in the Expression Values list box to change, because different objects have different property settings or events associated with them.

7 In the **Expression Categories** list box, verify that **<Form>** is selected. In the **Expression Values** list box, scroll down, double-click **Visible**, and then compare your screen with Figure 8.32.

The Expression Builder displays the correct syntax for the Visible property of the *8B Search Sessions Dialog Box*, which is a form. Instead of using the Expression Builder, you can type the expression in the Item box in the action block. An advantage of using the Expression Builder is that Access will insert square brackets and parentheses where they are required.

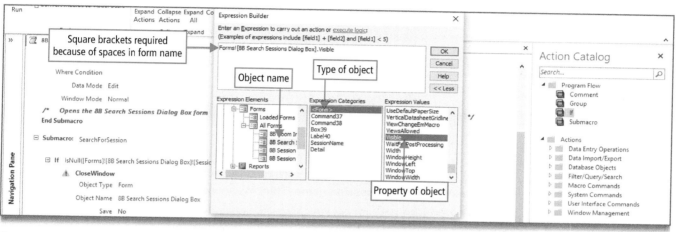

Figure 8.32

8 In the **Expression Builder**, click **OK**. In the **SetValue** action block, click in the **Expression** box, and then type **False**

This macro action sets the Visible property setting of the *8B Search Sessions Dialog Box* form to False; in other words, it will hide the *8B Search Sessions Dialog Box* form.

9 Add the following comment: **Hides the 8B Search Sessions Dialog Box form** Compare your screen with Figure 8.33.

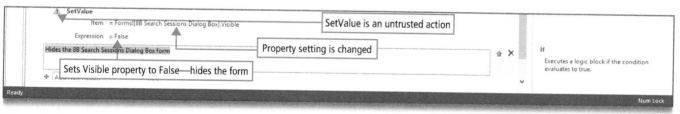

Figure 8.33

10 In the **Submacro**, add the **SelectObject** action. In the **SelectObject** action block, click the **Object Type arrow**, and then click **Form**. Click the **Object Name arrow**, and then click **8B Session Details**. Verify that the **In Database Window** box displays **No**. Add the following comment: **Changes the focus to the 8B Session Details form**

The SelectObject action is used to put the focus on a specified database object so that an action can be applied to that object. Recall that the *8B Session Details* form is automatically opened when the database is opened. Therefore, the In Database Window setting should be set to No. If the form is not open, Access needs to open it from the Navigation Pane, and the In Database Window setting should be set to Yes.

So far, the macro group will open the *8B Search Sessions Dialog Box* form and then check to see if the Sessions field displays data. If not, the macro stops executing. If data is displayed in the Sessions field, the *8B Search Sessions Dialog Box* form will be hidden, and the focus will shift to the *8B Session Details* form.

11 In the **Submacro**, add the **GoToControl** action. In the **GoToControl** action block, in the **Control Name** box, type **Title** Add the following comment: **Places focus on Title field on 8B Session Details form** Compare your screen with Figure 8.34.

In the previous action, the focus was changed to the *8B Session Details* form. With this action, the focus is placed on a specific text box control named *Title* on that form.

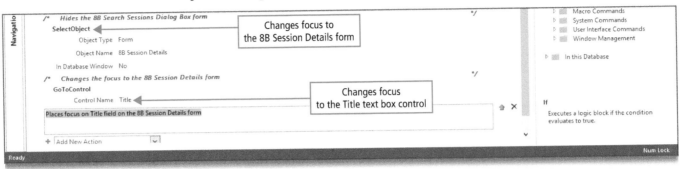

Figure 8.34

12 In the **Submacro**, add the **RunMenuCommand** action. In the **RunMenuCommand** action block, click the **Command arrow**, scroll down, and then click **SortAscending**. Add the following comment: **Sorts the session name (Title) in ascending order**

The RunMenuCommand action is used to execute an Access command, such as Sort Ascending or Save a Record.

13 In the **Submacro**, add the **FindRecord** action. In the **FindWhat** box, type **=[Forms]![8B Search Sessions Dialog Box]![SessionName]** selecting items as they appear in the list to reduce errors. Verify that you have entered the expression correctly. Click the **Match arrow**, and then click **Start of Field**. Point to each of the other argument boxes, reading the description of each argument and being sure not to change any of the settings. Add the following comment: **Finds the Title on the 8B Session Details form that matches the entry in the SessionName combo box on the 8B Search Sessions Dialog Box form** and then compare your screen with Figure 8.35.

The FindRecord action locates the first or next record that meets the specified search criteria; in this case, the data in the SessionName field of the *8B Search Sessions Dialog Box* form must match the data in the Title field of the *8B Session Details* form. This macro action is similar to using the Find button on the Home tab.

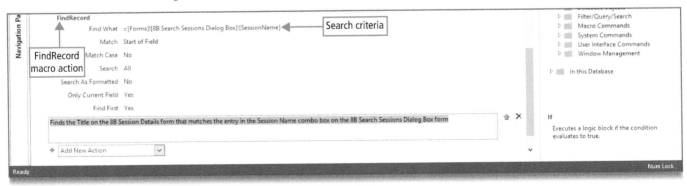

Figure 8.35

14 In the **Submacro**, add the **CloseWindow** action. In the **CloseWindow** action block, click the **Object Type arrow**, and then click **Form**. Click the **Object Name arrow**, and then click **8B Search Sessions Dialog Box**. Verify that **Prompt** appears in the **Save** box. Add the following comment: **Closes 8B Search Sessions Dialog Box form**

The Close action closes a specified object. If no object is specified in the Object Name box, the active object is closed.

15 In the **Submacro**, add the **MessageBox** action. In the **MessageBox** action block, click in the **Message** box, and then type **To display the records in their original sort order: On the Home tab, in the Sort & Filter group, click Remove Sort.** Click the **Type box arrow**, and then click **Information**. Click in the **Title** box, and then type **Search for Session Name** Add the following comment: **Displays a message with instructions for clearing the sort** Compare your screen with Figure 8.36.

Recall that if an individual filters or sorts records and closes the database, when the database is reopened, the filter or sort is still applied to the object.

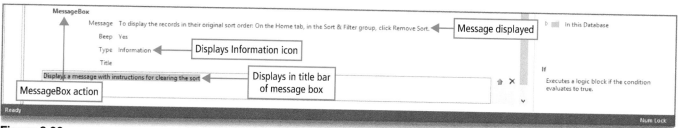

Figure 8.36

16 Save 💾 the macro group.

Activity 8.10 | Creating a Third Macro in a Macro Group

In this Activity, you will create a third and final macro in the macro group that will close the *8B Session Name Search* form.

1 In the **Macro Designer**, in the **Action Catalog pane**, double-click **Submacro**, and type **CancelSearch** to name the macro. Add the **CloseWindow** action. In the **CloseWindow** action block, click the **Object Type arrow**, and then click **Form**. Click the **Object Name arrow**, and then click **8B Search Sessions Dialog Box**. Verify that **Prompt** appears in the **Save** box. Add the following comment: **Closes 8B Search Sessions Dialog Box form when search is cancelled**

This macro will be used to close the *8B Search Sessions Dialog Box* form when the Cancel button on the form is clicked.

2 In the **Submacro**, add the **SelectObject** action. In the **SelectObject** action block, click the **Object Type arrow**, and then click **Form**. Click the **Object Name arrow**, and then click **8B Session Details**. Verify that the **In Database Window** box displays **No**. Add the following comment: **Changes the focus to 8B Session Details form** Compare your screen with Figure 8.37.

After the *8B Search Sessions Dialog Box* form is closed, the focus is placed on the *8B Session Details* form.

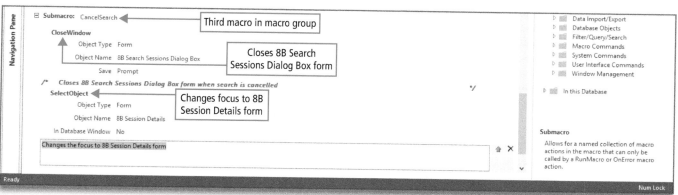

Figure 8.37

3 Save 🖫 the macro group. **Close** ✕ the Macro Designer, **Open** ≫ the **Navigation Pane**, and notice that under **Macros**, the macro group displays as one macro object.

> Double-clicking the macro does not cause this macro to execute because the macro has not been associated with the buttons on the *8B Session Details* form or the *8B Search Sessions Dialog Box* form.

Objective 6 | Associate a Macro with an Event

GO! Learn How
Video A8-6

Recall that an event is any action that can be detected by a program or computer system, such as clicking a button or closing an object. For example, clicking the Find Session button on the 8B Session Details form causes a system event, upon which Access can execute a macro.

Activity 8.11 | Associating a Command Button with a Macro

MOS
4.1.2

In this Activity, you will associate clicking the Find Session button on the *8B Session Details* form with a macro—the *8B Find Session Macro Group* macro. Clicking the Find Session button will cause the macro to execute.

1 In the **Navigation Pane**, under **Forms**, double-click **8B Session Details** to display the form in **Form** view. On the form, click the **Find Session** button, and notice that nothing happens because the button is not associated with any event.

2 **Close** ≪ the **Navigation Pane**, and then switch the form to **Design** view. In the **Form Header section**, right-click the **Find Session** button, and then click **Properties**. Verify that the **Property Sheet** displays *Selection type: Command Button* and that the **Selection type** box displays *cmdFindSession*.

3 On the **Property Sheet**, click the **Event tab**, if necessary. Click the **On Click property setting arrow**. Notice that the complete names of some of the macros do not display. Point to the **left edge** of the **Property Sheet** until the pointer ↔ displays. Drag to the left to the **7-inch mark on the horizontal ruler** or until the complete names display. Click the **On Click property setting arrow**, and then compare your screen with Figure 8.38.

> All of the macros that have been created display in the list.

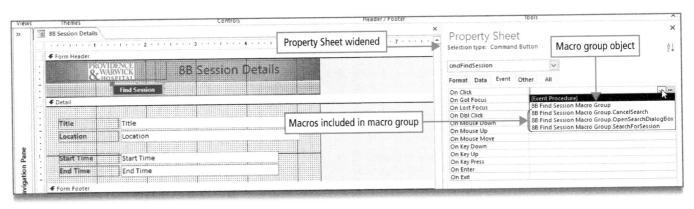

Figure 8.38

4 In the displayed list, click **8B Find Session Macro Group.OpenSearchDialogBox**.

> When you click on the Find Session button in the *8B Session Details* form, the OpenSearchDialogBox macro in the *8B Find Session Macro Group* will execute.

5 On the **Property Sheet**, click the **Format tab**. In the **Caption** property setting box, click to the left of **Find Session**, and then type **&**

> Recall that the ampersand (&) causes the letter that follows it to be underlined on the button, which will enable the user to use a shortcut key combination (Alt + the letter) to access the button instead of clicking on the button.

6 **Close** × the **Property Sheet**, **Save** 🖫 the form, and then switch to **Form** view. Notice that on the **Find Session** button, the letter **F** is underscored, which indicates that pressing Alt + F is the same action as clicking on the button.

7 Click the **Find Session** button, and then compare your screen with Figure 8.39.

> The Search Sessions dialog box displays, which is the *8B Search Sessions Dialog Box* form.

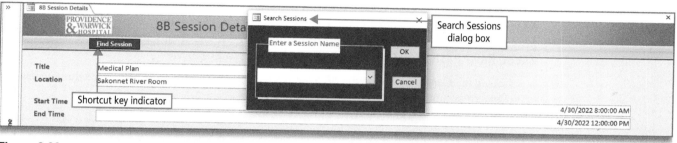

Figure 8.39

8 **Close** × the **Search Sessions** dialog box.

ALERT Did the Find and Replace dialog box display?

If you use the shortcut key and the Find and Replace dialog box displays instead of the Search Sessions dialog box, you held down Ctrl instead of Alt.

---

9 Do not close the **8B Session Details** form. **Open** » the **Navigation Pane**. Under **Forms**, right-click **8B Search Sessions Dialog Box** and then click **Design View**. **Close** « the **Navigation Pane**.

10 Right-click the **OK** button, and then click **Properties**. On the **Property Sheet**, click the **Event tab**. Click the **On Click property setting arrow**, and then click **8B Find Session Macro Group.SearchForSession**. On the **Property Sheet**, click the **Format tab**. In the **Caption** box, click to the left of **OK**, and then type **&** and then **Close** × the **Property Sheet**. **Save** 🖫 the form, and then switch the form to **Form** view.

> When the OK button is clicked or the user presses Alt + O, the second macro in the *8B Find Session Macro Group* executes.

11 In the **Enter a Session Name combo box**, click the **arrow**, and then click **Eye Care Plan**. Click **OK**, and then compare your screen with Figure 8.40.

> The macro executes, the *8B Session Details* form displays the first record—Record 3—with a session name (Title) of Eye Care Plan, and a message box displays, telling you to click the Remove Sort button to display the records in the original sort order.

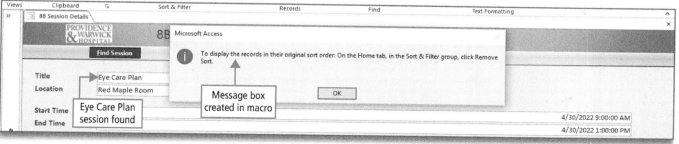

Figure 8.40

12 ▶ In the displayed message box, click **OK**. Press [Alt] + [F] to display the **Search Sessions** dialog box. In the **Search Sessions** dialog box, in the **Enter a Session Name** combo box, type **pr** and notice that Access displays Prescription Plan. Press [Alt] + [O]. In the displayed message box, click **OK**.

> Instead of selecting an item from the list, you can type the first few letters of the Session name. If Access finds the Session name in the list, it displays in the combo box. Record 7 is displayed.

13 ▶ On the **Home tab**, in the **Sort & Filter** group, click **Remove Sort**.

14 ▶ Open ⟩⟩ the **Navigation Pane**. Under **Forms**, open the **8B Search Sessions Dialog Box** form in **Design** view, and then **Close** ⟨⟨ the **Navigation Pane**.

15 ▶ Right-click the **Cancel** button, and then click **Properties**. On the **Property Sheet**, click the **Event tab**, click the **On Click property setting arrow**, and then click **8B Find Session Macro Group.CancelSearch**. Click the **Property Sheet Format tab**. In the **Caption** property setting box, click to the left of **Cancel**, type **&** and then **Close** ⊠ the **Property Sheet**. **Save** 🖫 the form, and then switch the form to **Form** view.

> Clicking the Cancel button on the *8B Search Sessions Dialog Box* form causes the third macro in the macro group to execute.

16 ▶ In the **Search Sessions** dialog box, click the **Cancel** button or press [Alt] + [C].

> The form closes, and the focus is placed on the *8B Session Details* form.

17 ▶ **Close** ⊠ the **8B Session Details** form.

Objective 7 | **Create a Data Macro**

GO! Learn How
Video A8-7

You have created macros using the Macro Designer and Macro Builder. Data macros are created and managed while you are viewing a table in Datasheet view. A *data macro* is a macro that is triggered by events, such as adding, updating, or deleting data within a table, form, or query. The macro is used to validate the accuracy of data in a table. It is also known as an event-driven macro.

Activity 8.12 | Creating an Event-Driven Macro

MOS
2.2.2

In this Activity, you will create an event-driven macro to determine the status of each session based on the # Enrolled.

1 ▶ Open ⟩⟩ the **Navigation Pane**. Under **Tables**, double-click **8B Sessions** to display the table in **Datasheet** view. Review the data displayed in the table. **Close** ⟨⟨ the **Navigation Pane**.

> The # Enrolled field displays how many employees have signed up for the session, and the Capacity field displays the maximum capacity in that room. The Status field will be used to display whether the session is still open for enrollment.

2 ▶ Under **Table Tools**, on the **Table tab**, in the **Before Events** group, click **Before Change** to display the **Macro Designer**.

3 ▶ In the **Macro Designer**, add the **If** action using one of the techniques you have learned. In the **If** action block, click in the **If** box, and type **[# Enrolled]>=[Capacity]** selecting items as they appear in the list to reduce errors.

> The conditional expression comparison is used to determine the action that will occur.

4 In the **If** action block, add the **SetField** action using one of the techniques you have learned. In the **SetField** action block, click in the **Name** box, and type **Status** Click in the **Value** box, type **"Closed"** and then compare your screen with Figure 8.41.

The SetField action will update the *Status* field if the condition is true.

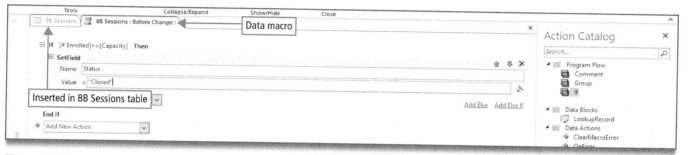

Figure 8.41

5 In the **If Arguments** block click **Add Else** on the right of the screen, below the arguments, to add an additional condition to the If Arguments block. In the **Else Arguments** block, add the **SetField** action using one of the techniques you have learned. In the **SetField** action block, click in the **Name** box, and type **Status** Click in the **Value** box, and type **"Open"**

The SetField action will update the *Status* field if the original conditional expression is false.

6 **Close** ☒ the **Macro Designer**. In the displayed message box, click **Yes** to save the changes made to the macro and to update the property. **Save** 🖫 the table.

7 In Record 7, click in the **# Enrolled** field, and type **30**. Press ⬇ to move to the next record, type **22** and then click in the first **ID** field. Notice the updates to the **Status** field. Compare your screen with Figure 8.42.

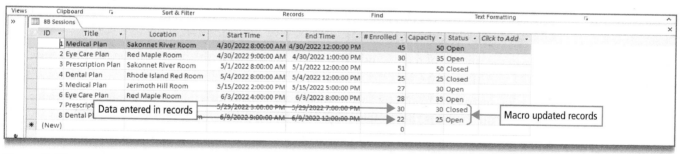

Figure 8.42

MORE KNOWLEDGE **Adding a Total Row to a Table**

A total row can be added to a table. On the Home tab, in the records group, click Totals. At the bottom of the table, under the field in which you want to add an aggregate function, click the empty box and then click the arrow. From the list of aggregate functions, click the one you wish to apply.

---

8 **Close** the table. **Open** ≫ the **Navigation Pane. Close** the database, and then **Close** Access.

For Non-MyLab Submissions: Determine What Your Instructor Requires for Submission

As directed by your instructor, submit your completed database file. If you are completing the optional activity, do so before submitting your database to your instructor.

9 In **MyLab IT**, locate and click the Grader Project **Access 8B Employee Benefits**. In **step 3**, under **Upload Completed Assignment**, click **Choose File**. In the **Open** dialog box, navigate to your **Access Chapter 8 folder**, and then click your **Student_Access_8B_Employee_Benefits** file one time to select it. In the lower right corner of the **Open** dialog box, click **Open**.

> The name of your selected file displays above the Upload button.

10 To submit your file to **MyLab IT** for grading, click **Upload**, wait a moment for a green **Success!** message, and then in **step 4**, click the blue **Submit for Grading** button. Click **Close Assignment** to return to your list of **Course Materials**.

ALERT   This Activity Is Optional

The following Activity is optional. Check with your instructor to see if you should complete this Activity. This Activity is not included in the **MyLab IT** Grader system for this project; however, you may want to practice this on your own.

Activity 8.13 | Printing Macro Group Details

In this Activity, you will use the Database Documenter to print out the details of the macro group that you have created in this project.

1 Start Access. Under *Recent*, click your **Access_8B_Employee_Benefits** file to open it.

2 **Close** 《 the **Navigation Pane**.

3 On the **Database Tools tab**, in the **Analyze group**, click **Database Documenter**.

> The Documenter dialog box displays tabs for each object type and a tab for the current database. Only standalone macros display on the Macros tab. Macros that are run are embedded with an object and will display as a property of the object.

4 In the **Documenter** dialog box, if necessary, click the **Macros tab**. Click **Options**. If necessary, click the **Permissions by User and Group** check box to clear it, and then click **OK**. In the **Documenter** dialog box, click **Select All**. Click **OK**.

5 Click in the middle of the document to zoom in to display the details of the **8B Find Session Macro Group** macro.

6 If you are instructed to submit this result, create a paper printout or PDF electronic image. On the **Print Preview tab**, in the **Close Preview group**, click **Close Print Preview**.

7 **Open** 》 the **Navigation Pane**. **Close** the database, and then **Close** Access.

For Non-MyLab Submissions: Determine What Your Instructor Requires for Submission
As directed by your instructor, submit your completed database file.

You have completed Project 8B **END**

wavebreakmedia/Shutterstock, Monkey Business Images/Fotolia, Ivanko80/Shutterstock, Monkey Business Images/Shutterstock

8

ACCESS

Microsoft Office Specialist (MOS) Skills in This Chapter	
Project 8A	**Project 8B**
4.1.1 Add, move, and remove form controls	**2.2.2** Add total rows
4.1.2 Set form control properties	**4.1.2** Set form control properties

Build Your E-Portfolio

An E-Portfolio is a collection of evidence, stored electronically, that showcases what you have accomplished while completing your education. Collecting and then sharing your work products with potential employees reflects your academic and career goals. Your completed documents from the following projects are good examples to show what you have learned: 8G, 8K, and 8L.

GO! For Job Success

Topic: Career Satisfaction

When students talk about career plans, they inevitably hear advice like, "Follow your passion!" or "Do what you love and you'll be successful." But is that really true? Should everyone expect that following their dreams will lead to a successful career? Are you a failure if you don't follow your passion?

With millions of people unemployed but millions of jobs going unfilled, many career experts believe a new way of thinking about "passion" is needed. More realistic advice might be to find a passion for the job you have rather than struggling to find a job that fits your passion. A particular skill or area of knowledge will result in a successful career only if there is a need for it in the market—employers and customers must be willing to pay you to do it.

g-stockstudio/Shutterstock

> Do you think it's possible to be happy in a job or career that you are not passionate about, but that you like or are good at?

> Do you think doing what you love is a requirement for a rewarding and successful career?

> If you have a passion for an activity or cause, do you think it's realistic that you could make a living devoted to it, and do you think you would continue to be passionate about it if you had to do it for a living every day?

End of Chapter

Summary

Macros are created to automate database tasks. A database must be trusted in order for all macro actions to be enabled. The Database Documenter is used to print details of objects, including macros.

Standalone macros can run from the Navigation Pane. An autoexec macro runs automatically when the database is opened. Macros can also be embedded within buttons; embedded macros do not display in the Navigation Pane.

A macro group is a set of submacros grouped together and displayed as a single macro in the Navigation Pane. Submacros can then be associated with the clicking of a button on a form or report.

Data macros are associated with a table and triggered by events, such as adding, updating, or deleting data in a table, form, or query. Data macros are used to validate the accuracy of data in a table.

GO! Learn It Online

Review the concepts, key terms, and MOS skills in this chapter by completing these online challenges, which you can find at **MyLab IT**.

Chapter Quiz: Answer matching and multiple choice questions to test what you learned in this chapter.

Lessons on the GO!: Learn how to use all the new apps and features as they are introduced by Microsoft.

MOS Quiz: Answer questions to review the MOS skills that you practiced in this chapter.

Project Guide for Access Chapter 8

Your instructor will assign Projects from this list to ensure your learning and assess your knowledge.

Project	Apply Skills from These Chapter Objectives	Project Type		Project Location
8A **MyLab IT**	Objectives 1–4 from Project 8A	**8A Instructional Project (Grader Project)** Guided instruction to learn the skills in Project 8A.	**Instruction**	In **MyLab IT** and in text
8B **MyLab IT**	Objectives 5–7 from Project 8B	**8B Instructional Project (Grader Project)** Guided instruction to learn the skills in Project 8B.	**Instruction**	In **MyLab IT** and in text
8C	Objectives 1–4 from Project 8A	**8C Chapter Review (Scorecard Grading)** A guided review of the skills from Project 8A.	**Review**	In text
8D	Objectives 5–7 from Project 8B	**8D Chapter Review (Scorecard Grading)** A guided review of the skills from Project 8B.	**Review**	In text
8E	Objectives 1–4 from Project 8A	**8E Mastery (Scorecard Grading)** **Mastery and Transfer of Learning** A demonstration of your mastery of the skills in Project 8A with extensive decision making.		In text
8F	Objectives 5–7 from Project 8B	**8F Mastery (Scorecard Grading)** **Mastery and Transfer of Learning** A demonstration of your mastery of the skills in Project 8B with extensive decision making.		In text
8G **MyLab IT**	Objectives 1–7 from Projects 8A and 8B	**8G Mastery (Grader Project)** **Mastery and Transfer of Learning** A demonstration of your mastery of the skills in Projects 8A and 8B with extensive decision making.		In **MyLab IT** and in text
8H	Combination of Objectives from Projects 8A and 8B	**8H GO! Fix It (Scorecard Grading)** **Critical Thinking** A demonstration of your mastery of the skills in Projects 8A and 8B by creating a correct result from a document that contains errors you must find.		Instructor Resource Center (IRC)
8I	Combination of Objectives from Projects 8A and 8B	**8I GO! Make It (Scorecard Grading)** **Critical Thinking** A demonstration of your mastery of the skills in Projects 8A and 8B by creating a result from a supplied picture.		IRC
8J	Combination of Objectives from Projects 8A and 8B	**8J GO! Solve It (Rubric Grading)** **Critical Thinking** A demonstration of your mastery of the skills in Projects 8A and 8B, your decision-making skills, and your critical thinking skills. A task-specific rubric helps you self-assess your result.		IRC
8K	Combination of Objectives from Projects 8A and 8B	**8K GO! Solve It (Rubric Grading)** **Critical Thinking** A demonstration of your mastery of the skills in Projects 8A and 8B, your decision-making skills, and your critical thinking skills. A task-specific rubric helps you self-assess your result.		In text
8L	Combination of Objectives from Projects 8A and 8B	**8L GO! Think (Rubric Grading)** **Critical Thinking** A demonstration of your understanding of the chapter concepts applied in a manner that you would use outside of college. An analytic rubric helps you and your instructor grade the quality of your work by comparing it to the work an expert in the discipline would create.		In text
8M	Combination of Objectives from Projects 8A and 8B	**8M GO! Think (Rubric Grading)** **Critical Thinking** A demonstration of your understanding of the chapter concepts applied in a manner that you would use outside of college. An analytic rubric helps you and your instructor grade the quality of your work by comparing it to the work an expert in the discipline would create.		IRC
8N	Combination of Objectives from Projects 8A and 8B	**8N You and GO! (Rubric Grading)** **Critical Thinking** A demonstration of your understanding of the chapter concepts applied in a manner that you would use in a personal situation. An analytic rubric helps you and your instructor grade the quality of your work.		IRC

Glossary

Glossary of Chapter Key Terms

Action A self-contained instruction that can be combined with other actions to automate tasks.

Argument A value that provides information to the macro action, such as the words to display in a message box or the control upon which to operate.

Code Builder A window used to type programming code in Microsoft Visual Basic.

Comment Explanatory information provided about the macro or the action.

Condition A statement that specifies that certain criteria must be met before the macro action executes.

Data macro A macro that is triggered by events, such as adding, updating, or deleting data within a table, form, or query. It is used to validate the accuracy of data in a table; also known as an event-driven macro.

Database Documenter An option used to create a report that contains detailed information about the objects in a database, including macros, and to create a paper record.

Debugging A logical process to find and reduce the number of errors in a program.

Embedded macro A macro that is stored in the properties of forms, reports, or controls.

Event Any action that can be detected by a program or computer system, such as clicking a button or closing an object.

Macro A series of actions grouped as a single command to accomplish a task or multiple tasks automatically to add functionality to your object or control.

Macro Designer Window that allows you to build the list of actions to be carried out when the macro runs.

Macro group A set of macros grouped by a common name that displays as one macro object on the Navigation Pane.

Modal window A child (secondary) window to a parent window—the original window that opened the modal window—that takes over control of the parent window.

Pop-up window A window that suddenly displays (pops up), usually contains a menu of commands, and stays on the screen only until the user selects one of the commands.

Single stepping Debugging a macro using a process that executes one action at a time.

Standalone macro A macro object that displays under Macros on the Navigation Pane.

Syntax The spelling, grammar, and sequence of characters of a programming language.

Chapter Review

Project 8C Supervisory Staff

Apply 8A skills from these Objectives:

1. Create a Standalone Macro with One Action
2. Add Multiple Actions to a Standalone Macro
3. Create an Embedded Macro
4. Print Macro Details

Maria Diaz, vice president of operations for Providence & Warwick Hospital, wants to customize her database of supervisory staff. In this project, you will create macros to automatically display a form and message box when the database is opened and embed macros within a form. Finally, you will display and print a report that documents the details of the macros you created. Your completed Navigation Pane will look similar to Figure 8.43.

Project Files

For Project 8C, you will need the following file:

a08C_Supervisory_Staff

You will save your database as:

Lastname_Firstname_8C_Supervisory_Staff

Project Results

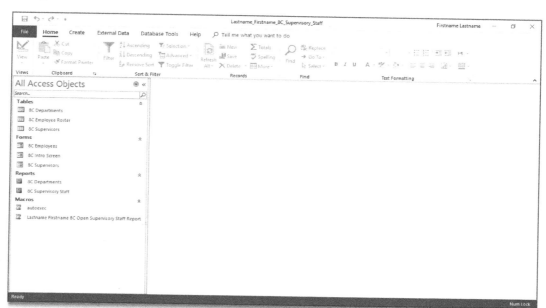

Figure 8.43

(continues on next page)

Chapter Review

1 Start Access. Locate and open the **a08C_Supervisory_Staff** file. Save the database in your **Access Chapter 8** folder as **Lastname_Firstname_8C_Supervisory_Staff** and then **Close** the **Navigation Pane**.

2 On the **Create tab**, in the **Macros & Code group**, click **Macro**.

a. In the **Macro Designer**, in the **Add New Action bar,** click the **arrow**, and then click **OpenReport**. In the **OpenReport** action block, in the **Report Name** box, click the **arrow**, and then click **8C Supervisory Staff**. In the **View** box, verify that **Report** is selected. The **Filter Name** and **Where Condition** boxes should be blank. In the **Window Mode** box, verify that the setting is **Normal**.

b. In the **Action Catalog pane**, double-click **Comment**, and type **Opens 8C Supervisory Staff report in Report view**

c. Under **Macro Tools**, on the **Design tab**, in the **Tools group**, click **Run**. In the displayed message box, click **Yes** to save the macro. In the **Save As** dialog box, type **Lastname Firstname 8C Open Supervisory Staff Report** and then click **OK**. **Close** the **8C Supervisory Staff** report, and then **Close** the Macro Designer.

3 **Open** the **Navigation Pane**. Under **Forms**, open the **8C Intro Screen** form in **Design** view. Under **Form Design Tools**, on the **Design tab**, in the **Tools group**, click **Property Sheet**. On the **Property Sheet Other tab**, click the **Pop Up property setting arrow**, and then click **Yes**. Click in the **Modal** property setting box, click the **arrow**, and then click **Yes**. **Close** the **Property Sheet**, and then **Close** the form, saving changes when prompted. **Close** the **Navigation Pane**.

4 On the **Create tab**, in the **Macros & Code group**, click **Macro**.

a. In the **Macro Designer**, add the **OpenForm** action. In the **OpenForm** action block, click the **Form Name arrow**, and then click **8C Intro Screen**. Add the following comment: **Opens 8C Intro Screen form**

b. On the **Quick Access Toolbar**, click **Save**. In the **Save As** dialog box, type **autoexec** and then click **OK**. **Close** the Macro Designer, and then **Open** the **Navigation Pane**. In the **Navigation Pane**, under **Macros**, double-click **autoexec** to run the macro. **Close** the form.

5 In the **Navigation Pane**, under **Macros**, right-click **autoexec**, and then click **Design View**. **Close** the **Navigation Pane**.

a. Add the **DisplayHourglassPointer** action. Notice that the default argument is *Yes*. Add the following comment: **Turns mouse pointer into a Busy icon**

b. Under **Macro Tools**, on the **Design tab**, in the **Show/Hide group**, click **Show All Actions**. In the **Macro Designer**, add the **Echo** action. In the **Echo** action block, click the **Echo On arrow**, and then click **No**. Click in the **Status Bar Text** box, and type **Macro is running** Add the following comment: **Hides the flickering screen as the macro runs**

c. Add the **RunMacro** action. In the **RunMacro** action block, click the **Macro Name arrow**, and then click your **8C Open Supervisory Staff Report**. The **Repeat Count** box and the **Repeat Expression** box should be blank. Add the following comment: **Runs 8C Open Supervisory Staff Report macro**

d. Add the **MessageBox** action. In the **MessageBox** action block, click in the **Message** box, and then type **Only supervisors at Providence & Warwick Hospital are authorized to access this database.** In the **Beep** box, verify that the Beep argument is **Yes**. Click the **Type box arrow**, and then click **Warning!** Click in the **Title** box, and then type **For Use by Providence & Warwick Hospital Supervisors Only!** Add the following comment: **Displays a warning message box**

e. In the **Macro Designer**, add the **DisplayHourglassPointer** action. In the **DisplayHourglassPointer** action block, click the **Hourglass On arrow**, and then click **No**. Add the following comment: **Restores the mouse pointer**

f. Add the **Echo** action. Add the following comment: **Screen displays results**

g. Scroll to the top of the **Action Argument** box. Click the **OpenForm** action to make it active, and then move the action below the comment **Runs 8C Open Supervisory Staff Report macro**.

h. Move the **OpenForm macro comment** below the **OpenForm action**.

i. **Save** the macro. Under **Macro Tools**, on the **Design tab**, in the **Tools group**, click **Run**. In the displayed message box, click **OK**. **Close** the **8C Intro Screen** form. On the **tab row**, right-click any tab, and then click **Close All**. **Open** the **Navigation Pane**.

(continues on next page)

Chapter Review

6 Open the **8C Supervisors** form in **Design** view. **Close** the **Navigation Pane**. Under **Form Design Tools**, on the **Design tab**, in the **Controls group**, click **Button**. In the **Details** section, align the plus sign (+) of the pointer at **3 inches on the horizontal ruler** and **2 inches on the vertical ruler**, and then click.

a. In the **Command Button Wizard** dialog box, click **Cancel**.

b. Right-click the button, and then click **Properties**. Verify that the **Property Sheet** displays *Selection type: Command Button* and the **Selection type** box displays *Command0* (your number may differ), identifying your command button. On the **Property Sheet Other tab**, in the **Name** property box, select the existing text and type **btnEmpl**

c. On the **Property Sheet Format tab**, in the **Caption** property box, select the existing text, type **Employee List** and then press Enter.

d. On the **Property Sheet Event tab**, in the **On Click** property setting box, click **Build**.

e. In the **Choose Builder** dialog box, click **Macro Builder**, if necessary, and then click **OK** to display the Macro Designer.

f. In the **Macro Designer**, add the **OpenForm** action using one of the techniques you have learned. In the **OpenForm** action block, click the **Form Name arrow**, and then click **8C Employees**. Click in the **Where Condition** box, and type **[Department]=[Forms]![8C Supervisors]![Department]** selecting items as they appear in the list to reduce errors.

g. In the **OpenForm** action block, click the **View arrow**, and then click **Datasheet**. Click the **Data Mode arrow**, and then click **Read Only**. Add the following comment: **Opens 8C Employees form for department indicated on 8C Supervisors form**

h. **Close** the **Macro Designer**. In the displayed message box, click **Yes** to save the changes made to the macro and to update the **On Click** property.

7 On the **Property Sheet**, click the **Format tab**. In the **Caption** box, click to the left of **Employee List**, and then type **&** to create a shortcut key using the letter

E. **Close** the **Property Sheet**, **Save** the form, and then switch the **8C Supervisors** form to **Form** view.

a. On the **8C Supervisors** form, click the **Employee List** button or press Alt + E.

b. **Close** the **8C Employees** form, and then **Close** the **8C Supervisors** form, saving changes, if necessary. **Open** the **Navigation Pane**.

8 Open the **8C Departments** report in **Design** view. **Close** the **Navigation Pane**. In the **Detail** section, right-click the **Dept ID** text box, and then click **Properties**. Verify that the **Property Sheet** displays *Selection type: Text Box* and the **Selection type** box displays *Dept ID*.

a. On the **Property Sheet Event tab**, in the **On Click** property setting box, click the **Build** button. In the **Choose Builder** dialog box, verify that **Macro Builder** is selected, and then click **OK** to display the Macro Designer.

b. In the **Macro Designer**, add the **OpenForm** action using one of the techniques you have learned. In the **OpenForm** action block, click the **Form Name arrow**, and then click **8C Supervisors** form. Click in the **Where Condition** box, type **[Dept ID]=[Reports]![8C Departments]![Dept ID]** selecting items as they appear in the list to reduce errors.

c. In the **OpenForm** action block, click the **Data Mode arrow**, and then click **Read Only**. Add the following comment: **Opens 8C Supervisors form for the Dept ID selected on 8C Departments report**

d. **Close** the **Macro Designer**. In the displayed message box, click **Yes** to save the changes made to the macro and to update the **On Click** property. **Close** the **Property Sheet**. **Save** the report.

e. Switch to **Report** view. On the **8C Departments** report, click the **Dept ID** text box for *1233-D* to run the macro.

f. **Close** the **8C Supervisors** form. **Close** the **8C Departments** report, saving changes.

9 **Open** the **Navigation Pane**. **Close** the database, and then **Close** Access.

10 As directed by your instructor, submit your database for grading.

You have completed Project 8C | END

Chapter Review

Skills Review | **Project 8D Hospital Departments**

Apply 8B skills from these Objectives:

5. Create a Macro Group
6. Associate a Macro with an Event
7. Create a Data Macro

Maria Diaz, vice president of operations for Providence & Warwick Hospital, wants to customize her database of department information, including automating the process to add new departments. You will associate command buttons with a macro group's submacros and create a data macro. Your completed Navigation Pane will look similar to Figure 8.44.

Project Files

For Project 8D, you will need the following file:

a08D_Hospital_Departments

You will save your database as:

Lastname_Firstname_8D_Hospital_Departments

Project Results

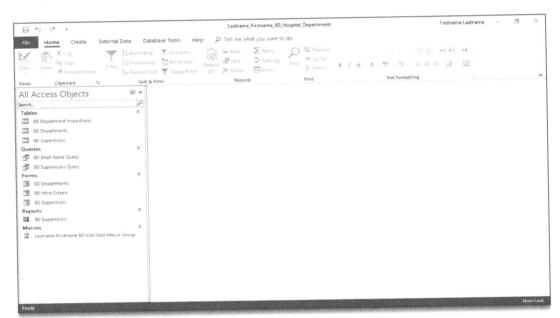

Figure 8.44

(continues on next page)

Chapter Review

1 Start Access. Locate and open the **a08D_Hospital_ Departments** file. Save the database in your **Access Chapter 8** folder as **Lastname_Firstname_8D_Hospital_ Departments** and then **Close** the **Navigation Pane**.

2 On the **Create tab**, in the **Macros & Code group**, click **Macro**. Under **Macro Tools**, on the **Design tab**, in the **Show/Hide group**, click **Show All Actions**.

a. In the **Action Catalog pane**, double-click **Group**. Click in the **Group** box, and type **Lastname Firstname 8D Add Dept Macro Group** Add the following comment: **Purpose: To enable a user to add a department using the 8D Departments form** On the **tab row**, right-click **Macro1**, click **Save**, and then type **Lastname Firstname 8D Add Dept Macro Group** Click **OK**.

b. In the **Action Catalog pane**, double-click **Submacro**, and type **GoToNewRecord** In the **Submacro**, add the **GoToRecord** action. In the **GoToRecord** action block, click the **Object Type arrow**, and then click **Form**. Click the **Object Name arrow**, and then click **8D Departments**. Verify that **New** appears in the **Record** box. Add the following comment: **Goes to new record in 8D Departments form**

c. In the submacro, add the **GoToControl** action. In the **GoToControl** action block, click in the **Control Name box**, and then type **Department ID** Add the following comment: **Changes focus from button to Department ID field**

d. In the submacro, add the **SetValue** action. In the **SetValue** action block, click in the **Item** box, and type **[Forms]![8D Departments]![cmdAddNew]. [Visible]** Click in the **Expression** box, and type **No** Add the following comment: **Hides the Add Dept button**

e. In the submacro, add the **SetValue** action. In the **SetValue** action block, click in the **Item** box, and type **[Forms]![8D Departments]![cmdShowAll]. [Visible]** Click in the **Expression** box and type **Yes** Add the following comment: **Displays the Show All button**

f. In the **Action Catalog pane**, double-click **Submacro**, and type **ShowAll** In the **ShowAll Submacro**, under **Add New Action**, click the arrow, and then click **ShowAllRecords**. Add the following comment: **Shows all records and exits data entry**

g. In the submacro, add the **GoToControl** action. In the **GoToControl** action block, click in the **Control Name** box, and type **Department ID** Add the following comment: **Changes focus from button to Department ID field**

h. In the submacro, add the **SetValue** action. In the **SetValue** action block, to the right of the **Item** box, click the **Builder** button. In the **Expression Builder**, select items or type **[Forms]![8D Departments]![cmdAddNew].[Visible]** and then click **OK**. Click in the **Expression** box, and type **Yes** Add the following comment: **Shows the Add Dept button**

i. In the submacro, add the **SetValue** action. In the **SetValue** action block, click in the **Item** box, and type **[Forms]![8D Departments]! [cmdShowAll]. [Visible]** Click in the **Expression** box, and then type **No** Add the following comment: **Hides the Show All button**

j. **Save** the macro group. **Close** the **Macro Designer**, and then **Open** the **Navigation Pane**.

3 In the **Navigation Pane**, **Open** the **8D Departments** form in **Design** view. **Close** the **Navigation Pane**.

a. In the **Form Header section**, right-click the **Add Dept** button, and then click **Properties**. Verify that the **Property Sheet** displays *Selection type: Command Button* and that the **Selection type** box displays *cmdAddNew*.

b. If necessary, point to the **left edge** of the **Property Sheet** until the pointer displays. Drag to the **7.25-inch mark** on the horizontal ruler.

c. On the **Property Sheet Event tab**, click the **On Click property setting arrow**. In the displayed list, click **Lastname Firstname 8D Add Dept Macro Group.GoToNewRecord**. On the **Property Sheet Format tab**, in the **Caption** property setting box, click to the left of **Add Dept**, and then type **&**

d. On the **Property Sheet**, in the **Selection type** box, click **cmdShowAll**. On the **Property Sheet Event tab**, click the **On Click property setting arrow**. In the displayed list, click **Lastname Firstname 8D Add Dept Macro Group.ShowAll**. On the **Property Sheet Format tab**, in the **Caption** property setting box, click to the left of **Show All**, and then type **&** and then **Close** the **Property Sheet**.

(continues on next page)

Chapter Review

e. Switch to **Form** view. Click the **Add Dept** button. In the **Department ID** field type **1236-D** Press Tab, and type **Dietary Services** Enter your information for all of the remaining fields except Super ID. In the **Super ID** field, type **417-Sup Close** the **8D Departments** form, saving changes.

4 ▶ **Open** the **8D Department Inspections** table in **Datasheet** view.

a. Under **Table Tools**, on the **Table tab**, in the **Before Events** group, click **Before Change** to display the Macro Designer.

b. In the **Macro Designer**, add the **If** action using one of the techniques you have learned. In the **If Arguments** action block, click in the **If** conditional expression box, and type **[FD Inspection]=Yes and [Safety Inspection]=Yes and [HD Inspection]=Yes** selecting items as they appear in the list to reduce errors.

c. In the **If Arguments Block**, add the **SetField** action using one of the techniques you have learned. In the

SetField action block, click in the **Name** box, and type **Inspection Status** Click in the **Value** box, and type **"Inspections Complete"**

d. In the **If Arguments Block**, click **Add Else** to add an additional action to the If Arguments Block. In the **Else Arguments Block**, add the **SetField** action using one of the techniques you have learned. In the **SetField** action block, click in the **Name** box, and type **Inspection Status** Click in the **Value** box, and type **"Schedule Necessary Inspections"**

e. **Close** the **Macro Designer**. In the displayed message box, click **Yes** to save the changes made to the macro and to update the property. **Save** the table.

f. In the **HD Inspections** field, click in the following Dept IDs: 1212-D, 1233-D, 1265-D, and 1459-D. Notice the updates to the **Inventory Status** field.

5 ▶ **Close** the database, and then **Close** Access.

6 ▶ As directed by your instructor, submit your database for grading

You have completed Project 8D   **END**

Content-Based Assessments (Mastery and Transfer of Learning)

| Mastering | Project 8E Gift Shop |

Apply 8A skills from these Objectives:

1. Create a Standalone Macro with One Action
2. Add Multiple Actions to a Standalone Macro
3. Create an Embedded Macro
4. Print Macro Details

Maria Diaz, vice president of operations for Providence & Warwick Hospital, wants to customize the gift shop database and automate common tasks. In this project, you will create a macro to automatically display a form and message box when the user opens the database. In addition, you will embed macros within a form and report. Your completed Navigation Pane will look similar to Figure 8.45.

Project Files

For Project 8E, you will need the following file:

a08E_Gift_Shop

You will save your database as:

Lastname_Firstname_8E_Gift_Shop

Project Results

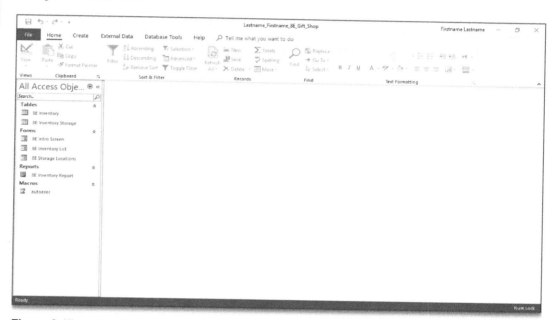

Figure 8.45

(continues on next page)

Content-Based Assessments (Mastery and Transfer of Learning)

Mastering: Project 8E Gift Shop (continued)

1 Start Access. Locate and open the **a08E_Gift_Shop** file. Save the database in your **Access Chapter 8** folder as **Lastname_Firstname_8E_Gift_Shop Close** the **Navigation Pane**.

2 Create a macro to open the **8E Intro Screen** form with a comment: **Opens 8E Intro Screen form** On the **Design tab**, in the **Show/Hide group**, verify that the **Show All Actions** button is active. **Save** the macro as **autoexec**

3 Modify the **autoexec** macro. Add the action **DisplayHourglassPointer** with the **Comment Displays the busy icon** Add the **Echo** action with the **Comment Hides the flickering screen as the macro runs** In the **Echo** action block, change the **Echo On** box to **No**. In the **Status Bar Text** box, type **Macro is running** Move the **OpenForm** action and comment below the **Echo** macro comment.

4 In the **Macro Designer**, at the bottom of the current list of actions, add a **MessageBox** action. Type a **Message** that displays **All gift shop inventory transfers must be recorded in the transfer log.** Add a **Beep**, and change the **Type** box to **Information**. Title the **Message** box **Inventory Transfers** Add a **Comment** that reads **Displays transfer procedure message**

5 In the **Macro Designer**, add an **Echo** action. In the **Echo** action block, verify the **Echo On** box is set to **Yes**. Add a **Comment** that says **Displays screen results**

6 In the **Macro Designer**, add a **DisplayHourglassPointer** action. In the **DisplayHourglassPointer** action block, change the **Hourglass On** box to **No**. Add a **Comment** that says **Restores the mouse pointer**

7 **Close** the Macro Designer, and **Save** the macro. **Open** the Navigation Pane.

8 Open the **8E Storage Locations** form in **Design** view. **Close** the **Navigation Pane**. In the **Detail** section, add a **Button** control at **1.5 inches on the horizontal ruler** and **0.25 inches on the vertical ruler**. In the **Command Button Wizard** dialog box, click **Cancel**. Right-click the button, and then click **Properties**. On the **Property Sheet Other tab**, change the **Name** to **btnInv** On the **Property Sheet Format tab**, change the **Caption**

to **Inventory List** On the **Property Sheet Event tab**, in the **On Click** property setting box, click the **Build** button. In the **Choose Builder** dialog box, verify that **Macro Builder** is selected, and then click **OK** to display the Macro Designer.

9 In the **Macro Designer**, add the **OpenForm** action to open the **8E Inventory List** form. In the **Where Condition** box, type **[Category]=[Forms]![8E Storage Locations]![Category]** For **View**, select **Datasheet**. For **Data Mode**, select **Read Only**. Add the comment: **Opens 8E Inventory List form for category indicated on 8E Storage Locations form Close** the **Macro Designer**, saving changes and updating the **On Click** property.

10 On the **Property Sheet Format tab**, in the **Caption** box, insert an **&** to the left of **Inventory List**. **Close** the **Property Sheet**, **Save** the form, and then switch **8E Storage Locations** to **Form** view. Click the **Inventory List** button. **Close** the **8E Inventory List** form. **Close** the **8E Storage Locations** form. **Open** the **Navigation Pane**.

11 Open the **8E Inventory Report** in **Design** view. **Close** the **Navigation Pane**. In the **Detail** section, display the **Property Sheet** for the **Category** text box. Verify that the **Property Sheet** displays *Selection type: Text Box* and the **Selection type** box displays *Category*. On the **Property Sheet Event tab**, in the **On Click** property setting box, click **Build**, and display the Macro Designer.

12 In the **Macro Designer**, add the **OpenForm** action to open the **8E Storage Locations** form. Add the **Where Condition [Category]=[Reports]![8E Inventory Report]![Category]** Change the **Data Mode** to **Read Only**. Add the comment: **Opens 8E Storage Locations form for the category selected on 8E Inventory Report Close** the **Macro Designer**, saving changes and updating the **On Click** property. **Close** the **Property Sheet**. **Save** the report.

13 Switch to **Report** view. On the **8E Inventory Report**, click the **Category** text box for *Perishable Food* to run the macro. **Close** the **8E Storage Locations** form. **Close** the **8E Inventory Report**, saving changes.

14 **Close** the database, and then **Close** Access.

15 As directed by your instructor, submit your database for grading.

You have completed Project 8E **END**

Content-Based Assessments (Mastery and Transfer of Learning)

> **Mastering** **Project 8F Orthopedic Supplies**

Apply 8B skills from these Objectives:

5. Create a Macro Group
6. Associate a Macro with an Event
7. Create a Data Macro

Maria Diaz, vice president of operations for Providence & Warwick Hospital, wants to customize the orthopedic supplies database using macros. In this project, you will create a macro group, associate command buttons with a macro, and create a data macro. Your completed Navigation Pane will look similar to Figure 8.46.

Project Files

For Project 8F, you will need the following file:

a08F_Orthopedic_Supplies

You will save your database as:

Lastname_Firstname_8F_Orthopedic_Supplies

Project Results

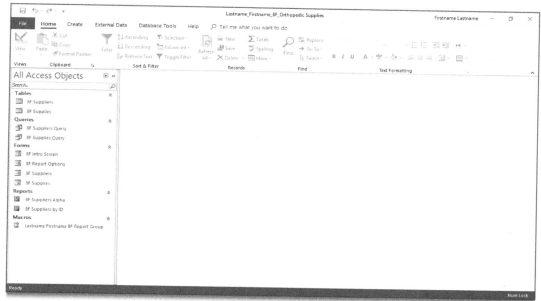

Figure 8.46

(continues on next page)

Mastering: Project 8F Orthopedic Supplies (continued)

1 Start Access. Locate and open the **a08F_ Orthopedic_Supplies** file. Save the database in your **Access Chapter 8** folder as **Lastname_Firstname_8F_ Orthopedic_Supplies Close** the **Navigation Pane.**

2 Create a **Macro Group** to print the reports. Name this macro group **Lastname Firstname 8F Report Group** with a comment: **Purpose: Allows users to select report printing options**

3 Create a **Submacro** named **Options** with the action **OpenForm** opening the **8F Report Options** form in Form view and Edit mode. Add the comment: **Opens 8F Report Options form**

4 Create a **Submacro** named **PrintReport** Add an If argument **1=[Forms]![8F Report Options]![Options]** and the **RunMacro** action for your **8F Report Group. ReportAlpha** macro. Add the comment: **Runs the macro for option 1** and then add the **StopMacro** action below the RunMacro action. In the submacro, below the first End If, add another **If** argument **2=[Forms]![8F Report Options]![Options]** and the **RunMacro** action for the **8F Report Group.ReportID** macro. Add the comment: **Runs the macro for option 2** and then add the **StopMacro** action.

5 Create a **Submacro** named **ReportAlpha** Add an action to **DisplayHourglassPointer**. Add the **RunMacro** for **8F Report Group.Cancel**, and add the comment: **Closes 8F Report Options form** Add the **OpenReport** action to open **8F Suppliers Alpha** report in Print Preview. Add the comment: **Opens report in print preview** Add the **SelectObject** action to select the **8F Suppliers Alpha** report, and add the comment: **Changes focus to 8F Suppliers Alpha report** Finally, add a macro action to turn off the hourglass with the comment: **Default mouse pointer displays**

6 Create a **Submacro** named **ReportID** Add an action to **DisplayHourglassPointer** with the comment: **Displays busy icon while macro is running** Add the **RunMacro** for **8F Report Group.Cancel**, and add the comment: **Closes 8F Report Options form** Next, add the **OpenReport** action to open the **8F Suppliers by ID** report in Print Preview. Add the comment: **Opens report in print preview** Add the **SelectObject** action to select the **8F Suppliers by ID** report, and add the comment:

Changes focus to 8F Suppliers by ID report Finally, add a macro action to turn off the hourglass with the comment: **Default mouse pointer displays**

7 Create a **Submacro** named **Cancel** Add the **CloseWindow** action to close the **8F Report Options** form. Add the comment: **Closes 8F Report Options form**

8 **Close** the **Macro Designer**, saving the group as **Lastname Firstname 8F Report Group**

9 Open the **8F Report Options** form in **Design** view. Open the **Property Sheet** for the **Print Report** button. On the **Property Sheet Event tab**, click the **On Click property setting box arrow**, and click **8F Report Group.PrintReport**. On the **Property Sheet Format tab**, click in the **Caption** property setting and type **&** before *Print Report*. On the Design grid, click the **Cancel** button. On the **Event tab**, in the **On Click** property setting, select **8F Report Group.Cancel**. On the **Property Sheet Format tab**, click in the **Caption** property setting and type **&** before *Cancel*. **Close** the **Property Sheet** and **Save** the form.

10 Switch to **Form** view, saving changes. Test each report option and **Close Print Preview**. **Close** the **8F Suppliers** form.

11 Open the **8F Supplies** table in **Datasheet** view. Add a data macro **Before Change**. Add the **If Arguments Block** with the condition **[# On Hand]<=36** Add the **SetField** action to set **Reorder Point** to **"Reorder Now"** In the **If Arguments Block**, add an **Else Arguments Block**, and then add the **SetField** action to set **Reorder Point** to **"Inventory OK"** **Close** the **Macro Designer**, saving changes. **Save** the table. In the record for **Supply ID** *519-Supp*, update the **# on Hand** to **70** In the record for *525-Supp*, update the **# on Hand** to **32** Click in the first field in the first record, and notice the updates to the **Reorder Point** field. View the table in **Print Preview**. If you are instructed to submit this result, create a paper printout or PDF electronic image in **Landscape** orientation. On the **Print Preview tab**, in the **Close Preview group**, click **Close Print Preview**.

12 **Close** the database, and then **Close** Access. As directed by your instructor, submit your database for grading.

You have completed Project 8F END

Content-Based Assessments (Mastery and Transfer of Learning)

MyLab IT Grader	Mastering	Project 8G Hospital Expansion

Apply 8A and 8B skills from these Objectives:

1. Create a Standalone Macro with One Action
2. Add Multiple Actions to a Standalone Macro
3. Create an Embedded Macro
4. Print Macro Details
5. Create a Macro Group
6. Associate a Macro with an Event
7. Create a Data Macro

Mara Bartello, facilities director of the Providence & Warwick Hospital in Providence, Rhode Island, is analyzing proposed expansion projects. In this project, you will create macros to automate the process. Your completed Navigation Pane will look similar to Figure 8.47.

Project Files for MyLab IT Grader

1. In your **MyLab IT** course, locate and click **Access 8G Hospital Expansion**, Download Materials, and then Download All Files.
2. Extract the zipped folder to your **Access Chapter 8** folder. Close the Grader download screens.
3. Take a moment to open the downloaded **Access_8G_Hospital_Expansion_Instructions**; note any recent updates to the book.

Project Results

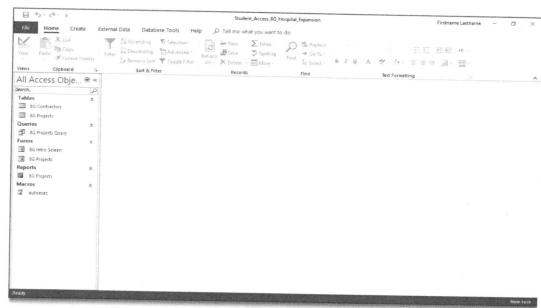

Figure 8.47

For Non-MyLab Submissions

For Project 8G, you will need:
a08G_Hospital_Expansion

Start with an Access Data File

In your Access Chapter 8 folder, save your database as:
Lastname_Firstname_8G_Hospital_Expansion

After you have saved your database, open it to launch Access. On the next page, begin with Step 2.
After Step 7, submit your database as directed by your instructor.

(continues on next page)

Mastering: Project 8G Hospital Expansion (continued)

1 Start Access. In the Access opening screen, click **Open Other Files**. Navigate to your **Access Chapter 8 folder**, and then double-click the Access file that you downloaded from **MyLab IT** that displays your name—**Student_Access_8G_Hospital_Expansion**.

2 Open the **8G Intro Screen** form in **Design** view. Change the **Pop Up** and **Modal** properties to **Yes**. **Save** and **Close** the form.

3 Create a macro to open the **8G Intro Screen** form with an appropriate comment. In the **Show/Hide group**, be sure the **Show All Actions** button is active. **Save** the macro as **autoexec**

4 Modify the **autoexec** macro. Add the action **OpenForm** to open the **8G Projects** form with an appropriate comment. Add the action **DisplayHourglassPointer** with the **Comment Displays the busy icon** Add the **Echo** action. In the **Echo** action block, change the **Echo On** box to **No**. Click in the **Status Bar Text** box, and then type **Macro is running** Add the **Comment Hides the flickering screen as the macro runs** Move the first **OpenForm** action and comment below the **Echo** macro comment. **Save** and **Close** the macro. **Close** the database, and then reopen it.

5 **Close** the **8G Intro Screen**. Switch the **8G Projects** form to **Design** view. In the **Form Header**, add a **Button** control at the **3-inch mark on the horizontal ruler** and **0.5-inch mark on the vertical ruler** with the caption **&Summary** Embed a macro to **Open** the **8G Projects** report in **Report** view. **Save** and **Close** the macro. **Save** the form. Switch to **Form** view, and test the macro. **Close** the report and the form.

6 Open the **8G Projects** table in **Datasheet** view. Add a data macro **Before Change**. Add the **If Arguments Block** with the condition [**Total Bid Amount**]<=[**Budget Amount**] Add the **SetField** action to set **Bid Status** to "**Accepted**" In the **If Arguments Block**, add an **Else Arguments Block**, and then add the **SetField** action to set **Bid Status** to "**Rejected**" **Close** the **Macro Designer**, saving changes. **Save** the table. In Record 6, update the **Total Bid Amount** to **86941000** In Record 7 update the **Total Bid Amount** to **100036** Click in the first field in the first record, and notice the updates to the **Bid Status** field.

7 Open the **Navigation Pane**. **Close** the database, and then **Close** Access.

8 In **MyLab IT**, locate and click the Grader Project **Access 8G Hospital Expansion**. In **step 3**, under **Upload Completed Assignment**, click **Choose File**. In the **Open** dialog box, navigate to your **Access Chapter 8 folder**, and then click your **Student_Access_8G_Hospital_Expansion** file one time to select it. In the lower right corner of the **Open** dialog box, click **Open**.

9 To submit your file to **MyLab IT** for grading, click **Upload**, wait a moment for a green **Success!** message, and then in **step 4**, click the blue **Submit for Grading** button. Click **Close Assignment** to return to your list of **Course Materials**.

You have completed Project 8G | **END**

Content-Based Assessments (Critical Thinking)

Apply a combination of the 8A and 8B skills.	GO! Fix It	**Project 8H Medical Transcription**	IRC
	GO! Make It	**Project 8I Recruiting Events**	IRC
	GO! Solve It	**Project 8J Dictation Department**	IRC
	GO! Solve It	**Project 8K Stay Length**	

Project Files

For Project 8K, you will need the following file:

a08K_Stay_Length

You will save your database as:

Lastname_Firstname_8K_Stay_Length

The vice president of operations at the Providence & Warwick Hospital, Maria Diaz, is preparing for the upcoming recruiting season. Open the **a08K_Stay_Length** database and save it as **Lastname_Firstname_8K_Stay_Length** Create an autoexec standalone macro to display the *8K Intro Screen* form. On the *8K Facilities* form, embed a macro in the Patients button to display the *8K Patients* form for the facility selected in Datasheet view. In the *8K Facility* table, create a Before Change data macro to display **Outpatient** in the Facility Type field if the Beds = 0; otherwise, it should display **Inpatient** Test the macro by entering **65** for the SMC facility and **0** for the WAC facility.

As directed by your instructor, submit your database for grading.

		Performance Level		
		Exemplary	**Proficient**	**Developing**
Performance Element	**Create autoexec macro**	Autoexec created with the correct actions, arguments, and comments	Autoexec created with no more than two missing actions, arguments, or comments	Autoexec created with more than two missing actions, arguments, or comments
	Create embedded macro in Patients button on 8K Facilities form	Embedded macro created with the correct actions, arguments, and comments	Embedded macro created with no more than two missing actions, arguments, or comments	Embedded macro created with more than two missing actions, arguments, or comments
	Create Before Change data macro in 8K Facility table	Data macro created with the correct actions, arguments, and comments	Data macro created with no more than two missing actions, arguments, or comments	Data macro created with more than two missing actions, arguments, or comments

You have completed Project 8K | END

Rubric

The following outcomes-based assessments are open-ended assessments. That is, there is no specific correct result; your result will depend on your approach to the information provided. Make Professional Quality your goal. Use the following scoring rubric to guide you in how to approach the problem and then to evaluate how well your approach solves the problem.

The *criteria*—Software Mastery, Content, Format and Layout, and Process—represent the knowledge and skills you have gained that you can apply to solving the problem. The *levels of performance*—Professional Quality, Approaching Professional Quality, or Needs Quality Improvements—help you and your instructor evaluate your result.

	Your completed project is of Professional Quality if you:	Your completed project is Approaching Professional Quality if you:	Your completed project Needs Quality Improvements if you:
1-Software Mastery	Choose and apply the most appropriate skills, tools, and features and identify efficient methods to solve the problem.	Choose and apply some appropriate skills, tools, and features, but not in the most efficient manner.	Choose inappropriate skills, tools, or features, or are inefficient in solving the problem.
2-Content	Construct a solution that is clear and well organized, contains content that is accurate, appropriate to the audience and purpose, and is complete. Provide a solution that contains no errors of spelling, grammar, or style.	Construct a solution in which some components are unclear, poorly organized, inconsistent, or incomplete. Misjudge the needs of the audience. Have some errors in spelling, grammar, or style, but the errors do not detract from comprehension.	Construct a solution that is unclear, incomplete, or poorly organized, contains some inaccurate or inappropriate content, and contains many errors of spelling, grammar, or style. Do not solve the problem.
3-Format and Layout	Format and arrange all elements to communicate information and ideas, clarify function, illustrate relationships, and indicate relative importance.	Apply appropriate format and layout features to some elements, but not others. Overuse features, causing minor distraction.	Apply format and layout that does not communicate information or ideas clearly. Do not use format and layout features to clarify function, illustrate relationships, or indicate relative importance. Use available features excessively, causing distraction.
4-Process	Use an organized approach that integrates planning, development, self-assessment, revision, and reflection.	Demonstrate an organized approach in some areas, but not others; or, use an insufficient process of organization throughout.	Do not use an organized approach to solve the problem.

Outcomes-Based Assessments (Critical Thinking)

Apply a combination of the 8A and 8B skills.

GO! Think **Project 8L Patient Charges**

Project Files

For Project 8L, you will need the following file:

a08L_Patient_Charges

You will save your database as:

Lastname_Firstname_8L_Patient_Charges

Paul Chin, CEO for Providence & Warwick Hospital, wants to study the patient charges accrued over the past few months at each of the facilities. Open the **a08L_Patient_Charges** database, close the Intro Screen, and save the database as **Lastname_Firstname_8L_Patient_Charges** Create a standalone macro that opens the *8L Patient Charges* report in Report view for the user to enter a facility name and then closes the *8L Display Charges* form. Save this macro as **Lastname Firstname 8L Charge Report** and associate the macro with the button on the *8L Display Charges* form. Using the form, generate the report for the P&W Rehab Center. Open the *8L Patient Charges* report in Design view and embed macros in both buttons in the Report Header. In the Display another facility button, embed a macro to close the current report without saving and open the *8L Display Charges* form to allow selection of a different facility. In the Close Database button, embed a macro to close the report without saving and close the database. As directed by your instructor, submit your database for grading.

You have completed Project 8L **END**

GO! Think **Project 8M Clinical Trials** **IRC**

You and GO! **Project 8N Club Directory** **IRC**

Integrating Access with Other Applications

9

ACCESS 2019

PROJECT 9A

Outcomes
Import data from and link to data in other Office applications.

Objectives
1. Import Data from a Word Table
2. Import Data from an Excel Workbook
3. Insert an Excel Chart into a Report
4. Import from and Link to Another Access Database

PROJECT 9B

Outcomes
Export data to Office applications, to HTML, and to XML files; create memos using mail merge.

Objectives
5. Export Data to Word
6. Use Mail Merge to Integrate Access and Word
7. Export Data to Excel
8. Export Data to an HTML File and an XML File

Jinning Li/Shutterstock

In This Chapter

 GO! To Work with Access

Using Access with other applications maximizes the efficiency of managing information. Data can be imported from another source or linked to data in an external source, such as a Word table, an Excel worksheet, or another Access database. Data can also be exported from an Access database into other applications and platforms. For example, Access data can be used to create individualized letters in Word or analyze data in Excel. In addition, tables, forms, queries, or reports can be exported using HTML, the markup language used to create webpages, or XML, a markup language similar to HTML.

Liberty Motors has one of eastern Missouri's largest preowned inventories of popular car brands, sport utility vehicles, hybrid cars, sports cars, and motorcycles. Liberty also offers extensive customization options for all types of vehicles through its accessories division. Its sales, service, and finance staff are all highly trained and knowledgeable about their products, and the company takes pride in its consistently high customer satisfaction ratings in both sales and service. Liberty Motors and its employees are active members of their local community, where they sponsor and participate in activities and events.

Project Activities

In Activities 9.01 through 9.08, you will assist Phillip Garrett, president of Liberty Motors, and Jeanine Thomas, finance manager, in bringing data from Word, Excel, and other Access databases into a new Access database to create queries and reports. They need to import data from Microsoft Word and Excel as well as link information from another Access database. Your completed Navigation Pane will look similar to Figure 9.1.

Project Files for MyLab IT Grader

1. In your storage location, create a folder named **Access Chapter 9**.
2. In your **MyLab IT** course, locate and click **Access 9A Liberty Motors**, Download Materials, and then Download All Files.
3. Extract the zipped folder to your Access Chapter 9 folder. Close the Grader download screens.
4. Take a moment to open the downloaded **Access_9A_Liberty_Motors_Instructions**; note any recent updates to the book.

Project Results

GO! Project 9A
Where We're Going

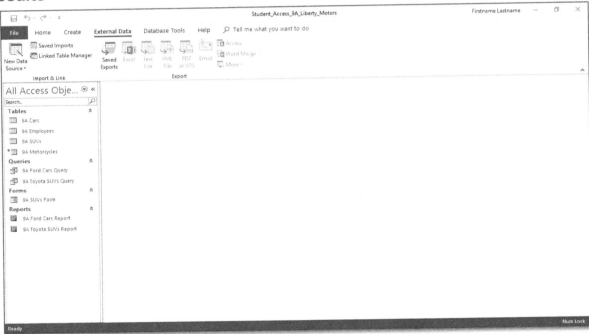

Figure 9.1 Project 9A Liberty Motors

For Non-MyLab Submissions

For Project 9A, you will need:
New blank Access database
a09A_Employees.docx
a09A_Used_Auto_Inventory.xlsx
a09A_Logo.jpg
a09A_Used_Auto_Chart.xlsx
a09A_SUVs_and_Motorcycles.accdb

After you have saved your database, open it to launch Access. On the next page, begin with Step 2.

Start with an Access Data File

In your storage location, create a folder named **Access Chapter 9**
In your Access Chapter 9 folder, save your database as:
Lastname_Firstname_9A_Liberty_Motors

Objective 1   Import Data from a Word Table

GO! Learn How
Video A9-1

When you create a database, you can type the records directly into a table. You can also *import* data from a variety of sources. Importing is the process used to bring in a copy of data from one source or application to another application. For example, you can import data from a Word table or Excel spreadsheet into an Access database.

Data can be imported in various ways. An imported table can overwrite an existing table or append data to an object with the same name in the existing database. Linked data can change the data in the database, and the change will be updated in the source document and vice versa; imported data will not be synchronized between the imported object and the source object.

Activity 9.01 | Preparing a Word Table for Importing

In this Activity, you will create an empty database to store an imported Word table and then prepare the Word table for the import process.

1 Start Access. In the Access opening screen, click **Open Other Files**. Navigate to your **Access Chapter 9** folder, and then double-click the Access file that you downloaded from **MyLab IT** that displays your name—**Student_Access_9A_Liberty_Motors**.

2 Notice the database is empty. **Close** the database, and then **Close** Access.

3 **Start** Word, and then, on the left, click **Open**. Under *Open*, click Browse, and then navigate to the location your **Access Chapter 9** folder. Locate and open the **a09A_Employees** file. Notice that employee data is saved in a table in this Word document.

4 Under **Table Tools**, click the **Layout tab**. In the **Data group**, click **Convert to Text**, and then compare your screen with Figure 9.2.

To import data from a Word table into an Access table, the data must be *converted* or changed to a *delimited file*—a file where each record displays on a separate line and the fields within the record are separated by a single character called a *delimiter*. A delimiter can be a paragraph mark, a tab, a comma, or another character.

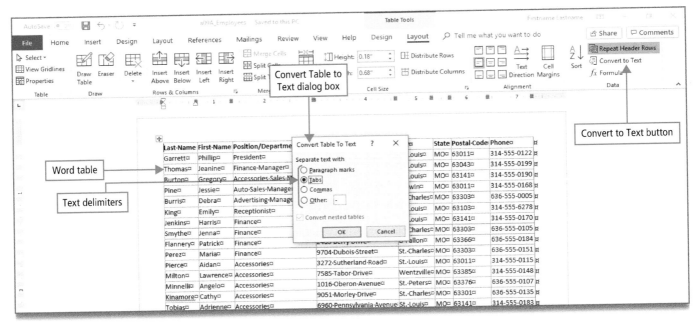

Figure 9.2

5 In the displayed **Convert Table to Text** dialog box, verify that the **Tabs** option button is selected—this is the delimiter character you will use to separate the data into fields—and then click **OK**.

6 On the **Home tab**, in the **Paragraph group**, click **Show/Hide** ¶ to display formatting marks if they are not already displayed. Click anywhere in the document to deselect the text, and then compare your screen with Figure 9.3.

Clicking Show/Hide enables you to see the tabs between the fields and the paragraph marks at the end of each line. Word also flags some proper names as spelling errors because they are not listed in the Word dictionary.

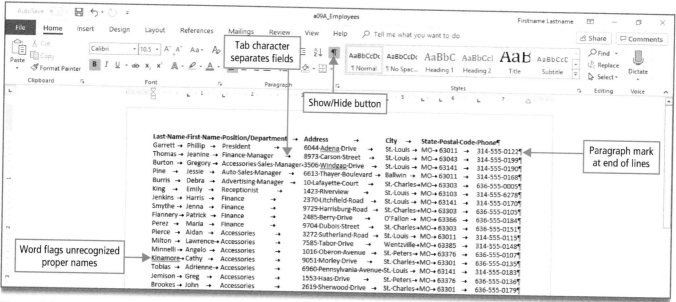

Figure 9.3

7 Click the **File tab**, click **Save As**, and then, under *Save As*, click **Browse**. In the **Save As** dialog box, navigate to the **Access Chapter 9** folder, and then, in the **File name** box, select the existing text, and then type **9A_Employees_Table** Click the **Save as type arrow**, and from the displayed list, scroll down, and then click **Plain Text**. In the **Save As** dialog box, click **Save**, and then compare your screen with Figure 9.4.

A Word table must be converted to a delimited text file and then saved as either *Plain Text* or Rich Text. Data stored in Plain Text format contains no formatting, such as bold or italics. Plain Text stores the data using the *ASCII*—American Standard Code for Information Interchange—character set. The File Conversion dialog box displays for you to confirm the conversion to a text file.

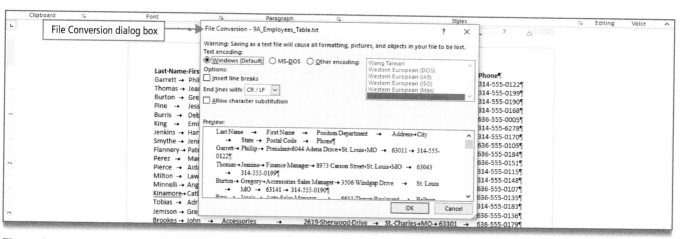

Figure 9.4

8 In the displayed **File Conversion** dialog box, accept the default settings by clicking **OK**. **Close** the document, and **Close** Word.

Activity 9.02 | Importing Data from a Word Table

2.1.1, 1.2.3, 2.4.5

In this Activity, you will import the Word table data that is stored in a delimited text file into your 9A_Liberty_Motors database.

1 **Start** Access. On the left side of the opening screen, under **Recent**, click **9A_Liberty_Motors** to open the empty database. Enable the content or add the Access Chapter 9 folder to the Trust Center. Notice that in the Navigation Pane, there are no tables in the database.

2 On the **External Data tab**, in the **Import & Link group**, click the **New Data Source arrow**. Point to **From File**, and then click **Text File**. In the displayed **Get External Data - Text File** dialog box, to the right of the **File name** box, click **Browse**. Navigate to the **Access Chapter 9** folder. In the **File Open** dialog box, double-click **9A_Employees_Table**, and then compare your screen with Figure 9.5.

The source file—the one being imported—is listed in the File name box. When importing, if a table with the same name as the imported table does not exist, Access creates the object. If a table with the same name exists in the database, Access may overwrite its contents with the imported data. If you modify data in the original text file, the data will not be updated in the Access database.

A *link* is a connection to data in another file. When linking, Access creates a table that maintains a link to the source data. You cannot change or delete data in a linked Access table; however, you can add new records.

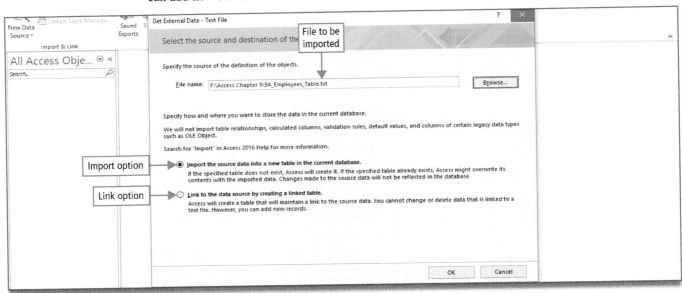

Figure 9.5

NOTE   **Importing Versus Linking Database Files**

Import when any of the following is true:
- The source file size is small and is changed infrequently.
- Data does not need to be shared with individuals using other database applications.
- You are replacing an old database application, and the data is no longer needed in the older format.
- You need to load data from another source to begin populating tables.
- You need the performance of Access 2019 while working with data from other database formats.

Link to a source when any of the following is true:
- The file is larger than the maximum capacity of a local Access database (2 gigabytes).
- The file is changed frequently, and the change needs to be reflected in the database.
- Data must be shared on a network with individuals using other database applications.
- The application is distributed to several individuals, and you need to make changes to the queries, forms, reports, and modules without changing the data already entered into the underlying tables.

3 In the **Get External Data - Text File** dialog box, verify that the **Import the source data into a new table in the current database** option button is selected, and then click **OK**. If a security message displays, click Open. Compare your screen with Figure 9.6.

The Import Text Wizard dialog box displays, indicating that the data seems to be in a delimited format, using a comma or tab to separate each field.

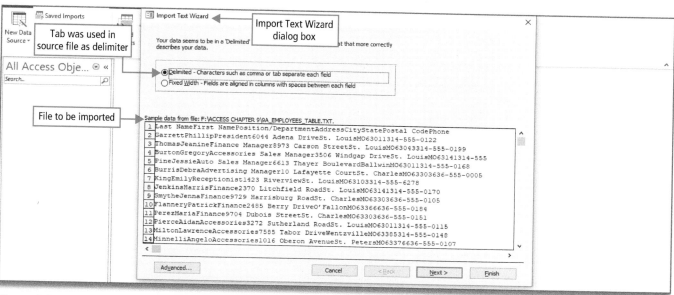

Figure 9.6

4 In the **Import Text Wizard** dialog box, verify that the **Delimited** option button is selected, and then click **Next**.

In this Import Text Wizard dialog box, you select the delimiter that you used when you created the text file.

5 Click each delimiter option button, and notice how the text is affected in the preview window. When you are finished, verify that the **Tab** option button is selected. Click the **First Row Contains Field Names** check box to convert the field names to column headings instead of first record data. Click the **Text Qualifier arrow**, and notice that a single quotation mark and a double quotation mark display. If you are working with a file that includes text in quotation marks, you would indicate this by selecting either the single quotation mark or the double quotation mark. Verify that **{none}** is selected, and then compare your screen with Figure 9.7.

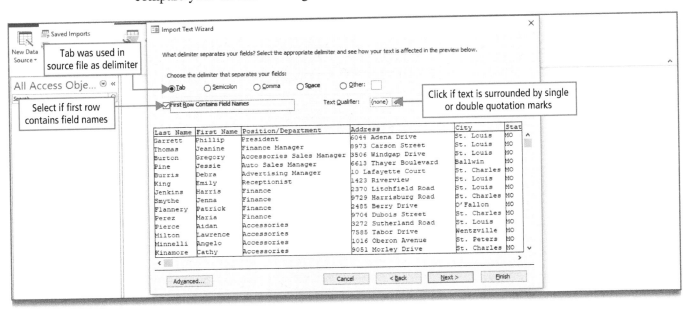

Figure 9.7

6 Click **Next**, and then compare your screen with Figure 9.8.

In this Import Text Wizard dialog box, under Field Options, you can change the field name, set the data type, index the field, or skip the importing of the field.

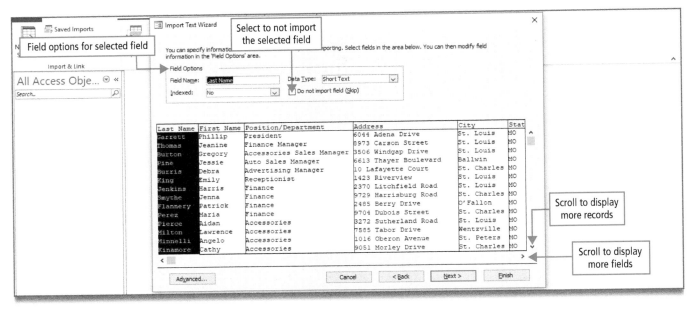

Figure 9.8

7 The Field Options for the **Last Name** field are correct. Use the horizontal scroll bar to display the fields on the right. Click in the **Postal Code** field to select the field. Under **Field Options**, click the **Data Type arrow**, and then click **Short Text**.

Because Access determined that the Postal Code field contained all numbers, it assigned a data type of Long Integer. Recall that fields containing numbers that are not used in calculations should have a data type of Short Text.

8 Click **Next** to display primary key options, and then compare your screen with Figure 9.9.

Notice the ID field displays to the left of the Last Name field. This is the primary key field that Access will add. It is an Autonumber field datatype.

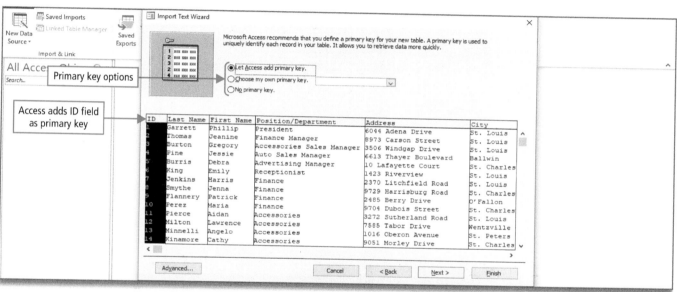

Figure 9.9

9 Verify that the **Let Access add primary key** option button is selected, and then click **Next**. In the **Import to Table** box, type **9A Employees** and then click **Finish**.

In this dialog box, you can accept the default name of the table or type a new name.

10 Because there are no errors in the imported file, the **Get External Data - Text File** dialog box displays, which enables you to save the import steps for future use.

When you import or export data in Access, you can save the settings you used so that you can repeat the process at any time without using the wizard. The name of the source file, the name of the destination database, primary key fields, field names, and all the other specifications you set are saved. Even though all of the specifications are saved, you can still change the name of the source file or destination file before running the import or export specification again. You cannot save the specifications for linking or exporting only a portion of a table.

11 Select the **Save import steps** check box to display additional options. Click in the **Description** box, and then type **Imports a tab-delimited file that was a Word table** Notice that if you are using Outlook, you can create an Outlook Task to remind you when to repeat the import operation. Click **Save Import**, and notice that in the **Navigation Pane**, the **9A Employees** table displays.

Access creates and saves the import specification in the current database. You cannot move or copy the specification to another database.

12 On the **External Data tab**, in the **Import & Link group**, click **Saved Imports**, and then compare your screen with Figure 9.10.

The Manage Data Tasks dialog box displays with two tabs—one for Saved Imports and one for Saved Exports. Clicking Run performs the operation using the selected specification. You can schedule execution by clicking Create Outlook Task or delete a specification by clicking Delete. You can change the name or description of a specification, change the source file in an import operation, or change the destination file in an export operation by clicking the appropriate section in the specification.

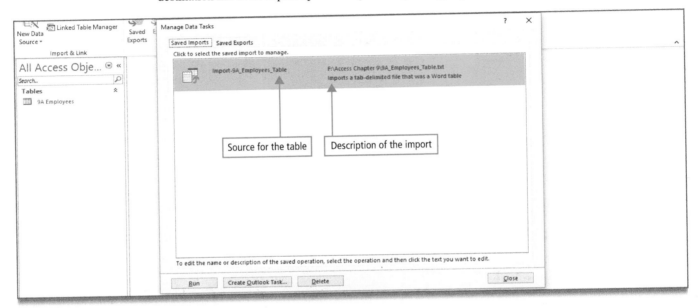

Figure 9.10

13 In the **Manage Data Tasks** dialog box, click **Close**.

14 Double-click **9A Employees** to open the table in **Datasheet** view, and then **Close** ⟪ the **Navigation Pane**. Apply **Best Fit** to adjust the widths of all of the fields to display all of the data and the entire field name for each field.

All of the data from the Word table, which was converted to a delimited file, has been imported successfully into a table within the database, saving you from typing the data.

MORE KNOWLEDGE **Importing from Other Applications**

If you have data in other applications that you would like to import or link to your Access database, explore the options on the External Data tab, in the Import & Link group, by clicking More. A *SharePoint List* is a list of documents maintained on a server running Microsoft Office SharePoint Server. A *SharePoint Server* enables you to share documents with others in your organization. You also can import data from other database applications, such as dBASE and ODBC databases. *ODBC* stands for *Open Database Connectivity*, a standard that enables databases using SQL statements to interface with one another. You can also import or link to an Outlook folder. Data can also be imported from or linked to an HTML—HyperText Markup Language—document or Web document. HTML is a language used to display webpages.

15 **Save** the table, and then **Close** ✕ the table.

Objective 2 | Import Data from an Excel Workbook

GO! Learn How
Video A9-2

Jessie Pine, the auto sales manager, keeps an inventory of used cars, SUVs, and motorcycles in an Excel workbook. A *workbook* is an Excel file that contains one or more worksheets. A *worksheet* is the primary document used in Excel to save and work with data that is arranged in columns and rows. You can import the data from an Excel workbook into Access by copying the data from an open worksheet and pasting it into an Access datasheet, by importing a worksheet into a new or existing Access table, or by creating a link to a worksheet from an Access database. There is no way to save the workbook as an Access database within Excel; the individual worksheets within a workbook must be imported into an Access database.

Activity 9.03 | Importing Data from an Excel Worksheet

MOS
1.2.3, 2.1.1

In this Activity, you will import an Excel worksheet containing the used car inventory, creating a new table in your database.

1 If necessary, click the **External Data tab**. In the **Import & Link group**, click the **New Data Source arrow**, point to **From File**, and then click **Excel**.

The Get External Data - Excel Spreadsheet dialog box displays, indicating that you can import the source data into a new table, append a copy of the records to an existing table, or link to the Excel worksheet.

2 In the **Get External Data - Excel Spreadsheet** dialog box, to the right of the **File name** box, click **Browse**. Navigate to your **Access Chapter 9** folder. Locate the **a09A_Used_Auto_Inventory** file, and then notice the icon to the left of the file name; it indicates the file is an Excel Worksheet file. Click **Open**.

3 In the **Get External Data - Excel Spreadsheet** dialog box, click **OK**, and then compare your screen with Figure 9.11.

The first Import Spreadsheet Wizard dialog box displays. A *spreadsheet* is another name for a worksheet. On this page you can select one worksheet—you can import only one worksheet at a time during an import operation. If you want to import several worksheets, save the import specification, and then change the source data. The first row displays column headings.

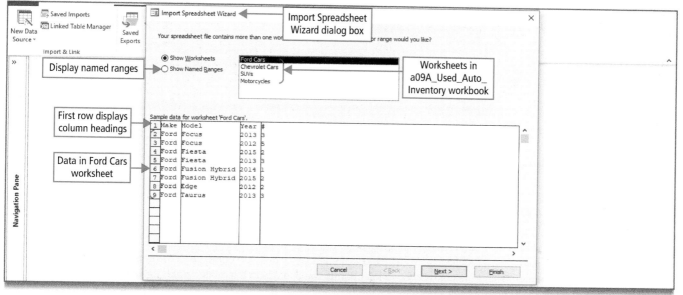

Figure 9.11

4 In the **Import Spreadsheet Wizard** dialog box, click the **Show Named Ranges** option button, and then in the box, click **Ford**.

This is the same data that displays in the *Ford Cars* worksheet, but without the column headings. If the Excel worksheet contains named ranges, you can select the Show Named Ranges option button. A *range* includes two or more selected cells on a worksheet that can be treated as a single unit. A *named range* is a range that has been given a name, making it easier to use the cells in calculations or modifications. A *cell* is the small box formed by the intersection of a column and a row.

5 Click the **Show Worksheets** option button, and verify that **Ford Cars** is selected. Click **Next** to display the second **Import Spreadsheet Wizard** dialog box. Notice that the wizard assumes that the first row contains column headings and that Access uses the column headings as field names.

6 Click **Next** to display the third **Import Spreadsheet Wizard** dialog box.

Just as you did when importing a text file, you can change the field name, index the field, set the data type, or remove the field from the import operation.

7 Click **Next**. In the fourth **Import Spreadsheet Wizard** dialog box, verify that **Let Access add primary key** is selected, and then click **Next**.

8 In the final **Import Spreadsheet Wizard** dialog box, in the **Import to Table** box, type **9A Cars** and then click **Finish**. Because you do not want to save the import steps, in the **Get External Data - Excel Spreadsheet** dialog box, click **Close**. Open ⊡ the **Navigation Pane**, and notice that the table displays under *Tables*.

9 In the **Navigation Pane**, double-click **9A Cars** to open the table in **Datasheet** view. Close ⊡ the **Navigation Pane**, and then compare your screen with Figure 9.12.

The data from the *Ford Cars* worksheet in the *a09A_Used_Auto_Inventory* Excel workbook has been imported into this new table.

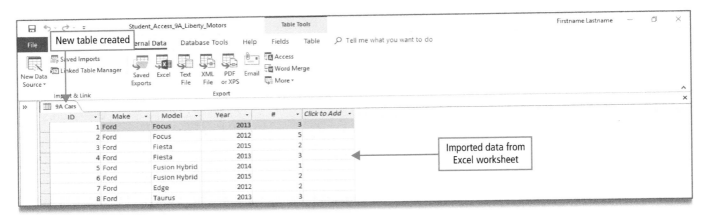

Figure 9.12

10 Close ⊡ the table.

MORE KNOWLEDGE **Importing from a Workbook That Contains a Chart**

If a workbook contains a chart on a separate worksheet, when you try to import any worksheet into Access, a message box displays stating that the wizard cannot access the information in the file and that you should check the file you want to import to see if it exists and if it is in the correct format. You should make a copy of the workbook, open the copied workbook, and then delete the worksheet containing the chart or move the chart to the sheet with the related data. Save the workbook, close it, and then import the data from any of the worksheets.

Activity 9.04 | Appending Data from Excel to an Access Table

1.1.1

In this Activity, you will append data from an Excel worksheet to the 9A Cars table. To append data, the table must already be created.

1 If necessary, click the **External Data tab**. In the **Import & Link group**, click the **New Data Source arrow**, point to **From File**, and then click **Excel**. In the **Get External Data - Excel Spreadsheet** dialog box, click **Browse**. If necessary, navigate to your Access Chapter 9 folder. Locate and **Open** the **a09A_Used_Auto_Inventory** file.

2 Under **Specify how and where you want to store the data in the current database**, click **Append a copy of the records to the table**. Click the **table name arrow** to display the names of the two tables that are saved in the database. Verify that **9A Cars** is selected, and then click **OK**.

3 In the first **Import Spreadsheet Wizard** dialog box, click the **Chevrolet Cars** worksheet, and then click **Next**. In the second **Import Spreadsheet Wizard** dialog box, notice that Access has determined that the first row matches the field names contained in the existing table and that you cannot clear the check box. Click **Next**.

4 In the **Import Spreadsheet Wizard** dialog box, click **Finish** to import the data into the **9A Cars** table in the current database.

5 In the **Get External Data - Excel Spreadsheet** dialog box, click **Close**, and then **Open** ⟩⟩ the **Navigation Pane**. Double-click **9A Cars** to display the table in **Datasheet** view. **Close** ⟨⟨ the **Navigation Pane**, and then compare your screen with Figure 9.13.

The data from the *Chevrolet Cars* worksheet in the *a09A_Used_Auto_Inventory* workbook is appended to the *9A Cars* table in your database.

	ke ▾	Model ▾	Year ▾	# ▾	Click to Add ▾
		Focus	2013	3	
2	Ford	Focus	2012	5	
3	Ford	Fiesta	2015	2	
4	Ford	Fiesta	2013	3	
5	Ford	Fusion Hybrid	2014	1	
6	Ford	Fusion Hybrid	2015	2	
7	Ford	Edge	2012	2	
8	Ford	Taurus	2013	3	
9	Chevrolet	Malibu	2014	10	
10	Chevrolet	Malibu	2015	7	
11	Chevrolet	Impala	2012	3	
12	Chevrolet	Impala	2014	6	
13	Chevrolet	Impala	2015	4	
14	Chevrolet	Impala	2012	8	
15	Chevrolet	Corvette	2006	3	
16	Chevrolet	Corvette	2012	8	
17	Chevrolet	Corvette	2014	10	
18	Chevrolet	Monte Carlo	2010	1	
19	Chevrolet	Monte Carlo	2012	4	
20	Chevrolet	Monte Carlo	2013	3	

Data imported and appended

Figure 9.13

6 **Close** ✕ the table.

Objective 3 Insert an Excel Chart into a Report

GO! Learn How
Video A9-3

A *chart* is a graphic representation of data. Data presented in a chart is easier to understand than a table of numbers. *Column charts* display comparisons among related numbers, *pie charts* display the contributions of parts to a whole amount, and *line charts* display trends over time. Excel is the best tool for creating a chart because there are a wide variety of chart types and formatting options.

Activity 9.05 | Creating a Query and a Report

MOS
3.1.6, 3.1.7,
5.2.1, 5.2.5,
5.2.6

In this Activity, you will create a query. Using the query, you will create a report that will be used in the next Activity.

1 On the **Create tab**, in the **Queries group**, click **Query Design**. In the **Show Table** dialog box, double-click **9A Cars** to add the table to the Query Design workspace, and then **Close** ☒ the **Show Table** dialog box.

2 In the field list, click **Make**. Hold down ⇧Shift, and then click **#** to select four fields. Drag the selected fields down into the first column of the design grid, and then compare your screen with Figure 9.14.

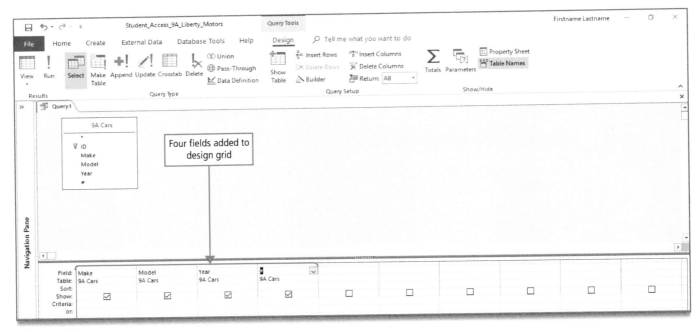

Figure 9.14

3 In the design grid, under **Make**, click in the **Criteria** box, type **Ford** and then press ⏎Enter.

4 Under **Query Tools**, on the **Design tab**, in the **Results group**, click **Run** to display only the Ford cars.

5 Switch the query to **Design** view. In the design grid, under **Make**, on the **Show** row, clear the check box, and then **Run** the query.

> Recall that clearing the Show check box hides the field from the query. Because this query only displays Ford cars, hiding this field is appropriate.

6 **Save** 💾 the query as **9A Ford Cars Query** and then **Close** ☒ the query. **Open** » the **Navigation Pane**, and then notice that the query displays in the Navigation Pane.

7 ▶ In the **Navigation Pane**, under **Queries**, click **9A Ford Cars Query** to select the query, and then **Close** ⟦«⟧ the **Navigation Pane**.

8 ▶ On the **Create tab**, in the **Reports group**, click **Report**. Switch to **Design** view.

9 ▶ In the **Report Header** section, in the **title**, double-click **Query** to select the word, and then type **Report** Press ⟦Enter⟧.

10 ▶ Click the image to the left of the title to select it. Under **Report Design Tools**, on the **Design tab**, in the **Header/Footer group**, click **Logo**. If necessary, navigate to the location where the data files for this chapter are saved, and then double-click **a09A_Logo** to insert the logo. In the **Tools group**, click **Property Sheet**, and then, if necessary, click the **Format tab**. Click in the **Size Mode** property box, and select **Zoom**. Resize the image so the right edge aligns with the **1-inch mark on the horizontal ruler**. In the **Report Footer**, click the Totals control. On the **Property Sheet Format tab**, click in the **Height** property box, and type **0.2** and then press ⟦Enter⟧. **Close** ⟦×⟧ the **Property Sheet**.

11 ▶ In the **Report Header** section, delete the **Date** and **Time text box controls** and placeholders, if necessary. In the **Page Footer** section, delete the **Page number text box control**. Resize the report to 6.5 inches wide. Compare your screen with Figure 9.15.

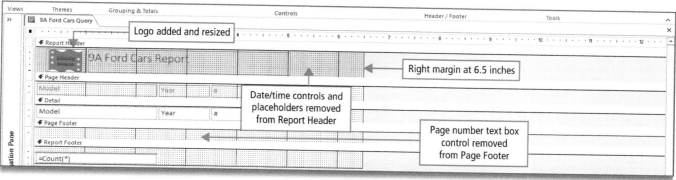

Figure 9.15

12 ▶ Save ⟦🖫⟧ the report as **9A Ford Cars Report**

Activity 9.06 | Inserting an Excel Chart into a Report

In this Activity, you will insert an Excel chart into the 9A Ford Cars Report.

1 ▶ In the report, in **Design** view, point to the top of the **Report Footer section bar** until the pointer displays. Drag the section down to the **3-inch mark on the vertical ruler** to increase the size of the Page Footer section.

2 **Start** Excel. From **Backstage** view, click **Open**. Navigate to your **Access Chapter 9** folder, and then double-click **a09A_Used_Auto_Chart** to open the workbook. Compare your screen with Figure 9.16.

The workbook opens with the *Cars* worksheet displaying. A pie chart has been saved in the worksheet and displays the percentage of cars for each model of Ford vehicles.

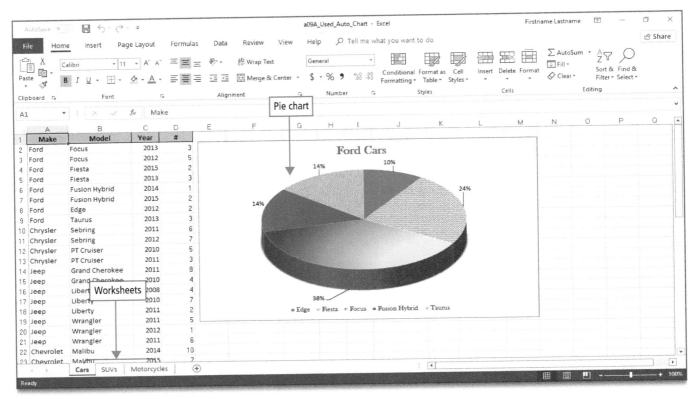

Figure 9.16

3 Click the outside edge of the **pie chart** to select the entire chart. On the **Home tab**, in the **Clipboard group**, click **Copy** to place a copy of the pie chart in the Office Clipboard. **Close** × Excel.

4 ▶ Click the **Access** icon [AB] on the taskbar to activate the 9A Ford Cars Report in the database. In the **9A Ford Cars Report**, right-click the **Page Footer section bar**, and then click **Paste**. Compare your screen with Figure 9.17.

The pie chart is pasted into the Page Footer section of the report.

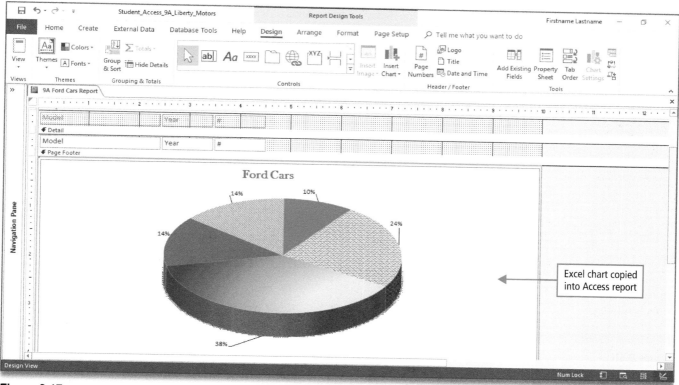

Figure 9.17

5 ▶ **Save** [💾] the report, and then switch to **Report** view. **Close** [×] the report.

Import from and Link to Another Access Database

GO! Learn How
Video A9-4

When you import data from another Access database, Access creates a copy of the source data without altering the source data. All of the objects in a database can be imported or copied to another Access database in a single operation. Import data from another Access database when you need to create similar tables or when you want to use the structure of the source database tables. Link to data in another Access database when the data is shared among multiple databases or if someone else needs to have the ability to add records and use the data, but not change the structure of the table.

Activity 9.07 | **Importing Data from Another Access Database**

MOS
2.1.3, 5.2.3

In this Activity, you will import the data contained in another Access database.

1 ▶ On the **External Data tab**, in the **Import & Link group**, click the **New Data Source arrow**, point to **From Database**, and then click **Access**. In the **Get External Data - Access Database** dialog box, click **Browse**. If necessary, navigate to your **Access Chapter 9** folder, and then double-click **a09A_SUVs_and_Motorcycles**.

The source database must be closed before you can import data from it. The destination database must be open. To import the data into a new database, you must create a blank database before starting the import operation.

2 Verify that the **Import tables, queries, forms, reports, macros, and modules into the current database** option button is selected, and then click **OK**. In the **Import Objects** dialog box, click the **Tables** tab, if necessary.

The Import Objects dialog box displays the two tables contained in the *a09A_SUVs_and_Motorcycles* database. To choose multiple types of objects, first select one object, click the relevant tab, and then click the desired object on that tab. To cancel a selected object, click the object again.

3 In the **Import Objects** dialog box, click **9A SUVs**, and then compare your screen with Figure 9.18.

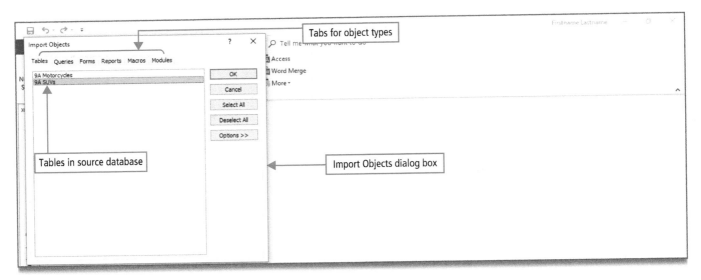

Figure 9.18

NOTE Importing Queries, Forms, and Reports

You can import table relationships, custom menus and toolbars, saved import/export specifications, and custom Navigation Pane groups. For tables, you can import the table definition and data or only the table definition. The *definition* is the structure of the database—the field names, data types, and field properties. You can import queries as queries or as tables. If you import a query as a query, you must also import the underlying table or tables used to create the query.

Importing a query, form, report, subform, or subreport does not automatically import the underlying record sources. If you create one of these objects using the data in two related tables, you must also import those two tables; otherwise, these objects will not open properly.

---

4 In the **Import Objects** dialog box, click the **Queries tab**, and then click **9A Toyota SUVs Query**. Click the **Forms tab**, and then click **9A SUVs Form**. Click the **Reports tab**, click **9A Toyota SUVs Report**, and then click **OK**.

The Get External Data - Access Database dialog box displays, enabling you to save the import steps. If Access encounters any errors in the import operation, messages will display.

5 In the **Get External Data - Access Database** dialog box, click **Close**.

6 Open 》 the **Navigation Pane**, and compare your screen with Figure 9.19.

A table, query, form, and report have been imported to the open database.

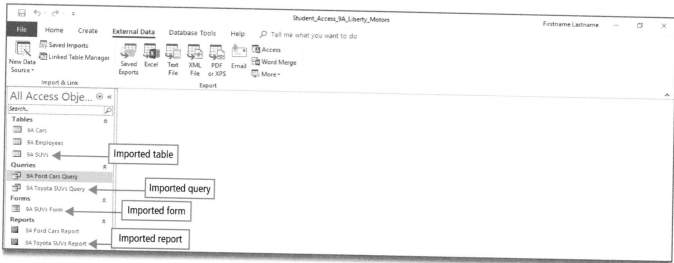

Figure 9.19

ALERT **Were all four objects not imported?**

If all four objects were not imported, you may not have clicked the object in the Import Objects dialog box. To correct this, run the import operation again, and select the missing object or objects. Do not select objects that were imported correctly. For example, if you correctly imported the *9A SUVs* table, and then you import it again, a second *9A SUVs* table will be imported and will be named *9A SUVs1*.

---

7 In the **Navigation Pane**, under **Reports**, right-click **9A Toyota SUVs Report**, and then click **Layout View**. Click the title one time to select it. Click the title placeholder to select it. Under **Report Layout Tools**, on the **Format tab**, in the **Font group**, click the **Background Color arrow**, and then, under **Theme Colors**, in the second row, select the fifth color.

8 Switch to **Report** view. **Save** 🖫 the report.

9 **Close** ✕ the report, and then **Close** 《 the **Navigation Pane**.

MORE KNOWLEDGE **Recover Data from a Backup File**

If you are missing objects or they have become corrupt, import the clean objects from the most recent backup file using the technique you practiced in this Activity.

Activity 9.08 | Linking to a Table in Another Access Database

2.1.2

In this Activity, you will link to the data in the 9A Motorcycles table in the *a09A_SUVs_and_Motorcycles* database. You can link only to tables in another Access database; you cannot link to queries, forms, reports, macros, or modules.

1 On the **External Data tab**, in the **Import & Link group**, click the **New Data Source arrow**, point to **From Database**, and then click **Access**. In the **Get External Data - Access Database** dialog box, **Browse** to your **Access Chapter 9** folder, and then double-click **a09A_SUVs_and_Motorcycles**.

2 In the **Get External Data - Access Database** dialog box, click the **Link to the data source by creating a linked table** option button, and then click **OK**.

Changes made to the data in Access will be propagated to the source data and vice versa. If the source database requires a password, that password is saved with the linked table. You cannot make changes to the structure of the table in the linked table.

3 In the **Link Tables** dialog box, on the **Tables tab**, click **9A Motorcycles**, and then click **OK**.

4 Open ⟩⟩ the **Navigation Pane**, if necessary, and then compare your screen with Figure 9.20.

The 9A Motorcycles linked table displays in the Navigation Pane under Tables. The arrow that displays to the left of the icon indicates that this is a linked object.

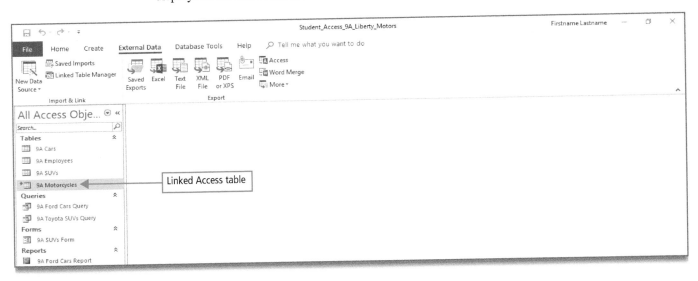

Figure 9.20

5 In the **Navigation Pane**, under **Tables**, double-click **9A Motorcycles** to display the table in **Datasheet** view. Apply **Best Fit** to adjust the columns widths as necessary.

6 **Close** ✕ the table, saving changes when prompted. **Close** ✕ the database, and then **Close** Access.

For Non-MyLab Submissions: Determine What Your Instructor Requires for Submission
As directed by your instructor, submit your completed database file.

7 In **MyLab IT**, locate and click the Grader Project **Access 9A Liberty Motors**. In **step 3**, under **Upload Completed Assignment**, click **Choose File**. In the **Open** dialog box, navigate to your **Access Chapter 9 folder**, and then click your **Student_Access_9A_ Liberty_Motors** file one time to select it. In the lower right corner of the **Open** dialog box, click **Open**.

The name of your selected file displays above the Upload button.

8 To submit your file to **MyLab IT** for grading, click **Upload**, wait a moment for a green **Success!** message, and then in **step 4**, click the blue **Submit for Grading** button. Click **Close Assignment** to return to your list of **Course Materials**.

You have completed Project 9A **END**

PROJECT

9B Used Inventory

Project Activities

In Activities 9.09 to 9.15, you will help the sales staff at Liberty Motors use information from Access databases in other applications. In addition, you need to help the webmaster include data on the company's website. Access enables you to export data from an Access database into other applications, such as Word, Excel, or another Access database, and merge data from an Access database with a Word document. You can also export data to be used on a webpage. Your completed Navigation Pane will look similar to Figure 9.21.

Project Files for MyLab IT Grader

1. In your **MyLab IT** course, locate and click **Access 9B Used Inventory**, Download Materials, and then Download All Files.
2. Extract the zipped folder to your **Access Chapter 9** folder. Close the Grader download screens.
3. Take a moment to open the downloaded **Access_9B_Used_Inventory_Instructions**; note any recent updates to the book.

Project Results

GO! Project 9B
Where We're Going

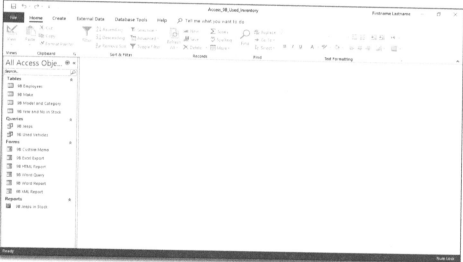

Figure 9.21 Project 9B Used Inventory

For Non-MyLab Submissions
For Project 9B, you will need:
a09B_Used_Inventory.accdb
a09B_Memo.docx

Start with an Access Data File
In your Access Chapter 9 folder, save your files as:
Lastname_Firstname_9B_Used_Inventory.accdb
Lastname_Firstname_9B_Jeeps_Exported.rtf
Lastname_Firstname_9B_Jeeps.docx
Lastname_Firstname_9B_Custom_Memo.docx
Lastname_Firstname_9B_Memo_Main.docx
Lastname_Firstname_9B_Used_Vehicles.xlsx
Lastname_Firstname_9B_Jeeps_in_Stock.html
Lastname_Firstname_9B_Jeeps_in_Stock.rtf
Lastname_Firstname_9B_XML_Jeeps.htm
Lastname_Firstname_9B_XML_Jeeps.xml
Lastname_Firstname_9B_XML_Jeeps.xsl

After you have saved your database, open it to launch Access. On the next page, begin with Step 2.

Objective 5 | Export Data to Word

GO! Learn How
Video A9-5

You can **export** a table, query, form, or report to Word 2019. Exporting is the process used to send out a copy of data from one source or application to another application. You can then email the Word document rather than the entire database. Exporting to Word is also helpful if you have a table that you want to format more than you can in an Access table. When you export an Access object, the Export Wizard creates a copy of the object's data in a Microsoft Word Rich Text Format file; an extension of .rtf is used. Hidden fields are not exported with tables, queries, and forms; visible fields and records display as a table in the Word document. When you export a report, the Export Wizard copies the report data and the design layout, making the Word document resemble the report as closely as possible.

Activity 9.09 | Exporting an Access Query to Word

MOS
1.3.2

In this Activity, you will export a query to Word 2019. The database must be open in Access to perform the export operation because there is no Access import feature in Word.

1 Start Access. In the Access opening screen, click **Open Other Files**. Navigate to your **Access Chapter 9 folder**, and then double-click the Access file that you downloaded from **MyLab IT** that displays your name—**Student_Access_9B_Used_Inventory**.

2 Under **Queries**, double-click **9B Jeeps** to run and display the query results.

The query displays the model name, the year of the vehicle, and the number of Jeeps in stock.

3 Switch the query to **Design** view, expand the field lists so all data displays fully, and then compare your screen with Figure 9.22.

The underlying source of this query is the *9B Used Vehicles* query. In the design grid, in the last column, the criteria is *Jeep*, which extracts records with this criteria in the Make field. The field is hidden from the results because the data is redundant.

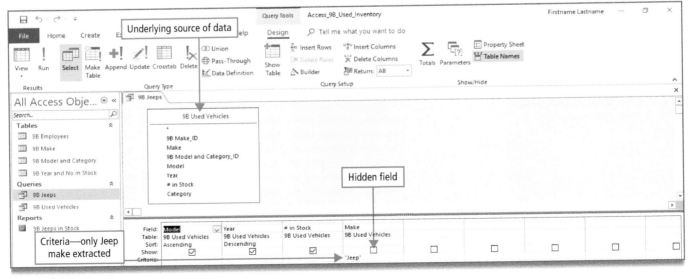

Figure 9.22

4 **Close** ☒ the query, saving changes. In the **Navigation Pane**, under **Queries**, right-click **9B Jeeps**, point to **Export**, and then click **Word RTF File**. Alternatively, click the External Data tab, and then in the Export group, click More, and then click Word. Compare your screen with Figure 9.23.

The Export - RTF File dialog box displays, which enables you to select the destination for the data you want to export. Because the Export Wizard always exports formatted data, this option is selected and inactive. An option is available to display the Word document after the export operation is complete. The last selection—*Export only the selected records*—is inactive. If you want to export some of the records, before you begin the export operation, open the object and select the records.

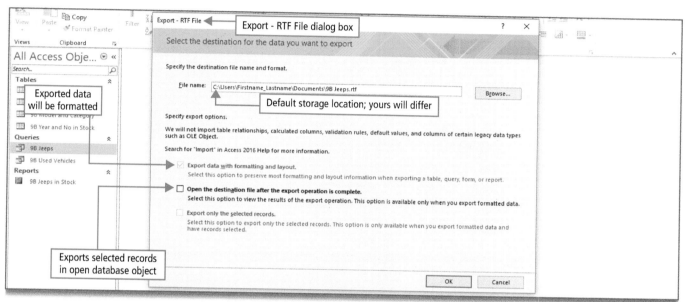

Figure 9.23

5 In the **Export - RTF File** dialog box, click **Browse**. Navigate to the **Access Chapter 9** folder. In the **File name** box, select the existing file name, type **9B _Jeeps_Exported** and then click **Save**.

NOTE   **Exporting Data into an Existing Word Document**

When you export from Access to Word, the data is always exported into a new Word document. If you select an existing document, the Export Wizard overwrites the Word document with the new data. To insert the data into an existing Word document, export the data from Access into a new Word document, and then copy the data from the new Word document and paste it into the existing Word document. Alternatively, copy rows directly from an Access table, query, form, or report, and then paste them into the existing Word document.

6 In the **Export - RTF File** dialog box, under **Specify export options**, select the **Open the destination file after the export operation is complete** check box, and then click **OK**. Compare your screen with Figure 9.24.

> The query data is exported to a Word document. Because the Word document did not exist, a new document was created. The data is displayed as a table in Word with the field names as column headings. The hidden field—Make—does not display. In the title bar of the Word document, *Compatibility Mode* displays because this document has an .rtf extension instead of the standard .docx extension.

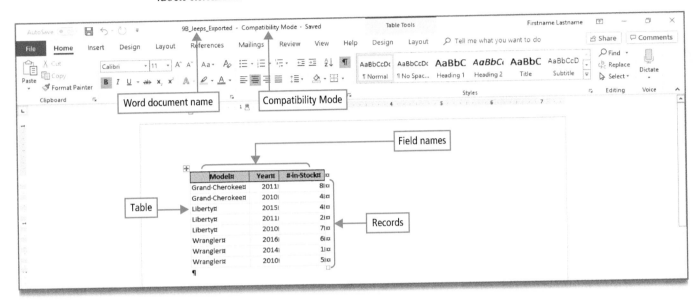

Figure 9.24

7 In Word, click the **Insert tab**. In the **Header & Footer group**, click **Header**. In the **Built-in** gallery, click **Austin**. Click the **[Document title]** text, and then type **9B Jeeps** to replace it. In the **Close group**, click **Close Header and Footer**.

8 On the **Quick Access Toolbar**, click **Save** 🖫, and then compare your screen with Figure 9.25.

> A message may display stating that a feature in the document is not supported by earlier versions of Word, meaning that a document with an .rtf extension cannot display the data in the same manner as Word. Although the summary is cryptic, in this case, an .rtf document cannot display content controls. If you click Continue, Word converts the header data to static text.

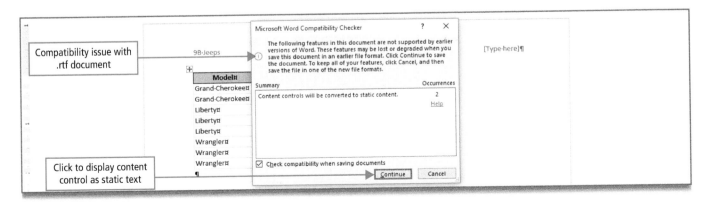

Figure 9.25

9 In the message box, click **Cancel**. Display **Backstage** view, and click **Save As**. In the **Access Chapter 9** folder, in the **Save As** dialog box, under the file name, click in the **Save as type** box, and select **Word Document (*.docx)**. Change the file name to **9B_Jeeps** and then click **Save**.

> A message box may display stating that you are about to save your document to one of the new file formats and that changes may be made in the layout of the document.

10 In the displayed message box, click **Continue**.

11 With the **Word** document displayed, use the **Snipping Tool** to create a screenshot of the window, and then **Save** the file as a **JPEG** using the file name **WordQuery**. **Close** the **Snipping Tool**, and **Close** ⊠ Word. In the **Export - RTF File** dialog box, click **Close**.

12 In the database, on the **Create tab**, in the **Forms group**, click **Form Design** to create a new form in **Design** view. Under **Form Design Tools**, on the **Design tab**, in the **Controls group**, click **Insert Image**, and then click **Browse**. Navigate to the location where you saved the **WordQuery** screenshot, and double-click the image file. Click in the upper left corner of the **Detail** section of the form to place the image.

13 **Save** the **Form** as **9B Word Query Close** ⊠ the **Form**.

Activity 9.10 | Exporting an Access Report to Word

MOS
1.3.2

In this Activity, you will export the 9B Jeeps in Stock report to a Word document.

1 In the **Navigation Pane**, under **Reports**, double-click **9B Jeeps in Stock** to open the report. Switch to **Layout** view. Click the title—**9B Jeeps in Stock**—two times to enter into editing mode. Click to the left of **9B**, type **Liberty Motors** and then press (Shift) + (Enter). Press (Enter), and then **Save** 🖫 the report.

> The report displays Jeep models, the year, and the number of vehicles in stock for each year of the model. Each model is counted and at the bottom of the report, the total number of Jeeps displays.

2 **Close** ⊠ the report. In the **Navigation Pane**, under **Reports**, right-click **9B Jeeps in Stock**, point to **Export**, and then click **Word RTF File**. Verify that the **File name** box displays the correct path to your **Access Chapter 9** folder. In the **File name** box, select the existing file name, and type **9B_Jeeps_in_Stock** Under **Specify export options**, click to select the **Open the destination file after the export operation is complete** check box, and then click **OK**. If a security message displays, click Open. Compare your screen with Figure 9.26.

> A message box displays, and then the document opens in Word. Although all of the data is exported, it is not aligned as nicely as it was in the Access report. You would probably want to do some further formatting in Word. All of the data is separated by tabs. The tab and paragraph marks only display if Show/Hide is active.

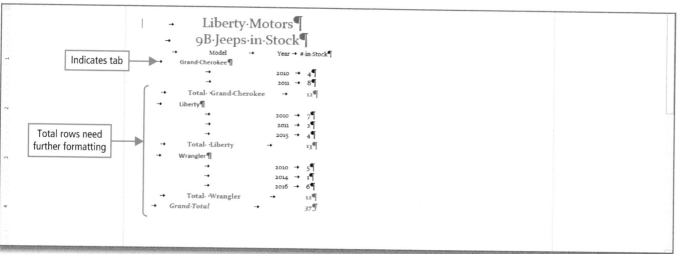

Figure 9.26

3 With the **Word** document displayed, use the **Snipping Tool** to create a screenshot of the window, and then **Save** the file as a **JPEG** using the file name **WordReport**. **Close** the **Snipping Tool**, and **Close** ☒ Word. In the **Export - RTF File** dialog box, click **Close**.

4 In the database, on the **Create tab**, in the **Forms group**, click **Form Design** to create a new form in **Design** view. Under **Form Design Tools**, on the **Design tab**, in the **Controls group**, click **Insert Image**, and then click **Browse**. Navigate to the location where you saved the **WordReport** screenshot, and double-click the image file. Click in the upper left corner of the **Detail** section of the form to place the image.

5 **Save** the **Form** as **9B Word Report Close** ☒ the **Form**.

Objective 6   Use Mail Merge to Integrate Access and Word

GO! Learn How
Video A9-6

Using Word's *mail merge* feature, letters or memos are created by combining, or *merging*, two documents—a *main document* and a *data source*. The main document contains the text of a letter or memo. The data source—an Access table or query—contains the names and addresses of the individuals to whom the letter, memo, or other document is being sent. Use the Mail Merge Wizard within Access to create a direct link between the table or query and the Word document.

Activity 9.11 | Merging an Access Table with a Word Document

MOS
1.3.2

In this Activity, you will create individual memos to the employees of Liberty Motors to inform them of an upcoming staff meeting. You will create the memos by merging the individual names and position or department in the 9B Employees Table with a memo created in Microsoft Word.

1 In the **Navigation Pane**, click the **9B Employees** table to select the table. On the **External Data tab**, in the **Export group**, click **Word Merge**. If a security message displays, click Open.

The Microsoft Word Mail Merge Wizard starts. In this first dialog box, you can link the data in the table to an existing Word document or create a new Word document and then link the data in the table to the new document.

2 Verify that **Link your data to an existing Microsoft Word document** is selected, and then click **OK**. In the **Select Microsoft Word Document** dialog box, navigate to the location where the student data files for this textbook are saved. Locate and open the **a09B_Memo** file; click the **Microsoft Word** icon on the taskbar to view the memo, and then compare your screen with Figure 9.27.

Microsoft Word opens with the memo on the left and the Mail Merge pane on the right.

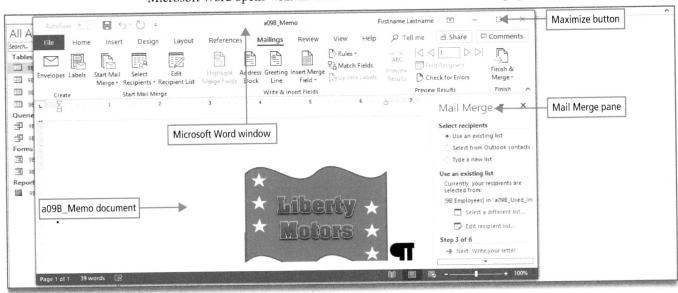

Figure 9.27

3 On the **Microsoft Word** title bar, click **Maximize** ☐. At the bottom of the **Mail Merge** pane, notice that the wizard is on **Step 3 of 6**.

Because you are using an existing Word document, the first two steps are already defined.

4 In the **Mail Merge** pane, under **Select recipients**, verify that the **Use an existing list** option button is selected. Under **Use an existing list**, click **Edit recipient list**, and then compare your screen with Figure 9.28.

The Mail Merge Recipients dialog box displays, enabling you to sort the list, filter the list, find duplicate entries, find a particular recipient or group of recipients, validate addresses, add recipients to the list, or remove recipients from the list.

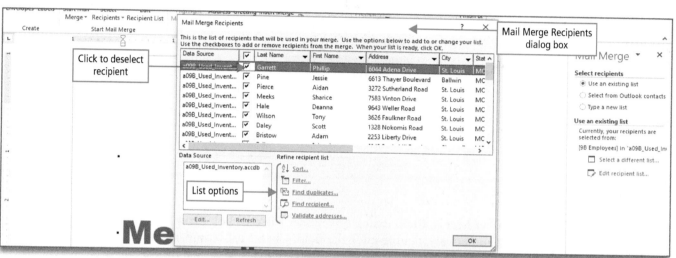

Figure 9.28

5 In the **Mail Merge Recipients** dialog box, on the row for **Phillip Garrett**, clear the **check box** to the left of **Garrett** to remove this record from the list of recipients. Click the **Last Name arrow**, and then click **Sort Ascending**. Click **OK**.

Because the memo is from Phillip Garrett, a memo should not be addressed to him.

6 In the **Mail Merge** pane, under **Step 3 of 6**, click **Next: Write your letter**. Take a moment to read the information in the **Mail Merge** pane. If necessary, on the Home tab, in the Paragraph group, click Show/Hide to display the paragraph marks. On the left side of the screen in the memo, click to the right of **To:** and to the left of the paragraph symbol, above the letter **P** in *Phillip*. In the **Mail Merge** pane, under **Write your letter**, click **More items**, and then compare your screen with Figure 9.29.

The Insert Merge Field dialog box displays, which enables you to select a field from the database to insert into the memo. The Match Fields button enables you to map the fields in the table to the mail merge fields that are built into Word. For example, this table contains a field named Position/Department that could be mapped to the Word mail merge field entitled Job Title.

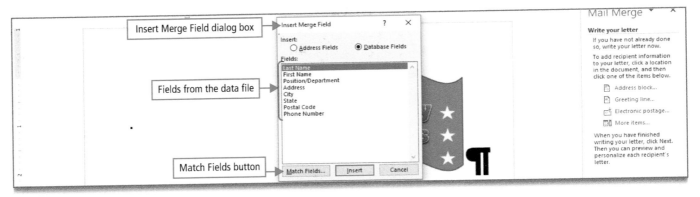

Figure 9.29

7 In the **Insert Merge Field** dialog box, under **Fields**, click **First Name**, and then click **Insert**. Alternatively, double-click the field. Click **Last Name**, and then click **Insert**. Click **Position/Department**, and then click **Insert**. Click **Close**, and then compare your screen with Figure 9.30.

Word inserts each field name surrounded with the characters << and >>. There are no spaces between the field names.

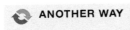 **ANOTHER WAY** Instead of inserting all of the fields together, you can insert each field from the Mailings tab. In the Write & Insert Fields group, click the Insert Merge Field arrow to view a list of available fields. Click the appropriate field desired as needed.

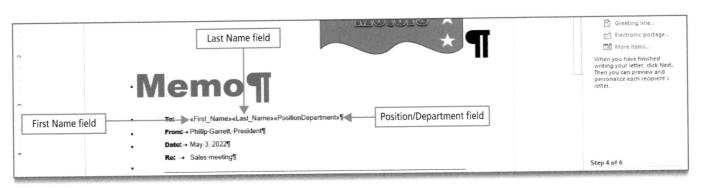

Figure 9.30

8 In the **memo**, click to the left of **<<Last_Name>>**, and then press ⟨Spacebar⟩ to insert a space between the First_Name and Last_Name fields. Click to the left of **<<PositionDepartment>>**, hold down ⟨Shift⟩, and then press ⟨Enter⟩ to move the field to the next line. Compare your screen with Figure 9.31.

Because the memo has built-in formatting, you must press ⟨Shift⟩ + ⟨Enter⟩ to insert a line break to align the Position/Department field directly under the First Name field. If you press ⟨Enter⟩ to insert a paragraph break, the Position/Department field will align at the left margin and a blank line will display above it.

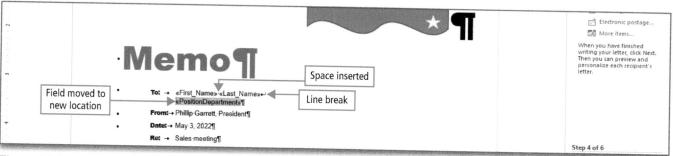

Figure 9.31

9 In the **Mail Merge** pane, under **Step 4 of 6**, click **Next: Preview your letters**. Notice that the first memo displays with a recipient name of *Adam Bristow*. In the **Mail Merge** pane, under **Preview your letters**, click the **Next recipient** ⟨>>⟩ button to display the memo for the next recipient. Continue clicking **Next recipient** until the letter addressed to *Sebastian Falk* (Recipient 10) displays.

10 In the **Mail Merge** pane, under **Step 5 of 6**, click **Next: Complete the merge**, and notice that in this step, you can either print the memos or edit the memos. In the **Mail Merge** pane, under **Merge**, click **Edit individual letters**.

By clicking *Edit individual letters*, you can customize one or more of the merged memos.

11 In the displayed **Merge to New Document** dialog box, click **Current record**, and then click **OK**.

The memo addressed to Sebastian Falk displays. At the end of the memo, a section break displays to demonstrate the end of the merged information for that record.

12 Press ⟨Ctrl⟩ + ⟨End⟩ to move to the end of the memo after the section break. Type **Please bring last month's service records to the meeting.** and then compare your screen with Figure 9.32.

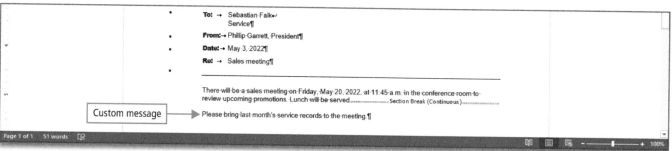

Figure 9.32

13 On the **Quick Access Toolbar**, click **Save** ⟨🖫⟩. In the **Save As** dialog box, navigate to your **Access Chapter 9** folder, and then save the Word document as **9B_Custom_Memo**

14 With the **Word** document displayed, use the **Snipping Tool** to create a screenshot of the window, and then **Save** the file as a **JPEG** using the file name **CustomMemo**

15 **Close** ⊠ Word to exit the custom document. Notice that the memo to Sebastian Falk without the custom message displays in the Mail Merge wizard.

16 From **Backstage** view, click **Save As**. In your **Chapter 9** folder, save the Word document as **9B_Memo_Main** and then **Close** ⊠ Word. If the database is not displayed, on the taskbar, click the **Microsoft Access** icon to restore the Access window to the screen.

17 In the database, on the **Create tab**, in the **Forms group**, click **Form Design** to create a new form in **Design** view. Under **Form Design Tools**, on the **Design tab**, in the **Controls group**, click **Insert Image**, and then click **Browse**. Navigate to the location where you saved the **CustomMemo** screenshot, and double-click the image file. Click in the upper left corner of the **Detail** section of the form to place the image.

18 Save the **Form** as **9B Custom Memo Close** ⊠ the **Form**.

Objective 7 | Export Data to Excel

GO! Learn How
Video A9-7

You can copy data from an Access database into a worksheet by exporting a table, form, or query to an Excel workbook; however, you cannot export reports, macros, or modules to Excel. When you export a table or form that contains a subdatasheet or a subform, only the main datasheet or main form is exported. You can export only one database object in a single export operation; however, you can merge the data in multiple worksheets in Excel after completing the individual export operations.

Export data to Excel if users share the data and some work with Access while others work with Excel. You can store the data in Access and then export it to Excel to analyze the data.

Activity 9.12 | Exporting Selected Records to Excel

3.1.7, 1.3.2

In this Activity, you will export selected records—Chevrolet vehicle data—from an Access query to an Excel workbook.

1 In the **Navigation Pane**, under **Queries**, double-click **9B Used Vehicles** to run the query and to display the results. **Close** « the **Navigation Pane**.

2 Click the arrow to the right of **Make** in the title row of the query results. Click the **Select All** check box to remove the check mark displaying all makes. Click the check box next to **Chevrolet** to filter the table to display only that make of vehicle. Click **OK**. Select those records, and then compare your screen with Figure 9.33.

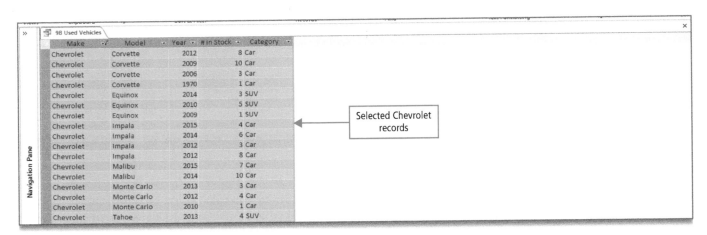

Figure 9.33

3 On the **External Data tab**, in the **Export group**, click **Excel**.

4 In the displayed **Export - Excel Spreadsheet** dialog box, in the **File name** box, verify that the path to your **Access Chapter 9** folder is correct. In the **File name** box, select the existing file name, and type **9B_Used_Vehicles** Notice that in the **File format** box, the file will be saved as an Excel Workbook with an extension of .xlsx, which is the extension used for Excel 2019.

5 In the **Export - Excel Spreadsheet** dialog box, under **Specify export options**, click the **Export data with formatting and layout** check box. Click the **Open the destination file after the export operation is complete** check box. Click the **Export only the selected records** check box.

6 In the **Export - Excel Spreadsheet** dialog box, click **OK**, and then compare your screen with Figure 9.34.

Excel opens and displays the exported data in a worksheet within the workbook. The worksheet name is the same as the query from which the data was exported. The workbook name displays in the Excel window title bar.

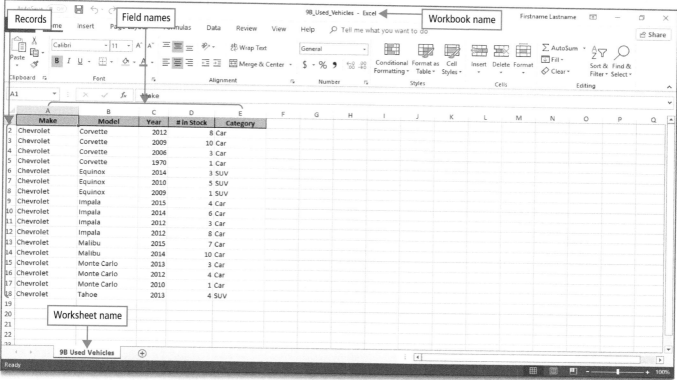

Figure 9.34

7 At the bottom of the worksheet, right-click the **Worksheet tab**, and then click **Rename**. Type **9B Chevrolet** and then press **Enter**. **Save** the workbook, and then **Minimize** ☐ the Excel workbook.

8 If necessary, click the **Microsoft Access** icon on the taskbar to restore the Access window and display the query.

Activity 9.13 | Copying Selected Records to an Existing Excel Workbook

In this Activity, you will export selected records—Toyota vehicle data—from an Access query to an Excel workbook by copying and pasting the records.

1 In the datasheet, using the techniques you practiced in the previous Activity, filter the table and then select all of the records displaying a **Make** of **Toyota**.

2 On the **Home tab**, in the **Clipboard group**, click **Copy** or press Ctrl + C.

3 On the taskbar, click the **Microsoft Excel** icon to make the Excel window active.

4 At the bottom of the worksheet, to the right of the **9B Chevrolet tab**, click **New sheet** ⊕. Compare your screen with Figure 9.35.

A blank worksheet is inserted to the right of the *9B Chevrolet* worksheet. A dark border displays around cell A1.

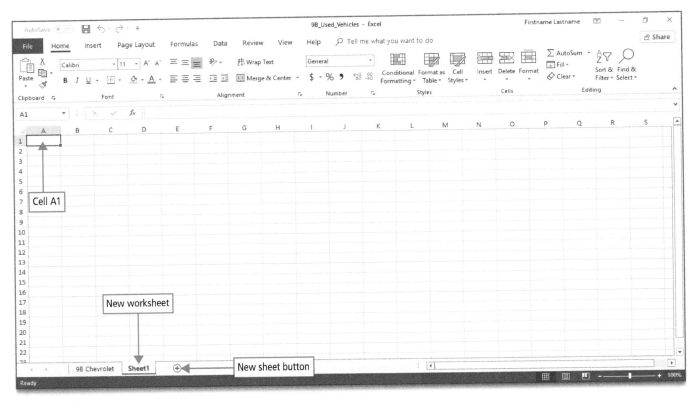

Figure 9.35

5 With cell **A1** selected, on the **Home tab**, in the **Clipboard group**, click **Paste** or press Ctrl + V.

The selected records are pasted into the *9B_Used_Vehicles* workbook on a separate worksheet.

NOTE   Exporting Data into an Existing Workbook

If you use the Export Wizard to export selected records into an existing workbook, the original data in the Excel workbook is overwritten.

---

6 Point to the column border between **B** and **C** until the pointer displays. Drag to the right until all of the data in cell **B12**—*Highlander*—displays on one line.

---

7 Using the techniques you practiced in the previous Activity, **Rename** the worksheet as **9B Toyota** and then compare your screen with Figure 9.36.

There are now two worksheets in the *9B_Used_Vehicles* workbook—*9B Chevrolet* and *9B Toyota*. The *9B Toyota* worksheet is active.

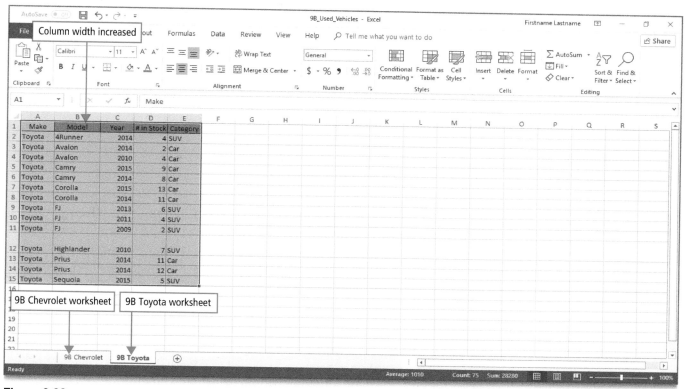

Figure 9.36

8 Save ▣ the workbook. On the **Insert tab**, in the **Text group**, click **Header & Footer**. In the center header box, type **9B Used Toyota Vehicles** Click anywhere in the worksheet to move the insertion point out of the header box.

9 At the bottom of the workbook, click the **9B Chevrolet tab**. Insert a **Header** of **9B Used Chevrolet Vehicles** and then click anywhere in the worksheet to move the insertion point out of the header box.

10 Save ▣ the workbook. With the **Chevrolet** workbook displayed, use the **Snipping Tool** to create a screenshot of the window, and then **Save** the file as a **JPEG** using the file name **ExcelExport Close** the **Snipping Tool**, and **Close** ⌧ Excel.

11 In the **Access** window, **Close** ⌧ the **9B Used Vehicles** query without saving.

12 In the database, on the **Create tab**, in the **Forms group**, click **Form Design** to create a new form in **Design** view. Under **Form Design Tools**, on the **Design tab**, in the **Controls group**, click **Insert Image**, and then click **Browse**. Navigate to the location where you saved the **ExcelExport** screenshot, and double-click the image file. Click in the upper left corner of the **Detail** section of the form to place the image.

13 Save the **Form** as **9B Excel Export** Close ⊠ the **Form**. Open ⟫ the **Navigation Pane**.

MORE KNOWLEDGE **Exporting Data to Another Access Database**

You can copy data from one Access database into another Access database. Copying and pasting is easiest, but exporting offers you more options. You can export all of the database objects into another database. However, to export selected records, you must copy and paste the records.

Exporting an object to another database is similar to importing the object from the first database, although you cannot export multiple objects in a single operation. If you want to export multiple objects, it is easier to open the destination database and perform an import operation. You cannot export table relationships, import and export specifications, custom menu bars, custom toolbars, or a query as a table.

Objective 8 | Export Data to an HTML File and an XML File

GO! Learn How
Video A9-8

If you need to display an Access object on a webpage, you can export the object to an *HTML* format, *HyperText Markup Language*—the language used to display webpages. Webpages are text files that contain text and codes—known as *tags*—that the web browser interprets as the page is loaded. A tag begins with the < character and ends with the > character; for example, to apply bold formatting to the word *Access* you would add a beginning and an ending tag to the word—Access. The tag identifies where the bold formatting begins. The tag identifies where the bold formatting ends.

XML, *Extensible Markup Language*, is the standard language for describing and delivering data on the web. Similar to HTML, XML uses tags to organize and present data. Unlike HTML, which uses standard tags, XML enables you to create your own set of tags. With an XML document, the data can be displayed on a webpage, included in a Word document, analyzed in Excel, imported into a different database, or imported into many other programs that recognize XML files.

Activity 9.14 | **Exporting a Report to an HTML File**

1.3.2

In this Activity, you will export the 9B Jeeps in Stock report to an HTML file.

1 In the **Navigation Pane**, under **Reports**, right-click **9B Jeeps in Stock**, point to **Export**, and then click **HTML Document**.

2 In the displayed **Export - HTML Document** dialog box, in the **File name** box, verify that the file will be saved in the **Access Chapter 9** folder. In the **File name** box, select the existing file name, and type **9B_Jeeps_in_Stock.html** Under **Specify export options**, select the **Open the destination file after the export operation is complete** check box, and then click **OK**.

3 In the displayed **HTML Output Options** dialog box, click **OK**, and then compare your screen with Figure 9.37.

> The document displays in Google Chrome or in your default web browser.

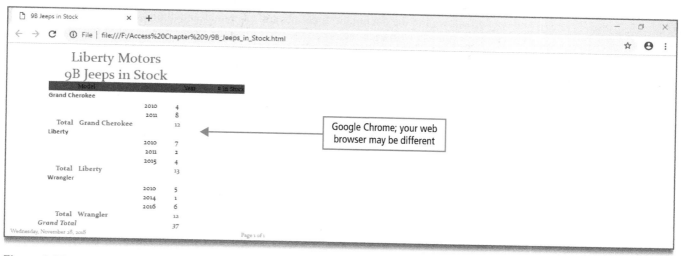

Google Chrome; your web browser may be different

Figure 9.37

4 With the web page displayed, use the **Snipping Tool** to create a screenshot of the window, and then **Save** the file as a **JPEG** using the file name **HTMLReport** Close the **Snipping Tool**, and then **Close** ☒ the web browser window. In the **Export - HTML Document** dialog box, click **Close**.

5 In the database, on the **Create tab**, in the **Forms group**, click **Form Design** to create a new form in **Design** view. Under **Form Design Tools**, on the **Design tab**, in the **Controls group**, click **Insert Image**, and then click **Browse**. Navigate to the location where you saved the **HTMLReport** screenshot, and double-click the image file. Click in the upper left corner of the **Detail** section of the form to place the image.

6 **Save** the form as **9B HTML Report** Close ☒ the form.

Activity 9.15 | Exporting a Report to an XML File

1.3.2

In this Activity, you will export the 9B Jeeps in Stock report to an XML file.

1 In the **Navigation Pane**, under **Reports**, right-click **9B Jeeps in Stock**, point to **Export**, and click **XML File**.

2 In the displayed **Export - XML File** dialog box, in the **File name** box, verify that the file will be saved in the **Access Chapter 9** folder. Select the file name, and then type **9B_XML_ Jeeps.xml** Click **OK**, and then compare your screen with Figure 9.38.

The Export XML dialog box displays. When you export data to XML, multiple files can be created. An *XML schema* is a document with an .xsd extension that defines the elements, entities, and content allowed in the document. It defines the tag names and defines the order, relationships, and data type you use with each tag. The schema is essential to ensure that all of the table relationships and data types are preserved when the data is imported into another database. An XML file cannot be viewed directly in a web browser. *XML presentation files* can be created so that the data can be viewed in a web browser.

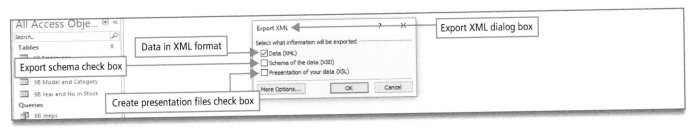

Figure 9.38

3 In the **Export XML** dialog box, verify that the **Data (XML)** check box is selected, and then click the **Presentation of your data (XSL)** check box. Click **OK**. In the **Export - XML File** dialog box, click **Close**.

Because XML files are typically imported into other applications, there is no option to view the file after the export operation.

4 On the taskbar, click the **File Explorer** icon. Navigate to the location where the **Access Chapter 9** folder is saved, and open the folder. Compare your screen with Figure 9.39.

In Details view, the name, size, and type of each file is displayed, in addition to the date and time the file was modified. Your dates and times will differ. The Type column shows two HTML documents—*9B_Jeeps_in_Stock* and *9B_XML_Jeeps*. *9B_Jeeps_in_Stock* is the HTML file that you created when you exported to an HTML file. *9B_XML_Jeeps* is an HTML presentation file that was created when you selected the *Presentation of your data (XSL)* check box while exporting to an XML file.

There is also an *XSL Stylesheet* file named *9B_XML_Jeeps*. This is the second presentation file that is used to create the HTML file. Finally, there is an XML document that stores the data that was exported.

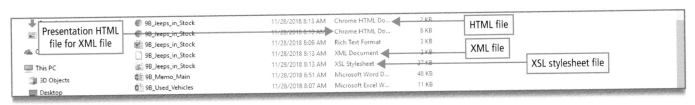

Figure 9.39

5 Locate the **9B_XML_Jeeps** file that displays a **Type** of **Chrome HTML Document** Right-click the file name, and then point to **Open with**. From the shortcut menu, click **Notepad**. Compare your screen with Figure 9.40.

The HTML code displays in a Notepad window. *Notepad* is a simple text editor that comes with the Windows operating system. This is the actual document that was exported. The web browser interprets the HTML tags and displays the text as a readable document. If you know HTML coding, you can format this document so that the column headings are more readable.

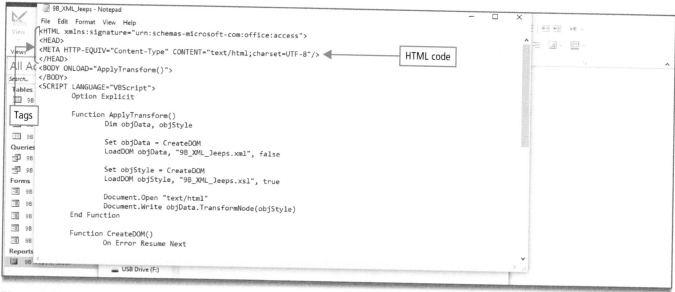

Figure 9.40

6 With the **Notepad** document displayed, use the **Snipping Tool** to create a screenshot of the screen, and then **Save** the file as a **JPEG** using the file name **XMLReport Close** the **Snipping Tool**, **Close Notepad**, and **Close File Explorer**.

7 In the database, on the **Create tab**, in the **Forms group**, click **Form Design** to create a new form in **Design** view. Under **Form Design Tools**, on the **Design tab**, in the **Controls group**, click **Insert Image**, and then click **Browse**. Navigate to the location where you saved the **XMLReport** screenshot, and double-click it to insert the image file in the **Detail** section of the form.

8 Save the form as **9B XML Report Close** ⊠ the form.

9 **Close** the database, and then **Close** Access.

MORE KNOWLEDGE **Exporting Data to Alternate Formats**

If you have data in your Access database that you would like to export to other applications, explore the options on the External Data tab, in the Export group.

- Objects can be shared with others as a PDF document or by emailing them in a format that the recipient can view and use. These export options do not require the recipient to have Access or any other database software.

- In the Export group, click More for additional export formats. A SharePoint List, as you recall, is a list of documents maintained on a server running Microsoft Office SharePoint Server. You also can export data to other database applications, such as ODBC databases. Recall that ODBC stands for Open Database Connectivity, a standard that enables databases using SQL statements to interface with one another.

10 In **MyLab IT**, locate and click the Grader Project **Access 9B Used Inventory**. In **step 3**, under **Upload Completed Assignment**, click **Choose File**. In the **Open** dialog box, navigate to your **Access Chapter 9 folder**, and then click your **Student_Access_9B_Used_ Inventory** file one time to select it. In the lower right corner of the **Open** dialog box, click **Open**.

The name of your selected file displays above the Upload button.

11 To submit your file to **MyLab IT** for grading, click **Upload**, wait a moment for a green **Success!** message, and then in **step 4**, click the blue **Submit for Grading** button. Click **Close Assignment** to return to your list of **Course Materials**.

You have completed Project 9B   END

wavebreakmedia/Shutterstock, Monkey Business Images/Fotolia, Ivanko80/Shutterstock, Monkey Business Images/Shutterstock

Microsoft Office Specialist (MOS) Skills in This Chapter	
Project 9A	**Project 9B**
1.1.1 Import objects or data from other sources	**1.3.2** Export objects to alternative formats
1.2.3 Set Primary Keys	**3.1.7** Run queries
2.1.1 Import data into tables	
2.1.2 Create linked tables from external sources	
2.1.3 Import tables from other databases	
2.4.5 Change field data types	
3.1.6 Save a query	
3.1.7 Run queries	
5.2.1 Format a report into multiple columns	
5.2.3 Format report elements	
5.2.5 Insert information in report headers and footers	
5.2.6 Insert images on reports	

Build Your E-Portfolio

An E-Portfolio is a collection of evidence, stored electronically, that showcases what you have accomplished while completing your education. Collecting and then sharing your work products with potential employers reflects your academic and career goals. Your completed Navigation Panes from the following projects are good examples to show what you have learned: 9G, 9K, and 9L.

GO! For Job Success

Topic: Workplace Bullying

Businesses devote a lot of resources to training and awareness of harassment in the workplace. Most managers and staff are aware that it is unprofessional, contrary to company policy, and often illegal to discriminate or create an inhospitable workplace based on gender, religion, or nationality. But it's more difficult to train for and control more generalized bullying. Bullying in the workplace might include undermining or humiliating a colleague or subordinate, excessive monitoring, unrealistic deadlines, and being isolated or treated differently from the rest of your group.

A tough but fair manager is not a bully, and being expected to do the job you were hired to do is not bullying. But persistent, targeted hostility and negative behaviors by people at work can have a devastating effect on employees' physical and mental health and the business's bottom line.

> What are some of the physical effects an employee might experience when bullied?

> Could bullying have an effect even on those not being directly targeted?

> What responsibility do you think a manager has if a member of their staff is bullying or being bullied?

g-stockstudio/Shutterstock

End of Chapter

Summary

Importing is the process of copying data in from another application. For example, a Word table can be converted to a text file for import, or data can come from an Excel worksheet or another database.

Linking is the process of connecting to data in another application. If a table exists in another database, it can be linked to share the table in the original database.

Exporting is the process of copying data to another application to use its features. For example, an Access query can be exported to perform a mail merge or selected records can be exported to Excel.

Access objects can be exported to HTML and XML files, formats used for viewing webpages. From File Explorer, files are opened using a web browser; however, the formatting differs from the Access report.

GO! Learn It Online

Review the concepts, key terms, and MOS skills in this chapter by completing these online challenges, which you can find at **MyLab IT**.

Chapter Quiz: Answer matching and multiple choice questions to test what you learned in this chapter.

Lessons on the GO!: Learn how to use all the new apps and features as they are introduced by Microsoft.

MOS Quiz: Answer questions to review the MOS skills that you practiced in this chapter.

Project Guide for Access Chapter 9

Your instructor will assign Projects from this list to ensure your learning and assess your knowledge.

Review and Assessment Guide for Access Chapter 9

Project	Apply Skills from These Chapter Objectives	Project Type		Project Location
9A MyLab IT	Objectives 1–4 from Project 9A	**9A Instructional Project (Grader Project)** Guided instruction to learn the skills in Project 9A.	**Instruction**	In **MyLab IT** and in text
9B MyLab IT	Objectives 5–8 from Project 9B	**9B Instructional Project (Grader Project)** Guided instruction to learn the skills in Project 9B.	**Instruction**	In **MyLab IT** and in text
9C	Objectives 1–4 from Project 9A	**9C Chapter Review** A guided review of the skills from Project 9A.	**Review**	In text
9D	Objectives 5–8 from Project 9B	**9D Chapter Review** A guided review of the skills from Project 9B.	**Review**	In text
9E	Objectives 1–4 from Project 9A	**9E Mastery (Scorecard Grading)** **Mastery and Transfer of Learning** A demonstration of your mastery of the skills in Project 9A with extensive decision making.		In text
9F	Objectives 5–8 from Project 9B	**9F Mastery (Scorecard Grading)** **Mastery and Transfer of Learning** A demonstration of your mastery of the skills in Project 9B with extensive decision making.		In text
9G MyLab IT	Objectives 1–8 from Projects 9A and 9B	**9G Mastery (Grader Project)** **Mastery and Transfer of Learning** A demonstration of your mastery of the skills in Projects 9A and 9B with extensive decision making.		In **MyLab IT** and in text
9H	Combination of Objectives from Projects 9A and 9B	**9H GO! Fix It (Scorecard Grading)** **Critical Thinking** A demonstration of your mastery of the skills in Projects 9A and 9B by creating a correct result from a document that contains errors you must find.		Instructor Resource Center (IRC)
9I	Combination of Objectives from Projects 9A and 9B	**9I GO! Make It (Scorecard Grading)** **Critical Thinking** A demonstration of your mastery of the skills in Projects 9A and 9B by creating a result from a supplied picture.		IRC
9J	Combination of Objectives from Projects 9A and 9B	**9J GO! Solve It (Rubric Grading)** **Critical Thinking** A demonstration of your mastery of the skills in Projects 9A and 9B, your decision making skills, and your critical thinking skills. A task-specific rubric helps you self-assess your result.		IRC
9K	Combination of Objectives from Projects 9A and 9B	**9K GO! Solve It (Rubric Grading)** **Critical Thinking** A demonstration of your mastery of the skills in Projects 9A and 9B, your decision making skills, and your critical thinking skills. A task-specific rubric helps you self-assess your result.		In text
9L	Combination of Objectives from Projects 9A and 9B	**9L GO! Think (Rubric Grading)** **Critical Thinking** A demonstration of your understanding of the chapter concepts applied in a manner that you would use outside of college. An analytic rubric helps you and your instructor grade the quality of your work by comparing it to the work an expert in the discipline would create.		In text
9M	Combination of Objectives from Projects 9A and 9B	**9M GO! Think (Rubric Grading)** **Critical Thinking** A demonstration of your understanding of the chapter concepts applied in a manner that you would use outside of college. An analytic rubric helps you and your instructor grade the quality of your work by comparing it to the work an expert in the discipline would create.		IRC
9N	Combination of Objectives from Projects 9A and 9B	**9N You and GO! (Rubric Grading)** **Critical Thinking** A demonstration of your understanding of the chapter concepts applied in a manner that you would use in a personal situation. An analytic rubric helps you and your instructor grade the quality of your work.		IRC

Glossary

Glossary of Chapter Key Terms

Appended When data is added to the end of an existing table.

ASCII An acronym for American Standard Code for Information Interchange, a character set.

Cell The small box formed by the intersection of a column and a row in a worksheet.

Chart A graphic representation of data.

Column chart A chart used to display comparisons among related numbers.

Converted Changed from one format to another.

Data source An Access table or query that contains the names and addresses of the individuals to whom a letter, memo, or other document is being sent in a mail merge.

Definition The structure of the table—the field names, data types, and field properties.

Delimited file A file in which each record displays on a separate line, and the fields within the record are separated by a single character.

Delimiter A single character; can be a paragraph mark, a tab, a comma, or another character to separate fields within a record.

Export The process used to send out a copy of data from one source or application to another application.

Extensible Markup Language The standard language for defining and storing data on the web.

HTML An acronym for HyperText Markup Language.

HyperText Markup Language The language used to display webpages.

Import The process used to bring in a copy of data from one source or application to another application.

Line chart A chart used to display trends over time.

Link A connection to data in another file.

Mail merge Letters or memos that are created by combining a document and a record source.

Main document The document that contains the text of a letter or memo for a mail merge.

Merging Combining two documents to create one.

Named range An Excel range that has been given a name, making it easier to use the cells in calculations or modifications.

Notepad A simple text editor that comes with the Windows operating systems.

ODBC An acronym for Open Database Connectivity.

Open Database Connectivity A standard that enables databases using SQL statements to interface with one another.

Pie chart A chart used to display the contributions of parts to a whole amount.

Plain Text A document format that contains no formatting, such as bold or italic.

Range An area that includes two or more selected cells on an Excel worksheet that can be treated as a single unit.

SharePoint List A list of documents maintained on a server running Microsoft Office SharePoint Server.

SharePoint Server A server that enables you to share documents with others in your organization.

Spreadsheet Another name for a worksheet.

Tags HTML codes that the web browser interprets as the page is loaded; they begin with the < character and end with the > character.

Workbook An Excel file that contains one or more worksheets.

Worksheet The primary document used in Excel to save and work with data that is arranged in columns and rows.

XML An acronym for Extensible Markup Language.

XML presentation files Files that can be created so that the data can be viewed in a web browser.

XML schema A document with an *.xsd* extension that defines the elements, entities, and content allowed in the document.

Chapter Review

Skills Review   Project 9C Cars and Motorcycles

Apply 9A skills from these Objectives:

1. Import Data from a Word Table
2. Import Data from an Excel Workbook
3. Insert an Excel Chart into a Report
4. Import from and Link to Another Access Database

Liberty Motors maintains many of its records in Word, Excel, and Access files. Phillip Garrett, president, and Jeanine Thomas, finance manager, want to bring the data from these files into an Access database to create queries and reports. In this project, you will import data from Word, Excel, and another Access database and create a link to data in another application. Your completed Navigation Pane will look similar to Figure 9.41.

Project Files

For Project 9C, you will need the following files:

New blank Access database

a09C_Used_Cars.accdb

a09C_Motorcycles.accdb

a09C_Logo.jpg

a09C_Domestic_Chart.xlsx

a09C_Customers.docx

a09C_Sports_Car_Sales.xlsx

You will save your files as:

Lastname_Firstname_9C_Cars_Motorcycles.accdb

Lastname_Firstname_9C_Customers_Table.txt

Project Results

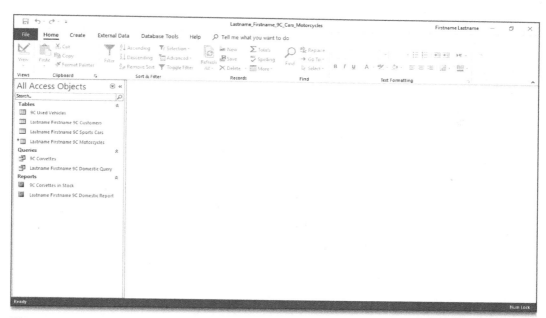

Figure 9.41

(continues on next page)

Chapter Review

1 **Start** Access. In the Access startup window, click **Blank database**. In the **Blank desktop database** dialog box, to the right of the **File Name** box, click **Browse**. In the **File New Database** dialog box, navigate to your **Access Chapter 9** folder. In the File New Database dialog box, click in the File name box, type **Lastname_ Firstname_9C_Cars_Motorcycles** and then press [Enter]. In the **Blank desktop database** dialog box, click **Create**. **Close** the displayed table.

2 **Start** Word. Click **Open Other Documents**. Click **Browse,** and then navigate to the location where the student data files for this textbook are saved. Locate and open the **a09C_Customers** file.

  a. Under **Table Tools**, on the **Layout tab**, in the **Data group**, click **Convert to Text**. In the dialog box, verify that the **Tabs** option button is selected, and then click **OK**. Click anywhere to deselect the text.

  b. Display **Backstage** view, double-click **Save As**, and then navigate to the **Access Chapter 9** folder. Save the file as **Lastname_Firstname_9C_Customers_ Table** Click the **Save as type arrow**, and from the displayed list click **Plain Text**. Click **Save**, and then click **OK**. **Close** Word.

3 Return to Access. On the **External Data tab**, in the **Import & Link group**, click **New Data Source**, click **From File**, and then click **Text File**. In the dialog box, to the right of the **File name** box, click **Browse**. Locate **9C_Customers_Table**, and double-click.

  a. Verify that the **Import the source data into a new table in the current database** option button is selected, and then click **OK**. In the **Import Text Wizard** dialog box, verify that the **Delimited** option button is selected. Click **Next**. Verify that the **Tab** option button is selected, and then click to select the **First Row Contains Field Names** check box. In the **Text Qualifier** box, verify that {**none**} is selected, and click **Next**.

  b. Click in the **Postal Code** field to select the field. Under **Field Options**, click the **Data Type arrow**, and then click **Short Text**. Click **Next**. Verify that the **Let Access add primary key** option button is selected, and then click **Next**. Change the name to **Lastname Firstname 9C Customers** Click **Finish**.

  c. Click the **Save import steps** check box. Click in the **Description** box, and then type **Imports a tab delimited text file that was a Word table** Click **Save Import**. On the **External Data tab**, in the

Import & Link group, click **Saved Imports**, and confirm that your import file is there. **Close** the dialog box.

4 In the **Navigation Pane**, double-click **9C Customers** to open it, and then **Close** the **Navigation Pane**.

  a. In **record 25**, add yourself as a customer. Apply **Best Fit** to adjust the column widths to fully display all of the data and field names.

  b. **Save**, and then **Close** the table.

5 On the **External Data tab**, in the **Import & Link group**, click **New Data Source**, point to **From File**, and then click **Excel**. In the dialog box, click **Browse**. Locate and open the **a09C_Sports_Car_Sales** file. Verify **Import the source data into a new table in the current database** is selected, and then click **OK**.

  a. In the **Import Spreadsheet Wizard** dialog box, verify that **Show Worksheets** is selected and **In Stock** is highlighted. Click **Next**.

  b. Verify that the **First Row Contains Column Headings** check box is selected. Click **Next** two times.

  c. Select **Choose my own primary key**. If necessary, click the **table name box arrow**, click **Vehicle#**, and then click **Next**. In the **Import to Table** box, type **Lastname Firstname 9C Sports Cars** and then click **Finish**. In the **Get External Data - Excel Spreadsheet** dialog box, click **Close**.

6 On the **External Data tab**, in the **Import & Link group**, click **New Data Source**, point to **From File**, and then click **Excel**. Locate and **Open** the **a09C_Sports_ Car_Sales** file.

  a. Click **Append a copy of the records to the table**. If necessary, click the **table name arrow** and select **9C Sports Cars**. Click **OK**. In the **Import Spreadsheet Wizard** dialog box, be certain that **Show Worksheets** is selected. Click **Special Order**, and then click **Next** two times. Click **Finish**. In the **Get External Data - Excel Spreadsheet** dialog box, click **Close**.

  b. **Open** the Navigation Pane. Double-click **9C Sport Cars** to open the table. If you are instructed to submit this result, create a paper printout or PDF electronic image of the table. **Close** the table, and then **Close** the **Navigation Pane**.

(continues on next page)

Chapter Review

Skills Review: Project 9C Cars and Motorcycles (continued)

7 On the **Create tab**, in the **Queries group**, click **Query Design**. In the **Show Table** dialog box, double-click **9C Sports Cars**, and then click **Close**. In the field list, click **Vehicle#**. Hold down Shift, and then click **Color**. Drag the fields down into the first column of the design grid. In the design grid, under **Domestic**, click in the **Criteria** box, type **Y** and then on the **Show** row, clear the check box. Under **Query Tools**, on the **Design tab**, in the **Results group**, click **Run**. **Save** the query as **Lastname Firstname 9C Domestic Query** and then **Close** the query.

8 Open the **Navigation Pane**. Under **Queries**, click **9C Domestic Query** to select the query, and then **Close** the **Navigation Pane**. On the **Create tab**, in the **Reports** group, click **Report**.

a. Switch to **Design** view. Click the image to the left of the title. Under **Report Design Tools**, on the **Design tab**, in the **Header/Footer group**, click **Logo**. Locate **a09C_Logo**, and then double-click. In the **Tools group**, click **Property Sheet**. On the **Property Sheet Format tab**, change the **Size Mode** property to **Zoom**. Change the **Height** to **0.75 Close** the **Property Sheet**. In the **Report Header** section, delete the **Date** and **Time text box controls** and placeholders. In the **Page Footer** section, delete the **Page number text box control**. In the **Report Footer** section, delete the **Count calculated control** and **line**, and then drag the bottom of the **Report Footer** section to the bottom of the section bar.

b. In the **Report Header**, in the **Title** control, replace *Query* with **Report** Click after your Firstname, and then press Delete to remove the space. Press Shift + Enter to move *9C Domestic Report* to a second line. Resize the report to the **6-inch mark on the horizontal ruler**. **Save** the report as **Lastname Firstname 9C Domestic Report** Point to the top of the **Report Footer section bar** until the pointer displays. Drag the section down to the **3-inch mark on the vertical ruler**.

c. **Start** Excel. If necessary, maximize the Excel window. Click **Open Other Workbooks**. Locate and open **a09C_Domestic_Chart**. Click the outside edge of the **column chart** to select the entire chart. Right-click the chart, and then click **Copy**. **Close** the workbook and **Close** Excel. In the **9C Domestic Report**, right-click the **Page Footer section bar**, and then click **Paste**. Remove any blank space in the Page Footer section. Resize the report to **6 inches** wide. **Save** the report, and then switch to **Report** view. **Close** the report, saving changes if necessary.

9 On the **External Data tab**, in the **Import & Link group**, click **New Data Source**, point to **From Database**, and then click **Access**. In the **Get External Data - Access Database** dialog box, click **Browse**. Locate and then double-click **a09C_Used_Cars**. Verify that the **Import tables, queries, forms, reports, macros, and modules into the current database** option button is selected, and then click **OK**.

a. In the **Import Objects** dialog box, click the **Tables tab**, and then click **9C Used Vehicles**. Click the **Queries tab**, and then click **9C Corvettes**. Click the **Reports tab**, click **9C Corvettes in Stock**, and then click **OK**.

b. In the dialog box, click **Close**. **Open** the **Navigation Pane**.

10 In the **Navigation Pane**, under **Reports**, right-click **9C Corvettes in Stock**, and then click **Layout View**. Click the title *9C Corvettes* one time to select the title. Click to the left of *9C*, type **Lastname Firstname** using your name, and then press Shift + Enter. Press Enter, and **Save** the report. **Close** the report.

11 On the **External Data tab**, in the **Import & Link group**, click **New Data Source**, point to **From Database**, and then click **Access**. In the **Get External Data - Access Database** dialog box, click **Browse** to locate and then double-click **a09C_Motorcycles**. Click the **Link to the data source by creating a linked table** option button, and then click **OK**.

a. In the **Link Tables** dialog box, click **9C Motorcycles**, and then click **OK**.

b. In the **Navigation Pane**, under **Tables**, right-click **9C Motorcycles**, and then click **Rename**. Click to the left of **9C**, type **Lastname Firstname** using your name, and then press Spacebar. Press Enter.

c. Double-click **9C Motorcycles** to display the table. Apply **Best Fit** to adjust the widths of all of the columns. If you submit this database electronically, also submit **a09C_Motorcycles** to view the linked objects properly. **Close** the table, saving changes when prompted.

12 Resize the **Navigation Pane** so all object names are fully visible. **Close** the database, and then **Close** Access.

13 As directed by your instructor, submit your database for grading.

You have completed Project 9C **END**

Chapter Review

Apply 9B skills from these Objectives:

5. Export Data to Word
6. Use Mail Merge to Integrate Access and Word
7. Export Data to Excel
8. Export Data to an HTML File and an XML File

The employees at Liberty Motors would like to be able to analyze their sports car inventory data in other applications in addition to Access. Access enables you to export data from an Access database into applications like Word and Excel, including merging Access data with a Word document. You can also export data to be displayed on a webpage. In this project, you will export data to several types of applications. Your completed Navigation Pane will look similar to Figure 9.42.

Project Files

For Project 9D, you will need the following files:

a09D_Sport_Vehicles.accdb

a09D_SC_Letter.docx

You will save your files as:

Lastname_Firstname_9D_Sport_Vehicles.accdb

Lastname_Firstname_9D_Imports_Query.rtf

Lastname_Firstname_9D_Letter.docx

Lastname_Firstname_9D_Letter_Main.docx

Lastname_Firstname_9D_Imports.docx

Lastname_Firstname_9D_Imports_Report.rtf

Lastname_Firstname_9D_15-16_Models.xlsx

Lastname_Firstname_9D_Corvettes_HTML

Lastname_Firstname_9D_Corvettes_XML.htm

Lastname_Firstname_9D_Corvettes_XML.xml

Lastname_Firstname_9D_Corvettes_XML.xsl

Project Results

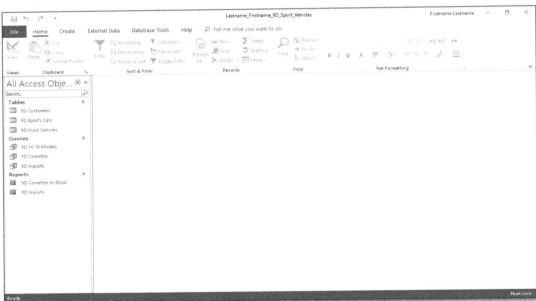

Figure 9.42

(continues on next page)

Chapter Review

1 ▶ **Start** Access. Navigate to the location where the student data files for this textbook are saved. Locate and open the **a09D_Sport_Vehicles** file. Save the database in your **Access Chapter 9** folder as **Lastname_Firstname_9D_Sport_Vehicles** Enable the content or add the Access Chapter 9 folder to the Trust Center.

2 ▶ In the **Navigation Pane**, under **Queries**, right-click **9D Imports**, point to **Export**, and then click **Word RTF File**. In the **Export - RTF File** dialog box, click **Browse**. Navigate to the **Access Chapter 9** folder. In the **File name** box, select the existing file name, type **Lastname_Firstname_9D_Imports_Query** and then click **Save**. In the **Export - RTF File** dialog box, under **Specify export options**, select the **Open the destination file after the export operation is complete** check box, and then click **OK**.

    a. On the **Insert tab,** in the **Header & Footer group**, click **Header**. In the **Built-in** gallery, click **Banded**. Click the **[DOCUMENT TITLE]** text, and then type **Lastname Firstname 9D Imported Sports Cars** In the **Close group**, click **Close Header and Footer**.

    b. Display **Backstage** view, click **Save As**, click **Browse**, and then navigate to the **Access Chapter 9** folder. Change the file name to **Lastname_Firstname_9D_Imports** In the **Save as type** box, select **Word Document**, which means the file will be given a .docx extension. In the **Save As** dialog box, click **Save**. In the displayed message box, click **OK**. **Close** Word. In the **Export - RTF File** dialog box, click **Close**.

3 ▶ Click the **9D Customers** table to select it. On the **External Data tab**, in the **Export group**, click **Word Merge**. Verify that **Link your data to an existing Microsoft Word document** is selected, and then click **OK**. In the **Select Microsoft Word Document** dialog box, locate and **Open** the **a09D_SC_Letter** file. Click the Microsoft Word icon on the taskbar, and **Maximize** the Word window.

    a. In the **Mail Merge** task pane, under **Select recipients**, verify that **Use an existing list** is selected. Under **Step 3 of 6**, click **Next: Write your letter**. Click to the right of **Dear**, and then press [Spacebar]. In the **Mail Merge** task pane, under **Write your letter**, click **More items**. In the **Insert Merge Field** dialog box under **Fields**, double-click **First Name**. Double-click **Last Name**, and then click **Close**. In the letter, click to the left of **<<Last_Name>>**, and then press [Spacebar]. Type a **colon** (:) after the **<<Last Name>>** field.

    b. In the **Mail Merge** task pane, click **Next: Preview your letters**; the first letter displays with a recipient name of **Thomas Walker**. In the **Mail Merge** task pane, under **Make changes**, click **Exclude this recipient**.

    c. In the **Mail Merge** task pane, click **Next: Complete the merge**. In the **Mail Merge** task pane, under **Merge**, click **Edit individual letters**. In the displayed **Merge to New Document** dialog box, click **From** and type **24** Under **To**, also type **24** Click **OK**. In the letter, click at the end of the paragraph that begins *Liberty Motors*, and then press [Enter] two times. Type **You will look great in a red Corvette!**

    d. On the **Quick Access Toolbar**, click **Save**. In the **Save As** dialog box, **Save** the Word document as **Lastname_Firstname_9D_Letter**

    e. **Close** the merged letters. **Save** the main document as **Lastname_Firstname_9D_Letter_Main Close** Word. If necessary, on the status bar, click the Microsoft Access icon to restore the Access window to the screen.

4 ▶ In the **Navigation Pane**, under **Reports**, double-click **9D Imports** to open the report. Switch to **Layout** view. Click the title—**9D Imports**—two times to enter into editing mode. Click to the left of **9D**, type **Lastname Firstname** using your own first and last names, and then press [Shift]+ [Enter]. Press [Enter], and then **Save** the report.

    a. **Close** the report. In the **Navigation Pane**, under **Reports**, right-click **9D Imports**, point to **Export**, and then click **Word RTF File**. Verify that the **File name** box displays the correct path to your **Access Chapter 9** folder. Rename the file **Lastname_Firstname_9D_Imports_Report** Under **Specify export options**, select the **Open the destination file after the export operation is complete** check box, and then click **OK**.

    b. **Close** the Word window. In the **Export - RTF File** dialog box, click **Close**.

5 ▶ In the **Navigation Pane**, under **Queries**, double-click **9D 14-16 Models** to open the query in Datasheet view. **Close** the **Navigation Pane**. In the title row of the query results, click the arrow to the right of **Year**. Click the **Select All** check box, and then click **2015** to filter the data to view only 2015 models. Click **OK**. Select all of the records displayed in the filtered query. Click the **External Data tab**, and in the **Export group**, click **Excel**.

(continues on next page)

Chapter Review

a. In the **Export - Excel Spreadsheet** dialog box, in the **File name** box, verify that the path to your **Access Chapter 9** folder is correct. In the **File name** box, select the existing file name, and type **Lastname_Firstname_9D_15-16_Models** Notice that in the **File format** box, the file will be saved as an Excel 2019 Workbook with an extension of .xlsx. Under **Specify export options**, click all three check boxes. Click **OK**.

b. At the bottom of the worksheet, right-click the **worksheet tab**, and then click **Rename**. Type **9D 2015 Models** and then press **Enter**. **Save** the workbook, and then **Minimize** Excel.

c. If necessary, on the taskbar, click the **Microsoft Access** icon to restore the Access window. Filter the query to display only the 2016 models. Select all of the displayed records. On the **Home tab**, in the **Clipboard group**, click **Copy**. On the taskbar, click the **Microsoft Excel** icon to make the Excel window active. At the bottom of the worksheet, to the right of the **9D 2015 Models** worksheet, click the **New sheet button**.

d. With cell **A1** selected, on the **Home tab**, in the **Clipboard group**, click **Paste**. Point to the column border between **B** and **C** until the pointer displays. Drag to the right until all of the data in cell **B1**—*Customer ID*—displays. Using the techniques you have practiced, **Rename** the worksheet as **9D 2016 Models Save** the workbook.

e. On the **Insert tab**, in the **Text group**, click **Header & Footer**. In the header box, type **Lastname Firstname 2016 Models** Click anywhere in the worksheet to move the insertion point out of the header box.

f. At the bottom of the workbook, click the **9D 2015 Models** tab. Insert a **Header** of **Lastname Firstname 2015 Models** and then click anywhere in the worksheet to move the insertion point out of the header box.

g. **Save** the workbook. **Close** Excel.

h. In the **Access** window, in the title row, click the arrow to the right of **Year**. Click the **Select All** check box to remove the filter, and click **OK**. **Close** the **9D 14-16 Models** query without saving, and then **Open** the **Navigation Pane**.

6 In the **Navigation Pane**, under **Reports**, right-click **9D Corvettes in Stock**, and open the report in **Design** view. Add your Lastname Firstname to the beginning of the report title, and press **Shift**+**Enter** to move **9D Corvettes in Stock** to the second line of the title. **Save** and **Close** the report. Right-click **9D Corvettes in Stock**, point to **Export**, and then click **HTML Document**.

a. In the **Export - HTML Document** dialog box, in the **File name** box, verify that the file will be saved in the **Access Chapter 9** folder. In the **File name** box, select the existing file name, and type **Lastname_Firstname_9D_Corvettes_HTML** Under **Specify export options**, select the **Open the destination file after the export operation is complete** check box, and then click **OK**. In the **HTML Output Options** dialog box, click **OK**.

b. If you are instructed to submit this result, create a paper printout or PDF electronic image of the webpage. **Close** the web browser window. In the **Export - HTML Document** dialog box, click **Close**.

7 In the **Navigation Pane**, under **Reports**, right-click **9D Corvettes in Stock**, point to **Export**, and then click **XML File**. In the **Export - XML File** dialog box, in the **File name** box, verify that the file will be saved in the **Access Chapter 9** folder. Select only the file name, and then type **Lastname_Firstname_9D_Corvettes_XML** Click **OK**. In the **Export XML** dialog box, verify that the **Data (XML)** check box is selected, and then click the **Presentation of your data (XSL)** check box. Click **OK**. In the **Export - XML File** dialog box, click **Close**.

8 Open **File Explorer**. Navigate to the location where the **Access Chapter 9** folder is saved, and open the folder. If necessary, click the View tab, and, in the Layout group, click Details. Maximize the window.

a. Locate the **9D_Corvettes_XML** file that displays a **Type** of HTM Document. Right-click the file name, click **Open with**, and then click **Notepad** to view the file.

b. **Close** the Notepad window, and then **Close** the Access Chapter 9 window.

9 **Close** the database, and then **Close** Access.

10 As directed by your instructor, submit your database for grading.

You have completed Project 9D | **END**

Content-Based Assessments (Mastery and Transfer of Learning)

Mastering   Project 9E Customized Cars

<table>
<tr><td>

Apply 9A skills from these Objectives:

1. Import Data from a Word Table
2. Import Data from an Excel Workbook
3. Insert an Excel Chart into a Report
4. Import from and Link to Another Access Database

</td><td>

Liberty Motors offers extensive customization options for all types of vehicles through its accessories division. In this project, you will import a Word table as a plain text file. You will import data from an Excel worksheet and create a report with an imported Excel chart. Your completed Navigation Pane will look similar to Figure 9.43.

Project Files

For Project 9E, you will need the following files:

New blank Access database
a09E_Custom_Features.docx
a09E_Package_Sales.xlsx
a09E_Employees.accdb
a09E_Logo.jpg

You will save your files as:

Lastname_Firstname_9E_Customized_Cars.accdb
Lastname_Firstname_9E_Custom_Features.txt

Project Results

</td></tr>
</table>

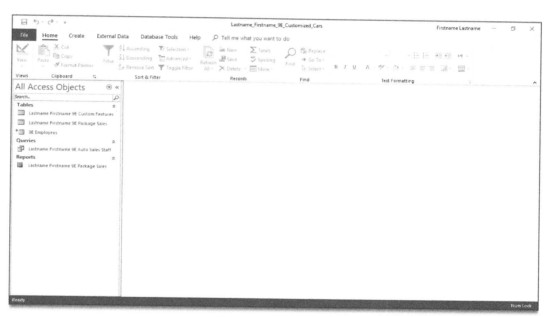

Figure 9.43

(continues on next page)

Mastering: Project 9E Customized Cars (continued)

1 **Start** Access. In your **Access Chapter 9** folder, create a new blank database called **Lastname_Firstname_9E_Customized_Cars Close** the displayed table.

2 **Start** Word. Locate and open the **a09E_Custom_Features** document. Under **Table Tools**, on the **Layout tab**, in the **Data group**, click **Convert to Text**. Separate the text with **Tabs**.

3 **Save** the file as **Plain Text** using the name **Lastname_Firstname_9E_Custom_Features** In the displayed **File Conversion** dialog box, accept the default settings, and then **Close** Word.

4 Return to the Access **9E_Customized_Cars** empty database. Import the **9E_Custom_Features** text file. Verify that the **Import the source data into a new table in the current database** option button is selected, and then click **OK**.

5 In the **Import Text Wizard** dialog box, verify that the **Delimited** option button is selected, and click **Next**. Verify that the **Tab** option button is selected. Select the **First Row Contains Field Names** check box. In the **Text Qualifier** box, verify that **{none}** is selected, and then click **Next**.

6 Change the **Data Type** in the **Customer Rating (1-5)** field to **Short Text**. Click **Next**. Verify that the **Let Access add primary key** option button is selected, and then click **Next**. Edit the table name by replacing the underscores with spaces. Click **Finish**.

7 Select the **Save import steps** check box to display additional options. Click in the **Description** box, type **Imports a tab-delimited text file that was a Word table** and then click **Save Import**.

8 Open the **9E Custom Features** table in **Datasheet** view, and apply **Best Fit** to adjust all of the column widths to fully display all of the data and field names.

9 **Save** and then **Close** the table.

10 Import the **a09E_Package_Sales** workbook file. Verify **Import the source data into a new table in the current database** is selected, and then click **OK**. In the **Import Spreadsheet Wizard** dialog box, verify that **Show Worksheets** is selected and **Packages** is highlighted. Click **Next**. Select the **First Row Contains Column Headings** check box. Click **Next** two times.

Verify that **Let Access add primary key** is selected, and then click **Next**. Name the table **Lastname Firstname 9E Package Sales** and then click **Finish**. In the **Get External Data - Excel Spreadsheet** dialog box, click **Close**.

11 Select the **9E Package Sales** table and create a new **Report**. Switch to **Design** view. Select the image placeholder to the left of the title and replace with the **a09E_Logo** file with a **Size Mode** property of **Zoom**. Resize the logo to approximately **1 inch** tall by **1 inch** wide. In the **Report Header** section, delete the **Date** and **Time text box controls** and the placeholder. Move **9E Package Sales** to the second line of the title. In the **Page Footer** section, delete the **Page number text box control**. In the **Report Footer** section, delete the **Count calculated control** and the **line**. Increase the size of the **Page Footer** section to the **2.75-inch mark** on the horizontal ruler. **Save** the report as **Lastname Firstname 9E Package Sales**

12 **Start** Excel. **Open** the **a09E_Package_Sales** workbook. In the **Package Totals** worksheet, select the entire chart. **Copy** the chart to the Office Clipboard. **Close** Excel. In the Access **9E Package Sales** report, **Paste** the chart in the **Page Footer**. Resize the report to **7 inches wide**. **Save** the report, and then switch to **Report** view. **Close** the report.

13 Import data from the **a09E_Employees** database. Click the **Link to the data source by creating a linked table** option button, and then click **OK**. In the **Link Tables** dialog box, click **9E Employees**, and then click **OK**.

14 Import data from the **a09E_Employees** database. Verify that the **Import tables, queries, forms, reports, macros, and modules into the current database** option button is selected, and then click **OK**. In the **Import Objects** dialog box, click the **Queries** tab, click **9E Auto Sales Staff**, and then click **OK**. Click **Close**. **Rename 9E Auto Sales Staff** by adding your **Lastname Firstname** to the beginning of the query name.

15 Resize the **Navigation Pane** so all object names are fully visible. **Close** Access.

16 As directed by your instructor, submit your database for grading.

You have completed Project 9E **END**

Content-Based Assessments (Mastery and Transfer of Learning)

| Mastering | Project 9F Custom Packages |

Apply 9B skills from these Objectives:

5. Export Data to Word
6. Use Mail Merge to Integrate Access and Word
7. Export Data to Excel
8. Export Data to an HTML File and an XML File

The accessories staff would like to be able to analyze data related to luxury features and package sales using Word and Excel. They would also like to be able to display data on the web. Access enables you to export data from an Access database into these applications and onto a webpage. In this project, you will export data to several types of applications, including merging Access data with a flyer created in Word. Your completed files will look similar to Figure 9.44.

Project Files

For Project 9F, you will need the following files:

a09F_Custom_Packages.accdb

a09F_Flyer.docx

You will save your files as:

Lastname_Firstname_9F_Custom_Packages.accdb
Lastname_Firstname_9F_Accessory_Staff.docx
Lastname_Firstname_9F_Flyers.docx
Lastname_Firstname_9F_Flyer_Main.docx
Lastname_Firstname_9F_Safety_Features.xlsx
Lastname_Firstname_9F_Package_Sales.html
Lastname_Firstname_9F_XML_Package_Features.xml
Lastname_Firstname_9F_XML_Package_Features.htm
Lastname_Firstname_9F_XML_Package_Features.xsl

Project Results

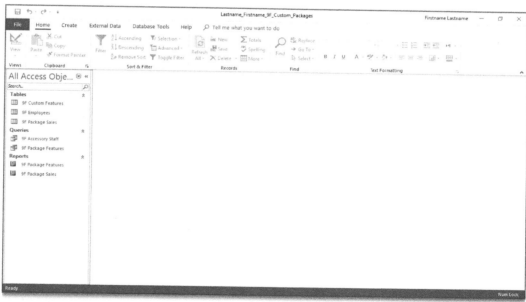

Figure 9.44

(continues on next page)

Mastering: Project 9F Custom Packages (continued)

1 **Start** Access. Locate and open the **a09F_Custom_ Packages** file. Save the database in your **Access Chapter 9** folder as **Lastname_Firstname_9F_Custom_Packages**

2 In the **Navigation Pane**, under **Queries**, right-click **9F Accessory Staff**, point to **Export**, and then click **Word RTF File**. Navigate to the **Access Chapter 9** folder, and name the file **Lastname_Firstname_9F_Accessory_Staff**

3 Under **Specify export options**, select the **Open the destination file after the export operation is complete** check box, and then click **OK**. In Word, click the **Insert tab**. In the **Header & Footer group**, click **Header**. In the **Built-in** gallery, click **Blank**, and then in the **Type text box**, type **Lastname Firstname 9F Accessory Staff Close** the header. Using the default file name, save the document as a **Word Document** in the **Access Chapter 9** folder. If necessary, in the displayed message box, click **OK**. **Close** the Word window. In the **Export - RTF File** dialog box, click **Close**.

4 Export the **9F Custom Features** table using **Word Merge**. Verify that **Link your data to an existing Microsoft Word document** is selected, and then click **OK**. Locate and open the **a09F_Flyer** file. Click the **Microsoft Word** icon on the taskbar, and maximize the Word window.

5 In the Word **Mail Merge** task pane, under **Select recipients**, verify that **Use an existing list** is selected, and then click **Next: Write your letter**. One at a time, click to the right of **Package Deal**, **Custom Feature**, and **Warranty**, inserting the appropriate field names. At the bottom of the flyer, replace *Firstname Lastname* with your first and last names. Preview and then complete the merge. Click **Edit Individual Letters**, and then merge records **3-4** only. Save your document in the **Access Chapter 9** folder as **Lastname_Firstname_9F_Flyers**

6 **Close** the merged document. **Save** the document as **Lastname_Firstname_9F_Flyer_Main** and **Close** Word. Restore the Access window to the screen.

7 In the **9F Custom Features** table, **Filter** the results to display only the *Safe & Secure Package Deal* records; select the records. On the **External Data tab**, in the **Export group**, click **Excel**.

8 **Save** the file in your **Access Chapter 9** folder as **Lastname_Firstname_9F_Safety_Features** Under **Specify export options**, select all three check boxes, and then click **OK**. **Rename** the worksheet **9F Safe & Secure** Insert a **Header** and, using your own name, type **Safe & Secure Package Sales Rep: Firstname Lastname Save** the workbook. **Close** the Excel workbook and **Close** Excel. In the Access window, **Close** the **9F Custom Features** table, but do not save the changes.

9 In the **Navigation Pane**, under **Reports**, open the **9F Package Sales** report in **Design** view. Add your **Lastname Firstname** to the beginning of the title, and move the rest of the title to a second line. **Save** and **Close** the report. Right-click the **9F Package Sales** report, point to **Export**, and then click **HTML Document**. Navigate to the **Access Chapter 9** folder, and name the file **Lastname_Firstname_9F_Package_Sales.html** Under **Specify export options**, click the **Open the destination file after the export operation is complete** check box, and then click **OK**. In the **HTML Output Options** dialog box, click **OK**. Click **OK** if you are prompted about the section width.

10 **Close** the web browser window. In the **Export - HTML Document** dialog box, click the **Close** button.

11 In the **Navigation Pane**, under **Reports**, open the **9F Package Features** report in **Design** view. Replace *Lastname Firstname* with your first and last names. **Save** and **Close** the report. Right-click **9F Package Features**, point to **Export**, and then click **XML File**. Save the file in the **Access Chapter 9** folder as **Lastname_Firstname_9F_XML_Package_Features.xml** and then click **OK**. In the **Export XML** dialog box, verify that the **Data (XML)** check box is selected, and then click the **Presentation of your data (XSL)** check box. Click **OK**. In the **Export - XML File** dialog box, click **Close**.

12 Locate the **9F_XML_Package_Features** file that displays a **Type** of **HTM Document** and display the source code in **Notepad**. **Close** the document window, and then **Close** the Access Chapter 9 window.

13 **Close** Access.

14 As directed by your instructor, submit your database for grading.

You have completed Project 9F END

Content-Based Assessments (Mastery and Transfer of Learning)

MyLab IT Grader	Mastering	Project 9G Monthly Promotions

Apply 9A and 9B skills from these Objectives:

1. Import Data from a Word Table
2. Import Data from an Excel Workbook
3. Insert an Excel Chart into a Report
4. Import from and Link to Another Access Database
5. Export Data to Word
6. Use Mail Merge to Integrate Access and Word
7. Export Data to Excel
8. Export Data to an HTML File and an XML File

Gregory Burton, accessories sales manager, and Jessie Pine, auto sales manager, at Liberty Motors have teamed up to offer special monthly promotions to encourage customers to revisit the showroom. In this project, you will import an Excel worksheet that contains the customer list and a Word table that contains the promotion details. You will use mail merge to inform the customers about the promotions. You will export a form created from the promotions table to an HTML file so it can be viewed as a webpage. Your completed Navigation Pane will look similar to Figure 9.45.

Project Files for MyLab IT Grader

1. In your **MyLab IT** course, locate and click **Access 9G Monthly Promotions**, Download Materials, and then Download All Files.
2. Extract the zipped folder to your Access Chapter 9 folder. Close the Grader download screens.
3. Take a moment to open the downloaded **Access_9G_Monthly_Promotions_Instructions**; note any recent updates to the book.

Project Results

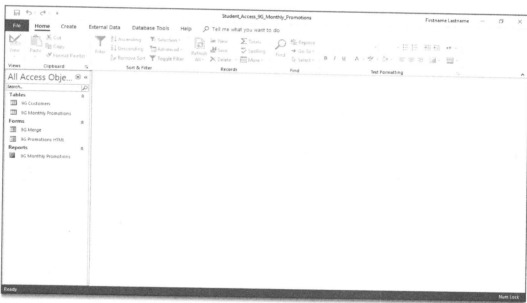

Figure 9.45

For Non-MyLab Submissions

For Project 9G, you will need these files:

a09G_Monthly_Promotions
a09G_Promotions_Letter.docx
a09G_Customers.xlsx
a09G_Monthly_Promotions.txt
a09G_Logo.jpg

After you have saved your database, open it to launch Access. On the next page, begin with Step 2.

After step 12, submit your database and the additional files for grading.

Start with an Access Data File

In your Access Chapter 9 folder, save your files as:

Lastname_Firstname_9G_Monthly_Promotions.accdb
Lastname_Firstname_9G_Promotions_Letter.docx
Lastname_Firstname_9G_Merged_Letters.docx
Lastname_Firstname_9G_Monthly_Promotions_HTML.html

(continues on next page)

Mastering: Project 9G Monthly Promotions (continued)

1 **Start** Access. **Create** a new blank database and save it in the **Access Chapter 9** folder as **9G_Monthly_ Promotions** **Close** the table.

2 Import **External Data** from the **a09G_Customers** Excel file into a new table in the **9G_Monthly_ Promotions** database. The **first row contains column headings**. Change the data type for the **Postal Code** field to **Short Text**. **Let Access add primary key**. Import to table **9G Customers**

3 Open the **9G Customers** table, and **Best Fit** all columns. **Save** and **Close** the table. Merge it with the existing Microsoft Word document **a09G_Promotions_ Letter**. The recipients will be selected from the existing list in the **9G Customers** table. Verify that **Show/Hide** is active. Place your insertion point at the beginning of the fifth blank line after the current date. Add the **Address Block**, and click **OK**. Insert the **First Name** and **Last Name** fields between the space and the colon in the salutation line. Place a space between these fields.

4 **Preview your letters** and **Complete the merge** for only the eighth record. Save the document as **9G_Merged_Letter** With the **Word** document displayed, use the **Snipping Tool** to create a screenshot of the screen, and then **Save** the file as a **JPEG** using the file name **MergeLetter** Close the **Snipping Tool**, **Close** the document, and **Close** Word.

5 In the database, create a blank form in **Design** view and then, in the **Detail** section, insert the image file **MergeLetter** Save the **Form** as **9G Merge** Close the **Form**.

6 Import **External Data** from the text file **a09G_ Monthly_Promotions**. Import the source data into a new table in the current database. Use the **tab delimiter**. The **first row contains field names**. The data types are correct. **Let Access add primary key**. Import this text to **9G Monthly Promotions** Do not save the import steps.

7 From the **9G Monthly Promotions** table, **Create** a report. In the **Title** of the report, add **Liberty Motors** in front of the title, and then move **9G Monthly**

Promotions to a second line. Add the **a09G_Logo** to the report header. With the **Size Mode** property set to **Zoom**, resize the **logo control** until it reaches the **1.5-inch mark on the horizontal ruler**. Delete the **Date** and **Time** controls and placeholder. Resize the report to **6.5 inches** wide. **Save** the report as **9G Monthly Promotions** and then **Close** the report.

8 Export the **9G Monthly Promotions** report as an **HTML Document**. Open the destination file after the export operation is complete. In the **HTML Output Options** dialog box, click **OK**.

9 Export the report as an HTML Document named **9G_Monthly_Promotions_HTML** Open the destination file after the export is complete, accepting all other default options. Use the **Snipping Tool** to create a screenshot of your screen, and save the file as a **JPEG** using the file name **HTMLPromo**

10 Create a blank form in **Design** view and then, in the **Detail** section, insert the image file **HTMLPromo** into it. Save the form as **9G Promotions HTML**

11 **Close** the browser window. In the **Export - HTML Document** dialog box, click **Close**.

12 Resize the **Navigation Pane** so all object names are fully visible. **Close** Access.

13 In **MyLab IT**, locate and click the Grader Project Access 9G Monthly Promotions. In **step 3**, under **Upload Completed Assignment**, click **Choose File**. In the **Open** dialog box, navigate to your **Access Chapter 9 folder**, and then click your **Student_Access_9G_ Monthly_Promotions** file one time to select it. In the lower right corner of the **Open** dialog box, click **Open**.

14 To submit your file to **MyLab IT** for grading, click **Upload**, wait a moment for a green **Success!** message, and then in **step 4**, click the blue **Submit for Grading** button. Click **Close Assignment** to return to your list of **Course Materials**.

You have completed Project 9G **END**

Content-Based Assessments (Critical Thinking)

Apply a combination of the 9A and 9B skills

GO! Fix It	Project 9H Customer Service	IRC
GO! Make It	Project 9I Sponsored Events	IRC
GO! Solve It	Project 9J Sales Data	IRC
GO! Solve It	Project 9K Advertisements	

Project Files

For Project 9K, you will need the following files:

a09K_Advertisements.accdb
a09K_Ad_Staff.txt

You will save your files as:

Lastname_Firstname_9K_Advertisements.accdb
Lastname_Firstname_9K_Ads_Workbook.xlsx

Jessie Pine, auto sales manager of Liberty Motors, explores many different venues to advertise the business. Most of the data for the advertisements is kept in a database. Some of the employees would like to see the data arranged in a worksheet to create a what-if analysis. Open the **a09K_Advertisements** database, and then save it as **Lastname_Firstname_9K_Advertisements** Import the **a09K_Ad_Staff.txt** file as a table, using the first row as field names, assigning a Short Text data type to the Postal Code field, and letting Access assign the primary key. Save the table as **Lastname Firstname 9K Ad Staff** and then Best Fit all columns in the table. Export the *9K Advertisements* table to an Excel workbook with formatting and layout. Save the workbook as **Lastname_Firstname_9K_Ads_Workbook** Rename the sheet tab **9K Data** If necessary, AutoFit the columns. Copy all of the data from the *9K Cost Analysis Summary* query to a second sheet in the same workbook. Rename this sheet **9K Analysis** AutoFit the columns. Type **Lastname Firstname 9K Advertisements** as a header for each of the sheets. As directed by your instructor, submit your database for grading.

Performance Criteria		Performance Level		
		Exemplary	**Proficient**	**Developing**
	Import the a09K_Ad_Staff.txt file as a table	Table created with correct fields and settings as directed.	Table created with no more than two missing fields or settings.	Table created with more than two missing fields or settings.
	Export the 9K Advertisements table to Excel	Worksheet created with correct fields and settings as directed.	Worksheet created with no more than two missing fields or settings.	Worksheet created with more than two missing fields or settings.
	Export the 9K Cost Analysis Summary query to Excel	Worksheet created with correct fields and settings as directed.	Worksheet created with no more than two missing fields or settings.	Worksheet created with more than two missing fields or settings.

You have completed Project 9K END

Outcomes-Based Assessments (Critical Thinking)

Rubric

The following outcomes-based assessments are open-ended assessments. That is, there is no specific correct result; your result will depend on your approach to the information provided. Make Professional Quality your goal. Use the following scoring rubric to guide you in how to approach the problem and then to evaluate how well your approach solves the problem.

The *criteria*—Software Mastery, Content, Format and Layout, and Process—represent the knowledge and skills you have gained that you can apply to solving the problem. The *levels of performance*—Professional Quality, Approaching Professional Quality, or Needs Quality Improvements—help you and your instructor evaluate your result.

	Your completed project is of Professional Quality if you:	Your completed project is Approaching Professional Quality if you:	Your completed project Needs Quality Improvements if you:
1-Software Mastery	Choose and apply the most appropriate skills, tools, and features and identify efficient methods to solve the problem.	Choose and apply some appropriate skills, tools, and features, but not in the most efficient manner.	Choose inappropriate skills, tools, or features, or are inefficient in solving the problem.
2-Content	Construct a solution that is clear and well organized, contains content that is accurate, appropriate to the audience and purpose, and is complete. Provide a solution that contains no errors of spelling, grammar, or style.	Construct a solution in which some components are unclear, poorly organized, inconsistent, or incomplete. Misjudge the needs of the audience. Have some errors in spelling, grammar, or style, but the errors do not detract from comprehension.	Construct a solution that is unclear, incomplete, or poorly organized, contains some inaccurate or inappropriate content, and contains many errors of spelling, grammar, or style. Do not solve the problem.
3-Format and Layout	Format and arrange all elements to communicate information and ideas, clarify function, illustrate relationships, and indicate relative importance.	Apply appropriate format and layout features to some elements, but not others. Overuse features, causing minor distraction.	Apply format and layout that does not communicate information or ideas clearly. Do not use format and layout features to clarify function, illustrate relationships, or indicate relative importance. Use available features excessively, causing distraction.
4-Process	Use an organized approach that integrates planning, development, self-assessment, revision, and reflection.	Demonstrate an organized approach in some areas, but not others; or, use an insufficient process of organization throughout.	Do not use an organized approach to solve the problem.

Outcomes-Based Assessments (Critical Thinking)

Apply a combination of the 9A and 9B skills

GO! Think Project 9L Employee Recognition

Project Files

For Project 9L, you will need the following files:

a09L_Employee_Recognition.accdb
a09L_Birthday_List.docx
a09L_Birthday_Card.docx

You will save your files as:

Lastname_Firstname_9L_Employee_Recognition.accdb
Lastname_Firstname_9L_Birthday_List.txt
Lastname_Firstname_9L_Birthday_Card.docx
Lastname_Firstname_9L_Card_Main.docx
Lastname_Firstname_9L_HTML_List.html

You have been asked to help with an employee recognition project at Liberty Motors. You will import the data from a Word table into a database table and then merge this table with cards created in Word. The birthday list will be uploaded to the company intranet, so it will need to be exported to HTML.

Open **a09L_Employee_Recognition** and save it as **Lastname_Firstname_9L_Employee_Recognition** Rename both tables to begin with your Lastname Firstname. Open **a09L_Birthday_List**, and then convert the table to text. Save as a text file named **Lastname_Firstname_9L_Birthday_List** and then import it into your database as a table named **Lastname Firstname 9L Birthday List** with the first row as field names and no primary key. Best fit all columns, and add your name and birthday to the table. Merge it with **a09L_Birthday_Card** so the person's full name appears on the line after *Happy Birthday* and their favorite cake appears before the word *Cake*. Adjust the spacing as necessary. Merge your card only (Record 13), and save it as **Lastname_Firstname_9L_Birthdy_Card** Save the main document as **Lastname_Firstname_9L_Card_Main**

Export the *9L Birthday List* table to HTML. Save the file as **Lastname_Firstname_9L_HTML_List.html** As directed by your instructor, submit your database for grading.

You have completed Project 9L | END

GO! Think Project 9M Service Records | IRC

You and GO! Project 9N Club Directory | IRC

Administering Databases and Writing SQL Statements

PROJECT 10A

Outcomes
Manage Access files.

Objectives
1. Create a Navigation Form
2. Use Microsoft Access Analysis Tools
3. Modify Access Views and Behaviors
4. Use the Database Splitter
5. Encrypt and Decrypt Databases
6. Create a Locked Database (ACCDE File)

PROJECT 10B

Outcomes
Write SQL statements.

Objectives
7. Modify a Query in SQL View
8. Create a Query in SQL View
9. Create a Union Query Using SQL
10. Create Calculated Fields and SQL Aggregate Functions

shutterpix/Shutterstock

In This Chapter

GO! To Work with Access

Throughout the life of a database, tables are added; design changes are made to queries, forms, and reports; and data is constantly updated and added. Understanding how to maintain a database is critical to the success of the individuals who rely on its data. Analysis tools enable users to identify potential problems and then fix them. Access also provides a set of security settings including password protection and a means to ensure the security of a database that you plan on sharing. Finally, Access provides a view for creating and modifying the SQL, or Structured Query Language, that makes all of its queries work.

Attorneys at **Loren-Renner Law Partners** counsel clients on a wide variety of issues including contracts, licensing, intellectual property, taxation, and the unique needs of the sports and entertainment industries. Entertainment clients include production companies, publishers, talent agencies, actors, writers, artists—anyone doing business in the entertainment industry. Sports clients include colleges and universities, professional sports teams, athletes, and venue operators. Increasingly, amateur and community sports coaches and organizations with concerns about liability are seeking the firm's specialized counsel.

PROJECT
10A Lawyer Recruitment

MyLab IT
Project 10A Grader for Instruction
Project 10A Simulation for Training and Review

Project Activities

Loren-Renner Law Partners uses Access databases to organize various operations. The firm uses one database to maintain its recruitment efforts and one that contains lawyer data, corporate client data, and corporate case data. In Activities 10.01 through 10.12, you will administer and secure the data by creating a navigation form, applying several file management tools, splitting a database, encrypting a database, and locking the database. Your Navigation Pane will look similar to the one in Figure 10.1.

 Project Files for MyLab IT Grader

1. In your storage location, create a folder named **Access Chapter 10**.
2. In your **MyLab IT** course, locate and click **Access 10A Lawyer Recruitment**, Download Materials, and then Download All Files.
3. Extract the zipped folder to your Access Chapter 10 folder. Close the Grader download screens.
4. Take a moment to open the downloaded **Access_10A_Lawyer_Recruitment_Instructions**; note any recent updates to the book.

Project Results

GO! Project 10A
Where We're Going

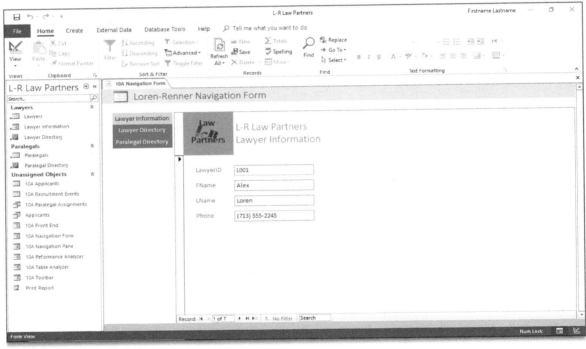

Figure 10.1 Project 10A Lawyer Recruitment

For Non-MyLab Submissions

For Project 10A, you will need:

a10A_Recruitment

a10A_Icon

a10A_Lawyers

Start with an Access Data File

In your storage location, create a folder named **Access Chapter 10**

In your Access Chapter 10 folder, save your database as:

Lastname_Firstname_10A_Recruitment

After you have saved your database, open it to launch Access. On the next page, begin with Step 2.

ALERT   Because Office 365 is a cloud-based subscription service that receives continuous updates, you may encounter some variations in what appears on your screen and what is shown in this instruction. Microsoft Office 365 is fully installed on your PC or Mac; no internet access is necessary to create or edit documents. When you *are* connected to the internet, you will receive monthly upgrades and new features, so you always have the latest versions of Office apps as soon as they are available. Your subscription gives you continuous free access to the latest innovations and refinements.

GO! Learn How
Video A10-1

A ***navigation form*** is a form that displays navigational controls that enable you to display forms and reports in your database. Navigation forms are useful when your database is web-based because browsers do not display the Access Navigation Pane. Navigation forms do not have to display controls for all of your database objects; you can design a navigation form for a specific purpose, such as managing recruitment events.

Activity 10.01 | Creating a Navigation Form Using the Navigation Form Tool

MOS
4.1.3

You can create a navigation form in Design or Layout view by using the Blank Form tool or by using the Navigation Form tool. In this Activity, you will create a navigation form to enable web access to one form and two reports in your Recruitment database.

1 Start Access. In the Access opening screen, click **Open Other Files**. Navigate to your **Access Chapter 10** folder, and then double-click the Access file that you downloaded from **MyLab IT** that displays your name—**Student_Access_10A_Recruitment**. Enable the content or add the Access Chapter 10 folder to the Trust Center.

2 On the **Create tab**, in the **Forms group**, click **Navigation**, and notice the six design layouts you can select for your navigation form. If necessary, close the Field List. Compare your screen with Figure 10.2.

Each layout provides tabs in different locations that you can use to switch to a database object.

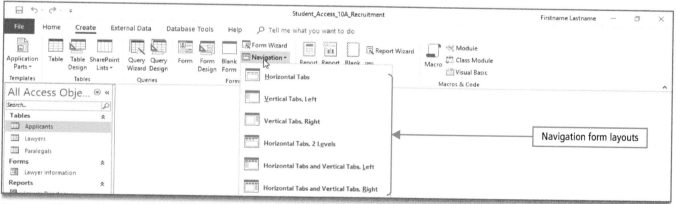

Figure 10.2

3 In the list, click **Vertical Tabs, Left**. If the Field List displays, close it. Compare your screen with Figure 10.3.

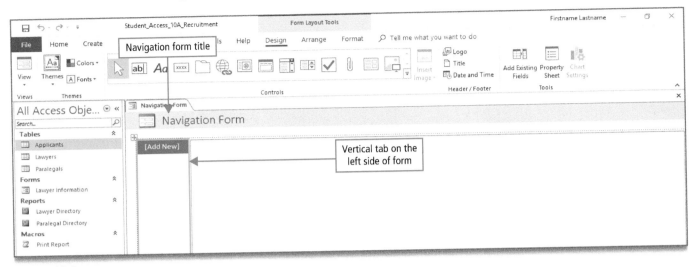

Figure 10.3

4 In the **Navigation Pane**, under **Forms**, point to **Lawyer Information**. Hold down the left mouse button, drag up and to the right to **[Add New]**, and then release the mouse button.

The Lawyer Information form is added to the navigation form as the first tab in the form.

5 Using the technique you just practiced, add the **Lawyer Directory** and the **Paralegal Directory** reports as the second and third tabs in the navigation form.

If you add an object as a tab in the navigation form by mistake, right-click the tab, and then click Delete.

6 At the top of the form, click the **Navigation Form** title to select it, and then click to the left of the *N* in *Navigation*. Type **Loren-Renner** press [Spacebar], and then press [Enter]. Compare your screen with Figure 10.4.

Figure 10.4

7 Save ⊟ the navigation form as **10A Navigation Form Close** « the **Navigation Pane**. Switch to **Form** view.

8 Close × the navigation form, and **Open** » the **Navigation Pane**.

Objective 2 | Use Microsoft Access Analysis Tools

GO! Learn How
Video A10-2

Microsoft Access contains several analysis tools that provide useful information to the database administrator. One tool scans tables for redundant data and then provides a mechanism to split them into smaller, related tables. Another tool analyzes all database objects and lists possible design flaws that decrease performance. Another analysis tool creates a highly detailed report listing the attributes for the entire database. These analysis tools are used to improve database performance and increase data reliability.

Activity 10.02 | Using the Table Analyzer

2.3.2, 1.2.3

Employees at Loren-Renner Law Partners notice that when they enter invoices into the database, they spend a significant amount of time typing the same recruitment information into multiple records. In this Activity, you will use the Table Analyzer to see if the table needs to be split. The ***Table Analyzer*** searches for repeated data in a table and then splits the table into two or more related tables to avoid data redundancy.

1 Open the **Applicants** table in **Datasheet** view. Click the **EventID column arrow**, and then click **Sort A to Z**. Scroll through the table, observe the duplicate entries in the EventID, Law School, and Event Date columns, and then **Close** ☒ the table, saving changes. **Close** ☒ the **Navigation Pane**.

> The data in the Applicants table repeats information numerous times within the table, making it redundant.

2 On the **Database Tools tab**, in the **Analyze group**, click **Analyze Table**. If a security message displays, click Open. In the Table Analyzer Wizard, with the *Table Analyzer: Looking At the Problem* information displayed, review the information, and click **Next** two times. Verify that the **Applicants** table is selected, and then compare your screen with Figure 10.5.

> If the *Show introductory pages?* check box is selected, two extra screens will display the next time the Table Analyzer is started. These two screens explain the normalization process.

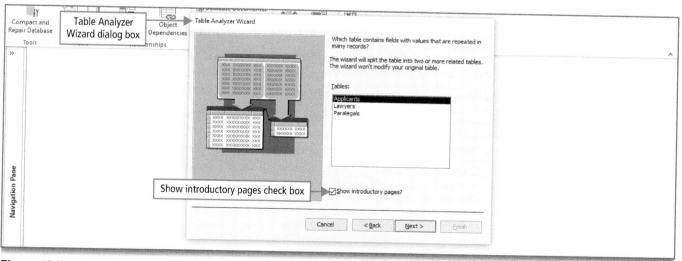

Figure 10.5

3 Click **Next**. In the displayed wizard dialog box, read the directions. Verify that the **Yes, let the wizard decide** option button is selected, and then click **Next**.

4 In the displayed wizard dialog box, read the directions. In the **Table1** field list, scroll down to display *Lookup to Table2*, and then compare your screen with Figure 10.6.

The wizard suggests placing the event data into a related table currently named Table2. It suggests using EventID as its primary key. In the proposal for Table1, a lookup field will be inserted to relate the two tables.

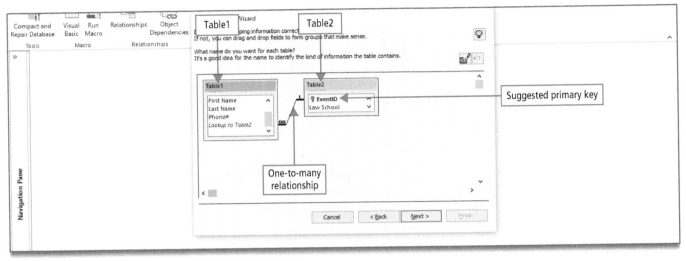

Figure 10.6

5 Double-click the **Table1** title bar. In the displayed dialog box, type **10A Applicants** and then click **OK**. If necessary, widen the field list until the entire table name is displayed.

6 Double-click the **Table2** title bar. In the displayed dialog box, type **10A Recruitment Events** and then click **OK**. If necessary, widen the field list until the entire table name is displayed.

7 Click **Next**, and then read the directions displayed in the wizard dialog box. In the **Applicants** table, click **Candidate#**, and then click **Set Unique Identifier** 🔑.

8 Use the **Snipping Tool** to create a screenshot of the window, and then **Save** the file as a **JPEG** using the file name **TableAnalyzer Close** ⊠ the **Snipping Tool**.

9 In the **Table Analyzer Wizard**, Click **Next**, and then read the directions displayed in the wizard dialog box. Verify that the **Yes, create the query** option button is selected, and then click **Finish. Close** ⊠ the displayed **Access Help** pane, and **Close** ⊠ the query.

10 On the **Create tab**, in the **Forms group**, click **Form Design** to create a new form in Design view. Under **Form Design Tools**, on the **Design tab**, in the **Controls group**, click **Insert Image**, and then click **Browse**. Navigate to the location where you saved the **TableAnalyzer** screenshot, and double-click the image file to place the image.

11 **Save** the form as **10A Table Analyzer Close** ⊠ the form.

12 Open [»] the **Navigation Pane**, and then compare your screen with Figure 10.7.

The two tables have been created and the original table has been renamed *Applicants_OLD*. A query named Applicants is created so that the reports and forms that relied on the old Applicants table will still work. The 10A Table Analyzer form also displays in the Navigation Pane.

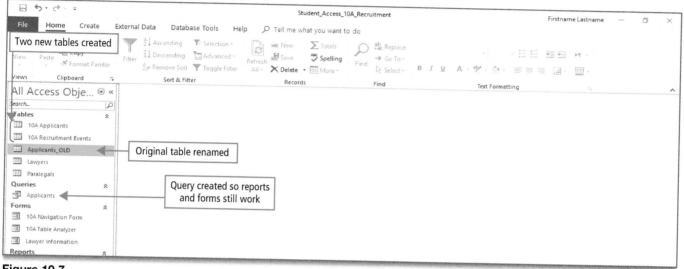

Figure 10.7

13 Close [«] the **Navigation Pane**.

NOTE **Preventing Accidental Deletion of Records During the Conversion Process**

Access creates the relationship between the Applicants and Recruitment Events tables with the Enforce Referential Integrity and Cascade Update Related Records options selected. The Cascade Delete Related Records is not selected so that you cannot accidentally delete any records.

Activity 10.03 | Using the Performance Analyzer

3.1.1, 3.1.6,
3.1.7

Poor database design impairs performance, especially when the database is used to store large amounts of data. Loren-Renner Law Partners needs to analyze its database to improve its performance. In this Activity, you will use the *Performance Analyzer* to identify and fix problems with the database. The Performance Analyzer is a wizard that analyzes database objects and then offers suggestions for improving them.

1 On the **Create tab**, in the **Queries group**, click **Query Design**. Add the **Paralegals** table and the **Lawyers** table, and then **Close** [×] the **Show Table** dialog box.

2 From the **Paralegals** table, add the **Paralegal** and **Phone** fields to the design grid. From the **Lawyers** table, add the **FName** and **LName** fields.

3 From the **Paralegals** table, drag **Lawyer** and drop it over **LawyerID** in the **Lawyers** table. Compare your screen with Figure 10.8.

An *indeterminate relationship* between the two tables is established using Lawyer as the common field. An indeterminate relationship is one that does not enforce referential integrity. The relationship applies to this query only and is not defined for the entire database.

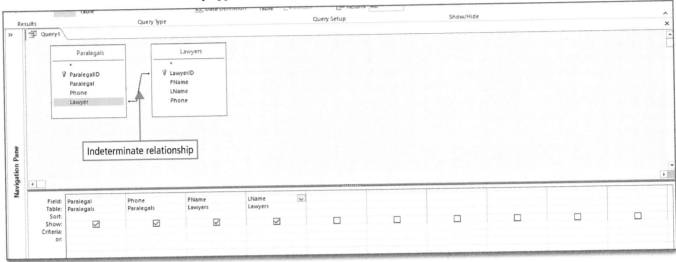

Figure 10.8

4 On the **Query Tools Design** tab, in the **Results group**, click **Run**. Click **Save** 🖫, type **10A Paralegal Assignments** and then click **OK**. **Close** ☒ the query.

5 On the **Database Tools tab**, in the **Analyze group**, click **Analyze Performance**.

6 In the displayed **Performance Analyzer** dialog box, click the **All Object Types** tab. Click **Select All**, and then click **OK**. When the Analysis Results display, compare your screen with Figure 10.9.

The Performance Analyzer provides three levels of suggestions: Recommendations, Suggestions, and Ideas. For this database, the Performance Analyzer has no recommendations, one suggestion, and several ideas.

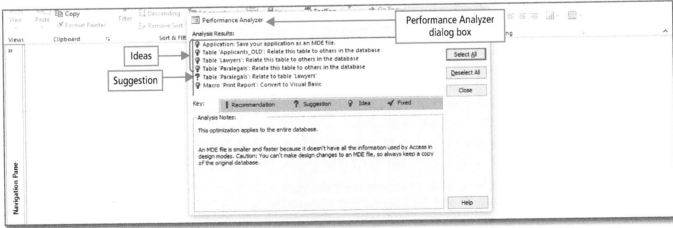

Figure 10.9

7 Under **Analysis Results**, click the suggestion **Table 'Paralegals': Relate to table 'Lawyers'**. Click **Optimize**.

A one-to-many relationship between the two tables is defined, and the Performance Analyzer displays a check mark next to the item.

8 Click the first item labeled with the **Idea** icon. Notice that Optimize is unavailable.

Access fixes only those problems identified as a recommendation or suggestion.

9 Use the **Snipping Tool** to create a screenshot of the window, and then **Save** the file as a **JPEG** using the file name **PerformanceAnalyzer Close** ⊠ the **Snipping Tool**.

10 In the database, read through the remaining ideas, and then click **Close**.

11 On the **Create tab**, in the **Forms group**, click **Form Design** to create a new form in **Design** view. Under **Form Design Tools**, on the **Design tab**, in the **Controls group**, click **Insert Image**, and then click **Browse**. Navigate to the location where you saved the **PerformanceAnalyzer** screenshot, and double-click the image file. Click in the upper left corner of the **Detail** section of the form to place the image.

12 **Save** the form as **10A Performance Analyzer Close** ⊠ the form.

Activity 10.04 | Viewing Object Dependencies

MOS
1.1.2

The Object Dependencies pane shows the dependencies between database objects. A *dependency* is an object that requires, or is dependent on, another database object. For example, several forms, reports, and queries may rely on a single table. Deleting that table would "break" those dependent objects. In this Activity, you will use the Object Dependencies pane to determine whether any objects depend on the Applicants_OLD table. If not, you will delete the table.

1 **Open** ⊠ the **Navigation Pane**. Click the **Lawyers** table to make it active. On the **Database Tools tab**, in the **Relationships group**, click **Object Dependencies**. If a message displays, click **OK**. On the right side of the Access window, notice that the Object Dependencies pane displays.

2 Widen the pane so all object names are visible. If necessary, click the *Objects that depend on me* option button. Compare your screen with Figure 10.10.

The Paralegals table, Paralegal Assignments query, Lawyer Information form, and Lawyer Directory report all depend on the Lawyers table.

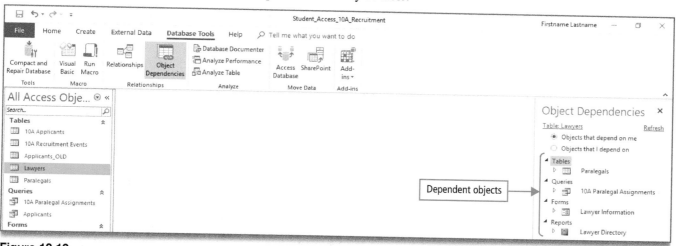

Figure 10.10

3 In the **Navigation Pane**, click the **Applicants_OLD** table, and then in the **Object Dependencies** pane, click **Refresh**. If a message displays, click **OK**. Notice that no database objects depend on the **Applicants_OLD** table.

4 **Close** ⊠ the **Object Dependencies** pane. With the **Applicants_OLD** table selected, press Delete. In the message box, click **Yes**.

Since no other objects in the database depend on the Applicants_OLD table, deleting the table will have no impact on the database.

MORE KNOWLEDGE | **Deleting Database Objects**

If there were objects dependent on the table that you deleted, they would no longer operate correctly. Any dependent objects will also need to be deleted or redesigned. Forms, reports, queries, and macros can all be deleted using the same technique.

5 On the **Database Tools tab**, in the **Analyze group**, click **Analyze Performance**. In the displayed **Performance Analyzer** dialog box, click the **All Object Types** tab, click the **Select All** button, and then click **OK**.

With the deletion of the old Applicants table, only two ideas are given by the Performance Analyzer.

6 In the **Performance Analyzer** dialog box, click **Close** ⊠. **Close** ⊠ the **Navigation Pane**.

Objective 3   Modify Access Views and Behaviors

GO! Learn How
Video A10-3

Access has many options that affect database views and behaviors. These options are changed using the Access Options dialog box. For example, there are options to alter colors and borders, options for how text is formatted, and settings that alter how windows display. The Access Options dialog box is also used to add and remove commands from the Quick Access Toolbar. You can create a custom interface by changing the options for the Navigation Pane. Hundreds of option settings are available to the database designer.

Activity 10.05 | Modifying Access Options

Loren-Renner Law Partners would like its database to have a unique look and feel. In this Activity, you will use the Access Options dialog box to customize the appearance of all databases opened on this computer.

1 Display **Backstage** view and click **Options**. If necessary, click General. Compare your screen with Figure 10.11.

The left pane displays several option groups that, when clicked, display their settings in the larger pane. The settings for the General option group currently display.

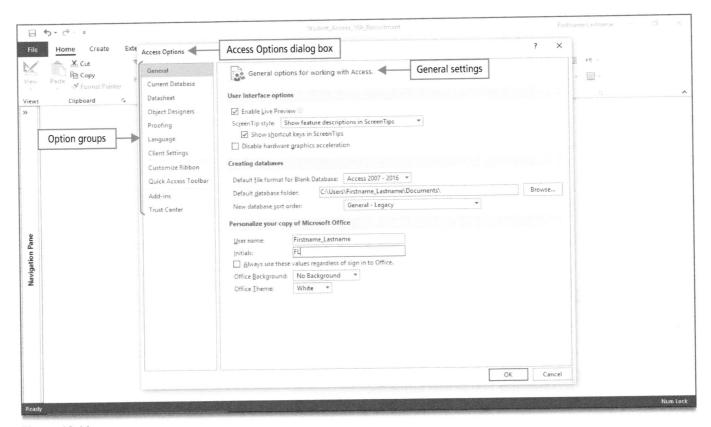

Figure 10.11

2 Under **Personalize your copy of Microsoft Office**, in the **User name** box, type **GO! Access** In the **Initials** box, type **GO!**

3 Under **Personalize your copy of Microsoft Office**, in the **Office Background** box, click the **Office Background box arrow**, and then click **Circuit**.

An *Office background* is a small graphic in the upper right corner of the Access application window used to personalize Office 2019.

4 Click **OK**, and then observe the changes to the top of the database application window.

These changes will affect every database opened on this computer as well as documents in the other Office 2019 applications.

5 Display **Backstage** view, and then click **Options**. In the left pane, click **Datasheet**.

6 Under **Gridlines and cell effects**, clear the **Horizontal** check box.

7 Under **Default font**, click the **Size arrow**, and then click **9**.

8 In the left pane, click **Object Designers**. Under **Table design view**, in the **Default text field size**, replace the existing value with **50**

The default field size for new text fields will be 50 instead of 255.

9 Click **OK**. Open ⏵ the **Navigation Pane**. Open the **Paralegals** table in **Datasheet** view, and compare your screen with Figure 10.12.

The horizontal gridlines no longer display between the records. The font size is smaller for the entire table, allowing the columns to be smaller and still display all of the data.

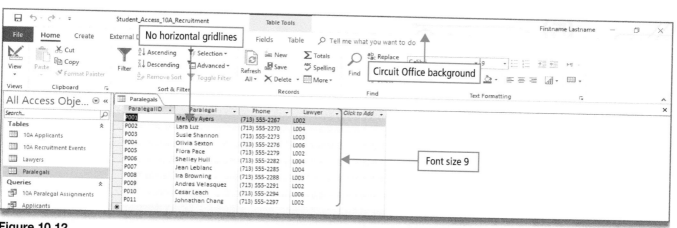

Figure 10.12

10 Close ✕ the **Paralegals** table. Close « the **Navigation Pane**.

Activity 10.06 | Customizing the Quick Access Toolbar

Any Access command, including those not available on the ribbon, can be added to the Quick Access Toolbar. Loren-Renner Law Partners would like to add its commonly used commands to the Quick Access Toolbar. In this Activity, you will use two different methods to customize the Quick Access Toolbar.

1 ▶ Display **Backstage** view, and then click **Options**. In the left pane, click **Quick Access Toolbar**. Compare your screen with Figure 10.13.

Under *Choose commands from*, the commands from the Popular Commands group display. Under *Customize Quick Access Toolbar*, the commands on the current Quick Access Toolbar are listed. The *Customize Quick Access Toolbar* menu provides two options—the Quick Access Toolbar can be modified for all databases or just the current database.

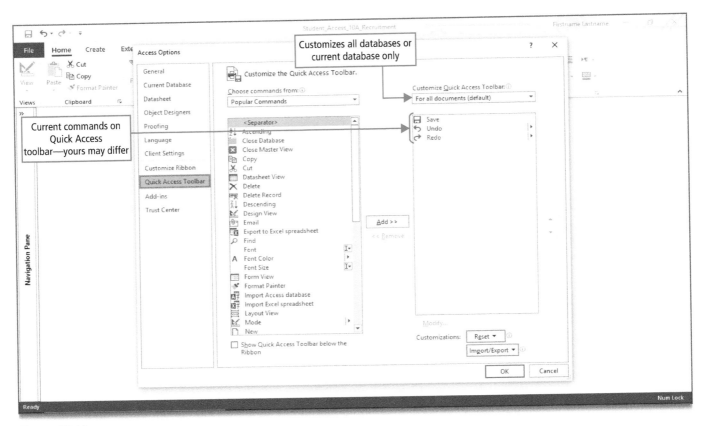

Figure 10.13

ANOTHER WAY On the Quick Access Toolbar, click the Customize Quick Access Toolbar arrow, and then click More Commands.

2 In the list below **Popular Commands**, click **Close Database,** and then click **Add**.

Loren-Renner Law Partners would like this button added for all databases opened on this computer.

3 In the upper-right corner, click the **Customize Quick Access Toolbar arrow**, and then click the path to the currently open database. In the list below **Popular Commands**, scroll down. Click **Quick Print**, and then click **Add**.

The firm would like this change for the currently opened database only.

4 Click **OK**, and then compare your screen with Figure 10.14.

The Close Database and Quick Print icons have been added to the Quick Access Toolbar. Icons added to just one database are placed to the right of the other icons.

Figure 10.14

5 Open [»] the **Navigation Pane**. Open the **Paralegals** table in **Datasheet** view.

6 Use the **Snipping Tool** to create a screenshot of the window, and then **Save** the file as a **JPEG** using the file name **QAToolbar Close** [×] the **Snipping Tool**.

7 In **Access, Close** [×] the **Paralegals** table.

8 On the **Create tab**, in the **Forms group**, click **Form Design** to create a new form in **Design** view. Under **Form Design Tools**, on the **Design tab**, in the **Controls group**, click **Insert Image**, and then click **Browse**. Navigate to the location where you saved the **QAToolbar** screenshot, and double-click the image file. Click in the upper left corner of the **Detail** section of the form to place the image.

9 **Save** the form as **10A Toolbar Close** [×] the form.

Activity 10.07 | Setting Current Database Options

The Current Database group provides several useful options you can change. These options enable the database designer to create the look and feel of a custom application. Loren-Renner Law Partners would like its database to have a unique look and feel, and the company does not want end users to make changes in Layout view. In this Activity, you will create a custom application title and application icon for the database, and then disable Layout view.

1 Display **Backstage** view, click **Options**, and then in the left pane, click **Current Database**.

2 Under **Application Options**, in the **Application Title** box, type **L-R Law Partners**

The *application title* is the text that displays in the Access title bar when that database is open. If the Application Title box is left blank, the file path, name, file, and application name display instead.

3 To the right of **Application Icon** box, click **Browse**. In the displayed **Icon Browser** dialog box, change the file type to **Bitmaps (*.bmp)**.

4 In the **Icon Browser** dialog box, navigate to where the student files for this project are stored. Locate and click **a10A_Icon**, and then click **OK**. Click to select the check box next to **Use as Form and Report Icon**.

5 To the right of the **Display Form** box, click the down-pointing arrow, and then click **10A Navigation Form** to display this form when the database is opened.

Because the Navigation Pane does not display in web-based databases, the navigation form should be set to display as the default form when the database is opened.

6 Under **Application Options**, select the **Compact on Close** check box.

With this option selected, the database will be compacted and repaired each time it is closed. As a database is used, it creates temporary files and doesn't automatically recapture space from deleted objects. These situations can make the database run slowly or experience problems. *Compact & Repair* is a process in which an Access file is rewritten to store the objects and data more efficiently.

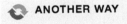 **ANOTHER WAY** Display Backstage view, and under Info, click Compact & Repair if you experience file problems while working with a database.

7 Clear the **Enable Layout View** check box to remove the check mark.

With the check mark removed, Layout view is disabled.

8 Click **OK**, read the displayed message, and then click **OK** again.

9 Display **Backstage** view, click **Close**, and then, under *Recent*, click **Student_Access_10A_Recruitment**.

> **10** ▶ **Close** ☒ the **10A Navigation Form**. **Open** the **Lawyer Directory** report in **Report** view, and then compare your screen with Figure 10.15.

> The application title displays in the title bar. The application icon displays in the report's tab. If the database file or icon image file is renamed or moved to another location, the icon will no longer display.

Figure 10.15

> **11** ▶ **Close** ☒ the report.

Activity 10.08 | Setting Navigation Options

The database designer can choose to customize the Navigation Pane to create a custom interface for the end user. Loren-Renner Law Partners would like its users to see objects in specialized groups in the Navigation Pane. In this Activity, you will customize the Navigation Pane by adding a custom category and two groups. You will then add forms and reports to their respective groups.

> **1** ▶ Display **Backstage** view, click **Options**, and then in the left pane, if necessary, click Current Database.

> **2** ▶ Under **Navigation**, click the **Navigation Options** button, and then compare your screen with Figure 10.16.

> The existing categories for the Navigation Pane display on the left and the groups for each existing category display on the right. Categories and Groups are edited using the buttons below the two columns.

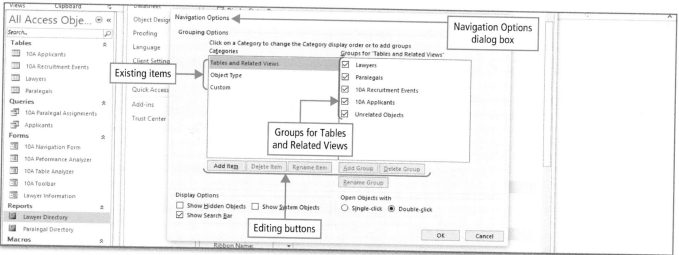

Figure 10.16

3 Click **Add Item**, type **L-R Law Partners** and then press Enter.

L-R Law Partners displays as a category. A *Navigation Pane category* is a top-level listing that displays when the Navigation Pane arrow is clicked.

4 With the **L-R Law Partners** category selected, click **Add Group**. Type **Lawyers** and then press Enter.

Lawyers displays as group. A *Navigation Pane group* is a second-level listing that displays when a Navigation Pane category is selected.

5 Click **Add Group**. Type **Paralegals** and then press Enter. Click **OK** twice to close the dialog boxes. Click **OK** to close the message box, if necessary.

6 Display **Backstage** view, and **Close** the database. Display **Backstage** view, under *Recent*, click **Student_Access_10A_Recruitment**. **Close** ⊠ the **10A Navigation Form**.

7 Click the **Navigation Pane arrow** ⊚, and then click **L-R Law Partners**. In the **Navigation Pane**, under **Unassigned Objects**, drag the **Lawyers** table and drop it over the **Lawyers** group. Drag the **Lawyer Information** form and drop it over the **Lawyers** group. Drag the **Lawyer Directory** report and drop it over the **Lawyers** group.

8 Drag the **Paralegals** table and drop it over the **Paralegals** group. Drag the **Paralegal Directory** report and drop it over the **Paralegals** group. Compare your screen with Figure 10.17.

The objects display as shortcuts within their respective Navigation Pane groups, and they are no longer listed under Unassigned Objects.

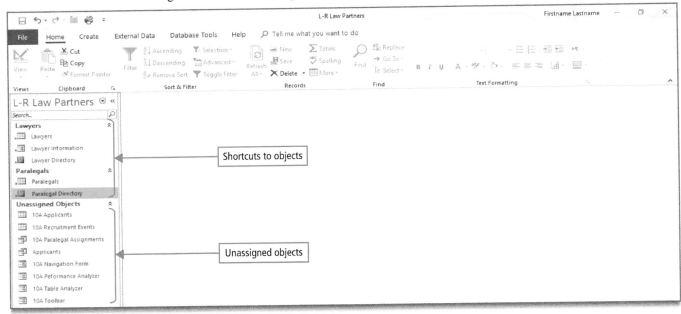

Figure 10.17

9 Display **Backstage** view, click **Options**, and then under **Navigation**, click the **Navigation Options** button. In the **Categories** column, click **L-R Law Partners**. In the **Groups** column, clear the **Unassigned Objects** check box, and then click **OK** two times to close the dialog boxes. Click **OK** to close the message box.

The two objects that you assigned earlier display in the Navigation Pane. You will need to close and reopen the database for the options to take effect.

10 Display **Backstage** view, and then click **Close**. From the **Backstage** view, under *Recent*, click **Student_Access_10A_Recruitment**.

11 Use the **Snipping Tool** to create a screenshot of the window, and then **Save** the file as a **JPEG** using the file name **Navigation Close** ⊠ the **Snipping Tool**.

12 In Access, on the **Quick Access Toolbar**, right-click the **Close Database button**, and then click **Remove from Quick Access Toolbar**. Use this same technique to remove the **Quick Print button** from the Quick Access Toolbar.

13 Display **Backstage** view, click **Options**, and then click **General**. Click the **Office Background arrow**, and then click **No Background**.

14 Click **Datasheet**. Click the **Default font size arrow**, and then click **11**. Under **Default gridlines showing**, select the **Horizontal** check box.

15 Click **Object Designers**, and then set the **Default text field size** back to **255**

16 Click **OK** to close the **Access Options** dialog box, and then click **OK** to close the message box.

17 On the **Create tab**, in the **Forms group**, click **Form Design** to create a new form in **Design** view. Under **Form Design Tools**, on the **Design tab**, in the **Controls group**, click **Insert Image**, and then click **Browse**. Navigate to the location where you saved the **Navigation** screenshot, and double-click the image file. Click in the upper left corner of the **Detail** section of the form to place the image.

18 **Save** the form as **10A Navigation Pane Close** ⨯ the form.

19 Display **Backstage** view, click **Options**, click **Current Database**, and then under **Navigation**, click the **Navigation Options** button. In the **Categories** column, click **L-R Law Partners**. In the **Groups** column, click the **Unassigned Objects** check box so it is displayed, and then click **OK** two times to close the dialog boxes. Click **OK** to close the message box.

> All objects display in the Navigation Pane. You will need to close and reopen the database for the options to take effect.

MORE KNOWLEDGE **Saving a Database as a Template**

Once you have personalized your database, you may choose to save it as a template to be used as the basis for future databases. Display Backstage view, click Save As. Under Save Database As, double-click Template. In the Create New Template from This Database dialog box, name the template, and add a description. Select any other options in the dialog box before clicking OK. To use the template, display Backstage view, and then click New. Under Suggested searches, click Personal to display the templates you have created. Click the template you wish to use, select a saving location, and name the database.

Objective 4 **Use the Database Splitter**

GO! Learn How
Video A10-4

Business databases are often divided into two parts—a back end and a front end. The **back end** consists of the database tables and their data. The back end is typically placed on a server and is not directly seen by the end user. In Access, the **front end** comprises the database forms, queries, reports, and macros. The end users open the front end to work with the data stored in the back-end tables. Dividing the database enables the database administrator to maintain a single source of data while designing multiple front ends to meet the needs of various departments in the company.

Activity 10.09 | Splitting a Database

A **split database** is an Access database that is split into two files—one containing the back end and one containing the front end. Several departments at Loren-Renner Law Partners need their own forms, reports, and queries. Instead of trying to coordinate separate databases, the company would like to place all of the database tables on a network server. Each department will then have its own custom front end that links to the tables in the back-end file. In this Activity, you will use the Split Database tool to create two separate files—one for the back end and one for the front end.

1 Start a second instance of Access so you can use your *Access_10A_Recruitment* database to insert your screen snips. In the Access opening screen, click **Open Other Files**. Navigate to your **Access Chapter 10** folder, and then double-click the Access file that you downloaded from **MyLab IT—a10A_Lawyers**.

2 On the **Database Tools tab**, in the **Move Data group**, click **Access Database**. Compare your screen with Figure 10.18.

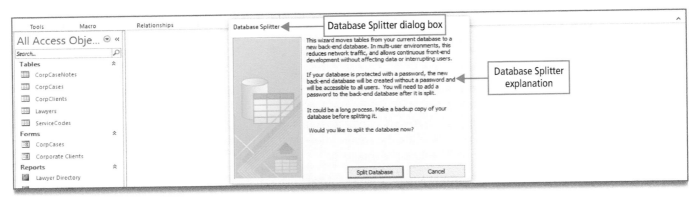

Figure 10.18

3 In the displayed **Database Splitter** dialog box, read the message, and then click **Split Database**. Compare your screen with Figure 10.19.

Figure 10.19

4 In the **Create Back-end Database** dialog box, if necessary, navigate to your **Access Chapter 10** folder. Notice the suggested file name, and then click **Split**. Read the displayed message, click **OK**, and then compare your screen with Figure 10.20.

In the Navigation Pane, the tables display the linked table icon and the other objects display as before. Recall that a linked table is a table that resides in a separate database file.

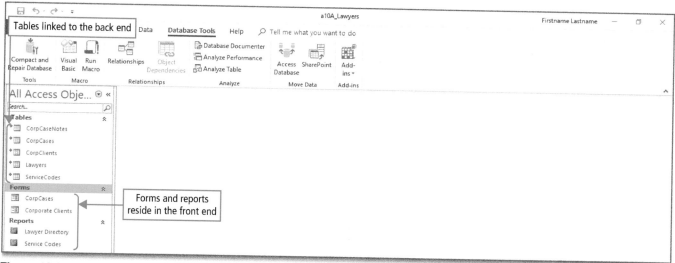

Figure 10.20

5 Use the **Snipping Tool** to create a screenshot of the window, and then **Save** the file as a **JPEG** using the file name **FrontEnd Close** [×] the **Snipping Tool**.

6 On the taskbar, click the **File Explorer** 🗔 icon. Navigate to the location where the **Access Chapter 10** folder is saved, and open the folder. Double-click **10A_Lawyers_be**. Compare your screen with Figure 10.21.

The five linked tables reside in this back-end database file. Typically, the file containing the back end would reside on a network server that all departments can access. Notice that none of the front-end objects in the Lawyers database were copied to this back-end file.

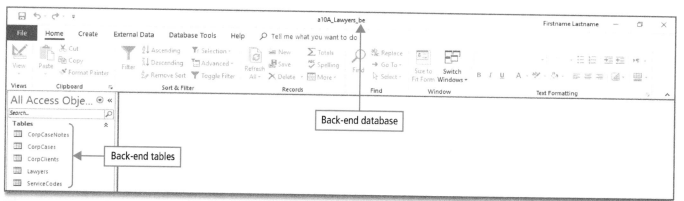

Figure 10.21

MORE KNOWLEDGE **Moving the Back End to a Microsoft SQL Server**

Instead of moving the back end into a separate Access database file, it can be placed on a Microsoft SQL Server. *Microsoft SQL Server* is a database application designed for high-end business uses. If a database contains thousands of records, or if it will be accessed by multiple users at the same time, moving the back-end files to a Microsoft SQL Server will dramatically improve performance.

7 ▸ **Close** the **10A_Lawyers_be** and this instance of Access.

8 ▸ With the **10A_Recruitment** database displayed, on the **Create tab**, in the **Forms group**, click **Form Design** to create a new form in **Design** view. Under **Form Design Tools**, on the **Design tab**, in the **Controls group**, click **Insert Image**, and then click **Browse**. Navigate to the location where you saved the **FrontEnd** screenshot, and double-click the image file. Click in the upper left corner of the **Detail** section of the form to place the image.

9 ▸ **Save** the form as **10A Front End Close** ⌧ the form.

10 ▸ **Close** the databases.

Objective 5 | Encrypt and Decrypt Databases

GO! Learn How
Video A10-5

The data stored in any company's database is one of that company's most valuable assets. If proprietary knowledge is made public, the company could lose its competitive advantage. Further, personal information stored in the database needs to be protected from unauthorized access. For these reasons, the data needs to be hidden until the correct password is entered. Only authorized users should know what that password is.

Activity 10.10 | Encrypting a Database with a Password

Loren-Renner Law Partners has a moral and legal responsibility to keep the data it collects hidden from unauthorized individuals. If one of the company computers or laptops is ever lost or stolen, the data should be unreadable to anyone outside of the company. In this Activity, you will make an Access 2019 database unreadable until a password is entered.

1 ▸ In **Backstage** view, click **Open Other Files**. Under Open, click **Browse**, and then locate and click **Student_Access_10A_Recruitment** one time. In the lower-right corner of the **Open** dialog box, click the **Open arrow**, and compare your screen with Figure 10.22.

Three additional open modes display. *Open Read-Only* opens the database so that all objects can be opened and viewed, but data and design changes cannot be made. *Open Exclusive* opens the database so that changes can be made, but no one else may open the database at the same time. *Open Exclusive Read-Only* opens the database in both Exclusive and Read-Only modes.

Figure 10.22

2 Click **Open Exclusive**. **Close** ⊠ the **10A Navigation Form**.

> The database must be opened in exclusive mode before it can be encrypted. To *encrypt* means to hide data by making the file unreadable until the correct password is entered.

3 Display **Backstage** view. Under *Info*, click **Encrypt with Password**. Compare your screen with Figure 10.23.

Figure 10.23

4 In the **Set Database Password** dialog box, in the **Password** box, type **GO!Access** Access passwords are case sensitive, so be sure to capitalize exactly as shown. In the **Verify** box, type **GO!Access**

> *Strong passwords* are created so they will be hard to guess and the database is secure. A strong password uses a combination of upper- and lowercase letters, special characters, numbers, and spaces in a character string. A *weak password* is a password that is easy to guess. Weak passwords may lead to costly losses of valuable data.

5 In **Access**, in the **Set Database Password** dialog box, click **OK**. If a message box displays, click **OK**. From **Backstage** view, click **Close**.

6 In **Backstage** view, under *Recent*, click your **Student_Access_10A_Recruitment** database to reopen it. In the displayed **Password Required** dialog box, type **GO!Access** and then click **OK**. Alternatively, type the password, and then press Enter.

> With encrypted Access 2019 files, individuals must enter a password to access the database. There is no way to retrieve a forgotten password to be able to open an encrypted database. Be sure to store passwords in a safe place away from the data they protect, in case locating it is ever necessary.

7 **Close** the database.

Activity 10.11 | Decrypting a Database with a Password

Loren-Renner Law Partners periodically resets the password used for its database to make it more secure. In this Activity, you will remove a password currently used to open the Lawyers database so it will be ready to reset later. When you no longer want a password to be required to open a database, you must *decrypt* the file or unset the password.

1 Using the technique you practiced in the previous exercise, open the **Student_Access_10A_Recruitment** database using the **Open Exclusive** option. In the **Password Required** dialog box, type **GO!Access** and click **OK**.

2 Display **Backstage** view. Under *Info*, click **Decrypt Database** to display the **Unset Database Password** dialog box. Compare your screen with Figure 10.24.

To prohibit any user from removing the password encryption applied to a database, the password must be entered to discontinue the password requirement for opening the current database.

Figure 10.24

3 Type **GO!Access** and then click **OK**. Alternatively, type the password, and then press Enter. From **Backstage** view, click **Close**.

4 Display **Backstage** view, and **Open** the **Student_Access_10A_Recruitment** database.

Notice the database opens without asking you to provide a password.

Objective 6 | Create a Locked Database (ACCDE File)

GO! Learn How
Video A10-6

A business may want to secure the design of certain objects in the database when providing a working copy of the database for staff. An *ACCDE file* is an Access 2016 file format that prevents users from creating forms and reports or making design changes to forms, reports, and macros while performing other regular database tasks. Because design changes might be necessary in the future, a copy of the original database should be stored in a secure place.

Activity 10.12 | Creating a Secure ACCDE File

Loren-Renner Law Partners wants to provide a locked-down version of its database so users cannot make any design changes. In this Activity, you will create and test an ACCDE file.

1 Open your **10A_Lawyers** database.

2 Display **Backstage** view, and click **Save As**. In the right column, under **Advanced**, double-click **Make ACCDE**. Compare your screen with Figure 10.25.

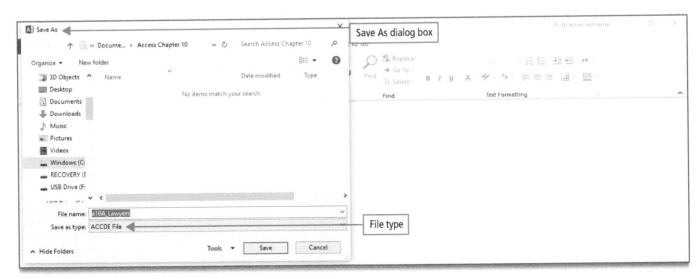

Figure 10.25

3 Verify that the path for your **Access Chapter 10** folder displays. In the **File name** box, change the file name to **10A_ACCDE** and then click **Save**.

4 **Close** Access. Switch to **File Explorer** and then compare your screen with Figure 10.26.

The Type description for the ACCDE file is Microsoft Access ACCDE Database. A padlock is added to the icon to indicate the file's "locked-down" status.

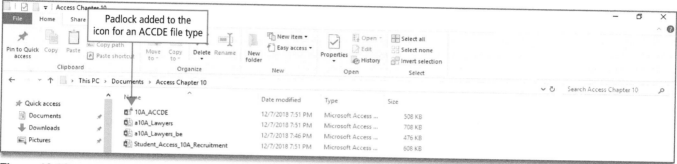

Figure 10.26

5 In the **File Explorer** window, double-click **10A_ACCDE**. If a security notice displays, click Open.

6 Click the **Create tab**, and then compare your screen with Figure 10.27.

The forms and reports creation tools are dimmed, indicating that new forms and reports cannot be created.

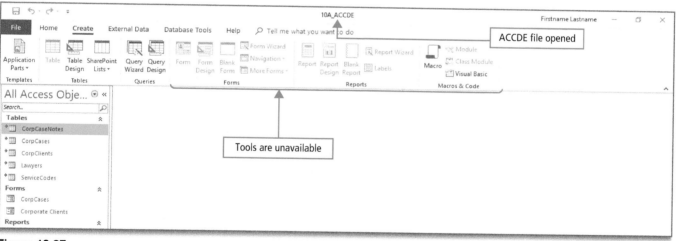

Figure 10.27

7 In the **Navigation Pane**, under **Reports**, right-click **Lawyer Directory**, and notice that the Design View command is dimmed. Design changes cannot be made in an ACCDE file.

8 Double-click the **Corporate Clients** form to open it in Form view. Add a new record using the following information. Replace **Firstname Lastname** with your first and last names. **Close** ☒ the form.

The form can be used for normal database tasks as long as no Design view features are used.

CorpID	C0025
OrgName	Little Elm Community College
Street	1010 South Main Street
City	Little Elm
State	TX
PostalCode	75068
Phone	(214) 555-5011
Representative	Firstname Lastname

9 **Close** the **10A_Lawyers** database. **Close** the **Student_Access_10A_Recruitment** database. **Close** all instances of Access.

For Non-MyLab Submissions: Determine What Your Instructor Requires for Submission
As directed by your instructor, submit your completed database file.

10 In **MyLab IT**, locate and click the Grader Project **Access 10A Lawyer Recruitment**. In **step 3**, under **Upload Completed Assignment**, click **Choose File**. In the **Open** dialog box, navigate to your **Access Chapter 10 folder**, and then click your **Student_Access_10A_ Recruitment** file one time to select it. In the lower right corner of the **Open** dialog box, click **Open**.

The name of your selected file displays above the Upload button.

11 To submit your file to **MyLab IT** for grading, click **Upload**, wait a moment for a green **Success!** message, and then in **step 4**, click the blue **Submit for Grading** button. Click **Close Assignment** to return to your list of **Course Materials**.

You have completed Project 10A END

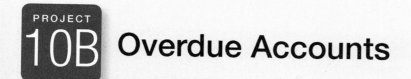

PROJECT

10B Overdue Accounts

MyLab IT
Project 10B Grader for Instruction
Project 10B Simulation for Training and Review

10
ACCESS

Project Activities

Loren-Renner Law Partners stores billing information in two unrelated tables. The firm needs queries that combine the data from both tables so it can call those clients that need to pay their bill. The only way to combine these two queries is to work in SQL view. The partners have given you several tables from their database, each with a small sample of data. Once the queries are working properly, they can be applied to the full data set. In Activities 10.13 through 10.18, you will write queries in SQL view. Using this view, you will be able to create queries that cannot be created in Design view. Your completed Navigation Pane will look similar to Figure 10.28.

Project Files for MyLab IT Grader

1. In your **MyLab IT** course, locate and click **Access 10B Accounts Due**, Download Materials, and then Download All Files.
2. Extract the zipped folder to your Access Chapter 10 folder. Close the Grader download screens.
3. Take a moment to open the downloaded **Access_10B_Accounts_Due_Instructions**; note any recent updates to the book.

Project Results

GO! Project 10B
Where We're Going

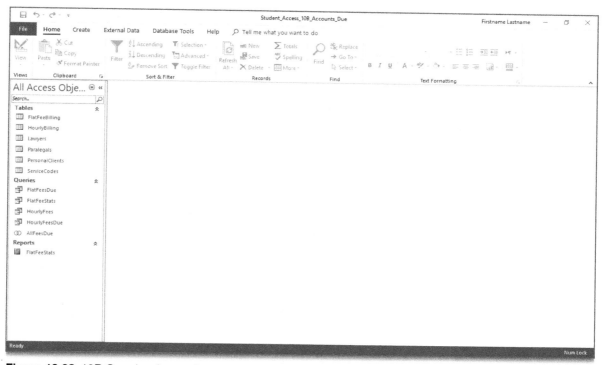

Figure 10.28 10B Overdue Accounts

For Non-MyLab Submissions
For Project 10B, you will need:
a10B_Accounts_Due

Start with an Access Data File
In your Access Chapter 10 folder, save your database as:
Lastname_Firstname_10B_Accounts_Due

After you have saved your database, open it to launch Access. On the next page, begin with Step 2.

Project 10B: Overdue Accounts | **Access** 727

Objective 7   Modify a Query in SQL View

GO! Learn How
Video A10-7

All Access queries use SQL. *SQL, or Structured Query Language*, is a language used by many database programs to view, update, and query data in relational databases. In Access, queries can be created in Design view and then modified in SQL view. Starting in Design view saves time and is a good way to become familiar with writing SQL.

Activity 10.13 │ Modifying a Query in SQL View

3.1.1, 3.1.5,
3.1.6, 3.1.7,
3.2.3, 3.2.2

Loren-Renner Law Partners needs a query that lists each client who was charged a flat fee and has not yet paid that fee. In this Activity, you will create that query in Design view and then modify it in SQL view.

1 ▶ Start Access. In the Access opening screen, click **Open Other Files**. Navigate to your **Access Chapter 10** folder, and then double-click the Access file that you downloaded from **MyLab IT** that displays your name—**Student_Access_10B_Accounts_Due**.

2 ▶ Enable the content, if necessary. **Close** ⟪ the **Navigation Pane**.

NOTE   Table and Field Naming Conventions

You will be creating queries by writing SQL. To simplify the SQL statements, database designers usually choose a naming convention where table and field names are abbreviated terms and do not contain any spaces. For this reason, this project follows what is known as the Upper Camel Case naming convention.

---

3 ▶ On the **Create tab**, in the **Queries group**, click **Query Design**. Using the techniques you have practiced, add the **PersonalClients** and **FlatFeeBilling** tables to the query design workspace. **Close** ✕ the **Show Table** dialog box. Resize the field lists to display all data.

4 ▶ From the **PersonalClients** table, add the following fields to the design grid: **PersonalID**, **FName**, **LName**, and **Phone**. From the **FlatFeeBilling** table, add the **Paid** field to the design grid. In the **Criteria** box for the **Paid** column, type **No**

When you type *No*, do not accept an autocomplete entry of *Now*. You may need to press the space bar after typing *No*.

5 ▶ Click **Save** 🖫, type **FlatFeesDue** and then click **OK**.

6 Locate the status bar in the lower-right corner of the database window, and then click **SQL View** 〘sqL〙. Click any blank area in the SQL workspace, and then compare your screen with Figure 10.29.

> When you work in Query Design view, Access builds the equivalent SQL statement. An **SQL statement** is an expression that defines the SQL commands that should be performed when the query is run. SQL statements typically contain several SQL clauses that begin with keywords. **Keywords** are commands built into the SQL programming language. Keywords are typically written using uppercase letters. In SQL view, statements are edited in the design grid.

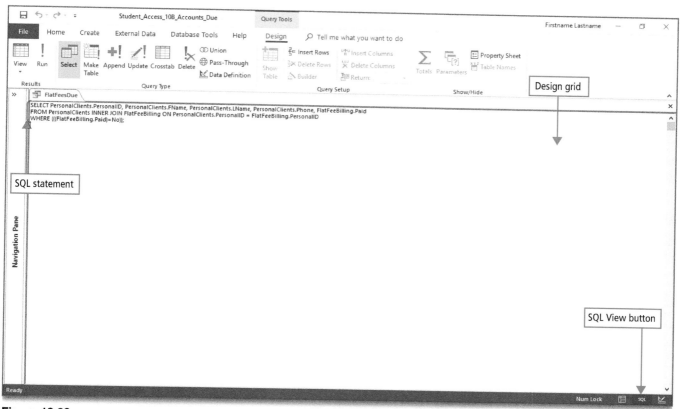

Figure 10.29

7 In the SQL statement, click to the left of the keyword *FROM*, and then press 〘Enter〙.

> This SQL statement starts with a SELECT clause. A **SELECT clause** lists which fields the query should display. The second clause in this SQL statement is a FROM clause. A **FROM clause** lists which tables hold the fields used in the SELECT clause.

8 Click to the left of the keyword *INNER*, and then press 〘Enter〙 two times.

> A **JOIN clause** defines the join type for a query. Recall that an inner join displays only those records that have a corresponding record in both of the related tables. A **WHERE clause** defines the criteria that should be applied when a query is run.

9 Click to the left of the keyword *WHERE*, and then press 〘Enter〙. In the **WHERE** clause, delete all six parentheses.

> These parentheses would be needed only if a more complex WHERE clause were written. Often, the SQL generated while in Design view will not be as efficient as the SQL written by a database designer in SQL view.

10 Click **Save** 💾. In the **Results group**, click **Run**. Click the **LName column arrow**, and then click **Sort A to Z**. Compare your screen with Figure 10.30.

> Brandi Dorsey and Faye Wiley are each listed two times. This type of duplication may lead to duplicate phone calls being made to the client.

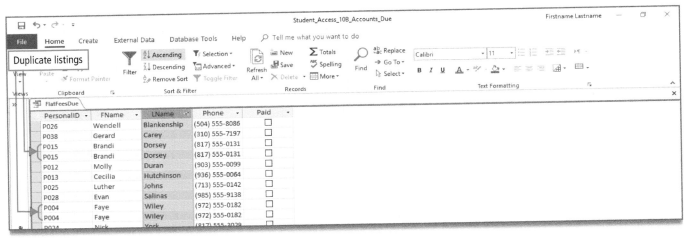

Figure 10.30

ALERT   Does your SQL code disappear?

Your SQL code may disappear when you click Save. The query will run, and the code will display after you run the query and click the SQL View button.

---

11 In the status bar, click the **SQL View** button 📄. Click to the right of the keyword SELECT, press [Spacebar], and then type **DISTINCT**

> The ***DISTINCT*** keyword returns only a single instance of any duplicate values in query results. It always follows the SELECT keyword, and is added only in SQL View.

12 **Run** the query and notice that duplicate records no longer display. **Save** 💾, and then **Close** ⊠ the query.

Objective 8   Create a Query in SQL View

GO! Learn How
Video A10-8

Many database designers find it easier to design their queries in SQL view. The typical SQL query uses the same three-step sequence. Understanding this sequence removes much of the complexity of the typical SQL statement. Working in SQL view enables the designer to write more efficient SQL and also provides more control than Design view. Several types of queries can be created only when working in SQL view.

Activity 10.14 | Creating an SQL Statement

MOS
3.1.1, 3.1.5,
3.1.6, 3.1.7, 3.2.3

Loren-Renner Law Partners needs a query that lists each client who was charged an hourly rate and has not yet paid the fee. Due to the nature of this query, you will need to work in SQL view to write a query not available in Design view. In this Activity, you will create that query in SQL view.

1 On the **Create tab**, in the **Queries group**, click **Query Design**. **Close** ⊠ the **Show Table** dialog box, and then in the status bar, click the **SQL View** button 📄.

> Because you started with a select query, the SELECT keyword displays followed by a semicolon. Semicolons are used to mark the end of SQL statements.

---

2 Click before the semicolon, press Spacebar, and then type the following: **PersonalClients. PersonalID, PersonalClients.FName, PersonalClients.LName, PersonalClients.Phone, HourlyBilling.Paid** Compare your screen with Figure 10.31.

In a SELECT clause, both the table name and field name are included and are separated by a period. Multiple fields must be separated by commas.

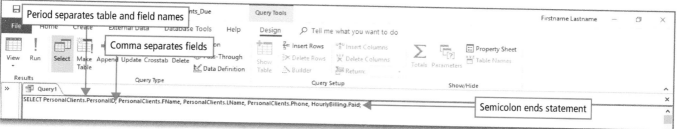

Figure 10.31

3 Press Enter, and then type the following FROM clause: **FROM PersonalClients, HourlyBilling**

All tables used in the SELECT clause must be listed in the FROM clause and are separated by commas.

4 Press Enter, and then type the following WHERE clause: **WHERE HourlyBilling.Paid=No**

Recall that in the WHERE statement, the criteria for the query is defined.

5 Be sure that the semicolon is at the end of the query. Click **Save** 🖫, and then type **HourlyFeesDue** Click **OK**.

6 Click **Run**, and then compare your screen with Figure 10.32. If you receive a message that the query has errors or the Enter Parameter Value dialog box displays, go back and check your typing very carefully.

The result of this query is a cross join query. Recall that in a cross join query, every possible combination of records between two related tables will be returned. If no join type is defined or if there is a mistake in the WHERE clause, SQL returns a cross join query. When tables contain a large number of records, cross join queries will take a very long time to run. In this query, the join type needs to be defined.

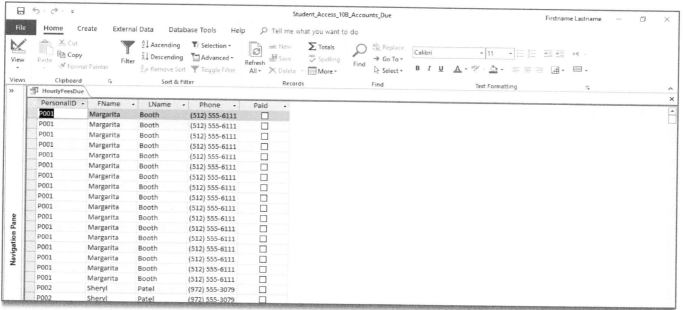

Figure 10.32

7 Save 🖫 your query, and then return to **SQL** view.

Activity 10.15 | Specifying the Join Type in SQL

MOS
3.1.5, 3.2.2

The Hourly Billing Due query currently returns a cross join. Once a join type is specified in the query, it will display one record per customer. In this Activity, you will add an SQL clause so that the two tables used in the query use an inner join.

1 In **SQL** view, in the **FROM** clause, click between *PersonalClients* and the comma, and then press Enter.

2 Press Delete to remove the comma.

3 Type the following JOIN clause, **INNER JOIN**

The INNER JOIN keyword instructs the query to use an inner join between two tables.

4 Click to the right of *HourlyBilling*, press Spacebar, and type the following ON clause: **ON PersonalClients.PersonalID = HourlyBilling.PersonalID**

The *ON* keyword is used to specify which field is common to two tables. The combination of the INNER JOIN and ON keywords creates a relationship between the two tables. In this query the PersonalID field is used to join the tables.

5 **Save** 📁, and then **Run** the query. Sort the **LName** column in alphabetical order, and then compare your screen with Figure 10.33.

The tables are joined correctly, but customers with more than one outstanding bill are listed two or more times.

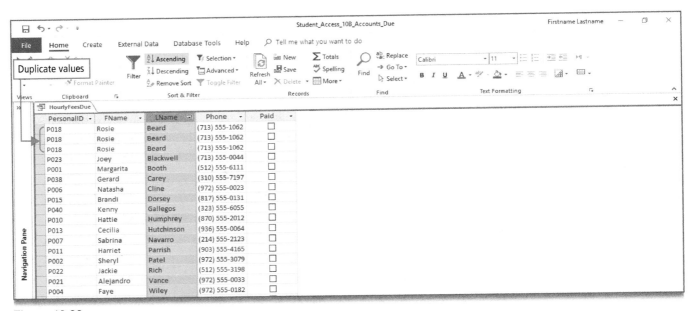

Figure 10.33

6 Return to **SQL** view. After the **SELECT** keyword, press Spacebar, and then type **DISTINCT**

7 **Run** the query. Check that no customer is listed more than once. **Save** 📁, and then **Close** ☒ the query.

Objective 9 | Create a Union Query Using SQL

GO! Learn How
Video A10-9

Using SQL, the results of two or more queries can be displayed in one query. A ***union query*** combines the results of two or more similar select queries. The combined queries must have the same number of columns and the same data types in each corresponding column. Union queries are created only in SQL view.

Activity 10.16 | Creating a Union Query in SQL View

MOS
3.1.5

Recall that Loren-Renner Law Partners needs a list of all personal clients with amounts owed. In earlier projects, you built two separate queries, one for flat fees and the other for hourly fees. In this Activity, you will use SQL to combine the results of both queries into a single query.

1 On the **Create tab**, in the **Queries group**, click **Query Design**. **Close** ✕ the **Show Table** dialog box.

2 On the **Query Tools Design tab**, in the **Query Type group**, click **Union**. Notice that the query switches to SQL view.

3 **Open** ⟫ the **Navigation Pane**. Open the **FlatFeesDue** query, and then in the status bar, click the **SQL View** button 🔲. With the entire SQL statement selected, right-click anywhere in the design grid, and then click **Copy**.

4 **Close** ✕ the **FlatFeesDue** query. In the union query, right-click anywhere in the design grid, and then click **Paste**.

5 At the end of the SQL statement, delete the semicolon, and then press Enter **two** times.

6 Type **UNION** and then press Enter **two** times. Compare your screen with Figure 10.34.

The *UNION* keyword is used to combine one or more queries in a union query.

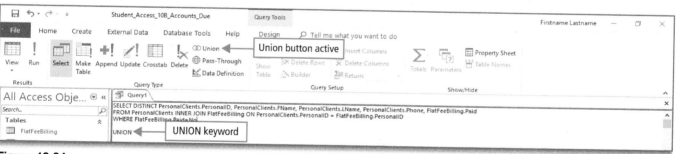

Figure 10.34

7 Open the **HourlyFeesDue** query, and then in the status bar, click the **SQL View** button 🔲. With the entire SQL statement selected, right-click anywhere in the design grid, and then click **Copy**.

8 **Close** ✕ the **HourlyFeesDue** query. In the union query that you are building, right-click next to the insertion point, and then click **Paste**.

9 Click **Save** 🔲, type **AllFeesDue** and then click **OK**.

10 In the **Navigation Pane**, notice the union query icon to the left of the query's name. On the **Query Tools Design tab**, in the **Results group**, click the **View arrow**, and notice that Design view is not available for this query.

11 **Run** the query, and then compare your results with Figure 10.35.

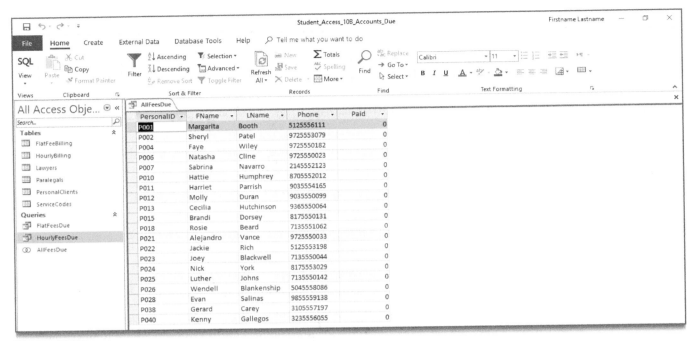

Figure 10.35

12 Click **Save** 🖫, and then **Close** ⊠ the query. **Close** « the **Navigation Pane**.

Objective 10 | Create Calculated Fields and SQL Aggregate Functions

SQL is a powerful language that does far more than create select queries. SQL provides commands to create calculated fields and summarize data using aggregate functions. Recall that an aggregate function performs a calculation on a column of data and returns a single value. When creating calculated fields, many developers prefer to work in SQL view because long expressions can be viewed without having to use the Zoom feature.

Activity 10.17 | Creating Calculated Fields in SQL

Loren-Renner Law Partners needs a list of total amounts due for the clients who were billed at an hourly rate. In this Activity, you will write an SQL statement with a field that calculates fees by multiplying the number of hours by the hourly rate.

1 On the **Create tab**, in the **Queries group**, click **Query Design**.

2 Use the displayed **Show Table** dialog box to add the **PersonalClients** and **HourlyBilling** tables, and then **Close** ⊠ the Show Table dialog box. Resize the field lists so all data displays.

3 From the **PersonalClients** table, add the **FName** field, and then add the **LName** field.

4 In the status bar, click the **SQL View** button 🔲.

> Starting this query in Design view saves you from having to type the SELECT, FROM, and INNER JOIN clauses.

---

5 To the right of the entire SELECT clause, type a comma, press [Spacebar], and then type the following: **HourlyBilling.Hours * HourlyBilling.Rate AS Fee**

A calculated field with the caption *Fee* will display the product of the Hours and Rate fields for each record. The *AS* keyword creates captions for fields.

6 At the end of the SQL statement, click to the left of the semicolon, press [Enter], and then type the following WHERE clause: **WHERE HourlyBilling.Paid = No**

7 Click **Save** [icon], type **HourlyFees** and then click **OK**.

8 **Run** the query, and then compare your screen with Figure 10.36.

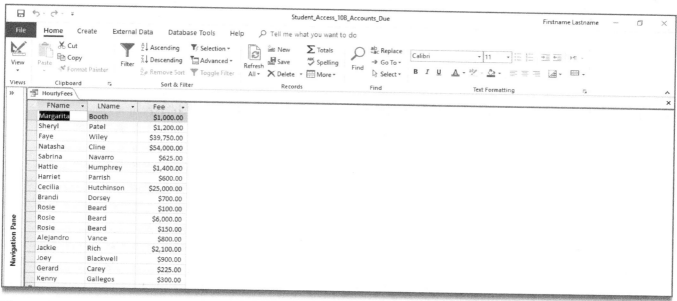

Figure 10.36

9 **Close** [×] the query.

Activity 10.18 | Writing SQL Aggregate Functions

MOS
3.1.1, 3.1.6,
3.1.7, 5.2.1

Loren-Renner Law Partners needs a report showing summary statistics for the amounts due from clients paying flat fees. In this Activity, you will use SQL aggregate functions to calculate summary statistics and then create a report based on the query.

1 On the **Create tab**, in the **Queries group**, click **Query Design**. **Close** [×] the displayed **Show Table** dialog box. In the status bar, click the **SQL View** button [icon].

2 In the design grid, click to the right of SELECT. Delete the semicolon, press [Spacebar], and then type the following: **Count(FlatFeeBilling.Fee) AS Count**

Count is an SQL aggregate function.

3 Press [Enter], and then type the following FROM clause: **FROM FlatFeeBilling**

4 Press [Enter], and then type the following WHERE clause: **WHERE FlatFeeBilling.Paid = No;**

5 Click **Save** [icon], type **FlatFeesStats** and then click **OK**.

6 Click **Run**, and then compare your screen with Figure 10.37.

The number of records in the query displays in a column that has *Count* as its caption.

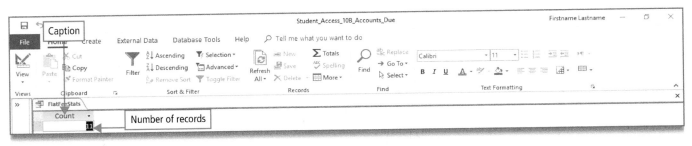

Figure 10.37

7 Return to **SQL View**. Click to the right of the entire **SELECT** clause, and then type a comma. Press Enter, and then type the following: **Avg(FlatFeeBilling.Fee) AS Average**, and then press Enter.

8 Continue adding to the SELECT clause by typing **Min(FlatFeeBilling.Fee) AS Minimum,** and then press Enter. Type **Max(FlatFeeBilling.Fee) AS Maximum**, and press Enter. Type **Sum(FlatFeeBilling.Fee) AS [Total Flat Fees]**

Because Total Flat Fees contains spaces, it must be enclosed in square brackets. In Access SQL statements, any table name or field name that has spaces must be enclosed in square brackets. If there are no spaces, then the square brackets are optional. After [Total Flat Fees], no comma is needed because it is the end of the SELECT clause.

9 Compare your screen with Figure 10.38. **Save** 🖫 and then **Run** the query. Apply **Best Fit** so all data is displayed.

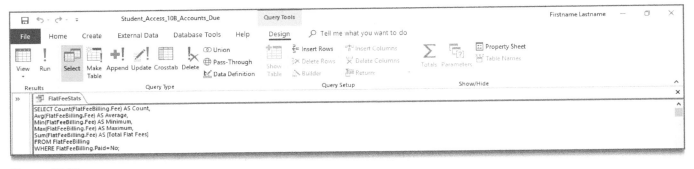

Figure 10.38

10 **Close** ⊠ the query, saving changes. **Open** ⨠ the **Navigation Pane**, and then click to select the **FlatFeesStats** query. On the **Create tab**, in the **Reports group**, click **Report**.

11 Click anywhere in the **Total Flat Fees** column to select the column. Under **Report Layout Tools**, on the **Design tab**, in the **Grouping & Totals group**, click **Totals**, and then click **Sum** to remove the second displayed total for that column. Click the **Total** line, and then press Delete.

12 Delete the **Date** and **Time** boxes in the **Report Header**, and then delete the placeholders. Change the report's title to **10B Flat Fees Statistics**

13 Click **Save** 🖫, and then accept the Report Name by clicking **OK**.

14 **Close** ⊠ the report, and then **Close** the database and **Close** Access.

For Non-MyLab Submissions: Determine What Your Instructor Requires for Submission
As directed by your instructor, submit your completed database file.

15 In **MyLab IT**, locate and click the Grader Project **Access 10B Overdue Accounts**. In **step 3**, under **Upload Completed Assignment**, click **Choose File**. In the **Open** dialog box, navigate to your **Access Chapter 10 folder**, and then click your **Student_Access_10B_Accounts_Due** file one time to select it. In the lower right corner of the **Open** dialog box, click **Open**.

The name of your selected file displays above the Upload button.

16 To submit your file to **MyLab IT** for grading, click **Upload**, wait a moment for a green **Success!** message, and then in **step 4**, click the blue **Submit for Grading** button. Click **Close Assignment** to return to your list of **Course Materials**.

You have completed Project 10B **END**

»»» GO! To Work

wavebreakmedia/Shutterstock, Monkey Business Images/Fotolia, Ivanko80/Shutterstock, Monkey Business Images/Shutterstock

Microsoft Office Specialist (MOS) Skills in this Chapter	
Project 10A	**Project 10B**
1.1.2 Delete database objects	**3.1.1** Create simple queries
1.1.3 Hide and display objects in the Navigation Pane	**3.1.5** Create basic multi-table queries
1.2.3 Set Primary Keys	**3.1.6** Save queries
2.3.2 Sort records	**3.1.7** Run queries
3.1.6 Save queries	**3.2.2** Sort data within queries
3.1.7 Run queries	**3.2.3** Filter data within queries
4.1.3 Add and modify form labels	**5.2.1** Format a report in multiple columns

Build Your E-Portfolio

An E-Portfolio is a collection of evidence, stored electronically, that showcases what you have accomplished while completing your education. Collecting and then sharing your work products with potential employers reflects your academic and career goals. Your completed documents from the following projects are good examples to show what you have learned: 10G, 10K, and 10L.

GO! For Job Success

Topic: Introverts and Extroverts

Psychology teaches that human beings have many personality aspects, but they generally lean one way or the other on the extroversion/introversion continuum. Extroverts focus on the outside world and may be talkative and energetic; introverts focus inward and may be seen as quiet or shy. Extroverts are energized by groups, teams, and interaction; introverts are energized by quiet introspection, time to think, and deep focus on work.

The typical business culture of meetings, open office arrangements, and teams is geared toward extroverts. Introverts may feel they have to hide their true personalities to fit in and be successful, but this can inhibit the contributions they make. Some businesses have started meetings with time for attendees to read the agenda and materials, focusing everyone on the subject and giving both extroverts and introverts time to collect their thoughts.

g-stockstudio/Shutterstock

> What are some other changes that could be made to business meetings that would make introverts feel more comfortable about sharing their ideas?

> Do you think you are an extrovert or an introvert, and how has this affected your participation in class assignments?

> In what other areas of your life, such as community service or family interactions, do you notice the difference between introverts and extroverts, and what changes could you make to make both types of people feel comfortable?

End of Chapter

Summary

A navigation form is a form that displays navigational controls to display forms and reports in your database; it is useful for a web-based database where the Navigation Pane is not displayed.

Analysis tools improve performance. The Table Analyzer and Performance Analyzer analyze objects and offer improvement ideas. Viewing object dependencies protects the database before deleting objects.

Access Options customize database views, including the Navigation Pane. Using a locked-down ACCDE file format, a split database with the back end stored on a server, or a password provides security.

SQL provides more control and flexibility than Design view when designing queries, and more options. SQL can be used to join two queries in a union query, create calculated fields, and create statistics.

GO! Learn It Online

Review the concepts, key terms, and MOS skills in this chapter by completing these online challenges, which you can find at **MyLab IT**.

Chapter Quiz: Answer matching and multiple choice questions to test what you learned in this chapter.

Lessons on the GO!: Learn how to use all the new apps and features as they are introduced by Microsoft.

MOS Prep Quiz: Answer questions to review the MOS skills you have practiced in this chapter.

Project Guide for Access Chapter 10

Your instructor will assign Projects from this list to ensure your learning and assess your knowledge.

	Review and Assessment Guide for Access Chapter 10		
Project	**Apply Skills from These Chapter Objectives**	**Project Type**	**Project Location**
10A **MyLab IT**	Objectives 1–6 from Project 10A	**10A Instructional Project (Grader Project)** Instruction Guided instruction to learn the skills in Project 10A.	In **MyLab IT** and in text
10B **MyLab IT**	Objectives 7–10 from Project 10B	**10B Instructional Project (Grader Project)** Instruction Guided instruction to learn the skills in Project 10B.	In **MyLab IT** and in text
10C	Objectives 1–6 from Project 10A	**10C Skills Review (Scorecard Grading)** Review A guided review of the skills from Project 10A.	In text
10D	Objectives 7–10 from Project 10B	**10D Skills Review (Scorecard Grading)** Review A guided review of the skills from Project 10B.	In text
10E	Objectives 1–6 from Project 10A	**10E Mastery (Scorecard Grading)** **Mastery and Transfer of Learning** A demonstration of your mastery of the skills in Project 10A with extensive decision making.	In text
10F	Objectives 7–10 from Project 10B	**10F Mastery (Scorecard Grading)** **Mastery and Transfer of Learning** A demonstration of your mastery of the skills in Project 10B with extensive decision making.	In text
10G **MyLab IT**	Objectives 1–10 from Projects 10A and 10B	**10G Mastery (Grader Project)** **Mastery and Transfer of Learning** A demonstration of your mastery of the skills in Projects 10A and 10B with extensive decision making.	In **MyLab IT** and in text
10H	Combination of Objectives from Projects 10A and 10B	**10H GO! Fix It (Scorecard Grading)** **Critical Thinking** A demonstration of your mastery of the skills in Projects 10A and 10B by creating a correct result from a document that contains errors you must find.	Instructor Resource Center (IRC)
10I	Combination of Objectives from Projects 10A and 10B	**10I GO! Make It (Scorecard Grading)** **Critical Thinking** A demonstration of your mastery of the skills in Projects 10A and 10B by creating a result from a supplied picture.	IRC
10J	Combination of Objectives from Projects 10A and 10B	**10J GO! Solve It (Rubric Grading)** **Critical Thinking** A demonstration of your mastery of the skills in Projects 10A and 10B, your decision-making skills, and your critical thinking skills. A task-specific rubric helps you self-assess your result.	IRC
10K	Combination of Objectives from Projects 10A and 10B	**10K GO! Solve It (Rubric Grading)** **Critical Thinking** A demonstration of your mastery of the skills in Projects 10A and 10B, your decision-making skills, and your critical thinking skills. A task-specific rubric helps you self-assess your result.	In text
10L	Combination of Objectives from Projects 10A and 10B	**10L GO! Think (Rubric Grading)** **Critical Thinking** A demonstration of your understanding of the chapter concepts applied in a manner that you would apply outside of college. An analytic rubric helps you and your instructor grade the quality of your work by comparing it to the work an expert in the discipline would create.	In text
10M	Combination of Objectives from Projects 10A and 10B	**10M GO! Think (Rubric Grading)** **Critical Thinking** A demonstration of your understanding of the chapter concepts applied in a manner that you would apply outside of college. An analytic rubric helps you and your instructor grade the quality of your work by comparing it to the work an expert in the discipline would create.	IRC
10N	Combination of Objectives from Projects 10A and 10B	**10N You and GO! (Rubric Grading)** **Critical Thinking** A demonstration of your understanding of the chapter concepts applied in a manner that you would apply in a personal situation. An analytic rubric helps you and your instructor grade the quality of your work.	IRC
Capstone Project for Access Chapters 1–10	Combination of Objectives from Projects in Chapters 1-10	A demonstration of your mastery of the skills in Chapters 1–10 with extensive decision making. **(Grader Project)**	IRC and in **MyLab IT**

Glossary

Glossary of Chapter Key Terms

ACCDE file An Access file format that prevents individuals from making design changes to forms, reports, and macros.

Application title The text that displays in the Access title bar when that database is open.

AS An SQL keyword that creates captions for fields.

Back end An Access database that consists of the database tables and their data. The back end is typically placed on a server and is not directly seen by the end user.

Compact & Repair A process where an Access file is rewritten to store the objects and data more efficiently.

Decrypt An action that removes a file's encryption or unsets a password.

Dependency An object that requires, or is dependent on, another database object.

DISTINCT An SQL keyword that returns only a single instance of any duplicate values in query results.

Encrypt A process to hide data by making the file unreadable until the correct password is entered.

FROM clause An SQL statement that lists which tables hold the fields used in the SELECT clause.

Front end An Access database that includes the database forms, queries, reports, and macros. The end users open the front end to work with the data stored in the back-end tables.

Indeterminate relationship A relationship that does not enforce referential integrity.

JOIN clause An SQL statement that defines the join type for a query.

Keywords Commands built into the SQL programming language.

Microsoft SQL Server A database application designed for high-end business uses.

Navigation form A form that displays navigational controls that enable you to display forms and reports in your database.

Navigation Pane category A top-level listing that displays when the Navigation Pane arrow is clicked.

Navigation Pane group A second-level listing that displays when a Navigation Pane category is selected.

Office background A small graphic in the upper-right corner of the Access application window used to personalize Office 2019.

ON An SQL keyword that is used to specify which field is common to two tables.

Open Exclusive An option that opens the database so that changes can be made, but no one else may open the database at the same time.

Open Exclusive Read-Only An option that opens the database in both Exclusive and Read-Only modes.

Open Read-Only An option that opens the database so that all objects can be opened and viewed, but data and design changes cannot be made.

Performance Analyzer A wizard that analyzes database objects, and then offers suggestions for improving them.

SELECT clause An SQL statement that lists which fields the query should display.

Split database An Access database that is split into two files—one containing the back end and one containing the front end.

SQL (Structured Query Language) A language used by many database programs to view, update, and query data in relational databases.

SQL statement An expression that defines the SQL commands that should be performed when the query is run.

Strong password A password that is very difficult to guess that may include upper and lowercase letters, numbers, and special characters.

Table Analyzer A wizard that searches for repeated data in a table, and then splits the table into two or more related tables.

UNION An SQL keyword that is used to combine one or more queries in a union query.

Union query A query type that combines the results of two or more similar select queries.

Weak password A password that is easy to guess.

WHERE clause An SQL statement that defines the criteria that should be applied when a query is run.

Chapter Review

Skills Review | Project 10C Paralegals

Apply 10A skills from these Objectives:

Apply 10A skills from these Objectives:

1. Create a Navigation Form
2. Use Microsoft Access Analysis Tools
3. Modify Access Views and Behaviors
4. Use the Database Splitter
5. Encrypt and Decrypt Databases
6. Create a Locked Database (ACCDE File)

Loren-Renner Law Partners wants to secure the database tables used by its paralegals. You will encrypt the database using a secure password, create a locked ACCDE file, and split the database to allow Human Resources to design separate front-end databases to be used by various departments. Your completed Navigation Pane will look like that shown in Figure 10.39.

Project Files

For Project 10C, you will need the following files:

a10C_Paralegals

a10C_Icon

You will save your files as:

Lastname_Firstname_10C_Paralegals

Lastname_Firstname_10C_Paralegals_ACCDE

Lastname_Firstname_10C_Paralegals_be

Project Results

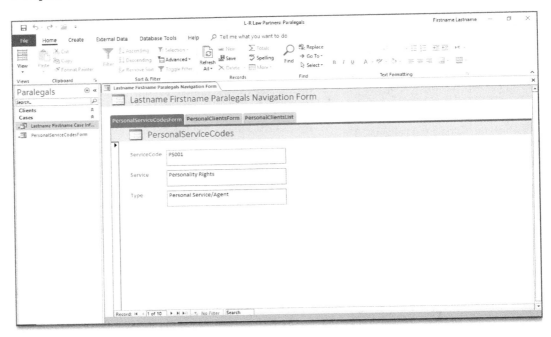

Figure 10.39

(continues on next page)

Chapter Review

Skills Review: Project 10C Paralegals (continued)

1 Start Access. Locate and then open the **a10C_Paralegals** file. Save the database in your **Access Chapter 10** folder as **Lastname_Firstname_10C_Paralegals** If necessary, add the Chapter 10 folder to the Trust Center or Enable Content.

2 On the **Create tab**, in the **Forms group**, click **Navigation**, and then click **Horizontal Tabs**. If the Field List displays, close it.

3 In the **Navigation Pane**, under **Forms**, point to **PersonalServiceCodesForm**, hold down the left mouse button, drag up and to the right to **[Add New]**, and then release the mouse button. Using the technique you practiced, add the **PersonalClientsForm** and the **PersonalClientsList** report as the second and third tabs in the navigation form.

  a. At the top of the form, edit the title to read **Lastname Firstname Paralegals Navigation Form**

  b. **Save** the navigation form as **Lastname Firstname Paralegals Navigation Form Close** the **Navigation Pane**. Switch to **Form** view. **Close** the **Paralegals Navigation Form**.

4 On the **Database Tools tab**, in the **Analyze group**, click **Analyze Table**. If the introductory page displays, click **Next** two times.

  a. Under **Tables**, verify that **Cases** is selected, and then click **Next**. Verify that **Yes, let the wizard decide** is selected, and then click **Next**.

  b. Double-click the **Table1** title bar, type **Lastname Firstname Cases** and then click **OK**. Double-click the **Table2** title bar, type **Lastname Firstname Paralegals** and then click **OK**.

  c. Click **Next**. In the **Cases** table, click **PCaseID**, and then click **Set Unique Identifier**.

  d. Click **Next**, and then click **Finish**. **Close** the **Access Help** window, and then **Close** the **Cases** query. **Open** the **Navigation Pane**.

5 Select the **Cases_OLD** table. On the **Database Tools tab**, in the **Relationships group**, click **Object Dependencies**. In the displayed message box, click **OK**. In **Access**, delete the **Cases_OLD** table. **Close** the **Object Dependencies** pane. **Close** the **Navigation Pane**.

6 On the **Create tab**, in the **Queries group**, click **Query Design**. Add the **Cases** and **PersonalServiceCodes** tables, and then **Close** the dialog box. Expand the field lists so all fields and table names display.

  a. From the **Cases** table, add the **PCaseID**, **Description**, and **Closed?** fields, and then from the **PersonalServiceCodes** table, add the **Service Code** field.

  b. **Save** the query as **Lastname Firstname Case Information** and then click **OK**. **Run**, and then apply **Best Fit** to all columns. **Save** and then **Close** the query.

7 On the **Database Tools tab**, in the **Analyze group**, click **Analyze Performance**. Click the **All Object Types tab**, click **Select All**, and then click **OK**.

  a. Under **Analysis Results**, click the Suggestion with the green question mark. Click **Optimize**.

  b. **Close** the **Performance Analyzer** dialog box.

8 From **Backstage** view, click **Options**. Click **Current Database**, and then in the **Application Title** box, type **L-R Law Partners: Paralegals**

  a. In the **Application Icon** box, browse to select **a10C_Icon**, a bitmap file, located within the student files. Click the **Use as Form and Report Icon** check box.

  b. Clear the **Display Status Bar** check box.

  c. In the **Display Form** box, click the arrow and then click the **Paralegals Navigation Form**.

9 Under **Navigation**, click the **Navigation Options** button.

  a. Click **Add Item**, type **Paralegals** and then press Enter.

  b. Click **Add Group**, type **Clients** and then press Enter.

  c. Click **Add Group**, type **Cases** and then press Enter. Click **OK** two times to close the dialog boxes.

  d. Read the displayed message, and then click **OK**.

  e. Display **Backstage** view, click **Close**, and then display **Backstage** view to reopen the database. **Close** the navigation form and **Open** the **Navigation Pane**.

10 Click the **Navigation Pane arrow**, and then click **Paralegals**.

  a. Drag the **PersonalClients** table and drop it into the **Clients** group. Drag the **PersonalClientsForm** and drop it into the **Clients** group. Drag the **PersonalClientsList** report and drop it into the **Clients** group.

(continues on next page)

Chapter Review

b. Drag the **Cases** table and drop it into the **Cases** group. Drag the **PersonalServiceCodes** table and drop it into the **Cases** group. Drag the **PersonalServiceCodesForm** and drop it into the **Cases** group. Drag the **Case Information** query and drop it into the **Cases** group.

11 Display **Backstage** view, and click **Options**. If necessary, click **Current Database**, and then under **Navigation**, click the **Navigation Options** button.

a. In the **Categories** column, click **Paralegals**. In the **Groups** column, clear the **Unassigned Objects** check box, and then click **OK** three times. **Close** and then **Open** the database.

12 Display **Backstage** view, click **Options**, and then click **Quick Access Toolbar**.

a. In the list of **Popular Commands**, scroll down, click **New**, and then click **Add**.

b. Click the **Customize Quick Access Toolbar arrow**, and then click the path for the current database. In the list below **Popular Commands**, click **Open**, and then click **Add**. Click **OK** twice to close the dialog and message boxes. **Close** and then **Open** the database. **Close** the **Paralegals Navigation Form**.

13 On the **Database Tools tab**, in the **Move Data** group, click **Access Database**.

a. In the **Database Splitter** dialog box, click the **Split Database** button.

b. In the **Create Back-end Database** dialog box, verify that your **Access Chapter 10** folder is open.

c. Click **Split**, accepting the default name for the back-end file, and then click **OK**. Click **OK** to close the message box.

14 In **Access**, on the **Quick Access Toolbar**, click the arrow. Click **New** to remove the icon from the Quick Access Toolbar.

a. Open the **PersonalServiceCodesForm**, and enter the following record:

ServiceCode	Service	Type
PS010	Insurance Disputes	Personal Service/ Agent

b. **Close** the form.

15 Display **Backstage** view, and then click **Close Database**.

a. Display **Backstage** view, click **Open**, and then click **Browse**. Navigate to your **Access Chapter 10** folder, and then click **Lastname_Firstname_10C_ Paralegals** one time.

b. In the lower-right corner of the **Open** dialog box, click the **Open arrow**, and then click **Open Exclusive**.

16 Display **Backstage** view, and click **Encrypt with Password**.

a. In the **Set Database Password** dialog box, in the **Password** box, type **GO!Access10C** In the **Verify** box, type **GO!Access10C** and then click **OK**. If a message box displays, click **OK** to close it.

b. Display **Backstage** view. **Close** and then reopen the **10C Paralegals** database. In the displayed **Password Required** dialog box, type **GO!Access10C** and click **OK** or press Enter.

17 Display **Backstage** view, click **Save As**, and then under Advanced, double-click **Make ACCDE**.

a. In the **Save As** dialog box, verify that your Access Chapter 10 folder is open. Save the locked database as Lastname_Firstname_10C_Paralegals_ACCDE

18 **Close** the database. **Close** Access.

19 As directed by your instructor, submit your databases for grading

You have completed Project 10C END

Chapter Review

Skills Review | Project 10D Top Accounts

Apply 10B skills from these Objectives:

7. Modify a Query in SQL View
8. Create a Query in SQL View
9. Create a Union Query Using SQL
10. Create Calculated Fields and SQL Aggregate Functions

Loren-Renner Law Partners wants a report that lists its top corporate accounts. To build the report, you will create two queries using SQL view. You will join the two queries into a union query. You will then create a query that summarizes the data in the union query and build the report from this query. Your completed Navigation Pane will look similar to the report shown in Figure 10.40.

Project Files

For Project 10D, you will need the following file:

a10D_Corporate_Accounts

You will save your database as:

Lastname_Firstname_10D_Corporate_Accounts

Project Results

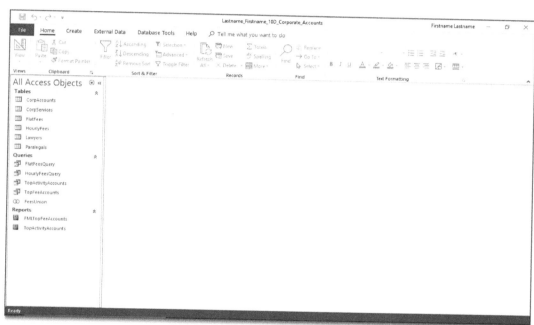

Figure 10.40

(continues on next page)

Chapter Review

1 Start Access. Locate and open the **a10D_ Corporate_Accounts** file. Save the database in your **Access Chapter 10** folder as **Lastname_Firstname_10D_ Corporate_Accounts** Enable content, if necessary.

2 On the **Create tab**, in the **Queries group**, click **Query Design**.

a. In the displayed **Show Table** dialog box, add the **CorpAccounts** and **FlatFees** tables to the query. Resize field lists so all fields are visible.

b. From the **CorpAccounts** table, add the **CorpName** field to the design grid. From the **FlatFees** table, add the **Fee** field to the design grid.

3 On the **Query Tools Design tab**, in the **Show/Hide group**, click **Totals**.

a. In the **Total** row for the **Fee** column, change **Group By** to **Sum**.

b. **Save** the query with the name **FlatFeesQuery**.

4 In the status bar, click the **SQL View** button.

a. After the *AS* keyword, replace the text *SumofFee* with **Totals**

b. In the **Results group**, click **Run**. View the results, and then click the **SQL View** button. Click **Save**.

5 On the **Create tab**, in the **Queries group**, click the **Query Design** button. **Close** the **Show Table** dialog box, and then click the **SQL View** button.

a. Replace the existing text with the following SELECT clause **SELECT CorpAccounts.CorpName, Rate * Hours AS Totals**

b. On a new line, enter the following FROM clause: **FROM CorpAccounts INNER JOIN HourlyFees ON CorpAccounts.CorpID = HourlyFees.CorpID;**

c. Click **Run** to test the query so far. **Save** the query as **HourlyFeesQuery**

6 Click the **SQL View** button. In the SELECT clause, replace the text *Rate * Hours* with **Sum(Rate * Hours)**

a. At the end of the SQL statement, click in front of the semicolon, press Enter, and then type the following clause: **GROUP BY CorpAccounts.CorpName**

b. Click **Run**, view the results, and then click **Save**.

7 On the **Create tab**, in the **Queries group**, click **Query Design**. Close the **Show Table** dialog box, and then in the **Query Type group**, click **Union**.

a. Display **FlatFeesQuery** in SQL view. Select the entire SQL statement, right-click, and then from the displayed shortcut menu, click **Copy**. Display the union query that you are building, right-click, and

then click **Paste**. Delete the semicolon, press Enter two times, and then type **UNION**

b. Display **HourlyFeesQuery** in SQL view, and then **Copy** the entire SQL statement. Display the union query, press Enter two times, and then press Ctrl + V.

c. **Save** the query with the name **FeesUnion** and then click the **Run** button. View the results, and then **Close** all three open queries, saving changes as needed.

8 On the **Create tab**, in the **Queries group**, click **Query Design**.

a. In the displayed **Show Table** dialog box, click the **Queries tab**, and then add the **FeesUnion** query to the query. **Close** the **Show Table** dialog box. Add the **CorpName** field to the design grid, and then add the **Totals** field.

b. In the **Show/Hide group**, click the **Totals** button. In the **Total** row for the **Totals** column, change **Group By** to **Sum**.

c. Click in the **Sort** row for the **Totals** column. Click the displayed arrow, and then click **Descending**.

d. **Save** the query with the name **TopFeeAccounts** Click the **Run** button and view the results. AutoFit columns as necessary.

9 Click the **SQL View** button. After the SELECT keyword, press Spacebar, and then type **TOP 10**

a. **Run** the query and view the results.

b. Click **Save**, and then **Close** the query.

10 In the **Navigation Pane**, click to select the **TopFeeAccounts** query. On the **Create tab**, in the **Reports group**, click the **Report** button.

a. In the **Report Header**, delete the **Date** and **Time** text box controls.

b. Change the report **Title** to **Lastname Firstname Top Accounts–Fees** Make adjustments so the title fits on one line. Change the **CorpName** label to **Corporation Name**

c. At the top of the **Totals** column, change the **SumofTotals** label to **Totals** At the bottom of the **Totals** column, click the text box that calculates the grand total, and then apply the **Currency** format. Resize the control so the total is visible.

d. **Save** the report with the name suggested by Access.

11 **Close** the report.

12 **Close** Access. As directed by your instructor, submit your database for grading.

You have completed Project 10D | END

Content-Based Assessments (Mastery and Transfer of Learning)

| Mastering | Project 10E Accountants |

Loren-Renner Law Partners wants to secure the databases used by its accounting and marketing departments. You will also create a new workgroup information file for the database used by the marketing department. Your completed Navigation Pane will look similar to that shown in Figure 10.41.

Apply 10A skills from these Objectives:

1. Create a Navigation Form
2. Use Microsoft Access Analysis Tools
3. Modify Access Views and Behaviors
4. Use the Database Splitter
5. Encrypt and Decrypt Databases
6. Create a Locked Database (ACCDE File)

Project Files

For Project 10E, you will need the following files:

a10E_Accountants

a10E_Icon

You will save your files as:

Lastname_Firstname_10E_Accountants

Lastname_Firstname_10E_Accountants_be

Lastname_Firstname_10E_ACCDE

Project Results

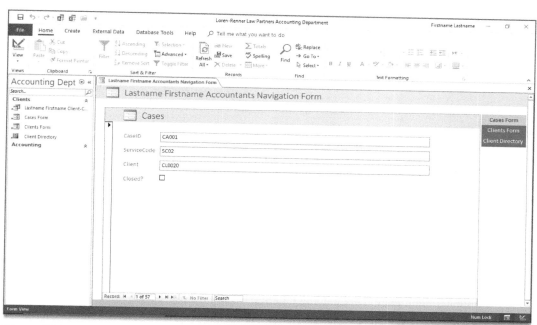

Figure 10.41

(continues on next page)

Content-Based Assessments (Mastery and Transfer of Learning)

1 Start Access. Locate and open the **a10E_ Accountants** file. **Save** the database in the **Access Chapter 10** folder as **Lastname_Firstname_10E_ Accountants** If necessary, enable content.

2 Create a navigation form, **Vertical Tabs, Right**. If the Field List displays, close it. Add the **Cases Form, Clients Form**, and **Client Directory** to the navigation form. Edit the title to read **Lastname Firstname Accountants Navigation Form Save** the navigation form as **Lastname Firstname Accountants Navigation Form**

3 **Close** the **Navigation Pane**. Switch to **Form** view and then **Close** the form.

4 Use the **Table Analyzer wizard** to analyze the **Billing** table. Have the wizard decide how to split the table, and then rename the suggested tables as follows:

Suggested Table	New Name
Table1	**Lastname Firstname Billing**
Table2	**Lastname Firstname Accountants**

5 In the **Billing** table, set **InvoiceID** as the **unique identifier**. Choose the option to create the query, and then **Finish** the wizard. **Close** the **Help** window, and **Close** the query.

6 Display all database objects that depend on the **Billing_OLD** table. Delete the **Billing_OLD** table.

7 Start a new query in **Query Design** view, and then add the **Clients** and **Cases** tables to the query. Resize the field lists so all fields and table names are visible. From the **Clients** table, add the **OrgName** field. From the **Cases** table, add the **CaseID** and **Closed?** fields. Create an indeterminate relationship between the **ClientID** field in the **Clients** table and the **Client** field in the **Cases** table, if necessary. Save the query as **Lastname Firstname Client-Cases Run** and then **Close** the query.

8 Run the **Performance Analyzer** wizard for **All Object Types**. Optimize the item with the **Suggestion** icon.

9 Display **Backstage** view, and then display the **Access Options** dialog box. Under **Current Database**, change the **Application Title** to **Loren-Renner Law Partners Accounting Department** For the **Application Icon**, assign **a10E_Icon**. Display the **Navigation Form**, and disable **Layout** view.

10 Edit the following **Navigation Pane** options: add a new item named **Accounting Dept** and then add two new groups: one named **Clients** and one named **Accounting Close** and then **Open** the database. In the **Navigation Pane**, display the **Accounting Dept** category. Drag the **Cases** and **Clients** tables into the **Clients** category. Drag the **Client-Cases** query into the **Clients** category. Drag the **Cases Form** and **Clients Form** into the **Clients** category. Drag the **Client Directory** report into the **Clients** category. Drag the **Accountants, Billing**, and **Services** tables into the **Accounting** category. Using the **Navigation** options, do not display Unassigned Objects in the Navigation Pane when the Accounting Dept category is selected. **Close** and then **Open** the database.

11 For the current database only, add the following commands to the Quick Access Toolbar: **Import Access database, Import Excel spreadsheet**, and **Open**.

12 Close all open dialog boxes and database objects.

13 Split the database into a back-end and front-end file. Save the back-end file in your **Access Chapter 10** folder with the name suggested by Access. **Close** the database.

14 Open **10E_Accountants** using the **Open Exclusive** command. Encrypt the database using the password **GO!10EAccess** Click **OK**, and then **Close** the database.

15 Open **10E_Accountants** using the password. Create a secure ACCDE version of the database file. Save the ACCDE file in your **Access Chapter 10** folder as **Lastname_Firstname_10E_ACCDE**

16 Close the database, and **Close** Access.

17 As directed by your instructor, submit your files for grading

You have completed Project 10E `END`

Content-Based Assessments (Mastery and Transfer of Learning)

Apply 10B skills from these Objectives:

7. Modify a Query in SQL View
8. Create a Query in SQL View
9. Create a Union Query Using SQL
10. Create Calculated Fields and SQL Aggregate Functions

Loren-Renner Law Partners wants a report that describes the various services that it provides to corporations and organizations. To build the report, you will create two queries using SQL view. You will join the two queries into a single query. You will then create a query that summarizes the data in the union query and build the report from this query. Your completed Navigation Pane will look similar to the report shown in Figure 10.42.

Project Files

For Project 10F, you will need the following file:

a10F_Legal_Services

You will save your database as:

Lastname_Firstname_10F_Legal_Services

Project Results

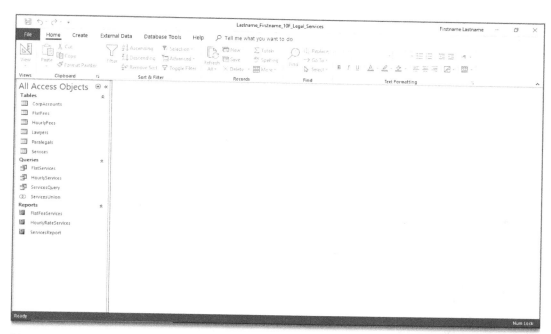

Figure 10.42

(continues on next page)

Mastering: Project 10F Legal Services (continued)

1 Start Access. Locate and open the **a10F_Legal_ Services** file. **Save** the database in the **Access Chapter 10** folder as **Lastname_Firstname_10F_Legal_Services** Enable content, if necessary.

2 Start a new query in **Design** view. Add the **Services** and **FlatFees** tables to the query. If necessary, expand the field lists to display all field names. From the **Services** table, add the **Service** field to the design grid. From the **FlatFees** table, add the **Fee** field.

3 In the **Show/Hide group**, click **Totals**. In the **Total** row for the **Fee** column, change **Group By** to **Avg**.

4 In **SQL** view, adapt the SELECT statement so that the calculated field's caption will display as **Average** **Run** the query and view the results. **Save** the query as **FlatServices**

5 Start a new query in **Design** view, and then switch to **SQL** view. Add a SELECT statement that displays the **Service** field from the **Services** table.

6 Add a calculated field to the SELECT statement that multiplies the **Rate** and **Hours** fields.

7 Add a FROM clause that joins the **Services** table to the **HourlyFees** table with an inner join that uses the **ServiceCode** fields from each table. If needed, use the FROM clause in the query created earlier in this project as your reference.

8 For the calculated field, add an SQL aggregate function that calculates the average (AVG) of the **Rate** field multiplied by the **Hours** field. Write the SQL

needed so that the calculated field's caption displays as Average Add a GROUP BY clause that groups the query by each **Service**. If needed, use the query created earlier in this project as your reference.

9 **Run** the query and view the results. **Save** the query as **HourlyServices**

10 Create a new **Union** query. **Copy** and **Paste** the SQL from the two queries created earlier and join them using the UNION keyword. **Run** the query, view the results, and then **Save** the query as **ServicesUnion**

11 Create a new query in **Design** view. In the displayed **Show Table** dialog box, click the **Queries tab**, add the **ServicesUnion** query, and then **Close** the dialog box. Add the **Service** field to the design grid, and then add the **Average** field.

12 In the **Show/Hide group**, click **Totals**. In the **Total** row for the **Average** column, change **Group By** to **Avg**. **Save** the query with the name **ServicesQuery** Click **Run**, view the results, and then **Close** all open queries.

13 Create a **Report** using the **ServicesQuery** query.

14 Change the **Title** to **Lastname Firstname Services** Change the **AvgofAverage** label to Average At the bottom of the **Average** column, delete the **total** and **line** controls.

15 **Save** the report as **ServicesReport Close** the report, and then **Close** Access.

16 As directed by your instructor, submit your database for grading.

You have completed Project 10F | END

Content-Based Assessments (Mastery and Transfer of Learning)

MyLab IT Grader		Mastering	Project 10G Bonuses

Apply 10A and 10B skills from these Objectives:

1. Create a Navigation Form
2. Use Microsoft Access Analysis Tools
3. Modify Access Views and Behaviors
4. Use the Database Splitter
5. Encrypt and Decrypt Databases
6. Create a Locked Database (ACCDE File)
7. Modify a Query in SQL View
8. Create a Query in SQL View
9. Create a Union Query Using SQL
10. Create Calculated Fields and SQL Aggregate Functions

The two lead partners, Alex Loren and David Renner, would like to customize this database. Then, you will create two queries using SQL view, join them in a union query, and then build another query summarizing the union query. Your completed Navigation Pane will look similar to Figure 10.43.

Project Files for MyLab IT Grader

1. In your **MyLab IT** course, locate and click **Access 10G Bonuses**, Download Materials, and then Download All Files.
2. Extract the zipped folder to your Access Chapter 10 folder. Close the Grader download screens.
3. Take a moment to open the downloaded **Access_10G_Bonuses_Instructions**; note any recent updates to the book.

Project Results

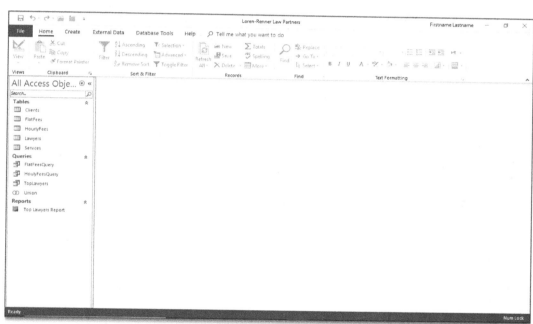

Figure 10.43

For Non-MyLab Submissions
For Project 10G, you will need:
a10G_Bonuses

Start with an Access Data File
In your Access Chapter 10 folder, save your databases as:
Lastname_Firstname_10G_Bonuses
Lastname_Firstname_10G_Bonuses_be

After you have saved your database, open it to launch Access. On the next page, begin with Step 2.
After Step 16, submit your database and any additional files for grading.

(continues on next page)

Content-Based Assessments (Mastery and Transfer of Learning)

1 Start Access. In the Access opening screen, click **Open Other Files**. Navigate to your **Access Chapter 10** folder, and then double-click the Access file that you downloaded from **MyLab IT** that displays your name—**Student_Access_10G_Bonuses**.

2 Set the **Application Title** as **Loren-Renner Law Partners**

3 For this database only, add the **Open** and **Close Database** commands to the Quick Access Toolbar.

4 Start a new query in **Design** view. Add the **Lawyers** and **FlatFees** tables to the query, expanding the field lists as necessary. From the **Lawyers** table, add the **FName** and **LName** fields to the design grid. From the **FlatFees** table, add the **Fee** field.

5 In the **Show/Hide group**, click **Totals**. In the **Total** row for the **Fee** column, change **Group By** to **Sum**.

6 In SQL view, change the caption for the calculated field to **Total Run** the query and view the results. **Save** the query as **FlatFeesQuery**

7 Start a new query in **Design** view, and then switch to **SQL** view. Using the earlier query as your guide, write a SELECT statement that displays the **FName** and **LName** fields from the **Lawyers** table.

8 Add a calculated field to the SELECT clause that multiplies the **Rate** and **Hours** fields from the **HourlyFees** table. Write the SQL needed so that the calculated field's caption displays as **Total**

9 For the calculated field, add an SQL aggregate function that calculates the sum of the **Rate** field multiplied by the **Hours** field.

10 Add a FROM clause that joins the **Lawyers** table to the **HourlyFees** table with an inner join that uses the **LawyerID** fields from each table.

11 Copy the GROUP BY clause from **FlatFeesQuery** and **Paste** it into the current query. **Run** the query and view the results. **Save** the query as **HourlyFeesQuery**

12 Create a new **Union** query. **Copy** and **Paste** the SQL statements from the two queries created earlier and join them using the UNION keyword. **Run** the query, view the results, and then **Save** the query as **Union Close** all open queries.

13 Create a new query in **Design** view, add the **Union** query, and then add the **FName, LName,** and **Total** fields to the design grid. Add the **Total** row to the design grid, and then in the **Total** row for the **Total** column, change **Group By** to **Sum**.

14 In the **Total** column, change the **Sort** row value to **Descending**. Display the **Property Sheet**, and then, on the **General** tab, change the **Format** to **Currency**.

15 In SQL view, after SELECT, add the **TOP 4** keyword. **Save** the query as **TopLawyers Run** the query, and then **Close** the query.

16 Create a report based on the **TopLawyers** query to display all fields. Change the report title to read **Top Four Lawyers** on one line. Change the **SumofTotal** label to read **Total** Remove the **Count** total and line control from under the **FName** field. In the **Report Header**, delete the **date** and **time** controls. **Save** the report as **Top Lawyers Report Close** the report and **Close** Access.

17 In **MyLab IT**, locate and click the Grader Project Access 10G Bonuses. In **step 3**, under **Upload Completed Assignment**, click **Choose File**. In the **Open** dialog box, navigate to your **Access Chapter 10 folder**, and then click your **Student_Access_10G_Bonuses** file one time to select it. In the lower right corner of the **Open** dialog box, click **Open**.

18 To submit your file to **MyLab IT** for grading, click **Upload**, wait a moment for a green **Success!** message, and then in **step 4**, click the blue **Submit for Grading** button. Click **Close Assignment** to return to your list of **Course Materials**.

You have completed Project 10G | **END**

Content-Based Assessments (Critical Thinking)

Apply a combination of the 10A and 10B skills.

GO! Fix It	Project 10H Annual Dinner	IRC
GO! Make It	Project 10I Professional Seminars	IRC
GO! Solve It	Project 10J Law Library	IRC
GO! Solve It	Project 10K Contracts	

Project Files

For Project 10K, you will need the following file:

a10K_Contracts

You will save your file as:

Lastname_Firstname_10K_Contracts

Open **a10K_Contracts**, and save it as **Lastname_Firstname_10K_Contracts**

Create a Navigation Form using a Horizontal tab style. Add the form and both reports to the Navigation Form. Edit the title to read **10K Navigation Form** Save the form using the same name. Close the Navigation Pane, and switch to Form view.

Using SQL, create a query that lists personal clients who have cases listed in the *Cases* table. List only the clients where the *ServiceCode* is equal to SC08. Include the *Name*, *Street*, *City*, *State*, and *PostalCode* fields. Add the necessary SQL command so that clients are not listed more than one time in the query's results. Save the query as **PersonalQuery**

Using SQL, create a query that lists corporate clients who have cases listed in the *Cases* table. List only the clients where the *ServiceCode* is equal to SC08. Include the *CompanyName*, *Street*, *City*, *State*, and *PostalCode* fields. Add the necessary SQL command so that clients are not listed more than one time in the query's results. Save the query as **CorporateQuery**

Create a union query that combines the two queries. Save the query as **AllClients**

As directed by your instructor, submit your files for grading.

		Performance Level		
		Exemplary	**Proficient**	**Developing**
Performance Criteria	**Create Contracts Navigation Form**	Form created with correct tabs and title.	Form created with no more than two missing elements.	Form created with more than two missing elements.
	Create PersonalQuery using SQL	Query created with correct syntax and format.	Query created with no more than two missing elements.	Query created with more than two missing elements.
	Create CorporateQuery using SQL	Query created with correct syntax and format.	Query created with no more than two missing elements.	Query created with more than two missing elements.
	Create AllClients union query using SQL	Query created with correct syntax and format.	Query created with no more than two missing elements.	Query created with more than two missing elements.

You have completed Project 10K | END

Outcomes-Based Assessments (Critical Thinking)

Rubric

The following outcomes-based assessments are open-ended assessments. That is, there is no specific correct result; your result will depend on your approach to the information provided. Make Professional Quality your goal. Use the following scoring rubric to guide you in how to approach the problem and then to evaluate how well your approach solves the problem.

The *criteria*—Software Mastery, Content, Format and Layout, and Process—represent the knowledge and skills you have gained that you can apply to solving the problem. The *levels of performance*—Professional Quality, Approaching Professional Quality, or Needs Quality Improvements—help you and your instructor evaluate your result.

	Your completed project is of Professional Quality if you:	Your completed project is Approaching Professional Quality if you:	Your completed project Needs Quality Improvements if you:
1-Software Mastery	Choose and apply the most appropriate skills, tools, and features and identify efficient methods to solve the problem.	Choose and apply some appropriate skills, tools, and features, but not in the most efficient manner.	Choose inappropriate skills, tools, or features, or are inefficient in solving the problem.
2-Content	Construct a solution that is clear and well organized, contains content that is accurate, appropriate to the audience and purpose, and is complete. Provide a solution that contains no errors of spelling, grammar, or style.	Construct a solution in which some components are unclear, poorly organized, inconsistent, or incomplete. Misjudge the needs of the audience. Have some errors in spelling, grammar, or style, but the errors do not detract from comprehension.	Construct a solution that is unclear, incomplete, or poorly organized, contains some inaccurate or inappropriate content, and contains many errors of spelling, grammar, or style. Do not solve the problem.
3-Format and Layout	Format and arrange all elements to communicate information and ideas, clarify function, illustrate relationships, and indicate relative importance.	Apply appropriate format and layout features to some elements, but not others. Overuse features, causing minor distraction.	Apply format and layout that does not communicate information or ideas clearly. Do not use format and layout features to clarify function, illustrate relationships, or indicate relative importance. Use available features excessively, causing distraction.
4-Process	Use an organized approach that integrates planning, development, self-assessment, revision, and reflection.	Demonstrate an organized approach in some areas, but not others; or, use an insufficient process of organization throughout.	Do not use an organized approach to solve the problem.

Outcomes-Based Assessments (Critical Thinking)

Apply a combination of the 10A and 10B skills.

GO! Think	Project 10L Case History

Project Files

For Project 10L, you will need the following files:

a10L_Case_History

a10L_Icon

You will save your files as:

Lastname_Firstname_10L_Case_History

Lastname_Firstname_10L_ACCDE

Loren-Renner Law Partners needs to secure the database containing a list of past cases. Open **a10L_Case_History** and save it as **Lastname_Firstname_10L_Case_History** Create an ACCDE file named **Lastname_Firstname_10L_ACCDE** At the beginning of each table name, add your own initials. Customize the Access Options so the Application Title **L-R Case History** displays along with the **a10L_Icon**. Add the Open and Close Database icons to the Quick Access Toolbar for this database only.

Using SQL, create a query that lists corporate clients who have past cases listed in the *Cases* table. List only the client name and how many cases they have had. Group the data by *CompanyName*, and then display the count as **PastCases** Save the query as **History**

As directed by your instructor, submit your files for grading.

You have completed Project 10L | **END**

GO! Think	Project 10M Phone List	IRC

You and GO!	Project 10N Club Directory	IRC

Appendix

	MICROSOFT OFFICE SPECIALIST ACCESS EXPERT 2019		
Obj Number	**Objective text**	**GO! Activity**	**Page Number**
1.0 Manage Databases			
1.1	**Modify database structure**		
1.1.1	Import objects or data from other sources	1.11, 2.17, 9.04, 9.06	121, 207, 657, 659
1.1.2	Delete database objects	1.05	112
1.1.3	Hide and display objects in the Navigation Pane	1.21, 10.08	146, 717
1.2	**Manage table relationship and keys**		
1.2.1	Understand relationships	2.02, 2.18, 5.18, 5.19	182, 208, 430, 432
1.2.2	Display relationships	2.04, 2.18, 3.01, 3.16, 5.11, 5.15	187, 208, 257, 286, 416, 424
1.2.3	Set Primary Keys	2.17, 4.03, 4.13, 6.01, 9.02, 9.03, 10.02	207, 332, 350, 457, 650, 655, 707
1.2.4	Enforce referential integrity	2.03, 2.18	185, 208
1.2.5	Set foreign keys	2.03, 2.18	185, 208
1.3	**Print and export data**		
1.3.1	Configure print options for records, forms, and reports	1.13, 1.15, 2.04, 3.15	126, 132, 187, 281
1.3.2	Export objects to alternative formats	9.09, 9.10, 9.11, 9.12, 9.14, 9.15	666, 669, 670, 674, 678, 679
2.0 Create and Modify Tables			
2.1	**Create tables**		
2.1.1	Import data into tables	1.07, 1.20, 4.04, 9.02, 9.03	114, 145, 333, 650, 655
2.1.2	Create linked tables from external sources	9.08	663
2.1.3	Import tables from other databases	4.06, 9.07	337, 661
2.2	**Manage tables**		
2.2.1	Hide fields in tables	6.11	479
2.2.2	Add total rows	8.12	622
2.2.3	Add table descriptions	1.09, 4.04	119, 333
2.3	**Manage table records**		
2.3.1	Find and replace data	3.05, 4.07, 4.08	263, 339, 341
2.3.2	Sort records	2.07, 2.08, 4.03, 5.15, 5.16, 5.17, 10.02	190, 191, 332, 424, 427, 428, 707
2.3.3	Filter records	3.06, 3.07, 3.08	264, 266, 268
2.4	**Create and modify fields**		
2.4.1	Add or remove fields	1.03, 1.08, 1.22, 4.03, 4.05, 4.09, 4.14	109, 117, 148, 332, 335, 342, 353
2.4.2	Add validation rules to fields	4.22	366

MICROSOFT OFFICE SPECIALIST ACCESS EXPERT 2019			
Obj Number	**Objective text**	**GO! Activity**	**Page Number**
2.4.3	Change field captions	1.04, 4.13	111, 350
2.4.4	Change field sizes	1.09, 4.13, 4.14	119, 350, 353
2.4.5	Change field data types	1.03, 1.04, 1.22, 2.17, 4.03, 4.05, 4.09, 4.11, 4.12, 4.13, 4.14, 4.15, 4.16, 4.18, 9.02	109, 111, 148, 207, 332, 335, 342, 345, 346, 350, 353, 355, 356, 360, 650
2.4.6	Configure fields to auto-increment	1.04	111
2.4.7	Set default values	4.22	366
2.4.8	Apply built-in input masks	4.17, 4.18	357, 360
3.0 Create and Modify Queries			
3.1	**Create and run queries**		
3.1.1	Create simple queries	2.09, 2.14, 2.15, 2.16, 2.19, 2.25, 2.23, 2.24, 2.26, 2.29, 5.03, 5.04, 5.05	193, 199, 201, 202, 210, 216, 213, 214, 218, 221, 399, 402, 405
3.1.2	Create basic crosstab queries	2.31, 5.06	223, 406
3.1.3	Create basic parameter queries	2.32, 5.09, 5.10	225, 411, 413
3.1.4	Create basic action queries	5.12, 5.13, 5.14, 5.15, 5.16, 5.17	417, 419, 421, 424, 427, 428
3.1.5	Create basic multi-table queries	2.24, 2.25, 5.04, 5.05, 5.09, 5.10, 5.11, 5.13, 5.17, 5.18, 10.13, 10.14, 10.15, 10.16, 10.17,	214, 216, 402, 405, 411, 413, 416, 419, 428, 430, 728, 730, 732, 733, 734
3.1.6	Save queries	1.14, 2.10, 2.12, 2.13, 2.14, 2.15, 2.16, 2.20, 2.21, 2.22, 2.23, 2.24, 2.26, 2.28, 2.30, 2.32, 5.01, 5.03, 5.04, 5.05, 5.10, 5.12, 5.13, 5.16, 5.18, 9.05, 10.03, 10.13, 10.14, 10.18	129, 194, 196, 198, 199, 201, 202, 210, 211, 212, 213, 214, 218, 220, 222, 225, 393, 399, 402, 405, 413, 417, 419, 427, 430, 658, 709, 728, 730, 735
3.1.7	Run queries	1.14, 2.10, 2.12, 2.13, 2.14, 2.15, 2.16, 2.19, 2.21, 2.22, 2.23, 2.24, 2.25, 2.26, 2.27, 2.29, 2.30, 2.32, 5.01, 5.03, 5.04, 5.05, 5.09, 5.10, 5.12, 5.13, 5.16, 5.17, 5.18, 5.19, 9.05, 9.12, 10.03, 10.13, 10.14, 10.17, 10.18	129, 194, 196, 198, 199, 201, 202, 210, 211, 212, 213, 214, 216, 218, 219, 221, 222, 225, 393, 399, 402, 405, 411, 413, 417, 419, 427, 428, 430, 432, 658, 674, 709, 728, 730, 734, 735
3.2	**Modify queries**		
3.2.1	Add, hide, and remove fields in queries	2.09, 2.12, 2.14, 2.15, 2.16, 2.19, 2.22, 2.23, 2.24, 2.25, 2.26, 2.27, 5.01, 5.03, 5.04, 5.05, 5.07, 5.08, 5.11, 5.13, 5.15, 5.16, 5.17, 5.18, 5.19	193, 196, 199, 201, 202, 210, 212, 213, 214, 216, 218, 219, 393, 399, 402, 405, 409, 410, 416, 419, 424, 427, 428, 430, 432

MICROSOFT OFFICE SPECIALIST ACCESS EXPERT 2019			
Obj Number	**Objective text**	**GO! Activity**	**Page Number**
3.2.2	Sort data within queries	2.13, 2.15, 2.16, 2.19, 2.24, 2.26, 2.30, 5.05, 5.15, 5.18, 10.13, 10.15,	198, 201, 202, 210, 214, 218, 222, 405, 424, 430, 728, 732
3.2.3	Filter data within queries	2.14, 2.15, 2.16, 2.19, 2.20, 2.21, 2.22, 2.23, 2.25, 2.32, 5.02, 5.07, 5.08, 5.09, 5.10, 5.11, 5.13, 5.15, 5.16, 5.17, 10.13, 10.14, 10.17	199, 201, 202, 210, 210, 211, 212, 213, 216, 225, 396, 409, 410, 411, 413, 416, 419, 424, 427, 428, 728, 730, 734
3.2.4	Format fields within queries	2.28, 2.29, 2.30, 5.02	220, 221, 222, 396
4.0 Modify Forms in Layout View			
4.1	**Configure from controls**		
4.1.1	Add, move, and remove form controls	1.15, 3.09, 3.12, 3.14, 6.01, 6.03, 6.04, 7.02, 7.03, 7.04, 7.05, 7.06, 7.07, 8.05, 8.06	132, 270, 274, 278, 457, 461, 463, 525, 530, 534, 535, 539, 543, 602, 607
4.1.2	Set form control properties	3.10, 3.12, 3.13, 3.14, 6.01, 6.03, 6.04, 6.05, 6.07, 6.08, 6.09, 6.10, 7.02, 7.05, 7.06, 8.02, 8.05, 8.06, 8.11	272, 274, 276, 278, 457, 461, 463, 466, 469, 471, 473, 474, 525, 535, 539, 593, 602, 607, 620
4.1.3	Add and modify form labels	3.11, 3.12, 3.13, 3.14, 6.04, 6.07, 7.07, 10.01	273, 274, 276, 278, 463, 469, 543, 705
4.2	**Format forms**		
4.2.1	Modify tab order on forms	6.1	457
4.2.2	Set records by form field	3.02, 3.03, 6.01, 6.03, 6.10, 7.02, 7.03	258, 260, 457, 461, 474, 525, 530
4.2.3	Modify form positioning	3.15, 6.10, 7.03	281, 474, 530
4.2.4	Insert information in form headers and footers	3.14, 6.02	278, 460
4.2.5	Insert images on forms	6.02, 6.04, 7.05	460, 463, 535
5.0 Modify Reports in Layout View			
5.1	**Configure report controls**		
5.1.1	Group and sort fields on reports	GO! Access Comprehensive 3.18, 3.19, 3.23, 6.17, 7.14	288, 291, 299, 488, 561
5.1.2	Add report controls	GO! Access Comprehensive 1.16, 3.17, 3.18, 3.19, 6.11, 6.13, 6.15, 6.18, 7.08, 7.09, 7.10, 7.11, 7.12	38, 287, 288, 291, 479, 482, 484, 491, 548, 550, 552, 553, 558
5.1.3	Add and modify labels on reports	GO! Access Comprehensive 1.16, 3.21, 3.22, 6.12, 6.14, 6.15, 6.18, 7.08, 7.09, 7.11, 7.12, 7.13, 7.14	38, 294, 297, 480, 483, 484, 491, 548, 550, 553, 558, 559, 561

MICROSOFT OFFICE SPECIALIST ACCESS EXPERT 2019			
Obj Number	**Objective text**	**GO! Activity**	**Page Number**
5.2	**Format reports**		
5.2.1	Format a report into multiple columns	3.18, 6.11, 9.05, 10.18	288, 479, 658, 735
5.2.2	Modify report positioning	3.21, 3.22, 6.13, 6.16, 6.17, 6.18, 7.11	294, 297, 482, 486, 488, 491, 553
5.2.3	Format report elements	1.16, 3.17, 3.20, 3.21, 3.22, 6.12, 6.13, 6.16, 7.10, 7.11, 7.12, 9.07	38, 287, 293, 294, 297, 480, 482, 486, 552, 553, 558, 661
5.2.4	Change report orientation	6.14, 6.16	483, 486
5.2.5	Insert information in report headers and footers	3.18, 7.11, 7.13	288, 553, 559
5.2.6	Insert images on reports	6.14, 6.16, 7.13	483, 486, 559

Glossary

ACCDE file An Access file format that prevents individuals from making design changes to forms, reports, and macros.

Action A self-contained instruction that can be combined with other actions to automate tasks.

Action query A query that creates a new table or changes data in an existing table.

Aggregate function A function that groups and performs calculations on multiple values.

Alphabetic index Grouping of items by a common first character.

AND condition A compound criteria used to display records that match all parts of the specified criteria.

Append To add on to the end of an object; for example, to add records to the end of an existing table.

Append query An action query that adds new records to an existing table by adding data from another Access database or from a table in the same database.

Application title The text that displays in the Access title bar when that database is open.

Argument A value that provides information to the macro action, such as the words to display in a message box or the control upon which to operate.

Arithmetic operators Mathematical symbols used in building expressions.

AS An SQL keyword that creates captions for fields.

Ascending order A sorting order that arranges text alphabetically (A to Z) and numbers from the lowest number to the highest number.

ASCII An acronym for American Standard Code for Information Interchange, a character set.

AutoNumber data type A data type that describes a unique sequential or random number assigned by Access as each record is entered and that is useful for data that has no distinct field that can be considered unique.

Back end An Access database that consists of the database tables and their data. The back end is typically placed on a server and is not directly seen by the end user.

Back up A feature that creates a copy of the original database to protect against lost data.

Bang operator The exclamation (!) mark that tells Access that what follows is an object that belongs to the object that precedes it in the expression.

Best Fit An Access command that adjusts the width of a column to accommodate the column's longest entry.

Between . . . And operator A comparison operator that looks for values within a range.

Blank desktop database A database that has no data and has no database tools—you must create the data and tools as you need them; the database is stored on your computer or other storage device.

Bound A term used to describe objects and controls that are based on data that is stored in tables.

Bound control A control that retrieves its data from an underlying table or query; a text box control is an example of a bound control.

Bound report A report that displays data from an underlying table, query, or SQL statement as specified in the report's Record Source property.

Button control A control that enables individuals to add a command button to a form or report that will perform an action when the button is clicked.

Calculated control A control that contains an expression, often a formula or function, that most often summarizes a field that contains numerical data.

Calculated field A field that obtains its data by using a formula to perform a calculation or computation.

Caption A property setting that displays a name for a field in a table, query, form, or report different from the one listed as the field name.

Cascade Delete Related Records A cascade option that enables you to delete a record in a table and also delete all of the related records in related tables.

Cascade options Relationship options that enable you to update records in related tables when referential integrity is enforced.

Cascade Update Related Fields A cascade option that enables you to change the data in the primary key field in the table on the *one* side of the relationship and update that change to any fields storing that same data in related tables.

Cell The small box formed by the intersection of a column and a row in a worksheet.

Chart A graphic representation of data.

Clipboard A temporary storage area in Windows that can hold up to 24 items.

Code Builder A window used to type programming code in Microsoft Visual Basic.

Column chart A chart used to display comparisons among related numbers.

Combo box A control that enables individuals to select from a list or to type a value.

Comment Explanatory information provided about the macro or the action.

Common field A field included in two or more tables that stores the same data.

Compact & Repair A process where an Access file is rewritten to store the objects and data more efficiently.

Comparison operators Symbols that are used to evaluate data in the field to determine if it is the same (=), greater than (>), less than (<), or in between a range of values as specified by the criteria.

Compound criteria Multiple conditions in a query or filter.

Concatenation Linking or joining strings.

Condition A statement that specifies that certain criteria must be met before the macro action executes.

Conditional formatting A way to apply formatting to specific controls based on a comparison to a rule set.

Control An object, such as a label or text box, in a form or report that enables individuals to view or manipulate information stored in tables or queries.

Control layout The grouped arrangement of controls on a form or report; for example, the Stacked layout.

ControlTip A message that displays descriptive text when the mouse pointer is paused over the control.

Converted Changed from one format to another.

Copy A command that duplicates a selection and places it on the Clipboard.

Criteria Conditions in a query that identify the specific records you are looking for.

Cross join A join that displays when each row from one table is combined with each row in a related table, usually created unintentionally when you do not create a join line between related tables.

Crosstab query A query that uses an aggregate function for data that is grouped by two types of information and displays the data in a compact, spreadsheet-like format. A crosstab query always has at least one row heading, one column heading, and one summary field.

Currency data type An Access data type that describes monetary values and numeric data that can be used in mathematical calculations involving values with one to four decimal places.

Custom web app A database that you can publish and share with others over the Internet.

Data Facts about people, events, things, or ideas.

Data entry The action of entering the data into a record in a database table or form.

Data macro A macro that is triggered by events, such as adding, updating, or deleting data within a table, form, or query. It is used to validate the accuracy of data in a table; also known as an event-driven macro.

Data source The table or tables from which a form, query, or report retrieves its data; also, an Access table or query that contains the names and addresses of the individuals to whom a letter, memo, or other document is being sent in a mail merge.

Data type Classification identifying the kind of data that can be stored in a field, such as numbers, text, or dates.

Data validation Rules that help prevent invalid data entries and ensure data is entered consistently.

Database An organized collection of facts about people, events, things, or ideas related to a specific topic or purpose.

Database Documenter An option used to create a report that contains detailed information about the objects in a database, including macros, and to create a paper record.

Database management system (DBMS) Database software that controls how related collections of data are stored, organized, retrieved, and secured; also known as a DBMS.

Database template A preformatted database that contains prebuilt tables, queries, forms, and reports that perform a specific task, such as tracking events.

Datasheet view The Access view that displays data organized in columns and rows similar to an Excel worksheet.

Date control A control on a form or report that inserts the current date each time the form or report is opened.

DBMS An acronym for database management system.

Debugging A logical process to find and reduce the number of errors in a program.

Decrypt An action that removes a file's encryption or unsets a password.

Default value A specified value to be automatically entered in a field in new records.

Definition The structure of the table—the field names, data types, and field properties.

Delete query An action query that removes records from an existing table in the same database.

Delimited file A file in which each record displays on a separate line, and the fields within the record are separated by a single character.

Delimiter A single character; can be a paragraph mark, a tab, a comma, or another character to separate fields within a record.

Dependency An object that requires, or is dependent on, another database object.

Descending order A sorting order that arranges text in reverse alphabetical order (Z to A) and numbers from the highest number to the lowest number.

Design grid The lower area of the query window that displays the design of the query.

Design view An Access view that displays the detailed structure of a table, query, form, or report. For forms and reports, may be the view in which some tasks must be performed, and only the controls, and not the data, display.

Destination table In an append query, the table to which you are appending records, attempting to match the fields.

Detail section The section of a form or report that displays the records from the underlying table or query.

DISTINCT An SQL keyword that returns only a single instance of any duplicate values in query results.

Dynamic An attribute applied to data in a database that changes.

Embedded macro A macro that is stored in the properties of forms, reports, or controls.

Encrypt A process to hide data by making the file unreadable until the correct password is entered.

Event Any action that can be detected by a program or computer system, such as clicking a button or closing an object.

Export The process used to send out a copy of data from one source or application to another application, such as an Access table into an Excel spreadsheet.

Expression A combination of functions, field values, constants, and operators that produces a result.

Expression Builder A feature used to create formulas (expressions) in calculated fields, query criteria, form and report controls, and table validation rules.

Extensible Markup Language The standard language for defining and storing data on the web.

Field A single piece of information that is stored in every record; represented by a column in a database table.

Field list A list of field names in a table.

Field properties Characteristics of a field that control how the field displays and how data can be entered in the field; vary for different data types.

Filter by Form An Access command that filters the records in a form based on one or more fields, or based on more than one value in the field.

Filter by Selection An Access command that displays only the records that contain the value in the selected field and hides the records that do not contain the value.

Filtering The process of displaying only a portion of the total records (a subset) based on matching specific values to provide a quick answer to a question.

Find Duplicates Query A query used to locate duplicate records in a table.

Find Unmatched Query A query used to locate unmatched records so they can be deleted from the table.

First principle of good database design A principle of good database design stating that data is organized in tables so that there is no redundant data.

Flagged Action of highlighting a word that Spell Check does not recognize from the Office dictionary.

Flat database A simple database file that is not related or linked to any other collection of data.

Focus A control that is selected and currently being acted upon.

Foreign key The field that is included in the related table so the field can be joined with the primary key in another table for the purpose of creating a relationship.

Form A database object that you can use to enter new records into a table, or to edit, delete, and display existing records in a table.

Form Footer Information at the bottom of the screen in Form view or Layout view that is printed after the last detail section on the last page of a printout.

Form Header Information such as a form's title that displays at the top of the screen in Form view or Layout view and is printed at the top of the first page when records are printed as forms.

Form selector The box in the upper left corner of a form in Design view where the rulers meet; used to select the entire form.

Form tool An Access tool that creates a form with a single mouse click, which includes all of the fields from the underlying data source (table or query).

Form view The Access view in which you can view, modify, delete, or add records in a table, but you cannot change the layout or design of the form.

Form Wizard An Access tool that walks you step by step through the creation of a form and that gives you more flexibility in the design, layout, and number of fields in a form.

FROM clause An SQL statement that lists which tables hold the fields used in the SELECT clause.

Front end An Access database that includes the database forms, queries, reports, and macros. The end users open the front end to work with the data stored in the back-end tables.

Group Footer Information printed at the end of each group of records; used to display summary information for the group.

Group Header Information printed at the beginning of each new group of records; for example, the group name.

Group, Sort, and Total pane A pane that displays at the bottom of the screen in which you can control how information is sorted and grouped in a report; provides the most flexibility for adding or modifying groups, sort orders, or totals options on a report.

HTML An acronym for HyperText Markup Language.

HyperText Markup Language The language used to display webpages.

Image control A control that enables individuals to insert an image into any section of a form or report.

Import The process of copying data from another file, such as a Word table or an Excel workbook, into a separate file, such as an Access database.

Indeterminate relationship A relationship that does not enforce referential integrity.

Index A special list created in Access to speed up searches and sorting.

Information Data that is accurate, timely, and organized in a useful manner.

Inner join A join that allows only the records where the common field exists in both related tables to be displayed in query results.

Innermost sort field When sorting on multiple fields in Datasheet view, the field that will be used for the second level of sorting.

Input Mask A field property that determines the data that can be entered, how the data displays, and how the data is stored.

Is Not Null A criteria that searches for fields that are not empty.

Is Null A criteria that searches for fields that are empty.

Join A relationship that helps a query return only the records from each table you want to see, based on how those tables are related to other tables in the query.

JOIN clause An SQL statement that defines the join type for a query.

Join line In the Relationships window, the line joining two tables that visually indicates the common fields and the type of relationship.

Junction table A table that breaks down the many-to-many relationship into two one-to-many relationships.

Keywords Commands built into the SQL programming language.

Label control A control on a form or report that contains descriptive information, usually a field name or title.

Layout selector A small symbol that displays in the upper left corner of a selected control layout in a form or report that is displayed in Layout view or Design view; used to move or format an entire group of controls.

Layout view The Access view in which you can make changes to a form or report while the object is running—the data from the underlying data source displays.

Left outer join A join used when you want to display all of the records on the *one* side of a one-to-many relationship, whether or not there are matching records in the table on the *many* side of the relationship.

Line chart A chart used to display trends over time.

Line control A control that enables an individual to insert a line into a form or report.

Link A connection to data in another file.

Linked form A form related to the main form that is not stored within the main form.

List box A control that enables individuals to select from a list but does not enable individuals to type anything that is not in the list.

Logical operators Operators that combine criteria using AND and OR. With two criteria, AND requires that both conditions be met and OR requires that either condition be met for the record to display in the query results.

Lookup Field A list retrieved from another table, query, or list of entered values from which a user can enter data in a table or form; the list may restrict entries in the field.

Macro A series of actions grouped as a single command to accomplish a task or multiple tasks automatically to add functionality to your object or control.

Macro Designer Window that allows you to build the list of actions to be carried out when the macro runs.

Macro group A set of macros grouped by a common name that displays as one macro object on the Navigation Pane.

Mail merge Letters or memos that are created by combining a document and a record source.

Main document The document that contains the text of a letter or memo for a mail merge.

Main form A form that contains a subform.

Main report A report that contains a subreport.

Make table query An action query that creates a new table by extracting data from one or more tables.

Many-to-many relationship A relationship between tables where one record in one table has many matching records in a second table, and a single record in the related table has many matching records in the first table.

Merging Combining two documents to create one.

Message Bar The area directly below the ribbon that displays information such as security alerts when there is potentially unsafe, active content in an Office document that you open.

Microsoft SQL Server A database application designed for high-end business uses.

Mini toolbar A miniature, semitransparent toolbar that is used to work with objects on the screen.

Modal window A child (secondary) window to a parent window—the original window that opened the modal window—that takes over control of the parent window.

Multi-page form A form that displays the data from the underlying table or query on more than one page.

Multiple-items form A form that enables you to display or enter multiple records in a table.

Multivalued field A field that holds multiple values.

Named range An Excel range that has been given a name, making it easier to use the cells in calculations or modifications.

Navigation area An area at the bottom of the Access window that indicates the number of records in the table and contains controls in the form of arrows that you click to move among the records.

Navigation form A form that displays navigational controls that enable you to display forms and reports in your database.

Navigation Pane An area of the Access window that displays and organizes the names of the objects in a database; from here, you open objects for use.

Navigation Pane category A top-level listing that displays when the Navigation Pane arrow is clicked.

Navigation Pane group A second-level listing that displays when a Navigation Pane category is selected.

Nested subform A subform that is embedded within another subform.

Normalization The process of applying design rules and principles to ensure that your database performs as expected.

Notepad A simple text editor that comes with the Windows operating systems.

Number data type An Access data type that represents a quantity, how much or how many, and may be used in calculations.

Object tab In the object window, a tab that identifies the object and which enables you to make an open object active.

Object window An area of the Access window that displays open objects, such as tables, queries, forms, or reports; by default, each object displays on its own tab.

Objects The basic parts of a database that you create to store your data and to work with your data; for example, tables, queries, forms, and reports.

ODBC An acronym for Open Database Connectivity.

Office background A small graphic in the upper right corner of the Access application window used to personalize Office 2019.

ON An SQL keyword that is used to specify which field is common to two tables.

One-to-many relationship A relationship between two tables where one record in the first table corresponds to many records in the second table— the most common type of relationship in Access.

Open Database Connectivity A standard that enables databases using SQL statements to interface with one another.

Open Exclusive An option that opens the database so that changes can be made, but no one else may open the database at the same time.

Open Exclusive Read-Only An option that opens the database in both Exclusive and Read-Only modes.

Open Read-Only An option that opens the database so that all objects can be opened and viewed, but data and design changes cannot be made.

OR condition A compound criteria used to display records that match at least one of the specified criteria.

Outer join A join that is typically used to display records from both tables, regardless of whether there are matching records.

Outermost sort field When sorting on multiple fields in Datasheet view, the field that will be used for the first level of sorting.

Page Footer Information printed at the bottom of every page in a report; most often includes the page number.

Page Header Information printed at the top of every page in a report.

Page number control A control on a form or report that inserts the page numbers when displayed in Print Preview or when printed.

Parameter A value that can be changed.

Parameter query A query that prompts you for one or more criteria before running.

Paste An action of placing text or other objects that have been copied or cut from one location to a new location.

Path The location of a folder or file on your computer or storage device.

Performance Analyzer A wizard that analyzes database objects, and then offers suggestions for improving them.

Picture Alignment property A property that determines where the background picture for a form displays on the form.

Picture Size Mode property A property that determines the proportion of a picture in a form.

Pie chart A chart used to display the contributions of parts to a whole amount.

Plain Text A document format that contains no formatting, such as bold or italic.

Point A measurement that is 1/72 of an inch.

Pop-up window A window that suddenly displays (pops up), usually contains a menu of commands, and stays on the screen only until the user selects one of the commands.

Populate The action of filling a database table with records.

Primary key A required field that uniquely identifies a record in a table; for example, a Student ID number at a college.

Propagate To disseminate or apply changes to an object.

Properties The characteristics that determine the appearance, structure, and behavior of an object.

Property Sheet A list of characteristics—properties—for fields or controls on a form or report in which you can make precise changes to each property associated with the field or control; also a pane that is available for every object on a form, including the form itself, to further enhance the object.

Property Update Options button An option button that displays when you make changes to the design of a table; it enables individuals to update the Property Sheet for a field in all objects that use a table as the record source.

Query A database object that retrieves specific data from one or more database objects—either tables or other queries—and then, in a single datasheet, displays only the data you specify.

Range An area that includes two or more selected cells on an Excel worksheet that can be treated as a single unit.

Record All of the categories of data pertaining to one person, place, event, thing, or idea; represented by a row in a database table.

Record selector bar The vertical bar at the left edge of a record when it is displayed in a form that is used to select an entire record.

Record selector box The small box at the left of a record in Datasheet view that, when clicked, selects the entire record.

Record source The tables or queries that provide the underlying data for a form or report.

Record Source property A property that enables you to specify the source of the data for a form or a report; the property setting can be a table name, a query name, or an SQL statement.

Redundant In a database, information that is duplicated in a manner that indicates poor database design.

Referential integrity A set of rules that Access uses to ensure that the data between related tables is valid.

Relational database A sophisticated type of database that has multiple collections of data within the file that are related to one another.

Relationship An association that you establish between two tables based on common fields.

Report A database object that summarizes the fields and records from a query or table in an easy-to-read format suitable for printing.

Report Footer Information printed at the bottom of the last page of a report.

Report Header Information printed on the first page of a report; used for logos, titles, and dates.

Report tool An Access tool that creates a report with one mouse click and displays all of the fields and records from the record source that you select.

Report Wizard An Access tool that walks you step by step through the creation of a report and that gives you more flexibility in the design, layout, and number of fields in a report.

Required A field property that ensures a field cannot be left empty.

Rich Text Format (RTF) A standard file format that contains some formatting such as underline, bold, font sizes, and colors. RTF documents can be opened in many applications.

Right outer join A join used when you want to display all of the records on the *many* side of a one-to-many relationship, whether or not there are matching records in the table on the *one* side of the relationship.

Run The process in which Access searches the records in the table(s) included in the query design, finds the records that match the specified criteria, and then displays the records in a datasheet; only the fields that have been included in the query design display.

Second principle of good database design A principle stating that appropriate database techniques are used to ensure the accuracy and consistency of data as it is entered into the table.

Section bar In Design view, a gray bar in a form or report that identifies and separates one section from another; used to select the section and to change the size of the section.

SELECT clause An SQL statement that lists which fields the query should display.

Select query A type of Access query that retrieves (selects) data from one or more tables or queries, displaying the selected data in a datasheet; also known as a simple select query.

SharePoint A Microsoft application used for setting up web sites to share and manage documents.

SharePoint List A list of documents maintained on a server running Microsoft Office SharePoint Server.

SharePoint Server A server that enables you to share documents with others in your organization.

Short Text data type An Access data type that describes text, a combination of text and numbers, or numbers that are not used in calculations, such as the Postal Code.

Simple select query Another name for a select query.

Single stepping Debugging a macro using a process that executes one action at a time.

Single-record form A form that enables you to display or enter one record at a time from a table.

Sorting The process of arranging data in a specific order based on the value in a field.

Source file When importing a file, refers to the file being imported.

Source table In a make table or append query, the table from which records are being extracted.

Split database An Access database that is split into two files—one containing the back end and one containing the front end.

Split form An object that displays data in two views—Form view and Datasheet view—on a single form.

Spreadsheet Another name for a worksheet.

SQL (Structured Query Language) A language used by many database programs to view, update, and query data in relational databases.

SQL statement An instruction using Structured Query Language.

Stacked layout A control layout format that is similar to a paper form, with label controls placed to the left of each text box control; the controls are grouped together for easy editing.

Standalone macro A macro object that displays under Macros on the Navigation Pane.

Static data Data that does not change.

Status Bar Text property A form property that enables individuals to enter text that will display in the status bar for a selected control.

String A series of characters.

Strong password A password that is very difficult to guess that may include upper and lowercase letters, numbers, and special characters.

Structure In Access, the underlying design of a table, including field names, data types, descriptions, and field properties.

Subdatasheet A format for displaying related records when you click the plus sign (+) next to a record in a table on the *one* side of the relationship.

Subform A form that is embedded within another form.

Subreport A report that is embedded within another report.

Subset A portion of the total records available.

Syntax The set of rules by which words and symbols in an expression are combined.

System tables Tables used to keep track of multiple entries in an attachment field that you cannot work with or view.

Tab control A control that is used to display data on the main form on different tabs, similar to the way database objects, such as forms and tables, display on different tabs.

Tab order The order in which the insertion point moves from one field to another in a form when you press the Tab key.

Table A format for information that organizes and presents text and data in columns and rows; the foundation of a database.

Table Analyzer A wizard that searches for repeated data in a table, and then splits the table into two or more related tables.

Table area The upper area of the query window that displays field lists for the tables that are used in a query.

Tables and Related Views An arrangement in the Navigation Pane that groups objects by the table to which they are related.

Tags HTML codes that the web browser interprets as the page is loaded; they begin with the < character and end with the > character.

Text box control A bound control on a form or report that displays the data from the underlying table or query.

Text string A sequence of characters.

Theme A predesigned set of colors, fonts, lines, and fill effects that look good together and that can be applied to all of the objects in the database or to individual objects in the database.

Totals query A query that calculates subtotals across groups of records.

Truncated Data that is cut off or shortened because the field or column is not wide enough to display all of the data or the field size is too small to contain all of the data.

Trust Center An area of Access where you can view the security and privacy settings for your Access installation.

Trusted source A person or organization that you know will not send you databases with malicious content.

Unbound control A control that does not have a source of data, such as the title in a form or report.

Unbound report A report that does not display data from an underlying table, query, or SQL statement and has an empty Record Source property setting.

Unequal join A join used to combine rows from two data sources based on field values that are not equal; can be created only in SQL view.

UNION An SQL keyword that is used to combine one or more queries in a union query.

Union query A query type that combines the results of two or more similar select queries.

Unmatched records Records in one table that have no matching records in a related table.

Update query An action query used to add, change, or delete data in fields of one or more existing records.

Validation rule An expression that precisely defines the range of data that will be accepted in a field.

Validation text The error message that displays when an individual enters a value prohibited by the validation rule.

Weak password A password that is easy to guess.

WHERE clause An SQL statement that defines the criteria that should be applied when a query is run.

Wizard A feature in Microsoft Office that walks you step by step through a process.

Wildcard character In a query, a character that represents one or more unknown characters in criteria; an asterisk (*) represents one or more unknown characters, and a question mark (?) represents a single unknown character.

Workbook An Excel file that contains one or more worksheets.

Worksheet The primary document used in Excel to save and work with data that is arranged in columns and rows.

XML An acronym for Extensible Markup Language.

XML presentation files Files that can be created so that the data can be viewed in a web browser.

XML schema A document with an *.xsd* extension that defines the elements, entities, and content allowed in the document.

Zero-length string An entry created by typing two quotation marks with no spaces between them ("") to indicate that no value exists for a required text or memo field.

Index

telephone numbers, 112
Tell Me feature, 41–44
Tell me more, 41–44
Tell me what you want to do box, 41
templates
   database, 106
   database creation from, 142–143
   defined, 4
testing
   field properties, 366–369
   table design, 366–369
text
   copying, 32
   cutting, 32
   editing, 11–14
   entering, 11–14
   formatting, 27–30
     with Format Painter, 30–32
text boxes, controls, 272, 284–285,
   291, 479
   defined, 269
text criteria, 199–200
text effects, applying, 18–19
Text Effects and Typography gallery, 19
text strings, 199
text wrapping, 22
theme colors, 28
   forms, 465
theme fonts, 28
themes
   applying
     to databases, 283
     to forms, 271
     to reports, 283
   colors, 28
   defined, 271
   PowerPoint, 326
This PC, 57, 71
3-D Models, 39
thumbnails, defined, 68
tiles, 56
   live, 51
Timeline, 69
title bars, 6, 66
toggle buttons, defined, 30
Toggle Filter button, 264, 267
toolbars, defined, 9
total records, in Design View, 486–495
total rows
   adding, to queries, 397–400
   adding, to tables, 620
   removing, 400
totals queries
   changing name of, 401
   creating, 400–402
   defined, 400
touch screens
   accessing shortcut menus, 57, 327
   accessing sign-in screen with, 50
   Snipping Tool and, 53–54
training videos, 44
triple-click, 29
truncation, defined, 118

Trust Center, 181, 329
   defined, 328
trusted databases, action queries and, 414
trusted locations
   adding file locations to, 328–330
   removing, 330
.txt file, 82
typing errors, correcting, 112

U

unbound controls, defined, 269
unbound reports, defined, 546
underlines, 29
undo, 18–19
unequal joins, 432
unhiding table fields, 342
union queries
   defined, 732
   in SQL view, 732–733
unmatched records
   finding, 406–409
   in tables with multivalued fields, 409
unzip, defined, 10
Up button, 57
update queries
   creating, 425–427
   defined, 425
   with expressions, 426–427
   restrictions for, 427
updating, tables with make table
   query, 417
USB flash drives, 54–55, 58, 84
   deleting files and, 87
   searching and, 87
Use Alignment guides, 23
user accounts
   Office 365, 59
   signed-in, 6
   in Windows 10, 47–49

V

validation rules
   creating, 364–366
   defined, 364
validation texts
   creating, 364–366
   defined, 364
variance, 399
viewing reports, 151

W

wallpapers, 52
Weather app, 67–68
web browsers, 11
wildcard characters, 215–216
   defined, 215
window control buttons, 6
window snip, 62
windows
   modal, 591

opening forms in, 591–594
   pop-up, 591
   snapping, 92–93
Windows 10, 46
   Home version, 55
   lock screen, 50
   sign-in screen, 50–51
   user accounts in, 47–49
   variations in appearance, 49
   variations organization and functionality,
     48
wizards
   creating forms with, 267–269
   creating reports with, 286–289
   crosstab queries, 404
   form, 532–533
   Form Wizard, 267–269
   Import Spreadsheet Wizard, 114, 145,
     206
   Input Mask, 356–357
   Query Wizard, 222–224
   Report Wizard, 286–289
   Simple Query Wizard, 129–130
   subreport, 546–548
Word, 101
   opening files with, 80–83
Word files
   exporting reports to, 297–298
   opening, 80–83
word tables, importing data from,
   645–652
WordPad Desktop app, 78
workbooks
   charts in, 654
   defined, 653
   importing data into Access tables from,
     114–117
   importing from, 114–117, 653–654
worksheets
   defined, 653
   importing from, 114–117, 653–654
wrapping text, 22

X

XML Paper Specification, 41
XPS files, 41

Z

zip, defined, 10
zipped files
   downloading and extracting, 11–14,
     65–66
   extracting with File Explorer, 73–74
zipped folders, 65
zoom, defined, 25
Zoom dialog box, calculated field
   creation in, 217–218
zoom levels
   changing, 25–26
   Page Width, 25–26
Zoom slider, 25–26